ADVANCES IN NEURAL INFORMATION PROCESSING SYSTEMS 8

ADVANCES IN NEURAL INFORMATION PROCESSING SYSTEMS

Published by Morgan-Kaufmann

NIPS-1
Advances in Neural Information Processing Systems: Proceedings of the 1988 Conference, David Touretzky, ed., 1989

NIPS-2
Advances in Neural Information Processing Systems: Proceedings of the 1989 Conference, David Touretzky, ed., 1990

NIPS-3
Advances in Neural Information Processing Systems: Proceedings of the 1990 Conference, Richard Lippmann, John E. Moody, and David S. Touretzky, eds., 1991

NIPS-4
Advances in Neural Information Processing Systems: Proceedings of the 1991 Conference, John E. Moody, Steve J. Hanson, and Richard P. Lippmann, eds., 1992

NIPS-5
Advances in Neural Information Processing Systems: Proceedings of the 1992 Conference, Stephen José Hanson, Jack D. Cowan, and C. Lee Giles, eds., 1993

NIPS-6
Advances in Neural Information Processing Systems: Proceedings of the 1993 Conference, Jack D. Cowan, Gerald Tesauro, and Joshua Alspector, eds., 1994

Published by The MIT Press

NIPS-7
Advances in Neural Information Processing Systems: Proceedings of the 1994 Conference, Gerald Tesauro, David Touretzky, and Todd Leen, eds., 1995

NIPS-8
Advances in Neural Information Processing Systems: Proceedings of the 1995 Conference, David S. Touretzky, Michael C. Mozer, and Michael E. Hasselmo, eds., 1996

ADVANCES IN NEURAL INFORMATION PROCESSING SYSTEMS 8

Proceedings of the 1995 Conference

edited by
David S. Touretzky, Michael C. Mozer, and Michael E. Hasselmo

A Bradford Book
The MIT Press
Cambridge, Massachusetts
London, England

© 1996 Massachusetts Institute of Technology

All rights reserved. No part of this book may be reproduced in any form by any electronic or mechanical means (including photocopying, recording, or information storage and retrieval) without permission in writing from the publisher.

This book was printed and bound in the United States of America.

ISSN: 1049-5258
ISBN: 0-262-20107-0

Contents

Preface	*xv*
Committees	*xvii*

PART I
COGNITIVE SCIENCE

Learning the Structure of Similarity J. B. TENENBAUM	*3*
A Model of Spatial Representations in Parietal Cortex Explains Hemineglect A. POUGET, T. J. SEJNOWSKI	*10*
Human Reading and the Curse of Dimensionality G. L. MARTIN	*17*
Extracting Tree-structured Representations of Trained Networks M. W. CRAVEN, J. W. SHAVLIK	*24*
Harmony Networks Do Not Work R. GOURLEY	*31*
Dynamics of Attention as Near Saddle-node Bifurcation Behavior H. NAKAHARA, K. DOYA	*38*
Rapid Quality Estimation of Neural Network Input Representations K. J. CHERKAUER, J. W. SHAVLIK	*45*
A Model of Auditory Streaming S. L. MCCABE, M. J. DENHAM	*52*

PART II
NEUROSCIENCE

Modeling Interactions of the Rat's Place and Head Direction Systems A.D. REDISH, D.S. TOURETZKY	*61*
Correlated Neuronal Response: Time Scales and Mechanisms W. BAIR, E. ZOHARY, C. KOCH	*68*
Information through a Spiking Neuron C. STEVENS, A. ZADOR	*75*
Reorganization of Somatosensory Cortex after Tactile Training R. S. PETERSEN, J. G. TAYLOR	*82*

A Dynamical Model of Context Dependencies for the Vestibulo-Ocular Reflex O. J. M. D. COENEN, T. J. SEJNOWSKI	89
The Role of Activity in Synaptic Competition at the Neuromuscular Junction S. R. H. JOSEPH, D. J. WILLSHAW	96
When Is an Integrate-and-fire Neuron like a Poisson Neuron? C. F. STEVENS, A. ZADOR	103
How Perception Guides Production in Birdsong Learning C. L. FRY	110
The Geometry of Eye Rotations and Listing's Law A. A. HANDZEL, T. FLASH	117
Temporal Coding in the Submillisecond Range: Model of *Barn Owl* Auditory Pathway R. KEMPTER, W. GERSTNER, J. L. VAN HEMMEN, H. WAGNER	124
Cholinergic Suppression of Transmission May Allow Combined Associative Memory Function and Self-organization in the Neocortex M. E. HASSELMO, M. CEKIC	131
A Predictive Switching Model of Cerebellar Movement Control A. G. BARTO, J. T. BUCKINGHAM, J. C. HOUK	138
Independent Component Analysis of Electroencephalographic Data S. MAKEIG, A. J. BELL, T.-P. JUNG, T. J. SEJNOWSKI	145
Simulation of a Thalamocortical Circuit for Computing Directional Heading in the Rat H. T. BLAIR	152
Plasticity of Center-Surround Opponent Receptive Fields in Real and Artificial Neural Systems of Vision S. YASUI, T. FURUKAWA, M. YAMADA, T. SAITO	159

PART III
THEORY

Learning Model Bias J. BAXTER	169
Statistical Theory of Overtraining—Is Cross-Validation Asymptotically Effective? S. AMARI, N. MURATA, K. R. MÜLLER, M. FINKE, H. YANG	176
A Bound on the Error of Cross Validation Using the Approximation and Estimation Rates, with Consequences for the Training-test Split M. KEARNS	183
Learning with Ensembles: How Overfitting Can Be Useful P. SOLLICH, A. KROGH	190

Contents

Neural Networks with Quadratic VC Dimension P. KOIRAN, E. D. SONTAG	*197*
Sample Complexity for Learning Recurrent Perceptron Mappings B. DASGUPTA, E. D. SONTAG	*204*
On the Computational Power of Noisy Spiking Neurons W. MAASS	*211*
A Realizable Learning Task Which Exhibits Overfitting S. BÖS	*218*
Stable Dynamic Parameter Adaptation S. M. RÜGER	*225*
Estimating the Bayes Risk from Sample Data R. R. SNAPP, T. XU	*232*
Recursive Estimation of Dynamic Modular RBF Networks V. KADIRKAMANATHAN, M. KADIRKAMANATHAN	*239*
On Neural Networks with Minimal Weights V. BOHOSSIAN, J. BRUCK	*246*
Modern Analytic Techniques to Solve the Dynamics of Recurrent Neural Networks A. C. C. COOLEN, S. N. LAUGHTON, D. SHERRINGTON	*253*
Implementation Issues in the Fourier Transform Algorithm Y. MANSOUR, S. SAHAR	*260*
Generalisation of a Class of Continuous Neural Networks J. SHAWE-TAYLOR, J. ZHAO	*267*
Gradient and Hamiltonian Dynamics Applied to Learning in Neural Networks J. W. HOWSE, C. T. ABDALLAH, G. L. HEILEMAN	*274*
Optimization Principles for the Neural Code M. DEWEESE	*281*
Strong Unimodality and Exact Learning of Constant Depth μ-Perceptron Networks M. MARCHAND, S. HADJIFARADJI	*288*
Active Learning in Multilayer Perceptrons K. FUKUMIZU	*295*
Dynamics of On-line Gradient Descent Learning for Multilayer Neural Networks D. SAAD, S. A. SOLLA	*302*
Worst-case Loss Bounds for Single Neurons D. P. HELMBOLD, J. KIVINEN, M. K. WARMUTH	*309*
Exponentially Many Local Minima for Single Neurons P. AUER, M. HERBSTER, M. K. WARMUTH	*316*

Adaptive Back-Propagation in On-line Learning of Multilayer Networks 323
A. H. L. WEST, D. SAAD

Optimizing Cortical Mappings 330
G. J. GOODHILL, S. FINCH, T.J. SEJNOWSKI

Quadratic-type Lyapunov Functions for Competitive Neural Networks with
Different Time-scales 337
A. MEYER-BÄSE

Examples of Learning Curves from a Modified VC-formalism 344
A. KOWALCZYK, J. SZYMANSKI, P. L. BARTLETT, R. C. WILLIAMSON

Bayesian Methods for Mixtures of Experts 351
S. WATERHOUSE, D. MACKAY, T. ROBINSON

Some Results on Convergent Unlearning Algorithm 358
S. A. SEMENOV, I. B. SHUVALOVA

Geometry of Early Stopping in Linear Networks 365
R. DODIER

Absence of Cycles in Symmetric Neural Networks 372
X. WANG, A. JAGOTA, F. BOTELHO, M. GARZON

PART IV
ALGORITHMS AND ARCHITECTURES

Adaptive Mixture of Probabilistic Transducers 381
Y. SINGER

REMAP: Recursive Estimation and Maximization of A Posteriori Probabilities—
Application to Transition-based Connectionist Speech Recognition 388
Y. KONIG, H. BOURLARD, N. MORGAN

Recurrent Neural Networks for Missing or Asynchronous Data 395
Y. BENGIO, F. GINGRAS

Family Discovery 402
S. M. OMOHUNDRO

Discriminant Adaptive Nearest Neighbor Classification and Regression 409
T. HASTIE, R. TIBSHIRANI

Clustering Data through an Analogy to the Potts Model 416
M. BLATT, S. WISEMAN, E. DOMANY

Generalized Learning Vector Quantization 423
A. SATO, K. YAMADA

Stochastic Hillclimbing as a Baseline Method for Evaluating Genetic
Algorithms 430
A. JUELS, M. WATTENBERG

Contents

Symplectic Nonlinear Component Analysis L. C. PARRA	437
A Unified Learning Scheme: Bayesian-Kullback Ying-Yang Machine L. XU	444
Universal Approximation and Learning of Trajectories Using Oscillators P. BALDI, K. HORNIK	451
A Smoothing Regularizer for Recurrent Neural Networks L. WU, J. MOODY	458
EM Optimization of Latent-Variable Density Models C. M. BISHOP, M. SVENSÉN, C. K. I. WILLIAMS	465
Factorial Hidden Markov Models Z. GHAHRAMANI, M. I. JORDAN	472
Boosting Decision Trees H. DRUCKER, C. CORTES	479
Exploiting Tractable Substructures in Intractable Networks L. K. SAUL, M. I. JORDAN	486
Hierarchical Recurrent Neural Networks for Long-term Dependencies S. E. HIHI, Y. BENGIO	493
Discovering Structure in Continuous Variables Using Bayesian Networks R. HOFMANN, V. TRESP	500
Using Pairs of Data Points to Define Splits for Decision Trees G. E. HINTON, M. REVOW	507
Gaussian Processes for Regression C. K. I. WILLIAMS, C. E. RASMUSSEN	514
Pruning with Generalization Based Weight Saliencies: γOBD, γOBS M. W. PEDERSEN, L. K. HANSEN, J. LARSEN	521
Fast Learning by Bounding Likelihoods in Sigmoid Type Belief Networks T. JAAKKOLA, L. K. SAUL, M., I. JORDAN	528
Generating Accurate and Diverse Members of a Neural-network Ensemble D. W. OPITZ, J. W. SHAVLIK	535
Improved Gaussian Mixture Density Estimates Using Bayesian Penalty Terms and Network Averaging D. ORMONEIT, V. TRESP	542
Explorations with the Dynamic Wave Model T. P. REBOTIER, J. L. ELMAN	549
The Capacity of a Bump G. W. FLAKE	556
Tempering Backpropagation Networks: Not All Weights Are Created Equal N. N. SCHRAUDOLPH, T. J. SEJNOWSKI	563

Investment Learning with Hierarchical PSOMs   *570*
J. WALTER, H. RITTER

Learning Long-term Dependencies Is Not as Difficult with NARX Networks   *577*
T. LIN, B. G. HORNE, P. TIÑO, C. L. GILES

Constructive Algorithms for Hierarchical Mixtures of Experts   *584*
S. R. WATERHOUSE, A. J. ROBINSON

An Information-theoretic Learning Algorithm for Neural Network Classification   *591*
D. MILLER, A. RAO, K. ROSE, A. GERSHO

A Practical Monte Carlo Implementation of Bayesian Learning   *598*
C. E. RASMUSSEN

From Isolation to Cooperation: An Alternative View of a System of Experts   *605*
S. SCHAAL, C. C. ATKESON

Finite State Automata that Recurrent Cascade-Correlation Cannot Represent   *612*
S. C. KREMER

SPERT-II: A Vector Microprocessor System and Its Application to Large Problems in Backpropagation Training   *619*
J. WAWRZYNEK, K. ASANOVIC, B. KINGSBURY, J. BECK, D. JOHNSON, N. MORGAN

Softassign versus Softmax: Benchmarks in Combinatorial Optimization   *626*
S. GOLD, A. RANGARAJAN

A Multiscale Attentional Framework for Relaxation Neural Networks   *633*
D. I. TSIOUTSIAS, E. MJOLSNESS

Is Learning the *n*-th Thing Any Easier Than Learning the First?   *640*
S. THRUN

Using Unlabeled Data for Supervised Learning   *647*
G. TOWELL

Learning Sparse Perceptrons   *654*
J. C. JACKSON, M. W. CRAVEN

Does the Wake-sleep Algorithm Produce Good Density Estimators?   *661*
B. J. FREY, G. E. HINTON, P. DAYAN

PART V
IMPLEMENTATIONS

Improved Silicon Cochlea Using Compatible Lateral Bipolar Transistors   *671*
A. VAN SCHAIK, E. FRAGNIÈRE, E. VITTOZ

Adaptive Retina with Center-Surround Receptive Field   *678*
S.-C. LIU, K. BOAHEN

Neuron-MOS Temporal Winner Search Hardware for Fully-parallel Data
Processing 685
T. SHIBATA, T. NAKAI, T. MORIMOTO, R. KAIHARA, T. YAMASHITA, T. OHMI

Analog VLSI Processor Implementing the Continuous Wavelet Transform 692
R. T. EDWARDS, G. CAUWENBERGHS

Silicon Models for Auditory Scene Analysis 699
J. LAZZARO, J. WAWRZYNEK

VLSI Model of Primate Visual Smooth Pursuit 706
R. ETIENNE-CUMMINGS, J. VAN DER SPIEGEL, P. MUELLER

Model Matching and SFMD Computation 713
S. REHFUSS, D. HAMMERSTROM

Parallel Analog VLSI Architectures for Computation of Heading Direction and
Time-to-contact 720
G. INDIVERI, J. KRAMER, C. KOCH

PART VI
SPEECH AND SIGNAL PROCESSING

Onset-based Sound Segmentation 729
L. S. SMITH

Laterally Interconnected Self-organizing Maps in Handwritten Digit
Recognition 736
Y. CHOE, J. SIROSH, R. MIIKKULAINEN

Forward-backward Retraining of Recurrent Neural Networks 743
A. SENIOR, T. ROBINSON

Context-dependent Classes in a Hybrid Recurrent Network-HMM Speech
Recognition System 750
D. KERSHAW, T. ROBINSON, M. HOCHBERG

A New Learning Algorithm for Blind Signal Separation 757
S. AMARI, A. CICHOCKI, H. H. YANG

Handwritten Word Recognition Using Contextual Hybrid Radial Basis Function
Network/Hidden Markov Models 764
B. LEMARIÉ, M. GILLOUX, M. LEROUX

Selective Attention for Handwritten Digit Recognition 771
E. ALPAYDIN

KODAK IMAGELINK™ OCR Alphanumeric Handprint Module 778
A. SHUSTOROVICH, C. W. THRASHER

The Gamma MLP for Speech Phoneme Recognition 785
S. LAWRENCE, A. C. TSOI, A. D. BACK

PART VII
VISION

A Framework for Nonrigid Matching and Correspondence S. PAPPU, S. GOLD, A. RANGARAJAN	795
Control of Selective Visual Attention: Modeling the "Where" Pathway E. NIEBUR, C. KOCH	802
Unsupervised Pixel-prediction W. R. SOFTKY	809
Learning to Predict Visibility and Invisibility from Occlusion Events J. A. MARSHALL, R. K. ALLEY, R. S. HUBBARD	816
Classifying Facial Action M. S. BARTLETT, P. A. VIOLA, T. J. SEJNOWSKI, B. A. GOLOMB, J. LARSEN, J. C. HAGER, P. EKMAN	823
Modeling Saccadic Targeting in Visual Search R. P. N. RAO, G. J. ZELINSKY, M. M. HAYHOE, D. H. BALLARD	830
A Model of Transparent Motion and Non-transparent Motion Aftereffects A. GRUNEWALD	837
A Neural Network Model of 3-D Lightness Perception L. PESSOA, W. D. ROSS	844
Empirical Entropy Manipulation for Real-world Problems P. VIOLA, N. N. SCHRAUDOLPH, T. J. SEJNOWSKI	851
Active Gesture Recognition Using Learned Visual Attention T. DARRELL, A. PENTLAND	858
SEEMORE: A View-based Approach to 3-D Object Recognition Using Multiple Visual Cues B. W. MEL	865

PART VIII
APPLICATIONS

Human Face Detection in Visual Scenes H. A. ROWLEY, S. BALUJA, T. KANADE	875
Improving Committee Diagnosis with Resampling Techniques B. PARMANTO, P. W. MUNRO, H. R. DOYLE	882
Primitive Manipulation Learning with Connectionism Y. MATSUOKA	889
Beating a Defender in Robotic Soccer: Memory-based Learning of a Continuous Function P. STONE, M. VELOSO	896

Visual Gesture-based Robot Guidance with a Modular Neural System 903
E. LITTMANN, A. DREES, H. RITTER

A Novel Channel Selection System in Cochlear Implants Using Artificial Neural Network 910
M. A. JABRI, R. J. WANG

Prediction of Beta Sheets in Proteins 917
A. KROGH, S. K. RIIS

A Neural Network Autoassociator for Induction Motor Failure Prediction 924
T. PETSCHE, A. MARCANTONIO, C. DARKEN, S. J. HANSON, G. M. KUHN, I. SANTOSO

Using Feedforward Neural Networks to Monitor Alertness from Changes in EEG Correlation and Coherence 931
S. MAKEIG, T.-P. JUNG, T. J. SEJNOWSKI

A Neural Network Classifier for the I1000 OCR Chip 938
J. C. PLATT, T. P. ALLEN

Predictive Q-Routing: A Memory-based Reinforcement Learning Approach to Adaptive Traffic Control 945
S. P. M. CHOI, D. YEUNG

Optimal Asset Allocation Using Adaptive Dynamic Programming 952
R. NEUNEIER

Using the Future to "Sort Out" the Present: Rankprop and Multitask Learning for Medical Risk Evaluation 959
R. CARUANA, S. BALUJA, T. MITCHELL

Stock Selection via Nonlinear Multi-factor Models 966
A. U. LEVIN

Experiments with Neural Networks for Real Time Implementation of Control 973
P. CAMPBELL, M. DALE, H. L. FERRÁ, A. KOWALCZYK

High-speed Airborne Particle Monitoring Using Artificial Neural Networks 980
A. FERGUSON, T. SABISCH, P. KAYE, L. C. DIXON, H. BOLOURI

PART IX
CONTROL

A Dynamical Systems Approach for a Learnable Autonomous Robot 989
J. TANI, N. FUKUMURA

Parallel Optimization of Motion Controllers via Policy Iteration 996
J. A. COELHO JR., R. SITARAMAN, R. A. GRUPEN

Learning Fine Motion by Markov Mixtures of Experts 1003
M. MEILA, M. I. JORDAN

Neural Control for Nonlinear Dynamic Systems 1010
S. YU, A. M. ANNASWAMY

Improving Elevator Performance Using Reinforcement Learning 1017
R. H. CRITES, A. G. BARTO

High-performance Job-Shop Scheduling with a Time-delay TD(λ) Network 1024
W. ZHANG, T. G. DIETTERICH

Competence Acquisition in an Autonomous Mobile Robot Using Hardware Neural Techniques 1031
G. JACKSON, A. F. MURRAY

Generalization in Reinforcement Learning: Successful Examples Using Sparse Coarse Coding 1038
R. S. SUTTON

Stable Linear Approximations to Dynamic Programming for Stochastic Control Problems with Local Transitions 1045
B. V. ROY, J. N. TSITSIKLIS

Stable Fitted Reinforcement Learning 1052
G. J. GORDON

Improving Policies without Measuring Merits 1059
P. DAYAN, S. P. SINGH

Memory-based Stochastic Optimization 1066
A. W. MOORE, J. SCHNEIDER

Temporal Difference in Learning in Continuous Time and Space 1073
K. DOYA

Reinforcement Learning by Probability Matching 1080
P. N. SABES, M. I. JORDAN

Author Index 1087
Keyword Index 1091

Preface

The interaction between neuroscience, cognitive science and theoretical work on information processing has increased rapidly over the past decade. In experimental work, the different levels of analysis and the complexity of the data require computational modeling in order to evaluate hypotheses and generate new experimentally testable predictions. At the same time, many information processing applications can draw inspiration from available data about the neural substrates of behavior. The papers in this volume contribute to this ongoing interaction between theory and experiment.

These papers summarize the talks and posters presented at the ninth annual conference on Neural Information Processing Systems (NIPS), held in Denver, Colorado from Nov. 27 to Nov. 30, 1995. The previous eight volumes of Advances in Neural Information Processing Systems have made an influential contribution to the field of biological and artificial neural networks. All papers presented at the conference were reviewed by three referees, with final acceptance of 152 out of the 462 papers submitted. Many excellent papers could not be accepted due to space limitations. The acceptance rate of this volume is lower than that for many journals—ensuring that it contains work of only the highest quality. All submitted papers received reviewer comments and feedback from NIPS conference participants which were incorporated in the revisions for final publication in this proceedings volume.

The field of computational neuroscience and neural network theory has drawn researchers from a range of more traditional disciplines. The papers in this volume describe how neuroscientists and cognitive scientists have used computational models of neural systems to test hypotheses and generate predictions to guide their work. This work includes models of how networks in the owl brainstem could be trained for complex localization function (Kempter et al.) how cellular activity may underlie rat navigation (Redish and Touretzky, Blair), how cholinergic modulation may regulate cortical reorganization (Hasselmo and Cekic), and how damage to parietal cortex results in neglect (Pouget and Sejnowski). Additional work concerns development of theoretical techniques important for understanding the dynamics of neural systems, including formation of cortical maps (Goodhill and Finch), analysis of recurrent networks (Coolen et al.), and analysis of self-supervised learning (Frey et al.). Other papers describe how engineers and computer scientists have approached problems of pattern recognition or speech recognition with the use of computational architectures inspired by the interaction of populations of neurons within the brain. For example, new neural network models have been applied to classical problems including handwritten character recognition (Lemarie et al., Choe et al) and object recognition (Mel, Rowley et al). Exciting new work has focused on building chips modeled after neural systems (Van Schaik et al., Lazzaro and Wawrzynek).

In addition to the papers in the main program, the NIPS conference was preceded by an excellent one-day tutorial program, and a popular two-day program of post-conference workshops took place in Vail. The workshop program has grown considerably in scale over the years. This year it covered topics ranging from "Vertebrate Neurophysiology and Neural Networks" to "Learning in Bayesian Networks."

The continued success of the NIPS conference can be attributed to the efforts of a large group of people, many of whom are listed on the following pages. We express our gratitude to the members of the organizing committee, program committee, publicity committee and foundation board, and the many referees who reviewed the 462 submissions to the conference. We especially thank Manavendra Misra for his smooth and cool handling of local arrangements, Christy Medina and Denise Pruell for their stellar efforts as professional conference administrators and registration coordinators, the many on-site student volunteers, John Angulo, Deb Miller, Mark Sitton, and Tim Tidwell II, students at the University of Colorado at Boulder who handled the monumental task of processing the conference submissions, and Mike Chang and Olivia Choe for assistance in assembling this volume. Finally, we thank the Colorado School of Mines for helping to finance the registration services, and the Advanced Research Projects Agency and Office of Naval Research for providing valuable financial support for many of the graduate students and young investigators who attend the meeting.

David S. Touretzky, Carnegie Mellon University
Michael C. Mozer, University of Colorado
Michael E. Hasselmo, Harvard University

January 18, 1996

Committees

**NIPS-95
ORGANIZING COMMITTEE**

General Chair	David Touretzky, Carnegie Mellon University
Program Chair	Michael Mozer, University of Colorado
Workshop Chair	Michael Perrone, IBM
Publicity Chair	David Cohn, MIT
Publications Chair	Michael Hasselmo, Harvard University
Treasurer	John Lazzaro, UC Berkeley
Government/Corporate Liaison	John Moody, Oregon Graduate Institute
Local Arrangements Chair	Manavendra Misra, Colorado School of Mines
Tutorials Chair	Jack Cowan, University of Chicago
Contracts	Steve Hanson, Siemens
	Scott Kirkpatrick, IBM
	Gerald Tesauro, IBM

**NIPS-95
PROGRAM COMMITTEE**

Program Chair	Michael Mozer, University of Colorado
Area Chairs	Yoshua Bengio, Universite de Montreal
	Terrence Fine, Cornell University
	John G. Harris, University of Florida
	Michael Kearns, AT&T Bell Labs
	Yann Le Cun, AT&T Bell Labs
	Stephen Omohundro, NEC Research Inst.
	Lori Pratt, Colorado School of Mines
	Jose Principe, University of Florida
	Allen Selverston, UC San Diego
	Satinder P. Singh, MIT
	Volker Tresp, Siemens AG
	Steven Zucker, McGill University

NIPS-95
PUBLICITY COMMITTEE

Publicity Chair   David Cohn, MIT
Overseas Liaisons
Australia, Singapore, India   Marwan Jabri, University of Sydney
Europe   Joachim Buhmann, University of Bonn
Hong Kong, China, Taiwan   Lei Xu, Chinese University of Hong Kong
Israel   Hava Siegelmann, Technion
Japan   Kenji Doya, ATR Research Laboratories
South America   Andreas Meier, Simon Bolivar University
Turkey   Ethem Alpaydin, Bogazici University
United Kingdom   Alan Murray, Edinburgh University

NIPS FOUNDATION
BOARD MEMBERS

President   Terry Sejnowski, Salk Institute
Vice President of Development   John Moody, Oregon Graduate Institute
Treasurer   Eric Mjolsness, UC San Diego
Secretary   Scott Kirkpatrick, IBM
Members   Leo Breiman, UC Berkeley
                                         Jack Cowan, University of Chicago
                                         Stephen Hanson, Siemens
                                         Richard Lippman, MIT
                                         Eve Marder, Brandeis
                                         Gerald Tesauro, IBM
NIPS95 General Chair   David Touretzky, Carnegie Mellon

NIPS-95
REFEREES

Subutai Ahmad	Herve Bourlard	Virginia de Sa
Luis Almeida	Jochen Braun	Bert deVries
Chuck Anderson	Timothy Brown	Thomas Dietterich
James Anderson	Joachim Buhmann	Allan Dobbins
Martin Anthony	John Byrne	Georg Dorffner
Chris Atkeson	Franco Callari	Gregory Dudek
Pierre Baldi	Ted Carnevale	Shimon Edelman
Etienne Barnard	Gert Cauwenberghs	Mark Fanty
Andrew Barron	Tzi-Dar Chiueh	Meir Feder
Peter Bartlett	Michael Cohen	Terrence Fine
Eric Baum	William Cohen	Gary Flake
Sue Becker	David Cohn	Bill Freeman
Yoshua Bengio	Corinna Cortes	Fabrizio Gabbiani
Avrim Blum	Gary Cottrell	Patrick Gallinari
Ulrich Bodenhausen	Christian Darken	Zoubin Ghahramani
Leon Bottou	Peter Dayan	Joumana Ghosn

Committees

C. Lee Giles
Federico Girosi
Hans Peter Graf
Vijaykumar Gullapalli
Patrick Haffner
Dan Hammerstrom
Tom Hancock
Catherine Harris
Michael Hasselmo
David Haussler
Simon Haykin
John Hertz
Haym Hirsh
Bill Horne
Don Hush
Nathan Intrator
Tommi Jaakkolla
Marwan Jabri
Robbie Jacobs
Allan Jepson
Dan Johnston
Leslie Pack
Michael Kearns
Dan Kersten
Christof Koch
Philip Kohn
Pascal Koiran
Adam Kowalczyk
Anders Krogh
Ramon Krosley
Kevin Lang
Steve Lawrence
John Lazzaro
M.D. Levine
Tsungnan Lin
Shawn Lockery

David Lowe
Stefan Manke
Bimal Mathur
Bartlett Mel
Stefan Miesbach
Kenneth Miller
Manavendra Misra
Melanie Mitchell
Martin Moller
F. Read Montague
Andrew Moore
Nelson Morgan
J. Anthony Movshon
Sayandev Mukherjee
Ralph Neuneier
Ernst Niebur
Steven Nowlan
Antonio Olmos-Gallo
Christian Omlin
Manfred Opper
Barak Pearlmutter
Fernando Pereira
Jim Peterson
Tony Plate
John Platt
David Plaut
Jordan Pollack
Dean Pomerleau
Larry Reeker
Steve Renals
Barry Richmond
Tony Robinson
Dana Ron
Eytan Ruppin
Philip Sabes
E. Sackinger

Majd Sakr
Lawrence Saul
Eric Saund
Terrence Sejnowski
Sebastian Seung
Robert Shapley
Noel Sharkey
Jude Shavlik
Tadashi Shibata
Patrice Simard
Yoram Singer
Massimo Sivilotti
Warren Smith
Padhraic Smyth
Bill Softky
David Standley
Martin Stemmler
Richard Sutton
Sebastian Thrun
Geoffrey Towell
Ah Chung Tsoi
Michael Turmon
Lyle Ungar
Santosh Venkatesh
Grace Wahba
DeLiang Wang
Chris Watkins
Raymond Watrous
John Wawrzynek
Ronald Williams
Robert Williamson
Charles Wilson
David Wolpert
Lei Xu
Hezy Yeshurun

ADVANCES IN NEURAL INFORMATION PROCESSING SYSTEMS 8

PART I
COGNITIVE SCIENCE

Learning the structure of similarity

Joshua B. Tenenbaum
Department of Brain and Cognitive Sciences
Massachusetts Institute of Technology
Cambridge, MA 02139
jbt@psyche.mit.edu

Abstract

The *additive clustering (ADCLUS)* model (Shepard & Arabie, 1979) treats the similarity of two stimuli as a weighted additive measure of their common features. Inspired by recent work in unsupervised learning with multiple cause models, we propose a new, statistically well-motivated algorithm for discovering the structure of natural stimulus classes using the ADCLUS model, which promises substantial gains in conceptual simplicity, practical efficiency, and solution quality over earlier efforts. We also present preliminary results with artificial data and two classic similarity data sets.

1 INTRODUCTION

The capacity to judge one stimulus, object, or concept as *similar* to another is thought to play a pivotal role in many cognitive processes, including generalization, recognition, categorization, and inference. Consequently, modeling subjective similarity judgments in order to discover the underlying structure of stimulus representations in the brain/mind holds a central place in contemporary cognitive science. Mathematical models of similarity can be divided roughly into two families: *spatial* models, in which stimuli correspond to points in a metric (typically Euclidean) space and similarity is treated as a decreasing function of distance; and *set-theoretic* models, in which stimuli are represented as members of salient subsets (presumably corresponding to natural classes or features in the world) and similarity is treated as a weighted sum of common and distinctive subsets.

Spatial models, fit to similarity judgment data with familiar *multidimensional scaling (MDS)* techniques, have yielded concise descriptions of homogeneous, perceptual domains (e.g. three-dimensional color space), often revealing the salient dimensions of stimulus variation (Shepard, 1980). Set-theoretic models are more general, in principle able to accomodate discrete conceptual structures typical of higher-level cognitive domains, as well as dimensional stimulus structures more common in perception (Tversky, 1977). In practice, however, the utility of set-theoretic models is limited by the hierarchical clustering techniques that underlie conventional methods for discovering the discrete features or classes of stimuli. Specifically, hierarchical clustering requires that any two classes of stimuli correspond to disjoint or properly inclusive subsets, while psychologically natural classes may correspond in general to arbitrarily overlapping subsets of stimuli. For example, the subjective similarity of two countries results from the interaction of multiple geographic and cultural factors, and there is no reason a priori to expect the subsets of communist, African, or French-speaking nations to be either disjoint or properly inclusive.

In this paper we consider the *additive clustering (ADCLUS)* model (Shepard & Arabie, 1979), the simplest instantiation of Tversky's (1977) general contrast model that accommodates the arbitrarily overlapping class structures associated with multiple causes of similarity. Here, the similarity of two stimuli is modeled as a weighted additive measure of their common clusters:

$$\hat{s}_{ij} = \sum_{k=1}^{K} w_k f_{ik} f_{jk} + c, \qquad (1)$$

where $\hat{s}_{ij}$ is the reconstructed similarity of stimuli i and j, the weight w_k captures the salience of cluster k, and the binary indicator variable f_{ik} equals 1 if stimulus i belongs to cluster k and 0 otherwise. The additive constant c is necessary because the similarity data are assumed to be on an interval scale.[1] As with conventional clustering models, ADCLUS recovers a system of discrete subsets of stimuli, weighted by salience, and the similarity of two stimuli increases with the number (and weight) of their common subsets. ADCLUS, however, makes none of the structural assumptions (e.g. that any two clusters are disjoint or properly inclusive) which limit the applicability of conventional set-theoretic models. Unfortunately this flexibility also makes the problem of fitting the ADCLUS model to an observed similarity matrix exceedingly difficult.

Previous attempts to fit the model have followed a heuristic strategy to minimize a squared-error energy function,

$$E = \sum_{i \neq j} (s_{ij} - \hat{s}_{ij})^2 = \sum_{i \neq j} (s_{ij} - \sum_k w_k f_{ik} f_{jk})^2, \qquad (2)$$

by alternately solving for the best cluster configurations f_{ik} given the current weights w_k and solving for the best weights given the current clusters (Shepard & Arabie, 1979; Arabie & Carroll, 1980). This strategy is appealing because given the cluster configuration, finding the optimal weights becomes a simple linear least-squares problem.[2] However, finding good cluster configurations is a difficult problem in combinatorial optimization, and this step has always been the weak point in previous work. The original ADCLUS (Shepard & Arabie, 1979) and later MAPCLUS (Arabie & Carroll, 1980) algorithms employ ad hoc techniques of combinatorial optimization that sometimes yield unexpected or uninterpretable final results. Certainly, no rigorous theory exists that would explain why these approaches fail to discover the underlying structure of a stimulus set when they do.

Essentially, the ADCLUS model is so challenging to fit because it generates similarities from the interaction of many independent underlying causes. Viewed this way, modeling the structure of similarity looks very similar to the multiple-cause learning

---

[1] In the remainder of this paper, we absorb c into the sum over k, taking the sum over $k = 0, \ldots, K$, defining $w_0 \equiv c$, and fixing $f_{i0} = 1, (\forall i)$.

[2] Strictly speaking, because the weights are typically constrained to be nonnegative, more elaborate techniques than standard linear least-squares procedures may be required.

problems that are currently a major focus of study in the neural computation literature (Ghahramani, 1995; Hinton, Dayan, et al., 1995; Saund, 1995; Neal, 1992). Here we propose a novel approach to additive clustering, inspired by the progress and promise of work on multiple-cause learning within the Expectation-Maximization (EM) framework (Ghahramani, 1995; Neal, 1992). Our EM approach still makes use of the basic insight behind earlier approaches, that finding $\{w_k\}$ given $\{f_{ik}\}$ is easy, but obtains better performance from treating the unknown cluster memberships probabilistically as hidden variables (rather than parameters of the model), and perhaps more importantly, provides a rigorous and well-understood theory. Indeed, it is natural to consider $\{f_{ik}\}$ as "unobserved" features of the stimuli, complementing the observed data $\{s_{ij}\}$ in the similarity matrix. Moreover, in some experimental paradigms, one or more of these features may be considered observed data, if subjects report using (or are requested to use) certain criteria in their similarity judgments.

2 ALGORITHM

2.1 Maximum likelihood formulation

We begin by formulating the additive clustering problem in terms of maximum likelihood estimation with unobserved data. Treating the cluster weights $w = \{w_k\}$ as model parameters and the unobserved cluster memberships $f = \{f_{ik}\}$ as hidden causes for the observed similarities $s = \{s_{ij}\}$, it is natural to consider a hierarchical generative model for the "complete data" (including observed and unobserved components) of the form $p(s, f|w) = p(s|f, w)p(f|w)$. In the spirit of earlier approaches to ADCLUS that seek to minimize a squared-error energy function, we take $p(s|f, w)$ to be gaussian with common variance σ^2:

$$p(s|f, w) \propto exp\{-\frac{1}{2\sigma^2} \sum_{i \neq j}(s_{ij} - \hat{s}_{ij})^2\} = exp\{-\frac{1}{2\sigma^2} \sum_{i \neq j}(s_{ij} - \sum_k w_k f_{ik} f_{jk})^2\}. \quad (3)$$

Note that $\log p(s|f, w)$ is equivalent to $-E/(2\sigma^2)$ (ignoring an additive constant), where E is the energy defined above. In general, priors $p(f|w)$ over the cluster configurations may be useful to favor larger or smaller clusters, induce a dependence between cluster size and cluster weight, or bias particular kinds of class structures, but only uniform priors are considered here. In this case $-E/(2\sigma^2)$ also gives the "complete data" loglikelihood $\log p(s, f|w)$.

2.2 The EM algorithm for additive clustering

Given this probabilistic model, we can now appeal to the EM algorithm as the basis for a new additive clustering technique. EM calls for iterating the following two-step procedure, in order to obtain successive estimates of the parameters w that are guaranteed never to decrease in likelihood (Dempster et al., 1977). In the E-step, we calculate

$$Q(w|w^{(n)}) = \sum_{f'} p(f'|s, w^{(n)}) \log p(s, f'|w) = \frac{1}{2\sigma^2} \langle -E \rangle_{s,w^{(n)}}. \quad (4)$$

$Q(w|w^{(n)})$ is equivalent to the expected value of E as a function of w, averaged over all possible configurations f' of the NK binary cluster memberships, given the observed data s and the current parameter estimates $w^{(n)}$. In the M-step, we maximize $Q(w|w^{(n)})$ with respect to w to obtain $w^{(n+1)}$.

Each cluster configuration f' contributes to the mean energy in proportion to its probability under the gaussian generative model in (3). Thus the number of configurations making significant contributions depends on the model variance σ^2. For large

σ^2, the probability is spread over many configurations. In the limiting case $\sigma^2 \to 0$, only the most likely configuration contributes, making EM effectively equivalent to the original approaches presented in Section 1 that use only the single best cluster configuration to solve for the best cluster weights at each iteration.

In line with the basic insight embodied less rigorously in these earlier algorithms, the M-step still reduces to a simple (constrained) linear least-squares problem, because the mean energy $\langle E \rangle = \sum_{i \neq j} \left(s_{ij}^2 - 2s_{ij} \sum_k w_k \langle f_{ik} f_{jk} \rangle + \sum_{kl} w_k w_l \langle f_{ik} f_{jk} f_{il} f_{jl} \rangle \right)$, like the energy E, is quadratic in the weights w_k. The E-step, which amounts to computing the expectations $m_{ijk} = \langle f_{ik} f_{jk} \rangle$ and $m_{ijkl} = \langle f_{ik} f_{jk} f_{il} f_{jl} \rangle$, is much more involved, because the required sums over all possible cluster configurations f' are intractable for any realistic case. We approximate these calculations using Gibbs sampling, a Monte Carlo method that has been successfully applied to learning similar generative models with hidden variables (Ghahramani, 1995; Neal 1992).[3]

Finally, the algorithm should produce not only estimates of the cluster weights, but also a final cluster configuration that may be interpreted as the psychologically natural features or classes of the relevant domain. Consider the expected cluster memberships $p_{ik} = \langle f_{ik} \rangle_{s,w^{(n)}}$, which give the probability that stimulus i belongs to cluster k, given the observed similarity matrix and the current estimates of the weights. Only when all p_{ik} are close to 0 or 1, i.e. when σ^2 is small enough that all the probability becomes concentrated on the most likely cluster configuration and its neighbors, can we fairly assert which stimuli belong to which classes.

2.3 Simulated annealing

Two major computational bottlenecks hamper the efficiency of the algorithm as described so far. First, Gibbs sampling may take a very long time to converge to the equilibrium distribution, particularly when σ^2 is small relative to the typical energy difference between neighboring cluster configurations. Second, the likelihood surfaces for realistic data sets are typically riddled with local maxima. We solve both problems by annealing on the variance. That is, we run Gibbs sampling using an effective variance σ_{eff}^2 initially much greater than the assumed model variance σ^2, and decrease σ_{eff}^2 towards σ^2 according to the following two-level scheme. We anneal within the nth iteration of EM to speed the convergence of the Gibbs sampling E-step (Neal, 1993), by lowering σ_{eff}^2 from some high starting value down to a target $\sigma_{Targ(n)}^2$ for the nth EM iteration. We also anneal between iterations of EM to avoid local maxima (Rose et al., 1990), by intializing $\sigma_{Targ(0)}^2$ at a high value and taking $\sigma_{Targ(n)}^2 \to \sigma^2$ as n increases.

3 RESULTS

In all of the examples below, one run of the algorithm consisted of 100-200 iterations of EM, annealed both within and between iterations. Within each E-step, 10-100 cycles of Gibbs sampling were carried out at the target temperature σ_{Targ} while the statistics for m_{ik} and m_{ijk} were recorded. These recorded cycles were preceeded by 20-200 unrecorded cycles, during which the system was annealed from a higher temperature (e.g. $8\sigma_{Targ}^2$) down to σ_{Targ}^2, to ensure that statistics were collected as close to equilibrium as possible. The precise numbers of recorded and unrecorded iterations were chosen as a compromise between the need for longer samples as the

---

[3]We generally also approximate $m_{ijkl} \approx m_{ijk} m_{ijl}$, which usually yields satisfactory results with much greater efficiency.

Table 1: Classes and weights recovered for the integers 0-9.

Rank	Weight	Stimuli in class	Interpretation
1	.444	2　4　　　8	powers of two
2	.345	0 1 2	small numbers
3	.331	3　　6　9	multiples of three
4	.291	6 7 8 9	large numbers
5	.255	2 3 4 5 6	middle numbers
6	.216	1　3　5　7　9	odd numbers
7	.214	1 2 3 4	smallish numbers
8	.172	4 5 6 7 8	largish numbers

Variance accounted for = 90.9% with 8 clusters (additive constant = .148).

number of hidden variables is increased and the need to keep computation times practical.

3.1 Artificial data

We first report results with artificial data, for which the true cluster memberships and weights are known, to verify that the algorithm does in fact find the desired structure. We generated 10 data sets by randomly assigning each of 12 stimuli independently and with probability 1/2 to each of 8 classes, and choosing random weights for the classes uniformly from $[0.1, 0.6]$. These numbers are grossly typical of the real data sets we examine later in this section. We then calculated the observed similarities from (1), added a small amount of random noise (with standard deviation equal to 5% of the mean noise-free similarity), and symmeterized the similarity matrix.

The crucial free parameter is K, the assumed number of stimulus classes. When the algorithm was configured with the correct number of clusters ($K = 8$), the original classes and weights were recovered during the first run of the algorithm on all 10 data sets, after an average of 58 EM iterations (low 30, high 92). When the algorithm was configured with $K = 7$ clusters, one less than the correct number, the seven classes with highest weight were recovered on 9/10 first runs. On these runs, the recovered weights and true weights had a mean correlation of 0.948 ($p < .05$ on each run). When configured with $K = 5$, the first run recovered either four of the top five classes (6/10 trials) or three of the top five (4/10 trials). When configured with too many clusters ($K = 12$), the algorithm typically recovered only 8 clusters with significantly non-zero weights, corresponding to the 8 correct classes. Comparable results are not available for ADCLUS or MAPCLUS, but at least we can be satisfied that our algorithm achieves a basic level of competence and robustness.

3.2 Judged similarities of the integers 0-9

Shepard et al. (1975) had subjects judge the similarities of the integers 0 through 9, in terms of the "abstract concepts" of the numbers. We analyzed the similarity matrix (Shepard, personal communication) obtained by pooling data across subjects and across three conditions of stimulus presentation (verbal, written-numeral, and written-dots). We chose this data set because it illustrates the power of additive clustering to capture a complex, overlapping system of classes, and also because it serves to compare the performance of our algorithm with the original ADCLUS algorithm. Observe first that two kinds of classes emerge in the solution. Classes 1, 3, and 6 represent familiar arithmetic concepts (e.g. "multiples of three", "odd numbers"), while the remaining classes correspond to subsets of consecutive integers

Table 2: Classes and weights recovered for the 16 consonant phonemes.

Rank	Weight	Stimuli in class	Interpretation
1	.800	f θ	front unvoiced fricatives
2	.572	d g	back voiced stops
3	.463	p k	unvoiced stops (omitting t)
4	.424	b v ð	front voiced
5	.357	p t k	unvoiced stops
6	.292	m n	nasals
7	.169	d g v ð z ž	voiced (omitting b)
8	.132	p t k f θ s	unvoiced (omitting š)

Variance accounted for = 90.2% with 8 clusters (additive constant = .047).

and thus together represent the dimension of numerical magnitude. In general, both arithmetic properties and numerical magnitude contribute to judged similarity, as every number has features of both types (e.g. 9 is a "large" "odd" "multiple of three"), except for 0, whose only property is "small." Clearly an overlapping clustering model is necessary here to accomodate the multiple causes of similarity.

The best solution reported for these data using the original ADCLUS algorithm consisted of 10 classes, accounting for 83.1% of the variance of the data (Shepard & Arabie, 1979).[4] Several of the clusters in this solution differed by only one or two members (e.g. three of the clusters were {0,1}, {0,1,2}, and {0,1,2,3,4}), which led us to suspect that a better fit might be obtained with fewer than 10 classes. Table 2 shows the best solution found in five runs of our algorithm, accounting for 90.9% of the variance with eight classes. Compared with our solution, the original ADCLUS solution leaves almost twice as much residual variance unaccounted for, and with 10 classes, is also less parsimonious.

3.3 Confusions between 16 consonant phonemes

Finally, we examine Miller & Nicely's (1955) classic data on the confusability of 16 consonant phonemes, collected under varying signal/noise conditions with the original intent of identifying the features of English phonology (compiled and reprinted in Carroll & Wish, 1974). Note that the recovered classes have reasonably natural interpretations in terms of the basic features of phonological theory, and a very different overall structure from the classes recovered in the previous example. Quite significantly, the classes respect a hierarchical structure almost perfectly, with class 3 included in class 5, classes 1 and 5 included in class 8, and so on. Only the absence of /b/ in class 7 violates the strict hierarchy.

These data also provide the only convenient oppportunity to compare our algorithm with the MAPCLUS approach to additive clustering (Arabie & Carroll, 1980). The published MAPCLUS solution accounts for 88.3% of the variance in this data, using eight clusters. Arabie & Carroll (1980) report being "substantively perturbed" (p. 232) that their algorithm does not recover a distinct cluster for the nasals /m n/, which have been considered a very salient subset in both traditional phonology (Miller & Nicely, 1955) and other clustering models (Shepard, 1980). Table 3 presents our eight-cluster solution, accounting for 90.2% of the variance. While this represents only a marginal improvement, our solution does contain a cluster for the nasals, as expected on theoretical grounds.

---

[4]Variance accounted for $= 1 - E/\sum_{i \neq j}(s_{ij} - \bar{s})^2$, where $\bar{s}$ is the mean of the set $\{s_{ij}\}$.

3.4 Conclusion

These examples show that ADCLUS can discover meaningful representations of stimuli with arbitrarily overlapping class structures (arithmetic properties), as well as dimensional structure (numerical magnitude) or hierarchical structure (phoneme families) when appropriate. We have argued that modeling similarity should be a natural application of learning generative models with multiple hidden causes, and in that spirit, presented a new probabilistic formulation of the ADCLUS model and an algorithm based on EM that promises better results than previous approaches. We are currently pursuing several extensions: enriching the generative model, e.g. by incorporating significant prior structure, and improving the fitting process, e.g. by developing efficient and accurate mean field approximations. More generally, we hope this work illustrates how sophisticated techniques of computational learning can be brought to bear on foundational problems of structure discovery in cognitive science.

Acknowledgements

I thank P. Dayan, W. Richards, S. Gilbert, Y. Weiss, A. Hershowitz, and M. Bernstein for many helpful discussions, and Roger Shepard for generously supplying inspiration and unpublished data. The author is a Howard Hughes Medical Institute Predoctoral Fellow.

References

Arabie, P. & Carroll, J. D. (1980). MAPCLUS: A mathematical programming approach to fitting the ADCLUS model. *Psychometrika* **45**, 211-235.

Carroll, J. D. & Wish, M. (1974) Multidimensional perceptual models and measurement methods. In *Handbook of Perception, Vol. 2*. New York: Academic Press, 391-447.

Dempster, A. P., Laird, N. M., & Rubin, D. B. (1977). Maximum likelihood estimation from incomplete data via the EM Algorithm (with discussion). *J. Roy. Stat. Soc.* **B39**, 1-38.

Ghahramani, Z. (1995). Factorial learning and the EM algorithm. In G. Tesauro, D. S. Touretzky, & T. K. Leen (eds.), *Advances in Neural Information Processing Systems 7*. Cambridge, MA: MIT Press, 617-624.

Hinton, G. E., Dayan, P., Frey, B. J., & Neal, R. M. (1995) The "wake-sleep" algorithm for unsupervised neural networks. *Science* **268**, 1158-1161.

Miller, G. A. & Nicely, P. E. (1955). An analysis of perceptual confusions among some English consonants. *J. Ac. Soc. Am.* **27**, 338-352.

Neal, R. M. (1992). Connectionist learning of belief networks. *Artif. Intell.* **56**, 71-113.

Neal, R. M. (1993). Probabilistic inference using Markov chain Monte Carlo methods. Technical Report CRG-TR-93-1, Dept. of Computer Science, U. of Toronto.

Rose, K., Gurewitz, F., & Fox, G. (1990). Statistical mechanics and phase transitions in clustering. *Physical Review Letters* **65**, 945-948.

Saund, E. (1995). A multiple cause mixture model for unsupervised learning. *Neural Computation* **7**, 51-71.

Shepard, R. N. & Arabie, P. (1979). Additive clustering: Representation of similarities as combinations of discrete overlapping properties. *Psychological Review* **86**, 87-123.

Shepard, R. N., Kilpatric, D. W., & Cunningham, J. P., (1975). The internal representation of numbers. *Cognitive Psychology* **7**, 82-138.

Shepard, R. N. (1980). Multidimensional scaling, tree-fitting, and clustering. *Science* **210**, 390-398.

Tversky, A. (1977). Features of similarity. *Psychological Review* **84**, 327-352.

A Model of Spatial Representations in Parietal Cortex Explains Hemineglect

Alexandre Pouget
Dept of Neurobiology
UCLA
Los Angeles, CA 90095-1763
alex@salk.edu

Terrence J. Sejnowski
Howard Hughes Medical Institute
The Salk Institute
La Jolla, CA 92037
terry@salk.edu

Abstract

We have recently developed a theory of spatial representations in which the position of an object is not encoded in a particular frame of reference but, instead, involves neurons computing basis functions of their sensory inputs. This type of representation is able to perform nonlinear sensorimotor transformations and is consistent with the response properties of parietal neurons. We now ask whether the same theory could account for the behavior of human patients with parietal lesions. These lesions induce a deficit known as hemineglect that is characterized by a lack of reaction to stimuli located in the hemispace contralateral to the lesion. A simulated lesion in a basis function representation was found to replicate three of the most important aspects of hemineglect: i) The models failed to cross the leftmost lines in line cancellation experiments, ii) the deficit affected multiple frames of reference and, iii) it could be object centered. These results strongly support the basis function hypothesis for spatial representations and provide a computational theory of hemineglect at the single cell level.

1 Introduction

According to current theories of spatial representations, the positions of objects are represented in multiple modules throughout the brain, each module being specialized for a particular sensorimotor transformation and using its own frame of reference. For instance, the lateral intraparietal area (LIP) appears to encode the location of objects in oculocentric coordinates, presumably for the control of saccadic eye movements. The ventral intraparietal cortex (VIP) and the premotor cortex, on the other hand, seem to use head-centered coordinates and might be

A Model of Spatial Representations in Parietal Cortex Explains Hemineglect

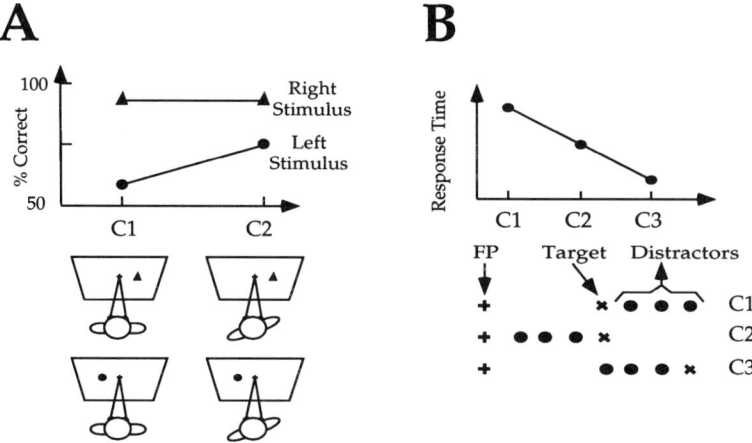

Figure 1: A. Retinotopic neglect modulated by egocentric position. B. Stimulus-centered neglect

involved in the control of hand movements toward the face.

This modular theory of spatial representations is not fully consistent with the behavior of patients with parietal or frontal lesions. Such lesions causes a syndrome known as hemineglect which is characterized by a lack of response to sensory stimuli appearing in the hemispace contralateral to the lesion [3]. According to the modular view, the deficit should be behavior dependent, e.g., oculocentric for eye movements, head-centered for reaching. However, experimental and clinical studies show that this is not the case. Instead, neglect affects multiple frames of reference simultaneously, and to a first approximation, independently of the task.

This point is particularly clear in an experiment by Karnath et al (1993) (Figure 1A). Subjects were asked to identify a stimulus that can appear on either side of the fixation point. In order to test whether the position of the stimuli with respect to the body affects performance, two conditions were tested: a control condition with head straight ahead (C1), and a second condition with head rotated 20 degrees on the right (or equivalently, with the trunk rotated 20 degrees on the left, see figure) (C2). In C2, both stimuli appeared further to the right of the trunk while being at the same location with respect to the head and retina than in C1. Moreover, the trunk-centered position of the left stimulus in C2 was the same than the trunk-centered position of the right stimulus in C1.

As expected, subjects with right parietal lesions performed better on the right stimulus in the control condition, a result consistent with both, retinotopic and trunk-centered neglect. To distinguish between the two frames of reference, one needs to compare performance across conditions.

If the deficit is purely retinocentric, the results should be identical in both conditions, since the retinotopic location of the stimuli does not vary. If, on the other hand, the deficit is purely trunk-centered, the performance on the left stimulus should improve when the head is turned right since the stimulus now appears further toward the right of the trunk-centered hemispace. Furthermore, performance on the right stimulus in the control condition should be the same as performance on the left stimulus in the rotated condition, since they share the same trunk-centered position in both cases.

Neither of these hypotheses can fully account for the data. As expected from a retinotopic neglect, subjects always performed better on the right stimulus in both conditions. However, performance on the left stimulus improved when the head was turned right (C2), though not sufficiently to match the level of performance on the right stimulus in the control condition (C1). Therefore, these results suggest a retinotopic neglect modulated by trunk-centered factors.

In addition, Karnath et al (1991) tested patients on a similar experiment in which subjects were asked to generate a saccade toward the target. The analysis of reaction time revealed the same type of results than the one found in the identification task, thereby demonstrating that the spatial deficit is, to a first approximation, independent of the task.

An experiment by Arguin and Bub (1993) suggests that neglect can be object-centered as well. As shown in figure 1B, they found that reaction times were faster when the target appeared on the right of a set of distractors (C2), as opposed to the left (C1), even though the target is at the same retinotopic location in both conditions. Interestingly, moving the target further to the right leads to even faster reaction times (C3), showing that hemineglect is not only object-centered but retinotopic as well in this task.

These results strongly support the existence of spatial representations using multiple frames of reference simultaneously shared by several behaviors. We have recently developed a theory [6] which has precisely these properties and we ask here whether a simulated lesion would lead to a deficit similar to hemineglect. Our theory posits that parietal neurons computes basis function (BF) of sensory signals, such as visual, or auditory inputs, and posture signals, such as eye or head position. The resulting representation, which we called a basis function map, can be used for performing nonlinear transformations of the sensory inputs, the type of transformations required for sensorimotor coordination.

2 Model Organization

The model contains two distinct parts: a network for performing sensorimotor transformations and a selection mechanism.

2.1 Network Architecture

We implemented a network using basis function units in the intermediate layer to perform a transformation from a visual retinotopic map to two motor maps in, respectively, head-centered and oculocentric coordinates (Figure 2). The input contains a retinotopic visual map analog to the one found in the early stages of visual processing, and a set of units encoding eye position, similar to the neurons found in the intralaminar nucleus of the thalamus. These input units project to a set of intermediate units shared by both transformations. Each intermediate unit computes a gaussian of the retinal location of object, r_x, multiplied by a sigmoid of eye position, e_x:

$$o_i = \frac{e^{-\frac{(r_x - r_{xi})^2}{2\sigma^2}}}{1 + e^{-\frac{e_x - e_{xi}}{t}}} \quad (1)$$

These units are organized in a map covering all possible combinations of retinal and eye position selectivities. As we have shown elsewhere [6], this type of response function is consistent with the response of single parietal neurons found in area 7a.

A Model of Spatial Representations in Parietal Cortex Explains Hemineglect

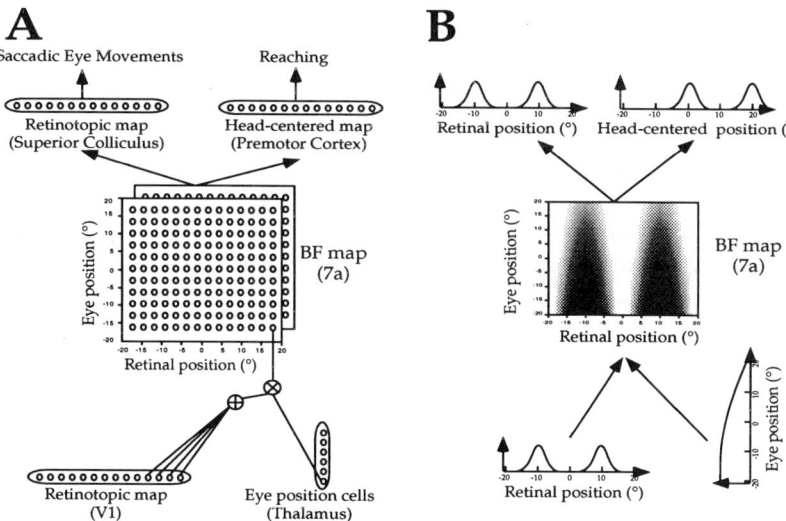

Figure 2: A. Network architecture B. Typical pattern of activity

The resulting map forms a basis function map which encodes the location of objects in head-centered and retinotopic coordinates simultaneously.

The activity of the unit in the output maps is computed by a simple linear combination of the BF unit activities. Appropriate values of the weights were found by using linear regression techniques.

This architecture mimics the pattern of projections of the parietal area 7a. 7a is known to project to, both, the superior colliculus and the premotor cortex (via the ventral parietal area, VIP), in which neurons have, respectively, retinotopic and head-centered visual receptive fields. Figure 2B shows a typical pattern of activity in the network when two stimuli are presented simultaneously while the eye fixated 10 degrees toward the right.

2.2 Hemispheric Biases and Lesion Model

Neurophysiological data indicate that both hemispheres contain neurons with all possible combinations of retinal and eye position selectivities, but with a contralateral bias. Hence, most neurons in the right parietal cortex (resp. left) have their retinal receptive field on the left hemiretina (resp. right). The bias for eye position is much weaker but a trend has been reported in several studies [1].

Therefore, spatial representations in a patient with a right parietal lesions are biased toward the right side of space. We modeled such a lesion by using a similar bias in the intermediate layer of our network. The BF map simply has more neurons tuned to *right retinal* and *eye positions*. We found that the exact profile of the neuronal gradient across the basis function maps did not matter as long as it was monotonic and contralateral for both eye position and retinal location.

2.3 Selection model

We also developed a selection mechanism to model the behavior of patients when presented with several stimuli simultaneously. The simultaneous presentation of stimuli induces multiple hills of activity in the network (see for instance the pattern of activity shown in figure 1B for two visual stimuli). Our selection mechanism operates on the peak values of these hills.

At each time step, the most active stimulus is selected according to a winner-take-all and its corresponding activity is set to zero (inhibition of return). At the next time step, the second highest stimuli is selected while the previously selected item is allowed to recover slowly. This procedure ensures that the most active item is not selected twice in a row, but because of the recovery process, stimulus with high activity might be selected again if displayed long enough.

This mechanism is such that the probability of selecting an item is proportional to two factors: the absolute amount of activity associated with the item, and the relative activity with respect to other competing items.

2.4 Evaluating network performance

We used this model to simulate several experiments in which patient performance was evaluated according to reaction time or percent of correct response.

Reaction time in the model was taken to be proportional to the number of time steps required by our selection mechanism to select a particular target. Performance on identification task was assumed to be proportional to the strength of the activity generated by the stimuli in the BF map.

3 Results

3.1 Line cancellation

We first tested the network on the line cancellation test, a test in which patients are asked to cross out short line segments uniformly spread over a page. To simulate this test, we presented the display shown in figure 3A and we ran the selection mechanism to determine which lines get selected by the network. As illustrated in figure 3A, the network crosses out only the lines located in the right half of the display, just as left neglect patients do in the same task. The rightward gradient introduced by the lesion biases the selection mechanism in favor of the most active lines, i.e., the ones on the right. As a result, the rightmost lines win the competition over and over, preventing the network from selecting the left lines.

3.2 Mixture of frames of reference

Next, we sought to determine the frame of reference of neglect in the model. Since Karnath et al (1993) manipulated head position, we simulated their experiment by using a BF map integrating visual inputs with head position, rather than eye position. We show in figure 3B the pattern of activity obtained in the retinotopic output layer of the network in the various experimental conditions (the other maps behaved in a similar way). In both conditions, head straight ahead (dotted lines) or turned on the side (solid lines), the right stimulus is associated with more activity than the left stimulus. This is the consequence of the larger number of cells in the basis function map for rightward position. In addition, the activity for the left stimulus increases when the head is turned to the right. This effect is related to the larger number of cells in the basis function maps tuned to right head positions.

Since network performance is proportional to activity strength, the overall pattern of performance was found to be similar to what has been reported in human patients

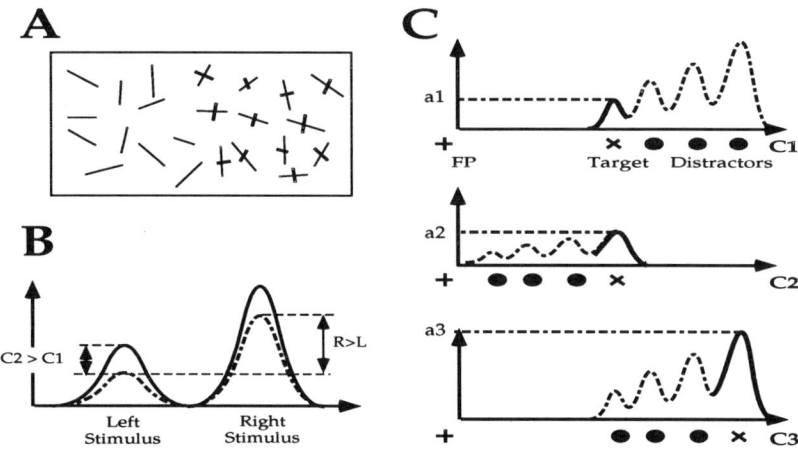

Figure 3: Network behavior in line cancellation task (A). Activity patterns in the retinotopic output layer when simulating the experiments by Karnath et al (1993) (B) and Arguin et al (1993) (C)

(figure 1A), namely: the right stimulus was better processed than the left stimulus and performance on the left stimulus increases when the head is rotated toward the right. Therefore, just like in human, neglect in the model is neither retinocentric nor trunk-centered alone, but both at the same time.

3.3 Object-centered effect

When simulating Arguin et al (1993) experiments, the network reaction times were found to follow the same trends than for human patients. Figure 3C illustrates the patterns of activity in the retinotopic output layer of the network when simulating the three conditions of Arguin experiments. Notice that the absolute activity associated with the target (solid lines) in conditions 1 and 2 is the same, but the activity of the distractors (dotted lines) differs in the two conditions. In condition 1, they have higher relative activity and thereby strongly delay the detection of the target by the selection mechanism. In condition 2, the distractors are now less active than the target and do not delay target processing as much as they do in condition 1. The reaction time decreases even more in condition 3, due to a higher absolute activity associated with the target. Therefore, the network exhibits retinocentric and object-centered neglect, just like parietal patients [2].

4 Discussion

The model of parietal cortex presented here was originally developed by considering the response properties of parietal neurons and the computational constraints inherent in sensorimotor transformations. It was not designed to model neglect, so its ability to account for a wide range of deficits is additional evidence in favor of the basis function hypothesis.

As we have shown, our model captures three essential aspects of the neglect syndrome: 1) It reproduces the pattern of line crossing reported in patients in line-cancellation experiments, 2) the deficit coexists in multiple frames of reference simultaneously, and 3) the model accounts for some of the object-based effects.

We can account for a very large number of studies beyond the ones we have considered here, using very similar computational principles. We can reproduce, in particular, the behavior of patients in line-bisection experiments and we can explain why neglect affects multiple cartesian frames of reference such as retinotopic, head-centered, trunk-centered, environment-centered (i.e. with respect to gravity), and object-centered.

It must be emphasized that these results have been obtained without using explicit representations of these various cartesian frames of reference (except for the retinotopy of the BF map). In fact, this is precisely because the lesion affected noncartesian representations that we have been able to reproduce these results. We have assumed that the lesion affects the functional space in which the basis functions are defined. This functional space shares common dimensions with cartesian spaces, but cannot be reduced to the latter. Hence, a basis function map integrating retinal location and head position is retinotopic, but not solely retinotopic. Consequently, any attempts to determine the cartesian space in which hemineglect operates is bound to lead to inconclusive results in which cartesian frames of reference appear to be mixed.

This study and previous research [6] suggests that the parietal cortex represents the position of objects by computing basis functions of the sensory and posture inputs. It would now be interesting to see if this hypothesis could also account for sensorimotor adaptation, such as learning to reach properly when wearing visual prisms. We predict that adaptation takes place in several frames of reference simultaneously, a prediction that is testable and would provide further support for the basis function framework.

References

[1] R.A. Andersen, C. Asanuma, G. Essick, and R.M. Siegel. Corticocortical connections of anatomically and physiologically defined subdivisions within the inferior parietal lobule. *Journal of Comparative Neurology*, 296(1):65–113, 1990.

[2] M. Arguin and D.N. Bub. Evidence for an independent stimulus-centered reference frame from a case of visual hemineglect. *Cortex*, 29:349–357, 1993.

[3] K.M. Heilman, R.T. Watson, and E. Valenstein. Neglect and related disorders. In K.M. Heilman and E. Valenstein, editors, *Clinical Neuropsychology*, pages 243–294. Oxford University Press, New York, 1985.

[4] H.O. Karnath, K. Christ, and W. Hartje. Decrease of contralateral neglect by neck muscle vibration and spatial orientation of trunk midline. *Brain*, 116:383–396, 1993.

[5] H.O. Karnath, P. Schenkel, and B. Fischer. Trunk orientation as the determining factor of the 'contralateral' deficit in the neglect syndrome and as the physical anchor of the internal representation of body orientation in space. *Brain*, 114:1997–2014, 1991.

[6] A. Pouget and T.J. Sejnowski. Spatial representations in the parietal cortex may use basis functions. In G. Tesauro, D.S. Touretzky, and T.K. Leen, editors, *Advances in Neural Information Processing Systems*, volume 7. MIT Press, Cambridge, MA, 1995.

Human Reading and the Curse of Dimensionality

Gale L. Martin
MCC Austin, TX 78613 galem@mcc.com

Abstract

Whereas optical character recognition (OCR) systems learn to classify single characters; people learn to classify long character strings in parallel, within a single fixation. This difference is surprising because high dimensionality is associated with poor classification learning. This paper suggests that the human reading system avoids these problems because the number of to-be-classified images is reduced by consistent and optimal eye fixation positions, and by character sequence regularities.

An interesting difference exists between human reading and optical character recognition (OCR) systems. The input/output dimensionality of character classification in human reading is much greater than that for OCR systems (see Figure 1). OCR systems classify one character at time; while the human reading system classifies as many as 8-13 characters per eye fixation (Rayner, 1979) and within a fixation, character category and sequence information is extracted in parallel (Blanchard, McConkie, Zola, and Wolverton, 1984; Reicher, 1969).

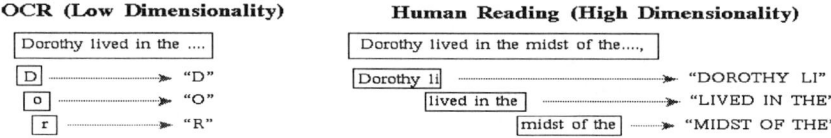

Figure 1: Character classification versus character sequence classification.

This is an interesting difference because high dimensionality is associated with poor classification learning–the so-called *curse of dimensionality* (Denker, et al; 1987; Geman, Bienenstock, & Doursat, 1992). OCR systems are designed to classify single characters to minimize such problems. The fact that most people learn to read quite well even with the high dimensional inputs and outputs, implies that variance is somehow lowered in this domain, thereby making accurate classification learning possible. The present paper reports on simulations of parallel character classification which suggest that variance is lowered through regularities in eye fixation positions and in character sequences making up valid words.

1 Training and Testing Materials

Training and testing materials were drawn from the story *The Wonderful Wizard of Oz* by L. Frank Baum. Images of text lines were created from 120 pages of text (about 160,000 characters, 33,000 total words, or 2,600 different words), which were divided into 6 different font and case conditions of 20 pages each. Three different fonts (variable and constant-width fonts), and two different cases (all upper-case or mixed-case characters) were used. Text line images were normalized with respect to height, but not width. All training and test sets contained an equal mix of the six font/case conditions. Two generalization sets were used, for test and cross-validation, and each consisted of about 14,000 characters.

> Dorothy lived in the midst of the great Kansas Prairies.
> DOROTHY LIVED IN THE MIDST OF THE GREAT KANSAS PRAIRIES.
> Dorothy lived in the midst of the great Kansas Prairies.
> DOROTHY LIVED IN THE MIDST OF THE GREAT KANSAS PRAIRIES.
> Dorothy lived in the midst of the great Kansas Prairies.
> DOROTHY LIVED IN THE MIDST OF THE GREAT KANSAS PRAIRIES.

Figure 2: Samples of the type font and case conditions used in the simulations

2 Network Architectures

The simulations used backpropagation networks (Rumelhart, Hinton & Williams, 1986) that extended the local receptive field, shared-weight architecture used in many character-based OCR neural networks (LeCun, et al, 1989; Martin & Pittman, 1991). In the previous single character-based approach, the input to the net is an image of a single character. The output is a vector representing the category of the character. Hidden nodes have local receptive fields that receive input from a spatially local region, (e.g., a 6x6 area) in the preceding layer. Groups of hidden nodes share their weights. Corresponding weights in each receptive field are initialized to the same value and updated by the same value. Different hidden nodes within a group learn to detect the same feature at different locations. A group is depicted as hidden nodes within a single plane of a cube that corresponds to a hidden layer. Different groups occupy different planes in the cube, and learn to detect different features. This architecture biases learning by reducing the number of free parameters available for representing a function. The fact that these nets usually train and generalize well in this domain, and that the local feature detectors that emerge are similar to the oriented-edge and -line detectors found in mammalian visual cortex (Hubel & Wiesel, 1979), suggests that the bias is at least roughly appropriate.

The extension of this character network to a character-sequence network is illustrated in Figure 3, where n (number of to-be-classified characters) is equal to 4. Each output node represents a character category (e.g., "D") in one of the nth ordinal positions (e.g., "First character on the left"). The size of the input window is expanded horizontally to cover at least the n widest characters ("WWWW"). When the character string is made up of relatively narrow characters, more than n characters will appear in the input window and the network must learn to ignore them. Increasing input/output dimensionality is accomplished by expanding the number of hidden nodes horizontally. Network capacity is described by the depth of each hidden layer (the number of different features detected), as well as by the width of each hidden layer (the spatial coverage of the network).

The network is potentially sensitive to both local and global visual information. Local receptive fields build in a sensitivity to letter features. Shared weights make learning transfer possible across representations of the same character at different positions. Output nodes are globally connected to all the nodes in the second hidden layer, but not with one another or with any word-level representations. Networks were trained until the training set accuracy failed to improve by at least .1% over 5 epochs, or overfitting became evident from periodic testing with the generalization test set.

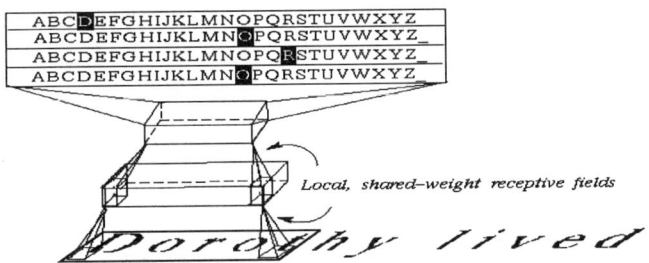

Figure 3: Net architecture for parallel character sequence classification, n=4 chars.

3 Effects of Dimensionality on Training Difficulty and Generalization

Experiment 1 provides a baseline measure of the impact of dimensionality. Increases in dimensionality result in exponential increases in the number of input and output patterns and the number of mapping functions. As a result, training problems arise due to limitations in network capacity or search scope. Generalization problems arise because it becomes impractical to use training sets large enough to obtain a good estimate of the underlying function. Four different levels of dimensionality were used (see Figure 4), from an input window of 20x20 pixels, with 1 to-be-classified character to an 80x20 window, with 4 to-be-classified characters). Input patterns were generated by starting the window at the left edge of the text line such that the first character was centered 10 pixels from the left of the window, and then successively scanning across the text line at each character position. Five training set sizes were used (about 700 samples to 50,000). Two relative network capacities were used (15 and 18 different feature detectors per hidden layer). Forty different

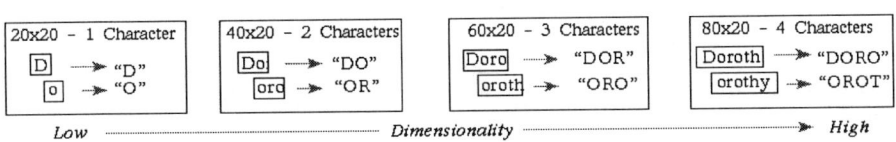

Figure 4: Four levels of input/output dimensionality used in the experiment.

networks were trained, one for each combination of dimensionality, training set size and relative network capacity (4x5x2). Training difficulty is described by asymptotic accuracy achieved on the training set and by amount of training required to reach the asymptote. Generalization is reported for both the test set (used to check for overfitting) and the cross-validation set. The results (see Figure 5) are consistent

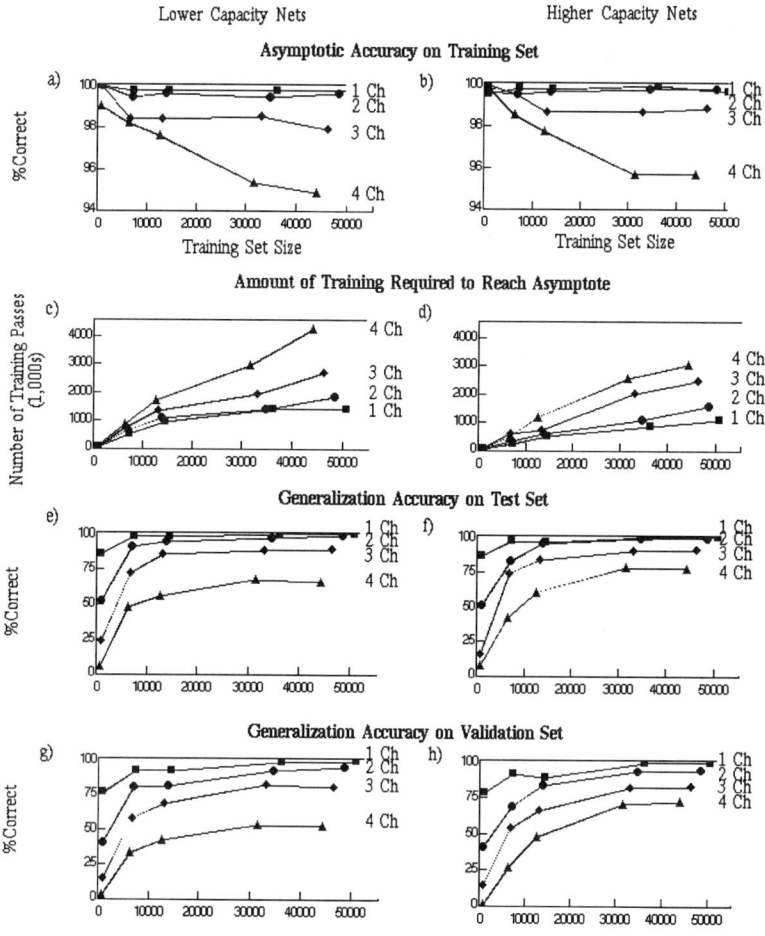

Figure 5: Impact of dimensionality on training and generalization.

with expectations. Increasing dimensionality results in increased training difficulty and lower generalization. Since the problems associated with high dimensionality occur in both training and test sets, and seem to be alleviated somewhat in the high capacity nets, they are presumably due to both capacity/search limitations and insufficient sample size.

4 Regularities in Window Positioning

One way human reading might reduce the problems associated with high dimensionality is to constrain eye fixation positions during reading; thereby reducing the number of different input images the system must learn to classify. Eye movement studies suggest that, although fixation positions within words do vary, there are consistencies Rayner, 1979). Moreover, the particular locations fixated, slightly to the left of the middle of words, appear to be optimal. People are most efficient at recognizing words at these locations (O'Regan & Jacobs, 1992). These fixation positions reduce variance by reducing the average variability in the positions of ordered characters within a word. Position variability increases as a function of distance from the fixated character. The average distance of characters within a word is minimized when the fixation position is toward the center of a word, as compared to when it is at the beginning or end of a word.

Experiment 2 simulated consistent and optimal positioning with an 80x20 input window fixated on the 3rd character. Only words of 3 or more characters were fixated (see Figure 6). The network learned to classify the first 4 characters in the word. This condition was compared to a *consistent positioning only* condition, in which the input window was fixated on the first character of a word. Two control conditions were also examined. They were replications of the 20x20-1Character and the 80x20-4 Character conditions of Experiment 1, except that in the first case, the network was trained and tested only on the first 4 characters in each word and in the second case, the network was trained as before but was tested with the window fixated on the first character of the word. Four levels of training set size were used and three replications of each training set size x window conditions were run (4 x 4 x 3 = 48 networks trained and tested). All networks employed 18 different feature detectors for each hidden layer. The results (see Figure 7) support the idea that

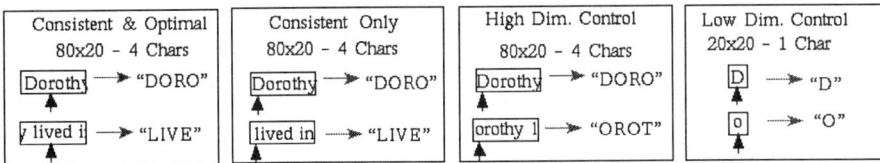

Figure 6: Window positioning and dimensionality manipulations in Experiment 2

consistent and optimal positioning reduces variance, as indicated by reductions in training difficulties and improved generalization. The consistent and optimal positioning networks achieved training and generalization results superior to the high dimensionality control condition, and equivalent to, or better than those for the low dimensionality control. They were also slightly better than the consistent positioning only nets.

5 Character Sequence Regularities

Since only certain character sequences are allowed in words, character sequence regularities in words may also reduce the number of distinct images the system must learn to classify. The system may also reduce variance by optimizing accuracy on highest frequency words. These hypotheses were tested by determining whether or not the three consistent and optimal positioning networks trained on the largest training set in Experiment 2, were more accurate in classifying high frequency words, as compared to low frequency words; and more accurate in classifying words as compared to pronounceable non-words or random character strings. The control condition used the networks trained in the low dimensional control (20x20 -1 Character) condition from Experiment 2. Human reading exhibits increased efficiency/accuracy in classifying high frequency as compared to low frequency words

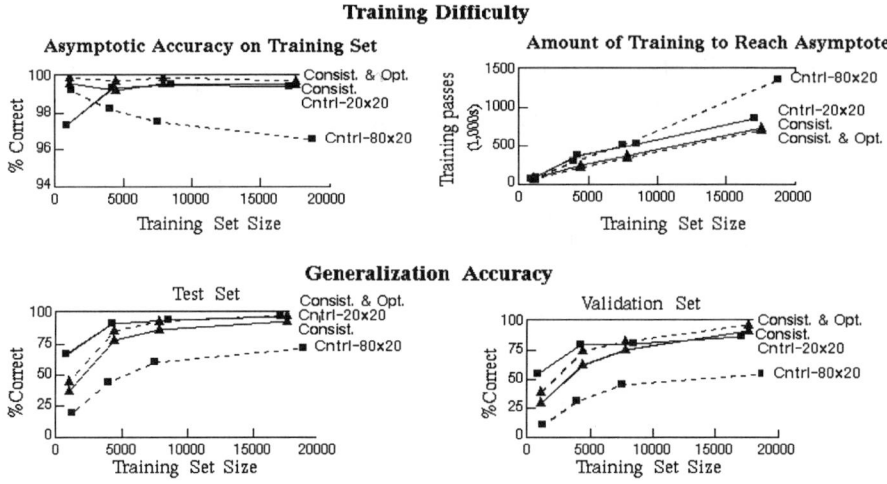

Figure 7: Impact of consistent & optimal window positions.

(Howes & Solomon, 1951; Solomon & Postman, 1952), and in classifying characters in words as compared to pronounceable non-words or random character strings (Baron & Thurston, 1973; Reicher, 1969). Experiment 3 involved creating a list of 30 4-letter words drawn from the Oz text, of which 15 occurred very frequently in the text (e.g., SAID), and 15 occurred infrequently (e.g., PAID), and creating a list of 30 4-letter pronounceable non-words (e.g., TOID) and a list of 30 4-letter random strings (e.g., SDIA). Each string was reproduced in each of the 6 font/case conditions and labeled to create a test set. One further condition involved creating a version of the word list in which the cases of the characters aLtErNaTeD. Psychologists used this manipulation to demonstrate that the advantages in processing words can not simply be due to the use of word-shape feature detectors, since the word advantage carries over to the alternating case condition, which destroys word-level features (McClelland, 1976).

Consistent with human reading (see Figure 8), the character-sequence-based networks were most accurate on high frequency words and least accurate for low frequency words. The character-sequence-based networks also showed a progressive decline in accuracy as the character string became less word-like. The advantage for word-like strings can not be due to the use of word shape feature detectors because accuracy on aLtErNaTiNg case words, where word shape is unfamiliar, remains quite high.

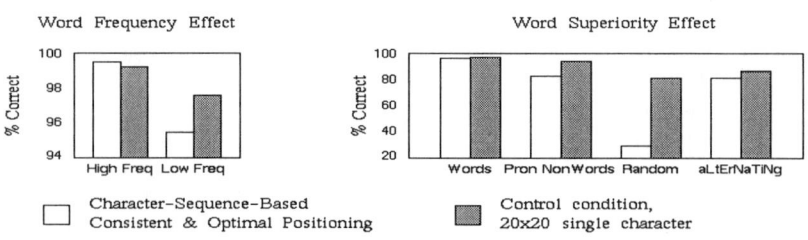

Figure 8: Sensitivity to word frequency and character sequence regularities

The present results raise questions about the role played by high dimensionality in determining reading disabilities and difficulties. Reading difficulties have been associated with reduced perceptual spans (Rayner, 1986; Rayner, et al., 1989), and with irregular eye fixation patterns (Rayner & Pollatsek, 1989). This suggests that some reading difficulties and disorders may be related to problems in generating the precise eye movements necessary to maintain consistent and optimal eye fixations. More generally, these results highlight the importance of considering the role of character classification in learning to read, particularly since content factors, such as word frequency, appear to influence even low-level classification operations.

References

Blanchard, H., McConkie, G., Zola, D., & Wolverton, G. (1984) Time course of visual information utilization during fixations in reading. *Jour. of Exp. Psych.: Human Perc. & Perf., 10*, 75-89.

Denker, J., Schwartz, D., Wittner, B., Solla, S., Howard, R., Jackel, L., & Hopfield, J. (1987) Large automatic learning, rule extraction and generalization, *Complex Systems, 1*, 877-933.

Geman, S., Bienenstock, E., and Doursat, R. (1992) Neural networks and the bias/variance dilemma. *Neural Computation, 4*, 1-58.

Howes, D. and Solomon, R. L. (1951) Visual duration threshold as a function of word probability. *Journal of Exp. Psych., 41*, 401-410.

Hubel, D. & Wiesel, T. (1979) Brain mechanisms of vision. *Sci. Amer., 241*, 150-162.

LeCun, Y., Boser, B., Denker, J., Henderson, D., Howard, R., Hubbard, W., & Jackel, L. (1990) Handwritten digit recognition with a backpropagation network. In *Adv. in Neural Inf. Proc. Sys. 2*, D. Touretzky (Ed) Morgan Kaufmann.

Martin, G. L. & Pittman, J. A. (1991) Recognizing hand-printed letters and digits using backpropagation learning. *Neural Computation, 3*, 258-267.

McClelland, J. L. (1976) Preliminary letter identification in the perception of words and nonwords. *Jour. of Exp. Psych.: Human Perc. & Perf., 2*, 80-91.

O'Regan, J. & Jacobs, A.(1992) Optimal viewing position effect in word recognition. *Jour. of Exp. Psych.: Human Perc.& Perf., 18*, 185-197.

Rayner, K. (1986) Eye movements and the perceptual span in beginning and skilled readers. *Jour. of Exp. Child Psych., 41*, 211-236.

Rayner, K. (1979) Eye guidance in reading. *Perception, 8*, 21-30.

Rayner, K., Murphy, L., Henderson, J. & Pollatsek, A. (1989) Selective attentional dyslexia. *Cognitive Neuropsych., 6*, 357-378.

Rayner, K. & Pollatsek, A. (1989) *The Psychology of reading.* Prentice Hall

Reicher, G. (1969) Perceptual recognition as a function of meaningfulness of stimulus material. *Jour. of Exp. Psych., 81*, 274-280.

Rumelhart, D., Hinton, G., and Williams, R. (1986) Learning internal representations by error propagation. In D. Rumelhart and J. McClelland, (Eds) *Parallel Distributed Processing, 1.* MIT Press.

Solomon, R. & Postman, L. (1952) Frequency of usage as a determinant of recognition thresholds for words. *Jour. of Exp. Psych., 43*, 195-210.

Extracting Tree-Structured Representations of Trained Networks

Mark W. Craven and Jude W. Shavlik
Computer Sciences Department
University of Wisconsin-Madison
1210 West Dayton St.
Madison, WI 53706
craven@cs.wisc.edu, shavlik@cs.wisc.edu

Abstract

A significant limitation of neural networks is that the representations they learn are usually incomprehensible to humans. We present a novel algorithm, TREPAN, for extracting comprehensible, symbolic representations from trained neural networks. Our algorithm uses queries to induce a decision tree that approximates the concept represented by a given network. Our experiments demonstrate that TREPAN is able to produce decision trees that maintain a high level of fidelity to their respective networks while being comprehensible and accurate. Unlike previous work in this area, our algorithm is general in its applicability and scales well to large networks and problems with high-dimensional input spaces.

1 Introduction

For many learning tasks, it is important to produce classifiers that are not only highly accurate, but also easily understood by humans. Neural networks are limited in this respect, since they are usually difficult to interpret after training. In contrast to neural networks, the solutions formed by "symbolic" learning systems (e.g., Quinlan, 1993) are usually much more amenable to human comprehension. We present a novel algorithm, TREPAN, for extracting comprehensible, symbolic representations from trained neural networks. TREPAN queries a given network to induce a decision tree that describes the concept represented by the network. We evaluate our algorithm using several real-world problem domains, and present results that demonstrate that TREPAN is able to produce decision trees that are accurate and comprehensible, and maintain a high level of fidelity to the networks from which they were extracted. Unlike previous work in this area, our algorithm is very general in its applicability, and scales well to large networks and problems with high-dimensional input spaces.

The task that we address is defined as follows: given a trained network and the data on which it was trained, produce a concept description that is comprehensible, yet classifies instances in the same way as the network. The concept description produced by our algorithm is a decision tree, like those generated using popular decision-tree induction algorithms (Breiman et al., 1984; Quinlan, 1993).

There are several reasons why the comprehensibility of induced concept descriptions is often an important consideration. If the designers and end-users of a learning system are to be confident in the performance of the system, they must understand how it arrives at its decisions. Learning systems may also play an important role in the process of scientific discovery. A system may discover salient features and relationships in the input data whose importance was not previously recognized. If the representations formed by the learner are comprehensible, then these discoveries can be made accessible to human review. However, for many problems in which comprehensibility is important, neural networks provide better generalization than common symbolic learning algorithms. It is in these domains that it is important to be able to extract comprehensible concept descriptions from trained networks.

2 Extracting Decision Trees

Our approach views the task of extracting a comprehensible concept description from a trained network as an inductive learning problem. In this learning task, the target concept is the function represented by the network, and the concept description produced by our learning algorithm is a decision tree that approximates the network. However, unlike most inductive learning problems, we have available an *oracle* that is able to answer queries during the learning process. Since the target function is simply the concept represented by the network, the oracle uses the network to answer queries. The advantage of learning with queries, as opposed to ordinary training examples, is that they can be used to garner information precisely where it is needed during the learning process.

Our algorithm, as shown in Table 1, is similar to conventional decision-tree algorithms, such as CART (Breiman et al., 1984), and C4.5 (Quinlan, 1993), which learn directly from a training set. However, TREPAN is substantially different from these conventional algorithms in number of respects, which we detail below.

The Oracle. The role of the oracle is to determine the class (as predicted by the network) of each instance that is presented as a query. Queries to the oracle, however, do not have to be complete instances, but instead can specify constraints on the values that the features can take. In the latter case, the oracle generates a complete instance by randomly selecting values for each feature, while ensuring that the constraints are satisfied. In order to generate these random values, TREPAN uses the training data to model each feature's marginal distribution. TREPAN uses frequency counts to model the distributions of discrete-valued features, and a kernel density estimation method (Silverman, 1986) to model continuous features. As shown in Table 1, the oracle is used for three different purposes: (i) to determine the class labels for the network's training examples; (ii) to select splits for each of the tree's internal nodes; (iii) and to determine if a node covers instances of only one class. These aspects of the algorithm are discussed in more detail below.

Tree Expansion. Unlike most decision-tree algorithms, which grow trees in a depth-first manner, TREPAN grows trees using a best-first expansion. The notion

Table 1: The TREPAN algorithm.

TREPAN($training\_examples, features$)
    $Queue := \emptyset$ /* sorted queue of nodes to expand */

    for each example $E \in training\_examples$ /* use net to label examples */
        class label for $E :=$ ORACLE(E)

    initialize the root of the tree, T, as a leaf node
    put $\langle T, training\_examples, \{\} \rangle$ into $Queue$

    while $Queue$ is not empty and size(T) < $tree\_size\_limit$ /* expand a node */
        remove node N from head of $Queue$
        $examples_N :=$ example set stored with N
        $constraints_N :=$ constraint set stored with N

        use $features$ to build set of candidate splits
        use $examples_N$ and calls to ORACLE($constraints_N$) to evaluate splits
        $S :=$ best binary split
        search for best m-of-n split, S', using S as a seed
        make N an internal node with split S'

        for each outcome, s, of S' /* make children nodes */
            make C, a new child node of N
            $constraints_C := constraints_N \cup \{S' = s\}$
            use calls to ORACLE($constraints_C$) to determine if C should remain a leaf
            otherwise
                $examples_C :=$ members of $examples_N$ with outcome s on split S'
                put $\langle C, examples_C, constraints_C \rangle$ into $Queue$

    return T

---

of the best node, in this case, is the one at which there is the greatest potential to increase the fidelity of the extracted tree to the network. The function used to evaluate node n is $f(n) = reach(n) \times (1 - fidelity(n))$, where $reach(n)$ is the estimated fraction of instances that reach n when passed through the tree, and $fidelity(n)$ is the estimated fidelity of the tree to the network for those instances.

Split Types. The role of internal nodes in a decision tree is to partition the input space in order to increase the separation of instances of different classes. In C4.5, each of these splits is based on a single feature. Our algorithm, like Murphy and Pazzani's (1991) ID2-of-3 algorithm, forms trees that use m-of-n expressions for its splits. An m-of-n expression is a Boolean expression that is specified by an integer threshold, m, and a set of n Boolean conditions. An m-of-n expression is satisfied when at least m of its n conditions are satisfied. For example, suppose we have three Boolean features, a, b, and c; the m-of-n expression 2-of-$\{a, \neg b, c\}$ is logically equivalent to $(a \wedge \neg b) \vee (a \wedge c) \vee (\neg b \wedge c)$.

Split Selection. Split selection involves deciding how to partition the input space at a given internal node in the tree. A limitation of conventional tree-induction algorithms is that the amount of training data used to select splits decreases with the depth of the tree. Thus splits near the bottom of a tree are often poorly chosen because these decisions are based on few training examples. In contrast, because TREPAN has an oracle available, it is able to use as many instances as desired to select each split. TREPAN chooses a split after considering at least S_{min} instances, where S_{min} is a parameter of the algorithm.

When selecting a split at a given node, the oracle is given the list of all of the previously selected splits that lie on the path from the root of the tree to that node. These splits serve as constraints on the feature values that any instance generated by the oracle can take, since any example must satisfy these constraints in order to reach the given node.

Like the ID2-of-3 algorithm, TREPAN uses a hill-climbing search process to construct its m-of-n splits. The search process begins by first selecting the best binary split at the current node; as in C4.5, TREPAN uses the *gain ratio* criterion (Quinlan, 1993) to evaluate candidate splits. For two-valued features, a binary split separates examples according to their values for the feature. For discrete features with more than two values, we consider binary splits based on each allowable value of the feature (e.g., *color=red?*, *color=blue?*, ...). For continuous features, we consider binary splits on thresholds, in the same manner as C4.5. The selected binary split serves as a seed for the m-of-n search process. This greedy search uses the *gain ratio* measure as its heuristic evaluation function, and uses the following two operators (Murphy & Pazzani, 1991):

- m-*of*-$n+1$: Add a new value to the set, and hold the threshold constant. For example, *2-of-*$\{a, b\} \implies$ *2-of-*$\{a, b, c\}$.
- $m+1$-*of*-$n+1$: Add a new value to the set, and increment the threshold. For example, *2-of-*$\{a, b, c\} \implies$ *3-of-*$\{a, b, c, d\}$.

Unlike ID2-of-3, TREPAN constrains m-of-n splits so that the same feature is not used in two or more disjunctive splits which lie on the same path between the root and a leaf of the tree. Without this restriction, the oracle might have to solve difficult satisfiability problems in order create instances for nodes on such a path.

Stopping Criteria. TREPAN uses two separate criteria to decide when to stop growing an extracted decision tree. First, a given node becomes a leaf in the tree if, with high probability, the node covers only instances of a single class. To make this decision, TREPAN determines the proportion of examples, p_c, that fall into the most common class at a given node, and then calculates a confidence interval around this proportion (Hogg & Tanis, 1983). The oracle is queried for additional examples until $prob(p_c < 1 - \epsilon) < \delta$, where ϵ and δ are parameters of the algorithm.

TREPAN also accepts a parameter that specifies a limit on the number of internal nodes in an extracted tree. This parameter can be used to control the comprehensibility of extracted trees, since in some domains, it may require very large trees to describe networks to a high level of fidelity.

3 Empirical Evaluation

In our experiments, we are interested in evaluating the trees extracted by our algorithm according to three criteria: (i) their predictive accuracy; (ii) their comprehensibility; (i) and their fidelity to the networks from which they were extracted. We evaluate TREPAN using four real-world domains: the Congressional voting data set (15 features, 435 examples) and the Cleveland heart-disease data set (13 features, 303 examples) from the UC-Irvine database; a promoter data set (57 features, 468 examples) which is a more complex superset of the UC-Irvine one; and a data set in which the task is to recognize protein-coding regions in DNA (64 features, 20,000 examples) (Craven & Shavlik, 1993b). We remove the `physician-fee-freeze` feature from the voting data set to make the problem more difficult. We conduct our experiments using a 10-fold cross validation methodology, except for in the protein-coding domain. Because of certain domain-specific characteristics of this data set, we use 4-fold cross-validation for our experiments with it.

We measure accuracy and fidelity on the examples in the test sets. Whereas accuracy is defined as the percentage of test-set examples that are correctly classified, *fidelity* is defined as the percentage of test-set examples on which the classification

Table 2: Test-set accuracy and fidelity.

domain	accuracy				fidelity
	networks	C4.5	ID2-of-3	TREPAN	TREPAN
heart	84.5%	71.0%	74.6%	81.8%	94.1%
promoters	90.6	84.4	83.5	87.6	85.7
protein coding	94.1	90.3	90.9	91.4	92.4
voting	92.2	89.2	87.8	90.8	95.9

made by a tree agrees with its neural-network counterpart. Since the comprehensibility of a decision tree is problematic to measure, we measure the syntactic complexity of trees and take this as being representative of their comprehensibility. Specifically, we measure the complexity of each tree in two ways: (i) the number of internal (i.e., non-leaf) nodes in the tree, and (ii) the number of *symbols* used in the splits of the tree. We count an ordinary, single-feature split as one symbol. We count an m-of-n split as n symbols, since such a split lists n feature values.

The neural networks we use in our experiments have a single layer of hidden units. The number of hidden units used for each network (0, 5, 10, 20 or 40) is chosen using cross validation on the network's training set, and we use a validation set to decide when to stop training networks. TREPAN is applied to each saved network. The parameters of TREPAN are set as follows for all runs: at least 1000 instances (training examples plus queries) are considered before selecting each split; we set the ϵ and δ parameters, which are used for the stopping-criterion procedure, to 0.05; and the maximum tree size is set to 15 internal nodes, which is the size of a complete binary tree of depth four.

As baselines for comparison, we also run Quinlan's (1993) C4.5 algorithm, and Murphy and Pazzani's (1991) ID2-of-3 algorithm on the same testbeds. Recall that ID2-of-3 is similar to C4.5, except that it learns trees that use m-of-n splits. We use C4.5's pruning method for both algorithms and use cross validation to select pruning levels for each training set. The cross-validation runs evaluate unpruned trees and trees pruned with confidence levels ranging from 10% to 90%.

Table 2 shows the test-set accuracy results for our experiments. It can be seen that, for every data set, neural networks generalize better than the decision trees learned by C4.5 and ID2-of-3. The decision trees extracted from the networks by TREPAN are also more accurate than the C4.5 and ID2-of-3 trees in all domains. The differences in accuracy between the neural networks and the two conventional decision-tree algorithms (C4.5 and ID2-of-3) are statistically significant for all four domains at the 0.05 level using a paired, two-tailed t-test. We also test the significance of the accuracy differences between TREPAN and the other decision-tree algorithms. Except for the promoter domain, these differences are also statistically significant. The results in this table indicate that, for a range of interesting tasks, our algorithm is able to extract decision trees which are more accurate than decision trees induced strictly from the training data.

Table 2 also shows the test-set fidelity measurements for the TREPAN trees. These results indicate that the trees extracted by TREPAN provide close approximations to their respective neural networks.

Table 3 shows tree-complexity measurements for C4.5, ID2-of-3, and TREPAN. For all four data sets, the trees learned by TREPAN have fewer internal nodes than the trees produced by C4.5 and ID2-of-3. In most cases, the trees produced by TREPAN and ID2-of-3 use more symbols than C4.5, since their splits are more

Table 3: Tree complexity.

domain	# internal nodes			# symbols		
	C4.5	ID2-of-3	TREPAN	C4.5	ID2-of-3	TREPAN
heart	17.5	15.7	11.8	17.5	48.8	20.8
promoters	11.2	12.6	9.2	11.2	47.5	23.8
protein coding	155.0	66.0	10.0	155.0	455.3	36.0
voting	20.1	19.2	11.2	20.1	77.3	20.8

complex. However, for most of the data sets, the TREPAN trees and the C4.5 trees are comparable in terms of their symbol complexity. For all data sets, the ID2-of-3 trees are more complex than the TREPAN trees. Based on these results, we argue that the trees extracted by TREPAN are as comprehensible as the trees learned by conventional decision-tree algorithms.

4 Discussion and Conclusions

In the previous section, we evaluated our algorithm along the dimensions of fidelity, syntactic complexity, and accuracy. Another advantage of our approach is its generality. Unlike numerous other extraction methods (Hayashi, 1991; McMillan et al., 1992; Craven & Shavlik, 1993a; Sethi et al., 1993; Tan, 1994; Tchoumatchenko & Ganascia, 1994; Alexander & Mozer, 1995; Setiono & Liu, 1995), the TREPAN algorithm does not place any requirements on either the architecture of the network or its training method. TREPAN simply uses the network as a black box to answer queries during the extraction process. In fact, TREPAN could be used to extract decision-trees from other types of opaque learning systems, such as nearest-neighbor classifiers.

There are several existing algorithms which do not require special network architectures or training procedures (Saito & Nakano, 1988; Fu, 1991; Gallant, 1993). These algorithms, however, assume that each hidden unit in a network can be accurately approximated by a threshold unit. Additionally, these algorithms do not extract m-of-n rules, but instead extract only conjunctive rules. In previous work (Craven & Shavlik, 1994; Towell & Shavlik, 1993), we have shown that this type of algorithm produces rule-sets which typically are far too complex to be comprehensible. Thrun (1995) has developed a general method for rule extraction, and has described how his algorithm can be used to *verify* that an m-of-n rule is consistent with a network, but he has not developed a rule-searching method that is able to find concise rule sets. A strength of our algorithm, in contrast, is its scalability. We have demonstrated that our algorithm is able to produce succinct decision-tree descriptions of large networks in domains with large input spaces.

In summary, a significant limitation of neural networks is that their concept representations are usually not amenable to human understanding. We have presented an algorithm that is able to produce comprehensible descriptions of trained networks by extracting decision trees that accurately describe the networks' concept representations. We believe that our algorithm, which takes advantage of the fact that a trained network can be queried, represents a promising advance towards the goal of general methods for understanding the solutions encoded by trained networks.

Acknowledgements

This research was partially supported by ONR grant N00014-93-1-0998.

References

Alexander, J. A. & Mozer, M. C. (1995). Template-based algorithms for connectionist rule extraction. In Tesauro, G., Touretzky, D., & Leen, T., editors, *Advances in Neural Information Processing Systems (volume 7)*. MIT Press.

Breiman, L., Friedman, J., Olshen, R., & Stone, C. (1984). *Classification and Regression Trees*. Wadsworth and Brooks, Monterey, CA.

Craven, M. & Shavlik, J. (1993a). Learning symbolic rules using artificial neural networks. In *Proc. of the 10th International Conference on Machine Learning*, (pp. 73–80), Amherst, MA. Morgan Kaufmann.

Craven, M. W. & Shavlik, J. W. (1993b). Learning to predict reading frames in *E. coli* DNA sequences. In *Proc. of the 26th Hawaii International Conference on System Sciences*, (pp. 773–782), Wailea, HI. IEEE Press.

Craven, M. W. & Shavlik, J. W. (1994). Using sampling and queries to extract rules from trained neural networks. In *Proc. of the 11th International Conference on Machine Learning*, (pp. 37–45), New Brunswick, NJ. Morgan Kaufmann.

Fu, L. (1991). Rule learning by searching on adapted nets. In *Proc. of the 9th National Conference on Artificial Intelligence*, (pp. 590–595), Anaheim, CA. AAAI/MIT Press.

Gallant, S. I. (1993). *Neural Network Learning and Expert Systems*. MIT Press.

Hayashi, Y. (1991). A neural expert system with automated extraction of fuzzy if-then rules. In Lippmann, R., Moody, J., & Touretzky, D., editors, *Advances in Neural Information Processing Systems (volume 3)*. Morgan Kaufmann, San Mateo, CA.

Hogg, R. V. & Tanis, E. A. (1983). *Probability and Statistical Inference*. MacMillan.

McMillan, C., Mozer, M. C., & Smolensky, P. (1992). Rule induction through integrated symbolic and subsymbolic processing. In Moody, J., Hanson, S., & Lippmann, R., editors, *Advances in Neural Information Processing Systems (volume 4)*. Morgan Kaufmann.

Murphy, P. M. & Pazzani, M. J. (1991). ID2-of-3: Constructive induction of M-of-N concepts for discriminators in decision trees. In *Proc. of the 8th International Machine Learning Workshop*, (pp. 183–187), Evanston, IL. Morgan Kaufmann.

Quinlan, J. (1993). *C4.5: Programs for Machine Learning*. Morgan Kaufmann.

Saito, K. & Nakano, R. (1988). Medical diagnostic expert system based on PDP model. In *Proc. of the IEEE International Conference on Neural Networks*, (pp. 255–262), San Diego, CA. IEEE Press.

Sethi, I. K., Yoo, J. H., & Brickman, C. M. (1993). Extraction of diagnostic rules using neural networks. In *Proc. of the 6th IEEE Symposium on Computer-Based Medical Systems*, (pp. 217–222), Ann Arbor, MI. IEEE Press.

Setiono, R. & Liu, H. (1995). Understanding neural networks via rule extraction. In *Proc. of the 14th International Joint Conference on Artificial Intelligence*, (pp. 480–485), Montreal, Canada.

Silverman, B. W. (1986). *Density Estimation for Statistics and Data Analysis*. Chapman and Hall.

Tan, A.-H. (1994). Rule learning and extraction with self-organizing neural networks. In *Proc. of the 1993 Connectionist Models Summer School*. Erlbaum.

Tchoumatchenko, I. & Ganascia, J.-G. (1994). A Bayesian framework to integrate symbolic and neural learning. In *Proc. of the 11th International Conference on Machine Learning*, (pp. 302–308), New Brunswick, NJ. Morgan Kaufmann.

Thrun, S. (1995). Extracting rules from artificial neural networks with distributed representations. In Tesauro, G., Touretzky, D., & Leen, T., editors, *Advances in Neural Information Processing Systems (volume 7)*. MIT Press.

Towell, G. & Shavlik, J. (1993). Extracting refined rules from knowledge-based neural networks. *Machine Learning*, 13(1):71–101.

Harmony Networks Do Not Work

René Gourley
School of Computing Science
Simon Fraser University
Burnaby, B.C., V5A 1S6, Canada
gourley@mprgate.mpr.ca

Abstract

Harmony networks have been proposed as a means by which connectionist models can perform symbolic computation. Indeed, proponents claim that a harmony network can be built that constructs parse trees for strings in a context free language. This paper shows that harmony networks do not work in the following sense: they construct many outputs that are not valid parse trees.

In order to show that the notion of systematicity is compatible with connectionism, Paul Smolensky, Geraldine Legendre and Yoshiro Miyata (Smolensky, Legendre, and Miyata 1992; Smolensky 1993; Smolensky, Legendre, and Miyata 1994) proposed a mechanism, "Harmony Theory," by which connectionist models purportedly perform structure sensitive operations without implementing classical algorithms. Harmony theory describes a "harmony network" which, in the course of reaching a stable equilibrium, apparently computes parse trees that are valid according to the rules of a particular context-free grammar.

Harmony networks consist of four major components which will be explained in detail in Section 1. The four components are,

Tensor Representation: A means to interpret the activation vector of a connectionist system as a parse tree for a string in a context-free language.

Harmony: A function that maps all possible parse trees to the non-positive integers so that a parse tree is valid if and only if its harmony is zero.

Energy: A function that maps the set of activation vectors to the real numbers and which is minimized by certain connectionist networks[1].

Recursive Construction: A system for determining the weight matrix of a connectionist network so that if its activation vector is interpreted as a parse

---

[1] Smolensky, Legendre and Miyata use the term "harmony" to refer to both energy and harmony. To distinguish between them, we will use the term that is often used to describe the Lyapunov function of dynamic systems, "energy" (see for example Golden 1986).

tree, then the network's energy is the negation of the harmony of that parse tree.

Smolensky et al. contend that, in the process of minimizing their energy values, harmony networks implicitly maximize the harmony of the parse tree represented by their activation vector. Thus, if the harmony network reaches a stable equilibrium where the energy is equal to zero, the parse tree that is represented by the activation vector must be a valid parse tree:

> When the lower-level description of the activation-spreading process satisfies certain mathematical properties, this process can be analyzed on a higher level as the construction of that structure including the given input structure which *maximizes Harmony*. (Smolensky 1993, p848, emphasis is original)

Unfortunately, harmony networks do not work — they do not always construct maximum-harmony parse trees. The problem is that the energy function is defined on the values of the activation vector. By contrast, the harmony function is defined on possible parse trees. Section 2 of this paper shows that these two domains are not equal, that is, there are some activation vectors that do not represent any parse tree.

The recursive construction merely guarantees that the energy function passes through zero at the appropriate points; its minima are unrestricted. So, while it may be the case that the energy and harmony functions are negations of one another, it is not always the case that a local minimum of one is a local maximum of the other. More succinctly, the harmony network will find minima that are not even trees, let alone valid parse trees.

The reason why harmony networks do not work is straightforward. Section 3 shows that the weight matrix must have only negative eigenvalues, for otherwise the network constructs structures which are not valid trees. Section 4 shows that if the weight matrix has only negative eigenvalues, then the energy function admits only a single zero — the origin. Furthermore, we show that the origin cannot be interpreted as a valid parse tree. Thus, the stable points of a harmony network are not valid parse trees.

1 HARMONY NETWORKS

1.1 TENSOR REPRESENTATION

Harmony theory makes use of tensor products (Smolensky 1990; Smolensky, Legendre, and Miyata 1992; Legendre, Miyata, and Smolensky 1991) to convolve symbols with their roles. The resulting products are then added to represent a labelled tree using the harmony network's activation vector. The particular tensor product used is very simple:

$$(a_1, a_2, \ldots, a_n) \otimes (b_1, b_2, \ldots, b_m) =$$
$$(a_1 b_1, a_1 b_2, \ldots, a_1 b_m, a_2 b_1, a_2 b_2, \ldots, a_2 b_m, \ldots, a_n b_m)$$

If two tensors of differing dimensions are to be added, then they are essentially concatenated.

Binary trees are represented with this tensor product using the following recursive rules:

1. The tensor representation of a tree containing no vertices is 0.

Table 1: Rules for determining harmony and the weight matrix. Let $G = (V, \Sigma, P, S)$ be a context-free grammar of the type suggested in section 1.2. The rules for determining the harmony of a tree labelled with V and Σ are shown in the second column. The rules for determining the system of equations for recursive construction are shown in the third column. (Smolensky, Legendre, and Miyata 1992; Smolensky 1993)

Grammar Element	Harmony Rule	Energy Equation
S	For every node labelled S add -1 to $H(T)$.	Include $(S+\vec{0}\otimes r_l)W_{root}(S+\vec{0}\otimes r_l) = 2$ in the system of equations
$x \in \Sigma$	For every node labelled x add -1 to $H(T)$.	Include $(x+\vec{0}\otimes r_l)W_{root}(x+\vec{0}\otimes r_l) = 2$ in the system of equations
$x \in V \setminus \{S\}$	For every node labelled x add -2 or -3 to $H(T)$ depending on whether or not x appears on the left of a production with two symbols on the right.	Include $(x+\vec{0}\otimes r_l)W_{root}(x+\vec{0}\otimes r_l) = 4$ or 6 in the system of equations, depending on whether or not x appears on the left of a production with two symbols on the right.
$x \to yz$ or $x \to y \in P$	For every edge where x is the parent and y is the left child add 2. Similarly, add 2 every time z is the right child of x.	Include in the system of equations, $(x+\vec{0}\otimes r_l)W_{root}(\vec{0}+y\otimes r_l) = -2$ $(\vec{0}+y\otimes r_l)W_{root}(x+\vec{0}\otimes r_l) = -2$ $(x+\vec{0}\otimes r_l)W_{root}(\vec{0}+z\otimes r_l) = -2$ $(\vec{0}+z\otimes r_l)W_{root}(x+\vec{0}\otimes r_l) = -2$

2. If A is the root of a tree, and T_L, T_R are the tensor product representations of its left subtree and right subtree respectively, then $A + T_L \otimes r_l + T_R \otimes r_r$ is the tensor representation of the whole tree.

The vectors, r_l, and r_r are called "role vectors" and indicate the roles of left child and right child.

1.2 HARMONY

Harmony (Legendre, Miyata, and Smolensky 1990; Smolensky, Legendre, and Miyata 1992) describes a way to determine the well-formedness of a potential parse tree with respect to a particular context free grammar. Without loss of generality, we can assume that the right-hand side of each production has at most two symbols, and if a production has two symbols on the right, then it is the only production for the variable on its left side. For a given binary tree, T, we compute the harmony of T, $H(T)$ by first adding the negative contributions of all the nodes according to their labels, and then adding the contributions of the edges (see first two columns of table 1).

1.3 ENERGY

Under certain conditions, some connectionist models are known to admit the following energy or Lyapunov function (see Legendre, Miyata, and Smolensky 1991):

$$E(a) = -\frac{1}{2}a^t W a$$

Here, W is the weight matrix of the connectionist network, and a is its activation vector. Every non-equilibrium change in the activation vector results in a strict decrease in the network's energy. In effect, the connectionist network serves to minimize its energy as it moves towards equilibrium.

1.4 RECURSIVE CONSTRUCTION

Smolensky, Legendre, and Miyata (1992) proposed that the recursive structure of their tensor representations together with the local nature of the harmony calculation could be used to construct the weight matrix for a network whose energy function is the negation of the harmony of the tree represented by the activation vector. First construct a matrix W_{root} which satisfies a system of equations. The system of equations is found by including equations for every symbol and production in the grammar, as shown in column three of table 1. Gourley (1995) shows that if W is constructed from copies of W_{root} according to a particular formula, and if a_T is a tensor representation for a tree, T, then $E(a_T) = -H(T)$.

2 SOME ACTIVATIONS ARE NOT TREES

As noted above, the reason why harmony networks do not work is that they seek minima in their state space which may not coincide with parse tree representations. One way to amelioarate this would be to make every possible activation vector represent some parse tree. If every activation vector represents some parse tree, then the rules that determine the weight matrix will ensure that the energy minima agree with the valid parse trees. Unfortunately, in that case, the system of equations used to determine W_{root} has no solution.

If every activation vector is to represent some parse tree, and the symbols of the grammar are two dimensional, then there are symbols represented by each vector, $(x_1, x_1), (x_1, x_2), (x_2, x_1)$, and (x_2, x_2), where $x_1 \neq x_2$. These symbols must satisfy the equations given in table 1, and so,

$$\left. \begin{array}{rcl} x_1^2(W_{root_{11}} + W_{root_{12}} + W_{root_{21}} + W_{root_{22}}) &=& h_1 \\ x_1^2 W_{root_{11}} + x_1 x_2 W_{root_{12}} + x_1 x_2 W_{root_{21}} + x_2^2 W_{root_{22}} &=& h_2 \\ x_2^2 W_{root_{11}} + x_1 x_2 W_{root_{12}} + x_1 x_2 W_{root_{21}} + x_1^2 W_{root_{22}} &=& h_3 \\ x_2^2(W_{root_{11}} + W_{root_{12}} + W_{root_{21}} + W_{root_{22}}) &=& h_4 \end{array} \right\} \text{where } h_i \in \{2, 4, 6\}$$

Because $h_i \in \{2, 4, 6\}$, there must be a pair h_i, h_j which are equal. In that case, it can be shown using Gaussian elimination that there is no solution for $W_{root_{11}}, W_{root_{12}}, W_{root_{21}}, W_{root_{22}}$. Similarly, if the symbols are represented by vectors of dimension three or greater, the same contradiction occurs.

Thus there are some activation vectors that do not represent any tree — valid or invalid. The question now becomes one of determining whether all of the harmony network's stable equilibria are valid parse trees.

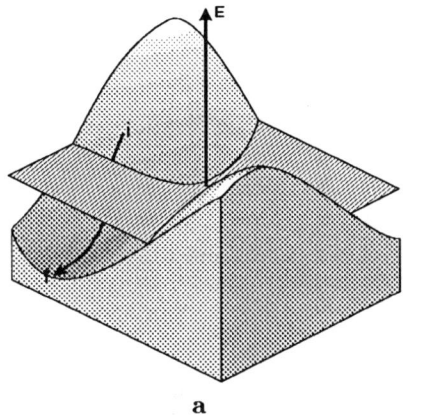 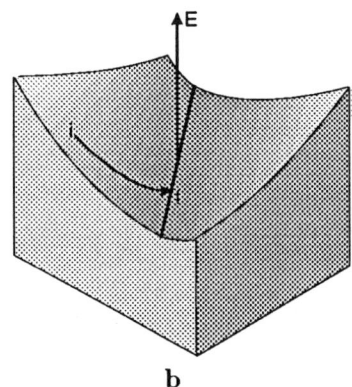

a b

Figure 1: Energy functions of two-dimensional harmony networks. In each case, the points i and f respectively represent an initial and a final state of the network. In **a**, one eigenvector is positive and the other is negative; the hashed plane represents the plane $E = 0$ which intersects the energy function and the vertical axis at the origin. In **b**, one eigenvalue is negative while the other is zero; The heavy line represents the intersection of the surface with the plane $E = 0$ and it intersects the vertical axis at the origin.

3 NON-NEGATIVE EIGENVECTORS YIELD NON-TREES

If any of the eigenvalues of the weight matrix, W, is positive, then it is easy to show that the harmony network will seek a stable equilibrium that does not represent a parse tree at all. Let $\lambda > 0$ be a positive eigenvalue of W, and let e be an eigenvector, corresponding to λ, that falls within the state space. Then,

$$E(e) = -\frac{1}{2}e^t W e = -\frac{1}{2}\lambda e^t e < 0.$$

Because the energy drops below zero, the harmony network would have to undergo an energy increase in order to find a zero-energy stable equilibrium. This cannot happen, and so, the network reaches an equilibrium with energy strictly less than zero.

Figure 1a illustrates the energy function of a harmony network where one eigenvalue is positive. Because harmony is the negation of energy, in this figure all the valid parse trees rest on the hashed plane, and all the invalid parse trees are above it. As we can see, the harmony network with positive eigenvalues will certainly find stable equilibria which are not valid parse tree representations.

Now, suppose W, the weight matrix, has a zero eigenvalue. If e is an eigenvector corresponding to that eigenvalue, then for every real α, $\alpha W e = 0$. Consequently, one of the following must be true:

1. αe is not a stable equilibrium. In that case, the energy function must drop below zero, yielding a sub-zero stable equilibrium — a stable equilibrium that does not represent any tree.

2. αe is a stable equilibrium. Then for every α, αe must be a valid tree representation. Such a situation is represented in fig-

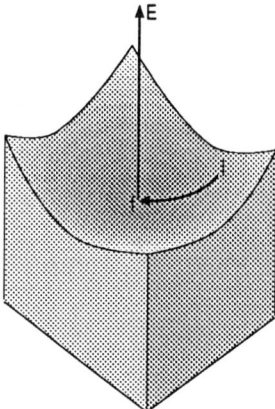

Figure 2: The energy function of a two-dimensional harmony network where both eigenvalues are negative. The vertical axis pierces the surface at the origin, and the points i and f respectively represent an initial and a final state of the network.

ure 1b where the set of all points αe is represented by the heavy line. This implies that there is a symbol, $(a_1, a_2, \ldots, a_n)$, such that $\alpha_1(a_1, a_2, \ldots, a_n), \alpha_2(a_1, a_2, \ldots, a_n), \ldots, \alpha_{n^2+1}(a_1, a_2, \ldots, a_n)$ are also all symbols. As before, this implies that W_{root} must satisfy the equation,

$$((a_1, \ldots, a_n) + \vec{0} \otimes r_l)^t W_{root}((a_1, \ldots, a_n) + \vec{0} \otimes r_l) = \frac{h_i}{\alpha_i^2}, \quad h_i \in \{2, 4, 6\}$$

for $i = 1 \ldots n^2 + 1$. Again using Gaussian elimination, it can be shown that there is no solution to this system of equations.

In either case, the harmony network admits stable equilibria that do not represent any tree. Thus, the eigenvalues must all be negative.

4 NEGATIVE EIGENVECTORS YIELD NON-TREES

If all the eigenvalues of the weight matrix are negative, then the energy function has a very special shape: it is a paraboloid centered on the origin and concave in the direction of positive energy. This is easily seen by considering the first and second derivatives of E:

$$\frac{\partial E(\vec{x})}{\partial x_i} = -\sum_j W_{i,j} x_i \qquad \frac{\partial^2 E(\vec{x})}{\partial x_i \partial x_j} = -W_{i,j}$$

Clearly, all the first derivatives are zero at the origin, and so, it is a critical point. Now the origin is a strict minimum if all the roots of the following well-known equation are positive:

$$0 = \det \begin{vmatrix} \frac{\partial^2 E(\vec{x})}{\partial x_1 \partial x_1} - \lambda & \frac{\partial^2 E(\vec{x})}{\partial x_1 \partial x_2} & \cdots \\ \frac{\partial^2 E(\vec{x})}{\partial x_2 \partial x_1} & \frac{\partial^2 E(\vec{x})}{\partial x_1 \partial x_2} - \lambda & \\ \vdots & & \ddots \end{vmatrix} = \det |-W - \lambda I|$$

$\det |-W - \lambda I|$ is the characteristic polynomial of $-W$. If λ is a root then it is an eigenvalue of $-W$, or equivalently, it is the negative of an eigenvalue of W. Because all of W's eigenvalues are negative, the origin is a strict minimum, and indeed it is the only minimum. Such a harmony network is illustrated in Figure 2.

Thus the origin is the only stable point where the energy is zero, but it cannot represent a parse tree which is valid for the grammar. If it does, then

$$S + T_L \otimes r_l + T_R \otimes r_r = (0, \ldots, 0)$$

where T_L, T_R are appropriate left and right subtree representations, and S is the start symbol of the grammar. Because each of the subtrees is multiplied by either r_l or r_r, they are not the same dimension as S, and are consequently concatenated instead of added. Therefore $S = \vec{0}$. But then, W_{root} must satisfy the equation

$$(\vec{0} + \vec{0} \otimes r_l) W_{root} (\vec{0} + \vec{0} \otimes r_l) = -2$$

This is impossible, and so, the origin is not a valid tree representation.

5 CONCLUSION

This paper has shown that in every case, a harmony network will reach stable equilibria that are not valid parse trees. This is not unexpected. Because the energy function is a very simple function, it would be more surprising if such a connectionist system could construct complicated structures such as parse trees for a context free grammar.

Acknowledgements

The author thanks Dr. Robert Hadley and Dr. Arvind Gupta, both of Simon Fraser University, for their invaluable comments on a draft of this paper.

References

Golden, R. (1986). The 'brain-state-in-a-box' neural model is a gradient descent algorithm. *Journal of Mathematical Psychology 30*, 73–80.

Gourley, R. (1995). Tensor represenations and harmony theory: A critical analysis. Master's thesis, Simon Fraser University, Burnaby, Canada. In preparation.

Legendre, G., Y. Miyata, and P. Smolensky (1990). Harmonic grammar – a formal multi-level connectionist theory of linguistic well-formedness: Theoretical foundations. In *Proceedings of the Twelfth National Conference on Cognitive Science*, Cambridge, MA, pp. 385–395. Lawrence Erlbaum.

Legendre, G., Y. Miyata, and P. Smolensky (1991). Distributedrecursive structure processing. In B. Mayoh (Ed.), *Proceedings of the 1991 Scandinavian Conference on Artificial Intelligence*, Amsterdam, pp. 47–53. IOS Press.

Smolensky, P. (1990). Tensor product variable binding and the representation of symbolic structures in connectionist systems. *Artificial Intelligence 46*, 159–216.

Smolensky, P. (1993). Harmonic grammars for formal languages. In S. Hanson, J. Cowan, and C. Giles (Eds.), *Advances in Neural Information Processing Systems 5*, pp. 847–854. San Mateo: Morgan Kauffman.

Smolensky, P., G. Legendre, and Y. Miyata (1992). Principles for an integrated connectionist/symbolic theory of higher cognition. Technical Report CU-CS-600-92, University of Colorado Computer Science Department.

Smolensky, P., G. Legendre, and Y. Miyata (1994). Integrating connectionist and symbolic computation for the theory of language. In V. Honavar and L. Uhr (Eds.), *Artificial Intelligence and Neural Networks: Steps Toward Principled Integration*, pp. 509–530. Boston: Academic Press.

Dynamics of Attention as Near Saddle-Node Bifurcation Behavior

Hiroyuki Nakahara*
General Systems Studies
University of Tokyo
3-8-1 Komaba, Meguro
Tokyo 153, Japan
nakahara@vermeer.c.u-tokyo.ac.jp

Kenji Doya
ATR Human Information Processing
Research Laboratories
2-2 Hikaridai, Seika, Soraku
Kyoto 619-02, Japan
doya@hip.atr.co.jp

Abstract

In consideration of attention as a means for goal-directed behavior in non-stationary environments, we argue that the dynamics of attention should satisfy two opposing demands: long-term maintenance and quick transition. These two characteristics are contradictory within the linear domain. We propose the near saddle-node bifurcation behavior of a sigmoidal unit with self-connection as a candidate of dynamical mechanism that satisfies both of these demands. We further show in simulations of the 'bug-eat-food' tasks that the near saddle-node bifurcation behavior of recurrent networks can emerge as a functional property for survival in non-stationary environments.

1 INTRODUCTION

Most studies of attention have focused on the selection process of incoming sensory cues (Posner et al., 1980; Koch et al., 1985; Desimone et al., 1995). Emphasis was placed on the phenomena of causing different percepts for the same sensory stimuli. However, the selection of sensory input itself is not the final goal of attention. We consider attention as a means for goal-directed behavior and survival of the animal. In this view, dynamical properties of attention are crucial. While attention has to be maintained long enough to enable robust response to sensory input, it also has to be shifted quickly to a novel cue that is potentially important. Long-term maintenance and quick transition are critical requirements for attention dynamics.

---

*currently at Dept. of Cognitive Science and Institute for Neural Computation, U. C. San Diego, La Jolla CA 92093-0515. hnakahar@cogsci.ucsd.edu

We investigate a possible neural mechanism that enables those dynamical characteristics of attention.

First, we analyze the dynamics of a network of sigmoidal units with self-connections. We show that both long-term maintenance and quick transition can be achieved when the system parameters are near a "saddle-node bifurcation" point. Then, we test if such a dynamical mechanism can actually be helpful for an autonomously behaving agent in simulations of a 'bug-eat-food' task. The result indicates that near saddle-node bifurcation behavior can emerge in the course of evolution for survival in non-stationary environments.

2 NEAR SADDLE-NODE BIFURCATION BEHAVIOR

When a pulse-like input is given to a linear system, the rising and falling phases of the response have the same time constants. This means that long-term maintenance and quick transition cannot be simultaneously achieved by linear dynamics. Therefore, it is essential to consider a nonlinear dynamical mechanism to achieve these two demands.

2.1 DYNAMICS OF A SELF-RECURRENT UNIT

First, we consider the dynamics of a single sigmoidal unit with the self-connection weight a and the bias b.

$$y(t+1) = F(ay(t) + b), \tag{1}$$

$$F(x) = \frac{1}{1 + \exp(-x)}. \tag{2}$$

The parameters (a, b) determine the qualitative behavior of the system such as the number of fixed points and their stabilities. As we change the parameters, the qualitative behavior of the system may suddenly change. This is referred to as "bifurcation" (Guckenheimer, et al., 1983). A typical example is a "saddle-node bifurcation" in which a pair of fixed points, one stable and one unstable, emerges. In our system, this occurs when the state transition curve $y(t+1) = F(ay(t)+b)$ is tangent to $y(t+1) = y(t)$. Let y^* be this point of tangency. We have the following condition for saddle-node bifurcation.

$$F(ay^* + b) = y^* \tag{3}$$

$$\left.\frac{dF(ay+b)}{dy}\right|_{y=y^*} = 1 \tag{4}$$

These equations can be solved, by noting $F'(x) = F(x)(1 - F(x))$, as

$$a = \frac{1}{y^*(1 - y^*)} \tag{5}$$

$$b = F^{-1}(y^*) - ay^* = F^{-1}(y^*) - \frac{1}{1 - y^*} \tag{6}$$

By changing the fixed point value y^* between 0 and 1, we can plot a curve in the parameter space (a, b) on which saddle-node bifurcation occurs, as shown in Figure 1 (left). A pair of a saddle point and a stable fixed point emerges or disappears when the parameters pass across the cusp like curve (cases 2 and 4). The system has only one stable fixed point when the parameters are outside the cusp (case 1) and three fixed points inside the cusp (case 3).

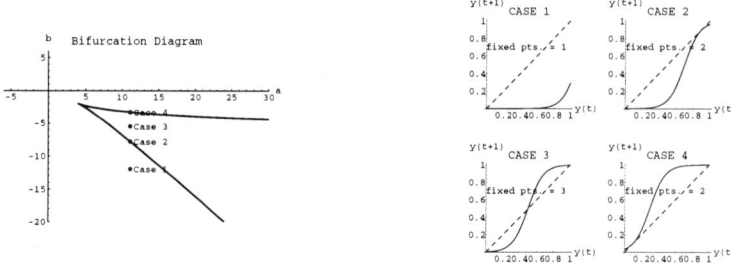

Figure 1: Bifurcation Diagram of a Self-Recurrent Unit. Left: the curve in the parameter space (a, b) on which saddle-node bifurcation is seen. Right: state transition diagrams for four different cases.

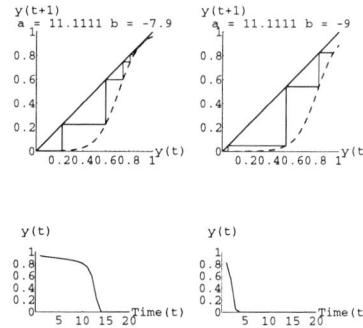

Figure 2: Temporal Responses of Self-Recurrent Units. Left: near saddle-node bifurcation. Right: far from bifurcation.

An interesting behavior can be seen when the parameters are just outside the cusp, as shown in Figure 2 (left). The system has only one fixed point near $y = 0$, but once the unit is activated ($y \simeq 1$), it stays "on" for many time steps and then goes back to the fixed point quickly. Such a mechanism may be useful in satisfying the requirements of attention dynamics: long-term maintenance and quick transition.

2.2 NETWORK OF SELF-RECURRENT UNITS

Next, we consider the dynamics of a network of the above self-recurrent units.

$$y_i(t+1) = F[ay_i(t) + b + \sum_{j, j \neq i} c_{ij} y_j(t) + d_i u_i(t)], \qquad (7)$$

where a is the self connection weight, b is the bias, c_{ij} is the cross connection weight, and d_i is the input connection weight, and $u_i(t)$ is the external input. The effect of lateral and external inputs is equivalent to the change in the bias, which slides the sigmoid curve horizontally without changing the slope.

For example, one parameter set of the bifurcation at $y^* = 0.9$ is $a = 11.11$ and $b \simeq -7.80$. Let $b = -7.90$ so that the unit has a near saddle-node bifurcation behavior when there is no lateral or external inputs. For a fixed $a = 11.11$, as we increase b, the qualitative behavior of the system appears as case 3 in Figure 1, and

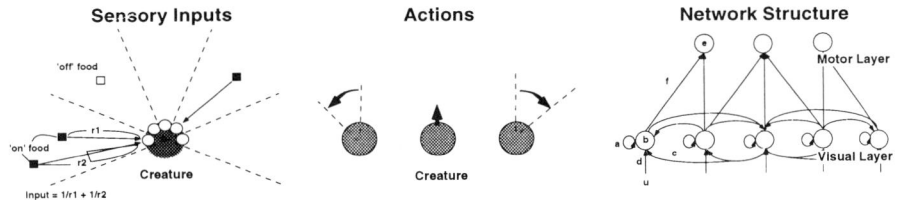

Figure 3: A Creature's Sensory Inputs(Left), Motor System(Center) and Network Architecture(Right)

then, it changes again at $b \simeq -3.31$, where the fixed point at $y = 0.1$, or another bifurcation point, appears as case 4 in Figure 1. Therefore, if the input sum is large enough, i.e. $\sum_{j, j \neq i} c_{ij} y_j + d_i u_j > -3.31 - (-7.90) \simeq 4.59$, the lower fixed point at $y = 0.1$ disappears and the state jumps up to the upper fixed point near $y = 1$, quickly turning the unit "on". If the lateral connections are set properly, this can in turn suppress the activation of other units. Once the external input goes away, as we see in Figure 2 (left), the state stays "on" for a long time until it returns to the fixed point near $y = 0$.

3 EVOLUTION OF NEAR BIFURCATION DYNAMICS

In the above section, we have theoretically shown the potential usefulness of near saddle-node bifurcation behavior for satisfying demands for attention dynamics. We further hypothesize that such behavior is indeed useful in animal behaviors and can be found in the course of learning and evolution of the neural system.

To test our hypothesis, we simulated a 'bug-eat-food' task. Our purpose in this simulation was to see whether the attention dynamics discussed in the previous section would help obtain better performance in a non-stationary environment. We used evolutionary programming (Fogel et al, 1990) to optimize the performance of recurrent networks and feedforward networks.

3.1 THE BUG AND THE WORLD

In our simulation, a simple creature traveled around a non-stationary environment. In the world, there were a certain number of food items. Each item was fixed at a certain place in the world but appeared or disappeared in a stochastic fashion, as determined by a two-state Markov system. In order to survive, A creature looked for food by traveling the world. The amount of food a creature found in a certain time period was the measure of its performance.

A creature had five sensory inputs, each of which detected food in the sector of 45 degrees (Figure 3, right). Its output level was given by $\sum_j \frac{1}{r_j}$, where r_j was the distance to the j-th food item within the sector. Note that the format of the input contained information about distance and also that the creature could only receive the amount of the input but could not distinguish each food from others.

For the sake of simplicity, we assumed that the creature lived in a grid-like world. On each time step, it took one of three motor commands: L: turn left (45 degrees),

Density of Food	0.05		0.10	
Markov Transition Matrix of each food	.5 .5 .5 .5	.8 .8 .2 .2	.5 .5 .5 .5	.8 .8 .2 .2
Random Walk	7.0	6.9	13.8	13.9
Nearest Visible	42.7	18.6	65.3	32.4
FeedForward	58.6	37.3	84.8	60.0
Recurrent	65.7	43.6	94.0	66.1
Nearest Visible/Invisible	97.7	97.1	129.1	128.8

Table 1: Performances of the Recurrent Network and Other Strategies.

C: step forward, and R: turn right (Figure 3, center). Simulations were run with different Markov transition matrices of food appearance and with different food densities. A creature got the food when it reached the food, whether it was visible or invisible. When a creature ate a food item, a new food item was placed randomly. The size of the world was 10x10 and both ends were connected as a torus.

A creature was composed of two layers: visual layer and motor layer (Figure 3, left). There were five units[1] in visual layer, one for each sensory input, and their dynamics were given by Equation (7). The self-connection a, the bias b and the input weight d_i were the same for all units. There were three units in motor layer, each coding one of three motor commands, and their state was given by

$$x_k(t) = e_k + \sum_i f_{ki} y_i(t), \qquad (8)$$

$$p_k(t) = \frac{\exp(x_k(t))}{\sum_l \exp(x_l(t))}, \qquad (9)$$

where e_k was the bias and f_{ki} was the feedforward connection weight.[2] One of the three motor commands (L,C,R) was chosen stochastically with the probability p_k (k=L,C,R). The activation pattern in visual layer was shifted when the creature made a turn, which should give proper mapping between the sensory input and the working memory.

3.2 EVOLUTIONARY PROGRAMMING

Each recurrent network was characterized by the parameters $(a, b, c_{ij}, d_i, e_k, f_{ki})$, some of which were symmetrically shared, e.g. $c_{12} = c_{21}$. For comparison, we also tested feedforward networks where recurrent connections were removed, i.e. $a = c_{ij} = 0$.

A population of 60 creatures was tested on each generation. The initial population was generated with random parameters. Each of the top twenty scoring creatures produced three offspring; one identical copy of the parameters of the parent's and two copies of these parameters with a Gaussian fluctuation. In this paper, we report the result after 60 generations.

3.3 PERFORMANCE

---

[1] We denote each unit in visual layer by u_1, u_2, u_3, u_4, u_5 from the left to the right for the later convenience

[2] In this simulation reported here, we set $e_k = 0$.

Dynamics of Attention as Near Saddle-node Bifurcation Behavior

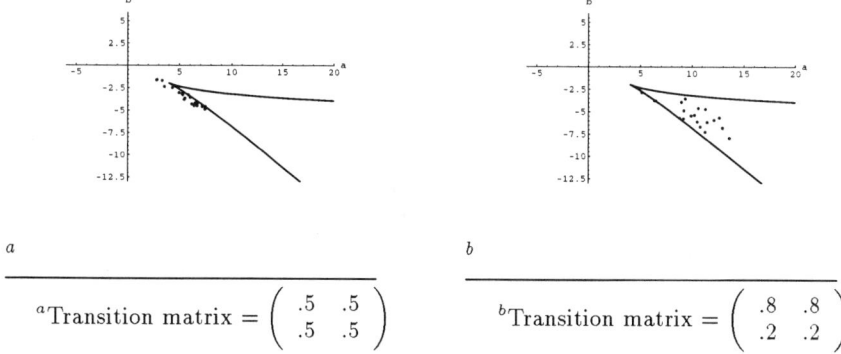

Figure 4: The Convergence of the Parameter of (a, b) by Evolutionary Programming Plotted in the Bifurcation Diagram. The food density is 0.10 in both examples above.

Table 1 shows the average of food found after 60 generations. As a reference of performance level, we also measured the performances of three other simple algorithms: 1) random walk: one of the three motor commands is taken randomly with equal probability. 2) nearest visible: move toward the nearest food visible at the time within the creature's field of view of (u_2, u_3, u_4). 3) nearest visible/invisible: move toward the nearest food within the view of (u_2, u_3, u_4) no matter if it is visible or not, which gives an upper bound of performance.

The performance of recurrent network is better than that of feedforward network and 'nearest visible'. This suggests that the ability of recurrent network to remember the past is advantageous.

The performance of feedforward network is better than that of 'nearest visible'. One reason is that feedforward network could cover a broader area to receive inputs than 'nearest visible'. In addition, two factors, the average time in which a creature reaches the food and the average time in which the food disappears, may influence the performance of feedforward network and 'nearest visible'. Feedforward network could optimize its output to adapt two factors with its broader view in evolution while 'nearest visible' did not have such adaptability.

It should be noted that both of 'nearest visible/invisible' and 'nearest visible' explicitly assumed the higher-order sensory processing: distinguishing each food item from the others and measuring the distance between each food and its body. Since its performance is so different regardless of its higher-order sensory processing, it implies the importance of remembering the past. We can regard recurrent network as compromising two characteristics, remembering the past as 'nearest visible/invisible' did and optimizing the sensitivity as feedforward network did, although recurrent network did not have a perfect memory as 'nearest visible/invisible'.

3.4 CONVERGENCE TO NEAR-BIFURCATION REGIME

We plotted the histogram of the performance in each generation and the history of the performance of a top-scoring creature over generations. Though they are not shown here, the performance was almost optimal after 60 generations.

Figure 4 shows that two examples of a graph in which we plotted the parameter set (a, b) of top twenty scoring creatures in the 60th generation in the bifurcation diagram. In the left graph, we can see the parameter set has converged to a regime that gives a near saddle-node bifurcation behavior. On the other hand, in the right graph, the parameter set has converged into the inside of cusp. It is interesting to note that the area inside of the cusp gives bistable dynamics. Hence, if the input is higher than a repelling point, it goes up and if the input is lower, it goes down. The reason of the convergence to that area is because of the difference of the world setting, that is, a Markov transition matrix. Since food would disappear more quickly and stay invisible longer in the setting of the right graph, it should be beneficial for a creature to remember the direction of higher inputs longer. In most of cases reported in Table 1, we obtained the convergence into our predicted regime and/or the inside of the cusp.

4 DISCUSSION

Near saddle-node bifurcation behavior can have the long-term maintenance and quick transition, which characterize attention dynamics. A recurrent network has better performance than memoryless systems for tasks in our simulated non-stationary environment. Clearly, near saddle-node bifurcation behavior helped a creature's survival and in fact, creatures actually evolved to our expected parameter regime. However, we also obtained the convergence into another unexpected regime which gives bistable dynamics. How the bistable dynamics are used remains to be investigated.

Acknowledgments

H.N. is grateful to Ed Hutchins for his generous support, to John Batali and David Fogel for their advice on the implementation of evolutionary programming and to David Rogers for his comments on the manuscript of this paper.

References

R. Desimone, E. K. Miller, L. Chelazzi, & A. Lueschow. (1995) Multiple Memory Systems in the Visual Cortex. In M. Gazzaniga (ed.), *The Cognitive Neurosciences*, 475-486. MIT Press.

D. B. Fogel, L. J. Fogel, & V. W. Porto. (1990) Evolving Neural Networks. *Biological cybernetics* **63**:487-493.

J. Guckenheimer & P. Homes. (1983) *Nonlinear Oscillations, Dynamical Systems, and Bifurcation of Vector Fields*

C. Koch & S. Ullman. (1985) Shifts in selective visual attention:towards the underlying neural circuitry. *Human Neurobiology* **4**:219-227.

M. Posner, C. .R .R. Snyder, & B. J. Davidson. (1980) Attention and the detection of signals. *Journal of Experimental Psychology: General* **109**:160-174

Rapid Quality Estimation of Neural Network Input Representations

Kevin J. Cherkauer   Jude W. Shavlik
Computer Sciences Department, University of Wisconsin-Madison
1210 W. Dayton St., Madison, WI 53706
{cherkauer,shavlik}@cs.wisc.edu

Abstract

The choice of an input representation for a neural network can have a profound impact on its accuracy in classifying novel instances. However, neural networks are typically computationally expensive to train, making it difficult to test large numbers of alternative representations. This paper introduces fast quality measures for neural network representations, allowing one to quickly and accurately estimate which of a collection of possible representations for a problem is the best. We show that our measures for ranking representations are more accurate than a previously published measure, based on experiments with three difficult, real-world pattern recognition problems.

1 Introduction

A key component of successful artificial neural network (ANN) applications is an input representation that suits the problem. However, ANNs are usually costly to train, preventing one from trying many different representations. In this paper, we address this problem by introducing and evaluating three new measures for quickly estimating ANN input representation quality. Two of these, called *ID3leaves* and *Min(leaves)*, consistently outperform Rendell and Ragavan's (1993) *blurring* measure in accurately ranking different input representations for ANN learning on three difficult, real-world datasets.

2 Representation Quality

Choosing good input representations for supervised learning systems has been the subject of diverse research in both connectionist (Cherkauer & Shavlik, 1994; Kambhatla & Leen, 1994) and symbolic paradigms (Almuallim & Dietterich, 1994;

Caruana & Freitag, 1994; John et al., 1994; Kira & Rendell, 1992). Two factors of representation quality are well-recognized in this work: the ability to separate examples of different classes (*sufficiency* of the representation) and the number of features present (representational *economy*). We believe there is also a third important component that is often overlooked, namely the ease of learning an accurate concept under a given representation, which we call *transparency*. We define transparency as the density of concepts that are both accurate (generalize well) *and* simple (of low complexity) in the space of possible concepts under a given input representation and learning algorithm. Learning an accurate concept will be more likely if the concept space is rich in accurate concepts that are also simple, because simple concepts require less search to find and less data to validate.

In this paper, we introduce fast transparency measures for ANN input representations. These are orders of magnitude faster than the *wrapper* method (John et al., 1994), which would evaluate ANN representations by training and testing the ANNs themselves. Our measures are based on the strong assumption that, for a fixed input representation, information about the density of accurate, simple concepts under a (fast) decision-tree learning algorithm will transfer to the concept space of an ANN learning algorithm. Our experiments on three real-world datasets demonstrate that our transparency measures are highly predictive of representation quality for ANNs, implying that the transfer assumption holds surprisingly well for some pattern recognition tasks even though ANNs and decision trees are believed to work best on quite different types of problems (Quinlan, 1994).[1] In addition, our Exper. 1 shows that transparency does not depend on representational sufficiency. Exper. 2 verifies this conclusion and also demonstrates that transparency does not depend on representational economy. Finally, Exper. 3 examines the effects of redundant features on the transparency measures, demonstrating that the *ID3leaves* measure is robust in the face of such features.

2.1 Model-Based Transparency Measures

We introduce three new "model-based" measures that estimate representational transparency by sampling instances of roughly accurate concept models from a decision-tree space and measuring their complexities. If simple, accurate models are abundant, the average complexity of the sampled models will be low. If they are sparse, we can expect a higher complexity value.

Our first measure, *avg(leaves)*, estimates the expected complexity of accurate concepts as the average number of leaves in n randomly constructed decision trees that correctly classify the training set:

$$avg(leaves) \equiv \frac{1}{n} \sum_{t=1}^{n} leaves(t)$$

where $leaves(t)$ is the number of leaves in tree t. Random trees are built top-down; features are chosen with uniform probability from those which further partition the training examples (ignoring example class). Tree building terminates when each leaf achieves class purity (i.e., the tree correctly classifies all the training examples). High values of *avg(leaves)* indicate high concept complexity (i.e., low transparency).

The second measure, *min(leaves)*, finds the minimum number of leaves over the n randomly constructed trees instead of the average to reflect the fact that learning systems try to make intelligent, not random, model choices:

$$min(leaves) \equiv \min_{t=1,n} \{leaves(t)\}$$

---

[1] We did not preselect datasets based on whether our experiments upheld the transfer assumption. We report the results for all datasets that we have tested our transparency measures on.

Table 1: Summary of datasets used.

Dataset	Examples	Classes	Cross Validation Folds
DNA	20,000	6	4
NIST	3,471	10	10
Magellan	625	2	4

The third measure, *ID3leaves*, simply counts the number of leaves in the tree grown by Quinlan's (1986) ID3 algorithm:

$$ID3leaves \equiv leaves(ID3\ tree)$$

We always use the full ID3 tree (100% correct on the training set). This measure assumes the complexity of the concept ID3 finds depends on the density of simple, accurate models in its space and thus reflects the true transparency.

All these measures fix tree training-set accuracy at 100%, so simpler trees imply more accurate generalization (Fayyad, 1994) as well as easier learning. This lets us estimate transparency without the multiplicative additional computational expense of cross validating each tree. It also lets us use all the training data for tree building.

2.2 "Blurring" as a Transparency Measure

Rendell and Ragavan (1993) address ease of learning explicitly and present a metric for quantifying it called *blurring*. In their framework, the less a representation requires the use of feature interactions to produce accurate concepts, the more transparent it is. *Blurring* heuristically estimates this by measuring the average information content of a representation's individual features. *Blurring* is equivalent to the (negation of the) average information gain (Quinlan, 1986) of a representation's features with respect to a training set, as we show in Cherkauer and Shavlik (1995).

3 Evaluating the Transparency Measures

We evaluate the transparency measures on three problems: DNA (predicting gene reading frames; Craven & Shavlik, 1993), NIST (recognizing handwritten digits; "F13" distribution), and Magellan (detecting volcanos in radar images of the planet Venus; Burl et al., 1994).[2] The datasets are summarized in Table 1.

To assess the different transparency measures, we follow these steps for each dataset in Exper. 1 and 2:

1. Construct several different input representations for the problem.
2. Train ANNs using each representation and test the resulting generalization accuracy via cross validation (CV). This gives us a (costly) ground-truth ranking of the relative qualities of the different representations.
3. For each transparency measure, compute the transparency score of each representation. This gives us a (cheap) predicted ranking of the representations from each measure.
4. For each transparency measure, compute Spearman's rank correlation coefficient between the ground-truth and predicted rankings. The higher this correlation, the better the transparency measure predicts the true ranking.

---

[2] On these problems, we have found that ANNs generalize 1–6 percentage points better than decision trees using identical input representations, motivating our desire to develop fast measures of ANN input representation quality.

Table 2: User CPU seconds on a Sun SPARCstation 10/30 for the largest representation of each dataset. Parenthesized numbers are standard deviations over 10 runs.

Dataset	Blurring	ID3leaves	Min/Avg(leaves)	Backprop
DNA	1.68 (2.38)	1,245 (3.96)	13,444 (56.25)	212,900
NIST	2.69 (2.31)	221 (2.75)	1,558 (5.00)	501,400
Magellan	0.21 (0.15)	1 (0.07)	12 (0.13)	6,300

In Exper. 3 we rank only two representations at a time, so instead of computing a rank correlation in step 4, we just count the number of pairs ranked correctly.

We created input representations (step 1) with an algorithm we call RS ("Representation Selector"). RS first constructs a large pool of plausible, domain-specific Boolean features (5,460 features for DNA, 251,679 for NIST, 33,876 for Magellan). For each CV fold, RS sorts the features by information gain on the entire training set. Then it scans the list, selecting each feature that is not strongly pairwise dependent on any feature already selected according to a standard χ^2 independence test using the X^2 statistic.

This produces a single reasonable input representation, R_1.[3] To obtain the additional representations needed for the ranking experiments, we ran RS several times with successively smaller subsets of the initial feature pool, created by deleting features whose training-set information gains were above different thresholds. For each dataset, we made nine additional representations of varying qualities, labeled R_2–R_{10}, numbered from least to most "damaged" initial feature pool.

To get the ground-truth ranking (step 2), we trained feed-forward ANNs with backpropagation using each representation and one output unit per class. We tried several different numbers of hidden units in one layer and used the best CV accuracy among these (Fig. 1, left) to rank each input representation for ground truth.

Each transparency measure also predicted a ranking of the representations (step 3). A CPU time comparison is in Table 2. This table and the experiments below report $min(leaves)$ and $avg(leaves)$ results from sampling 100 random trees, but sampling only 10 trees (giving a factor 10 speedup) yields similar ranking accuracy.

Finally, in Exper. 1 and 2 we evaluate each transparency measure (step 4) using Spearman's rank correlation coefficient, $r_S = 1 - \frac{6 \cdot \sum_{i=1}^{m} d_i^2}{m(m^2-1)}$, between the ground-truth and predicted rankings (m is the number of representations (10); d_i is the ground-truth rank (an integer between 1 and 10) minus the transparency rank). We evaluate the transparency measures in Exper. 3 by counting the number (out of ten) of representation pairs each measure orders the same as ground truth.

4 Experiment 1—Transparency vs. Sufficiency

This experiment demonstrates that our transparency measures are good predictors of representation quality and shows that transparency does not depend on representational sufficiency (ability to separate examples). In this experiment we used transparency to rank ten representations for each dataset and compared the rankings to the ANN ground truth using the rank correlation coefficient. RS created the representations by adding features until each representation could completely separate the training data into its classes. Thus, representational sufficiency was

---

[3]Though feature selection is not the focus of this paper, note that similar feature selection algorithms have been used by others for machine learning applications (Baim, 1988; Battiti, 1994).

Rapid Quality Estimation of Neural Network Input Representations

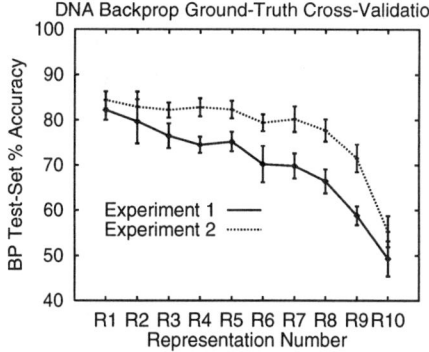

DNA Dataset		
Measure	Exp1 r_S	Exp2 r_S
ID3leaves	0.99	0.95
Min(leaves)	0.94	0.99
Avg(leaves)	0.78	0.96
Blurring	0.78	0.81

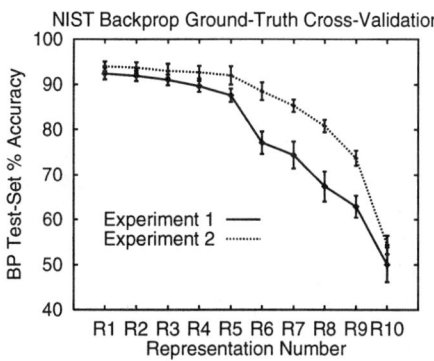

NIST Dataset		
Measure	Exp1 r_S	Exp2 r_S
ID3leaves	1.00	1.00
Min(leaves)	1.00	1.00
Avg(leaves)	1.00	1.00
Blurring	1.00	1.00

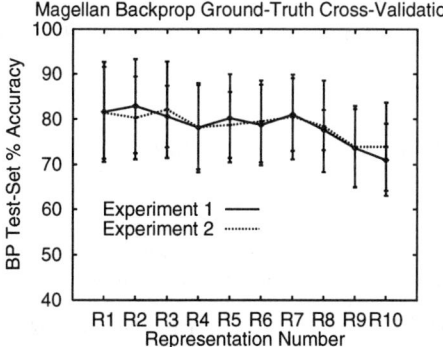

Magellan Dataset		
Measure	Exp1 r_S	Exp2 r_S
ID3leaves	0.81	0.78
Min(leaves)	0.83	0.76
Avg(leaves)	0.71	0.71
Blurring	0.48	0.73

Figure 1: **Left:** Exper. 1 and 2 ANN CV test-set accuracies (y axis; error bars are 1 SD) used to rank the representations (x axis). **Right:** Exper. 1 and 2, transparency rankings compared to ground truth. r_S: rank correlation coefficient (see text).

held constant. (The number of features could vary across representations.)

The rank correlation results are shown in Fig. 1 (right). *ID3leaves* and *min(leaves)* outperform the less sophisticated *avg(leaves)* and *blurring* measures on datasets where there is a difference. On the NIST data, all measures produce perfect rankings. The confidence that a true correlation exists is greater than 0.95 for all measures and datasets except *blurring* on the Magellan data, where it is 0.85.

The high rank correlations we observe imply that our transparency measures capture a predictive factor of representation quality. This factor does not depend on representational sufficiency, because sufficiency was equal for all representations.

Table 3: Exper. 3 results: correct rankings (out of 10) by the transparency measures of the corresponding representation pairs, R_i vs. R'_i, from Exper. 1 and Exper. 2.

Dataset	ID3leaves	Min(leaves)	Avg(leaves)	Blurring
DNA	10	0	0	0
NIST	10	0	0	0
Magellan	6	5	4	4

5 Experiment 2—Transparency vs. Economy

This experiment shows that transparency does not depend on representational economy (number of features), and it verifies Exper. 1's conclusion that it does not depend on sufficiency. It also reaffirms the predictive power of the measures.

In Exper. 1, sufficiency was held constant, but economy could vary. Exper. 2 demonstrates that transparency does not depend on economy by equalizing the number of features and redoing the comparison. In Exper. 2, RS added extra features to each representation used in in Exper. 1 until they all contained a fixed number of features (200 for DNA, 250 for NIST, 100 for Magellan). Each Exper. 2 representation, R'_i ($i = 1, \ldots, 10$), is thus a proper superset of the corresponding Exper. 1 representation, R_i. All representations for a given dataset in Exper. 2 have an identical number of features and allow perfect classification of the training data, so neither economy nor sufficiency can affect the transparency scores now.

The results (Fig. 1, right) are similar to Exper. 1's. The notable changes are that *blurring* is not as far behind *ID3leaves* and *min(leaves)* on the Magellan data as before, and *avg(leaves)* has joined the accuracy of the other two model-based measures on the DNA. The confidence that correlations exist is above 0.95 in all cases.

Again, the high rank correlations indicate that transparency is a good predictor of representation quality. Exper. 2 shows that transparency does not depend on representational economy or sufficiency, as both were held constant here.

6 Experiment 3—Redundant Features

Exper. 3 tests the transparency measures' predictions when the number of redundant features varies, as ANNs can often use redundant features to advantage (Sutton & Whitehead, 1993), an ability generally not attributed to decision trees.

Exper. 3 reuses the representations R_i and R'_i ($i = 1, \ldots, 10$) from Exper. 1 and 2. Recall that $R'_i \supset R_i$. The extra features in each R'_i are redundant as they are not needed to separate the training data. We show the number of R_i vs. R'_i representation pairs each transparency measure ranks correctly for each dataset (Table 3). For DNA and NIST, the redundant representations always improved ANN generalization (Fig. 1, left; 0.05 significance). Only *ID3leaves* predicted this correctly, finding smaller trees with the increased flexibility afforded by the extra features. The other measures were always incorrect because the lower quality redundant features degraded the random trees *(avg(leaves), min(leaves))* and the average information gain *(blurring)*. For Magellan, ANN generalization was only significantly different for one representation pair, and all measures performed near chance.

7 Conclusions

We introduced the notion of *transparency* (the prevalence of *simple and accurate* concepts) as an important factor of input representation quality and developed inexpensive, effective ways to measure it. Empirical tests on three real-world datasets demonstrated these measures' accuracy at ranking representations for ANN learning at much lower computational cost than training the ANNs themselves. Our next step will be to use transparency measures as scoring functions in algorithms that apply extensive search to find better input representations.

Acknowledgments

This work was supported by ONR grant N00014-93-1-0998, NSF grant CDA-9024618 (for CM-5 use), and a NASA GSRP fellowship held by KJC.

References

Almuallim, H. & Dietterich, T. (1994). Learning Boolean concepts in the presence of many irrelevant features. *Artificial Intelligence*, 69(1–2):279–305.

Baim, P. (1988). A method for attribute selection in inductive learning systems. *IEEE Transactions on Pattern Analysis & Machine Intelligence*, 10(6):888–896.

Battiti, R. (1994). Using mutual information for selecting features in supervised neural net learning. *IEEE Transactions on Neural Networks*, 5(4):537–550.

Burl, M., Fayyad, U., Perona, P., Smyth, P., & Burl, M. (1994). Automating the hunt for volcanoes on Venus. In *IEEE Computer Society Conf on Computer Vision & Pattern Recognition: Proc*, Seattle, WA. IEEE Computer Society Press.

Caruana, R. & Freitag, D. (1994). Greedy attribute selection. In *Machine Learning: Proc 11th Intl Conf*, (pp. 28–36), New Brunswick, NJ. Morgan Kaufmann.

Cherkauer, K. & Shavlik, J. (1994). Selecting salient features for machine learning from large candidate pools through parallel decision-tree construction. In Kitano, H. & Hendler, J., eds., *Massively Parallel Artificial Intel*. MIT Press, Cambridge, MA.

Cherkauer, K. & Shavlik, J. (1995). Rapidly estimating the quality of input representations for neural networks. In *Working Notes, IJCAI Workshop on Data Engineering for Inductive Learning*, (pp. 99–108), Montréal, Canada.

Craven, M. & Shavlik, J. (1993). Learning to predict reading frames in *E. coli* DNA sequences. In *Proc 26th Hawaii Intl Conf on System Science*, (pp. 773–782), Wailea, HI. IEEE Computer Society Press.

Fayyad, U. (1994). Branching on attribute values in decision tree generation. In *Proc 12th Natl Conf on Artificial Intel*, (pp. 601–606), Seattle, WA. AAAI/MIT Press.

John, G., Kohavi, R., & Pfleger, K. (1994). Irrelevant features and the subset selection problem. In *Machine Learning: Proc 11th Intl Conf*, (pp. 121–129), New Brunswick, NJ. Morgan Kaufmann.

Kambhatla, N. & Leen, T. (1994). Fast non-linear dimension reduction. In *Advances in Neural Info Processing Sys (vol 6)*, (pp. 152–159), San Francisco, CA. Morgan Kaufmann.

Kira, K. & Rendell, L. (1992). The feature selection problem: Traditional methods and a new algorithm. In *Proc 10th Natl Conf on Artificial Intel*, (pp. 129–134), San Jose, CA. AAAI/MIT Press.

Quinlan, J. (1986). Induction of decision trees. *Machine Learning*, 1:81–106.

Quinlan, J. (1994). Comparing connectionist and symbolic learning methods. In Hanson, S., Drastal, G., & Rivest, R., eds., *Computational Learning Theory & Natural Learning Systems (vol I: Constraints & Prospects)*. MIT Press, Cambridge, MA.

Rendell, L. & Ragavan, H. (1993). Improving the design of induction methods by analyzing algorithm functionality and data-based concept complexity. In *Proc 13th Intl Joint Conf on Artificial Intel*, (pp. 952–958), Chambéry, France. Morgan Kaufmann.

Sutton, R. & Whitehead, S. (1993). Online learning with random representations. In *Machine Learning: Proc 10th Intl Conf*, (pp. 314–321), Amherst, MA. Morgan Kaufmann.

A MODEL OF AUDITORY STREAMING

Susan L. McCabe & Michael J. Denham
Neurodynamics Research Group
School of Computing
University of Plymouth
Plymouth PL4 8AA, U.K.

ABSTRACT

An essential feature of intelligent sensory processing is the ability to focus on the part of the signal of interest against a background of distracting signals, and to be able to direct this focus at will. In this paper the problem of auditory scene segmentation is considered and a model of the early stages of the process is proposed. The behaviour of the model is shown to be in agreement with a number of well known psychophysical results. The principal contribution of this model lies in demonstrating how streaming might result from interactions between the tonotopic patterns of activity of input signals and traces of previous activity which feedback and influence the way in which subsequent signals are processed.

1 INTRODUCTION

The appropriate segmentation and grouping of incoming sensory signals is important in enabling an organism to interact effectively with its environment (Llinas, 1991). The formation of associations between signals, which are considered to arise from the same external source, allows the organism to recognise significant patterns and relationships within the signals from each source without being confused by accidental coincidences between unrelated signals (Bregman, 1990). The intrinsically temporal nature of sound means that in addition to being able to focus on the signal of interest, perhaps of equal significance, is the ability to predict how that signal is expected to progress; such expectations can then be used to facilitate further processing of the signal. It is important to remember that perception is a creative act (Luria, 1980). The organism creates its interpretation of the world in response to the current stimuli, within the context of its current state of alertness, attention, and previous experience. The creative aspects of perception are exemplified in the auditory system where peripheral processing decomposes acoustic stimuli. Since the frequency spectra of complex sounds generally overlap, this poses a complicated problem for the auditory system : which parts of the signal belong together, and which of the subgroups should be associated with each other from one moment to the next, given the extra complication of possible discontinuities and occlusion of sound signals? The process of streaming effectively acts to to associate those sounds emitted from the same source and may be seen as an accomplishment, rather than the breakdown of some integration mechanism (Bregman, 1990).

The cognitive model of streaming, proposed by (Bregman, 1990), is based primarily on Gestalt principles such as common fate, proximity, similarity and good continuation. Streaming is seen as a multistage process, in which an initial, preattentive process partitions the sensory input, causing successive sounds to be associated depending on the relationship between pitch proximity and presentation rate. Further refinement of these sound streams is thought to involve the use of attention and memory in the processing of single streams over longer time spans.

Recently a number of computational models which implement these concepts of streaming have been developed. A model of streaming in which pitch trajectories are used as the basis of sequential grouping is proposed by (Cooke, 1992). In related work, (Brown, 1992) uses data-driven grouping schema to form complex sound groups from frequency components with common periodicity and simultaneous onset. Sequential associations are then developed on the basis of pitch trajectory. An alternative approach suggests that the coherence of activity within networks of coupled oscillators, may be interpreted to indicate both simultaneous and sequential groupings (Wang, 1995), (Brown, 1995), and can, therefore, also model the streaming of complex stimuli. Sounds belonging to the same stream, are distinguished by synchronous activity and the relationship between frequency proximity and stream formation is modelled by the degree of coupling between oscillators.

A model, which adheres closely to auditory physiology, has been proposed by (Beauvois, 1991). Processing is restricted to two frequency channels and the streaming of pure tones. The model uses competitive interactions between frequency channels and leaky integrator model neurons in order to replicate a number of aspects of human psychophysical behaviour. The model, described here, used Beauvois' work as a starting point, but has been extended to include multichannel processing of complex signals. It can account for the relationship streaming and frequency difference and time interval (Beauvois, 1991), the temporal development and variability of streaming perceptions (Anstis, 1985), the influence of background organisation on foreground perceptions (Bregman, 1975), as well as a number of other behavioural results which have been omitted due to space limitations.

2 THE MODEL

We assume the existence of tonotopic maps, in which frequency is represented as a distributed pattern of activity across the map. Interactions between the excitatory tonotopic patterns of activity reflecting stimulus input, and the inhibitory tonotopic masking patterns, resulting from previous activity, form the basis of the model. In order to simulate behavioural experiments, the relationship between characteristic frequency and position across the arrays is determined by equal spacing within the ERB scale (Glasberg, 1990). The pattern of activation across the tonotopic axis is represented in terms of a Gaussian function with a time course which reflects the onset-type activity found frequently within the auditory system.

Input signals therefore take the form:

$$i(x, t) = c_1(t - t_{Onset})e^{-c_2(t-t_{Onset})}e^{\frac{-1}{2\alpha^2}(f_c(x)-f_s)^2} \quad [1]$$

where $i(x,t)$ is the probability of input activity at position x, time t. c_1 and c_2 are constants, t_{Onset} is the starting time of the signal, $f_c(x)$ is the characteristic frequency at position x, f_s is the stimulus frequency, and α determines the spread of the activation.

In models where competitive interactions within a single network are used to model the streaming process, such as (Beauvois, 1991), it is difficult to see how the organisation of background sounds can be used to improve foreground perceptions (Bregman, 1975) since the strengthening of one stream generally serves to weaken others. To overcome this problem, the model of preattentive streaming proposed here, consists of two interacting networks, the foreground and background networks, F and B; illustrated in figure 1. The output from F indicates the activity, if any, in the foreground, or attended stream, and the output from B reflects any other activity. The interaction between the two eventually ensures that those signals appearing in the output from F, i.e. in the foreground stream, do not appear in the output from B, the background; and vice versa. In the model, strengthening of the organisation of the background sounds, results in the 'sharpening' of the foreground stream due to the enhanced inhibition produced by a more coherent background.

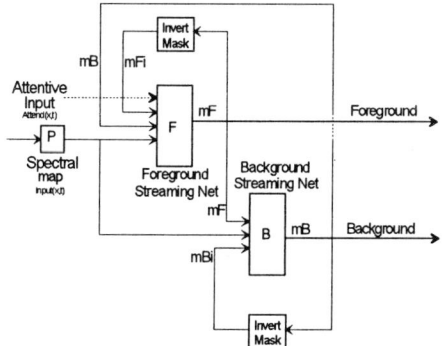

Figure 1 : Connectivity of the Streaming Networks.

Neurons within each array do not interact with each other but simply perform a summation of their input activity. A simplified neuron model with low-pass filtering of the inputs, and output representing the probability of firing, is used:

$$p(x, t) = \sigma[\sum_j v_j(x, t)], \text{ where } \sigma(y) = \frac{1}{1+e^{-y}} \quad [2]$$

The inputs to the foreground net are:
$$v_1(x, t) = (1 - \tfrac{dt}{\tau_1})v_1(x, t - dt) + V_1.\phi(i(x, t)).dt \quad [3]$$

$$v_2(x, t) = (1 - \tfrac{dt}{\tau_2})v_2(x, t - dt) + V_2.\phi(mFi(x, t - dt)).dt \quad [4]$$

$$v_3(x, t) = (1 - \tfrac{dt}{\tau_3})v_3(x, t - dt) + V_3.\phi(mB(x, t - dt)).dt \quad [5]$$

where x is the position across the array, time t, sampling rate dt. τ_i are time constants which determine the rate of decay of activity, V_i are weights on each of the inputs, and $\phi(y)$ is a function used to simulate the stochastic properties of nerve firing which returns a value of 1 or 0 with probability y.

A Model of Auditory Streaming

The output activity pattern in the foreground net and its 'inverse', $mF(x,t)$ and $mFi(x,t)$, are found by:

$$mF(x,t) = \sigma[v_1(x,t) - \eta(v_2(x,t),n) - \eta(v_3(x,t),n)] \qquad [6]$$

$$mFi(x,t) = \max\{[\frac{1}{N}\sum_{i=1}^{N} mF(x_i, t-dt)] - mF(x, t-dt), 0\} \qquad [7]$$

where $\eta(v(x,t),n)$ is the mean of the activity within neighbourhood n of position x at time t and N is the number of frequency channels. Background inputs are similarly calculated.

To summarise, the current activity in response to the acoustic stimulus forms an excitatory input to both the foreground and background streaming arrays, F and B. In addition, F receives inhibitory inputs reflecting the current background activity, and the inverse of the current foreground activity. The interplay between the excitatory and inhibitory activities causes the model to gradually focus the foreground stream and exclude extraneous stimuli. Since the patterns of inhibitory input reflect the distributed patterns of activity in the input, the relationship between frequency difference and streaming, results simply from the graded inhibition produced by these patterns. The relationship between tone presentation rate and streaming is determined by the time constants in the model which can be tuned to alter the rate of decay of activity.

To enable comparisons with psychophysical results, we view the judgement of coherence or streaming made by the model as the difference between the strength of the foreground response to one set of tones compared to the other. The strength of the response to a given frequency, $Resp(f,t)$, is a weighted sum of the activity within a window centred on the frequency:

$$Resp(f,t) = \sum_{i=-W}^{W} mF(x(f)+i, t) * e^{-\frac{i^2}{2\alpha^2}} \qquad [8]$$

where W determines the size of the window centred on position, $x(f)$, the position in the map corresponding to frequency f, and α determines the spread of the weighting function about position $x(f)$.

The degree of coherence between two tones, say f_1 and f_2, is assumed to depend on the difference in strength of foreground response to the two:

$$Coh(f_1, f_2, t) = 1 - \left|\frac{Resp(f_1,t) - Resp(f_2,t)}{Resp(f_1,t) + Resp(f_2,t)}\right| \qquad [9]$$

where $Coh(f_1,f_2,t)$ ranges between 0, when $Resp(f_1,t)$ or $Resp(f_2,t)$ vanishes and the difference between the responses is a maximum, indicating maximum streaming, and 1, when the responses are equal and maximally coherent. Values between these limits are interpreted as the *degree of coherence*, analogous to the probability of human subjects making a judgement of coherence (Anstis, 1985), (Beauvois, 1991).

3 RESULTS

Experiments exploring the effect of frequency interval and tone presentation rate and streaming are described in (Beauvois, 1991). Subjects were required to listen to an alternating sequence of tones, ABABAB... for 15 seconds, and then to judge whether at the end of the sequence they perceived an oscillating, trill-like, temporally coherent sequence, or two separate streams, one of interrupted high tones, the other of interrupted low tones. Their results showed clearly an increasing tendency towards stream segmentation both with increasing frequency difference between A and B, and increasing tone presentation rate, results the model manages substantially to reproduce; as may be seen in figure 2.

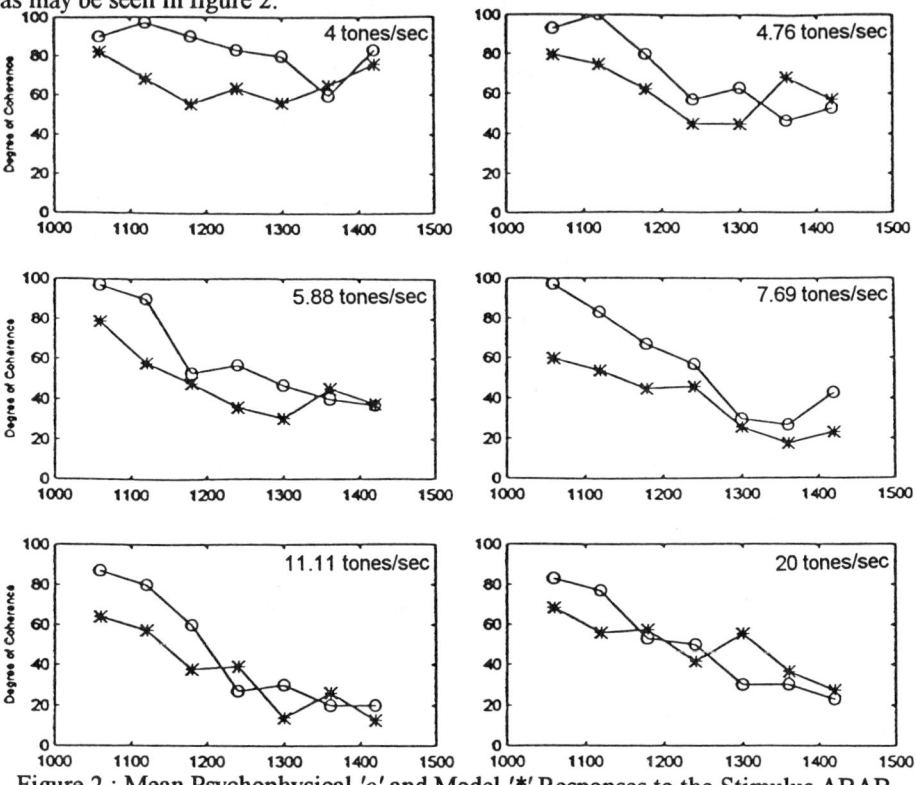

Figure 2 : Mean Psychophysical 'o' and Model '*' Responses to the Stimulus ABAB... (A=1000 Hz, B as indicated along X axis (Hz), tone presentation rates, as shown.)

In investigating the temporal development of stream segmentation, (Anstis, 1985) used a similar stimulus to the experiment described above, but in this case subjects were required to indicate continuously whether they were perceiving a coherent or streaming signal. As can be seen in figure 3, the model clearly reproduces the principal features found in their experiments, i.e. the probability of hearing a single, fused, stream declines during each run, the more rapid the tone presentation rate, the quicker stream segmentation occurs, and the judgements made were quite variable during each run.

In an experiment to investigate whether the organisation of the background sounds affects the foreground, subjects were required to judge whether tone A was higher or lower than B (Bregman, 1975). This judgement was easy when the two tones were presented in isolation, but performance degraded significantly when the distractor tones, X, were included. However, when a series of 'captor' tones, C, with frequency close to X were added, the judgement became easier, and the degree of improvement was inversely related to the difference in frequency between X and C. In the experiment, subjects received an initial priming AB stimulus, followed by a set of 9 tones : CCCXABXCC. The frequency of the captor tones, was manipulated to investigate how the proximity of 'captor' to 'distractor' tones affected the required AB order judgement.

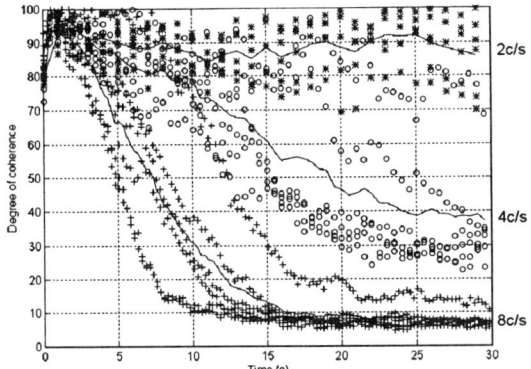

Figure 3 : The Probability of Perceptual Coherence as a Function of Time in Response to Two Alternating Tones. Symbols: '*' 2 tones/s, 'o' 4 tones/s, '+' 8 tones/s.

In order to model this experiment and the effect of priming, an 'attentive' input, focussed on the region of the map corresponding to the A and B tones, was included. We assume, as argued by Bregman, that subjects' performance in this task is related to the degree to which they are able to stream the AB pair separately. His D parameter is a measure of the degree to which AB/BA can be discriminated. The model's performance is then given by the strength of the foreground response to the AB pair as compared to the distractor tones, and $Coh([A\ B],X)$ is used to measure this difference. The model exhibits a similar sensitivity to the distractor/captor frequency difference to that of human subjects, and it appears that the formation of a coherent background stream allows the model to distinguish the foreground group more clearly.

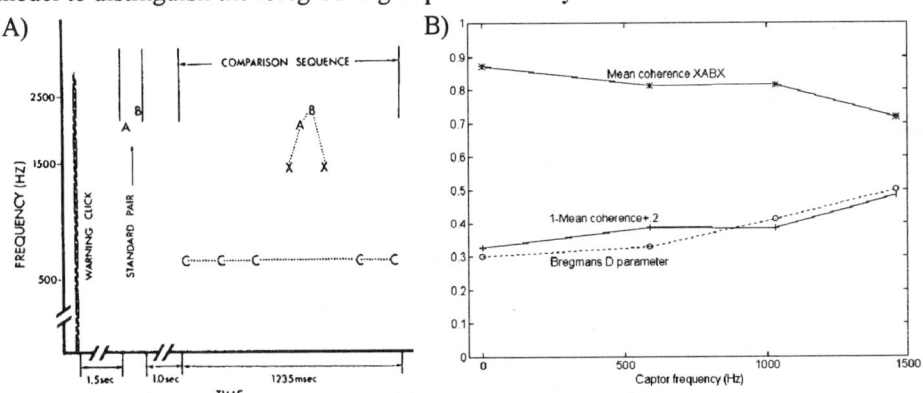

Figure 4 : A) Experiment to Demonstrate the Formation of Multiple Streams, (Bregman, 1975). B) Model Response; '*' Mean Degree of Doherence to XABX, 'o', Bregman's D Parameter, '+' Model's Judgement of Coherence.

4 DISCUSSION

The model of streaming which we have presented here is essentially a very simple one, which can, nevertheless, successfully replicate a wide range of psychophysical experiments. Embodied in the model is the idea that the characteristics of the incoming sensory signals result in activity which modifies the way in which subsequent incoming signals are processed. The inhibitory feedback signals effectively comprise expectations against which later signals are processed. Processing in much of the auditory system seems to be restricted to processing within frequency 'channels'. In this model, it is shown how local interactions, restricted almost entirely to within-channel activity, can form a global computation of stream formation. It is not known where streaming occurs in the auditory system, but feedback projections both within and between nuclei are extensive, perhaps allowing an iterative refinement of streams. Longer range projections, originating from attentive processes or memory, may modify local interactions to facilitate the extraction of recognised or interesting sounds.

The relationship between streaming and frequency interval, could be modelled by systematically graded inhibitory weights between frequency channels. However, in the model this relationship arises directly from the distributed incoming activity patterns, which seems a more robust and plausible solution, particularly if one takes the need to cope with developmental changes into account. Although to simplify the simulations peripheral auditory processing was not included in the model, the activity patterns assumed as input can be produced by the competitive processing of the output from a cochlear model.

An important aspect of intelligent sensory processing is the ability to focus on signals of interest against a background of distracting signals, thereby enabling the perception of significant temporal patterns. Artificial sensory systems, with similar capabilities, could act as robust pre-processors for other systems, such as speech recognisers, fault detection systems, or any other application which required the dynamic extraction and temporal linking of subsets of the overall signal.

Values Used For Model Parameters

$\alpha=.005$, $c_1=75$, $c_2=100$, $V=[100\ 5\ 5\ 5\ 5]$, $\tau=[.05\ .6\ .6\ .6\ .6]$, $n=2$, $N=100$

References

Anstis, S., Saida, S., J. (1985) Exptl Psych, 11(3), pp257-271

Beauvois, M.W., Meddis, R. (1991) J. Exptl Psych, 43A(3), pp517-541

Bregman, A.S., Rudnicky, A.I. (1975) J. Exptl Psych, 1(3), pp263-267

Bregman, A.S. (1990) 'Auditory scene analysis', MIT Press

Brown, G.J. (1992) University of Sheffield Research Reports, CS-92-22

Brown, G.J., Cooke, M. (1995) submitted to IJCAI workshop on Computational Auditory Scene Analysis

Cooke, M.P. (1992) Computer Speech and Language 6, pp 153-173

Glasberg, B.R., Moore, B.C.J. (1990) Hearing Research, 47, pp103-138

Llinas, R.R., Pare, D. (1991) Neuroscience, 44(3), pp521-535

Luria, A. (1980) 'Higher cortical functions in man', NY:Basic

van Noorden, L.P.A.S. (1975) doctoral dissertation, published by Institute for Perception Research, PO Box 513, Eindhoven, NL

Wang, D.L. (1995) in 'Handbook of brain theory and neural networks', MIT Press

PART II
NEUROSCIENCE

Modeling Interactions of the Rat's Place and Head Direction Systems

A. David Redish and David S. Touretzky
Computer Science Department & Center for the Neural Basis of Cognition
Carnegie Mellon University, Pittsburgh PA 15213-3891
Internet: {dredish,dst}@cs.cmu.edu

Abstract

We have developed a computational theory of rodent navigation that includes analogs of the place cell system, the head direction system, and path integration. In this paper we present simulation results showing how interactions between the place and head direction systems can account for recent observations about hippocampal place cell responses to doubling and/or rotation of cue cards in a cylindrical arena (Sharp *et al.*, 1990).

Rodents have multiple internal representations of their relationship to their environment. They have, for example, a representation of their location (place cells in the hippocampal formation, see Muller *et al.*, 1991), and a location-independent representation of their heading (head direction cells in the postsubiculum and the anterior thalamic nuclei, see Taube *et al.*, 1990; Taube, 1995).

If these representations are to be used for navigation, they must be aligned consistently whenever the animal reenters a familiar environment. This process was examined in a set of experiments by Sharp *et al.* (1990).

1 The Sharp *et al.*, 1990 experiment

Rats spent multiple sessions finding food scattered randomly on the floor of a black cylindrical arena with a white cue card along the wall subtending 90° of arc. The animals were not disoriented before entering the arena, and they always entered at the same location: the northwest corner. See Figure 3a. Hippocampal place fields were mapped by single-cell recording. A variety of probe trials were then introduced. When an identical second cue

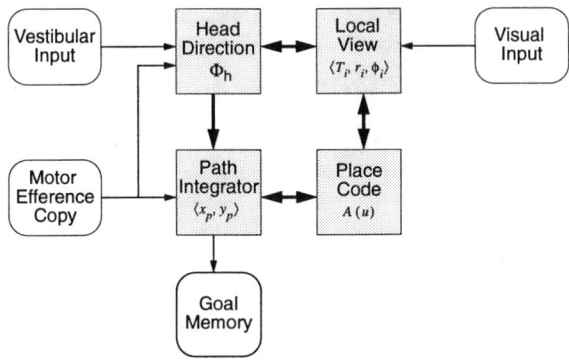

Figure 1: Organization of the rodent navigation model.

card was added opposite the first (Figure 3c), most place fields did not double.[1] Instead, the cells continued to fire at their original locations. However, if the rat was introduced into the double-card environment at the *southeast* corner (Figure 3d), the place fields rotated by 180°. But rotation did not occur in single-card probe trials with a southeast entry point (Figure 3b). When tested with cue cards rotated by ±30°, Sharp *et al.* observed that place field locations were controlled by an interaction of the choice of entry point with the cue card positions (Figure 3f.)

2 The CRAWL model

In earlier work (Wan *et al.*, 1994a; Wan *et al.*, 1994b; Redish and Touretzky, 1996) we described a model of rodent navigation that includes analogs of both place cells and the head direction system. This model also includes a local view module representing egocentric spatial information about landmarks, and a separate metric representation of location which serves as a substrate for path integration. The existence of a path integration faculty in rodents is strongly supported by behavioral data; see Maurer and Seguinot (1995) for a discussion. Hypotheses about the underlying neural mechanismss are presently being explored by several researchers, including us.

The structure of our model is shown in Figure 1. Visual inputs are represented as triples of form $\langle T_i, r_i, \theta_i \rangle$, each denoting the type, distance, and egocentric bearing of a landmark. The experiments reported here used two point-type landmarks representing the left and right edges of the cue card, and one surface-type landmark representing the arena wall. For the latter, r_i and θ_i define the normal vector between the rat and the surface. In the local view module, egocentric bearings θ_i are converted to allocentric form ϕ_i by adding the current value represented in the head direction system, denoted as Φ_h. The visual angle α_{ij} between pairs of landmarks is also part of the local view, and can be used to help localize the animal when its head direction is unknown. See Figure 2.

---

[1] Five of the 18 cells recorded by Sharp *et al.* changed their place fields over the various recording sessions. Our model does not reproduce these effects, since it does not address changes in place cell tuning. Such changes could occur due to variations in the animal's mental state from one trial to the next, or as a result of learning across trials.

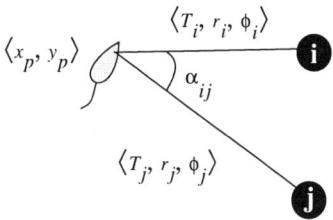

Figure 2: Spatial variables used in tuning a place cell to two landmarks i and j when the animal is at path integrator coordinates $\langle x_p, y_p \rangle$.

Our simulated place units are radial basis functions tuned to combinations of individual landmark bearings and distances, visual angles between landmark pairs, and path integrator coordinates. Place units can be driven by visual input alone when the animal is trying to localize itself upon initial entry at a random spot in the environment, or by the path integrator alone when navigating in the dark. But normally they are driven by both sources simultaneously. A key role of the place system is to maintain associations between the two representations, so that either can be reconstructed from the other. The place system also maintains a record of allocentric bearings of landmarks when viewed from the current position; this enables the local view module to compare perceived with remembered landmark bearings, so that drift in the head direction system can be detected and corrected.

In computer simulations using a single parameter set, the model reproduces a variety of behavioral and neurophysiological results including control of place fields by visual landmarks, persistence of place fields in the dark, and place fields drifting in synchrony with drift in the head direction system. Its predictions for open-field landmark-based navigation behavior match many of the experimental results of Collett et al. (1986) for gerbils.

2.1 Entering a familiar environment

Upon entering a familiar environment, the model's four spatial representations (local view, head direction, place code, and path integrator coordinates) must be aligned with the current sensory input and with each other. Note that local view information is completely determined given the visual input and head direction, and place cell activity is completely determined given the local view and path integrator representations. Thus, the alignment process manipulates just two variables: head direction and path integrator coordinates. When the animal enters the environment with initial estimates for them, the alignment process can produce four possible outcomes: (1) Retain the initial values of both variables, (2) Reset the head direction, (3) Reset the path integrator, or (4) Reset both head direction and the path integrator.

2.2 Prioritizing the outcomes

When the animal was placed at the northwest entry point and there were two cue cards (Figure 3c), we note that the orientation of the wall segment adjacent to the place field is identical with that in the training case. This suggests that the animal's head direction did not change. The spatial relationship between the entry point and place field was also unchanged: notice that the distance from the entry point to the center of the field is the same as in Figure 3a. Therefore, we conclude that the initially estimated path integrator coordinates were retained. Alternatively, the animal could have changed both its head direction (by 180°) and its path integrator coordinates (to those of the southeast corner) and produced consistent results, but to the experimenter the place field would appear to have flipped to the other card. Because no flip was observed, the first outcome must have priority over the fourth.

In panel d, where the place field has flipped to the northwest corner, the orientation of the segment of wall adjacent to the field has changed, but the spatial relationship between the entry point and field center has not. Resetting the path integrator and not the head direction would also give a solution consistent with this local view, but with the place field unflipped (as in panel b). We conclude that the second outcome (reset head direction) must have priority over the third (reset the path integrator).

The third and fourth outcomes are demonstrated in Figures 3b and 3f. In panel b, the orientation of the wall adjacent to the place field is unchanged from panel a, but the spatial relationship between the entry point and the place field center is different, as evidenced by the fact that the distance between them is much reduced. This is outcome 3. In panel f, both variables have changed (outcome 4).

Finally, the fact that place fields are stable over an entire session, even when there are multiple cue cards (and therefore multiple consistent pairings of head directions and path integrator coordinates) implies that animals do not reset their head direction or path integrator in visually ambiguous environments as long as the current values are reasonably consistent with the local view. We therefore assume that outcome 1 is preferred over the others.

This analysis establishes a partial ordering over the four outcomes: 1 is preferred over 4 by Figure 3c, and over the others by the stability of place fields, and outcome 2 is preferred over 3 by Figure 3d. This leaves open the question of whether outcome 3 or 4 has priority over the other. In this experiment, after resetting the path integrator it's always safe for the animal to attempt to reset its head direction. If the head direction does not change by more than a few degrees, as in panel b, we observe outcome 3; if it does change substantially, as in panel f, we observe outcome 4.

2.3 Consistency

The viability of an outcome is a function of the *consistency* between the local view and path integrator representations. The place system maintains the association between the two representations and mediates the comparison between them.

The activity $A(u)$ of a place unit is the product of a local view term $LV(u)$ and a path integrator term $C(u)$. $LV(u)$ is in turn a product of five Gaussians: two tuned to bearings and two to distances (for the same pair of landmarks), and one tuned to the retinal angle between a pair of landmarks. $C(u)$ is a Gaussian tuned to the path integrator coordinates of the center of the place field.

If the two representations agree, then the place units activated by path integrator input will be the same as those activated by the local view module, so the product $A(u)$ computed by those units will be significantly greater than zero. The consistency κ of the association between path integrator and local view representations is given by: $\kappa = \sum_u A(u) / \sum_u C(u)$. Because $A(u) < C(u)$ for all place units, κ ranges between 0 and 1. When the current local view is compatible with that predicted by the current path integrator coordinates, κ will be high; when the two are not compatible, κ will be low.

Earlier we showed that the navigation system should choose the highest priority viable outcome. If the consistency of an outcome is more than κ^* better than all higher-priority outcomes, that outcome is a viable choice and higher-priority ones are not. κ^* is an empirically derived constant that we have set equal to 0.04.

3 Discussion

Our results match all of the cases already discussed. (See Figure 3, panels a through d as well as f and h.) Sharp et al. (1990) did not actually test the rotated cue cards with a northwest entry point, so our result in panel e is a prediction.

When the animals entered from the northwest, but only one cue card was available at 180°, Sharp et al. report that the place field did not rotate. In our model the place field does rotate, as a result of outcome 4. This discrepancy can be explained by the fact that this particular manipulation was the last one in the sequence done by Sharp et al. McNaughton et al. (1994) and Knierim et al. (1995) have shown that if rats experience the cue card moving over a number of sessions, they eventually come to ignore it and it loses control over place fields. When we tested our model without a cue card (equivalent to a card being present but ignored), the resulting place field was more diffuse than normal but showed no rotation; see Figure 3g. We thus predict that if this experiment had been done before the other manipulations rather than after, the place field would have followed the cue card.

In the Sharp et al. experiment, the animals were always placed in the environment at the same location during training. Therefore, they could reliably estimate their initial path integrator coordinates. They also had a reliable head direction estimate because they were not disoriented. We predict that were the rats trained with a variety of entry points instead of just one, using an environment with a single cue card at 0° (the training environment used by Sharp et al.), and then tested with two cue cards at 0° and 180°, the place field would not rotate no matter what entry point was used. This is because when trained with a variable entry point, the animal would not learn to anticipate its path integrator coordinates upon entry; a path integrator reset would have to be done every time in order to establish the animal's coordinates. The reset mechanism uses allocentric bearing information derived from the head direction estimate, and in this task the resulting path integrator coordinates will be consistent with the initial head direction estimate. Hence, outcome 3 will always prevail.

If the animal is disoriented, however, then both the path integrator and the head direction system must be reset upon entry (because consistency will be low with a faulty head direction), and the animal must choose one cue card or the other to match against its memory. So with disorientation and a variable entry point, the place field will be controlled by one or the other cue card with a 50/50 probability. This was found to be true in a related behavioral experiment by Cheng (1986).

Our model shows how interactions between the place and head direction systems handle the various combinations of entry point, number of cue cards, and amount of cue card rotation. It predicts that head direction reset will be observed in certain tasks and not in others. In experiments such as the single cue card task with an entry in the southeast, it predicts the place code will shift from an initial value corresponding to the northwest entry point to the value for the southeast entry point, but the head direction will *not* change. This could be tested by recording simultaneously from place cells and head direction cells.

References

Cheng, K. (1986). A purely geometric module in the rat's spatial representation. *Cognition*, 23:149–178.

Collett, T., Cartwright, B. A., and Smith, B. A. (1986). Landmark learning and visuospatial memories in gerbils. *Journal of Comparative Physiology A*, 158:835–851.

Knierim, J. J., Kudrimoti, H. S., and McNaughton, B. L. (1995). Place cells, head direction cells, and the learning of landmark stability. *Journal of Neuroscience*, 15:1648–59.

Maurer, R. and Seguinot, V. (1995). What is modelling for? A critical review of the models of path integration. *Journal of Theoretical Biology*, 175:457–475.

McNaughton, B. L., Mizumori, S. J. Y., Barnes, C. A., Leonard, B. J., Marquis, M., and Green, E. J. (1994). Cortical rpresentation of motion during unrestrained spatial navigation in the rat. *Cerebral Cortex*, 4(1):27–39.

Muller, R. U., Kubie, J. L., Bostock, E. M., Taube, J. S., and Quirk, G. J. (1991). Spatial firing correlates of neurons in the hippocampal formation of freely moving rats. In Paillard, J., editor, *Brain and Space*, chapter 17, pages 296–333. Oxford University Press, New York.

Redish, A. D. and Touretzky, D. S. (1996). Navigating with landmarks: Computing goal locations from place codes. In Ikeuchi, K. and Veloso, M., editors, *Symbolic Visual Learning*. Oxford University Press. In press.

Sharp, P. E., Kubie, J. L., and Muller, R. U. (1990). Firing properties of hippocampal neurons in a visually symmetrical environment: Contributions of multiple sensory cues and mnemonic processes. *Journal of Neuroscience*, 10(9):3093–3105.

Taube, J. S. (1995). Head direction cells recorded in the anterior thalamic nuclei of freely moving rats. *Journal of Neuroscience*, 15(1):1953–1971.

Taube, J. S., Muller, R. I., and Ranck, Jr., J. B. (1990). Head direction cells recorded from the postsubiculum in freely moving rats. I. Description and quantitative analysis. *Journal of Neuroscience*, 10:420–435.

Wan, H. S., Touretzky, D. S., and Redish, A. D. (1994a). Computing goal locations from place codes. In *Proceedings of the 16th annual conference of the Cognitive Science society*, pages 922–927. Lawrence Earlbaum Associates, Hillsdale NJ.

Wan, H. S., Touretzky, D. S., and Redish, A. D. (1994b). Towards a computational theory of rat navigation. In Mozer, M., Smolensky, P., Touretzky, D., Elman, J., and Weigend, A., editors, *Proceedings of the 1993 Connectionist Models Summer School*, pages 11–19. Lawrence Earlbaum Associates, Hillsdale NJ.

Modeling Interactions of the Rat's Place and Head Direction Systems

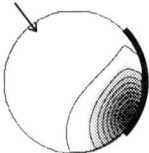

(a) 1 cue card at 0° (East)
entry in Northwest corner
angle of rotation (Sharp *et al.*) = 2.7°
precession of HD system = 0°

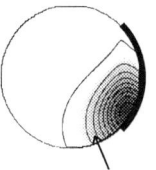

(b) 1 cue card at 0°
entry in Southeast corner
angle of rotation (Sharp *et al.*) = −6.0°
precession of HD system = 2°

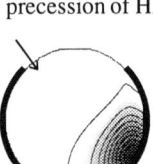

(c) 2 cue cards at 0° (East) & 180° (West)
entry in Northwest corner
angle of rotation (Sharp *et al.*) = −2.3°
precession of HD system = 0°

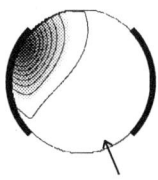

(d) 2 cue cards at 0° & 180°
entry in Southeast corner
angle of rotation (Sharp *et al.*) = 182.5°
precession of HD system = 178°

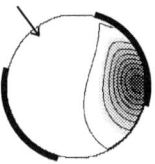

(e) 2 cue cards at 330° & 150°
entry in Northwest corner
not done by Sharp et al.
precession of HD system = 331°

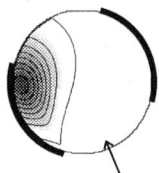

(f) 2 cue cards at 330° & 150°
entry in Southeast corner
angle of rotation (Sharp *et al.*) = 158.3°
precession of HD system = 151°

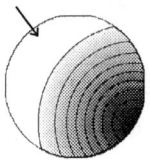

(g) 1 cue card at 180° (West)
entry in Northwest corner
angle of rotation (Sharp *et al.*) = −5.5°
precession of HD system = 0°

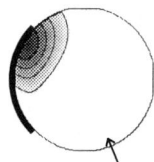

(h) 1 cue card at 180°
entry in Southeast corner
angle of rotation (Sharp *et al.*) = 182.2°
precession of HD system = 179°

Figure 3: Computer simulations of the Sharp *et al.* (1990) experiment showing that place fields are controlled by both cue cards (thick arcs) and entry point (arrowhead). "Angle of rotation" is the angle at which the correlation between the probe and training case place fields is maximal. Because head direction and place code are tightly coupled in our model, precession of HD is an equivalent measure in our model.

Correlated Neuronal Response: Time Scales and Mechanisms

Wyeth Bair
Howard Hughes Medical Inst.
NYU Center for Neural Science
4 Washington Pl., Room 809
New York, NY 10003

Ehud Zohary
Dept. of Neurobiology
Institute of Life Sciences
The Hebrew University, Givat Ram
Jerusalem, 91904 ISRAEL

Christof Koch
Computation and Neural Systems
Caltech, 139-74
Pasadena, CA 91125

Abstract

We have analyzed the relationship between correlated spike count and the peak in the cross-correlation of spike trains for pairs of simultaneously recorded neurons from a previous study of area MT in the macaque monkey (Zohary et al., 1994). We conclude that common input, responsible for creating peaks on the order of ten milliseconds wide in the spike train cross-correlograms (CCGs), is also responsible for creating the correlation in spike count observed at the two second time scale of the trial. We argue that both common excitation and inhibition may play significant roles in establishing this correlation.

1 INTRODUCTION

In a previous study of pairs of MT neurons recorded using a single extracellular electrode, it was found that the spike count during two seconds of visual motion stimulation had an average correlation coefficient of $r = 0.12$ and that this correlation could significantly limit the usefulness of pooling across increasingly large populations of neurons (Zohary et al., 1994). However, correlated spike count between two neurons could in principle occur at several time-scales. Correlated drifts in the excitability of the cells, for example due to normal biological changes or electrode induced changes, could cause correlation at a time scale of many minutes. Alternatively, attentional or priming effects from higher areas could change the responsivity of the cells at the time scale of an experimental trial. Or, as suggested here, common input that changes on the order of milliseconds could cause correlation in spike count. The first section determines the time scale at which the neurons are correlated by analyzing the relationship between the peak in the spike train cross-correlograms (CCGs) and the correlation between the spike counts using a construct we call the *trial* CCG. The second section examines temporal structure that is indicative of correlated suppression of firing, perhaps due to inhibition, which may also contribute to the spike count correlation.

2 THE TIME SCALE OF CORRELATION

At the time scale of the single trial, the correlation, r_{sc}, of spike counts x and y from two neurons recorded during nominally identical two second stimuli was computed using Pearson's correlation coefficient,

$$r_{sc} = \frac{E[xy] - ExEy}{\sigma_x \sigma_y}, \tag{1}$$

where E is expected value and σ^2 is variance. If spike counts are converted to z-scores, i.e., zero mean and unity variance, then $r_{sc} = E[xy]$, and r_{sc} may be interpreted as the zero-lag value of the cross-correlation of the z-scored spike counts. The *trial* CCGs resulting from this procedure are shown for two pairs of neurons in Fig. 1.

To distinguish between cases like the two shown in Fig. 1, the correlation was broken into a long-term component, r_{lt}, the average value (computed using a Gaussian window of standard deviation 4 trials) surrounding the zero-lag value, and a short-term component, r_{st}, the difference between the zero-lag value and r_{lt}. Across 92 pairs of neurons from three monkeys, the average r_{st} was 0.10 (s.d. 0.17) while r_{lt} was not significantly different from zero (mean 0.01, s.d. 0.11). The mean of r_{st} was similar to the overall correlation of 0.12 reported by Zohary et al. (1994).

Under certain assumptions, including that the time scale of correlation is less than the trial duration, r_{st} can be estimated from the area under the spike train CCG and the areas under the autocorrelations (derivation omitted). Under the additional assumption that the spike trains are individually Poisson and have no peak in the autocorrelation except that which occurs by definition at lag zero, the correlation coefficient for spike count can be estimated by

$$r_{peak} \approx \sqrt{\lambda_A \lambda_B} \text{Area}, \tag{2}$$

where λ_A and λ_B are the mean firing rates of neurons A and B, and *Area* is the area under the spike train CCG peak, like that shown in Fig. 2 for one pair of neurons. Taking *Area* to be the area under the CCG between ±32 msec gives a good estimate of short-term r_{st}, as shown in Fig. 3. In addition to the strong correlation ($r = 0.71$) between r_{peak} and r_{st}, r_{peak} is a less noisy measure, having standard deviation (not shown) on average one fourth as large as those of r_{st}.

We conclude that the common input that causes the peaks in the spike train CCGs is also responsible for the correlation in spike count that has been previously reported.

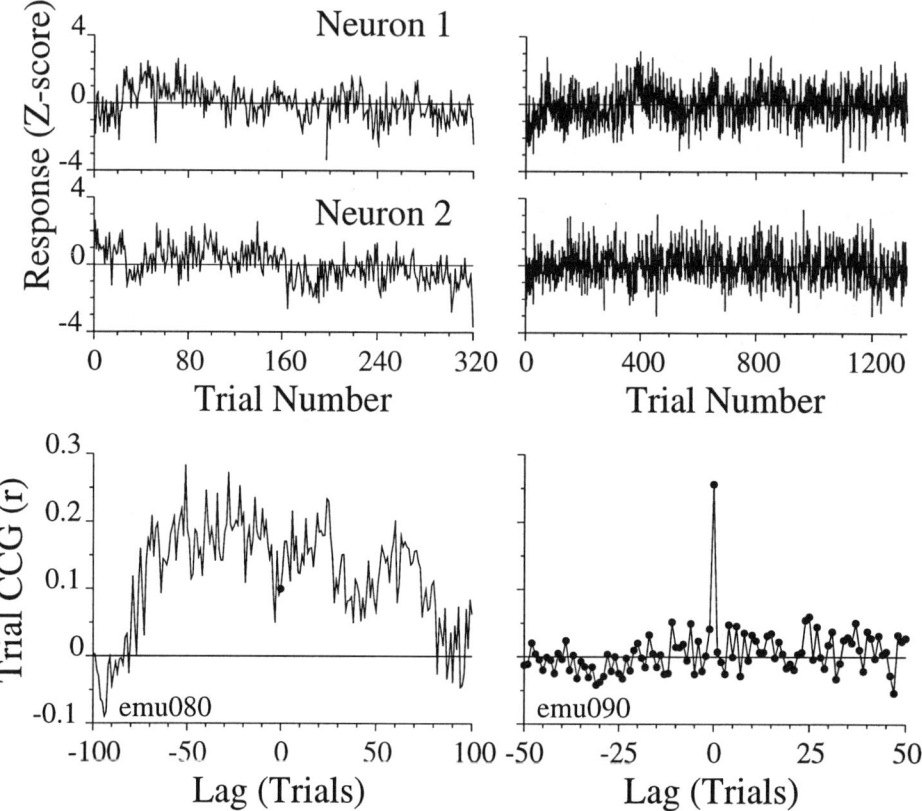

Figure 1: Normalized responses for two pairs of neurons and their trial cross-correlograms (CCGs). The upper traces show the z-scored spike counts for all trials in the order they occurred. Spikes were counted during the 2 sec stimulus, but trials occurred on average 5 sec apart, so 100 trials represents about 2.5 minutes. The lower traces show the trial CCGs. For the pair of cells in the left panel, responsivity drifts during the experiment. The CCG (lower left) shows that the drift is correlated between the two neurons over nearly 100 trials. For the pair of cells in the right panel, the trial CCG shows a strong correlation only for simultaneous trials. Thus, the measured correlation coefficient (trial CCG at zero lag) seems to occur at a long time scale on the left but a short time scale (less than or equal to one trial) on the right. The zero-lag value can be broken into two components, r_{st} and r_{lt} (short term and long term, respectively, see text). The short-term component, r_{st}, is the value at zero lag minus the weighted average value at surrounding lag times. On the left, $r_{st} \approx 0$, while on the right, $r_{lt} \approx 0$.

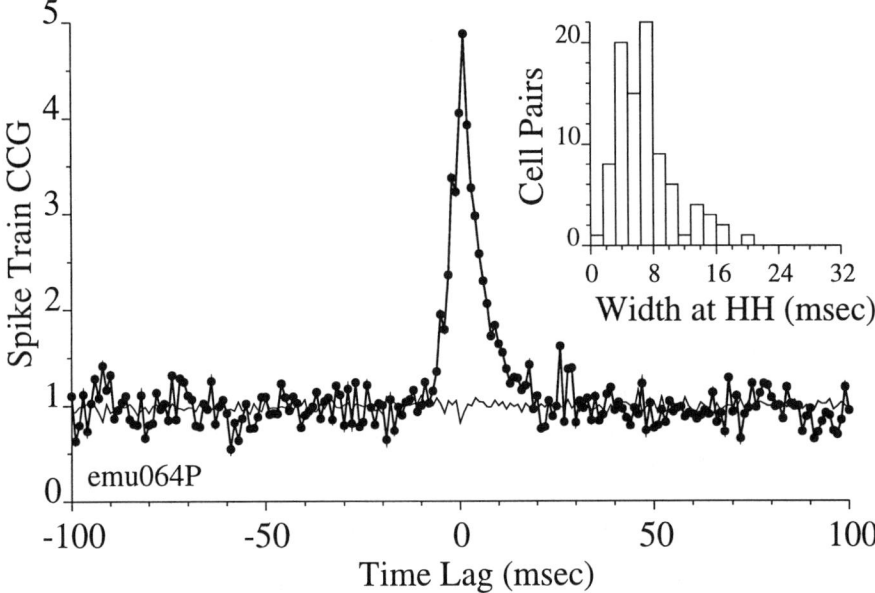

Figure 2: A spike train CCG with central peak. The frequency histogram of widths at half-height is shown (inset) for 92 cell pairs from three monkeys. The area of the central peak measured between ±32 msec is used to predict the correlation coefficients, r_{peak}, plotted in Fig. 3. The y-axis indicates the probability of a coincidence relative to that expected for Poisson processes at the measured firing rates.

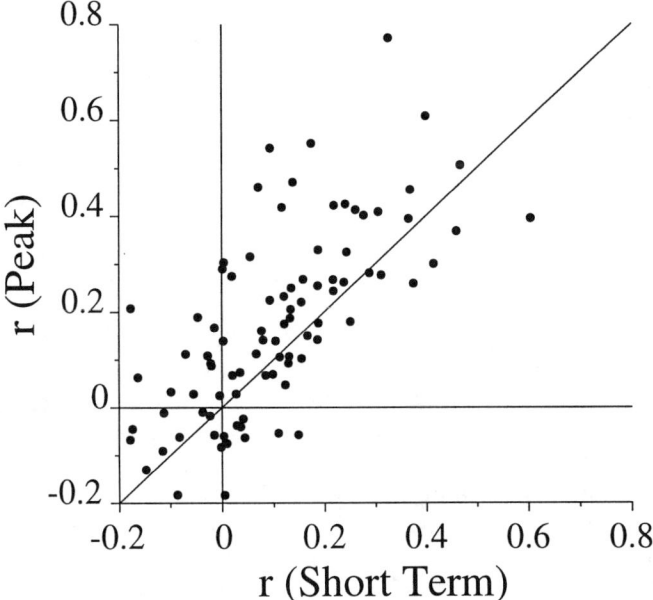

Figure 3: The area of the peak of the spike train CCG yields a prediction, r_{peak} (see Eqn. 2), that is strongly correlated ($r = 0.71$, $p < 0.00001$), with the short-term spike count correlation coefficient, r_{st}. The absence of points in the lower right corner of the plot indicates that there are no cases of a pair of cells being strongly correlated without having a peak in the spike train CCG.

In Fig. 3, there are no pairs of neurons that have a short-term correlation and yet do not have a peak in the ±32 msec range of the spike train CCG.

3 CORRELATED SUPPRESSION

There is little doubt that common excitatory input causes peaks like the one shown in Fig. 2 and therefore results in the correlated spike count at the time scale of the trial. However, we have also observed correlated periods of suppressed firing that may point to inhibition as another contribution to the CCG peaks and consequently to the correlated spike count.

Fig. 4 **A** and **B** show the response of one neuron to coherent preferred and null direction motion, respectively. Excessively long inter-spike intervals (ISIs), or *gaps*, appear in the response to preferred motion, while bursts appear in the response to null motion. Across a database of 84 single neurons from a previous study (Britten et al., 1992), the occurrence of the gaps and bursts has a symmetrical time course—both are most prominent on average from 600–900 msec post-stimulus onset, although there are substantial variations from cell to cell (Bair, 1995). The gaps, roughly 100 msec long, are not consistent with the slow, steady adaptation (presumably due to potassium currents) which is observed under current injection in neocortical pyramidal neurons, e.g., the RS_1 and RS_2 neurons of Agmon and Connors (1992).

Fig. 4 **C** shows spike trains from two simultaneously recorded neurons stimulated with preferred direction motion. The longest gaps appear to occur at about the same time. To assess the correlation with a cross-correlogram, we first transform the spike trains to *interval* trains, shown in Fig. 4 **D** for the spike trains in **C**. This emphasizes the presence of long ISIs and removes some of the information regarding the precise occurrence times of action potentials. The interval cross-correlation (ICC) between each pair of interval trains is computed and averaged over all trials, and the average shift predictor is subtracted. Fig. 4 **E** and **F** show ICCs (thick lines) for two different pairs of neurons. In 17 of 31 pairs (55%), there were peaks in the raw ICC that were at least 4 standard errors above the level of the shift predictor. The peaks were on average centered (mean 4.3 msec, SD 54 msec) and had mean width at half-height of 139 msec (SD 59 msec).

To isolate the cause of the peaks, the *long* intervals in the trains were set to the mean of the *short* intervals. Long intervals were defined as those that accounted for 30% of the duration of the data and were longer than all short intervals. Note that this is only a small fraction of the number of ISIs in the spike train (typically less than about 10%), since a few long intervals consume the same amount of time as many short intervals. Data from 300–1950 msec was processed, avoiding the on-transient and the lack of final interval. With the longest intervals neutralized, the peaks were pushed down to the level of the noise in the ICC (thin lines, Fig. 4 **E**, **F**). Thus, 90% of the action potentials may serve to set a mean rate, while a few periods of long ISIs dominate the ICC peaks.

The correlated gaps are consistent with common inhibition to neurons in a local region of cortex, and this inhibition adds area to the spike train CCG peaks in the form of a broader base (not shown). The data analyzed here is from behaving animals, so the gaps may be related to small saccades (within the 0.5 degree

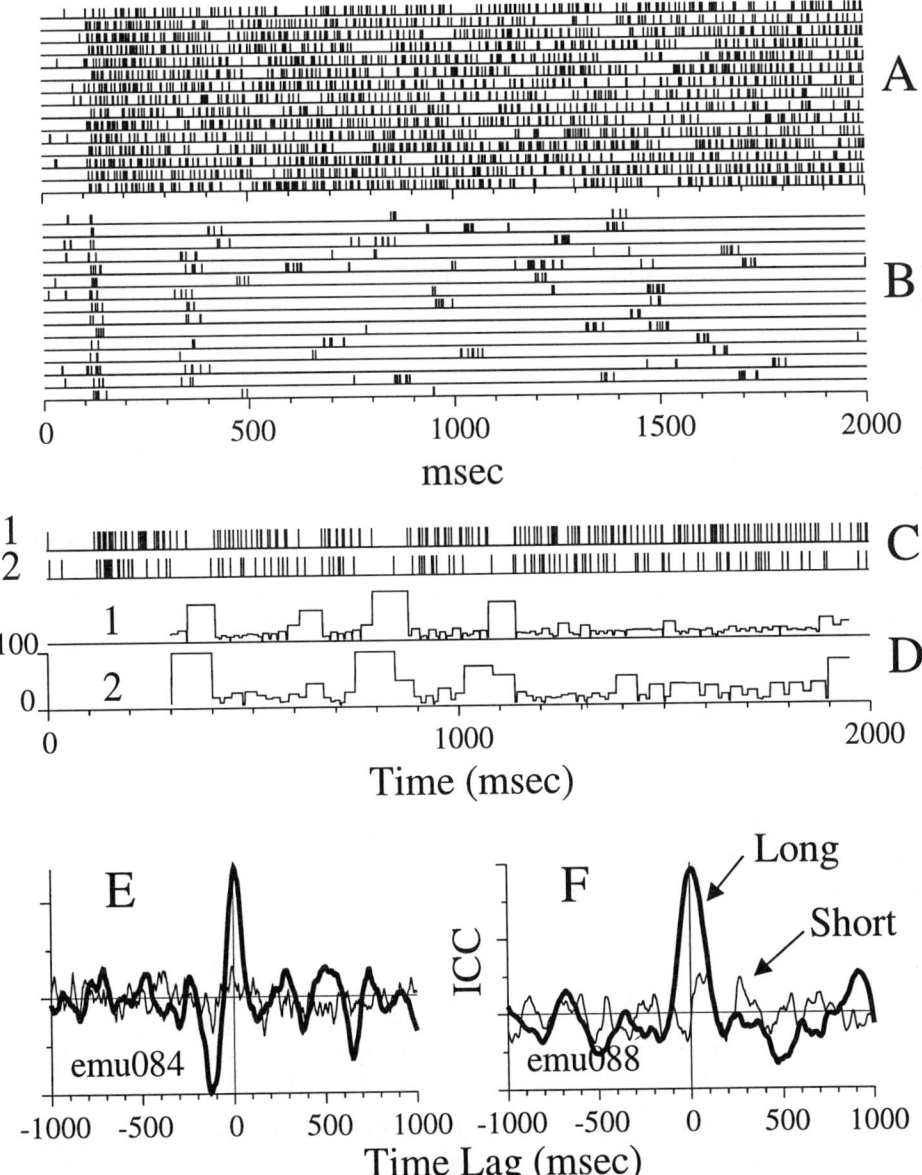

Figure 4: (A) The brisk response to coherent preferred direction motion is interrupted by occasional excessively long inter-spike intervals, i.e., gaps. (B) The suppressed response to null direction motion is interrupted by bursts of spikes. (C) Simultaneous spike trains from two neurons show correlated gaps in the preferred direction response. (D) The interval representation for the spike trains in C. (E,F) Interval cross-correlograms have peaks indicating that the gaps are correlated (see text).

fixation window) or eyelid blink. It has been hypothesized that blink suppression and saccadic visual suppression may operate through the same pathways and are of neuronal origin (Ridder and Tomlinson, 1993). An alternative hypothesis is that the gaps and bursts arise in cortex from intrinsic circuitry arranged in an opponent fashion.

4 CONCLUSION

Common input that causes central peaks on the order of tens of milliseconds wide in spike train CCGs is also responsible for causing the correlation in spike count at the time scale of two second long trials. Long-term correlation due to drifts in responsivity exists but is zero on average across all cell pairs and may represent a source of noise which complicates the accurate measurement of cell-to-cell correlation. The area of the peak of the spike train CCG within a window of ± 32 msec is the basis of a good prediction of the spike count correlation coefficient and provides a less noisy measure of correlation between neurons. Correlated gaps observed in the response to coherent preferred direction motion is consistent with common inhibition and contributes to the area of the spike train CCG peak, and thus to the correlation between spike count. Correlation in spike count is an important factor that can limit the useful pool-size of neuronal ensembles (Zohary et al., 1994; Gawne and Richmond, 1993).

Acknowledgements

We thank William T. Newsome, Kenneth H. Britten, Michael N. Shadlen, and J. Anthony Movshon for kindly providing data that was recorded in previous studies and for helpful discussion. This work was funded by the Office of Naval Research and the Air Force Office of Scientific Research. W. B. was supported by the L. A. Hanson Foundation and the Howard Hughes Medical Institute.

References

Agmon A, Connors BW (1992) Correlation between intrinsic firing patterns and thalamocortical synaptic responses of neurons in mouse barrel cortex. *J Neurosci* **12**:319–329.

Bair W (1995) *Analysis of Temporal Structure in Spike Trains of Visual Cortical Area MT*. Ph.D. thesis, California Institute of Technology.

Britten KH, Shadlen MN, Newsome WT, Movshon JA (1992) The analysis of visual motion: a comparison of neuronal and psychophysical performance. *J Neurosci* **12**:4745–4765.

Gawne TJ, Richmond BJ (1993) How independent are the messages carried by adjacent inferior temporal cortical neurons? *J Neurosci* **13**:2758–2771.

Ridder WH, Tomlinson A (1993) Suppression of contrasts sensitivity during eyelid blinks. *Vision Res* **33**:1795–1802.

Zohary E, Shadlen MN, Newsome WT (1994) Correlated neuronal discharge rate and its implications for psychophysical performance. *Nature* **370**:140–143.

Information through a Spiking Neuron

Charles F. Stevens and Anthony Zador
Salk Institute MNL/S
La Jolla, CA 92037
zador@salk.edu

Abstract

While it is generally agreed that neurons transmit information about their synaptic inputs through spike trains, the code by which this information is transmitted is not well understood. An upper bound on the information encoded is obtained by hypothesizing that the precise timing of each spike conveys information. Here we develop a general approach to quantifying the information carried by spike trains under this hypothesis, and apply it to the leaky integrate-and-fire (IF) model of neuronal dynamics. We formulate the problem in terms of the probability distribution $p(T)$ of interspike intervals (ISIs), assuming that spikes are detected with arbitrary but finite temporal resolution. In the absence of added noise, all the variability in the ISIs could encode information, and the information rate is simply the entropy of the ISI distribution, $H(T) = \langle -p(T) \log_2 p(T) \rangle$, times the spike rate. $H(T)$ thus provides an *exact* expression for the information rate. The methods developed here can be used to determine experimentally the information carried by spike trains, even when the lower bound of the information rate provided by the stimulus reconstruction method is not tight. In a preliminary series of experiments, we have used these methods to estimate information rates of hippocampal neurons in slice in response to somatic current injection. These pilot experiments suggest information rates as high as 6.3 bits/spike.

1 Information rate of spike trains

Cortical neurons use spike trains to communicate with other neurons. The output of each neuron is a stochastic function of its input from the other neurons. It is of interest to know how much each neuron is telling other neurons about its inputs.

How much information does the spike train provide about a signal? Consider noise $n(t)$ added to a signal $s(t)$ to produce some total input $y(t) = s(t) + n(t)$. This is then passed through a (possibly stochastic) functional $\mathcal{F}$ to produce the output spike train $\mathcal{F}[y(t)] \to z(t)$. We assume that *all* the information contained in the spike train can be represented by the list of spike times; that is, there is no extra information contained in properties such as spike height or width. Note, however, that many characteristics of the spike train such as the mean or instantaneous rate can be derived from this representation; if such a derivative property turns out to be the relevant one, then this formulation can be specialized appropriately.

We will be interested, then, in the mutual information $I(S(t); Z(t))$ between the input signal ensemble $S(t)$ and the output spike train ensemble $Z(t)$. This is defined in terms of the entropy $H(S)$ of the signal, the entropy $H(Z)$ of the spike train, and their joint entropy $H(S, Z)$,

$$I(S; Z) = H(S) + H(Z) - H(S, Z). \tag{1}$$

Note that the mutual information is symmetric, $I(S; Z) = I(Z; S)$, since the joint entropy $H(S, Z) = H(Z, S)$. Note also that if the signal $S(t)$ and the spike train $Z(t)$ are completely independent, then the mutual information is 0, since the joint entropy is just the sum of the individual entropies $H(S, Z) = H(S) + H(Z)$. This is completely in line with our intuition, since in this case the spike train can provide no information about the signal.

1.1 Information estimation through stimulus reconstruction

Bialek and colleagues (Bialek et al., 1991) have used the *reconstruction method* to obtain a strict lower bound on the mutual information in an experimental setting. This method is based on an expression mathematically equivalent to eq. (1) involving the conditional entropy $H(S|Z)$ of the signal given the spike train,

$$\begin{aligned} I(S; Z) &= H(S) - H(S|Z) \\ &\geq H(S) - H_{\text{est}}(S|Z), \end{aligned} \tag{2}$$

where $H_{\text{est}}(S|Z)$ is an upper bound on the conditional entropy obtained from a reconstruction $s_{\text{est}}(t)$ of the signal. The entropy is estimated from the second order statistics of the reconstruction error $e(t) \triangleq s(t) - s_{\text{est}}(t)$; from the maximum entropy property of the Gaussian this is an upper bound. Intuitively, the first equation says that the information gained about the spike train by observing the stimulus is just the initial uncertainty of the signal (in the absence of knowledge of the spike train) minus the uncertainty that remains about the signal once the spike train is known, and the second equation says that this second uncertainty must be greater for any particular estimate than for the optimal estimate.

1.2 Information estimation through spike train reliability

We have adopted a different approach based an equivalent expression for the mutual information:

$$I(S; Z) = H(Z) - H(Z|S). \tag{3}$$

The first term $H(Z)$ is the entropy of the spike train, while the second $H(Z|S)$ is the conditional entropy of the spike train given the signal; intuitively this like the inverse *repeatability* of the spike train given repeated applications of the same signal. Eq. (3) has the advantage that, if the spike train is a deterministic function of the input, it permits *exact* calculation of the mutual information. This follows from an important difference between the conditional entropy term here and in eq. 2: whereas $H(S|Z)$ has both a deterministic and a stochastic component, $H(Z|S)$ has only a stochastic component. Thus in the absence of added noise, the discrete entropy $H(Z|S) = 0$, and eq. (3) reduces to $I(S; Z) = H(Z)$.

If ISIs are independent, then the $H(Z)$ can be simply expressed in terms of the entropy of the (discrete) ISI distribution $p(T)$,

$$H(T) = -\sum_{i=0}^{\infty} p(T_i) \log_2 p(T_i) \tag{4}$$

as $H(Z) = nH(T)$, where n is the number of spikes in Z. Here $p(T_i)$ is the probability that the spike occurred in the interval $(i)\Delta t$ to $(i+1)\Delta t$. The assumption of finite timing precision Δt keeps the potential information finite. The advantage of considering the ISI distribution $p(T)$ rather than the full spike train distribution $p(Z)$ is that the former is univariate while the latter is multivariate; estimating the former requires much less data.

Under what conditions are ISIs independent? Correlations between ISIs can arise either through the stimulus or the spike generation mechanism itself. Below we shall guarantee that correlations do not arise from the spike-generator by considering the *forgetful integrate-and-fire* (IF) model, in which all information about the previous spike is eliminated by the next spike. If we further limit ourselves to temporally uncorrelated stimuli (*i.e.* stimuli drawn from a white noise ensemble), then we can be sure that ISIs are independent, and eq. (4) can be applied.

In the presence of noise, $H(Z|T)$ must also be evaluated, to give

$$I(S;T) = H(T) - H(T|S). \tag{5}$$

$H(T|S)$ is the conditional entropy of the ISI given the signal,

$$H(T|S) = -\left\langle \sum_{j=1}^{\infty} p(T_j|s_i(t)) \log_2 p(T_j|s_i(t)) \right\rangle_{s_i(t)} \tag{6}$$

where $p(T_j|s_i(t))$ is the probability of obtaining an ISI of T_j in response to a particular stimulus $s_i(t)$ in the presence of noise $n(t)$. The conditional entropy can be thought of as a quantification of the reliability of the spike generating mechanism: it is the average trial-to-trial variability of the spike train generated in response to repeated applications of the same stimulus.

1.3 Maximum spike train entropy

In what follows, it will be useful to compare the information rate for the IF neuron with the limiting case of an exponential ISI distribution, which has the maximum entropy for any point process of the given rate (Papoulis, 1984). This provides an upper bound on the information rate possible for any spike train, given the spike rate and the temporal precision. Let $f(T) = \bar{r}e^{-\bar{r}T}$ be an exponential distribution with a mean spike rate $\bar{r}$. Assuming a temporal precision of Δt, the entropy/spike is $H(T) = \log_2 \frac{e}{\bar{r}\Delta t}$, and the entropy/time for a rate $\bar{r}$ is $\bar{r}H(T) = \bar{r}\log_2 \frac{e}{\bar{r}\Delta t}$. For example, if $\bar{r} = 1$ Hz and $\Delta t = 0.001$ sec, this gives (11.4 bits/second) (1 spike/second) = 11.4 bits/spike. That is, if we discretize a 1 Hz spike train into 1 msec bins, it is not possible for it to transmit more than 11.4 bits/second. If we reduce the bin size two-fold, the rate increases by $\log_2 1/2 = 1$ bit/spike to 12.4 bits/spike, while if we double it we lose one bit/s to get 10.4 bit/s. Note that at a different firing rate, e.g. $\bar{r} = 2$ Hz, halving the bin size still increases the entropy/spike by 1 bit/spike, but because the spike rate is twice as high, this becomes a 2 bit/second increase in the information rate.

1.4 The IF model

Now we consider the functional $\mathcal{F}$ describing the forgetful leaky IF model of spike generation. Suppose we add some noise $n(t)$ to a signal $s(t)$, $y(t) = n(t) + s(t)$, and threshold the sum to produce a spike train $z(t) = \mathcal{F}[s(t) + n(t)]$. Specifically, suppose the voltage $v(t)$ of the neuron obeys $\dot{v}(t) = -v(t)/\tau + y(t)$, where τ is the membrane time constant, both $s(t)$ and $n(t)$ have a white Gaussian distributions and $y(t)$ has mean μ and variance σ^2. If the voltage reaches the threshold θ_0 at some time t, the neuron emits a spike at that time and resets to the initial condition v_0.

In the language of neurobiology, this model can be thought of (Tuckwell, 1988) as the limiting case of a neuron with a leaky IF spike generating mechanism receiving many excitatory and inhibitory synaptic inputs. Note that since the input $y(t)$ is white, there are no correlations in the spike train induced by the signal, and *since the neuron resets after each spike there are no correlations induced by the spike-generating mechanism.* Thus ISIs are independent, and eq. (4) can be applied.

We will estimate the mutual information $I(S, Z)$ between the ensemble of input signals S and the ensemble of outputs Z. Since in this model ISIs are independent by construction, we need only evaluate $H(T)$ and $H(T|S)$; for this we must determine $p(T)$, the distribution of ISIs, and $p(T|s_i)$, the conditional distribution of ISIs for an ensemble of signals $s_i(t)$. Note that $p(T)$ corresponds to the first passage time distribution of the Ornstein-Uhlenbeck process (Tuckwell, 1988).

The neuron model we are considering has two regimes determined by the relation of the asymptotic membrane potential (in the absence of threshold) $\mu\tau$ and the threshold θ. In the *suprathreshold* regime, $\mu\tau > \theta$, threshold crossings occur even if the signal variance is zero ($\sigma^2 = 0$). In the *subthreshold* regime, $\mu\tau \leq \theta$, threshold crossings occur only if $\sigma^2 > 0$. However, in the limit that $E\{T\} \gg \tau$, *i.e.* the mean firing rate is low compared with the integration time constant (this can only occur in the subthreshold regime), the ISI distribution is exponential, and its coefficient of variation (CV) is unity (cf. (Softky and Koch, 1993)). In this low-rate regime the firing is *deterministically Poisson*; by this we mean to distinguish it from the more usual usage of *Poisson neuron*, the stochastic situation in which the instantaneous firing rate parameter (the probability of firing over some interval) depends on the stimulus (*i.e.* $\bar{r} \propto s(t)$). In the present case the exponential ISI distribution arises from a deterministic mechanism.

At the border between these regimes, when the threshold is just equal to the asymptotic potential, $\theta_0 = \mu\tau$, we have an explicit and exact solution for the entire ISI distribution (Sugiyama et al., 1970)

$$p(T) = \frac{(\mu\tau)(\tau/2)^{-3/2}}{(2\pi)^{1/2}\sigma}[e^{2T/\tau} - 1]^{-3/2}\exp(2T/\tau - \frac{(\mu\tau)^2}{(\sigma^2\tau)(e^{2T/\tau} - 1)}). \quad (7)$$

This is the special case where, in the absence of fluctuations ($\sigma^2 = 0$), the membrane potential hovers just subthreshold. Its neurophysiological interpretation is that the excitatory inputs just balance the inhibitory inputs, so that the neuron hovers just on the verge of firing.

1.5 Information rates for noisy and noiseless signals

Here we compare the information rate for a IF neuron at the "balance point" $\mu\tau = \theta$ with the maximum entropy spike train. For simplicity and brevity we consider only the zero-noise case, *i.e.* $n(t) = 0$. Fig. 1A shows the information per spike as a function of the firing rate calculated from eq. (7), which was varied by changing the signal variance σ^2. We assume that spikes can be resolved with a temporal resolution of 1 msec, *i.e.* that the ISI distribution has bins 1 msec wide. The *dashed* line shows the theoretical upper bound given by the exponential distribution; this limit can be approached by a neuron operating far below threshold, in the Poisson limit. For both the IF model and the upper bound, the information per spike is a monotonically decreasing function of the spike rate; the model almost achieves the upper bound when the mean ISI is just equal to the membrane time constant. In the model the information saturates at very low firing rates, but for the exponential distribution the information increases without bound. At high firing rates the information goes to zero when the firing rate is too fast for individual ISIs to be resolved at the temporal resolution. Fig. 1B shows that the information rate (information per second) when the neuron is at the balance point goes through a maximum as the firing rate increases. The maximum occurs at a lower firing rate than for the exponential distribution (*dashed line*).

1.6 Bounding information rates by stimulus reconstruction

By construction, eq. (3) gives an exact expression for the information rate in this model. We can therefore compare the lower bound provided by the stimulus reconstruction method eq. (2) (Bialek et al., 1991). That is, we can assess how tight a lower bound it provides. Fig. 2 shows the lower bound provided by the reconstruction (*solid line*) and the reliability (*dashed line*) methods as a function of the firing rate. The firing rate was increased by increasing the mean μ of the input stimulus $y(t)$, and noise was set to 0. At low firing rates the two estimates are nearly identical, but at high firing rates the reconstruction method substantially underestimates the information rate. The amount of the underestimate depends on the model parameters, and decreases as noise is added to the stimulus. The tightness of the bound is therefore an empirical question. While Bialek and colleagues (1996) show that under the conditions of their experiments the underestimate is less than a factor of two, it is clear that the potential for underestimate under different conditions or in different systems is greater.

2 Discussion

While it is generally agreed that spike trains encode information about a neuron's inputs, it is not clear how that information is encoded. One idea is that it is the mean firing rate alone that encodes the signal, and that variability about this mean is effectively noise. An alternative view is that it is the variability itself that encodes the signal, *i.e.* that the information is encoded in the precise times at which spikes occur. In this view the information can be expressed in terms of the interspike interval (ISI) distribution of the spike train. This encoding scheme yields much higher information rates than one in which only the mean rate (over some interval longer than the typical ISI) is considered. Here we have quantified the information content of spike trains under the latter hypothesis for a simple neuronal model.

We consider a model in which by construction the ISIs are independent, so that the information rate (in bits/sec) can be computed directly from the information per spike (in bits/spike) and the spike rate (in spikes/sec). The information per spike in turn depends on the temporal precision with which spikes can be resolved (if precision were infinite, then the information content would be infinite as well, since any message could for example be encoded in the decimal expansion of the precise arrival time of a single spike), the reliability of the spike transduction mechanism, and the entropy of the ISI distribution itself. For low firing rates, when the neuron is in the subthreshold limit, the ISI distribution is close to the theoretically maximal exponential distribution.

Much of the recent interest in information theoretic analyses of the neural code can attributed to the seminal work of Bialek and colleagues (Bialek et al., 1991; Rieke et al., 1996), who measured the information rate for sensory neurons in a number of systems. The present results are in broad agreement with those of DeWeese (1996), who considered the information rate of a linear-filtered threshold crossing[1] (LFTC) model. DeWeese developed a functional expansion, in which the first term describes the limit in which spike times (not ISIs) are independent, and the second term is a correction for correlations. The LFTC model differs from the present IF model mainly in that it does not "reset" after each spike. Consequently the "natural"

---

[1] In the LFTC model, Gaussian signal and noise are convolved with a linear filter; the times at which the resulting waveform crosses some threshold are called "spikes".

representation of the spike train in the LFTC model is as a sequence $t_0 \ldots t_n$ of firing times, while in the IF model the "natural" representation is as a sequence $T_1 \ldots T_n$ of ISIs. The choice is one of convenience, since the two representations are equivalent.

The two models are complementary. In the LFTC model, results can be obtained for colored signals and noise, while such conditions are awkward in the IF model. In the IF model by contrast, a class of highly correlated spike trains can be conveniently considered that are awkward in the LFTC model. That is, the indendent-ISI condition required in the IF model is less restrictive than the independent-spike condition of the LFTC model—spikes are independent iff ISIs are indepennndent *and* the ISI distribution $p(T)$ is exponential. In particular, at high firing rates the ISI distribution can be far from exponential (and therefore the spikes far from independent) even when the ISIs themselves are independent.

Because we have assumed that the input $s(t)$ is white, its entropy is infinite, and the mutual information can grow without bound as the temporal precision with which spikes are resolved improves. Nevertheless, the spike train is transmitting only a minute fraction of the total available information. The signal thereby saturates the capacity of the spike train. While it is not at all clear whether this is how real neurons actually behave, it is not implausible: a typical cortical neuron receives as many as 10^4 synaptic inputs, and if the information rate of each input is the same as the target, then the information rate impinging upon the target is 10^4-fold greater (neglecting synaptic unreliability, which could decrease this substantially) than its capacity.

In a preliminary series of experiments, we have used the reliability method to estimate the information rate of hippocampal neuronal spike trains in slice in response to somatic current injection (Stevens and Zador, *unpublished*). Under these conditions ISIs appear to be independent, so the method developed here can be applied. In these pilot experiments, an information rates as high as 6.3 bits/spike was observed.

References

Bialek, W., Rieke, F., de Ruyter van Steveninck, R., and Warland, D. (1991). Reading a neural code. *Science*, 252:1854–1857.

DeWeese, M. (1996). Optimization principles for the neural code. In Hasselmo, M., editor, *Advances in Neural Information Processing Systems, vol. 8*. MIT Press, Cambridge, MA.

Papoulis, A. (1984). *Probability, random variables and stochastic processes, 2nd edition*. McGraw-Hill.

Rieke, F., Warland, D., de Ruyter van Steveninck, R., and Bialek, W. (1996). *Neural Coding*. MIT Press.

Softky, W. and Koch, C. (1993). The highly irregular firing of cortical cells is inconsistent with temporal integration of random epsps. *J. Neuroscience.*, 13:334–350.

Sugiyama, H., Moore, G., and Perkel, D. (1970). Solutions for a stochastic model of neuronal spike production. *Mathematical Biosciences*, 8:323–341.

Tuckwell, H. (1988). *Introduction to theoretical neurobiology (2 vols.)*. Cambridge.

Information Through a Spiking Neuron

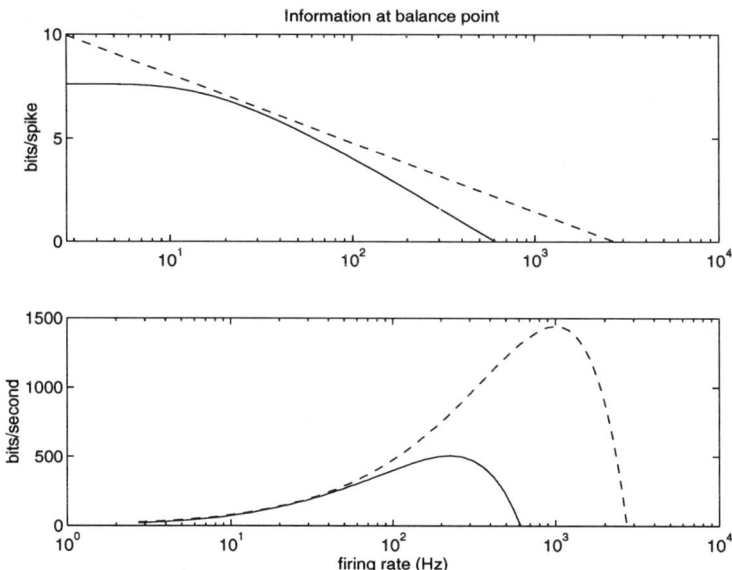

Figure 1: Information rate at balance point. (A; *top*) The information per spike decreases monotonically with the spike rate (*solid line*). It is bounded above by the entropy of the exponential limit (*dashed line*), which is the highest entropy ISI distribution for a given mean rate; this limit is approached for the IF neuron in the subthreshold regime. The information rate goes to 0 when the firing rate is of the same order as the temporal resolution Δt. The information per spike at the balance point is nearly optimal when $E\{T\} \approx \tau$. ($\tau = 50$ msec; $\Delta t = 1$ msec); (B; *bottom*) Information per second for above conditions. The information rate for both the balance point (*solid curve*) and the exponential distribution (*dashed curve*) pass through a maximum, but the maximum is greater and occurs at an higher rate for the latter. For firing rates much smaller than τ, the rates are almost indistinguishable. ($\tau = 50$ msec; $\Delta t = 1$ msec)

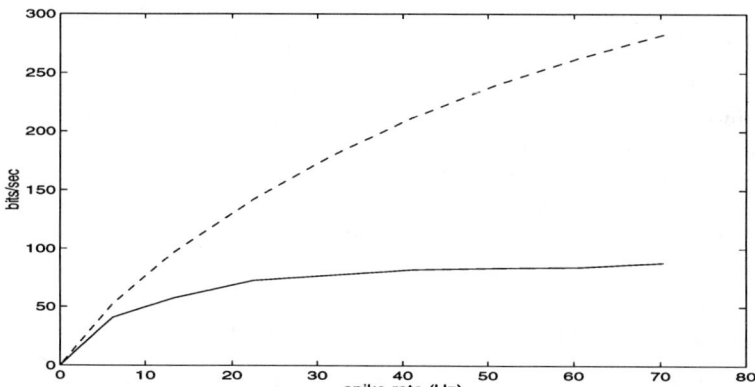

Figure 2: Estimating information by stimulus reconstruction. The information rate estimated by the reconstruction method *solid line* and the exact information rate *dashed line* are shown as a function of the firing rate. The reconstruction method significantly underestimates the actual information, particularly at high firing rates. The firing rate was varied through the mean input μ. The parameters were: membrane time constant $\tau = 20$ msec; spike bin size $\Delta t = 1$ msec; signal variance $\sigma_s^2 = 0.8$; threshold $Q = 10$.

Reorganisation of Somatosensory Cortex after Tactile Training

Rasmus S. Petersen   John G. Taylor
Centre for Neural Networks, King's College London
Strand, London WC2R 2LS, UK

Abstract

Topographic maps in primary areas of mammalian cerebral cortex reorganise as a result of behavioural training. The nature of this reorganisation seems consistent with the behaviour of competitive neural networks, as has been demonstrated in the past by computer simulation. We model tactile training on the hand representation in primate somatosensory cortex, using the Neural Field Theory of Amari and his colleagues. Expressions for changes in both receptive field size and magnification factor are derived, which are consistent with owl monkey experiments and make a prediction which goes beyond them.

1. INTRODUCTION

The primary cortical areas of mammals are now known to be plastic throughout life; reviewed recently by Kaas(1995). The problem of how and why the underlying learning processes work is an exciting one, for which neural network modelling appears well suited. In this contribution, we model the long-term effects of tactile training (Jenkins et al, 1990) on the functional organisation of monkey primary somatosensory cortex, by perturbing a topographic net (Takeuchi and Amari, 1979).

1.1 ADAPTATION IN ADULT SOMATOSENSORY CORTEX

Light touch activates skin receptors which in primates are mapped, largely topographically, in area 3b. In a series of papers, Merzenich and colleagues describe how area 3b becomes reorganised following peripheral nerve damage (Merzenich et al, 1983a; 1983b) or digit amputation (Merzenich et al, 1984). The underlying learning processes may also explain the phenomenon of phantom limb "telescoping" (Haber, 1955). Recent advances in brain scanning are beginning to make them observable even in the human brain (Mogilner et al, 1993).

1.2 ADAPTATION ASSOCIATED WITH TACTILE TRAINING

Jenkins et al trained owl monkeys to maintain contact with a rotating disk. The apparatus was arranged so that success eventually involved touching the disk with only the digit tips. Hence these regions received selective stimulation. Some time after training had been completed electro-physiological recordings were made from area 3b. These revealed an increase in Magnification Factor (MF) for the stimulated skin and a decrease in the size of Receptive Fields (RFs) for that region. The net territory gained for light touch of the digit tips came from area 3a and/or the face region of area 3b, but details of any changes in these representations were not reported.

2. THEORETICAL FRAMEWORK

2.1 PREVIOUS WORK

Takeuchi and Amari(1979), Ritter and Schulten(1986), Pearson et al(1987) and Grajski and Merzenich(1990) have all modelled amputation/denervation by computer simulation of competitive neural networks with various Hebbian weight dynamics. Grajski and Merzenich(1990) also modelled the data of Jenkins et al. We build on this research within the *Neural Field Theory* framework (Amari, 1977; Takeuchi and Amari, 1979; Amari, 1980) of the *Neural Activity Model* of Willshaw and von der Malsburg(1976).

2.2 NEURAL ACTIVITY MODEL

Consider a "cortical" network of simple, laterally connected neurons. Neurons sum inputs linearly and output a sigmoidal function of this sum. The lateral connections are excitatory at short distances and inhibitory at longer ones. Such a network is competitive: the steady state consists of blobs of activity centred around those neurons locally receiving the greatest afferent input (Amari, 1977). The range of the competition is limited by the range of the lateral inhibition.

Suppose now that the afferent synapses adapt in a Hebbian manner to stimuli that are localised in the sensory array; the lateral ones are fixed. Willshaw and von der Malsburg(1976) showed by computer simulation that this network is able to form a topographic map of the sensory array. Takeuchi and Amari(1979) amended the Willshaw-Malsburg model slightly: neurons possess an *adaptive firing threshold* in order to prevent synaptic weight explosion, rather than the more usual mechanism of weight normalisation. They proved that a topographic mapping is stable under certain conditions.

2.3 TAKEUCHI-AMARI THEORY

Consider a one-dimensional model. The membrane dynamics are:

$$\frac{\partial u(x,y,t)}{\partial t} = -u(x,y,t) + \int s(x,y',t)a(y-y')dy' - \\ s_0(x,t)a_0 + \int w(x-x')\mathrm{f}[u(x',y,t)]dx' - h \quad (1)$$

Here $u(x,y,t)$ is the membrane potential at time t for point x when a stimulus centred at y is being presented; h is a positive resting potential; $w(z)$ is the lateral inhibitory weight between two points in the neural field separated by a distance z - positive for small $|z|$ and negative for larger $|z|$; $s(x,y,t)$ is the excitatory synaptic weight from y to x at time t and $s_0(x,t)$ is an inhibitory weight from a tonically active inhibitory input a_0 to x at time t - it is the adaptive firing threshold. $\mathrm{f}[u]$ is a binary threshold function that maps positive membrane potentials to 1 and non-positive ones to 0.

Idealised, point-like stimuli are assumed, which "spread out" somewhat on the sensory surface or subcortically. The spreading process is assumed to be independent of y and is described in the same coordinates. It is represented by the function $a(y-y')$, which describes the effect of a point input at y spreading to the point y'. This is a decreasing, positive, symmetric function of $|y-y'|$. With this type of input, the steady-state activity of the network is a single blob, localised around the neuron with maximum afferent input.

The afferent synaptic weights adapt in a leaky Hebbian manner but with a time constant much larger than that of the membrane dynamics (1). Effectively this means that learning occurs on the steady state of the membrane dynamics. The following averaged weight dynamics can be justified (Takeuchi and Amari, 1979; Geman 1979):

$$\frac{\partial s(x,y,t)}{\partial t} = -s(x,y,t) + b \int p(y')a(y-y')f[\hat{u}(x,y')]dy'$$

$$\frac{\partial s_0(x,y,t)}{\partial t} = -s_0(x,y,t) + b' a_0 \int p(y')f[\hat{u}(x,y')]dy'$$

(2)

where $\hat{u}(x,y')$ is the steady-state of the membrane dynamics at x given a stimulus at y' and $p(y')$ is the probability of a stimulus at y'; b, b' are constants.

Empirically, the "classical" Receptive Field (RF) of a neuron is defined as the region of the input field within which localised stimulation causes change in its activity. This concept can be modelled in neural field theory as: the RF of a neuron at x is the portion of the input field within which a stimulus evokes a positive membrane potential (inhibitory RFs are not considered). If the neural field is a continuous map of the sensory surface then the RF of a neuron is fully described by its two borders $r_1(x), r_2(x)$, defined formally:

$$\hat{u}(x, r_i(x)) = 0 \qquad i = 1,2 \qquad (3)$$

which are illustrated in figure 1.

Let RF size and RF position be denoted respectively by the functions $r(x)$ and $m(x)$, which represent experimentally measurable quantities. In terms of the border functions they can be expressed:

$$r(x) = r_2(x) - r_1(x)$$
$$m(x) = \tfrac{1}{2}(r_1(x) + r_2(x))$$

(4)

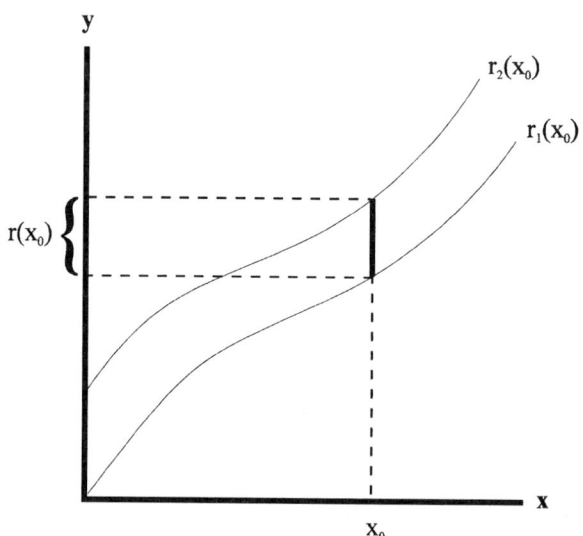

Figure 1: RF boundaries as a function of position in the neural field, for a topographically ordered network. Only the region in-between $r_1(x)$ and $r_2(x)$ has positive steady-state membrane potential $\hat{u}(x,y)$. $r_1(x)$ and $r_2(x)$ are defined by the condition $\hat{u}(x,r_i(x))=0$ for $i=1,2$.

Using (1), (2) and the definition (3), Takeuchi and Amari(1979) derived dynamical equations for the change in RF borders due to learning. In the case of uniform stimulus probability, they found solutions for the steady-state RF border functions. With periodic boundary conditions, the basic solution is a linear map with constant RF size:

$$r(x) = r_0 = \text{const} \qquad r_1^{uni}(x) = \rho x$$
$$m(x) = \rho x + \tfrac{1}{2} r_0 \qquad r_2^{uni}(x) = \rho x + r_0 \qquad (5)$$

This means that both RF size and activity blob size are uniform across the network and that RF position $m(x)$ is a linear function of network location. (The value of ρ is determined by boundary conditions; r_0 is then determined from the joint equilibrium of (1), (2)). The inverse of the RF position function, denoted by $m^{-1}(y)$, is the centre of the cortical active region caused by a stimulus centred at y. The change in $m^{-1}(y)$ over a unit interval in the input field is, by empirical definition, the cortical magnification factor (MF). Here we model MF as the rate of change of $m^{-1}(y)$. The MF for the system described by (5) is:

$$\frac{d}{dy} m^{-1}(y) = \rho^{-1} \qquad (6)$$

3. ANALYSIS OF TACTILE TRAINING

3.1 TRAINING MODEL AND ASSUMPTIONS

Jenkins et al's training sessions caused an increase in the relative frequency of stimulation to the finger tips, and hence a decrease in relative frequency of stimulation elsewhere. Over a long time, we can express this fact as a localised change in stimulus probability (figure 2). (This is not sufficient to cause cortical reorganisation - Recanzone et al(1992) showed that attention to the stimulation is vital. We consider only attended stimulation in this model). To account for such data it is clearly necessary to analyse *non-uniform stimulus probabilities*, which demands extending the results of Takeuchi and Amari. Unfortunately, it seems to be hard to obtain general results. However, a perturbation analysis around the uniform probability solution (5) is possible.

To proceed in this way, we must be able to assume that the change in the stimulus probability density function away from uniformity is small. This reasoning is expressed by the following equation:

$$p(y) = p_0 + \varepsilon \tilde{p}(y) \qquad (7)$$

where $p(y)$ is the new stimulus probability in terms of the uniform one and a perturbation due to training: ε is a small constant. The effect of the perturbation is to ease the weight dynamics (2) away from the solution (5) to a new steady-state. Our goal is to discover the effect of this on the RF border functions, and hence for RF size and MF.

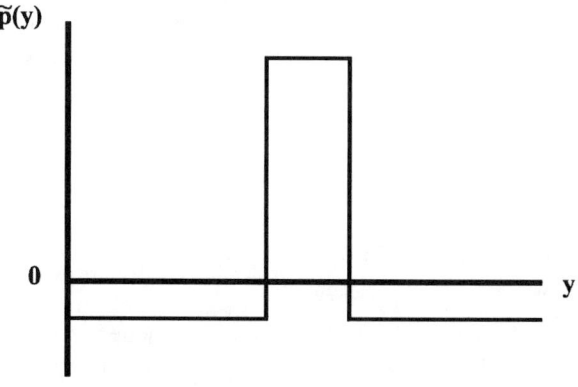

Figure 2: The type of change in stimulus probability density that we assume to model the effects of behavioural training.

3.2 PERTURBATION ANALYSIS

3.2.1 General Case

For a small enough perturbation, the effect on the RF borders and on the activity blob size ought also to be small. We consider effects to first order in ε, seeking new solutions of the form:

$$r_i^{per}(x) = r_i^{uni}(x) + \varepsilon \tilde{r}_i(x) \quad i = 1,2 \qquad \begin{array}{l} \tilde{r}(x) = \tilde{r}_2(x) - \tilde{r}_1(x) \\ \tilde{m}(x) = \tfrac{1}{2}(\tilde{r}_1(x) + \tilde{r}_2(x)) \end{array} \qquad (8)$$

where the superscript *per* denotes the new, perturbed equilibrium and *uni* denotes the unperturbed, uniform probability equilibrium. Using (1) and (2) in (3) for the post-training RF borders, expanding to first order in ε, a pair of difference equations may be obtained for the changes in RF borders. It is convenient to define the following terms:

$$A_1(x) = \int_0^{r_0} \tilde{p}(y + \rho x) k(y) dy - b' a_0^2 \int_{r_1^{uni}(x)}^{r_2^{uni}(x)} \tilde{p}(y) dy$$

$$A_2(x) = \int_{-r_0}^{0} \tilde{p}(y + \rho x + r_0) k(y) dy - b' a_0^2 \int_{r_1^{uni}(x)}^{r_2^{uni}(x)} \tilde{p}(y) dy$$

$$k(y) = b \int a(y - y') a(y') dy' \qquad (9)$$

$$B = b' a_0^2 p_0 - k(r_0) p_0 > 0$$

$$C = w(\rho^{-1} r_0) \rho^{-1} < 0$$

where the signs of B and C arise due to stability conditions (Amari, 1977; Takeuchi and Amari, 1979). In terms of RF size and RF position (4), the general result is:

$$B\Delta^2 \tilde{r}(x) = \Delta(\Delta+1) A_1(x) - \Delta A_2(x)$$
$$BC\Delta^2 \tilde{m}(x) = (B - C - \tfrac{1}{2}C\Delta)(\Delta+1) A_1(x) + (C - B + \tfrac{1}{2}(C - 2B)\Delta) A_2(x) \qquad (10)$$

where Δ is the difference operator:

$$\Delta f(x) = f(x + \rho^{-1} r_0) - f(x) \qquad (11)$$

3.2.2 Particular Case

The second order difference equations (10) are rather opaque. This is partly due to coupling in y caused by the auto-correlation function $k(y)$: (10) simplifies considerably if very narrow stimuli are assumed - $a(y) = \delta(y)$ (see also Amari, 1980). For periodic boundary conditions:

$$\frac{\tilde{r}(x)}{r_0} = -\frac{1}{p_0 r_0} \int_{r_1^{uni}(x)}^{r_2^{uni}(x)} \tilde{p}(y) dy$$

$$\frac{d}{dy} \tilde{m}^{-1}(y) \approx \frac{1}{2 p_0 \rho r_0} \int_{y-r_0}^{y+r_0} \tilde{p}(y') dy' - \frac{ba(0)^2}{w(\rho^{-1} r_0) r_0} \tilde{p}(y) \qquad (12)$$

where:

$$m^{-1\,post}(y) = m^{-1\,pre}(y) + \varepsilon \tilde{m}^{-1}(y)$$
$$= \rho^{-1}(y - \tfrac{1}{2} r_0) + \varepsilon \tilde{m}^{-1}(y) \tag{13}$$

and we have used the crude approximation:

$$\frac{d}{dx} \tilde{m}(x) \approx \frac{1}{l_0} \Delta m(x - \tfrac{1}{2} \rho^{-1} r_0) \tag{14}$$

which demands smoothness on the scale of l_0. However, for perturbations like that sketched in figure 2, this is sufficient to tell us about the constant regions of MF. (We would not expect to be able to model the data in the transition region in any case, as its form is too dependent upon fine detail of the model).

Our results (12) show that the change in RF size of a neuron is simply minus the total change in stimulus probability over its RF. Hence RF size decreases where p(y) increases and *vice versa*. Conversely, the change in MF at a given stimulus location is roughly the local average change in stimulus probability there. Note that changes in RF size correlate inversely with changes in MF. Figure 3 is a sketch of these results for the perturbation of figure 2.

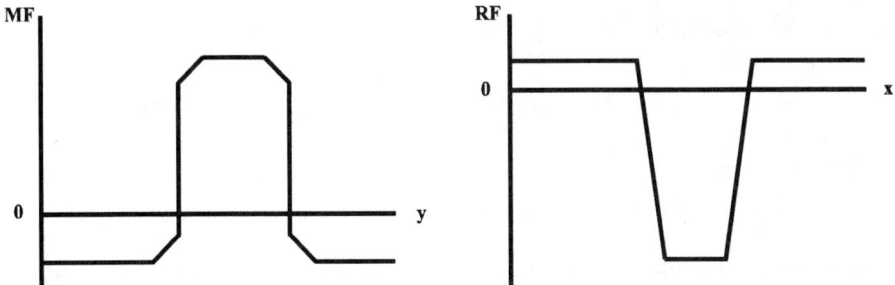

Figure 3: Results of perturbation analysis for how behavioural training (figure 2) changes RF size and MF respectively, in the case where stimulus width can be neglected. For MF - due to the approximation (14) - predictions do not apply near the transitions.

4. DISCUSSION

Equations (12) are the results of our model for RF size and MF after area 3b has fully adapted to the behavioural task, in the case where stimulus width can be neglected. They appear to be fully consistent with the data of Jenkins et al described above: RF size decreases in the region of cortex selective for the stimulated body part and the MF for this body part increases. Our analysis also makes a specific prediction that goes beyond Jenkins et al's data, directly due to the inverse relationship between changes in RF size and those in MF. Within the regions that *surrender* territory to the entrained finger tips (sometimes the face region), for which MF decreases, RF sizes should *increase*.

Surprisingly perhaps, these changes in RF size are *not* due to adaptation of the afferent weights $s(x,y)$. The changes are rather due to the *adaptive threshold* term $s_0(x)$. This point will be discussed more fully elsewhere.

A limitation of our analysis is the assumption that the change in stimulus probability is in some sense small. Such an approximation may be reasonable for behavioural training but seems less so as regards important experimental protocols like amputation or denervation. Evidently a more general analysis would be highly desirable.

5. CONCLUSION

We have analysed a system with three interacting features: lateral inhibitory interactions; Hebbian adaptivity of afferent synapses and an adaptive firing threshold. Our results indicate that such a system can account for the data of Jenkins et al, concerning the response of adult somatosensory cortex to the changing environmental demands imposed by tactile training. The analysis also brings out a prediction of the model, that may be testable.

Acknowledgements

RSP is very grateful for a travel stipend from the NIPS Foundation and for a Nick Hughes bursary from the School of Physical Sciences and Engineering, King's College London, that enabled him to participate in the conference.

References

Amari S. (1977) *Biol. Cybern.* **27** 77-87

Amari S. (1980) *Bull. Math. Biology* **42** 339-364

Geman S. (1979) *SIAM J. App. Math.* **36** 86-105

Grajski K.A., Merzenich M.M. (1990) in *Neural Information Processing Systems* **2** Touretzky D.S. (Ed) 52-59

Haber W.B. (1955) *J. Psychol.* **40** 115-123

Jenkins W.M., Merzenich M.M., Ochs M.T., Allard T., Guíc-Robles E. (1990) *J. Neurophysiol.* **63** 82-104

Kaas J.H. (1995) in *The Cognitive Neurosciences* Gazzaniga M.S. (Ed ic) 51-71

Merzenich M.M., Kaas J.H., Wall J.T., Nelson R.J., Sur M., Felleman D.J. (1983a) *Neuroscience* **8** 35-55

Merzenich M.M., Kaas J.H., Wall J.T., Sur M., Nelson R.J., Felleman D.J. (1983b) *Neuroscience* **10** 639-665

Merzenich M.M., Nelson R.J., Stryker M.P., Cynader M.S., Schoppmann A., Zook J.M. (1984) *J. Comp. Neurol.* **224** 591-605

Mogilner A., Grossman A.T., Ribrary V., Joliot M., Volmann J., Rapaport D., Beasley R., Llinás R. (1993) *Proc. Natl. Acad. Sci. USA* **90** 3593-3597

Pearson J.C., Finkel L.H., Edelman G.M. (1987) *J. Neurosci.* **12** 4209-4223

Recanzone G.H., Merzenich M.M., Jenkins W.M., Grajski K.A., Dinse H.R. (1992) *J. Neurophysiol.* **67** 1031-1056

Ritter H., Schulten K. (1986) *Biol. Cybern.* **54** 99-106

Takeuchi A., Amari S. (1979) *Biol. Cybern.* **35** 63-72

Willshaw D.J., von der Malsburg C. (1976) *Proc. R. Soc. Lond.* **B194** 203-243

A Dynamical Model of Context Dependencies for the Vestibulo-Ocular Reflex

Olivier J.M.D. Coenen*   Terrence J. Sejnowski[†]

Computational Neurobiology Laboratory
Howard Hughes Medical Institute
The Salk Institute for Biological Studies
10010 North Torrey Pines Road
La Jolla, CA 92037, U.S.A.

Departments of [†]Biology and [*†]Physics
University of California, San Diego
La Jolla, CA 92093, U.S.A
{olivier,terry}@salk.edu

Abstract

The vestibulo-ocular reflex (VOR) stabilizes images on the retina during rapid head motions. The gain of the VOR (the ratio of eye to head rotation velocity) is typically around -1 when the eyes are focused on a distant target. However, to stabilize images accurately, the VOR gain must vary with context (eye position, eye vergence and head translation). We first describe a kinematic model of the VOR which relies solely on sensory information available from the semicircular canals (head rotation), the otoliths (head translation), and neural correlates of eye position and vergence angle. We then propose a dynamical model and compare it to the eye velocity responses measured in monkeys. The dynamical model reproduces the observed amplitude and time course of the modulation of the VOR and suggests one way to combine the required neural signals within the cerebellum and the brain stem. It also makes predictions for the responses of neurons to multiple inputs (head rotation and translation, eye position, etc.) in the oculomotor system.

1 Introduction

The VOR stabilizes images on the retina during rapid head motions: Rotations and translations of the head in three dimensions must be compensated by appropriate rotations of the eye. Because the head's rotation axis is not the same as the eye's rotation axis, the calculations for proper image stabilization of an object must take into account diverse variables such as object distance from each eye, gaze direction, and head translation (Viire et al., 1986). The stabilization is achieved by integrating information from different sources: head rotations from the semicircular canals of the inner ear, head translations from the otolith organs, eye positions, viewing distance, as well as other context information, such as posture (head tilts) or activity (walking, running) (Snyder and King, 1992; Shelhamer et al.,1992; Grossman et al., 1989). In this paper we concentrate on the context modulation of the VOR which can be described by the kinematics of the reflex, i.e. eye position, eye vergence and head translation.

2 The Vestibulo-Ocular Reflex: Kinematic Model

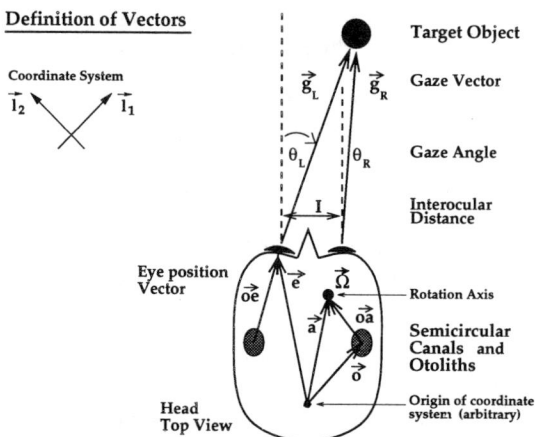

Figure 1: Diagram showing the definition of the vectors used in the equation of the kinematic model of the vestibulo-ocular reflex.

The ideal VOR response is a compensatory eye movement which keeps the image fixed on the retina for any head rotations and translations. We therefore derived an equation for the eye rotation velocity by requiring that a target remains stationary on the retina. The velocity of the resulting compensatory eye rotation can be written as (see fig. 1):

$$\vec{\omega} = -\vec{\Omega}_c + \frac{\hat{g}}{|g|} \times \left[\vec{oe}_j \times \vec{\Omega}_c - \vec{T}_{o_j}\right] \qquad (1)$$

where $\vec{\Omega}_c$ is the head rotation velocity sensed by the semicircular canals, $\vec{T}_{o_j}$ is the head translation velocity sensed by the otoliths, $\vec{oe}_j \equiv (\vec{e} - \vec{o}_j)$, $\vec{e}$ is a constant vector specifying the location of an eye in the head, $\vec{o}_j$ is the position of either the left or right otolith, $\hat{g}$ and $|g|$ are the unit vector and amplitude of the gaze vector: $\hat{g}$ gives the eye position (orientation of the eye relative to the head), and $|g|$ gives the distance from the eye to the object, and the symbol × indicates the cross-product between two vectors. $\vec{\omega}$ and $\vec{\Omega}_c$ are rotation vectors which describe the instantaneous angular velocity of the eye and head, respectively. A rotation vector lies along the instantaneous axis of rotation; its magnitude indicates the speed of rotation around the axis, and its direction is given by the right-hand screw rule. A motion of the head combining rotation ($\vec{\Omega}$) and translation ($\vec{T}$) is sensed as the combination of a rotation velocity $\vec{\Omega}_c$ measured by the semicircular canals and a translation velocity $\vec{T}_o$ sensed by the otoliths. The rotation vectors are equal ($\vec{\Omega} = \vec{\Omega}_c$), and the translation velocity vector as measured by the otoliths is given by: $\vec{T}_{o_j} = \vec{oa}_j \times \vec{\Omega} + \vec{T}$, where $\vec{oa}_j \equiv (\vec{a} - \vec{o}_j)$, and $\vec{a}$ is the position vector of the axis of rotation.

The special case where the gaze is horizontal and the rotation vector is vertical (horizontal head rotation) has been studied extensively in the literature. We used this special case in the simulations. In that case $\vec{w}$ may be simplify by writing its equation with dot products. Since $\hat{g}$ and $\vec{\Omega}_c$ are then perpendicular ($\hat{g} \cdot \vec{\Omega}_c = 0$), the first term of the following expression in brackets is zero:

$$\vec{w} = -\vec{\Omega}_c + \frac{1}{|g|} \left[\vec{oe}(\hat{g} \cdot \vec{\Omega}_c) - \vec{\Omega}_c(\hat{g} \cdot \vec{oe}) - \hat{g} \times \vec{T}_o \right] \quad (2)$$

The semicircular canals decompose and report acceleration and velocity of head rotation $\vec{\Omega}$ by its components along the three canals on each side of the head $\vec{\Omega}_c$: horizontal, anterior and posterior. The two otolith organs on each side report the dynamical inertial forces generated during linear motion (translation) in two perpendicular plane, one vertical and the other horizontal relative to the head. Here we assume that a translation velocity signal ($\vec{T}_o$) derived from or reported by the otolith afferents is available. The otoliths encode as well the head orientation relative to the gravity vector force, but was not included in this study.

To complete the correspondence between the equation and a neural correlate, we need to determine a physiological source for $\hat{g}$ and $\frac{1}{|g|}$. The eye position $\hat{g}$ is assumed to be given by the output of the velocity-to-position transformation or so-called "neural integrator" which provides eye position information and which is necessary for the activation of the motoneuron to sustain the eye in a fixed position. The integrator for horizontal eye position appears to be located in the nucleus prepositus hypoglossi in the pons, and the vertical integrator in the midbrain interstitial nucleus of Cajal. (Crawford, Cadera and Vilis, 1991; Cannon and Robinson, 1987). We assume that the eye position is given as the coordinates of the unit vector $\hat{g}$ along the $\vec{l}_1$ and $\vec{l}_2$ of fig. 1. The eye position depends on the eye velocity according to $\frac{d\hat{g}}{dt} = \hat{g} \times \vec{w}$. For the special case $\vec{w}(t) = w(t)\hat{z}$, i.e. for horizontal head rotation, the eye position coordinates are given by:

$$\hat{g}_1(t) = \hat{g}_1(0) + \int_0^t \hat{g}_2(\tau)w(\tau)\,d\tau$$
$$\hat{g}_2(t) = \hat{g}_2(0) - \int_0^t \hat{g}_1(\tau)w(\tau)\,d\tau \quad (3)$$

This is a set of two negatively coupled integrators. The "neural integrator" therefore does not integrate the eye velocity directly but a product of eye position and eye velocity. The distance from eye to target $\frac{1}{|g|}$ can be written using the gaze angles in the horizontal plane of the head:

$$\text{Right eye:} \quad \frac{1}{|g_R|} = \frac{\sin(\theta_R - \theta_L)}{I \cos(\theta_L)} = \frac{1}{I}\sec(\theta_L)\sin(\theta_R - \theta_L) \quad (4)$$

$$\text{Left eye:} \quad \frac{1}{|g_L|} = \frac{\sin(\theta_R - \theta_L)}{I \cos(\theta_R)} = \frac{1}{I}\sec(\theta_R)\sin(\theta_R - \theta_L) \quad (5)$$

where $(\theta_R - \theta_L)$ is the vergence angle, and I is the interocular distance; the angles are measured from a straight ahead gaze, and take on negative values when the eyes are turned towards the right. Within the oculomotor system, the vergence angle and speed are encoded by the mesencephalic reticular formation neurons (Judge and Cumming, 1986; Mays, 1984). The nucleus reticularis tegmenti pontis with reciprocal connections to the flocculus, oculomotor vermis, paravermis of the cerebellum also contains neurons which activity varies linearly with vergence angle (Gamlin and Clarke, 1995).

We conclude that it is possible to perform the computations needed to obtain an ideal VOR with signals known to be available physiologically.

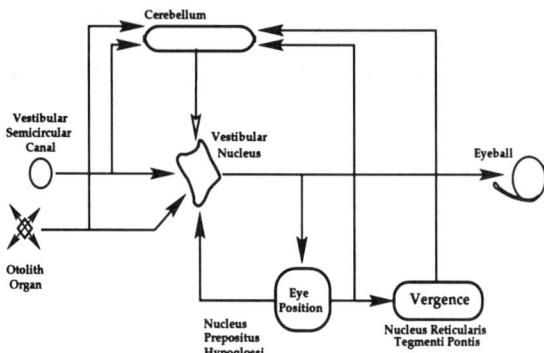

Figure 2: Anatomical connections considered in the dynamical model. Only the left side is shown, the right side is identical and connected to the left side only for the calculation of vergence angle. The nucleus prepositus hypoglossi and the nucleus reticularis tegmenti pontis are meant to be representative of a class of nuclei in the brain stem carrying eye position or vergence signal. All connections are known to exist except the connection between the prepositus nucleus to the reticularis nucleus which has not been verified. Details of the cerebellum are in fig. 3 and of the vestibular nucleus in fig. 4.

3 Dynamical Model

Snyder & King (1992) studied the effect of viewing distance and location of the axis of rotation on the VOR in monkeys; their main results are reproduced in fig. 5. In an attempt to reproduce their data and to understand how the signals that we have described in section 2 may be combined in time, we constructed a dynamical model based on the kinematic model. Its basic anatomical structure is shown in fig. 2. Details of the model are shown in fig. 3, and fig. 4 where all constants are written using a millisecond time scale. The results are presented in fig. 5. The dynamical variables represent the change of average firing rate from resting level of activity. The firing rate of the afferents has a tonic component proportional to the velocity and a phasic component proportional to the acceleration of movement. Physiologically, the afferents have a wide range of phasic and tonic amplitudes. This is reflected by a wide selection of parameters in the numerators in the boxes of fig. 3 and fig. 4. The Laplace transform of the integration operator in equation (3) of the eye position coordinates is $\frac{1}{s}$. Following Robinson (1981), we modeled the neural integrator with a gain and a time constant of 20 seconds. We therefore replaced the pure integrator $\frac{1}{s}$ with $\frac{20000}{20000s+1}$ in the calculations of eye position. The term $\frac{1}{g}$ in fig. 3 is calculated by using equations (4) and (5), and by using the integrator $\frac{20000}{20000s+1}$ on the eye velocity motor command to find the angles θ_L and θ_R.

The dynamical model is based on the assumption that the cerebellum is required for context modulation, and that because of its architecture, the cerebellum is more likely to implement complex functions of multiple signals than other relevant nuclei. The major contributions of vergence and eye position modulation on the VOR are therefore mediated by the cerebellum. Smaller and more transient contributions from eye position are assumed to be mediated through the vestibular nucleus as shown in fig. 4. The motivation for combining eye position as in fig. 4 are, first, the evidence for eye response oscillations; second, the theoretical consideration that linear movement information ($\vec{T}_o$) is useless without eye position information for proper VOR.

The parameters in the dynamical model were adjusted by hand after observing the behavior of the different components of the model and noting how these combine to produce the oscillations observed

A Dynamical Model of Context Dependencies for the Vestibulo-Ocular Reflex

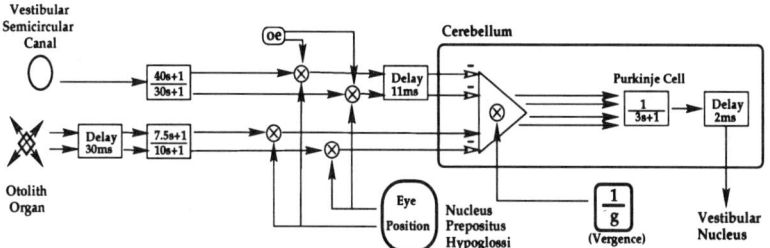

Figure 3: Contribution of the cerebellum to the dynamical model. Filtered velocity inputs from the canals and otoliths are combined with eye position according to equation (2). These calculations could be performed either outside the cerebellum in one or multiple brain stem nuclei (as shown) or possibly inside the cerebellum. The only output is to the vestibular nucleus. The Laplace notation is used in each boxes to represent a leaky integrator with a time constant, input derivative and input gain. The term oe are the coordinates of the vector $\vec{oe}$ shown in fig. 1. The × indicates a multiplication. The term $\frac{1}{g}$ multiplies each inputs individually. The open arrows indicate inhibitory (negative) connections.

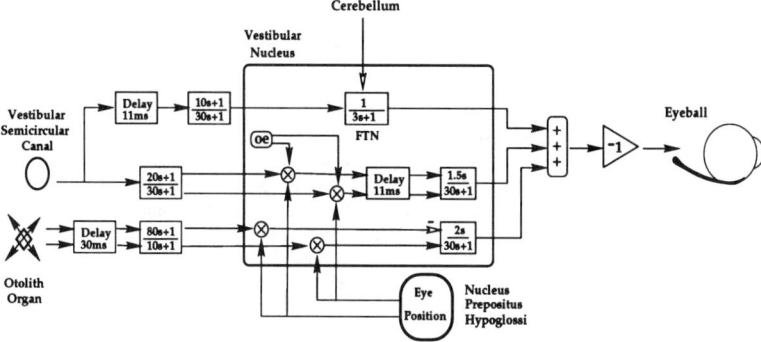

Figure 4: Contribution of the vestibular nucleus to the dynamical model. Three pathways in the vestibular nucleus process the canal and otolith inputs to drive the eye. The first pathway is modulated by the output of the cerebellum through a FTN (Flocculus Target Neuron). The second and third pathways report transient information from the inputs which are combined with eye position in a manner identical to fig. 3. The location of these calculations is hypothetical.

in the data. Even though the number of parameters in the model is not small, it was not possible to fit any single response in fig. 5 without affecting most of the other eye responses. This puts severe limits on the set of parameters allowed in the model.

The dynamical model suggests that the oscillations present in the data reflect: 1) important acceleration components in the neural signals, both rotational and linear, 2) different time delays between the canal and otolith signal processing, and 3) antagonistic or synergistic action of the canal and otolith signals with different axes of rotation, as described by the two terms in the bracket of equation (2).

4 Discussion

By fitting the dynamical model to the data, we tested the hypothesis that the VOR has a response close to ideal taking into account the time constraints imposed by the sensory inputs and the neural networks performing the computations. The vector computations that we used in the model may not

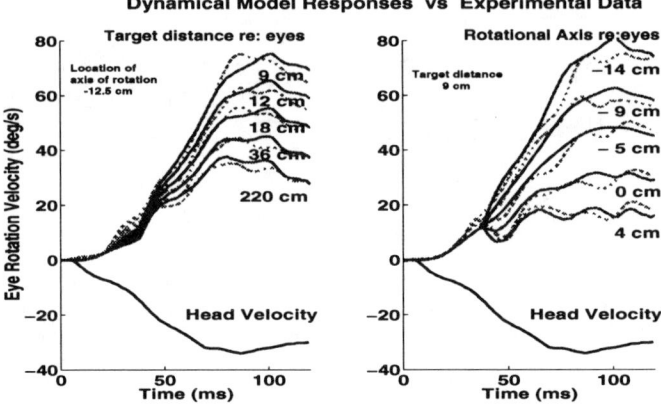

Figure 5: Comparison between the dynamical model and monkey data. The dotted lines show the effect of viewing distance and location of the axis of rotation on the VOR as recorded by Snyder & King (1992) from monkeys in the dark. The average eye velocity response (of left and right eye) to a sudden change in head velocity is shown for different target distances (left) and rotational axes (right). On the left, the location of the axis of rotation was in the midsagittal plane 12.5 cm behind the eyes (-12.5 cm), and the target distance was varied between 220 cm and 9 cm. On the right, the target distance was kept constant at 9 cm in front of the eye, and the location of the axis of rotation was varied from 14 cm behind to 4 cm in front of the eyes (-14 cm to 4 cm) in the midsagittal plane. The solid lines show the model responses. The model replicates many characteristics of the data. On the left the model captures the eye velocity fluctuations between 20-50 ms, followed by a decrease and an increase which are both modulated with target distance (50-80 ms). The later phase of the response (80-100 ms) is almost exact for 220 cm, and one peak is seen at the appropriate location for the other distances. On the right the closest fits were obtained for the 4 cm and 0 cm locations. The mean values are in good agreement and the waveforms are close, but could be shifted in time for the other locations of the axis of rotations. Finally, the latest peak ($\sim$ 100 ms) in the data appears in the model for -14 cm and 9 cm location.

be the representation used in the oculomotor system. Mathematically, the vector representation is only one way to describe the computations involved. Other representations exist such as the quaternion representation which has been studied in the context of the saccadic system (Tweed and Vilis, 1987; see also Handzel and Flash, 1996 for a very general representation). Detailed comparisons between the model and recordings from neurons will be require to settle this issue.

Direct comparison between Purkinje cell recordings (L.H. Snyder & W.M. King, unpublished data) and predictions of the model could be used to determine more precisely the different inputs to some Purkinje cells. The model can therefore be an important tool to gain insights difficult to obtain directly with experiments.

The question of how the central nervous system learns the transformations that we described still remains. The cerebellum may be one site of learning for these transformations, and its output may modulate the VOR in real time depending on the context. This view is compatible with the results of Angelaki and Hess (1995) which indicate that the cerebellum is required to correctly perform an otolith transformation. It is also consistent with adaptation results in the VOR. To test this hypothesis, we have been working on a model of the cerebellum which learns to anticipate sensory inputs and feedbacks, and use these signals to modulate the VOR. The learning in the cerebellum and vestibular nuclei is mediated by the climbing fibers which report a reinforcement signal of the prediction error (Coenen and Sejnowski, in preparation).

5 Conclusion

Most research on the VOR has assumed forward gaze focussed at infinity. The kinematics of off-center gaze and fixation at finite distance necessitates nonlinear corrections that require the integration of a variety of sensory inputs. The dynamical model studied here is a working hypothesis for how these corrections could be computed and is generally consistent with what is known about the cerebellum and brain stem nuclei. We are, however, far from knowing the mechanisms underlying these computations, or how they are learned through experience.

6 Acknowledgments

The first author was supported by a McDonnell-Pew Graduate Fellowship during this research. We would like to thank Paul Viola for helpful discussions.

References

Angelaki, D. E. and Hess, B. J. (1995). Inertial representation of angular motion in the vestibular system of rhesus monkeyus. II. Otolith-controlled transformation that depends on an intact cerebellar nodulus. *Journal of Neurophysiology*, 73(5):1729–1751.

Cannon, S. C. and Robinson, D. A. (1987). Loss of the neural integrator of the oculomotor system from brain stem lesions in monkey. *Journal of Neurophysiology*, 57(5):1383–1409.

Crawford, J. D., Cadera, W., and Vilis, T. (1991). Generation of torsional and vertical eye position signals by the interstitial nucleus of Cajal. *Science*, 252:1551–1553.

Gamlin, P. D. R. and Clarke, R. J. (1995). Single-unit activity in the primate nucleus reticularis tegmenti pontis related to vergence and ocular accomodation. *Journal of Neurophysiology*, 73(5):2115–2119.

Grossman, G. E., Leigh, R. J., Bruce, E. N., Huebner, W. P., and Lanska, D. J. (1989). Performance of the human vestibuloocular reflex during locomotion. *Journal of Neurophysiology*, 62(1):264–272.

Handzel, A. A. and Flash, T. (1996). The geometry of eye rotations and listing's law. In Touretzky, D., Mozer, M., and Hasselmo, M., editors, *Advances in Neural Information Processing Systems 8*, Cambridge, MA. MIT Press.

Judge, S. J. and Cumming, B. G. (1986). Neurons in the monkey midbrain with activity related to vergence eye movement and accomodation. *Journal of Neurophysiology*, 55:915–930.

Mays, L. E. (1984). Neural control of vergence eye movements: Convergence and divergence neurons in midbrain. *Journal of Neurophysiology*, 51:1091–1108.

Robinson, D. A. (1981). The use of control systems analysis in the neurophysiology of eye movements. *Ann. Rev. Neurosci.*, 4:463–503.

Shelhamer, M., Robinson, D. A., and Tan, H. S. (1992). Context-specific adaptation of the gain of the vestibulo-ocular reflex in humans. *Journal of Vestibular Research*, 2:89–96.

Snyder, L. H. and King, W. M. (1992). Effect of viewing distance and location of the axis of head rotation on the monkey's vestibuloocular reflex I. eye movement response. *Journal of Neurophysiology*, 67(4):861–874.

Tweed, D. and Vilis, T. (1987). Implications of rotational kinematics for the oculomotor system in three dimensions. *Journal of Neurophysiology*, 58(4):832–849.

Viire, E., Tweed, D., Milner, K., and Vilis, T. (1986). A reexamination of the gain of the vestibuloocular reflex. *Journal of Neurophysiology*, 56(2):439–450.

The Role of Activity in Synaptic Competition at the Neuromuscular Junction

Samuel R. H. Joseph
Centre for Cognitive Science
Edinburgh University
Edinburgh, U.K.
email: sam@cns.ed.ac.uk

David J. Willshaw
Centre for Cognitive Science
Edinburgh University
Edinburgh, U.K.
email: david@cns.ed.ac.uk

Abstract

An extended version of the dual constraint model of motor endplate morphogenesis is presented that includes activity dependent and independent competition. It is supported by a wide range of recent neurophysiological evidence that indicates a strong relationship between synaptic efficacy and survival. The computational model is justified at the molecular level and its predictions match the developmental and regenerative behaviour of real synapses.

1 INTRODUCTION

The neuromuscular junction (NMJ) of mammalian skeletal muscle is one of the most extensively studied areas of the nervous system. One aspect of its development that it shares with many other parts of the nervous system is its achievement of single innervation, one axon terminal connecting to one muscle fibre, after an initial state of polyinnervation. The presence of electrical activity is associated with this transition, but the exact relationship is far from clear. Understanding how activity interacts with the morphogenesis of neural systems could provide us with insights into methods for constructing artificial neural networks. With that in mind, this paper examines how some of the conflicting ideas about the development of neuromuscular connections can be resolved.

2 EXPERIMENTAL FINDINGS

The extent to which a muscle is innervated can be expressed in terms of the motor unit size - the number of fibres contacted by a given motor axon. Following removal of some motor axons at birth, the average size of the remaining motor units after withdrawal of polyinnervation is larger than normal (Fladby & Jansen, 1987). This strongly suggests that individual motor axons successfully innervate more fibres as a result of the absence of their neighbours. It is appealing to interpret this as a competitive process where terminals from different axons compete for the same muscle endplate. Since each terminal is made up of a number of synapses the process can be viewed as the co-existence of synapses from the same terminal and the elimination of synapses from different terminals on the same endplate.

2.1 THE EFFECTS OF ELECTRICAL ACTIVITY

There is a strong activity dependent component to synapse elimination. Paralysis or stimulation of selected motor units appears to favour the more active motor terminals (Colman & Lichtman, 1992), while inactive axon terminals tend to coexist. Recent work also shows that active synaptic sites can destabilise inactive synapses in their vicinity (Balice-Gordon & Lichtman, 1994). These findings support the idea that more active terminals have a competitive advantage over their inactive fellows, and that this competition takes place at a synaptic level.

Activity independent competition has been demonstrated in the rat lumbrical muscle (Ribchester, 1993). This muscle is innervated by the sural and the lateral plantar nerves. If the sural nerve is damaged the lateral plantar nerve will expand its territory to the extent that it innervates the entire muscle. On subsequent reinnervation the regenerating sural nerve may displace some of the lateral plantar nerve terminals. If the muscle is paralysed during reinnervation more lateral plantar nerve terminals are displaced than in the normal case, indicating that competition between inactive terminals does take place, and that paralysis can give an advantage to some terminals.

3 MODELS AND MECHANISMS

If the nerve terminals are competing with each other for dominance of motor endplates, what is the mechanism behind it? As mentioned above, activity is thought to play an important role in affecting the competitive chances of a terminal, but in most models the terminals compete for some kind of trophic resource (Gouze et al., 1983; Willshaw, 1981). It is possible to create models that use competition for either a postsynaptic (endplate) resource or a presynaptic (motor axon) resource. Both types of model have advantages and disadvantages, which leads naturally to the possibility of combining the two into a single model.

3.1 BENNET AND ROBINSON'S DUAL CONSTRAINT MODEL

The dual constraint model (DCM) (Bennet & Robinson, 1989), as extended by Rasmussen & Willshaw (1993), is based on a reversible reaction between molecules from a presynaptic resource A and a postsynaptic resource B. This reaction takes place in the synaptic cleft and produces a binding complex C which is essential for the terminal's survival. Each motor axon and muscle fibre has a limited amount of their particular resource and the size of each terminal is proportional to the amount of the binding complex at that terminal. The model achieves single innervation and a perturbation analysis performed by Rasmussen & Willshaw (1993) showed that this single innervation state is stable. However, for the DCM to function the forward rate of the reaction had to be made proportional to the size of the terminal, which was difficult to justify other than suggesting it was related to electrical activity.

3.2 SELECTIVE MECHANISMS

While the synapses in the surviving presynaptic terminal are allowed to coexist, synapses from other axons are eliminated. How do synapses make a distinction between synapses in their own terminal and those in others? There are two possibilities: (i) Synchronous transmitter release in the synaptic boutons of a motor neuron could distinguish synapses, allowing them to compete as cartels rather than individuals (Colman & Lichtman, 1992). (ii) The synapses could be employing selective recognition mechanisms, e.g the 'induced-fit' model (Ribchester & Barry, 1994).

A selective mechanism implies that all the synapses of a given motor neuron can be identified by a molecular substrate. In the induced-fit model each motor neuron is associated with a specific isoform of a cellular adhesion molecule (CAM); the synapses compete by attempting to induce all the CAMs on the endplate into the conformation associated with their neuron. This kind of model can be used to account for much of the developmental and regenerative processes of the NMJ. However, it has difficulty explaining Balice-Gordon & Lichtman's (1994) focal blockade experiments which show competition between synapses distinguished only by the presence of activity. If, instead, activity is responsible for the distinction of friend from foe, how can competition take place at the terminal level when activity is not present? Could we resolve this dilemma by extending the dual constraint model?

4 EXTENDING THE DUAL CONSTRAINT MODEL

Tentative suggestions can be made for the identity of the 'mystery molecules' in the DCM. According to McMahan (1990) a protein called agrin is synthesised in the cell bodies of motor neurons and transported down their axons to the muscle. When this protein binds to the surface of the developing muscle, it causes acetylcholine receptors (AChRs), and other components of the postsynaptic apparatus, to aggregate on the myotube surface in the vicinity of the activated agrin.

Other work (Wallace, 1988) has provided insights into the mechanism used by agrin to cause the aggregation of the postsynaptic apparatus. Initially, AChR aggregates, or 'speckles', are free to diffuse laterally in the myotube plasma membrane (Axelrod et al., 1976). When agrin binds to an agrin-specific receptor, AChR speckles in the immediate vicinity of the agrin-receptor complex are immobilised. As more speckles are trapped larger patches are formed, until a steady state is reached. Such a patch will remain so long as agrin is bound to its receptor and Ca^{++} and energy supplies are available.

Following AChR activation by acetylcholine, Ca^{++} enters the postsynaptic cell. Since Ca^{++} is required for both the formation and maintenance of AChR aggregates, a feedback loop is possible whereby the bigger a patch is the more Ca^{++} it will have available when the receptors are activated. Crucially, depolarisation of non-junctional regions blocks AChR expression (Andreose et al., 1995) and it is AChR activation at the NMJ that causes depolarisation of the postsynaptic cell. So it seems that agrin is a candidate for molecule A, but what about B or C? It is tempting to posit AChR as molecule B since it is the critical postsynaptic resource. However, since agrin does not bind directly to the acetylcholine receptor, a different sort of reaction is required.

4.1 A DIFFERENT SORT OF REACTION

If AChR is molecule B, and one agrin molecule can attract at least 160 AChRs (Nitkin et al., 1987) the simple reversible reaction of the DCM is ruled out. Alternatively, AChR could exist in either free, B_f, or bound, B_b states, being converted through the mediation of A. B_b would now play the role of C in the DCM. It is possible to devise a rate equation for the change in the number of receptors at a nerve terminal over time:

$$\frac{dB_b}{dt} = \alpha A B_f - \beta B_b \qquad (1)$$

where α and β are rate constants. The increase in bound AChR over time is proportional to the amount of agrin at a junction and the number of free receptors in the endplate area, while the decrease is proportional to the amount of bound AChRs. The rate equation (1) can be used as the basis of an extended DCM if four other factors are considered: (i) Agrin stays active as receptors accumulate, so the conservation equations for A and B are:

$$A_0 = A_n + \sum_{j=1}^{M} A_{nj} \qquad B_0 = B_{mf} + \sum_{i=1}^{N} B_{imb} \qquad (2)$$

where the subscript 0 indicates the fixed resource available to each muscle or neuron, the lettered subscripts indicate the amount of that substance that is present in the neuron n, muscle fibre m and terminal nm, and there are N motor neurons and M muscle fibres. (ii) The size of a terminal is proportional to the number of bound AChRs, so if we assume the anterograde flow is evenly divided between the ν_n terminals of neuron n, the transport equation for agrin is:

$$\frac{dA_{nm}}{dt} = \lambda \frac{A_n}{\nu_n} - \delta \frac{A_{nm}}{B_{nmb}} \qquad (3)$$

where λ and δ are transport rate constants and the retrograde flow is assumed proportional to the amount of agrin at the terminal and inversely proportional to the size of the terminal. (iii) AChRs are free to diffuse laterally across the surface of the muscle, so the forward reaction rate will be related to the probability of an AChR speckle intersecting a terminal, which is itself proportional to the terminal diameter. (iv) The influx of Ca^{++} through AChRs on the surface of the endplate will also affect the forward reaction rate in proportion to the area of the terminal. Taking B_b to be proportional to the volume of the postsynaptic apparatus, these last two terms are proportional to $B_b^{1/3}$ and $B_b^{2/3}$ respectively. This gives the final rate equation:

$$\frac{dB_{nmb}}{dt} = \alpha A_{nm} B_{mf} B_{nmb}^{1/3} B_{nmb}^{2/3} - \beta B_{nmb} = \alpha A_{nm} B_{mf} B_{nmb} - \beta B_{nmb} \qquad (4)$$

Equations (3) and (4) are similar to those in the original DCM, only now we have been able to justify the dependence of the forward reaction rate on the size of the terminal, B_{nmb}. We can also resolve the distinction paradox, as follows.

4.2 RESOLVING THE DISTINCTION PARADOX

In terms of distinguishing between synapses it seems plausible that concurrently active synapses (i.e. those belonging to the same neuron) will protect themselves from the negative effects of depolarisation. In paralysed systems, synapses will benefit from the AChR accumulating affects of the agrin molecules in those synapses nearby (i.e. those in the same terminal). It was suggested (Jennings, 1994) that competition between synapses of the same terminal was seen after focal blockade because active AChRs help stabilise the receptors around them and suppress those further away. This fits in with the stabilisation role of Ca^{++} in this model and the suppressive effects of depolarisation, as well as the physical range of these effects during 'heterosynaptic suppression' (Lo & Poo, 1991). It seems that Jenning's mechanism, although originally speculative, is actually quite a plausible explanation and one that fits in well with the extended DCM. The critical effect in the XDCM is that if the system is paralysed during development there is a change in the dependency of the forward reaction rate on the size of an individual terminal. This gives the reinnervating terminals a small initial advantage due to their more competitive diameter/volume ratios. As we shall see in the next section, this allows us to demonstrate activity independent competition.

5 SIMULATING THE EXTENDED DCM

In terms of achieving single innervation the extended DCM performs just as well as the original, and when subjected to the same perturbation analysis it has been demonstrated to be stable. Simulating a number of systems with as many muscle fibres and motor neurons as found in real muscles allowed a direct comparison of model findings with experimental data (figure 1).

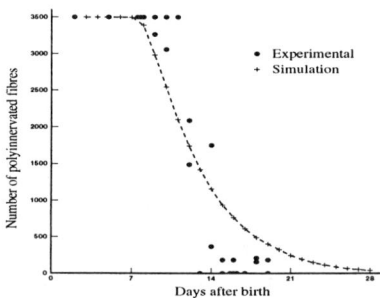

Figure 1: Elimination of Polyinnervation in Rat soleus muscle and Simulation

Figure 2 shows nerve dominance histograms of reinnervation in both the rat lumbrical muscle and its extended DCM simulation. Both compare the results produced when the system is paralysed from the outset of reinnervation (removal of $B_{nmb}^{2/3}$

term from equation (4)) with the normal situation. Note that in both the simulation and the experiment the percentage of fibres singly innervated by the reinnervating sural nerve is increased in the paralysis case. Inactive sural nerve terminals are displacing more inactive lateral plantar nerve terminals (activity independent competition). They can achieve this because during paralysis the terminals with the largest diameters capture more receptors, while the terminals with the largest volumes lose more agrin; so small reinnervating terminals do a little better. However, if activity is present the receptors are captured in proportion to a terminal's volume, so there's no advantage to a small terminal's larger diameter/volume ratio.

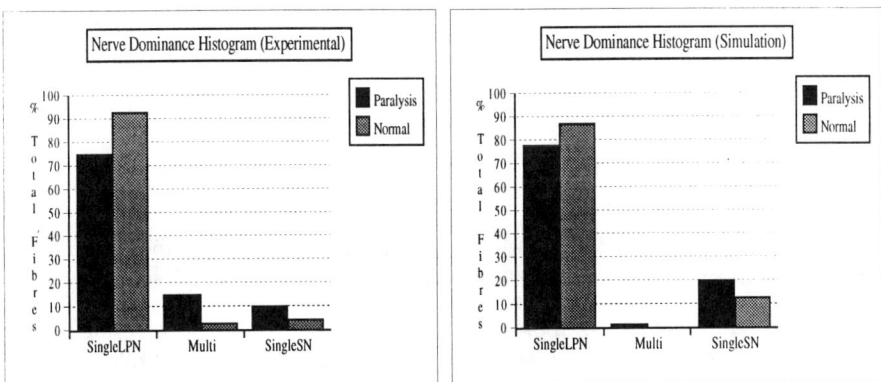

Figure 2: Types of Innervation by Lateral Plantar and Sural Nerves

6 DISCUSSION

The extensions to the DCM outlined here demonstrate both activity dependent and independent competition and provide greater biochemical plausibility. However this is still only a phenomenological demonstration and further experimental work is required to ascertain its validity. There is a need for illumination concerning the specific chemical mechanisms that underlie agrin's aggregational effects and the roles that both Ca^{++} and depolarisation play in junctional dynamics. An important connection made here is one between synaptic efficiency and junctional survival. Ca^{++} and NO have both been implicated in Hebbian mechanisms (Bliss & Collingridge, 1993) and perhaps some of the principles uncovered here may be applicable to neuroneuronic synapses. This work should be followed up with a direct model of synaptic interaction at the NMJ that includes the presynaptic effects of depolarisation, allowing the efficacy of the synapse to be related to its biochemistry; an important step forward in our understanding of nervous system plasticity. Relating changes in synaptic efficiency to neural morphogenesis may also give insights into the construction of artificial neural networks.

Acknowledgements

We are grateful to Michael Joseph and Bruce Graham for critical reading of the manuscript and to the M.R.C. for funding this work.

References

Andreose J. S., Fumagalli G. & Lømo T. (1995) Number of junctional acetylcholine receptors: control by neural and muscular influences in the rat. *Journal of Physiology* **483.2**:397-406.

Axelrod D., Ravdin P., Koppel D. E., Schlessinger J., Webb W. W., Elson E. L. & Podleski T. R. (1976) Lateral motion of fluorescently labelled acetylcholine receptors in membranes of developing muscle fibers. *Proc. Natl. Acad. Sci. USA* **73**:4594-4598.

Balice-Gordon R. J. & Lichtman J. W. (1994) Long-term synapse loss induced by focal blockade of postsynaptic receptors. *Nature* **372**:519-524.

Bennett M. R. & Robinson J. (1989) Growth and elimination of nerve terminals during polyneuronal innervation of muscle cells: a trophic hypothesis. *Proc. Royal Soc. Lond. [Biol]* **235**:299-320.

Bliss T. V. P. & Collingridge G. L. (1993) A synaptic model of memory: long-term potentiation in the hippocampus. *Nature* **361**:31-39.

Colman H. & Lichtman J. W. (1992) 'Cartellian' competition at the neuromuscular junction. *Trends in Neuroscience* **15, 6**:197-199.

Fladby T. & Jansen J. K. S. (1987) Postnatal loss of synaptic terminals in the partially denervated mouse soleus muscle. *Acta. Physiol. Scand* **129**:239-246.

Gouze J. L., Lasry J. M. & Changeux J. -P. (1983) Selective stabilization of muscle innervation during development: A mathematical model. *Biol Cybern.* **46**:207-215.

Jennings C. (1994) Death of a synapse. *Nature* **372**:498-499.

Lo Y. J. & Poo M. M. (1991) Activity-dependent synapse competition in vitro: heterosynaptic suppression of developing synapses. *Science* **254**:1019-1022.

McMahan U. J. (1990) The Agrin Hypothesis. *Cold Spring Harbour Symp. Quant. Biol.* **55**:407-419.

Nitkin R. M., Smith M. A., Magill C., Fallon J. R., Yao Y. -M. M., Wallace B. G. & McMahan U. J. (1987) Identification of agrin, a synaptic organising protein from Torpedo electric organ. *Journal Cell Biology* **105**:2471-2478.

Rasmussen C. E. & Willshaw D. J. (1993) Presynaptic and postsynatic competition in models for the development of neuromuscular connections. *B. Cyb.* **68**:409-419.

Ribchester R. R. (1993) Co-existence and elimination of convergent motor nerve terminals in reinnervated and paralysed adult rat skeletal muscle. *J. Phys.* **466**: 421-441.

Ribchester R. R. & Barry J. A. (1994) Spatial Versus Consumptive Competition at Polyneuronally Innervated Neuromuscular Junctions. *Exp. Physiology* **79**:465-494.

Wallace B. G. (1988) Regulation of agrin-induced acetylcholine receptor aggregation by Ca^{++} and phorbol ester. *Journal of Cell Biol.* **107**:267-278.

Willshaw D. J. (1981) The establishment and the subsequent elimination of polyneuronal innervation of developing muscle: theoretical considerations. *Proc. Royal Soc. Lond.* **B212**: 233-252.

When is an Integrate-and-fire Neuron like a Poisson Neuron?

Charles F. Stevens
Salk Institute MNL/S
La Jolla, CA 92037
cfs@salk.edu

Anthony Zador
Salk Institute MNL/S
La Jolla, CA 92037
zador@salk.edu

Abstract

In the Poisson neuron model, the output is a rate-modulated Poisson process (Snyder and Miller, 1991); the time varying rate parameter $r(t)$ is an instantaneous function $G[.]$ of the stimulus, $r(t) = G[s(t)]$. In a Poisson neuron, then, $r(t)$ gives the instantaneous firing rate—the instantaneous probability of firing at any instant t—and the output is a stochastic function of the input. In part because of its great simplicity, this model is widely used (usually with the addition of a refractory period), especially in *in vivo* single unit electrophysiological studies, where $s(t)$ is usually taken to be the value of some sensory stimulus. In the integrate-and-fire neuron model, by contrast, the output is a filtered and thresholded function of the input: the input is passed through a low-pass filter (determined by the membrane time constant τ) and integrated until the membrane potential $v(t)$ reaches threshold θ, at which point $v(t)$ is reset to its initial value. By contrast with the Poisson model, in the integrate-and-fire model the ouput is a deterministic function of the input. Although the integrate-and-fire model is a caricature of real neural dynamics, it captures many of the qualitative features, and is often used as a starting point for conceptualizing the biophysical behavior of single neurons. Here we show how a slightly modified Poisson model can be derived from the integrate-and-fire model with noisy inputs $y(t) = s(t) + n(t)$. In the modified model, the transfer function $G[.]$ is a sigmoid (erf) whose shape is determined by the noise variance σ_n^2. Understanding the equivalence between the dominant *in vivo* and *in vitro* simple neuron models may help forge links between the two levels.

1 Introduction

In the Poisson neuron model, the output is a rate-modulated Poisson process; the time varying rate parameter $r(t)$ is an instantaneous function $G[.]$ of the stimulus, $r(t) = G[s(t)]$. In a Poisson neuron, then, $r(t)$ gives the instantaneous firing rate—the instantaneous probability of firing at any instant t—and the output is a stochastic function of the input. In part because of its great simplicity, this model is widely used (usually with the addition of a refractory period), especially in *in vivo* single unit electrophysiological studies, where $s(t)$ is usually taken to be the value of some sensory stimulus.

In the integrate-and-fire neuron model, by contrast, the output is a filtered and thresholded function of the input: the input is passed through a low-pass filter (determined by the membrane time constant τ) and integrated until the membrane potential $v(t)$ reaches threshold θ, at which point $v(t)$ is reset to its initial value. By contrast with the Poisson model, in the integrate-and-fire model the ouput is a deterministic function of the input. Although the integrate-and-fire model is a caricature of real neural dynamics, it captures many of the qualitative features, and is often used as a starting point for conceptualizing the biophysical behavior of single neurons (Softky and Koch, 1993; Amit and Tsodyks, 1991; Shadlen and Newsome, 1995; Shadlen and Newsome, 1994; Softky, 1995; DeWeese, 1995; DeWeese, 1996; Zador and Pearlmutter, 1996).

Here we show how a slightly modified Poisson model can be derived from the integrate-and-fire model with noisy inputs $y(t) = s(t) + n(t)$. In the modified model, the transfer function $G[.]$ is a sigmoid (erf) whose shape is determined by the noise variance σ_n^2. Understanding the equivalence between the dominant *in vivo* and *in vitro* simple neuron models may help forge links between the two levels.

2 The integrate-and-fire model

Here we describe the the forgetful leaky integrate-and-fire model. Suppose we add a signal $s(t)$ to some noise $n(t)$,

$$y(t) = n(t) + s(t),$$

and threshold the sum to produce a spike train

$$z(t) = \mathcal{F}[s(t) + n(t)],$$

where $\mathcal{F}$ is the thresholding functional and $z(t)$ is a list of firing times generated by the input. Specifically, suppose the voltage $v(t)$ of the neuron obeys

$$\dot{v}(t) = -\frac{v(t)}{\tau} + y(t) \tag{1}$$

where τ is the membrane time constant. We assume that the noise $n(t)$ has 0-mean and is white with variance σ_n^2. Thus $y(t)$ can be thought of as a Gaussian white process with variance σ_n^2 and a time-varying mean $s(t)$. If the voltage reaches the threshold θ_0 at some time t, the neuron emits a spike at that time and resets to the initial condition v_0. This is therefore a 5 parameter model: the membrane time constant τ, the mean input signal μ, the variance of the input signal σ^2, the threshold θ, and the reset value v_0. Of course, if $n(t) = 0$, we recover a purely deterministic integrate-and-fire model.

In order to forge the link between the integrate-and-fire neuron dynamics and the Poisson model, we will treat the firing times T probabilistically. That is, we will express the output of the neuron to some particular input $s(t)$ as a conditional distribution $p(T|s(t))$, i.e. the probability of obtaining any firing time T given some particular input $s(t)$.

Under these assumptions, $p(T)$ is given by the first passage time distribution (FPTD) of the Ornstein-Uhlenbeck process (Uhlenbeck and Ornstein, 1930; Tuckwell, 1988). This means that the time evolution of the voltage prior to reaching threshold is given by the Fokker-Planck equation (FPE),

$$\frac{\partial}{\partial t} g(t,v) = \frac{\sigma_y^2}{2} \frac{\partial^2}{\partial v^2} g(t,v) - \frac{\partial}{\partial v}[(s(t) - \frac{v(t)}{\tau})g(t,v)], \qquad (2)$$

where $\sigma_y = \sigma_n$ and $g(t,v)$ is the distribution at time t of voltage $-\infty < v \leq \theta_0$. Then the first passage time distribution is related to $g(v,t)$ by

$$p(T) = -\frac{\partial}{\partial t} \int_{-\infty}^{\theta_0} g(t,v) dv. \qquad (3)$$

The integrand is the fraction of all paths that have not yet crossed threshold. $p(T)$ is therefore just the interspike interval (ISI) distribution for a given signal $s(t)$. A general eigenfunction expansion solution for the ISI distribution is known, but it converges slowly and its terms offer little insight into the behavior (at least to us).

We now derive an expression for the probability of crossing threshold in some very short interval Δt, starting at some v. We begin with the "free" distribution of g (Tuckwell, 1988): the probability of the voltage jumping to v' at time $t' = t + \Delta t$, given that it was at v at time t, assuming von Neumann boundary conditions at plus and minus infinity,

$$g(t', v'|t, v) = \frac{1}{\sqrt{2\pi \, q(\Delta t; \sigma_y)}} \exp\left[-\frac{(v' - m(\Delta t; \sigma_y))^2}{2 \, q(\Delta t; \sigma_y)}\right], \qquad (4)$$

with

$$q_\Delta = \sigma_y^2 \tau(1 - e^{-2 \Delta t/\tau})$$

and

$$m(\Delta t) = v e^{-\Delta t/\tau} + s(t) * \tau(1 - e^{-\Delta t/\tau}),$$

where $*$ denotes convolution. The free distribution is a Gaussian with a time-dependent mean $m(\Delta t)$ and variance $q(\Delta t; \sigma_y)$. This expression is valid for all Δt. The probability of making a jump

$$\Delta v = v' - v$$

in a short interval $\Delta t \ll \tau$ depends only on Δv and Δt,

$$g_\Delta(\Delta t, \Delta v; \sigma_y) = \frac{1}{\sqrt{2\pi \, q_\Delta(\sigma_y)}} \exp\left[-\frac{\Delta v^2}{2 \, q_\Delta(\sigma_y)}\right]. \qquad (5)$$

For small Δt, we expand to get

$$q_\Delta(\sigma_y) \approx 2\sigma_y^2 \Delta t,$$

which is independent of τ, showing that the leak can be neglected for short times.

Now the probability P_Δ that the voltage exceeds threshold in some short Δt, given that it started at v, depends on how far v is from threshold; it is

$$\Pr[v + \Delta v \geq \theta] = \Pr[\Delta v \geq \theta - v].$$

Thus

$$P_\Delta = \int_{\theta-v}^{\infty} dv g_\Delta(\Delta t, v; \sigma_y) \tag{6}$$

$$= \frac{1}{2}\text{erfc}\left(\frac{\theta - v}{\sqrt{2q_\Delta(\sigma_y)}}\right)$$

$$\approx \frac{1}{2}\text{erfc}\left(\frac{\theta - v}{\sigma_y\sqrt{2\Delta t}}\right)$$

where $\text{erfc}(x) = 1 - \frac{2}{\sqrt{\pi}}\int_0^x e^{-t^2} dt$ goes from $[2:0]$. This then is the key result: it gives the instantaneous probability of firing as a function of the instantaneous voltage v. erfc is sigmoidal with a slope determined by σ_y, so a smaller noise yields a steeper (more deterministic) transfer function; in the limit of 0 noise, the transfer function is a step and we recover a completely deterministic neuron.

Note that P_Δ is actually an instantaneous function of $v(t)$, not the stimulus itself $s(t)$. If the noise is large compared with $s(t)$ we must consider the distribution $g_s(v, t; \sigma_y)$ of voltages reached in response to the input $s(t)$:

$$P_Y(t) = \int_{-\infty}^{\theta} g_s(\gamma, t; \sigma_y) \int_{\theta-\gamma}^{\infty} g_\Delta(\Delta t, \eta; \sigma_y) d\eta d\gamma \tag{7}$$

$$= \int_{-\infty}^{\theta} g_s(\gamma, t; \sigma_y) \left[\frac{1}{2}\text{erfc}\left(\frac{\theta - \gamma}{\sqrt{2q_\Delta(\sigma_y)}}\right)\right] d\gamma$$

3 Ensemble of Signals

What if the inputs $s(t)$ are themselves drawn from an ensemble? If their distribution is also Gaussian and white with mean μ and variance σ_s^2, and if the firing rate is low ($E[T] \gg \tau$), then the output spike train is Poisson. Why is firing Poisson only in the slow firing limit? The reason is that, by assumption, immediately following a spike the membrane potential resets to 0; it must then rise (assuming $\mu > 0$) to some asymptotic level that is independent of the initial conditions. During this rise the firing rate is lower than the asymptotic rate, because on average the membrane is farther from threshold, and its variance is lower. The rate at which the asymptote is achieved depends on τ. In the limit as $t \gg \tau$, some asymptotic distribution of voltage $q_\infty(v)$, is attained. Note that if we make the reset v_0 stochastic, with a distribution given by $q_\infty(v)$, then the firing probability would be the same even immediately after spiking, and firing would be Poisson for all firing rates.

A Poisson process is characterized by its mean alone. We therefore solve the FPE (eq. 2) for the steady-state by setting $\frac{\partial}{\partial t}g(t, v) = 0$ (we consider only threshold crossings from initial values $t \gg \tau$; neglecting the early events results in only a small error, since we have assumed $E\{T\} \gg \tau$). Thus with the absorbing boundary at θ the distribution at time $t \gg \tau$ (given here for $\mu = 0$) is

$$g_\infty(v;\sigma_y) = k_1 \left(1 - k_2 \text{erfi}\left[\frac{v}{\sigma_y\sqrt{\tau}}\right]\right) \exp\left[\frac{-v^2}{\sigma_y^2 \tau}\right], \tag{8}$$

where $\sigma_y^2 = \sigma_s^2 + \sigma_n^2$, $\text{erfi}(z) = -i\text{erf}(iz)$, k_1 determines the normalization (the sign of k_1 determines whether the solution extends to positive or negative infinity) and $k_2 = 1/\text{erfi}(\theta/(\sigma_y\sqrt{\tau}))$ is determined by the boundary. The instantaneous Poisson rate parameter is then obtained through eq. (7),

$$\begin{aligned} P_Y &= \int_{-\infty}^{\theta} g_\infty(\gamma;\sigma_y) \int_{\theta-\gamma}^{\infty} g_\Delta(\Delta t, \eta;\sigma_y) d\eta d\gamma \tag{9} \\ &= \int_{-\infty}^{\theta} g_\infty(\gamma;\sigma_y) \left[\frac{1}{2}\text{erfc}\left(\frac{\theta-\gamma}{\sqrt{2q_\Delta(\sigma_y)}}\right)\right] d\gamma \end{aligned}$$

Fig. 1 tests the validity of the exponential approximation. The top graph shows the ISI distribution near the "balance point", when the excitation is in balance with the inhibition and the membrane potential hovers just subthreshold. The bottom curves show the ISI distribution far below the balance point. In both cases, the exponential distribution provides a good approximation for $t \gg \tau$.

4 Discussion

The main point of this paper is to make explicit the relation between the Poisson and integrate-and-fire models of neuronal acitivity. The key difference between them is that the former is stochastic while the latter is deterministic. That is, given exactly the same stimulus, the Poisson neuron produces different spike trains on different trials, while the integrate-and-fire neuron produces exactly the same spike train each time. It is therefore clear that if some degree of stochasticity is to be obtained in the integrate-and-fire model, it must arise from noise in the stimulus itself.

The relation we have derived here is purely formal; we have intentionally remained agnostic about the deep issues of what is signal and what is noise in the inputs to a neuron. We observe nevertheless that although we derive a limit (eq. 9) where the spike train of an integrate-and-fire neuron is a Poisson process—i.e. the probability of obtaining a spike in any interval is independent of obtaining a spike in any other interval (except for very short intervals)—from the point of view of information processing it is a very different process from the purely stochastic rate-modulated Poisson neuron. In fact, in this limit the spike train is *deterministically Poisson* if $\sigma_y = \sigma_s$, i.e. when $n(t) = 0$; in this case the output is a purely deterministic function of the input, but the ISI distribution is exponential.

References

Amit, D. and Tsodyks, M. (1991). Quantitative study of attractor neural network retrieving at low spike rates. i. substrate-spikes, rates and neuronal gain. *Network: Computation in Neural Systems*, 2:259–273.

DeWeese, M. (1995). *Optimization principles for the neural code*. PhD thesis, Dept of Physics, Princeton University.

DeWeese, M. (1996). Optimization principles for the neural code. In Hasselmo, M., editor, *Advances in Neural Information Processing Systems, vol. 8*. MIT Press, Cambridge, MA.

Shadlen, M. and Newsome, W. (1994). Noise, neural codes and cortical organization. *Current Opinion in Neurobiology*, 4:569–579.

Shadlen, M. and Newsome, W. (1995). Is there a signal in the noise? [comment]. *Current Opinion in Neurobiology*, 5:248–250.

Snyder, D. and Miller, M. (1991). *Random Point Processes in Time and Space*, 2nd edition. Springer-Verlag.

Softky, W. (1995). Simple codes versus efficient codes. *Current Opinion in Neurobiology*, 5:239–247.

Softky, W. and Koch, C. (1993). The highly irregular firing of cortical cells is inconsistent with temporal integration of random epsps. *J. Neuroscience.*, 13:334–350.

Tuckwell, H. (1988). *Introduction to theoretical neurobiology (2 vols.)*. Cambridge.

Uhlenbeck, G. and Ornstein, L. (1930). On the theory of brownian motion. *Phys. Rev.*, 36:823–841.

Zador, A. M. and Pearlmutter, B. A. (1996). VC dimension of an integrate and fire neuron model. *Neural Computation*, 8(3). In press.

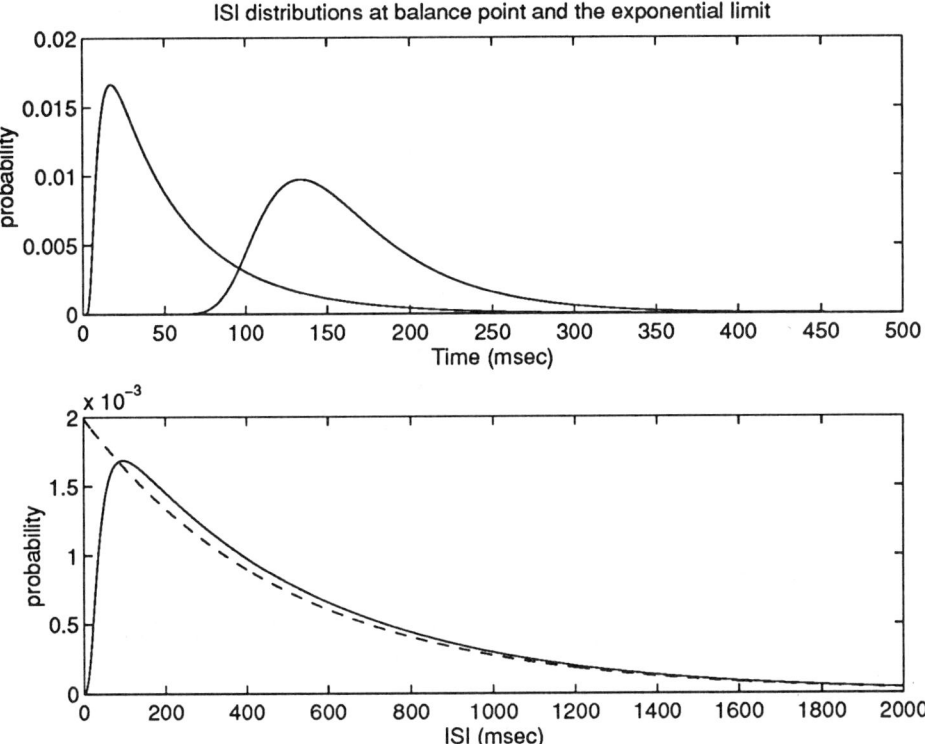

Figure 1: ISI distributions. (A; *top*) ISI distribution for leaky integrate-and-fire model at the balance point, where the asymptotic membrane potential is just subthreshold, for two values of the signal variance σ^2. Increasing σ^2 shifts the distribution to the left. For the left curve, the parameters were chosen so that $E\{T\} \approx \tau$, giving a nearly exponential distribution; for the *right* curve, the distribution would be hard to distinguish experimentally from an exponential distribution with a refractory period. ($\tau = 50$ msec; *left*: $E\{T\} = 166$ msec; *right*: $E\{T\} = 57$ msec). (B; *bottom*) In the subthreshold regime, the ISI distribution (*solid*) is nearly exponential (*dashed*) for intervals greater than the membrane time constant. ($\tau = 50$ msec; $E\{T\} = 500$ msec)

How Perception Guides Production in Birdsong Learning

Christopher L. Fry
cfry@cogsci.ucsd.edu
Department of Cognitive Science
University of California at San Diego
La Jolla, CA 92093-0515

Abstract

A computational model of song learning in the song sparrow (*Melospiza melodia*) learns to categorize the different syllables of a song sparrow song and uses this categorization to train itself to reproduce song. The model fills a crucial gap in the computational explanation of birdsong learning by exploring the organization of perception in songbirds. It shows how competitive learning may lead to the organization of a specific nucleus in the bird brain, replicates the song production results of a previous model (Doya and Sejnowski, 1995), and demonstrates how perceptual learning can guide production through reinforcement learning.

1 INTRODUCTION

The *passeriformes* or songbirds make up more than half of all bird species and are divided into two groups: the *oscines* which learn their songs and *sub-oscines* which do not. *Oscines* raised in isolation sing degraded species typical songs similar to wild song. Deafened *oscines* sing completely degraded songs (Konishi, 1965), while deafened *sub-oscines* develop normal songs (Kroodsma and Konishi, 1991) indicating that auditory feedback is crucial in *oscine* song learning.

Innate structures in the bird brain regulate song learning. For example, song sparrows show innate preferences for their own species' songs and song structure (Marler, 1991). Innate preferences are thought to be encoded in an **auditory template** which limits the sounds young birds may copy. According to the **auditory template hypothesis** birds go through two phases during song learning, a **memorization phase** and a **motor phase**. In the **memorization phase**, which lasts from approximately 20 to 50 days after birth in the song sparrow, the bird selects which sounds to copy based on an innate template and refines the template based

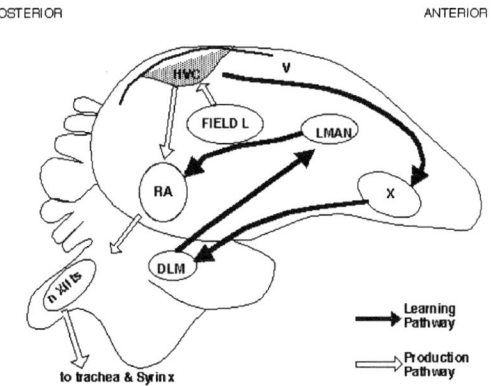

Figure 1: A simplified sketch of a saggital section of the songbird brain. **Field L** (Field L) receives auditory input and projects to the production pathway: **HVc** (formerly the caudal nucleus of the hyperstriatum), **RA** (robust nucleus of archistriatum), **nXIIts** (hypoglossal nerve), the syrinx (vocal organ) and the learning pathway: **X** (area X), **DLM** (medial nucleus of the dorsolateral thalamus), **LMAN** (lateral magnocellular nucleus of the anterior neostriatum), **RA** (Konishi, 1989; Vicario, 1994). **V** is the lateral ventricle.

on the sounds it hears. In the **motor phase** (from approximately 272 to 334 days after birth) the template provides feedback during singing. Learning to sing the memorized, template song is a gradual process of refining the produced song to match memory (Marler, 1991).

A song is made up of phrases, phrases of syllables and syllables of notes. Syllables, usually separated by periods of silence, are the main units of analysis. Notes typically last from 10-100 msecs and are used to construct syllables (100-200 msecs) which are reused to produce trills and other phrases.

2 NEUROBIOLOGY OF SONG

The two main neural pathways that govern song are the motor and learning pathways seen in figure 1 (Konishi, 1989). Lesions to the motor pathway interrupt singing throughout life while lesions to the learning pathway disrupt early song learning. Although these pathways seem to have segregated functions, recordings of neurons during song playback have shown that cells throughout the song system respond to song (Konishi, 1989).

Studies of song perception have shown the best auditory stimulus that will evoke a response in the song system is the bird's own song (Margoliash, 1986). The song specific neurons in **HVc** of the white-crowned sparrow often require a sequence of two syllables to respond (Margoliash, 1986; Margoliash and Fortune, 1992) and are made up of two main types in **HVc**. One type is sensitive to temporal combinations of stimuli while the other is sensitive to harmonic characteristics (Margoliash and Fortune, 1992).

3 COMPUTATION

Previous computational work on birdsong learning predicted individual neural responses using back-propagation (Margoliash and Bankes, 1993) and modelled motor mappings for song production (Doya and Sejnowski, 1995). The current work de-

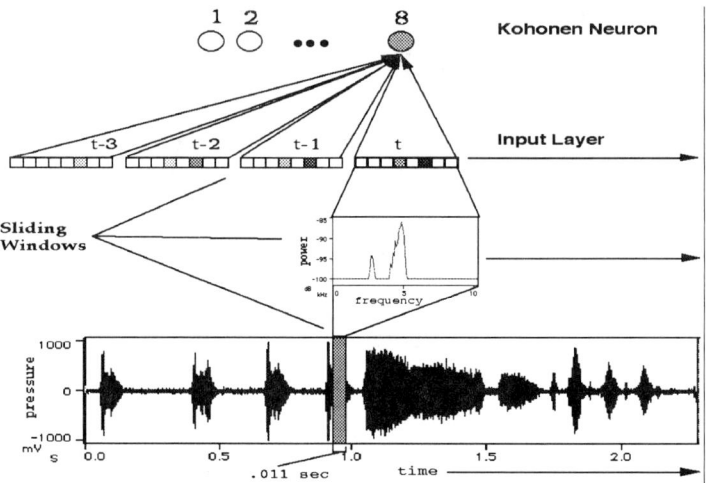

Figure 2: Perceptual network input encoding. The song is converted into frequency bins which are presented to the Kohonen layer over four time steps.

velops a model of birdsong syllable perception which extends Doya and Sejnowski's (1995) model of birdsong learning. Birdsong syllable segmentation is accomplished using an unsupervised system and this system is used to train the network to reproduce its input using reinforcement learning.

The model implements the two phases of the auditory template hypothesis, **memorization** and **motor**. In the first phase the template song is segmented into syllables by an unsupervised Kohonen network (Kohonen, 1984). In the second phase the syllables are reproduced using a reinforcement learning paradigm based on Doya and Sejnowski (1995).

The model extends previous work in three ways: 1) a self-organizing network picks out syllables in the song; 2) the self-organizing network provides feedback during song production; and 3) a more biologically plausible model of the syrinx is used to generate song.

3.1 Perception

Recognizing a syllable involves identifying a short sequence of notes. Kohonen networks use an unsupervised learning method to categorize an input space based on similar neural responses. Thus a Kohonen network is a natural candidate for identifying the syllables in a song.

One song from the repertoire of a song sparrow was chosen as the training song for the network. The song was encoded by passing a sliding window across the training waveform (sampled at 22.255 kHz) of the selected song. At each time step, a non-overlapping 256 point ($\approx$ .011 sec) fast fourier transform (FFT) was used to generate a power spectrum (figure 2). The power spectrum was divided into 8 bins. Each bin was mapped to a real number using a gaussian summation procedure with the peak of the gaussian at the center of each frequency bin. Four time-steps were passed to each Kohonen neuron.

The network's task was to identify similar syllables in the input song. The input song was broken down into syllables by looking for points where the power at all

How Perception Guides Production in Birdsong Learning

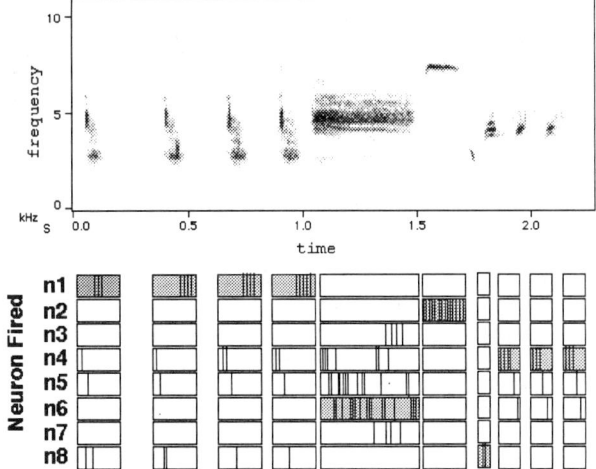

Figure 3: Categorization of song syllables by a Kohonen network. The power-spectrum of the training song is at the top. The responses of the Kohonen neurons are at the bottom. For each time-step the winning neuron is shown with a vertical bar. The shaded areas indicate the neuron that fired the most during the presentation of the syllable.

frequencies dropped below a threshold. A syllable was defined as sound of duration greater than .011 seconds bounded by two low-power points. The network was not trained on the noise between syllables. The song was played for the network ten times (1050 training vectors), long enough for a stable response pattern to emerge.

The activation of a neuron was: $Net_j = \Sigma x_i w_{ij}$. Where: Net_j = output of neuron j, w_{ij} = the weight connecting $input_i$ to $neuron_j$, $x_i = input_i$. The Kohonen network was trained by initializing the connection weights to $1/\sqrt{number\ of\ neurons}$ + small random component (r $\leq$ .01), normalizing the inputs, and updating the weights to the winning neuron by the following rule: $\mathbf{w}_{new} = \mathbf{w}_{old} + \alpha(\mathbf{x} - \mathbf{w}_{old})$ where: α = $training\ rate$ = .20. If the same neuron won twice in a row the training rate was decreased by 1/2. Only the winning neuron was reinforced resulting in a non-localized feature map.

3.1.1 Perceptual Results

The Kohonen network was able to assign a unique neuron to each type of syllable (figure 3). Of the eight neurons in the network, the one that fired the most frequently during the presentation of a syllable uniquely identified the type of syllable. The first four syllables of the input song sound alike, contain similar frequencies, and are coded by the first neuron (**N1**). The last three syllables sound alike, contain similar frequencies, and are coded by the fourth neuron (**N4**). Syllable five was coded by neuron six (**N6**), syllable six by neuron two (**N2**) and syllable seven by neuron eight (**N8**).

Figure 4 shows the frequency sensitivity of each neuron (1-8, figure 3) plotted against each time step (1-4). This plot shows the harmonic and temporally sensitive neurons that developed during the learning phase of the Kohonen network. Neuron 2 is sensitive to only one frequency at approximately 6-7 kHz, indicated by the solid white band across the 6-7 kHz frequency range in figure 4. Neuron 4 is sensitive to mid-range frequencies of short duration. Note that in figure 4 **N4** responds

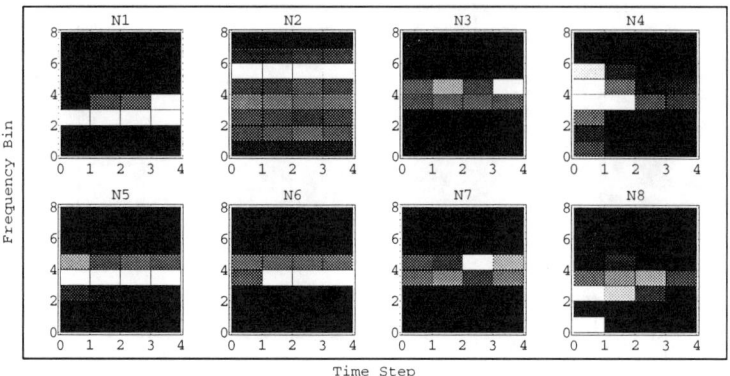

Figure 4: The values of the weights mapping frequency bins and time steps to Kohonen neurons. White is maximum, Black is minimum.

maximally to mid-range frequencies only in the first two time steps. It uses this temporal sensitivity to distinguish between the last three syllables and the fifth syllable (figure 3) by keying off the length of time mid-range frequencies are present. Contrast this early response sensitivity with neuron 6, which is sensitive to mid-range frequencies of long duration, but responds only *after* one time step. It uses this temporal sensitivity to respond to the long sustained frequency of syllable four. Considered together, neurons 2,4,6 and 8 illustrate the two types of neurons (temporal and harmonic) found in **HVc** by Margoliash and Fortune (1993). Competitive learning may underly the formation of these neurons in **HVc**.

3.2 Production

After competitive learning trains the perceptual part of the network to categorize the song into syllables, the perceptual network can be used to train the production side of the network to sing.

The first step in modelling song production is to create a model of the avian vocal apparatus, the syrinx. In the syrinx sounds arise when air flows through the syringeal passage and causes the tympanic membrane to vibrate. The frequency is controlled by the tension of the membrane controlled by the syringeal musculature. The amplitude is dependent on the area of the syringeal orifice which is dependent on the tension of the labium. The interactions of this system were modelled by modulated sine waves. Four parameters governed the fundamental frequency(**p**), frequency modulation(**tm**), amplitude (**ex**) and frequency of amplitude modulation(**l**). The range of the parameters was set according to calculations in Greenwalt (1968). The parameters were combined in the following equation (based on Greenwalt, 1968), $f(ex, l, p, tm, t) = \mathbf{ex} \cos(2\pi t\ \mathbf{l}) \cos(2\pi t\ \mathbf{p} + cos(2\pi t\ \mathbf{tm}))$.

Using this equation song can be generated over time by making assumptions about the response properties of neurons in **RA**. Following Doya and Sejnowski (1995) it was assumed that pools of **RA** neurons have different temporal response profiles. Syllable like temporal responses can be generated by modifying the weights from the Kohonen layer (**HVc**) to the production layer (**RA**).

How Perception Guides Production in Birdsong Learning

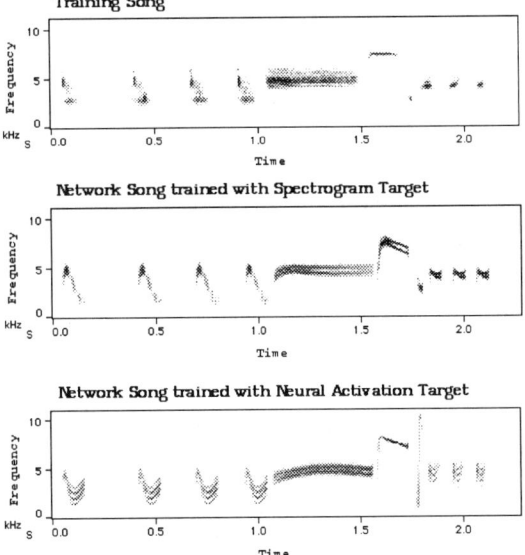

Figure 5: Training song and two songs produced with different representations of the training song.

The production side of the network was trained using the reinforcement learning paradigm described in Doya and Sejnowski (1995). Each syllable was presented in the order it occurred in the training song to the Kohonen layer, which turned on a single neuron. A random vector was added to the weights from the Kohonen layer to the output layer and a syllable was produced. The produced syllable was compared to the stored representation of the template song which was used to generate an error signal and an estimate of the gradient. If the evaluation of the produced syllable was better than a threshold the weights were kept, otherwise they were discarded.

Two experiments were done using different representations of the template song. In the first experiment the template song was the stored power spectrum of each syllable and the error signal was the cosine of the angle between the power spectrum of the produced syllable and the template syllable. In the second experiment the template song was the stored neural responses to song (recorded during the memorization phase) and the error signal was the Euclidean distance between neural responses to the produced syllable and the neural responses to the template song.

3.2.1 Production Results

Figure 5 shows the output of the production network after training with different representations of the training song. The network was able to replicate the major frequency components of the training song to a high degree of accuracy. The song trained with the spectrogram target was learned to a 90% average cosine between the spectrograms of the produced song and the training song on each syllable with the best syllable learned to 100% accuracy and the worst to 85% after 1000 trials. A crucial aspect to achieving performance was smoothing the template spectrogram. The third song shows that the network was able to learn the template song using the neural responses of the perceptual system to generate the reinforcement signal. The average distance between the initial randomly produced syllables and the training song was reduced by 50%.

4 DISCUSSION

This work fills a crucial gap in the computational explanation of song learning left by prior work. Doya and Sejnowski (1995) showed how song could be produced but left unanswered the questions of how song is perceived and how the perceptual system provides feedback during song production. This study shows a time-delay Kohonen network can learn to categorize the syllables of a sample song and this network can train song production with no external teacher. The Kohonen network explains how neurons sensitive to temporal and harmonic structure could arise in the songbird brain through competitive learning. Taken as a whole, the model presents a concrete proposal of the computational principles governing the **Auditory Template Hypothesis** and how a song is memorized and used to train song production. Future work will flesh out the effects of innate structure on learning by examining how the settings of the initial weights on the network affect song learning and predict experimental effects of deafening and isolation.

Acknowledgements

Thanks to S. Vehrencamp for providing the song data, J. Batali, J. Elman, J. Bradbury and T. Sejnowski for helpful comments, and K. Doya for advice on replicating his model.

References

Doya, K. and Sejnowski, T.J. (1995). A novel reinforcement model of birdsong vocalization learning. In Tesauro, G., Touretzky, D. S. and Leen, T.K., editors, *Advances in Neural Information Processing Systems 7*. MIT Press, Cambridge, MA.

Greenwalt, C.H. (1968). Bird Song: Acoustics and Physiology. Smithsonian Institution Press. Wash., D.C.

Kohonen, T. (1984). *Self-organization and Associative Memory, Vol. 8*. Springer-Verlag, Berlin.

Konishi, M. (1965). The role of auditory feedback in the control of vocalization in the white-crowned sparrow. *Zeitschrift fur Tierpsychogie*, 22,770-783.

Konishi, M. (1989). Birdsong for Neurobiologists. *Neuron*, 3, 541-549.

Kroodsma, D.E. and Konishi, M. (1991). A suboscine bird (eastern phoebe, Sayonoris phoebe) develops normal song without auditory feedback. *Animal Behavior*, 42, 477-487.

Marler, P. (1991). The instinct to learn. In *The Epigenesis of Mind: Essays on Biology and Cognition*, eds. S. Carey and R. Gelman. Lawrence Erlbaum Associates.

Margoliash, D. (1986). Preference for autogenous song by auditory neurons in a song system nucleus of the white-crowned sparrow. *Journal of Neuroscience*, 6,1643-1661.

Margoliash, D. and Bankes, S.C. (1993). Computations in the Ascending Auditory Pathway in Songbirds Related to Song Learning. *American Zoologist*, 33, 94-103.

Margoliash, D. and Fortune, E. (1992). Temporal and Harmonic Combination-Sensitive Neurons in the Zebra Finch's HVc. *Journal of Neuroscience*, 12, 4309-4326.

Vicario, D. (1994). Motor Mechanisms Relevant to Auditory-Vocal Interactions in Songbirds. *Brain, Behavior and Evolution*,44, 265-278.

The Geometry of Eye Rotations and Listing's Law

Amir A. Handzel*   **Tamar Flash[†]**
Department of Applied Mathematics and Computer Science
Weizmann Institute of Science
Rehovot, 76100 Israel

Abstract

We analyse the geometry of eye rotations, and in particular saccades, using basic Lie group theory and differential geometry. Various parameterizations of rotations are related through a unifying mathematical treatment, and transformations between co-ordinate systems are computed using the Campbell–Baker–Hausdorff formula. Next, we describe Listing's law by means of the Lie algebra $so(3)$. This enables us to demonstrate a direct connection to Donders' law, by showing that eye orientations are restricted to the quotient space $SO(3)/SO(2)$. The latter is equivalent to the sphere $\mathcal{S}^2$, which is exactly the space of gaze directions. Our analysis provides a mathematical framework for studying the oculomotor system and could also be extended to investigate the geometry of multi-joint arm movements.

1 INTRODUCTION

1.1 SACCADES AND LISTING'S LAW

Saccades are fast eye movements, bringing objects of interest into the center of the visual field. It is known that eye positions are restricted to a subset of those which are anatomically possible, both during saccades and fixation (Tweed & Vilis, 1990). According to Donders' law, the eye's gaze direction determines its orientation uniquely, and moreover, the orientation does not depend on the history of eye motion which has led to the given gaze direction. A precise specification of the "allowed" subspace of position is given by Listing's law: the observed orientations of the eye are those which can be reached from the distinguished orientation called *primary*

---

*hand@wisdom.weizmann.ac.il
[†]tamar@wisdom.weizmann.ac.il

position through a single rotation about an axis which lies in the plane perpendicular to the gaze direction at the primary position (Listing's plane). We say then that the orientation of the eye has zero torsion. Recently, the domain of validity of Listing's law has been extended to include eye vergence by employing a suitable mathematical treatment (Van Rijn & Van Den Berg, 1993).

Tweed and Vilis used quaternion calculus to demonstrate, in addition, that in order to move from one allowed position to another in a single rotation, the rotation axis itself lies outside Listing's plane (Tweed & Vilis, 1987). Indeed, normal saccades are performed approximately about a single axis. However, the validity of Listing's law does not depend on the rotation having a single axis, as was shown in double-step target displacement experiments (Minken, Van Opstal & Van Gisbergen, 1993): even when the axis of rotation itself changes during the saccade, Listing's law is obeyed at each and every point along the trajectory which is traced by the eye.

Previous analyses of eye rotations (and in particular of Listing's law) have been based on various representations of rotations: quaternions (Westheimer, 1957), rotation vectors (Hepp, 1990), spinors (Hestenes, 1994) and 3×3 rotation matrices; however, they are all related through the same underlying mathematical object — the three dimensional (3D) rotation group. In this work we analyse the geometry of saccades using the Lie algebra of the rotation group and the group structure. Next, we briefly describe the basic mathematical notions which will be needed later. This is followed by Section 2 in which we analyse various parameterizations of rotations from the point of view of group theory; Section 3 contains a detailed mathematical analysis of Listing's law and its connection to Donders' law based on the group structure; in Section 4 we briefly discuss the issue of angular velocity vectors or axes of rotation ending with a short conclusion.

1.2 THE ROTATION GROUP AND ITS LIE ALGEBRA

The group of rotations in three dimensions, $G = SO(3)$, (where 'SO' stands for special orthogonal transformations) is used both to describe actual rotations and to denote eye positions by means of a unique virtual rotation from the primary position. The identity operation leaves the eye at the primary position, therefore, we identify this position with the unit element of the group $e \in SO(3)$. A rotation can be parameterized by a 3D axis and the angle of rotation about it. Each axis "generates" a continuous set of rotations through increasing angles. Formally, if n is a unit axis of rotation, then

$$\text{EXP}(\theta \cdot n) \qquad (1)$$

is a continuous one-parameter subgroup (in G) of rotations through angles θ in the plane that is perpendicular to n. Such a subgroup is denoted as $SO(2) \subset SO(3)$. We can take an explicit representation of n as a matrix and the exponent can be calculated as a Taylor series expansion. Let us look, for example, at the one parameter subgroup of rotations in the $y-z$ plane, i.e. rotations about the x axis which is represented in this case by the matrix

$$L_x = \begin{pmatrix} 0 & 0 & 0 \\ 0 & 0 & 1 \\ 0 & -1 & 0 \end{pmatrix}. \qquad (2)$$

A direct computation of this rotation by an angle θ gives

$$\text{EXP}(\theta L_x) = I + \theta L_x + \frac{1}{2!}(\theta L_x)^2 + \ldots + \frac{1}{n!}(\theta L_x)^n + \ldots = \begin{pmatrix} 1 & 0 & 0 \\ 0 & \cos\theta & \sin\theta \\ 0 & -\sin\theta & \cos\theta \end{pmatrix} \qquad (3)$$

The Geometry of Eye Rotations and Listing's Law

where I is the identity matrix. Thus, the rotation matrix $R(\theta)$ can be constructed from the axis and angle of rotation. The same rotation, however, could also be achieved using λL_x instead of L_x, where λ is any scalar, while rescaling the angle to θ/λ. The collection of matrices λL_x is a one dimensional linear space whose elements are the *generators* of rotations in the $y-z$ plane.

The set of all the generators constitutes the *Lie algebra* of a group. For the full space of 3D rotations, the Lie algebra is the three dimensional vector space that is spanned by the standard orthonormal basis comprising the three direction vectors of the principal axes:

$$g = so(3) = Span\{\mathbf{e}_x, \mathbf{e}_y, \mathbf{e}_z\}. \tag{4}$$

Every axis $\mathbf{n}$ can be expressed as a linear combination of this basis. Elements of the Lie algebra can also be represented in matrix form and the corresponding basis for the matrix space is

$$L_x = \begin{pmatrix} 0 & 0 & 0 \\ 0 & 0 & 1 \\ 0 & -1 & 0 \end{pmatrix} \quad L_y = \begin{pmatrix} 0 & 0 & 1 \\ 0 & 0 & 0 \\ -1 & 0 & 0 \end{pmatrix} \quad L_z = \begin{pmatrix} 0 & 1 & 0 \\ -1 & 0 & 0 \\ 0 & 0 & 0 \end{pmatrix}; \tag{5}$$

hence we have the isomorphism

$$\begin{pmatrix} 0 & \theta_z & \theta_y \\ -\theta_z & 0 & \theta_x \\ -\theta_y & -\theta_x & 0 \end{pmatrix} \longleftrightarrow \begin{pmatrix} \theta_x \\ \theta_y \\ \theta_z \end{pmatrix}. \tag{6}$$

Thanks to its linear structure, the Lie algebra is often more convenient for analysis than the group itself. In addition to the linear structure, the Lie algebra has a bilinear antisymmetric operation defined between its elements which is called the *bracket* or *commutator*. The bracket operation between vectors in g is the usual vector cross product. When the elements of the Lie algebra are written as matrices, the bracket operation becomes a commutation relation, i.e.

$$[A, B] \equiv AB - BA. \tag{7}$$

As expected, the commutation relations of the basis matrices of the Lie algebra (of the 3D rotation group) are equivalent to the vector product:

$$[L_i, L_j] = \epsilon_{ijk} L_k \tag{8}$$

Finally, in accordance with (1), every rotation matrix is obtained by exponentiation:

$$R(\theta) = \text{EXP}(\theta_x L_x + \theta_y L_y + \theta_z L_z). \tag{9}$$

where θ stands for the three component angles.

2 CO-ORDINATE SYSTEMS FOR ROTATIONS

In linear spaces the "position" of a point is simply parameterized by the co-ordinates w.r.t. the principal axes (a chosen orthonormal basis). For a non-linear space (such as the rotation group) we define local co-ordinate charts that look like pieces of a vector space $\mathbb{R}^n$. Several co-ordinate systems for rotations are based on the fact that group elements can be written as exponents of elements of the Lie algebra (1). The angles θ appearing in the exponent serve as the co-ordinates. The underlying property which is essential for comparing these systems is the non-commutativity of rotations. For usual real numbers, e.g. c_1 and c_2, commutativity implies $\exp^{c_1} \exp^{c_2} = \exp^{c_1+c_2}$. A corresponding equation for non-commuting elements is the Campbell-Baker-Hausdorff formula (CBH) which is a Taylor series expansion using repeated commutators between the elements of the Lie algebra. The expansion to third order is (Choquet-Bruhat et al., 1982):

$$\text{EXP}(x_1)\text{EXP}(x_2) = \text{EXP}\left(x_1 + x_2 + \frac{1}{2}[x_1, x_2] + \frac{1}{12}[x_1 - x_2, [x_1, x_2]]\right) \quad (10)$$

where x_1, x_2 are variables that stand for elements of the Lie algebra.

One natural parameterization uses the representation of a rotation by the axis and the angle of rotation. The angles which appear in (9) are then called *canonical co-ordinates of the first kind* (Varadarajan, 1974). Gimbal systems constitute a second type of parameterization where the overall rotation is obtained by a series of consecutive rotations about the principal axes. The component angles are then called *canonical co-ordinates of the second kind*. In the present context, the first type of co-ordinates are advantageous because they correspond to single axis rotations which in turn represent natural eye movements. For convenience, we will use the name *canonical* co-ordinates for those of the first kind, whereas those of the second type will simply be called gimbals. The gimbals of Fick and Helmholtz are commonly used in the study of oculomotor control (Van Opstal, 1993). A rotation matrix in Fick gimbals is

$$R_F(\theta_x, \theta_y, \theta_z) = \text{EXP}(\theta_z L_z) \cdot \text{EXP}(\theta_y L_y) \cdot \text{EXP}(\theta_x L_x), \quad (11)$$

and in Helmholtz gimbals the order of rotations is different:

$$R_H(\theta_x, \theta_y, \theta_z) = \text{EXP}(\theta_y L_y) \cdot \text{EXP}(\theta_z L_z) \cdot \text{EXP}(\theta_x L_x). \quad (12)$$

The CBH formula (10) can be used as a general tool for obtaining transformations between various co-ordinate systems (Gilmore, 1974) such as (9,11,12). In particular, we apply (10) to the product of the two right-most terms in (11) and then again to the product of the result with the third term. We thus arrive at an expression whose form is the same as the right hand side of (10). By equating it with the expression for canonical angles (9) and then taking the *log* of the exponents on both sides of the equation, we obtain the transformation formula from Fick angles to canonical angles. Repeating this calculation for (12) gives the equivalent formula for Helmholtz angles[1]. Both transformations are given by the following three equations where $\theta^{F,H}$ stands for an angle either in Fick or in Helmholtz co-ordinates; for Helmholtz angles there is a plus sign in front of the last term of the first equation and a minus sign in the case of Fick angles:

$$\theta_x^C = \theta_x^{F,H}\left(1 - \frac{1}{12}\left((\theta_y^{F,H})^2 + (\theta_z^{F,H})^2\right)\right) \pm \frac{1}{2}\theta_y^{F,H}\theta_z^{F,H}$$

$$\theta_y^C = \theta_y^{F,H}\left(1 - \frac{1}{12}\left((\theta_z^{F,H})^2 + (\theta_x^{F,H})^2\right)\right) + \frac{1}{2}\theta_z^{F,H}\theta_x^{F,H} \quad (13)$$

$$\theta_z^C = \theta_z^{F,H}\left(1 - \frac{1}{12}\left((\theta_x^{F,H})^2 + (\theta_y^{F,H})^2\right)\right) - \frac{1}{2}\theta_x^{F,H}\theta_y^{F,H}$$

The error caused by the above approximation is smaller than 0.1 degree within most of the oculomotor range.

We mention in closing two additional parameterizations, namely quaternions and rotation vectors. Unit quaternions lie on the 3D sphere S^3 (embedded in $\mathbb{R}^4$) which constitutes the same manifold as the group of unitary rotations $SU(2)$. The latter is the double covering group of $SO(3)$ having the same local structure. This enables to use quaternions to parameterize rotations. The popular rotation vectors (written as $\tan(\theta/2)\mathbf{n}$, $\mathbf{n}$ being the axis of rotation and θ its angle) are closely related to

---

[1] In contrast to this third order expansion, second order approximations usually appear in the literature; see for example equation B2 in (Van Rijn & Van Den Berg, 1993).

The Geometry of Eye Rotations and Listing's Law

quaternions because they are central (gnomonic) projections of a hemisphere of S^3 onto the 3D affine space tangent to the quaternion $q_e = (1,0,0,0) \in \mathbb{R}^4$. [2]

3   LISTING'S LAW AND DONDERS' LAW

A customary choice of a head fixed coordinate system is the following: e_x is in the straight ahead direction in the horizontal plane, e_y is in the lateral direction and e_z points upwards in the vertical direction. e_x and e_z thus define the midsagittal plane; e_y and e_z define the coronal plane. The principal axes of rotations (L_x, L_y, L_z) are set parallel to the head fixed co-ordinate system. A reference eye orientation called the primary position is chosen with the gaze direction being $(1,0,0)$ in the above co-ordinates. How is Listing's law expressed in terms of the Lie algebra of $SO(3)$? The allowed positions are generated by linear combinations of L_z and L_y only. This 2D subspace of the Lie algebra,

$$l = \text{Span}\{L_y, L_z\}, \tag{14}$$

is Listing's plane. Denoting $\text{Span}\{L_x\}$ by h, we have a decomposition of the Lie algebra $so(3)$ into a direct sum of two linear subspaces:

$$g = l \oplus h. \tag{15}$$

Every vector $v \in g$ can be projected onto its component which is in l:

$$v = v_l + v_h \xrightarrow{proj.} v_l. \tag{16}$$

Until now, only the linear structure has been considered. In addition, h is closed under the bracket operation:

$$[L_x, L_x] = 0 \in h, \tag{17}$$

and because h is closed both under vector addition and the Lie bracket, it is a subalgebra of g. In contrast, l is not a subalgebra because it is not closed under commutation (8). The fact that h stands as an algebra on its own implies that it has a corresponding group H, just as $g = so(3)$ corresponds to $G = SO(3)$. The subalgebra h generates rotations about the x axis, and therefore H is $SO(2)$, the group of rotations in a plane.

The group $G = SO(3)$ does not have a linear structure. We may still ask whether some kind of decomposition and projection can be achieved in G in analogy to (15,16). The answer is positive and the projection is performed as follows: take any element of the group, $a \in G$, and multiply it by all the elements of the subgroup H. This gives a subset in G which is considered as a single object $\tilde{a}$ called a *coset*:

$$\tilde{a} = \{ab \mid b \in H\}. \tag{18}$$

The set of all cosets constitutes the *quotient space*. It is written as

$$S \equiv G/H = SO(3)/SO(2) \tag{19}$$

because mapping the group to the quotient space can be understood as dividing G by H. The quotient space is not a group, and this corresponds to the fact that the subspace l above (14) is not a subalgebra. The quotient space has been constructed algebraically but is difficult to visualize; however, it is mathematically equivalent

---

[2] Geometrically, each point $q \in S^3$ can be connected to the center of the sphere by a line. Another line runs from q_e in the direction parallel to the vector part of q within the tangent space. The intersection of the two lines is the projected point. Numerically, one simply takes the vector part of q divided by its scalar part.

Table 1: Summary table of biological notions and the corresponding mathematical representation, both in terms of the rotation group and its Lie algebra.

Biological notion	Lie Algebra	Rotation Group
general eye position	$g = so(3) = h \oplus l$	$G = SO(3)$
primary position	$0_g \in g$	$e \in G$
eye torsion	$h = \text{Span}\{L_x\}$	$H = SO(2)$
"allowed" eye positions	$l = \text{Span}\{L_y, L_z\}$ (Listing's plane)	$S = G/H = SO(3)/SO(2)$ $\cong S^2$ (Donders' sphere of gaze directions)

to another space — the unit sphere S^2 (embedded in $\mathbb{R}^3$). This equivalence can be seen in the following way: a unit vector in $\mathbb{R}^3$, e.g. $e = (1, 0, 0)$, can be rotated so that its head reaches every point on the unit sphere S^2; however, for any such point there are infinitely many rotations by which the point can be reached. Moreover, all the rotations around the x axis leave the vector e above invariant. We therefore have to "factor out" these rotations (of $H = SO(2)$) in order to eliminate the above degeneracy and to obtain a one-to-one correspondence between the required subset of rotations and the sphere. This is achieved by going to the quotient space.

The matrix of a torsionless rotation (generated by elements in Listing's plane) is obtained by setting $\theta_x = 0$ in (9):

$$R = \begin{pmatrix} \cos\theta & \sin\theta\sin\phi & \sin\theta\cos\phi \\ -\sin\theta\sin\phi & \cos\theta + (1-\cos\theta)\cos^2\phi & \cos\phi\sin\phi(1-\cos\theta) \\ -\sin\theta\cos\phi & \cos\phi\sin\phi(1-\cos\theta) & \cos\theta + (1-\cos\theta)\sin^2\phi \end{pmatrix}, \quad (20)$$

where $\theta = \sqrt{\theta_y^2 + \theta_z^2}$ is the total angle of rotation and ϕ is the angle between θ and the y axis in the $\theta_y - \theta_z$ plane, i.e. (θ, ϕ) are polar co-ordinates in Listing's plane. Notice that the first column on the left constitutes the Cartesian co-ordinates of a point on a sphere of unit radius (Gilmore, 1974).

As we have just seen, there is an exact correspondence between the group level and the Lie algebra level. In fact, the two describe the same reality, the former in a global manner and the latter in an infinitesimal one. Table 1 summarizes the important biological notions concerning Listing's law together with their corresponding mathematical representations. The connection between Donders' law and Listing's law can now be seen in a clear and intuitive way. The sphere, which was obtained by eliminating torsion, is the space of gaze directions. Recall that Donders' law states that the orientation of the eye is determined uniquely by its gaze direction. Listing's law implies that we need only take into consideration the gaze direction and disregard torsion. In order to emphasize this point, we use the fact that *locally*, $SO(3)$ looks like a product of topological spaces: [3]

$$P = U \times SO(2) \quad \text{where} \quad U \subset S^2. \quad (21)$$

U parameterizes gaze direction and $SO(2)$ — torsion. Donders' law restricts eye orientation to an unknown 2D submanifold of the product space P. Listing's law shows that the submanifold is U, a piece of the sphere. This representation is advantageous for biological modelling, because it mathematically sets apart the degrees of freedom of gaze orientation from torsion, which also differ functionally.

---

[3] $SO(3)$ is a principal bundle over S^2 with fiber $SO(2)$.

4 AXES OF ROTATION FOR LISTING'S LAW

As mentioned in the introduction, moving between two (non-primary) positions requires a rotation whose axis (i.e. angular velocity vector) lies outside Listing's plane. This is a result of the group structure of $SO(3)$. Had the axis of rotation been contained within Listing's plane, the matrices of the quotient space (20) should have been closed under multiplication so as to form a subgroup of $SO(3)$. In other words, if r_i and r_f are matrices representing the current and target orientations of the eye corresponding to axes in Listing's plane, then $r_f \cdot r_i^{-1}$ should have been a matrix of the same form (20); however, as explained in Section 3, this condition is not fulfilled.

Finally, since normal saccades involve rotations about a single axis, they are one-parameter subgroups generated by a single element of the Lie algebra (1). In addition, they have the property of being geodesic curves in the group manifold under the natural metric which is given by the bilinear Cartan-Killing form of the group (Choquet-Bruhat et al., 1982).

5 CONCLUSION

We have analysed the geometry of eye rotations using basic Lie group theory and differential geometry. The unifying view presented here can serve to improve the understanding of the oculomotor system. It may also be extended to study the three dimensional rotations of the joints of the upper limb.

Acknowledgements

We would like to thank Stephen Gelbart, Dragana Todorić and Yosef Yomdin for instructive conversations on the mathematical background and Dario Liebermann for fruitful discussions. Special thanks go to Stan Gielen for conversations which initiated this work.

References

Choquet-Bruhat Y., De Witt-Morette C. & Dillard-Bleick M., *Analysis, Manifolds and Physics*, North-Holland (1982).

Gilmore R., *LieGroups, Lie Algebras, and Some of Their Applications*, Wiley (1974).

Hepp K., *Commun. Math. Phys.* **132** (1990) 285-292.

Hestenes D., *Neural Networks* **7**, No. 1 (1994) 65-77.

Minken A.W.H. Van Opstal A.J. & Van Gisbergen J.A.M., *Exp. Brain Research* **93** (1993) 521-533.

Tweed, D. & Vilis T., *J. Neurophysiology* **58** (1987) 832-849.

Tweed D. & Vilis T., *Vision Research* **30** (1990) 111-127.

Van Opstal J., "Representations of Eye Positions in Three Dimensions", in *Multisensory Control of Movement*, ed. Berthoz A., (1993) 27-41.

Van Rijn L.J. & Van Den Berg A.V., *Vision Research* **33**, No. 5/6 (1993) 691-708.

Varadarajan V.S., *Lie Groups, Lie Algebras, and Their Reps.*, Prentice-Hall (1974).

Westheimer G., *Journal of the Optical Society of America* **47** (1957) 967-974.

Temporal coding in the sub-millisecond range: Model of *barn owl* auditory pathway

Richard Kempter[*]
Institut für Theoretische Physik
Physik-Department der TU München
D-85748 Garching bei München
Germany

Wulfram Gerstner
Institut für Theoretische Physik
Physik-Department der TU München
D-85748 Garching bei München
Germany

J. Leo van Hemmen
Institut für Theoretische Physik
Physik-Department der TU München
D-85748 Garching bei München
Germany

Hermann Wagner
Institut für Zoologie
Fakultät für Chemie und Biologie
D-85748 Garching bei München
Germany

Abstract

Binaural coincidence detection is essential for the localization of external sounds and requires auditory signal processing with high temporal precision. We present an integrate-and-fire model of spike processing in the auditory pathway of the barn owl. It is shown that a temporal precision in the microsecond range can be achieved with neuronal time constants which are at least one magnitude longer. An important feature of our model is an unsupervised Hebbian learning rule which leads to a temporal fine tuning of the neuronal connections.

---

[*]email: kempter,wgerst,lvh @ physik.tu-muenchen.de

1 Introduction

Owls are able to locate acoustic signals based on extraction of interaural time difference by coincidence detection [1, 2]. The spatial resolution of sound localization found in experiments corresponds to a temporal resolution of auditory signal processing well below one millisecond. It follows that both the firing of spikes and their transmission along the so-called time pathway of the auditory system must occur with high temporal precision.

Each neuron in the nucleus magnocellularis, the second processing stage in the ascending auditory pathway, responds to signals in a narrow frequency range. Its spikes are phase locked to the external signal (Fig. 1a) for frequencies up to 8 kHz [3]. Axons from the nucleus magnocellularis project to the nucleus laminaris where signals from the right and left ear converge. Owls use the interaural phase difference for azimuthal sound localization. Since barn owls can locate signals with a precision of one degree of azimuthal angle, the temporal precision of spike encoding and transmission must be at least in the range of some 10 μs.

This poses at least two severe problems. First, the neural architecture has to be adapted to operating with high temporal precision. Considering the fact that the total delay from the ear to the nucleus magnocellularis is approximately 2-3 ms [4], a temporal precision of some 10 μs requires some fine tuning, possibly based on learning. Here we suggest that Hebbian learning is an appropriate mechanism. Second, neurons must operate with the necessary temporal precision. A firing precision of some 10 μs seems truly remarkable considering the fact that the membrane time constant is probably in the millisecond range. Nevertheless, it is shown below that neuronal spikes can be transmitted with the required temporal precision.

2 Neuron model

We concentrate on a single frequency channel of the auditory pathway and model a neuron of the nucleus magnocellularis. Since synapses are directly located on the *soma*, the spatial structure of the neuron can be reduced to a single compartment. In order to simplify the dynamics, we take an integrate-and-fire unit. Its membrane potential changes according to

$$\frac{d}{dt}u = -\frac{u}{\tau_0} + I(t) \tag{1}$$

where $I(t)$ is some input and τ_0 is the membrane time constant. The neuron fires, if $u(t)$ crosses a threshold $\vartheta = 1$. This defines a firing time t_0. After firing u is reset to an initial value $u_0 = 0$. Since auditory neurons are known to be fast, we assume a membrane time constant of 2 ms. Note that this is shorter than in other areas of the brain, but still a factor of 4 longer than the period of a 2 kHz sound signal.

The magnocellular neuron receives input from several presynaptic neurons $1 \le k \le K$. Each input spike at time t_k^f generates a current pulse which decays exponentially with a fast time constant $\tau_r = 0.02$ ms. The magnitude of the current pulse depends on the coupling strength J_k. The total input is

$$I(t) = \sum_{k,f} J_k \exp(\frac{t - t_k^f}{\tau_r}) \theta(t - t_k^f) \tag{2}$$

where $\theta(x)$ is the unit step function and the sum runs over all input spikes.

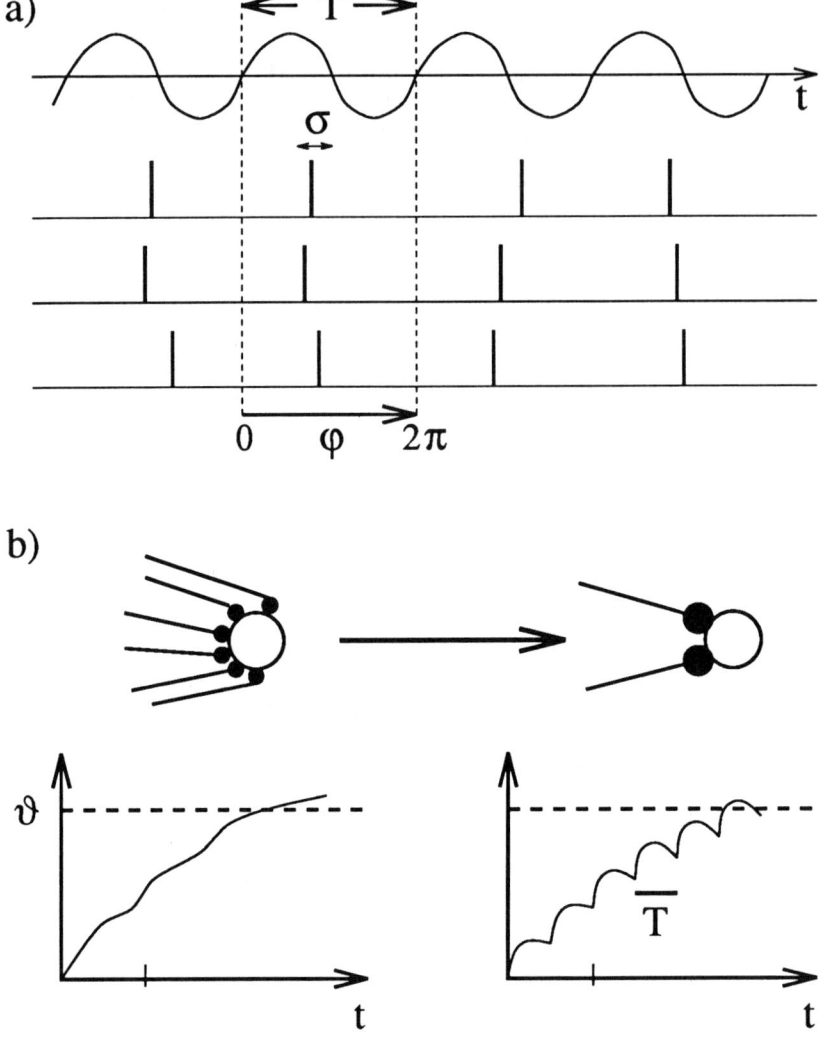

Fig. 1. *Principles of phase locking and learning.* a) The stimulus consists of a sound wave (top). Spikes of auditory nerve fibers leading to the nucleus magnocellularis are phase-locked to the periodic wave, that is, they occur at a preferred phase in relation to the sound, but with some jitter σ. Three examples of phase-locked spike trains are indicated. b) Before learning (left), many auditory input fibers converge to a neuron of the nucleus magnocellularis. Because of axonal delays which vary between different fibers, spikes *arrive* incoherently even though they are generated in a phase locked fashion. Due to averaging over several incoherent inputs, the total postsynaptic potential (bottom left) of a magnocellular neuron follows a rather smooth trajectory with no significant temporal structure. After learning (right) most connections have disappeared and only a few strong contacts remain. Input spikes now arrive coherently and the postsynaptic potential exhibits a clear oscillatory structure. Note that firing must occur during the rising phase of the oscillation. Thus output spikes will be phase locked.

All input signals belong to the same frequency channel with a carrier frequency of 2 kHz (period $T = 0.5$ ms), but the inputs arise from different presynaptic neurons ($1 \leq k \leq K$). Their axons have different diameter and length leading to a signal transmission delay Δ_k which varies between 2 and 3 ms [4]. Note that a delay as small as 0.25 ms shifts the signal by half a period.

Each input signal consists of a periodic spike train subject to two types of noise. First, a presynaptic neuron may not fire regularly every period but, on average, every n^{th} period only where $n \approx 1/(\nu T)$ and ν is the mean firing rate of the neuron. For the sake of simplicity, we set $n = 1$. Second, the spikes may occur slightly too early or too late compared to the mean delay Δ. Based on experimental results, we assume a typical shift $\sigma = \pm 0.05$ ms [3]. Specifically we assume in our model that inputs from a presynaptic neuron k arrive with the probability density

$$P(t_k^f) = \frac{1}{\sqrt{2\pi}\sigma} \sum_{n=-\infty}^{\infty} \exp\left[\frac{-(t_k^f - nT - \Delta_k)^2}{2\sigma^2}\right] \quad (3)$$

where Δ_k is the axonal transmission delay of input k (Fig. 1).

3 Temporal tuning through learning

We assume a developmental period of unsupervised learning during which a fine tuning of the temporal characteristics of signal transmission takes place (Fig. 1b). Before learning the magnocellular neuron receives many inputs ($K = 50$) with weak coupling ($J_k = 1$). Due to the broad distribution of delays the total input (2) has, apart from fluctuations, no temporal structure. After learning, the magnocellular neuron receives input from two or three presynaptic neurons only. The connections to those neurons have become very effective; cf. Fig. 2.

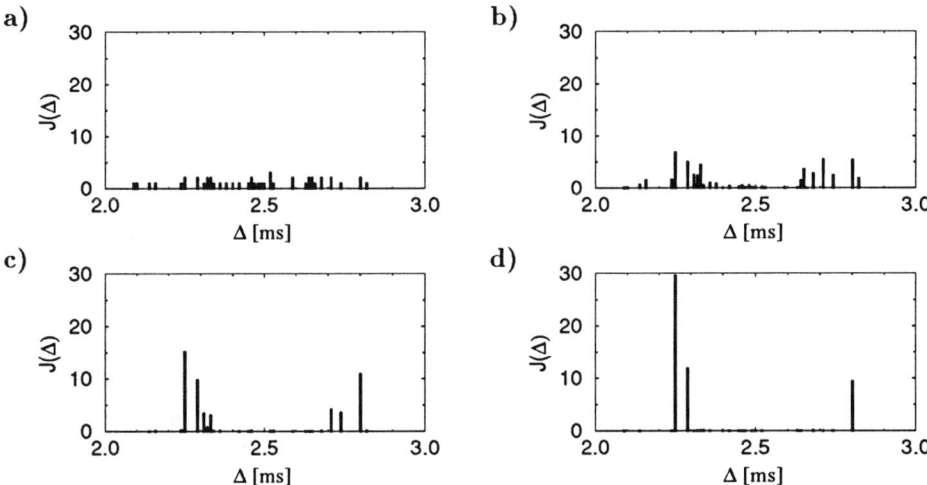

Fig. 2. *Learning. We plot the number of synaptic contacts (y-axis) for each delay Δ (x-axis). (a) At the beginning, the neuron has contacts to 50 presynaptic neurons with delays $2\,ms \leq \Delta \leq 3\,ms$. (b) and (c) During learning, some presynaptic neurons increase their number of contacts, other contacts disappear. (d) After learning, contacts to three presynaptic neurons with delays 2.25, 2.28, and 2.8 ms remain. The remaining contacts are very strong.*

The constant J_k measures the *total* coupling strength between a presynaptic neuron k and the postsynaptic neuron. Values of J_k larger than one indicate that several synapses have been formed. It has been estimated from anatomical data that a fully developed magnocellular neuron receives inputs from as few as 1-4 presynaptic neurons, but each presynaptic axon shows multiple branching near the postsynaptic soma and makes up to one hundred synaptic contacts on the soma of the magnocellular neuron[5]. The result of our simulation study is consistent with this finding. In our model, learning leads to a final state with a few but highly effective inputs. The remaining inputs all have the same time delay modulo the period T of the stimulus. Thus, learning leads to reduction of the number of input neurons contacts with a nucleus magnocellularis neuron. This is the fine tuning of the neuronal connections necessary for precise temporal coding (see below, section 4).

a)

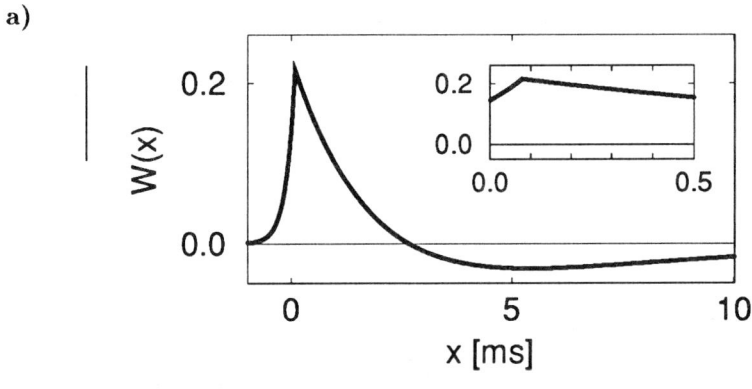

b)

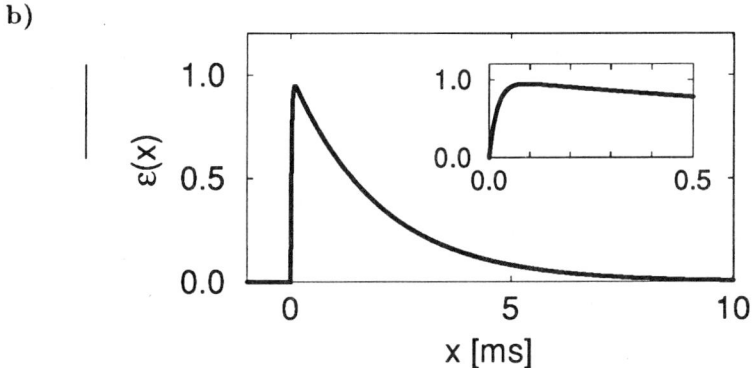

Fig. 3. *(a) Time window of learning $W(x)$. Along the x-axis we plot the time difference between presynaptic and postsynaptic fiing $x = t_i^f - t^k$. The window function $W(x)$ has a positive and a negative phase. Learning is most effective, if the postsynaptic spike is late by 0.08 ms (inset). (b) Postsynaptic potential $\epsilon(x)$. Each input spike evoked a postsynaptic potential which decays with a time constant of 2 ms. Since synapses are located directly at the soma, the rise time is very fast (see inset). Our learning scenario requires that the rise time of $\epsilon(x)$ should be approximately equal to the time x where $W(x)$ has its maximum.*

In our model, temporal tuning is achieved by a variant of Hebbian learning. In standard Hebbian learning, synaptic weights are changed if pre- and postsynaptic activity occurs simultaneously. In the context of temporal coding by spikes, the concept of 'simultaneous activity' has to be refined. We assume that a synapse k is changed, if a presynaptic spike t_k^f and a postsynaptic spike t_0 occur within a *time window* $W(t_k^f - t_0)$. More precisely, each pair of presynaptic and postsynaptic spikes changes a synapse J_k by an amount

$$\Delta J_k = \gamma W(t_k^f - t_0) \qquad (4)$$

with a prefactor $\gamma = 0.2$. Depending on the sign of $W(x)$, a contact to a presynaptic neuron is either increased or decreased. A decrease below $J_k = 0$ is not allowed. In our model, we assume a function $W(x)$ with two phases; cf. Fig. 3. For $x \approx 0$, the function $W(x)$ is positive. This leads to a strengthening (potentiation) of the contact with a presynaptic neuron k which is active shortly before or after a postsynaptic spike. Synaptic contacts which become active more than 3 ms later than the postsynaptic spike are decreased. Note that the time window spans several cycles of length T. The combination of decrease and increase balances the average effects of potentiation and depression and leads to a normalization of the number and weight of synapses. Learning is stopped after 50.000 cycles of length T.

4 Temporal coding after learning

After learning contacts remain to a small number of presynaptic neurons. Their axonal transmission delays coincide or differ by multiples of the period T. Thus the spikes arriving from the few different presynaptic neurons have approximately the same phase and add up to an input signal (2) which retains, apart from fluctuations, the periodicity of the external sound signal (Fig.4a).

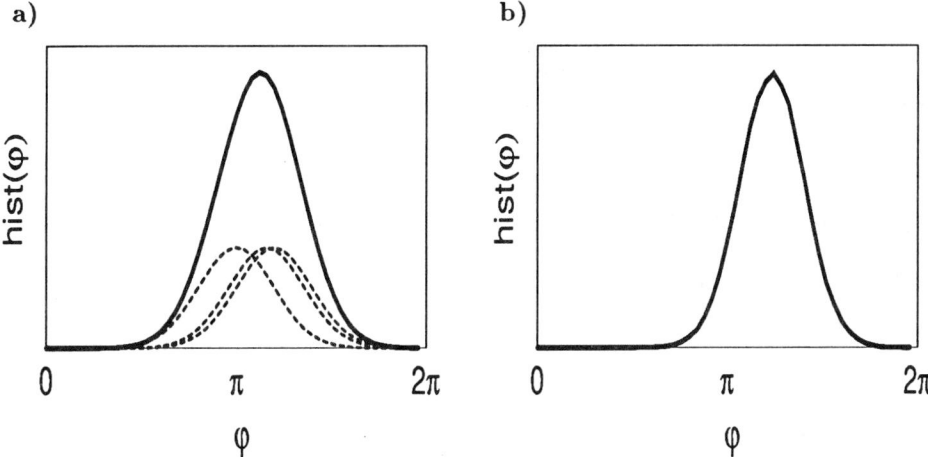

Fig. 4. *(a) Distribution of input phases after learning. The solid line shows the number of instances that an input spike with phase φ has occured (arbitrary units). The input consists of spikes from the three presynaptic neurons which have survived after learning; cf. Fig. 1d. Due to the different delays, the mean input phase varies slightly between the three input channels. The dashed curves show the phase distribution of the individual channels, the solid line is the sum of the three dashed curves. (b) Distribution of output phases after learning. The histogram of output phases is sharply peaked. Comparison of the position of the maxima of the solid curves in (a) and (b) shows that the output is phase locked to the input with a relative delay $\delta\varphi$ which is related to the rise time of the postsynaptic potential.*

Output spikes of the magnocellular neuron are generated by the integrate-and-fire process (1). In Fig.4b we show a histogram of the phases of the output spikes. We find that the phases have a narrow distribution around a peak value. Thus the output is phase locked to the external signal. The width of the phase distribution corresponds to a precision of 0.084 phase cycles which equals 42 μs for a 2 kHz stimulus. Note that the temporal precision of the output has improved compared to the input where we had three channels with slightly different mean phases and a variation of $\sigma = 50\mu$s each. The increase in the precision is due to the average over three uncorrelated input signals.

We assume that the same principles are used during the following stages along the auditory pathway. In the nucleus laminaris several hundred signals are combined. This improves the signal-to-noise ratio further and a temporal precision below 10 μs could be achieved.

5 Discussion

We have demonstrated that precise temporal coding in the microsecond range is possible despite neuronal time constants in the millisecond range. Temporal refinement has been achieved through a slow developmental learning rule. It is a correlation based rule with a time window W which spans several milliseconds. Nevertheless learning leads to a fine tuning of the connections supporting temporal coding with a resolution of 42 μs. The membrane time constant was set to 2 ms. This is nearly two orders of magnitudes longer than the achieved resolution. In our model, there is only one fast time constant which describes the typical duration of a input current pulse evoked by a presynaptic spike. Our value of $\tau_r = 20$ μs corresponds to a rise time of the postsynaptic potential of 100 μs. This seems to be realistic for auditory neurons since synaptic contacts are located directly on the *soma* of the postsynaptic neuron. The basic results of our model can also be applied to other areas of the brain and can shed new light on some aspects of temporal coding with slow neurons.

Acknowledgments: R.K. holds scholarship of the state of Bavaria. W.G. has been supported by the Deutsche Forschungsgemeinschaft (DFG) under grant number He 1729/2-2. H.W. is a Heisenberg fellow of the DFG.

References

[1] L. A. Jeffress, J. Comp. Physiol. Psychol. **41**, 35 (1948).

[2] M. Konishi, Trends Neurosci. **9**, 163 (1986).

[3] C. E. Carr and M. Konishi, J. Neurosci. **10**, 3227 (1990).

[4] W. E. Sullivan and M. Konishi, J. Neurosci. **4**, 1787 (1984).

[5] C. E. Carr and R. E. Boudreau, J. Comp. Neurol. **314**, 306 (1991).

Cholinergic suppression of transmission may allow combined associative memory function and self-organization in the neocortex.

Michael E. Hasselmo and Milos Cekic
Department of Psychology and Program in Neurosciences,
Harvard University, 33 Kirkland St., Cambridge, MA 02138
hasselmo@katla.harvard.edu

Abstract

Selective suppression of transmission at feedback synapses during learning is proposed as a mechanism for combining associative feedback with self-organization of feedforward synapses. Experimental data demonstrates cholinergic suppression of synaptic transmission in layer I (feedback synapses), and a lack of suppression in layer IV (feedforward synapses). A network with this feature uses local rules to learn mappings which are not linearly separable. During learning, sensory stimuli and desired response are simultaneously presented as input. Feedforward connections form self-organized representations of input, while suppressed feedback connections learn the transpose of feedforward connectivity. During recall, suppression is removed, sensory input activates the self-organized representation, and activity generates the learned response.

1 INTRODUCTION

The synaptic connections in most models of the cortex can be defined as either associative or self-organizing on the basis of a single feature: the relative influence of modifiable synapses on post-synaptic activity during learning (figure 1). In associative memories, post-synaptic activity during learning is determined by nonmodifiable afferent input connections, with no change in the storage due to synaptic transmission at modifiable synapses (Anderson, 1983; McNaughton and Morris, 1987). In self-organization, post-synaptic activity is predominantly influenced by the modifiable synapses, such that modification of synapses influences subsequent learning (Von der Malsburg, 1973; Miller et al., 1990). Models of cortical function must combine the capacity to form new representations and store associations between these representations. Networks combining self-organization and associative memory function can learn complex mapping functions with more biologically plausible learning rules (Hecht-Nielsen, 1987; Carpenter et al., 1991; Dayan et al.,

1995), but must control the influence of feedback associative connections on self-organization. Some networks use special activation dynamics which prevent feedback from influencing activity unless it coincides with feedforward activity (Carpenter et al., 1991). A new network alternately shuts off feedforward and feedback synaptic transmission (Dayan et al., 1995).

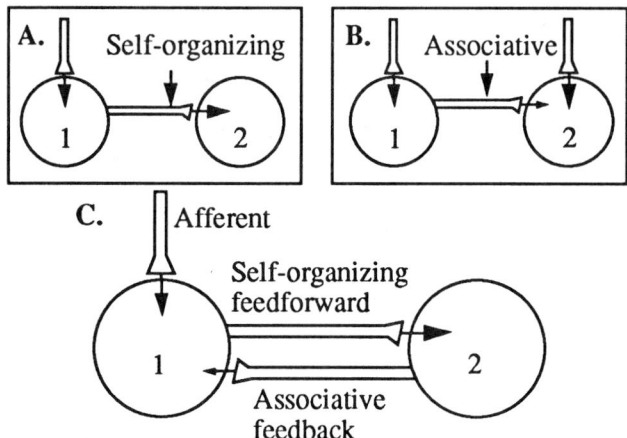

Figure 1 - Defining characteristics of self-organization and associative memory. A. At self-organizing synapses, post-synaptic activity during learning depends predominantly upon transmission at the modifiable synapses. B. At synapses mediating associative memory function, post-synaptic activity during learning does not depend primarily on the modifiable synapses, but is predominantly influenced by separate afferent input. C. Self-organization and associative memory function can be combined if associative feedback synapses are selectively suppressed during learning but not recall.

Here we present a model using selective suppression of feedback synaptic transmission during learning to allow simultaneous self-organization and association between two regions. Previous experiments show that the neuromodulator acetylcholine selectively suppresses synaptic transmission within the olfactory cortex (Hasselmo and Bower, 1992; 1993) and hippocampus (Hasselmo and Schnell, 1994). If the model is valid for neocortical structures, cholinergic suppression should be stronger for feedback but not feedforward synapses. Here we review experimental data (Hasselmo and Cekic, 1996) comparing cholinergic suppression of synaptic transmission in layers with predominantly feedforward or feedback synapses.

2. BRAIN SLICE PHYSIOLOGY

As shown in Figure 2, we utilized brain slice preparations of the rat somatosensory neocortex to investigate whether cholinergic suppression of synaptic transmission is selective for feedback but not feedforward synaptic connections. This was possible because feedforward and feedback connections show different patterns of termination in neocortex. As shown in Figure 2, Layer I contains primarily feedback synapses from other cortical regions (Cauller and Connors, 1994), whereas layer IV contains primarily afferent synapses from the thalamus and feedforward synapses from more primary neocortical structures (Van Essen and Maunsell, 1983). Using previously developed techniques (Cauller and Connors, 1994; Li and Cauller, 1995) for testing of the predominantly feedback connections in layer I, we stimulated layer I and recorded in layer I (a cut prevented spread of activity from layers II and III). For testing the predominantly feedforward connections terminating in layer IV, we elicited synaptic potentials by stimulating the white matter deep to layer VI and recorded in layer IV. We tested suppression by measuring the change in height of synaptic potentials during perfusion of the cholinergic agonist carbachol at 100μM. Figure 3 shows that perfusion of carbachol caused much stronger suppression of synaptic transmission in layer I as compared to layer IV (Hasselmo and Cekic, 1996), suggesting that cholinergic suppression of transmission is selective for feedback synapses and not for feedforward synapses.

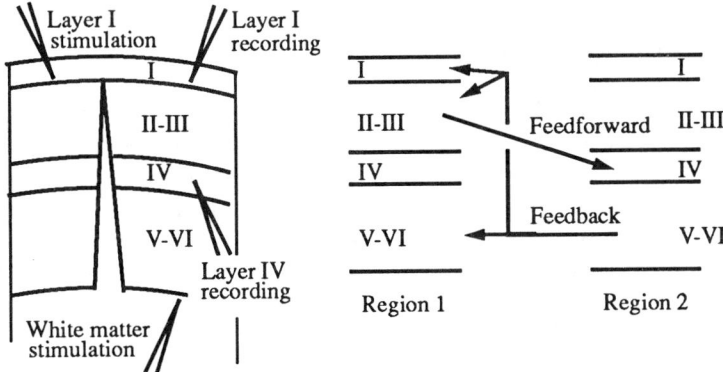

Figure 2. A. Brain slice preparation of somatosensory cortex showing location of stimulation and recording electrodes for testing suppression of synaptic transmission in layer I and in layer IV. Experiment based on procedures developed by Cauller (Cauller and Connors, 1994; Li and Cauller, 1995). B. Anatomical pattern of feedforward and feedback connectivity within cortical structures (based on Van Essen and Maunsell, 1983).

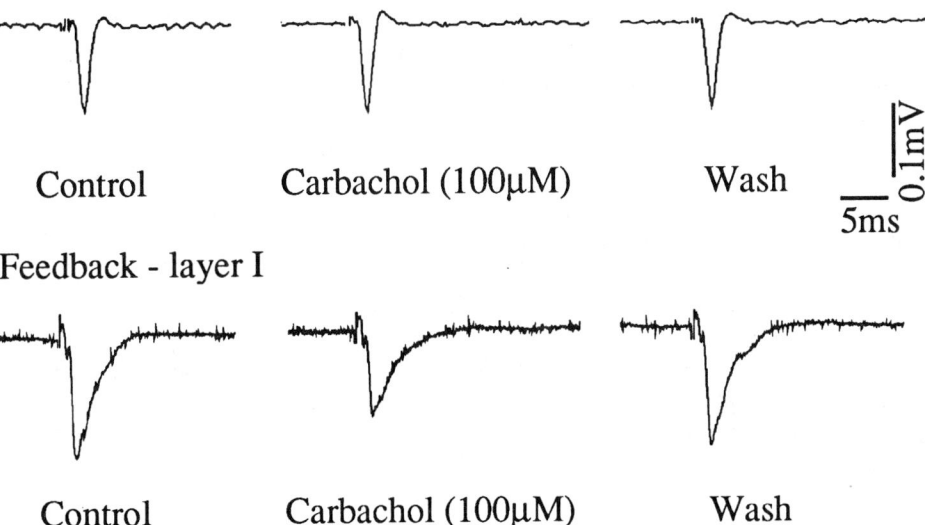

Figure 3 - Suppression of transmission in somatosensory neocortex. Top: Synaptic potentials recorded in layer IV (where feedforward and afferent synapses predominate) show little effect of 100μM carbachol. Bottom: Synaptic potentials recorded in layer I (where feedback synapses predominate) show suppression in the presence of 100μM carbachol.

3. COMPUTATIONAL MODELING

These experimental results supported the use of selective suppression in a computational model (Hasselmo and Cekic, 1996) with self-organization in its feedforward synaptic connections and associative memory function in its feedback synaptic connections (Figs 1 and 4). The proposed network uses local, Hebb-type learning rules supported by evidence on the physiology of long-term potentiation in the hippocampus (Gustafsson and Wigstrom, 1986). The learning rule for each set of connections in the network takes the form:

$$\Delta W_{ij}^{(x,y)} = \eta \, (a_i^{(y)} - \theta^{(y)}) \, g \, (a_j^{(x)})$$

Where $W^{(x,y)}$ designates the connections from region x to region y, θ is the threshold of synaptic modification in region y, η is the rate of modification, and the output function is $g(a_i^{(x)}) = [\tanh(a_j^{(x)} - \mu^{(x)})]_+$ where $[]_+$ represents the constraint to positive values only. Feedforward connections ($W_{ij}^{(x<y)}$) have self-organizing properties, while feedback connections ($W_{ij}^{(x>=y)}$) have associative memory properties. This difference depends entirely upon the selective suppression of feedback synapses during learning, which is implemented in the activation rule in the form (1-c). For the entire network, the activation rule takes the form:

$$a_i^{(y)} = A_i^{(y)} + \sum_{x=1}^{M} \sum_{k=1}^{n(x)} W_{ik}^{(x<y)} g(a_k^{(x)}) + \sum_{x=1}^{N} \sum_{k=1}^{n(x)} (1-c) W_{ik}^{(x \geq y)} g(a_k^{(x)}) - \sum_{k=1}^{n(y)} H_{ik}^{(y)} (g(a_k^{(y)}))$$

where $a_i^{(y)}$ represents the activity of each of the $n^{(y)}$ neurons in region y, $a_k^{(x)}$ is the activity of each of the $n^{(x)}$ neurons in other regions x, M is the total number of regions providing feedforward input, N is the total number of regions providing feedback input, $A_i^{(y)}$ is the input pattern to region y, $H^{(y)}$ represents the inhibition between neurons in region y, and (1 - c) represents the suppression of synaptic transmission. During learning, c takes a value between 0 and 1. During recall, suppression is removed, c = 0. In this network, synapses (W) between regions only take positive values, reflecting the fact that long-range connections between cortical regions consist of excitatory synapses arising from pyramidal cells. Thus, inhibition mediated by the local inhibitory interneurons within a region is represented by a separate inhibitory connectivity matrix H.

After each step of learning, the total weight of synaptic connections is normalized pre-synaptically for each neuron j in each region:

$$W_{ij}(t+1) = [W_{ij}(t) + \Delta W_{ij}(t)] / \left(\sqrt{\sum_{i=1}^{n} [W_{ij}(t) + \Delta W_{ij}(t)]^2} \right)$$

Synaptic weights are then normalized post-synaptically for each neuron i in each region (replacing i with j in the sum in the denominator in equation 3). This normalization of synaptic strength represents slower cellular mechanisms which redistribute pre and post-synaptic resources for maintaining synapses depending upon local influences.

In these simulations, both the sensory input stimuli and the desired output response to be learned are presented as afferent input to the neurons in region 1. Most networks using error-based learning rules consist of feedforward architectures with separate layers of input and output units. One can imagine this network as an auto-encoder network folded back on itself, with both input and output units in region 1, and hidden units in region 2.

As an example of its functional properties, the network presented here was trained on the XOR problem. The XOR problem has previously been used as an example of the capability of error based training schemes for solving problems which are not linearly separable. The specific characteristics of the network and patterns used for this simulation are shown in figure 4. The two logical states of each component of the XOR problem are represented by two separate units (designated on or off in figures 4 and 5), ensuring that activation of the network is equal for each input condition. The problem has the appearance of two XOR problems with inverse logical states being solved simultaneously.

As shown in figure 4, the input and desired output of the network are presented simultaneously during learning to region 1. The six neurons in region 1 project along feedforward connections to four neurons in region 2, the hidden units of the network. These four neurons project along feedback connections to the six neurons in region 1. All connections take random initial weights. During learning, the feedforward connections undergo self-organization which ultimately causes the hidden units to become feature detectors responding to each of the four patterns of input to region 1. Thus, the rows of the feedforward synaptic connectivity matrix gradually take the form of the individual input patterns.

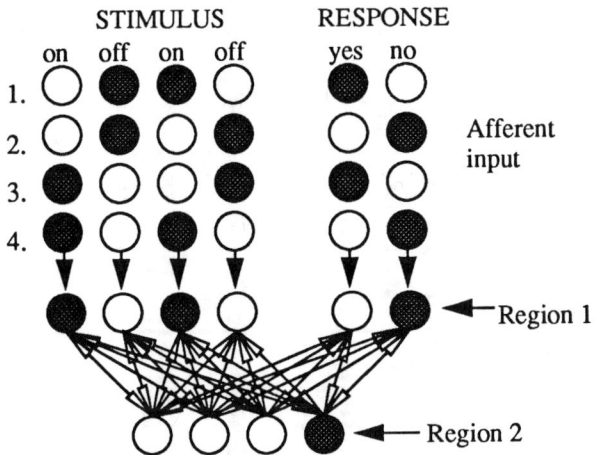

Figure 4 - Network for learning the XOR problem, with 6 units in region 1 and 4 units in region 2. Four different patterns of afferent input are presented successively to region 1. The input stimuli of the XOR problem are represented by the four units on the left, and the desired output designation of XOR or not-XOR is represented by the two units on the right. The XOR problem has four basic states: on-off and off-on on the input is categorized by yes on the output, while on-on and off-off on the input is categorized by no on the output.

Modulation is applied during learning in the form of selective suppression of synaptic transmission along feedback connections (this suppression need not be complete), giving these connections associative memory function. Hebbian synaptic modification causes these connections to link each of the feature detecting hidden units in region 2 with the cells in region 1 activated by the pattern to which the hidden unit responds. Gradually, the feedback synaptic connectivity matrix becomes the transpose of the feedforward connectivity matrix. (Parameters used in simulation: $A_j(1) = 0$ or 1, $h = 2.0$, $q(1) = 0.5$, $q(2) = 0.6$, $(1) = 0.2$, $(2) = 0.5$, $c = 1.0$ and $H_{ik}(2) = 0.6$). Function was similar and convergence was obtained more rapidly with $c = 0.5$. Feedback synaptic transmission prevented convergence during learning when c = 0.367).

During recall, modulation of synaptic transmission is removed, and the various input stimuli of the XOR problem are presented to region 1 without the corresponding output pattern. Activity spreads along the self-organized feedforward connections to activate the specific hidden layer unit responding to that pattern. Activity then spreads back along feedback connections from that particular unit to activate the desired output units. The activity in the two regions settles into a final pattern of recall. Figure 5 shows the settled recall of the network at different stages of learning. It can be seen that the network initially may show little recall activity, or erroneous recall activity, but after several cycles of learning, the network settles into the proper response to each of the XOR problem states. Convergence during learning and recall have been obtained with other problems, including recognition of whether on units were on the left or right, symmetry of on units, and number of on units. In addition, larger scale problems involving multiple feedforward and feedback layers have been shown to converge.

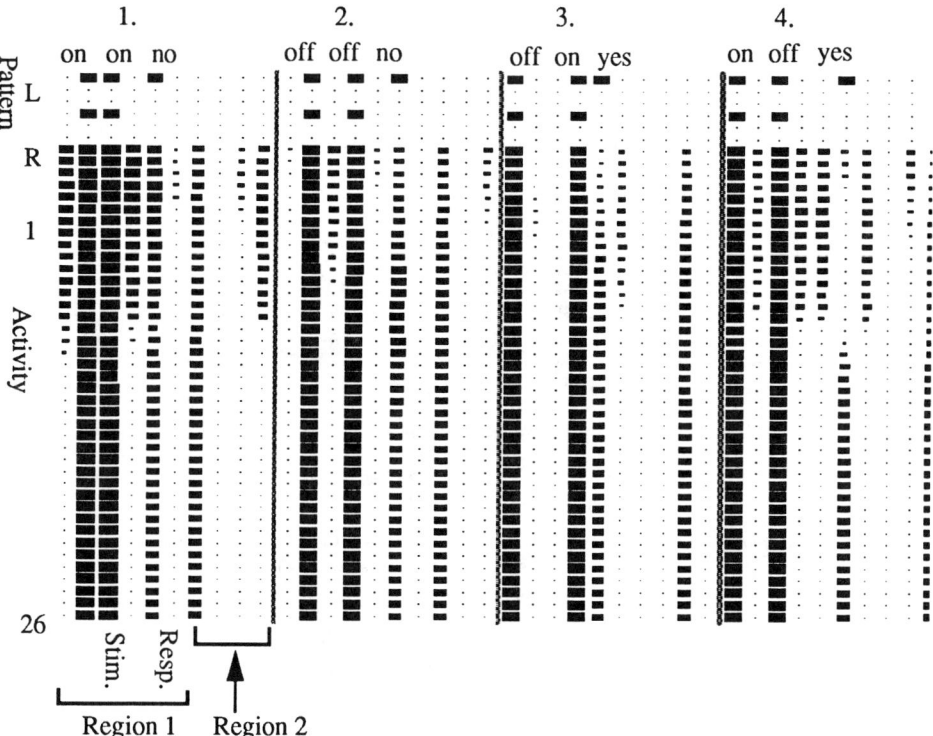

Figure 5 - Output neuronal activity in the network shown at different learning steps. The four input patterns are shown at top. Below these are degraded patterns presented during recall, missing the response components of the input pattern. The output of the 6 region 1 units and the 4 region 2 units are shown at each stage of learning. As learning progresses, gradually one region 2 unit starts to respond selectively to each input pattern, and the correct output unit becomes active in response to the degraded input. Note that as learning progresses the response to pattern 4 changes gradually from incorrect (yes) to correct (no).

References

Anderson, J.A. (1983) Cognitive and psychological computation with neural models. IEEE Trans. Systems, Man, Cybern. SMC-13, 799-815.

Carpenter, G.A., Grossberg, S. and Reynolds, J.H. (1991) ARTMAP: Supervised real-time learning and classification of nonstationary data by a self-organizing neural network. Neural Networks 4: 565-588.

Cauller, L.J. and Connors, B.W. (1994) Synaptic physiology of horizontal afferents to layer I in slices of rat SI neocortex. J. Neurosci. 14: 751-762.

Dayan, P., Hinton, G.E., Neal, R.M. and Zemel, R.S. (1995) The Helmholtz machine. Neural Computation .

Gustafsson, B. and Wigstrom, H. (1988) Physiological mechanisms underlying long-term potentiation. Trends Neurosci. 11: 156-162.

Hasselmo, M.E. (1993) Acetylcholine and learning in a cortical associative memory. Neural Computation. 5(1): 32-44.

Hasselmo M.E. and Bower J.M. (1992) Cholinergic suppression specific to intrinsic not afferent fiber synapses in rat piriform (olfactory) cortex. J. Neurophysiol. 67: 1222-1229.

Hasselmo, M.E. and Bower, J.M. (1993) Acetylcholine and Memory. Trends Neurosci. 26: 218-222.

Hasselmo, M.E. and Cekic, M. (1996) Suppression of synaptic transmission may allow combination of associative feedback and self-organizing feedforward connections in the neocortex. Behav. Brain Res. in press.

Hasselmo M.E., Anderson B.P. and Bower J.M. (1992) Cholinergic modulation of cortical associative memory function. J. Neurophysiol. 67: 1230-1246.

Hasselmo M.E. and Schnell, E. (1994) Laminar selectivity of the cholinergic suppression of synaptic transmission in rat hippocampal region CA1: Computational modeling and brain slice physiology. J. Neurosci. 15: 3898-3914.

Hecht-Nielsen, R. (1987) Counterpropagation networks. Applied Optics 26: 4979-4984.

Li, H. and Cauller, L.J. (1995) Acetylcholine modulation of excitatory synaptic inputs from layer I to the superficial layers of rat somatosensory neocortex in vitro. Soc. Neurosci. Abstr. 21: 68.

Linsker, R. (1988) Self-organization in a perceptual network. Computer 21: 105-117.

McNaughton B.L. and Morris R.G.M. (1987) Hippocampal synaptic enhancement and information storage within a distributed memory system. Trends in Neurosci. 10:408-415.

Miller, K.D., Keller, J.B. and Stryker, M.P. (1989) Ocular dominance column development: Analysis and simulation. Science 245: 605-615.

van Essen, D.C. and Maunsell, J.H.R. (1983) Heirarchical organization and functional streams in the visual cortex. Trends Neurosci. 6: 370-375.

von der Malsburg, C. (1973) Self-organization of orientation sensitive cells in the striate cortex. Kybernetik 14: 85-100.

A Predictive Switching Model of Cerebellar Movement Control

Andrew G. Barto
Jay T. Buckingham
Department of Computer Science
University of Massachusetts
Amherst, MA 01003-4610
barto@cs.umass.edu

James C. Houk
Department of Physiology
Northwestern University Medical School
303 East Chicago Ave
Chicago, Illinois 60611-3008
houk@acns.nwu.edu

Abstract

We present a hypothesis about how the cerebellum could participate in regulating movement in the presence of significant feedback delays without resorting to a forward model of the motor plant. We show how a simplified cerebellar model can learn to control endpoint positioning of a nonlinear spring–mass system with realistic delays in both afferent and efferent pathways. The model's operation involves prediction, but instead of predicting sensory input, it directly regulates movement by reacting in an anticipatory fashion to input patterns that include delayed sensory feedback.

1 INTRODUCTION

The existence of significant delays in sensorimotor feedback pathways has led several researchers to suggest that the cerebellum might function as a forward model of the motor plant in order to predict the sensory consequences of motor commands before actual feedback is available; e.g., (Ito, 1984; Keeler, 1990; Miall et al., 1993). While we agree that there are many potential roles for forward models in motor control systems, as discussed, e.g., in (Wolpert et al., 1995), we present a hypothesis about how the cerebellum could participate in regulating movement in the presence of significant feedback delays without resorting to a forward model. We show how a very simplified version of the adjustable pattern generator (APG) model being developed by Houk and colleagues (Berthier et al., 1993; Houk et al., 1995) can learn to control endpoint positioning of a nonlinear spring–mass system with significant delays in both afferent and efferent pathways. Although much simpler than a multilink dynamic arm, control of this spring–mass system involves some of the challenges critical in the control of a more realistic motor system and serves to illustrate the principles we propose. Preliminary results appear in (Buckingham et al., 1995).

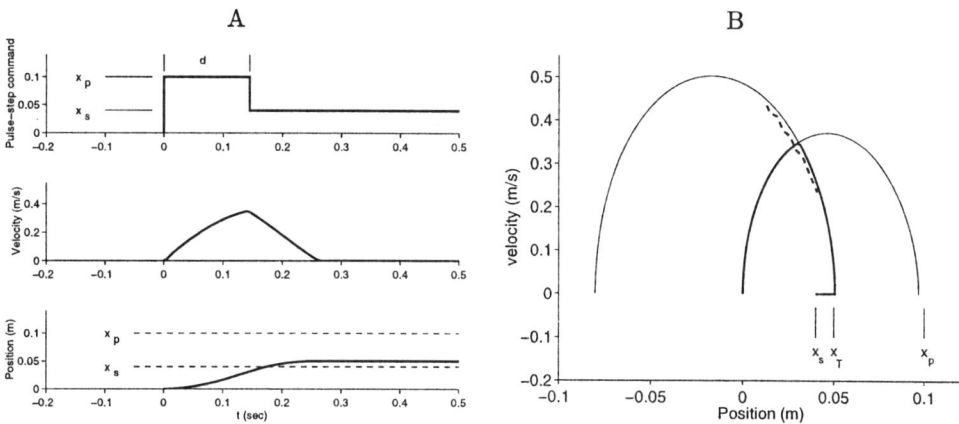

Figure 1: Pulse–step control of a movement from initial position $x_0 = 0$ to target endpoint position $x_T = .05$. Panel A: Top—The pulse–step command. Middle—Velocity as a function of time. Bottom—Position as a function of time. Panel B: Switching curve. The dashed line plots states of the spring–mass system at which the command should switch from pulse to step so that the mass will stick at the endpoint $x_T = .05$ starting from different initial states. The bold line shows the phase–plane trajectory of the movement shown in Panel A.

2 NONLINEAR VISCOSITY

An important aspect of the model is that the plant being contolled has a form of nonlinear viscosity, brought about in animals through a combination of muscle and spinal reflex properties. To illustrate this, we use a nonlinear spring–mass model based on studies of human wrist movement (Wu et al., 1990):

$$m\ddot{x} + b\dot{x}^{\frac{1}{5}} + k(x - x_{eq}) = 0, \qquad (1)$$

where x is the position (in meters) of an object of mass m (kg) attached to the spring, x_{eq} is the resting, or equilibrium, position, b is a damping coefficient, and k is the spring's stiffness. Setting $m = 1$, $b = 4$, and $k = 60$ produces trajectories that are qualitatively similar to those observed in human wrist movement (Wu et al., 1990).

This one–fifth power law viscosity gives the system the potential to produce fast movements that terminate with little or no oscillation. However, the principle of setting the equilibrium position to the desired movement endpoint does not work in practice because the system tends to "stick" at non–equilibrium positions, thereafter drifting extremely slowly toward the equilibrium position, x_{eq}. We call the position at which the mass sticks (which we define as the position at which its absolute velocity falls and remains below .005m/s) the *endpoint* of a movement, denoted x_e. Thus, endpoint control of this system is not entirely straightforward. The approach taken by our model is to switch the value of the control signal, x_{eq}, at a precisely–placed point during a movement. This is similar to virtual trajectory control, except that here the commanded equilibrium position need not equal the desired endpoint either before or after the switch.

Panel A of Fig. 1 shows an example of this type of control. The objective is to move the mass from an initial position $x_0 = 0$ to a target endpoint $x_T = .05$. The control signal is the pulse–step shown in the top graph, where $x_p = .1$ and $x_s = .04$

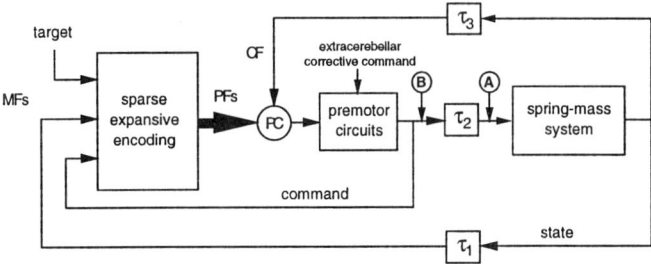

Figure 2: The simplified model. PC, Purkinje cell; MFs, mossy fibers; PFs, parallel fibers; CF, climbing fiber. The labels A and B mark places in the feedback loop to which we refer in discussing the model's behavior.

respectively denote the pulse and step values, and d denotes the pulse duration. The mass sticks near the target endpoint $x_T = .05$, which is different from both equilibrium positions. If the switch had occurred sooner (later), the mass would have undershot (overshot) the target endpoint.

The bold trajectory in Panel B of Fig. 1 is the phase–plane portrait of this movement. During its initial phase, the state follows the trajectory that would eventually lead to equilibrium position x_p. When the pulse ends, the state switches to the trajectory that would eventually lead to equilibrium position x_s, which allows a rapid approach to the target endpoint $x_T = .05$, where the mass sticks before reaching x_s. The dashed line plots pairs of positions and velocities at which the switch should occur so that movements starting from different initial states will reach the endpoint $x_T = .05$. This *switching curve* has to vary as a function of the target endpoint.

3 THE MODEL'S ARCHITECTURE

The simplified model (Fig. 2) consists of a unit representing a Purkinje cell (PC) whose input is derived from a sparse expansive encoding of mossy fiber (MF) input representing the target position, x_T, which remains fixed throughout a movement, delayed information about the state of the spring–mass system, and the current motor command, x_{eq}.[1] Patterns of MF activity are recoded to form sparse activity patterns over a large number (here 8000) of binary parallel fibers (PFs) which synapse upon the PC unit, along the lines suggested by Marr (Marr, 1969) and the CMAC model of Albus (Albus, 1971). While some liberties have been taken with this representation, the delay distributions are within the range observed for the intermediate cerebellum of the monkey (Van Kan et al., 1993).

Also as in Marr and Albus, the PC unit is trained by a signal representing the activity of a climbing fiber (CF), whose response properties are described below. Occasional corrective commands, also discussed below, are assumed to be generated

---

[1] In this model, 256 Gaussian radial basis function (RBF) units represent the target position, 400 RBF units represent the position of the mass (i.e., the length of the spring), with centers distributed uniformly across an appropriate range of positions and with delays distributed according to a Gaussian of mean 15msec and standard deviation 6msec. This distribution is truncated so that the minimum delay is 5msec. This delay distribution is represented by τ_1 in Fig. 2. Another 400 RBF units similarly represent mass velocity. An additional 4 MF inputs are efference copy signals that simply copy the current motor command.

by an extracerebellar system. The PC's output determines the motor command through a simple transformation. The model includes an efferent and CF delays, both equal to 20msec (τ_2 and τ_3, respectively, in Fig. 2). These delays are also within the physiological range for these pathways (Gellman et al., 1983). How this model is related to the full APG model and its justification in terms of the anatomy and physiology of the cerebellum and premotor circuits are discussed extensively elsewhere (Berthier et al., 1993; Houk et al., 1995).

The PC unit is a linear threshold unit with hysteresis. Let $s(t) = \sum_i w_i(t)\phi_i(t)$, where $\phi_i(t)$ denotes the activity of PF i at time t and $w_i(t)$ is the weight at time step t of the synapse by which PF i influences the PC unit. The output of the PC unit at time t, denoted $y(t)$, is the PC's activity state, high or low, at time t, which represents a high or a low frequency of simple spike activity. PC activation depends on two thresholds: θ_{high} and $\theta_{low} < \theta_{high}$. The activity state switches from low to high when $s(t) > \theta_{high}$, and it switches from high to low when $s(t) < \theta_{low}$. If $\theta_{high} = \theta_{low}$, the PC unit is the usual linear threshold unit. Although hysteresis is not strictly necessary for the control task we present here, it accelerates learning: A PC can more easily learn when to switch states than it can learn to maintain the correct output on a moment–to–moment basis. The bistability of this PC unit is a simplified representation of multistability that could be produced by dendritic zones of hysteresis arising from ionic mechanisms (Houk et al., 1995).

Because PC activity inhibits premotor circuits, PC state low corresponds to the pulse phase of the motor command, which sets a "far" equilibrium position, x_p; PC state high corresponds to the step phase, which sets a "near" equilibrium position, x_s. Thus, the pulse ends when the PC state switches from low to high. Because the precise switching point determines where the mass sticks, this single binary PC can bring the mass to any target endpoint in a considerable range by switching state at the right moment during a movement.

4 LEARNING

Learning is based on the idea that corrective movements following inaccurate movements provide training information by triggering CF responses. These responses are presumed to be proprioceptively triggered by the onset of a corrective movement, being suppressed during the movement itself. Corrective movements can be generated when a cerebellar module generates an additional pulse phase of the motor command, or through the action of a system other than the cerebellum. The second, extracerebellar, source of corrective movements only needs to operate when small corrections are needed.

The learning mechanism has to adjust the PC weights, w_i, so that the PC switches state at the correct moment during a movement. This is difficult because training information is significantly delayed due to the combined effects of movement duration and delays in the relevant feedback pathways. The relevant PC activity is completed well before a corrective movement triggers a CF response. To learn under these conditions, the learning mechanism needs to modify synaptic actions that occurred prior to the CF's discharge. The APG model adopts Klopf's (Klopf, 1982) idea of a synaptic "eligibility trace" whereby appropriate synaptic activity sets up a synaptically–local memory trace that renders the synapse "eligible" for modification if and when the appropriate training information arrives within a short time period.

The learning rule has two components: one implments a form of long–term depression (LTD); the other implements a much weaker form of long–term potentiation

(LTP). It works as follows. Whenever the CF fires ($c(t) = 1$), the weights of all the *eligible* synapses decrease. A synapse is eligible if its presynaptic parallel fiber was active in the past when the PC switched from low to high, with the degree of eligibility decreasing with the time since that state switch. This makes the PC less likely to switch to high in future situations represented by patterns of PF activity similar to the pattern present when the eligibility–initiating switch occurred. This has the effect of increasing the duration of the PC pause, which increases the duration of the pulse phase of the motor command. Superimposed on weight decreases are much smaller weight increases that occur for any synapse whose presynaptic PF is active when the PC switches from low to high, irrespective of CF activity. This makes the PC more likely to switch to high under similar circumstances in the future, which decreases the duration of the pulse phase of the movement command.

To define this mathematically, let $\eta(t)$ detect when the PC's activity state switches from low to high: $\eta(t) = 0$ unless $y(t-1) = $ low and $y(t) = $ high, in which case $\eta(t) = 1$. The eligibility trace for synapse i at time step t, denoted $e_i(t)$, is set to 1 whenever $\eta(t) = 1$ and thereafter decays geometrically toward zero until it is reset to 1 when η is again set to 1 by another upward switch of PC activity level. Then the learning rule is given for $t = 1, 2, \ldots$, by:

$$\Delta w_i(t) = -\alpha c(t) e_i(t) + \beta \eta(t) \phi_i(t),$$

where α and β, with $\alpha \gg \beta$, are positive parameters respectively determining the rate of LTD and LTP. See (Houk et al., 1995) for a discussion of this learning rule in light of physiological data and cellular mechanisms.

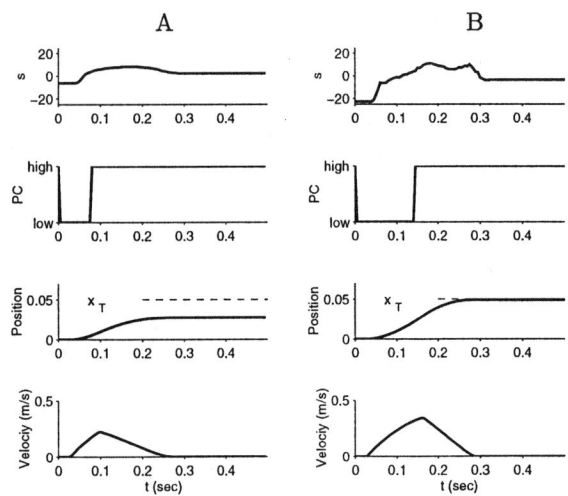

Figure 3: Model behavior. Panel A: early in learning; Panel B: late in learning. Assume that at time step 0, x_T has just been switched from 0 to .05. Shown are the time courses of the PC's weighted sum, s, activation state, y, and the position and velocity of the mass.

5 SIMULATIONS

We performed a number of simulations of the simplified APG model learning to control the nonlinear spring–mass system. We trained each version of the model to move the mass from initial positions selected randomly from the interval $[-.02, .02]$ to a target position randomly set to .03, .04, or .05. We set the pulse height, x_p, and the step height, x_s, to .1 and .04 respectively. Each simulation consisted of a series of trial movements. The parameters of the learning rule, which were not optimized, were $\alpha = .0004$ and $\beta = .00004$. Eligibility traces decayed 1% per time step.

Figure 3 shows time courses of relevant variables at different stages in learning to move to target endpoint $x_T = .05$ from initial position $x_0 = 0$. Early in learning (Panel A), the PC has learned to switch to low at the beginning of the trial but switches back to high too soon, which causes the mass to undershoot the target. Because of this undershoot, the CF fires at the end of the movement due to a final very small corrective movement generated by an extracerebellar system. The mass sticks at $x_e = .027$. Late in learning (Panel B), the mass sticks at $x_e = .049$, and the CF does not fire. Note that to accomplish this, the PC state has to switch to high well before (about 150ms) the endpoint is reached.

Figure 4 shows three representations of the switching curve learned by a version of the model for target $x_T = .05$. As an aid to understanding the model's behavior, all the proprioceptive signals in this version of the model had the same delay of 30ms (τ_1 in Fig. 2) instead of the more realistic distribution of delays described above. Hence the total loop delay ($\tau_1 + \tau_2$) was 50ms. The curve labeled "spring switch", which closely coincides with the optimal switching curve (also shown), plots states that the spring–mass system passes through when the command input to the spring switches. In other words, this is the switching curve as seen from the point marked A in Fig. 2. That this coincides with the optimal switching curve shows that the model learned to behave correctly. The movement trajectory crosses this curve about 150ms before the movement ends.

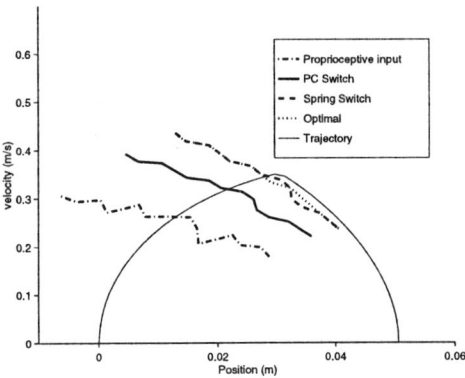

Figure 4: Phase–plane portraits of switching curves implemented by the model after learning. Four switching curves and one movement trajectory are shown. See text for explanation.

The curve labeled "PC switch", on the other hand, plots states that the spring–mass system passes through when the PC unit switches state: it is the switching curve as seen from the point marked B in Fig. 2 (assuming the expansive encoding involves no delay). The state of the spring–mass system crosses this curve 20ms before it reaches the "spring switch" curve. One can see, therefore, that the PC unit learned to switch its activity state 20ms before the motor command must switch state at the spring itself, appropriately compensating for the 20ms latency of the efferent pathway.

We can also ask what is the state of the spring–mass system that the PC actually "sees", via proprioceptive signals, when it has to switch state. When the PC has to switch states, that is, when the spring–mass state reaches switching curve "PC switch", the PC is actually receiving via its PF input a description of the system state that occurred a significant time earlier ($\tau_1 = 30$ms in Fig. 2). Switching curve "proprioceptive input" in Fig. 4 is the locus of system states that the PC is sensing when it has to switch. The PC has learned to do this by learning, on the basis of delayed CF training information, to switch when it sees PF patterns that code spring–mass states that lie on curve "proprioceptive input".

6 DISCUSSION

The model we have presented is most closely related to adaptive control methods known as direct predictive adaptive controllers (Goodwin & Sin, 1984). Feedback delays pose no particular difficulties despite the fact that no use is made of a forward model of the motor plant. Instead of producing predictions of proprioceptive feedback, the model uses its predictive capabilities to directly produce appropriately timed motor commands. Although the nonlinear viscosity of the spring–mass system renders linear control principles inapplicable, it actually makes the control problem easier for an appropriate controller. Fast movements can be performed with little or no oscillation. We believe that similar nonlinearities in actual motor plants have significant implications for motor control. A critical feature of this model's learning mechanism is its use of eligibility traces to bridge the temporal gap between a PC's activity and the consequences of this activity on the movement endpoint. Cellular studies are needed to explore this important issue. Although nothing in the present paper suggests how this might extend to more complex control problems, one of the objectives of the full APG model is to explore how the collective behavior of multiple APG modules might accomplish more complex control.

Acknowledgements

This work was supported by NIH 1-50 MH 48185-04.

References

Albus, JS (1971). A theory of cerebellar function. *Mathematical Biosciences,* **10**, 25–61.

Berthier, NE, Singh, SP, Barto, AG, & Houk, JC (1993). Distributed representations of limb motor programs in arrays of adjustable pattern generators. *Cognitive Neuroscience,* **5**, 56–78.

Buckingham, JT, Barto, AG, & Houk, JC (1995). Adaptive predictive control with a cerebellar model. In: *Proceedings of the 1995 World Congress on Neural Networks,* I-373–I-380.

Gellman, R, Gibson, AR, & Houk, JC (1983). Somatosensory properties of the inferior olive of the cat. *J. Comp. Neurology,* **215**, 228–243.

Goodwin, GC & Sin, KS (1984). *Adaptive Filtering Prediction and Control.* Englewood Cliffs, N.J.: Prentice-Hall.

Houk, JC, Buckingham, JT, & Barto, AG (1995). Models of the cerebellum and motor learning. *Brain and Behavioral Sciences,* in press.

Ito, M (1984). *The Cerebellum and Neural Control.* New York: Raven Press.

Keeler, JD (1990). A dynamical system view of cerebellar function. *Physica D,* **42**, 396–410.

Klopf, AH (1982). *The Hedonistic Neuron: A Theory of Memory, Learning, and Intelligence.* Washington, D.C.: Hemishere.

Marr, D (1969). A theory of cerebellar cortex. *J. Physiol. London,* **202**, 437–470.

Miall, RC, Weir, DJ, Wolpert, DM, & Stein, JF (1993). Is the cerebellum a smith predictor? *Journal of Motor Behavior,* **25**, 203–216.

Van Kan, PLE, Gibson, AR, & Houk, JC (1993). Movement-related inputs to intermediate cerebellum of the monkey. *Journal of Physiology,* **69**, 74–94.

Wolpert, DM, Ghahramani, Z, & Jordan, MI (1995). Foreward dynamic models in human motor control: Psychophysical evidence. In: *Advances in Neural Information Processing Systems 7,* (G Tesauro, DS Touretzky, & TK Leen, eds) , Cambridge, MA: MIT Press.

Wu, CH, Houk, JC, Young, KY, & Miller, LE (1990). Nonlinear damping of limb motion. In: *Multiple Muscle Systems: Biomechanics and Movement Organization,* (J Winters & S Woo, eds). New York: Springer–Verlag.

Independent Component Analysis of Electroencephalographic Data

Scott Makeig
Naval Health Research Center
P.O. Box 85122
San Diego CA 92186-5122
scott@cpl_mmag.nhrc.navy.mil

Anthony J. Bell
Computational Neurobiology Lab
The Salk Institute, P.O. Box 85800
San Diego, CA   92186-5800
tony@salk.edu

Tzyy-Ping Jung
Naval Health Research Center and
Computational Neurobiology Lab
The Salk Institute, P.O. Box 85800
San Diego, CA   92186-5800
jung@salk.edu

Terrence J. Sejnowski
Howard Hughes Medical Institute and
Computational Neurobiology Lab
The Salk Institute, P.O. Box 85800
San Diego, CA   92186-5800
terry@salk.edu

Abstract

Because of the distance between the skull and brain and their different resistivities, *electroencephalographic* (EEG) data collected from any point on the human scalp includes activity generated within a large brain area. This spatial smearing of EEG data by volume conduction does not involve significant time delays, however, suggesting that the *Independent Component Analysis* (ICA) algorithm of Bell and Sejnowski [1] is suitable for performing blind source separation on EEG data. The ICA algorithm separates the problem of source identification from that of source localization. First results of applying the ICA algorithm to EEG and *event-related potential* (ERP) data collected during a sustained auditory detection task show: (1) ICA training is insensitive to different random seeds. (2) ICA may be used to segregate obvious artifactual EEG components (line and muscle noise, eye movements) from other sources. (3) ICA is capable of isolating overlapping EEG phenomena, including alpha and theta bursts and spatially-separable ERP components, to separate ICA channels. (4) Nonstationarities in EEG and behavioral state can be tracked using ICA via changes in the amount of residual correlation between ICA-filtered output channels.

1 Introduction

1.1 Separating What from Where in EEG Source Analysis

The joint problems of EEG source segregation, identification, and localization are very difficult, since the problem of determining brain electrical sources from potential patterns recorded on the scalp surface is mathematically underdetermined. Recent efforts to identify EEG sources have focused mostly on performing spatial segregation and localization of source activity [4]. By applying the ICA algorithm of Bell and Sejnowski [1], we attempt to completely separate the twin problems of source identification (What) and source localization (Where). The ICA algorithm derives independent sources from highly correlated EEG signals statistically and without regard to the physical location or configuration of the source generators. Rather than modeling the EEG as a unitary output of a multidimensional dynamical system, or as "the roar of the crowd" of independent microscopic generators, we suppose that the EEG is the output of a number of statistically independent but spatially fixed potential-generating systems which may either be spatially restricted or widely distributed.

1.2 Independent Component Analysis

Independent Component Analysis (ICA) [1, 3] is the name given to techniques for finding a matrix, $\mathbf{W}$ and a vector, w, so that the elements, $\mathbf{u} = [u_1 \ldots u_N]^T$, of the linear transform $\mathbf{u} = \mathbf{W}\mathbf{x} + w$ of the random vector, $\mathbf{x} = [x_1 \ldots x_N]^T$, are statistically independent. In contrast with decorrelation techniques such as Principal Components Analysis (PCA) which ensure that $\langle u_i u_j \rangle = 0, \forall ij$, ICA imposes the much stronger criterion that the multivariate probability density function (p.d.f.) of $\mathbf{u}$ factorizes: $f_\mathbf{u}(\mathbf{u}) = \prod_{i=1}^{N} f_{u_i}(u_i)$. Finding such a factorization involves making the mutual information between the u_i go to zero: $I(u_i, u_j) = 0, \forall ij$. Mutual information is a measure which depends on all higher-order statistics of the u_i while decorrelation only takes account of 2nd-order statistics.

In [1], a new algorithm was proposed for carrying out ICA. The only prior assumption is that the unknown independent components, u_i, each have the same form of cumulative density function (c.d.f.) after scaling and shifting, and that we know this form, call it $F_u(u)$. ICA can then be performed by maximizing the entropy, $H(\mathbf{y})$, of a non-linearly transformed vector: $\mathbf{y} = F_u(\mathbf{u})$. This yields stochastic gradient ascent rules for adjusting $\mathbf{W}$ and w:

$$\Delta \mathbf{W} \propto [\mathbf{W}^T]^{-1} + \hat{\mathbf{y}}\mathbf{x}^T, \Delta w \propto \hat{\mathbf{y}} \tag{1}$$

where $\hat{\mathbf{y}} = [\hat{y}_1 \ldots \hat{y}_N]^T$, the elements of which are:

$$\hat{y}_i = \frac{\partial}{\partial y_i} \frac{\partial y_i}{\partial u_i} \quad [\text{which if } \mathbf{y} = F_u(\mathbf{u})] \quad = \frac{\partial f_u(u_i)}{\partial F_u(u_i)} \tag{2}$$

It can be shown that an ICA solution is a stable point of the relaxation of eqs.(1-2). In practical tests on separating mixed speech signals, good results were found when using the logistic function, $y_i = (1 + e^{-u_i})^{-1}$, instead of the known c.d.f., F_u, of the speech signals. In this case $\hat{y}_i = 1 - 2y_i$, and the algorithm has a simple form. These results were obtained despite the fact that the p.d.f. of the speech signals was not exactly matched by the gradient of the logistic function. In the experiments in this paper, we also used the speedup technique of prewhitening described in [2].

1.3 Applying ICA to EEG Data

The ICA technique appears ideally suited for performing source separation in domains where, (1) the sources are independent, (2) the propagation delays of the 'mixing medium' are negligible, (3) the sources are analog and have p.d.f.'s not too unlike the gradient of a logistic sigmoid, and (4) the number of independent signal sources is the same as the number of sensors, meaning if we employ N sensors, using the ICA algorithm we can separate N sources. In the case of EEG signals, N scalp electrodes pick up correlated signals and we would like to know what effectively 'independent brain sources' generated these mixtures. If we assume that the complexity of EEG dynamics can be modeled, at least in part, as a collection of a modest number of statistically independent brain processes, the EEG source analysis problem satisfies ICA assumption (1). Since volume conduction in brain tissue is effectively instantaneous, ICA assumption (2) is also satisfied. Assumption (3) is plausible, but assumption (4), that the EEG is a linear mixtures of exactly N sources, is questionable, since we do not know the effective number of statistically independent brain signals contributing to the EEG recorded from the scalp. The foremost problem in interpreting the output of ICA is, therefore, determining the proper dimension of input channels, and the physiological and/or psychophysiological significance of the derived ICA source channels.

Although the ICA model of the EEG ignores the known variable synchronization of separate EEG generators by common subcortical or corticocortical influences [5], it appears promising for identifying concurrent signal sources that are either situated too close together, or are too widely distributed to be separated by current localization techniques. Here, we report a first application of the ICA algorithm to analysis of 14-channel EEG and ERP recordings during sustained eyes-closed performance of an auditory detection task, and give evidence suggesting that the ICA algorithm may be useful for identifying psychophysiological state transitions.

2 Methods

EEG and behavioral data were collected to develop a method of objectively monitoring the alertness of operators of complex systems [8]. Ten adult volunteers participated in three or more half-hour sessions, during which they pushed one button whenever they detected an above-threshold auditory target stimulus (a brief increase in the level of the continuously-present background noise). To maximize the chance of observing alertness decrements, sessions were conducted in a small, warm, and dimly-lit experimental chamber, and subjects were instructed to keep their eyes closed. Auditory targets were 350 ms increases in the intensity of a 62 dB white noise background, 6 dB above their threshold of detectability, presented at random time intervals at a mean rate of 10/min, and superimposed on a continuous 39-Hz click train evoking a 39-Hz *steady-state response* (SSR). Short, and task-irrelevant probe tones of two frequencies (568 and 1098 Hz) were interspersed between the target noise bursts at 2-4 s intervals. EEG was collected from thirteen electrodes located at sites of the International 10-20 System, referred to the right mastoid, at a sampling rate of 312.5 Hz. A bipolar diagonal electrooculogram (EOG) channel was also recorded for use in eye movement artifact correction and rejection. Target Hits were defined as targets responded to within a 100-3000 ms window, while Lapses were targets not responded to. Two sessions each from three of the subjects were selected for analysis based on their containing at least 50 response Lapses. A continuous performance measure, local error rate, was computed by convolving the irregularly-sampled performance index time series (Hit=0/Lapse=1) with a 95 s smoothing window advanced for 1.64 s steps.

The ICA algorithm in eqs.(1-2) was applied to the 14 EEG recordings. The time index was permuted to ensure signal stationarity, and the 14-dimensional time point vectors were presented to a 14 → 14 ICA network one at a time. To speed convergence, we first pre-whitened the data to remove first- and second-order statistics. The learning rate was annealed from 0.03 to 0.0001 during convergence. After each pass through the whole training set, we checked the amount of correlation between the ICA output channels and the amount of change in weight matrix, and stopped the training procedure when, (1) the mean correlation among all channel pairs was below 0.05, and (2) the ICA weights had stopped changing appreciably.

3 Results

A small (4.5 s) portion of the resulting ICA-transformed EEG time series is shown in Figure 1. As expected, correlations between the ICA traces are close to zero. The dominant theta wave (near 7 Hz) spread across many EEG channels (*left panel*) is more or less isolated to ICA trace 1 (*upper right*), both in the epoch shown and throughout the session. Alpha activity (near 10 Hz) not obvious in the EEG data is uncovered in ICA trace 2, which here and throughout the session contains alpha bursts interspersed with quiescent periods. Other ICA traces (3-8) contain brief oscillatory bursts which are not easy to characterize, but clearly display different dynamics from the activity in ICA trace 1 which dominates the raw EEG record. ICA trace 10 contains near-DC changes associated with eye slow movements in the EOG and most frontal (Fpz) EEG channels. ICA trace 13 contains mostly line noise (60 Hz), while ICA traces 9 and 14 have a broader high frequency (50-100 Hz) spectrum, suggesting that their source is likely to be high-frequency activity generated by scalp muscles.

Apparently, the ICA source solution for this data does not depend strongly on learning rate or initial conditions. When the same portion of one session was used to train two ICA networks with different random starting weights, data presentation orders, and learning rates, the two final ICA weight matrices were very close to one another. Filtering another segment of EEG data from the same session using each ICA matrix produced two ICA source transforms in which 11 of the 14 best-correlated output channel pairs correlated above 0.95 and none correlated less than 0.894.

While ICA training minimized mutual information, and therefore also correlations between output channels during the initial (alert) ICA training period, output data channels filtered by the same ICA weight matrix became more correlated during the drowsy portion of the session, and then reverted to their initial levels of (de)correlation when the subject again became alert. Conversely, filtering the same session's data with an ICA weight matrix trained on the drowsy portion of the session produced output channels that were more correlated during the alert portions of the session than during the drowsy training period. Presumably, these changes in residual correlation among ICA outputs reflect changes in the dynamics and topographic structure of the EEG signals in alert and drowsy brain states.

An important problem in human electrophysiology is to determine a means of objectively identifying overlapping ERP subcomponents. Figure 3 (*right panel*) shows an ICA decomposition of (*left panel*) ERPs to detected (Hit) and undetected (Lapse) targets by the same subject. ICA spatial filtering produces two channels (S[1-2]) separating out the 39-Hz *steady-state response* (SSR) produced by the continuous 39-Hz click stimulation during the session. Note the stimulus-induced perturbation in SSR amplitude previously identified in [6]. Three channels (H[1-3]) pass time-limited components of the detected target response, while four others (L[1-4])

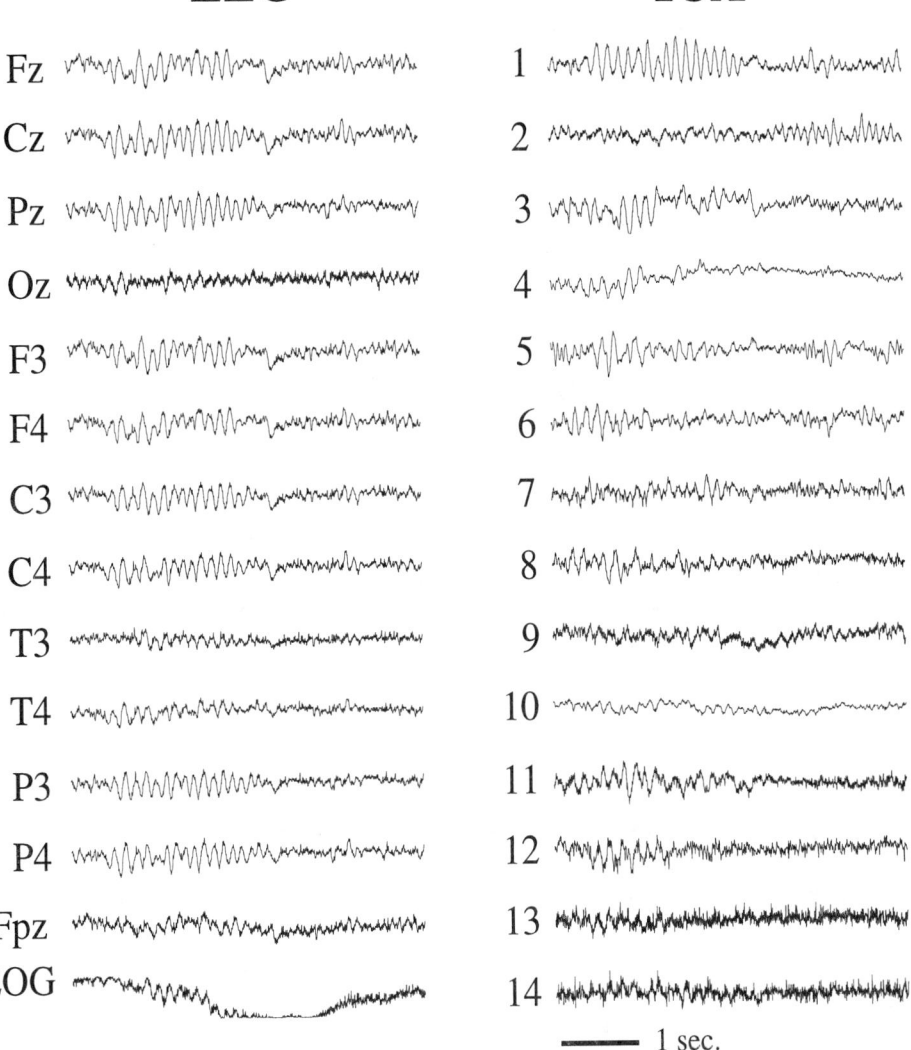

Figure 1: Left: 4.5 seconds of 14-channel EEG data. Right: an ICA transform of the same data, using weights trained on 6.5 minutes of similar data from the same session.

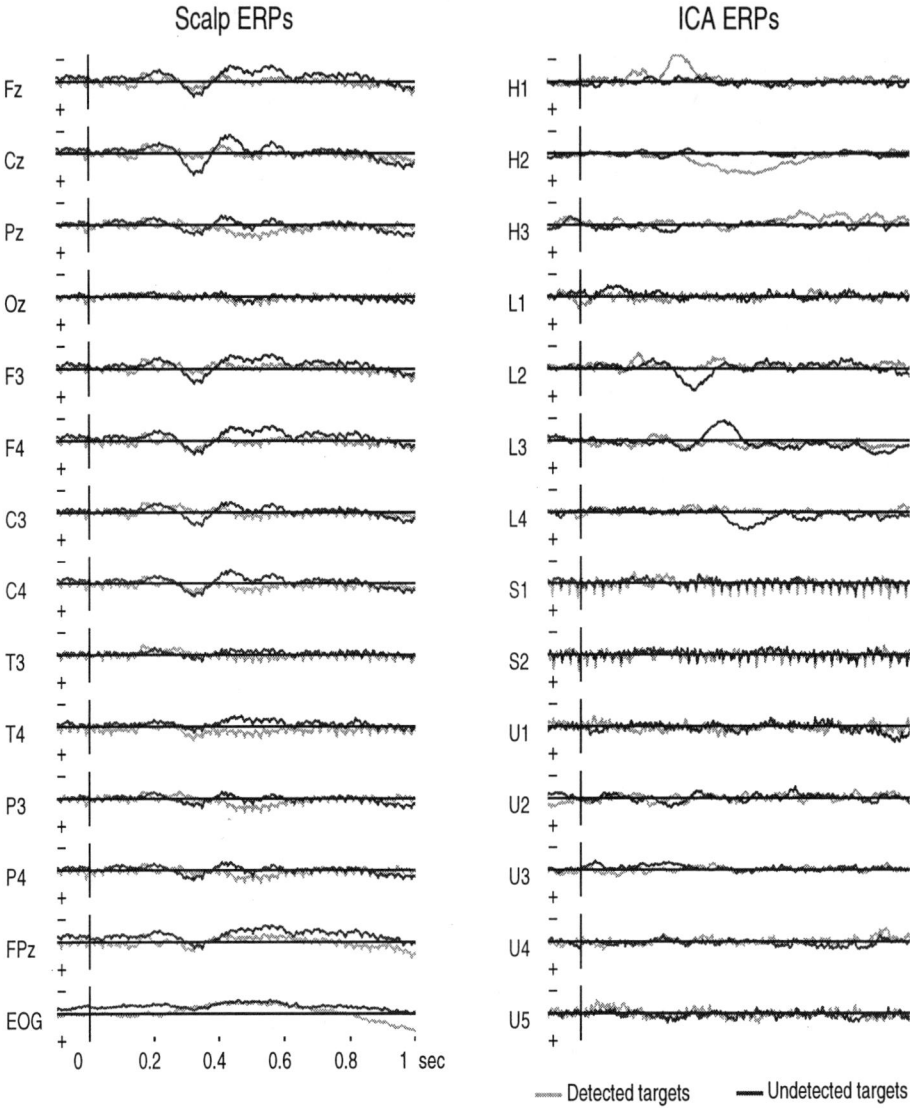

Figure 2: *Left panel*: Event-related potentials (ERPs) in response to undetected (*bold traces*) and detected (*faint traces*) noise targets during two half-hour sessions. *Right panel*: Same ERP signals filtered using an ICA weight matrix trained on the ERP data.

components of the (larger) undetected target response. We suggest these represent the time course of the locus (either focal or distributed) of brain response activity, and may represent a solution to the longstanding problem of objectively dividing evoked responses into neurobiologically meaningful, temporally overlapping subcomponents.

4 Conclusions

ICA appears to be a promising new analysis tool for human EEG and ERP research. It can isolate a wide range of artifacts to a few output channels while removing them from remaining channels. These may in turn represent the time course of activity in longlasting or transient independent 'brain sources' on which the algorithm converges reliably. By incorporating higher-order statistical information, ICA avoids the non-uniqueness associated with decorrelating decompositions. The algorithm also appears to be useful for decomposing evoked response data into spatially distinct subcomponents, while measures of nonstationarity in the ICA source solution may be useful for observing brain state changes.

Acknowledgments

This report was supported in part by a grant (ONR.Reimb.30020.6429) to the Naval Health Research Center by the Office of Naval Research. The views expressed in this article are those of the authors and do not reflect the official policy or position of the Department of the Navy, Department of Defense, or the U.S. Government. Dr. Bell is supported by grants from the Office of Naval Research and the Howard Hughes Medical Institute.

References

[1] A.J. Bell & T.J. Sejnowski (1995). An information-maximization approach to blind separation and blind deconvolution, *Neural Computation* 7:1129-1159.

[2] A.J. Bell & T.J. Sejnowski (1995). Fast blind separation based on information theory, in *Proc. Intern. Symp. on Nonlinear Theory and Applications (NOLTA)*, Las Vegas, Dec. 1995.

[3] P. Comon (1994) Independent component analysis, a new concept? *Signal processing* 36:287-314.

[4] A.M. Dale & M.I. Sereno (1993) EEG and MEG source localization: a linear approach. *J. Cogn. Neurosci.* 5:162.

[5] R. Galambos & S. Makeig. (1989) Dynamic changes in steady-state potentials. In Erol Basar (ed.), *Dynamics of Sensory and Cognitive Processing of the Brain*, 102-122. Berlin:Springer-Verlag.

[6] S. Makeig & R. Galambos. (1989) The CERP: Event-related perturbations in steady-state responses. In E. Basar & T.H. Bullock (ed.), *Brain Dynamics: Progress and Perspectives*, 375-400. Berlin:Springer-Verlag.

[7] T-P. Jung, S. Makeig, M. Stensmo, & T. Sejnowski. Estimating alertness from the EEG power spectrum. Submitted for publication.

[8] S. Makeig & M. Inlow (1993) Lapses in alertness: Coherence of fluctuations in performance and EEG spectrum. *Electroencephalog. clin. Neurophysiolog.* **86**:23-35.

Simulation of a Thalamocortical Circuit for Computing Directional Heading in the Rat

Hugh T. Blair*
Department of Psychology
Yale University
New Haven, CT 06520-8205
tadb@minerva.cis.yale.edu

Abstract

Several regions of the rat brain contain neurons known as *head-direction cells*, which encode the animal's directional heading during spatial navigation. This paper presents a biophysical model of head-direction cell activity, which suggests that a thalamocortical circuit might compute the rat's head direction by integrating the angular velocity of the head over time. The model was implemented using the neural simulator NEURON, and makes testable predictions about the structure and function of the rat head-direction circuit.

1 HEAD-DIRECTION CELLS

As a rat navigates through space, neurons called *head-direction cells* encode the animal's directional heading in the horizontal plane (Ranck, 1984; Taube, Muller, & Ranck, 1990). Head-direction cells have been recorded in several brain areas, including the postsubiculum (Ranck, 1984) and anterior thalamus (Taube, 1995). A variety of theories have proposed that head-direction cells might play an important role in spatial learning and navigation (Brown & Sharp, 1995; Burgess, Recce, & O'Keefe, 1994; McNaughton, Knierim, & Wilson, 1995; Wan, Touretzky, & Redish, 1994; Zhang, 1995).

1.1 BASIC FIRING PROPERTIES

A head-direction cell fires action potentials only when the rat's head is facing in a particular direction with respect to the static surrounding environment, regardless of the animal's location within that environment. Head-direction cells are *not* influenced by the position of the rat's head with respect to its body, they are only influenced by the direction of the

---

*Also at the Yale Neuroengineering and Neuroscience Center (NNC), 5 Science Park North, New Haven, CT 06511

Simulation of Thalamocortical Circuit for Computing Directional Heading in Rats

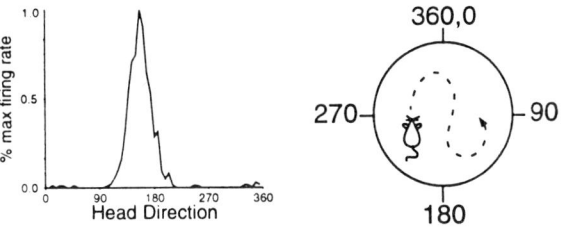

Figure 1: Directional Tuning Curve of a Head-Direction Cell

head with respect to the stationary reference frame of the spatial environment. Each head-direction cell has its own directional preference, so that together, the entire population of cells can encode any direction that the animal is facing.

Figure 1 shows an example of a head-direction cell's *directional tuning curve*, which plots the firing rate of the cell as a function of the rat's momentary head direction. The tuning curve shows that this cell fires maximally when the rat's head is facing in a preferred direction of about 160 degrees. The cell fires less rapidly for directions close to 160 degrees, and stops firing altogether for directions that are far from 160 degrees.

1.2 THE VELOCITY INTEGRATION HYPOTHESIS

McNaughton, Chen, & Markus (1991) have proposed that head-direction cells might rely on a process of *dead-reckoning* to calculate the rat's current head direction, based on the previous head direction and the angular velocity at which the head is turning. That is, head-direction cells might compute the directional position of the head by integrating the angular velocity of the head over time. This velocity integration hypothesis is supported by three experimental findings. First, several brain regions that are associated with head-direction cells contain *angular velocity cells*, neurons that fire in proportion to the angular head velocity (McNaughton et al., 1994; Sharp, in press). Second, some head-direction cells in postsubiculum are modulated by angular head velocity, such that their peak firing rate is higher if the head is turning in one direction than in the other (Taube et al., 1990). Third, it has recently been found that head-direction cells in the anterior thalamus, but not the postsubiculum, anticipate the *future* direction of the rat's head (Blair & Sharp, 1995).

1.3 ANTICIPATORY HEAD-DIRECTION CELLS

Blair and Sharp (1995) discovered that head-direction cells in the anterior thalamus shift their directional preference to the left during clockwise turns, and to the right during counterclockwise turns. They showed that this shift occurs systematically as a function of head velocity, in a way that allows these cells anticipate the future direction of the rat's head. To illustrate this, consider a cell that fires whenever the head will be facing a specific direction, θ, in the near future. How would such a cell behave? There are three cases to consider. First, imagine that the rat's head is turning clockwise, approaching the direction θ from the left side. In this case, the anticipatory cell must fire when the head is facing to the left of θ, because being to the left of θ and turning clockwise predicts arrival at θ in the near future. Second, when the head is turning counterclockwise and approaching θ from the right side, the anticipatory cell must fire when the head is to the right of θ. Third, if the head is still, then the cell should only fire if the head is presently facing θ.

In summary, an anticipatory head direction cell should shift its directional preference to the left during clockwise turns, to the right during counterclockwise turns, and not at all when the head is still. This behavior can be formalized by the equation

$$\mu(v) = \theta - v\tau, \qquad [1]$$

where μ denotes the cell's preferred present head direction, ν denotes the angular velocity of the head, θ denotes the future head direction that the cell anticipates, and τ is a constant time delay by which the cell's activity anticipates arrival at θ. Equation 1 assumes that μ is measured in degrees, which increase in the clockwise direction, and that ν is positive for clockwise head turns, and negative for counterclockwise head turns. Blair & Sharp (1995) have demonstrated that Equation 1 provides a good approximation of head-direction cell behavior in the anterior thalamus.

1.3 ANTICIPATORY TIME DELAY (τ)

Initial reports suggested that head-direction cells in the anterior thalamus anticipate the future head direction by an average time delay of $\tau = 40$ msec, whereas postsubicular cells encode the present head direction, and therefore "anticipate" by $\tau = 0$ msec (Blair & Sharp, 1995; Taube & Muller, 1995). However, recent evidence suggests that individual neurons in the anterior thalamus may be temporally tuned to anticipate the rat's future head-direction by different time delays between 0-100 msec, and that postsubicular cells may "lag behind" the present head-direction by about 10 msec (Blair & Sharp, 1996).

2 A BIOPHYSICAL MODEL

This section describes a biophysical model that accounts for the properties of head-direction cells in postsubiculum and anterior thalamus, by proposing that they might be connected to form a thalamocortical circuit. The next section presents simulation results from an implementation of the model, using the neural simulator NEURON (Hines, 1993).

2.1 NEURAL ELEMENTS

Figure 2 illustrates a basic circuit for computing the rat's head-direction. The circuit consists of five types of cells: 1) *Present Head-Direction* (PHD) Cells encode the present direction of the rat's head, 2) *Anticipatory Head-Direction* (AHD) Cells encode the future direction of the rat's head, 3) *Angular-Velocity* (AV) Cells encode the angular velocity of the rat's head (the CLK AV Cell is active during clockwise turns, and the CNT AV Cell is active during counterclockwise turns), 4) the *Angular Speed* (AS) Cell fires in inverse proportion to the angular speed of the head, regardless of the turning direction (that is, the AS Cell fires at a lower rate during fast turns, and at a higher rate during slow turns), 5) *Angular-Velocity Modulated Head-Direction* (AVHD) Cells are head-direction cells that fire

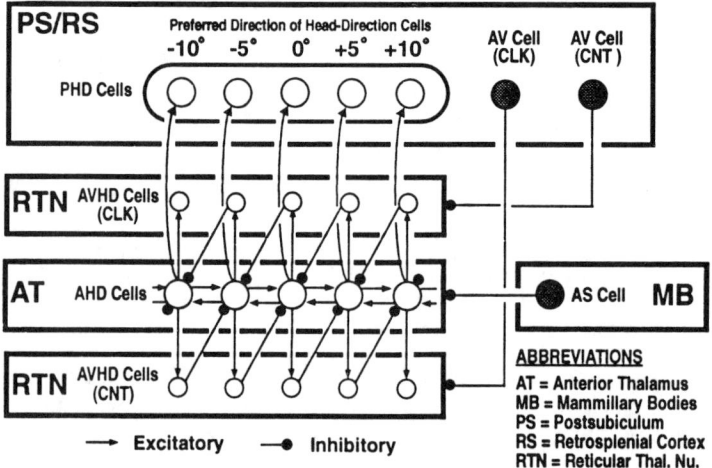

Figure 2: A Model of the Rat Head-Direction System

only when the head is turning in one direction and not the other (the CLK AVHD Cell fires in its preferred direction only when the head is turning clockwise, and the CNT AVHD Cell fires in its preferred direction only when the head turns counterclockwise).

2.2 FUNCTIONAL CHARACTERISTICS

In the model, AHD Cells directly excite their neighbors on either side, but indirectly inhibit these same neighbors via the AVHD Cells, which act as inhibitory interneurons. AHD Cells also send excitatory feedback connections to themselves (omitted from Figure 2 for clarity), so that once they become active, they remain active until they are turned off by inhibitory input (the rate of firing can also be modulated by inhibitory input). When the rat is not turning its head, the cell representing the current head direction fires constantly, both exciting and inhibiting its neighbors. In the steady-state condition (i.e., when the rat is not turning its head), lateral inhibition exceeds lateral excitation, and therefore activity does not spread in either direction through the layer of AHD Cells. However, when the rat begins turning its head, some of the AVHD Cells are turned off, allowing activity to spread in one direction. For example, during a clockwise head turn, the CLK AV Cell becomes active, and inhibits the layer of CNT AVHD Cells. As a result, AHD Cells stop inhibiting their right neighbors, so activity spreads to the right through the layer of AHD Cells. Because AHD Cells continue to inhibit their neighbors to the left, activity is shut down in the leftward direction, in the wake of the activity spreading to the right.

The speed of propagation through the AHD layer is governed by the AS Cell. During slow head turns, the AS Cell fires at a high rate, strongly inhibiting the AHD Cells, and thereby slowing the speed of propagation. During fast head turns, the AS Cell fires at a low rate, weakly inhibiting the AHD Cells, allowing activity to propagate more quickly. Because of inhibition from AS cells, AHD cells fire faster when the head is turning than when it is still (see Figure 4), in agreement with experimental data (Blair & Sharp, 1995).

AHD Cells send a topographic projection to PHD Cells, such that each PHD Cell receives excitatory input from an AHD Cell that anticipates when the head will soon be facing in the PHD Cell's preferred direction. AHD Cell activity anticipates PHD Cell activity because there is a transmission delay between the AHD and PHD Cells (assumed to be 5 msec in the simulations presented below). Also, the weights of the connections from AHD Cells to PHD Cells are small, so each AHD Cell must fire several action potentials before its targeted PHD Cell can begin to fire. The time delay between AHD and PHD Cells accounts for anticipatory firing, and corresponds to the τ parameter in Equation 1.

2.3 ANATOMICAL CHARACTERISTICS

Each component of the model is assumed to reside in a specific brain region. AHD and PHD Cells are assumed to reside in anterior thalamus (AT) and postsubiculum (PS), respectively. AS Cells have been observed in PS (Sharp, in press) and retrosplenial cortex (RS) (McNaughton, Green, & Mizumori, 1986), but the model predicts that they may also be found in the mammillary bodies (MB), since MB receives input from PS and RS (Shibata, 1989), and MB projects to ATN. AVHD Cells have been observed in PS (Taube et al., 1990), but the model predicts that they may also be found in the reticular thalamic nucleus (RTN), because RTN receives input from PS/RS (Lozsadi, 1994), and RTN inhibits AT. It should be noted that lateral excitation between ATN cells has not been shown, so this feature of the model may be incorrect. Table 1 summarizes anatomical evidence.

3 SIMULATION RESULTS

The model illustrated in Figure 2 has been implemented using the neural simulator NEURON (Hines, 1993). Each neural element was represented as a single spherical compart-

Table 1: Anatomical Features of the Model

FEATURE OF MODEL	REFERENCE
PHD Cells in PS/RS	Chen et al., 1990; Ranck, 1984
AHD Cells in AT	Blair & Sharp, 1995
AV Cells in PS/RS	McNaughton et al., 1994; Sharp, in press
AT projects to PS	van Groen & Wyss, 1990
AT projects to RTN	Shibata, 1992
PS/RS projects to RTN	Lozsadi, 1994
AVHD Cells in RTN	PREDICTION OF MODEL
AS Cells in MB	PREDICTION OF MODEL

ment, 30 µm in diameter, with RC time constants ranging between 15 and 30 msec. Synaptic connections were simulated using triggered alpha-function conductances. The results presented here demonstrate the behavior of the model, and compare the properties of the model with experimental data.

To begin each simulation, a small current was injected in to one of the AHD Cells, causing it to initiate sustained firing. This cell represented the simulated rat's initial head direction. Head-turning behavior was simulated by injecting current into the AV and AS Cells, with an amplitude that yielded firing proportional to the desired angular head velocity.

3.1 ACTIVITY OF HEAD-DIRECTION CELLS

Figure 3 presents a simple simulation, which illustrates the behavior of head-direction cells in the model. The simulated rat begins by facing in the direction of 0 degrees. Over the course of 250 msec, the rat quickly turns its head 60 degrees to the right, and then returns to the initial starting position of 0 degrees. The average velocity of the head in this simulation was 480 degrees/sec, which is similar to the speed at which an actual rat performs a fast head turn (Blair & Sharp, 1995). Over the course of the simulation, neural activation propagates from the 0-degree cell to the 60-degree cell, and then back to the 0-degree cell.

3.2 COMPARISON WITH EXPERIMENTAL DATA

To examine how well the model reproduces firing properties of PS and AT cells, another simple simulation was performed. The firing rate the model's PHD and AHD Cells was examined while the simulated rat performed several 360-degree revolutions in both the clockwise and counterclockwise directions. Results are summarized in Figure 4, which

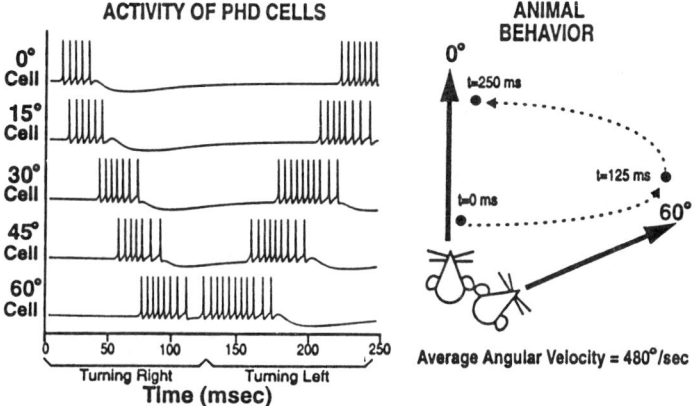

Figure 3: Simulation Example

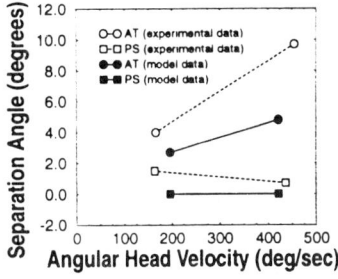 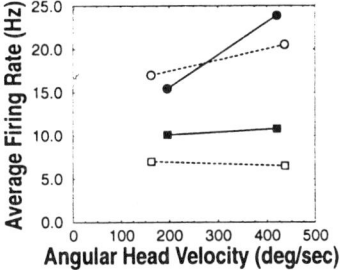

Figure 4: Compared Properties of Real and Simulated Head-Direction Cells

compares simulation data with experimental data. The experimental data in Figure 4 shows averaged results for 21 cells recorded in AT, and 19 cells recorded in PS.

Because AT cells anticipate the future head direction, they exhibit an angular separation between their clockwise and counterclockwise directional preference, whereas as no such separation occurs for PS cells (see section 2.4). For AT cells, the magnitude of the angular separation is proportional to angular head velocity, with greater separation occurring for fast turns, and less separation for slow turns (see Eq. 1). The left panel of Figure 4 shows that the model's PHD and AHD Cells exhibit a similar pattern of angular separation.

Blair & Sharp (1995) reported that the firing rates of AT and PS cells differ in two ways: 1) AT cells fire at a higher rate than PS cells, and 2) AT cells have a higher rate during fast turns than during slow turns, whereas PS cells fire at the same rate, regardless of turning speed. In Figure 4 (right panel), it can be seen that the model reproduces these findings.

4 DISCUSSION AND CONCLUSIONS

In this paper, I have presented a neural model of the rat head-direction system. The model includes neural elements whose firing properties are similar to those of actual neurons in the rat brain. The model suggests that a thalamocortical circuit might compute the directional position of the rat's head, by integrating angular head velocity over time.

4.1 COMPARISON WITH OTHER MODELS

McNaughton et al. (1991) proposed that neurons encoding head-direction and angular velocity might be connected to form a linear associative mapping network. Skaggs et al. (1995) have refined this idea into a theoretical circuit, which incorporates head-direction and angular velocity cells. However, the Skaggs et al. (1995) circuit does not incorporate anticipatory head-direction cells, like those found in AT. A model that does incorporate anticipatory cells has been developed by Elga, Redish, & Touretzky (unpublished manuscript). Zhang (1995) has recently presented a theoretical analysis of the head-direction circuit, which suggests that anticipatory head-direction cells might be influenced by both the angular velocity and angular acceleration of the head, whereas non-anticipatory cells may be influenced by the angular velocity only, and not the angular acceleration.

4.2 LIMITATIONS OF THE MODEL

In its current form, the model suffers some significant limitations. For example, the directional tuning curves of the model's head-direction cells are much narrower than those of actual head-direction cells. Also, in its present form, the model can accurately track the rat's head-direction over a rather limited range of angular head velocities. These limitations are presently being addressed in a more advanced version of the model.

Acknowledgments

This work was supported by NRSA fellowship number 1 F31 MH11102-01A1 from NIMH, a Yale Fellowship, and the Yale Neuroengineering and Neuroscience Center (NNC). I thank Michael Hines, Patricia Sharp, and Steve Fisher for their assistance.

References

Blair, H.T., & Sharp, P.E. (1995). Anticipatory head-direction cells in anterior thalamus: Evidence for a thalamocortical circuit that integrates angular head velocity to compute head direction. *Journal of Neuroscience, 15,* 6260-6270.

Blair, H.T., & Sharp (1996). Temporal Tuning of Anticipatory Head-Direction Cells in the Anterior Thalamus of the Rat. *Submitted.*

Brown, M. & Sharp, P.E. (1995). Simulation of spatial learning in the morris water maze by a neural network model of the hippocampal formation and nucleus accumbens. *Hippocampus, 5,* 171-188.

Burgess, N., Recce, M., & O'Keefe, J. (1994). A model of hippocampal function. *Neural Networks, 7,* 1065-1081.

Elga, A.N., Redish, A.D., & Touretzky, D.S. (1995). A model of the rodent head-direction system. *Unpublished Manuscript.*

Hines, M. (1993). NEURON: A program for simulation of nerve equations. In F. Eckman (Ed.), *Neural Systems: Analysis and Modeling,* Norwell, MA : Kluwer Academic Publishers, pp. 127-136.

Lozsadi, D.A. (1994). Organization of cortical afferents to the rostral, limbic sector of the rat thalamic reticular nucleus. *The Journal of Comparative Neurology, 341,* 520-533.

McNaughton, B.L., Chen, L.L., & Markus, E.J. (1991). Dead reckoning, landmark learning, and the sense of direction: a neurophysiological and computational hypothesis. *Journal of Cognitive Neuroscience, 3,* 190-202.

McNaughton, B.L., Green, E.J., & Mizumori, S.J.Y. (1986). Representation of body motion trajectory by rat sensory motor cortex neurons. *Society for Neuroscience Abstracts,* 12, 260.

McNaughton, B.L., Knierim, J.J., & Wilson, M.A. (1995). Vector encoding and the vestibular foundations of spatial cognition: neurophysiological and computational mechanisms. In M. Gazzaniga (Ed.), *The Cognitive Neurosciences.* Cambridge: MIT Press.

McNaughton, B.L., Mizumori, S.Y.J., Barnes, C.A., Leonard, B.J., Marquis, M., & Green, B.J. (1994). Coritcal representation of motion during unrestrained spatial navigaton in the rat. *Cerebral Cortex, 4,* 27-39.

Ranck, J.B. (1984). Head-direction cells in the deep cell layers of dorsal presubiculum in freely moving rats. *Society for Neuroscience Abstracts, 12,* 1524.

Shibata, H. (1989). Descending projections to the mammillary nuclei in the rat, as studied by retrograde and anterograde transport of wheat germ agglutinin-horseradish peroxidase. *The Journal of Comparative Neurology, 285,* 436-452.

Shibata, H. (1992). Topographic organization of subcortical projections to the anterior thalamic nuclei in the rat. *The Journal of Comparative Neurology, 323,* 117-127.

Sharp, P.E. (in press). Multiple spatial/behavioral corrrelates for cells in the rat postsubiculum: multiple regression analysis and comparison to other hippocampal areas. *Cerebral Cortex.*

Skaggs, W.E., Knierim, J.J., Kudrimoti, H.S., & McNaughton, B.L. (1995). A model of the neural basis of the rat's sense of direction. In G. Tesauro, D.S. Touretzky, & T.K. Leen (Eds.), *Advances in Neural Information Processing Systems 7.* MIT Press.

Taube, J.S. (1995). Head-direction cells recorded in the anterior thalamic nuclei of freely-moving rats. *Journal of Neuroscience, 15,* 70-86.

Taube, J.S., & Muller, R.U. (1995). Head-direction cell activity in the anterior thalamus, but not the postsubiculum, predicts the animal's future directional heading. *Society for Neuroscience Abstracts, 21,* 946.

Taube, J.S., Muller, R.U., & Ranck, J.B. (1990). Head-direction cells recorded from the postsubiculum in freely moving rats, I. Description and quantitative analysis. *Jounral of Neuroscience, 10,* 420-435.

van Groen, T., & Wyss, J.M. (1990). The postsubicular cortex in the rat: characterization of the fourth region of subicular cortex and its connections. *Journal of Comparative Neurology, 216,* 192-210.

Wan, H.S., Touretzky, D.S., & Redish, D.S. (1994). A rodent navigation model that combines place code, head-direction, and path integration information. *Society for Neuroscience Abstracts, 20,* 1205.

Zhang, K. (1995). Representation of spatial orientation by the intrinsic dynamics of the head-direction cell ensemble: A theory. *Submitted.*

Plasticity of Center-Surround Opponent Receptive Fields in Real and Artificial Neural Systems of Vision

S. Yasui
Kyushu Institute of Technology
Iizuka 820, Japan

T. Furukawa
Kyushu Institute of Technology
Iizuka 820, Japan

M. Yamada
Electrotechnical Laboratory
Tsukuba 305, Japan

T. Saito
Tsukuba University
Tsukuba 305, Japan

Abstract

Despite the phylogenic and structural differences, the visual systems of different species, whether vertebrate or invertebrate, share certain functional properties. The center-surround opponent receptive field (CSRF) mechanism represents one such example. Here, analogous CSRFs are shown to be formed in an artificial neural network which learns to localize contours (edges) of the luminance difference. Furthermore, when the input pattern is corrupted by a background noise, the CSRFs of the hidden units becomes shallower and broader with decrease of the signal-to-noise ratio (SNR). The same kind of SNR-dependent plasticity is present in the CSRF of real visual neurons; in bipolar cells of the carp retina as is shown here experimentally, as well as in large monopolar cells of the fly compound eye as was described by others. Also, analogous SNR-dependent plasticity is shown to be present in the biphasic flash responses (BPFR) of these artificial and biological visual systems. Thus, the spatial (CSRF) and temporal (BPFR) filtering properties with which a wide variety of creatures see the world appear to be optimized for detectability of changes in space and time.

1 INTRODUCTION

A number of learning algorithms have been developed to make synthetic neural machines be trainable to function in certain optimal ways. If the brain and nervous systems that we see in nature are best answers of the evolutionary process, then one might be able to find some common 'softwares' in real and artificial neural systems. This possibility is examined in this paper, with respect to a basic visual mechanism relevant to detection of brightness contours (edges). In most visual systems of vertebrate and invertebrate, one finds interneurons which possess center-surround opponent receptive fields (CSRFs). CSRFs underlie the mechanism of lateral inhibition which produces edge enhancement effects such as Mach band. It has also been shown in the fly compound eye that the CSRF of large monopolar cells (LMCs) changes its shape in accordance with SNR; the CSRF becomes wider with increase of the noise level in the sensory environment. Furthermore, whereas CSRFs describe a filtering function in space, an analogous observation has been made in LMCs as regards the filtering property in the time domain; the biphasic flash response (BPFR) lasts longer as the noise level increases (Dubs, 1982; Laughlin, 1982).

A question that arises is whether similar SNR-dependent spatio-temporal filtering properties might be present in vertebrate visual cells. To investigate this, we made an intracellular recording experiment to measure the CSRF and BPFR profiles of bipolar cells in the carp retina under appropriate conditions, and the results are described in the first part of this paper. In the second part, we ask the same question in a 3-layer feedforward artificial neural network (ANN) trained to detect and localize spatial and temporal changes in simulated visual inputs corrupted by noise. In this case, the ANN wiring structure evolves from an initial random state so as to minimize the detection error, and we look into the internal ANN organization that emerges as a result of training. The findings made in the real and artificial neural systems are compared and discussed in the final section.

In this study, the backpropagation learning algorithm was applied to update the synaptic parameters of the ANN. This algorithm was used as a means for the computational optimization. Accordingly, the present choice is not necessarily relevant to the question of whether the error backpropagation pathway actually might exist in real neural systems(cf. Stork & Hall, 1989).

2 THE CASE OF A REAL NEURAL SYSTEM: RETINAL BIPOLAR CELL

Bipolar cells occur as a second order neuron in the vertebrate retina, and they have a good example of CSRF Here we are interested in the possibility that the CSRF and BPFR of bipolar cells might change their size and shape as a function of the visual environment, particularly as regards the dark- versus light-adapted retinal states which correspond to low versus high SNR conditions as explained later. Thus, the following intracellular recording experiment was carried out.

2.1 MATERIAL AND METHOD

The retina was isolated from the carp which had been kept in complete darkness for 2 hrs before being pithed for sacrifice. The specimen was then mounted on a chamber with the receptor side up, and it was continuously superfused with a Ringer solution composed of (in mM) 102 NaCl, 28 $NaHCO_3$, 2.6 KCl, 1 $CaCl_2$, 1 $MgCl_2$ and 5 glucose, maintained at pH=7.6 and aerated with a gas mixture of 95% O_2 and 5% CO_2. Glass micropipettes filled with 3M KCl and having tip resistances of about 150 MΩ were used to record the membrane potential. Identification of bipolar cell units was made on the basis of presence or absence of CSRF. For this preliminary test, the center and peripheral responses were examined by using flashes of a small centered spot and a narrow annular ring. To map their receptive field profile, the stimulus was given as flashes of a narrow slit presented at discrete positions 60 μm apart on the retina. The slit of white light was 4 mm long and 0.17 mm wide, and its flash had intensity of 7.24 $\mu W/cm^2$ and duration of 250 msec. The CSRF measurement was made under dark- and light- adapted conditions. A

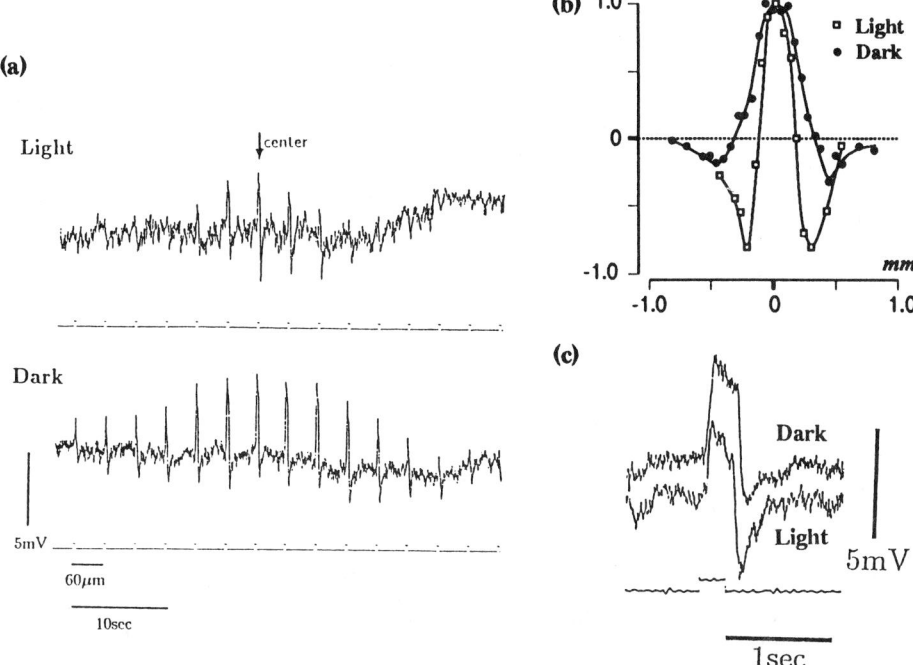

Figure 1: (a) Intracellular recordings from an ON-center bipolar cell of the carp retina with moving slit stimuli under light and dark adapted condition. (b) The receptive field profiles plotted from the recordings. (c) The response recorded when the slit was positioned at the receptive field center.

steady background light of 0.29 $\mu W/cm^2$ was provided for light adaptation.

2.2 RESULTS

Fig.1a shows a typical set of records obtained from a bipolar cell. The response to each flash of slit was biphasic (i.e., BPFR), consisting of a depolarization (ON) followed by a hyperpolarization(OFF). The ON response was the major component when the slit was positioned centrally on the receptive field, whereas the OFF response was dominant at peripheral locations and somewhat sluggish. The CSRF pattern was portrayed by plotting the response membrane potential measured at the time just prior to the cessation of each test flash. The result compiled from the data of Fig.1a is presented in Fig.1b, showing that the CSRF of the dark-adapted state was shallow and broad as opposed to the sharp profile produced during light adaptation. The records with the slit positioned at the receptive field center are enlarged in Fig.1c, indicating that the OFF part of the BPFR waveform was shallower and broader when the retina was dark adapted than when light adapted.

3 THE CASE OF ARTIFICIAL NEURAL NETWORKS

Visual pattern recognition and imagery data processing have been a traditional application area of ANNs. There are also ANNs that deal with time series signals. These both types of ANNs are considered here, and they are trained to detect and localize spatial or temporal changes of the input signal corrupted by noise.

3.1 PARADIGMS AND METHODS

The ANN models we used are illustrated in Figs.2. The model of Fig.2a deals with one-dimensional spatial signals. It consists of three layers (input, hidden, output), each having the same number of 12 or 20 neuronal units. The pattern given to the input layer represents the brightness distribution of light. The network was trained by means of the standard backpropagation algorithm, to detect and localize step-wise changes (edges) which were distributed on each training pattern in a random fashion with respect to the number, position and height. The mean level of the whole pattern was varied randomly as well. In addition, there was a background noise (not illustrated in Figs.2); independent noise signals of the same statistics were given to the all input units, and the maximum noise amplitude (NL: noise level) remained constant throughout each training session. The teacher signal was the "true" edge positions which were subject to obscuration due to the background noise; the learning was supervised such that each output unit would respond with 1 when a step-wise change not due to the background noise occurred at the corresponding position, and respond with −1 otherwise. The value of each synaptic weight parameter was given randomly at the outset and updated by using the backpropagation algorithm after presentation of each training pattern. The training session was terminated when the mean square error stopped decreasing.

To process time series inputs, the ANN model of Fig.2b was constructed with the backpropagation learning algorithm. This temporal model also has three layers, but the meaning of this is quite different from the spatial network model of Fig.2a. That is, whereas each unit of each layer in the spatial model is an anatomical entity, this is not the case with respect to the temporal model. Thus, each layer represents a single neuron so that there are actually only three neuronal elements, i.e., a receptor, an interneuron, and an output cell. And, the units in the same layer represent activity states of one neuron at different time slices; the rightmost unit for the present time, the next one for one time unit ago, and so on. As is apparent from Fig.2b, therefore, there is no convergence from the future (right) to the past (left). Each cell has memory of T-units time. Accordingly, the network requires $2T - 1$ units in the input layer, T units in the hidden layer and 1 units in the output layer to calculate the output at present time. The input was a discrete time series in which step-wise changes took place randomly in a manner analogous to the spatial input of Fig.2a. As in the spatial case, there was a background noise

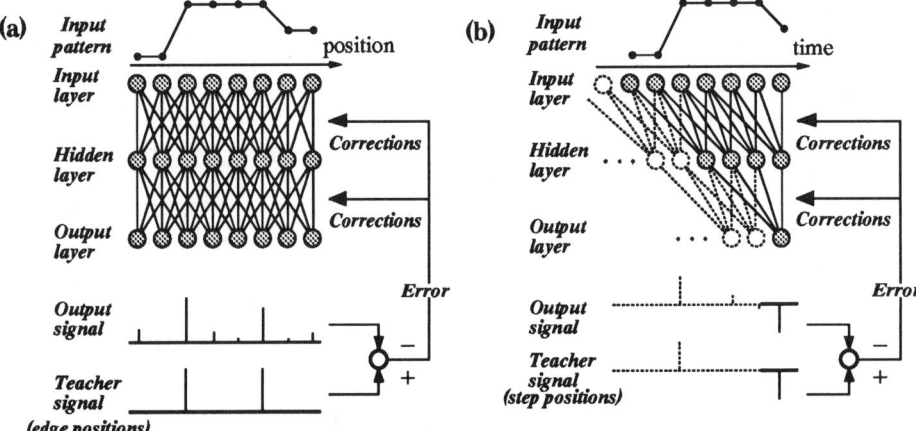

Figure 2: The neural network architectures. Spatial (a) and temporal model (b).

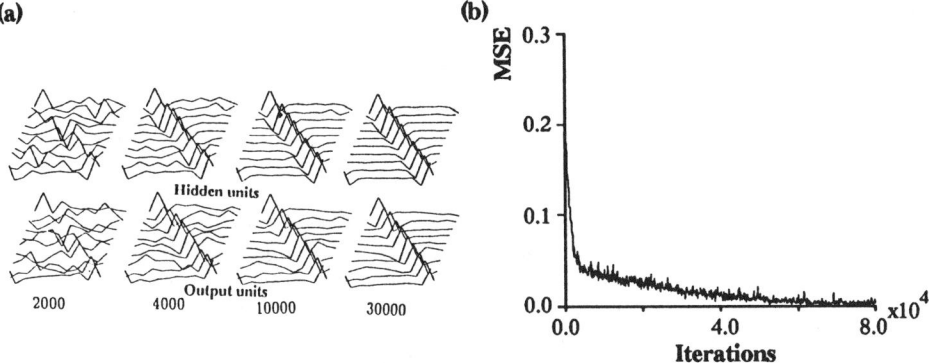

Figure 3: Development of receptive fields. Synaptic weights (a) and mean square error (b), both as a function of the number of iterations.

added to the input. The network was trained to respond with $+1/-1$ when the original input signal increased/decreased, and to respond with 0 otherwise.

3.2 RESULTS

Spatial case: Emergence of CSRFs with SNR-dependent plasticity

As regards the edge detection learning by the ANN model of Fig.2a, the results without the background noise are described first (Furukawa & Yasui, 1990; Joshi & Lee, 1993). Fig.3a illustrates how the synaptic connections developed from the initial random state. If the final distribution of synaptic weight parameters is examined from input units to any hidden unit and also from hidden units to any output unit, then it can be seen in either case that the central and peripheral connections are opposite in the polarity of their weight parameters; the central group had either positive (ON-center) or negative (OFF-center) values, but the reversed profiles are

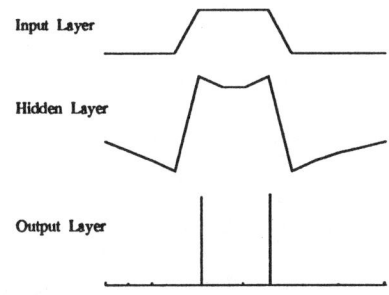

Figure 4: A Sample of activity pattern of each layer

shown in the drawing of Fig.3a for the OFF-center case. In any event, CSRFs were formed inside the network as a result of the edge detection learning. Fig.3b shows the performance improvement during a learning session. Fig.4 shows the activation pattern of each layer in response to a sample input, and edge enhancement like the Mach band effect can be observed in the hidden layer. Fig.5a presents sample input patterns corrupted by the background noise of various NL values, and Fig.5b shows how a hidden unit was connected to the input layer at the end of training. CSRFs were still formed when the environment suffered from the noise. However, the structure of the center-surround antagonism changed as a function of NL; the CSRFs became shallow and broad as NL increased, i.e., as the SNR decreased.

Temporal case: Emergence of BPFRs with SNR-dependent plasticity

With reference to the learning paradigm of Fig.2b, Fig.5c reveals how a representative hidden unit made synaptic connections with the input units as a function of NL; the weight parameters are plotted against the elapsed time. Each trace would correspond to the response of the hidden unit to a flash of light, and it consists of two phases of ON and OFF, i.e., BPFRs (biphasic flash responses) emerged in this ANN as a result of learning, and the biphasic time course changed depending on NL; the negative-going phase became shallower and longer with decrease of SNR.

4 DISCUSSION: Common Receptive Field Properties in Vertebrate, Invertebrate and Artificial Systems

A CSRF profile emerges after differentiating twice in space a small patch of light, and CSRF is a kind of point spreading function. Accordingly, the response to any input distribution can be obtained by convolving the input pattern with CSRF. The double differentiation of this spatial filtering acts to locate edge positions. On the other hand, the waveform of BPFR appears by differentiating once in time a short flash of light. Thus, the BPFR is an impulse response function with which to convolve the given input time series to obtain the response waveform. This is a derivative filtering, which subserves detection of temporal changes in the input visual signal. While both CSRF and BPFR occur in visual neurons of a wide variety of vertebrates and invertebrates, the first part of the present study shows that these spatial and temporal filtering functions can develop autonomously in our ANNs.

The neural system of visual signal processing encounters various kinds of noise. There are non-biological ones such as a background noise in the visual input itself and the photon noise which cannot be ignored when the light intensity is low. Endogenous sources of noise include spontaneous photoisomerization in photoreceptor cells, quantal transmitter release at synaptic sites, open/close activities of ion channels and so on. Generally speaking, therefore, since the surroundings are dim when the retina is dark adapted, SNR in the neuronal environment tends to be low during dark adaptation. According to the present experiment on the carp retina, the CSRF of bipolar cells widens in space and the BPFR is prolonged in time when the retina is dark adapted, that is, when SNR is presumably low. Interestingly, the same SNR-dependent properties have also been described in connection with the CSRF and BPFR of large monopolar cells in the fly compound eye. These spatial and temporal observations are both in accord with a notion that a method to remove noise is smoothing which requires averaging for a sufficiently long interval. In other words, when SNR is low, the signal averaging takes place over a large portion of the spatio-temporal domain comprised of CSRF and BPFR. Smoothing and differentiation are entirely opposite in the signal processing role. The SNR dependency of the CSRF and BPFR profiles can be viewed as a compromise between these two operations, for the need to detect signal changes in the presence of noise. These

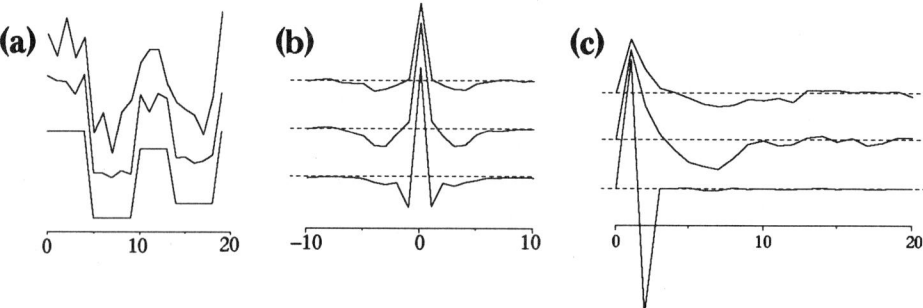

Figure 5: (a) A sample set of training patterns with different background noise levels (NLs). The NLs are 0.0, 0.4, 1.0 from bottom to top. The receptive field profiles (b) and flash responses (c) after training with each NL. The ordinate scale is linear but in arbitrary unit, with the zero level indicated by dotted lines.

points parallel the results of information-theoretic analysis by Atick and Redlich (1992) and by Laughlin (1982).

5 CONCLUDING REMARKS

We have learnt from this study that the same software is at work for the SNR-dependent control of the spatio-temporal visual receptive field in entirely different hardwares; namely, vertebrate, invertebrate and artificial neural systems. In other words, the plasticity scheme represents nature's optimum answer to the visual functional demand, not a result of compromise with other factors such as metabolism or morphology. Some mention needs to be made of the standard regularization theory. If the theory is applied to the edge detection problem, then one obtains the Laplacian-Gaussian filter which is a well-known CSRF example(Torre & Poggio, 1980). And, the shape of this spatial filter can be made wide or narrow by manipulating the value of a constant usually referred to as the regularization parameter. This parameter choice corresponds to the compromise that our ANN finds autonomously between smoothing and differentiation. The present type of research aided by trainable artificial neural networks seems to be a useful top-down approach to gain insight into the brain and neural mechanisms. Earlier, Lehky and Sejnowski (1988) were able to create neuron-like units similar to the complex cells of the visual cortex by using the backpropagation algorithm, however, the CSRF mechanism was given *a priori* to an early stage in their ANN processor. It should also be noted that Linsker (1986) succeeded in self-organization of CSRFs in an ANN model that operates under the learning law of Hebb. Perhaps, it remains to be examined whether the CSRFs formed in such an unsupervised learning paradigm might also possess an SNR-dependent plasticity similar to that described in this paper.

References

Atick, J.J. & Redlich, A.N. (1992) What does the retina know about natural scenes? *Neural Computation, 4*, 196-210.

Dubs, A. (1982) The spatial integration of signals in the retina and lamina of the fly compound eye under different conditions of luminance. *J. Comp. Physiol A, 146*, 321-334.

Furukawa, T. & Yasui, S. (1990) Development of center-surround opponent receptive fields in a neural network through backpropagation training. *Proc. Int. Conf. Fuzzy Logic & Neural Networks* (Iizuka, Japan) 473-490.

Joshi, A. & Lee, C.H. (1993) Backpropagation learns Marr's operator *Biol. Cybern., 70*, 65-73.

Laughlin, S. B. (1982) Matching coding to scenes to enhance efficiency. In Braddick OJ, Sleigh AC(eds) *The physical and biological processing of images* (pp.42-52). Springer, Berlin, Heidelberg New York.

Lehky, S. R. & Sejnowski, T. J. (1988) Network model of shape-from shading: neural function arises from both receptive and projective fields. *Nature, 333*, 452-454.

Linsker, R. (1986) From basic network principles to neural architecture: Emergence of spatial-opponent cells. Proc. Natl. Acad. Sci. USA, 83, 7508-7512.

Stork, D. G. & Hall, J. (1989) Is backpropagation biologically plausible? *International Join Conf. Neural Networks, II (Washington DC)*, 241-246.

Torre, V. & Poggio, T. A. (1986) On edge detection. *IEEE Trans. Pattern Anal. Machine Intel., PAMI-8*, 147-163.

PART III
THEORY

Learning Model Bias

Jonathan Baxter
Department of Computer Science
Royal Holloway College, University of London
jon@dcs.rhbnc.ac.uk

Abstract

In this paper the problem of *learning* appropriate domain-specific bias is addressed. It is shown that this can be achieved by learning many related tasks from the same domain, and a theorem is given bounding the number tasks that must be learnt. A corollary of the theorem is that if the tasks are known to possess a common *internal representation* or *preprocessing* then the number of examples required per task for good generalisation when learning n tasks simultaneously scales like $O(a + \frac{b}{n})$, where $O(a)$ is a bound on the minimum number of examples requred to learn a single task, and $O(a + b)$ is a bound on the number of examples required to learn each task independently. An experiment providing strong qualitative support for the theoretical results is reported.

1 Introduction

It has been argued (see [6]) that the main problem in machine learning is the biasing of a learner's hypothesis space sufficiently well to ensure good generalisation from a small number of examples. Once suitable biases have been found the actual learning task is relatively trivial. Exisiting methods of bias generally require the input of a human expert in the form of heuristics, hints [1], domain knowledge, *etc.* Such methods are clearly limited by the accuracy and reliability of the expert's knowledge and also by the extent to which that knowledge can be transferred to the learner. Here I attempt to solve some of these problems by introducing a method for *automatically learning* the bias.

The central idea is that in many learning problems the learner is typically embedded within an *environment* or *domain* of related learning tasks and that the bias appropriate for a single task is likely to be appropriate for other tasks within the same environment. A simple example is the problem of handwritten character recognition. A preprocessing stage that identifies and removes any (small) rotations, dilations and translations of an image of a character will be advantageous for recognising all characters. If the set of all individual character recognition problems is viewed as an environment of learning tasks, this preprocessor represents a bias that is appropriate to all tasks in the environment. It is likely that there are many other currently unknown biases that are also appropriate for this environment. We would like to be able to learn these automatically.

Bias that is appropriate for all tasks must be learnt by sampling from many tasks. If only a single task is learnt then the bias extracted is likely to be specific to that task. For example, if a network is constructed as in figure 1 and the output nodes are simultaneously trained on many similar problems, then the hidden layers are more likely to be useful in learning a novel problem of the same type than if only a single problem is learnt. In the rest of this paper I develop a general theory of bias learning based upon the idea of learning multiple related tasks. The theory shows that a learner's generalisation performance can be greatly improved by learning related tasks and that if sufficiently many tasks are learnt the learner's bias can be extracted and used to learn novel tasks.

Other authors that have empirically investigated the idea of learning multiple related tasks include [5] and [8].

2 Learning Bias

For the sake of argument I consider learning problems that amount to minimizing the mean squared error of a function h over some training set D. A more general formulation based on statistical decision theory is given in [3]. Thus, it is assumed that the learner receives a training set of (possibly noisy) *input-output* pairs $D = \{(x_1, y_1), \ldots, (x_m, y_m)\}$, drawn according to a probability distribution P on $X \times Y$ (X being the input space and Y being the output space) and searches through its hypothesis space $\mathcal{H}$ for a function $h: X \to Y$ minimizing the *empirical error*,

$$\hat{E}(h, D) = \frac{1}{m} \sum_{i=1}^{m} (h(x_i) - y_i)^2. \tag{1}$$

The *true error* or *generalisation error* of h is the expected error under P:

$$E(h, P) = \int_{X \times Y} (h(x) - y)^2 \, dP(x, y). \tag{2}$$

The hope of course is that an h with a small empirical error on a large enough training set will also have a small true error, *i.e.* it will *generalise* well.

I model the *environment* of the learner as a pair $(\mathcal{P}, Q)$ where $\mathcal{P} = \{P\}$ is a set of learning tasks and Q is a probability measure on $\mathcal{P}$. The learner is now supplied not with a single hypothesis space $\mathcal{H}$ but with a *hypothesis space family* $\mathbb{H} = \{\mathcal{H}\}$. Each $\mathcal{H} \in \mathbb{H}$ represents a different bias the learner has about the environment. For example, one $\mathcal{H}$ may contain functions that are very smooth, whereas another $\mathcal{H}$ might contain more wiggly functions. Which hypothesis space is best will depend on the kinds of functions in the environment. To determine the best $\mathcal{H} \in \mathbb{H}$ for $(\mathcal{P}, Q)$, we provide the learner not with a single training set D but with n such training sets $D_1, \ldots, D_n$. Each D_i is generated by first sampling from $\mathcal{P}$ according to Q to give P_i and then sampling m times from $X \times Y$ according to P_i to give $D_i = \{(x_{i1}, y_{i1}), \ldots, (x_{im}, y_{im})\}$. The learner searches for the hypothesis space $\mathcal{H} \in \mathbb{H}$ with minimal empirical error on $D_1, \ldots, D_n$, where this is defined by

$$\hat{E}^*(\mathcal{H}, D_1, \ldots, D_n) = \frac{1}{n} \sum_{i=1}^{n} \inf_{h \in \mathcal{H}} \hat{E}(h, D_i). \tag{3}$$

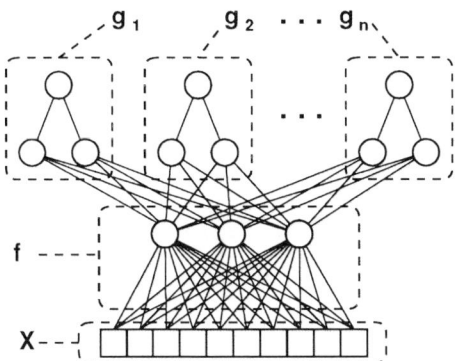

Figure 1: Net for learning multiple tasks. Input x_{ij} from training set D_i is propagated forwards through the *internal representation* f and then only through the output network g_i. The error $[g_i(f(x_{ij})) - y_{ij}]^2$ is similarly backpropagated only through the output network g_i and then f. Weight updates are performed after all training sets $D_1, \ldots, D_n$ have been presented.

The hypothesis space $\mathcal{H}$ with smallest empirical error is the one that is best able to learn the n data sets on average.

There are *two* ways of measuring the true error of a bias learner. The first is how well it generalises on the n tasks $P_1, \ldots, P_n$ used to generate the training sets. Assuming that in the process of minimising (3) the learner generates n functions $h_1, \ldots, h_n \in \mathcal{H}$ with minimal empirical error on their respective training sets[1], the learner's true error is measured by:

$$E^n(h_1, \ldots, h_n, P_1, \ldots, P_n) = \frac{1}{n} \sum_{i=1}^{n} E(h_i, P_i). \tag{4}$$

Note that in this case the learner's empirical error is given by $\hat{E}^n(h_1, \ldots, h_n, D_1, \ldots, D_n) = \frac{1}{n} \sum_{i=1}^{n} \hat{E}(h_i, D_i)$. The second way of measuring the generalisation error of a bias learner is to determine how good $\mathcal{H}$ is for learning *novel tasks* drawn from the environment $(\mathcal{P}, Q)$:

$$E^*(\mathcal{H}, Q) = \int_{\mathcal{P}} \inf_{h \in \mathcal{H}} E(h, P) \, dQ(P) \tag{5}$$

A learner that has found an $\mathcal{H}$ with a small value of (5) can be said to have *learnt to learn* the tasks in $\mathcal{P}$ in general. To state the bounds ensuring these two types of generalisation a few more definitions must be introduced.

Definition 1 *Let $\mathbb{H} = \{\mathcal{H}\}$ be a hypothesis space family. Let $\mathbb{H}_\sigma = \{h \in \mathcal{H} : \mathcal{H} \in \mathbb{H}\}$. For any $h : X \to Y$, define a map $h : X \times Y \to [0, 1]$ by $h(x, y) = (h(x) - y)^2$. Note the abuse of notation: h stands for two different functions depending on its argument. Given a sequence of n functions $\vec{h} = (h_1, \ldots, h_n)$ let $\vec{h} : (X \times Y)^n \to [0, 1]$ be the function $(x_1, y_1, \ldots, x_n, y_n) \mapsto \frac{1}{n} \sum_{i=1}^{n} h_i(x_i, y_i)$. Let $\mathcal{H}^n$ be the set of all such functions where the h_i are all chosen from $\mathcal{H}$. Let $\mathbb{H}^n = \{\mathcal{H}^n : \mathcal{H} \in H\}$. For each $\mathcal{H} \in \mathbb{H}$ define $\mathcal{H}^* : \mathcal{P} \to [0, 1]$ by $\mathcal{H}^*(P) = \inf_{h \in \mathcal{H}} E(h, P)$ and let $\mathbb{H}^* = \{\mathcal{H}^* : \mathcal{H} \in \mathbb{H}\}$.*

---

[1] This assumes the infimum in (3) is attained.

Definition 2 *Given a set of functions $\mathcal{H}$ from any space Z to $[0,1]$, and any probability measure on Z, define the pseudo-metric d_P on $\mathcal{H}$ by*

$$d_P(h, h') = \int_Z |h(z) - h'(z)| \, dP(z).$$

Denote the smallest ε-cover of $(\mathcal{H}, d_P)$ by $\mathcal{N}(\varepsilon, \mathcal{H}, d_P)$. Define the ε-capacity of $\mathcal{H}$ by

$$\mathcal{C}(\varepsilon, \mathcal{H}) = \sup_P \mathcal{N}(\varepsilon, \mathcal{H}, d_P)$$

where the supremum is over all discrete probability measures P on Z.

Definition 2 will be used to define the ε-capacity of spaces such as $\mathbb{H}^*$ and $[\mathbb{H}^n]_\sigma$, where from definition 1 the latter is $[\mathbb{H}^n]_\sigma = \{\vec{h} \in \mathcal{H}^n : \mathcal{H} \in \mathbb{H}\}$.

The following theorem bounds the number of tasks and examples per task required to ensure that the hypothesis space learnt by a bias learner will, with high probability, contain good solutions to novel tasks in the same environment[2].

Theorem 1 *Let the n training sets $D_1, \ldots, D_n$ be generated by sampling n times from the environment $\mathcal{P}$ according to Q to give $P_1, \ldots, P_n$, and then sampling m times from each P_i to generate D_i. Let $\mathbb{H} = \{\mathcal{H}\}$ be a hypothesis space family and suppose a learner chooses $\hat{\mathcal{H}} \in \mathbb{H}$ minimizing (3) on $D_1, \ldots, D_n$. For all $\varepsilon > 0$ and $0 < \delta < 1$, if*

$$n = O\left(\frac{1}{\varepsilon^2} \ln \frac{\mathcal{C}(\varepsilon, \mathbb{H}^*)}{\delta}\right),$$

$$\text{and} \quad m = O\left(\frac{1}{n\varepsilon^2} \ln \frac{\mathcal{C}(\varepsilon, [\mathbb{H}^m]_\sigma)}{\delta}\right)$$

then

$$\Pr\left\{D_1, \ldots, D_n : |\hat{E}^*(\hat{\mathcal{H}}, D_1, \ldots, D_n) - E^*(\hat{\mathcal{H}}, Q)| > \varepsilon\right\} \leq \delta.$$

The bound on m in theorem 1 is the also the number of examples required per task to ensure generalisation of the first kind mentioned above. That is, it is the number of examples required in each data set D_i to ensure good generalisation on average across all n tasks when using the hypothesis space family $\mathbb{H}$. If we let $m(\mathbb{H}, n, \varepsilon, \delta)$ be the number of examples required per task to ensure that $\Pr\left\{D_1, \ldots, D_n : |\hat{E}^n(h_1, \ldots, h_n, D_1, \ldots, D_n) - E^n(h_1, \ldots, h_n, P_1, \ldots, P_n)| > \varepsilon\right\} \leq \delta$, where all $h_i \in \mathcal{H}$ for some fixed $\mathcal{H} \in \mathbb{H}$, then

$$G(\mathbb{H}, n, \varepsilon, \delta) = \frac{m(\mathbb{H}, 1, \varepsilon, \delta)}{m(\mathbb{H}, n, \varepsilon, \delta)}$$

represents the advantage in learning n tasks as opposed to one task (the ordinary learning scenario). Call $G(\mathbb{H}, n, \varepsilon, \delta)$ the *n-task gain* of $\mathbb{H}$. Using the fact [3] that

$$\mathcal{C}(\varepsilon, \mathbb{H}_\sigma) \leq \mathcal{C}(\varepsilon, [\mathbb{H}^n]_\sigma) \leq \mathcal{C}(\varepsilon, \mathbb{H}_\sigma)^n,$$

and the formula for m from theorem 1, we have,

$$1 \leq G(\mathbb{H}, n, \varepsilon, \delta) \leq n.$$

---

[2]The bounds in theorem 1 can be improved to $O\left(\frac{1}{\varepsilon}\right)$ if all $\mathcal{H} \in H$ are convex and the error is the squared loss [7].

Thus, at least in the worst case analysis here, learning n tasks in the same environment can result in anything from no gain at all to an n-fold reduction in the number of examples required per task. In the next section a very intuitive analysis of the conditions leading to the extreme values of $G(H, n, \varepsilon, \delta)$ is given for the situation where an internal representation is being learnt for the environment. I will also say more about the bound on the number of tasks (n) in theorem 1.

3 Learning Internal Representations with Neural Networks

In figure 1 n tasks are being learnt using a common representation f. In this case $[\mathbb{H}^n]_\sigma$ is the set of all possible networks formed by choosing the weights in the representation and output networks. $\mathbb{H}_\sigma$ is the same space with a single output node. If the n tasks were learnt independently (*i.e.* without a common representation) then each task would use its own copy of H_σ, *i.e.* we wouldn't be forcing the tasks to all use the same representation.

Let W_R be the total number of weights in the representation network and W_O be the number of weights in an individual output network. Suppose also that all the nodes in each network are *Lipschitz bounded*[3]. Then it can be shown [3] that $\ln \mathcal{C}\left(\varepsilon, [\mathbb{H}^n]_\sigma\right) = O\left(\left(W_O + \frac{W_R}{n}\right) \ln \frac{1}{\varepsilon}\right)$ and $\ln \mathcal{C}(\varepsilon, \mathbb{H}^*) = O\left(W_R \ln \frac{1}{\varepsilon}\right)$. Substituting these bounds into theorem 1 shows that to generalise well on average on n tasks using a common representation requires $m = O\left(\frac{1}{\varepsilon^2}\left[\left(W_O + \frac{W_R}{n}\right) \ln \frac{1}{\varepsilon} + \frac{1}{n} \ln \frac{1}{\delta}\right]\right) = O\left(a + \frac{b}{n}\right)$ examples of each task. In addition, if $n = O\left(\frac{1}{\varepsilon^2} W_R \ln \frac{1}{\varepsilon}\right)$ then with high probability the resulting representation will be good for learning novel tasks from the same environment. Note that this bound is very large. However it results from a worst-case analysis and so is highly likely to be beaten in practice. This is certainly borne out by the experiment in the next section.

The *learning gain* $G(H, n, \varepsilon)$ satisfies $G(H, n, \varepsilon) \approx \frac{W_O + W_R}{W_O + \frac{W_R}{n}}$. Thus, if $W_R \gg W_O$, $G \approx n$, while if $W_O \gg W_R$ then $G \approx 1$. This is perfectly intuitive: when $W_O \gg W_R$ the representation network is hardly doing any work, most of the power of the network is in the ouput networks and hence the tasks are effectively being learnt independently. However, if $W_R \gg W_O$ then the representation network dominates; there is very little extra learning to be done for the individual tasks once the representation is known, and so each example from every task is providing full information to the representation network. Hence the gain of n.

Note that once a representation has been learnt the sampling burden for learning a novel task will be reduced to $m = O\left(\frac{1}{\varepsilon^2}\left[W_O \ln \frac{1}{\varepsilon} + \ln \frac{1}{\delta}\right]\right)$ because only the output network has to be learnt. If this theory applies to human learning then the fact that we are able to learn words, faces, characters, *etc* with relatively few examples (a single example in the case of faces) indicates that our "output networks" are very small, and, given our large ignorance concerning an appropriate representation, the representation network for learning in these domains would have to be large, so we would expect to see an n-task gain of nearly n for learning within these domains.

---

[3] A node $a: \mathbb{R}^p \to \mathbb{R}$ is *Lipschitz bounded* if there exists a constant c such that $|a(x) - a(x')| < c \|x - x'\|$ for all $x, x' \in \mathbb{R}^p$. Note that this rules out threshold nodes, but sigmoid squashing functions are okay as long as the weights are bounded.

4 Experiment: Learning Symmetric Boolean Functions

In this section the results of an experiment are reported in which a neural network was trained to learn *symmetric*[4] Boolean functions. The network was the same as the one in figure 1 except that the output networks g_i had no hidden layers. The input space $X = \{0,1\}^{10}$ was restricted to include only those inputs with between one and four ones. The functions in the environment of the network consisted of all possible *symmetric* Boolean functions over the input space, except the trivial "constant 0" and "constant 1" functions. Training sets $D_1, \ldots, D_n$ were generated by first choosing n functions (with replacement) uniformly from the fourteen possible, and then choosing m input vectors by choosing a random number between 1 and 4 and placing that many 1's at random in the input vector. The training sets were learnt by minimising the empirical error (3) using the backpropagation algorithm as outlined in figure 1. Separate simulations were performed with n ranging from 1 to 21 in steps of four and m ranging from 1 to 171 in steps of 10. Further details of the experimental procedure may be found in [3], chapter 4.

Once the network had sucessfully learnt the n training sets its generalization ability was tested on all n functions used to generate the training set. In this case the generalisation error (equation (4)) could be computed exactly by calculating the network's output (for all n functions) for each of the 385 input vectors. The generalisation error as a function of n and m is plotted in figure 2 for two independent sets of simulations. Both simulations support the theoretical result that the number of examples m required for good generalisation decreases with increasing n (*cf* theorem 1). For training sets $D_1, \ldots, D_n$ that led to a generalisation error of less than

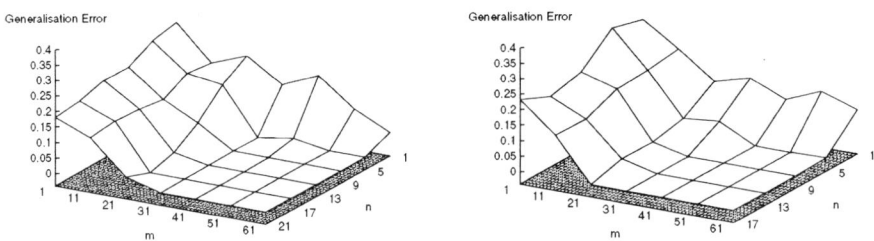

Figure 2: Learning *surfaces* for two independent simulations.

0.01, the representation network f was extracted and tested for its *true error*, where this is defined as in equation (5) (the hypothesis space $\mathcal{H}$ is the set of all networks formed by attaching any output network to the fixed representation network f). Although there is insufficient space to show the representation error here (see [3] for the details), it was found that the representation error monotonically decreased with the number of tasks learnt, verifying the theoretical conclusions.

The representation's output for all inputs is shown in figure 3 for sample sizes $(n,m) = (1,131), (5,31)$ and $(13,31)$. All outputs corresponding to inputs from the same category (*i.e.* the same number of ones) are labelled with the same symbol. The network in the $n=1$ case generalised perfectly but the resulting representation does not capture the symmetry in the environment and also does not distinguish the inputs with 2, 3 and 4 "1's" (because the function learnt didn't), showing that

---

[4]A symmetric Boolean function is one that is invariant under interchange of its inputs, or equivalently, one that only depends on the number of "1's" in its input (*e.g.* parity).

learning a single function is not sufficient to learn an appropriate representation. By $n = 5$ the representation's behaviour has improved (the inputs with differing numbers of 1's are now well separated, but they are still spread around a lot) and by $n = 13$ it is perfect. As well as reducing the sampling burden for the n tasks in

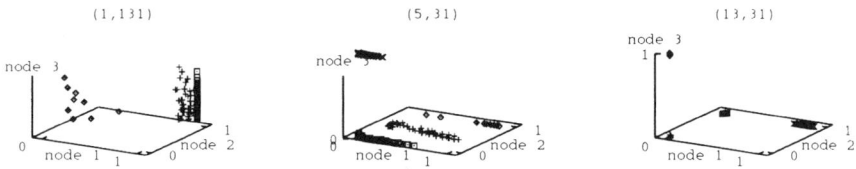

Figure 3: Plots of the output of a representation generated from the indicated (n, m) sample.

the training set, a representation learnt on sufficiently many tasks should be good for learning novel tasks and should greatly reduce the number of examples required for new tasks. This too was experimentally verified although there is insufficient space to present the results here (see [3]).

5 Conclusion

I have introduced a formal model of bias learning and shown that (under mild restrictions) a learner can sample sufficiently many times from sufficiently many tasks to learn bias that is appropriate for the entire environment. In addition, the number of examples required per task to learn n tasks independently was shown to be upper bounded by $O(a + b/n)$ for appropriate environments. See [2] for an analysis of bias learning within an Information theoretic framework which leads to an exact $a + b/n$-type bound.

References

[1] Y. S. Abu-Mostafa. Learning from Hints in Neural Networks. *Journal of Complecity*, 6:192–198, 1989.

[2] J. Baxter. A Bayesian Model of Bias Learning. Submitted to COLT 1996, 1995.

[3] J. Baxter. *Learning Internal Representations*. PhD thesis, Department of Mathematics and Statistics, The Flinders University of South Australia, 1995. Draft copy in Neuroprose Archive under "/pub/neuroprose/Thesis/baxter.thesis.ps.Z".

[4] J. Baxter. Learning Internal Representations. In *Proceedings of the Eighth International Conference on Computational Learning Theory*, Santa Cruz, California, 1995. ACM Press.

[5] R. Caruana. Learning Many Related Tasks at the Same Time with Backpropagation. In *Advances in Neural Information Processing 5*, 1993.

[6] S. Geman, E. Bienenstock, and R. Doursat. Neural networks and the bias/variance dilemma. *Neural Comput.*, 4:1–58, 1992.

[7] W. S. Lee, P. L. Bartlett, and R. C. Williamson. Sample Complexity of Agnostic Learning with Squared Loss. In preparation, 1995.

[8] T. M. Mitchell and S. Thrun. Learning One More Thing. Technical Report CMU-CS-94-184, CMU, 1994.

Statistical Theory of Overtraining – Is Cross-Validation Asymptotically Effective?

S. Amari, N. Murata, K.-R. Müller*
Dept. of Math. Engineering and Inf. Physics, University of Tokyo
Hongo 7-3-1, Bunkyo-ku, Tokyo 113, Japan

M. Finke
Inst. f. Logik, University of Karlsruhe
76128 Karlsruhe, Germany

H. Yang
Lab. f. Inf. Representation, RIKEN,
Wakoshi, Saitama, 351-01, Japan

Abstract

A statistical theory for overtraining is proposed. The analysis treats realizable stochastic neural networks, trained with Kullback-Leibler loss in the *asymptotic* case. It is shown that the asymptotic gain in the generalization error is small if we perform early stopping, even if we have access to the optimal stopping time. Considering cross-validation stopping we answer the question: In what ratio the examples should be divided into training and testing sets in order to obtain the optimum performance. In the non-asymptotic region cross-validated early stopping always decreases the generalization error. Our large scale simulations done on a CM5 are in nice agreement with our analytical findings.

1 Introduction

Training multilayer neural feed-forward networks, there is a folklore that the generalization error decreases in an early period of training, reaches the minimum and then increases as training goes on, while the training error monotonically decreases. Therefore, it is considered advantageous to stop training at an adequate time or to use regularizers (Hecht-Nielsen [1989], Hassoun [1995], Wang et al. [1994], Poggio and Girosi [1990], Moody [1992], LeCun et al. [1990] and others). To avoid overtraining, the following stopping rule has been proposed based on cross-validation:

---

*Permanent address: GMD FIRST, Rudower Chaussee 5, 12489 Berlin, Germany. E-mail: Klaus@first.gmd.de

Divide all the available examples into two disjoint sets. One set is used for training. The other set is used for testing such that the behavior of the trained network is evaluated by using the test examples and training is stopped at the point that minimizes the testing error.

The present paper gives a mathematical analysis of the so-called overtraining phenomena to elucidate the folklore. We analyze the asymptotic case where the number t of examples are very large. Our analysis treats 1) a realizable stochastic machine, 2) Kullback-Leibler loss (negative of the log likelihood loss), 3) asymptotic behavior where the number t of examples is sufficiently large (compared with the number m of parameters). We firstly show that asymptotically the gain of the generalization error is small even if we could find the optimal stopping time. We then answer the question: In what ratio, the examples should be divided into training and testing sets in order to obtain the optimum performance. We give a definite answer to this problem. When the number m of network parameters is large, the best strategy is to use almost all t examples in the training set and to use only $1/\sqrt{2m}$ examples in the testing set, e.g. when $m = 100$, this means that only 7% of the training patterns are to be used in the set determining the point for early stopping.

Our analytic results were confirmed by large-scale computer simulations of three-layer continuous feedforward networks where the number m of modifiable parameters are $m = 100$. When $t > 30m$, the theory fits well with simulations, showing cross-validation is not necessary, because the generalization error becomes worse by using test examples to obtain an adaequate stopping time. For an intermediate range, where $t < 30m$ overtraining occurs surely and the cross-validation stopping improves the generalization ability strongly.

2 Stochastic feedforward networks

Let us consider a stochastic network which receives input vector $\mathbf{x}$ and emits output vector $\mathbf{y}$. The network includes a modifiable vector parameter $\mathbf{w} = (w_1, \cdots, w_m)$ and is denoted by $N(\mathbf{w})$. The input-output relation of the network $N(\mathbf{w})$ is specified by the conditional probability $p(\mathbf{y}|\mathbf{x};\mathbf{w})$. We assume (a) that there exists a teacher network $N(\mathbf{w}_0)$ which generates training examples for the student $N(\mathbf{w})$. And (b) that the Fisher information matrix $G_{ij}(\mathbf{w}) = E\left[\frac{\partial}{\partial w_i}\log p(\mathbf{x},\mathbf{y};\mathbf{w})\frac{\partial}{\partial w_j}\log p(\mathbf{x},\mathbf{y};\mathbf{w})\right]$ exists, is non-degenerate and is smooth in $\mathbf{w}$, where E denotes the expectation with respect to $p(\mathbf{x},\mathbf{y};\mathbf{w}) = q(\mathbf{x})p(\mathbf{y}|\mathbf{x};\mathbf{w})$. The training set $D_t = \{(\mathbf{x}_1,\mathbf{y}_1),\cdots,(\mathbf{x}_t,\mathbf{y}_t)\}$ consists of t independent examples generated by the distribution $p(\mathbf{x},\mathbf{y};\mathbf{w}_0)$ of $N(\mathbf{w}_0)$. The maximum likelihood estimator (m.l.e.) $\hat{\mathbf{w}}$ is the one that maximizes the likelihood of producing D_t, or equivalently minimizes the training error or *empirical* risk function

$$R_{\text{train}}(\mathbf{w}) = -\frac{1}{t}\sum_{i=1}^{t}\log p(\mathbf{x}_i,\mathbf{y}_i;\mathbf{w}). \qquad (2.1)$$

The generalization error or risk function $R(\mathbf{w})$ of network $N(\mathbf{w})$ is the expectation with respect to the true distribution,

$$R(\mathbf{w}) = -E_0[\log p(\mathbf{x},\mathbf{y};\mathbf{w})] = H_0 + D(\mathbf{w}_0 \parallel \mathbf{w}) = H_0 + E_0\left[\log\frac{p(\mathbf{x},\mathbf{y};\mathbf{w}_0)}{p(\mathbf{x},\mathbf{y};\mathbf{w})}\right], \qquad (2.2)$$

where E_0 denotes the expectation with respect to $p(\mathbf{x},\mathbf{y};\mathbf{w}_0)$, H_0 is the entropy of the teacher network and $D(\mathbf{w}_0 \parallel \mathbf{w})$ is the Kullback-Leibler divergence from probability distribution $p(\mathbf{x},\mathbf{y};\mathbf{w}_0)$ to $p(\mathbf{x},\mathbf{y};\mathbf{w})$ or the divergence of $N(\mathbf{w})$ from $N(\mathbf{w}_0)$. Hence, minimizing $R(\mathbf{w})$ is equivalent to minimizing $D(\mathbf{w}_0 \parallel \mathbf{w})$, and the minimum is attained at $\mathbf{w} = \mathbf{w}_0$. The asymptotic theory of statistics proves that the m.l.e. $\hat{\mathbf{w}}_t$ is asymptotically subject to the normal distribution with mean $\mathbf{w}_0$ and variance G^{-1}/t, where G^{-1} is the inverse of the Fisher information matrix G. We can expand for example the risk $R(\mathbf{w}) = H_0 + \frac{1}{2}(\mathbf{w} - \mathbf{w}_0)^T G(\mathbf{w}_0)(\mathbf{w} - \mathbf{w}_0) + O\left(\frac{1}{t^2}\right)$ to obtain

$$\langle R_{\text{gen}}(\hat{\mathbf{w}}) \rangle = H_0 + \frac{m}{2t} + O\left(\frac{1}{t^2}\right), \quad \langle R_{\text{train}}(\hat{\mathbf{w}}) \rangle = H_0 - \frac{m}{2t} + O\left(\frac{1}{t^2}\right), \quad (2.3)$$

as asymptotic result for training and test error (see Murata et al. [1993] and Amari and Murata [1990]). An extension of (2.3) including higher order corrections was recently obtained by Müller et al. [1995].

Let us consider the gradient descent learning rule (Amari [1967], Rumelhart et al. [1986], and many others), where the parameter $\hat{\mathbf{w}}(n)$ at the nth step is modified by

$$\hat{\mathbf{w}}(n+1) = \hat{\mathbf{w}}(n) - \varepsilon \frac{\partial R_{\text{train}}(\hat{\mathbf{w}}_n)}{\partial \mathbf{w}}, \quad (2.4)$$

and where ε is a small positive constant. This is batch learning where all the training examples are used for each iteration of modifying $\hat{\mathbf{w}}(n)$.[1] The batch process is deterministic and $\hat{\mathbf{w}}(n)$ converges to $\hat{\mathbf{w}}$, provided the initial $\mathbf{w}(0)$ is included in its basin of attraction. For large n we can argue, that $\hat{\mathbf{w}}(n)$ is approaching $\hat{\mathbf{w}}$ isotropically and the learning trajectory follows a linear ray towards $\hat{\mathbf{w}}$ (for details see Amari et al. [1995]).

3 Virtual optimal stopping rule

During learning as the parameter $\hat{\mathbf{w}}(n)$ approaches $\hat{\mathbf{w}}$, the generalization behavior of network $N\{\hat{\mathbf{w}}(n)\}$ is evaluatled by the sequence $R(n) = R\{\hat{\mathbf{w}}(n)\}, \quad n = 1, 2, \ldots$ The folklore says that $R(n)$ decreases in an early period of learning but it increases later. Therefore, there exists an optimal stopping time n at which $R(n)$ is minimized. The stopping time n_{opt} is a random variable depending on $\hat{\mathbf{w}}$ and the initial $\mathbf{w}(0)$. We now evaluate the ensemble average of $\langle R(n_{\text{opt}}) \rangle$.

The true $\mathbf{w}_0$ and the m.l.e. $\hat{\mathbf{w}}$ are in general different, and they are apart of order $1/\sqrt{t}$. Let us compose a sphere S of which the center is at $(1/2)(\mathbf{w}_0 + \hat{\mathbf{w}})$ and which passes through both $\mathbf{w}_0$ and $\hat{\mathbf{w}}$, as shown in Fig.1b. Its diameter is denoted by d, where $d^2 = |\hat{\mathbf{w}} - \mathbf{w}_0|^2$ and

$$E_0[d^2] = E_0[(\hat{\mathbf{w}} - \mathbf{w}_0)^T G^{-1}(\hat{\mathbf{w}} - \mathbf{w}_0)] = \frac{1}{t}\text{tr}(G^{-1}G) = \frac{m}{t}. \quad (3.1)$$

Let A be the ray, that is the trajectory $\hat{\mathbf{w}}(n)$ starting at $\hat{\mathbf{w}}(0)$ which is not in the neighborhood of $\mathbf{w}_0$. The optimal stopping point $\mathbf{w}^*$ that minimizes

$$R(n) = H_0 + \frac{1}{2}|\hat{\mathbf{w}}(n) - \mathbf{w}_0|^2 \quad (3.2)$$

is given by the first intersection of the ray A and the sphere S.

Since $\mathbf{w}^*$ is the point on A such that $\mathbf{w}_0 - \mathbf{w}^*$ is orthogonal to A, it lies on the sphere S (Fig.1b). When ray A' is approaching $\hat{\mathbf{w}}$ from the opposite side of $\mathbf{w}_0$ (the right-hand side in the figure), the first intersection point is $\hat{\mathbf{w}}$ itself. In this case, the optimal stopping never occurs until it converges to $\hat{\mathbf{w}}$.

Let θ be the angle between the ray A and the diameter $\mathbf{w}_0 - \hat{\mathbf{w}}$ of the sphere S. We now calculate the distribution of θ when the rays are isotropically distributed.

---

[1] We can alternatively use on-line learning, studied by Amari [1967], Heskes and Kappen [1991], and recently by Barkai et al. [1994] and Solla and Saard [1995].

Lemma 1. When ray A is approaching $\hat{\mathbf{w}}$ from the side in which $\mathbf{w}_0$ is included, the probability density of θ, $0 \le \theta \le \pi/2$, is given by

$$r(\theta) = \frac{1}{I_{m-2}} \sin^{m-2} \theta, \quad \text{where} \quad I_m = \int_0^{\pi/2} \sin^m \theta \, d\theta. \tag{3.3}$$

The detailed proof of this lemma can be found in Amari et al. [1995]. Using the density of θ given by Eq.(3.3) and we arrive at the following theorem.

Theorem 1. The average generalization error at the optimal stopping point is given by

$$\langle R(n_{\text{opt}}) \rangle = H_0 + \frac{1}{2t}(m - \frac{1}{2}). \tag{3.4}$$

Proof. When ray A is at angle θ, $0 \le \theta < \pi/2$, the optimal stopping point $\mathbf{w}^*$ is on the sphere S. It is easily shown that $|\mathbf{w}^* - \mathbf{w}_0| = d \sin \theta$. This is the case where A is from the same side as $\mathbf{w}_0$ (from the left-hand side in Fig.1b), which occurs with probability 0.5, and the average of $(d \sin \theta)^2$ is

$$E_0[(d \sin \theta)^2] = \frac{E_0[d^2]}{I_{m-2}} \int_0^{\pi/2} \sin^2 \theta \sin^{m-2} \theta \, d\theta = \frac{m}{t} \frac{I_m}{I_{m-2}} = \frac{m}{t}(1 - \frac{1}{m}).$$

When θ is $\pi/2 \le \theta \le \pi$, that is A approaches $\hat{\mathbf{w}}$ from the opposite side, it does not stop until it reaches $\hat{\mathbf{w}}$, so that $|\mathbf{w}^* - \mathbf{w}_0|^2 = |\hat{\mathbf{w}} - \mathbf{w}_0| = d^2$. This occurs with probability 0.5. Hence, we proved the theorem.

The theorem shows that, if we could know the optimal stopping time n_{opt} for each trajectory, the generalization error decreases by $1/2t$, which has an effect of decreasing the effective dimensions by $1/2$. This effect is neglegible when m is large. The optimal stopping time is of the order $\log t$. However, it is impossible to know the optimal stopping time. If we stop learning at an estimated optimal time $\hat{n}_{\text{opt}}$, we have a small gain when the ray A is from the same side as $\mathbf{w}_0$ but we have some loss when ray A is from the opposite direction. This shows that the gain is even smaller if we use a common stopping time $\bar{n}_{\text{opt}}$ independent of $\hat{\mathbf{w}}$ and $\mathbf{w}(0)$ as proposed by Wang et al. [1994]. However, the point is that there is neither direct means to estimate n_{opt} nor $\bar{n}_{\text{opt}}$ rather than for example cross-validation. Hence, we analyze cross-validation stopping in the following.

4 Optimal stopping by cross-validation

The present section studies asymptotically two fundamental problems: 1) Given t examples, how many examples should be used in the training set and how many in the testing set? 2) How much gain can one expect by the above cross-validated stopping?

Let us divide t examples into rt examples of the training set and $r't$ examples of the testing set, where $r + r' = 1$. Let $\hat{\mathbf{w}}$ be the m.l.e. from rt training examples, and let $\tilde{\mathbf{w}}$ be the m.l.e. from the other $r't$ testing examples. Since the training examples and testing examples are independent, $\hat{\mathbf{w}}$ and $\tilde{\mathbf{w}}$ are subject to independent normal distributions with mean $\mathbf{w}_0$ and covariance matrices $G^{-1}/(rt)$ and $G^{-1}/(r't)$, respectively.

Let us compose the triangle with vertices $\mathbf{w}_0$, $\hat{\mathbf{w}}$ and $\tilde{\mathbf{w}}$. The trajectory A starting at $\mathbf{w}(0)$ enters $\hat{\mathbf{w}}$ linearly in the neighborhood. The point $\mathbf{w}^*$ on the trajectory A which minimizes the testing error is the point on A that is closest to $\tilde{\mathbf{w}}$, since the testing error defined by

$$R_{\text{test}}(\mathbf{w}) = \frac{1}{r't} \sum_i \{-\log p(\mathbf{x}_i, \mathbf{y}_i; \mathbf{w})\}, \tag{4.1}$$

where summation is taken over $r't$ testing examples, can be expanded as

$$R_{\text{test}}(\mathbf{w}) = H_0 - \frac{1}{2}|\tilde{\mathbf{w}} - \mathbf{w}_0|^2 + \frac{1}{2}|\mathbf{w} - \tilde{\mathbf{w}}|^2. \tag{4.2}$$

Let S be the sphere centered at $(\hat{\mathbf{w}} + \tilde{\mathbf{w}})/2$ and passing through both $\hat{\mathbf{w}}$ and $\tilde{\mathbf{w}}$. It's diameter is given by $d = |\hat{\mathbf{w}} - \tilde{\mathbf{w}}|$. Then, the optimal stopping point $\mathbf{w}^*$ is given by the intersection of the trajectory A and sphere S. When the trajectory comes from the opposite side of $\tilde{\mathbf{w}}$, it does not intersect S until it converges to $\hat{\mathbf{w}}$, so that the optimal point is $\mathbf{w}^* = \hat{\mathbf{w}}$ in this case. Omitting the detailed proof, the generalization error of $\mathbf{w}^*$ is given by Eq.(??), so that we calculate the expectation

$$E[|\mathbf{w}^* - \mathbf{w}_0|^2] = \frac{m}{tr} - \frac{1}{2t}\left(\frac{1}{r} - \frac{1}{r'}\right).$$

Lemma 2. The average generalization error by the optimal cross-validated stopping is

$$\langle R(\mathbf{w}^*, r)\rangle = H_0 + \frac{2m-1}{4rt} + \frac{1}{4r't} \tag{4.3}$$

We can then calculate the optimal division rate

$$r_{\text{opt}} = 1 - \frac{\sqrt{2m-1}-1}{2(m-1)} \quad \text{and} \quad r_{\text{opt}} = 1 - \frac{1}{\sqrt{2m}} \quad (\text{large } m \text{ limit}). \tag{4.4}$$

of examples, which minimizes the generalization error. So for large m only $(1/\sqrt{2m}) \times 100\%$ of examples should be used for testing and all others for training. For example, when $m = 100$, this shows that 93% of examples are to be used for training and only 7% are to be kept for testing. From Eq.(4.4) we obtain as optimal generalization error for large m

$$\langle R(\mathbf{w}^*, r_{\text{opt}})\rangle = H_0 + \frac{m}{2t}\left(1 + \sqrt{\frac{2}{m}}\right). \tag{4.5}$$

This shows that the generalization error asymptotically *increases* slightly by cross-validation compared with non-stopped learning which is using *all* the examples for training.

5 Simulations

We use standard feed-forward classifier networks with N inputs, H sigmoid hidden units and M softmax outputs (classes). The output activity O_l of the lth output unit is calculated via the softmax squashing function

$$p(\mathbf{y} = C_l|\mathbf{x}; \mathbf{w}) = O_l = \frac{\exp(h_l)}{1 + \sum_k \exp(h_k)}, \quad l = 1, \cdots, M, \quad O_0 = \frac{1}{1 + \sum_k \exp(h_k)},$$

where $h_l^O = \sum_j w_{lj}^O s_j - \vartheta_l^O$ is the local field potential. Each output O_l codes the a-posteriori probability of being in class C_l, O_0 denotes a zero class for normalization purposes. The m network parameters consist of biases ϑ and weights $\mathbf{w}$. When $\mathbf{x}$ is input, the activity of the j-th hidden unit is

$$s_j = [1 + \exp(-\sum_{k=1}^{N} w_{jk}^H x_k - \vartheta_j^H)]^{-1}, \quad j = 1, \cdots, H.$$

The input layer is connected to the hidden layer via $\mathbf{w}^H$, the hidden layer is connected to the output layer via $\mathbf{w}^O$, but no short-cut connections are present. Although the network is completely deterministic, it is constructed to approximate

class conditional probabilities (Finke and Müller [1994]).
The examples $\{(\mathbf{x}_1, \mathbf{y}_1), \cdots, (\mathbf{x}_t, \mathbf{y}_t)\}$ are produced randomly, by drawing $\mathbf{x}_i$, $i = 1, \cdots, t$, from a uniform distribution independently and producing the labels $\mathbf{y}_i$ stochastically from the teacher classifier. Conjugate gradient learning with linesearch on the empirical risk function Eq.(2.1) is applied, starting from some random initial vector. The generalization ability is measured using Eq. (2.2) on a large test set (50000 patterns). Note that we use Eq. (2.1) on the cross-validation set, because only the empirical risk is available on the cross-validation set in a practical situation. We compare the generalisation error for the settings: exhaustive training (no stopping), early stopping (controlled by the cross-validation set) and optimal stopping (controlled by the large testset). The simulations were performed on a parallel computer (CM5). Every curve in the figures takes about 8h of computing time on a 128 respectively 256 partition of the CM5, i.e. we perform 128-256 parallel trials. This setting enabled us to do extensive statistics (cf. Amari et al. [1995]). Fig. 1a shows the results of simulations, where $N = 8$, $H = 8$, $M = 4$, so that the number m of modifiable parameters is $m = (N+1)H + (H+1)M = 108$. We observe clearly, that saturated learning without early stopping is the best in the asymptotic range of $t > 30m$, a range which is due to the limited size of the data sets often unaccessible in practical applications. Cross-validated early stopping does not improve the generalization error here, so that no overtraining is observed on the average in this range. In the asymptotic area (figure 1) we observe that the smaller the percentage of the training set, which is used to determine the point of early stopping, the better the performance of the generalization ability. When we use cross-validation, the optimal size of the test set is about 7% of all the examples, as the theory predicts.

Clearly, early stopping does improve the generalization ability to a large extent in an intermediate range for $t < 30m$ (see Müller et al. [1995]). Note, that our theory also gives a good estimate of the optimal size of the early stopping set in this intermediate range.

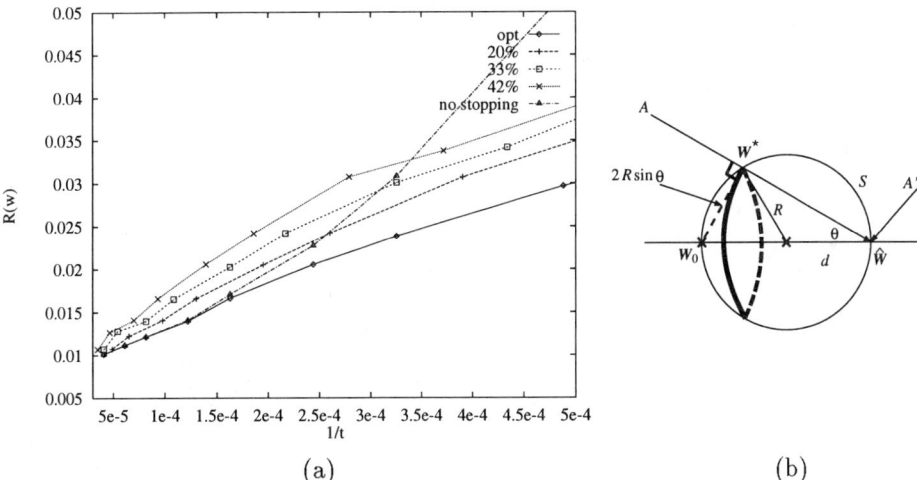

Figure 1: *(a) $R(\mathbf{w})$ plotted as a function of $1/t$ for different sizes r' of the early stopping set for an 8-8-4 classifier network. opt. denotes the use of a very large cross-validation set (50000) and no stopping adresses the case where 100% of the training set is used for exhaustive learning. (b) Geometrical picture to determine the optimal stopping point $\mathbf{w}^*$.*

6 Conclusion

We proposed an asymptotic theory for overtraining. The analysis treats realizable stochastic neural networks, trained with Kullback-Leibler loss.

It is demonstrated both theoretically and in simulations that *asymptotically* the gain in the generalization error is small if we perform early stopping, even if we have access to the optimal stopping time. For cross-validation stopping we showed for large m that optimally only $r'_{opt} = 1/\sqrt{2m}$ examples should be used to determine the point of early stopping in order to obtain the best performance. For example, if $m = 100$ this corresponds to using 93% of the t training patterns for training and only 7% for testing where to stop. Yet, even if we use r_{opt} for cross-validated stopping the generalization error is always increased comparing to exhaustive training. Nevertheless note, that this range is due to the limited size of the data sets often unaccessible in practical applications.

In the non-asymptotic region simulations show that cross-validated early stopping always helps to enhance the performance since it decreases the generalization error. In this intermediate range our theory also gives a good estimate of the optimal size of the early stopping set. In future we will consider higher order correction terms to extend our theory to give also a quantitative description of the non-asymptotic region.

Acknowledgements: We would like to thank Y. LeCun, S. Bös and K. Schulten for valuable discussions. K. -R. M. thanks K. Schulten for warm hospitality during his stay at the Beckman Inst. in Urbana, Illinois. We acknowledge computing time on the CM5 in Urbana (NCSA) and in Bonn, supported by the National Institutes of Health (P41RR0 5969) and the EC S & T fellowship (FTJ3-004, K. -R. M.).

References

Amari, S. [1967], *IEEE Trans.*, **EC-16**, 299–307.

Amari, S., Murata, N. [1993], *Neural Computation* 5, 140

Amari, S., Murata, N., Müller, K.-R., Finke, M., Yang, H. [1995], Statistical Theory of Overtraining and Overfitting, Univ. of Tokyo Tech. Report 95-06, submitted

Barkai, N. and Seung, H. S. and Sompolinski, H. [1994], On-line learning of dichotomies, NIPS'94

Finke, M. and Müller, K.-R. [1994] in Proc. of the 1993 Connectionist Models summer school, Mozer, M., Smolensky, P., Touretzky, D.S., Elman, J.L. and Weigend, A.S. (Eds.), Hillsdale, NJ: Erlenbaum Associates, 324

Hassoun, M. H. [1995], Fundamentals of Artificial Neural Networks, MIT Press.

Hecht-Nielsen, R. [1989], Neurocomputing, Addison-Wesley.

Heskes, T. and Kappen, B. [1991], *Physical Review*, **A44**, 2718–2762.

LeCun, Y., Denker, J.S., Solla, S. [1990], Optimal brain damage, NIPS'89

Moody, J. E. [1992], The effective number of parameters: An analysis of generalization and regularization in nonlinear learning systems, NIPS 4

Murata, N., Yoshizawa, S., Amari, S. [1994], *IEEE Trans.*, **NN5**, 865–872.

Müller, K.-R., Finke, M., Murata, N., Schulten, K. and Amari, S. [1995] A numerical study on learning curves in stochastic multilayer feed-forward networks, Univ. of Tokyo Tech. Report METR 95-03 and *Neural Computation* in Press

Poggio, T. and Girosi, F. [1990], *Science*, **247**, 978–982.

Rissanen, J. [1986], *Ann. Statist.*, **14**, 1080–1100.

Rumelhart, D., Hinton, G. E., Williams, R. J. [1986], in PDP, Vol.1, MIT Press.

Saad, D., Solla, S. A. [1995], *PRL*, **74**, 4337 and *Phys. Rev. E*, 52, 4225

Wang, Ch., Venkatesh, S. S., Judd, J. S. [1994], Optimal stopping and effective machine complexity in learning, to appear, (revised and extended version of NIPS'93).

A Bound on the Error of Cross Validation Using the Approximation and Estimation Rates, with Consequences for the Training-Test Split

Michael Kearns
AT&T Research

1 INTRODUCTION

We analyze the performance of cross validation [1] in the context of model selection and complexity regularization. We work in a setting in which we must choose the right number of parameters for a hypothesis function in response to a finite training sample, with the goal of minimizing the resulting generalization error. There is a large and interesting literature on cross validation methods, which often emphasizes asymptotic statistical properties, or the exact calculation of the generalization error for simple models. Our approach here is somewhat different, and is primarily inspired by two sources. The first is the work of Barron and Cover [2], who introduced the idea of bounding the error of a model selection method (in their case, the Minimum Description Length Principle) in terms of a quantity known as the *index of resolvability*. The second is the work of Vapnik [5], who provided extremely powerful and general tools for uniformly bounding the deviations between training and generalization errors.

We combine these methods to give a new and general analysis of cross validation performance. In the first and more formal part of the paper, we give a rigorous bound on the error of cross validation in terms of two parameters of the underlying model selection problem: the *approximation rate* and the *estimation rate*. In the second and more experimental part of the paper, we investigate the implications of our bound for choosing γ, the fraction of data withheld for testing in cross validation. The most interesting aspect of this analysis is the identification of several qualitative properties of the optimal γ that appear to be invariant over a wide class of model selection problems:

- When the target function complexity is small compared to the sample size, the performance of cross validation is relatively insensitive to the choice of γ.
- The importance of choosing γ optimally increases, and the optimal value for γ decreases, as the target function becomes more complex relative to the sample size.
- There is nevertheless a single *fixed* value for γ that works *nearly* optimally for a wide range of target function complexity.

2 THE FORMALISM

We consider model selection as a two-part problem: choosing the appropriate number of parameters for the hypothesis function, and tuning these parameters. The training sample is used in both steps of this process. In many settings, the tuning of the parameters is determined by a fixed learning algorithm such as backpropagation, and then model selection reduces to the problem of choosing the architecture. Here we adopt an idealized version of this division of labor. We assume a nested sequence of function classes $H_1 \subset \cdots \subset H_d \cdots$, called the *structure* [5], where H_d is a class of boolean functions of d parameters, each

---
[1]Perhaps in conflict with accepted usage in statistics, here we use the term "cross validation" to mean the simple method of saving out an independent test set to perform model selection. Precise definitions will be stated shortly.

function being a mapping from some input space X into $\{0, 1\}$. *For simplicity, in this paper we assume that the Vapnik-Chervonenkis (VC) dimension [6, 5] of the class H_d is $O(d)$.* To remove this assumption, one simply replaces all occurrences of d in our bounds by the VC dimension of H_d. We assume that we have in our possession a learning algorithm L that on input any training sample S and any value d will output a hypothesis function $h_d \in H_d$ that minimizes the training error over H_d — that is, $\epsilon_t(h_d) = \min_{h \in H_d}\{\epsilon_t(h)\}$, where $\epsilon_t(h)$ is the fraction of the examples in S on which h disagrees with the given label. In many situations, training error minimization is known to be computationally intractable, leading researchers to investigate heuristics such as backpropagation. The extent to which the theory presented here applies to such heuristics will depend in part on the extent to which they approximate training error minimization for the problem under consideration.

Model selection is thus the problem of choosing the best value of d. More precisely, we assume an arbitrary *target function f* (which may or may not reside in one of the function classes in the structure $H_1 \subset \cdots \subset H_d \cdots$), and an input distribution P; f and P together define the *generalization error* function $\epsilon_g(h) = \Pr_{x \in P}[h(x) \neq f(x)]$. We are given a training sample S of f, consisting of m random examples drawn according to P and labeled by f (with the labels possibly corrupted by a noise process that randomly complements each label independently with probability $\eta < 1/2$). The goal is to minimize the *generalization* error of the hypothesis selected.

In this paper, we will make the rather mild but very useful assumption that the structure has the property that for any sample size m, there is a value $d_{max}(m)$ such that $\epsilon_t(h_{d_{max}(m)}) = 0$ for any labeled sample S of m examples. We call the function $d_{max}(m)$ the *fitting number* of the structure. The fitting number formalizes the simple notion that with enough parameters, we can always fit the training data perfectly, a property held by most sufficiently powerful function classes (including multilayer neural networks). We typically expect the fitting number to be a linear function of m, or at worst a polynomial in m. The significance of the fitting number for us is that no reasonable model selection method should choose h_d for $d \geq d_{max}(m)$, since doing so simply adds complexity without reducing the training error.

In this paper we concentrate on the simplest version of cross validation. We choose a parameter $\gamma \in [0, 1]$, which determines the split between training and test data. Given the input sample S of m examples, let S' be the subsample consisting of the first $(1 - \gamma)m$ examples in S, and S'' the subsample consisting of the last γm examples. In cross validation, rather than giving the entire sample S to L, we give only the smaller sample S', resulting in the sequence $h_1, \ldots, h_{d_{max}((1-\gamma)m)}$ of increasingly complex hypotheses. Each hypothesis is now obtained by training on only $(1 - \gamma)m$ examples, which implies that we will only consider values of d smaller than the corresponding fitting number $d_{max}((1 - \gamma)m)$; let us introduce the shorthand d_{max}^γ for $d_{max}((1 - \gamma)m)$. Cross validation chooses the h_d satisfying $h_d = \min_{i \in \{1,\ldots,d_{max}^\gamma\}}\{\epsilon_t''(h_i)\}$ where $\epsilon_t''(h_i)$ is the error of h_i on the subsample S''. Notice that we are not considering multifold cross validation, or other variants that make more efficient use of the sample, because our analyses will require the independence of the test set. However, we believe that many of the themes that emerge here may apply to these more sophisticated variants as well.

We use $\epsilon_{cv}(m)$ to denote the generalization error $\epsilon_g(h_d)$ of the hypothesis h_d chosen by cross validation when given as input a sample S of m random examples of the target function. Obviously, $\epsilon_{cv}(m)$ depends on S, the structure, f, P, and the noise rate. *When bounding $\epsilon_{cv}(m)$, we will use the expression "with high probability" to mean with probability $1 - \delta$ over the sample S, for some small fixed constant $\delta > 0$.* All of our results can also be stated with δ as a parameter at the cost of a $\log(1/\delta)$ factor in the bounds, or in terms of the expected value of $\epsilon_{cv}(m)$.

3 THE APPROXIMATION RATE

It is apparent that any nontrivial bound on $\epsilon_{cv}(m)$ must take account of some measure of the "complexity" of the unknown target function f. The correct measure of this complexity is less obvious. Following the example of Barron and Cover's analysis of MDL performance in the context of density estimation [2], we propose the *approximation rate* as a natural measure of the complexity of f and P in relation to the chosen structure $H_1 \subset \cdots \subset H_d \cdots$. Thus we define the approximation rate function $\epsilon_g(d)$ to be $\epsilon_g(d) = \min_{h \in H_d}\{\epsilon_g(h)\}$. The function $\epsilon_g(d)$ tells us the best generalization error that can be achieved in the class H_d, and it is a nonincreasing function of d. If $\epsilon_g(s) = 0$ for some sufficiently large s, this means that the target function f, at least with respect to the input distribution, is realizable in the class H_s, and thus s is a coarse measure of how complex f is. More generally, even if $\epsilon_g(d) > 0$ for all d, the rate of decay of $\epsilon_g(d)$ still gives a nice indication of how much representational power we gain with respect to f and P by increasing the complexity of our models. Still missing, of course, is some means of determining the extent to which this representational power can be realized by training on a finite sample of a given size, but this will be added shortly. First we give examples of the approximation rate that we will examine following the general bound on $\epsilon_{cv}(m)$.

The Intervals Problem. In this problem, the input space X is the real interval $[0, 1]$, and the class H_d of the structure consists of all boolean step functions over $[0, 1]$ of at most d steps; thus, each function partitions the interval $[0, 1]$ into at most d disjoint segments (not necessarily of equal width), and assigns alternating positive and negative labels to these segments. The input space is one-dimensional, but the structure contains arbitrarily complex functions over $[0, 1]$. It is easily verified that our assumption that the VC dimension of H_d is $O(d)$ holds here, and that the fitting number obeys $d_{max}(m) \leq m$. Now suppose that the input density P is uniform, and suppose that the target function f is the function of s alternating segments of equal width $1/s$, for some s (thus, f lies in the class H_s). We will refer to these settings as the *intervals problem*. Then the approximation rate is $\epsilon_g(d) = (1/2)(1 - d/s)$ for $1 \leq d < s$ and $\epsilon_g(d) = 0$ for $d \geq s$ (see Figure 1).

The Perceptron Problem. In this problem, the input space X is $\Re^N$ for some large natural number N. The class H_d consists of all perceptrons over the N inputs in which at most d weights are nonzero. If the input density is spherically symmetric (for instance, the uniform density on the unit ball in $\Re^N$), and the target function is the function in H_s with all s nonzero weights equal to 1, then it can be shown that the approximation rate is $\epsilon_g(d) = (1/\pi)\cos^{-1}(\sqrt{d/s})$ for $d < s$ [4], and of course $\epsilon_g(d) = 0$ for $d \geq s$ (see Figure 1).

Power Law Decay. In addition to the specific examples just given, we would also like to study reasonably natural parametric forms of $\epsilon_g(d)$, to determine the sensitivity of our theory to a plausible range of behaviors for the approximation rate. This is important, because in practice we do not expect to have precise knowledge of $\epsilon_g(d)$, since it depends on the target function and input distribution. Following the work of Barron [1], who shows a c/d bound on $\epsilon_g(d)$ for the case of neural networks with one hidden layer under a squared error generalization measure (where c is a measure of target function complexity in terms of a Fourier transform integrability condition) [2], we can consider approximation rates of the form $\epsilon_g(d) = (c/d)^\alpha + \epsilon_{min}$, where $\epsilon_{min} \geq 0$ is a parameter representing the "degree of unrealizability" of f with respect to the structure, and $c, \alpha > 0$ are parameters capturing the rate of decay to ϵ_{min} (see Figure 1).

4 THE ESTIMATION RATE

For a fixed f, P and $H_1 \subset \cdots \subset H_d \cdots$, we say that a function $\rho(d, m)$ is an *estimation rate bound* if for all d and m, with high probability over the sample S we have $|\epsilon_t(h_d) - \epsilon_g(h_d)| \leq \rho(d, m)$, where as usual h_d is the result of training error minimization on S within H_d. Thus $\rho(d, m)$ simply bounds the deviation between the training error and the generalization error of h_d. Note that the best such bound may depend in a complicated way on all of the elements of the problem: f, P and the structure. Indeed, much of the recent work on the statistical physics theory of learning curves has documented the wide variety of behaviors that such deviations may assume [4, 3]. However, for many natural problems

---

[2] Since the bounds we will give have straightforward generalizations to real-valued function learning under squared error, examining behavior for $\epsilon_g(d)$ in this setting seems reasonable.

it is both convenient and accurate to rely on a *universal* estimation rate bound provided by the powerful theory of uniform convergence: Namely, for any f, P and any structure, the function $\rho(d,m) = \sqrt{(d/m)\log(m/d)}$ is an estimation rate bound [5]. Depending upon the details of the problem, it is sometimes appropriate to omit the $\log(m/d)$ factor, and often appropriate to refine the $\sqrt{d/m}$ behavior to a function that interpolates smoothly between d/m behavior for small ϵ_t to $\sqrt{d/m}$ for large ϵ_t. Although such refinements are both interesting and important, many of the qualitative claims and predictions we will make are invariant to them as long as the deviation $|\epsilon_t(h_d) - \epsilon_g(h_d)|$ is well-approximated by a power law $(d/m)^\alpha$ ($\alpha > 0$); it will be more important to recognize and model the cases in which power law behavior is grossly violated.

Note that this universal estimation rate bound holds only under the assumption that the training sample is noise-free, but straightforward generalizations exist. For instance, if the training data is corrupted by random label noise at rate $0 \leq \eta < 1/2$, then $\rho(d,m) = \sqrt{(d/(1-2\eta)^2 m)\log(m/d)}$ is again a universal estimation rate bound.

5   THE BOUND

Theorem 1 *Let $H_1 \subset \cdots \subset H_d \cdots$ be any structure, where the VC dimension of H_d is $O(d)$. Let f and P be any target function and input distribution, let $\epsilon_g(d)$ be the approximation rate function for the structure with respect to f and P, and let $\rho(d,m)$ be an estimation rate bound for the structure with respect to f and P. Then for any m, with high probability*

$$\epsilon_{cv}(m) \leq \min_{1 \leq d \leq d_{max}^\gamma} \{\epsilon_g(d) + \rho(d, (1-\gamma)m)\} + O\left(\sqrt{\frac{\log(d_{max}^\gamma)}{\gamma m}}\right) \quad (1)$$

where γ is the fraction of the training sample used for testing, and d_{max}^γ is the fitting number $d_{max}((1-\gamma)m)$. Using the universal estimation bound rate and the rather weak assumption that $d_{max}(m)$ is polynomial in m, we obtain that with high probability

$$\epsilon_{cv}(m) \leq \min_{1 \leq d \leq d_{max}^\gamma} \left\{\epsilon_g(d) + O\left(\sqrt{\frac{d}{(1-\gamma)m}\log\left(\frac{m}{d}\right)}\right)\right\} + O\left(\sqrt{\frac{\log((1-\gamma)m)}{\gamma m}}\right). \quad (2)$$

Straightforward generalizations of these bounds for the case where the data is corrupted by classification noise can be obtained, using the modified estimation rate bound given in Section 4 [3].

We delay the proof of this theorem to the full paper due to space considerations. However, the central idea is to appeal twice to uniform convergence arguments: once within each class H_d to bound the generalization error of the resulting training error minimizer $h_d \in H_d$, and a second time to bound the generalization error of the h_d minimizing the error on the test set of γm examples.

In the bounds given by (1) and (2), the $\min\{\cdot\}$ expression is analogous to Barron and Cover's index of resolvability [2]; the final term in the bounds represents the error introduced by the testing phase of cross validation. These bounds exhibit tradeoff behavior with respect to the parameter γ: as we let γ approach 0, we are devoting more of the sample to training the h_d, and the estimation rate bound term $\rho(d, (1-\gamma)m)$ is decreasing. However, the test error term $O(\sqrt{\log(d_{max}^\gamma)/(\gamma m)})$ is increasing, since we have less data to accurately estimate the $\epsilon_g(h_d)$. The reverse phenomenon occurs as we let γ approach 1.

While we believe Theorem 1 to be enlightening and potentially useful in its own right, we would now like to take its interpretation a step further. More precisely, suppose we

---
[3] The main effect of classification noise at rate η is the replacement of occurrences in the bound of the sample size m by the smaller "effective" sample size $(1-\eta)^2 m$.

assume that the bound is an approximation to the actual behavior of $\epsilon_{cv}(m)$. Then in principle we can optimize the bound to obtain the best value for γ. Of course, in addition to the assumptions involved (the main one being that $\rho(d, m)$ is a good approximation to the training-generalization error deviations of the h_d), this analysis can only be carried out given information that we should not expect to have in practice (at least in exact form) — in particular, the approximation rate function $\epsilon_g(d)$, which depends on f and P. However, we argue in the coming sections that several interesting qualitative phenomena regarding the choice of γ are largely invariant to a wide range of natural behaviors for $\epsilon_g(d)$.

6 A CASE STUDY: THE INTERVALS PROBLEM

We begin by performing the suggested optimization of γ for the intervals problem. Recall that the approximation rate here is $\epsilon_g(d) = (1/2)(1 - d/s)$ for $d < s$ and $\epsilon_g(d) = 0$ for $d \geq s$, where s is the complexity of the target function. Here we analyze the behavior obtained by assuming that the estimation rate $\rho(d, m)$ actually behaves as $\rho(d, m) = \sqrt{d/(1 - \gamma)m}$ (so we are omitting the log factor from the universal bound), and to simplify the formal analysis a bit (but without changing the qualitative behavior) we replace the term $\sqrt{\log((1 - \gamma)m)/(\gamma m)}$ by the weaker $\sqrt{\log(m)/m}$. Thus, if we define the function $F(d, m, \gamma) = \epsilon_g(d) + \sqrt{d/(1 - \gamma)m} + \sqrt{\log(m)/(\gamma m)}$ then following Equation (1), we are approximating $\epsilon_{cv}(m)$ by $\epsilon_{cv}(m) \approx \min_{1 \leq d \leq d_{max}^{\gamma}}\{F(d, m, \gamma)\}$ [4].

The first step of the analysis is to fix a value for γ and differentiate $F(d, m, \gamma)$ with respect to d to discover the minimizing value of d; the second step is to differentiate with respect to γ. It can be shown (details omitted) that the optimal choice of γ under the assumptions is $\gamma_{opt} = (\log(m)/s)^{1/3}/(1 + (\log(m)/s)^{1/3})$. It is important to remember at this point that despite the fact that we have derived a precise expression for γ_{opt}, due to the assumptions and approximations we have made in the various constants, any quantitative interpretation of this expression is meaningless. However, we can reasonably expect that this expression captures the qualitative way in which the optimal γ changes as the amount of data m changes in relation to the target function complexity s. On this score the situation initially appears rather bleak, as the function $(\log(m)/s)^{1/3}/(1 + (\log(m)/s)^{1/3})$ is quite sensitive to the ratio $\log(m)/s$, which is something we do not expect to have the luxury of knowing in practice. However, it is both fortunate and interesting that γ_{opt} does not tell the entire story. In Figure 2, we plot the function $F(s, m, \gamma)$ as a function of γ for $m = 10000$ and for several different values of s (note that for consistency with the later experimental plots, the x axis of the plot is actually the training fraction $1 - \gamma$). Here we can observe four important qualitative phenomena, which we list in order of increasing subtlety: (A) When s is small compared to m, the predicted error is relatively insensitive to the choice of γ: as a function of γ, $F(s, m, \gamma)$ has a wide, flat bowl, indicating a wide range of γ yielding essentially the same near-optimal error. (B) As s becomes larger in comparison to the fixed sample size m, the relative superiority of γ_{opt} over other values for γ becomes more pronounced. In particular, large values for γ become progressively worse as s increases. For example, the plots indicate that for $s = 10$ (again, $m = 10000$), even though $\gamma_{opt} = 0.524 \cdots$ the choice $\gamma = 0.75$ will result in error quite near that achieved using γ_{opt}. However, for $s = 500$, $\gamma = 0.75$ is predicted to yield greatly suboptimal error. Note that for very large s, the bound predicts vacuously large error for all values of γ, so that the choice of γ again becomes irrelevant. (C) Because of the insensitivity to γ for s small compared to m, there is a *fixed* value of γ which seems to yield reasonably good performance for a wide range of values for s. This value is essentially the value of γ_{opt} for the case where s is large but nontrivial generalization is still possible, since choosing the best value for γ is more important there than for the small s case. (D) The value of γ_{opt} is decreasing as s increases. This is slightly difficult to confirm from the plot, but can be seen clearly from the precise expression for γ_{opt}.

---

[4] Although there are hidden constants in the $O(\cdot)$ notation of the bounds, it is the *relative* weights of the estimation and test error terms that is important, and choosing both constants equal to 1 is a reasonable choice (since both terms have the same Chernoff bound origins).

In Figure 3, we plot the results of experiments in which labeled random samples of size $m = 5000$ were generated for a target function of s equal width intervals, for $s = 10, 100$ and 500. The samples were corrupted by random label noise at rate $\eta = 0.3$. For each value of γ and each value of d, $(1 - \gamma)m$ of the sample was given to a program performing training error minimization within H_d; the remaining γm examples were used to select the best h_d according to cross validation. The plots show the true generalization error of the h_d selected by cross validation as a function of γ (the generalization error can be computed exactly for this problem). Each point in the plots represents an average over 10 trials.

While there are obvious and significant quantitative differences between these experimental plots and the theoretical predictions of Figure 2, the properties (A), (B) and (C) are rather clearly borne out by the data: (A) In Figure 3, when s is small compared to m, there is a wide range of acceptable γ; it appears that any choice of γ between 0.10 and 0.50 yields nearly optimal generalization error. (B) By the time $s = 100$, the sensitivity to γ is considerably more pronounced. For example, the choice $\gamma = 0.50$ now results in clearly suboptimal performance, and it is more important to have γ close to 0.10. (C) Despite these complexities, there does indeed appear to be single value of γ — approximately 0.10 — that performs nearly optimally for the entire range of s examined.

The property (D) — namely, that the optimal γ decreases as the target function complexity is increased relative to a fixed m — is certainly not refuted by the experimental results, but any such effect is simply too small to be verified. It would be interesting to verify this prediction experimentally, perhaps on a different problem where the predicted effect is more pronounced.

7 CONCLUSIONS

For the cases where the approximation rate $\epsilon_g(d)$ obeys either power law decay or is that derived for the perceptron problem discussed in Section 3, the behavior of $\epsilon_{cv}(m)$ as a function of γ predicted by our theory is largely the same (for example, see Figure 4). In the full paper, we describe some more realistic experiments in which cross validation is used to determine the number of backpropagation training epochs. Figures similar to Figures 2 through 4 are obtained, again in rough accordance with the theory.

In summary, our theory predicts that although significant quantitative differences in the behavior of cross validation may arise for different model selection problems, the properties (A), (B), (C) and (D) should be present in a wide range of problems. At the very least, the behavior of our *bounds* exhibits these properties for a wide range of problems. It would be interesting to try to identify natural problems for which one or more of these properties is strongly violated; a potential source for such problems may be those for which the underlying learning curve deviates from classical power law behavior [4, 3].

Acknowledgements: I give warm thanks to Yishay Mansour, Andrew Ng and Dana Ron for many enlightening conversations on cross validation and model selection. Additional thanks to Andrew Ng for his help in conducting the experiments.

References

[1] A. Barron. Universal approximation bounds for superpositions of a sigmoidal function. *IEEE Transactions on Information Theory*, 19:930–944, 1991.

[2] A. R. Barron and T. M. Cover. Minimum complexity density estimation. *IEEE Transactions on Information Theory*, 37:1034–1054, 1991.

[3] D. Haussler, M. Kearns, H.S. Seung, and N. Tishby. Rigourous learning curve bounds from statistical mechanics. In *Proceedings of the Seventh Annual ACM Confernce on Computational Learning Theory*, pages 76–87, 1994.

[4] H. S. Seung, H. Sompolinsky, and N. Tishby. Statistical mechanics of learning from examples. *Physical Review*, A45:6056–6091, 1992.

[5] V. N. Vapnik. *Estimation of Dependences Based on Empirical Data*. Springer-Verlag, New York, 1982.

[6] V. N. Vapnik and A. Y. Chervonenkis. On the uniform convergence of relative frequencies of events to their probabilities. *Theory of Probability and its Applications*, 16(2):264–280, 1971.

A Bound on the Error of Cross Validation

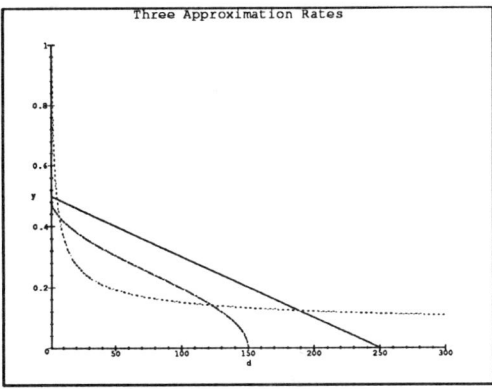

Figure 1: Plots of three approximation rates: for the intervals problem with target complexity $s = 250$ intervals (linear plot intersecting d-axis at 250), for the perceptron problem with target complexity $s = 150$ nonzero weights (nonlinear plot intersecting d-axis at 150), and for power law decay asymptoting at $\epsilon_{min} = 0.05$.

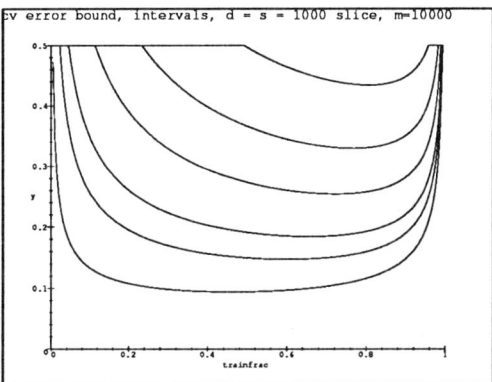

Figure 2: Plot of the predicted generalization error of cross validation for the intervals model selection problem, as a function of the fraction $1 - \gamma$ of data used for training. (In the plot, the fraction of training data is 0 on the left ($\gamma = 1$) and 1 on the right ($\gamma = 0$)). The fixed sample size $m = 10,000$ was used, and the 6 plots show the error predicted by the theory for target function complexity values $s = 10$ (bottom plot), 50, 100, 250, 500, and 1000 (top plot).

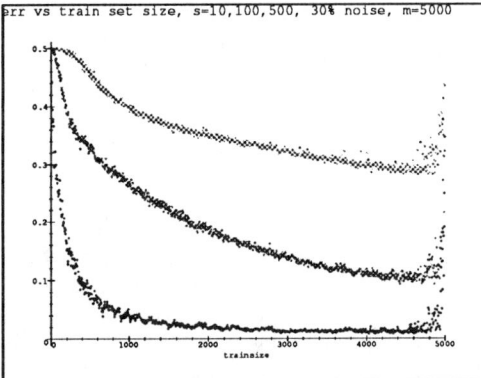

Figure 3: Experimental plots of cross validation generalization error in the intervals problem as a function of training set size $(1-\gamma)m$. Experiments with the three target complexity values $s = 10, 100$ and 500 (bottom plot to top plot) are shown. Each point represents performance averaged over 10 trials.

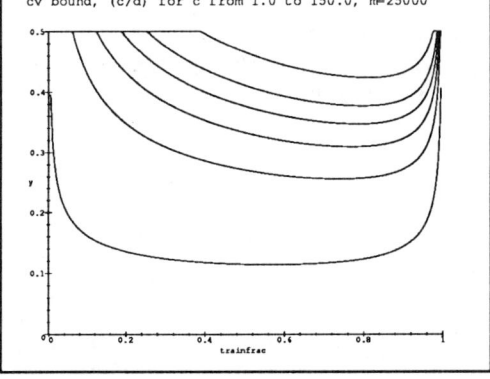

Figure 4: Plot of the predicted generalization error of cross validation for the power law case $\epsilon_g(d) = (c/d)$, as a function of the fraction $1-\gamma$ of data used for training. The fixed sample size $m = 25,000$ was used, and the 6 plots show the error predicted by the theory for target function complexity values $c = 1$ (bottom plot), 25, 50, 75, 100, and 150 (top plot).

Learning with ensembles: How over-fitting can be useful

Peter Sollich
Department of Physics
University of Edinburgh, U.K.
P.Sollich@ed.ac.uk

Anders Krogh[*]
NORDITA, Blegdamsvej 17
2100 Copenhagen, Denmark
krogh@sanger.ac.uk

Abstract

We study the characteristics of learning with ensembles. Solving exactly the simple model of an ensemble of linear students, we find surprisingly rich behaviour. For learning in large ensembles, it is advantageous to use under-regularized students, which actually over-fit the training data. Globally optimal performance can be obtained by choosing the training set sizes of the students appropriately. For smaller ensembles, optimization of the ensemble weights can yield significant improvements in ensemble generalization performance, in particular if the individual students are subject to noise in the training process. Choosing students with a wide range of regularization parameters makes this improvement robust against changes in the unknown level of noise in the training data.

1 INTRODUCTION

An ensemble is a collection of a (finite) number of neural networks or other types of predictors that are trained for the same task. A combination of many different predictors can often improve predictions, and in statistics this idea has been investigated extensively, see *e.g.* [1, 2, 3]. In the neural networks community, ensembles of neural networks have been investigated by several groups, see for instance [4, 5, 6, 7]. Usually the networks in the ensemble are trained independently and then their predictions are combined.

In this paper we study an ensemble of linear networks trained on different but overlapping training sets. The limit in which all the networks are trained on the full data set and the one where all the data sets are different has been treated in [8]. In this paper we treat the case of intermediate training set sizes and overlaps

---

[*]Present address: The Sanger Centre, Hinxton, Cambs CB10 1RQ, UK.

2 GENERAL FEATURES OF ENSEMBLE LEARNING

We consider the task of approximating a target function f_0 from R^N to R. It will be assumed that we can only obtain noisy samples of the function, and the (now stochastic) target function will be denoted $y(\mathbf{x})$. The inputs $\mathbf{x}$ are taken to be drawn from some distribution $P(\mathbf{x})$. Assume now that an ensemble of K independent predictors $f_k(\mathbf{x})$ of $y(\mathbf{x})$ is available. A weighted ensemble average is denoted by a bar, like

$$\overline{f}(\mathbf{x}) = \sum_k w_k f_k(\mathbf{x}), \tag{1}$$

which is the final output of the ensemble. One can think of the weight w_k as the belief in predictor k and we therefore constrain the weights to be positive and sum to one. For an input $\mathbf{x}$ we define the error of the ensemble $\epsilon(\mathbf{x})$, the error of the kth predictor $\epsilon_k(\mathbf{x})$, and its *ambiguity* $a_k(\mathbf{x})$

$$\epsilon(\mathbf{x}) = (y(\mathbf{x}) - \overline{f}(\mathbf{x}))^2 \tag{2}$$
$$\epsilon_k(\mathbf{x}) = (y(\mathbf{x}) - f_k(\mathbf{x}))^2 \tag{3}$$
$$a_k(\mathbf{x}) = (f_k(\mathbf{x}) - \overline{f}(\mathbf{x}))^2. \tag{4}$$

The ensemble error can be written as $\epsilon(\mathbf{x}) = \overline{\epsilon}(\mathbf{x}) - \overline{a}(\mathbf{x})$ [7], where $\overline{\epsilon}(\mathbf{x}) = \sum_k w_k \epsilon_k(\mathbf{x})$ is the average error over the individual predictors and $\overline{a}(\mathbf{x}) = \sum_k w_k a_k(\mathbf{x})$ is the average of their ambiguities, which is the variance of the output over the ensemble. By averaging over the input distribution $P(\mathbf{x})$ (and implicitly over the target outputs $y(\mathbf{x})$), one obtains the ensemble *generalization error*

$$\epsilon = \overline{\epsilon} - \overline{a} \tag{5}$$

where $\epsilon(\mathbf{x})$ averaged over $P(\mathbf{x})$ is simply denoted ϵ, and similarly for $\overline{\epsilon}$ and $\overline{a}$. The first term on the right is the weighted average of the generalization errors of the individual predictors, and the second is the weighted average of the ambiguities, which we refer to as the ensemble ambiguity. An important feature of equation (5) is that it separates the generalization error into a term that depends on the generalization errors of the individual students and another term that contains *all correlations* between the students. The latter can be estimated entirely from *unlabeled data*, i.e., without any knowledge of the target function to be approximated. The relation (5) also shows that the more the predictors differ, the lower the error will be, provided the individual errors remain constant.

In this paper we assume that the predictors are trained on a sample of p examples of the target function, $(\mathbf{x}^\mu, y^\mu)$, where $y^\mu = f_0(\mathbf{x}^\mu) + \eta^\mu$ and η^μ is some additive noise ($\mu = 1, \ldots, p$). The predictors, to which we refer as students in this context because they learn the target function from the training examples, need not be trained on all the available data. In fact, since training on different data sets will generally increase the ambiguity, it is possible that training on subsets of the data will *improve* generalization. An additional advantage is that, by holding out for each student a different part of the total data set for the purpose of testing, one can use the whole data set for training the ensemble while still getting an unbiased estimate of the ensemble generalization error. Denoting this estimate by $\hat{\epsilon}$, one has

$$\hat{\epsilon} = \overline{\epsilon_{\text{test}}} - \hat{\overline{a}} \tag{6}$$

where $\overline{\epsilon_{\text{test}}} = \sum_k w_k \epsilon_{\text{test},k}$ is the average of the students' test errors. As already pointed out, the estimate $\hat{\overline{a}}$ of the ensemble ambiguity can be found from unlabeled data.

So far, we have not mentioned how to find the weights ω_k. Often uniform weights are used, but optimization of the weights in some way is tempting. In [5, 6] the training set was used to perform the optimization, *i.e.*, the weights were chosen to minimize the ensemble training error. This can easily lead to over-fitting, and in [7] it was suggested to minimize the estimated generalization error (6) instead. If this is done, the estimate (6) acquires a bias; intuitively, however, we expect this effect to be small for large ensembles.

3 ENSEMBLES OF LINEAR STUDENTS

In preparation for our analysis of learning with ensembles of linear students we now briefly review the case of a single linear student, sometimes referred to as 'linear perceptron learning'. A linear student implements the input-output mapping

$$f(\mathbf{x}) = \frac{1}{\sqrt{N}}\mathbf{w}^T\mathbf{x}$$

parameterized in terms of an N-dimensional parameter vector $\mathbf{w}$ with real components; the scaling factor $1/\sqrt{N}$ is introduced here for convenience, and $\ldots^T$ denotes the transpose of a vector. The student parameter vector $\mathbf{w}$ should not be confused with the ensemble weights ω_k. The most common method for training such a linear student (or parametric inference models in general) is minimization of the sum-of-squares training error

$$E = \sum_\mu (y^\mu - f(\mathbf{x}^\mu))^2 + \lambda \mathbf{w}^2$$

where $\mu = 1, \ldots, p$ numbers the training examples. To prevent the student from fitting noise in the training data, a weight decay term $\lambda \mathbf{w}^2$ has been added. The size of the weight decay parameter λ determines how strongly large parameter vectors are penalized; large λ corresponds to a stronger *regularization* of the student.

For a linear student, the global minimum of E can easily be found. However, in practical applications using non-linear networks, this is generally not true, and training can be thought of as a stochastic process yielding a different solution each time. We crudely model this by considering white noise added to gradient descent updates of the parameter vector $\mathbf{w}$. This yields a limiting distribution of parameter vectors $P(\mathbf{w}) \propto \exp(-E/2T)$, where the 'temperature' T measures the amount of noise in the training process.

We focus our analysis on the 'thermodynamic limit' $N \to \infty$ at constant normalized number of training examples, $\alpha = p/N$. In this limit, quantities such as the training or generalization error become self-averaging, *i.e.*, their averages over all training sets become identical to their typical values for a particular training set. Assume now that the training inputs $\mathbf{x}^\mu$ are chosen randomly and independently from a Gaussian distribution $P(\mathbf{x}) \propto \exp(-\frac{1}{2}\mathbf{x}^2)$, and that training outputs are generated by a linear target function corrupted by additive noise, *i.e.*, $y^\mu = \mathbf{w}_0^T\mathbf{x}^\mu/\sqrt{N} + \eta^\mu$, where the η^μ are zero mean noise variables with variance σ^2. Fixing the length of the parameter vector of the target function to $\mathbf{w}_0^2 = N$ for simplicity, the generalization error of a linear student with weight decay λ and learning noise T becomes [9]

$$\epsilon = (\sigma^2 + T)G + \lambda(\sigma^2 - \lambda)\frac{\partial G}{\partial \lambda}. \tag{7}$$

On the r.h.s. of this equation we have dropped the term arising from the noise on the target function alone, which is simply σ^2, and we shall follow this convention throughout. The 'response function' G is [10, 11]

$$G = G(\alpha, \lambda) = (1 - \alpha - \lambda + \sqrt{(1 - \alpha - \lambda)^2 + 4\lambda})/2\lambda. \tag{8}$$

Learning with Ensembles: How Overfitting Can Be Useful

For zero training noise, $T = 0$, and for any α, the generalization error (7) is minimized when the weight decay is set to $\lambda = \sigma^2$; its value is then $\sigma^2 G(\alpha, \sigma^2)$, which is the minimum achievable generalization error [9].

3.1 ENSEMBLE GENERALIZATION ERROR

We now consider an ensemble of K linear students with weight decays λ_k and learning noises T_k ($k = 1\ldots K$). Each student has an ensemble weight w_k and is trained on $N\alpha_k$ training examples, with students k and l sharing $N\alpha_{kl}$ training examples (of course, $\alpha_{kk} = \alpha_k$). As above, we consider noisy training data generated by a linear target function. The resulting ensemble generalization error can be calculated by diagrammatic [10] or response function [11] methods. We refer the reader to a forthcoming publication for details and only state the result:

$$\epsilon = \sum_{kl} w_k w_l \epsilon_{kl} \tag{9}$$

where

$$\epsilon_{kl} = \frac{\rho_k \rho_l + \sigma^2 (1 - \rho_k)(1 - \rho_l)\alpha_{kl}/(\alpha_k \alpha_l)}{1 - (1 - \rho_k)(1 - \rho_l)\alpha_{kl}/(\alpha_k \alpha_l)} + \frac{T_k}{\lambda_k} \rho_k \delta_{kl}. \tag{10}$$

Here ρ_k is defined as $\rho_k = \lambda_k G(\alpha_k, \lambda_k)$. The Kronecker delta in the last term of (10) arises because the training noises of different students are uncorrelated. The generalization errors and ambiguities of the individual students are

$$\epsilon_k = \epsilon_{kk} \qquad a_k = \epsilon_{kk} - 2\sum_l w_l \epsilon_{kl} + \sum_{lm} w_l w_m \epsilon_{lm};$$

the result for the ϵ_k can be shown to agree with the single student result (7). In the following sections, we shall explore the consequences of the general result (9). We will concentrate on the case where the training set of each student is sampled randomly from the total available data set of size $N\alpha$. For the overlap of the training sets of students k and l ($k \neq l$) one then has $\alpha_{kl}/\alpha = (\alpha_k/\alpha)(\alpha_l/\alpha)$ and hence

$$\alpha_{kl} = \alpha_k \alpha_l / \alpha \tag{11}$$

up to fluctuations which vanish in the thermodynamic limit. For finite ensembles one can construct training sets for which $\alpha_{kl} < \alpha_k \alpha_l / \alpha$. This is an advantage, because it results in a smaller generalization error, but for simplicity we use (11).

4 LARGE ENSEMBLE LIMIT

We now use our main result (9) to analyse the generalization performance of an ensemble with a large number K of students, in particular when the size of the training sets for the individual students are chosen optimally. If the ensemble weights w_k are approximately uniform ($w_k \approx 1/K$) the off-diagonal elements of the matrix (ϵ_{kl}) dominate the generalization error for large K, and the contributions from the training noises T_k are suppressed. For the special case where all students are identical and are trained on training sets of identical size, $\alpha_k = (1 - c)\alpha$, the ensemble generalization error is shown in Figure 1(left). The minimum at a nonzero value of c, which is the fraction of the total data set held out for testing each student, can clearly be seen. This confirms our intuition: when the students are trained on smaller, less overlapping training sets, the increase in error of the individual students can be more than offset by the corresponding increase in ambiguity.

The optimal training set sizes α_k can be calculated analytically:

$$c_k \equiv 1 - \alpha_k/\alpha = \frac{1 - \lambda_k/\sigma^2}{1 + G(\alpha, \sigma^2)}. \tag{12}$$

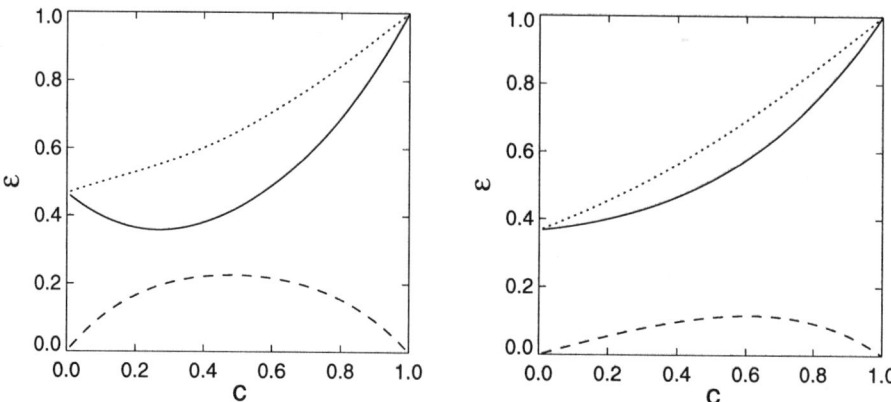

Figure 1: Generalization error and ambiguity for an infinite ensemble of identical students. Solid line: ensemble generalization error, ϵ; dotted line: average generalization error of the individual students, $\bar{\epsilon}$; dashed line: ensemble ambiguity, $\bar{a}$. For both plots $\alpha = 1$ and $\sigma^2 = 0.2$. The left plot corresponds to under-regularized students with $\lambda = 0.05 < \sigma^2$. Here the generalization error of the ensemble has a minimum at a nonzero value of c. This minimum exists whenever $\lambda < \sigma^2$. The right plot shows the case of over-regularized students ($\lambda = 0.3 > \sigma^2$), where the generalization error is minimal at $c = 0$.

The resulting generalization error is $\epsilon = \sigma^2 G(\alpha, \sigma^2) + O(1/K)$, which is the globally minimal generalization error that can be obtained using all available training data, as explained in Section 3. Thus, *a large ensemble with optimally chosen training set sizes can achieve globally optimal generalization performance.* However, we see from (12) that a valid solution $c_k > 0$ exists only for $\lambda_k < \sigma^2$, i.e., if the ensemble is under-regularized. This is exemplified, again for an ensemble of identical students, in Figure 1(right), which shows that for an over-regularized ensemble the generalization error is a monotonic function of c and thus minimal at $c = 0$.

We conclude this section by discussing how the adaptation of the training set sizes could be performed in practice, for simplicity confining ourselves to an ensemble of identical students, where only one parameter $c = c_k = 1 - \alpha_k/\alpha$ has to be adapted. If the ensemble is under-regularized one expects a minimum of the generalization error for some nonzero c as in Figure 1. One could, therefore, start by training all students on a large fraction of the total data set (corresponding to $c \approx 0$), and then gradually and randomly remove training examples from the students' training sets. Using (6), the generalization error of each student could be estimated by their performance on the examples on which they were not trained, and one would stop removing training examples when the estimate stops decreasing. The resulting estimate of the generalization error will be slightly biased; however, for a large enough ensemble the risk of a strongly biased estimate from systematically testing all students on too 'easy' training examples seems small, due to the random selection of examples.

5 REALISTIC ENSEMBLE SIZES

We now discuss some effects that occur in learning with ensembles of 'realistic' sizes. In an over-regularized ensemble nothing can be gained by making the students more diverse by training them on smaller, less overlapping training sets. One would also

Learning with Ensembles: How Overfitting Can Be Useful

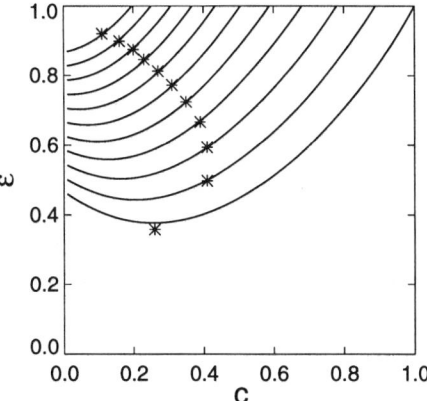

Figure 2: The generalization error of an ensemble with 10 identical students as a function of the test set fraction c. From bottom to top the curves correspond to training noise $T = 0, 0.1, 0.2, \ldots, 1.0$. The star on each curve shows the error of the optimal single perceptron (i.e., with optimal weight decay for the given T) trained on all examples, which is independent of c. The parameters for this example are: $\alpha = 1$, $\lambda = 0.05$, $\sigma^2 = 0.2$.

expect this kind of 'diversification' to be unnecessary or even counterproductive when the training noise is high enough to provide sufficient 'inherent' diversity of students. In the large ensemble limit, we saw that this effect is suppressed, but it does indeed occur in finite ensembles. Figure 2 shows the dependence of the generalization error on c for an ensemble of 10 identical, under-regularized students with identical training noises $T_k = T$. For small T, the minimum of ϵ at nonzero c persists. For larger T, ϵ is monotonically increasing with c, implying that further diversification of students beyond that caused by the learning noise is wasteful. The plot also shows the performance of the optimal single student (with λ chosen to minimize the generalization error at the given T), demonstrating that the ensemble can perform significantly better by effectively averaging out learning noise.

For realistic ensemble sizes the presence of learning noise generally reduces the potential for performance improvement by choosing optimal *training set sizes*. In such cases one can still adapt the *ensemble weights* to optimize performance, again on the basis of the estimate of the ensemble generalization error (6). An example is

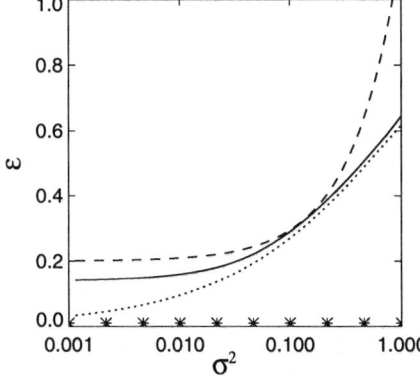
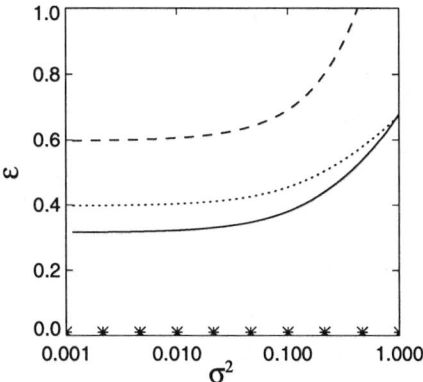

Figure 3: The generalization error of an ensemble of 10 students with different weight decays (marked by stars on the σ^2-axis) as a function of the noise level σ^2. Left: training noise $T = 0$; right: $T = 0.1$. The dashed lines are for the ensemble with uniform weights, and the solid line is for optimized ensemble weights. The dotted lines are for the optimal single perceptron trained on all data. The parameters for this example are: $\alpha = 1$, $c = 0.2$.

shown in Figure 3 for an ensemble of size $K = 10$ with the weight decays λ_k equally spaced on a logarithmic axis between 10^{-3} and 1. For both of the temperatures T shown, the ensemble with uniform weights performs worse than the optimal single student. With weight optimization, the generalization performance approaches that of the optimal single student for $T = 0$, and is actually better at $T = 0.1$ over the whole range of noise levels σ^2 shown. Even the best single student from the ensemble can never perform better than the optimal single student, so combining the student outputs in a weighted ensemble average is superior to simply choosing the best member of the ensemble by cross-validation, *i.e.*, on the basis of its estimated generalization error. The reason is that the ensemble average suppresses the learning noise on the individual students.

6 CONCLUSIONS

We have studied ensemble learning in the simple, analytically solvable scenario of an ensemble of linear students. Our main findings are: In large ensembles, one should use under-regularized students in order to maximize the benefits of the variance-reducing effects of ensemble learning. In this way, the globally optimal generalization error on the basis of *all* the available data can be reached by optimizing the training set sizes of the individual students. At the same time an estimate of the generalization error can be obtained. For ensembles of more realistic size, we found that for students subjected to a large amount of noise in the training process it is unnecessary to increase the diversity of students by training them on smaller, less overlapping training sets. In this case, optimizing the ensemble weights can still yield substantially better generalization performance than an optimally chosen single student trained on all data with the same amount of training noise. This improvement is most insensitive to changes in the unknown noise levels σ^2 if the weight decays of the individual students cover a wide range. We expect most of these conclusions to carry over, at least qualitatively, to ensemble learning with nonlinear models, and this correlates well with experimental results presented in [7].

References

[1] C. Granger, Journal of Forecasting **8**, 231 (1989).
[2] D. Wolpert, Neural Networks **5**, 241 (1992).
[3] L. Breimann, Tutorial at *NIPS 7* and personal communication.
[4] L. Hansen and P. Salamon, IEEE Trans. Pattern Anal. and Mach. Intell. **12**, 993 (1990).
[5] M. P. Perrone and L. N. Cooper, in *Neural Networks for Speech and Image processing*, ed. R. J. Mammone (Chapman-Hall, 1993).
[6] S. Hashem: Optimal Linear Combinations of Neural Networks. Tech. Rep. PNL-SA-25166, submitted to Neural Networks (1995).
[7] A. Krogh and J. Vedelsby, in *NIPS 7*, ed. G. Tesauro *et al.*, p. 231 (MIT Press, 1995).
[8] R. Meir, in *NIPS 7*, ed. G. Tesauro *et al.*, p. 295 (MIT Press, 1995).
[9] A. Krogh and J. A. Hertz, J. Phys. A **25**, 1135 (1992).
[10] J. A. Hertz, A. Krogh, and G. I. Thorbergsson, J. Phys. A **22**, 2133 (1989).
[11] P. Sollich, J. Phys. A **27**, 7771 (1994).

Neural Networks with Quadratic VC Dimension

Pascal Koiran[*]
Lab. de l'Informatique du Parallélisme
Ecole Normale Supérieure de Lyon – CNRS
69364 Lyon Cedex 07, France

Eduardo D. Sontag[†]
Department of Mathematics
Rutgers University
New Brunswick, NJ 08903, USA

Abstract

This paper shows that neural networks which use continuous activation functions have VC dimension at least as large as the square of the number of weights w. This result settles a long-standing open question, namely whether the well-known $O(w \log w)$ bound, known for hard-threshold nets, also held for more general sigmoidal nets. Implications for the number of samples needed for valid generalization are discussed.

1 Introduction

One of the main applications of artificial neural networks is to pattern classification tasks. A set of labeled training samples is provided, and a network must be obtained which is then expected to correctly classify previously unseen inputs. In this context, a central problem is to estimate the amount of training data needed to guarantee satisfactory learning performance. To study this question, it is necessary to first formalize the notion of learning from examples.

One such formalization is based on the paradigm of *probably approximately correct (PAC) learning*, due to Valiant (1984). In this framework, one starts by fitting some function f, chosen from a predetermined class $\mathcal{F}$, to the given training data. The class $\mathcal{F}$ is often called the "hypothesis class", and for purposes of this discussion it will be assumed that the functions in $\mathcal{F}$ take binary values $\{0,1\}$ and are defined on a common domain X. (In neural networks applications, typically $\mathcal{F}$ corresponds to the set of all neural networks with a given architecture and choice of activation functions. The elements of X are the inputs, possibly multidimensional.) The training data consists of labeled samples (x_i, ε_i), with each $x_i \in X$ and each $\varepsilon_i \in \{0, 1\}$, and

[*]koiran@lip.ens-lyon.fr.
[†]sontag@hilbert.rutgers.edu.

"fitting" by an f means that $f(x_i) = \varepsilon_i$ for each i. Given a new example x, one uses $f(x)$ as a guess of the "correct" classification of x. Assuming that both training inputs and future inputs are picked according to the same probability distribution on X, one needs that the space of possible inputs be well-sampled by the training data, so that f is an accurate fit. We omit the details of the formalization of PAC learning, since there are excellent references available, both in textbook (e.g. Anthony and Biggs (1992), Natarajan (1991)) and survey paper (e.g. Maass (1994)) form, and the concept is by now very well-known.

After the work of Vapnik (1982) in statistics and of Blumer et. al. (1989) in computational learning theory, one knows that a certain combinatorial quantity, called the *Vapnik-Chervonenkis (VC) dimension* VC($\mathcal{F}$) of the class $\mathcal{F}$ of interest completely characterizes the sample sizes needed for learnability in the PAC sense. (The appropriate definitions are reviewed below. In Valiant's formulation one is also interested in quantifying the computational effort required to actually fit a function to the given training data, but we are ignoring that aspect in the current paper.) Very roughly speaking, the number of samples needed in order to learn reliably is proportional to VC($\mathcal{F}$). Estimating VC($\mathcal{F}$) then becomes a central concern. Thus from now on, we speak exclusively of VC dimension, instead of the original PAC learning problem.

The work of Cover (1988) and Baum and Haussler (1989) dealt with the computation of VC($\mathcal{F}$) when the class $\mathcal{F}$ consists of networks built up from hard-threshold activations and having w weights; they showed that VC($\mathcal{F}$)= $O(w \log w)$. (Conversely, Maass (1993) showed that there is also a lower bound of this form.) It would appear that this definitely settled the VC dimension (and hence also the sample size) question.

However, the above estimate assumes an architecture based on hard-threshold ("Heaviside") neurons. In contrast, the usually employed gradient descent learning algorithms ("backpropagation" method) rely upon *continuous* activations, that is, neurons with graded responses. As pointed out in Sontag (1989), the use of analog activations, which allow the passing of rich (not just binary) information among levels, may result in higher memory capacity as compared with threshold nets. This has serious potential implications in learning, essentially because more memory capacity means that a given function f may be able to "memorize" in a "rote" fashion too much data, and less generalization is therefore possible. Indeed, Sontag (1992) showed that there are conceivable (though not very practical) neural architectures with extremely high VC dimensions. Thus the problem of studying VC($\mathcal{F}$) for analog networks is an interesting and relevant issue. Two important contributions in this direction were the papers by Maass (1993) and by Goldberg and Jerrum (1995), which showed upper bounds on the VC dimension of networks that use piecewise polynomial activations. The last reference, in particular, established for that case an upper bound of $O(w^2)$, where, as before, w is the number of weights. However it was an open problem (specifically, "open problem number 7" in the recent survey by Maass (1993) if there is a matching w^2 lower bound for such networks, and more generally for arbitrary continuous-activation nets. It could have been the case that the upper bound $O(w^2)$ is merely an artifact of the method of proof in Goldberg and Jerrum (1995), and that reliable learning with continuous-activation networks is still possible with far smaller sample sizes, proportional to $O(w \log w)$. But this is not the case, and in this paper we answer Maass' open question in the affirmative.

Assume given an activation σ which has different limits at $\pm\infty$, and is such that there is at least one point where it has a derivative and the derivative is nonzero (this last condition rules out the Heaviside activation). Then there are architectures with arbitrary large numbers of weights w and VC dimension proportional to w^2. The proof relies on first showing that networks consisting of two types of activations, Heavisides and linear, already have this power. This is a somewhat surprising result, since purely linear networks result in VC dimension proportional to w, and purely threshold nets have, as per the results quoted above, VC dimension bounded by $w \log w$. Our construction was originally motivated by a related one, given in Goldberg and Jerrum (1995), which showed that real-number programs (in the Blum-Shub-Smale (1989) model of computation) with running time T have VC dimension $\Omega(T^2)$. The desired result on continuous activations is then obtained, approximating Heaviside gates by σ-nets with large weights and approximating linear gates by σ-nets with small weights. This result applies in particular to the standard sigmoid $1/(1+e^{-x})$. (However, in contrast with the piecewise-polynomial case, there is still in that case a large gap between our $\Omega(w^2)$ lower bound and the $O(w^4)$ upper bound which was recently established in Karpinski and Macintyre (1995).) A number of variations, dealing with Boolean inputs, or weakening the assumptions on σ, are discussed. The full version of this paper also includes some remarks on thresholds networks with a constant number of linear gates, and threshold-only nets with "shared" weights.

Basic Terminology and Definitions

Formally, a (first-order, feedforward) *architecture* or *network* $\mathcal{A}$ is a connected directed acyclic graph together with an assignment of a function to a subset of its nodes. The nodes are of two types: those of fan-in zero are called *input nodes* and the remaining ones are called *computation nodes* or *gates*. An *output node* is a node of fan-out zero. To each gate g there is associated a function $\sigma_g : \mathbb{R} \to \mathbb{R}$, called the *activation* or *gate function* associated to g.

The *number of weights* or *parameters* associated to a gate g is the integer n_g equal to the fan-in of g plus one. (This definition is motivated by the fact that each input to the gate will be multiplied by a weight, and the results are added together with a "bias" constant term, seen as one more weight; see below.) The *(total) number of weights* (or parameters) of $\mathcal{A}$ is by definition the sum of the numbers n_g, over all the gates g of $\mathcal{A}$. The *number of inputs* m of $\mathcal{A}$ is the total number of input nodes (one also says that "$\mathcal{A}$ has inputs in $\mathbb{R}^m$"); it is assumed that $m > 0$. The *number of outputs* p of $\mathcal{A}$ is the number of output nodes (unless otherwise mentioned, we assume by default that all nets considered have one-dimensional outputs, that is, $p = 1$).

Two examples of gate functions that are of particular interest are the identity or *linear* gate: $\mathrm{Id}(x) = x$ for all x, and the *threshold* or *Heaviside* function: $H(x) = 1$ if $x \geq 0$, $H(x) = 0$ if $x < 0$.

Let $\mathcal{A}$ be an architecture. Assume that nodes of $\mathcal{A}$ have been linearly ordered as $\pi_1, \ldots, \pi_m, g_1, \ldots, g_l$, where the π_j's are the input nodes and the g_j's the gates. For simplicity, write $n_i := n_{g_i}$, for each $i = 1, \ldots, l$. Note that the total number of parameters is $n = \sum_{i=1}^{l} n_i$ and the fan-in of each g_i is $n_i - 1$. To each architecture $\mathcal{A}$ (strictly speaking, an architecture together with such an ordering of nodes) we associate a function
$$F : \mathbb{R}^m \times \mathbb{R}^n \to \mathbb{R}^p,$$
where p is the number of outputs of $\mathcal{A}$, defined by first assigning an "output" to each node, recursively on the distance from the the input nodes. Assume given an input $x \in \mathbb{R}^m$ and a vector of weights $w \in \mathbb{R}^n$. We partition w into blocks $(w_1, \ldots, w_l)$ of sizes $n_1, \ldots, n_l$ respectively. First the coordinates of x are assigned as the outputs of the input nodes $\pi_1, \ldots, \pi_m$ respectively. For each of the other gates g_i, we proceed as follows. Assume that outputs $y_1, \ldots, y_{n_i-1}$ have already

been assigned to the predecessor nodes of g_i (these are input and/or computation nodes, listed consistently with the order fixed in advance). Then the output of g_i is by definition

$$\sigma_{g_i}(w_{i,0} + w_{i,1}y_1 + w_{i,2}y_2 + \ldots + w_{i,n_i-1}y_{n_i-1}),$$

where we are writing $w_i = (w_{i,0}, w_{i,1}, w_{i,2}, \ldots, w_{i,n_i-1})$. The value of $F(x, w)$ is then by definition the vector (scalar if $p = 1$) obtained by listing the outputs of the output nodes (in the agreed-upon fixed ordering of nodes). We call F the *function computed by the architecture* $\mathcal{A}$. For each choice of weights $w \in \mathbb{R}^n$, there is a function $F_w : \mathbb{R}^m \to \mathbb{R}^p$ defined by $F_w(x) := F(x, w)$; by abuse of terminology we sometimes call this also the function computed by $\mathcal{A}$ (if the weight vector has been fixed).

Assume that $\mathcal{A}$ is an architecture with inputs in $\mathbb{R}^m$ and scalar outputs, and that the (unique) output gate has range $\{0, 1\}$. A subset $A \subseteq \mathbb{R}^m$ is said to be *shattered* by $\mathcal{A}$ if for each Boolean function $\beta : A \to \{0, 1\}$ there is some weight $w \in \mathbb{R}^n$ so that $F_w(x) = \beta(x)$ for all $x \in A$. The *Vapnik-Chervonenkis (VC) dimension* of $\mathcal{A}$ is the maximal size of a subset $A \subseteq \mathbb{R}^m$ that is shattered by $\mathcal{A}$. If the output gate can take non-binary values, we implicitly assume that the result of the computation is the sign of the output. That is, when we say that a subset $A \subseteq \mathbb{R}^m$ is shattered by $\mathcal{A}$, we really mean that A is shattered by the architecture $\bar{H}(\mathcal{A})$ in which the output of $\mathcal{A}$ is fed to a sign gate.

2 Networks Made up of Linear and Threshold Gates

Proposition 1 *For every $n \geq 1$, there is a network architecture $\mathcal{A}$ with inputs in $\mathbb{R}^2$ and $O(\sqrt{N})$ weights that can shatter a set of size $N = n^2$. This architecture is made only of linear and threshold gates.*

Proof. Our architecture has n parameters $W_1, \ldots, W_n$; each of them is an element of $T = \{0.w_1 \ldots w_n; w_i \in \{0, 1\}\}$. The shattered set will be $S = [n]^2 = \{1, \ldots, n\}^2$.

For a given choice of $W = (W_1, \ldots, W_n)$, $\mathcal{A}$ will compute the boolean function $f_W : S \to \{0, 1\}$ defined as follows: $f_W(x, y)$ is equal to the x-th bit of W_y. Clearly, for any boolean function f on S, there exists a (unique) W such that $f = f_W$.

We first consider the obvious architecture which computes the function:

$$f_W^1(y) = W_1 + \sum_{z=2}^{n}(W_z - W_{z-1})H(y - z + 1/2) \qquad (1)$$

sending each point $y \in [n]$ to W_y. This architecture has $n - 1$ threshold gates, $3(n - 1) + 1$ weights, and just one linear gate.

Next we define a second multi-output net which maps $w \in T$ to its binary representation $f^2(w) = (w_1, \ldots, w_n)$. Assume by induction that we have a net $\mathcal{N}_i^2$ that maps w to $(w_1, \ldots, w_i, 0.w_{i+1} \ldots w_n)$. Since $w_{i+1} = H(0.w_{i+1} \ldots w_n - 1/2)$ and $0.w_{i+2} \ldots w_n = 2 \times 0.w_{i+1} \ldots w_n - w_{i+1}$, $\mathcal{N}_{i+1}^2$ can be obtained by adding one threshold gate and one linear gate to $\mathcal{N}_i^2$ (as well as 4 weights). It follows that $\mathcal{N}_n^2$ has n threshold gates, n linear gates and $4n$ weights.

Finally, we define a net $\mathcal{N}^3$ which takes as input $x \in [n]$ and $w = (w_1, \ldots, w_n) \in \{0, 1\}^n$, and outputs w_x. We would like this network to be as follows:

$$f^3(x, w) = w_1 + \sum_{z=2}^{n} w_z H(x - z + 1/2) - \sum_{z=2}^{n} w_{z-1} H(x - z + 1/2).$$

This is not quite possible, because the products between the w_i's (which are inputs in this context) and the Heavisides are not allowed. However, since we are dealing with binary variables one can write $uv = H(u+v-1.5)$. Thus $\mathcal{N}_3$ has one linear gate, $4(n-1)$ threshold gates and $12(n-1)+n$ weights. Note that $f_W(x,y) = f^3(x, f^2(f_W^1(y)))$. This can be realized by means of a net that has $n+2$ linear gates, $(n-1)+n+4(n-1) = 6n-5$ threshold gates, and $(3n-2)+4n+(12n-11) = 19n-13$ weights. □

The following is the main result of this section:

Theorem 1 *For every $n \geq 1$, there is a network architecture $\mathcal{A}$ with inputs in $\mathbb{R}$ and $O(\sqrt{N})$ weights that can shatter a set of size $N = n^2$. This architecture is made only of linear and threshold gates.*

Proof. The shattered set will be $S = \{0, 1, \ldots, n^2 - 1\}$. For every $x \in S$, there are unique integers $x, y \in \{0, 1, \ldots, n-1\}$ such that $u = nx + y$. The idea of the construction is to compute x and y, and then feed $(x+1, y+1)$ to the network constructed in Proposition 1. Note that x is the unique integer such that $u - nx \in \{0, 1, \ldots, n-1\}$. It can therefore by computed by brute force search as follows:

$$x = \sum_{k=0}^{n-1} kH[H(u-nk) + H(n-1-(u-nk)) - 1.5].$$

This network has $3n$ threshold gates, one linear gate and $8n$ weights. Then of course $y = u - nx$. □

A Boolean version is as follows.

Theorem 2 *For every $d \geq 1$, there is a network architecture $\mathcal{A}$ with $O(\sqrt{N})$ weights that can shatter the $N = 2^{2d}$ points of $\{0,1\}^{2d}$. This architecture is made only of linear and threshold gates.*

Proof. Given $u \in \{0,1\}^{2d}$, one can compute $x = 1 + \sum_{i=1}^{d} 2^{i-1} u_i$ and $y = 1 + \sum_{i=1}^{d} 2^{i-1} u_{i+d}$ with two linear gates. Then (x,y) can be fed to the network of Proposition 1 (with $n = 2^d$). □

In other words, there is a network architecture with 2^d weights that can compute all boolean functions on $2d$ variables.

3 Arbitrary Sigmoids

We now extend the preceding VC dimension bounds to networks that use just one activation function σ (instead of both linear and threshold gates). All that is required is that the gate function have a sigmoidal shape and satisfy a very weak smoothness property:

1. σ is differentiable at some point x_0 (i.e., $\sigma(x_0 + h) = \sigma(x_0) + \sigma'(x_0)h + o(h)$) where $\sigma'(x_0) \neq 0$.
2. $\lim_{x \to -\infty} \sigma(x) = 0$ and $\lim_{x \to +\infty} \sigma(x) = 1$ (the limits 0 and 1 can be replaced by any distinct numbers).

A function satisfying these two conditions will be called *sigmoidal*. Given any such σ, we will show that networks using only σ gates provide quadratic VC dimension.

Theorem 3 *Let σ be an arbitrary sigmoidal function. There exist architectures $\mathcal{A}_1$ and $\mathcal{A}_2$ with $O(\sqrt{N})$ weights made only of σ gates such that:*

- *$\mathcal{A}_1$ can shatter a subset of $\mathbb{R}$ of cardinality $N = n^2$;*
- *$\mathcal{A}_2$ can shatter the $N = 2^{2d}$ points of $\{0,1\}^{2d}$.*

This follows directly from Theorems 1 and 2, together with the following simulation result:

Theorem 4 *Let σ be a an arbitrary sigmoidal function. Let $\mathcal{N}$ be a network of T threshold and L linear gates, with a threshold gate at the output. Then $\mathcal{N}$ can be simulated on any given finite set of inputs by a network $\mathcal{N}'$ of $T+L$ gates that all use the activation function σ (except the output gate which is still a threshold). Moreover, if $\mathcal{N}$ has n weights then $\mathcal{N}'$ has $O(n)$ weights.*

Proof. Let S be a finite set of inputs. We can assume, by changing the thresholds of threshold gates if necessary, that the net input $I_g(x)$ to any threshold gate g of $\mathcal{N}$ is different from 0 for all inputs $x \in S$.

Given $\epsilon > 0$, let $\mathcal{N}_\epsilon$ be the net obtained by replacing the output functions of all gates by the new output function $x \mapsto \sigma(x/\epsilon)$ if this output function is the sign function, and by $x \mapsto \sigma_\epsilon(x) = [\sigma(x_0+\epsilon x) - \sigma(x_0)]/[\epsilon\sigma'(x_0)]$ if it is the identity function. Note that for any $a > 0$, $\lim_{\epsilon \to 0+} \sigma(x/\epsilon) = H(x)$ uniformly for $x \in]-\infty, -a] \cup [a, +\infty]$ and $\lim_{\epsilon \to 0} \sigma_\epsilon(x) = x$ uniformly for $x \in [-1/a, 1/a]$.

This implies by induction on the depth of g that for any gate g of $\mathcal{N}$ and any input $x \in S$, the net input $I_{g,\epsilon}(x)$ to g in the transformed net $\mathcal{N}_\epsilon$ satisfies $\lim_{\epsilon \to 0} I_{g,\epsilon}(x) = I_g(x)$ (here, we use the fact that the output function of every g is continuous at $I_g(x)$). In particular, by taking g to be the output gate of $\mathcal{N}$, we see that $\mathcal{N}$ and $\mathcal{N}_\epsilon$ compute the same function on S if ϵ is small enough. Such a net $\mathcal{N}_\epsilon$ can be transformed into an equivalent net $\mathcal{N}'$ that uses only σ as gate function by a simple transformation of its weights and thresholds. The number of weights remains the same, except at most for a constant term that must be added to each net input to a gate; thus if $\mathcal{N}$ has n weights, $\mathcal{N}'$ has at most $2n$ weights. □

4 More General Gate Functions

The objective of this section is to establish results similar to Theorem 3, but for even more arbitrary gate functions, in particular weakening the assumption that limits exist at infinity. The main result is, roughly, that any σ which is piecewise twice (continuously) differentiable gives at least quadratic VC dimension, save for certain exceptional cases involving functions that are almost everywhere linear.

A function $\sigma : \mathbb{R} \to \mathbb{R}$ is said to be *piecewise C^2* if there is a finite sequence $a_1 < a_2 < \ldots < a_p$ such that on each interval I of the form $]-\infty, a_1[$, $]a_i, a_{i+1}[$ or $]a_p, +\infty[$, $\sigma_{|I}$ is C^2.

(Note: our results hold even if it is only assumed that the second derivative exists in each of the above intervals; we do not use the continuity of these second derivatives.)

Theorem 5 *Let σ be a piecewise C^2 function. For every $n \geq 1$, there exists an architecture made of σ-gates, and with $O(n)$ weights, that can shatter a subset of $\mathbb{R}^2$ of cardinality n^2, except perhaps in the following cases:*

1. *σ is piecewise-constant, and in this case the VC dimension of any architecture of n weights is $O(n \log n)$;*

2. σ is affine, and in this case the VC dimension of any architecture of n weights is at most n.

3. there are constants $a \neq 0$ and b such that $\sigma(x) = ax + b$ except at a finite nonempty set of points. In this case, the VC dimension of any architecture of n weights is $O(n^2)$, and there are architectures of VC dimension $\Omega(n \log n)$.

Due to the lack of space, the proof cannot be included in this paper. Note that the upper bound of the first special case is tight for threshold nets, and that of the second special case is tight for linear functions in $\mathbb{R}^n$.

Acknowledgements

Pascal Koiran was supported by an INRIA fellowship, DIMACS, and the International Computer Science Institute. Eduardo Sontag was supported in part by US Air Force Grant AFOSR-94-0293.

References

M. ANTHONY AND N.L. BIGGS (1992) *Computational Learning Theory: An Introduction*, Cambridge U. Press.

E.B. BAUM AND D. HAUSSLER (1989) *What size net gives valid generalization?*, Neural Computation 1, pp. 151-160.

L. BLUM, M. SHUB AND S. SMALE (1989) *On the theory of computation and complexity over the real numbers: NP-completeness, recursive functions and universal machines*, Bulletin of the AMS 21, pp. 1–46.

A. BLUMER, A. EHRENFEUCHT, D. HAUSSLER, AND M. WARMUTH (1989) *Learnability and the Vapnik-Chervonenkis dimension*, J. of the ACM 36, pp. 929-965.

T.M. COVER (1988) *Capacity problems for linear machines*, in: Pattern Recognition, L. Kanal ed., Thompson Book Co., pp. 283-289.

P. GOLDBERG AND M. JERRUM (1995) *Bounding the Vapnik-Chervonenkis dimension of concept classes parametrized by real numbers*, Machine Learning 18, pp. 131-148.

M. KARPINSKI AND A. MACINTYRE (1995) *Polynomial bounds for VC dimension of sigmoidal neural networks*, in Proc. 27th ACM Symposium on Theory of Computing, pp. 200-208.

W. MAASS (1993) *Bounds for the computational power and learning complexity of analog neural nets*, in Proc. of the 25th ACM Symp. Theory of Computing, pp. 335-344.

W. MAASS (1994) *Perspectives of current research about the complexity of learning in neural nets*, in Theoretical Advances in Neural Computation and Learning, V.P. Roychowdhury, K.Y. Siu, and A. Orlitsky, editors, Kluwer, Boston, pp. 295-336.

B.K. NATARAJAN (1991) *Machine Learning: A Theoretical Approach*, M. Kaufmann Publishers, San Mateo, CA.

E.D. SONTAG (1989) *Sigmoids distinguish better than Heavisides*, Neural Computation 1, pp. 470-472.

E.D. SONTAG (1992) *Feedforward nets for interpolation and classification*, J. Comp. Syst. Sci 45, pp. 20-48.

L.G. VALIANT (1984) *A theory of the learnable*, Comm. of the ACM 27, pp. 1134–1142

V.N. VAPNIK (1982) *Estimation of Dependencies Based on Empirical Data*, Springer, Berlin.

Sample Complexity for Learning Recurrent Perceptron Mappings

Bhaskar Dasgupta
Department of Computer Science
University of Waterloo
Waterloo, Ontario N2L 3G1
CANADA
bdasgupt@daisy.uwaterloo.ca

Eduardo D. Sontag
Department of Mathematics
Rutgers University
New Brunswick, NJ 08903
USA
sontag@control.rutgers.edu

Abstract

Recurrent perceptron classifiers generalize the classical perceptron model. They take into account those correlations and dependences among input coordinates which arise from linear digital filtering. This paper provides tight bounds on sample complexity associated to the fitting of such models to experimental data.

1 Introduction

One of the most popular approaches to binary pattern classification, underlying many statistical techniques, is based on *perceptrons* or *linear discriminants*; see for instance the classical reference (Duda and Hart, 1973). In this context, one is interested in classifying k-dimensional input patterns

$$v = (v_1, \ldots, v_k)$$

into two disjoint classes A^+ and A^-. A perceptron P which classifies vectors into A^+ and A^- is characterized by a vector (of "weights") $\vec{c} \in \mathbb{R}^k$, and operates as follows. One forms the inner product

$$\vec{c}.v = c_1 v_1 + \ldots c_k v_k.$$

If this inner product is positive, v is classified into A^+, otherwise into A^-.

In signal processing and control applications, the size k of the input vectors v is typically very large, so the number of samples needed in order to accurately "learn" an appropriate classifying perceptron is in principle very large. On the other hand, in such applications the classes A^+ and A^- often can be separated by means of a dynamical system of fairly small dimensionality. The existence of such a dynamical system reflects the fact that the signals of interest exhibit context dependence and correlations, and this prior information can help in narrowing down the search for a classifier. Various dynamical system models for classification appear from instance when learning finite automata and languages (Giles *et. al.*, 1990) and in signal processing as a channel equalization problem (at least in the simplest 2-level case) when modeling linear channels transmitting digital data from a quantized source, e.g. (Baksho et. al., 1991) and (Pulford *et. al.*, 1991).

When dealing with linear dynamical classifiers, the inner product $\vec{c}.v$ represents a convolution by a separating vector $\vec{c}$ that is the impulse-response of a recursive digital filter of some order $n \ll k$. Equivalently, one assumes that the data can be classified using a $\vec{c}$ that is *n-recursive*, meaning that there exist real numbers $r_1, \ldots, r_n$ so that

$$c_j = \sum_{i=1}^{n} c_{j-i} r_i, \quad j = n+1, \ldots, k.$$

Seen in this context, the usual perceptrons are nothing more than the very special subclass of "finite impulse response" systems (all poles at zero); thus it is appropriate to call the more general class "recurrent" or "IIR (infinite impulse response)" perceptrons. Some authors, particularly Back and Tsoi (Back and Tsoi, 1991; Back and Tsoi, 1995) have introduced these ideas in the neural network literature. There is also related work in control theory dealing with such classifying, or more generally quantized-output, linear systems; see (Delchamps, 1989; Koplon and Sontag, 1993).

The problem that we consider in this paper is: if one assumes that there is an n-recursive vector $\vec{c}$ that serves to classify the data, and one knows n but not the particular vector, how many labeled samples $v^{(i)}$ are needed so as to be able to reliably estimate $\vec{c}$? More specifically, we want to be able to guarantee that any classifying vector consistent with the seen data will classify "correctly with high probability" the unseen data as well. This is done by computing the VC dimension of the related concept class and then applying well-known results from computational learning theory. Very roughly speaking, the main result is that the number of samples needed is proportional to the logarithm of the length k (as opposed to k itself, as would be the case if one did not take advantage of the recurrent structure). Another application of our results, again by appealing to the literature from computational learning theory, is to the case of "noisy" measurements or more generally data not exactly classifiable in this way; for example, our estimates show roughly that if one succeeds in classifying 95% of a data set of size $\log q$, then with confidence ≈ 1 one is assured that the prediction error rate will be < 90% on future (unlabeled) samples.

Section 5 contains a result on polynomial-time learnability: for n constant, the class of concepts introduced here is PAC learnable. Generalizations to the learning of real-valued (as opposed to Boolean) functions are discussed in Section 6. For reasons of space we omit many proofs; the complete paper is available by electronic mail from the authors.

2 Definitions and Statements of Main Results

Given a set $\mathbb{X}$, and a subset X of $\mathbb{X}$, a *dichotomy* on X is a function

$$\delta : X \to \{-1, 1\}.$$

Assume given a class $\mathcal{F}$ of functions $\mathbb{X} \to \{-1, 1\}$, to be called the class of *classifier* functions. The subset $X \subseteq \mathbb{X}$ is *shattered* by $\mathcal{F}$ if each dichotomy on X is the restriction to X of some $\phi \in \mathcal{F}$. The *Vapnik-Chervonenkis dimension* VC $(\mathcal{F})$ is the supremum (possibly infinite) of the set of integers κ for which there is some subset

$X \subseteq \mathbb{X}$ of cardinality κ which can be shattered by $\mathcal{F}$. Due to space limitations, we omit any discussion regarding the relevance of the VC dimension to learning problems; the reader is referred to the excellent surveys in (Maass, 1994; Turán, 1994) regarding this issue.

Pick any two integers $n > 0$ and $q \geq 0$. A sequence
$$\vec{c} = (c_1, \ldots, c_{n+q}) \in \mathbb{R}^{n+q}$$
is said to be *n-recursive* if there exist real numbers $r_1, \ldots, r_n$ so that
$$c_{n+j} = \sum_{i=1}^{n} c_{n+j-i} r_i, \quad j = 1, \ldots, q.$$

(In particular, every sequence of length n is n-recursive, but the interesting cases are those in which $q \neq 0$, and in fact $q \gg n$.) Given such an n-recursive sequence $\vec{c}$, we may consider its associated *perceptron* classifier. This is the map
$$\phi_{\vec{c}} : \mathbb{R}^{n+q} \to \{-1, 1\} : (x_1, \ldots, x_{n+q}) \mapsto \operatorname{sign}\left(\sum_{i=1}^{n+q} c_i x_i\right)$$
where the sign function is understood to be defined by $\operatorname{sign}(z) = -1$ if $z \leq 0$ and $\operatorname{sign}(z) = 1$ otherwise. (Changing the definition at zero to be $+1$ would not change the results to be presented in any way.) We now introduce, for each two fixed n, q as above, a class of functions:
$$\mathcal{F}_{n,q} := \{ \phi_{\vec{c}} \mid \vec{c} \in \mathbb{R}^{n+q} \text{ is } n\text{-recursive} \}.$$
This is understood as a function class with respect to the input space $\mathbb{X} = \mathbb{R}^{n+q}$, and we are interested in estimating $\operatorname{vc}(\mathcal{F}_{n,q})$.

Our main result will be as follows (all logs in base 2):

Theorem 1

$$\boxed{\max\left\{n, n \lfloor \log(\lfloor 1 + \tfrac{q-1}{n} \rfloor) \rfloor \right\} \leq \operatorname{vc}(\mathcal{F}_{n,q}) \leq \min\{n+q, 18n + 4n \log(q+1)\}}$$

Note that, in particular, when $q > \max\{2 + n^2, 32\}$, one has the tight estimates
$$\frac{n}{2} \log q \leq \operatorname{vc}(\mathcal{F}_{n,q}) \leq 8n \log q.$$

The organization of the rest of the paper is as follows. In Section 3 we state an abstract result on VC-dimension, which is then used in Section 4 to prove Theorem 1. Finally, Section 6 deals with bounds on the sample complexity needed for identification of linear dynamical systems, that is to say, the real-valued functions obtained when not taking "signs" when defining the maps $\phi_{\vec{c}}$.

3 An Abstract Result on VC Dimension

Assume that we are given two sets $\mathbb{X}$ and Λ, to be called in this context the set of *inputs* and the set of *parameter values* respectively. Suppose that we are also given a function
$$F : \Lambda \times \mathbb{X} \to \{-1, 1\}.$$
Associated to this data is the class of functions
$$\mathcal{F} := \{ F(\lambda, \cdot) : \mathbb{X} \to \{-1, 1\} \mid \lambda \in \Lambda \}$$

obtained by considering F as a function of the inputs alone, one such function for each possible parameter value λ. Note that, given the same data one could, dually, study the class
$$\mathcal{F}^* : \{F(\cdot, \xi) : \Lambda \to \{-1, 1\} \mid \xi \in \mathbb{X}\}$$
which obtains by fixing the elements of $\mathbb{X}$ and thinking of the parameters as inputs. It is well-known (and in any case, a consequence of the more general result to be presented below) that $\text{VC}(\mathcal{F}) \geq \lfloor \log(\text{VC}(\mathcal{F}^*)) \rfloor$, which provides a lower bound on $\text{VC}(\mathcal{F})$ in terms of the "dual VC dimension." A sharper estimate is possible when Λ can be written as a product of n sets
$$\Lambda = \Lambda_1 \times \Lambda_2 \times \ldots \times \Lambda_n \tag{1}$$
and that is the topic which we develop next.

We assume from now on that a decomposition of the form in Equation (1) is given, and will define a variation of the dual VC dimension by asking that only certain dichotomies on Λ be obtained from $\mathcal{F}^*$. We define these dichotomies only on "rectangular" subsets of Λ, that is, sets of the form
$$L = L_1 \times \ldots \times L_n \subseteq \Lambda$$
with each $L_i \subseteq \Lambda_i$ a nonempty subset. Given any index $1 \leq \kappa \leq n$, by a κ-axis dichotomy on such a subset L we mean any function $\delta : L \to \{-1, 1\}$ which depends only on the κth coordinate, that is, there is some function $\phi : L_\kappa \to \{-1, 1\}$ so that $\delta(\lambda_1, \ldots, \lambda_n) = \phi(\lambda_\kappa)$ for all $(\lambda_1, \ldots, \lambda_n) \in L$; an axis dichotomy is a map that is a κ-axis dichotomy for some κ. A rectangular set L will be said to be *axis-shattered* if every axis dichotomy is the restriction to L of some function of the form $F(\cdot, \xi) : \Lambda \to \{-1, 1\}$, for some $\xi \in \mathbb{X}$.

Theorem 2 *If $L = L_1 \times \ldots \times L_n \subseteq \Lambda$ can be axis-shattered and each set L_i has cardinality r_i, then $\text{VC}(\mathcal{F}) \geq \lfloor \log(r_1) \rfloor + \ldots + \lfloor \log(r_n) \rfloor$.*

(In the special case $n=1$ one recovers the classical result $\text{VC}(\mathcal{F}) \geq \lfloor \log(\text{VC}(\mathcal{F}^*)) \rfloor$.) The proof of Theorem 2 is omitted due to space limitations.

4 Proof of Main Result

We recall the following result; it was proved, using Milnor-Warren bounds on the number of connected components of semi-algebraic sets, by Goldberg and Jerrum:

Fact 4.1 (Goldberg and Jerrum, 1995) *Assume given a function $F : \Lambda \times \mathbb{X} \to \{-1, 1\}$ and the associated class of functions $\mathcal{F} := \{F(\lambda, \cdot) : \mathbb{X} \to \{-1, 1\} \mid \lambda \in \Lambda\}$. Suppose that $\Lambda = \mathbb{R}^k$ and $\mathbb{X} = \mathbb{R}^n$, and that the function F can be defined in terms of a Boolean formula involving at most s polynomial inequalities in $k+n$ variables, each polynomial being of degree at most d. Then, $\text{VC}(\mathcal{F}) \leq 2k \log(8eds)$.* □

Using the above Fact and bounds for the standard "perceptron" model, it is not difficult to prove the following Lemma.

Lemma 4.2 $\text{VC}(\mathcal{F}_{n,q}) \leq \min\{n + q, 18n + 4n \log(q + 1)\}$

Next, we consider the lower bound of Theorem 1.

Lemma 4.3 $\text{VC}(\mathcal{F}_{n,q}) \geq \max\{n, n\lfloor \log(\lfloor 1 + \frac{q-1}{n} \rfloor) \rfloor\}$

Proof. As $\mathcal{F}_{n,q}$ contains the class of functions $\phi_{\vec{c}}$ with $\vec{c} = (c_1, \ldots, c_n, 0, \ldots, 0)$, which in turn being the set of signs of an n-dimensional linear space of functions, has VC dimension n, we know that $\text{VC}(\mathcal{F}_{n,q}) \geq n$. Thus we are left to prove that if $q > n$ then $\text{VC}(\mathcal{F}_{n,q}) \geq n \lfloor \log(\lfloor 1 + \frac{q-1}{n} \rfloor) \rfloor$.

The set of n-recursive sequences of length $n+q$ includes the set of sequences of the following special form:

$$c_j = \sum_{i=1}^{n} l_i^{j-1}, \quad j = 1, \ldots, n+q \qquad (2)$$

where $\alpha_i, l_i \in \mathbb{R}$ for each $i = 1, \ldots, n$. Hence, to prove the lower bound, it is sufficient to study the class of functions induced by

$$F : \mathbb{R}^n \times \mathbb{R}^{n+q} \to \{-1, 1\}, \quad (\lambda_1, \ldots, \lambda_n, x_1, \ldots, x_{n+q}) \mapsto \text{sign}\left(\sum_{i=1}^{n}\sum_{j=1}^{n+q} \lambda_i^{j-1} x_j\right).$$

Let $r = \lfloor \frac{q+n-1}{n} \rfloor$ and let $L_1, \ldots, L_n$ be n disjoint sets of real numbers (if desired, integers), each of cardinality r. Let $L = \bigcup_{i=1}^{n} L_i$. In addition, if $rn < q+n-1$, then select an additional set B of $(q+n-rn-1)$ real numbers disjoint from L.

We will apply Theorem 2, showing that the rectangular subset $L_1 \times \ldots \times L_n$ can be axis-shattered. Pick any $\kappa \in \{1, \ldots, n\}$ and any $\phi : L_\kappa \to \{-1, 1\}$. Consider the (unique) interpolating polynomial

$$p(\lambda) = \sum_{j=1}^{n+q} x_j \lambda^{j-1}$$

in λ of degree $q+n-1$ such that

$$p(\lambda) = \begin{cases} \phi(\lambda) & \text{if } \lambda \in L_\kappa \\ 0 & \text{if } \lambda \in (L \cup B) - L_\kappa. \end{cases}$$

Now pick $\xi = (x_1, \ldots, x_{n+q-1})$. Observe that

$$F(l_1, l_2, \ldots, l_n, x_1, \ldots, x_{n+q}) = \text{sign}\left(\sum_{i=1}^{n} p(l_i)\right) = \phi(l_\kappa)$$

for all $(l_1, \ldots, l_n) \in L_1 \times \ldots \times L_n$, since $p(l) = 0$ for $l \notin L_\kappa$ and $p(l) = \phi(l)$ otherwise. It follows from Theorem 2 that $\text{VC}(\mathcal{F}_{n,q}) \geq n \lfloor \log(r) \rfloor$, as desired. ∎

5 The Consistency Problem

We next briefly discuss polynomial time learnability of recurrent perceptron mappings. As discussed in e.g. (Turán, 1994), in order to formalize this problem we need to first choose a *data structure* to represent the hypotheses in $\mathcal{F}_{n,q}$. In addition, since we are dealing with complexity of computation involving real numbers, we must also clarify the meaning of "finding" a hypothesis, in terms of a suitable notion of polynomial-time computation. Once this is done, the problem becomes that of solving the *consistency problem*:

> Given a set of $s \geq s(\varepsilon, \delta)$ inputs $\xi_1, \xi_2, \ldots, \xi_s \in \mathbb{R}^{n+q}$, and an arbitrary dichotomy $\Delta : \{\xi_1, \xi_2, \ldots, \xi_s\} \to \{-1, 1\}$ find a representation of a hypothesis $\phi_{\vec{c}} \in \mathcal{F}_{n,q}$ such that the restriction of $\phi_{\vec{c}}$ to the set $\{\xi_1, \xi_2, \ldots, \xi_s\}$ is identical to the dichotomy Δ (or report that no such hypothesis exists).

Sample Complexity for Learning Recurrent Perceptron Mappings

The representation to be used should provide an "efficient encoding" of the values of the parameters $r_1, \ldots, r_n, c_1, \ldots, c_n$: given a set of inputs $(x_1, \ldots, x_{n+q}) \in \mathbb{R}^{n+q}$, one should be able to efficiently check concept membership (that is, compute $\text{sign}\left(\sum_{i=1}^{n+q} c_i x_i\right)$). Regarding the precise meaning of polynomial-time computation, there are at least two models of complexity possible: the *unit cost model* which deals with algebraic complexity (arithmetic and comparison operations take unit time) and the *logarithmic cost model* (computation in the Turing machine sense; inputs $(x_1, \ldots, x_{n+q})$ are rationals, and the time involved in finding a representation of $r_1, \ldots, r_n, c_1, \ldots, c_n$ is required to be polynomial on the number of bits L.

Theorem 3 *For each fixed $n > 0$, the consistency problem for $\mathcal{F}_{n,q}$ can be solved in time polynomial in q and s in the unit cost model, and time polynomial in q, s, and L in the logarithmic cost model.*

Since $\text{VC}(\mathcal{F}_{n,q}) = O(n + n\log(q+1))$, it follows from here that the class $\mathcal{F}_{n,q}$ is learnable in time polynomial in q (and L in the log model). Due to space limitations, we must omit the proof; it is based on the application of recent results regarding computational complexity aspects of the first-order theory of real-closed fields.

6 Pseudo-Dimension Bounds

In this section, we obtain results on the learnability of linear systems dynamics, that is, the class of functions obtained if one does *not* take the sign when defining recurrent perceptrons. The connection between VC dimension and sample complexity is only meaningful for classes of Boolean functions; in order to obtain learnability results applicable to real-valued functions one needs metric entropy estimates for certain spaces of functions. These can be in turn bounded through the estimation of Pollard's pseudo-dimension. We next briefly sketch the general framework for learning due to Haussler (based on previous work by Vapnik, Chervonenkis, and Pollard) and then compute a pseudo-dimension estimate for the class of interest.

The basic ingredients are two complete separable metric spaces $\mathbb{X}$ and $\mathbb{Y}$ (called respectively the sets of inputs and outputs), a class $\mathcal{F}$ of functions $f : \mathbb{X} \to \mathbb{Y}$ (called the decision rule or hypothesis space), and a function $\ell : \mathbb{Y} \times \mathbb{Y} \to [0, r] \subset \mathbb{R}$ (called the loss or cost function). The function ℓ is so that the class of functions $(x, y) \mapsto \ell(f(x), y)$ is "permissible" in the sense of Haussler and Pollard. Now, one may introduce, for each $f \in \mathcal{F}$, the function

$$A_{f,\ell} : \mathbb{X} \times \mathbb{Y} \times \mathbb{R} \to \{-1, 1\} : (x, y, t) \mapsto \text{sign}\left(\ell(f(x), y) - t\right)$$

as well as the class $\mathcal{A}_{\mathcal{F},\ell}$ consisting of all such $A_{f,\ell}$. The *pseudo-dimension* of $\mathcal{F}$ with respect to the loss function ℓ, denoted by $\text{PD}[\mathcal{F}, \ell]$, is defined as:

$$\text{PD}[\mathcal{F}, \ell] := \text{VC}(\mathcal{A}_{\mathcal{F},\ell}).$$

Due to space limitations, the relationship between the pseudo-dimension and the sample complexity of the class $\mathcal{F}$ will not be discussed here; the reader is referred to the references (Haussler, 1992; Maass, 1994) for details.

For our application we define, for any two nonnegative integers n, q, the class

$$\mathcal{F}'_{n,q} := \left\{ \widehat{\phi}_{\vec{c}} \,\middle|\, \vec{c} \in \mathbb{R}^{n+q} \text{ is } n\text{-recursive} \right\}$$

where $\widehat{\phi}_{\vec{c}} : \mathbb{R}^{n+q} \to \mathbb{R} : (x_1, \ldots, x_{n+q}) \mapsto \sum_{i=1}^{n+q} c_i x_i$. The following Theorem can be proved using Fact 4.1.

Theorem 4 *Let p be a positive integer and assume that the loss function ℓ is given by $\ell(y_1, y_2) = |y_1 - y_2|^p$. Then, $\text{PD}[\mathcal{F}'_{n,q}, \ell] \leq 18n + 4n\log(p(q+1))$.*

Acknowledgements

This research was supported in part by US Air Force Grant AFOSR-94-0293.

References

A.D. BACK AND A.C. TSOI, *FIR and IIR synapses, a new neural network architecture for time-series modeling*, Neural Computation, 3 (1991), pp. 375–385.

A.D. BACK AND A.C. TSOI, *A comparison of discrete-time operator models for nonlinear system identification*, Advances in Neural Information Processing Systems (NIPS'94), Morgan Kaufmann Publishers, 1995, to appear.

A.M. BAKSHO, S. DASGUPTA, J.S. GARNETT, AND C.R. JOHNSON, *On the similarity of conditions for an open-eye channel and for signed filtered error adaptive filter stability*, Proc. IEEE Conf. Decision and Control, Brighton, UK, Dec. 1991, IEEE Publications, 1991, pp. 1786–1787.

A. BLUMER, A. EHRENFEUCHT, D. HAUSSLER, AND M. WARMUTH, *Learnability and the Vapnik-Chervonenkis dimension*, J. of the ACM, 36 (1989), pp. 929-965.

D.F. DELCHAMPS, *Extracting State Information from a Quantized Output Record*, Systems and Control Letters, 13 (1989), pp. 365-372.

R.O. DUDA AND P.E. HART, *Pattern Classification and Scene Analysis*, Wiley, New York, 1973.

C.E. GILES, G.Z. SUN, H.H. CHEN, Y.C. LEE, AND D. CHEN, *Higher order recurrent networks and grammatical inference*, Advances in Neural Information Processing Systems 2, D.S. Touretzky, ed., Morgan Kaufmann, San Mateo, CA, 1990.

P. GOLDBERG AND M. JERRUM, *Bounding the Vapnik-Chervonenkis dimension of concept classes parameterized by real numbers*, Mach Learning, 18, (1995): 131-148.

D. HAUSSLER, *Decision theoretic generalizations of the PAC model for neural nets and other learning applications*, Information and Computation, 100, (1992): 78-150.

R. KOPLON AND E.D. SONTAG, *Linear systems with sign-observations*, SIAM J. Control and Optimization, 31(1993): 1245 - 1266.

W. MAASS, *Perspectives of current research about the complexity of learning in neural nets*, in *Theoretical Advances in Neural Computation and Learning*, V.P. Roychowdhury, K.Y. Siu, and A. Orlitsky, eds., Kluwer, Boston, 1994, pp. 295-336.

G.W. PULFORD, R.A. KENNEDY, AND B.D.O. ANDERSON, *Neural network structure for emulating decision feedback equalizers*, Proc. Int. Conf. Acoustics, Speech, and Signal Processing, Toronto, Canada, May 1991, pp. 1517–1520.

E.D. SONTAG, *Neural networks for control*, in *Essays on Control: Perspectives in the Theory and its Applications* (H.L. Trentelman and J.C. Willems, eds.), Birkhauser, Boston, 1993, pp. 339-380.

GYÖRGY TURÁN, *Computational Learning Theory and Neural Networks:A Survey of Selected Topics*, in *Theoretical Advances in Neural Computation and Learning*, V.P. Roychowdhury, K.Y. Siu,and A. Orlitsky, eds., Kluwer, Boston, 1994, pp. 243-293.

L.G. VALIANT *A theory of the learnable*, Comm. ACM, 27, 1984, pp. 1134–1142.

V.N.VAPNIK, *Estimation of Dependencies Based on Empirical Data*, Springer, Berlin, 1982.

On the Computational Power of Noisy Spiking Neurons

Wolfgang Maass

Institute for Theoretical Computer Science, Technische Universitaet Graz
Klosterwiesgasse 32/2, A-8010 Graz, Austria, e-mail: maass@igi.tu-graz.ac.at

Abstract

It has remained unknown whether one can in principle carry out reliable digital computations with networks of biologically realistic models for neurons. This article presents rigorous constructions for simulating in real-time arbitrary given boolean circuits and finite automata with arbitrarily high reliability by networks of noisy spiking neurons.

In addition we show that with the help of "shunting inhibition" even networks of very unreliable spiking neurons can simulate in real-time any McCulloch-Pitts neuron (or "threshold gate"), and therefore any multilayer perceptron (or "threshold circuit") in a reliable manner. These constructions provide a possible explanation for the fact that biological neural systems can carry out quite complex computations within 100 msec.

It turns out that the assumption that these constructions require about the shape of the EPSP's and the behaviour of the noise are surprisingly weak.

1 Introduction

We consider networks that consist of a finite set V of *neurons*, a set $E \subseteq V \times V$ of *synapses*, a *weight* $w_{u,v} \geq 0$ and a *response function* $\varepsilon_{u,v} : \mathbf{R}^+ \to \mathbf{R}$ for each synapse

$\langle u, v \rangle \in E$ (where $\mathbf{R}^+ := \{x \in \mathbf{R} : x \geq 0\}$), and a *threshold function* $\Theta_v : \mathbf{R}^+ \to \mathbf{R}^+$ for each neuron $v \in V$.

If $F_u \subseteq \mathbf{R}^+$ is the set of *firing times* of a neuron u, then the *potential* at the trigger zone of neuron v at time t is given by $P_v(t) := \sum_{u \,:\, \langle u, v \rangle \in E} \sum_{s \in F_u \,:\, s < t} w_{u,v} \cdot \varepsilon_{u,v}(t - s)$. The threshold function $\Theta_v(t - t')$ quantifies the "reluctance" of v to fire again at time t, if its last previous firing was at time t'. We assume that $\Theta_v(0) \in (0, \infty)$, $\Theta_v(x) = \infty$ for $x \in (0, \tau_{ref}]$ (for some constant $\tau_{ref} > 0$, the "absolute refractory period"), and $\sup\{\Theta_v(x) : x \geq \tau\} < \infty$ for any $\tau > \tau_{ref}$.

In a *deterministic* model for a spiking neuron (Maass, 1995a, 1996) one can assume that a neuron v fires exactly at those time points t when $P_v(t)$ reaches (from below) the value $\Theta_v(t - t')$. We consider in this article a biologically more realistic model, where as in (Gerstner, van Hemmen, 1994) the size of the difference $P_v(t) - \Theta_v(t-t')$ just governs the *probability* that neuron v fires. The choice of the exact firing times is left up to some unknown stochastic processes, and it may for example occur that v does *not* fire in a time interval I during which $P_v(t) - \Theta_v(t-t') > 0$, or that v fires "spontaneously" at a time t when $P_v(t) - \Theta_v(t-t') < 0$. We assume that (apart from their communication via potential changes) the stochastic processes for different neurons v are independent. It turns out that the assumptions that one has to make about this stochastic firing mechanism in order to prove our results are surprisingly weak. We assume that there exist two arbitrary functions $L, \mathcal{U} : \mathbf{R} \times \mathbf{R}^+ \to [0, 1]$ so that $L(\Delta, \ell)$ provides a *lower* bound (and $\mathcal{U}(\Delta, \ell)$ provides an *upper* bound) for the probability that neuron v fires during a time interval I of length ℓ with the property that $P_v(t) - \Theta_v(t-t') \geq \Delta$ (respectively $P_v(t) - \Theta_v(t-t') \leq \Delta$) for all $t \in I$ up to the next firing of v (t' denotes the last firing time of v before I). We just assume about these functions L and $\mathcal{U}$ that they are non-decreasing in each of their two arguments (for any fixed value of the other argument), that $\lim_{\Delta \to -\infty} \mathcal{U}(\Delta, \ell) = 0$ for any fixed $\ell > 0$, and that $\lim_{\Delta \to \infty} L(\Delta, \ell) > 0$ for any fixed $\ell \geq R/6$ (where R is the assumed length of the rising segment of an EPSP, see below). The neurons are allowed to be "arbitrarily noisy" in the sense that the difference $\lim_{\Delta \to \infty} L(\Delta, \ell) - \lim_{\Delta \to -\infty} \mathcal{U}(\Delta, \ell)$ can be arbitrarily small. Hence our constructions also apply to neurons that exhibit persistent firing failures, and they also allow for synapses that fail with a rather high probability. Furthermore a detailed analysis of our constructions shows that we can relax the somewhat dubious assumption that the noise-distributions for different neurons are independent. Thus we are also able to deal with "systematic noise" in the distribution of firing times of neurons in a pool (e.g. caused by changes in the biochemical environment that simultaneously affect *many* neurons in a pool).

It turns out that it suffices to assume only the following rather weak properties of the other functions involved in our model:

1) Each response function $\varepsilon_{u,v} : \mathbf{R}^+ \to \mathbf{R}$ is either excitatory or inhibitory (and for the sake of biological realism one may assume that each neuron u induces only one type of response). All excitatory response functions $\varepsilon_{u,v}(x)$ have the value

0 for $x \in [0, \Delta_{u,v})$, and the value $\varepsilon^E(x - \Delta_{u,v})$ for $x \geq \Delta_{u,v}$, where $\Delta_{u,v} \geq 0$ is the *delay* for this synapse between neurons u and v, and ε^E is the common shape of all excitatory response functions ("EPSP's"). Corresponding assumptions are made about the inhibitory response functions ("IPSP's"), whose common shape is described by some function $\varepsilon^I : \mathbf{R}^+ \to \{x \in \mathbf{R} : x \leq 0\}$.

2) ε^E is continuous, $\varepsilon^E(0) = 0$, $\varepsilon^E(x) = 0$ for all sufficiently large x, and there exists some parameter $R > 0$ such that ε^E is non-decreasing in $[0, R]$, and some parameter $\rho > 0$ such that $\varepsilon^E(x + R/6) \geq \rho + \varepsilon^E(x)$ for all $x \in [0, 2R/3]$.

3) $-\varepsilon^I$ satisfies the same conditions as ε^E.

4) There exists a source BN^- of negative *"background noise"*, that contributes to the potential $P_v(t)$ of each neuron v an additive term that deviates for an arbitrarily long time interval by an arbitrarily small percentage from its average value $w_v^- \leq 0$ (which we can choose). One can delete this assumption if one assumes that the firing threshold of neurons can be shifted by some other mechanism.

In section 3 we will assume in addition the availability of a corresponding *positive* background noise BN^+ with average value $w_v^+ \geq 0$.
In a biological neuron v one can interpret BN^- and BN^+ as the combined effect of a continuous bombardment with a very large number of IPSP's (EPSP's) from randomly firing neurons that arrive at remote synapses on the dendritic tree of v.

We assume that *we* can choose the values of delays $\Delta_{u,v}$ and weights $w_{u,v}, w_v^+, w_v^-$. We refer to all assumptions specified in this section as our *"weak assumptions"* about noisy spiking neurons. It is easy to see that the most frequently studied *concrete* model for noisy spiking neurons, the *spike response model* (Gerstner and van Hemmen, 1994) satisfies these weak assumptions, and is hence a special case. However not even for the more concrete spike response model (or any other model for noisy spiking neurons) there exist any rigorous results about *computations* in these models. In fact, one may view this article as being the first that provides results about the computational complexity of neural networks for a neuron model that is acceptable to many neurobiologistis as being reasonably realistic.

In this article we only address the problem of reliable *digital* computing with noisy spiking neurons. For details of the proofs we refer to the forthcoming journal-version of this extended abstract. For results about *analog* computations with noisy spiking neurons we refer to Maass, 1995b.

2 Simulation of Boolean Circuits and Finite Automata with Noisy Spiking Neurons

Theorem 1: *For any deterministic finite automaton D one can construct a network $N(D)$ consisting of any type of noisy spiking neurons that satisfy our weak assumptions, so that $N(D)$ can simulate computations of D of any given length with arbitrarily high probability of correctness.*

Idea of the **proof**: Since the behaviour of a *single* noisy spiking neuron is completely unreliable, we use instead *pools* $A, B, \ldots$ of neurons as the basic building blocks in our construction, where all neurons v in the same pool receive approximately the same "input potential" $P_v(t)$. The intricacies of our stochastic neuron model allow us only to employ a *"weak coding"* of bits, where a "1" is represented by a pool A during a time interval I, if *at least* $p_1 \cdot |A|$ neurons in A fire (at least once) during I (where $p_1 > 0$ is a suitable constant), and "0" is represented if *at most* $p_0 \cdot |A|$ firings of neurons occur in A during I, where p_0 with $0 < p_0 < p_1$ is another constant (that can be chosen arbitrarily small in our construction).

The described coding scheme is *weak* since it provides no useful *upper* bound (e.g. $1.5 \cdot p_1 \cdot |A|$) on the number of neurons that fire during I if A represents a "1" (nor on the number of firings of a single neuron in A). It also does not impose constraints on the *exact timing* of firings in A *within* I. However a "0" can be represented more precisely in our model, by choosing p_0 sufficiently small.

The proof of Theorem 1 shows that this weak coding of bits suffices for reliable digital computations. The idea of these simulations is to introduce artificial negations into the computation, which allow us to exploit that "0" has a more precise representation than "1". It is apparently impossible to simulate an AND-gate in a straightforward fashion for a weak coding of bits, but one can simulate a NOR-gate in a reliable manner. ∎

Corollary 2: *Any boolean function can be computed by a sufficiently large network of noisy spiking neurons (that satisfy our weak assumptions) with arbitrarily high probability of correctness.*

3 Fast Simulation of Threshold Circuits via Shunting Inhibition

For biologically realistic parameters, each computation step in the previously constructed network takes around 25 msec (see point *b*) in section 4). However it is well-known that biological neural systems can carry out complex computations within just 100 msec (Churchland, Sejnowski, 1992). A closer inspection of the preceding construction shows, that one can simulate with the same speed also OR- and NOR-gates with a much larger fan-in than just 2. However wellknown results from theoretical computer science (see the results about the complexity class AC^0 in the survey article by Johnson in (van Leeuwen, 1990)) imply that for *any fixed* number of layers the computational power of circuits with gates for OR, NOR, AND, NOT remains very weak, even if one allows *any* polynomial size fan-in for such gates.

In contrast to that, the construction in this section will show that by using a biologically more realistic model for a noisy spiking neuron, one can in principle simulate within 100 msec 3 or more layers of a boolean circuit that employs substantially more powerful boolean gates: *threshold gates* (i.e. "Mc Culloch-Pitts neurons", also called "perceptrons"). The use of these gates provides a giant leap in computational power for boolean circuits with a small number of layers: In spite of many years of intensive research, one has not been able to exhibit a *single concrete computational problem in the complexity classes P or NP* that can be shown to be *not* computable by a polynomial size threshold circuit with 3 layers (for threshold circuits with integer weights of *unbounded* size the same holds already for just 2 layers).

In the neuron model that we have employed so far in this article, we have assumed (as it is common in the spike response model) that the potential $P_v(t)$ at the trigger zone of neuron v depends *linearly* on all the terms $w_{u,v} \cdot \varepsilon_{u,v}(t-s)$. There exists however ample biological evidence that this assumption is not appropriate for certain types of synapses. An example are synapses that carry out *shunting inhibition* (see. e.g. (Abeles, 1991) and (Shepherd, 1990)). When a synapse of this type (located on the dendritic tree of a neuron v) is activated, it basically erases (through a short circuit mechanism) for a short time all EPSP's that pass the location of this synapse on their way to the trigger zone of v. However in contrast to those IPSP's that occur linearly in the formula for $P_v(t)$, the activation of such synapse for *shunting* inhibition has *no impact* on those EPSP's that travel to the trigger zone of v through another part of its dendritic tree. We model shunting inhibition in our framework as follows. We write Γ for the subset of all neurons γ in V that can "veto" other synapses $\langle u,v \rangle$ via shunting inhibition (we assume that the neurons in Γ have no other role apart from that). We allow in our formal model that certain γ in Γ are assigned as *label* to certain synapses $\langle u,v \rangle$ that have an *excitatory* response function $\varepsilon_{u,v}$. If γ is a label of $\langle u,v \rangle$, then this models the situation that γ can intercept EPSP's from u on their way to the trigger zone of v via shunting inhibition. We then define

$$P_v(t) = \sum_{u \in V : \langle u,v \rangle \in E} \left(\sum_{s \in F_u : s < t} w_{u,v} \cdot \varepsilon_{u,v}(t-s) \cdot \prod_{\gamma \text{ is label of } \langle u,v \rangle} S_\gamma(t) \right),$$

where we assume that $S_\gamma(t) \in [0,1]$ is arbitrarily close to 0 for a short time interval after neuron γ has fired, and else equal to 1. The firing mechanism for neurons $\gamma \in \Gamma$ is defined like for all other neurons.

Theorem 3: *One can simulate any threshold circuit T by a sufficiently large network $N(T)$ of noisy spiking neurons with shunting inhibition (with arbitrarily high probability of correctness). The computation time of $N(T)$ does not depend on the number of gates in each layer, and is proportional to the number of layers in the threshold circuit T.*

Idea of the **proof** *of Theorem 3:* It is already impossible to simulate in a straightforward manner an AND-gate with *weak coding* of bits. The same difficulties arise in an even more drastic way if one wants to simulate a threshold gate with large fan-in.

The left part of Figure 1 indicates that with the help of shunting inhibition one can transform via an intermediate pool of neurons B_1 the bit that is weakly encoded by

A_1 into a contribution to $P_v(t)$ for neurons $v \in C$ that is throughout a time interval J arbitrarily close to 0 if A_1 encodes a "0", and *arbitrarily close to some constant $P^* > 0$* if A_1 encodes a "1" (we will call this a *"strong coding"* of a bit). Obviously it is rather easy to realize a threshold gate if one can make use of such *strong coding* of bits.

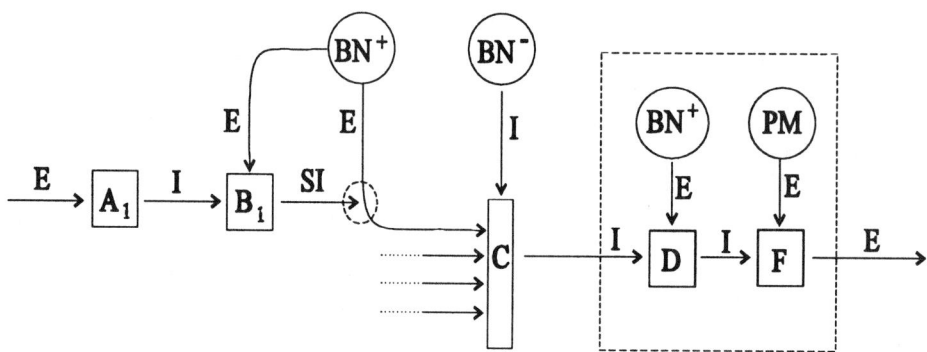

Figure 1: *Realization of a threshold gate G via shunting inhibition (SI)*.

The task of the module in Figure 1 is to simulate with noisy spiking neurons a given boolean threshold gate G that outputs 1 if $\sum_{i=1}^{n} \alpha_i x_i \geq \Theta$, and 0 else. For simplicity Figure 1 shows only the pool A_1 whose firing activity encodes (in weak coding) the first input bit x_1. The other input bits are represented (in weak coding) simultaneously in pools $A_2, \ldots, A_n$ parallel to A_1. If $x_1 = 0$, then the firing activity in pool A_1 is low, hence the shunting inhibition from pool B_1 intercepts those EPSP's that are sent from BN^+ to each neuron v in pool C. More precisely, we assume that each pool B_i associated with a different input bit x_i carries out shunting inhibition on a *different* subtree of the dendritic tree of such neuron v (where each such subtree receives EPSP's from BN^+). If $x_1 = 1$, the higher firing activity in pool A_1 inhibits the neurons in B_1 for some time period. Hence during the relevant time interval BN^+ contributes an almost constant positive summand to the potential $P_v(t)$ of neurons v in C. By choosing w_v^+ and w_v^- appropriately, one can achieve that during this time interval the potential $P_v(t)$ of neurons v in C is arbitrarily much positive if $\sum_{i=1}^{n} \alpha_i x_i \geq \Theta$, and arbitrarily much negative if $\sum_{i=1}^{n} \alpha_i x_i < \Theta$. Hence the activity level of C encodes the output bit of the threshold gate G (in *weak* coding). The purpose of the subsequent pools D and F is to synchronize (with the help of "double-negation") the output of this module via a pacemaker or synfire chain PM. In this way one can achieve that all input "bits" to another module that simulates a threshold gate on the next layer of circuit T arrive simultaneously. ∎

4 Conclusion

Our constructions throw new light on various experimental data, and on our attempts to understand neural computation and coding:

a) If one would record all firing times of a few arbitrarily chosen neurons in our networks during many repetitions of the same computation, one is likely to see that each run yields quite different seemingly random firing sequences, where however a few firing patterns will occur more frequently than could be explained by mere chance. This is consistent with the experimental results reported in (Abeles, 1991), and one should also note that the *synfire chains* of (Abeles, 1991) have many features in common with the here constructed networks.

b) If one plugs in biologically realistic values (see (Shepherd, 1990), (Churchland, Sejnowski, 1992)) for the length of transmission delays (around 5 msec) and the duration of EPSP's and IPSP's (around 15 msec for fast PSP's), then the computation time of our modules for NOR- and threshold gates comes out to be not more than 25 msec. Hence in principle a multi-layer perceptron with up to 4 layers can be simulated within 100 msec.

c) Our constructions provide new hypotheses about the computational roles of regular and shunting *inhibition*, that go far beyond their usually assumed roles.

d) We provide new hypotheses regarding the computational role of randomly firing neurons, and of EPSP's and IPSP's that arrive through synapses at distal parts of biological neurons (see the use of BN^+ and BN^- in our constructions).

References:

M. Abeles. (1991) Corticonics: Neural Circuits of the Cerebral Cortex. *Cambridge University Press*.

P. S. Churchland, T. J. Sejnowski. (1992) The Computational Brain. *MIT-Press*.

W. Gerstner, J. L. van Hemmen. (1994) How to describe neuronal activity: spikes, rates, or assemblies? *Advances in Neural Information Processing Systems, vol. 6, Morgan Kaufmann*: 463-470.

W. Maass. (1995a) On the computational complexity of networks of spiking neurons (extended abstract). *Advances in Neural Information Processing Systems, vol. 7 (Proceedings of NIPS '94), MIT-Press*, 183-190.

W. Maass. (1995b) An efficient implementation of sigmoidal neural nets in temporal coding with noisy spiking neurons. *IGI-Report 422 der Technischen Universität Graz*, submitted for publication.

W. Maass. (1996) Lower bounds for the computational power of networks of spiking neurons. *Neural Computation* 8:1, to appear.

G. M. Shepherd. (1990) The Synaptic Organization of the Brain. *Oxford University Press*.

J. van Leeuwen, ed. (1990) Handbook of Theoretical Computer Science, vol. A: Algorithms and Complexity. *MIT-Press*.

A Realizable Learning Task which Exhibits Overfitting

Siegfried Bös
Laboratory for Information Representation, RIKEN,
Hirosawa 2-1, Wako-shi, Saitama, 351-01, Japan
email: boes@zoo.riken.go.jp

Abstract

In this paper we examine a perceptron learning task. The task is realizable since it is provided by another perceptron with identical architecture. Both perceptrons have nonlinear sigmoid output functions. The gain of the output function determines the level of nonlinearity of the learning task. It is observed that a high level of nonlinearity leads to overfitting. We give an explanation for this rather surprising observation and develop a method to avoid the overfitting. This method has two possible interpretations, one is learning with noise, the other cross–validated early stopping.

1 Learning Rules from Examples

The property which makes feedforward neural nets interesting for many practical applications is their ability to approximate functions, which are given only by examples. Feed-forward networks with at least one hidden layer of nonlinear units are able to approximate each continuous function on a N-dimensional hypercube arbitrarily well. While the existence of neural function approximators is already established, there is still a lack of knowledge about their practical realizations. Also major problems, which complicate a good realization, like overfitting, need a better understanding.

In this work we study overfitting in a one–layer perceptron model. The model allows a good theoretical description while it exhibits already a qualitatively similar behavior as the multilayer perceptron.

A one–layer perceptron has N input units and one output unit. Between input and output it has one layer of adjustable weights $W_i, (i = 1, \ldots, N)$. The output z is a possibly nonlinear function of the weighted sum of inputs x_i, i.e.

$$z = g(h), \quad \text{with} \quad h = \frac{1}{\sqrt{N}} \sum_{i=1}^{N} W_i x_i. \tag{1}$$

The quality of the function approximation is measured by the difference between the correct output z_* and the net's output z averaged over all possible inputs. In the *supervised learning* scheme one trains the network using a set of examples $\underline{x}^\mu$ ($\mu = 1, \ldots, P$), for which the correct output is known. It is the learning task to minimize a certain cost function, which measures the difference between the correct output z_*^μ and the net's output z^μ averaged over all examples.

Using the mean squared error as a suitable measure for the difference between the outputs, we can define the *training error* E_T and the *generalization error* E_G as

$$E_T := \frac{1}{2P} \sum_{\mu=1}^{P} [z_*(\underline{x}^\mu) - z(\underline{x}^\mu)]^2, \qquad E_G := \frac{1}{2} < [z_*(\underline{x}) - z(\underline{x})]^2 >_{\{\underline{x}\}}. \quad (2)$$

The development of both errors as a function of the number P of trained examples is given by the *learning curves*. Training is conventionally done by gradient descend.

For theoretical purposes it is very useful to study learning tasks, which are provided by a second network, the so-called *teacher network*. This concept allows a more transparent definition of the difficulty of the learning task. Also the monitoring of the training process becomes clearer, since it is always possible to compare the student network and the teacher network directly.

Suitable quantities for such a comparison are, in the perceptron case, the following *order parameters*,

$$r := \frac{1}{||\underline{W}||} \sum_{i=1}^{N} W_i^* W_i, \qquad q := ||\underline{W}|| = \sqrt{\sum_{i=1}^{N}(W_i)^2}. \quad (3)$$

Both have a very transparent interpretation, r is the normalized overlap between the weight vectors of teacher and student, and q is the norm of the student's weight vector. These order parameters can also be used in multilayer learning, but their number increases with the number of all possible permutations between the hidden units of teacher and student.

2 The Learning Task

Here we concentrate on the case in which a student perceptron has to learn a mapping provided by another perceptron. We choose identical networks for teacher and student. Both have the same sigmoid output function, i.e. $g_*(h) = g(h) = \tanh(\gamma h)$. Identical network architectures of teacher and student are *realizable* tasks. In principle the student is able to learn the task provided by the teacher exactly. *Unrealizable* tasks can not be learnt exactly, there remains always a finite error.

If we use uniformally distributed random inputs $\underline{x}$ and weights $\underline{W}$, the weighted sum h in (1) can be assumed as Gaussian distributed. Then we can express the generalization error (2) by the order parameters (3),

$$E_G = \int Dz_1 \int Dz_2 \, \frac{1}{2} \left\{ \tanh[\gamma z_1] - \tanh\left[q(rz_1 + \sqrt{1-r^2}\, z_2)\right] \right\}^2, \quad (4)$$

with the Gaussian measure

$$\int Dz := \int_{-\infty}^{+\infty} \frac{dz}{\sqrt{2\pi}} \exp\left(-\frac{z^2}{2}\right). \quad (5)$$

From equation (4) we can see how the student learns the gain γ of the teachers output function. It adjusts the norm q of its weights. The gain γ plays an important role since it allows to tune the function $\tanh(\gamma h)$ between a linear function ($\gamma \ll 1$) and a highly nonlinear function ($\gamma \gg 1$). Now we want to determine the learning curves of this task.

3 Emergence of Overfitting

3.1 Explicit Expression for the Weights

Below the storage capacity of the perceptron, i.e. $\alpha = 1$, the minimum of the training error E_T is zero. A zero training error implies that every example has been learnt exactly, thus

$$E_T = 0 \quad \Rightarrow \quad z^\mu = z^\mu_* \quad \Rightarrow \quad h^\mu = g^{-1}(g_*(h^\mu_*)) = h^\mu_*. \tag{6}$$

The weights with minimal norm that fulfill this condition are given by the *Pseudoinverse* (see Hertz et al. 1991),

$$W_i = \sum_{\mu,\nu=1}^{P} h^\mu_* (C^{-1})_{\mu\nu} x^\nu_i, \qquad C_{\mu\nu} = \frac{1}{N} \sum_{i=1}^{N} x^\mu_i x^\nu_i. \tag{7}$$

Note, that the weights are completely independent of the output function $g(h) = g_*(h)$. They are the same as in the simplest realizable case, linear perceptron learns linear perceptron.

3.2 Statistical Mechanics

The calculation of the order parameters can be done by a method from statistical mechanics which applies the commonly used *replica method*. For details about the replica approach see Hertz et al. (1991). The solution of the continuous perceptron problem can be found in Bös et al. (1993). Since the results of the statistical mechanics calculations are exact only in the thermodynamic limit, i.e. $N \to \infty$, the variable α is the more natural measure. It is defined as the fraction of the number of patterns P over the system size N, i.e. $\alpha := P/N$. In the thermodynamic limit N and P are infinite, but α is still finite. Normally, reasonable system sizes, such as $N \geq 100$, are already well described by this theory.

Usually one concentrates on the zero temperature limit, because this implies that the training error E_T accepts its absolute minimum for every number of presented examples P. The corresponding order parameters for the case, linear perceptron learns linear student, are

$$q = \gamma \sqrt{\alpha}, \qquad r = \sqrt{\alpha}. \tag{8}$$

The zero temperature limit can also be called *exhaustive training*, since the student net is trained until the absolute minimum of E_T is reached.

For small α and high gains γ, i.e levels of nonlinearity, exhaustive training leads to overfitting. That means the generalization error $E_G(\alpha)$ is not, as it should, monotonously decreasing with α. It is one reason for overfitting, that the training follows too strongly the examples. The *critical gain* γ_c, which determines whether the generalization error $E_G(\alpha)$ is increasing or decreasing function for small values of α, can be determined by a linear approximation. For small α, both order parameters (3) are small, and the student's tanh–function in (4) can be approximated by a linear function. This simplifies the equation (4) to the following expression,

$$E_G(\epsilon) = E_G(0) - \frac{\epsilon}{2}[2H(\gamma) - \gamma], \quad \text{with} \quad H(\gamma) := \int Dz \, \tanh(\gamma z) \, z. \tag{9}$$

Since the function $H(\gamma)$ has an upper bound, i.e. $\sqrt{2/\pi}$, the critical gain is reached if $\gamma_c = 2H(\gamma_c)$. The numerical solution gives $\gamma_c = 1.3371$. If γ is higher, the slope of $E_G(\alpha)$ is positive for small α. In the following considerations we will use always the gain $\gamma = 5$ as an example, since this is an intermediate level of nonlinearity.

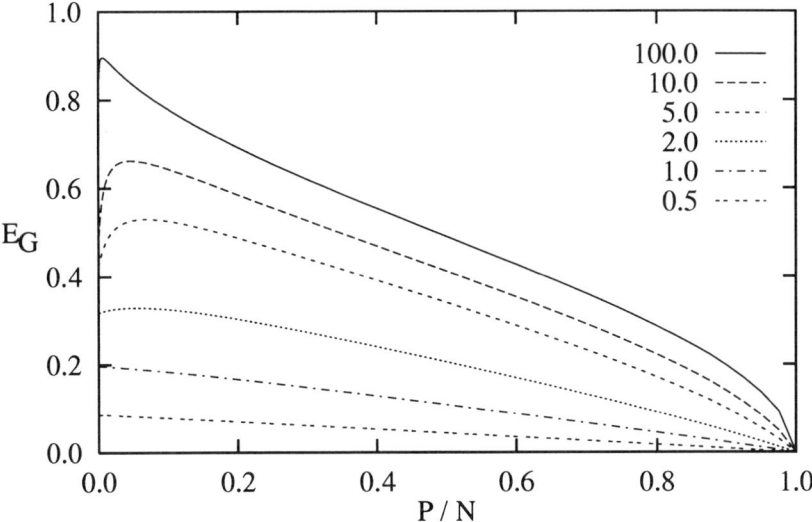

Figure 1: Learning curves $E(\alpha)$ for the problem, tanh–perceptron learns tanh–perceptron, for different values of the gain γ. Even in this realizable case, exhaustive training can lead to overfitting, if the gain γ is high enough.

3.3 How to Understand the Emergence of Overfitting

Here the evaluation of the generalization error in dependence of the order parameters r and q is helpful. Fig. 2 shows the function $E_G(r,q)$ for r between 0 and 1 and q between 0 and 1.2γ.

The exhaustive training in realizable cases follows always the line $q(r) = \gamma r$ independent of the actual output function. That means, training is guided only by the training error and not by the generalization error. If the gain γ is higher than γ_c, the line $E_G = E_G(0,0)$ starts with a lower slope than $q(r) = \gamma r$, which results in overfitting.

4 How to Avoid Overfitting

From Fig. 2 we can guess already that q increases too fast compared to r. Maybe the ratio between q and r is better during the training process. So we have to develop a description for the training process first.

4.1 Training Process

We found already that the order parameters for finite temperatures $(T > 0)$ of the statistical mechanics approach are a good description of the training process in an unrealizable learning task (Bös 1995). So we use the finite temperature order parameters also in this task. These are, again taken from the task 'linear perceptron learns linear perceptron',

$$q(\alpha, a) = \gamma \sqrt{\left(\frac{\alpha}{a}\right)\frac{(1+\alpha)a - 2\alpha}{a^2 - \alpha}}, \quad r(\alpha, a) = \sqrt{\left(\frac{\alpha}{a}\right)\frac{a^2 - \alpha}{(1+\alpha)a - 2\alpha}}, \qquad (10)$$

with the temperature dependent variable

$$a := 1 + [\beta(Q - q)]^{-1}. \qquad (11)$$

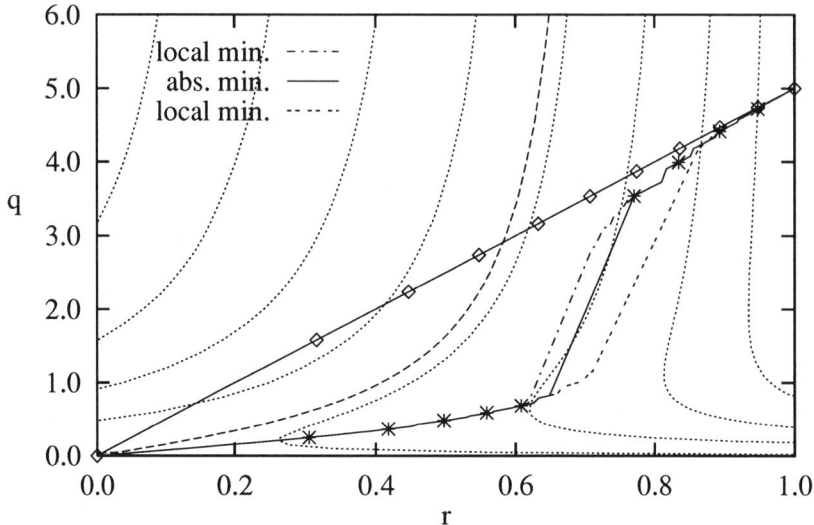

Figure 2: Contour plot of $E_G(r,q)$ defined by (4), the generalization error as a function of the two order parameters. Starting from the minimum $E_G = 0$ at $(r,q) = (1,5)$ the contour lines for $E_G = 0.1, 0.2, ..., 0.8$ are given (dotted lines). The dashed line corresponds to $E_G(0,0) = 0.42$. The solid lines are parametric curves of the order parameters (r,q) for certain training strategies. The straight line illustrates exhaustive training, the lower ones the optimal training, which will be explained in Fig. 3. Here the gain $\gamma = 5$.

The zero temperature limit corresponds to $a = 1$. We will show now that the decrease of the temperature dependent parameter a from ∞ to 1, describes the evolution of the order parameters during the training process. In the training process the natural parameter is the number of parallel training steps t. In each parallel training step all patterns are presented once and all weights are updated. Fig. 3 shows the evolution of the order parameters (10) as parametric curves (r,q).

The exhaustive learning curve is defined by $a = 1$ with the parameter α (solid line). For each α the training ends on this curve. The dotted lines illustrate the training process, a runs from infinity to 1. Simulations of the training process have shown that this theoretical curve is a good description, at least after some training steps. We will now use this description of the training process for the definition of an optimized training strategy.

4.2 Optimal temperature

The optimized training strategy chooses not $a = 1$ or the corresponding temperature $T = 0$, but the value of a (i.e. temperature), which minimizes the generalization error E_G. In the lower solid curve indicating the parametric curve (r,q) the value of a is chosen for every α, which minimizes E_G. The function $E_G(a)$ has two minima between $\alpha = 0.5$ and 0.7. The solid line indicates always the absolute minimum. The parametric curves corresponding to the local minima are given by the double dashed and dash–dotted lines. Note, that the optimized value a is always related to an optimized temperature through equation (11). But the parameter a is also related to the number of training steps t.

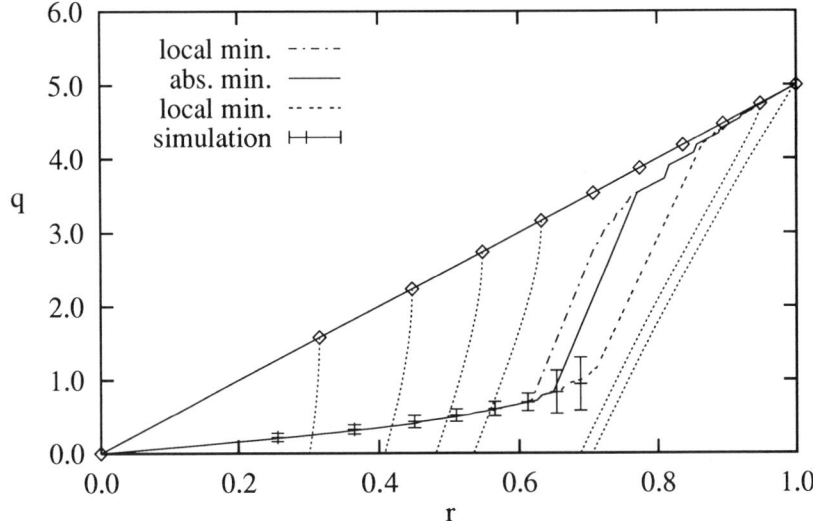

Figure 3: Training process. The order parameters (10) as parametric curves (r, q) with the parameters α and a. The straight solid line corresponds to exhaustive learning, i.e. $a = 1$ (marks at $\alpha = 0.1, 0.2, \ldots 1.0$). The dotted lines describe the training process for fixed α. Iterative training reduces the parameter a from ∞ to 1. Examples for $\alpha = 0.1, 0.2, 0.3, 0.4, 0.9, 0.99$ are given. The lower solid line is an optimized learning curve. To achieve this curve the value of a is chosen, which minimizes E_G absolutely. Between $\alpha \simeq 0.5$ and 0.7 the error E_G has two minima; the double–dashed and dash–dotted lines indicate the second, local minimum of E_G. Compare with Fig. 2, to see which is the absolute and which the local minimum of E_G. A naive early stopping procedure ends always in the minimum with the smaller q, since it is the first minimum during the training process (see simulation indicated with errorbars).

4.3 Early Stopping

Fig. 3 and Fig. 2 together indicate that an earlier stopping of the training process can avoid the overfitting. But in order to determine the stopping point one has to know the actual generalization error during the training. *Cross–validation* tries to provide an approximation for the real generalization error. The cross–validation error E_{CV} is defined like E_T, see (2), on a set of examples, which are not used during the training. Here we calculate the optimum using the real generalization error, given by r and q, to determine the optimal point for early stopping. It is a lower bound for training with finite cross–validation sets. Some preliminary tests have shown that already small cross–validation sets approximate the real E_G quite well. Training is stopped, when E_G increases. The resulting curve is given by the errorbars in Fig. 3. The errorbars indicate the standard deviation of a simulation with $N = 100$ averaged over 50 trials.

In Fig. 4 the same results are shown as learning curves $E_G(\alpha)$. There one can see clearly that the early stopping strategy avoids the overfitting.

5 Summary and outlook

In this paper we have shown that overfitting can also emerge in realizable learning tasks. The calculation of a critical gain and the contour lines in Fig. 2 imply, that

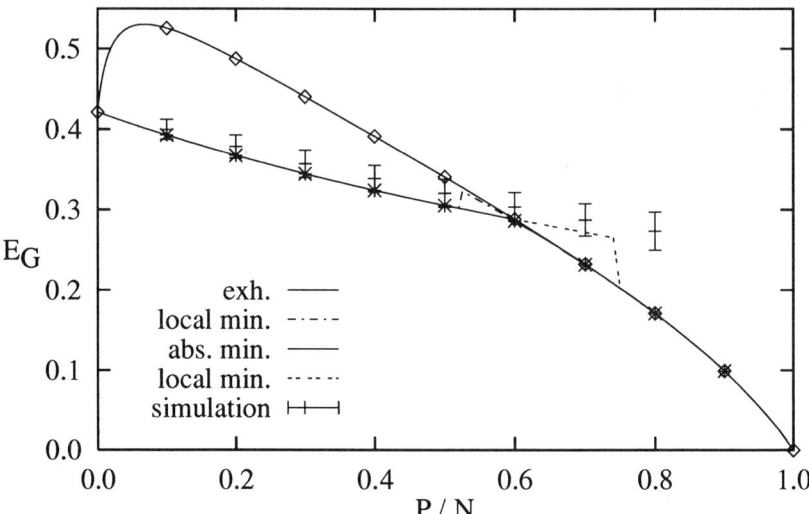

Figure 4: Learning curves corresponding to the parametric curves in Fig. 3. The upper solid line shows again exhaustive training. The optimized finite temperature curve is the lower solid line. From $\alpha = 0.6$ exhaustive and optimal training lead to identical results (see marks). The simulation for early stopping (errorbars) finds the first minimum of E_G.

the reason for the overfitting is the nonlinearity of the problem. The network adjusts slowly to the nonlinearity of the task. We have developed a method to avoid the overfitting, it can be interpreted in two ways.

Training at a finite temperature reduces overfitting. It can be realized, if one trains with noisy examples. In the other interpretation one learns without noise, but stops the training earlier. The early stopping is guided by cross-validation. It was observed that early stopping is not completely simple, since it can lead to a local minimum of the generalization error. One should be aware of this possibility, before one applies early stopping.

Since multilayer perceptrons are built of nonlinear perceptrons, the same effects are important for multilayer learning. A study with large scale simulations (Müller et al. 1995) has shown that overfitting occurs also in realizable multilayer learning tasks.

Acknowledgments

I would like to thank S. Amari and M. Opper for stimulating discussions, and M. Herrmann for hints concerning the presentation.

References

S. Bös. (1995) Avoiding overfitting by finite temperature learning and cross-validation. *International Conference on Artificial Neural Networks'95* Vol.2, p.111.
S. Bös, W. Kinzel & M. Opper. (1993) Generalization ability of perceptrons with continuous outputs. *Phys. Rev. E* **47**:1384–1391.
J. Hertz, A. Krogh & R. G. Palmer. (1991) *Introduction to the Theory of Neural Computation.* Reading: Addison–Wesley.
K. R. Müller, M. Finke, N. Murata, K. Schulten & S. Amari. (1995) On large scale simulations for learning curves, *Neural Computation* in press.

Stable Dynamic Parameter Adaptation

Stefan M. Rüger
Fachbereich Informatik, Technische Universität Berlin
Sekr. FR 5-9, Franklinstr. 28/29
10 587 Berlin, Germany
async@cs.tu-berlin.de

Abstract

A stability criterion for dynamic parameter adaptation is given. In the case of the learning rate of backpropagation, a class of stable algorithms is presented and studied, including a convergence proof.

1 INTRODUCTION

All but a few learning algorithms employ one or more parameters that control the quality of learning. Backpropagation has its learning rate and momentum parameter; Boltzmann learning uses a simulated annealing schedule; Kohonen learning a learning rate and a decay parameter; genetic algorithms probabilities, etc. The investigator always has to set the parameters to specific values when trying to solve a certain problem. Traditionally, the metaproblem of adjusting the parameters is solved by relying on a set of well-tested values of other problems or an intensive search for good parameter regions by restarting the experiment with different values. In this situation, a great deal of expertise and/or time for experiment design is required (as well as a huge amount of computing time).

1.1 DYNAMIC PARAMETER ADAPTATION

In order to achieve dynamic parameter adaptation, it is necessary to modify the learning algorithm under consideration: evaluate the performance of the parameters in use from time to time, compare them with the performance of nearby values, and (if necessary) change the parameter setting on the fly. This requires that there exist a measure of the quality of a parameter setting, called performance, with the following properties: the performance depends continuously on the parameter set under consideration, and it is possible to evaluate the performance locally, i.e., at a certain point within an inner loop of the algorithm (as opposed to once only at the end of the algorithm). This is what *dynamic parameter adaptation* is all about.

Dynamic parameter adaptation has several virtues. It is automatic; and there is no need for an extra schedule to find what parameters suit the problem best. When the notion of what the good values of a parameter set are changes during learning, dynamic parameter adaptation keeps track of these changes.

1.2 EXAMPLE: LEARNING RATE OF BACKPROPAGATION

Backpropagation is an algorithm that implements gradient descent in an error function $E: \mathbb{R}^n \to \mathbb{R}$. Given $w^o \in \mathbb{R}^n$ and a fixed $\eta > 0$, the iteration rule is $w^{t+1} = w^t - \eta \nabla E(w^t)$. The learning rate η is a local parameter in the sense that at different stages of the algorithm different learning rates would be optimal. This property and the following theorem make η especially interesting.

Trade-off theorem for backpropagation. *Let $E: \mathbb{R}^n \to \mathbb{R}$ be the error function of a neural net with a regular minimum at $w^* \in \mathbb{R}^n$, i.e., E is expansible into a Taylor series about w^* with vanishing gradient $\nabla E(w^*)$ and positive definite Hessian matrix $H(w^*)$. Let λ denote the largest eigenvalue of $H(w^*)$. Then, in general, backpropagation with a fixed learning rate $\eta > 2/\lambda$ cannot converge to w^*.*

Proof. Let U be an orthogonal matrix that diagonalizes $H(w^*)$, i.e., $D := U^T H(w^*) U$ is diagonal. Using the coordinate transformation $x = U^T(w - w^*)$ and Taylor expansion, $E(w) - E(w^*)$ can be approximated by $F(x) := x^T D x / 2$. Since gradient descent does not refer to the coordinate system, the asymptotic behavior of backpropagation for E near w^* is the same as for F near 0. In the latter case, backpropagation calculates the weight components $x_i^t = x_i^o (1 - D_{ii} \eta)^t$ at time step t. The diagonal elements D_{ii} are the eigenvalues of $H(w^*)$; convergence for all geometric sequences $t \mapsto x_i^t$ thus requires $\eta < 2/\lambda$. ∎

The trade-off theorem states that, given η, a large class of minima cannot be found, namely, those whose largest eigenvalue of the corresponding Hessian matrix is larger than $2/\eta$. Fewer minima might be overlooked by using a smaller η, but then the algorithm becomes intolerably slow. Dynamic learning-rate adaptation is urgently needed for backpropagation!

2 STABLE DYNAMIC PARAMETER ADAPTATION

Transforming the equation for gradient descent, $w^{t+1} = w^t - \eta \nabla E(w^t)$, into a differential equation, one arrives at $\partial w^t / \partial t = -\eta \nabla E(w^t)$. Gradient descent with constant step size η can then be viewed as Euler's method for solving the differential equation. One serious drawback of Euler's method is that it is unstable: each finite step leaves the trajectory of a solution without trying to get back to it. Virtually any other differential-equation solver surpasses Euler's method, and there are even some featuring dynamic parameter adaptation [5].

However, in the context of function minimization, this notion of stability ("do not drift away too far from a trajectory") would appear to be too strong. Indeed, differential-equation solvers put much effort into a good estimation of points that are as close as possible to the trajectory under consideration. What is really needed for minimization is *asymptotic stability*: ensuring that the performance of the parameter set does not decrease at the end of learning. This weaker stability criterion allows for greedy steps in the initial phase of learning.

There are several successful examples of dynamic learning-rate adaptation for backpropagation: Newton and quasi-Newton methods [2] as an adaptive η-tensor; individual learning rates for the weights [3, 8]; conjugate gradient as a one-dimensional η-estimation [4]; or straightforward η-adaptation [1, 7].

Stable Dynamic Parameter Adaptation

A particularly good example of dynamic parameter adaptation was proposed by Salomon [6, 7]: let $\zeta > 1$; at every step t of the backpropagation algorithm test two values for η, a somewhat smaller one, η_t/ζ, and a somewhat larger one, $\eta_t\zeta$; use as η_{t+1} the value with the better performance, i.e., the smaller error:

$$\eta_{t+1} = \begin{cases} \eta_t/\zeta & \text{if } E(w^t - \eta_t/\zeta \cdot \nabla E(w^t)) \leq E(w^t - \eta_t\zeta \cdot \nabla E(w^t)) \\ \eta_t\zeta & \text{otherwise} \end{cases}$$

The setting of the new parameter ζ proves to be uncritical (all values work, especially sensible ones being those between 1.2 and 2.1). This method outperforms many other gradient-based algorithms, but it is nonetheless unstable.

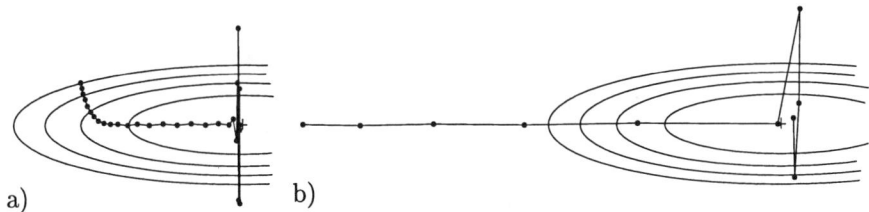

Figure 1: Unstable Parameter Adaptation

The problem arises from a rapidly changing length and direction of the gradient, which can result in a huge leap away from a minimum, although the latter may have been almost reached. Figure 1a shows the niveau lines of a simple quadratic error function $E: \mathbb{R}^2 \to \mathbb{R}$ along with the weight vectors $w^0, w^1, \ldots$ (bold dots) resulting from the above algorithm. This effect was probably the reason why Salomon suggested using the normalized gradient instead of the gradient, thus getting rid of the changes in the length of the gradient. Although this works much better, Figure 1b shows the instability of this algorithm due to the change in the gradient's direction.

There is enough evidence that these algorithms converge for a purely quadratic error function [6, 7]. Why bother with stability? One would like to prove that an algorithm asymptotically finds the minimum, rather than occasionally leaping far away from it and thus leaving the region where the quadratic Hessian term of a globally nonquadratic error function dominates.

3 A CLASS OF STABLE ALGORITHMS

In this section, a class of algorithms is derived from the above ones by adding stability. This class provides not only a proof of asymptotic convergence, but also a significant improvement in speed.

Let $E: \mathbb{R}^n \to \mathbb{R}$ be an error function of a neural net with random weight vector $w^0 \in \mathbb{R}^n$. Let $\zeta > 1$, $\eta_0 > 0$, $0 < c \leq 1$, and $0 < a \leq 1 \leq b$. At step t of the algorithm, choose a vector g^t restricted only by the conditions $g^t \nabla E(w^t)/|g^t||\nabla E_{w^t}| \geq c$ and that it either holds for all t that $1/|g^t| \in [a, b]$ or that it holds for all t that $|\nabla E(w^t)|/|g^t| \in [a, b]$, i.e., the vectors g^t have a minimal positive projection onto the gradient and either have a uniformly bounded length or are uniformly bounded by the length of the gradient. Note that this is always possible by choosing g^t as the gradient or the normalized gradient.

Let $e: \eta \mapsto E(w^t - \eta g^t)$ denote a one-dimensional error function given by E, w^t and g^t. Repeat (until the gradient vanishes or an upper limit of t or a lower limit $E_{\min}$

of E is reached) the iteration $w^{t+1} = w^t - \eta_{t+1} g^t$ with

$$\eta_{t+1} = \begin{cases} \eta^* := \dfrac{\eta_t \zeta/2}{1 + \dfrac{e(\eta_t \zeta) - e(0)}{\eta_t \zeta g^t \nabla E(w^t)}} & \text{if } e(0) < e(\eta_t \zeta) \\ \eta_t/\zeta & \text{if } e(\eta_t/\zeta) \leq e(\eta_t \zeta) \leq e(0) \\ \eta_t \zeta & \text{otherwise.} \end{cases} \qquad (1)$$

The first case for η_{t+1} is a stabilizing term η^*, which definitely decreases the error when the error surface is quadratic, i.e., near a minimum. η^* is put into effect when the error $e(\eta_t \zeta)$, which would occur in the next step if $\eta_{t+1} = \eta_t \zeta$ was chosen, exceeds the error $e(0)$ produced by the present weight vector w^t. By construction, η^* results in a value less than $\eta_t \zeta/2$ if $e(\eta_t \zeta) > e(0)$; hence, given $\zeta < 2$, the learning rate is decreased as expected, no matter what E looks like. Typically, (if the values for ζ are not extremely high) the other two cases apply, where $\eta_t \zeta$ and η_t/ζ compete for a lower error.

Note that, instead of gradient descent, this class of algorithms proposes a "g^t descent," and the vectors g^t may differ from the gradient. A particular algorithm is given by a specification of how to choose g^t.

4 PROOF OF ASYMPTOTIC CONVERGENCE

Asymptotic convergence. Let $E: w \mapsto \sum_{i=1}^n \lambda_i w_i^2 / 2$ with $\lambda_i > 0$. For all $\zeta > 1$, $0 < c \leq 1$, $0 < a \leq 1 \leq b$, $\eta_o > 0$, and $w^o \in \mathbb{R}^n$, every algorithm from Section 3 produces a sequence $t \mapsto w^t$ that converges to the minimum 0 of E with an at least exponential decay of $t \mapsto E(w^t)$.

Proof. This statement follows if a constant $q < 1$ exists with $E(w^{t+1}) \leq q E(w^t)$ for all t. Then, $\lim_{t \to \infty} w^t = 0$, since $w \mapsto \sqrt{E(w)}$ is a norm in $\mathbb{R}^n$.

Fix a w^t, η_t, and a g^t according to the premise. Since E is a positive definite quadratic form, $e: \eta \mapsto E(w^t - \eta g^t)$ is a one-dimensional quadratic function with a minimum at, say, η^*. Note that $e(0) = E(w^t)$ and $e(\eta_{t+1}) = E(w^{t+1})$. e is completely determined by $e(0)$, $e'(0) = -g^t \nabla E(w^t)$, $\eta_t \zeta$, and $e(\eta_t \zeta)$. Omitting the algebra, it follows that η^* can be identified with the stabilizing term of (1).

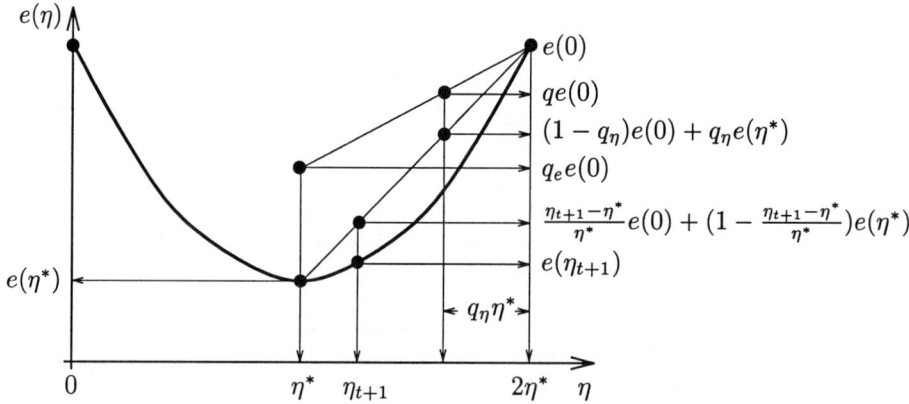

Figure 2: Steps in Estimating a Bound q for the Improvement of E.

If $e(\eta_t\zeta) > e(0)$, by (1) η_{t+1} will be set to η^*; hence, w^{t+1} has the smallest possible error $e(\eta^*)$ along the line given by g^t. Otherwise, the three values 0, η_t/ζ, and $\eta_t\zeta$ cannot have the same error e, as e is quadratic; $e(\eta_t\zeta)$ or $e(\eta_t/\zeta)$ must be less than $e(0)$, and the argument with the better performance is used as η_{t+1}. The sequence $t \mapsto E(w^t)$ is strictly decreasing; hence, a $q \leq 1$ exists. The rest of the proof shows the existence of a $q < 1$.

Assume there are two constants $0 < q_e, q_\eta < 1$ with

$$\eta_{t+1}/\eta^* \in [q_\eta, 2-q_\eta] \qquad (2)$$
$$e(\eta^*) \leq q_e e(0). \qquad (3)$$

Let $\eta_{t+1} \geq \eta^*$; using first the convexity of e, then (2), and (3), one obtains

$$\begin{aligned}
e(\eta_{t+1}) &= e\left(\frac{\eta_{t+1}-\eta^*}{\eta^*}2\eta^* + \left(1 - \frac{\eta_{t+1}-\eta^*}{\eta^*}\right)\eta^*\right) \\
&\leq \frac{\eta_{t+1}-\eta^*}{\eta^*}e(0) + \left(1 - \frac{\eta_{t+1}-\eta^*}{\eta^*}\right)e(\eta^*) \\
&\leq (1-q_\eta)e(0) + q_\eta e(\eta^*) \\
&\leq (1 - q_\eta(1-q_e))e(0).
\end{aligned}$$

Figure 2 shows how the estimations work. The symmetric case $0 < \eta_{t+1} \leq \eta^*$ has the same result $E(w^{t+1}) \leq qE(w^t)$ with $q := 1 - q_\eta(1-q_e) < 1$.

Let $\lambda^< := \min\{\lambda_i\}$ and $\lambda^> := \max\{\lambda_i\}$. A straightforward estimation for q_e yields

$$q_e := 1 - c^2\frac{\lambda^<}{\lambda^>} < 1.$$

Note that η^* depends on w^t and g^t. A careful analysis of the recursive dependence of $\eta^{t+1}/\eta^*(w^t, g^t)$ on $\eta^t/\eta^*(w^{t-1}, g^{t-1})$ uncovers an estimation

$$q_\eta := \min\left\{\frac{2}{\zeta^2+1}, \frac{2\zeta}{\zeta^2+1}\frac{ca}{b}\left(\frac{\lambda^<}{\lambda^>}\right)^{3/2}, \frac{\eta_0\zeta\lambda^<}{b\max\{1, \sqrt{2\lambda^> E(w^\circ)}\}}\right\} > 0. \qquad \blacksquare$$

5 NON-GRADIENT DIRECTIONS CAN IMPROVE CONVERGENCE

It is well known that the sign-changed gradient of a function is not necessarily the best direction to look for a minimum. The momentum term of a modified back-propagation version uses old gradient directions; Newton or quasi-Newton methods explicitly or implicitly exploit second-order derivatives for a change of direction; another choice of direction is given by conjugate gradient methods [5].

The algorithms from Section 3 allow almost any direction, as long as it is not nearly perpendicular to the gradient. Since they estimate a good step size, these algorithms can be regarded as a sort of "trial-and-error" line search without bothering to find an exact minimum in the given direction, but utilizing any progress made so far.

One could incorporate the Polak-Ribiere rule, $d^{t+1} = \nabla E(w^{t+1}) + \alpha\beta d^t$, for conjugate directions with $d^\circ = \nabla E(w^\circ), \alpha = 1$, and

$$\beta = \frac{(\nabla E(w^{t+1}) - \nabla E(w^t))\nabla E(w^{t+1})}{(\nabla E(w^t))^2}$$

to propose vectors $g^t := d^t/|d^t|$ for an explicit algorithm from Section 3. As in the conjugate gradient method, one should reset the direction d^t after each n (the number of weights) updates to the gradient direction. Another reason for resetting the direction arises when g^t does not have the minimal positive projection c onto the normalized gradient.

$\alpha = 0$ sets the descent direction g^t to the normalized gradient $\nabla E(w^t)/|\nabla E(w^t)|$; this algorithm proves to exhibit a behavior very similar to Salomon's algorithm with normalized gradients. The difference lies in the occurrence of some stabilization steps from time to time, which, in general, improve the convergence.

Since comparisons of Salomon's algorithm to many other methods have been published [7], this paper confines itself to show that significant improvements are brought about by non-gradient directions, e. g., by Polak-Ribiere directions ($\alpha = 1$).

Table 1: Average Learning Time for Some Problems

PROBLEM	E_{min}	$\alpha = 0$	$\alpha = 1$
(a) 3-2-4 regression	10^0	195 ± 95%	58 ± 70%
(b) 3-2-4 approximation	10^{-4}	1070 ± 140%	189 ± 115%
(c) Pure square ($n = 76$)	10^{-16}	464 ± 17%	118 ± 9%
(d) Power 1.8 ($n = 76$)	10^{-4}	486 ± 29%	84 ± 23%
(e) Power 3.8 ($n = 76$)	10^{-16}	28 ± 10%	37 ± 14%
(f) 8-3-8 encoder	10^{-4}	1380 ± 60%	300 ± 60%

Table 1 shows the average number of epochs of two algorithms for some problems. The average was taken over many initial random weight vectors and over values of $\zeta \in [1.7, 2.1]$; the root mean square error of the averaging process is shown as a percentage. Note that, owing to the two test steps for η_t/ζ and $\eta_t\zeta$, one epoch has an overhead of around 50% compared to a corresponding epoch of backpropagation. $\alpha \neq 0$ helps: it could be chosen by dynamic parameter adaptation.

Problems (a) and (b) represent the approximation of a function known only from some example data. A neural net with 3 input, 2 hidden, and 4 output nodes was used to generate the example data; artificial noise was added for problem (a). The same net with random initial weights was then used to learn an approximation. These problems for feedforward nets are expected to have regular minima.

Problem (c) uses a pure square error function $E: w \mapsto \sum_{i=1}^{n} i|w_i|^p/2$ with $p = 2$ and $n = 76$. Note that conjugate gradient needs exactly n epochs to arrive at the minimum [5]. However, the few additional epochs that are needed by the $\alpha = 1$ algorithm to reach a fairly small error (here 118 as opposed to 76) must be compared to the overhead of conjugate gradient (one line search per epoch).

Powers other than 2, as used in (d) or (e), work well as long as, say, $p > 1.5$. A power $p < 1$ will (if $n \geq 2$) produce a "trap" for the weight vector at a location near a coordinate axis, where, owing to an infinite gradient component, no gradient-based algorithm can escape[1]. Problems are expected even for p near 1: the algorithms of Section 3 exploit the fact that the gradient vanishes at a minimum, which in turn is numerically questionable for a power like 1.1. Typical minima, however, employ powers $2, 4, \ldots$ Even better convergence is expected and found for large powers.

---

[1]Dynamic parameter adaptation as in (1) can cope with the square-root singularity ($p = 1/2$) in one dimension, because the adaptation rule allows a fast enough decay of the learning rate; the ability to minimize this one-dimensional square-root singularity is somewhat overemphasized in [7].

The 8-3-8 encoder (f) was studied, because the error function has global minima at the boundary of the domain (one or more weights with infinite length). These minima, though not covered in Section 4, are quickly found. Indeed, the ability to increase the learning rate geometrically helps these algorithms to approach the boundary in a few steps.

6 CONCLUSIONS

It has been shown that implementing asymptotic stability *does* help in the case of the backpropagation learning rate: the theoretical analysis has been simplified, and the speed of convergence has been improved. Moreover, the presented framework allows descent directions to be chosen flexibly, e. g., by the Polak-Ribiere rule. Future work includes studies of how to apply the stability criterion to other parametric learning problems.

References

[1] R. Battiti. Accelerated backpropagation learning: Two optimization methods. *Complex Systems*, 3:331–342, 1989.

[2] S. Becker and Y. le Cun. Improving the convergence of back-propagation learning with second order methods. In D. Touretzky, G. Hinton, and T. Sejnowski, editors, *Proceedings of the 1988 Connectionist Models Summer School*, pages 29–37. Morgan Kaufmann, San Mateo, 1989.

[3] R. Jacobs. Increased rates of convergence through learning rate adaptation. *Neural Networks*, 1:295–307, 1988.

[4] A. Kramer and A. Sangiovanni-Vincentelli. Efficient parallel learning algorithms for neural networks. In D. Touretzky, editor, *Advances in Neural Information Processing Systems 1*, pages 40–48. Morgan Kaufmann, San Mateo, 1989.

[5] W. H. Press, B. P. Flannery, S. A. Teukolsky, and W. T. Vetterling. *Numerical Recipes in C*. Cambridge University Press, 1988.

[6] R. Salomon. *Verbesserung konnektionistischer Lernverfahren, die nach der Gradientenmethode arbeiten*. PhD thesis, TU Berlin, October 1991.

[7] R. Salomon and J. L. van Hemmen. Accelerating backpropagation through dynamic self-adaptation. *Neural Networks*, 1996 (in press).

[8] F. M. Silva and L. B. Almeida. Speeding up backpropagation. In *Proceedings of NSMS - International Symposium on Neural Networks for Sensory and Motor Systems*, Amsterdam, 1990. Elsevier.

Estimating the Bayes Risk from Sample Data

Robert R. Snapp* and **Tong Xu**
Computer Science and Electrical Engineering Department
University of Vermont
Burlington, VT 05405

Abstract

A new nearest-neighbor method is described for estimating the Bayes risk of a multiclass pattern classification problem from sample data (e.g., a classified training set). Although it is assumed that the classification problem can be accurately described by sufficiently smooth class-conditional distributions, neither these distributions, nor the corresponding prior probabilities of the classes are required. Thus this method can be applied to practical problems where the underlying probabilities are not known. This method is illustrated using two different pattern recognition problems.

1 INTRODUCTION

An important application of artificial neural networks is to obtain accurate solutions to pattern classification problems. In this setting, each pattern, represented as an n-dimensional feature vector, is associated with a discrete pattern class, or state of nature (Duda and Hart, 1973). Using available information, (e.g., a statistically representative set of labeled feature vectors $\{(\mathbf{x}_i, \ell_i)\}$, where $\mathbf{x}_i \in \mathbb{R}^n$ denotes a feature vector and $\ell_i \in \mathbb{L} = \{\omega_1, \omega_2, \ldots, \omega_C\}$, its correct pattern class), one desires a function (e.g., a neural network classifier) that assigns new feature vectors to pattern classes with the smallest possible misclassification cost.

If the classification problem is stationary, such that the patterns from each class are generated according to known probability distributions, then it is possible to construct an optimal classifier that assigns each pattern to a class with minimal expected risk. Although our method can be generalized to problems in which different types of classification errors incur different costs, we shall simplify our discussion by assuming that all errors are equal. In this case, a *Bayes classifier* assigns each feature vector to a class with maximum posterior probability. The expected risk of this classifier, or *Bayes risk* then reduces to the probability of error

$$R_B = \int_S \left[1 - \sup_{\ell \in \mathbb{L}} P(\ell|\mathbf{x}) \right] f(\mathbf{x}) \, d\mathbf{x}, \tag{1}$$

---
* E-mail: snapp@emba.uvm.edu

(Duda and Hart, 1973). Here, $P(\ell|\mathbf{x})$ denotes the posterior probability of class ℓ conditioned on observing the feature vector $\mathbf{x}$, $f(\mathbf{x})$ denotes the unconditional mixture density of the feature vector $\mathbf{x}$, and $S \subset \mathbb{R}^n$ denotes the probability-one support of f.

Knowing how to estimate the value of the Bayes risk of a given classification problem with a specific input representation, may facilitate the design of more accurate classifiers. For example, since the value of R_B depends upon the set of features chosen to represent each pattern (e.g., the significance of the input units in a neural network classifier), one might compare estimates of the Bayes risk for a number of different feature sets, and then select the representation that yields the smallest value. Unfortunately, it is necessary to know the explicit probability distributions to evaluate (1). Thus with the possible exception of trivial examples, the Bayes risk cannot be determined exactly for practical classification problems.

Lacking the means to evaluate the Bayes risk exactly, motivates the development of statistical estimators of R_B. In this paper, we use a recent asymptotic analysis of the finite-sample risk of the k-nearest-neighbor classifier to obtain a new procedure for estimating the Bayes risk from sample data. Section 2 describes the k-nearest-neighbor algorithm, and briefly describes how estimates of its finite-sample risk have been used to estimate R_B. Section 3 describes how a recent asymptotic analysis of the finite-sample risk can be applied to obtain new statistical estimators of the Bayes risk. In Section 4 the k-nearest-neighbor algorithm is used to estimate the Bayes risk of two example problems. Section 5 contains some concluding remarks.

2 THE k-NEAREST-NEIGHBOR CLASSIFIER

Due to its analytic tractability, and its nearly optimal performance in the large sample limit, the k-nearest-neighbor classifier has served as a useful framework for estimating the Bayes risk from classified samples. Recall, that the k-nearest-neighbor algorithm (Fix and Hodges, 1951) classifies an n-dimensional feature vector $\mathbf{x}$ by consulting a reference sample of m correctly classified feature vectors $\mathcal{X}_m = \{(\mathbf{x}_i, \ell_i) : i = 1, \ldots m\}$. First, the algorithm identifies the k nearest neighbors of $\mathbf{x}$, i.e., the k feature vectors within $\mathcal{X}_m$ that lie closest to $\mathbf{x}$ with respect to a given metric. Then, the classifier assigns $\mathbf{x}$ to the most frequent class label represented by the k nearest neighbors. (A variety of procedures can be used to resolve ties.) In the following, C denotes the number of pattern classes.

The *finite-sample risk* of this algorithm, R_m, equals the probability that the k-nearest-neighbor classifier assigns $\mathbf{x}$ to an incorrect class, averaged over all input vectors $\mathbf{x}$, and all m-samples, $\mathcal{X}_m$. The following properties have been shown to be true under weak assumptions:

Property 1 *(Cover and Hart, 1967): For fixed k,*
$$R_m \to R_\infty(k), \quad \text{as} \quad m \to \infty$$
with
$$R_B \leq R_\infty(1) \leq R_B\left(2 - \frac{C}{C-1} R_B\right). \tag{2}$$

Property 2 *(Devroye, 1981): If $k \geq 5$, and $C = 2$, then there exist universal constants $\alpha = 0.3399\cdots$, and $\beta = 0.9749\cdots$ such that $R_\infty(k)$ is bounded by*
$$R_B \leq R_\infty(k) \leq (1 + a_k) R_B, \quad \text{where} \quad a_k = \frac{\alpha\sqrt{k}}{k - 3.25}\left(1 + \frac{\beta}{\sqrt{k-3}}\right).$$

More generally, if $C = 2$, then
$$R_B \leq R_\infty(k) \leq \left(1 + \sqrt{\frac{2}{k}}\right) R_B. \tag{3}$$

By the latter property, this algorithm is said to be *Bayes consistent* in that for any $\epsilon > 0$, it is possible to construct a k-nearest-neighbor classifier such that $|R_m - R_B| < \epsilon$ if m and k are sufficiently large. Bayes consistency is also evident in other nonparametric pattern classifiers.

Several methods for estimating R_B from sample data have previously been proposed, e.g., (Devijver, 1985), (Fukunaga, 1985), (Fukunaga and Hummels, 1987), (Garnett and Yau, 1977), and (Loizou and Maybank, 1987). Typically, these methods involve constructing sequences of k-nearest neighbor classifiers, with increasing values of k and m. The misclassification rates are estimated using an independent test sample, from which upper and lower bounds to R_B are obtained. Because these experiments are necessarily performed with finite reference samples, these bounds are often imprecise. This is especially true for problems in which R_m converges to $R_\infty(k)$ at a slow rate. In order to remedy this deficiency, it is necessary to understand the manner in which the limit in Property 1 is achieved. In the next section we describe how this information can be used to construct new estimators for the Bayes risk of sufficiently smooth classification problems.

3 NEW ESTIMATORS OF THE BAYES RISK

For a subset of multiclass classification problems that can be described by probability densities with uniformly bounded partial derivatives up through order $N + 1$ (with $N \geq 2$), the finite-sample risk of a k-nearest-neighbor classifier that uses a weighted L_p metric can be represented by the truncated asymptotic expansion

$$R_m = R_\infty(k) + \sum_{j=2}^{N} c_j m^{-j/n} + O\left(m^{-(N+1)/n}\right), \tag{4}$$

(Psaltis, Snapp, and Venkatesh, 1994), and (Snapp and Venkatesh, 1995). In the above, n equals the dimensionality of the feature vectors, and $R_\infty(k), c_2, \ldots, c_N$, are the expansion coefficients that depend upon the probability distributions that define the pattern classification problem.

This asymptotic expansion provides a parametric description of how the finite-sample risk R_m converges to its infinite sample limit $R_\infty(k)$. Using a large sample of classified data, one can obtain statistical estimates of the finite-sample risk $\hat{R}_m$ for different values of m. Specifically, let $\{m_i\}$ denote a sequence of M different sample sizes, and select fixed values for k and N. For each value of m_i, construct an ensemble of k-nearest-neighbor classifiers, i.e., for each classifier construct a random reference sample $\mathcal{X}_{m_i}$ by selecting m_i patterns with replacement from the original large sample. Estimate the empirical risk of each classifier in the ensemble with an independently drawn set of "test" vectors. Let $\hat{R}_{m_i}$ denote the average empirical risk of the i-th ensemble. Then, using the resulting set of data points $\{(m_i, \hat{R}_{m_i})\}$, find the values of the coefficients $R_\infty(k)$, and c_2 through c_N, that minimizes the sum of the squares:

$$\sum_{i=1}^{M} \left(\hat{R}_{m_i} - R_\infty(k) - \sum_{j=2}^{N} c_j m_i^{-j/n} \right)^2 \tag{5}$$

Several inequalities can then be used obtain approximations of R_B from the estimated value of $R_\infty(k)$. For example, if $k = 1$, then Cover and Hart's inequality in Property 1 implies that

$$\frac{R_\infty(1)}{2} \leq R_B \leq R_\infty(1).$$

To enable an estimate of R_B with precision ϵ, choose $k > 2/\epsilon^2$, and estimate $R_\infty(k)$ by the above method. Then Devroye's inequality (3) implies

$$R_\infty(k) - \epsilon \leq R_\infty(k)(1 - \epsilon) \leq R_B \leq R_\infty(k).$$

4 EXPERIMENTAL RESULTS

The above procedure for estimating R_B was applied to two pattern recognition problems. First consider the synthetic, two-class problem with prior probabilities $P_1 = P_2 = 1/2$, and normally distributed, class-conditional densities

$$f_\ell(\mathbf{x}) = \frac{1}{(2\pi)^{n/2}} e^{-\frac{1}{2}\left((x_1+(-1)^\ell)^2 + \sum_{i=2}^n x_i^2\right)},$$

for $\ell = 1$ and 2. Pseudorandom labeled feature vectors $(\mathbf{x}, \ell)$ were numerically generated in accordance with the above for dimensions $n = 1$ and $n = 5$. Twelve sample sizes between 10 and 3000 were examined. For each dimension and sample size the risks R_m of many independent k-nearest-neighbor classifiers with $k = 1, 7$, and 63 were empirically estimated. (Because the asymptotic expansion (4) does not accurately describe the very small sample behavior of the k-nearest-neighbor classifier, sample sizes smaller than $2k$ were not included in the fit.)

Estimates of the coefficients in (5) for six different fits appear in the first equation of each cell in the third and fourth columns of Table 1. For reference, the second column contains the values of $R_\infty(k)$ that were obtained by numerically evaluating an exact integral expression (Cover and Hart, 1967). Estimates of the Bayes risk appear in the second equation of each cell in the third and fourth columns. Cover and Hart's inequality (2) was used for the experiments that assumed $k = 1$, and Devroye's inequality (3) was used if $k \geq 7$. For this problem, formula (1) evaluates to $R_B = (1/2)\,\text{erfc}(1/\sqrt{2}) = 0.15865$.

Table 1: Estimates of the model coefficients and Bayes error for a classification problem with two normal classes.

k	$R_\infty(k)$	$n = 1$ $(N = 2)$	$n = 5$ $(N = 6)$
1	0.2248	$R_m = 0.2287 + \dfrac{0.6536}{m^2}$ $R_B = 0.172 \pm 0.057$	$R_m = 0.2287 + \dfrac{0.1121}{m^{2/5}} + \dfrac{0.2001}{m^{4/5}} - \dfrac{0.0222}{m^{6/5}}$ $R_B = 0.172 \pm 0.057$
7	0.1746	$R_m = 0.1744 + \dfrac{4.842}{m^2}$ $R_B = 0.152 \pm 0.023$	$R_m = 0.1700 + \dfrac{0.2218}{m^{2/5}} - \dfrac{1.005}{m^{4/5}} + \dfrac{3.782}{m^{6/5}}$ $R_B = 0.148 \pm 0.022$
63	0.1606	$R_m = 0.1606 + \dfrac{20.23}{m^2}$ $R_B = 0.157 \pm 0.004$	$R_m = 0.1595 + \dfrac{0.1002}{m^{2/5}} - \dfrac{1.426}{m^{4/5}} + \dfrac{10.96}{m^{6/5}}$ $R_B = 0.156 \pm 0.004$

The second pattern recognition problem uses natural data; thus the underlying probability distributions are not known. A pool of 2^{22} classified multispectral pixels were was extracted from a seven band satellite image. Each pixel was represented by five spectral components, $\mathbf{x} = (x_1, \ldots, x_5)$, each in the range $0 \leq x_\nu \leq 255$. (Thus, $n = 5$.) The class label of each pixel was determined by one of the remaining spectral components, $0 \leq y \leq 255$. Two pattern classes were then defined: $\omega_1 = \{y < \theta\}$, and $\omega_2 = \{y \geq \theta\}$, where θ was a predetermined threshold. (This particular problem was chosen to test the feasibility of this method. In future work, we will examine more interesting pixel classification problems.)

Table 2: Coefficients that minimize the squared error fit for different N. Note that $c_3 = 0$ and $c_5 = 0$ in (2) if $n \geq 4$ (Psaltis, Snapp, and Venkatesh, 1994).

N	$R_\infty(1)$	c_2	c_4	c_6
2	0.0757133	0.126214		
4	0.0757846	0.124007	0.0132804	
6	0.0766477	0.0785847	0.689242	−2.68818

With $k = 1$, a large number of Bernoulli trials (e.g., 200—1000) were performed for each value of m_i. Each trial began by constructing a reference sample of m_i classified pixels chosen at random from the pool. The risk of each reference sample was then estimated by classifying t pixels with the nearest-neighbor algorithm under a Euclidean metric. Here, the t pixels, with $2000 \leq t \leq 20000$, were chosen independently, with replacement, from the pool. The risk $\hat{R}_{m_i}$ was then estimated as the average risk of each reference sample of size m_i. (The number of experiments performed for each value of m_i, and the values of t, were chosen to ensure that the variance of $\hat{R}_{m_i}$ was sufficiently small, less than 10^{-4} in this case.) This process was repeated for $M = 33$ different values of m_i in the range $100 \leq m_i \leq 15000$. Results of these experiments are displayed in Table 2 and Figure 1 for three different values of N. Note that the robustness of the fit begins to dissolve, for this data, at $N = 6$, either the result of overfitting, or insufficient smoothness in the underlying probability distributions. However, the estimate for $R_\infty(1)$ appears to be stable. For this classification problem, we thus obtain $R_B = 0.0568 \pm 0.0190$.

5 CONCLUSION

The described method for estimating the Bayes risk is based on a recent asymptotic analysis of the finite-sample risk of the k-nearest-neighbor classifier (Snapp and Venkatesh, 1995). Representing the finite-sample risk as a truncated asymptotic series enables an efficient estimation of the infinite-sample risk $R_\infty(k)$ from the classifier's finite-sample behavior. The Bayes risk can then be estimated by the Bayes consistency of the k-nearest-neighbor algorithm. Because such finite-sample analyses are difficult, and consequently rare, this new method has the potential to evolve into a useful algorithm for estimating the Bayes risk. Further improvements in efficiency may be obtained by incorporating principles of optimal experimental design, cf., (Elfving, 1952) and (Federov, 1972).

It is important to emphasize, however, that the validity of (4) rests on several rather strong smoothness assumptions, including a high-degree of differentiability of the class-conditional probability densities. For problems that do not satisfy these conditions, other finite-sample descriptions need to be constructed before this method can be applied. Nevertheless, there is much evidence that nature favors smoothness. Thus, these restrictive assumptions may still be applicable to many important problems.

Acknowledgments

The work reported here was supported in part by the National Science Foundation under Grant No. NSF OSR-9350540 and by Rome Laboratory, Air Force Material Command, USAF, under grant number F30602-94-1-0010.

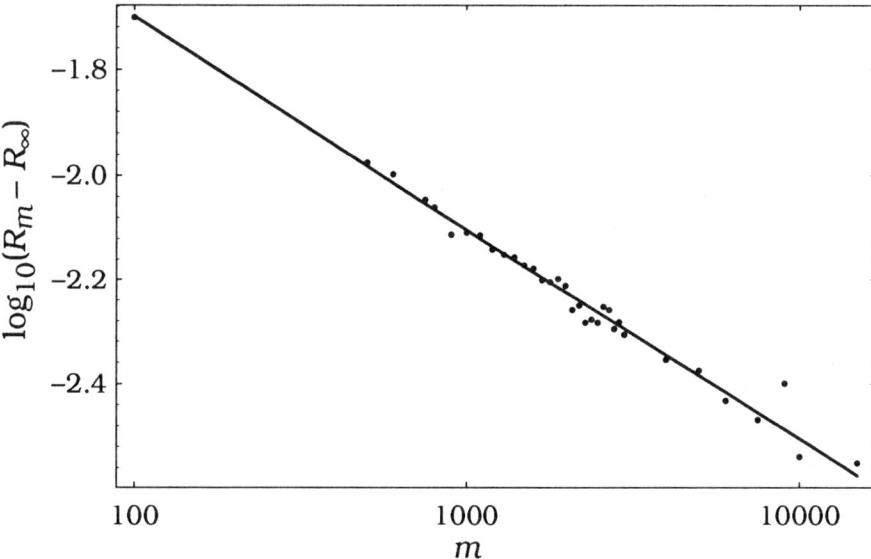

Figure 1: The best fourth-order ($N = 4$) fit of Eqn. (5) to 33 empirical estimates of $\hat{R}_{m_i}$ for a pixel classification problem obtained from a multispectral Landsat image. Using $R_\infty = 0.0758$, the fourth-order fit, $R_m = 0.0758 + 0.124 m^{-2/5} + 0.0133 m^{-4/5}$, is plotted on a log-log scale to reveal the significance of the $j = 2$ term.

References

T. M. Cover and P. E. Hart, "Nearest neighbor pattern classification," *IEEE Trans. Inform. Theory*, vol. IT–13, 1967, pp. 21–27.

P. A. Devijver, "A multiclass, $k - NN$ approach to Bayes risk estimation," *Pattern Recognition Letters*, vol. 3, 1985, pp. 1–6.

L. Devroye, "On the asymptotic probability of error in nonparametric discrimination," *Annals of Statistics*, vol. 9, 1981, pp. 1320–1327.

R. O. Duda and P. E. Hart, *Pattern Classification and Scene Analysis*. New York, New York: John Wiley & Sons, 1973.

G. Elfving, "Optimum allocation in linear regression theory," *Ann. Math. Statist.*, vol. 23, 1952, pp. 255–262.

V. V. Federov, *Theory of Optimal Experiments*, New York, New York: Academic Press, 1972.

E. Fix and J. L. Hodges, "Discriminatory Analysis: Nonparametric Discrimination: Consistency Properties," from *Project 21–49–004, Report Number 4*, UASF School of Aviation Medicine, Randolf Field, Texas, 1951, pp. 261–279.

K. Fukunaga, "The estimation of the Bayes error by the k-nearest neighbor approach," in L. N. Kanal and A. Rosenfeld (ed.), *Progress in Pattern Recognition*, vol. 2, Elesvier Science Publishers B.V. (North Holland), 1985, pp. 169–187.

K. Fukunaga and D. Hummels, "Bayes error estimation using Parzen and k-NN procedures," *IEEE Transactions on Pattern Analysis and Machine Intelligence*, vol. 9, 1987, pp. 634–643.

J. M. Garnett, III and S. S. Yau, "Nonparametric estimation of the Bayes error of feature extractors using ordered nearest neighbor sets," *IEEE Transactions on Computers*, vol. 26, 1977, pp. 46–54.

G. Loizou and S. J. Maybank, "The nearest neighbor and the Bayes error rate," *IEEE Transactions on Pattern Analysis and Machine Intelligence*, vol. 9, 1987, pp. 254–262.

D. Psaltis, R. R. Snapp, and S. S. Venkatesh, "On the finite sample performance of the nearest neighbor classifier," *IEEE Trans. Inform. Theory*, vol. IT–40, 1994, pp. 820—837.

R. R. Snapp and S. S. Venkatesh, "k Nearest Neighbors in Search of a Metric," 1995, (submitted).

Recursive Estimation of Dynamic Modular RBF Networks

Visakan Kadirkamanathan
Automatic Control & Systems Eng. Dept.
University of Sheffield, Sheffield S1 4DU, UK
visakan@acse.sheffield.ac.uk

Maha Kadirkamanathan
Dragon Systems UK
Cheltenham GL52 4RW, UK
maha@dragon.co.uk

Abstract

In this paper, recursive estimation algorithms for dynamic modular networks are developed. The models are based on Gaussian RBF networks and the gating network is considered in two stages: At first, it is simply a time-varying scalar and in the second, it is based on the state, as in the mixture of local experts scheme. The resulting algorithm uses Kalman filter estimation for the model estimation and the gating probability estimation. Both, 'hard' and 'soft' competition based estimation schemes are developed where in the former, the most probable network is adapted and in the latter all networks are adapted by appropriate weighting of the data.

1 INTRODUCTION

The problem of learning multiple modes in a complex nonlinear system is increasingly being studied by various researchers [2, 3, 4, 5, 6]. The use of a mixture of local experts [5, 6], and a conditional mixture density network [3] have been developed to model various modes of a system. The development has mainly been on model estimation from a given set of block data, with the model likelihood dependent on the input to the networks. A recursive algorithm for this static case is the approximate iterative procedure based on the block estimation schemes [6].

In this paper, we consider dynamic systems – developing a recursive algorithm is difficult since mode transitions have to be detected on-line whereas in the block scheme, search procedures allow optimal detection. Block estimation schemes for general architectures have been described in [2, 4]. However, unlike in those schemes, the algorithm developed here uses relationships based on Bayes law and Kalman filters and attempts to describe the dynamic system explicitly. The modelling is carried out by radial basis function (RBF) networks for their property that by pre-selecting the centres and widths, the problem can be reduced to a linear estimation.

2 DYNAMIC MODULAR RBF NETWORK

The dynamic modular RBF network consists of a number of models (or experts) to represent each nonlinear mode in a dynamical system. The models are based on the RBF networks with Gaussian function, where the RBF centre and width parameters are chosen *a priori* and the unknown parameters are only the linear coefficients **w**. The functional form of the RBF network can be expressed as,

$$f(\mathbf{x}; \mathbf{p}) = \sum_{k=1}^{K} w_k g_k(\mathbf{x}) = \mathbf{w}^T \mathbf{g} \tag{1}$$

where $\mathbf{w} = [\ldots, w_k, \ldots]^T \in \Re^K$ is the linear weight vector and $\mathbf{g} = [\ldots, g_k(\mathbf{x}), \ldots]^T \in \Re_+^K$ are the radial basis functions, where,

$$g_k(\mathbf{x}) = \exp\{-0.5 r^{-2} \|\mathbf{x} - \mathbf{m}_k\|^2\} \tag{2}$$

$\mathbf{m}_k \in \Re^M$ are the RBF centres or means and r the width. The RBF networks are used for their property that having chosen appropriate RBF centre and width parameters $\mathbf{m}_k$, r, only the linear weights **w** need to be estimated for which fast, efficient and optimal algorithms exist.

Each model has an associated probability score of being the current underlying model for the given observation. In the first stage of the development, this probability is not determined from parametrised gating network as in the mixture of local experts [5] and the mixture density network [3], but is determined on-line as it varies with time. In dynamic systems, time information must be taken into account whereas the mixture of local experts use only the state information which is not sufficient in general, unless the states contain the necessary information. In the second stage, the probability is extended to represent both the time and state information explicitly using the expressions from the mixture of local experts. Recently, time and state information have been combined in developing models for dynamic systems such as the mixture of controllers [4] and the Input – Output HMM [2]. However, the scheme developed here is more explicit and is not as general as the above schemes and is recursive as opposed to block estimation.

3 RECURSIVE ESTIMATION

The problem of recursive estimation with RBF networks have been studied previously [7, 8] and the algorithms developed here is a continuation of that process. Let the set of input – output observations from which the model is to be estimated be,

$$\mathcal{Z}_N = \{z_n \mid n = 1, \ldots, N\} \tag{3}$$

where, $\mathcal{Z}_N$ includes all observations upto the Nth data and z_n is the nth data,

$$z_n = \{(\mathbf{x}_n, y_n) \mid \mathbf{x}_n \in \Re^M, y_n \in \Re\} \tag{4}$$

The underlying system generating the observations are assumed to be multi-modal (with known H modes), with each observation satisfying the nonlinear relation,

$$y = f_h(\mathbf{x}) + \eta \tag{5}$$

where η is the noise with unknown distribution and $f_h(\cdot) : \Re^M \mapsto \Re$ is the unknown underlying nonlinear function for the hth mode which generated the observation. Under assumptions of zero mean Gaussian noise and that the model can approximate the underlying function arbitrarily closely, the probability distribution,

$$p(z_n | \mathbf{w}^h, \mathcal{M}^n = \mathcal{M}_h, \mathcal{Z}_{n-1}) = (2\pi)^{-\frac{1}{2}} R_0^{-\frac{1}{2}} \exp\left\{-\frac{1}{2} R_0^{-1} \left|y_n - f_h(\mathbf{x}_n; \mathbf{w}^h)\right|^2\right\} \tag{6}$$

is Gaussian. This is the *likelihood* of the observation z_n for the model $\mathcal{M}_h$, which in our case is the GRBF network, given model parameters $\mathbf{w}$ and that the nth observation was generated by $\mathcal{M}_h$. R_0 is the variance of the noise η. In general however, the model generating the nth observation is unknown and the likelihood of the nth observation is expanded to include γ_n^h the *indicator variable*, as in [6],

$$p(z_n, \gamma_n | \mathbf{W}, \mathcal{M}, \mathcal{Z}_{n-1}) = \prod_{h=1}^{H} [p(z_n | \mathbf{w}^h, \mathcal{M}^n = \mathcal{M}_h, \mathcal{Z}_{n-1}) p(\mathcal{M}^n = \mathcal{M}_h | \mathbf{x}_n, \mathcal{Z}^{n-1})]^{\gamma_n^h} \quad (7)$$

Bayes law can be applied to the on-line or recursive parameter estimation,

$$p(\mathbf{W} | \mathcal{Z}_n, \mathcal{M}) = \frac{p(z_n | \mathbf{W}, \mathcal{M}, \mathcal{Z}_{n-1}) p(\mathbf{W} | \mathcal{Z}_{n-1}, \mathcal{M})}{p(z_n | \mathcal{Z}_{n-1}, \mathcal{M})} \quad (8)$$

and the above equation is applied recursively for $n = 1, \ldots, N$. The term $p(z_n | \mathcal{Z}_{n-1}, \mathcal{M})$ is the *evidence*. If the underlying system is unimodal, this will result in the optimal Kalman estimator and if we assign the *prior* probability distribution for the model parameters $p(\mathbf{w}^h | \mathcal{M}_h)$ to be Gaussian with mean $\mathbf{w}_0$ and covariance matrix (positive definite) $\mathbf{P}_0 \in \Re^{K \times K}$, which combines the likelihood and the prior to give the *posterior* probability distribution which at time n is given by $p(\mathbf{w}^h | \mathcal{Z}_n, \mathcal{M}_h)$ which is also Gaussian,

$$p(\mathbf{w}^h | \mathcal{Z}_n, \mathcal{M}_h) = (2\pi)^{-\frac{K}{2}} |\mathbf{P}_n^h|^{-\frac{1}{2}} \exp\left\{-\frac{1}{2} (\mathbf{w}^h - \mathbf{w}_n^h)^T \mathbf{P}_n^{h^{-1}} (\mathbf{w}^h - \mathbf{w}_n^h)\right\} \quad (9)$$

In the multimodal case also, the estimation for the individual model parameters decouple naturally with the only modification being that the likelihood used for the parameter estimation is now based on weighted data and given by,

$$p(z_n | \mathbf{w}^h, \mathcal{M}_h, \mathcal{Z}_{n-1}) = (2\pi)^{-\frac{1}{2}} (R_0 \gamma_n^{h^{-1}})^{-\frac{1}{2}} \exp\left\{-\frac{1}{2} R_0^{-1} \gamma_n^h |y_n - f_h(\mathbf{x}_n; \mathbf{w}^h)|^2\right\} \quad (10)$$

The Bayes law relation (8) applies to each model. Hence, the only modification in the Kalman filter algorithm is that the noise variance for each model is set to R_0/γ_n^h and the resulting equations can be found in [7]. It increases the apparent uncertainty in the measurement output according to how likely the model is to be the true underlying mode, by increasing the noise variance term of the Kalman filter algorithm. Note that the term $p(\mathcal{M}^n = \mathcal{M}_h | \mathbf{x}_n, \mathcal{Z}^{n-1})$ is a time-varying scalar and does not influence the parameter estimation process.

The evidence term can also be determined directly from the Kalman filter,

$$p(z_n | \mathcal{M}_h, \mathcal{Z}_{n-1}) = (2\pi)^{-\frac{1}{2}} R_n^{h^{-\frac{1}{2}}} \exp\left\{-\frac{1}{2} R_n^{h^{-1}} |e_n^h|^2\right\} \quad (11)$$

where the e_n^h is the prediction error and R_n^h is the innovation variance with,

$$e_n^h = y_n - \mathbf{w}_{n-1}^{h^T} \mathbf{g}_n \quad (12)$$

$$R_n^h = R_0 \gamma_n^{h^{-1}} + \mathbf{g}_n^T \mathbf{P}_{n-1}^h \mathbf{g}_n \quad (13)$$

This is also the likelihood of the nth observation given the model $\mathcal{M}$ and the past observations $\mathcal{Z}_{n-1}$. The above equation shows that the evidence term used in Bayesian model selection [9] is computed recursively, but for the specific priors R_0, $\mathbf{P}_0$. On-line Bayesian model selection can be carried out by choosing many different priors, effectively sampling the prior space, to determine the best model to fit the given data, as discussed in [7].

4 RECURSIVE MODEL SELECTION

Bayes law can be invoked to perform recursive or on-line model selection and this has been used in the derivation of the *multiple model algorithm* [1]. The multiple model algorithm has been used for the recursive identification of dynamical nonlinear systems [7]. Applying Bayes law gives the following relation:

$$p(\mathcal{M}_h|\mathcal{Z}_n) = \frac{p(z_n|\mathcal{M}_h, \mathcal{Z}_{n-1})p(\mathcal{M}_h|\mathcal{Z}_{n-1})}{p(z_n|\mathcal{Z}_{n-1})} \qquad (14)$$

which can be computed recursively for $n = 1, \ldots, N$. $p(z_n|\mathcal{M}_h, \mathcal{Z}_{n-1})$ is the likelihood given in (11) and $p(\mathcal{M}_h|\mathcal{Z}_n)$ is the posterior probability of model $\mathcal{M}_h$ being the underlying model for the nth data given the observations $\mathcal{Z}_n$. The term $p(z_n|\mathcal{Z}_{n-1})$ is the normalising term given by,

$$p(z_n|\mathcal{Z}_{n-1}) = \sum_{h=1}^{H} p(z_n|\mathcal{M}_h, \mathcal{Z}_{n-1})p(\mathcal{M}_h|\mathcal{Z}_{n-1}) \qquad (15)$$

The initial prior probabilities for models are assigned to be equal to $1/H$. The equations (11), (14) combined with the Kalman filter estimation equations is known as the multiple model algorithm [1].

Amongst all the networks that are attempting to identify the underlying system, the identified model is the one with the highest posterior probability $p(\mathcal{M}_h|\mathcal{Z}_n)$ at each time n, ie.,

$$\mathcal{M}^n = \arg\max_{\mathcal{M}_h} p(\mathcal{M}_h|\mathcal{Z}_n) \qquad (16)$$

and hence can vary from time to time. This is preferred over the averaging of all the H models as the likelihood is multimodal and hence modal estimates are sought. Predictions are based on this most probable model.

Since the system is dynamical, if the underlying model for the dynamics is known, it can be used to predict the estimates at the next time instant based on the current estimates, prior to observing the next data. Here, a first order Markov assumption is made for the mode transitions. Given that at the time instant $n - 1$ the given mode is j, it is predicted that the probability of the mode at time instant n being h is the transition probability P_{hj}. With H modes, $\sum P_{hj} = 1$. The predicted probability of the mode being h at time n therefore is given by,

$$p_{n|n-1}(\mathcal{M}_h|\mathcal{Z}_{n-1}) = \sum_{j=1}^{H} P_{hj} p(\mathcal{M}_j|\mathcal{Z}_{n-1}) \qquad (17)$$

This can be viewed as the prediction stage of the model selection algorithm. The predicted output of the system is obtained from the output of the model that has the highest predicted probability.

Given the observation z_n, the correction is achieved through the multiple model algorithm of (14) with the following modification:

$$p(\mathcal{M}_h|\mathcal{Z}_n) = \frac{p(z_n|\mathcal{M}_h, \mathcal{Z}_{n-1})p_{n|n-1}(\mathcal{M}_h|\mathcal{Z}_{n-1})}{p(z_n|\mathcal{Z}_{n-1})} \qquad (18)$$

where modification to the prior has been made. Note that this probability is a time-varying scalar value and does not depend on the states.

5 HARD AND SOFT COMPETITION

The development of the estimation and model selection algorithms have thus far assumed that the indicator variable γ_n^h is known. The γ_n^h is unknown and an expected value must be used in the algorithm, which is given by,

$$\beta_n^h = \frac{p(z_n|\mathcal{M}^n = \mathcal{M}_h, \mathcal{Z}_{n-1})p_{n|n-1}(\mathcal{M}^n = \mathcal{M}_h|\mathcal{Z}_{n-1})}{p(z_n|\mathcal{Z}_{n-1})} \quad (19)$$

Two possible methodologies can be used for choosing the values for γ_n^h. In the first scheme,

$$\gamma_n^h = 1 \quad \text{if} \quad \beta_n^h > \beta_n^j \text{ for all } j \neq h, \quad \text{and} \quad 0 \quad \text{otherwise} \quad (20)$$

This results in *'hard' competition* where, only the model with the highest predicted probability undergoes adaptation using the Kalman filter algorithm while all other models are prevented from adapting. Alternatively, the expected value can be used in the algorithm,

$$\gamma_n^h = \beta_n^h \quad (21)$$

which results in *'soft' competition* and all models are allowed to undergo adaptation with appropriate data weighting as outlined in section 3. This scheme is slightly different from that presented in [7]. Since the posterior probabilities of each mode effectively indicate which mode is dominant at each time n, changes can then be used as means of detecting mode transitions.

6 EXPERIMENTAL RESULTS

The problem chosen for the experiment is learning the inverse robot kinematics used in [3]. This is a two link rigid arm manipulator for which, given joint arm angles (θ_1, θ_2), the end effector position in cartesian co-ordinates is given by,

$$\begin{aligned} x_1 &= L_1 \cos(\theta_1) - L_2 \cos(\theta_1 + \theta_2) \\ x_2 &= L_1 \sin(\theta_1) - L_2 \sin(\theta_1 + \theta_2) \end{aligned} \quad (22)$$

$L_1 = 0.8$, $L_2 = 0.2$ being the arm lengths. The inverse kinematics learning problem requires the identification of the underlying mapping from $(x_1, x_2) \rightarrow (\theta_1, \theta_2)$, which is bi-modal. Since the algorithm is developed for the identification of dynamical systems, the data are generated with the joint angles being excited sinusoidally with differing frequencies within the intervals $[0.3, 1.2] \times [\pi/2, 3\pi/2]$. The first 1000 observations are used for training and the next 1000 observations are used for testing with the adaptation turned off. The models use 28 RBFs chosen with fixed parameters, the centres being uniformly placed on a 7×4 grid.

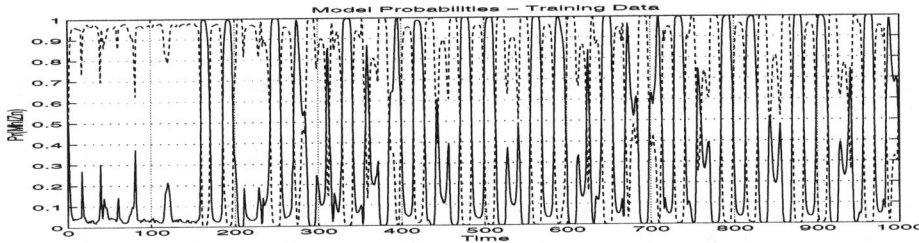

Figure 1: Learning inverse kinematics ('hard' competition): Model probabilities.

Figure 1 shows the model probabilities during training and shows the switching taking place between the two modes.

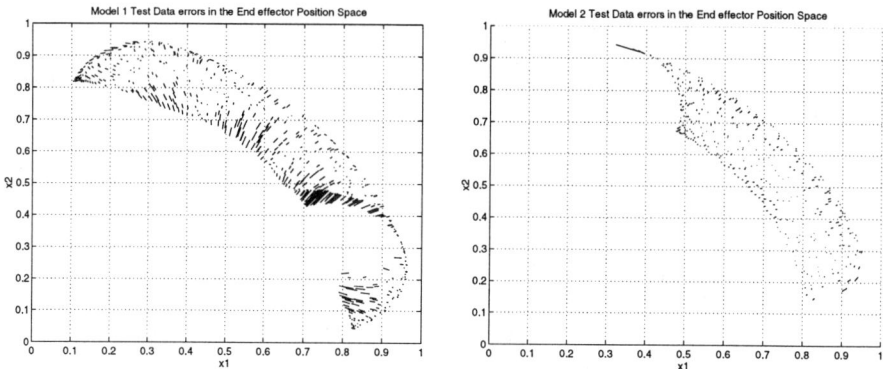

Figure 2: End effector position errors (test data) ('hard' competition): (a) Model 1 prediction (b) Model 2 prediction.

Figure 2 show the end effector position errors on the test data by both models 1 and 2 separately under the 'hard' competition scheme. The figure indicates the errors achieved by the best model used in the prediction – both models predicting in the centre of the input space where the function is multi-modal. This demonstrates the successful operation of the algorithm in the two RBF networks capturing some elements of the two underlying modes of the relationship. The best results on this learning task are: The RMSE on test data for this problem by the Mixture Density

Table 1: Learning Inverse Kinematics: Results

	Hard Competition	Soft Competition
RMSE (Train)	0.0213	0.0442
RMSE (Test)	0.0084	0.0212

Network is 0.0053 and by a single network is 0.0578 [3]. Note however that the algorithm here did not use state information and used only the time dependency.

7 PARAMETRISED GATING NETWORKS

The model parameters were determined explicitly based on the time information in the dynamical system. If the gating model probabilities are expressed as a function of the states, similar to [6],

$$p(\mathcal{M}_h|\mathbf{x}_n, \mathcal{Z}_{n-1}) = \exp\{\mathbf{a}^{h^T}\mathbf{g}\} / \sum_{h=1}^{H} \exp\{\mathbf{a}^{h^T}\mathbf{g}\} = \alpha_n^h \qquad (23)$$

where $\mathbf{a}^h$ are the gating network parameters. Note that the gating network shares the same basis functions as the expert models.

This extension to the gating networks does not affect the model parameter estimation procedure. The likelihood in (7) decomposes into a part for model parameter estimation involving output prediction error and a part for gating parameter estimation involving the indicator variable γ_n. The second part can be approximated to a Gaussian of the form,

$$p(\gamma_n|\mathbf{x}_n, \mathbf{a}^h, \mathcal{Z}_{n-1}) \approx (2\pi)^{-\frac{1}{2}} R_{go}^{h^{-\frac{1}{2}}} \exp\left\{-\frac{1}{2}R_{go}^{h^{-1}}|\gamma_n^h - \alpha_n^h|^2\right\} \qquad (24)$$

This approximation allows the extended Kalman filter algorithm to be used for gating network parameter estimation. The model selection equations of section 4 can be applied without any modification with the new gating probabilities. The choice of the indicator variable γ_n^h can be based as before, resulting in either hard or soft competition. The necessary expressions in (21) are obtained through the Kalman filter estimates and the evidence values, for both the model and gating parameters. Note that this is different from the estimates used in [6] in the sense that, marginalisation over the model and gating parameters have been done here.

8 CONCLUSIONS

Recursive estimation algorithms for dynamic modular RBF networks have been developed. The models are based on Gaussian RBF networks and the gating is simply a time-varying scalar. The resulting algorithm uses Kalman filter estimation for the model parameters and the multiple model algorithm for the gating probability. Both, 'hard' and 'soft' competition based estimation schemes are developed where in the former, the most probable network is adapted and in the latter all networks are adapted by appropriate weighting of the data. Experimental results are given that demonstrate the capture of the switching in the dynamical system by the modular RBF networks. Extending the method to include the gating probability to be a function of the state are then outlined briefly. Work is currently in progress to experimentally demonstrate the operation of this extension.

References

[1] Bar–Shalom, Y. and Fortmann, T. E. *Tracking and data association*, Academic Press, New York, 1988.

[2] Bengio, Y. and Frasconi, P. "An input output HMM architecture", In G. Tesauro, D. S. Touretzky and T. K. Leen (eds.) *Advances in Neural Information Processing Systems 7*, Morgan Kaufmann, CA: San Mateo, 1995.

[3] Bishop, C. M. "Mixture density networks", *Report NCRG/4288*, Computer Science Dept., Aston University, UK, 1994.

[4] Cacciatore, C. W. and Nowlan, S. J. "Mixtures of controllers for jump linear and nonlinear plants", In J. Cowan, G. Tesauro, and J. Alspector (eds.) *Advances in Neural Information Processing Systems 6*, Morgan Kaufmann, CA: San Mateo, 1994.

[5] Jacobs, R. A., Jordan, M. I., Nowlan, S. J. and Hinton, G. E. "Adaptive mixtures of local experts", *Neural Computation*, *3*: 79-87, 1991.

[6] Jordan, M. I. and Jacobs, R. A. "Hierarchical mixtures of experts and the EM algorithm", *Neural Computation*, *6*: 181-214, 1994.

[7] Kadirkamanathan, V. "Recursive nonlinear identification using multiple model algorithm", In *Proceedings of the IEEE Workshop on Neural Networks for Signal Processing V*, 171-180, 1995.

[8] Kadirkamanathan, V. "A statistical inference based growth criterion for the RBF network", In *Proceedings of the IEEE Workshop on Neural Networks for Signal Processing IV*, 12-21, 1994.

[9] MacKay, D. J. C. "Bayesian interpolation", *Neural Computation*, *4*: 415-447, 1992.

On Neural Networks with Minimal Weights

Vasken Bohossian   Jehoshua Bruck

California Institute of Technology
Mail Code 136-93
Pasadena, CA 91125
E-mail: {vincent, bruck}@paradise.caltech.edu

Abstract

Linear threshold elements are the basic building blocks of artificial neural networks. A linear threshold element computes a function that is a sign of a weighted sum of the input variables. The weights are arbitrary integers; actually, they can be very big integers—exponential in the number of the input variables. However, in practice, it is difficult to implement big weights. In the present literature a distinction is made between the two extreme cases: linear threshold functions with polynomial-size weights as opposed to those with exponential-size weights. The main contribution of this paper is to fill up the gap by further refining that separation. Namely, we prove that the class of linear threshold functions with polynomial-size weights can be divided into subclasses according to the degree of the polynomial. In fact, we prove a more general result—that there exists a minimal weight linear threshold function for any arbitrary number of inputs and any weight size. To prove those results we have developed a novel technique for constructing linear threshold functions with minimal weights.

1 Introduction

Human brains are by far superior to computers for solving hard problems like combinatorial optimization and image and speech recognition, although their basic building blocks are several orders of magnitude slower. This observation has boosted interest in the field of artificial neural networks [Hopfield 82], [Rumelhart 82]. The latter are built by interconnecting multiple artificial neurons (or linear threshold gates), whose behavior is inspired by that of biological neurons. Artificial neural networks have found promising applications in pattern recognition, learning and other data processing tasks. However most of the research has been oriented towards the practical aspect of neural networks, simulating or building networks for particular tasks and then comparing their performance with that of more traditional methods for those particular tasks. To compare neural networks to other computational models one needs to develop the theoretical settings in which to estimate their capabilities and limitations.

1.1 Linear Threshold Gate

The present paper focuses on the study of a single linear threshold gate (artificial neuron) with binary inputs and output as well as integer weights (synaptic coefficients). Such a gate is mathematically described by a *linear threshold function*.

Definition 1 (Linear Threshold Function)
A linear threshold function of n variables is a Boolean function $f : \{-1,1\}^n \to \{-1,1\}$ that can be written as

$$f(\vec{x}) = sgn(F(\vec{x})) = \begin{cases} 1 & \text{, for } F(\vec{x}) \geq 0 \\ -1 & \text{, otherwise} \end{cases} \text{, where } F(\vec{x}) = \vec{w} \cdot \vec{x} = \sum_{i=1}^{n} w_i x_i$$

for any $\vec{x} \in \{-1,1\}^n$ and a fixed $\vec{w} \in Z^n$.

Although we could allow the weights w_i to be real numbers, it is known [Muroga 71], [Raghavan 88] that for a, binary input neuron, one needs $O(n \log n)$ bits per weight, where n is the number of inputs. So in the rest of the paper, we will assume without loss of generality that all weights are integers.

1.2 Motivation

Many experimental results in the area of neural networks have indicated that the magnitudes of the coefficients in the linear threshold elements grow very fast with the size of the inputs and therefore limit the practical use of the network. One natural question to ask is the following. How limited is the computational power of the network if one limits oneself to threshold elements with only "small" growth in the size of the coefficients? To answer that question we have to define a measure of the magnitudes of the weights. Note that, given a function f, the weight vector $\vec{w}$ is not unique (see Example 1 below).

Definition 2 (Weight Space)
Given a linear threshold function f we define W as the set of all weights that satisfy Definition 1, that is $W = \{\vec{w} \in Z^n : \forall \vec{x} \in \{-1,1\}^n, sgn(\vec{w} \cdot \vec{x}) = f(\vec{x})\}$.

Here follows a measure of the size of the weights.

Definition 3 (Minimal Weight Size)
We define the size of a weight vector as the sum of the absolute values of the weights. The minimal weight size of a linear threshold function is defined as :

$$S[f] = \min_{\vec{w} \in W} (\sum_{i=1}^{n} |w_i|)$$

The particular vector that achieves the minimum is called a minimal weight vector.

Naturally, $S[f]$ is a function of n.

It has been shown [Hastad 94], [Myhill 61], [Shawe-Taylor 92], [Siu 91] that there exists a linear threshold function that can be implemented by a single threshold element with exponentially growing weights, $S[f] \sim 2^n$, but cannot be implemented by a threshold element with smaller : polynomialy growing weights, $S[f] \sim n^d$, d constant. In light of that result the above question was dealt with by defining a class within the set of linear threshold functions : the class of functions with "small" (i.e. polynomialy growing) weights [Siu 91]. Most of the recent research focuses on the power of circuits with small weights, relative to circuits with arbitrary weights [Goldmann 92], [Goldman 93]. Rather than dealing with circuits we are interested in studying a single threshold gate. The main contribution of the present paper is to further refine the division of small versus arbitrary weights. We separate the set of functions with small weights into classes indexed by d, the degree of polynomial growth and show that all of them are non-empty. In particular, we develop a technique for proving that a weight vector is minimal. We use that technique to construct a function of size $S[f] = s$ for an arbitrary s.

1.3 Approach

The main difficulty in analyzing the size of the weights of a threshold element is due to the fact that a single linear threshold function can be implemented by different sets of weights as shown in the following example.

Example 1 (A Threshold Function with Minimal Weights)
Consider the following two sets of weights (weight vectors).

$$\vec{w}_1 = (1\ 2\ 4), \quad F_1(\vec{x}) = x_1 + 2x_2 + 4x_3$$

$$\vec{w}_2 = (2\ 4\ 8), \quad F_2(\vec{x}) = 2x_1 + 4x_2 + 8x_3$$

They both implement the same threshold function

$$f(\vec{x}) = sgn(F_2(\vec{x})) = sgn(2F_1(\vec{x})) = sgn(F_1(\vec{x}))$$

A closer look reveals that $f(\vec{x}) = sgn(x_3)$, implying that none of the above weight vectors has minimal size. Indeed, the minimal one is $\vec{w}_3 = (0\ 0\ 1)$ and $S[f] = 1$.

It is in general difficult to determine if a given set of weights is minimal [Amaldi 93], [Willis 63]. Our technique consists of limiting the study to only a particular subset of linear threshold functions, a subset for which it is possible to prove that a given weight vector is minimal. That subset is loosely defined by the requirement that there exist input vectors for which $f(\vec{x}) = f(-\vec{x})$. The existence of such a vector, called a *root* of f, puts a constraint on the weight vector used to implement f. The larger the set of roots – the larger the constraint on the set of weight vectors, which in turn helps determine the minimal one. A detailed description of the technique is given in Section 2.

1.4 Organization

Here follows a brief outline of the rest of the paper. Section 2 mathematically defines the setting of the problem as well as derives some basic results on the properties of functions that admit roots. Those results are used as building blocks for the proof of the main results in Section 3. It also introduces a construction method for functions with minimal weights. Section 3 presents the main result : for any weight size, s, and any number of inputs, n, there exists an n-input linear threshold function that requires weights of size $S[f] = s$. Section 4 presents some applications of the result of Section 3 and indicates future research directions.

2 Construction of Minimal Threshold Functions

The present section defines the mathematical tools used to construct functions with minimal weights.

2.1 Mathematical setting

We are interested in constructing functions for which the minimal weight is easily determined. Finding the minimal weight involves a search, we are therefore interested in finding functions with a constrained weight spaces. The following tools allows us to put constraints on W.

Definition 4 (Root Space of a Boolean Function)
A vector $\vec{v} \in \{-1,1\}^n$ such that $f(\vec{v}) = f(-\vec{v})$ is called a root of f. We define the root space, R, as the set of all roots of f.

Definition 5 (Root Generator Matrix)
For a given weight vector $\vec{w} \in W$ and a root $\vec{v} \in R$, the root generator matrix, $G = (g_{ij})$, is a $(n \times k)$-matrix, with entries in $\{-1, 0, 1\}$, whose rows $\vec{g}$ are orthogonal to $\vec{w}$ and equal to $\vec{v}$ at all non-zero coordinates, namely,

1. $G\vec{w} = \vec{0}$

2. $g_{ij} = 0$ or $g_{ij} = v_j$ for all i and j.

Example 2 (Root Generator Matrix)
Suppose that we are given a linear threshold function specified by a weight vector $\vec{w} = (1, 1, 2, 4, 1, 1, 2, 4)$. By inspection we determine one root $\vec{v} = (1, 1, 1, 1, -1, -1, -1, -1)$. Notice that $w_1 + w_2 - w_7 = 0$ which can be written as $\vec{g} \cdot \vec{w} = 0$, where $\vec{g} = (1, 1, 0, 0, 0, 0, -1, 0)$ is a row of G. Set $\vec{r} = \vec{v} - 2\vec{g}$. Since $\vec{g}$ is equal to $\vec{v}$ at all non-zero coordinates, $\vec{r} \in \{-1, 1\}^n$. Also $\vec{r} \cdot \vec{w} = \vec{v} \cdot \vec{w} + \vec{g} \cdot \vec{w} = 0$. We have generated a new root : $\vec{r} = (-1, -1, 1, 1, -1, -1, 1, -1)$.

Lemma 6 (Orthogonality of G and W)
For a given weight vector $\vec{w} \in W$ and a root $\vec{v} \in R$

$$\vec{u}G^T = \vec{0}$$

holds for any weight vector $\vec{u} \in W$.

Proof. For an arbitrary $\vec{u} \in W$ and an arbitrary row, $\vec{g}_i$, of G, let $\vec{v}' = \vec{v} - 2\vec{g}_i$. By definition of $\vec{g}_i$, $\vec{v}' \in \{-1, 1\}^n$ and $\vec{v}' \cdot \vec{w} = 0$. That implies $f(\vec{v}') = f(-\vec{v}')$: $\vec{v}'$ is a root of f. For any weight vector $\vec{u} \in W$, $sgn(\vec{u} \cdot \vec{v}') = sgn(-\vec{u} \cdot \vec{v}')$. Therefore $\vec{u} \cdot (\vec{v} - 2\vec{g}_i) = 0$ and finally, since $\vec{v} \cdot \vec{u} = 0$ we get $\vec{u} \cdot \vec{g}_i = 0$. □

Lemma 7 (Minimality)
For a given weight vector $\vec{w} \in W$ and a root $\vec{v} \in R$ if $rank(G) = n - 1$ (i.e. G has $n-1$ independent rows) and $|w_i| = 1$ for some i, then $\vec{w}$ is the minimal weight vector.

Proof. From Lemma 6 any weight vector $\vec{u}$ satisfies $\vec{u}G^T = \vec{0}$. $rank(G) = n - 1$ implies that $dim(W) = 1$, i.e. all possible weight vectors are integer multiples of each other. Since $|w_i| = 1$, all vectors are of the form $\vec{u} = k\vec{w}$, for $k \geq 1$. Therefore $\vec{w}$ has the smallest size. □

We complete Example 2 with an application of Lemma 7.

Example 3 (Minimality)
Given $\vec{w} = (1, 1, 2, 4, 1, 1, 2, 4)$ and $\vec{v} = (1, 1, 1, 1, -1, -1, -1, -1)$ we can construct :

$$G = \begin{pmatrix} 1 & 0 & 0 & 0 & -1 & 0 & 0 & 0 \\ 0 & 1 & 0 & 0 & 0 & -1 & 0 & 0 \\ 0 & 0 & 1 & 0 & 0 & 0 & -1 & 0 \\ 0 & 0 & 0 & 1 & 0 & 0 & 0 & -1 \\ 1 & 0 & 0 & 0 & 0 & -1 & 0 & 0 \\ 1 & 1 & 0 & 0 & 0 & 0 & -1 & 0 \\ 1 & 1 & 1 & 0 & 0 & 0 & 0 & -1 \end{pmatrix}$$

It is easy to verify that $rank(G) = n - 1 = 7$ and therefore, by Lemma 7, $\vec{w}$ is minimal and $S[f] = 16$.

2.2 Construction of minimal weight vectors

In Example 3 we saw how, given a weight vector, one can show that it is minimal. In this section we present an example of a linear threshold function with minimal weight size, with an arbitrary number of input variables.

We would like to construct a weight vector and show that it is minimal. Let the number of inputs, n, be even. Let $\vec{w}$ consist of two identical blocks : $(w_1, w_2, ..., w_{n/2}, w_1, w_2, ..., w_{n/2})$. Clearly, $\vec{v} = (1, 1, ..., 1, -1, -1, ..., -1)$ is a root and G is the corresponding generator matrix.

$$G = \begin{pmatrix} 1 & 0 & 0 & 0 & \cdots & 0 & 0 & 0 & -1 & 0 & 0 & 0 & \cdots & 0 & 0 & 0 \\ 0 & 1 & 0 & 0 & \cdots & 0 & 0 & 0 & 0 & -1 & 0 & 0 & \cdots & 0 & 0 & 0 \\ 0 & 0 & 1 & 0 & \cdots & 0 & 0 & 0 & 0 & 0 & -1 & 0 & \cdots & 0 & 0 & 0 \\ \vdots & & & & & & & & & & & & & & & \vdots \\ 0 & 0 & 0 & 0 & \cdots & 0 & 1 & 0 & 0 & 0 & 0 & 0 & \cdots & 0 & -1 & 0 \\ 0 & 0 & 0 & 0 & \cdots & 0 & 0 & 1 & 0 & 0 & 0 & 0 & \cdots & 0 & 0 & -1 \end{pmatrix}$$

3 The Main Result

The following theorem states that given an integer s and a number of variables n there exists a function of n variables and minimal weight size s.

Theorem 8 (Main Result)
For any pair (s, n) that satisfies

1. $n \leq s \leq \begin{cases} 2^{\frac{n}{2}} & \text{, for } n \text{ even} \\ 2^{\frac{n-1}{2}} + 2^{\frac{n-3}{2}} & \text{, for } n \text{ odd} \end{cases}$

2. s even

there exists a linear threshold function of n variables, f, with minimal weight size $S[f] = s$.

Proof. Given a pair (s, n), that satisfies the above conditions we first construct a weight vector $\vec{w}$ that satisfies $\sum_{i=1}^{n} |w_i| = s$, then show that it is the minimal weight vector of the function $f(x) = sgn(\vec{w} \cdot \vec{x})$. The proof is shown only for n even.

CONSTRUCTION.

1. Define $(a_1, a_2, ..., a_{n/2}) = (1, 1, ..., 1)$.

2. If $\sum_{i=1}^{n/2} a_i < s/2$ then increase by one the smallest a_i such that $a_i < 2^{i-2}$. (In the case of a tie take the w_i with smallest index i).

3. Repeat the previous step until $\sum_{i=1}^{n/2} a_i = s/2$ or $(a_1, a_2, ..., a_N) = (1, 1, 2, 4, ..., 2^{\frac{n}{2}-2})$.

4. Set $\vec{w} = (a_1, a_2, ..., a_{n/2}, a_1, a_2, ..., a_{n/2})$.

Because we increase the size by one unit at a time the algorithm will converge to the desired result for any integer s that satisfies $n \leq s \leq 2^{\frac{n}{2}}$. We have a construction for any valid (s, n) pair. Let us show that $\vec{w}$ is minimal.

MINIMALITY. Given that $\vec{w} = (a_1, a_2, ..., a_{n/2}, a_1, a_2, ..., a_{a/2})$ we find a root $\vec{v} = (1, 1, ..., 1, -1, -1, ..., -1)$ and $n/2$ rows of the generator matrix G corresponding to the equations $w_i = w_{i+\frac{n}{2}}$. To form additional rows note that the first k a_i's are powers of two (where k depends on s and n). Those can be written as $a_i = \sum_{j=1}^{i-1} a_j$ and generate $k-1$ rows. And finally note that all other a_i, $i > k$, are smaller than 2^{k+1}. Hence, they can be written as a binary expansion $a_i = \sum_{j=1}^{k} \alpha_{ij} a_j$ where $\alpha_{ij} \in \{0, 1\}$. There are $\frac{n}{2} - k$ such weights. G has a total of $n - 1$ independent rows. $rank(G) = n - 1$ and $w_1 = 1$, therefore by Lemma 7, $\vec{w}$ is minimal and $S[f] = s$. □

Example 4 (A Function of 10 variables and size $S[f] = 26$)
We start with $\vec{a} = (1, 1, 1, 1, 1)$. We iterate : $(1, 1, 2, 1, 1)$, $(1, 1, 2, 2, 1)$, $(1, 1, 2, 2, 2)$, $(1, 1, 2, 3, 2)$, $(1, 1, 2, 3, 3)$, $(1, 1, 2, 4, 3)$, $(1, 1, 2, 4, 4)$, and finally $(1, 1, 2, 4, 5)$. The construction algorithm converges to $\vec{a} = (1, 1, 2, 4, 5)$. We claim that $\vec{w} = (\vec{a}, \vec{a}) = (1, 1, 2, 4, 5, 1, 1, 2, 4, 5)$ is minimal. Indeed, $\vec{v} = (1, 1, 1, 1, 1, -1, -1, -1, -1, -1)$ and

$$G = \begin{pmatrix} 1 & 0 & 0 & 0 & 0 & -1 & 0 & 0 & 0 & 0 \\ 0 & 1 & 0 & 0 & 0 & 0 & -1 & 0 & 0 & 0 \\ 0 & 0 & 1 & 0 & 0 & 0 & 0 & -1 & 0 & 0 \\ 0 & 0 & 0 & 1 & 0 & 0 & 0 & 0 & -1 & 0 \\ 0 & 0 & 0 & 0 & 1 & 0 & 0 & 0 & 0 & -1 \\ 1 & 0 & 0 & 0 & 0 & 0 & -1 & 0 & 0 & 0 \\ 1 & 1 & 0 & 0 & 0 & 0 & 0 & -1 & 0 & 0 \\ 1 & 1 & 1 & 0 & 0 & 0 & 0 & 0 & -1 & 0 \\ 1 & 0 & 0 & 1 & 0 & 0 & 0 & 0 & 0 & -1 \end{pmatrix}$$

is a matrix of rank 9.

Example 5 (Functions with Polynomial Size)
This example shows an application of Theorem 8. We define $\widehat{LT}^{(d)}$ as the set of linear threshold functions for which $S[f] \leq n^d$. The Theorem states that for any even n there exists a function f of n variables and minimum weight $S[f] = n^d$. The implication is that for all d, $\widehat{LT}^{(d-1)}$ is a proper subset of $\widehat{LT}^{(d)}$

4 Conclusions

We have shown that for any reasonable pair of integers (n, s), where s is even, there exists a linear threshold function of n variables with minimal weight size $S[f] = s$. We have developed a novel technique for constructing linear threshold functions with minimal weights that is based on the existence of root vectors. An interesting application of our method is the computation of a lower bound on the number of linear threshold functions [Smith 66]. In addition, our technique can help in studying the trade-offs between a number of important parameters associated with linear threshold (neural) circuits, including, the number of elements, the number of layers, the fan-in, fan-out and the size of the weights.

Acknowledgements

This work was supported in part by the NSF Young Investigator Award CCR-9457811, by the Sloan Research Fellowship, by a grant from the IBM Almaden Research Center, San Jose, California, by a grant from the AT&T Foundation and by the center for Neuromorphic Systems Engineering as a part of the National Science Foundation Engineering Research Center Program; and by the California Trade and Commerce Agency, Office of Strategic Technology.

References

[Amaldi 93] E. Amaldi and V. Kann. The complexity and approximability of finding maximum feasible subsystems of linear relations. Ecole Polytechnique Federale De Lausanne Technical Report, *ORWP 93/11*, August 1993.

[Goldmann 92] M. Goldmann, J. Hastad, and A. Razborov. Majority gates vs. general weighted threshold gates. *Computational Complexity*, (2):277–300, 1992.

[Goldman 93] M. Goldmann and M. Karpinski. Simulating threshold circuits by majority circuits. In *Proc. 25th ACM STOC*, pages pp. 551–560, 1993.

[Hastad 94] J. Hastad. On the size of weights for threshold gates. *SIAM. J. Disc. Math.*, 7:484–492, 1994.

[Hopfield 82] J. Hopfield. Neural networks and physical systems with emergent collective computational abilities. *Proc. of the USA National Academy of Sciences*, 79:2554–2558, 1982.

[Muroga 71] M. Muroga. *Threshold Logic and its Applications*. Wiley-Interscience, 1971.

[Myhill 61] J. Myhill and W. H. Kautz. On the size of weights required for linear-input switching functions. *IRE Trans. Electronic Computers*, (EC10):pp. 288–290, 1961.

[Raghavan 88] P. Raghavan. Learning in threshold networks: a computational model and applications. Technical Report RC 13859, IBM Research, July 1988.

[Rumelhart 82] D. Rumelhart and J. McClelland. Parallel distributed processing: Explorations in the microstructure of cognition. *MIT Press*, 1982.

[Shawe-Taylor 92] J. S. Shawe-Taylor, M. H. G. Anthony, and W. Kern. Classes of feedforward neural networks and their circuit complexity. *Neural Networks*, Vol. 5:pp. 971–977, 1992.

[Siu 91] K. Siu and J. Bruck. On the power of threshold circuits with small weights. *SIAM J. Disc. Math.*, Vol. 4(No. 3):pp. 423–435, August 1991.

[Smith 66] D. R. Smith. Bounds on the number of threshold functions. *IEEE Transactions on Electronic Computers*, June 1966.

[Willis 63] D. G. Willis. Minimum weights for threshold switches. In *Switching Theory in Space Techniques*. Stanford University Press, Stanford, Calif., 1963.

Modern Analytic Techniques to Solve the Dynamics of Recurrent Neural Networks

A.C.C. Coolen
Dept. of Mathematics
King's College London
Strand, London WC2R 2LS, U.K.

S.N. Laughton
Dept. of Physics - Theoretical Physics
University of Oxford
1 Keble Road, Oxford OX1 3NP, U.K.

D. Sherrington [*]
Center for Non-linear Studies
Los Alamos National Laboratory
Los Alamos, New Mexico 87545

Abstract

We describe the use of modern analytical techniques in solving the dynamics of symmetric and nonsymmetric recurrent neural networks near saturation. These explicitly take into account the correlations between the post-synaptic potentials, and thereby allow for a reliable prediction of transients.

1 INTRODUCTION

Recurrent neural networks have been rather popular in the physics community, because they lend themselves so naturally to analysis with tools from equilibrium statistical mechanics. This was the main theme of physicists between, say, 1985 and 1990. Less familiar to the neural network community is a subsequent wave of theoretical physical studies, dealing with the dynamics of symmetric and nonsymmetric recurrent networks. The strategy here is to try to describe the processes at a reduced level of an appropriate small set of dynamic macroscopic observables. At first, progress was made in solving the dynamics of extremely diluted models (Derrida et al, 1987) and of fully connected models away from saturation (for a review see (Coolen and Sherrington, 1993)). This paper is concerned with more recent approaches, which take the form of dynamical replica theories, that allow for a reliable prediction of transients, even near saturation. Transients provide the link between initial states and final states (equilibrium calculations only provide

---
[*] On leave from Department of Physics - Theoretical Physics, University of Oxford

information on the possible final states). In view of the technical nature of the subject, we will describe only basic ideas and results for simple models (full details and applications to more complicated models can be found elsewhere).

2 RECURRENT NETWORKS NEAR SATURATION

Let us consider networks of N binary neurons $\sigma_i \in \{-1, 1\}$, where neuron states are updated sequentially and stochastically, driven by the values of post-synaptic potentials h_i. The probability to find the system at time t in state $\boldsymbol{\sigma} = (\sigma_1, \ldots, \sigma_N)$ is denoted by $p_t(\boldsymbol{\sigma})$. For the rates $w_i(\boldsymbol{\sigma})$ of the transitions $\sigma_i \to -\sigma_i$ and for the potentials $h_i(\boldsymbol{\sigma})$ we make the usual choice

$$w_i(\boldsymbol{\sigma}) = \frac{1}{2}\left[1 - \sigma_i \tanh[\beta h_i(\boldsymbol{\sigma})]\right] \qquad h_i(\boldsymbol{\sigma}) = \sum_{j \neq i} J_{ij}\sigma_j$$

The parameter β controls the degree of stochasticity: the $\beta = 0$ dynamics is completely random, whereas for $\beta = \infty$ we find the deterministic rule $\sigma_i \to \text{sgn}[h_i(\boldsymbol{\sigma})]$. The evolution in time of $p_t(\boldsymbol{\sigma})$ is given by the master equation

$$\frac{d}{dt}p_t(\boldsymbol{\sigma}) = \sum_{k=1}^{N}\left[p_t(F_k\boldsymbol{\sigma})w_k(F_k\boldsymbol{\sigma}) - p_t(\boldsymbol{\sigma})w_k(\boldsymbol{\sigma})\right] \qquad (1)$$

with $F_k\Phi(\boldsymbol{\sigma}) = \Phi(\sigma_1, \ldots, -\sigma_k, \ldots, \sigma_N)$. For symmetric models, where $J_{ij} = J_{ji}$ for all (ij), the dynamics (1) leads asymptotically to the Boltzmann equilibrium distribution $p_{\text{eq}}(\boldsymbol{\sigma}) \sim \exp\left[-\beta E(\boldsymbol{\sigma})\right]$, with the energy $E(\boldsymbol{\sigma}) = -\sum_{i<j}\sigma_i J_{ij}\sigma_j$.

For associative memory models with Hebbian-type synapses, required to store a set of p random binary patterns $\boldsymbol{\xi}^\mu = (\xi_1^\mu, \ldots, \xi_N^\mu)$, the relevant macroscopic observable is the overlap m between the current microscopic state $\boldsymbol{\sigma}$ and the pattern to be retrieved (say, pattern 1): $m = \frac{1}{N}\sum_i \xi_i^1 \sigma_i$. Each post-synaptic potential can now be written as the sum of a simple signal term and an interference-noise term, e.g.

$$J_{ij} = \frac{1}{N}\sum_{\mu=1}^{p=\alpha N}\xi_i^\mu \xi_j^\mu \qquad h_i(\boldsymbol{\sigma}) = m\xi_i^1 + \frac{1}{N}\sum_{\mu>1}\xi_i^\mu\sum_{j\neq i}\xi_j^\mu\sigma_j \qquad (2)$$

All complications arise from the noise terms.

The 'Local Chaos Hypothesis' (LCH) consists of assuming the noise terms to be independently distributed Gaussian variables. The macroscopic description then consists of the overlap m and the width Δ of the noise distribution (Amari and Maginu, 1987). This, however, works only for states near the nominated pattern, see also (Nishimori and Ozeki, 1993). In reality the noise components in the potentials have far more complicated statistics[1]. Due to the build up of correlations between the system state and the non-nominated patterns, the noise components can be highly correlated and described by bi-modal distributions. Another approach involves a description in terms of correlation- and response functions (with two time-arguments). Here one builds a generating functional, which is a sum over all possible trajectories in state space, averaged over the distribution of the non-nominated patterns. One finds equations which are exact for $N \to \infty$, but, unfortunately, also rather complicated. For the typical neural network models solutions are known only in equilibrium (Rieger et al, 1988); information on transients has so far only been obtained through cumbersome approximation schemes (Horner et al, 1989). We now turn to a theory that takes into account the non-trivial statistics of the post-synaptic potentials, yet involves observables with one time-argument only.

---

[1] Correlations are negligible only in extremely diluted (asymmetric) networks (Derrida et al, 1987), and in networks with independently drawn (asymmetric) random synapses

3 DYNAMICAL REPLICA THEORIES

The evolution of macroscopic observables $\Omega(\sigma) = (\Omega_1(\sigma), \ldots, \Omega_K(\sigma))$ can be described by the so-called Kramers-Moyal expansion for the corresponding probability distribution $P_t(\Omega)$ (derived directly from (1)). Under certain conditions on the sensitivity of Ω to single-neuron transitions $\sigma_i \to -\sigma_i$, one finds on finite time-scales and for $N \to \infty$ the macroscopic state Ω to evolve deterministically according to:

$$\frac{d}{dt}\Omega = \frac{\sum_\sigma p_t(\sigma) \delta[\Omega - \Omega(\sigma)] \sum_i w_i(\sigma) [\Omega(F_i\sigma) - \Omega(\sigma)]}{\sum_\sigma p_t(\sigma) \delta[\Omega - \Omega(\sigma)]} \quad (3)$$

This equation depends explicitly on time through $p_t(\sigma)$. However, there are two natural ways for (3) to become autonomous: (i) by the term $\sum_i w_i(\sigma) [\Omega(F_i\sigma) - \Omega(\sigma)]$ depending on σ only through $\Omega(\sigma)$ (as for attractor networks away from saturation), or (ii) by (1) allowing for solutions of the form $p_t(\sigma) = f_t[\Omega(\sigma)]$ (as for extremely diluted networks). In both cases $p_t(\sigma)$ drops out of (3). Simulations further indicate that for $N \to \infty$ the macroscopic evolution usually depends only on the statistical properties of the patterns $\{\xi^\mu\}$, not on their microscopic realisation ('self-averaging'). This leads us to the following closure assumptions:

1. Probability equipartitioning in the Ω subshells of the ensemble: $p_t(\sigma) \sim \delta[\Omega_t - \Omega(\sigma)]$. If Ω indeed obeys closed equations, this assumption is safe.
2. Self-averaging of the Ω flow with respect to the microscopic details of the non-nominated patterns: $\frac{d}{dt}\Omega \to \langle \frac{d}{dt}\Omega \rangle_{\text{patt}}$.

Our equations (3) are hereby transformed into the *closed* set:

$$\frac{d}{dt}\Omega = \langle \frac{\sum_\sigma \delta[\Omega - \Omega(\sigma)] \sum_i w_i(\sigma) [\Omega(F_i\sigma) - \Omega(\sigma)]}{\sum_\sigma \delta[\Omega - \Omega(\sigma)]} \rangle_{\text{patt}}$$

The final observation is that the tool for averaging fractions is replica theory:

$$\frac{d}{dt}\Omega = \lim_{n\to 0} \lim_{N\to\infty} \sum_{\sigma^1 \ldots \sigma^n} \langle \sum_i w_i(\sigma^1) [\Omega(F_i\sigma^1) - \Omega(\sigma^1)] \prod_{\alpha=1}^n \delta[\Omega - \Omega(\sigma^\alpha)] \rangle_{\text{patt}} \quad (4)$$

The choice to be made for the observables $\Omega(\sigma)$, crucial for the closure assumptions to make sense, is constrained by requiring the theory to be exact in specific limits:

$$\text{exactness for } \alpha \to 0: \quad \Omega = (m, \ldots)$$
$$\text{exactness for } t \to \infty: \quad \Omega = (E, \ldots) \quad \text{(for symmetric models only)}$$

4 SIMPLE VERSION OF THE THEORY

For the Hopfield model (2) the simplest two-parameter theory which is exact for $\alpha \to 0$ and for $t \to \infty$ is consequently obtained by choosing $\Omega = (m, E)$. Equivalently we can choose $\Omega = (m, r)$, where $r(\sigma)$ measures the 'interference energy':

$$m = \frac{1}{N} \sum_i \xi_i^1 \sigma_i \qquad E = -\frac{1}{2}[m^2 + \alpha r] \qquad r = \frac{1}{\alpha} \sum_{\mu > 1} [\frac{1}{N} \sum_i \xi_i^\mu \sigma_i]^2$$

The result of working out (4) for $\Omega = (m, r)$ is:

$$\frac{d}{dt}m = \int dz\, D_{m,r}[z] \tanh \beta(m+z) - m$$

$$\frac{1}{2}\frac{d}{dt}r = \frac{1}{\alpha} \int dz\, D_{m,r}[z] z \tanh \beta(m+z) + 1 - r$$

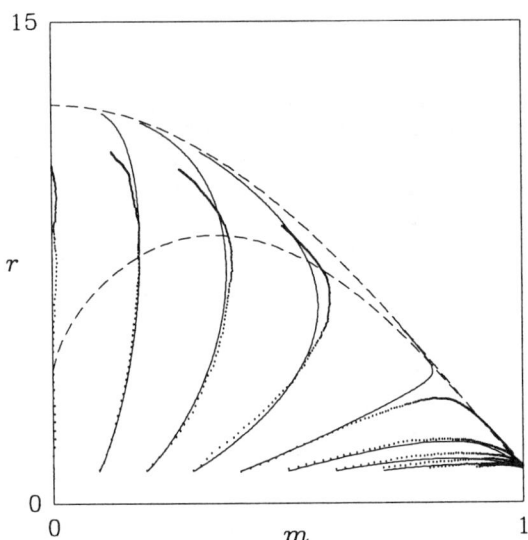

Figure 1: Simulations ($N = 32000$, dots) versus simple RS theory (solid lines), for $\alpha = 0.1$ and $\beta = \infty$. Upper dashed line: upper boundary of the physical region. Lower dashed line: upper boundary of the RS region (the AT instability).

in which $D_{m,r}[z]$ is the distribution of 'interference-noise' terms in the PSP's, for which the replica calculation gives the outcome (in so-called RS ansatz):

$$D_{m,r}[z] = \frac{e^{-\frac{1}{2\alpha r}(\Delta+z)^2}}{2\sqrt{2\pi\alpha r}}\left\{1 - \int Dy\ \tanh\left[\lambda y\left[\frac{\Delta}{\alpha\rho r}\right]^{\frac{1}{2}} + (\Delta+z)\frac{\lambda^2}{\alpha\rho r} + \mu\right]\right\}$$
$$+ \frac{e^{-\frac{1}{2\alpha r}(\Delta-z)^2}}{2\sqrt{2\pi\alpha r}}\left\{1 - \int Dy\ \tanh\left[\lambda y\left[\frac{\Delta}{\alpha\rho r}\right]^{\frac{1}{2}} + (\Delta-z)\frac{\lambda^2}{\alpha\rho r} - \mu\right]\right\}$$

with $Dy = [2\pi]^{-\frac{1}{2}}e^{-\frac{1}{2}y^2}dy$, $\Delta = \alpha\rho r - \lambda^2/\rho$ and $\lambda = \rho\sqrt{\alpha q}[1-\rho(1-q)]^{-1}$, and with the remaining parameters $\{q, \mu, \rho\}$ to be solved from the coupled equations:

$$m = \int Dy\ \tanh[\lambda y + \mu] \qquad q = \int Dy\ \tanh^2[\lambda y + \mu] \qquad r = \frac{1-\rho(1-q)^2}{[1-\rho(1-q)]^2}$$

Here we only give (partly new) results of the calculation; details can be found in (Coolen and Sherrington, 1994). The noise distribution is not Gaussian (in agreement with simulations, in contrast to LCH). Our simple two-parameter theory is found to be exact for $t \sim 0$, $t \to \infty$ and for $\alpha \to 0$. Solving numerically the dynamic equations leads to the results shown in figures 1 and 2. We find a nice agreement with numerical simulations in terms of the flow in the (m, r) plane. However, for trajectories leading away from the recall state $m \sim 1$, the theory fails to reproduce an overall slowing down. These deviations can be quantified by comparing cumulants of the noise distributions (Ozeki and Nishimori, 1994), or by applying the theory to exactly solvable models (Coolen and Franz, 1994). Other recent applications include spin-glass models (Coolen and Sherrington, 1994) and more general classes of attractor neural network models (Laughton and Coolen, 1995). The simple two-parameter theory always predicts adequately the location of the transients in the order parameter plane, but overestimates the relaxation speed. In fact, figure 2 shows a remarkable resemblance to the results obtained for this model in (Horner et al, 1989) with the functional integral formalism; the graphs of $m(t)$ are almost identical, but here they are derived in a much simpler way.

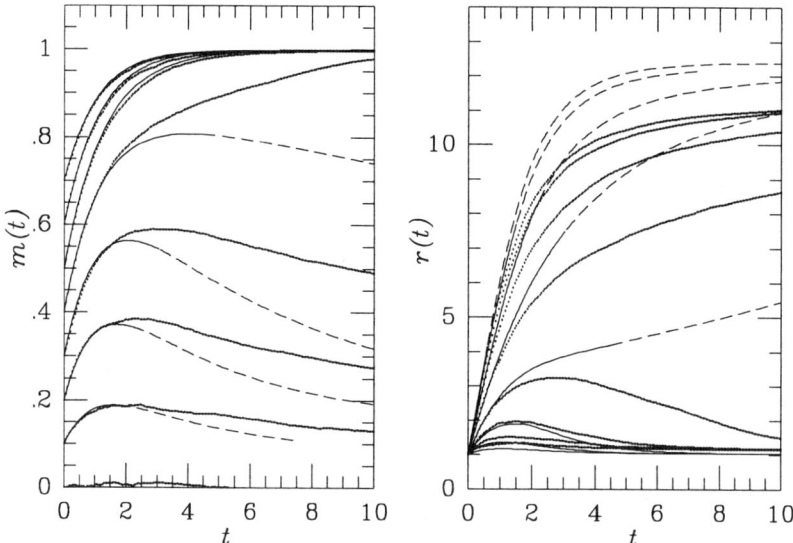

Figure 2: Simulations ($N = 32000$, dots) versus simple RS theory (RS stable: solid lines, RS unstable: dashed lines), now as functions of time, for $\alpha = 0.1$ and $\beta = \infty$.

5 ADVANCED VERSION OF THE THEORY

Improving upon the simple theory means expanding the set Ω beyond $\Omega = (m, E)$. Adding a finite number of observables will only have a minor impact; a qualitative step forward, on the other hand, results from introducing a dynamic order parameter *function*. Since the microscopic dynamics (1) is formulated entirely in terms of neuron states and post-synaptic potentials we choose for $\Omega(\boldsymbol{\sigma})$ the joint distribution:

$$D[\zeta, h](\boldsymbol{\sigma}) = \frac{1}{N} \sum_i \delta[\zeta - \sigma_i] \delta[h - h_i(\boldsymbol{\sigma})]$$

This choice has the advantages that (a) both m and (for symmetric systems) E are integrals over $D[\zeta, h]$, so the advanced theory automatically inherits the exactness at $t = 0$ and $t = \infty$ of the simple one, (b) it applies equally well to symmetric and nonsymmetric models and (c) as with the simple version, generalisation to models with continuous neural variables is straightforward. Here we show the result of applying the theory to a model of the type (1) with synaptic interactions:

$$J_{ij} = \frac{J_0}{N} \xi_i \xi_j + \frac{J}{\sqrt{N}} \left[\cos(\frac{\omega}{2}) x_{ij} + \sin(\frac{\omega}{2}) y_{ij} \right]$$

$x_{ij} = x_{ji}$, $y_{ij} = -y_{ji}$ (independent random Gaussian variables)

(describing a nominated pattern being stored on a 'messy' synaptic background). The parameter ω controls the degree of synaptic symmetry (e.g. $\omega = 0$: symmetric, $\omega = \pi$: anti-symmetric). Equation (4) applied to the observable $D[\zeta, h](\boldsymbol{\sigma})$ gives:

$$\frac{\partial}{\partial t} D_t[\zeta, h] = J^2 \left[1 - \langle \sigma \tanh(\beta H) \rangle_{D_t} \right] \frac{\partial^2}{\partial h^2} D_t[\zeta, h] + \frac{\partial}{\partial h} A[\zeta, h; D_t]$$

$$+ \frac{\partial}{\partial h} \left\{ D_t[\zeta, h] \left[h - J_0 \langle \tanh(\beta H) \rangle_{D_t} \right] \right\}$$

$$+ \frac{1}{2} [1 + \zeta \tanh(\beta h)] D_t[-\zeta, h] - \frac{1}{2} [1 - \zeta \tanh(\beta h)] D_t[\zeta, h]$$

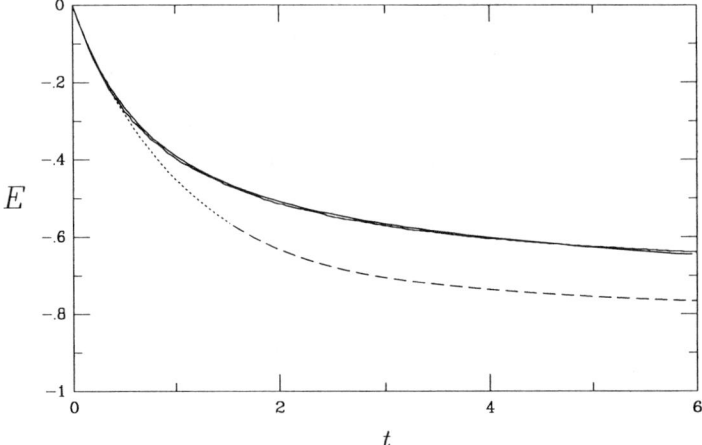

Figure 3: Comparison of simulations ($N = 8000$, solid line), simple two-parameter theory (RS stable: dotted line, RS unstable: dashed line) and advanced theory (solid line), for the $\omega = 0$ (symmetric background) model, with $J_0 = 0$, $\beta = \infty$. Note that the two solid lines are almost on top of each other at the scale shown.

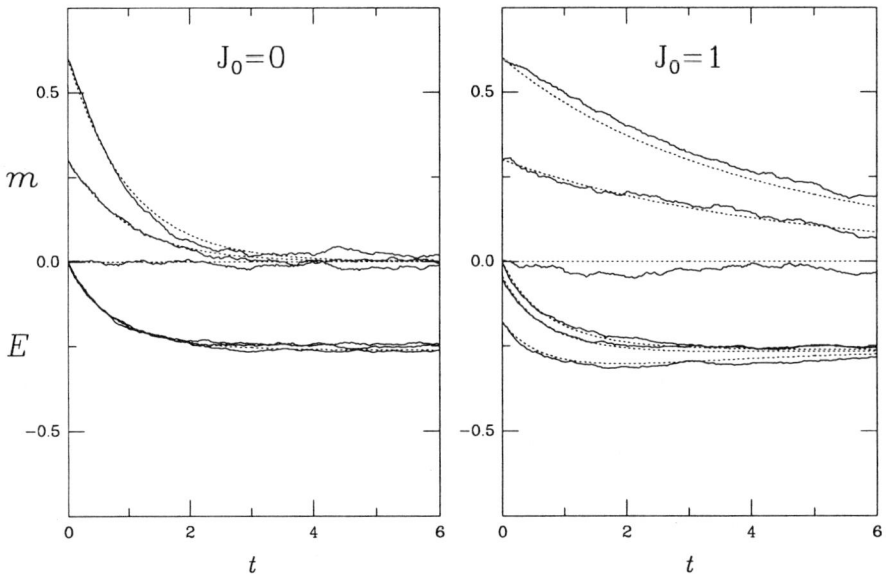

Figure 4: Advanced theory versus $N = 5600$ simulations in the $\omega = \frac{1}{2}\pi$ (asymmetric background) model, with $\beta = \infty$ and $J = 1$. Solid: simulations; dotted: solving the RS diffusion equation.

with $\langle f(\sigma, H)\rangle_D = \sum_\sigma \int dH\, D[\sigma, H] f(\sigma, H)$. All complications are concentrated in the kernel $\mathcal{A}[\zeta, h; D]$, which is to be solved from a nontrivial set of equations emerging from the replica formalism. Some results of solving these equations numerically are shown in figures 3 and 4 (for details of the calculations and more elaborate comparisons with simulations we refer to (Laughton, Coolen and Sherrington, 1995; Coolen, Laughton and Sherrington, 1995)). It is clear that the advanced theory quite convincingly describes the transients of the simulation experiments, including the hitherto unexplained slowing down, for symmetric and nonsymmetric models.

6 DISCUSSION

In this paper we have described novel techniques for studying the dynamics of recurrent neural networks near saturation. The simplest two-parameter theory (exact for $t = 0$, for $t \to \infty$ and for $\alpha \to 0$), which employs as dynamic order parameters the overlap with a pattern to be recalled and the total 'energy' per neuron, already describes quite accurately the location of the transients in the order parameter plane. The price paid for simplicity is that it overestimates the relaxation speed. A more advanced version of the theory, which describes the evolution of the joint distribution for neuron states and post-synaptic potentials, is mathematically more involved, but predicts the dynamical data essentially perfectly, as far as present applications allow us conclude. Whether this latter version is either exact, or just a very good approximation, still remains to be seen.

In this paper we have restricted ourselves to models with binary neural variables, for reasons of simplicity. The theories generalise in a natural way to models with analogue neurons (here, however, already the simple version will generally involve order parameter functions as opposed to a finite number of order parameters). Ongoing work along these lines includes, for instance, the analysis of analogue and spherical attractor networks and networks of coupled oscillators near saturation.

References

B. Derrida, E. Gardner and A. Zippelius (1987), *Europhys. Lett.* **4**: 167-173

A.C.C. Coolen and D. Sherrington (1993), in J.G. Taylor (ed.), *Mathematical Approaches to Neural Networks*, 293-305. Amsterdam: Elsevier.

S. Amari and K. Maginu (1988), *Neural Networks* **1**: 63-73

H. Nishimori and T. Ozeki (1993), *J. Phys. A* **26**: 859-871

H. Rieger, M. Schreckenberg and J. Zittartz (1988), *Z. Phys. B* **72**: 523-533

H. Horner, D. Bormann, M. Frick, H. Kinzelbach and A. Schmidt (1989), *Z. Phys. B* **76**: 381-398

A.C.C. Coolen and D. Sherrington (1994), *Phys. Rev. E* **49**(3): 1921-1934

H. Nishimori and T. Ozeki (1994), *J. Phys. A* **27**: 7061-7068

A.C.C. Coolen and S. Franz (1994), *J. Phys. A* **27**: 6947-9954

A.C.C. Coolen and D. Sherrington (1994), *J. Phys. A* **27**: 7687-7707

S.N. Laughton and A.C.C. Coolen (1995), *Phys. Rev. E* **51**: 2581-2599

S.N. Laughton, A.C.C. Coolen and D. Sherrington (1995), J. Phys. A (in press)

A.C.C. Coolen, S.N. Laughton and D. Sherrington (1995), Phys. Rev. B (in press)

Implementation Issues in the Fourier Transform Algorithm

Yishay Mansour* Sigal Sahar[†]
Computer Science Dept.
Tel-Aviv University
Tel-Aviv, ISRAEL

Abstract

The Fourier transform of boolean functions has come to play an important role in proving many important learnability results. We aim to demonstrate that the Fourier transform techniques are also a useful and practical algorithm in addition to being a powerful theoretical tool. We describe the more prominent changes we have introduced to the algorithm, ones that were crucial and without which the performance of the algorithm would severely deteriorate. One of the benefits we present is the confidence level for each prediction which measures the likelihood the prediction is correct.

1 INTRODUCTION

Over the last few years the Fourier Transform (**FT**) representation of boolean functions has been an instrumental tool in the computational learning theory community. It has been used mainly to demonstrate the learnability of various classes of functions with respect to the uniform distribution. The first connection between the Fourier representation and learnability of boolean functions was established in [6] where the class AC^0 was learned (using its FT representation) in $O(n^{poly-log(n)})$ time. The work of [5] developed a very powerful algorithmic procedure: given a function and a threshold parameter it finds in polynomial time all the Fourier coefficients of the function larger than the threshold. Originally the procedure was used to learn decision trees [5], and in [8, 2, 4] it was used to learn polynomial size DNF. The FT technique applies naturally to the uniform distribution, though some of the learnability results were extended to product distribution [1, 3].

---

*e-mail: mansour@cs.tau.ac.il
[†]e-mail: gales@cs.tau.ac.il

A great advantage of the FT algorithm is that it does not make any assumptions on the function it is learning. We can apply it to *any* function and hope to obtain "large" Fourier coefficients. The prediction function simply computes the sum of the coefficients with the corresponding basis functions and compares the sum to some threshold. The procedure is also immune to some noise and will be able to operate even if a fraction of the examples are maliciously misclassified. Its drawback is that it requires to query the target function on randomly selected inputs.

We aim to demonstrate that the FT technique is not only a powerful theoretical tool, but also a practical one. In the process of implementing the Fourier algorithm we enhanced it in order to improve the accuracy of the hypothesis we generate while maintaining a desirable run time. We have added such feartures as the detection of inaccurate approximations "on the fly" and immediate correction of the errors incurred at a minimal cost. The methods we devised to choose the "right" parameters proved to be essential in order to achieve our goals. Furthermore, when making predictions, it is extremely beneficial to have the prediction algorithm supply an indicator that provides the confidence level we have in the prediction we made. Our algorithm provides us naturally with such an indicator as detailed in Section 4.1.

The paper is organized as follows: section 2 briefly defines the FT and describes the algorithm. In Section 3 we describe the experiments and their outcome and in Section 4 the enhancements made. We end with our conclusions in Section 5.

2 FOURIER TRANSFORM (FT) THEORY

In this section we briefly introduce the FT theory and algorithm. its connection to learning and the algorithm that finds the large coefficients. A comprehensive survey of the theoretical results and proofs can be found in [7].

We consider boolean functions of n variables: $f : \{0,1\}^n \to \{-1,1\}$. We define the inner product: $<g,f>= 2^{-n}\sum_{x \in \{0,1\}^n} f(x)g(x) = E[g \cdot f]$, where E is the expected value with respect to the uniform distribution. The basis is defined as follows: for each $z \in \{0,1\}^n$, we define the *basis function* $\chi_z(x_1, \cdots, x_n) = (-1)^{\sum_{i=1}^{n} x_i z_i}$. Any function of n boolean inputs can be uniquely expressed as a linear combination of the basis functions. For a function f, the zth *Fourier coefficient* of f is denoted by $\hat{f}(z)$, i.e., $f(x) = \sum_{z \in \{0,1\}^n} \hat{f}(z)\chi_z(x)$. The Fourier coefficients are computed by $\hat{f}(z) =<f, \chi_z>$ and we call z the *coefficient-name* of $\hat{f}(z)$. We define a *t-sparse function* to be a function that has at most t non-zero Fourier coefficients.

2.1 PREDICTION

Our aim is to approximate the target function f by a t-sparse function h. In many cases h will simply include the "large" coefficients of f. That is, if $\Lambda = \{z_1, \ldots, z_m\}$ is the set of z's for which $\hat{f}(z_i)$ is "large", we set $h(x) = \sum_{z_i \in \Lambda} a_i \chi_{z_i}(x)$, where a_i is our approximation of $\hat{f}(z_i)$. The hypothesis we generate using this process, $h(x)$, does not have a boolean output. In order to obtain a boolean prediction we use $Sign(h(x))$, i.e., output $+1$ if $h(x) \geq 0$ and -1 if $h(x) < 0$. We want to bound the error we get from approximating f by h using the expected error squared, $E[(f-h)^2]$. It can be shown that bounding it bounds the boolean prediction error probability, i.e., $\Pr[f(x) \neq sign(h(x))] \leq E[(f-h)^2]$. For a given t, the t-sparse hypothesis h that minimizes $E[(f-h)^2]$ simply includes the t largest coefficients of f. Note that the more coefficients we include in our approximation and the better we approximate their values, the smaller $E[(f-h)^2]$ is going to be. This provides us with the motivation to find the "large" coefficients.

2.2 FINDING THE LARGE COEFFICIENTS

The algorithm that finds the "large" coefficients receives as inputs a function f (a black-box it can query) and an interest threshold parameter $\theta > 0$. It outputs a list of coefficient-names that (1) includes all the coefficients-names whose corresponding coefficients are *"large"*, i.e., at least θ, and (2) does not include "too many" coefficient-names. The algorithm runs in polynomial time in both $1/\theta$ and n.

```
SUBROUTINE search(α)
    IF TEST[f, α, θ] THEN IF |α| = n THEN OUTPUT α
                    ELSE search(α0); search(α1);
```

Figure 1: Subroutine search

The basic idea of the algorithm is to perform a search in the space of the coefficient-names of f. Throughout the search algorithm (see Figure (1)) we maintain a prefix of a coefficient-name and try to estimate whether *any* of its extensions can be a coefficient-name whose value is "large". The algorithm commences by calling search(λ) where λ is the empty string. On each invocation it computes the predicate $TEST[f, \alpha, \theta]$. If the predicate is true, it recursively calls search($\alpha 0$) and search($\alpha 1$). Note that if $TEST$ is very permissive we may reach all the coefficients, in which case our running time will not be polynomial; its implementation is therefore of utmost interest. Formally, $TEST[f, \alpha, \theta]$ computes whether

$$E_{x \in \{0,1\}^{n-k}} E^2_{y \in \{0,1\}^k}[f(yx)\chi_\alpha(y)] \geq \theta^2, \quad \text{where } k = \|\alpha\|. \tag{1}$$

Define $f_\alpha(x) = \sum_{\beta \in \{0,1\}^{n-k}} \hat{f}(\alpha\beta)\chi_\beta(x)$. It can be shown that the expected value in (1) is exactly the sum of the squares of the coefficients whose prefix is α, i.e., $E_{x \in \{0,1\}^{n-k}} E^2_{y \in \{0,1\}^k}[f(yx)\chi_\alpha(y)] = E_x[f_\alpha^2(x)] = \sum_{\beta \in \{0,1\}^{n-k}} \hat{f}^2(\alpha\beta)$, implying that if there exists a coefficient $|\hat{f}(\alpha\beta)| \geq \theta$, then $E[f_\alpha^2] \geq \theta^2$. This condition guarantees the correctness of our algorithm, namely that we reach all the "large" coefficients. We would like also to bound the number of recursive calls that search performs. We can show that for at most $1/\theta^2$ of the prefixes of size k, $TEST[f, \alpha, \theta]$ is true. This bounds the number of recursive calls in our procedure by $O(n/\theta^2)$.

In $TEST$ we would like to compute the expected value, but in order to do so efficiently we settle for an approximation of its value. This can be done as follows: (1) choose m_1 random $x_i \in \{0,1\}^{n-k}$, (2) choose m_2 random $y_{i,j} \in \{0,1\}^k$, (3) query f on $y_{i,j}x_i$ (which is why we need the query model—to query f on many points with the same prefix x_i) and receive $f(y_{i,j}x_i)$, and (4) compute the estimate as, $B_\alpha = \frac{1}{m_1} \sum_{i=1}^{m_1} \left(\frac{1}{m_2} \sum_{j=1}^{m_2} f(y_{i,j}x_i)\chi_\alpha(y_{i,j}) \right)^2$. Again, for more details see [7].

3 EXPERIMENTS

We implemented the FT algorithm (Section 2.2) and went forth to run a series of experiments. The parameters of each experiment include the target function, θ, m_1

and m_2. We briefly introduce the parameters here and defer the detailed discussion. The parameter θ determines the threshold between "small" and "large" coefficients, thus controlling the number of coefficients we will output. The parameters $\mathbf{m_1}$ and $\mathbf{m_2}$ determine how accurately we approximate the $TEST$ predicate. Failure to approximate it accurately may yield faulty, even random, results (e.g., for a ludicrous choice of $m_1 = 1$ and $m_2 = 1$) that may cause the algorithm to fail (as detailed in Section 4.3). An intelligent choice of m_1 and m_2 is therefore indispensable. This issue is discussed in greater detail in Sections 4.3 and 4.4.

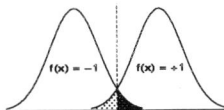

Figure 2: **Typical frequency plots and typical errors.** Errors occur in two cases: (1) the algorithm predicts a $+1$ response when the actual response is -1 (the lightly shaded area), and (2) the algorithm predicts a -1 response, while the true response is $+1$ (the darker shaded area).

Figures (3)-(5) present representative results of our experiments in the form of graphs that evaluate the output hypothesis of the algorithm on randomly chosen test points. The target function, f, returns a boolean response, ± 1, while the FT hypothesis returns a real response. We therefore present, for each experiment, a graph constituting of two curves: the frequency of the values of the hypothesis, $h(x)$, when $f(x) = +1$, and the second curve for $f(x) = -1$. If the two curves intersect, their intersection represents the inherent error the algorithm makes.

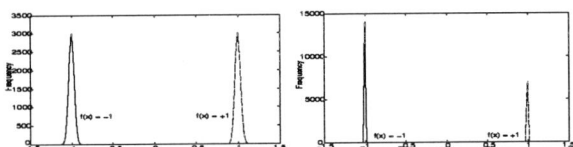

Figure 3: **Decision trees of depth 5 and 3 with 41 variables.** The 5-deep (3-deep) decision tree returns -1 about 50% (62.5%) of the time. The results shown above are for values $\theta = 0.03$, $m_1 = 100$ and $m_2 = 5600$ ($\theta = 0.06$, $m_1 = 100$ and $m_2 = 1300$). Both graphs are disjoint, signifying 0% error.

4 RESULTS AND ALGORITHM ENHANCEMENTS

4.1 CONFIDENCE LEVELS

One of our most consistent and interesting empirical findings was the distribution of the error versus the value of the algorithm's hypothesis: its shape is always that of a bell shaped curve. Knowing the error distribution permits us to determine with a high (often 100%) confidence level the result for most of the instances, yielding the much sought after confidence level indicator. Though this simple logic thus far has not been supported by any theoretical result, our experimental results provide overwhelming evidence that this is indeed the case.

Let us demonstrate the strength of this technique: consider the results of the 16-term DNF portrayed in Figure (4). If the algorithm's hypothesis outputs 0.3 (translated

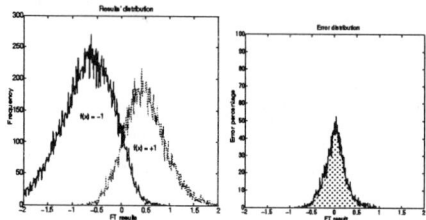

Figure 4: **16 term DNF.** This (randomly generated) DNF of 40 variables returns -1 about 61% of the time. The results shown above are for the values of $\theta = 0.02$, $m_2 = 12500$ and $m_1 = 100$. The hypothesis uses 186 non-zero coefficients. A total of 9.628% error was detected.

into 1 in boolean terms by the **Sign** function), we know with an 83% confidence level that the prediction is correct. If the algorithm outputs -0.9 as its prediction, we can virtually guarantee that the response is correct. Thus, although the total error level is over 9% we can supply a confidence level for each prediction. This is an indispensable tool for practical usage of the hypothesis.

4.2 DETERMINING THE THRESHOLD

Once the list of large coefficients is built and we compute the hypothesis $h(x)$, we still need to determine the threshold, a, to which we compare $h(x)$ (i.e., predict $+1$ iff $h(x) > a$). In the theoretical work it is assumed that $a = 0$, since a priori one cannot make a better guess. We observed that fixing a's value according to our hypothesis, improves the hypothesis. a is chosen to minimize the error with respect to a number of random examples.

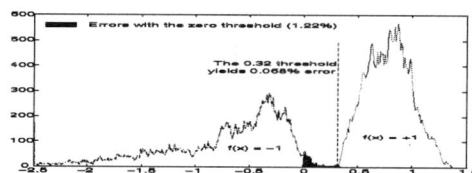

Figure 5: **8 term DNF.** This (randomly generated) DNF of 40 variables returns -1 about 43% of the time. The results shown above are for the values of $\theta = 0.03$, $m_2 = 5600$ and $m_1 = 100$. The hypothesis consists of 112 non-zero coefficients.

For example, when trying to learn an 8-term DNF with the zero threshold we will receive a total of 1.22% overall error as depicted in Figure (5). However, if we choose the threshold to be 0.32, we will get a diminished error of 0.068%.

4.3 ERROR DETECTION ON THE FLY - RETRY

During our experimentations we have noticed that at times the estimate B_α for $E[f_\alpha^2]$ may be inaccurate. A faulty approximation may result in the abortion of the traversal of "interesteees" subtreees, thus decreasing the hypothesis' accuracy, or in traversal of "uninteresting" subtrees, thereby needlessly increasing the algorithm's runtime. Since the properties of the FT guarantee that $E[f_\alpha^2] = E[f_{\alpha 0}^2] + E[f_{\alpha 1}^2]$, we expect $B_\alpha \approx B_{\alpha 0} + B_{\alpha 1}$. Whenever this is not true, we conclude that at least one of our approximations is somewhat lacking. We can remedy the situation by

Implementation Issues in the Fourier Transform Algorithm

running the **search** procedure again on the children, i.e., *retry* node α. This solution increases the probability of finding all the "large" coefficients. A brute force implementation may cost us an inordinate amount of time since we may retraverse subtrees that we have previously visited. However, since any discrepancies between the parent and its children are discovered—and corrected—as soon as they appear, we can circumvent any retraversal. Thus, we correct the errors without any superfluous additions to the run time.

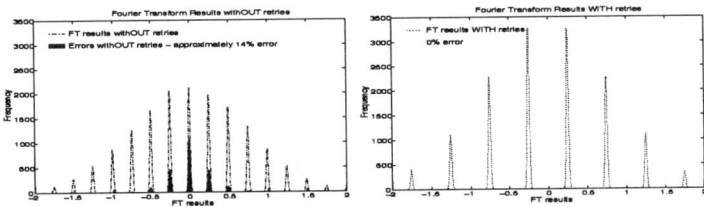

Figure 6: **Majority function** of 41 variables. The result portrayed are for values $m_1 = 100, m_2 = 800$ and $\theta = 0.08$. Note the majority-function characteristic distribution of the results[1].

We demonstrate the usefulness of this approach with an example of learning the majority function of 41 boolean variables. With*out* the retry mechanism, 8 (of a total of 42) large coefficients were missed, giving rise to 13.724% error represented by the shaded area in Figure (6). *With* the retries *all* the correct coefficients were found, yielding perfect (flawless) results represented in the dotted curve in Figure (6).

4.4 DETERMINING THE PARAMETERS

One of our aims was to determine the values of the different parameters, m_1, m_2 and θ. Recall that in our algorithm we calculate B_α, the approximation of $E_x[f_\alpha^2(x)]$ where m_1 is the number of times we sample x in order to make this approximation. We sample y randomly m_2 times to approximate $f_\alpha(x_i) = E_y[f(yx_i)\chi_\alpha(y)]$, for each x_i. This approximation of $f_\alpha(x_i)$ has a standard deviation of approximately $\frac{1}{\sqrt{m_2}}$. Assume that the true value is β_i, i.e. $\beta_i = f_\alpha(x_i)$, then we expect the contribution of the ith element to B_α to be $(\beta_i \pm \frac{1}{\sqrt{m_2}})^2 = \beta_i^2 \pm \frac{2\beta_i}{\sqrt{m_2}} + \frac{1}{m_2}$. The algorithm tests $B_\alpha = \frac{1}{m_1}\sum \beta_i^2 \geq \theta^2$, therefore, to ensure a low error, based on the above argument, we choose $m_2 = \frac{5}{\theta^2}$.

Choosing the right value for m_2 is of great importance. We have noticed on more than one occasion that *increasing* the value of m_2 actually *decreases* the overall run time. This is not obvious at first: seemingly, any increase in the number of times we loop in the algorithm only increases the run time. However, a more accurate value for m_2 means a more accurate approximation of the *TEST* predicate, and therefore less chance of redundant recursive calls (the run time is linear in the number of recursive calls). We can see this exemplified in Figure (7) where the number of recursive calls increase drastically as m_2 *decreases*. In order to present Figure (7),

---

[1] The "peaked" distribution of the results is not coincidental. The FT of the majority function has 42 large equal coefficients, labeled c_{maj}: one for each singleton (a vector of the form 0..010..0) and one for parity (the all-ones vector). The zeros of an input vector with z zeros we will contribute $\pm |(2z - 41) * c_{maj}|$ to the result and the parity will contribute $\pm c_{maj}$ (depending on whether z is odd or even), so that the total contribution is an even factor of c_{maj}. Since $c_{maj} = \binom{40}{20}\frac{1}{2^{40}} \sim 0.12$, we have peaks around factors of 0.24. The distribution around the peaks is due to the fact we only approximate each coefficient and get a value close to c_{maj}.

we learned the same 3 term DNF always using $\theta = 0.05$ and $m_1 * m_2 = 100000$. The trials differ in the specific values chosen in each trial for m_2.

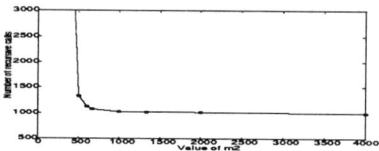

Figure 7: **Determining m_2**. Note that the number of recursive calls grows dramatically as m_2's value decreases. For example, for $m_2 = 400$, the number of recursive calls is $14,433$ compared with only $1,329$ recursive calls for $m_2 = 500$.

SPECIAL CASES: When $k = \|\alpha\|$ is either very small or very large, the values we choose for m_1 and m_2 can be self-defeating: when $k \sim n$ we still loop m_1 ($\gg 2^{n-k}$) times, though often without gaining additional information. The same holds for very small values of k, and the corresponding m_2 ($\gg 2^k$) values. We therefore add the following feature: for small and large values of k we calculate exactly the expected value thereby decreasing the run time and increasing accuracy.

5 CONCLUSIONS

In this work we implemented the FT algorithm and showed it to be a useful practical tool as well as a powerful theoretical technique. We reviewed major enhancements the algorithm underwent during the process. The algorithm successfully recovers functions in a reasonable amount of time. Furthermore, we have shown that the algorithm naturally derives a confidence parameter. This parameter enables the user in many cases to conclude that the prediction received is accurate with extremely high probability, even if the overall error probability is not negligible.

Acknowledgements

This research was supported in part by The Israel Science Foundation administered by The Israel Academy of Science and Humanities and by a grant of the Israeli Ministry of Science and Technology.

References

[1] Mihir Bellare. A technique for upper bounding the spectral norm with applications to learning. In *5th Annual Workshop on Computational Learning Theory*, pages 62–70, July 1992.

[2] Avrim Blum, Merrick Furst, Jeffrey Jackson, Michael Kearns, Yishay Mansour, and Steven Rudich. Weakly learning DNF and characterizing statistical query learning using fourier analysis. In *The 26th Annual ACM Symposium on Theory of Computing*, pages 253 – 262, 1994.

[3] Merrick L. Furst, Jeffrey C. Jackson, and Sean W. Smith. Improved learning of AC^0 functions. In *4th Annual Workshop on Computational Learning Theory*, pages 317–325, August 1991.

[4] J. Jackson. An efficient membership-query algorithm for learning DNF with respect to the uniform distribution. In *Annual Symposium on Switching and Automata Theory*, pages 42 – 53, 1994.

[5] E. Kushilevitz and Y. Mansour. Learning decision trees using the fourier spectrum. *SIAM Journal on Computing* 22(6): 1331–1348, 1993.

[6] N. Linial, Y. Mansour, and N. Nisan. Constant depth circuits, fourier transform and learnability. *JACM* 40(3):607–620, 1993.

[7] Y. Mansour. Learning Boolean Functions via the Fourier Transform. *Advances in Neural Computation*, edited by V.P. Roychodhury and K-Y. Siu and A. Orlitsky, Kluwer Academic Pub. 1994. Can be accessed via ftp://ftp.math.tau.ac.il/pub/mansour/PAPERS/LEARNING/fourier-survey.ps.Z.

[8] Yishay Mansour. An $o(n^{\log \log n})$ learning algorihm for DNF under the uniform distribution. *J. of Computer and System Science*, 50(3):543–550, 1995.

Generalisation of A Class of Continuous Neural Networks

John Shawe-Taylor
Dept of Computer Science,
Royal Holloway, University of London,
Egham, Surrey TW20 0EX, UK
Email: john@dcs.rhbnc.ac.uk

Jieyu Zhao[*]
IDSIA, Corso Elvezia 36,
6900-Lugano, Switzerland
Email: jieyu@carota.idsia.ch

Abstract

We propose a way of using boolean circuits to perform real valued computation in a way that naturally extends their boolean functionality. The functionality of multiple fan in threshold gates in this model is shown to mimic that of a hardware implementation of continuous Neural Networks. A Vapnik-Chervonenkis dimension and sample size analysis for the systems is performed giving best known sample sizes for a real valued Neural Network. Experimental results confirm the conclusion that the sample sizes required for the networks are significantly smaller than for sigmoidal networks.

1 Introduction

Recent developments in complexity theory have addressed the question of complexity of computation over the real numbers. More recently attempts have been made to introduce some computational cost related to the accuracy of the computations [5]. The model proposed in this paper weakens the computational power still further by relying on classical boolean circuits to perform the computation using a simple encoding of the real values. Using this encoding we also show that TC_0 circuits interpreted in the model correspond to a Neural Network design referred to as Bit Stream Neural Networks, which have been developed for hardware implementation [8].

With the perspective afforded by the general approach considered here, we are also able to analyse the Bit Stream Neural Networks (or indeed any other adaptive system based on the technique), giving VC dimension and sample size bounds for PAC learning. The sample sizes obtained are very similar to those for threshold networks,

---

[*]Work performed while at Royal Holloway, University of London

despite their being derived by very different techniques. They give the best bounds for neural networks involving smooth activation functions, being significantly lower than the bounds obtained recently for sigmoidal networks [4, 7].

We subsequently present simulation results showing that Bit Stream Neural Networks based on the technique can be used to solve a standard benchmark problem. The results of the simulations support the theoretical finding that for the same sample size generalisation will be better for the Bit Stream Neural Networks than for classical sigmoidal networks. It should also be stressed that the approach is very general – being applicable to any boolean circuit – and by its definition employs compact digital hardware. This fact motivates the introduction of the model, though it will not play an important part in this paper.

2 Definitions and Basic Results

A *boolean circuit* is a directed acyclic graph whose nodes are referred to as *gates*, with a single *output* node of out-degree zero. The nodes with in-degree zero are termed *input* nodes. The nodes that are not input nodes are *computational* nodes. There is a boolean function associated with each computational node of arity equal to its in-degree. The function computed by a boolean network is determined by assigning (input) values to its input nodes and performing the function at each computational node once its input values are determined. The result is the value at the output node. The class TC_0 is defined to be those functions that can be computed by a family of polynomially sized Boolean circuits with unrestricted fan-in and constant depth, where the gates are either NOT or THRESHOLD.

In order to use the boolean circuits to compute with real numbers we use the method of stochastic computing to encode real numbers as bit streams. The encoding we will use is to consider the stream of binary bits, for which the 1's are generated independently at random with probability p, as representing the number p. This is referred to as a Bernoulli sequence of probability p. In this representation, the multiplication of two independently generated streams can be achieved by a simple AND gate, since the probability of a 1 on the output stream is equal to $p_1 p_2$, where p_1 is the probability of a 1 on the first input stream and p_2 is the probability of a 1 on the second input stream. Hence, in this representation the boolean circuit consisting of a single AND gate can compute the product of its two inputs.

More background information about stochastic computing can be found in the work of Gaines [1]. The analysis we provide is made by treating the calculations as exact real valued computations. In a practical (hardware) implementation real bit streams would have to be generated [3] and the question of the accuracy of a delivered result arises.

In the applications considered here the output values are used to determine a binary value by comparing with a threshold of 0.5. Unless the actual output is exactly 1 or 0 (which can happen), then however many bits are collected at the output there is a slight probability that an incorrect classification will be made. Hence, the number of bits required is a function of the difference between the actual output and 0.5 and the level of confidence required in the correctness of the classification.

Definition 1 *The real function computed by a boolean circuit C, which computes the boolean function*
$$f_C : \{0,1\}^n \longrightarrow \{0,1\},$$
is the function
$$g_C : [0,1]^n \longrightarrow [0,1],$$

Generalisation of a Class of Continuous Neural Networks

obtained by coding each input independently as a Bernoulli sequence and interpreting the output as a similar sequence.

Hence, by the discussion above we have for the circuit C consisting of a single AND gate, the function g_C is given by $g_C(x_1, x_2) = x_1 x_2$.

We now give a proposition showing that the definition of real computation given above is well-defined and generalises the Boolean computation performed by the circuit.

Proposition 2 *The bit stream on the output of a boolean circuit computing a real function is a Bernoulli sequence. The real function g_C computed by an n input boolean circuit C can be expressed in terms of the corresponding boolean function f_C as follows:*

$$g_C(x) = \sum_{\alpha \in \{0,1\}^n} P_x(\alpha) f_C(\alpha), \quad \text{where} \quad P_x(\alpha) = \prod_{i=1}^n x_i^{\alpha_i}(1-x_i)^{(1-\alpha_i)}.$$

In particular, $g_C|_{\{0,1\}^n} = f_C$.

Proof: The output bit stream is a Bernoulli sequence, since the behaviour at each time step is independent of the behaviour at previous time sequences, assuming the input sequences are independent. Let the probability of a 1 in the output sequence be p. Hence, $g_C(x) = p$. At any given time the input to the circuit must be one of the 2^n possible binary vectors α. $P_x(\alpha)$ gives the probability of the vector α occurring. Hence, the expected value of the output of the circuit is given in the proposition statement, but by the properties of a Bernoulli sequence this value is also p. The final claim holds since $P_\alpha(\alpha) = 1$, while $P_\alpha(\alpha') = 0$ for $\alpha \neq \alpha'$. ∎

Hence, the function computed by a circuit can be denoted by a polynomial of degree n, though the representation given above may involve exponentially many terms. This representation will therefore only be used for theoretical analysis.

3 Bit Stream Neural Networks

In this section we describe a neural network model based on stochastic computing and show that it corresponds to taking TC_0 circuits in the framework considered in Section 2.

A Stochastic Bit Stream Neuron is a processing unit which carries out very simple operations on its input bit streams. All input bit streams are combined with their corresponding weight bit streams and then the weighted bits are summed up. The final total is compared to a threshold value. If the sum is larger than the threshold the neuron gives an output 1, otherwise 0.

There are two different versions of the Stochastic Bit Stream Neuron corresponding to the different data representations. The definitions are given as follows.

Definition 3 *(AND-SBSN):* A n-input AND version Stochastic Bit Stream Neuron has n weights in the range $[-1,1]$ and n inputs in the range $[0,1]$, which are all unipolar representations of Bernoulli sequences. An extra sign bit is attached to each weight Bernoulli sequence. The threshold θ is an integer lying between $-n$ to n which is randomly generated according to the threshold probability density function $\phi(\theta)$. The computations performed during each operational cycle are

(1) combining respectively the n bits from n input Bernoulli sequences with the corresponding n bits from n weight Bernoulli sequences using the AND operation.

(2) assigning n weight sign bits to the corresponding output bits of the AND gate, summing up all the n signed output bits and then comparing the total with the randomly generated threshold value. If the total is not less than the threshold value, the AND-SBSN outputs 1, otherwise it outputs 0.

We can now present the main result characterising the functionality of a Stochastic Bit Stream Neural Network as the real function of an TC_0 circuit.

Theorem 4 *The functionality of a family of feedforward networks of Bit Stream Neurons with constant depth organised into layers with interconnections only between adjacent layers corresponds to the function g_C for an TC_0 circuit C of depth twice that of the network. The number of input streams is equal to the number of network inputs while the number of parameters is at most twice the number of weights.*

Proof: Consider first an individual neuron. We construct a circuit whose real functionality matches that of the neuron. The circuit has two layers. The first consists of a series of AND gates. Each gate links one input line of the neuron with its corresponding weight input. The outputs of these gates are linked into a threshold gate with fixed threshold $2d$ for the AND-SBSN, where d is the number of input lines to the neuron. The threshold distribution of the AND SBSN is now simulated by having a series of $2d$ additional inputs to the threshold gate. The number of additional input streams required to simulate the threshold depends on how general a distribution is allowed for the threshold. We consider three cases:

1. If the threshold is fixed (i.e. not programmable), then no additional inputs are required, since the actual threshold can be suitably adapted.

2. If the threshold distribution is always focussed on one value (which can be varied), then an additional $\lceil \log_2(2d) \rceil$ ($\lceil \log_2(d) \rceil$) inputs are required to specify the binary value of this number. A circuit feeding the corresponding number of 1's to the threshold gate is not hard to construct.

3. In the fully general case any series of $2d + 1$ ($d + 1$) numbers summing to one can be assigned as the probabilities of the possible values
$$\phi(0), \phi(1), \ldots, \phi(t),$$
where $t = 2d$ for the AND SBSN. We now construct a circuit which takes t input streams and passes the 1-bits to the threshold gate of all the inputs up to the first input stream carrying a 0. No further input is passed to the threshold gate. In other words

   Threshold gate receives s bits of input $\Leftrightarrow$ Input streams $1, \ldots, s$ have bit 1 and either $s = t$ or input stream $s + 1$ has input 0.

   We now set the probability p_s of stream s as follows;
$$p_1 = 1 - \phi(0)$$
$$p_s = \frac{1 - \sum_{i=0}^{s-1} \phi(i)}{1 - \sum_{i=0}^{s-2} \phi(i)}$$
$$\text{for } s = 2, \ldots, t$$

   With these values the probability of the threshold gate receiving s bits is $\phi(s)$ as required.

This completes the replacement of a single neuron. Clearly, we can replace all neurons in a network in the same manner and construct a network with the required properties provided connections do not 'shortcut' layers, since this would create interactions between bits in different time slots. ∎

4 VC Dimension and Sample Sizes

In order to perform a VC Dimension and sample size analysis of the Bit Stream Neural Networks described in the previous section we introduce the following general framework.

Definition 5 *For a set $\mathcal{G}$ of smooth functions $f : \mathcal{R}^n \times \mathcal{R}^\ell \to \mathcal{R}$, the class $\mathcal{F}$ is defined as*
$$\mathcal{F} = \mathcal{F}_\mathcal{G} = \{f_w | f_w(x) = f(x, w), f \in \mathcal{G}\}.$$
The corresponding classification class obtained by taking a fixed set of s of the functions from $\mathcal{G}$, thresholding the corresponding functions from $\mathcal{F}$ at 0 and combining them (with the same parameter vector) in some logical formula will be denoted $H_s(\mathcal{F})$. We will denote $H_1(\mathcal{F})$ by $H(\mathcal{F})$.

In our case we will consider a set of circuits $\mathcal{C}$ each with $n + \ell$ input connections, n labelled as the input vector and ℓ identified as parameter input connections. Note that if circuits have too few input connections, we can pad them with dummy ones. The set $\mathcal{G}$ will then be the set
$$\mathcal{G} = \mathcal{G}_\mathcal{C} = \{g_C | C \in \mathcal{C}\},$$
while $\mathcal{F}_{\mathcal{G}_\mathcal{C}}$ will be denoted by $\mathcal{F}_\mathcal{C}$.

We now quote some of the results of [7] which uses the techniques of Karpinski and MacIntyre [4] to derive sample sizes for classes of smoothly parametrised functions.

Proposition 6 *[7] Let $\mathcal{G}$ be the set of polynomials p of degree at most d with $p : \mathcal{R}^n \times \mathcal{R}^\ell \to \mathcal{R}$ and*
$$\mathcal{F} = \mathcal{F}_\mathcal{G} = \{p_w | p_w(x) = p(x, w), p \in \mathcal{G}\}.$$
Hence, there are ℓ adjustable parameters and the input dimension is n. Then the VC-dimension of the class $H_s(\mathcal{F}_\mathcal{C})$ is bounded above by
$$\log_2(2(2d)^\ell) + 17\ell \log_2(s).$$

Corollary 7 *For a set of circuits $\mathcal{C}$, with n input connections and ℓ parameter connections, the VC-dimension of the class $H_s(\mathcal{F}_\mathcal{C})$ is bounded above by*
$$1 + \ell(1 + \log_2(n + \ell) + 17 \log_2(s)).$$

Proof: By Proposition 2 the function g_C computed by a circuit C with t input connections has the form
$$g_C(x) = \sum_{\alpha \in \{0,1\}^t} P_x(\alpha) f_C(\alpha), \quad \text{where} \quad P_x(\alpha) = \prod_{i=1}^t x_i^{\alpha_i}(1 - x_i)^{(1-\alpha_i)}.$$

Hence, $g_C(x)$ is a polynomial of degree t. In the case considered the number t of input connections is $n + \ell$. The result follows from the proposition. ∎

Proposition 8 *[7] Let $\mathcal{G}$ be the set of polynomials p of degree at most d with $p : \mathcal{R}^n \times \mathcal{R}^\ell \to \mathcal{R}$ and*

$$\mathcal{F} = \mathcal{F}_\mathcal{G} = \{p_w | p_w(x) = p(x, w), p \in \mathcal{G}\}.$$

Hence, there are ℓ adjustable parameters and the input dimension is n. If a function $h \in H_s(\mathcal{F})$ correctly computes a function on a sample of m inputs drawn independently according to a fixed probability distribution, where

$$m \geq m_0(\epsilon, \delta) = \frac{1}{\epsilon(1 - \sqrt{\epsilon})} \left[2\ell \ln \left(\frac{4e\sqrt{sd}}{\epsilon} \right) + \ln \left(\frac{2\ell/(\ell - 1)}{\delta} \right) \right]$$

then with probability at least $1 - \delta$ the error rate of h will be less than ϵ on inputs drawn according to the same distribution.

Corollary 9 *For a set of circuits $\mathcal{C}$, with n input connections and ℓ parameter connections, If a function $h \in H_s(\mathcal{F}_\mathcal{C})$ correctly computes a function on a sample of m inputs drawn independently according to a fixed probability distribution, where*

$$m \geq m_0(\epsilon, \delta) = \frac{1}{\epsilon(1 - \sqrt{\epsilon})} \left[2\ell \ln \left(\frac{4e\sqrt{s(n + \ell)}}{\epsilon} \right) + \ln \left(\frac{2\ell/(\ell - 1)}{\delta} \right) \right]$$

then with probability at least $1 - \delta$ the error rate of h will be less than ϵ on inputs drawn according to the same distribution.

Proof: As in the proof of the previous corollary, we need only observe that the functions g_C for $C \in \mathcal{C}$ are polynomials of degree at most $n + \ell$. ∎

Note that the best known sample sizes for threshold networks are given in [6]:

$$m \geq m_0(\epsilon, \delta) = \frac{1}{\epsilon(1 - \sqrt{\epsilon})} \left[2W \ln \left(\frac{6\sqrt{N}}{\epsilon} \right) + \ln \left(\frac{\ell/(\ell - 1)}{\delta} \right) \right],$$

where W is the number of adaptable weights (parameters) and N is the number of computational nodes in the network. Hence, the bounds given above are almost identical to those for threshold networks, despite the underlying techniques used to derive them being entirely different.

One surprising fact about the above results is that the VC dimension and sample sizes are independent of the complexity of the circuit (except in as much as it must have the required number of inputs). Hence, additional layers of fixed computation cannot increase the sample complexity above the bound given).

5 Simulation Results

The Monk's problems which were the basis of a first international comparison of learning algorithms, are derived from a domain in which each training example is represented by six discrete-valued attributes. Each problem involves learning a binary function defined over this domain, from a sample of training examples of this function. The 'true' concepts underlying each Monk's problem are given by:

MONK-1: $(attribute_1 = attribute_2)$
        or $(attribute_5 = 1)$
MONK-2: $(attribute_i = 1)$
        for EXACTLY TWO $i \in \{1, 2, ..., 6\}$
MONK-3: $(attribute_5 = 3$ and $attribute_4 = 1)$
        or $(attribute_5 \neq 4$ and $attribute_2 \neq 3)$

There are 124, 169 and 122 samples in the training sets of MONK-1, MONK-2 and MONK-3 respectively. The testing set has 432 patterns. The network had 17 input units, 10 hidden units, 1 output unit, and was fully connected. Two networks were used for each problem. The first was a standard multi-layer perceptron with sigmoid activation function trained using the backpropagation algorithm (BP Network).

The second network had the same architecture, but used bit stream neurons in place of sigmoid ones (BSN Network). The functionality of the neurons was simulated using probability generating functions to compute the probability values of the bit streams output at each neuron. The backpropagation algorithm was adapted to train these networks by computing the derivative of the output probability value with respect to the individual inputs to that neuron [8].

Experiments were performed with and without noise in the training examples. There is 5% additional noise (misclassifications) in the training set of MONK-3. The results for the Monk's problems using the moment generating function simulation are shown as follows:

	BP Network		BSN Network	
	training	testing	training	testing
MONK-1	100%	86.6%	100%	97.7%
MONK-2	100%	84.2%	100%	100%
MONK-3	97.1%	83.3%	98.4%	98.6%

It can be seen that the generalisation of the BSN network is much better than that of a general multilayer backpropagation network. The results on MONK-3 problem is extremely good. The results reported by Hassibi and Stork [2] using a sophisticated weight pruning technique are only 93.4% correct for the training set and 97.2% correct for the testing set.

References

[1] B. R. Gaines, Stochastic Computing Systems, Advances in Information Systems Science 2 (1969) pp37-172.

[2] B. Hassibi and D.G. Stork, Second order derivatives for network pruning: Optimal brain surgeon, Advances in Neural Information Processing System, Vol 5 (1993) 164–171.

[3] P. Jeavons, D.A. Cohen and J. Shawe-Taylor, Generating Binary Sequences for Stochastic Computing, IEEE Trans on Information Theory, 40 (3) (1994) 716–720.

[4] M. Karpinski and A. MacIntyre, Bounding VC-Dimension for Neural Networks: Progress and Prospects, Proceedings of EuroCOLT'95, 1995, pp. 337–341, Springer Lecture Notes in Artificial Intelligence, 904.

[5] P. Koiran, A Weak Version of the Blum, Shub and Smale Model, ESPRIT Working Group NeuroCOLT Technical Report Series, NC-TR-94-5, 1994.

[6] J. Shawe-Taylor, Threshold Network Learning in the Presence of Equivalences, Proceedings of NIPS 4, 1991, pp. 879–886.

[7] J. Shawe-Taylor, Sample Sizes for Sigmoidal Networks, to appear in the Proceedings of Eighth Conference on Computational Learning Theory, COLT'95, 1995.

[8] John Shawe-Taylor, Peter Jeavons and Max van Daalen, "Probabilistic Bit Stream Neural Chip : Theory", Connection Science, Vol 3, No 3, 1991.

Gradient and Hamiltonian Dynamics Applied to Learning in Neural Networks

James W. Howse   Chaouki T. Abdallah   Gregory L. Heileman

Department of Electrical and Computer Engineering
University of New Mexico
Albuquerque, NM 87131

Abstract

The process of machine learning can be considered in two stages: model selection and parameter estimation. In this paper a technique is presented for constructing dynamical systems with desired qualitative properties. The approach is based on the fact that an n-dimensional nonlinear dynamical system can be decomposed into one gradient and (n − 1) Hamiltonian systems. Thus, the model selection stage consists of choosing the gradient and Hamiltonian portions appropriately so that a certain behavior is obtainable. To estimate the parameters, a stably convergent learning rule is presented. This algorithm has been proven to converge to the desired system trajectory for all initial conditions and system inputs. This technique can be used to design neural network models which are guaranteed to solve the trajectory learning problem.

1 Introduction

A fundamental problem in mathematical systems theory is the identification of dynamical systems. System identification is a dynamic analogue of the functional approximation problem. A set of input-output pairs $\{u(t), y(t)\}$ is given over some time interval $t \in [\mathcal{T}_i, \mathcal{T}_f]$. The problem is to find a model which for the given input sequence returns an approximation of the given output sequence. Broadly speaking, solving an identification problem involves two steps. The first is choosing a class of identification models which are capable of emulating the behavior of the actual system. The second is selecting a method to determine which member of this class of models best emulates the actual system. In this paper we present a class of nonlinear models and a learning algorithm for these models which are guaranteed to learn the trajectories of an example system. Algorithms to learn given trajectories of a continuous time system have been proposed in [6], [8], and [7] to name only a few. To our knowledge, no one has ever proven that the error between the learned and desired trajectories vanishes for any of these algorithms. In our trajectory learning system this error is guaranteed to vanish. Our models extend the work in [1] by showing that Cohen's systems are one instance of the class of models generated by decomposing the dynamics into a component normal to some surface and a set of components tangent to the same surface. Conceptually this formalism can be used to design dynamical systems with a variety of desired qualitative properties. Furthermore, we propose a provably convergent learning algorithm which allows the parameters of Cohen's models to be learned from examples rather than being programmed in advance. The algorithm is

Gradient and Hamiltonian Dynamics Applied to Learning in Neural Networks

convergent in the sense that the error between the model trajectories and the desired trajectories is guaranteed to vanish. This learning procedure is related to one discussed in [5] for use in linear system identification.

2 Constructing the Model

First some terminology will be defined. For a system of n first order ordinary differential equations, the *phase space* of the system is the n-dimensional space of all state components. A solution *trajectory* is a curve in phase space described by the differential equations for one specific starting point. At every point on a trajectory there exists a tangent vector. The space of all such tangent vectors for all possible solution trajectories constitutes the *vector field* for this system of differential equations.

The trajectory learning models in this paper are systems of first order ordinary differential equations. The form of these equations will be obtained by considering the system dynamics as motion relative to some surface. At each point in the state space an arbitrary system trajectory will be decomposed into a component normal to this surface and a set of components tangent to this surface. This approach was suggested to us by the results in [4], where it is shown that an arbitrary n-dimensional vector field can be decomposed locally into the sum of one gradient vector field and $(n-1)$ Hamiltonian vector fields. The concept of a potential function will be used to define these surfaces. A *potential function* $V(x)$ is any scalar valued function of the system states $x = [x_1, x_2, \ldots, x_n]^\dagger$ which is at least twice continuously differentiable (i.e. $V(x) \in C^r : r \geq 2$). The operation $[\cdot]^\dagger$ denotes the transpose of the vector. If there are n components in the system state, the function $V(x)$, when plotted with respect all of the state components, defines a surface in an $(n+1)$-dimensional space. There are two curves passing through every point on this potential surface which are of interest in this discussion, they are illustrated in Figure 1(a). The dashed curve is

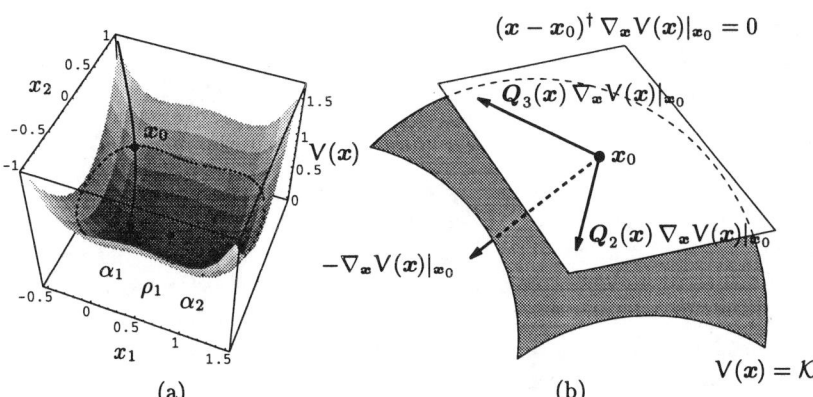

Figure 1: (a) The potential function $V(x) = x_1^2 (x_1 - 1)^2 + x_2^2$ plotted versus its two dependent variables x_1 and x_2. The dashed curve is called a level surface and is given by $V(x) = 0.5$. The solid curve follows the path of steepest descent through x_0. (b) The partitioning of a 3-dimensional vector field at the point x_0 into a 1-dimensional portion which is normal to the surface $V(x) = \mathcal{K}$ and a 2-dimensional portion which is tangent to $V(x) = \mathcal{K}$. The vector $-\nabla_x V(x)|_{x_0}$ is the normal vector to the surface $V(x) = \mathcal{K}$ at the point x_0. The plane $(x - x_0)^\dagger \nabla_x V(x)|_{x_0} = 0$ contains *all* of the vectors which are tangent to $V(x) = \mathcal{K}$ at x_0. Two linearly independent vectors are needed to form a basis for this tangent space, the pair $Q_2(x) \nabla_x V(x)|_{x_0}$ and $Q_3(x) \nabla_x V(x)|_{x_0}$ that are shown are just one possibility.

referred to as a *level surface*, it is a surface along which $V(x) = \mathcal{K}$ for some constant $\mathcal{K}$. Note that in general this level surface is an n-dimensional object. The solid curve moves downhill along $V(x)$ following the path of steepest descent through the point x_0. The vector which is tangent to this curve at x_0 is normal to the level surface at x_0. The system dynamics will be designed as motion relative to the level surfaces of $V(x)$. The results in [4] require n different local potential functions to achieve arbitrary dynamics. However, the results in [1] suggest that a considerable number of dynamical systems can be achieved using only a single global potential function.

A system which is capable of traversing any downhill path along a given potential surface $V(x)$, can be constructed by decomposing each element of the vector field into a vector normal to the level surface of $V(x)$ which passes through each point and a set of vectors tangent to the level surface of $V(x)$ which passes through the same point. So the potential function $V(x)$ is used to partition the n-dimensional phase space into two subspaces. The first contains a vector field normal to some level surface $V(x) = \mathcal{K}$ for $\mathcal{K} \in \mathbb{R}$, while the second subspace holds a vector field tangent to $V(x) = \mathcal{K}$. The subspace containing all possible normal vectors to the n-dimensional level surface at a given point, has dimension one. This is equivalent to the statement that every point on a smooth surface has a unique normal vector. Similarly, the subspace containing all possible tangent vectors to the level surface at a given point has dimension $(n - 1)$. An example of this partition in the case of a 3-dimensional system is shown in Figure 1(b). Since the space of all tangent vectors at each point on a level surface is $(n - 1)$-dimensional, $(n - 1)$ linearly independent vectors are required to form a basis for this space.

Mathematically, there is a straightforward way to construct dynamical systems which either move downhill along $V(x)$ or remain at a constant height on $V(x)$. In this paper, dynamical systems which always move downhill along some potential surface are called *gradient-like systems*. These systems are defined by differential equations of the form

$$\dot{x} = -P(x)\nabla_x V(x), \tag{1}$$

where $P(x)$ is a matrix function which is symmetric (i.e. $P^\dagger = P$) and positive definite at every point x, and where $\nabla_x V(x) = [\frac{\partial V}{\partial x_1}, \frac{\partial V}{\partial x_2}, \ldots, \frac{\partial V}{\partial x_n}]^\dagger$. These systems are similar to the gradient flows discussed in [2]. The trajectories of the system formed by Equation (1) always move downhill along the potential surface defined by $V(x)$. This can be shown by taking the time derivative of $V(x)$ which is $\dot{V}(x) = -[\nabla_x V(x)]^\dagger P(x)[\nabla_x V(x)] \leq 0$. Because $P(x)$ is positive definite, $\dot{V}(x)$ can only be zero where $\nabla_x V(x) = 0$, elsewhere $\dot{V}(x)$ is negative. This means that the trajectories of Equation (1) always move toward a level surface of $V(x)$ formed by "slicing" $V(x)$ at a lower height, as pointed out in [2]. It is also easy to design systems which remain at a constant height on $V(x)$. Such systems will be denoted *Hamiltonian-like systems*. They are specified by the equation

$$\dot{x} = Q(x)\nabla_x V(x), \tag{2}$$

where $Q(x)$ is a matrix function which is skew-symmetric (i.e. $Q^\dagger = -Q$) at every point x. These systems are similar to the Hamiltonian systems defined in [2]. The elements of the vector field defined by Equation (2) are always tangent to some level surface of $V(x)$. Hence the trajectories of this system remain at a constant height on the potential surface given by $V(x)$. Again this is indicated by the time derivative of $V(x)$, which in this case is $\dot{V}(x) = [\nabla_x V(x)]^\dagger Q(x)[\nabla_x V(x)] = 0$. This indicates that the trajectories of Equation (2) always remain on the level surface on which the system starts. So a model which can follow an arbitrary downhill path along the potential surface $V(x)$ can be designed by combining the dynamics of Equations (1) and (2). The dynamics in the subspace normal to the level surfaces of $V(x)$ can be

Gradient and Hamiltonian Dynamics Applied to Learning in Neural Networks

defined using one equation of the form in Equation (1). Similarly the dynamics in the subspace tangent to the level surfaces of $V(x)$ can be defined using $(n-1)$ equations of the form in Equation (2). Hence the total dynamics for the model are

$$\dot{x} = -P(x)\nabla_x V(x) + \sum_{i=2}^{n} Q_i(x)\nabla_x V(x). \qquad (3)$$

For this model the number and location of equilibria is determined by the function $V(x)$, while the manner in which the equilibria are approached is determined by the matrices $P(x)$ and $Q_i(x)$.

If the potential function $V(x)$ is bounded below (i.e. $V(x) > B_l \; \forall \; x \in \mathbb{R}^n$, where B_l is a constant), eventually increasing (i.e. $\lim_{\|x\| \to \infty} V(x) \to \infty$), and has only a finite number of isolated local maxima and minima (i.e. in some neighborhood of every point where $\nabla_x V(x) = 0$ there are no other points where the gradient vanishes), then the system in Equation (3) satisfies the conditions of Theorem 10 in [1]. Therefore the system will converge to one of the points where $\nabla_x V(x) = 0$, called the *critical points* of $V(x)$, for all initial conditions. Note that this system is capable of all downhill trajectories along the potential surface only if the $(n-1)$ vectors $Q_i(x)\nabla_x V(x) \; \forall \; i = 2, \ldots, n$ are linearly independent at every point x. It is shown in [1] that the potential function

$$V(x) = C \int_{\mathcal{X}_1}^{x_1} \mathcal{L}_1(\gamma)\, d\gamma + \sum_{i=2}^{n} \left[\frac{1}{2}(x_i - \mathcal{L}_i(x_1))^2 + \frac{1}{2}\int_{\mathcal{X}_i}^{x_1} \mathcal{L}_1(\gamma)\,[\mathcal{L}'_i(\gamma)]^2\, d\gamma \right] \qquad (4)$$

satisfies these three criteria. In this equation $\mathcal{L}_i(x_1) \; \forall \; i = 1, \ldots, n$ are interpolation polynomials, C is a real positive constant, $\mathcal{X}_i \; \forall \; i = 1, \ldots, n$ are real constants chosen so that the integrals are positive valued, and $\mathcal{L}'_i(x_1) \equiv \frac{d\mathcal{L}_i}{dx_1}$.

3 The Learning Rule

In Equation (3) the number and location of equilibria can be controlled using the potential function $V(x)$, while the manner in which the equilibria are approached can be controlled with the matrices $P(x)$ and $Q_i(x)$. If it is assumed that the locations of the equilibria are known, then a potential function which has local minima and maxima at these points can be constructed using Equation (4). The problem of trajectory learning is thereby reduced to the problem of parameterizing the matrices $P(x)$ and $Q_i(x)$ and finding the parameter values which cause this model to best emulate the actual system. If the elements $P(x)$ and $Q_i(x)$ are correctly chosen, then a learning rule can be designed which makes the model dynamics converge to that of the actual system. Assume that the dynamics given by Equation (3) are a parameterized model of the actual dynamics. Using this model and samples of the actual system states, an estimator for states of the actual system can be designed. The behavior of the model is altered by changing its parameters, so a parameter estimator must also be constructed. The following theorem provides a form for both the state and parameter estimators which guarantees convergence to a set of parameters for which the error between the estimated and target trajectories vanishes.

Theorem 3.1. *Given the model system*

$$\dot{x} = \sum_{i=1}^{k} A_i\, f_i(x) + B\, g(u) \qquad (5)$$

where $A_i \in \mathbb{R}^{n \times n}$ and $B \in \mathbb{R}^{n \times m}$ are unknown, and $f_i(\cdot)$ and $g(\cdot)$ are known smooth functions such that the system has bounded solutions for bounded inputs $u(t)$. Choose a state estimator of the form

$$\dot{\hat{x}} = \mathcal{R}_s(\hat{x} - x) + \sum_{i=1}^{k} \hat{A}_i f_i(x) + \hat{B} g(u) \tag{6}$$

where $\mathcal{R}_s$ is an $(n \times n)$ matrix of real constants whose eigenvalues must all be in the left half plane, and $\hat{A}_i$ and $\hat{B}$ are the estimates of the actual parameters. Choose parameter estimators of the form

$$\begin{aligned} \dot{\hat{A}}_i &= -\mathcal{R}_p(\hat{x} - x) [f_i(x)]^\dagger \ \forall \ i = 1, \ldots, k \\ \dot{\hat{B}} &= -\mathcal{R}_p(\hat{x} - x) [g(u)]^\dagger \end{aligned} \tag{7}$$

where $\mathcal{R}_p$ is an $(n \times n)$ matrix of real constants which is symmetric and positive definite, and $(\hat{x} - x)[\cdot]^\dagger$ denotes an outer product. For these choices of state and parameter estimators $\lim_{t \to \infty} (\hat{x}(t) - x(t)) = 0$ for all initial conditions. Furthermore, this remains true if any of the elements of $\hat{A}_i$ or $\hat{B}$ are set to 0, or if any of these matrices are restricted to being symmetric or skew-symmetric.

The proof of this theorem appears in [3]. Note that convergence of the parameter estimates to the actual parameter values is not guaranteed by this theorem. The model dynamics in Equation (3) can be cast in the form of Equation (5) by choosing each element of $P(x)$ and $Q_i(x)$ to have the form

$$P_{rs} = \sum_{j=1}^{n} \sum_{k=0}^{l-1} \xi_{rsjk} \vartheta_k(x_j) \quad \text{and} \quad Q_{rs} = \sum_{j=1}^{n} \sum_{k=0}^{l-1} \lambda_{rsjk} \varrho_k(x_j), \tag{8}$$

where $\{\vartheta_0(x_j), \vartheta_1(x_j), \ldots, \vartheta_{l-1}(x_j)\}$ and $\{\varrho_0(x_j), \varrho_1(x_j), \ldots, \varrho_{l-1}(x_j)\}$ are a set of l orthogonal polynomials which depend on the state x_j. There is a set of such polynomials for every state x_j, $j = 1, 2, \ldots, n$. The constants ξ_{rsjk} and λ_{rsjk} determine the contribution of the kth polynomial which depends on the jth state to the value of P_{rs} and Q_{rs} respectively. In this case the dynamics in Equation (3) become

$$\dot{x} = \sum_{j=1}^{n} \sum_{k=0}^{l-1} \left\{ \Xi_{jk} \left[\vartheta_k(x_j) \nabla_x V(x) \right] + \sum_{i=2}^{n} \Lambda_{ijk} \left[\varrho_{ik}(x_j) \nabla_x V(x) \right] \right\} + \Upsilon g(u(t)) \tag{9}$$

where Ξ_{jk} is the $(n \times n)$ matrix of all values ξ_{rsjk} which have the same value of j and k. Likewise Λ_{ijk} is the $(n \times n)$ matrix of all values λ_{rsjk}, having the same value of j and k, which are associated with the ith matrix $Q_i(x)$. This system has m inputs, which may explicitly depend on time, that are represented by the m-element vector function $u(t)$. The m-element vector function $g(\cdot)$ is a smooth, possibly nonlinear, transformation of the input function. The matrix Υ is an $(n \times m)$ parameter matrix which determines how much of input $s \in \{1, \ldots, m\}$ effects state $r \in \{1, \ldots, n\}$. Appropriate state and parameter estimators can be designed based on Equations (6) and (7) respectively.

4 Simulation Results

Now an example is presented in which the parameters of the model in Equation (9) are trained, using the learning rule in Equations (6) and (7), on one input signal and then are tested on a different input signal. The actual system has three equilibrium points, two stable points located at $(1, 3)$ and $(3, 5)$, and a saddle point located at $(2 - \frac{\sqrt{3}}{3}, 4 + \frac{\sqrt{3}}{3})$. In this example the dynamics of both the actual system and the model are given by

$$\begin{pmatrix} \dot{x}_1 \\ \dot{x}_2 \end{pmatrix} = \begin{pmatrix} p_1 + p_2 x_1^2 + p_3 x_2^2 & 0 \\ 0 & p_4 + p_5 x_1^2 + p_6 x_2^2 \end{pmatrix} \begin{pmatrix} \frac{\partial V}{\partial x_1} \\ \frac{\partial V}{\partial x_2} \end{pmatrix} + \begin{pmatrix} 0 & -\{p_7 + p_8 x_1 + p_9 x_2\} \\ p_7 + p_8 x_1 + p_9 x_2 & 0 \end{pmatrix} \begin{pmatrix} \frac{\partial V}{\partial x_1} \\ \frac{\partial V}{\partial x_2} \end{pmatrix} + \begin{pmatrix} p_{10} \\ 0 \end{pmatrix} u(t) \tag{10}$$

where $V(x)$ is defined in Equation (4) and $u(t)$ is a time varying input. For the actual system the parameter values were $\mathcal{P}_1 = \mathcal{P}_4 = -4$, $\mathcal{P}_2 = \mathcal{P}_5 = -2$, $\mathcal{P}_3 = \mathcal{P}_6 = -1$, $\mathcal{P}_7 = 1$, $\mathcal{P}_8 = 3$, $\mathcal{P}_9 = 5$, and $\mathcal{P}_{10} = 1$. In the model the 10 elements $\mathcal{P}_i$ are treated as the unknown parameters which must be learned. Note that the first matrix function is positive definite if the parameters $\mathcal{P}_1$–$\mathcal{P}_6$ are all negative valued. The second matrix function is skew-symmetric for all values of $\mathcal{P}_7$–$\mathcal{P}_9$. The two input signals used for training and testing were $u_1 = 10000\,(\sin\frac{1}{3}1000\,t + \sin\frac{2}{3}1000\,t)$ and $u_2 = 5000\sin 1000\,t$. The phase space responses of the actual system to the inputs u_1 and u_2 are shown by the solid curves in Figures 3(b) and 3(a) respectively. Notice that both of these inputs produce a periodic attractor in the phase space of Equation (10). In order to evaluate the effectiveness of the learning algorithm the Euclidean distance between the actual and learned state and parameter values was computed and plotted versus time. The results are shown in Figure 2. Figure 2(a) shows these statistics when

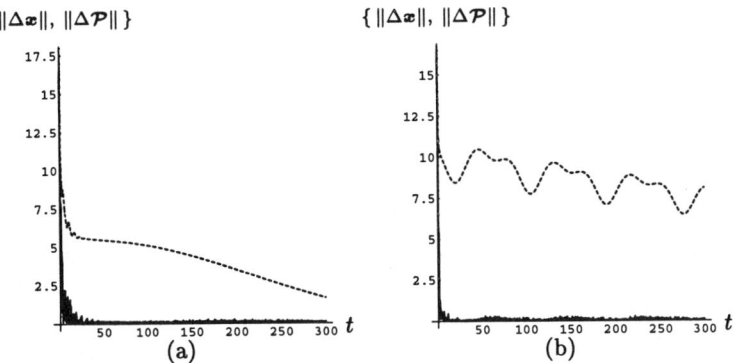

Figure 2: (a) The state and parameter errors for training using input signal u_1. The solid curve is the Euclidean distance between the state estimates and the actual states as a function of time. The dashed curve shows the distance between the estimated and actual parameter values versus time.
(b) The state and parameter errors for training using input signal u_2.

training with input u_1, while Figure 2(b) shows the same statistics for input u_2. The solid curves are the Euclidean distance between the learned and actual system states, and the dashed curves are the distance between the learned and actual parameter values. These statistics have two noteworthy features. First, the error between the learned and desired states quickly converges to very small values, regardless of how well the actual parameters are learned. This result was guaranteed by Theorem 3.1. Second, the final error between the learned and desired parameters is much lower when the system is trained with input u_1. Intuitively this is because input u_1 excites more frequency modes of the system than input u_2. Recall that in a nonlinear system the frequency modes excited by a given input do not depend solely on the input because the system can generate frequencies not present in the input. The quality of the learned parameters can be qualitatively judged by comparing the phase plots using the learned and actual parameters for each input, as shown in Figure 3. In Figure 3(a) the system was trained using input u_1 and tested with input u_2, while in Figure 3(b) the situation was reversed. The solid curves are the system response using the actual parameter values, and the dashed curves are the response for the learned parameters. The Euclidean distance between the target and test trajectories in Figure 3(a) is in the range $(0, 0.64)$ with a mean distance of 0.21 and a standard deviation of 0.14. The distance between the the target and test trajectories in Figure 3(b) is in the range $(0, 4.53)$ with a mean distance of 0.98 and a standard deviation of 1.35. Qualitatively, both sets of learned parameters give an accurate response for non-training inputs.

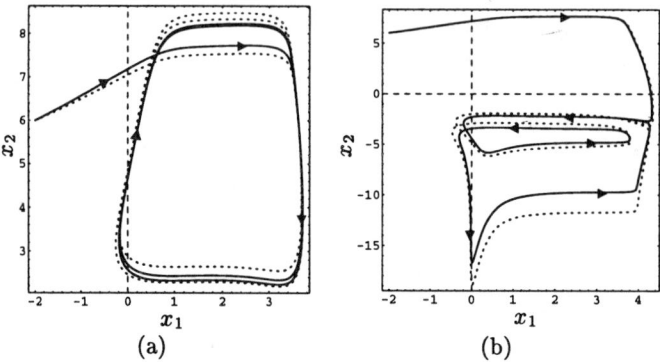

Figure 3: (a) A phase plot of the system response when trained with input u_1 and tested with input u_2. The solid line is the response to the test input using the actual parameters. The dotted line is the system response using the learned parameters. (b) A phase plot of the system response when trained with input u_2 and tested with input u_1.

Note that even when the error between the learned and actual parameters is large, the periodic attractor resulting from the learned parameters appears to have the same "shape" as that for the actual parameters.

5 Conclusion

We have presented a conceptual framework for designing dynamical systems with specific qualitative properties by decomposing the dynamics into a component normal to some surface and a set of components tangent to the same surface. We have presented a specific instance of this class of systems which converges to one of a finite number of equilibrium points. By parameterizing these systems, the manner in which these equilibrium points are approached can be fitted to an arbitrary data set. We present a learning algorithm to estimate these parameters which is guaranteed to converge to a set of parameter values for which the error between the learned and desired trajectories vanishes.

Acknowledgments

This research was supported by a grant from Boeing Computer Services under Contract W-300445. The authors would like to thank Vangelis Coutsias, Tom Caudell, and Bill Horne for stimulating discussions and insightful suggestions.

References

[1] M.A. Cohen. The construction of arbitrary stable dynamics in nonlinear neural networks. *Neural Networks*, 5(1):83–103, 1992.

[2] M.W. Hirsch and S. Smale. *Differential equations, dynamical systems, and linear algebra*, volume 60 of *Pure and Applied Mathematics*. Academic Press, Inc., San Diego, CA, 1974.

[3] J.W. Howse, C.T. Abdallah, and G.L. Heileman. A gradient-hamiltonian decomposition for designing and learning dynamical systems. Submitted to *Neural Computation*, 1995.

[4] R.V. Mendes and J.T. Duarte. Decomposition of vector fields and mixed dynamics. *Journal of Mathematical Physics*, 22(7):1420–1422, 1981.

[5] K.S. Narendra and A.M. Annaswamy. *Stable adaptive systems*. Prentice-Hall, Inc., Englewood Cliffs, NJ, 1989.

[6] B.A. Pearlmutter. Learning state space trajectories in recurrent neural networks. *Neural Computation*, 1(2):263–269, 1989.

[7] D. Saad. Training recurrent neural networks via trajectory modification. *Complex Systems*, 6(2):213–236, 1992.

[8] M.-A. Sato. A real time learning algorithm for recurrent analog neural networks. *Biological Cybernetics*, 62(2):237–241, 1990.

Optimization Principles for the Neural Code

Michael DeWeese
Sloan Center, Salk Institute
La Jolla, CA 92037
deweese@salk.edu

Abstract

Recent experiments show that the neural codes at work in a wide range of creatures share some common features. At first sight, these observations seem unrelated. However, we show that these features arise naturally in a linear filtered threshold crossing (LFTC) model when we set the threshold to maximize the transmitted information. This maximization process requires neural adaptation to not only the DC signal level, as in conventional light and dark adaptation, but also to the statistical structure of the signal and noise distributions. We also present a new approach for calculating the mutual information between a neuron's output spike train and any aspect of its input signal which does not require reconstruction of the input signal. This formulation is valid provided the correlations in the spike train are small, and we provide a procedure for checking this assumption. This paper is based on joint work (DeWeese [1], 1995). Preliminary results from the LFTC model appeared in a previous proceedings (DeWeese [2], 1995), and the conclusions we reached at that time have been reaffirmed by further analysis of the model.

1 Introduction

Most sensory receptor cells produce analog voltages and currents which are smoothly related to analog signals in the outside world. Before being transmitted to the brain, however, these signals are encoded in sequences of identical pulses called action potentials or spikes. We would like to know if there is a universal principle at work in the choice of these coding strategies. The existence of such a potentially powerful theoretical tool in biology is an appealing notion, but it may not turn out to be useful. Perhaps the function of biological systems is best seen as a complicated compromise among constraints imposed by the properties of biological materials, the need to build the system according to a simple set of development rules, and the fact that current systems must arise from their ancestors by evolution through random change and selection. In this view, biology is history, and the search for principles (except for evolution itself) is likely to be futile. Obviously, we hope that this view is wrong, and that at least some of biology is understandable in terms of the same sort of universal principles that have emerged in the physics of the inanimate world.

Adrian noticed in the 1920's that every peripheral neuron he checked produced discrete, identical pulses no matter what input he administered (Adrian, 1928). From the work of Hodgkin and Huxley we know that these pulses are stable non-linear waves which emerge from the non-linear dynamics describing the electrical properties of the nerve cell membrane These dynamics in turn derive from the molecular dynamics of specific ion channels in the cell membrane. By analogy with other non-linear wave problems, we thus understand that these signals have propagated over a long distance — e.g. $\approx$ one meter from touch receptors in a finger to their targets in the spinal cord — so that every spike has the same shape. This is an important observation since it implies that all information carried by a spike train is encoded in the arrival times of the spikes. Since a creature's brain is connected to all of its sensory systems by such axons, all the creature knows about the outside world must be encoded in spike arrival times.

Until recently, neural codes have been studied primarily by measuring changes in the rate of spike production by different input signals. Recently it has become possible to characterize the codes in information-theoretic terms, and this has led to the discovery of some potentially universal features of the code (Bialek, 1996) (or see (Bialek, 1993) for a brief summary). They are:

1. *Very high information rates.* The record so far is 300 bits per second in a cricket mechanical sensor.

2. *High coding efficiency.* In cricket and frog vibration sensors, the information rate is within a factor of 2 of the entropy per unit time of the spike train.

3. *Linear decoding.* Despite evident non-linearities of the nervous system, spike trains can be *decoded* by simple linear filters. Thus we can write an estimate of the analog input signal $s(t)$ as $s_{est}(t) = \sum_i K_1(t - t_i)$, with K_1 chosen to minimize the mean-squared errors $\langle \chi^2 \rangle$ in the estimate. Adding non-linear $K_2(t - t_i, t - t_j)$ terms does not significantly reduce χ^2.

4. *Moderate signal-to-noise ratios (SNR).* The SNR in these experiments was defined as the ratio of power spectra of the input signal to the noise referred back to the input; the power spectrum of the noise was approximated by χ^2 defined above. All these examples of high information transmission rates have SNR of order unity over a broad bandwidth, rather than high SNR in a narrow band.

We will try to tie all of these observations together by elevating the first to a principle: The neural code is chosen to maximize information transmission where information is quantified following Shannon. We apply this principle in the context of a simple model neuron which converts analog signals into spike trains. Before we consider a specific model, we will present a procedure for expanding the information rate of any point process encoding of an analog signal about the limit where the spikes are uncorrelated. We will briefly discuss how this can be used to measure information rates in real neurons.

This work will also appear in Network.

2 Information Theory

In the 1940's, Shannon proposed a quantitative definition for "information" (Shannon, 1949). He argued first that the average amount of information gained by observing some event x is the entropy of the distribution from which x is chosen, and then showed that this is the only definition consistent with several plausible requirements. This definition implies that the amount of information one signal can provide about some other signal is the difference between the entropy of the first signal's *a priori* distribution and the entropy of its conditional distribution. The average of this quantity is called the mutual (or transmitted) information. Thus, we can write the amount of information that the spike train, $\{t_i\}$, tells us about the time dependent signal, $s(t)$, as

$$I = -\int \frac{\mathcal{D}t_i}{N!} P[\{t_i\}] \log_2 P[\{t_i\}] - \left\langle -\int \frac{\mathcal{D}t_i}{N!} P[\{t_i\}|s()] \log_2 P[\{t_i\}|s()] \right\rangle_s, \quad (1)$$

where $\int \mathcal{D}t_i$ is shorthand for integration over all arrival times $\{t_i\}$ from 0 to T and summation over the total number of spikes, N (we have divided the integration measure by $N!$ to prevent over counting due to equivalent permutations of the spikes, rather than absorb this factor into the probability distribution as we did in (DeWeese [1], 1995)). $< \cdots >_s \equiv \int \mathcal{D}s P[s()] \cdots$ denotes integration over the space of functions $s(t)$ weighted by the signal's *a priori* distribution, $P[\{t_i\}|s()]$ is the probability distribution for the spike train when the signal is fixed and $P[\{t_i\}]$ is the spike train's average distribution.

3 Arbitrary Point Process Encoding of an Analog Signal

In order to derive a useful expression for the information given by Eq. (1), we need an explicit representation for the conditional distribution of the spike train. If we choose to represent each spike as a Dirac delta function, then the spike train can be defined as

$$\rho(t) \equiv \sum_{i=1}^{N} \delta(t - t_i). \quad (2)$$

This is the output spike train for our cell, so it must be a functional of both the input signal, $s(t)$, and all the noise sources in the cell which we will lump together and call $\eta(t)$. Choosing to represent the spikes as delta functions allows us to think of $\rho(t)$ as the probability of finding a spike at time t when both the signal and noise are specified. In other words, if the noise were not present, ρ would be the cell's firing rate, singular though it is. This implies that in the presence of noise the cell's observed firing rate, $r(t)$, is the noise average of $\rho(t)$:

$$r(t) = \int \mathcal{D}\eta P[\eta()|s()]\rho(t) \equiv \langle \rho(t) \rangle_\eta. \quad (3)$$

Notice that by averaging over the conditional distribution for the noise rather than its *a priori* distribution as we did in (DeWeese [1], 1995), we ensure that this expression is still valid if the noise is signal dependent, as is the case in many real neurons.

For any particular realization of the noise, the spike train is completely specified which means that the distribution for the spike train when both the signal and noise are fixed is a modulated Poisson process with a singular firing rate, $\rho(t)$. We emphasize that this is true even though we have assumed nothing about the encoding of the signal in the spike train when the noise is not fixed. One might then assume that the conditional distribution for the spike train for fixed signal would be the noise average of the familiar formula for a modulated Poisson process:

$$P[\{t_i\}|s()] \approx \left\langle e^{-\int_0^T dt\, \rho(t)} \prod_{i=1}^N \rho(t_i) \right\rangle_\eta . \qquad (4)$$

However, this is only approximately true due to subtleties arising from the singular nature of $\rho(t)$. One can derive the correct expression (DeWeese [1], 1995) by carefully taking the continuum limit of an approximation to this distribution defined for discrete time. The result is the same sum of noise averages over products of ρ's produced by expanding the exponential in Eq. (4) in powers of $\int dt\, \rho(t)$ except that all terms containing more than one factor of $\rho(t)$ at equal times are not present. The exact answer is:

$$P[\{t_i\}|s()] = \left\langle e^{-\int dt\, \rho(t)} \prod_{i=1}^N \rho(t_i) \right\rangle_\eta^-, \qquad (5)$$

where the superscripted minus sign reminds us to remove all terms containing products of coincident ρ's after expanding everything in the noise average in powers of ρ.

4 Expanding About the Poisson Limit

An exact solution for the mutual information between the input signal and spike train would be hopeless for all but a few coding schemes. However, the success of linear decoding coupled with the high information rates seen in the experiments suggests to us that the spikes might be transmitting roughly independent information (see (DeWeese [1], 1995) or (Bialek, 1993) for a more fleshed out argument on this point). If this is the case, then the spike train should approximate a Poisson process. We can explicitly show this relationship by performing a cluster expansion on the right hand side of Eq. (5):

$$\begin{aligned} P[\{t_i\}|s()] &= e^{-\int r(t)dt} \prod_{i=1}^N r(t_i) \left\langle e^{-\int \Delta\rho(t)dt} \prod_{i=1}^N \left(1 + \frac{\Delta\rho(t_i)}{r(t_i)}\right) \right\rangle_\eta^- \qquad (6) \\ &= e^{-\int r(t)dt} \prod_{i=1}^N r(t_i) \left[1 + \sum_{m=2}^\infty C_\eta(m)\right], \end{aligned}$$

where we have defined $\Delta\rho(t) \equiv \rho(t) - <\rho(t)>_\eta = \rho(t) - r(t)$ and introduced $C_\eta(m)$ which collects all terms containing m factors of $\Delta\rho$. For example,

$$C_\eta(2) \equiv \frac{1}{2} \sum_{i \neq j} \frac{\langle \Delta\rho_i \Delta\rho_j \rangle_\eta^-}{r_i r_j} - \int dt' \sum_{i=1}^N \frac{\langle \Delta\rho' \Delta\rho_i \rangle_\eta^-}{r_i} + \frac{1}{2} \int dt' dt'' \langle \Delta\rho' \Delta\rho'' \rangle_\eta^- . \qquad (7)$$

Clearly, if the correlations between spikes are small in the noise distribution, then the C_η's will be small, and the spike train will nearly approximate a modulated Poisson process when the signal is fixed.

Optimization Principles for the Neural Code

Performing the cluster expansion on the signal average of Eq. (5) yields a similar expression for the average distribution for the spike train:

$$P[\{t_i\}] = e^{-T\bar{r}}\bar{r}^N \left[1 + \sum_{m=2}^{\infty} C_{\eta,s}(m)\right], \quad (8)$$

where T is the total duration of the spike train, $\bar{r}$ is the average firing rate, and $C_{\eta,s}(m)$ is identical to $C_\eta(m)$ with these substitutions: $r(t) \to \bar{r}$, $\Delta\rho(t) \to \bar{\Delta}\rho(t) \equiv \rho(t) - \bar{r}$, and $\langle\cdots\rangle_\eta^- \to \langle\langle\cdots\rangle_\eta^-\rangle_s$. In this case, the distribution for a homogeneous Poisson process appears in front of the square brackets, and inside we have 1 + corrections due to correlations in the average spike train.

5 The Transmitted Information

Inserting these expressions for $P[\{t_i\}|s()]$ and $P[\{t_i\}]$ (taken to *all* orders in $\Delta\rho$ and $\bar{\Delta}\rho$, respectively) into Eq. (1), and expanding to second non-vanishing order in $\bar{r}\tau_c$ results in a useful expression for the information (DeWeese [1], 1995):

$$\begin{aligned}
I &= \int_0^T dt \left\langle r(t)\log_2\left(\frac{r(t)}{\bar{r}(t)}\right)\right\rangle_s \\
&\quad + \frac{1}{2}\int_0^T dt \int_0^T dt' \left[\left\langle\langle\rho\rho'\rangle_\eta^- \log_2\left(\frac{\bar{r}\bar{r}'\langle\rho\rho'\rangle_\eta^-}{rr'\langle\langle\rho\rho'\rangle_\eta^-\rangle_s}\right)\right\rangle_s \right. \\
&\quad \left. - \frac{\langle\langle\Delta\rho\Delta\rho'\rangle_\eta^-\rangle_s}{\ln 2} + \frac{\langle\langle\bar{\Delta}\rho\bar{\Delta}\rho'\rangle_\eta^-\rangle_s}{\ln 2}\right] + \mathcal{O}\left[(\bar{r}\tau_c)^2\right].
\end{aligned} \quad (9)$$

where we have suppressed the explicit time notation in the correction term inside the double integral. If the signal and noise are stationary then we can replace the $\int_0^T dt$ in front of each of these terms by T illustrating that the information does indeed grow linearly with the duration of the spike train.

The leading term, which is exact if there are no correlations between the spikes, depends only on the firing rate, and is never negative. The first correction is positive when the correlations between pairs of spikes are being used to encode the signal, and negative when individual spikes carry redundant information. This correction term is cumbersome but we present it here because it is experimentally accessible, as we now describe.

This formula can be used to measure information rates in real neurons without having to assume any method of reconstructing the signal from the spike train. In the experimental context, averages over the (conditional) noise distribution become repeated trials with the same input signal, and averages over the signal are accomplished by summing over all trials. $r(t)$, for example, is the histogram of the spike trains resulting from the same input signal, while $\bar{r}(t)$ is the histogram of all spike trains resulting from all input signals. If the signal and noise are stationary, then $\bar{r}$ will not be time dependent. $\langle\rho(t)\rho(t')\rangle_\eta$ is in general a 2-dimensional histogram which is signal dependent: It is equal to the number of spike trains resulting from some specific input signal which simultaneously contain a spike in the time bins containing t and t'. If the noise is stationary, then this is a function of only $t - t'$, and it reduces to a 1-dimensional histogram.

In order to measure the full amount of information contained in the spike train, it is crucial to bin the data in small enough time bins to resolve all of the structure in

$r(t)$, $\langle \rho(t)\rho(t')\rangle_\eta$, and so on. We have assumed nothing about the noise or signal; in fact, they can even be correlated so that the noise averages are signal dependent without changing the experimental procedure. The experimenter can also choose to fix only some aspects of the sensory data during the noise averaging step, thus measuring the mutual information between the spike train and only these aspects of the input. The only assumption we have made up to this point is that the spikes are roughly uncorrelated which can be checked by comparing the leading term to the first correction, just as we do for the model we discuss in the next section.

6 The Linear Filtered Threshold Crossing Model

As we reported in a previous proceedings (DeWeese [2], 1995) (and see (DeWeese [1], 1995) for details), the leading term in Eq. (9) can be calculated exactly in the case of a linear filtered threshold crossing (LFTC) model when the signal and noise are drawn from independent Gaussian distributions. Unlike the Integrate and Fire (IF) model, the LFTC model does not have a "renewal process" which resets the value of the filtered signal to zero each time the threshold is reached. Stevens and Zador have developed an alternative formulation for the information transmission which is better suited for studying the IF model under some circumstances (Stevens, 1995), and they give a nice discussion on the way in which these two formulations compliment each other.

For the LFTC model, the leading term is a function of only three variables: 1) The threshold height; 2) the ratio of the variances of the filtered signal and the filtered noise, $\langle s^2(t)\rangle_s / \langle \eta^2(t)\rangle_\eta$, which we refer to as the SNR; 3) and the ratio of correlation times of the filtered signal and the filtered noise, τ_s/τ_η, where $\tau_s^2 \equiv \langle s^2(t)\rangle_s / \langle \dot{s}^2(t)\rangle_s$ and similarly for the noise. In the equations in this last sentence, and in what follows, we absorb the linear filter into our definitions for the power spectra of the signal and noise. Near the Poisson limit, the linear filter can only affect the information rate through its generally weak influence on the ratios of variances and correlation times of the signal and noise, so we focus on the threshold to understand adaptation in our model cell.

When the ratio of correlation times of the signal and noise is moderate, we find a maximum for the information rate near the Poisson limit — the leading term $\approx 10\times$ the first correction. For the interesting and physically relevant case where the noise is slightly more broadband than the signal as seen through the cell's prefiltering, we find that the maximum information rate is achieved with a threshold setting which does not correspond to the maximum average firing rate illustrating that this optimum is non-trivial. Provided the SNR is about one or less, linear decoding does well — a lower bound on the information rate based on optimal linear reconstruction of the signal is within a factor of two of the total available information in the spike train. As SNR grows unbounded, this lower bound asymptotes to a constant. In addition, the required timing resolution for extracting the information from the spike train is quite modest — discretizing the spike train into bins which are half as wide as the correlation time of the signal degrades the information rate by less than 10%. However, at maximum information transmission, the information *per spike* is low — $R_{max}/\bar{r} \approx .7$ bits/spike, much lower than 3 bits/spike seen in the cricket. This low information rate drives the efficiency down to 1/3 of the experimental values despite the model's robustness to timing jitter. Aside from the low information rate, the optimized model captures all the experimental features we set out to explain.

7 Concluding Remarks

We have derived a useful expression for the transmitted information which can be used to measure information rates in real neurons provided the correlations between spikes are shorter range than the average inter-spike interval. We have described a method for checking this hypothesis experimentally. The four seemingly unrelated features that were common to several experiments on a variety of neurons are actually the natural consequences of maximizing the transmitted information. Specifically, they are all due to the relation between $\bar{r}$ and τ_c that is imposed by the optimization. We reiterate our previous prediction (DeWeese [2], 1995; Bialek, 1993): Optimizing the code requires that the threshold adapt not only to cancel DC offsets, but it must adapt to the statistical structure of the signal and noise. Experimental hints at adaptation to statistical structure have recently been seen in the fly visual system (de Ruyter van Steveninck, 1994) and in the salamander retina (Warland, 1995).

8 References

M. DeWeese 1995 *Optimization Principles for the Neural Code* (Dissertation, Princeton University)

M. DeWeese and W. Bialek 1995 Information flow in sensory neurons *Il Nuovo Cimento* **17D** 733-738

E. D. Adrian 1928 *The Basis of Sensation* (New York: W. W. Norton)

F. Rieke, D. Warland, R. de Ruyter van Steveninck, and W. Bialek 1996 *Neural Coding* (Boston: MIT Press)

W. Bialek, M. DeWeese, F. Rieke, and D. Warland 1993 Bits and Brains: Information Flow in the Nervous System *Physica A* **200** 581-593

C. E. Shannon 1949 Communication in the presence of noise, *Proc. I. R. E.* **37** 10-21

C. Stevens and A. Zador 1996 *Information Flow Through a Spiking Neuron* in M. Hasselmo ed *Advances in Neural Information Processing Systems, Vol 8* (Boston: MIT Press) (this volume)

R.R. de Ruyter van Steveninck, W. Bialek, M. Potters, R.H. Carlson 1994 Statistical adaptation and optimal estimation in movement computation by the blowfly visual system, in *IEEE International Conference On Systems, Man, and Cybernetics* pp 302-307

D. Warland, M. Berry, S. Smirnakis, and M. Meister 1995 personal communication

Strong Unimodality and Exact Learning of Constant Depth μ-Perceptron Networks

Mario Marchand
Department of Computer Science
University of Ottawa
Ottawa, Ont., Canada K1N 6N5
marchand@csi.uottawa.ca

Saeed Hadjifaradji
Department of Physics
University of Ottawa
Ottawa, Ont., Canada K1N 6N5
saeed@physics.uottawa.ca

Abstract

We present a statistical method that exactly learns the class of constant depth μ-perceptron networks with weights taken from $\{-1, 0 + 1\}$ and arbitrary thresholds when the distribution that generates the input examples is member of the family of product distributions. These networks (also known as nonoverlapping perceptron networks or read-once formulas over a weighted threshold basis) are loop-free neural nets in which each node has only one outgoing weight. With arbitrary high probability, the learner is able to exactly identify the connectivity (or skeleton) of the target μ-perceptron network by using a new statistical test which exploits the strong unimodality property of sums of independent random variables.

1 INTRODUCTION

From a computational learning theory perspective, it is well known that efficient learning of non trivial (or non simple) neural network function classes is possible only when either (1) the learner is able to use membership queries or (2) the distribution that generates the input examples is not arbitrary but member of some well defined family. Following several positive learnability results on different classes of *read-once* Boolean formulas, a membership query algorithm has been recently proposed [4] for learning the class of *nonoverlapping* perceptron networks. These networks (also known as μ-perceptron networks or read-once formulas over a weighted threshold basis) are loop-free neural nets in which each node has only one outgoing weight. If membership queries are not permitted (as we assume throughout this paper), learning this class becomes intractable [6] under arbitrary input distributions. However, under the *uniform* distribution, a PAC learning algorithm has been proposed recently [2] for a quite restricted subclass called *generalized µ-perceptron decision lists*. As an important step towards the learnability of the whole class of µ-perceptron networks under "simple" distributions, we present in this paper a statistical method that exactly learns the class of constant depth µ-perceptron networks under the family of *product distributions*, *i.e.* distributions in which the setting of each input variable is chosen independently of the other variables. Eventhough the depth of the network must be fixed to a constant, we satisfy here a harder learning criterion than the one proposed by the PAC model [9]. Indeed, with arbitrary high probability, the proposed algorithm is able to *exactly identify* [1] the target function. Moreover, because of its statistical nature [7], the proposed algorithm can tolerate a classification noise rate η up to the information theoretic limit of $\eta = 1/2$.

There exist other statistical methods to learn other classes of read-once formulas under particular distributions [1] and product distributions [8]. They all basically differ in the statistical tests they use to identify the gate parameters and the formula's skeleton. Our key novel contribution is to introduce a new test (for discovering the network's connectivity) which exploits the *strong unimodality* [5] property of sums of independent random variables.

2 DEFINITIONS

We consider the problem of learning Boolean functions of the Boolean domain $\{0,1\}^n$. Let $X = \{x_1, x_2 \cdots, x_n\}$ be the set of n input variables and $\mathbf{x} \in \{0,1\}^n$ be some assignment of these n variables, we denote by $\mathbf{x}_V$ the restriction of assignment $\mathbf{x}$ on the variables in $V \subseteq X$. A *perceptron* g on V is defined by a vector of $v = |V|$ weights w_i and a single threshold θ. As usual, for any $\mathbf{x}_V \in \{0,1\}^v$, the output of $g(\mathbf{x}_V)$ is 1 whenever $\sum_{i \in V} w_i x_i > \theta$ and 0 otherwise.

We restrict ourselves to the case where each $w_i \in \{-1, 0, +1\}$ but the thresholds are arbitrary so that, without loss of generality (w.l.o.g.), $\theta \in \{-v-1, \cdots v\}$. A perceptron is said to be *positive* if all its incoming weights are $+1$. The learning algorithm will use the following classification for positive perceptrons.
T1 perceptrons: These are perceptrons which output 1 iff one or more of its inputs are set to 1. These are OR gates of multiple inputs.
T0 perceptrons: These are perceptrons which output 0 iff one or more of its inputs are set to 0. These are AND gates of multiple inputs.
T11 perceptrons: These are perceptrons which output 1 iff two or more of its inputs are set to 1. These include majority gates of three inputs.
T00 perceptrons: These are perceptrons which output 0 iff two or more of its inputs are set to 0. These include majority gates of four variables.
TG perceptrons: All the perceptrons which do not belong to any one of the above four categories. They must, therefore, have at least five inputs.

Each perceptron can have variables and/or other perceptrons as inputs. Hence, a *node* will denote either a variable or a perceptron. The class of *µ-perceptron networks* is the set of all Boolean functions that can be represented as a loop-free network of perceptrons where each node (including input units) has only one outgoing weight. The output unit of a network will often be referred as the *root node*. We say that a node is a *child* of the *parent* perceptron g if it is an immediate input to perceptron g. Children of the same perceptron are called *siblings*. A perceptron is said to be a *bottom level perceptron* if all its children are variables. The *depth* of a node is defined as the number of perceptrons (including the parent of the node and the root node) on the path from the parent of the node to the root. The perceptrons on this path are called the *ancestors* of that node. The *descendants* of perceptron g, denoted by desc(g), is the set of nodes that have perceptron g as an ancestor. The depth of a network is defined as the depth of the deepest variable in the net. The *least common ancestor* of a set V of nodes, denoted by lca(V), is defined as the deepest ancestor which is common to every node in V. Variables $\{x_i, x_j, x_k\}$ are said to *meet* at perceptron g, *iff* lca(x_i, x_j) = lca(x_i, x_k) = lca(x_j, x_k) = g. If there does not exist a perceptron g having this property, then variables $\{x_i, x_j, x_k\}$ are said not to meet.

In this paper, we use a learning criterion which is more ambitious than the PAC criterion introduced by Valiant [9]. We consider that each training example **x** is generated by an unknown product distribution D on $\{0,1\}^n$ and then labeled according to an unknown target Boolean function f representable as a μ-perceptron network. After observing a set of such examples, the goal of the learning algorithm is to produce an hypothesis function h which is the exact equivalent of f. More formally we say that algorithm A *exactly learns* (or exactly identifies) a class F of of Boolean functions *iff* for any $0 < \delta < 1$, any product distribution D on $\{0,1\}^n$, and any target function $f \in F$, algorithm A outputs, with probability at least $1-\delta$ an hypothesis function h such that $h(\mathbf{x}) = f(\mathbf{x}) \ \forall \ \mathbf{x} \in \{0,1\}^n$.

The learning algorithm will perform several statistical tests to build its hypothesis. Namely, for each variable x_i, it will estimate its *influence*, defined as:

$$\text{Infl}(x_i) \stackrel{\text{def}}{=} \Pr(f = 1 | x_i = 1) - \Pr(f = 1 | x_i = 0) \tag{1}$$

where all probabilities (here and in the sequel) are defined with respect to the (unknown) training product distribution D. The empirical estimate of $\Pr(A)$ will be denoted as $\hat{\Pr}(A)$. We will also use, $\text{Infl}_g(x_i)$ to denote the influence of x_i on the subformula of f which is rooted at perceptron g. Also, $\text{Infl}(x_i|x_j = a)$ will denote the influence of x_i given that variable x_j is fixed to value a. To discover the skeleton of the target function, the learner will compute the *coinfluence* of several triples of variables, defined as:

$$C_{i,j}^k \stackrel{\text{def}}{=} \frac{\text{Infl}(x_j|x_i = 1, x_k = 0)}{\text{Infl}(x_j|x_i = 0, x_k = 0)} - \frac{\text{Infl}(x_j|x_i = 1, x_k = 1)}{\text{Infl}(x_j|x_i = 0, x_k = 1)} \tag{2}$$

Because h must make zero error with f, the learner must produce an hypothesis h which contains all the input variables and all the perceptrons of f (except those variables and perceptrons which are fixed to a constant value). Consequently, for a target f defined on n input variables x_i and containing r perceptrons g_k, we define ϵ_s as:

$$\epsilon_s \stackrel{\text{def}}{=} \min\left\{\Pr(x_i = a)_{i \in \{0, \cdots n\}, a \in \{0,1\}}, \Pr(g_k = b)_{k \in \{0, \cdots r\}, b \in \{0,1\}}\right\} \tag{3}$$

Hence, $\forall \ i \in \{0, \cdots n\}$ we have: $\epsilon_s \leq \Pr(x_i = 1) \leq 1 - \epsilon_s$ and $\forall \ k \in \{0, \cdots r\}$ we have: $\epsilon_s \leq \Pr(g_k = 1) \leq 1 - \epsilon_s$. To exactly learn the class of constant depth μ-percepton networks, the proposed algorithm needs a number of examples which is polynomial in $1/\epsilon_s$ (see the algorithm **LearnNPN**).

3 THE LEARNING ALGORITHM

We first perform some simplifying reductions that hold for any target μ-perceptron net f. (1) We can assume, w.l.o.g., that only input variables have a negative outgoing weight. Indeed, if a perceptron g has a -1 outgoing weight, we can replace it by a perceptron which has all its incoming weights negated and a $+1$

outgoing weight; this leaves the computation by f unchanged when we add $+1$ to the threshold of g's parent. In this manner, all -1 weights are pushed to the input variables. (2) $T1$ perceptrons do not have $T1$ perceptrons as children since such nodes can always be merged. The same remark is true for $T0$ perceptrons. (3) Because the output of each node is Boolean valued, each perceptron has at least two inputs. This implies that f has at most $n-1$ perceptrons.

The first step of the algorithm is to identify the weight w_i that springs out of each input variable x_i. For this we appeal to the following lemma:

Lemma 1 *Let f be any μ-perceptron network with weights taken from $\{-1, 0, +1\}$ and arbitrary thresholds. Let D be any product distribution on $\{0,1\}^n$. Let g be any perceptron with v weights and for which $\rho \leq \Pr(g=1) \leq 1-\rho$. Let input variable x_i be a child of g. Then:*

$$\mathrm{Infl}_g(x_i) \begin{cases} > +\rho/(2v) & \text{if } w_i = +1 \\ = 0 & \text{if } w_i = 0 \\ < -\rho/(2v) & \text{if } w_i = -1 \end{cases}$$

Moreover, if x_i has depth d, then, we have:

$$|\mathrm{Infl}(x_i)| > \left(\frac{\epsilon_s}{2n}\right)^d$$

Thus $\mathrm{Infl}(x_i)$ has a gap of $O([\epsilon_s/n]^d)$ that separates the three possible values for w_i. From Chernoff bounds [3], this implies that a sample size polynomial in ϵ_s/n is sufficient to find, with high probability, the *exact* value of w_i when d is fixed. After having identified all the weights in this manner, we transform the target function into its *positive form* simply by changing x_i to $1-x_i$ (and adding $+1$ to the threshold of x_i's parent) whenever $w_i = -1$.

To find the skeleton of the target function, the algorithm will first find all the bottom level perceptrons (*i.e.* perceptrons whose children are all variables). Then, after finding the *exact* thresholds (for TG perceptrons), we will consider these bottom level perceptrons as new "meta" variables (that replace their children) from which we can find their parent perceptrons. In this manner similar to Schapire's algorithm [8], we will build every perceptron of the net until we reach the root.

The coinfluence function will enable the learner to determine if certain variables are siblings of a perceptron g and if g is fed by other perceptrons. This is possible because the distribution of a sum of independent random variables is strongly unimodal [5]. More specifically, we have (and need) here a stronger property:

Lemma 2 *Let $\{x_1, x_2 \cdots, x_v\}$ be v independent random Boolean variables, each with $\Pr(x_i = 1) = q_i$ and let $S \stackrel{\mathrm{def}}{=} \sum_{i=1}^v x_i$. Then for any $\{q_1 \cdots, q_v\}$ and any $k \in \{1, \cdots, v\}$:*

$$\frac{\Pr(S=k-1)}{\Pr(S=k)} - \frac{\Pr(S=k-2)}{\Pr(S=k-1)} \geq \frac{\Pr(S=0)}{\Pr(S=1)} = \frac{1}{v<\alpha>_v}$$

where $\alpha_i \stackrel{\mathrm{def}}{=} q_i/(1-q_i)$ and $<\alpha>_v \stackrel{\mathrm{def}}{=} \sum_{i=1}^v \alpha_i/v$.

Proof: Omitted from this abstract but one can easily verify its exactness in the case where $q_i = q$ for all $i = 1 \cdots, v$. □.

The next lemma constitutes our main tool for finding the connectivity of f. It is expressed in terms of what we call the *strong unimodal gap* γ_n:

$$\gamma_n \stackrel{\mathrm{def}}{=} \min\left\{\frac{1}{n<\alpha>_n}, \frac{1}{n<1/\alpha>_n}\right\}$$

where: $<1/\alpha>_n \stackrel{\text{def}}{=} \sum_{i=1}^n \alpha_i^{-1}/n$.

Lemma 3 *Let $\{x_i, x_j, x_k\}$ be any triple of variables such that each is a child of some TG perceptron. Then:*

1. *$C_{i,j}^k \geq \gamma_n$ if $\{x_i, x_j, x_k\}$ are siblings of a perceptron g.*

2. *$C_{i,j}^k = 0$ if $x_k \notin \text{desc}(\text{lca}(x_i, x_j))$*

3. *$C_{i,j}^k = C_{i,l}^k$ if $\{x_i, x_j, x_k\}$ meet at a perceptron g that has a perceptron g_j as a child with the property that both x_j and x_l feed g_j.*

4. *If $\{$ $C_{i,j}^k \geq \gamma_n$ and x_l feeds $\text{lca}(x_i, x_j)$ through a perceptron g_l which is not fed by (x_i, x_j) $\}$ Then $C_{i,j}^l > \gamma_n^3 \cdot \text{Infl}(x_l)$*

Proof sketch: If $\{x_i, x_j, x_k\}$ are siblings of a perceptron g of threshold θ, then $C_{i,j}^k = [\Pr(S = \theta - 1)/\Pr(S = \theta)] - [\Pr(S = \theta - 2)/\Pr(S = \theta - 1)]$ which, from lemma 2, establishes fact 1. Let $g = \text{lca}(x_i, x_j)$. Then, if $x_k \notin \text{desc}(\text{lca}(x_i, x_j))$, $\text{Infl}(x_j|x_i = a, x_k = b) = \text{Infl}(g|x_k = b) \cdot \text{Infl}_g(x_j|x_i = a)$ which establishes fact 2. The proofs for fact 3 and 4 are omitted from this abstract. □

The constraints on x_i and x_k in lemma 3 are to avoid vanishing denominators in $C_{i,j}^k$. This does not create any problems since by using simpler tools, we can always find the children of the $T0, T1, T00, T11$ perceptrons before those of the TG perceptrons. In the following we also explain how to identify the non-TG bottom level perceptrons.

Lemma 4 *Variable x_i is a child of a $T1$ perceptron iff there exist x_j such that $\text{Infl}(x_j|x_i = 1) = 0$. Otherwise $\text{Infl}(x_j|x_i = 1) > \text{Infl}(x_j) \cdot \gamma_n$ for all $x_j \neq x_i$.*

Moreover, a set W of variables, each of which is a child of a $T1$ perceptron, is a set of siblings iff $\text{Infl}(x_j|x_i = 1) = 0$ $\forall$ $\{x_i, x_j\} \in W$.

Moreover, If $\{$ $W \subseteq V$ is a set of variables, all siblings of a $T1$ perceptron g, such that no children of g is in $V - W$ $\}$ Then $\{$ g is a bottom level perceptron with respect to V iff $\text{Infl}(x_k|x_i = 1) > \text{Infl}(x_k) \cdot \gamma_n$ for all $x_k \in V - W, x_i \in W$. Otherwise there exist $x_k \in V - W$ and $x_i \in W$ such that $\text{Infl}(x_k|x_i = 1) = 0$ $\}$.

The lemma is valid when we replace $T1$ by $T0$ if the condition $x_i = 1$ is replaced by $x_i = 0$.

Proof idea: Directly follows from lemma 2, the definitions of $T1$ and $T0$ and from the fact that no two consecutive $T1$ (nor $T0$) perceptrons occur in f. □

From this lemma, we define a routine, **Find-bl-T1**(V), that finds all $T1$ perceptrons which are bottom level with respect to the set V of variables (or meta variables). It achieves this by testing, for each pair of variables, if $\hat{\text{Infl}}(x_j|x_i = 1)/\hat{\text{Infl}}(x_j) > \gamma_n/2$. (By using Chernoff bounds, we find the probability of making the correct decision for each variable as a function of the sample size m.) Moreover, the output of this routine is a set V' which consists of the original set V from which the siblings have been replaced by their bottom level $T1$ parents (with their children connected) as new meta variables. It also tags those variables in V that are children of some non-bottom level $T1$ perceptron. This is to warn the subsequent routines of not using these variables to find out if they are children of other types of perceptrons. An identical definition and a similar operation applies for **Find-bl-T0**(V). The same applies also for **Find-bl-T11**(V), **Find-bl-T00**(V) and **Find-bl-TG**(V) but for them, we need to use the following lemmas.

Lemma 5 Let x_i and x_j be variables which neither is a child of a T1 or a T0 perceptron. Then $\{x_i, x_j\}$ are siblings of a T11 perceptron iff there exist x_k such that $\text{Infl}(x_k | x_i = x_j = 1) = 0$. Otherwise $\text{Infl}(x_k | x_i = x_j = 1) > \text{Infl}(x_k) \cdot \gamma_n^2$ for all $x_k \notin \{x_i, x_j\}$.

Moreover, let V be a set of variables for which no one is a child of some T0 or T1 perceptron. Let $W \subseteq V$ be a set of variables, all siblings of a T11 perceptron g and such that no children of g is in $V - W$. Then g is a bottom level perceptron with respect to V iff $C_{i,j}^k = 0$ for all $x_k \in V - W$ and $\{x_i, x_j\} \in W$. Otherwise there exist $x_k \in V - W$ and $\{x_i, x_j\} \in W$ such that $C_{i,j}^k > \text{Infl}(x_k) \cdot \gamma_n^3$.

The lemma is valid when we replace T11 by T00 if the condition $x_i = x_j = 1$ is replaced by $x_i = x_j = 0$.

Proof idea: Follows from lemmas 2 and 3 and from the definitions of T11 and T00 perceptrons. □

Lemma 6 Let V be a set of variables, each of which is a child of some TG perceptron. Let $W \subseteq V$ be a set of variables for which $C_{i,j}^k \geq \gamma_n \; \forall \; \{x_i, x_j, x_k\} \in W$. Then W is a set of siblings of a bottom level TG perceptron g (and thus g is bottom level with respect to V) iff there does not exist any $\{l, m\} \in V - W$ and $\{i, j\} \in W$ for which all of these properties hold:

1. $C_{i,j}^l > \gamma_n^3 \cdot \text{Infl}(x_l)$ and $C_{i,j}^m > \gamma_n^3 \cdot \text{Infl}(x_m)$

2. $C_{l,m}^i = C_{l,m}^j = 0$

Moreover, the threshold θ of a bottom level TG perceptron g (in positive form) is obtained by the value of k for which $\Pr(f = 1 | S = k+1) - \Pr(f = 1 | S = k) \geq \text{Infl}(x_j)$ where x_j can be any child of g and S denotes the sum over all its children. This difference is zero if $k \neq \theta$.

Having sketched the action of the different **Find-bl-T*** routines, we now propose the following learning algorithm.

Algorithm LearnNPN(n, ϵ_s, δ)

1. Call $m = \left(\dfrac{64}{\epsilon_s^2 \gamma_n^5}\right)^2 \left(\dfrac{2n}{\epsilon_s}\right)^{4d} \ln\left(\dfrac{32 d n^3}{\delta}\right)$ training examples.

2. For every $x_i \in X$, let $w_i = +1$ if $\hat{\text{Infl}}(x_i) > \epsilon_s/4n$, let $w_i = -1$ if $\hat{\text{Infl}}(x_i) < -\epsilon_s/4n$ and let $w_i = 0$ otherwise. Let $x_i = 1 - x_i$ whenever $w_i = -1$ (conversion into the positive form). Let $V = X$.

3. Repeat {
      Repeat {
        Repeat {
          Repeat {Let $V_i = V$; $V = $ **Find-bl-T1**(**Find-bl-T0**(V_i))
          } Until $V = V_i$
          Let $V_i = V$; $V = $ **Find-bl-T00**(V_i)
        } Until $V = V_i$
        Let $V_i = V$; $V = $ **Find-bl-T11**(V_i)
      } Until $V = V_i$
      $V = $ **Find-bl-TG**(V)
   } Until only one meta-variable remains in V

4. Return this meta-variable (with all the others attached to it) as our hypothesis network h and convert from positive to normal form.

The nested loops insure that, every time the set V of meta-variables is updated, all bottom level $T0$ and $T1$ perceptrons are found before the $T00$ and $T11$ perceptrons which are themselves found before the TG perceptrons. This is essential in order that the **Find-bl-T*** routines make proper use of lemma 5 and 6.

Theorem 1 *Under product distributions, the algorithm* **LearnNPN** *exactly learns the class of μ-perceptrons networks of depth at most d with weights taken from $\{-1, 0, +1\}$ and arbitrary thresholds. The algorithm runs in time of $O(m \times d \times n^3)$.*

Proof idea: By using Chernoff bounds [3], one can verify that the above sample of m examples is sufficient to ensure that all probabilities are estimated with enough precision to have $h(\mathbf{x}) = f(\mathbf{x}) \; \forall \mathbf{x} \in \{0,1\}^n$ with probability at least $1 - \delta$.

Acknowledgments

We thank Mostefa Golea and Hans U. Simon for useful comments and discussions about technical points. M. Marchand is supported by NSERC grant OGP0122405. Saeed Hadjifaradji is supported by the MCHE of Iran.

References

[1] Goldman S., Kearns M.J., & Schapire R., (1990). "Exact identification of circuits using fixed points of amplification functions. *Proceedings of the 31st Symposium on Foundations of Computer Science*, Los Alamitos, CA: IEEE Computer Society Press.

[2] Golea M., Marchand M., & Hancock T.R., (1995) "On Learning μ-Perceptron Networks On the Uniform Distribution", to appear in *Neural Networks*. For a short version see: *Advances in Neural Information Processing Systems 5*, pp. 591–598, San Mateo CA, Morgan Kaufmann Publishers, (1993). Also: *Computational Learning Theory: EuroCOLT'93*, pp. 47–60, Oxford University Press, (1994).

[3] Hagerup T. & Rub C. (1989) "A Guided Tour to Chernoff Bounds", *Info. Proc. Lett.*, Vol. 33, 305–308.

[4] Hancock T.R., Golea M., & Marchand M., (1994) "Learning Nonoverlapping Perceptron Networks from Examples and Membership Queries", *Machine Learning*, vol. 16, pp. 161–183.

[5] Ibragimov I.A., (1956) "On the composition of unimodal distributions", *Theor. Probability Appl.* vol. 1, 255–266. *Also:* Keilson J. & Gerber H., (1971) "Some results for discrete unimodality", *J. Amer. Statist. Assoc.*, vol. 66, 386–389.

[6] Kearns M.J., Li M., Pitt L. & Valiant L. G., (1987). "On the learnability of boolean formulae" *Proceedings of the Nineteenth Annual ACM Symposium on Theory of Computing* (pp. 285–295). New York: ACM Press.

[7] Kearns M. (1993). "Efficient Noise-Tolerant Learning from Statistical Queries", *Proceedings of the Twenty Fifth Annual ACM Symposium on the Theory of Computation*, p. 392.

[8] Schapire R., (1994) "Learning probabilistic read-once formulas on product distributions" *Machine Learning* vol. 14, 47–81. San Mateo, CA: Morgan Kaufman.

[9] Valiant L.G. (1984) "A Theory of the Learnable", *Comm. ACM*, Vol. 27, 1134–1142.

Active Learning in Multilayer Perceptrons

Kenji Fukumizu
Information and Communication R&D Center, Ricoh Co., Ltd.
3-2-3, Shin-yokohama, Yokohama, 222 Japan
E-mail: fuku@ic.rdc.ricoh.co.jp

Abstract

We propose an active learning method with hidden-unit reduction, which is devised specially for multilayer perceptrons (MLP). First, we review our active learning method, and point out that many Fisher-information-based methods applied to MLP have a critical problem: the information matrix may be singular. To solve this problem, we derive the singularity condition of an information matrix, and propose an active learning technique that is applicable to MLP. Its effectiveness is verified through experiments.

1 INTRODUCTION

When one trains a learning machine using a set of data given by the true system, its ability can be improved if one selects the training data actively. In this paper, we consider the problem of active learning in multilayer perceptrons (MLP). First, we review our method of active learning (Fukumizu el al., 1994), in which we prepare a probability distribution and obtain training data as samples from the distribution. This methodology leads us to an information-matrix-based criterion similar to other existing ones (Fedorov, 1972; Pukelsheim, 1993).

Active learning techniques have been recently used with neural networks (MacKay, 1992; Cohn, 1994). Our method, however, as well as many other ones has a crucial problem: the required inverse of an information matrix may not exist (White, 1989).

We propose an active learning technique which is applicable to three-layer perceptrons. Developing a theory on the singularity of a Fisher information matrix, we present an active learning algorithm which keeps the information matrix nonsingular. We demonstrate the effectiveness of the algorithm through experiments.

2 STATISTICALLY OPTIMAL TRAINING DATA

2.1 A CRITERION OF OPTIMALITY

We review the criterion of statistically optimal training data (Fukumizu et al., 1994). We consider the regression problem in which the target system maps a given input x to y according to
$$y = f(x) + Z,$$
where $f(x)$ is a deterministic function from $\mathbf{R}^L$ to $\mathbf{R}^M$, and Z is a random variable whose law is a normal distribution $N(0, \sigma^2 I_M)$, (I_M is the unit $M \times M$ matrix). Our objective is to estimate the true function f as accurately as possible.

Let $\{f(x;\theta)\}$ be a parametric model for estimation. We use the maximum likelihood estimator (MLE) $\hat{\theta}$ for training data $\{(x^{(\nu)}, y^{(\nu)})\}_{\nu=1}^N$, which minimizes the sum of squared errors in this case. In theoretical derivations, we assume that the target function f is included in the model and equal to $f(\cdot;\theta_0)$.

We make a training example by choosing $x^{(\nu)}$ to try, observing the resulting output $y^{(\nu)}$, and pairing them. The problem of active learning is how to determine input data $\{x^{(\nu)}\}_{\nu=1}^N$ to minimize the estimation error after training. Our approach is a statistical one using a *probability for training*, $r(x)$, and choosing $\{x^{(\nu)}\}_{\nu=1}^N$ as independent samples from $r(x)$ to minimize the expectation of the MSE *in the actual environment*:

$$\text{EMSE} = \text{E}_{\{(x^{(\nu)}, y^{(\nu)})\}} \left[\int \int \|y - f(x; \hat{\theta})\|^2 p(y|x) dy dQ \right]. \quad (1)$$

In the above equation, Q is *the environmental probability* which gives input vectors to the true system in the actual environment, and $\text{E}_{\{(x^{(\nu)}, y^{(\nu)})\}}$ means the expectation on training data. Eq.(1), therefore, shows the average error of the trained machine that is used as a substitute of the true function in the actual environment.

2.2 REVIEW OF AN ACTIVE LEARNING METHOD

Using statistical asymptotic theory, Eq.(1) is approximated as follows:

$$\text{EMSE} = \sigma^2 + \frac{\sigma^2}{N} \text{Tr}\left[I(\theta_0) J^{-1}(\theta_0)\right] + O(N^{-3/2}), \quad (2)$$

where the matrixes I and J are (*Fisher*) *information matrixes* defined by

$$I_{ab}(x;\theta) = \frac{\partial f^T(x;\theta)}{\partial \theta_a} \frac{\partial f(x;\theta)}{\partial \theta_b}, \quad I(\theta) = \int I(x;\theta) dQ(x), \quad J(\theta) = \int I(x;\theta) r(x) dx.$$

The essential part of Eq.(2) is $\text{Tr}[I(\theta_0) J^{-1}(\theta_0)]$, computed by the unavailable parameter θ_0. We have proposed a practical algorithm in which we replace θ_0 with $\hat{\theta}$, prepare a family of probability $\{r(x;v) \mid v : \text{paramater}\}$ to choose training samples, and optimize v and $\hat{\theta}$ iteratively (Fukumizu et al., 1994).

Active Learning Algorithm

1. Select an initial training data set $D_{[0]}$ from $r(x; v_{[0]})$, and compute $\hat{\theta}_{[0]}$.
2. $k := 1$.
3. Compute the optimal $v = v_{[k]}$ to minimize $\text{Tr}[I(\hat{\theta}_{[k-1]}) J^{-1}(\hat{\theta}_{[k-1]})]$.

4. Choose N_k new training data from $r(x; v_{[k]})$ and let $D_{[k]}$ be a union of $D_{[k-1]}$ and the new data.

5. Compute the MLE $\hat{\theta}_{[k]}$ based on the training data set $D_{[k]}$.

6. $k := k + 1$ and go to 3.

The above method utilizes a probability to generate training data. It has the advantage of making many data in one step compared to existing ones in which only one data is chosen in each step, though their criterions are similar to each other.

3 SINGULARITY OF AN INFORMATION MATRIX

3.1 A PROBLEM ON ACTIVE LEARNING IN MLP

Hereafter, we focus on active learning in three-layer perceptrons with H hidden units, $\mathcal{N}_H = \{f(x, \theta)\}$. The map $f(x; \theta)$ is defined by

$$f_i(x; \theta) = \sum_{j=1}^{H} w_{ij} s(\sum_{k=1}^{L} u_{jk} x_k + \zeta_j) + \eta_i, \quad (1 \leq i \leq M), \quad (3)$$

where $s(t)$ is the sigmoidal function: $s(t) = 1/(1 + e^{-t})$.

Our active learning method as well as many other ones requires the inverse of an information matrix J. The information matrix of MLP, however, is not always invertible (White, 1989). Any statistical algorithms utilizing the inverse, then, cannot be applied directly to MLP (Hagiwara et al., 1993). Such problems do not arise in linear models, which almost always have a nonsingular information matrix.

3.2 SINGULARITY OF AN INFORMATION MATRIX OF MLP

The following theorem shows that the information matrix of a three-layer perceptron is singular if and only if the network has redundant hidden units. We can deduce that if the information matrix is singular, we can make it nonsingular by eliminating redundant hidden units without changing the input-output map.

Theorem 1 *Assume $r(x)$ is continuous and positive at any x. Then, the Fisher information matrix J is singular if and only if at least one of the following three conditions is satisfied:*
(1) $u_j := (u_{j1}, \ldots, u_{jL})^T = 0$, for some j.
(2) $w_j := (w_{1j}, \ldots, w_{Mj}) = 0^T$, for some j.
(3) For different j_1 and j_2, $(u_{j_1}^T, \zeta_{j_1}) = (u_{j_2}^T, \zeta_{j_2})$ or $(u_{j_1}^T, \zeta_{j_1}) = -(u_{j_2}^T, \zeta_{j_2})$.

The rough sketch of the proof is shown below. The complete proof will appear in a forthcoming paper (Fukumizu, 1996).
Rough sketch of the proof. We know easily that an information matrix is singular if and only if $\{\frac{\partial f(x;\theta)}{\partial \theta_a}\}_a$ are linearly dependent. The sufficiency can be proved easily. To show the necessity, we show that the derivatives are linearly independent if none of the three conditions is satisfied. Assume a linear relation:

$$\sum_{i=1}^{M} \sum_{j=1}^{H} \alpha_{ij} \frac{\partial f}{\partial w_{ij}} + \sum_{i=1}^{M} \alpha_{i0} \frac{\partial f}{\partial \eta_i} + \sum_{j=1}^{H} \sum_{k=1}^{L} \beta_{jk} \frac{\partial f}{\partial u_{jk}} + \sum_{j=1}^{H} \beta_{j0} \frac{\partial f}{\partial \zeta_j} = 0. \quad (4)$$

We can show there exists a basis of $\mathbf{R}^L$, $\langle x^{(1)}, \ldots, x^{(L)} \rangle$, such that $u_j \cdot x^{(l)} \neq 0$ for $\forall j$, $\forall l$, and $u_{j_1} \cdot x^{(l)} + \zeta_{j_1} \neq \pm(u_{j_2} \cdot x^{(l)} + \zeta_{j_2})$ for $j_1 \neq j_2, \forall l$. We replace x in eq.(4) by $x^{(l)}t$ ($t \in \mathbf{R}$). Let $m_j^{(l)} := u_j \cdot x^{(l)}$, $S_j^{(l)} := \{z \in \mathbf{C} \mid z = ((2n+1)\pi\sqrt{-1} - \zeta_j)/m_j^{(l)}, n \in \mathbf{Z}\}$, and $D^{(l)} := \mathbf{C} - \cup_j S_j^{(l)}$. The points in $S_j^{(l)}$ are the singularities of $s(m_j^{(l)}z + \zeta_j)$. We define holomorphic functions on $D^{(l)}$ as

$$\Psi_i^{(l)}(z) := \sum_{j=1}^{H}\alpha_{ij}s(m_j^{(l)}z + \zeta_j) + \alpha_{i0} + \sum_{j=1}^{H}\sum_{k=1}^{L}\beta_{jk}w_{ij}s'(m_j^{(l)}z + \zeta_j)x_k^{(l)}z$$
$$+ \sum_{j=1}^{H}\beta_{j0}w_{ij}s'(m_j^{(l)}z + \zeta_j), \qquad (1 \leq i \leq M).$$

From eq.(4), we have $\Psi_i^{(l)}(t) = 0$ for all $t \in \mathbf{R}$. Using standard arguments on isolated singularities of holomorphic functions, we know $S_j^{(l)}$ are removable singularities of $\Psi_i^{(l)}(z)$, and finally obtain

$$w_{ij}\sum_{k=1}^{L}\beta_{jk}x_k^{(l)} = 0, \qquad w_{ij}\beta_{j0} = 0, \qquad \alpha_{ij} = 0, \qquad \alpha_{i0} = 0.$$

It is easy to see $\beta_{jk} = 0$. This completes the proof.

3.3 REDUCTION PROCEDURE

We introduce the following *reduction procedure* based on Theorem 1. Used during BP training, it eliminates redundant hidden units and keeps the information matrix nonsingular. The criterion of elimination is very important, because excessive elimination of hidden units degrades the approximation capacity. We propose an algorithm which does not increase the mean squared error on average. In the following, let $\hat{s}_j := s(\hat{u}_j \cdot x + \hat{\eta}_j)$ and $\varepsilon(N) = A/N$ for a positive number A.

Reduction Procedure

1. If $\quad \|\hat{w}_j\|^2 \int (\hat{s}_j - s(\hat{\zeta}_j))^2 dQ < \varepsilon(N)$, then eliminate the jth hidden unit, and $\hat{\eta}_i \to \hat{\eta}_i + \hat{w}_{ij}s(\hat{\zeta}_j)$ for all i.

2. If $\quad \|\hat{w}_j\|^2 \int (\hat{s}_j)^2 dQ < \varepsilon(N)$, then eliminate the jth hidden unit.

3. If $\quad \|\hat{w}_{j_2}\|^2 \int (\hat{s}_{j_2} - \hat{s}_{j_1})^2 dQ < \varepsilon(N) \quad$ for different j_1 and j_2, then eliminate the j_2th hidden unit and $\hat{w}_{ij_1} \to \hat{w}_{ij_1} + \hat{w}_{ij_2}$ for all i.

4. If $\quad \|\hat{w}_{j_2}\|^2 \int (1 - \hat{s}_{j_2} - \hat{s}_{j_1})^2 dQ < \varepsilon(N) \quad$ for different j_1 and j_2, then eliminate the j_2th hidden unit and $\hat{w}_{ij_1} \to \hat{w}_{ij_1} - \hat{w}_{ij_2}$, $\hat{\eta}_i \to \hat{\eta}_i + \hat{w}_{ij_2}$ for all i.

From Theorem 1, we know that $\hat{w}_j$, $\hat{u}_j$, $(\hat{u}_{j_2}^T, \hat{\zeta}_{j_2}) - (\hat{u}_{j_1}^T, \hat{\zeta}_{j_1})$, or $(\hat{u}_{j_2}^T, \hat{\zeta}_{j_2}) + (\hat{u}_{j_1}^T, \hat{\zeta}_{j_1})$ can be reduced to 0 if the information matrix is singular. Let $\tilde{\theta} \in \mathcal{N}_K$ denote the reduced parameter from $\hat{\theta}$ according to the above procedure. The above four conditions are, then, given by calculating $\int \|f(x; \tilde{\theta}) - f(x; \hat{\theta})\|^2 dQ$.

We briefly explain how the procedure keeps the information matrix nonsingular and does not increase EMSE in high probability. First, suppose $\det J(\theta_0) = 0$, then there exists $\theta_0^K \in \mathcal{N}_K$ ($K < H$) such that $f(x; \theta_0) = f(x; \theta_0^K)$ and $\det J(\theta_0^K) \neq 0$ in $\mathcal{N}_K$. The elimination of hidden units up to K, of course, does not increase the EMSE. Therefore, we have only to consider the case in which $\det J(\theta_0) \neq 0$ and hidden units are eliminated.

Suppose $\int \|f(x; \theta_0^K) - f(x; \theta_0)\|^2 dQ > O(N^{-1})$ for any reduced parameter θ_0^K from θ_0. The probability of satisfying $\int \|f(x; \hat{\theta}) - f(x; \tilde{\theta})\|^2 dQ < A/N$ is very small for a sufficiently small A. Thus, the elimination of hidden units occurs in very tiny probability. Next, suppose $\int \|f(x;\theta_0^K) - f(x;\theta_0)\|^2 dQ = O(N^{-1})$. Let $\tilde{\theta} \in \mathcal{N}_K$ be a reduced parameter made from $\hat{\theta}$ with the same procedure as we obtain θ_0^K from θ_0. We will show for a sufficiently small A,

$$\mathrm{E}\left[\int \|f(x;\hat{\theta}^K) - f(x;\theta_0)\|^2 dQ\right] \leq \mathrm{E}\left[\int \|f(x;\hat{\theta}) - f(x;\theta_0)\|^2 dQ\right],$$

where $\hat{\theta}^K$ is MLE computed in $\mathcal{N}_K$. We write $\theta = (\theta^{(1)}, \theta^{(2)})$ in which $\theta^{(2)}$ is changed to 0 in reduction, changing the coordinate system if necessary. The Taylor expansion and asymptotic theory give

$$\mathrm{E}\left[\int \|f(x;\hat{\theta}^K) - f(x;\theta_0)\|^2 dQ\right] \approx \int \|f(x;\theta_0^K) - f(x;\theta_0)\|^2 dQ + \frac{\sigma^2}{N} \mathrm{Tr}[I_{11}(\theta_0^K) J_{11}^{-1}(\theta_0^K)],$$

$$\mathrm{E}\left[\int \|f(x;\tilde{\theta}) - f(x;\hat{\theta})\|^2 dQ\right] \approx \int \|f(x;\theta_0^K) - f(x;\theta_0)\|^2 dQ + \frac{\sigma^2}{N} \mathrm{Tr}[I_{22}(\theta_0^K) J_{22}^{-1}(\theta_0)],$$

where I_{ii} and J_{ii} denote the local information matrixes w.r.t. $\theta^{(i)}$ ($i = 1, 2$). Thus,

$$\mathrm{E}\left[\int \|f(x;\hat{\theta}) - f(x;\theta_0)\|^2 dQ\right] - \mathrm{E}\left[\int \|f(x;\hat{\theta}^K) - f(x;\theta_0)\|^2 dQ\right]$$

$$\approx -\mathrm{E}\left[\int \|f(x;\tilde{\theta}) - f(x;\hat{\theta})\|^2 dQ\right] + \frac{\sigma^2}{N} \mathrm{Tr}[I_{22}(\theta_0^K) J_{22}^{-1}(\theta_0)]$$

$$- \frac{\sigma^2}{N} \mathrm{Tr}[I_{11}(\theta_0^K) J_{11}^{-1}(\theta_0^K)] + \mathrm{E}\left[\int \|f(x;\hat{\theta}) - f(x;\theta_0)\|^2 dQ\right].$$

Since the sum of the last two terms is positive, the l.h.s is positive if $\mathrm{E}[\int \|f(x;\hat{\theta}^K) - f(x;\hat{\theta})\|^2 dQ] < B/N$ for a sufficiently small B. Although we cannot know the value of this expectation, we can make the probability of holding this enequality very high by taking a small A.

4 ACTIVE LEARNING WITH REDUCTION PROCEDURE

The reduction procedure keeps the information matrix nonsingular and makes the active learning algorithm applicable to MLP even with surplus hidden units.

Active Learning with Hidden Unit Reduction

1. Select initial training data set D_0 from $r(x; v_{[0]})$, and compute $\hat{\theta}_{[0]}$.
2. $k := 1$, and do REDUCTION PROCEDURE.
3. Compute the optimal $v = v_{[k]}$ to minimize $\mathrm{Tr}[I(\hat{\theta}_{[k-1]}) J^{-1}(\hat{\theta}_{[k-1]})]$, using the steepest descent method.
4. Choose N_k new training data from $r(x; v_{[k]})$ and let $D_{[k]}$ be a union of $D_{[k-1]}$ and the new data.
5. Compute the MLE $\hat{\theta}_{[k]}$ based on the training data $D_{[k]}$ using BP with REDUCTION PROCEDURE.
6. $k := k + 1$ and go to 3.

The BP with reduction procedure is applicable not only to active learning, but to a variety of statistical techniques that require the inverse of an information matrix. We do not discuss it in this paper, however.

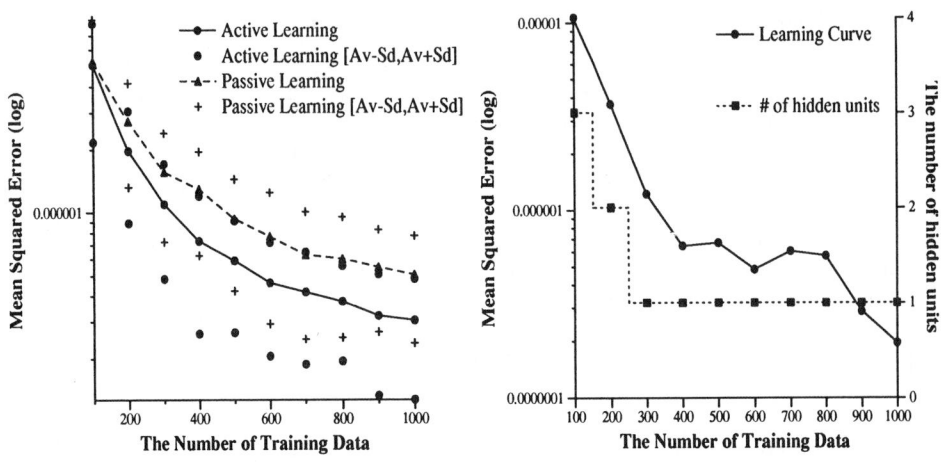

Figure 1: Active/Passive Learning : $f(x) = s(x)$

5 EXPERIMENTS

We demonstrate the effect of the proposed active learning algorithm through experiments. First we use a three-layer model with 1 input unit, 3 hidden units, and 1 output unit. The true function f is a MLP network with 1 hidden unit. The information matrix is singular at θ_0, then. The environmental probability, Q, is a normal distribution $N(0, 4)$. We evaluate the generalization error in the actual environment using the following mean squared error of the function values:

$$\int \|f(x; \hat{\theta}) - f(x)\|^2 dQ.$$

We set the deviation in the true system $\sigma = 0.01$. As a family of distributions for training $\{r(x; v)\}$, a mixture model of 4 normal distributions is used. In each step of active learning, 100 new samples are added. A network is trained using online BP, presented with all training data 10000 times in each step, and operated the reduction procedure once a 100 cycles between 5000th and 10000th cycle. We try 30 trainings changing the seed of random numbers. In comparison, we train a network passively based on training samples given by the probability Q.

Fig.1 shows the averaged learning curves of active/passive learning and the number of hidden units in a typical learning curve. The advantage of the proposed active learning algorithm is clear. We can find that the algorithm has expected effects on a simple, ideal approximation problem.

Second, we apply the algorithm to a problem in which the true function is not included in the MLP model. We use MLP with 4 input units, 7 hidden units, and 1 output unit. The true function is given by $f(x) = \mathrm{erf}(x_1)$, where $\mathrm{erf}(t)$ is the *error function*. The graph of the error function resembles that of the sigmoidal function, while they never coincide by any affine transforms. We set $Q = N(0, 25 \times I_4)$. We train a network actively/passively based on 10 data sets, and evaluate MSE's of function values. Other conditions are the same as those of the first experiment.

Fig.2 shows the averaged learning curves and the number of hidden units in a typical learning curve. We find that the active learning algorithm reduces the errors though the theoretical condition is not perfectly satisfied in this case. It suggests the robustness of our active learning algorithm.

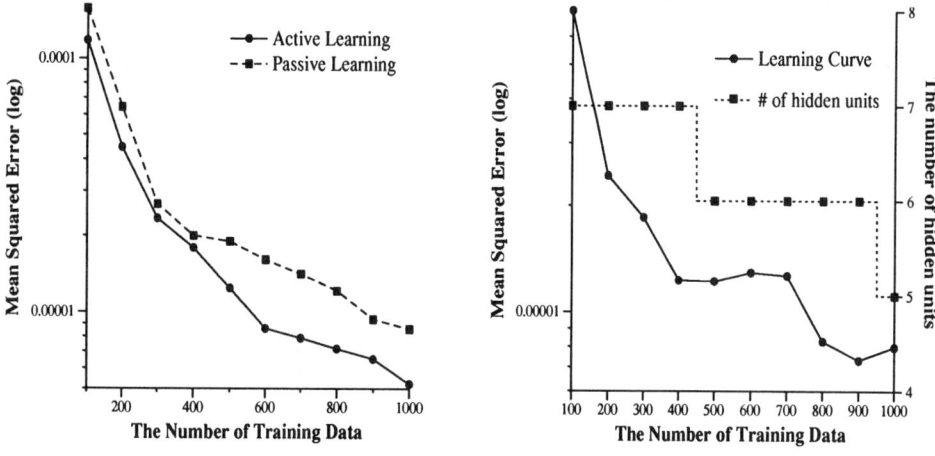

Figure 2: Active/Passive Learning : $f(x) = \text{erf}(x_1)$

6 CONCLUSION

We review statistical active learning methods and point out a problem in their application to MLP: the required inverse of an information matrix does not exist if the network has redundant hidden units. We characterize the singularity condition of an information matrix and propose an active learning algorithm which is applicable to MLP with any number of hidden units. The effectiveness of the algorithm is verified through computer simulations, even when the theoretical assumptions are not perfectly satisfied.

References

D. A. Cohn. (1994) Neural network exploration using optimal experiment design. In J. Cowan et al. (ed.), *Advances in Neural Information Processing Systems 6*, 679-686. San Mateo, CA: Morgan Kaufmann.

V. V. Fedorov. (1972) *Theory of Optimal Experiments*. NY: Academic Press.

K. Fukumizu. (1996) A Regularity Condition of the Information Matrix of a Multilayer Perceptron Network. *Neural Networks*, to appear.

K. Fukumizu, & S. Watanabe. (1994) Error Estimation and Learning Data Arrangement for Neural Networks. *Proc. IEEE Int. Conf. Neural Networks* :777-780.

K. Hagiwara, N. Toda, & S. Usui. (1993) On the problem of applying AIC to determine the structure of a layered feed-forward neural network. *Proc. 1993 Int. Joint Conf. Neural Networks* :2263-2266.

D. MacKay. (1992) Information-based objective functions for active data selection, *Neural Computation* 4(4):305-318.

F. Pukelsheim. (1993) *Optimal Design of Experiments*. NY: John Wiley & Sons.

H. White. (1989) Learning in artificial neural networks: A statistical perspective *Neural Computation* 1(4):425-464.

Dynamics of On-Line Gradient Descent Learning for Multilayer Neural Networks

David Saad[*]
Dept. of Comp. Sci. & App. Math.
Aston University
Birmingham B4 7ET, UK

Sara A. Solla[†]
CONNECT, The Niels Bohr Institute
Blegdamsdvej 17
Copenhagen 2100, Denmark

Abstract

We consider the problem of on-line gradient descent learning for general two-layer neural networks. An analytic solution is presented and used to investigate the role of the learning rate in controlling the evolution and convergence of the learning process.

Learning in layered neural networks refers to the modification of internal parameters $\{\mathbf{J}\}$ which specify the strength of the interneuron couplings, so as to bring the map $f_\mathbf{J}$ implemented by the network as close as possible to a desired map $\tilde{f}$. The degree of success is monitored through the *generalization error*, a measure of the dissimilarity between $f_\mathbf{J}$ and $\tilde{f}$.

Consider maps from an N-dimensional input space $\boldsymbol{\xi}$ onto a scalar ζ, as arise in the formulation of classification and regression tasks. Two-layer networks with an arbitrary number of hidden units have been shown to be universal approximators [1] for such N-to-one dimensional maps. Information about the desired map $\tilde{f}$ is provided through independent examples $(\boldsymbol{\xi}^\mu, \zeta^\mu)$, with $\zeta^\mu = \tilde{f}(\boldsymbol{\xi}^\mu)$ for all μ. The examples are used to train a student network with N input units, K hidden units, and a single linear output unit; the target map $\tilde{f}$ is defined through a teacher network of similar architecture except for the number M of hidden units. We investigate the emergence of generalization ability in an *on-line* learning scenario [2], in which the couplings are modified after the presentation of each example so as to minimize the corresponding error. The resulting changes in $\{\mathbf{J}\}$ are described as a dynamical evolution; the number of examples plays the role of time.

In this paper we limit our discussion to the case of the soft-committee machine [2], in which all the hidden units are connected to the output unit with positive couplings of unit strength, and only the input-to-hidden couplings are adaptive.

---

[*]D.Saad@aston.ac.uk
[†]On leave from AT&T Bell Laboratories, Holmdel, NJ 07733, USA

Consider the student network: hidden unit i receives information from input unit r through the weight J_{ir}, and its activation under presentation of an input pattern $\boldsymbol{\xi} = (\xi_1,\ldots,\xi_N)$ is $x_i = \mathbf{J}_i \cdot \boldsymbol{\xi}$, with $\mathbf{J}_i = (J_{i1},\ldots,J_{iN})$ defined as the vector of incoming weights onto the i-th hidden unit. The output of the student network is $\sigma(\mathbf{J},\boldsymbol{\xi}) = \sum_{i=1}^{K} g(\mathbf{J}_i \cdot \boldsymbol{\xi})$, where g is the activation function of the hidden units, taken here to be the error function $g(x) \equiv \mathrm{erf}(x/\sqrt{2})$, and $\mathbf{J} \equiv \{\mathbf{J}_i\}_{1 \leq i \leq K}$ is the set of input-to-hidden adaptive weights.

Training examples are of the form $(\boldsymbol{\xi}^\mu, \zeta^\mu)$. The components of the independently drawn input vectors $\boldsymbol{\xi}^\mu$ are uncorrelated random variables with zero mean and unit variance. The corresponding output ζ^μ is given by a deterministic teacher whose internal structure is the same as for the student network but may differ in the number of hidden units. Hidden unit n in the teacher network receives input information through the weight vector $\mathbf{B}_n = (B_{n1},\ldots,B_{nN})$, and its activation under presentation of the input pattern $\boldsymbol{\xi}^\mu$ is $y_n^\mu = \mathbf{B}_n \cdot \boldsymbol{\xi}^\mu$. The corresponding output is $\zeta^\mu = \sum_{n=1}^{M} g(\mathbf{B}_n \cdot \boldsymbol{\xi}^\mu)$. We will use indices $i,j,k,l\ldots$ to refer to units in the student network, and $n,m,\ldots$ for units in the teacher network.

The error made by a student with weights $\mathbf{J}$ on a given input $\boldsymbol{\xi}$ is given by the quadratic deviation

$$\epsilon(\mathbf{J},\boldsymbol{\xi}) \equiv \frac{1}{2}[\sigma(\mathbf{J},\boldsymbol{\xi}) - \zeta]^2 = \frac{1}{2}\left[\sum_{i=1}^{K} g(x_i) - \sum_{n=1}^{M} g(y_n)\right]^2 . \quad (1)$$

Performance on a typical input defines the generalization error $\epsilon_g(\mathbf{J}) \equiv \langle \epsilon(\mathbf{J},\boldsymbol{\xi}) \rangle_{\{\boldsymbol{\xi}\}}$ through an average over all possible input vectors $\boldsymbol{\xi}$, to be performed implicitly through averages over the activations $\mathbf{x} = (x_1,\ldots,x_K)$ and $\mathbf{y} = (y_1,\ldots,y_M)$. Note that both $\langle x_i \rangle = \langle y_n \rangle = 0$; second order correlations are given by the overlaps among the weight vectors associated with the various hidden units: $\langle x_i x_k \rangle = \mathbf{J}_i \cdot \mathbf{J}_k \equiv Q_{ik}$, $\langle x_i y_n \rangle = \mathbf{J}_i \cdot \mathbf{B}_n \equiv R_{in}$, and $\langle y_n y_m \rangle = \mathbf{B}_n \cdot \mathbf{B}_m \equiv T_{nm}$. Averages over $\mathbf{x}$ and $\mathbf{y}$ are performed using the resulting multivariate Gaussian probability distribution, and yield an expression for the generalization error in terms of the parameters Q_{ik}, R_{in}, and T_{nm} [3]. For $g(x) \equiv \mathrm{erf}(x/\sqrt{2})$ the result is:

$$\epsilon_g(\mathbf{J}) = \frac{1}{\pi}\left\{\sum_{ik} \arcsin \frac{Q_{ik}}{\sqrt{1+Q_{ii}}\sqrt{1+Q_{kk}}} + \sum_{nm} \arcsin \frac{T_{nm}}{\sqrt{1+T_{nn}}\sqrt{1+T_{mm}}} \right.$$
$$\left. -2 \sum_{in} \arcsin \frac{R_{in}}{\sqrt{1+Q_{ii}}\sqrt{1+T_{nn}}}\right\}. \quad (2)$$

The parameters T_{nm} are characteristic of the task to be learned and remain fixed. The overlaps Q_{ik} and R_{in}, which characterize the correlations among the various student units and their degree of specialization towards the implementation of the desired task, are determined by the student weights $\mathbf{J}$ and evolve during training.

A gradient descent rule for the update of the student weights results in $\mathbf{J}_i^{\mu+1} = \mathbf{J}_i^\mu + \frac{\eta}{N} \delta_i^\mu \boldsymbol{\xi}^\mu$, where the learning rate η has been scaled with the input size N, and

$$\delta_i^\mu \equiv g'(x_i^\mu)\left[\sum_{n=1}^{M} g(y_n^\mu) - \sum_{j=1}^{K} g(x_j^\mu)\right] \quad (3)$$

is defined in terms of both the activation function g and its derivative g'. The time evolution of the overlaps R_{in} and Q_{ik} can be explicitly written in terms of similar difference equations. In the large N limit the normalized number of examples $\alpha = \mu/N$ can be interpreted as a continuous time variable, leading to the equations of motion

$$\frac{dR_{in}}{d\alpha} = \eta < \delta_i\, y_n >_{\{\xi\}},$$

$$\frac{dQ_{ik}}{d\alpha} = \eta < \delta_i\, x_k >_{\{\xi\}} + \eta < \delta_k\, x_i >_{\{\xi\}} + \eta^2 < \delta_i\, \delta_k >_{\{\xi\}}, \qquad (4)$$

to be averaged over all possible ways in which an example can be chosen at a given time step. The dependence on the current input ξ is only through the activations **x** and **y**; the corresponding averages can be performed analytically for $g(x) = \mathrm{erf}(x/\sqrt{2})$, resulting in a set of coupled first-order differential equations [3]. These dynamical equations are exact, and provide a novel tool used here to analyze the learning process for a general soft-committee machine with an arbitrary number K of hidden units, trained to implement a task defined through a teacher of similar architecture except for the number M of hidden units. In what follows we focus on uncorrelated teacher vectors of unit length, $T_{nm} = \delta_{nm}$.

The time evolution of the overlaps R_{in} and Q_{ik} follows from integrating the equations of motion (4) from initial conditions determined by a random initialization of the student vectors $\{\mathbf{J}_i\}_{1 \leq i \leq K}$. Random initial norms Q_{ii} for the student vectors are taken here from a uniform distribution in the $[0, 0.5]$ interval. Overlaps Q_{ik} between independently chosen student vectors $\mathbf{J}_i$ and $\mathbf{J}_k$, or R_{in} between $\mathbf{J}_i$ and an unknown teacher vector $\mathbf{B}_n$ are small numbers, of order $1/\sqrt{N}$ for $N \gg K, M$, and taken here from a uniform distribution in the $[0, 10^{-12}]$ interval.

We show in Fig. 1a-c the evolution of the overlaps and generalization error for a *realizable* case: $K = M = 3$ and $\eta = 0.1$. This example illustrates the successive regimes of the learning process. The system quickly evolves into a symmetric subspace controlled by an unstable suboptimal solution which exhibits no differentiation among the various student hidden units. Trapping in the symmetric subspace prevents the specialization needed to achieve the optimal solution, and the generalization error remains finite, as shown by the plateau in Fig. 1c. The symmetric solution is unstable, and the perturbation introduced through the random initialization of the overlaps R_{in} eventually takes over: the student units become specialized and the matrix R of student-teacher overlaps tends towards the matrix T, except for a permutational symmetry associated with the arbitrary labeling of the student hidden units. The generalization error plateau is followed by a monotonic decrease towards zero once the specialization begins and the system evolves towards the optimal solution. The evolution of the overlaps and generalization error for the *unrealizable* case $K < M$ is characterized by qualitatively similar stages, except that the asymptotic behavior is controlled by a suboptimal solution which reflects the differences between student and teacher architectures.

Curves for the time evolution of the generalization error for different values of η shown in Fig. 1d for $K = M = 3$ identify trapping in the symmetric subspace as a small η phenomenon. We therefore consider the equations of motion (4) in the small η regime. The term proportional to η^2 is neglected and the resulting truncated equations of motion are used to investigate a phase characterized by students of similar norms: $Q_{ii} = Q$ for all $1 \leq i \leq K$, similar correlations among themselves: $Q_{ik} = C$ for all $i \neq k$, and similar correlations with the teacher vectors: $R_{in} = R$ for all $1 \leq i \leq K$, $1 \leq n \leq M$. The resulting dynamical equations exhibit a fixed point solution at

$$Q^* = C^* = \frac{M}{K^2} \frac{M - K^2 + \sqrt{K^4 - K^2 + M^2}}{2M - 1} \quad \text{and} \quad R^* = \sqrt{\frac{Q^*}{M}} \qquad (5)$$

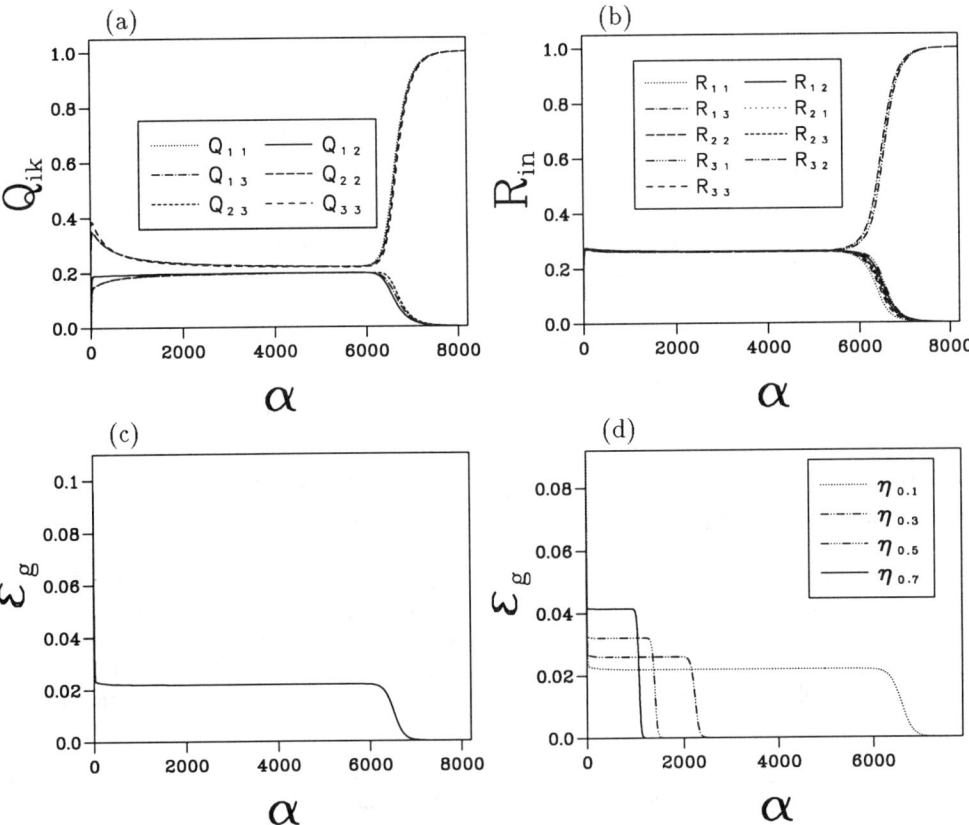

Figure 1: Dependence of the overlaps and the generalization error on the normalized number of examples α for a three-node student learning a three-node teacher characterized by $T_{nm} = \delta_{nm}$. Results for $\eta = 0.1$ are shown for (a) student-student overlaps Q_{ik} and (b) student-teacher overlaps R_{in}. The generalization error is shown in (c), and again in (d) for different values of the learning rate.

for the general case, which reduces to

$$Q^* = C^* = \frac{1}{2K-1} \quad \text{and} \quad R^* = \sqrt{\frac{Q^*}{K}} = \frac{1}{\sqrt{K(2K-1)}} \tag{6}$$

in the realizable case ($K = M$), where the corresponding generalization error is given by

$$\epsilon_g^* = \frac{K}{\pi}\left\{\frac{\pi}{6} - K\arcsin\left(\frac{1}{2K}\right)\right\}. \tag{7}$$

A simple geometrical picture explains the relation $Q^* = C^* = M(R^*)^2$ at the symmetric fixed point. The learning process confines the student vectors $\{\mathbf{J}_i\}$ to the subspace $\mathcal{S}_B$ spanned by the set of teacher vectors $\{\mathbf{B}_n\}$. For $T_{nm} = \delta_{nm}$ the teacher vectors form an orthonormal set: $\mathbf{B}_n = \mathbf{e}_n$, with $\mathbf{e}_n \cdot \mathbf{e}_m = \delta_{nm}$ for $1 \leq n, m \leq M$, and provide an expansion for the weight vectors of the trained student: $\mathbf{J}_i^* = \sum_n R_{in}\mathbf{e}_n$. The student-teacher overlaps R_{in} are independent of i in the symmetric phase and independent of n for an isotropic teacher: $R_{in} = R^*$ for all $1 \leq i \leq K$ and $1 \leq n \leq M$. The expansion $\mathbf{J}_i^* = R^*\sum_n \mathbf{e}_n$ for all i results in $Q^* = C^* = M(R^*)^2$.

The length of the symmetric plateau is controlled by the degree of asymmetry in the initial conditions [2] and by the learning rate η. The small η analysis predicts trapping times inversely proportional to η, in quantitative agreement with the shrinking plateau of Fig. 1d. The increase in the height of the plateau with decreasing η is a second order effect, as the truncated equations of motion predict a unique value: $\epsilon_g^* = 0.0203$ for $K = M = 3$. The mechanism for the second order effect is revealed by an examination of Fig. 1a: the student-student overlaps do agree with the prediction $C^* = 0.2$ of the small η analysis for $K = M = 3$, but the norms of the student vectors remain larger, at $Q = Q^* + \Delta$. The gap Δ between diagonal and off-diagonal elements is observed numerically to increase with increasing η, and is responsible for the excess generalization error. A first order expansion in Δ at $R = R^*$, $C = C^*$, and $Q = Q^* + \Delta$ yields

$$\epsilon_g = \frac{K}{\pi} \left\{ \frac{\pi}{6} - K \arcsin\left(\frac{1}{2K}\right) + \sqrt{\frac{2K-1}{2K+1}} \Delta \right\}, \tag{8}$$

in agreement with the trend observed in Fig. 1d for the realizable case.

The excess norm Δ of the student vectors corresponds to a residual component in $\mathbf{J}_i$ not confined to the subspace $\mathcal{S}_B$. The weight vectors of the trained student can be written as $\mathbf{J}_i = R^* \sum_n \mathbf{e}_n + \mathbf{J}_i^\perp$, with $\mathbf{J}_i^\perp \cdot \mathbf{e}_n = 0$ for all $1 \leq n \leq M$. Student weight vectors are not constrained to be identical; they differ through orthogonal components $\mathbf{J}_i^\perp$ which are typically uncorrelated: $\mathbf{J}_i^\perp \cdot \mathbf{J}_k^\perp = 0$ for $i \neq k$. Correlations $Q_{ik} = C$ do satisfy $C = C^* = M(R^*)^2$, but norms $Q_{ii} = Q$ are given by $Q = Q^* + \Delta$, with $\Delta = \|\mathbf{J}^\perp\|^2$. Learning at very small η tends to eliminate $\mathbf{J}^\perp$ and confine the student vectors to $\mathcal{S}_B$.

Escape from the symmetric subspace signals the onset of hidden unit specialization. As shown in Fig. 1b, the process is driven by a breaking of the uniformity of the student-teacher correlations: each student node becomes increasingly specialized to a specific teacher node, while its overlap with the remaining teacher nodes decreases and eventually decays to its asymptotic value. In the realizable case this asymptotic value is zero, while in the unrealizable case two different non-zero asymptotic values distinguish weak overlaps with teacher nodes imitated by other student vectors from more significant overlaps with those teacher nodes not specifically imitated by any of the student vectors.

The matrix of student-teacher overlaps can no longer be characterized by a unique parameter, as we need to distinguish between a dominant overlap R between a given student node and the teacher node it begins to imitate, secondary overlaps S between the same student node and the teacher nodes to which other student nodes are being assigned, and residual overlaps U with the remaining teacher nodes. The student hidden nodes can be relabeled so as to bring the matrix of student-teacher overlaps to the form $R_{in} = R\delta_{in} + S(1 - \delta_{in})\Theta(K - n) + U(1 - \Theta(K - n))$, where the step function Θ is 0 for negative arguments and 1 otherwise. The emerging differentiation among student vectors results in a decrease of the overlaps $Q_{ik} = C$ for $i \neq k$, while their norms $Q_{ii} = Q$ increase. The matrix of student-student overlaps takes the form $Q_{ik} = Q\delta_{ik} + C(1 - \delta_{ik})$.

Here we limit our description of the onset of specialization to the realizable case, for which $R_{in} = R\delta_{in} + S(1 - \delta_{in})$. The small η analysis is extended to allow for $S \neq R$ in order to describe the escape from the symmetric subspace. The resulting dynamical equations are linearized around the fixed point solution at $Q^* = C^* = 1/(2K-1)$ and $R^* = S^* = 1/\sqrt{K(2K-1)}$, and the generalization error is expanded around its fixed point value (7) to first order in the corresponding deviations q, c, r, and s. The analysis identifies a relevant perturbation with $q = c = 0$ and $s = -r/(K-1)$, which

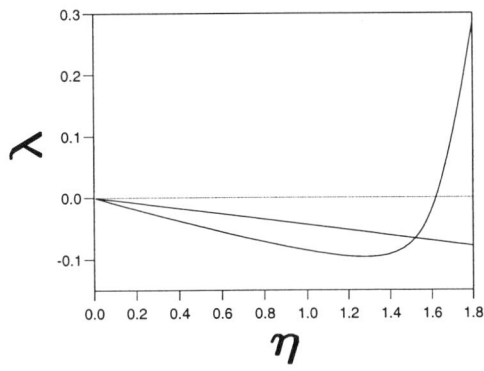

Figure 2: Dependence of the two leading decay eigenvalues on the learning rate η in the realizable case: λ_1 (curved line) and λ_2 (straight line) are shown for $M = K = 3$.

leaves the generalization error unchanged and explains the behavior illustrated in Fig. 1a-b. It is the differentiation between R and S which signals the escape from the symmetric subspace; the differentiation between Q and C occurs for larger values of α. The relevant perturbation corresponds to an enhancement of the overlap $R = R^* + r$ between a given student node and the teacher node it is learning to imitate, while the overlap $S = S^* + s$ between the same student node and the remaining teacher nodes is weakened. The time constant associated with this mode is $\tau = (\pi/2K)(2K-1)^{1/2}(2K+1)^{3/2}$, with $\tau \sim 2\pi K$ in the large K limit.

It is in the subsequent convergence to an asymptotic solution that the realizable and unrealizable cases exhibit fundamental differences. We examine first the realizable scenario, in which the system converges to an optimal solution with perfect generalization.

As the specialization continues, the dominant overlaps R grow, and the secondary overlaps S decay to zero. Further specialization involves the decay to zero of the student-student correlations C and the growth of the norms Q of the student vectors. To investigate the convergence to the optimal solution we linearize the equations of motion around the asymptotic fixed point at $S^* = C^* = 0$, $R^* = Q^* = 1$, with $\epsilon_g^* = 0$. We describe convergence to the optimal solution by applying the full equations of motion (4) to a phase characterized by $R_{in} = R\delta_{in} + S(1 - \delta_{in})$ and $Q_{ik} = Q\delta_{ik} + C(1 - \delta_{in})$.

Linearization of the full equations of motion around the asymptotic fixed point results in four eigenvalues; the dependence of the two largest eigenvalues on η is shown in Fig. 2 for $M = K = 3$. An initially slow mode corresponds to the eigenvalue λ_2, which remains negative for all values of η, while the eigenvalue λ_1 for the initially fast mode becomes positive as η exceeds η_{max}, given by

$$\eta_{max} = \frac{\pi}{K}\frac{75 - 42\sqrt{3}}{25\sqrt{3} - 42} \tag{9}$$

to first order in $1/K$. The optimal solution with $\epsilon_g^* = 0$ is not accessible for $\eta > \eta_{max}$. Exponential convergence of R, S, C, and Q to their optimal values is guaranteed for all learning rates in the range $(0, \eta_{max})$; in this regime the generalization error decays exponentially to $\epsilon_g^* = 0$, with a rate controlled by the slowest decay mode. An expansion of ϵ_g in terms of $r = 1 - R$, s, c, and $q = 1 - Q$ reveals that of the leading modes whose eigenvalues are shown in Fig. 2 only the mode associated with λ_1 contributes to the decay of the linear term, while the decay of the second order term is controlled by the mode associated with λ_2 and dominates the convergence if $2\lambda_2 < \lambda_1$. The learning rate η_{opt} which guarantees fastest asymptotic decay for the generalization error follows from $\lambda_1(\eta_{opt}) = 2\lambda_2(\eta_{opt})$.

The asymptotic convergence of unrealizable learning is an intrinsically more complicated process that cannot be described in closed analytic form. The asymptotic values of the order parameters and the generalization error depend on the learning rate η; convergence to an optimal solution with minimal generalization error requires $\eta \to 0$ as $\alpha \to \infty$. Optimal values for the order parameters follow from a small η analysis, equivalent to neglecting $\mathbf{J}^\perp$ and assuming student vectors confined to $\mathcal{S}_B$. The resulting expansion $\mathbf{J}_i = \sum_{n=1}^{M} R_{in}\mathbf{e}_n$, with $R_{ii} = R$, $R_{in} = S$ for $1 \leq n \leq K$, $n \neq i$, and $R_{in} = U$ for $K+1 \leq n \leq M$, leads to

$$Q = R^2 + (K-1)S^2 + (M-K)U^2 \, , \quad C = 2RS + (K-2)S^2 = (M-K)U^2 \, . \quad (10)$$

The equations of motion for the remaining parameters R, S, and U exhibit a fixed point solution which controls the asymptotic behavior. This solution cannot be obtained analytically, but numerical results are well approximated to order $(1/K^3)$ by

$$R^* = 1 - \frac{6\sqrt{3}-3}{8}\frac{L}{K^2}\left(1 - \frac{1}{K}\right) \, ,$$

$$S^* = \left(1 - \frac{\sqrt{3}}{6}\right)\frac{L}{K^3} \, , \quad U^* = \frac{1}{K}\left(1 - \frac{1}{2K^2}\right) \, , \quad (11)$$

where $L \equiv M - K$. The corresponding fixed point values Q^* and C^* follow from Eq. (10). Note that R^* is lower than for the realizable case, and that correlations U^* (significant) and S^* (weaker) between student vectors and the teacher vectors they do not imitate are not eliminated. The asymptotic generalization error is given by

$$\epsilon_g^* = \frac{1}{24\pi}\frac{L}{K^2}\left[4K^2(\pi - 3) + 4K(2\sqrt{3} - 3) + 1\right] \quad (12)$$

to order $(1/K^2)$. Note its proportionality to the mismatch L between teacher and student architectures.

Learning at fixed and sufficiently small η results in exponential convergence to an asymptotic solution whose fixed point coordinates are shifted from the values discussed above. The solution is suboptimal; the resulting increase in ϵ_g^* from its optimal value (12) is easily obtained to first order in η, and it is also proportional to L. We have investigated convergence to the optimal solution (12) for schedules of the form $\eta(\alpha) = \eta_0/(\alpha - \alpha_0)^z$ for the decay of the learning rate. A constant rate η_0 is used for $\alpha \leq \alpha_0$; the monotonic decrease of η for $\alpha > \alpha_0$ is switched on after specialization begins. Asymptotic convergence requires $0 < z \leq 1$; fastest decay of the generalization error is achieved for $z = 1/2$.

Specialization as described here and illustrated in Fig.1 is a simultaneous process in which each student node acquires a strong correlation with a specific teacher node while correlations to other teacher nodes decrease. Such synchronous escape from the symmetric phase is characteristic of learning scenarios where the target task is defined through an isotropic teacher. In the case of a graded teacher we find that specialization occurs through a sequence of escapes from the symmetric subspace, ordered according to the relevance of the corresponding teacher nodes [3].

Acknowledgement The work was supported by the EU grant CHRX-CT92-0063.

References

[1] G. Cybenko, *Math. Control Signals and Systems* **2**, 303 (1989).

[2] M. Biehl and H. Schwarze, *J. Phys. A* **28**, 643 (1995).

[3] D. Saad and S. A. Solla, *Phys. Rev. E*, **52**, 4225 (1995).

Worst-case Loss Bounds for Single Neurons

David P. Helmbold
Department of Computer Science
University of California, Santa Cruz
Santa Cruz, CA 95064
USA

Jyrki Kivinen
Department of Computer Science
P.O. Box 26 (Teollisuuskatu 23)
FIN-00014 University of Helsinki
Finland

Manfred K. Warmuth
Department of Computer Science
University of California, Santa Cruz
Santa Cruz, CA 95064
USA

Abstract

We analyze and compare the well-known Gradient Descent algorithm and a new algorithm, called the Exponentiated Gradient algorithm, for training a single neuron with an arbitrary transfer function. Both algorithms are easily generalized to larger neural networks, and the generalization of Gradient Descent is the standard back-propagation algorithm. In this paper we prove worst-case loss bounds for both algorithms in the single neuron case. Since local minima make it difficult to prove worst-case bounds for gradient-based algorithms, we must use a loss function that prevents the formation of spurious local minima. We define such a matching loss function for any strictly increasing differentiable transfer function and prove worst-case loss bound for any such transfer function and its corresponding matching loss. For example, the matching loss for the identity function is the square loss and the matching loss for the logistic sigmoid is the entropic loss. The different structure of the bounds for the two algorithms indicates that the new algorithm out-performs Gradient Descent when the inputs contain a large number of irrelevant components.

1 INTRODUCTION

The basic element of a neural network, a *neuron*, takes in a number of real-valued input variables and produces a real-valued output. The input-output mapping of a neuron is defined by a *weight vector* $\mathbf{w} \in \mathbf{R}^N$, where N is the number of input variables, and a *transfer function* ϕ. When presented with input given by a vector $\mathbf{x} \in \mathbf{R}^N$, the neuron produces the output $\hat{y} = \phi(\mathbf{w} \cdot \mathbf{x})$. Thus, the weight vector regulates the influence of each input variable on the output, and the transfer function can produce nonlinearities into the input-output mapping. In particular, when the transfer function is the commonly used logistic function, $\phi(p) = 1/(1 + e^{-p})$, the outputs are bounded between 0 and 1. On the other hand, if the outputs should be unbounded, it is often convenient to use the identity function as the transfer function, in which case the neuron simply computes a linear mapping. In this paper we consider a large class of transfer functions that includes both the logistic function and the identity function, but not discontinuous (e.g. step) functions.

The goal of *learning* is to come up with a weight vector $\mathbf{w}$ that produces a desirable input-output mapping. This is achieved by considering a sequence $S = ((\mathbf{x}_1, y_1), \ldots, (\mathbf{x}_\ell, y_\ell))$ of *examples*, where for $t = 1, \ldots, \ell$ the value $y_t \in \mathbf{R}$ is the desired output for the input vector $\mathbf{x}_t$, possibly distorted by noise or other errors. We call $\mathbf{x}_t$ the tth *instance* and y_t the tth *outcome*. In what is often called batch learning, all ℓ examples are given at once and are available during the whole training session. As noise and other problems often make it impossible to find a weight vector $\mathbf{w}$ that would satisfy $\phi(\mathbf{w} \cdot \mathbf{x}_t) = y_t$ for all t, one instead introduces a *loss function* L, such as the *square loss* given by $L(y, \hat{y}) = (y - \hat{y})^2/2$, and finds a weight vector $\mathbf{w}$ that minimizes the empirical loss (or training error)

$$\mathrm{Loss}(\mathbf{w}, S) = \sum_{t=1}^{\ell} L(y_t, \phi(\mathbf{w} \cdot \mathbf{x}_t)) \ . \tag{1}$$

With the square loss and identity transfer function $\phi(p) = p$, this is the well-known linear regression problem. When ϕ is the logistic function and L is the *entropic loss* given by $L(y, \hat{y}) = y \ln(y/\hat{y}) + (1 - y) \ln((1 - y)/(1 - \hat{y}))$, this can be seen as a special case of logistic regression. (With the entropic loss, we assume $0 \leq y_t, \hat{y}_t \leq 1$ for all t, and use the convention $0 \ln 0 = 0 \ln(0/0) = 0$.)

In this paper we use an *on-line prediction* (or life-long learning) approach to the learning problem. It is well known that on-line performance is closely related to batch learning performance (Littlestone, 1989; Kivinen and Warmuth, 1994). Instead of receiving all the examples at once, the training algorithm begins with some fixed start vector $\mathbf{w}_1$, and produces a sequence $\mathbf{w}_1, \ldots, \mathbf{w}_{\ell+1}$ of weight vectors. The new weight vector $\mathbf{w}_{t+1}$ is obtained by applying a simple *update rule* to the previous weight vector $\mathbf{w}_t$ and the single example $(\mathbf{x}_t, y_t)$. In the on-line prediction model, the algorithm uses its tth weight vector, or *hypothesis*, to make the *prediction* $\hat{y}_t = \phi(\mathbf{w}_t \cdot \mathbf{x}_t)$. The training algorithm is then charged a loss $L(y_t, \hat{y}_t)$ for this tth *trial*. The performance of a training algorithm A that produces the weight vectors $\mathbf{w}_t$ on an example sequence S is measured by its total (cumulative) loss

$$\mathrm{Loss}(A, S) = \sum_{t=1}^{\ell} L(y_t, \phi(\mathbf{w}_t \cdot \mathbf{x}_t)) \ . \tag{2}$$

Our main results are bounds on the cumulative losses for two on-line prediction algorithms. One of these is the standard *Gradient Descent* (GD) algorithm. The other one, which we call $\mathrm{EG}^\pm$, is also based on the gradient but uses it in a different manner than GD. The bounds are derived in a worst-case setting: we make no assumptions about how the instances are distributed or the relationship between each instance $\mathbf{x}_t$ and its corresponding outcome y_t. Obviously, some assumptions are needed in order to obtain meaningful bounds. The approach we take is to compare the total losses, Loss(GD, S) and Loss(EG$^\pm$, S), to the least achievable empirical loss, $\inf_\mathbf{w}$ Loss($\mathbf{w}, S$). If the least achievable empirical loss is high, the dependence between the instances and outcomes in S cannot be tracked by any neuron using the transfer function, so it is reasonable that the losses of the algorithms are also high. More interestingly, if some weight vector achieves a low empirical loss, we also require that the losses of the algorithms are low. Hence, although the algorithms always predict based on an initial segment of the example sequence, they must perform almost as well as the best fixed weight vector for the whole sequence.

The choice of loss function is crucial for the results that we prove. In particular, since we are using gradient-based algorithms, the empirical loss should not have spurious local minima. This can be achieved for any differentiable increasing transfer function ϕ by using the loss function L_ϕ defined by

$$L_\phi(y, \hat{y}) = \int_{\phi^{-1}(y)}^{\phi^{-1}(\hat{y})} (\phi(z) - y) \, dz \; . \tag{3}$$

For $y < \hat{y}$ the value $L_\phi(y, \hat{y})$ is the area in the $z \times \phi(z)$ plane below the function $\phi(z)$, above the line $\phi(z) = y$, and to the left of the line $z = \phi^{-1}(\hat{y})$. We call L_ϕ the *matching* loss function for transfer function ϕ, and will show that for any example sequence S, if $L = L_\phi$ then the mapping from $\mathbf{w}$ to Loss($\mathbf{w}, S$) is convex. For example, if the transfer function is the logistic function, the matching loss function is the entropic loss, and if the transfer function is the identity function, the matching loss function is the square loss. Note that using the logistic activation function with the square loss can lead to a very large number of local minima (Auer et al., 1996). Even in the batch setting there are reasons to use the entropic loss with the logistic transfer function (see, for example, Solla et al., 1988).

How much our bounds on the losses of the two algorithms exceed the least empirical loss depends on the maximum slope of the transfer function we use. More importantly, they depend on various norms of the instances and the vector $\mathbf{w}$ for which the least empirical loss is achieved. As one might expect, neither of the algorithms is uniformly better than the other. Interestingly, the new EG$^\pm$ algorithm is better when most of the input variables are irrelevant, i.e., when some weight vector $\mathbf{w}$ with $w_i = 0$ for most indices i has a low empirical loss. On the other hand, the GD algorithm is better when the weight vectors with low empirical loss have many nonzero components, but the instances contain many zero components.

The bounds we derive concern only single neurons, and one often combines a number of neurons into a multilayer feedforward neural network. In particular, applying the Gradient Descent algorithm in the multilayer setting gives the famous back propagation algorithm. Also the EG$^\pm$ algorithm, being gradient-based, can easily be generalized for multilayer feedforward networks. Although it seems unlikely that our loss bounds will generalize to multilayer networks, we believe that the intuition gained from the single neuron case will provide useful insight into the relative performance of the two algorithms in the multilayer case. Furthermore, the EG$^\pm$ algorithm is less sensitive to large numbers of irrelevant attributes. Thus it might be possible to avoid multilayer networks by introducing many new inputs, each of which is a non-linear function of the original inputs. Multilayer networks remain an interesting area for future study.

Our work follows the path opened by Littlestone (1988) with his work on learning thresholded neurons with sparse weight vectors. More immediately, this paper is preceded by results on linear neurons using the identity transfer function (Cesa-Bianchi et al., 1996; Kivinen and Warmuth, 1994).

2 THE ALGORITHMS

This section describes how the Gradient Descent training algorithm and the new Exponentiated Gradient training algorithm update the neuron's weight vector.

For the remainder of this paper, we assume that the transfer function ϕ is increasing and differentiable, and Z is a constant such that $\phi'(p) \leq Z$ holds for all $p \in \mathbf{R}$. For the loss function L_ϕ defined by (3) we have

$$\frac{\partial L_\phi(y, \phi(\mathbf{w} \cdot \mathbf{x}))}{\partial w_i} = (\phi(\mathbf{w} \cdot \mathbf{x}) - y)x_i \ . \qquad (4)$$

Treating $L_\phi(y, \phi(\mathbf{w} \cdot \mathbf{x}))$ for fixed $\mathbf{x}$ and y as a function of $\mathbf{w}$, we see that the Hessian H of the function is given by $H_{ij} = \phi'(\mathbf{w} \cdot \mathbf{x})x_i x_j$. Then $\mathbf{v}^T H \mathbf{v} = \phi'(\mathbf{w} \cdot \mathbf{x})(\mathbf{v} \cdot \mathbf{x})^2$, so H is positive definite. Hence, for an arbitrary fixed S, the empirical loss $\text{Loss}(\mathbf{w}, S)$ defined in (1) as a function of $\mathbf{w}$ is convex and thus has no spurious local minima.

We first describe the Gradient Descent (GD) algorithm, which for multilayer networks leads to the back-propagation algorithm. Recall that the algorithm's prediction at trial t is $\hat{y}_t = \phi(\mathbf{w}_t \cdot \mathbf{x}_t)$, where $\mathbf{w}_t$ is the current weight vector and $\mathbf{x}_t$ is the input vector. By (4), performing gradient descent in weight space on the loss incurred in a single trial leads to the update rule

$$\mathbf{w}_{t+1} = \mathbf{w}_t - \eta(\hat{y}_t - y_t)\mathbf{x}_t \ .$$

The parameter η is a positive *learning rate* that multiplies the gradient of the loss function with respect to the weight vector $\mathbf{w}_t$. In order to obtain worst-case loss bounds, we must carefully choose the learning rate η. Note that the weight vector $\mathbf{w}_t$ of GD always satisfies $\mathbf{w}_t = \mathbf{w}_1 + \sum_{i=1}^{t-1} a_i \mathbf{x}_i$ for some scalar coefficients a_i. Typically, one uses the zero initial vector $\mathbf{w}_1 = \mathbf{0}$.

A more recent training algorithm, called the Exponentiated Gradient (EG) algorithm (Kivinen and Warmuth, 1994), uses the same gradient in a different way. This algorithm makes multiplicative (rather than additive) changes to the weight vector, and the gradient appears in the exponent. The basic version of the EG algorithm also normalizes the weight vector, so the update is given by

$$w_{t+1,i} = w_{t,i} e^{-\eta(\hat{y}_t - y_t)x_{t,i}} \Big/ \sum_{j=1}^{N} w_{t,j} e^{-\eta(\hat{y}_t - y_t)x_{t,j}} \ .$$

The start vector is usually chosen to be uniform, $\mathbf{w}_1 = (1/N, \ldots, 1/N)$. Notice that it is the logarithms of the weights produced by the EG training algorithm (rather than the weights themselves) that are essentially linear combinations of the past examples. As can be seen from the update, the EG algorithm maintains the constraints $w_{t,i} > 0$ and $\sum_i w_{t,i} = 1$. In general, of course, we do not expect that such constraints are useful. Hence, we introduce a modified algorithm EG$^\pm$ by employing a linear transformation of the inputs. In addition to the learning rate η, the EG$^\pm$ algorithm has a *scaling factor* $U > 0$ as a parameter. We define the behavior of EG$^\pm$ on a sequence of examples $S = ((\mathbf{x}_1, y_1), \ldots, (\mathbf{x}_\ell, y_\ell))$ in terms of the EG algorithm's behavior on a transformed example sequence $S' = ((\mathbf{x}'_1, y_1), \ldots, (\mathbf{x}'_\ell, y_\ell))$

where $\mathbf{x}' = (Ux_1, \ldots, Ux_N, -Ux_1, \ldots, -Ux_N)$. The EG algorithm uses the uniform start vector $(1/(2N), \ldots, 1/(2N))$ and learning rate supplied by the EG$^\pm$ algorithm. At each time time t the N-dimensional weight vector $\mathbf{w}$ of EG$^\pm$ is defined in terms of the $2N$-dimensional weight vector $\mathbf{w}'$ of EG as

$$w_{t,i} = U(w'_{t,i} - w'_{t,N+i}).$$

Thus EG$^\pm$ with scaling factor U can learn any weight vector $\mathbf{w} \in \mathbf{R}^N$ with $||\mathbf{w}||_1 < U$ by having the embedded EG algorithm learn the appropriate $2N$-dimensional (nonnegative and normalized) weight vector $\mathbf{w}'$.

3 MAIN RESULTS

The loss bounds for the GD and EG$^\pm$ algorithms can be written in similar forms that emphasize how different algorithms work well for different problems. When $L = L_\phi$, we write $\text{Loss}_\phi(\mathbf{w}, S)$ and $\text{Loss}_\phi(A, S)$ for the empirical loss of a weight vector $\mathbf{w}$ and the total loss of an algorithm A, as defined in (1) and (2). We give the upper bounds in terms of various norms. For $\mathbf{x} \in \mathbf{R}^N$, the 2-norm $||\mathbf{x}||_2$ is the Euclidean length of the vector $\mathbf{x}$, the 1-norm $||\mathbf{x}||_1$ the sum of the absolute values of the components of $\mathbf{x}$, and the ∞-norm $||\mathbf{x}||_\infty$ the maximum absolute value of any component of $\mathbf{x}$. For the purposes of setting the learning rates, we assume that before training begins the algorithm gets an upper bound for the norms of instances. The GD algorithm gets a parameter X_2 and EG a parameter X_∞ such that $||\mathbf{x}_t||_2 \leq X_2$ and $||\mathbf{x}_t||_\infty \leq X_\infty$ hold for all t. Finally, recall that Z is an upper bound on $\phi'(p)$. We can take $Z = 1$ when ϕ is the identity function and $Z = 1/4$ when ϕ is the logistic function.

Our first upper bound is for GD. For any sequence of examples S and any weight vector $\mathbf{u} \in \mathbf{R}^N$, when the learning rate is $\eta = 1/(2X_2^2 Z)$ we have

$$\text{Loss}_\phi(\text{GD}, S) \leq 2\text{Loss}_\phi(\mathbf{u}, S) + 2(||\mathbf{u}||_2 X_2)^2 Z .$$

Our upper bounds on the EG$^\pm$ algorithm require that we restrict the one-norm of the *comparison class*: the set of weight vectors competed against. The comparison class contains all weight vectors $\mathbf{u}$ such that $||\mathbf{u}||_1$ is at most the scaling factor, U. For any scaling factor U, any sequence of examples S, and any weight vector $\mathbf{u} \in \mathbf{R}^N$ with $||\mathbf{u}||_1 \leq U$, we have

$$\text{Loss}_\phi(\text{EG}^\pm, S) \leq \frac{4}{3}\text{Loss}_\phi(\mathbf{u}, S) + \frac{16}{3}(UX_\infty)^2 Z \ln(2N)$$

when the learning rate is $\eta = 1/(4(UX_\infty)^2 Z)$.

Note that these bounds depend on both the unknown weight vector $\mathbf{u}$ and some norms of the input vectors. If the algorithms have some further prior information on the sequence S they can make a more informed choice of η. This leads to bounds with a constant of 1 before the the $\text{Loss}_\phi(\mathbf{u}, S)$ term at the cost of an additional square-root term (for details see the full paper, Helmbold et al., 1996).

It is important to realize that we bound the total loss of the algorithms over *any* adversarially chosen sequence of examples where the input vectors satisfy the norm bound. Although we state the bounds in terms of loss on the data, they imply that the algorithms must also perform well on new unseen examples, since the bounds still hold when an adversary adds these additional examples to the end of the sequence. A formal treatment of this appears in several places (Littlestone, 1989;

Kivinen and Warmuth, 1994). Furthermore, in contrast to standard convergence proofs (e.g. Luenberger, 1984), we bound the loss on the *entire* sequence of examples instead of studying the convergence behavior of the algorithm when it is arbitrarily close to the best weight vector.

Comparing these loss bounds we see that the bound for the $EG^{\pm}$ algorithm grows with the maximum component of the input vectors and the one-norm of the best weight vector from the comparison class. On the other hand, the loss bound for the GD algorithm grows with the two-norm (Euclidean length) of both vectors. Thus when the best weight vector is sparse, having few significant components, and the input vectors are dense, with several similarly-sized components, the bound for the $EG^{\pm}$ algorithm is better than the bound for the GD algorithm. More formally, consider the noise-free situation where $\text{Loss}_\phi(\mathbf{u}, S) = 0$ for some $\mathbf{u}$. Assume $\mathbf{x}_t \in \{-1, 1\}^N$ and $\mathbf{u} \in \{-1, 0, 1\}^N$ with only k nonzero components in $\mathbf{u}$. We can then take $X_2 = \sqrt{N}$, $X_\infty = 1$, $\|\mathbf{u}\|_2 = \sqrt{k}$, and $U = k$. The loss bounds become $(16/3)k^2 Z \ln(2N)$ for $EG^{\pm}$ and $2kZN$ for GD, so for $N \gg k$ the $EG^{\pm}$ algorithm clearly wins this comparison. On the other hand, the GD algorithm has the advantage over the EG algorithm when each input vector is sparse and the best weight vector is dense, having its weight distributed evenly over its components. For example, if the inputs $\mathbf{x}_t$ are the rows of an $N \times N$ unit matrix and $\mathbf{u} \in \{-1, 1\}^N$, then $X_2 = X_\infty = 1$, $\|\mathbf{u}\|_2 = \sqrt{N}$, and $U = N$. Thus the upper bounds become $(16/3)N^2 Z \ln(2N)$ for $EG^{\pm}$ and $2NZ$ for GD, so here GD wins the comparison.

Of course, a comparison of the upper bounds is meaningless unless the bounds are known to be reasonably tight. Our experiments with artificial random data suggest that the upper bounds are not tight. However, the experimental evidence also indicates that $EG^{\pm}$ is much better than GD when the best weight vector is sparse. Thus the upper bounds do predict the relative behaviors of the algorithms.

The bounds we give in this paper are very similar to the bounds Kivinen and Warmuth (1994) obtained for the comparison class of linear functions and the square loss. They observed how the relative performances of the GD and $EG^{\pm}$ algorithms relate to the norms of the input vectors and the best weight vector in the linear case.

Our methods are direct generalizations of those applied for the linear case (Kivinen and Warmuth, 1994). The key notion here is a *distance function* d for measuring the distance $d(\mathbf{u}, \mathbf{w})$ between two weight vectors $\mathbf{u}$ and $\mathbf{w}$. Our main distance measures are the Squared Euclidean distance $\frac{1}{2}\|\mathbf{u} - \mathbf{w}\|_2^2$ and the Relative Entropy distance (or Kullback-Leibler divergence) $\sum_{i=1}^N u_i \ln(u_i/w_i)$. The analysis exploits an invariant over t and $\mathbf{u}$ of the form

$$aL_\phi(y_t, \mathbf{w}_t \cdot \mathbf{x}_t) - bL_\phi(y_t, \mathbf{u} \cdot \mathbf{x}_t) \leq d(\mathbf{u}, \mathbf{w}_t) - d(\mathbf{u}, \mathbf{w}_{t+1}) \ ,$$

where a and b are suitably chosen constants. This invariant implies that at each trial, if the loss of the algorithm is much larger than that of an arbitrary vector $\mathbf{u}$, then the algorithm updates its weight vector so that it gets closer to $\mathbf{u}$. By summing the invariant over all trials we can bound the total loss of the algorithms in terms of $\text{Loss}_\phi(\mathbf{u}, S)$ and $d(\mathbf{u}, \mathbf{w}_1)$. Full details will be contained in a technical report (Helmbold et al., 1996).

4 OPEN PROBLEMS

Although the presence of local minima in multilayer networks makes it difficult to obtain worst case bounds for gradient-based algorithms, it may be possible to analyze slightly more complicated settings than just a single neuron. One likely candidate is to generalize the analysis to logistic regression with more than two classes. In this case each class would be represented by one neuron.

As noted above, the matching loss for the logistic transfer function is the entropic loss, so this pair does not create local minima. No bounded transfer function matches the square loss in this sense (Auer et al., 1996), and thus it seems impossible to get the same kind of strong loss bounds for a bounded transfer function and the square loss as we have for any (increasing and differentiable) transfer function and its matching loss function.

As the bounds for $EG^\pm$ depend only logarithmically on the input dimension, the following approach may be feasible. Instead of using a multilayer net, use a single (linear or sigmoided) neuron on top of a large set of basis functions. The logarithmic growth of the loss bounds in the number of such basis functions mean that large numbers of basis functions can be tried.

Note that the bounds of this paper are only worst-case bounds and our experiments on artificial data indicate that the bounds may not be tight when the input values and best weights are large. However, we feel that the bounds do indicate the relative merits of the algorithms in different situations. Further research needs to be done to tighten the bounds. Nevertheless, this paper gives the first worst-case upper bounds for neurons with nonlinear transfer functions.

References

P. Auer, M. Herbster, and M. K. Warmuth (1996). Exponentially many local minima for single neurons. In *Advances in Neural Information Processing Systems 8*.

N. Cesa-Bianchi, P. Long, and M. K. Warmuth (1996). Worst-case quadratic loss bounds for on-line prediction of linear functions by gradient descent. *IEEE Transactions on Neural Networks*. To appear. An extended abstract appeared in *COLT '93*, pp. 429–438.

D. P. Helmbold, J. Kivinen, and M. K. Warmuth (1996). Worst-case loss bounds for single neurons. Technical Report UCSC-CRL-96-2, Univ. of Calif. Computer Research Lab, Santa Cruz, CA, 1996. In preparation.

J. Kivinen and M. K. Warmuth (1994). Exponentiated gradient versus gradient descent for linear predictors. Technical Report UCSC-CRL-94-16, Univ. of Calif. Computer Research Lab, Santa Cruz, CA, 1994. An extended abstract appeared in *STOC '95*, pp. 209-218.

N. Littlestone (1988). Learning when irrelevant attributes abound: A new linear-threshold algorithm. *Machine Learning*, 2:285-318.

N. Littlestone (1989). From on-line to batch learning. In *Proc. 2nd Annual Workshop on Computational Learning Theory*, pages 269–284. Morgan Kaufmann, San Mateo, CA.

D. G. Luenberger (1984). *Linear and Nonlinear Programming*. Addison-Wesley, Reading, MA.

S. A. Solla, E. Levin, and M. Fleisher (1988). Accelerated learning in layered neural networks. *Complex Systems*, 2:625–639.

Exponentially many local minima for single neurons

Peter Auer Mark Herbster Manfred K. Warmuth

Department of Computer Science
Santa Cruz, California
{pauer,mark,manfred}@cs.ucsc.edu

Abstract

We show that for a single neuron with the logistic function as the transfer function the number of local minima of the error function based on the square loss can grow exponentially in the dimension.

1 INTRODUCTION

Consider a single artificial neuron with d inputs. The neuron has d weights $\mathbf{w} \in \mathbf{R}^d$. The output of the neuron for an input pattern $\mathbf{x} \in \mathbf{R}^d$ is $\hat{y} = \phi(\mathbf{x} \cdot \mathbf{w})$, where $\phi : \mathbf{R} \to \mathbf{R}$ is a *transfer* function. For a given sequence of training *examples* $\langle(\mathbf{x}_t, y_t)\rangle_{1 \le t \le m}$, each consisting of a pattern $\mathbf{x}_t \in \mathbf{R}^d$ and a desired output $y_t \in \mathbf{R}$, the goal of the *training phase* for neural networks consists of minimizing the error function with respect to the weight vector $\mathbf{w} \in \mathbf{R}^d$. This function is the sum of the losses between outputs of the neuron and the desired outputs summed over all training examples. In notation, the error function is

$$E(\mathbf{w}) = \sum_{t=1}^{m} L(y_t, \phi(\mathbf{x}_t \cdot \mathbf{w})) \, ,$$

where $L : \mathbf{R} \times \mathbf{R} \to [0, \infty)$ is the loss function.

A common example of a transfer function is the logistic function $\text{logistic}(z) = \frac{1}{1+e^{-z}}$ which has the bounded range $(0, 1)$. In contrast, the identity function $id(z) = z$ has unbounded range. One of the most common loss functions is the square loss $L(y, \hat{y}) = (y - \hat{y})^2$. Other examples are the absolute loss $|y - \hat{y}|$ and the entropic loss $y \ln \frac{y}{\hat{y}} + (1-y) \ln \frac{1-y}{1-\hat{y}}$.

We show that for the square loss and the logistic function the error function of a single neuron for n training examples may have $\lfloor n/d \rfloor^d$ local minima. More generally, this holds for any loss and transfer function for which the composition of the loss function with the transfer function (in notation $L(y, \phi(\mathbf{x} \cdot \mathbf{w}))$) is continuous and has bounded range. This

Exponentially Many Local Minima for Single Neurons

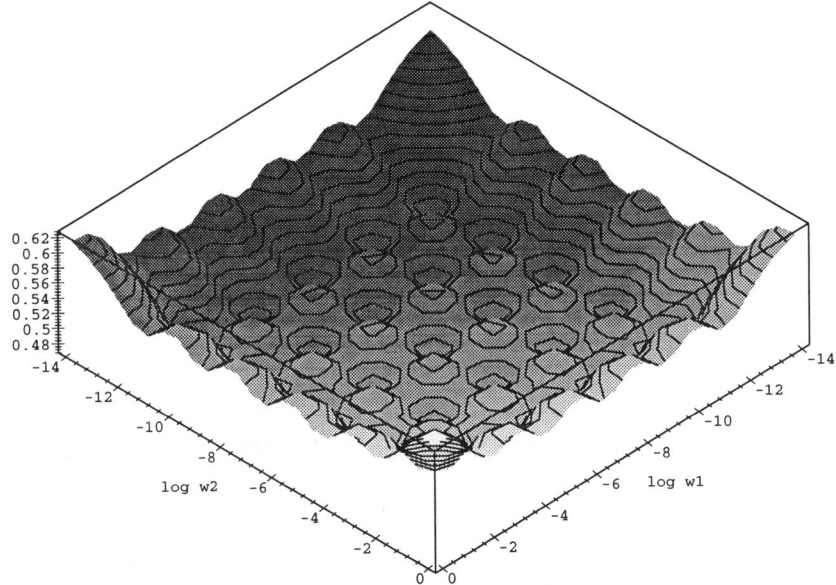

Figure 1: Error Function with 25 Local Minima (16 Visible), Generated by 10 Two-Dimensional Examples.

proves that for any transfer function with bounded range exponentially many local minima can occur when the loss function is the square loss.

The sequences of examples that we use in our proofs have the property that they are *non-realizable* in the sense that there is no weight vector $\mathbf{w} \in \mathbf{R}^d$ for which the error function is zero, i.e. the neuron cannot produce the desired output for all examples. We show with some minimal assumptions on the loss and transfer functions that for a single neuron there can be no local minima besides the global minimum if the examples are realizable.

If the transfer function is the logistic function then it has often been suggested in the literature to use the entropic loss in artificial neural networks in place of the square loss [BW88, WD88, SLF88, Wat92]. In that case the error function of a single neuron is convex and thus has only one minimum even in the non-realizable case. We generalize this observation by defining a *matching loss* for any differentiable increasing transfer functions ϕ:

$$L_\phi(y, \hat{y}) = \int_{\phi^{-1}(y)}^{\phi^{-1}(\hat{y})} (\phi(z) - y) \, dz \; .$$

The loss is the area depicted in Figure 2a. If ϕ is the identity function then L_ϕ is the square loss likewise if ϕ is the logistic function then L_ϕ is the entropic loss. For the matching loss the gradient descent update for minimizing the error function for a sequence of examples is simply

$$\mathbf{w}_{new} := \mathbf{w}_{old} - \eta \left(\sum_{t=1}^{m} (\phi(\mathbf{x}_t \cdot \mathbf{w}_{old}) - y_t)\mathbf{x}_t \right) ,$$

where η is a positive learning rate. Also the second derivatives are easy to calculate for this general setting: $\frac{L_\phi(y_t, \phi(\mathbf{x}_t \cdot \mathbf{w}))}{\partial w_i \partial w_j} = \phi'(\mathbf{x}_t \cdot \mathbf{w})x_{t,i}x_{t,j}$. Thus, if $H_t(w)$ is the Hessian of $L_\phi(y_t, \phi(\mathbf{x}_t \cdot \mathbf{w}))$ with respect to $\mathbf{w}$ then $\mathbf{v}^T H_t(\mathbf{w})\mathbf{v} = \phi'(\mathbf{x}_t \cdot \mathbf{w})(\mathbf{v} \cdot \mathbf{x}_t)^2$. Thus

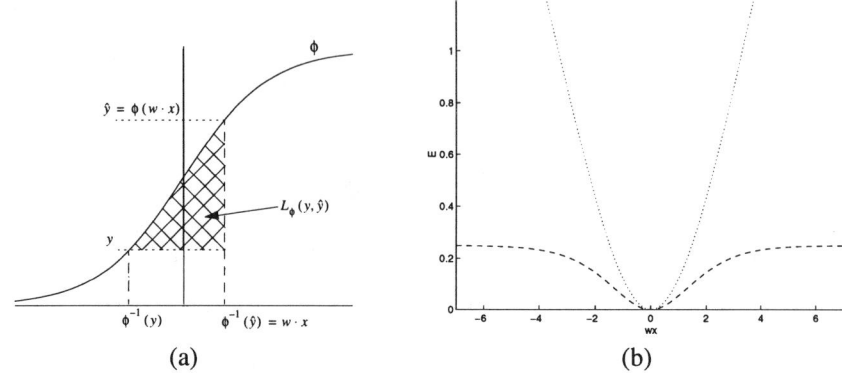

Figure 2: (a) The Matching Loss Function L_ϕ.
(b) The Square Loss becomes Saturated, the Entropic Loss does not.

H_t is positive semi-definite for any increasing differentiable transfer function. Clearly $\sum_{t=1}^{m} H_t(\mathbf{w})$ is the Hessian of the error function $E(\mathbf{w})$ for a sequence of m examples and it is also positive semi-definite. It follows that for any differentiable increasing transfer function the error function with respect to the matching loss is always convex.

We show that in the case of one neuron the logistic function paired with the square loss can lead to exponentially many minima. It is open whether the number of local minima grows exponentially for some natural data. However there is another problem with the pairing of the logistic and the square loss that makes it hard to optimize the error function with gradient based methods. This is the problem of flat regions. Consider one example $(\mathbf{x}, y)$ consisting of a pattern $\mathbf{x}$ (such that $\mathbf{x}$ is not equal to the all zero vector) and the desired output y. Then the square loss $(\text{logistic}(\mathbf{x} \cdot \mathbf{w}) - y)^2$, for $y \in [0, 1]$ and $\mathbf{w} \in \mathbf{R}^d$, turns flat as a function of $\mathbf{w}$ when $\hat{y} = \text{logistic}(\mathbf{x} \cdot \mathbf{w})$ approaches zero or one (for example see Figure 2b where $d = 1$ and $y = 0$). It is easy to see that for all bounded transfer functions with a finite number of minima and corresponding bounded loss functions, the same phenomenon occurs. In other words, the composition $L(y, \phi(\mathbf{x} \cdot \mathbf{w}))$ of the square loss with any bounded transfer function ϕ which has a finite number of extrema turns flat as $|\mathbf{x} \cdot \mathbf{w}|$ becomes large. Similarly, for multiple examples the error function $E(\mathbf{w})$ as defined above becomes flat. In flat regions the gradients with respect to the weight vector $\mathbf{w}$ are small, and thus gradient-based updates of the weight vector may have a hard time moving the weight vector out of these flat regions. This phenomenon can easily be observed in practice and is sometimes called "saturation" [Hay94]. In contrast, if the logistic function is paired with the entropic loss (see Figure 2b), then the error function turns flat only at the global minimum. The same holds for any increasing differentiable transfer function and its matching loss function.

A number of previous papers discussed conditions necessary and sufficient for multiple local minima of the error function of single neurons or otherwise small networks [WD88, SS89, BRS89, Blu89, SS91, GT92]. This previous work only discusses the occurrence of multiple local minima whereas in this paper we show that the number of such minima can grow exponentially with the dimension. Also the previous work has mainly been limited to the demonstration of local minima in networks or neurons that have used the hyperbolic tangent or logistic function with the square loss. Here we show that exponentially many minima occur whenever the composition of the loss function with the transfer function is continuous and bounded.

The paper is outlined as follows. After some preliminaries in the next section, we give formal

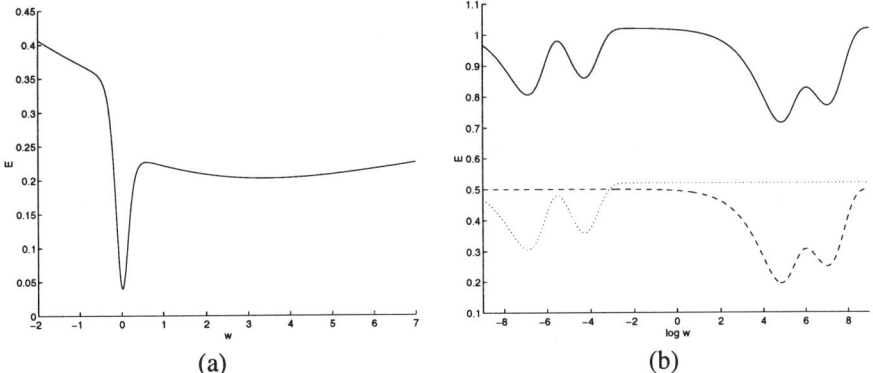

Figure 3: (a) Error Function for the Logistic Transfer Function and the Square Loss with Examples $\langle(10, .55), (.7, .25)\rangle$
(b) Sets of Minima can be Combined.

statements and proofs of the results mentioned above in Section 3. At first (Section 3.1) we show that n one-dimensional examples might result in n local minima of the error function (see e.g. Figure 3a for the error function of two one-dimensional examples). From the local minima in one dimension it follows easily that n d-dimensional examples might result in $\lfloor n/d \rfloor^d$ local minima of the error function (see Figure 1 and discussion in Section 3.2).

We then consider neurons with a bias (Section 4), i.e. we add an additional input that is clamped to one. The error function for a sequence of examples $\mathcal{S} = \langle(\mathbf{x}_t, y_t)\rangle_{1 \leq t \leq m}$ is now

$$E_\mathcal{S}(B, \mathbf{w}) = \sum_{t=1}^{m} L(y_t, \phi(B + \mathbf{w}\mathbf{x}_t)),$$

where B denotes the bias, i.e. the weight of the input that is clamped to one. We can prove that the error function might have $\lfloor n/2d \rfloor^d$ local minima if loss and transfer function are symmetric. This holds for example for the square loss and the logistic transfer function. The proofs are omitted due to space constraints. They are given in the full paper [AHW96], together with additional results for general loss and transfer functions.

Finally we show in Section 5 that with minimal assumptions on transfer and loss functions that there is only one minimum of the error function if the sequence of examples is realizable by the neuron.

The essence of the proofs is quite simple. At first observe that if loss and transfer function are bounded and the domain is unbounded, then there exist areas of saturation where the error function is essentially flat. Furthermore the error function is "additive" i.e. the error function produced by examples in $\mathcal{S} \cup \mathcal{S}'$ is simply the error function produced by the examples in $\mathcal{S}$ added to the error function produced by the examples in $\mathcal{S}'$, $E_{\mathcal{S} \cup \mathcal{S}'} = E_\mathcal{S} + E_{\mathcal{S}'}$. Hence the local minima of $E_\mathcal{S}$ remain local minima of $E_{\mathcal{S} \cup \mathcal{S}'}$ if they fall into an area of saturation of $E_{\mathcal{S}'}$. Similarly, the local minima of $E_{\mathcal{S}'}$ remain local minima of $E_{\mathcal{S} \cup \mathcal{S}'}$ as well (see Figure 3b). In this way sets of local minima can be combined.

2 PRELIMINARIES

We introduce the notion of *minimum-containing* set which will prove useful for counting the minima of the error function.

Definition 2.1 Let $f : \mathbf{R}^d \to \mathbf{R}$ be a continuous function. Then an open and bounded set $U \in \mathbf{R}^d$ is called a *minimum-containing set* for f if for each w on the boundary of U there is a $w^* \in U$ such that $f(w^*) < f(w)$.

Obviously any minimum-containing set contains a local minimum of the respective function. Furthermore each of n disjoint minimum-containing sets contains a distinct local minimum. Thus it is sufficient to find n disjoint minimum-containing sets in order to show that a function has at least n local minima.

3 MINIMA FOR NEURONS WITHOUT BIAS

We will consider transfer functions ϕ and loss functions L which have the following property:

(P1): The transfer function $\phi : \mathbf{R} \to \mathbf{R}$ is non-constant. The loss function $L : \phi(\mathbf{R}) \times \phi(\mathbf{R}) \to [0, \infty)$ has the property that $L(y, y) = 0$ and $L(y, \hat{y}) > 0$ for all $y \neq \hat{y} \in \phi(\mathbf{R})$. Finally the function $L(\cdot, \phi(\cdot)) : \phi(\mathbf{R}) \times \mathbf{R} \to [0, \infty)$ is continuous and bounded.

3.1 ONE MINIMUM PER EXAMPLE IN ONE DIMENSION

Theorem 3.1 Let ϕ and L satisfy (P1). Then for all $n \geq 1$ there is a sequence of n examples $\mathcal{S} = \langle (x_1, y), \ldots, (x_n, y) \rangle$, $x_t \in \mathbf{R}$, $y \in \phi(\mathbf{R})$, such that $E_{\mathcal{S}}(w)$ has n distinct local minima.

Since $L(y, \phi(w))$ is continuous and non-constant there are $w^-, w^*, w^+ \in \mathbf{R}$ such that the values $\phi(w^-), \phi(w^*), \phi(w^+)$ are all distinct. Furthermore we can assume without loss of generality that $0 < w^- < w^* < w^+$. Now set $y = \phi(w^*)$. If the error function $L(y, \phi(w))$ has infinitely many local minima then Theorem 3.1 follows immediately, e.g. by setting $x_1 = \cdots = x_n = 1$. If $L(y, \phi(w))$ has only finitely many minima then $\lim_{w \to \infty} L(y, \phi(w)) = L(y, \phi(\infty))$ exists since $L(y, \phi(w))$ is bounded and continuous. We use this fact in the following lemma. It states that we get a new minimum-containing set by adding an example in the area of saturation of the error function.

Lemma 3.2 Assume that $\lim_{w \to \infty} L(y, \phi(w))$ exists. Let $\mathcal{S} = \langle (x_1, y_1), \ldots, (x_n, y_n) \rangle$ be a sequence of examples and $0 < w_1^- < w_1^* < w_1^+ < \cdots < w_n^- < w_n^* < w_n^+$ such that $E_{\mathcal{S}}(w_t^-) > E_{\mathcal{S}}(w_t^*)$ and $E_{\mathcal{S}}(w_t^*) < E_{\mathcal{S}}(w_t^+)$ for $t = 1, \ldots, n$. Let $\mathcal{S}' = \langle (x_0, y), (x_1, y_1), \ldots, (x_n, y_n) \rangle$ where x_0 is sufficiently large. Furthermore let $w_0^* = w^*/x_0$ and $w_0^\pm = w^\pm/x_0$ (where $w^-, w^*, w^+, y = \phi(w^*)$ are as above). Then $0 < w_0^- < w_0^* < w_0^+ < w_1^- < w_1^* < w_1^+ < \cdots < w_n^- < w_n^* < w_n^+$ and

$$E_{\mathcal{S}'}(w_t^-) > E_{\mathcal{S}'}(w_t^*) \text{ and } E_{\mathcal{S}'}(w_t^*) < E_{\mathcal{S}'}(w_t^+), \text{ for } t = 0, \ldots, n. \tag{1}$$

Proof. We have to show that for all x_0 sufficiently large condition (1) is satisfied, i.e. that

$$\lim_{x_0 \to \infty} E_{\mathcal{S}'}(w_t^*) < \lim_{x_0 \to \infty} E_{\mathcal{S}'}(w_t^\pm), \text{ for } t = 0, \ldots, n. \tag{2}$$

We get

$$\lim_{x_0 \to \infty} E_{\mathcal{S}'}(w_0^*) = L(y, \phi(w^*)) + \lim_{x_0 \to \infty} E_{\mathcal{S}}(w^*/x_0) = L(y, \phi(w^*)) + E_{\mathcal{S}}(0),$$

recalling that $w_0^* = w^*/x_0$ and $\mathcal{S}' = \mathcal{S} \cup (x_0, y)$. Analogously

$$\lim_{x_0 \to \infty} E_{\mathcal{S}'}(w_0^\pm) = L(y, \phi(w^\pm)) + E_{\mathcal{S}}(0).$$

Thus equation (2) holds for $t = 0$. For $t = 1, \ldots, n$ we get

$$\lim_{x_0 \to \infty} E_{\mathcal{S}'}(w_t^*) = \lim_{x_0 \to \infty} L(y, \phi(w_t^* x_0)) + E_{\mathcal{S}}(w_t^*) = L(y, \phi(\infty)) + E_{\mathcal{S}}(w_t^*)$$

and

$$\lim_{x_0 \to \infty} E_{\mathcal{S}'}(w_t^\pm) = \lim_{x_0 \to \infty} L(y, \phi(w_t^\pm x_0)) + E_{\mathcal{S}}(w_t^\pm) = L(y, \phi(\infty)) + E_{\mathcal{S}}(w_t^\pm).$$

Since $E_{\mathcal{S}}(w_t^*) < E_{\mathcal{S}}(w_t^\pm)$ for $t = 1, \cdots, n$, the lemma follows. □

Proof of Theorem 3.1. The theorem follows by induction from Lemma 3.2 since each interval (w_t^-, w_t^+) is a minimum-containing set for the error function. □

Remark. Though the proof requires the magnitude of the examples to be arbitrarily large[1] in practice local minima show up for even moderately sized w (see Figure 3a).

3.2 CURSE OF DIMENSIONALITY: THE NUMBER OF MINIMA MIGHT GROW EXPONENTIALLY WITH THE DIMENSION

We show how the 1-dimensional minima of Theorem 3.1 can be combined to obtain d-dimensional minima.

Lemma 3.3 *Let $f : \mathbf{R} \to \mathbf{R}$ be a continuous function with n disjoint minimum-containing sets $U_1, \ldots, U_n$. Then the sets $U_{t_1} \times \cdots \times U_{t_d}$, $t_j \in \{1, \ldots, n\}$, are n^d disjoint minimum-containing sets for the function $g : \mathbf{R}^d \to \mathbf{R}$, $g(x_1, \ldots, x_d) = f(x_1) + \cdots + f(x_d)$.*

Proof. Omitted. □

Theorem 3.4 *Let ϕ and L satisfy (P1). Then for all $n \geq 1$ there is a sequence of examples $S = \langle (\mathbf{x}_1, y), \ldots, (\mathbf{x}_n, y) \rangle$, $\mathbf{x}_t \in \mathbf{R}^d$, $y \in \phi(\mathbf{R})$, such that $E_{\mathcal{S}}(\mathbf{w})$ has $\lfloor \frac{n}{d} \rfloor^d$ distinct local minima.*

Proof. By Lemma 3.2 there exists a sequence of one-dimensional examples $S' = \langle (x_1, y), \ldots, (x_{\lfloor \frac{n}{d} \rfloor}, y) \rangle$ such that $E_{\mathcal{S}'}(w)$ has $\lfloor \frac{n}{d} \rfloor$ disjoint minimum-containing sets. Thus by Lemma 3.3 the error function $E_{\mathcal{S}}(\mathbf{w})$ has $\lfloor \frac{n}{d} \rfloor^d$ disjoint minimum-containing sets where $S = \langle ((x_1, 0, \ldots, 0), y), \ldots, ((x_{\lfloor \frac{n}{d} \rfloor}, 0, \ldots, 0), y), \ldots, ((0, \ldots, x_1), y), \ldots, ((0, \ldots, x_{\lfloor \frac{n}{d} \rfloor}), y) \rangle$. □

4 MINIMA FOR NEURONS WITH A BIAS

Theorem 4.1 *Let the transfer function ϕ and the loss function L satisfy $\phi(B_0 + z) - \phi_0 = \phi_0 - \phi(B_0 - z)$ and $L(\phi_0 + y, \phi_0 + \hat{y}) = L(\phi_0 - y, \phi_0 - \hat{y})$ for some $B_0, \phi_0 \in \mathbf{R}$ and all $z \in \mathbf{R}$, $y, \hat{y} \in \phi(\mathbf{R})$. Furthermore let ϕ have a continuous second derivative and assume that the first derivative of ϕ at B_0 is non-zero. At last let $\frac{\partial^2}{\partial \hat{y}^2} L(y, \hat{y})$ be continuous in y and $\hat{y}$, $L(y, y) = 0$ for all $y \in \phi(\mathbf{R})$, and $\left(\frac{\partial^2}{\partial \hat{y}^2} L(y, \hat{y}) \right)(\phi_0, \phi_0) > 0$. Then for all $n \geq 1$ there is a sequence of examples $S = \langle (\mathbf{x}_1, y_1), \ldots, (\mathbf{x}_n, y_n) \rangle$, $\mathbf{x}_t \in \mathbf{R}^d$, $y_t \in \phi(\mathbf{R})$, such that $E_{\mathcal{S}}(B, \mathbf{w})$ has $\lfloor \frac{n}{2d} \rfloor^d$ distinct local minima.*

Note that the square loss along with either the hyperbolic or logistic transfer function satisfies the conditions of the theorem.

---
[1] There is a parallel proof where the magnitudes of the examples may be arbitrarily small.

5 ONE MINIMUM IN THE REALIZABLE CASE

We show that when transfer and loss function are monotone and the examples are *realizable* then there is only a single minimal surface. A sequence of examples $\mathcal{S}$ is realizable if $E_\mathcal{S}(\mathbf{w}) = 0$ for some $\mathbf{w} \in \mathbf{R}^d$.

Theorem 5.1 *Let ϕ and L satisfy (P1). Furthermore let ϕ be monotone and L such that $L(y, y + r_1) \leq L(y, y + r_2)$ for $0 \leq r_1 \leq r_2$ or $0 \geq r_1 \geq r_2$. Assume that for some sequence of examples $\mathcal{S}$ there is a weight vector $\mathbf{w}_0 \in \mathbf{R}^d$ such that $E_\mathcal{S}(\mathbf{w}_0) = 0$. Then for each $\mathbf{w}_1 \in \mathbf{R}^d$ the function $h(\alpha) = E_\mathcal{S}((1 - \alpha)\mathbf{w}_0 + \alpha \mathbf{w}_1)$ is increasing for $\alpha \geq 0$.*

Thus each minimum $\mathbf{w}_1$ can be connected with $\mathbf{w}_0$ by the line segment $\overline{\mathbf{w}_0\mathbf{w}_1}$ such that $E_\mathcal{S}(\mathbf{w}) = 0$ for all $\mathbf{w}$ on $\overline{\mathbf{w}_0\mathbf{w}_1}$.

Proof of Theorem 5.1. Let $\mathcal{S} = \langle (\mathbf{x}_1, y_1), \ldots, (\mathbf{x}_n, y_n) \rangle$. Then $h(\alpha) = \sum_{t=1}^n L(y_t, \phi(\mathbf{w}_0\mathbf{x}_t + \alpha(\mathbf{w}_1 - \mathbf{w}_0)\mathbf{x}_t))$. Since $y_t = \phi(\mathbf{w}_0\mathbf{x}_t)$ it suffices to show that $L(\phi(z), \phi(z+\alpha r))$ is monotonically increasing in $\alpha \geq 0$ for all $z, r \in \mathbf{R}$. Let $0 \leq \alpha_1 \leq \alpha_2$. Since ϕ is monotone we get $\phi(z + \alpha_1 r) = \phi(z) + r_1$, $\phi(z + \alpha_2 r) = \phi(z) + r_2$ where $0 \leq r_1 \leq r_2$ or $0 \geq r_1 \geq r_2$. Thus $L(\phi(z), \phi(z + \alpha_1 r)) \leq L(\phi(z), \phi(z + \alpha_2 r))$. □

Acknowledgments

We thank Mike Dooley, Andrew Klinger and Eduardo Sontag for valuable discussions. Peter Auer gratefully acknowledges support from the FWF, Austria, under grant J01028-MAT. Mark Herbster and Manfred Warmuth were supported by NSF grant IRI-9123692.

References

[AHW96] P. Auer, M. Herbster, and M. K. Warmuth. Exponentially many local minima for single neurons. Technical Report UCSC-CRL-96-1, Univ. of Calif. Computer Research Lab, Santa Cruz, CA, 1996. In preperation.

[Blu89] E.K. Blum. Approximation of boolean functions by sigmoidal networks: Part i: Xor and other two-variable functions. *Neural Computation*, 1:532–540, February 1989.

[BRS89] M.L. Brady, R. Raghavan, and J. Slawny. Back propagation fails to separate where perceptrons succeed. *IEEE Transactions On Circuits and Systems*, 36(5):665–674, May 1989.

[BW88] E. Baum and F. Wilczek. Supervised learning of probability distributions by neural networks. In D.Z. Anderson, editor, *Neural Information Processing Systems*, pages 52–61, New York, 1988. American Insitute of Physics.

[GT92] Marco Gori and Alberto Tesi. On the problem of local minima in backpropagation. *IEEE Transaction on Pattern Analysis and Machine Intelligence*, 14(1):76–86, 1992.

[Hay94] S. Haykin. *Neural Networks: a Comprehensive Foundation*. Macmillan, New York, NY, 1994.

[SLF88] S. A. Solla, E. Levin, and M. Fleisher. Accelerated learning in layered neural networks. *Complex Systems*, 2:625–639, 1988.

[SS89] E.D. Sontag and H.J. Sussmann. Backpropagation can give rise to spurious local minima even for networks without hidden layers. *Complex Systems*, 3(1):91–106, February 1989.

[SS91] E.D. Sontag and H.J. Sussmann. Back propagation separates where perceptrons do. *Neural Networks*, 4(3), 1991.

[Wat92] R. L. Watrous. A comparison between squared error and relative entropy metrics using several optimization algorithms. *Complex Systems*, 6:495–505, 1992.

[WD88] B.S. Wittner and J.S. Denker. Strategies for teaching layered networks classification tasks. In D.Z. Anderson, editor, *Neural Information Processing Systems*, pages 850–859, New York, 1988. American Insitute of Physics.

Adaptive Back-Propagation in On-Line Learning of Multilayer Networks

Ansgar H. L. West[1,2] and David Saad[2]
[1]Department of Physics, University of Edinburgh
Edinburgh EH9 3JZ, U.K.
[2]Neural Computing Research Group, University of Aston
Birmingham B4 7ET, U.K.

Abstract

An adaptive back-propagation algorithm is studied and compared with gradient descent (standard back-propagation) for on-line learning in two-layer neural networks with an arbitrary number of hidden units. Within a statistical mechanics framework, both numerical studies and a rigorous analysis show that the adaptive back-propagation method results in faster training by breaking the symmetry between hidden units more efficiently and by providing faster convergence to optimal generalization than gradient descent.

1 INTRODUCTION

Multilayer feedforward perceptrons (MLPs) are widely used in classification and regression applications due to their ability to learn a range of complicated maps [1] from examples. When learning a map f_o from N-dimensional inputs $\boldsymbol{\xi}$ to scalars ζ the parameters $\{\boldsymbol{W}\}$ of the *student* network are adjusted according to some training algorithm so that the map defined by these parameters f_W approximates the *teacher* f_o as close as possible. The resulting performance is measured by the *generalization error* ϵ_g, the average of a suitable error measure ϵ over all possible inputs $\epsilon_g = \langle \epsilon \rangle_\xi$. This error measure is normally defined as the squared distance between the output of the network and the desired output, i.e.,

$$\epsilon = \frac{1}{2}[f_W(\boldsymbol{\xi}) - f_o(\boldsymbol{\xi})]^2. \tag{1}$$

One distinguishes between two learning schemes: *batch learning*, where training algorithms are generally based on minimizing the above error on the whole set of given examples, and *on-line learning*, where single examples are presented serially and the training algorithm adjusts the parameters after the presentation of each example. We measure the efficiency of these training algorithms by how fast (or whether at all) they converge to an "acceptable" generalization error.

This research has been motivated by recent work [2] investigating an on-line learning scenario of a general two-layer student network trained by gradient descent on a task defined by a teacher network of similar architecture. It has been found that in the early stages of training the student is drawn into a suboptimal symmetric phase, characterized by each student node imitating all teacher nodes with the same degree of success. Although the symmetry between the student nodes is eventually broken and the student converges to the minimal achievable generalization error, the majority of the training time may be spent with the system trapped in the symmetric regime, as one can see in Fig. 1. To investigate possible improvements we introduce an adaptive back-propagation algorithm, which improves the ability of the student to distinguish between hidden nodes of the teacher. We compare its efficiency with that of gradient descent in training two-layer networks following the framework of [2]. In this paper we present numerical studies and a rigorous analysis of both the breaking of the symmetric phase and the convergence to optimal performance. We find that adaptive back-propagation can significantly reduce training time in both regimes by breaking the symmetry between hidden units more efficiently and by providing faster exponential convergence to zero generalization error.

2 DERIVATION OF THE DYNAMICAL EQUATIONS

The student network we consider is a soft committee machine [3], consisting of K hidden units which are connected to N-dimensional inputs ξ by their weight vectors $\boldsymbol{W} = \{\boldsymbol{W}_i\}$ $(i = 1, \ldots, K)$. All hidden units are connected to the linear output unit by couplings of unit strength and the implemented mapping is therefore $f_W(\xi) = \sum_{i=1}^{K} g(x_i)$, where $x_i = \boldsymbol{W}_i \cdot \xi$ is the activation of hidden unit i and $g(\cdot)$ is a sigmoidal transfer function. The map f_o to be learned is defined by a teacher network of the same architecture except for a possible difference in the number of hidden units M and is defined by the weight vectors $\boldsymbol{B} = \{\boldsymbol{B}_n\}$ $(n = 1, \ldots, M)$. Training examples are of the form (ξ^μ, ζ^μ), where the components of the input vectors ξ^μ are drawn independently from a zero mean unit variance Gaussian distribution; the outputs are $\zeta^\mu = \sum_{n=1}^{M} g(y_n^\mu)$, where $y_n^\mu = \boldsymbol{B}_n \cdot \xi^\mu$ is the activation of teacher hidden unit n.

An on-line training algorithm $\mathcal{A}$ is defined by the update of each weight in response to the presentation of an example (ξ^μ, ζ^μ), which can take the general form $\boldsymbol{W}_i^{\mu+1} = \boldsymbol{W}_i^\mu + \mathcal{A}_i(\{\gamma\}, \boldsymbol{W}^\mu, \xi^\mu, \zeta^\mu)$, where $\{\gamma\}$ defines parameters adjustable by the user. In the case of standard back-propagation, i.e., gradient descent on the error function defined in Eq. (1): $\mathcal{A}_i^{\text{gd}}(\eta, \boldsymbol{W}^\mu, \xi^\mu, \zeta^\mu) = (\eta/N)\delta_i^\mu \xi^\mu$ with

$$\delta_i^\mu = \delta^\mu g'(x_i^\mu) = [\zeta^\mu - f_W(\xi^\mu)]\, g'(x_i^\mu), \qquad (2)$$

where the only user adjustable parameter is the learning rate η scaled by $1/N$. One can readily see that the only term that breaks the symmetry between different hidden units is $g'(x_i^\mu)$, i.e., the derivative of the transfer function $g(\cdot)$. The fact that a prolonged symmetric phase can exist indicates that this term is not significantly different over the hidden units for a typical input in the symmetric phase.

The rationale of the adaptive back-propagation algorithm defined below is therefore to alter the g'-term, in order to magnify small differences in the activation between hidden units. This can be easily achieved by altering $g'(x_i)$ to $g'(\beta x_i)$, where β plays the role of an inverse "temperature". Varying β changes the range of hidden unit activations relevant for training, e.g., for $\beta > 1$ learning is more confined to small activations, when compared to gradient descent ($\beta = 1$). The whole adaptive back-propagation training algorithm is therefore:

$$\mathcal{A}_i^{\text{abp}}(\eta, \beta, \boldsymbol{W}^\mu, \boldsymbol{\xi}^\mu, \boldsymbol{\zeta}^\mu) = \frac{\eta}{N} \delta^\mu g'(\beta x_i^\mu) \boldsymbol{\xi}^\mu = \frac{\eta}{N} \widetilde{\delta_i^\mu} \boldsymbol{\xi}^\mu \qquad (3)$$

with δ^μ as in Eq. (2). To compare the adaptive back-propagation algorithm with normal gradient descent, we follow the statistical mechanics calculation in [2]. Here we will only outline the main ideas and present the results of the calculation.

As we are interested in the typical behaviour of our training algorithm we average over all possible instances of the examples $\boldsymbol{\xi}$. We rewrite the update equations (3) in $\boldsymbol{W}_i$ as equations in the order parameters describing the overlaps between student nodes $Q_{ij} = \boldsymbol{W}_i \cdot \boldsymbol{W}_j$, student and teacher nodes $R_{in} = \boldsymbol{W}_i \cdot \boldsymbol{B}_n$ and teacher nodes $T_{nm} = \boldsymbol{B}_n \cdot \boldsymbol{B}_m$. The generalization error ϵ_g, measuring the typical performance, can be expressed in these variables only [2]. The order parameters Q_{ij} and R_{in} are the new dynamical variables, which are self-averaging with respect to the randomness in the training data in the thermodynamic limit ($N \to \infty$). If we interpret the normalized example number $\alpha = \mu/N$ as a continuous time variable, the update equations for the order parameters become first order coupled differential equations

$$\frac{dR_{in}}{d\alpha} = \eta \left\langle \widetilde{\delta}_i y_n \right\rangle_\xi,$$

$$\frac{dQ_{ij}}{d\alpha} = \eta \left\langle \widetilde{\delta}_i x_j + \widetilde{\delta}_j x_i \right\rangle_\xi + \eta^2 \left\langle \widetilde{\delta}_i \widetilde{\delta}_j \right\rangle_\xi. \qquad (4)$$

All the integrals in Eqs. (4) and the generalization error can be calculated explicitly if we choose $g(x) = \text{erf}(x/\sqrt{2})$ as the sigmoidal activation function [2]. The exact form of the resulting dynamical equations for adaptive back-propagation is similar to the equations in [2] and will be presented elsewhere [4]. They can easily be integrated numerically for any number of K student and M teacher hidden units. For the remainder of the paper, we will however focus on the realizable case ($K = M$) and uncorrelated isotropic teachers of unit length $T_{nm} = \delta_{nm}$.

The dynamical evolution of the overlaps Q_{ij} and R_{in} follows from integrating the equations of motion (4) from initial conditions determined by the random initialization of the student weights $\boldsymbol{W}$. Whereas the resulting norms Q_{ii} of the student vector will be order $\mathcal{O}(1)$, the overlaps Q_{ij} between student vectors, and student-teacher vectors R_{in} will be only order $\mathcal{O}(1/\sqrt{N})$. The random initialization of the weights is therefore simulated by initializing the norms Q_{ii} and the overlaps Q_{ij} and R_{in} from uniform distributions in the $[0, 0.5]$ and $[0, 10^{-12}]$ interval respectively.

In Fig. 1 we show the difference of a typical evolution of the overlaps and the generalization error for $\beta = 12$ and $\beta = 1$ (gradient descent) for $K = 3$ and $\eta = 0.01$. In both cases, the student is drawn quickly into a suboptimal symmetric phase, characterized by a finite generalization error (Fig. 1e) and no differentiation between the hidden units of the student: the student norms Q_{ii} and overlaps Q_{ij} are similar (Figs. 1b,1d) and the overlaps of each student node with all teacher nodes R_{in} are nearly identical (Figs. 1a,1c). The student trained by gradient descent (Figs. 1c,1d) is trapped in this unstable suboptimal solution for most of the training time, whereas adaptive back-propagation (Figs. 1a,1b) breaks the symmetry significantly earlier. The convergence phase is characterized by a specialization of the different student nodes and the evolution of the overlap matrices $\boldsymbol{Q}$ and $\boldsymbol{R}$ to their optimal value $\boldsymbol{T}$, except for the permutational symmetry due to the arbitrary labeling of the student nodes. Clearly, the choice $\beta = 12$ is suboptimal in this regime. The student trained with $\beta = 1$ converges faster to zero generalization error (Fig. 1e). In order to optimize β seperately for both the symmetric and the convergence phase, we will examine the equations of motions analytically in the following section.

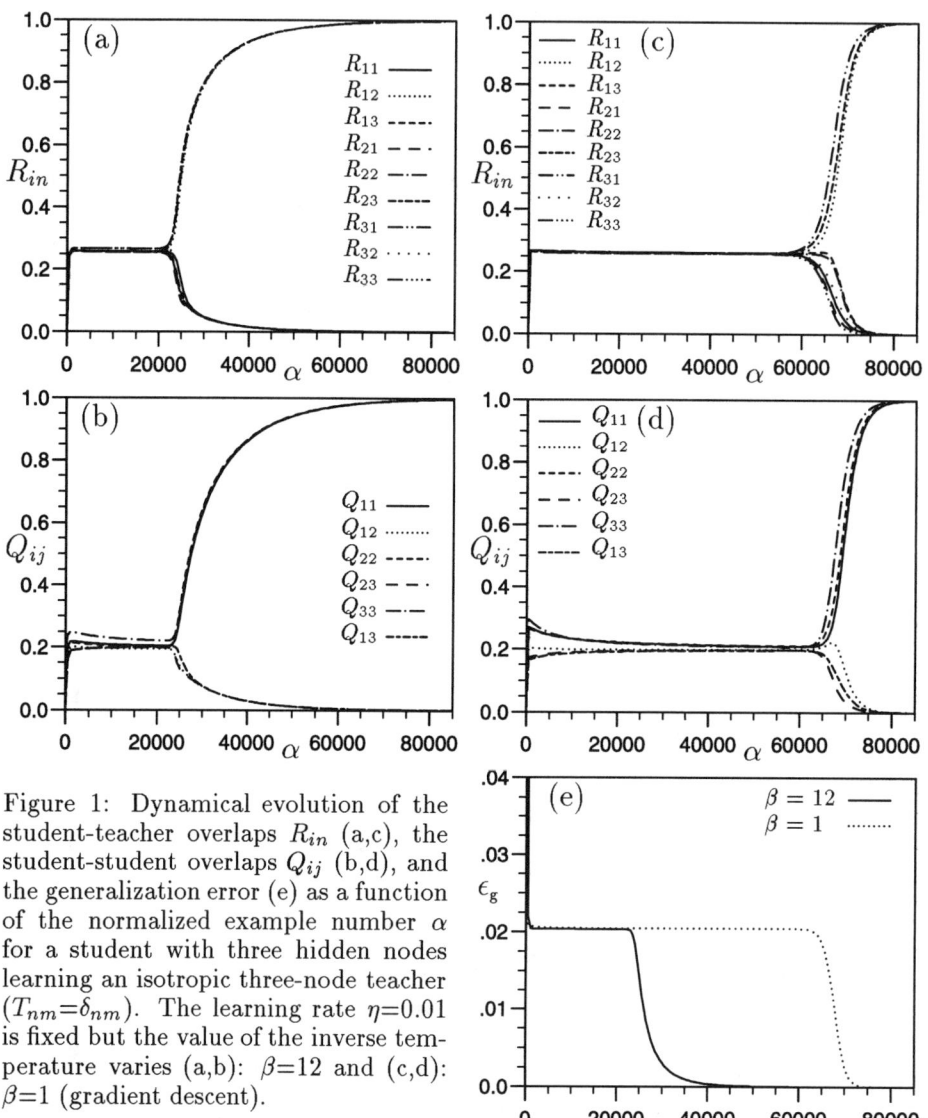

Figure 1: Dynamical evolution of the student-teacher overlaps R_{in} (a,c), the student-student overlaps Q_{ij} (b,d), and the generalization error (e) as a function of the normalized example number α for a student with three hidden nodes learning an isotropic three-node teacher ($T_{nm}=\delta_{nm}$). The learning rate $\eta=0.01$ is fixed but the value of the inverse temperature varies (a,b): $\beta=12$ and (c,d): $\beta=1$ (gradient descent).

3 ANALYSIS OF THE DYNAMICAL EQUATIONS

In the case of a realizable learning scenario ($K=M$) and isotropic teachers ($T_{nm}=\delta_{nm}$) the order parameter space can be very well characterized by similar diagonal and off-diagonal elements of the overlap matrices $\mathbf{Q}$ and $\mathbf{R}$, i.e., $Q_{ij} = Q\delta_{ij} + C(1-\delta_{ij})$ for the student-student overlaps and, apart from a relabeling of the student nodes, by $R_{in} = R\delta_{in} + S(1-\delta_{in})$ for the student-teacher overlaps. As one can see from Fig. 1, this approximation is particularly good in the symmetric phase and during the final convergence to perfect generalization.

3.1 SYMMETRIC PHASE AND ONSET OF SPECIALIZATION

Numerical integration of the equations of motion for a range of learning scenarios show that the length of the symmetric phase is especially prolonged by isotropic teachers and small learning rates η. We will therefore optimize the dynamics (4) in the symmetric phase with respect to β for isotropic teachers in the small η regime, where terms proportional to η^2 can be neglected. The fixed point of the truncated equations of motion

$$Q^* = C^* = \frac{1}{2K-1} \quad \text{and} \quad R^* = S^* = \sqrt{\frac{Q^*}{K}} = \frac{1}{\sqrt{K(2K-1)}} \tag{5}$$

is independent of β and thus identical to the one obtained in [2]. However, the symmetric solution is an unstable fixed point of the dynamics and the small perturbations introduced by the generically nonsymmetric initial conditions will eventually drive the student towards specialization.

To study the onset of specialization, we expand the truncated differential equations to first order in the deviations $q = Q - Q^*$, $c = C - C^*$, $r = R - R^*$, and $s = S - S^*$ from the fixed point values (5). The linearized equations of motion take the form $d\boldsymbol{v}/d\alpha = \mathbf{M}\cdot\boldsymbol{v}$, where $\boldsymbol{v} = (q,c,r,s)$ and $\mathbf{M}$ is a 4×4 matrix whose elements are the first derivatives of the truncated update equations (4) at the fixed point with respect to $\boldsymbol{v}$. Perturbations or *modes* which are proportional to the *eigenvectors* $\boldsymbol{v}_i$ of $\mathbf{M}$ will therefore decrease or increase exponentially depending on whether the corresponding *eigenvalue* λ_i is negative or positive. For the onset of specialization only the modes are relevant which are amplified by the dynamics, i.e., the ones with positive eigenvalue. For them we can identify the inverse eigenvalue as a typical escape time τ_i from the symmetric phase.

We find only one relevant perturbation for $q = c = 0$ and $s = -r/(K-1)$. This can be confirmed by a closer look at Fig. 1. The onset of specialization is signaled by the breaking of the symmetry between the student-teacher overlaps, whereas significant differences from the symmetric fixed point values of the student norms and overlaps occur later. The escape time τ associated with the above perturbation is

$$\tau(\beta) = \frac{\pi}{2\eta} \frac{\sqrt{2K-1}(2K+\beta)^{3/2}}{K\beta}. \tag{6}$$

Minimization of τ with respect to β yields $\beta^{\text{opt}} = 4K$, i.e., the optimal β scales with the number of hidden units, and

$$\tau^{\text{opt}} = \frac{9\pi}{2\eta} \frac{\sqrt{2K-1}}{\sqrt{6K}}. \tag{7}$$

Trapping in the symmetric phase is therefore always inversely proportional to the learning rate η. In the large K limit it is proportional to the number of hidden nodes K ($\tau \sim 2\pi K/\eta$) for gradient descent, whereas it is independent of K [$\tau \sim 3\sqrt{3}\pi/(2\eta)$] for the optimized adaptive back-propagation algorithm.

3.2 CONVERGENCE TO OPTIMAL GENERALIZATION

In order to predict the optimal learning rate η^{opt} and inverse temperature β^{opt} for the convergence, we linearize the full equations of motion (4) around the zero generalization error fixed point $R^* = Q^* = 1$ and $S^* = C^* = 0$. The matrix $\mathbf{M}$ of the resulting system of four coupled linear differential equations in $q = 1 - Q$, $c = C$, $r = 1 - R$, and $s = S$ is very complicated for arbitrary β, K and η, and its eigenvalues and eigenvectors can therefore only be analysed numerically.

We illustrate the solution space with $K = 3$ and two β values in Fig. 2a. We find that the dynamics decompose into four modes: two slow modes associated with eigenvalues λ_1 and λ_2 and two fast modes associated with eigenvalues λ_3 and λ_4, which are negative for all learning rates and whose magnitude is significantly larger.

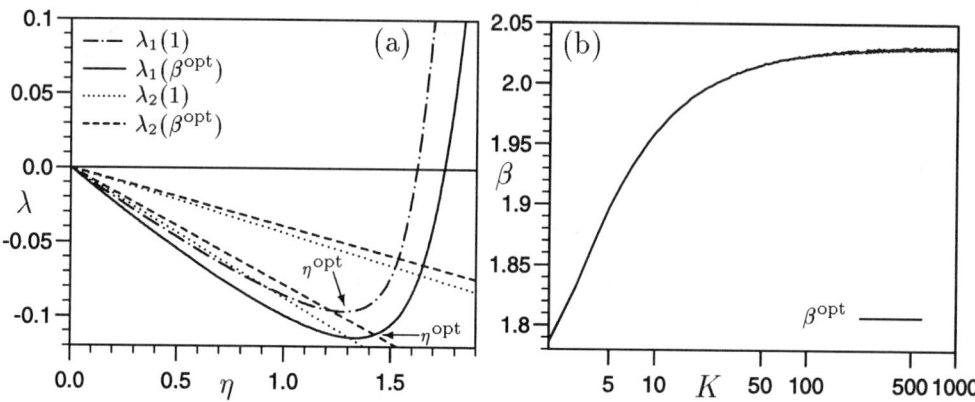

Figure 2: (a) The eigenvalues λ_1, λ_2 (see text) as a function of the learning rate η at $K = 3$ for two values of β: $\beta = 1$, and $\beta = \beta^{\text{opt}} = 1.8314$. For comparison we plot $2\lambda_2$ and find that the optimal learning rate η^{opt} is given by the condition $\lambda_1 = 2\lambda_2$ for β^{opt}, but by the minimum of λ_1 for $\beta = 1$. (b) The optimal inverse temperature β^{opt} as a function of the number of hidden units K saturates for large K.

The fast modes decay quickly and their influence on the long-time dynamics is negligible. They are therefore excluded from Fig. 2a and the following discussion. The eigenvalue λ_2 is negative and linear in η. The eigenvalue λ_1 is a non-linear function of both β and η and negative for small η. For large η, λ_1 becomes positive and training does not converge to the optimal solution defining the maximum learning rate $\eta_{\max}$ as $\lambda_1(\eta_{\max}) = 0$. For all $\eta < \eta_{\max}$ the generalization error decays exponentionally to $\epsilon_g^* = 0$.

In order to identify the corresponding convergence time τ, which is inversely proportional to the modulus of the eigenvalue associated with the slowest decay mode, we expand the generalization error to second order in q, c, r and s. We find that the mode associated with the linear eigenvalue λ_2 does not contribute to first order terms, and controls only second order term in a decay rate of $2\lambda_2$. The learning rate η^{opt} which provides the fastest asymptotic decay rate λ^{opt} of the generalization error is therefore either given by the condition $\lambda_1(\eta^{\text{opt}}) = 2\lambda_2(\eta^{\text{opt}})$ or alternatively by $\min_\eta(\lambda_1)$ if $\lambda_1 > 2\lambda_2$ at the minimum of λ_1 (see Fig. 2a).

We can further optimize convergence to optimal generalization by minimizing the decay rate $\lambda^{\text{opt}}(\beta)$ with respect to β (see Fig. 2b). Numerically, we find that the optimal inverse temperature β^{opt} saturates for large K at $\beta^{\text{opt}} \approx 2.03$. For large K, we find an associated optimal convergence time $\tau^{\text{opt}}(\beta^{\text{opt}}) \sim 2.90K$ for adaptive back-propagation optimized with respect to η and β, which is an improvement by 17% when compared to $\tau^{\text{opt}}(1) \sim 3.48K$ for gradient descent optimized with respect to η. The optimal and maximal learning rates show an asymptotic $1/K$ behaviour and $\eta^{\text{opt}}(\beta^{\text{opt}}) \sim 4.78/K$, which is an increase by 20% compared to gradient descent. Both algorithms are quite stable as the maximal learning rates, for which the learning process diverges, are about 30% higher than the optimal rates.

4 SUMMARY AND DISCUSSION

This research has been motivated by the dominance of the suboptimal symmetric phase in on-line learning of two-layer feedforward networks trained by gradient descent [2]. This trapping is emphasized for inappropriate small learning rates but exists in all training scenarios, effecting the learning process considerably. We proposed an adaptive back-propagation training algorithm [Eq. (3)] parameterized by an inverse temperature β, which is designed to improve specialization of the student nodes by enhancing differences in the activation between hidden units. Its performance has been compared to gradient descent for a soft-committee student network with K hidden units trying to learn a rule defined by an isotropic teacher ($T_{nm} = \delta_{nm}$) of the same architecture.

A linear analysis of the equations of motion around the symmetric fixed point for small learning rates has shown that optimized adaptive back-propagation characterized by $\beta^{\mathrm{opt}} = 4K$ breaks the symmetry significantly faster. The effect is especially pronounced for large networks, where the trapping time of gradient descent grows $\tau \propto K/\eta$ compared to $\tau \propto 1/\eta$ for β^{opt}. With increasing network size it seems to become harder for a student node trained by gradient descent to distinguish between the many teacher nodes and to specialize on one of them. In the adaptive back-propagation algorithm this effect can be eliminated by choosing $\beta^{\mathrm{opt}} \propto K$.

An open question is how the choice of the optimal inverse temperature is effected for large learning rates, where η^2-terms cannot be neglected, as unbounded increase of the learning rate causes uncontrolled growth of the student norms. However, the full equations of motion are very difficult to analyse in the symmetric phase. Numerical studies indicate that β^{opt} is smaller but still scales with K and yields an overall decrease in training time which is still significant. We also find that the optimal learning rate η^{opt}, which exhibits the shortest symmetric phase, is significantly lower in this regime than during convergence [4].

During convergence, independent of which algorithm is used, the time constant for decay to zero generalization error scales with K, due to the necessary rescaling of the learning rate by $1/K$ as the typical quadratic deviation between teacher and student output increases proportional to K. The reduction in training time with adaptive back-propagation is 17% and independent of the number of hidden units in contrast to the symmetric phase, where a factor K is gained. This can be explained by the fact that each student node is already specialized on one teacher node and the effect of other nodes in inhibiting further specialization is negligible. In fact, at first it seems rather surprising that anything can be gained by not changing the weights of the network according to their error gradient. The optimal setting of $\beta > 1$, together with training at a larger learning rate, speeds up learning for small activations and slows down learning for highly activated nodes. This is equivalent to favouring rotational changes of the weight vectors over pure length changes to a degree determined by β.

We believe that the adaptive back-propagation algorithm investigated here will be beneficial for any multilayer feedforward network and hope that this work will motivate further theoretical research into the efficiency of training algorithms and their systematic improvement.

References

[1] C. Cybenko, *Math. Control Signals and Systems* **2**, 303 (1989).

[2] D. Saad and S. A. Solla, *Phys. Rev. E* **52**, 4225 (1995).

[3] M. Biehl and H. Schwarze, *J. Phys. A* **28**, 643 (1995).

[4] A. West and D. Saad, in preparation (1995).

Optimizing Cortical Mappings

Geoffrey J. Goodhill
The Salk Institute
10010 North Torrey Pines Road
La Jolla, CA 92037, USA

Steven Finch
Human Communication Research Centre
University of Edinburgh, 2 Buccleuch Place
Edinburgh EH8 9LW, GREAT BRITAIN

Terrence J. Sejnowski
The Howard Hughes Medical Institute
The Salk Institute for Biological Studies
10010 North Torrey Pines Road, La Jolla, CA 92037, USA
&
Department of Biology, University of California San Diego
La Jolla, CA 92037, USA

Abstract

"Topographic" mappings occur frequently in the brain. A popular approach to understanding the structure of such mappings is to map points representing input features in a space of a few dimensions to points in a 2 dimensional space using some self-organizing algorithm. We argue that a more general approach may be useful, where similarities between features are not constrained to be geometric distances, and the objective function for topographic matching is chosen explicitly rather than being specified implicitly by the self-organizing algorithm. We investigate analytically an example of this more general approach applied to the structure of interdigitated mappings, such as the pattern of ocular dominance columns in primary visual cortex.

1 INTRODUCTION

A prevalent feature of mappings in the brain is that they are often "topographic". In the most straightforward case this simply means that neighbouring points on a two-dimensional sheet (e.g. the retina) are mapped to neighbouring points in a more central two-dimensional structure (e.g. the optic tectum). However a more complex case, still often referred to as topographic, is the mapping from an abstract space of features (e.g. position in the visual field, orientation, eye of origin etc) to

Optimizing Cortical Mappings

the cortex (e.g. layer 4 of V1). In many cortical sensory areas, the preferred sensory stimuli of neighbouring neurons changes slowly, except at discontinuous jumps, suggestive of an optimization principle that attempts to match "similar" features to nearby points in the cortex. In this paper, we (1) discuss what might constitute an appropriate measure of similarity between features, (2) outline an optimization principle for matching the similarity structure of two abstract spaces (i.e. a measure of the degree of topography of a mapping), and (3) use these ideas to analyse the case where two equivalent input variables are mapped onto one target structure, such as the "ocular dominance" mapping from the right and left eyes to V1 in the cat and monkey.

2 SIMILARITY MEASURES

A much-investigated computational approach to the study of mappings in V1 is to consider the input features as points in a multidimensional euclidean space [1, 5, 9]. The input dimensions then consist of e.g. spatial position, orientation, ocular dominance, and so on. Some distribution of points in this space is assumed which attempts, in some sense, to capture the statistics of these features in the visual world. For instance, in [5], distances between points in the space are interpreted as a decreasing function of the degree to which the corresponding features are correlated over an ensemble of images. Some self-organizing algorithm is then applied which produces a mapping from the high-dimensional feature space to a two-dimensional sheet representing the cortex, such that nearby points in the feature space map to nearby points in the two-dimensional sheet.[1]

However, such approaches assume that the dissimilarity structure of the input features is well-captured by euclidean distances in a geometric space. There is no particular reason why this should be true. For instance, such a representation implies that the dissimilarity between features can become arbitrarily large, an unlikely scenario. In addition, it is difficult to capture higher-order relationships in such a representation, such as that two oriented line-segment detectors will be more correlated if the line segments are co-linear than if they are not. We propose instead that, for a set of features, one could construct directly from the statistics of natural stimuli a feature *matrix* representing similarities or dissimilarities, without regard to whether the resulting relationships can be conveniently captured by distances in a euclidean feature space. There are many ways this could be done; one example is given below. Such a similarity matrix for features can then be optimally matched (in some sense) to a similarity matrix for positions in the output space.

A disadvantage from a computational point of view of this generalized approach is that the self-organizing algorithms of e.g. [6, 2] can no longer be applied, and possibly less efficient optimization techniques are required. However, an advantage of this is that one may now explore the consequences of optimizing a whole range of objective functions for quantifying the quality of the mapping, rather than having to accept those given explicitly or implicitly by the particular self-organizing algorithm.

---

[1]We mean this in a rather loose sense, and wish to include here the principles of mapping nearby points in the sheet to nearby points in the feature space, mapping distant points in the feature space to distant points in the sheet, and so on.

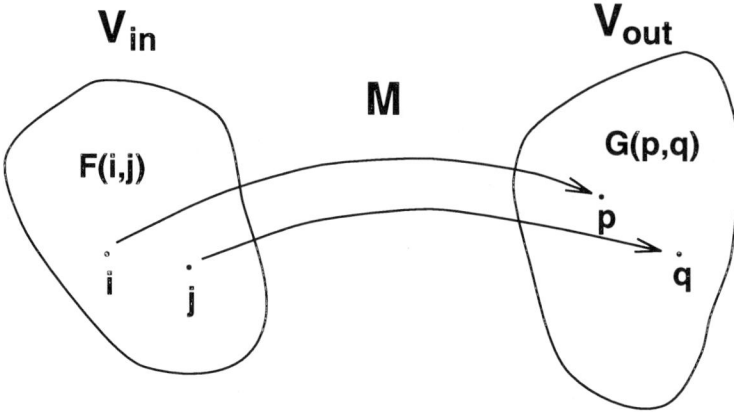

Figure 1: The mapping framework.

3 OPTIMIZATION PRINCIPLES

We now outline a general framework for measuring to what degree a mapping matches the structure of one similarity matrix to that of another. It is assumed that input and output matrices are of the same (finite) dimension, and that the mapping is bijective. Consider an input space V_{in} and an output space V_{out}, each of which contains N points. Let M be the mapping from points in V_{in} to points in V_{out} (see figure 1). We use the word "space" in a general sense: either or both of V_{in} and V_{out} may not have a geometric interpretation. Assume that for each space there is a symmetric "similarity" function which, for any given pair of points in the space, specifies how similar (or dissimilar) they are. Call these functions F for V_{in} and G for V_{out}. Then we define a cost functional C as follows

$$C = \sum_{i=1}^{N} \sum_{j<i} F(i,j) G(M(i), M(j)), \qquad (1)$$

where i and j label points in V_{in}, and M(i) and M(j) are their respective images in V_{out}. The sum is over all possible pairs of points in V_{in}. Since M is a bijection it is invertible, and C can equivalently be written

$$C = \sum_{i=1}^{N} \sum_{j<i} F(M^{-1}(i), M^{-1}(j)) G(i,j), \qquad (2)$$

where now i and j label points in V_{out}, and M^{-1} is the inverse map. A good (i.e. highly topographic) mapping is one with a high value of C. However, if one of F or G were given as a dissimilarity function (i.e. increasing with decreasing similarity) then a good mapping would be one with a low value of C. How F and G are defined is problem-specific.

C has a number of important properties that help to justify its adoption as a measure of the degree of topography of a mapping (for more details see [3]). For instance, it can be shown that if a mapping that *preserves ordering relationships* between two similarity matrices exists, then maximizing C will find it. Such maps are homeomorphisms. However not all homeomorphisms have this property, so we refer to such "perfect" maps as "topographic homeomorphisms". Several previously defined optimization principles, such as minimum path and minimum wiring [1], are special cases of C. It is also closely related (under the assumptions above) to Luttrell's minimum distortion measure [7], if F is euclidean distance in a geometric input space, and G gives the noise process in the output space.

4 INTERDIGITATED MAPPINGS

As a particular application of the principles discussed so far, we consider the case where the similarity structure of V_{in} can be expressed in matrix form as

$$\begin{pmatrix} Q_S & Q_C \\ Q_C & Q_S \end{pmatrix}$$

where Q_S and Q_C are of dimension $N/2$. This means that V_{in} consists of two halves, each with the same internal similarity structure, and an in general different similarity structure between the two halves. The question is how best to match this dual similarity structure to a single similarity structure in V_{out}. This is of mathematical interest since it is one of the simplest cases of a mismatch between the similarity structures of V_{in} and V_{out}, and of biological interest since it abstractly represents the case of input from two equivalent sets of receptors coming together in a single cortical sheet, e.g. ocular dominance columns in primary visual cortex (see e.g. [8, 5]). For simplicity we consider only the case of two one-dimensional retinae mapping to a one-dimensional cortex.

The feature space approach to the problem presented in [5] says that the dissimilarities in V_{in} are given by squared euclidean distances between points arranged in two parallel rows in a two-dimensional space. That is,

$$F(i,j) = \begin{cases} |i-j|^2 & : \quad i,j \text{ in same half of } V_{in} \\ |i-j-N/2|^2 + k^2 & : \quad i,j \text{ in different halves of } V_{in} \end{cases} \quad (3)$$

assuming that indices $1 \ldots N/2$ give points in one half and indices $N/2+1 \ldots N$ give points in the other half. $G(i,j)$ is given by

$$G(i,j) = \begin{cases} 1 & : \quad i,j \text{ neighbouring} \\ 0 & : \quad \text{otherwise} \end{cases} \quad (4)$$

It can be shown that the globally optimal mapping (i.e. minimum of C) when $k > 1$ is to keep the two halves of V_{in} entirely separate in V_{out} [5]. However, there is also a local minimum for an interdigitated (or "striped") map, where the interdigitations have width $n = 2k$. By varying the value of k it is thus possible to smoothly vary the periodicity of the locally optimal striped map. Such behavior predicted the outcome of a recent biological experiment [4]. For $k < 1$ the globally optimal map is stripes of width $n = 2$.

However, in principle many alternative ways of measuring the similarity in V_{in} are possible. One obvious idea is to assume that similarity is given directly by the degree of correlation between points within and between the two eyes. A simple assumption about the form of these correlations is that they are a gaussian function of physical distance between the receptors (as in [8]). That is,

$$F(i,j) = \begin{cases} e^{-\alpha|i-j|^2} & : \quad i,j \text{ in same half of } V_{in} \\ ce^{-\beta|i-j-N/2|^2} & : \quad i,j \text{ in different halves of } V_{in} \end{cases} \quad (5)$$

with $c < 1$. We assume for ease of analysis that G is still as given in equation 4. This directly implements an intuitive notion put forward to account for the interdigitation of the ocular dominance mapping [4]: that the cortex tries to represent similar inputs close together, that similarity is given by the degree of correlation between the activities of points (cells), and additionally that natural visual scenes impose a correlational structure of the same qualitative form as equation 5. We now calculate C analytically for various mappings (c.f. [5]), and compare the cost of a map that keeps the two halves of V_{in} entirely separate in V_{out} to those which interdigitate the two halves of V_{in} with some regular periodicity. The map of the first type we consider will be refered to as the "up and down" map: moving from one end of V_{out} to the other implies moving entirely through one half of V_{in}, then back in the opposite direction through the other half. For this map, the cost C_{ud} is given by

$$C_{ud} = 2(N-1)e^{-\alpha} + c. \qquad (6)$$

For an interdigitated (striped) map where the stripes are of width $n \geq 2$:

$$C_s(n) = N\left[2\left(1 - \frac{1}{n}\right)e^{-\alpha} + \frac{c}{n}\left(e^{-\beta f(n)} + e^{-\beta g(n)}\right)\right] \qquad (7)$$

where for n even $f(n) = g(n) = \left(\frac{n-2}{2}\right)^2$ and for n odd $f(n) = \left(\frac{n-1}{2}\right)^2$, $g(n) = \left(\frac{n-3}{2}\right)^2$. To characterize this system we now analyze how the n for which $C_s(n)$ has a local maximum varies with c, α, β, and when this local maximum is also a global maximum. Setting $\frac{dC_s(n)}{dn} = 0$ does not yield analytically tractable expressions (unlike [5]). However, more direct methods can be used: there is a local maximum at n if $C_s(n-1) < C_s(n) > C_s(n+1)$. Using equation 7 we derive conditions on c for this to be true. For n odd, we obtain the condition $c_1 < c < c_2$ where $c_1 = c_2$; that is, there are no local maxima at odd values of n. For n even, we also obtain $c_1 < c < c_2$ where now

$$c_1 = \frac{2e^{-\alpha}}{ne^{-\beta(\frac{n-4}{2})^2} - (n-2)e^{-\beta(\frac{n-2}{2})^2}}$$

and $c_2(n) = c_1(n+2)$. $c_1(n)$ and $c_2(n)$ are plotted in figure 2, from which one can see the ranges of c for which particular n are local maxima. As β increases, maxima for larger values of n become apparent, but the range of c for which they exist becomes rather small. It can be shown that C_{ud} is always the global maximum, except when $e^{-\alpha} > c$, when $n = 2$ is globally optimal. As c decreases the optimal stripe width gets wider, analogously to k increasing in the dissimilarities given by equation 3. When β is such that there is no local maximum the only optimum is stripes as wide as possible. This fits with the intuitive idea that if corresponding points in the two halves of V_{in} (i.e. $|i - j| \approx N/2$) are sufficiently similar then it is favorable to interdigitate the two halves in V_{out}, otherwise the two halves are kept completely separate.

The qualitative behavior here is similar to that for equation 3. $n = 2$ is a global optimum for large c (small k), then as c decreases (k increases) $n = 2$ first becomes a local optimum, then the position of the local optimum shifts to larger n. However, an important difference is that in equation 3 the dissimilarities increase without limit with distance, whereas in equation 5 the similarities tend to zero with distance. Thus for equation 5 the extra cost of stripes one unit wider rapidly becomes negligible, whereas for equation 3 this extra cost keeps on increasing by ever larger amounts. As $n \to \infty$, $C_{ud} \sim C_s(n)$ for the similarities defined by equation 5 (i.e. there is the same cost for traversing the two blocks in the same direction as in the opposite direction), whereas for the dissimilarities defined by equation 3 there is a quite different cost in these two cases. That F and G should tend to a bounded value as i and j become ever more distant neighbors seems biologically more plausible than that they should be potentially unbounded.

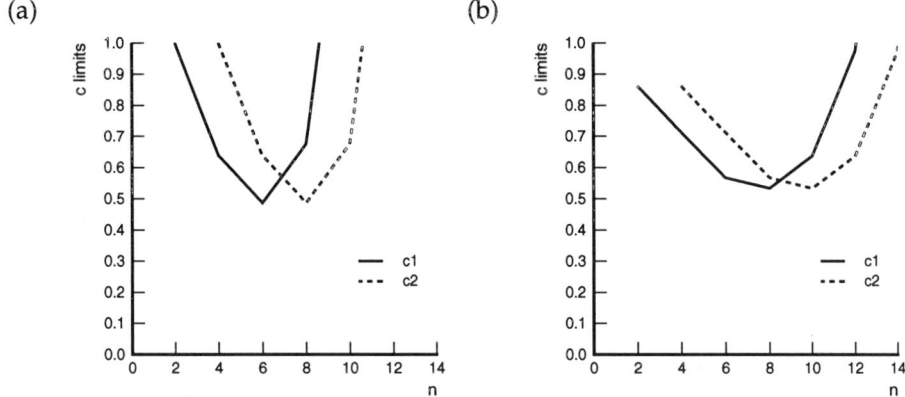

Figure 2: The ranges of c for which particular n are local maxima. (a) $\alpha = \beta = 0.25$. (b) $\alpha = 0.25$, $\beta = 0.1$. When the c_2 (dashed) line is below the c_1 (solid) line no local maxima exist. For each (even) value of n to the left of the crossing point, the vertical range between the two lines gives the values of c for which that n is a local maximum. Below the solid line and to the right of the crossing point the only maximum is stripes as wide as possible.

Issues such as those we have addressed regarding the transition from "striped" to "blocked" solutions for combining two sets of inputs distinguished by their intra- and inter-population similarity structure may be relevant to understanding the spatial representation of functional attributes across cortex. The results suggest the hypothesis that two variables are interdigitated in the same area rather than being represented separately in two distinct areas if the inter-population similarity is sufficiently high. An interesting point is that the striped solutions are often only local optima. It is possible that in reality developmental constraints (e.g. a chemically defined bias towards overlaying the two projections) impose a bias towards finding a striped rather than blocked solution, even though the latter may be the global optimum.

5 DISCUSSION

We have argued that, in order to understand the structure of mappings in the brain, it could be useful to examine more general measures of similarity and of topographic matching than those implied by standard feature space models. The consequences of one particular alternative set of choices has been examined for the case of an interdigitated map of two variables. Many alternative objective functions for topographic matching are of course possible; this topic is reviewed in [3]. Two issues we have not discussed are the most appropriate way to define the features of interest, and the most appropriate measures of similarity between features (see [10] for an interesting discussion).

A next step is to apply these methods to more complex structures in V1 than just the ocular dominance map. By examining more of the space of possibilities than that occupied by the current feature space models, we hope to understand more about the optimization strategies that might be being pursued by the cortex. Feature space models may still turn out to be more or less the right answer; however even if this is true, our approach will at least give a deeper level of understanding why.

Acknowledgements

We thank Gary Blasdel, Peter Dayan and Paul Viola for stimulating discussions.

References

[1] Durbin, R. & Mitchison, G. (1990). A dimension reduction framework for understanding cortical maps. *Nature,* **343,** 644-647.

[2] Durbin, R. & Willshaw, D.J. (1987). An analogue approach to the travelling salesman problem using an elastic net method. *Nature,* **326,** 689-691.

[3] Goodhill, G. J., Finch, S. & Sejnowski, T. J. (1995). Quantifying neighbourhood preservation in topographic mappings. Institute for Neural Computation Technical Report Series, No. INC-9505, November 1995. Available from ftp://salk.edu/pub/geoff/goodhill_finch_sejnowski_tech95.ps.Z or http://cnl.salk.edu/~geoff.

[4] Goodhill, G.J. & Löwel, S. (1995). Theory meets experiment: correlated neural activity helps determine ocular dominance column periodicity. *Trends in Neurosciences,* **18,** 437-439.

[5] Goodhill, G.J. & Willshaw, D.J. (1990). Application of the elastic net algorithm to the formation of ocular dominance stripes. *Network,* **1,** 41-59.

[6] Kohonen, T. (1982). Self-organized formation of topologically correct feature maps. *Biol. Cybern.,* **43,** 59-69.

[7] Luttrell, S.P. (1990). Derivation of a class of training algorithms. *IEEE Trans. Neural Networks,* **1,** 229-232.

[8] Miller, K.D., Keller, J.B. & Stryker, M.P. (1989). Ocular dominance column development: Analysis and simulation. *Science,* **245,** 605-615.

[9] Obermayer, K., Blasdel, G.G. & Schulten, K. (1992). Statistical-mechanical analysis of self-organization and pattern formation during the development of visual maps. *Phys. Rev. A,* **45,** 7568-7589.

[10] Weiss, Y. & Edelman, S. (1995). Representation of similarity as a goal of early sensory coding. *Network,* **6,** 19-41.

Quadratic–Type Lyapunov Functions for Competitive Neural Networks with Different Time–Scales

Anke Meyer–Bäse
Institute of Technical Informatics
Technical University of Darmstadt
Darmstadt, Germany 64283

Abstract

The dynamics of complex neural networks modelling the self–organization process in cortical maps must include the aspects of long and short–term memory. The behaviour of the network is such characterized by an equation of neural activity as a fast phenomenon and an equation of synaptic modification as a slow part of the neural system. We present a quadratic–type Lyapunov function for the flow of a competitive neural system with fast and slow dynamic variables. We also show the consequences of the stability analysis on the neural net parameters.

1 INTRODUCTION

This paper investigates a special class of laterally inhibited neural networks. In particular, we have examined the dynamics of a restricted class of laterally inhibited neural networks from a rigorous analytic standpoint.

The network models for retinotopic and somatotopic cortical maps are usually composed of several layers of neurons from sensory receptors to cortical units, with feedforward excitations between the layers and lateral (or recurrent) connection within the layer. Standard techniques include (1) Hebbian rule and its variations for modifying synaptic efficacies, (2) lateral inhibition for establishing topographical organization of the cortex, and (3) adiabatic approximation in decoupling the dynamics of relaxation (which is on the fast time scale) and the dynamics of learning (which is on the slow time scale) of the network. However, in most cases, only computer simulation results were obtained and therefore provided limited mathematical understanding of the self–organizing neural response fields.

The networks under study model the dynamics of both the neural activity levels, the short–term memory (STM), and the dynamics of synaptic modifications, the long–term memory (LTM). The actual network models under consideration may be considered extensions of Grossberg's shunting network [Gro76] or Amari's model for primitive neuronal competition [Ama82]. These earlier networks are considered pools of mutually inhibitory neurons with **fixed** synaptic connections. Our results extended these earlier studies to systems where the synapses can be modified by external stimuli. The dynamics of competitive systems may be extremely complex, exhibiting convergence to point attractors and periodic attractors. For networks which model only the dynamic of the neural activity levels Cohen and Grossberg [CG83] found a Lyapunov function as a necessary condition for the convergence behavior to point attractors.

In this paper we apply the results of the theory of Lyapunov functions for singularly perturbed systems on large–scale neural networks, which have two types of state variables (LTM and STM) describing the slow and the fast dynamics of the system. So we can find a Lyapunov function for the neural system with different time–scales and give a design concept of storing desired pattern as stable equilibrium points.

2 THE CLASS OF NEURAL NETWORKS WITH DIFFERENT TIME–SCALES

This section defines the network of differential equations characterizing laterally inhibited neural networks. We consider a laterally inhibited network with a deterministic signal Hebbian learning law [Heb49] and is similar to the spatiotemporal system of Amari [Ama83].

The general neural network equations describe the temporal evolution of the STM (activity modification) and LTM states (synaptic modification). For the jth neuron of a N–neuron network these equations are:

$$\dot{x}_j = -a_j x_j + \sum_{i=1}^{N} D_{ij} f(x_i) + B_j S_j \tag{1}$$

$$\dot{S}_j = -S_j + |\mathbf{y}|^2 f(x_j) \tag{2}$$

where x_j is the current activity level, a_j is the time constant of the neuron, B_j is the contribution of the external stimulus term, $f(x_i)$ is the neuron's output, D_{ij} is the lateral inhibition term and y_i is the external stimulus. The dynamic variable S_j represents the synaptic modification state and $|\mathbf{y}|^2|$ is defined as $|\mathbf{y}|^2 = \mathbf{y}^T \mathbf{y}$.

We will assume that the input stimuli are normalized vectors of unit magnitude $|\mathbf{y}|^2 = 1$. These systems will be subject to our analysis considerations regarding the stability of their equilibrium points.

3 ASYMPTOTIC STABILITY OF NEURAL NETWORKS WITH DIFFERENT TIME–SCALES

We show in this section that it is possible to determine the asymptotic stability of this class of neural networks interpreting them as nonlinear singularly perturbed systems. While singular perturbation theory, a traditional tool of fluid dynamics and nonlinear mechanics, embraces a wide variety of dynamic phenomena possesing slow and fast modes, we show that singular perturbations are present in many neurodynamical problems. In this sense we apply in this paper the results of this valuable analysis tool on the dynamics of laterally inhibited networks.

In [SK84] is shown that a quadratic–type Lyapunov function for a singularly perturbed system is obtained as a weighted sum of quadratic–type Lyapunov functions of two lower order systems: the so–called reduced and the boundary–layer systems. Assuming that each of the two systems is asymptotically stable and has a Lyapunov function, conditions are derived to guarantee that, for a sufficiently small perturbation parameter, asymptotic stability of the singularly perturbed system can be established by means of a Lyapunov function which is composed as a weighted sum of the Lyapunov functions of the reduced and boundary–layer systems.

Adopting the notations from [SK84] we will consider the singularly perturbed system [2]

$$\dot{\mathbf{x}} = \mathbf{f}(\mathbf{x}, \mathbf{y}) \quad \mathbf{x} \in \mathbf{B_x} \subset \mathbf{R^n} \tag{3}$$

$$\epsilon \dot{\mathbf{y}} = \mathbf{g}(\mathbf{x}, \mathbf{y}, \epsilon) \quad \mathbf{y} \in \mathbf{B_y} \subset \mathbf{R^m}, \epsilon > 0 \tag{4}$$

We assume that, in $\mathbf{B_x}$ and $\mathbf{B_y}$, the origin ($\mathbf{x} = \mathbf{y} = \mathbf{0}$) is the unique equilibrium point and (3) and (4) has a unique solution. A reduced system is defined by setting $\epsilon = 0$ in (3) and (4) to obtain

$$\dot{\mathbf{x}} = \mathbf{f}(\mathbf{x}, \mathbf{y}) \tag{5}$$

$$\mathbf{0} = \mathbf{g}(\mathbf{x}, \mathbf{y}, 0) \tag{6}$$

Assuming that in $\mathbf{B_x}$ and $\mathbf{B_y}$, (6) has a unique root $\mathbf{y} = \mathbf{h}(\mathbf{x})$, the reduced system is rewritten as

$$\dot{\mathbf{x}} = \mathbf{f}(\mathbf{x}, \mathbf{h}(\mathbf{x})) = \mathbf{f_r}(\mathbf{x}) \tag{7}$$

A boundary–layer system is defined as

$$\frac{\partial \mathbf{y}}{\partial \tau} = \mathbf{g}(\mathbf{x}, \mathbf{y}(\tau), 0) \tag{8}$$

where $\tau = t/\epsilon$ is a stretching time scale. In (8) the vector $\mathbf{x} \in \mathbf{R^n}$ is treated as a fixed unknown parameter that takes values in $\mathbf{B_x}$. The aim is to establish the stability properties of the singularly perturbed system (3) and (4), for small ϵ, from those of the reduced system (7) and the boundary–layer system (8). The Lyapunov functions for system 7 and 8 are of quadratic–type. In [SK84] it is shown that under mild assumptions, for sufficiently small ϵ, any weighted sum of the Lyapunov functions of the reduced and boundary–layer system is a quadratic–type Lyapunov function for the singularly perturbed system (3) and (4).

The necessary assumptions are stated now [SK84]:

1. The reduced system (7) has a Lyapunov function $V : \mathbf{R^n} \rightarrow \mathbf{R_+}$ such that for all $\mathbf{x} \in \mathbf{B_x}$

$$(\nabla_x V(\mathbf{x}))^T \mathbf{f_r}(\mathbf{x}) \leq -\alpha_1 \psi^2(\mathbf{x}) \quad \alpha_1 > 0 \tag{9}$$

where $\psi(\mathbf{x})$ is a scalar–valued function of $\mathbf{x}$ that vanishes at $\mathbf{x} = \mathbf{0}$ and is different from zero for all other $\mathbf{x} \in \mathbf{B_x}$. This condition guarantees that $\mathbf{x} = \mathbf{0}$ is an asymptotically stable equilibrium point of the reduced system (7).

---

[2] The symbol $\mathbf{B_x}$ indicates a closed sphere centered at $\mathbf{x} = \mathbf{0}$; $\mathbf{B_y}$ is defined in the same way.

2. The boundary–layer system (8) has a Lyapunov function $W(\mathbf{x}, \mathbf{y}) : \mathbf{R}^n \times \mathbf{R}^m \to \mathbf{R}_+$ such that for all $\mathbf{x} \in \mathbf{B_x}$ and $\mathbf{y} \in \mathbf{B_y}$

$$(\nabla_y W(\mathbf{x}, \mathbf{y}))^T \mathbf{g}(\mathbf{x}, \mathbf{y}, 0) \leq -\alpha_2 \phi^2 (\mathbf{y} - \mathbf{h}(\mathbf{x})) \quad \alpha_2 > 0 \tag{10}$$

where $\phi(\mathbf{y} - \mathbf{h}(\mathbf{x}))$ is a scalar-valued function $(\mathbf{y} - \mathbf{h}(\mathbf{x})) \in \mathbf{R}^m$ that vanishes at $\mathbf{y} = \mathbf{h}(\mathbf{x})$ and is different from zero for all other $\mathbf{x} \in \mathbf{B_x}$ and $\mathbf{y} \in \mathbf{B_y}$. This condition guarantees that $\mathbf{y} = \mathbf{h}(\mathbf{x})$ is an asymptotically stable equilibrium point of the boundary–layer system (8).

3. The following three inequalities hold $\forall \mathbf{x} \in \mathbf{B_x}$ and $\forall \mathbf{y} \in \mathbf{B_y}$:

a.)
$$(\nabla_x W(\mathbf{x}, \mathbf{y}))^T \mathbf{f}(\mathbf{x}, \mathbf{y}) \leq c_1 \phi^2 (\mathbf{y} - \mathbf{h}(\mathbf{x})) + c_2 \psi(\mathbf{x}) \phi(\mathbf{y} - \mathbf{h}(\mathbf{x})) \tag{11}$$

b.)
$$(\nabla_x V(\mathbf{x}))^T [\mathbf{f}(\mathbf{x}, \mathbf{y}) - \mathbf{f}(\mathbf{x}, \mathbf{h}(\mathbf{x}))] \leq \beta_1 \psi(\mathbf{x}) \phi(\mathbf{y} - \mathbf{h}(\mathbf{x})) \tag{12}$$

c.)
$$(\nabla_y W(\mathbf{x}, \mathbf{y}))^T [\mathbf{g}(\mathbf{x}, \mathbf{y}, \epsilon) - \mathbf{g}(\mathbf{x}, \mathbf{y}, 0)] \leq \\ \epsilon K_1 \phi^2(\mathbf{y} - \mathbf{h}(\mathbf{x})) + \epsilon K_2 \psi(\mathbf{x}) \phi(\mathbf{y} - \mathbf{h}(\mathbf{x})) \tag{13}$$

The constants c_1, c_2, β_1, K_1 and K_2 are nonnegative. The inequalities above determine the permissible interaction between the slow and fast variables. They are basically smoothness requirements of f and g.

After these introductory remarks the stability criterion is now stated:

Theorem: *Suppose that conditions 1–3 hold; let d be a positive number such that $0 < d < 1$, and let $\epsilon^*(d)$ be the positive number given by*

$$\epsilon^*(d) = \frac{\alpha_1 \alpha_2}{\alpha_1 \gamma + [\beta_1(1-d) + \beta_2 d]^2 / 4d(1-d)} \tag{14}$$

where $\beta_2 = K_2 + C_2$, $\gamma = K_1 + C_1$, then for all $\epsilon < \epsilon^*(d)$, the origin $(\mathbf{x} = \mathbf{y} = 0)$ is an asymptotically stable equilibrium point of (3) and (4) and

$$v(\mathbf{x}, \mathbf{y}) = (1 - d)V(\mathbf{x}) + dW(\mathbf{x}, \mathbf{y}) \tag{15}$$

is a Lyapunov function of (3) and (4).

If we put $\epsilon = \frac{1}{A}$ as a global neural time constant in equation (1) then we have to determine two Lyapunov functions: one for the boundary–layer system and the other for the reduced–order system.

In [CG83] is mentioned a global Lyapunov function for a competitive neural network with only an activation dynamics.

$$V(x) = -\sum_{i=1}^{n} \int_0^{x_i} b_i(\zeta_i) f_i'(\zeta_i) d\zeta_i + \frac{1}{2} \sum_{j,k=1}^{n} m_{jk} f_j(x_j) f_k(x_k) \tag{16}$$

under the constraints: $m_{ij} = m_{ji}$, $a_i(x_i) \geq 0$, $f_j(x_j) \geq 0$.

This Lyapunov–function can be taken as one for the boundary–layer system (STM–equation), if the LTM contribution S_i is considered as a fixed unknown parameter:

$$W(\mathbf{x},\mathbf{S}) = \sum_{j=1}^{N} \int_{0}^{x_j} a_j(\zeta_j) f_j'(\zeta_j) d\zeta_j - \sum_{j=1}^{N} B_j S_j \int_{0}^{x_j} f_j'(\zeta_j) d\zeta_j - \frac{1}{2}\sum_{j=1}^{N} D_{ij} f_j(x_j) f_k(x_k) \quad (17)$$

For the reduced-order system (LTM-equation) we can take as a Lyapunov-function:

$$V(\mathbf{S}) = \frac{1}{2}\mathbf{S}^T\mathbf{S} = \sum_{i=1}^{N} S_i^2 \quad (18)$$

The Lyapunov-function for the coupled STM and LTM dynamics is the sum of the two Lyapunov-function:

$$v(\mathbf{x},\mathbf{S}) = (1-d)V(\mathbf{S}) + dW(\mathbf{x},\mathbf{S}) \quad (19)$$

4 DESIGN OF STABLE COMPETITIVE NEURAL NETWORKS

Competitive neural networks with learning rules have moving equilibria during the learning process. The concept of asymptotic stability derived from matrix perturbation theory can capture this phenomenon.

We design in this section a competitive neural network that is able to store a desired pattern as a stable equilibrium.

The theoretical implications are illustrated in an example of a two neuron network.

Example: Let $N = 2$, $a_i = A$, $B_j = B$, $D_{ii} = \alpha > 0$, $D_{ij} = -\beta < 0$ and the nonlinearity be a linear function $f(x_j) = x_j$ in equations (1) and (2).

We get for the boundary-layer system:

$$\dot{x}_j = -Ax_j + \sum_{i=1}^{N} D_{ij} f(x_i) + BS_j \quad (20)$$

and for the reduced-order system:

$$\dot{S}_j = S_j[\frac{B}{A-\alpha} - 1] - \frac{C}{A-\alpha} \quad (21)$$

Then we get for the Lyapunov-functions:

$$V(\mathbf{S}) = \frac{1}{2}(S_1^2 + S_2^2) \quad (22)$$

and

$$W(\mathbf{x},\mathbf{S}) = \frac{A}{2}x_1^2 + \frac{A}{2}x_2^2 - BS_1x_1 - BS_2x_2 - \frac{1}{2}[\alpha x_1^2 + \alpha x_2^2 - 2\beta x_1 x_2] \quad (23)$$

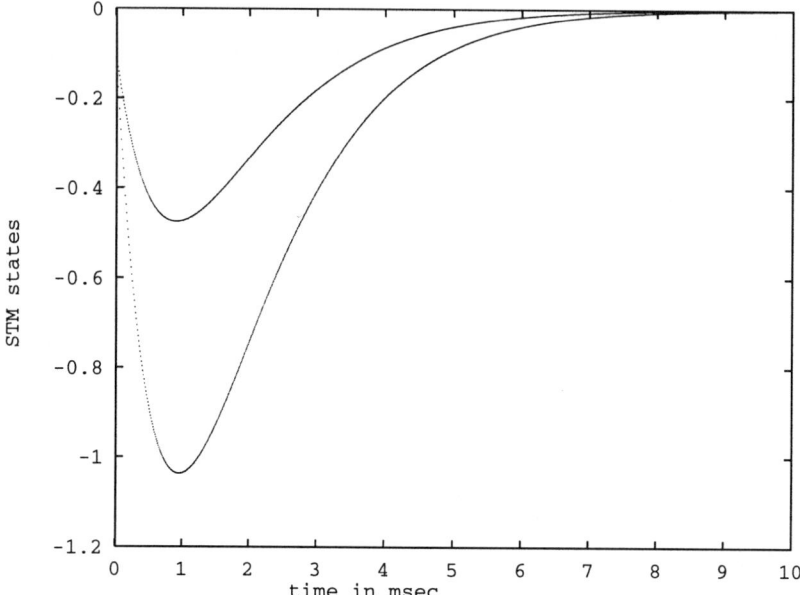

Figure 1: Time histories of the neural network with the origin as an equilibrium point: STM states.

For the nonnegative constants we get: $\alpha_1 = 1 - \frac{B}{A-\alpha}$, $\alpha_2 = (A-\alpha)^2$, $c_1 = \gamma = -B$, with $B < 0$, and $c_2 = \beta_1 = \beta_2 = 1$ and $K_1 = K_2 = 0$.

We get some interesting implications from the above results as: $A-\alpha > B$, $A-\alpha > 0$ and $B < 0$.

The above impications can be interpreted as follows: To achieve a stable equilibrium point $(0,0)$ we should have a negative contribution of the external stimulus term and the sum of the excitatory and inhibitory contribution of the neurons should be less than the time constant of a neuron. An evolution of the trajectories of the STM and LTM states for a two neuron system is shown in figure 1 and 2. The STM states exhibit first an oscillation from the expected equilibrium point, while the LTM states reach monotonically the equilibrium point. We can see from the pictures that the equilibrium point $(0,0)$ is reached after 5 msec by the STM- and LTM-states.

Choosing $B = -5$, $A = 1$ and $\alpha = 0.5$ we obtain for $\epsilon^*(d)$: $\epsilon^*(d) = \frac{11 \cdot 0.5^2}{55 + \frac{1}{4d(1-d)}}$. From the above formula we can see that $\epsilon^*(d)$ has a maximum at $d = d^* = 0.5$.

5 CONCLUSIONS

We presented in this paper a quadratic-type Lyapunov function for analyzing the stability of equilibrium points of competitive neural networks with fast and slow dynamics. This global stability analysis method is interpreting neural networks as nonlinear singularly perturbed systems. The equilibrium point is constrained to a neighborhood of $(0,0)$. This technique supposes a monotonically increasing non-linearity and a symmetric lateral inhibition matrix. The learning rule is a deterministic Hebbian. This method gives an upper bound on the perturbation

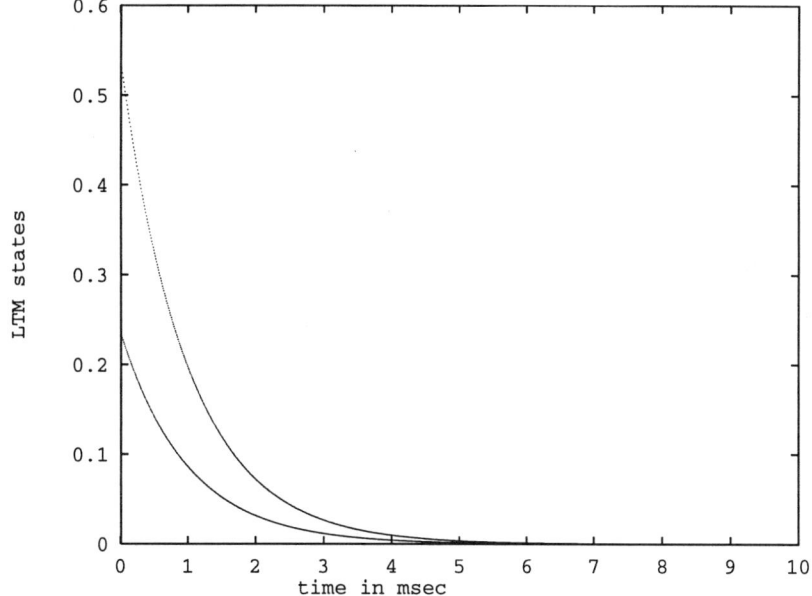

Figure 2: Time histories of the neural network with the origin as an equilibrium point: LTM states.

parameter and such an estimation of a maximal positive neural time-constant. The practical implication of the theoretical problem is the design of a competitive neural network that is able to store a desired pattern as a stable equilibrium.

References

[Ama82] S. Amari. *Competitive and cooperative aspects in dynamics of neural excitation and self-organization. Competition and cooperation in neural networks*, 20:1–28, 7 1982.

[Ama83] S. Amari. *Field theory of self-organizing neural nets. IEEE Transactions on systems, machines and communication*, SMC-13:741–748, 7 1983.

[CG83] A. M. Cohen und S. Grossberg. *Absolute Stability of Global Pattern Formation and Parallel Memory Storage by Competitive Neural Networks. IEEE Transactions on Systems, Man and Cybernetics*, SMC-13:815–826, 9 1983.

[Gro76] S. Grossberg. *Adaptive Pattern Classification and Universal Recording. Biological Cybernetics*, 23:121–134, 1 1976.

[Heb49] D. O. Hebb. *The Organization of Behavior*. J. Wiley Verlag, 1949.

[SK84] Ali Saberi und Hassan Khalil. *Quadratic-Type Lyapunov Functions for Singularly Perturbed Systems. IEEE Transactions on Automatic Control*, pp. 542–550, June 1984.

Examples of learning curves from a modified VC-formalism.

A. Kowalczyk & J. Szymański
Telstra Research Laboratories
770 Blackburn Road,
Clayton, Vic. 3168, Australia
{a.kowalczyk,j.szymanski}@trl.oz.au

P.L. Bartlett & R.C. Williamson
Department of Systems Engineering
Australian National University
Canberra, ACT 0200, Australia
{bartlett,williams}@syseng.anu.edu.au

Abstract

We examine the issue of evaluation of model specific parameters in a modified VC-formalism. Two examples are analyzed: the 2-dimensional homogeneous perceptron and the 1-dimensional higher order neuron. Both models are solved theoretically, and their learning curves are compared against true learning curves. It is shown that the formalism has the potential to generate a variety of learning curves, including ones displaying "phase transitions."

1 Introduction

One of the main criticisms of the Vapnik-Chervonenkis theory of learning [15] is that the results of the theory appear very loose when compared with empirical data. In contrast, theory based on statistical physics ideas [1] provides tighter numerical results as well as qualitatively distinct predictions (such as "phase transitions" to perfect generalization). (See [5, 14] for a fuller discussion.) A question arises as to whether the VC-theory can be modified to give these improvements. The general direction of such a modification is obvious: one needs to sacrifice the universality of the VC-bounds and introduce model (e.g. distribution) dependent parameters. This obviously can be done in a variety of ways. Some specific examples are VC-entropy [15], empirical VC-dimensions [16], efficient complexity [17] or (μ, C)-uniformity [8, 9] in a VC-formalism with error shells. An extension of the last formalism is of central interest to this paper. It is based on a refinement of the "fundamental theorem of computational learning" [2] and its main innovation is to split the set of partitions of a training sample into separate "error shells", each composed of error vectors corresponding to the different error values.

Such a split introduces a whole range of new parameters (the average number of patterns in each of a series of error shells) in addition to the VC dimension. The difficulty of determining these parameters then arises. There are some crude, "obvious" upper bounds on them which lead to both the VC-based estimates [2, 3, 15] and the statistical physics based formalism (with phase transitions) [5] as specific cases of this novel theory. Thus there is an obvious potential for improvement of the theory with tighter bounds. In particular we find that the introduction of a single parameter (order of uniformity), which in a sense determines shifts in relative sizes of error shells, leads to a full family of shapes of learning curves continuously ranging in behavior from decay proportional to the inverse of the training sample size to "phase transitions" (sudden drops) to perfect generalization in small training sample sizes. We present initial comparison of the learning curves from this new formalism with "true" learning curves for two simple neral networks.

2 Overview of the formalism

The presentation is set in the typical PAC-style; the notation follows [2]. We consider a space X of samples with a probability measure μ, a subspace H of binary functions $X \to \{0, 1\}$ (dichotomies) (called the *hypothesis space*) and a *target hypothesis* $t \in H$. For each $h \in H$ and each m-sample $\vec{x} = (x_1, ..., x_m) \in X^m$ ($m \in \{1, 2, ...\}$), we denote by $\epsilon_{h,\vec{x}} \stackrel{def}{=} \frac{1}{m} \sum_{i=1}^{m} |t-h|(x_i)$ the *empirical error* of h on $\vec{x}$, and by $\epsilon_h \stackrel{def}{=} \int_X |t-h|(x)\mu(dx)$ the *expected error* of $h \in H$.

For each $m \in \{1, 2, ...\}$ let us consider the random variable

$$\epsilon_H^{max}(\vec{x}) \stackrel{def}{=} \max_{h \in H} \{\epsilon_h \,;\, \epsilon_{h,\vec{x}} = 0\} \qquad (\vec{x} \in X^m) \tag{1}$$

defined as the maximal expected error of an hypothesis $h \in H$ consistent with t on $\vec{x}$. The *learning curve of* H, defined as the expected value of ϵ_H^{max},

$$\epsilon_H^{av}(m) \stackrel{def}{=} E_{X^m}[\epsilon_H^{max}] = \int_{X^m} \epsilon_H^{max}(\vec{x}) \mu^m(d\vec{x}) \qquad (\vec{x} \in X^m) \tag{2}$$

is of central interest to us. Upper bounds on it can be derived from basic PAC-estimates as follows. For $\epsilon \geq 0$ we denote by $H_\epsilon \stackrel{def}{=} \{h \in H \,;\, \epsilon_h \geq \epsilon\}$ the subset of ϵ-*bad hypotheses* and by

$$Q_\epsilon^m \stackrel{def}{=} \{\vec{x} \in X^m \,;\, \exists_{h \in H_\epsilon} \, \epsilon_{h,\vec{x}} = 0\} = \{\vec{x} \in X^m \,;\, \exists_{h \in H} \, \epsilon_{h,\vec{x}} = 0 \,\&\, \epsilon_h \geq \epsilon\} \tag{3}$$

the subset of m-samples for which there exists an ϵ-bad hypothesis consistent with the target t.

Lemma 1 *If $\mu^m(Q_\epsilon^m) \leq \psi(\epsilon, m)$, then $\epsilon_H^{av}(m) \leq \int_0^1 \min(1, \psi(\epsilon, m))\mu(d\epsilon)$, and equality in the assumption implies equality in the conclusion.* $\square$

Proof outline. If the assumption holds, then $\Psi(\epsilon, m) \stackrel{def}{=} 1 - \min(1, \psi(\epsilon, m))$ is a lower bound on the cumulative distribution of the random variable (1). Thus $E_{X^m}[\epsilon_H^{max}] \leq \int_0^1 \epsilon \frac{d}{d\epsilon} \Psi(\epsilon, m) d\epsilon$ and integration by parts yields the conclusion.
$\square$

Given $\vec{x} = (x_1, ..., x_m) \in X^m$, let us introduce the transformation (projection) $\pi_{t,\vec{x}} : H \to \{0, 1\}^m$ allocating to each $h \in H$ the vector

$$\pi_{t,\vec{x}}(h) \stackrel{def}{=} (|h(x_1) - t(x_1)|, ..., |h(x_m) - t(x_m)|)$$

called *the error pattern* of h on $\vec{x}$. For a subset $G \subset H$, let $\pi_{t,\vec{x}}(G) = \{\pi_{t,\vec{x}}(h) : h \in G\}$. The space $\{0, 1\}^m$ is the disjoint union of *error shells* $\mathcal{E}_i^m \stackrel{def}{=} \{(\xi_1, ..., \xi_m) \in \{0, 1\}^m \,;\, \xi_1 + \cdots + \xi_m = i\}$ for $i = 0, 1, ..., m$, and $|\pi_{t,\vec{x}}(H_\epsilon) \cap \mathcal{E}_i^m|$ is the number of different error patterns with i errors which can be obtained for $h \in H_\epsilon$. We shall employ the following notation for its average:

$$|H_\epsilon|_i^m \stackrel{def}{=} E_{X^m}[|\pi_{t,\vec{x}}(H_\epsilon) \cap \mathcal{E}_i^m|] = \int_{X^m} |\pi_{t,\vec{x}}(H_\epsilon) \cap \mathcal{E}_i^m| \mu^m(d\vec{x}). \qquad (4)$$

The central result of this paper, which gives a bound on the probability of the set Q_ϵ^m as in Lemma 1 in terms of $|H_\epsilon|_i^m$, will be given now. It is obtained by modification of the proof of [8, Theorem 1] which is a refinement of the proof of the "fundamental theorem of computational learning" in [2]. It is a simplified version (to the consistent learning case) of the basic estimate discussed in [9, 7].

Theorem 2 *For any integer $k \geq 0$ and $0 \leq \epsilon, \gamma \leq 1$*

$$\mu^m(Q_\epsilon^m) \leq A_{\epsilon,k,\gamma} \sum_{j \geq \gamma k}^{k} \binom{k}{j} \binom{m+k}{j}^{-1} |H_\epsilon|_j^{m+k}, \qquad (5)$$

where $A_{\epsilon,k,\gamma} \stackrel{def}{=} \left(1 - \sum_{j=0}^{\lfloor \gamma k \rfloor} \binom{k}{j} \epsilon^j (1-\epsilon)^{k-j}\right)^{-1}$, for $k > 0$ and $A_{\epsilon,0,\gamma} \stackrel{def}{=} 1$. □

Since error shells are disjoint we have the following relation:

$$\bar{P}_H(m) \stackrel{def}{=} 2^{-m} \int_{X^m} |\pi_{\vec{x}}(H)| \mu^m(d\vec{x}) = 2^{-m} \sum_{i=0}^{m} |H|_i^m \leq \Pi_H(m)/2^m \qquad (6)$$

where $\pi_{\vec{x}}(h) \stackrel{def}{=} \pi_{0,\vec{x}}(h)$, $|H|_i^m \stackrel{def}{=} |H_0|_i^m$ and $\Pi_H(m) \stackrel{def}{=} \max_{\vec{x} \in X^m} |\pi_{\vec{x}}(H)|$ is the growth function [2] of H. (Note that assuming that the target $t \equiv 0$ does not affect the cardinality of $\pi_{t,\vec{x}}(H)$.) If the VC-dimension of H, $d = d_{VC}(H)$, is finite, we have the well-known estimate [2]

$$\Pi_H(m) \leq \Phi(d,m) \stackrel{def}{=} \sum_{j=0}^{d} \binom{m}{j} \leq (em/d)^d. \qquad (7)$$

Corollary 3 *(i) If the VC-dimension d of H is finite and $m > 8/\epsilon$, then $\mu^m(Q_\epsilon^m) \leq 2^{2-m\epsilon/2}(2em/d)^d$.*

(ii) If H has finite cardinality, then $\mu^m(Q_\epsilon^m) \leq \sum_{h \in H_\epsilon}(1-\epsilon_h)^m$.

Proof. (i) Use the estimate $A_{\epsilon,k,\epsilon/2} \leq 2$ for $k \geq 8/\epsilon$ resulting from the Chernoff bound and set $\gamma = \epsilon/2$ and $k = m$ in (5). (ii) Substitute the following crude estimate:

$$|H_\epsilon|_i^m \leq \sum_{i=0}^{m} |H_\epsilon|_i^m \leq \sum_{i=0}^{m} |H|_i^m \leq P_H \leq (em/d)^d,$$

into the previous estimate. (iii) Set $k = 0$ into (i) and use the estimate

$$|H|_i^m \leq \sum_{h \in H_\epsilon} Pr_{X^m}(\epsilon_{h,\vec{x}} = i/m) = \sum_{h \in H_\epsilon} (1-\epsilon_h)^{m-i} \epsilon_h^i. \qquad □$$

The inequality in Corollary 3.i (ignoring the factor of 2) is the basic estimate of the VC-formalism (c.f. [2]); the inequality in Corollary 3.ii is the union bound which is the starting point for the statistical physics based formalism developed in [5]. In this sense both of these theories are unified in estimate (5) and all their conclusions (including the prediction

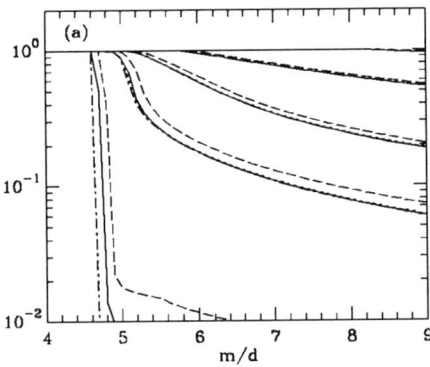
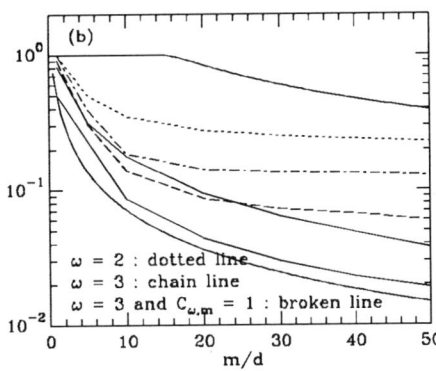

Figure 1: **(a)** Examples of upper bounds on the learning curves for the case of finite VC-dimension $d = d_{VC}(H)$ implied by Corollary 4.ii for $C_{\omega,m} \equiv$ const. They split into five distinct "bands" of four curves each, according to the values of the order of uniformity $\omega = 2, 3, 4, 5, 10$ (in the top-down order). Each band contains a solid line ($C_{\omega,m} \equiv 1, d = 100$), a dotted line ($C_{\omega,m} \equiv 100, d = 100$), a chain line ($C_{\omega,m} \equiv 1, d = 1000$) and a broken line ($C_{\omega,m} \equiv 100, d = 1000$).
(b) Various learning curves for the 2-dimensional homogeneous perceptron. Solid lines (top to bottom): *(i)* - for the VC-theory bound (Corollary 3.ii) with VC-dimension $d = 2$; *(ii)* - for the bound (for Eqn. 5 and Lemma 1) with $\gamma = \epsilon$, $k = m$ and the upper bounds $|H_\epsilon|_i^m \leq |H|_i^m = 2$ for $i = 1, ..., m-1$ and $|H_\epsilon|_i^m \leq |H|_i^m = 1$ for $i = 0, m$; *(iii)* - as in *(ii)* but with the exact values for $|H_\epsilon|_i^m$ as in (11); *(iv)* - true learning curve (Eqn. 13). The ω-uniformity bound for $\omega = 2$ (with the minimal $C_{\omega,m}$ satisfying (9), which turn out to be = const = 1) is shown by dotted line; for $\omega = 3$ the chain line gives the result for minimal $C_{\omega,m}$ and the broken line for $C_{\omega,m}$ set to 1.

of phase transitions to perfect generalization for the Ising perceptron for $\alpha = m/d < 1.448$ in the thermodynamic limit [5]) can be derived from this estimate, and possibly improved with the use of tighter estimates on $|H_\epsilon|_i^m$.

We now formally introduce a family of estimates on $|H_\epsilon|_i^m$ in order to discuss a potential of our formalism. For any m, ϵ and $\omega \geq 1.0$ there exists $C_{\omega,m} > 0$ such that

$$|H_\epsilon|_i^m \leq |H|_i^m \leq C_{\omega,m} \binom{m}{i} \bar{P}_H(m)^{1-|1-2i/m|^\omega} \qquad \text{(for } 0 \leq i \leq m\text{)}. \tag{8}$$

We shall call such an estimate *an ω-uniformity bound*.

Corollary 4 *(i)* If an ω-uniformity bound (8) holds, then

$$\mu^m(Q_\epsilon^m) \leq A_{\epsilon,m,\gamma} C_{\omega,m} \sum_{j \geq \gamma m}^{m} \binom{m}{j} \bar{P}_H(2m)^{1-|1-j/m|^\omega}; \tag{9}$$

(ii) if additionally $d = d_{VC}(H) < \infty$, then

$$\mu^m(Q_\epsilon^m) \leq A_{\epsilon,m,\gamma} C_{\omega,m} \sum_{j \geq \gamma m}^{m} \binom{m}{j} \left(2^{-2m}(2em/d)^d\right)^{1-|1-j/m|^\omega} . \square \tag{10}$$

3 Examples of learning curves

In this section we evaluate the above formalism on two examples of simple neural networks.

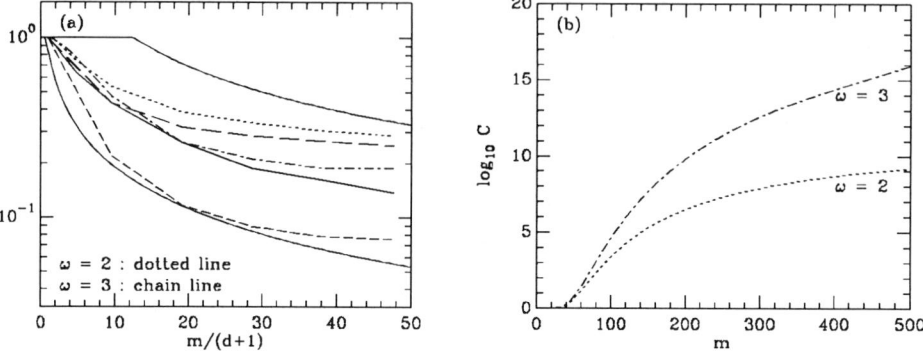

Figure 2: **(a)** Different learning curves for the higher order neuron (analogous to Fig. 1.b). Solid lines (top to bottom) *(i)* - for the VC-theory bound (Corollary 3.ii) with VC-dimension $d+1 = 21$; *(ii)* - for the bound (5) with $\gamma = \epsilon$ and the upper bounds $|H_\epsilon|_i^m \leq |H|_i^m$ with $|H|_i^m$ given by (15); *(iii)* - true learning curve (the upper bound given by (18)). The ω-uniformity bound/approximation are plotted as chain and dotted lines for the minimal $C_{\omega,m}$ satisfying (8), and as broken (long broken) line for $C_{\omega,m} = \text{const} = 1$ with $\omega = 2$ ($\omega = 3$). **(b)** Plots of the minimal value of $C_{\omega,m}$ satisfying condition of ω-uniformity bound (8) for higher order neuron and selected values of ω.

3.1 2-dimensional homogeneous perceptron

We consider $X \stackrel{def}{=} \mathbf{R}^2$ and H defined as the family of all functions $(\xi_1, \xi_2) \mapsto \theta(\xi_1 w_1 + \xi_2 w_2)$, where $(w_1, w_2) \in \mathbf{R}^2$ and $\theta(\tau)$ is defined as 1 if $\tau \geq 0$ and 0, otherwise, and the probability measure μ on $\mathbf{R}^2$ has rotational symmetry with respect to the origin. Fix an arbitrary target $t \in H$. In such a case

$$|H_\epsilon|_i^m = \begin{cases} 2(1-\epsilon)^m - (1-2\epsilon)^m & \text{(for } i=0 \text{ and } 0 \leq \epsilon \leq 1/2\text{)}, \\ 1 & \text{(for } i=m\text{)}, \\ 2\sum_{j=0}^{i} \binom{m}{j} \epsilon^j (1-\epsilon)^{m-j} & \text{(otherwise)}. \end{cases} \quad (11)$$

In particular we find that $|H|_i^m = 1$ for $i = 0, m$ and $|H|_i^m = 2$, otherwise, and

$$\bar{P}_H(m) = \sum_{i=0}^{m} |H|_i^m / 2^m = (1 + 2 + \cdots + 2 + 1)/2^m = m/2^{m-1}. \quad (12)$$

and the true learning curve is

$$\epsilon_H^{av}(m) = 1.5(m+1)^{-1}. \quad (13)$$

The latter expression results from Lemma 1 and the equality

$$\mu^m(Q_\epsilon^m) = \begin{cases} 2(1-\epsilon)^m - (1-2\epsilon)^m & \text{(for } 0 \leq \epsilon \leq 1/2\text{)}, \\ 2(1-\epsilon)^m & \text{(for } 1/2 < \epsilon \leq 1\text{)}, \end{cases} \quad (14)$$

Different learning curves (bounds and approximations) for homogeneous perceptron are plotted in Figure 1.b.

3.2 1-dimensional higher order neuron

We consider $X \stackrel{def}{=} [0,1] \subset \mathbf{R}$ with a continuous probability distribution μ. Define the hypothesis space $H \subset \{0,1\}^X$ as the set of all functions of the form $\theta \circ p(x)$ where p is a

Examples of Learning Curves from a Modified VC-formalism   349

polynomial of degree $\leq d$ on $\mathbf{R}$. Let the target be constant, $t \equiv 1$. It is easy to see that H restricted to a finite subset of $[0, 1]$ is exactly the restriction of the family of all functions $\tilde{H} \subset \{0, 1\}^{[0,1]}$ with up to d "jumps" from 0 to 1 or 1 to 0 and thus $d_{VC}(H) = d+1$. With probability 1 an m-sample $\vec{x} = (x_1, ..., x_m)$ from X^m is such that $x_i \neq x_j$ for $i \neq j$. For such a generic $\vec{x}$, $|\pi_{t,\vec{x}}(H) \cap \mathcal{E}_i^m| = const = |H|_i^m$. This observation was used to derive the following relations for the computation of $|H|_i^m$:

$$|H|_i^m = \sum_{\delta=0}^{\min(d, m-1)} |\tilde{H}^{(\delta)}|_i^m + |\tilde{H}^{(\delta)}|_{m-i}^m, \qquad (15)$$

for $0 \leq i \leq m$, where $|\tilde{H}^{(\delta)}|_i^m$, for $\delta = 0, 1, ..., d$, is defined as follows. We initialize $|\tilde{H}^{(0)}|_0^m = |\tilde{H}^{(1)}|_i^m \stackrel{def}{=} 1$ for $i = 1, ..., m-1$, $|\tilde{H}^{(1)}|_0^m = |\tilde{H}^{(1)}|_m^m \stackrel{def}{=} 0$ and $|\tilde{H}^{(\delta)}|_i^m \stackrel{def}{=} 0$ for $i = 0, 1, ..., m$, $\delta = 2, 3, ..., d$, and then, recurrently, for $\delta \geq 2$ we set $|\tilde{H}^{(\delta)}|_i^m \stackrel{def}{=} \sum_{k=\max(\delta, m-i)}^{m-1} |\tilde{H}^{(\delta-1)}|_{i-m+k}^k$ if δ is odd and $|\tilde{H}^{(\delta)}|_i^m \stackrel{def}{=} \sum_{k=\delta}^{m-1} |\tilde{H}^{(\delta-1)}|_i^k$ if δ is even. (Here $|\tilde{H}^{(\delta)}|_i^m$ is defined by the relation (4) with the target $t \equiv 1$ for the hypothesis space $H^{(\delta)} \subset \tilde{H}$ composed of functions having the value 1 near 0 and exactly δ jumps in $(0, 1)$, exactly at entries of $\vec{x}$; similarly as for H, $|H^{(\delta)}|_i^m = |\pi_{1,\vec{x}} H^{(\delta)} \cap \mathcal{E}_i^m|$ for a generic m-sample $\vec{x} \in (0, 1)^m$.)

Analyzing an embedding of $\mathbf{R}$ into $\mathbf{R}^d$, and using an argument based on the Vandermonde determinant as in [6, 13], it can be proved that the partition function Π_H is given by Cover's counting function [4], and that

$$\bar{P}_H(m) = \sum_{i=0}^{m} |H|_i^m / 2^m = \Pi_H(m)/2^m = 2 \sum_{i=0}^{d} \binom{m-1}{i} / 2^m. \qquad (16)$$

For the uniform distribution on $[0, 1]$ and a generic $\vec{x} \in [0, 1]^m$ let $\lambda_k(\vec{x})$ denote the sum of k largest segments of the partition of $[0, 1]$ into $m+1$ segments by the entries of $\vec{x}$. Then

$$\lambda_{\lfloor d/2 \rfloor}(\vec{x}) \leq \epsilon_H^{max}(\vec{x}) \leq \lambda_{\lfloor d/2 \rfloor + 1}(\vec{x}). \qquad (17)$$

An explicit expression for the expected value of λ_k is known [11], thus a very tight bound on the true learning curve $\epsilon_H^{av}(m)$ defined by (2) can be obtained:

$$\frac{\lfloor d/2 \rfloor}{m+1}\left(1 + \sum_{j=\lfloor d/2 \rfloor + 1}^{m+1} \frac{1}{j}\right) \leq \epsilon_H^{av}(m) \leq \frac{\lfloor d/2 \rfloor + 1}{m+1}\left(1 + \sum_{j=\lfloor d/2 \rfloor + 2}^{m+1} \frac{1}{j}\right). \qquad (18)$$

Numerical results are shown in Figure 2.

4 Discussion and conclusions

The basic estimate (5) of Theorem 1 has been used to produce upper bounds on the learning curve (via Lemma 1) in three different ways: (i) using the exact values of coefficients $|H_\epsilon|_i^m$ (Fig. 1a), (ii) using the estimate $|H_\epsilon|_i^m \leq |H|_i^m$ and the values of $|H|_i^m$ and (iii) using the ω-uniformity bound (8) with minimal value of $C_{\omega,m}$ and as an "approximation" with $C_{\omega,m} = const = 1$. Both examples of simple learning tasks considered in the paper allowed us to compare these results with the true learning curves (or their tight bounds) which can serve as benchmarks.

Figure 1.a implies that values of parameter ω in the ω-uniformity bound (approximation) governing a distribution of error patterns between different error shells (c.f. [10]) has a significant impact on learning curve shapes, changing from slow decrease to rapid jumps ("phase transitions") in generalization.

Figure 1.b proves that one loses tightness of the bound by using $|H|_i^m$ rather than $|H_\epsilon|_i^m$, and even more is lost if ω-uniformity bounds (with variable $C_{\omega,m}$) are employed. Inspecting Figures 1.b and 2.a we find that approximate approaches consisting of replacing $|H_\epsilon|_i^m$ by a simple estimate (ω-uniformity) can produce learning curves very close to $|H|_i^m$-learning curves suggesting that an application of this formalism to learning systems where neither $|H_\epsilon|_i^m$ nor $|H|_i^m$ can by calculated might be possible. This could lead to a sensible approximate theory capturing at least certain qualitative properties of learning curves for more complex learning tasks.

Generally, the results of this paper show that by incorporating the limited knowledge of the statistical distribution of error patterns in the sample space one can dramatically improve bounds on the learning curve with respect to the classical universal estimates of the VC-theory. This is particularly important for "practical" training sample sizes ($m \leq 12\times$ VC-dimension) where the VC-bounds are void.

Acknowledgement. The permission of Director, Telstra Research Laboratories, to publish this paper is gratefully acknowledged. A.K. acknowledges the support of the Australian Research Council.

References

[1] S. Amari, N. Fujita, and S. Shinomoto. Four types of learning curves. *Neural Computation*, 4(4):605–618, 1992.

[2] M. Anthony and N. Biggs. *Computational Learning Theory*. Cambridge University Press, 1992.

[3] A. Blumer, A. Ehrenfeucht, D. Haussler, and M.K. Warmuth. Learnability and the Vapnik-Chervonenkis dimensions. *Journal of the ACM*, **36**:929–965, (Oct. 1989).

[4] T.M. Cover. Geometrical and statistical properties of linear inequalities with applications to pattern recognition. *IEEE Trans. Elec. Comp.*, **EC-14**:326–334, 1965.

[5] D. Haussler, M. Kearns, H.S. Seung, and N. Tishby. Rigorous learning curve bounds from statistical mechanics. In *Proc. 7th Ann. ACM Conf. on Comp. Learn. Theory*, pages 76–87, 1994.

[6] A. Kowalczyk. Estimates of storage capacity of multi-layer perceptron with threshold logic hidden units. *Neural Networks*, to appear.

[7] A. Kowalczyk. VC-formalism with explicit bounds on error shells size distribution. A manuscript, 1994.

[8] A. Kowalczyk and H. Ferra. Generalisation in feedforward networks. *Adv. in NIPS 7, The MIT Press*, Cambridge, 1995.

[9] A. Kowalczyk, J. Szymanski, and H. Ferra. Combining statistical physics with VC-bounds on generalisation in learning systems. In *Proc. ACNN'95*, Sydney, 1995. University of Sydney.

[10] A. Kowalczyk, J. Szymanski, and R.C. Williamson. Learning curves from a modified vc-formalism: a case study. In *Proceedings of ICNN'95, Perth (CD-ROM)*, volume VI, pages 2939–2943, Rundle Mall, South Australia, 1995. IEEE/Causal Production.

[11] J.G. Mauldon. Random division of an interval. *Proc. Cambridge Phil. Soc.*, **47**:331–336, 1951.

[12] K.R. Muller, M. Finke, N. Murata, and S. Amari. On large scale simulations for learning curves. In *Proc. ACNN'95*, pages 45–48, Sydney, 1995. University of Sydney.

[13] A. Sakurai. n-h-1 networks store no less $n\ h + 1$ examples but sometimes no more. In *Proceedings of the 1992 International Conference on Neural Networks*, pages III-936–III-941. IEEE, June 1992.

[14] H. Sompolinsky, H.S. Seung, and N. Tishby. Statistical mechanics of learning curves. *Physical Reviews*, **A45**:6056–6091, 1992.

[15] V. Vapnik. *Estimation of Dependences Based on Empirical Data*. Springer-Verlag, 1982.

[16] V. Vapnik, E. Levin, and Y. Le Cun. Measuring the VC-dimension of a learning machine. *Neural Computation*, **6** (5):851–876, 1994.

[17] C. Wang and S.S. Venkantesh. Temporal dynamics of generalisation in neural networks. *Adv. in NIPS 7, The MIT Press*, Cambridge, 1995.

Bayesian Methods for Mixtures of Experts

Steve Waterhouse
Cambridge University
Engineering Department
Cambridge CB2 1PZ
England
Tel: [+44] 1223 332754
srw1001@eng.cam.ac.uk

David MacKay
Cavendish Laboratory
Madingley Rd.
Cambridge CB3 0HE
England
Tel: [+44] 1223 337238
mackay@mrao.cam.ac.uk

Tony Robinson
Cambridge University
Engineering Department
Cambridge CB2 1PZ
England.
Tel: [+44] 1223 332815
ajr@eng.cam.ac.uk

ABSTRACT

We present a Bayesian framework for inferring the parameters of a mixture of experts model based on ensemble learning by variational free energy minimisation. The Bayesian approach avoids the over-fitting and noise level under-estimation problems of traditional maximum likelihood inference. We demonstrate these methods on artificial problems and sunspot time series prediction.

INTRODUCTION

The task of estimating the parameters of adaptive models such as artificial neural networks using Maximum Likelihood (ML) is well documented eg. Geman, Bienenstock & Doursat (1992). ML estimates typically lead to models with high variance, a process known as "over-fitting". ML also yields over-confident predictions; in regression problems for example, ML underestimates the noise level. This problem is particularly dominant in models where the ratio of the number of data points in the training set to the number of parameters in the model is low. In this paper we consider inference of the parameters of the hierarchical mixture of experts (HME) architecture (Jordan & Jacobs 1994). This model consists of a series of "experts," each modelling different processes assumed to be underlying causes of the data. Since each expert may focus on a different subset of the data which may be arbitrarily small, the possibility of over-fitting of each process is increased. We use Bayesian methods (MacKay 1992a) to avoid over-fitting by specifying prior belief in various aspects of the model and marginalising over parameter uncertainty.

The use of regularisation or "weight decay" corresponds to the prior assumption that the model should have smooth outputs. This is equivalent to a prior $P(\theta|\alpha)$ on the parameters θ of the model, where α are the *hyperparameters* of the prior. Given a set of priors we may specify a *posterior* distribution of the parameters given data D,

$$P(\theta|D, \alpha, \mathcal{H}) \propto P(D|\theta, \mathcal{H})P(\theta|\alpha, \mathcal{H}), \tag{1}$$

where the variable $\mathcal{H}$ encompasses the assumptions of model architecture, type of regularisation used and assumed noise model. Maximising the posterior gives us the *most probable* parameters θ_{MP}. We may then set the hyperparameters either by cross-validation, or by finding the maximum of the posterior distribution of the hyperparameters $P(\alpha|D)$, also known as the "evidence" (Gull 1989). In this paper we describe a method, motivated by the Expectation Maximisation (EM) algorithm of Dempster, Laird & Rubin (1977) and the principle of ensemble learning by variational free energy minimisation (Hinton & van Camp 1993, Neal & Hinton 1993) which achieves simultaneous optimisation of the parameters *and* hyperparameters of the HME. We then demonstrate this algorithm on two simulated examples and a time series prediction task. In each task the use of the Bayesian methods prevents over-fitting of the data and gives better prediction performance. Before we describe this algorithm, we will specify the model and its associated priors.

MIXTURES OF EXPERTS

The mixture of experts architecture (Jordan & Jacobs 1994) consists of a set of "experts" which perform local function approximation. The expert outputs are combined by a "gate" to form the overall output. In the hierarchical case, the experts are themselves mixtures of further experts, thus extending the network in a tree structured fashion. The model is a generative one in which we assume that data are generated in the domain by a series of J independent processes which are selected in a stochastic manner. We specify a set of *indicator* variables $Z = \{z_j^{(n)} : j = 1 \ldots J, n = 1 \ldots N\}$, where $z_j^{(n)}$ is 1 if the output $y^{(n)}$ was generated by expert j and zero otherwise. Consider the case of regression over a data set $D = \{x^{(n)} \in \Re^k, y^{(n)} \in \Re^p, n = 1 \ldots N\}$ with $p = 1$. We specify that the conditional probability of the scalar output $y^{(n)}$ given the input vector $x^{(n)}$ at exemplar (n) is

$$P(y^{(n)}|x^{(n)}, \theta) = \sum_{j=1}^{J} P(z_j^{(n)}|x^{(n)}, \xi_j) P(y^{(n)}|x^{(n)}, \mathbf{w}_j, \beta_j), \qquad (2)$$

where $\{\xi_j \in \Re^k\}$ is the set of gate parameters, and $\{(\mathbf{w}_j \in \Re^k), \beta_j\}$ the set of expert parameters. In this case, $P(y^{(n)}|x^{(n)}, \mathbf{w}_j, \beta_j)$ is a Gaussian:

$$\phi_j^{(n)} \equiv P(y^{(n)}|x^{(n)}, \mathbf{w}_j, \beta_j) = \left(\frac{2\pi}{\beta_j}\right)^{-\frac{1}{2}} \exp\left(-\frac{\beta_j}{2}\left(y^{(n)} - \hat{y}_j^{(n)}\right)^2\right), \qquad (3)$$

where $1/\beta_j$ is the variance of expert j,[1] and $\hat{y}_j^{(n)} = f_j(x^{(n)}, \mathbf{w}_j)$ is the output of expert j, giving a probabilistic mixture model. In this paper we restrict the expert output to be a linear function of the input, $f_j(x^{(n)}, \mathbf{w}_j) = \mathbf{w}_j^T x^{(n)}$. We model the action of selecting process j with the gate, the outputs of which are given by the softmax function of the inner products of the input vector[2] and the gate parameter vectors. The conditional probability of selecting expert j given input $x^{(n)}$ is thus:

$$g_j^{(n)} \equiv P(z_j^{(n)} = 1|x^{(n)}, \xi_j) = \exp(\xi_j^T x^{(n)}) \bigg/ \sum_{i=1}^{J} \exp(\xi_i^T x^{(n)}) \qquad (4)$$

A straightforward extension of this model also gives us the conditional probability $h_j^{(n)}$ of expert j having been selected given input $x^{(n)}$ and output $y^{(n)}$,

$$h_j^{(n)} \equiv P(z_j^{(n)} = 1|y^{(n)}, x^{(n)}, \theta) = g_j^{(n)} \phi_j^{(n)} \bigg/ \sum_{i=1}^{J} g_i^{(n)} \phi_i^{(n)} . \qquad (5)$$

---

[1] Although β_j is a parameter of expert j, in common with MacKay (1992a) we consider it as a hyperparameter on the Gaussian noise prior.

[2] In all notation, we assume that the input vector is augmented by a constant term, which avoids the need to specify a "bias" term in the parameter vectors.

PRIORS

We assume a separable prior on the parameters θ of the model:

$$P(\theta|\alpha) = \prod_{j=1}^{J} P(\xi_j|\mu)P(\mathbf{w}_j|\alpha_j) \qquad (6)$$

where $\{\alpha_j\}$ and $\{\mu\}$ are the hyperparameters for the parameter vectors of the experts and the gate respectively. We assume Gaussian priors on the parameters of the experts $\{\mathbf{w}_j\}$ and the gate $\{\xi_j\}$, for example:

$$P(\mathbf{w}_j|\alpha_j) = \left(\frac{\alpha_j}{2\pi}\right)^{\frac{k}{2}} \exp\left(-\frac{\alpha_j}{2}\mathbf{w}_j^T\mathbf{w}_j\right) \qquad (7)$$

For simplicity of notation, we shall refer to the set of all smoothness hyperparameters as $\alpha = \{\mu, \alpha_j\}$ and the set of all noise level hyperparameters as $\beta = \{\beta_j\}$.

Finally, we assume Gamma priors on the hyperparameters $\{\mu, \alpha_j, \beta_j\}$ of the priors, for example:

$$P(\log \beta_j | \rho_\beta, v_\beta) = \frac{1}{\Gamma(\rho_\beta)} \left(\frac{\beta_j}{v_\beta}\right)^{\rho_\beta} \exp(-\beta_j / v_\beta), \qquad (8)$$

where v_β, ρ_β are the *hyper*-hyperparameters which specify the range in which we expect the noise levels β_j to lie.

INFERRING PARAMETERS USING ENSEMBLE LEARNING

The EM algorithm was used by Jordan & Jacobs (1994) to train the HME in a maximum likelihood framework. In the EM algorithm we specify a complete data set $\{D, Z\}$ which includes the observed data D and the set of indicator variables Z. Given $\theta^{(m-1)}$, the E step of the EM algorithm computes a distribution $P(Z|D, \theta^{(m-1)})$ over Z. The M step then maximises the expected value of the *complete* data likelihood $P(D, Z|\theta)$ over this distribution. In the case of the HME, the indicator variables $Z = \{\{z_j^{(n)}\}_{j=1}^{J}\}_{n=1}^{N}$ specify which expert was responsible for generating the data at each time.

We now outline an algorithm for the simultaneous optimisation of the parameters θ and hyperparameters α and β, using the framework of ensemble learning by variational free energy minimisation (Hinton & van Camp 1993). Rather than optimising a point estimate of θ, α and β, we optimise a distribution over these parameters. This builds on Neal & Hinton's (1993) description of the EM algorithm in terms of variational free energy minimisation.

We first specify an approximating *ensemble* $Q(\mathbf{w}, \xi, \alpha, \beta, Z)$ which we optimise so that it approximates the posterior distribution $P(\mathbf{w}, \xi, \alpha, \beta, Z|D, \mathcal{H})$ well. The objective function chosen to measure the quality of the approximation is the *variational free energy*,

$$F(Q) = \int d\mathbf{w}\, d\xi\, d\alpha\, d\beta\, dZ\, Q(\mathbf{w}, \xi, \alpha, \beta, Z) \log \frac{Q(\mathbf{w}, \xi, \alpha, \beta, Z)}{P(\mathbf{w}, \xi, \alpha, \beta, Z, D|\mathcal{H})}, \qquad (9)$$

where the joint probability of parameters $\{\mathbf{w}, \xi\}$, hyperparameters, $\{\alpha, \beta\}$, missing data Z and observed data D is given by,

$$P(\mathbf{w}, \xi, \alpha, \beta, Z, D|\mathcal{H}) =$$

$$P(\mu)\prod_{j=1}^{J} P(\xi_j|\mu)P(\alpha_j)P(\mathbf{w}_j|\alpha_j)P(\beta_j|\rho_j, v_j) \prod_{n=1}^{N} \left(P(z_j^{(n)} = 1|\mathbf{x}^{(n)}, \xi_j)P(y^{(n)}|\mathbf{x}^{(n)}, \mathbf{w}_j, \beta_j)\right)^{z_j^{(n)}} \quad (10)$$

The free energy can be viewed as the sum of the negative log evidence $-\log P(D|\mathcal{H})$ and the Kullback-Leibler divergence between Q and $P(\mathbf{w}, \xi, \alpha, \beta, Z|D, \mathcal{H})$. F is bounded below by $-\log P(D|\mathcal{H})$, with equality when $Q = P(\mathbf{w}, \xi, \alpha, \beta, Z|D, \mathcal{H})$.

We constrain the approximating ensemble Q to be separable in the form $Q(\mathbf{w}, \xi, \alpha, \beta, Z) = Q(\mathbf{w})Q(\xi)Q(\alpha)Q(\beta)Q(Z)$. We find the optimal separable distribution Q by considering separately the optimisation of F over each separate ensemble component $Q(\cdot)$ with all other components fixed.

Optimising $Q_w(\mathbf{w})$ and $Q_\xi(\xi)$.

As a functional of $Q_w(\mathbf{w})$, F is

$$F = \int d\mathbf{w}\, Q_w(\mathbf{w}) \left[\sum_j \frac{\bar{\alpha}_j}{2} \mathbf{w}_j^T \mathbf{w}_j + \sum_{n=1}^{N} \bar{z}_j^{(n)} \frac{\bar{\beta}_j}{2} (y^{(n)} - \hat{y}_j^{(n)})^2 + \log Q_w(\mathbf{w})\right] + \text{const} \quad (11)$$

where for any variable a, $\bar{a}$ denotes $\int da\, Q(a)\, a$. Noting that the $\mathbf{w}$ dependent terms are the log of a posterior distribution and that a divergence $\int Q \log(Q/\tilde{P})$ is minimised by setting $Q = \tilde{P}$, we can write down the distribution $Q_w(\mathbf{w})$ that minimises this expression. For given data and $Q_\alpha, Q_\beta, Q_z, Q_\xi$, the optimising distribution $Q_w^{\text{opt}}(\mathbf{w})$ is

$$Q_w^{\text{opt}}(\mathbf{w}) = \prod_j Q_{w_j}^{\text{opt}}(w_j) = \prod_j \exp\left(-\frac{\bar{\alpha}_j}{2} \mathbf{w}_j^T \mathbf{w}_j - \sum_n \bar{z}_j^{(n)} \frac{\bar{\beta}_j}{2} (y^{(n)} - \hat{y}_j^{(n)})^2\right) \Big/ \text{const} \quad (12)$$

This is a set of J Gaussian distributions with means $\{\bar{w}_j\}$, which can be found exactly by quadratic optimisation. We denote the variance covariance matrices of $Q_{w_j}^{\text{opt}}(\mathbf{w}_j)$ by $\{\Sigma_{w_j}\}$. The analogous expression for the gates $Q_\xi^{\text{opt}}(\xi)$ is obtained in a similar fashion and is given by

$$Q_\xi^{\text{opt}}(\xi) = \prod_j Q_{\xi_j}^{\text{opt}}(\xi_j) = \prod_j \exp\left(-\frac{\bar{\mu}_j}{2} \xi_j^T \xi_j + \sum_n \bar{z}_j^{(n)} \log g_j^{(n)}\right) \Big/ \text{const.} \quad (13)$$

We approximate each $Q_{\xi_j}^{\text{opt}}(\xi_j)$ by a Gaussian distribution fitted at its maximum $\xi_j = \bar{\xi}_j$ with variance covariance matrix Σ_{ξ_j}.

Optimising $Q_z(Z)$

By a similar procedure, the optimal distribution $Q_z^{\text{opt}}(Z)$ is given by

$$Q_z^{\text{opt}}(Z) = \prod_n \prod_j \left\{ \exp(s_j^{(n)}) \Big/ \sum_{i=1}^{J} \exp(s_i^{(n)}) \right\} \quad (14)$$

$$\text{where} \quad s_j^{(n)} = \bar{\xi}_j^T \mathbf{x}^{(n)} - \frac{\bar{\beta}_j}{2}\left[(y^{(n)} - \hat{y}_j^{(n)}(\mathbf{w}_j^{MP}))^2 + \mathbf{x}^{(n)} \Sigma_{w_j}^{-1} \mathbf{x}^{(n)}\right] \quad (15)$$

and $\bar{\xi}_j$ is the value of ξ_j computed above. The standard E-step gives us a distribution of Z given a fixed value of parameters and the data, as shown in equation (5). In this case, by finding the optimal $Q_z(Z)$ we obtain the alternative expression of (15), with dependencies on the uncertainty of the experts' predictions. Ideally (if we did not made the assumption of a separable distribution Q) Q_z might be expected to contain an additional effect of the uncertainty in the gate parameters. We can introduce this by the method of MacKay (1992b) for marginalising classifiers, in the case of binary gates.

Optimising $Q_\alpha(\alpha)$ and $Q_\beta(\beta)$

Finally, for the hyperparameter distributions, the optimal values of ensemble functions give values for α_j and β_j as

$$\frac{1}{\bar{\alpha}_j} = \frac{\mathbf{w}_j^T \mathbf{w}_j + 2/v_{\alpha_j} + \text{Trace}\Sigma_{\mathbf{w}_j}}{k + 2\rho_{\alpha_j}}, \quad \frac{1}{\bar{\beta}_j} = \frac{\sum_n \left[\bar{z}_j^{(n)}(y^{(n)} - \hat{y}_j^{(N+1)})^2 + \mathbf{x}^{(n)T}\Sigma_{\mathbf{w}_j}\mathbf{x}^{(n)}\right] + 2/v_{\beta_j}}{\sum_n \bar{z}_j^{(n)} + 2\rho_{\beta_j}}. \quad (16)$$

An analogous procedure is used to set the hyperparameters $\{\mu\}$ of the gate.

MAKING PREDICTIONS

In order to make predictions using the model, we must *marginalise* over the parameters and hyperparameters to get the predictive distribution. We use the optimal distributions $Q^{\text{opt}}(\cdot)$ to approximate the posterior distribution.

For the experts, the marginalised outputs are given by $\tilde{y}_j^{(N+1)} = f_j(\mathbf{x}^{(N+1)}, \mathbf{w}_j^{MP})$, with variance $\sigma^2_{y|\alpha_j,\beta_j} = \mathbf{x}^{(N+1)T}\Sigma_{\mathbf{w}_j}\mathbf{x}^{(N+1)} + \sigma_j^2$, where $\sigma_j^2 = 1/\bar{\beta}_j$. We may also marginalise over the gate parameters (MacKay 1992b) to give marginalised outputs for the gates. The predictive distribution is then a mixture of Gaussians, with mean and variance given by its first and second moments,

$$\tilde{y}^{(N+1)} = \sum_{i=1}^{J} g_i^{(N+1)} \tilde{y}_i^{(N+1)}; \quad \sigma^2_{y|\alpha,\beta} = \sum_{i=1}^{J} g_i^{(N+1)}(\sigma^2_{y|\alpha_i,\beta_i} + (\tilde{y}_i^{(N+1)})^2) - (\tilde{y}^{(N+1)})^2. \quad (17)$$

SIMULATIONS
Artificial Data

In order to test the performance of the Bayesian method, we constructed two artificial data sets. Both data sets consist of a known function corrupted by additive zero mean Gaussian noise. The first data set, shown in Figure (1a) consists of 100 points from a piecewise linear function in which the leftmost portion is corrupted with noise of variance 3 times greater than the rightmost portion. The second data set, shown in Figure (1b) consists of 100 points from the function $g(t) = 4.26(e^{-t} - 4e^{-2t} + 3e^{-3t})$, corrupted by Gaussian noise of constant variance 0.44. We trained a number of models on these data sets, and they provide a typical set of results for the maximum likelihood and Bayesian methods, together with the error bars on the Bayesian solutions. The model architecture used was a 6 deep binary hierarchy of linear experts. In both cases, the ML solutions tend to overfit the noise in the data set. The Bayesian solutions, on the other hand, are both smooth functions which are better approximations to the underlying functions.

Time Series Prediction

The Bayesian method was also evaluated on a time series prediction problem. This consists of yearly readings of sunspot activity from 1700 to 1979, and was first

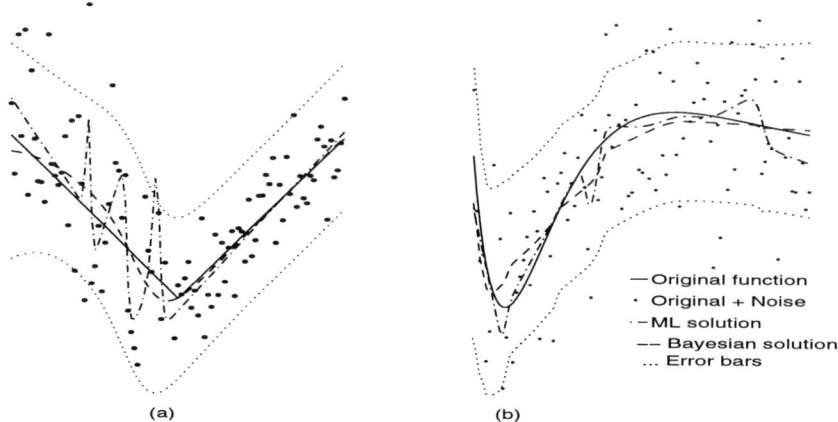

Figure 1: The effect of regularisation on fitting known functions corrupted with noise.

considered in the connectionist community by Weigend, Huberman & Rumelhart (1990), who used an MLP with 8 hidden tanh units, to predict the coming year's activity based on the activities of the previous 12 years. This data set was chosen since it consists of a relatively small number of examples and thus the probability of over-fitting sizeable models is large. In previous work, we considered the use of a mixture of 7 experts on this problem. Due to the problems of over-fitting inherent in ML however, we were constrained to using cross validation to stop the training early. This also constrained the selection of the model order, since the branches of deep networks tend to become "pinched off" during ML training, resulting in local minima during training. The Bayesian method avoids this over-fitting of the gates and allows us to use very large models.

Table 1: Single step prediction on the Sunspots data set using a lag vector of 12 years. NMSE is the mean squared prediction error normalised by the variance of the entire record from 1700 to 1979. The models used were; WHR: Weigend et al's MLP result; 1HME_7_CV: mixture of 7 experts trained via maximum likelihood and using a 10 % cross validation scheme; 8HME2_ML & 8HME2_Bayes: 8 deep binary HME,trained via maximum likelihood (ML) and Bayesian method (Bayes).

MODEL	Train NMSE	Test NMSE	
	1700-1920	1921-1955	1956-1979
WHR	0.082	0.086	0.35
1HME7_CV	0.061	0.089	0.27
8HME2_ML	0.052	0.162	0.41
8HME2_Bayes	0.079	0.089	0.26

Table 1 shows the results obtained using a variety of methods on the sunspots task. The Bayesian method performs significantly better on the test sets than the maximum likelihood method (8HME2_ML), and is competitive with the MLP of Weigend et al (WHR). It should be noted that even though the number of parameters in the 8 deep binary HME (4992) used is much larger than the number of training examples (209), the Bayesian method still avoids over-fitting of the data. This allows us to specify large models and avoids the need for prior architecture selection, although in some cases such selection may be advantageous, for example if the number of processes inherent in the data is known *a-priori*.

In our experience with linear experts, the smoothness prior on the output function of the expert does not have an important effect; the prior on the gates and the Bayesian inference of the noise level are the important factors. We expect that the smoothness prior would become more important if the experts used more complex basis functions.

DISCUSSION

The EM algorithm is a special case of the ensemble learning algorithm presented here: the EM algorithm is obtained if we constrain $Q_\Theta(\Theta)$ and $Q_\beta(\beta)$ to be delta functions and fix $\alpha = 0$. The Bayesian ensemble works better because it includes regularization and because the uncertainty of the parameters is taken into account when predictions are made. It could be of interest in future work to investigate how other models trained by EM could benefit from the ensemble learning approach such as hidden Markov models.

The Bayesian method of avoiding over-fitting has been shown to lend itself naturally to the mixture of experts architecture. The Bayesian approach can be implemented practically with only a small computational overhead and gives significantly better performance than the ML model.

References

Dempster, A. P., Laird, N. M. & Rubin, D. B. (1977), 'Maximum likelihood from incomplete data via the EM algorithm', *Journal of the Royal Statistical Society, Series B* **39**, 1–38.

Geman, S., Bienenstock, E. & Doursat, R. (1992), 'Neural networks and the bias / variance dilemma', *Neural Computation* **5**, 1–58.

Gull, S. F. (1989), Developments in maximum entropy data analysis, *in* J. Skilling, ed., 'Maximum Entropy and Bayesian Methods, Cambridge 1988', Kluwer, Dordrecht, pp. 53–71.

Hinton, G. E. & van Camp, D. (1993), Keeping neural networks simple by minimizing the description length of the weights, To appear in: *Proceedings of COLT-93*.

Jordan, M. I. & Jacobs, R. A. (1994), 'Hierarchical Mixtures of Experts and the EM algorithm', *Neural Computation* **6**, 181–214.

MacKay, D. J. C. (1992*a*), 'Bayesian interpolation', *Neural Computation* **4**(3), 415–447.

MacKay, D. J. C. (1992*b*), 'The evidence framework applied to classification networks', *Neural Computation* **4**(5), 698–714.

Neal, R. M. & Hinton, G. E. (1993), 'A new view of the EM algorithm that justifies incremental and other variants'. Submitted to Biometrika. Available at URL:ftp://ftp.cs.toronto.edu/pub/radford/www.

Weigend, A. S., Huberman, B. A. & Rumelhart, D. E. (1990), 'Predicting the future: a connectionist approach', *International Journal of Neural Systems* **1**, 193–209.

Some results on convergent unlearning algorithm

Serguei A. Semenov & Irina B. Shuvalova
Institute of Physics and Technology
Prechistenka St. 13/7
Moscow 119034, Russia

Abstract

In this paper we consider probabilities of different asymptotics of convergent unlearning algorithm for the Hopfield-type neural network (Plakhov & Semenov, 1994) treating the case of unbiased random patterns. We show also that failed unlearning results in total memory breakdown.

1 INTRODUCTION

In the past years the unsupervised learning schemes arose strong interest among researchers but for the time being a little is known about underlying learning mechanisms, as well as still less rigorous results like convergence theorems were obtained in this field. One of promising concepts along this line is so called "unlearning" for the Hopfield-type neural networks (Hopfield et al, 1983, van Hemmen & Klemmer, 1992, Wimbauer et al, 1994). Elaborating that elegant ideas the convergent unlearning algorithm has recently been proposed (Plakhov & Semenov, 1994), executing without patterns presentation. It is aimed at to correct initial Hebbian connectivity in order to provide extensive storage of arbitrary correlated data.

This algorithm is stated as follows. Pick up at iteration step m, $m = 0, 1, 2, \ldots$ a random network state $S^{(m)} = (S_1^{(m)}, \ldots, S_N^{(m)})$, with the values $S_i^{(m)} = \pm 1$ having equal probability 1/2, calculate local fields generated by $S^{(m)}$

$$h_i^{(m)} = \sum_{i=1}^{N} J_{ij}^{(m)} S_j^{(m)}, \quad i = 1, \ldots, N,$$

and then update the synaptic weights by

$$J_{ij}^{(m+1)} = J_{ij}^{(m)} - \varepsilon N^{-1} h_i^{(m)} h_j^{(m)}, \quad i, j = 1, \ldots, N. \tag{1}$$

Some Results on Convergent Unlearning Algorithm

Here $\varepsilon > 0$ stands for the unlearning strength parameter. We stress that self-interactions, J_{ii}, are necessarily involved in the iteration process. The initial condition for (1) is given by the Hebb matrix, $J_{ij}^{(0)} = J_{ij}^H$:

$$J_{ij}^H = N^{-1} \sum_{\mu=1}^{p} \xi_i^\mu \xi_j^\mu \qquad (2)$$

with arbitrary (± 1)-patterns ξ^μ, $\mu = 1, \ldots, p$.

For $\varepsilon < \varepsilon_c$, the (rescaled) synaptic matrix has been proven to converge with probability one to the projection one on the linear subspace spanned by maximal subset of linearly independent patterns (Plakhov & Semenov, 1994). As the sufficient condition for that convergence to occur, the value of unlearning strength ε should be less than $\varepsilon_c = \lambda_{\max}^{-1}$ where $\lambda_{\max}$ denotes the largest eigenvalue of the Hebb matrix. Very often in real-world situations there are no means to know ε_c in advance, and therefore it is of interest to explore asymptotic behaviour of iterated synaptic matrix for arbitrary values of ε. As it is seen, there are only three possible limiting behaviours of the normalized synaptic matrix (Plakhov 1995, Plakhov & Semenov, 1995). The corresponding convergence theorems relate corresponding spectrum dynamics to limiting behaviour of normalized synaptic matrix $\tilde{J} = J/\|J\|$ ($\|J\| = (\sum_{i,j=1}^{N} J_{ij}^2)^{1/2}$) which can be described in terms of $\lambda_{\min}^{(m)}$ the smallest eigenvalues of $J^{(m)}$:

I. if $\lambda_{\min}^{(m)} = 0$ for every $m = 0, 1, 2, \ldots$, with multiplicity of zero eigenvalue being fixed, then

$$(A) \qquad \lim_{m \to \infty} \tilde{J}_{ij}^{(m)} = s^{-1/2} P_{ij}$$

where P marks the projection matrix on the linear subspace $\mathcal{L} \subset \mathbf{R}^N$ spanned by the nominated patterns set ξ^μ, $\mu = 1, \ldots, p$, $s = \dim \mathcal{L} \leq p$;

II. if $\lambda_{\min}^{(m)} = 0$, $m = 0, 1, 2, \ldots$, besides at some (at least one) steps multiplicity of zero eigenvalue increases, then

$$(B) \qquad \lim_{m \to \infty} \tilde{J}_{ij}^{(m)} = s'^{-1/2} P'_{ij}$$

where P' is the projector on some subspace $\mathcal{L}' \subset \mathcal{L}$, $s' = \dim \mathcal{L}' < s$;

III. if $\lambda_{\min}^{(m)} < 0$ starting from some value of m, then

$$(C) \qquad \lim_{m \to \infty} \tilde{J}_{ij}^{(m)} = -\xi_i \xi_j \qquad (3)$$

with some (not a ± 1) unity random vector $\xi = (\xi_1, \ldots, \xi_N)$.

These three cases exhaust all possible asymptotic behaviours of $\tilde{J}_{ij}^{(m)}$, that is their total probability is unity: $P_A + P_B + P_C = 1$. The patterns set is supposed to be fixed.

The convergence theorems say nothing about relative probabilities to have specific asymptotics depending on model parameters. In this paper we present some general results elucidating this question and verify them by numerical simulation.

We show further that the limiting synaptic matrix for the case (C) which is the projector on $-\xi \in \mathcal{L}$ cannot maintain any associative memory. Brief discussion on the retrieval properties of the intermediate case (B) is also given.

2 PROBABILITIES OF POSSIBLE LIMITING BEHAVIOURS OF $\tilde{J}^{(m)}$

The unlearning procedure under consideration is stochastic in nature. Which result of iteration process, $(A), (B)$ or (C), will realize depends upon the value of ε, size and statistical properties of the patterns set $\{\xi^\mu, \mu = 1, \ldots, p\}$, and realization of unlearning sequence $\{S^{(m)}, m = 0, 1, 2, \ldots\}$.

Under fixed patterns set probabilities of appearance of each limiting behaviour of synaptic matrix is determined by the value of unlearning strength ε only. In this section we consider these probabilities as a function of ε.

Generally speaking, considered probabilities exhibit strong dependence on patterns set, making impossible to calculate them explicitly. It is possible however to obtain some general knowledge concerning that probabilities, namely: $P_A(\varepsilon) \to 1$ as $\varepsilon \to 0+$, and hence, $P_{B,C}(\varepsilon) \to 0$, otherwise $P_C(\varepsilon) \to 1$ as $\varepsilon \to \infty$, and $P_{A,B}(\varepsilon) \to 0$, because of $P_A + P_B + P_C = 1$. This means that the risk to have failed unlearning rises when ε increases. Specifically, we are able to prove the following:

Proposition. *There exist positive ε_1 and ε_2 such that $P_A(\varepsilon) = 1$, $0 < \varepsilon < \varepsilon_1$, and $P_C(\varepsilon) = 1$, $\varepsilon_2 < \varepsilon$.*

Before passing to the proof we bring forward an alternative formulation of the above stated classification. After multiplying both sides of (1) by $S_i^{(m)} S_j^{(m)}$ and summing up over all i and j, we obtain in the matrix notation

$$S^{(m)T} J^{(m+1)} S^{(m)} = \Delta_m S^{(m)T} J^{(m)} S^{(m)} \qquad (4)$$

where the contraction factor $\Delta_m = 1 - \varepsilon N^{-1} S^{(m)T} J^{(m)} S^{(m)}$ controls the asymptotics of $\tilde{J}^{(m)}$, as it is suggested by detailed analysis (Plakhov & Semenov, 1995). (Here and below superscript T designates the transpose.) The hypothesis of convergence theorems can be thus restated in terms of Δ_m, instead of $\lambda_{\min}^{(m)}$, respectively: I. $\Delta_m > 0 \ \forall m$; II. $\Delta_m = 0$ for l steps $m_1, \ldots, m_l$; III. $\Delta_m < 0$ at some step m.

Proof. It is obvious that $\Delta_m \geq 1 - \varepsilon \lambda_{\max}^{(m)}$ where $\lambda_{\max}^{(m)}$ marks the largest eigenvalue of $J^{(m)}$. From (4), it follows that the sequence $\{\lambda_{\max}^{(m)}, m = 0, 1, 2, \ldots\}$ is nonincreasing, and consequently $\Delta_m \geq 1 - \varepsilon \lambda_{\max}^{(0)}$ with

$$\lambda_{\max}^{(0)} = \sup_{|x|=1} x^T J^H x = \sup_{|x|=1} N^{-1} \sum_{\mu=1}^{p} \left(\sum_i \xi_i^\mu x_i \right)^2$$

$$\leq \sup_{|x|=1} N^{-1} \sum_{\mu=1}^{p} \sum_{i=1}^{N} (\xi_i^\mu)^2 \sum_{i=1}^{N} x_i^2 = p.$$

From this, it is straightforward to see that, if $\varepsilon < p^{-1}$, then $\Delta_m > 0$ for any m. By convergence theorem (Plakhov & Semenov, 1995) iteration process (1) thus leads to the limiting relation (A).

Let by definition $\gamma = \min_S N^{-1} S^T J^H S$ where minimum is taken over such (± 1)-vectors S for which $J^H S \neq 0$ ($\gamma > 0$, in view of positive semidefiniteness of J^H), and put $\varepsilon > \gamma^{-1}$. Let us further denote by n the iteration step such that $J^H S^{(m)} = 0$, $m = 0, 1, \ldots, n - 1$ and $J^H S^{(n)} \neq 0$. Needless to say that this condition may be satisfied even for the initial step $n = 0$: $J^H S^{(0)} \neq 0$. At step n one has

$$\Delta_n = 1 - \varepsilon N^{-1} S^{(n)T} J^H S^{(n)} \leq 1 - \varepsilon \gamma < 0.$$

The latter implies loss of positive semidefiniteness of $J^{(m)}$, what results in asymptotics (C) (Plakhov, 1995, Plakhov & Semenov, 1995). By choosing $\varepsilon_1 = p^{-1}$ and $\varepsilon_2 = \gamma^{-1}$ we come to the statement of Proposition.

Comparison of numerical estimates of considered probabilities with analytical approximations can be done on simple patterns statistics. In what follows the patterns are assumed to be random and unbiased.

The dependence $P(\varepsilon)$ has been found in computer simulation with unbiased random patterns. It is worth noting, by passing, that calculation Δ_m using current simulation data supplies a good control of unlearning process owing to an alternative formulation of convergence theorems. In simulation we calculate $P_A^N(\varepsilon)$ averaged over the sets of unbiased random patterns, as well as over the realizations of unlearning sequence. As N increases, with $\alpha = p/N$ remaining fixed, the curves slope steeply down approaching step function $P_A^\infty(\varepsilon) = \theta(\varepsilon - \alpha^{-1})$ (Plakhov & Semenov, 1995). Without presenting of derivation or proof we will advance the reasoning suggestive of it. First it can be checked that Δ_m is a selfaveraging quantity with mean $1 - \varepsilon N^{-1} \text{Tr} J^{(m)}$ and variance vanishing as N goes to infinity. Initially one has $N^{-1} \text{Tr} J^H = \alpha$, and obviously the sequence $\{\text{Tr} J^{(m)}, m = 0, 1, 2, \ldots\}$ is nonincreasing. Therefore $\Delta_0 = 1 - \varepsilon \alpha$, and all others Δ_m are not less than Δ_0. If one chooses $\varepsilon < \alpha^{-1}$, then all Δ_m will be positive, and the case (A) will realize. On the other hand, when $\varepsilon > \alpha^{-1}$, we have $\Delta_0 < 0$, and the case (C) will take place.

What is probability for asymptotics (B) to appear? We will adduce an argument (detailed analysis (Plakhov & Semenov, 1995) is rather cumbersome and omitted here) indicating that this probability is quite small. First note that given patterns set it is nonzero for isolated values of ε only. Under the assumption that the patterns are random and unbiased, we have calculated probability of l-fold appearance $\Delta_m = 0$ summed up over that isolated values of ε. Using Gaussian approximation at large N, we have found that probability scales with N as $N^{l/2 + 2 - 2^{l+m+1}}$. The total probability can then be obtained through summing up over integer values $l : 0 < l < s$ and all the iteration steps $m = 0, 1, 2, \ldots$. As a result, the main contribution to the total probability comes from $m = 0$ term which is of the order $N^{-3/2}$.

3 LIMITING RETRIEVAL PROPERTIES

How does reduction of dimension of "memory space" in the case (B), $s \to s' = s - l$, affect retrieval properties of the system? They may vary considerably depending on l. In the most probable case $l = 1$ it is expected that there will be a slight decrease in storage capacity but the size of attraction basins will change negligibly. This is corroborated by calculating the stability parameter for each pattern μ

$$\kappa_i^\mu = \xi_i^\mu \sum_{j \neq i} P'_{ij} \xi_j^\mu. \tag{5}$$

Let $S^{(m_1)}$ be the state vector with normalized projection on $\mathcal{L}$ given by $V = PS^{(m_1)}/|PS^{(m_1)}|$ such that

$$|PS^{(m_1)}| = \sqrt{\alpha N}, \quad V_i \sim N^{-1/2}, \quad \sum_{i=1}^N V_i \xi_i^\mu \sim 1.$$

Then the stability parameter (5) is estimated by

$$\kappa_i^\mu = \xi_i^\mu \sum_{j \neq i} (P_{ij} - V_i V_j) \xi_j^\mu = (1 - P_{ii}) - \left(V_i \xi_i^\mu \sum_{j=1}^N V_j \xi_j^\mu - V_i^2 \right) \approx 1 - P_{ii} + O(N^{-1/2}).$$

Since P_{ii} has mean α and variance vanishing as $N \to \infty$, we thus conclude that the stability parameter only slightly differs from that calculated for the projector rule ($s = s'$) (Kanter & Sompolinsky, 1987).

On the other hand, in the situation $0 < s'/s \ll 1$ (the possible case $s' = 0$ is trivial) the system will be capable retrieving only a few nominated patterns which ones we cannot specify beforehand. As mentioned above, this case realizes with very small but finite probability.

The main effect of self-interactions J_{ii} lies in substantial decrease in storage capacity (Kanter & Sompolinsky, 1987). This is relevant when considering the cases (A) and (B). In the case (C) the system possesses an interesting dynamics exhibiting permanent walk over the state space. There are no fixed points at all. To show this, we write down the fixed point condition for arbitrary state S : $S_i \sum_{j=1}^{N} J_{ij} S_j > 0$, $i = 1, \ldots, N$. By using the explicit expression for limiting matrix $\tilde{J}_{ij}$ (3) and summing up over i's, we get as a result $(\sum_j S_j \xi_j)^2 < 0$, what is impossible.

If self-interactions are excluded from local fields at the stage of network dynamics, it is then driven by the energy function of the form $H = -(2N)^{-1} \sum_{i \neq j} J_{ij} S_i S_j$. (Zero-temperature sequential dynamics either random or regular one is assumed.) In the rest of this section we examine dynamics of the network equiped with limiting synaptic matrix (C) (3). We will show that in this limit the system lacks any associative memory. There are a single global maximum of H given by $S_i = \text{sgn}(\xi_i)$ and exponentially many shallow minima concentrated close to the hyperplane orthogonal to ξ. Moreover it is turned out that all the metastable states are unstable against single spin flip only, whatever the realization of limiting vector ξ. Therefore after a spin flips the system can relax into a new nearby energy minimum. Through a sequence of steps each consisting of a single spin flip followed by relaxation one can, in principle, pass from one metastable state to the other one.

We will prove in what follows that *any given metastable state S' one can pass to any other one S through a sequence of steps each consisting of a single spin flip and subsequent relaxation to a some new metastable state.* Note that this general statement gives no indications concerning the order of spin flips when moving along a particular trajectory in the state space.

Now on we turn to the proof. Let us enumerate the spins in increasing order in absolute values of vector components $0 \leq |\xi_1| \leq \ldots \leq |\xi_N|$. The proof is carried out by induction on $j = 1, \ldots, N$ where j is the maximal index for which $S^1_j \neq S_j$.

For $j = 1$ the statement is evident. Assuming that it holds for $1, \ldots, j - 1$ ($2 \leq j \leq N$), let us prove it for j. One has $j = \max\{i : S^1_i \neq S_i\}$. With flipping spin j in the state S^1, we next allow relaxation by flipping spins $1, \ldots, j-1$ only. The system finally reaches the state S^2 realizing conditional energy minimum under fixed $S_j, \ldots, S_N$.

Show that S^2 is true energy minimum. There are two possibilities:

(i) For some i, $1 \leq i \leq j-1$, one has $\text{sgn}(\xi_i S^2_i) = \text{sgn}(\xi^T S^2)$. The fixed point condition for S^2 can be then written as

$$|\xi^T S^2| \leq \min\{|\xi_i| : 1 \leq i \leq j-1, \text{sgn}(\xi_i S^2_i) = \text{sgn}(\xi^T S^2)\}.$$

¿From this, in view of increasing order of $|\xi_i|$'s, one gets immediately

$$|\xi^T S^2| \leq \min\{|\xi_i| : 1 \leq i \leq N, \text{sgn}(\xi_i S^2_i) = \text{sgn}(\xi^T S^2)\},$$

what implies S^2 is true energy minimum.

(ii) $\text{sgn}(\xi_i S_i^2) \neq \text{sgn}(\xi^T S^2)$ for all $1 \leq i \leq j-1$.

If $\xi^T S^2 = 0$, the fixed point condition for S^2 is automatically satisfied. Otherwise, for $1 \leq i \leq j-1$ one has

$$\xi_i S_i^2 = -\text{sgn}(\xi^T S^2)|\xi_i|,$$

and

$$\xi^T S^2 = -\text{sgn}(\xi^T S^2) \sum_{i=1}^{j-1} |\xi_i| + \sum_{i=j}^{N} \xi_i S_i. \tag{6}$$

For the sake of definiteness, we set $\xi^T S > 0$. (The opposite case is treated analogously.) In this case $\xi^T S^2 > 0$, since otherwise, according to (6), it should be

$$0 \geq \xi^T S^2 = \sum_{i=1}^{j-1} |\xi_i| + \sum_{i=j}^{N} \xi_i S_i \geq \xi^T S,$$

what contradicts our setting.

One thus obtains

$$\xi^T S^2 = -\sum_{i=1}^{j-1} |\xi_i| + \sum_{i=j}^{N} \xi_i S_i \leq \xi^T S, \tag{7}$$

and using the fixed point condition for S one gets

$$\xi^T S \leq \min\{|\xi_i| : \xi_i S_i > 0\} \leq \min\{|\xi_i| : j \leq i \leq N, \xi_i S_i > 0\}$$
$$= \min\{|\xi_i| : \xi_i S_i^2 > 0\}. \tag{8}$$

In the latter inequality of (8) one uses that $\xi_i S_i^2 < 0$, $1 \leq i \leq j-1$ and $S_i^2 = S_i$, $j \leq i \leq N$. Taking into account (7) and (8), as a result we come to the condition for S^2 to be true energy minimum

$$0 < \xi^T S^2 \leq \min\{|\xi_i| : \xi_i S_i^2 > 0\}.$$

According to inductive hypothesis, since $S_i^2 = S_i$, $j \leq i \leq N$, from the state S^2 one can pass to S, and therefore from S' through S^2 to S. This proves the statement.

In general, metastable states may be grouped in clusters surrounded by high energy barriers. The meaning of proven statement resides in excluding the possibility of even such type a memory. Conversely, allowing a sequence of single spin flips (for instance, this can be done at finite temperatures) it is possible to walk through the whole set of metastable states.

4 CONCLUSION

In this paper we have begun studying on probabilities of different asymptotics of convergent unlearning algorithm considering the case of unbiased random patterns. We have shown also that failed unlearning results in total memory breakdown.

References

Hopfield, J.J., Feinstein, D.I. & Palmer, R.G. (1983) "Unlearning" has a stabilizing effect in collective memories. *Nature* 304:158-159.

van Hemmen, J.L. & Klemmer, N. (1992) Unlearning and its relevance to REM sleep: Decorrelating correlated data. In J. G. Taylor et al (eds.), *Neural Network Dynamics*, pp. 30-43. London: Springer.

Wimbauer, U., Klemmer, N. & van Hemmen, J.L. (1994) Universality of unlearning. *Neural Networks* **7**:261-270.

Plakhov, A.Yu. & Semenov, S.A. (1994) Neural networks: iterative unlearning algorithm converging to the projector rule matrix. *J. Phys.I France* **4**:253-260.

Plakhov, A.Yu. (1995) private communication

Plakhov, A.Yu. & Semenov, S.A. (1995) preprint IPT.

Kanter, I. & Sompolinsky, H. (1987) Associative recall of memory without errors. *Phys. Rev. A* **35**:380-392.

Geometry of Early Stopping in Linear Networks

Robert Dodier [*]
Dept. of Computer Science
University of Colorado
Boulder, CO 80309

Abstract

A theory of early stopping as applied to linear models is presented. The backpropagation learning algorithm is modeled as gradient descent in continuous time. Given a training set and a validation set, all weight vectors found by early stopping must lie on a certain quadric surface, usually an ellipsoid. Given a training set and a candidate early stopping weight vector, all validation sets have least-squares weights lying on a certain plane. This latter fact can be exploited to estimate the probability of stopping at any given point along the trajectory from the initial weight vector to the least-squares weights derived from the training set, and to estimate the probability that training goes on indefinitely. The prospects for extending this theory to nonlinear models are discussed.

1 INTRODUCTION

'Early stopping' is the following training procedure:

> Split the available data into a training set and a "validation" set. Start with initial weights close to zero. Apply gradient descent (backpropagation) on the training data. If the error on the validation set increases over time, stop training.

This training method, as applied to neural networks, is of relatively recent origin. The earliest references include Morgan and Bourlard [4] and Weigend *et al.* [7].

---
[*]Address correspondence to: dodier@cs.colorado.edu

Finnoff et al. [2] studied early stopping empirically. While the goal of a theory of early stopping is to analyze its application to nonlinear approximators such as sigmoidal networks, this paper will deal mainly with linear systems and only marginally with nonlinear systems. Baldi and Chauvin [1] and Wang et al. [6] have also analyzed linear systems.

The main result of this paper can be summarized as follows. It can be shown (see Sec. 5) that the most probable stopping point on a given trajectory (fixing the training set and initial weights) is the same no matter what the size of the validation set. That is, the most probable stopping point (considering all possible validation sets) for a finite validation set is the same as for an infinite validation set. (If the validation data is unlimited, then the validation error is the same as the true generalization error.) However, for finite validation sets there is a dispersion of stopping points around the best (most probable and least generalization error) stopping point, and this increases the expected generalization error. See Figure 1 for an illustration of these ideas.

2 MATHEMATICAL PRELIMINARIES

In what follows, backpropagation will be modeled as a process in continuous time. This corresponds to letting the learning rate approach zero. This continuum model simplifies the necessary algebra while preserving the important properties of early stopping. Let the inputs be denoted $\mathbf{X} = (x_{ij})$, so that x_{ij} is the j'th component of the i'th observation; there are p components of each of the n observations. Likewise, let $\mathbf{y} = (y_i)$ be the (scalar) outputs observed when the inputs are $\mathbf{X}$. Our regression model will be a linear model, $y_i = \mathbf{w}'\mathbf{x}_i + \epsilon_i$, $i = 1,\ldots,n$. Here ϵ_i represents independent, identically distributed (i.i.d.) Gaussian noise, $\epsilon_i \sim N(0,\sigma^2)$. Let $E(\mathbf{w}) = \frac{1}{2}\|\mathbf{X}\mathbf{w} - \mathbf{y}\|^2$ be one–half the usual sum of squared errors.

The error gradient with respect to the weights is $\nabla E(\mathbf{w}) = \mathbf{w}'\mathbf{X}'\mathbf{X} - \mathbf{y}'\mathbf{X}$. The backprop algorithm is modeled as $\dot{\mathbf{w}} = -\nabla E(\mathbf{w})$. The least-squares solution, at which $\nabla E(\mathbf{w}) = 0$, is $\mathbf{w}_{LS} = (\mathbf{X}'\mathbf{X})^{-1}\mathbf{X}'\mathbf{y}$. Note the appearence here of the input correlation matrix, $\mathbf{X}'\mathbf{X} = (\sum_{k=1}^n x_{ki}x_{kj})$. The properties of this matrix determine, to a large extent, the properties of the least-squares solutions we find. It turns out that as the number of observations n increases without bound, the matrix $\sigma^2(\mathbf{X}'\mathbf{X})^{-1}$ converges with probability one to the population covariance matrix of the weights. We will find that the correlation matrix plays an important role in the analysis of early stopping.

We can rewrite the error E using a diagonalization of the correlation matrix $\mathbf{X}'\mathbf{X} = \mathbf{S}\Lambda\mathbf{S}'$. Omitting a few steps of algebra,

$$E(\mathbf{w}) = \frac{1}{2}\sum_{k=1}^{p} \lambda_k v_k^2 + \frac{1}{2}\mathbf{y}'(\mathbf{y} - \mathbf{X}\mathbf{w}_{LS}) \qquad (1)$$

where $\mathbf{v} = \mathbf{S}'(\mathbf{w} - \mathbf{w}_{LS})$ and $\Lambda = \mathrm{diag}(\lambda_1,\ldots,\lambda_p)$. In this sum we see that the magnitude of the k'th term is proportional to the corresponding characteristic value, so moving $\mathbf{w}$ toward $\mathbf{w}_{LS}$ in the direction corresponding to the largest characteristic value yields the greatest reduction of error. Likewise, moving in the direction corresponding to the smallest characteristic value gives the least reduction of error.

So far, we have implicitly considered only one set of data; we have assumed all data is used for training. Now let us distinguish training data, $\mathbf{X}_t$ and $\mathbf{y}_t$, from validation data, $\mathbf{X}_v$ and $\mathbf{y}_v$; there are n_t training and n_v validation data. Now each set of data has its own least-squares weight vector, $\mathbf{w}_t$ and $\mathbf{w}_v$, and its own error gradient, $\nabla E_t(\mathbf{w})$ and $\nabla E_v(\mathbf{w})$. Also define $\mathbf{M}_t = \mathbf{X}_t'\mathbf{X}_t$ and $\mathbf{M}_v = \mathbf{X}_v'\mathbf{X}_v$ for convenience. The early stopping method can be analyzed in terms of the these pairs of matrices, gradients, and least-squares weight vectors.

3 THE MAGIC ELLIPSOID

Consider the early stopping criterion, $\frac{dE_v}{dt}(\mathbf{w}) = 0$. Applying the chain rule,

$$\frac{dE_v}{dt} = \frac{dE_v}{d\mathbf{w}} \cdot \frac{d\mathbf{w}}{dt} = \nabla E_v \cdot -\nabla E_t, \qquad (2)$$

where the last equality follows from the definition of gradient descent. So the early stopping criterion is the same as saying

$$\nabla E_t \cdot \nabla E_v = 0, \qquad (3)$$

that is, at an early stopping point, the training and validation error gradients are perpendicular, if they are not zero.

Consider now the set of all points in the weight space such that the training and validation error gradients are perpendicular. These are the points at which early stopping may stop. It turns out that this set of points has an easily described shape. The condition given by Eq. 3 is equivalent to

$$0 = \nabla E_t \cdot \nabla E_v = (\mathbf{w} - \mathbf{w}_t)'\mathbf{M}_t\mathbf{M}_v'(\mathbf{w} - \mathbf{w}_v). \qquad (4)$$

Note that all correlation matrices are symmetric, so $\mathbf{M}_t\mathbf{M}_v' = \mathbf{M}_t\mathbf{M}_v$. We see that Eq. 4 gives a quadratic form. Let us put Eq. 4 into a standard form. Toward this end, let us define some useful terms. Let

$$\begin{aligned}
\mathbf{M} &= \mathbf{M}_t\mathbf{M}_v, & (5)\\
\bar{\mathbf{M}} &= \tfrac{1}{2}(\mathbf{M} + \mathbf{M}') = \tfrac{1}{2}(\mathbf{M}_t\mathbf{M}_v + \mathbf{M}_v\mathbf{M}_t), & (6)\\
\bar{\mathbf{w}} &= \tfrac{1}{2}(\mathbf{w}_t + \mathbf{w}_v), & (7)\\
\Delta\mathbf{w} &= \mathbf{w}_t - \mathbf{w}_v, & (8)
\end{aligned}$$

and

$$\tilde{\mathbf{w}} = \bar{\mathbf{w}} - \tfrac{1}{4}\bar{\mathbf{M}}^{-1}(\mathbf{M} - \mathbf{M}')\Delta\mathbf{w}. \qquad (9)$$

Now an important result can be stated. The proof is omitted.

Proposition 1. $\nabla E_t \cdot \nabla E_v = 0$ is equivalent to

$$(\mathbf{w} - \tilde{\mathbf{w}})'\bar{\mathbf{M}}(\mathbf{w} - \tilde{\mathbf{w}}) = \tfrac{1}{4}\Delta\mathbf{w}[\bar{\mathbf{M}} + \tfrac{1}{4}(\mathbf{M}' - \mathbf{M})\bar{\mathbf{M}}^{-1}(\mathbf{M} - \mathbf{M}')]\Delta\mathbf{w}. \quad \square \qquad (10)$$

The matrix $\bar{\mathbf{M}}$ of the quadratic form given by Eq. 10 is "usually" positive definite. As the number of observations n_t and n_v of training and validation data increase without bound, $\bar{\mathbf{M}}$ converges to a positive definite matrix. In what follows it will always be assumed that $\bar{\mathbf{M}}$ is indeed positive definite. Given this, the locus defined by $\nabla E_t \perp \nabla E_v$ is an ellipsoid. The centroid is $\widetilde{\mathbf{w}}$, the orientation is determined by the characteristic vectors of $\bar{\mathbf{M}}$, and the length of the k'th semiaxis is $\sqrt{c/\bar{\lambda}_k}$, where c is the constant on the righthand side of Eq. 10 and $\bar{\lambda}_k$ is the k'th characteristic value of $\bar{\mathbf{M}}$.

4 THE MAGIC PLANE

Given the least-squares weight vector $\mathbf{w}_t$ derived from the training data and a candidate early stopping weight vector $\mathbf{w}_{es}$, any least-squares weight vector $\mathbf{w}_v$ from a validation set must lie on a certain plane, the 'magic plane.' The proof of this statement is omitted.

Proposition 2. The condition that $\mathbf{w}_t$, $\mathbf{w}_v$, and $\mathbf{w}_{es}$ all lie on the magic ellipsoid,

$$(\mathbf{w}_t - \widetilde{\mathbf{w}})'\bar{\mathbf{M}}(\mathbf{w}_t - \widetilde{\mathbf{w}}) = (\mathbf{w}_v - \widetilde{\mathbf{w}})'\bar{\mathbf{M}}(\mathbf{w}_v - \widetilde{\mathbf{w}}) = (\mathbf{w}_{es} - \widetilde{\mathbf{w}})'\bar{\mathbf{M}}(\mathbf{w}_{es} - \widetilde{\mathbf{w}}) = c, \quad (11)$$

implies

$$(\mathbf{w}_t - \mathbf{w}_{es})'\mathbf{M}\mathbf{w}_v = (\mathbf{w}_t - \mathbf{w}_{es})'\mathbf{M}\mathbf{w}_{es}. \quad \Box \quad (12)$$

This shows that $\mathbf{w}_v$ lies on a plane, the magic plane, with normal $\mathbf{M}'(\mathbf{w}_t - \mathbf{w}_{es})$. The reader will note a certain difficulty here, namely that $\mathbf{M} = \mathbf{M}_t \mathbf{M}_v$ depends on the particular validation set used, as does $\mathbf{w}_v$. However, we can make progress by considering only a fixed correlation matrix $\mathbf{M}_v$ and letting $\mathbf{w}_v$ vary. Let us suppose the inputs $(x_1, x_2, \ldots, x_p)$ are i.i.d. Gaussian random variables with mean zero and some covariance Σ. (Here the inputs are random but they are observed exactly, so the error model $y = \mathbf{w}'\mathbf{x} + \epsilon$ still applies.) Then

$$\langle \mathbf{M}_v \rangle = \langle \mathbf{X}_v' \mathbf{X}_v \rangle = n_v \Sigma,$$

so in Eq. 12 let us replace $\mathbf{M}_v$ with its expected value $n_v \Sigma$. That is, we can approximate Eq. 12 with

$$(\mathbf{w}_t - \mathbf{w}_{es})'\mathbf{M}_t \Sigma \mathbf{w}_v = (\mathbf{w}_t - \mathbf{w}_{es})'\mathbf{M}_t \Sigma \mathbf{w}_{es}. \quad (13)$$

Now consider the probability that a particular point $\mathbf{w}(t)$ on the trajectory from $\mathbf{w}(0)$ to $\mathbf{w}_t$ is an early stopping point, that is, $\nabla E_t(\mathbf{w}(t)) \cdot \nabla E_v(\mathbf{w}(t)) = 0$. This is exactly the probability that Eq. 12 is satisfied, and approximately the probability that Eq. 13 is satisfied. This latter approximation is easy to calculate: it is the mass of an infinitesimally–thin slab cutting through the distribution of least-squares validation weight vectors. Given the usual additive noise model $y = \mathbf{w}'\mathbf{x} + \epsilon$ with ϵ being i.i.d. Gaussian distributed noise with mean zero and variance σ^2, the least-squares weights are approximately distributed as

$$\mathbf{w} - \mathbf{w}^* \sim N(0, \sigma^2 (\mathbf{X}'\mathbf{X})^{-1}) \quad (14)$$

when the number of data is large.

Consider now the plane $\Omega = \{\mathbf{w} : \mathbf{w}'\hat{\mathbf{n}} = k\}$. The probability mass on this plane as it cuts through a Gaussian distribution $N(\mu, \mathbf{C})$ is then

$$p_\Omega(k, \hat{\mathbf{n}}) = (2\pi \hat{\mathbf{n}}' \mathbf{C} \hat{\mathbf{n}})^{-1/2} \exp(-\frac{1}{2} \frac{(k - \mu'\hat{\mathbf{n}})^2}{\hat{\mathbf{n}}' \mathbf{C} \hat{\mathbf{n}}}) \, ds \quad (15)$$

where ds denotes an infinitesimal arc length. (See, for example, Sec. VIII-9.3 of von Mises [3].)

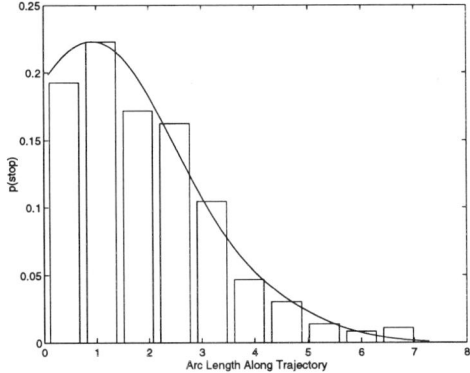

Figure 1: Histogram of early stopping points along a trajectory, with bins of equal arc length. An approximation to the probability of stopping (Eq. 16) is superimposed. Altogether 1000 validation sets were generated for a certain training set; of these, 288 gave "don't start" solutions, 701 gave early stopping solutions (which are binned here) somewhere on the trajectory, and 11 gave "don't stop" solutions.

5 PROBABILITY OF STOPPING AT A GIVEN POINT

Let us apply Eq. 15 to the problem at hand. Our normal is $\hat{\mathbf{n}} = n_v \Sigma \mathbf{M}_t (\mathbf{w}_t - \mathbf{w}_{es})$ and the offset is $k = \hat{\mathbf{n}}' \mathbf{w}_{es}$. A formal statement of the approximation of p_Ω can now be made.

Proposition 3. Assuming the validation correlation matrix $\mathbf{X}_v' \mathbf{X}_v$ equals the mean correlation matrix $n_v \Sigma$, the probability of stopping at a point $\mathbf{w}_{es} = \mathbf{w}(t)$ on the trajectory from $\mathbf{w}(0)$ to $\mathbf{w}_t$ is approximately

$$p_\Omega(t) = p_\Omega(k(t), \hat{\mathbf{n}}(t)) = (2\pi \hat{\mathbf{n}}' \mathbf{C} \hat{\mathbf{n}})^{-1/2} \exp(-\frac{1}{2} \frac{(\hat{\mathbf{n}}'(\mathbf{w}_{es} - \mathbf{w}^*))^2}{\hat{\mathbf{n}}' \mathbf{C} \hat{\mathbf{n}}}), \quad (16)$$

with

$$\hat{\mathbf{n}}' \mathbf{C} \hat{\mathbf{n}} = n_v \sigma^2 (\mathbf{w}_t - \mathbf{w}_{es})' \mathbf{M}_t \Sigma \mathbf{M}_t (\mathbf{w}_t - \mathbf{w}_{es}). \quad \square \quad (17)$$

How useful is this approximation? Simulations were carried out in which the initial weight vector $\mathbf{w}(0)$ and the training data ($n_t = 20$) were fixed, and many validation sets of size $n_v = 20$ were generated (without fixing $\mathbf{X}_v' \mathbf{X}_v$). The trajectory was divided into segments of equal length and histograms of the number of early stopping weights on each segment were constructed. A typical example is shown in Figure 1. It can be seen that the empirical histogram is well-approximated by Eq. 16.

If for some $\mathbf{w}(t)$ on the trajectory the magic plane cuts through the true weights $\mathbf{w}^*$, then p_Ω will have a peak at t. As the number of validation data n_v increases, the variance of $\mathbf{w}_v$ decreases and the peak narrows, but the position $\mathbf{w}(t)$ of the peak does not move. As $n_v \to \infty$ the peak becomes a spike at $\mathbf{w}(t)$. That is, the peak of p_Ω for a finite validation set is the same as if we had access to the true generalization error. In this sense, early stopping does the right thing.

It has been observed that when early stopping is employed, the validation error may decrease forever and never rise – thus the 'early stopping' procedure yields the least-squares weights. How common is this phenomenon? Let us consider a fixed training set and a fixed initial weight vector, so that the trajectory is fixed. Letting the validation set range over all possible realizations, let us denote by $P_\Omega(t) = P_\Omega(k(t), \hat{\mathbf{n}}(t))$ the probability that training stops at time t or later. $1 - P_\Omega(0)$ is the probability that validation error rises immediately upon beginning training, and let us agree that $P_\Omega(\infty)$ denotes the probability that validation error never increases. This $P_\Omega(t)$ is approximately the mass that is "behind" the plane $\hat{\mathbf{n}}'\mathbf{w}_v = \hat{\mathbf{n}}'\mathbf{w}_{es}$, "behind" meaning the points $\mathbf{w}_v$ such that $(\mathbf{w}_v - \mathbf{w}_{es})'\hat{\mathbf{n}} < 0$. (The identification of P_Ω with the mass to one side of the plane is not exact because intersections of magic planes are ignored.) As Eq. 15 has the form of a Gaussian p.d.f., it is easy to show that

$$P_\Omega(k, \hat{\mathbf{n}}) = G\left(\frac{k - \hat{\mathbf{n}}'\mathbf{w}^*}{(\hat{\mathbf{n}}'\mathbf{C}\hat{\mathbf{n}})^{1/2}}\right) \tag{18}$$

where G denotes the standard Gaussian c.d.f., $G(z) = (2\pi)^{-1/2}\int_{-\infty}^{z}\exp(-t^2/2)dt$. Recall that we take the normal $\hat{\mathbf{n}}$ of the magic plane through $\mathbf{w}_{es}$ as $\hat{\mathbf{n}} = \Sigma\mathbf{M}_t(\mathbf{w}_t - \mathbf{w}_{es})$. For $t = 0$ there is no problem with Eq. 18 and an approximation for the "never-starting" probability is stated in the next proposition.

Proposition 4. *The probability that validation error increases immediately upon beginning training ("never starting"), assuming the validation correlation matrix $\mathbf{X}_v'\mathbf{X}_v$ equals the mean correlation matrix $n_v\Sigma$, is approximately*

$$1 - P_\Omega(0) = 1 - G\left(\frac{\sqrt{n_v}}{\sigma}\frac{(\mathbf{w}^* - \mathbf{w}(0))'\mathbf{M}_t\Sigma(\mathbf{w}_t - \mathbf{w}(0))}{[(\mathbf{w}_t - \mathbf{w}(0))'\mathbf{M}_t\Sigma\mathbf{M}_t(\mathbf{w}_t - \mathbf{w}(0))]^{1/2}}\right). \quad \Box \tag{19}$$

With similar arguments we can develop an approximation to the "never-stopping" probability.

Proposition 5. *The probability that training continues indefinitely ("never stopping"), assuming the validation correlation matrix $\mathbf{X}_v'\mathbf{X}_v$ equals the mean correlation matrix $n_v\Sigma$, is approximately*

$$P_\Omega(\infty) = G\left(\frac{\sqrt{n_v}}{\sigma}\frac{(\mathbf{w}^* - \mathbf{w}_t)'\mathbf{M}_t\Sigma(\pm\mathbf{s}^*)}{\lambda^*[(\mathbf{s}^*)'\Sigma\mathbf{s}^*]^{1/2}}\right). \tag{20}$$

In Eq. 20 pick $+\mathbf{s}^*$ if $(\mathbf{w}_t - \mathbf{w}(0))'\mathbf{s}^* > 0$, otherwise pick $-\mathbf{s}^*$. $\Box$

Simulations are in good agreement with the estimates given by Propositions 4 and 5.

6 EXTENDING THE THEORY TO NONLINEAR SYSTEMS

It may be possible to extend the theory presented in this paper to nonlinear approximators. The elementary concepts carry over unchanged, although it will be more difficult to describe them algebraically. In a nonlinear early stopping problem, there will be a surface corresponding to the magic ellipsoid on which $\nabla E_t \perp \nabla E_v$, but this surface may be nonconvex or not simply connected. Likewise, corresponding to the magic plane there will be a surface on which least-squares validation weights must fall, but this surface need not be flat or unbounded.

It is customary in the world of statistics to apply results derived for linear systems to nonlinear systems by assuming the number of data is very large and various regularity conditions hold. If the errors ϵ are additive, the least-squares weights again have a Gaussian distribution. As in the linear case, the Hessian of the total error appears as the inverse of the covariance of the least-squares weights. In this asymptotic (large data) regime, the standard results for linear regression carry over to nonlinear regression mostly unchanged. This suggests that the linear theory of early stopping will also apply to nonlinear regression models, such as sigmoidal networks, when there is much data.

However, it should be noted that the asymptotic regression theory is purely local – it describes only what happens in the neighborhood of the least-squares weights. As the outcome of early stopping depends upon the initial weights and the trajectory taken through the weight space, any local theory will not suffice to analyze early stopping. Nonlinear effects such as local minima and non-quadratic basins cannot be accounted for by a linear or asymptotically linear theory, and these may play important roles in nonlinear regression problems. This may invalidate direct extrapolations of linear results to nonlinear networks, such as that given by Wang and Venkatesh [5].

7 ACKNOWLEDGMENTS

This research was supported by NSF Presidential Young Investigator award IRI-9058450 and grant 90-21 from the James S. McDonnell Foundation to Michael C. Mozer.

References

[1] Baldi, P., and Y. Chauvin. "Temporal Evolution of Generalization during Learning in Linear Networks," *Neural Computation* **3**, 589–603 (Winter 1991).

[2] Finnoff, W., F. Hergert, and H. G. Zimmermann. "Extended Regularization Methods for Nonconvergent Model Selection," in *Advances in NIPS 5*, S. Hanson, J. Cowan, and C. L. Giles, eds., pp 228–235. San Mateo, CA: Morgan Kaufmann Publishers. 1993.

[3] von Mises, R. *Mathematical Theory of Probability and Statistics.* New York: Academic Press. 1964.

[4] Morgan, N., and H. Bourlard. "Generalization and Parameter Estimation in Feedforward Nets: Some Experiments," in *Advances in NIPS 2*, D. Touretzky, ed., pp 630–637. San Mateo, CA: Morgan Kaufmann. 1990.

[5] Wang, C., and S. Venkatesh. "Temporal Dynamics of Generalization in Neural Networks," in *Advances in NIPS 7*, G. Tesauro, D. Touretzky, and T. Leen, eds. pp 263–270. Cambridge, MA: MIT Press. 1995.

[6] Wang, C., S. Venkatesh, J. S. Judd. "Optimal Stopping and Effective Machine Complexity in Learning," in *Advances in NIPS 6*, J. Cowan, G. Tesauro, and J. Alspector, eds., pp 303–310. San Francisco: Morgan Kaufmann. 1994.

[7] Weigend, A., B. Huberman, and D. Rumelhart. "Predicting the Future: A Connectionist Approach," *Int'l J. Neural Systems* **1**, 193–209 (1990).

Absence of Cycles in Symmetric Neural Networks

Xin Wang
Computer Science Dept
UCLA
Los Angeles, CA 90024
xwang@cs.ucla.edu

Arun Jagota, Fernanda Botelho, Max Garzon
Dept of Mathematical Sciences
University of Memphis
Memphis, TN 38152
jagota, botelhof, garzonm@hermes.msci.memst.edu

Abstract

For a given recurrent neural network, a discrete-time model may have asymptotic dynamics different from the one of a related continuous-time model. In this paper, we consider a discrete-time model that discretizes the continuous-time leaky integrator model and study its parallel and sequential dynamics for symmetric networks. We provide sufficient (and necessary in many cases) conditions for the discretized model to have the same cycle-free dynamics of the corresponding continuous-time model in symmetric networks.

1 INTRODUCTION

For an n-neuron recurrent network, a much-studied and widely-used continuous-time (CT) model is the leaky integrator model (Hertz, et al., 1991; Hopfield, 1984), given by a system of nonlinear differential equations:

$$\tau_i \frac{dx_i}{dt} = -x_i + \sigma_i(\sum_{j=1}^{n} w_{ij} x_j + I_i), \quad t \geq 0, \quad i = 1, ..., n, \quad (1)$$

and a related discrete-time (DT) version is the sigmoidal model (Hopfield, 1982; Marcus & Westervelt, 1989), specified by a system of nonlinear difference equations:

$$x_i(t+1) = \sigma_i(\sum_{j=1}^{n} w_{ij} x_j(t) + I_i), \quad t = 0, 1, ..., \quad i = 1, ..., n, \quad (2)$$

where $x_i(t)$, taking values in a compact interval $[a, b]$, represents the state of neuron i at time t, τ_i is the time constant, $W = [w_{ij}]$ is the real-valued weight matrix, $\sigma_i : \Re \to [a, b]$ is the activation function which often takes a sigmoidal form and I_i

Absence of Cycles in Symmetric Neural Networks

is the constant external input to neuron i. When the network is symmetric (i.e., W is symmetric), the dynamics of both models have been well understood: the CT model (1) is always convergent, namely, every initial state will approach a fixed point asymptotically (Hirsch, 1989; Hertz, et al., 1991; Hopfield, 1984), and the DT model (2) is either convergent or approaches a periodic orbit of period 2 (i.e., a 2-cycle) (Goles, et al., 1985; Marcus & Westervelt, 1989; Koiran, 1994). For results and analyses of fixed points and cycles in networks that are not necessarily symmetric, see (Brown, 1992; Bruck, 1990; Goles, 1986).

For a given symmetric network (n, W, σ_i, I_i), the existence of possible 2-cycles in its discrete-time operation is sometimes trouble-some and undesirable, especially in associative memory and neural optimization applications where only fixed points are used to represent memory patterns (Hopfield, 1982) or to encode feasible solutions (Hertz, et al., 1991). Originally in (Hopfield, 1982) a type of sequential dynamics (in which only one randomly chosen neuron updates its state at any time) had to be employed in order to ensure the convergent dynamics of (2). A great deal of work on asymptotic behavior of (2) has focused on constraining the symmetric matrix W so that the model exhibits only convergent dynamics. It was shown in (Goles, et al., 1985) that, for σ_i equal to the $-1/+1$ signum function, if W is positive definite on the set $\{-1, 0, 1\}^n$, then the model (2) is convergent only to fixed points. In (Marcus & Westervelt, 1989), a similar condition on W and neuron gains was derived for networks with differentiable σ_i's (see also (Marcus, et al., 1990; Waugh & Westervelt, 1993)). Nevertheless, the fact remains as that not all symmetric networks that are convergent in (1) show the same convergent dynamics in (2).

Such implausibility of the DT model (2) in fully inheriting the dynamics of the CT model (1) leads to study of another DT model in this paper, which generalizes (2) with some new parameters. For symmetric networks, this model has the same types of parallel and sequential dynamics of (2). But, under some conditions on the new parameters (rather than on the weight matrix itself), this model has the same global convergent parallel dynamics and the same local stability around fixed points of (1). Moreover, with these new parameters as bifurcation parameters, the existence of possible 2-cycles can be understood in this model as resulting from the existence of possible period-doubling bifurcation when the parameters are varied. Finally, it is this model, rather than (2), that is used more often in practice as a discrete-time approximation of (1). Based on all of the above, the DT model studied here is a more appropriate discrete-time model of neural networks for purposes of theoretical investigation, numerical simulation and practical application.

2 A DISCRETE-TIME MODEL

The DT model that is studied in this paper is

$$x_i(t+1) = (1 - \alpha_i)x_i(t) + \alpha_i \sigma_i(\sum_{j=1}^{n} w_{ij}x_j(t) + I_i), \quad t = 0, 1, ..., \quad i = 1, ..., n, \quad (3)$$

where α_i's are newly introduced parameters, taking values in $(0, 1]$. This model is based on the Euler discretization of the CT model (1) with all $\tau_i = 1$ [1], with $x_i(s)$ and $(x_i(s+1) - x_i(s))/\alpha_i$ approximating $x_i(t)$ and $dx_i(t)/dt$ in (1), respectively, at $t = s * \alpha_i$. It takes the model (2) as its special case of all $\alpha_i = 1$. The new neuron state $x_i(t+1)$ is now a linear combination of the activation function value

---

[1] When (1) is globally convergent to fixed points, neglecting all τ_i does not change its dynamics.

$\sigma_i(\sum_{j=1}^n w_{ij}x_j(t)+I_i)$ and the old state $x_i(t)$. Because of $\alpha_i \in (0,1]$, the model (3) is well defined, in that the iterative maps resulting from the model,

$$F_i(x) = (1-\alpha_i)x_i + \alpha_i\sigma_i(\sum_{j=1}^n w_{ij}x_j + I_i), \qquad (4)$$

preserve neuron states in the compact interval $[a,b]$.

For the purposes of this paper, neuron activation functions σ_i are assumed to satisfy the following constraints:

(i) σ_i have continuous first-order derivatives $\sigma_i'(y)$ for all $y \in \Re$;
(ii) σ_i are monotone increasing with $\sigma_i'(y) > 0$;
(iii) $\sigma_i'(y) \to 0$ as $y \to \pm\infty$; and
(iv) $\sigma_i'(y)$ take maximal values μ_i, which are usually referred to as *neuron gains*.

Such functions are fairly general, including often-used $[-1,1]$- and $[0,1]$-sigmoids, such as $tanh(\mu_i y)$, $2/\pi \tan^{-1}(\pi\mu_i y/2)$, and $1/(1+e^{-\mu_i y})$. The constraints on σ_i's are sufficient for the functions defined by

$$G_i(x_i) = \int_0^{x_i} \sigma_i^{-1}(y)dy. \qquad (5)$$

to have the following properties that will be used subsequently in proofs of several propositions of this paper:

(i) $G_i'(y) = \sigma_i^{-1}(y)$, and particularly $G_i'(\Delta x_i(t)/\alpha_i + x_i(t)) = \sum_j w_{ij}x_i(t) + I_i$;
(ii) $G_i(y) - G_i(z) \leq G'(y)(y-z) - 1/(2\mu_i)(y-z)^2 \leq G'(y)(y-z)$;
(iii) $G_i''(y) = 1/\sigma_i'(\sigma_i^{-1}(y))$; and
(iv) $G_i'(y_0 + y_1) - G_i'(y_0) \geq (\min_z G_i''(z))y_1 = y_1/\mu_i$,

where $\Delta x_i(t) = x_i(t+1) - x_i(t)$.

3 PARALLEL AND SEQUENTIAL DYNAMICS

In parallel dynamics, also called synchronous dynamics, all neurons update their states in each time step. In sequential dynamics, a single neuron updates its state in each time step in such a way that each neuron updates its state infinitely-many times, over all time steps t. The most widely studied special case of sequential dynamics is called asynchronous dynamics (Hopfield, 1982), in which the neuron whose state is updated is chosen at random. This models asynchronous evolution of a neural network circuit composed of autonomous neurons.

It is easy to see that the discretized DT model (3) shares the same set of fixed points with the CT model (1); that is, a point x^* is a fixed point of (3) (i.e., $x_i^* = F_i(x^*)$ with F_i given in (4)), if and only if it is a fixed point of (1) (i.e., $-x_i^* + \sigma_i(\sum_{ij} w_{ij}x_j^* + I_i) = 0$).

However, as the result of discretization, fixed points may have different asymptotic stability (Wang & Blum, 1992) and periodic points that are not fixed points may occur (Blum & Wang, 1992; Marcus & Westervelt, 1989) in the DT model, especially when all $\alpha_i = 1$. Nevertheless, the discretized DT model retains the same type of the global parallel dynamics and sequential dynamics of (2), as stated in the following two propositions. These results extend the results for all $\alpha_i = 1$ in (Marcus & Westervelt, 1989) to $\alpha_i \in (0,1]$.

Proposition 1 *If W is symmetric, any trajectory in parallel dynamics of (3) tends to either a fixed point or a 2-cycle.*

Proof. Consider the following function:

$$E(t) = -\sum_{i,j} w_{ij} x_i(t) x_j(t-1) - \sum_i I_i[x_i(t) + x_i(t-1)]$$
$$+ \sum_i (2-\alpha_i) G_i(x_i(t-1)) + \sum_i \alpha_i G_i(\Delta x_i(t-1)/\alpha_i + x_i(t-1)).$$

When $\alpha_i = 1$, this function is the one used in (Goles, et al., 1985; Marcus & Westervelt, 1989). It can be shown (the details is omitted due to space limitation) that the one-step change of $E(t)$, $\Delta E(t) = E(t+1) - E(t)$, is always less than or equal to 0 and $\Delta E(t) = 0$ implies that the two-step change $\Delta_2 x(t) = x(t+1) - x(t-1)$ is necessarily equal to zero. As $E(t)$ is bounded from below, the network is therefore convergent to either a fixed point or a 2-cycle. □

Proposition 2 *If W is symmetric with all $w_{ii} > -(2-\alpha_i)/(\alpha_i \mu_i)$, the DT model (3) has the sequential dynamics convergent to fixed points for any $\alpha_i \in (0,1]$.*

Proof. Consider the function used in (Hopfield, 1984; Marcus & Westervelt, 1989),

$$L(t) = -\frac{1}{2} \sum_{i,j} w_{ij} x_i(t) x_j(t) - \sum_i I_i x_i(t) + \sum_i G_i(x_i(t)). \quad (6)$$

If at time t only neuron i is chosen to update its state and all the others remain unchanged, then $L(t)$ is not increasing, and it is strictly decreasing when the one-step change in $x_i(t)$, $\Delta x_i(t)$, is not 0. (The derivation is omitted due to space limitation.) Hence, any sequential trajectory tends to some fixed point. □

4 GLOBAL CONVERGENCE

Call a model of a neural network *cycle-free* if it is globally convergent to fixed points only. The following proposition provides a condition that eliminates the possible "spurious" periodic dynamic behaviors of the discretized DT model (3).

Proposition 3 *If W is symmetric, a sufficient condition for (3) to be cycle-free in parallel dynamics is*

the matrix $W + (2I - A)A^{-1}M^{-1}$ is positive definite, $\quad (7)$

where $A = diag(\alpha_i)$ and $M = diag(\mu_i)$ are the diagonal matrices formed by the parameters α_i and the neuron gains μ_i.

Proof. Use the energy function $L(t)$ used in the proof of Proposition 2. The one-step difference $\Delta L(t)$ of $L(t)$ along any trajectory $x(t)$ has an upper bound

$$\Delta L(t) \leq -\frac{1}{2} \Delta x(t)^T (W + (2I - A)A^{-1}M^{-1}) \Delta x(t). \quad (8)$$

The condition (7) implies that the upper bound is negative and hence the parallel dynamics is globally convergent. □

In a simple case where all gains $\mu_i = 1$ (e.g., $\sigma_i(z) = \tanh(z)$) and $\alpha_i = \alpha$, this proposition says that the model is cycle-free if the matrix $W + [(2-\alpha)/\alpha]I$ is positive definite.

The sufficient condition (7) generalizes many existing conditions for the cycle-free dynamics in the literature. When $\alpha_i = 1$, it reduces to that matrix $W + M^{-1}$ is positive definite, which is the one presented in (Marcus & Westervelt, 1989) (with all $R_i = 1$ in their model) for the DT model (2) to be cycle-free. Moreover, when $\mu \to \infty$ the sigmoidal functions tend to the signum function. If in this case $\alpha_i \geq \epsilon$ for some fixed positive ϵ, the condition (7) reduces to that the weight matrix W be positive definite, which is the one in (Goles, et al., 1985), except that in the latter case W need be positive definite only on the set $\{-1, 0, 1\}^n$.

When α_i are sufficiently small, the matrix in (7) will be dominated by its positive diagonal entries and become positive definite. In fact,

Corollary 1 *Let λ_{min} be the minimum eigenvalue of the symmetric matrix W. If either (i) $\lambda_{min} > 0$ (i.e., W is positive definite itself) and α_i are arbitrary in $(0, 1]$, or (ii) $\lambda_{min} \leq 0$ and all α_i's satisfy $(2 - \alpha_i)/(\alpha_i \mu_i) > -\lambda_{min}$, then the model (3) is cycle-free.*

Proof. Let $W = P^\mathsf{T} \Lambda P$ be an orthogonal decomposition of W; that is, Λ is a diagonal matrix formed by the eigenvalues of W and P is some orthogonal matrix with its transpose $P^\mathsf{T} = P^{-1}$. The condition (7) is equivalent to that the diagonal matrix

$$\Lambda + (2I - A)A^{-1}M^{-1} \text{ is positive definite.}$$

The later condition can be fulfilled by either condition (i) or (ii). The conclusion then follows from Proposition (3). □

This corollary implies that if the weight matrix W is formed according to the Hebb rule as constructed in (Hopfield, 1982), then the model is cycle-free. This is because W is an outer-product $W = VV^\mathsf{T} - mI$ of a collection of some "memory" vectors $V = [v_1, ..., v_m]$, and it is positive definite.

5 LOCAL ASYMPTOTIC STABILITY

When all $\alpha_i = \alpha$, the condition (7) in Proposition 3 becomes

$$\text{the matrix } W + \frac{2-\alpha}{\alpha}M^{-1} \text{ is positive definite.}$$

This is the one given in (Wang & Blum, 1992) that ensures consistency of the DT model (3) with the CT model (1) on local asymptotic dynamics around fixed points for symmetric networks. The consistency means that any fixed point has exactly the same asymptotic stability in both (3) and (1). If these two models are consistent in this regard, a fixed point is an attractor (saddle point or repellor, respectively) of (3) if and only if it is an attractor (saddle point or repellor) of (1). This answers the issue raised in (Marcus & Westervelt, 1989) on why a stable fixed point of (1) is also stable in (2), if a specific version of the condition (7) is met. For symmetric networks, the consistency condition on the local asymptotic dynamics between the CT and DT models turns out to be a consistency condition between them on the global convergent dynamics as well. It is certainly interesting to see if this type of relationship between the local and global consistencies can be extended to general (non-symmetric) networks.

6 PERIOD-DOUBLING BIFURCATION

In many cases, the condition (7) in Proposition 3 is also necessary for the network to be cycle-free. This can be addressed from a bifurcation point of view by treating the parameters α_i as bifurcation parameters. Essentially, the condition (7) gives no room for existence of period-doubling bifurcation, which is the source of generating possible 2-cycles.

Proposition 4 *Let the activation functions σ_i be symmetric, i.e., $\sigma_i : \Re \to [-a,a]$, and satisfy*
$$\sigma_i(0) = 0, \quad \sigma_i'(0) = \mu_i.$$
Let the external bias vector $I = 0$. Then condition (7) is also a necessary condition for the network to be cycle-free.

Proof. Define $C = \{(\alpha_1, \ldots, \alpha_n) \mid W + (2I - A)A^{-1}M^{-1} \text{ is positive definite}\}$. Let C_i denote the projection of the ith components of the n-tuples in C. Because $\alpha < \alpha' \in C_i$ implies $\alpha \in C_i$, each C_i is either the entire interval $(0, 1]$ or an open interval $(0, c_{i_0})$ for some $0 < c_{i_0} < 1$. Notice that 0 is a fixed point of the network.

The Jacobian of the iterative maps in (4) at the fixed point 0 is
$$(I - A) + AMW. \quad (9)$$
Notice that the condition (7) is equivalent to that the eigenvalues of $(2I - A) + AMW$ are all positive, which is further equivalent to that the Jacobian (9) has all eigenvalues $\lambda \geq -1$.

If $C = (0, 1]^n$, the model has no cycles, according to Proposition 3, for any $(\alpha_1, \ldots, \alpha_n) \in (0, 1]^n$. However, if $C_i = (0, c_{i_0})$ for some i and $c_{i_0} < 1$, some eigenvalue of the Jacobian (9) becomes less than -1 when α_i exceeds the "threshold" c_{i_0}. During this course of changing α_i, the network undergoes generically a period-doubling bifurcation (Ruelle, 1989), resulting in emergence of some 2-cycles. Thus, in this case the condition (7) in Proposition 3 is also necessary to prevent this type of period-doubling bifurcation from happening around fixed points and hence to eliminate possibility of generating 2-cycles. □

Examples of σ_i's satisfying hypotheses of Proposition 4 are $\tanh_{\mu_i} : \Re \to [-1, 1]$ with $\tanh_{\mu_i}(z) = \tanh(\mu_i z)$.

7 EFFECT OF NEURON GAINS IN NEURAL COMPUTATIONS

Considerable research has been conducted on using (1) in neural computations such as solving optimization problems approximately; see (Hertz, et al., 1991, Chapter 4) for an overview. Often, the neuron gains μ_i are also modified while the network is evolving. A popular algorithm of this kind uses mean field annealing (MFA) (Peterson & Anderson, 1988) to solve optimization problems, in which small neuron gains are used initially, and increased gradually. Similar situations also happen in some learning algorithms.

In practice, a discretized model such as (3) is used instead. Proposition 3 gives some criterion on how to choose the "discretization step-sizes" α_i as functions of μ_i. If efficiency, for example, were the paramount consideration, one might want to choose α_i as large as possible while ensuring that the sufficient condition of Proposition 3 is met.

The effect of changing μ on the largest sufficing α can be examined as follows. For simplicity, consider the case where all neuron gains μ_i equal μ and all α_i equal to α. Let c_i, $i = 1, 2$, be the respective supremums of α's such that $W + (2-\alpha)/(\alpha d_i)I$ are positive definite when the neuron gains μ are equal to two different values d_1 and

d_2. Then c_1 and c_2 satisfy $(2-c_1)/(c_1 d_1) = (2-c_2)(c_2 d_2)$. Letting $\beta = d_2/d_1$, the above gives $c_2 = 2c_1/(c_1 + \beta(2-c_1))$. Clearly, c_2 is proportional to the reciprocal of the ratio β. Thus, when μ is small, α can be taken larger than when μ is large. This may be used to evolve the network efficiently in the beginning and slow it down later, while ensuring that 2-cycles are never retrieved.

References

E.K. Blum & X. Wang. (1992) Stability of fixed points and periodic orbits and bifurcations in analog neural networks. *Neural Networks*, 5:577–587.

D.P. Brown. (1992) Matrix tests for period 1 and 2 limit cycles in discrete threshold networks. *IEEE Trans. on Systems, Man, & Cybernetics*, 22:552–554.

J. Bruck. (1990) On the convergence properties of the Hopfield model. *Proc. IEEE*, 78:1579–1585.

E. Goles, F. Fogelman-Soulie & D. Pellegrin. (1985) Decreasing energy functions as a tool for studying threshold networks. *Discrete Applied Mathematics*, 12:261–277.

E. Goles. (1982) Fixed point behaviour of threshold functions on a finite set. *SIAM J. of Algorithmic Discrete Methods*, 3:529–531.

E. Goles. (1986) Antisymmetrical neural networks. *Discrete Applied Mathematics*, 13:97–100.

J. Hertz, A. Krogh & R.G. Palmer. (1991) *Introduction to the Theory of Neural Computation*. Addison-Wesley.

M.W. Hirsch. (1989) Convergent activation dynamics in continuous time networks. *Neural Networks*, 2:331–349.

J.J. Hopfield. (1982) Neural networks and physical systems with collective computational abilities. *Proc. of the National Academy of Sciences, USA*, 79:2554–2558.

J.J. Hopfield. (1984) Neurons with graded response have collective computational properties like those of two-state neurons. *Proc. of the National Academy of Sciences, USA*, 81:3088–3092.

P. Koiran. (1994) Dynamics of discrete time, continuous state Hopfield networks. *Neural Computation*, 6:459–468.

C.M. Marcus & R.M. Westervelt. (1989) Dynamics of iterated-map neural networks. *Physical Review A*, 40:501–504.

C. Peterson & J.R. Anderson. (1988) Neural networks and NP-complete optimization problems; a performance study on the graph bisection problem. *Complex Systems*, 2:59–89.

D. Ruelle. (1989) *Elements of Differentiable dynamics and Bifurcation Theory*. Academic Press, Inc.

X. Wang & E.K. Blum. (1992) Discrete-time versus continuous-time neural networks. *J. of Computer and System Sciences*, 49:1–17.

F.R. Waugh & R.M. Westervelt. (1993) Analog neural networks with local competition. I. Dynamics and stability. *Physical Review E*, 47:4524–4536.

PART IV
ALGORITHMS AND ARCHITECTURES

Adaptive Mixture of Probabilistic Transducers

Yoram Singer
AT&T Bell Laboratories
singer@research.att.com

Abstract

We introduce and analyze a mixture model for supervised learning of probabilistic transducers. We devise an online learning algorithm that efficiently infers the structure and estimates the parameters of each model in the mixture. Theoretical analysis and comparative simulations indicate that the learning algorithm tracks the best model from an arbitrarily large (possibly infinite) pool of models. We also present an application of the model for inducing a noun phrase recognizer.

1 Introduction

Supervised learning of a probabilistic mapping between temporal sequences is an important goal of natural sequences analysis and classification with a broad range of applications such as handwriting and speech recognition, natural language processing and DNA analysis. Research efforts in supervised learning of probabilistic mappings have been almost exclusively focused on estimating the parameters of a *predefined* model. For example, in [5] a second order recurrent neural network was used to induce a finite state automata that classifies input sequences and in [1] an input-output HMM architecture was used for similar tasks.

In this paper we introduce and analyze an alternative approach based on a *mixture* model of a new subclass of probabilistic transducers, which we call suffix tree transducers. The mixture of experts architecture has been proved to be a powerful approach both theoretically and experimentally. See [4, 8, 6, 10, 2, 7] for analyses and applications of mixture models, from different perspectives such as connectionism, Bayesian inference and computational learning theory. By combining techniques used for compression [13] and unsupervised learning [12], we devise an online algorithm that efficiently updates the mixture weights *and* the parameters of *all* the possible models from an arbitrarily large (possibly infinite) pool of suffix tree transducers. Moreover, we employ the mixture estimation paradigm to the estimation of the parameters of each model in the pool and achieve an efficient estimate of the free parameters of each model. We present theoretical analysis, simulations and experiments with real data which show that the learning algorithm indeed tracks the best model in a *growing* pool of models, yielding an accurate approximation of the source. All proofs are omitted due to the lack of space

2 Mixture of Suffix Tree Transducers

Let Σ_{in} and Σ_{out} be two finite alphabets. A *Suffix Tree Transducer* T over $(\Sigma_{in}, \Sigma_{out})$ is a rooted, $|\Sigma_{in}|$-ary tree where every internal node of T has one child for each symbol in Σ_{in}. The nodes of the tree are labeled by pairs (s, γ_s), where s is the string associated with the path (sequence of symbols in Σ_{in}) that leads from the root to that node, and $\gamma_s : \Sigma_{out} \to [0, 1]$ is the output probability function. A suffix tree transducer (stochastically) maps arbitrarily long input sequences over Σ_{in} to output sequences over Σ_{out} as follows. The probability that $\mathcal{T}$ will output a string $y_1, y_2, \ldots, y_n$ in Σ_{out}^n given an input string $x_1, x_2, \ldots, x_n$ in Σ_{in}^n, denoted by $P_{\mathcal{T}}(y_1, y_2, \ldots, y_n | x_1, x_2, \ldots, x_n)$, is $\prod_{k=1}^{n} \gamma_{s^k}(y_k)$, where $s^1 = x_1$, and for $1 \leq j \leq n-1$, s^j is the string labeling the *deepest* node reached by taking the path corresponding to $x_j, x_{j-1}, x_{j-2}, \ldots$ starting at the root of $\mathcal{T}$. A suffix tree transducer is therefore a probabilistic mapping that induces a measure over the possible output strings given an input string. Examples of suffix tree transducers are given in Fig. 1.

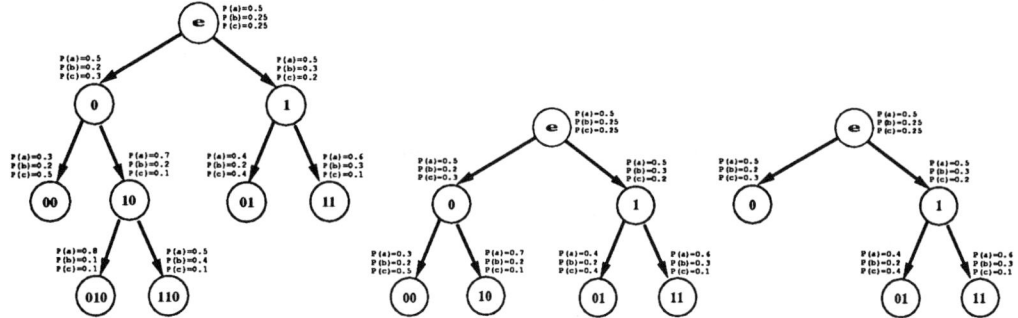

Figure 1: A suffix tree transducer (left) over $(\Sigma_{in}, \Sigma_{out}) = (\{0,1\}, \{a,b,c\})$ and two of its possible sub-models (subtrees). The strings labeling the nodes are the suffixes of the input string used to predict the output string. At each node there is an output probability function defined for each of the possible output symbols. For instance, using the suffix tree transducer depicted on the left, the probability of observing the symbol b given that the input sequence is $\ldots, 0, 1, 0$, is 0.1. The probability of the current output, when each transducer is associated with a weight (prior), is the weighted sum of the predictions of each transducer. For example, assume that the weights of the trees are 0.7 (left tree), 0.2 (middle), and 0.1, then the probability that the output $y_n = $ a given that $(x_{n-2}, x_{n-1}, x_n) = (0,1,0)$ is $0.7 \cdot P_{\mathcal{T}_1}(a|010) + 0.2 \cdot P_{\mathcal{T}_2}(a|10) + 0.1 \cdot P_{\mathcal{T}_3}(a|0) = 0.7 \cdot 0.8 + 0.2 \cdot 0.7 + 0.1 \cdot 0.5 = 0.75$.

Given a suffix tree transducer $\mathcal{T}$ we are interested in the prediction of the mixture of *all* possible subtrees of $\mathcal{T}$. We associate with each subtree (including $\mathcal{T}$) a weight which can be interpreted as its prior probability. We later show how the learning algorithm of a mixture of suffix tree transducers adapts these weights with accordance to the performance (the *evidence* in Bayesian terms) of each subtree on past observations. Direct calculation of the mixture probability is infeasible since there might be exponentially many such subtrees. However, the technique introduced in [13] can be generalized and applied to our setting. Let $\mathcal{T}'$ be a subtree of $\mathcal{T}$. Denote by n_1 the number of the internal nodes of $\mathcal{T}'$ and by n_2 the number of leaves of $\mathcal{T}'$ which are *not* leaves of $\mathcal{T}$. For example, $n_1 = 2$ and $n_2 = 1$, for the tree depicted on the right part of Fig. 1, assuming that $\mathcal{T}$ is the tree depicted on the left part of the figure. The prior weight of a tree $\mathcal{T}'$, denoted by $P_0(\mathcal{T}')$ is defined to be $(1-\alpha)^{n_1} \alpha^{n_2}$, where $\alpha \in (0,1)$. Denote by $Sub(\mathcal{T})$ the set of all possible subtrees of $\mathcal{T}$ including $\mathcal{T}$ itself. It can be easily verified that this definition of the weights is a proper measure, i.e., $\sum_{\mathcal{T}' \in Sub(\mathcal{T})} P_0(\mathcal{T}') = 1$. This distribution over trees can be extended to unbounded trees assuming that the largest tree is an *infinite* $|\Sigma_{in}|$-ary suffix tree transducer and using the following randomized recursive process. We start with a suffix tree that includes only the root node. With probability α we stop the process and with probability $1 - \alpha$ we add all the possible $|\Sigma_{in}|$ sons of the node and continue the process recursively for each of the sons. Using this recursive prior the suffix tree transducers, we can calculate the prediction of the mixture at step n in time that is linear in n, as follows,

$$\alpha \gamma_e(y_n) + (1-\alpha)\left(\alpha \gamma_{x_n}(y_n) + (1-\alpha)\left(\alpha \gamma_{x_{n-1}x_n}(y_n) + (1-\alpha)\right)\ldots\right)$$

Therefore, the prediction time of a single symbol is bounded by the maximal depth of $\mathcal{T}$, or the length of the input sequence if $\mathcal{T}$ is infinite. Denote by $\tilde{\gamma}_s(y_n)$ the prediction of the mixture of subtrees rooted at s, and let $Leaves(\mathcal{T})$ be the set of leaves of $\mathcal{T}$. The above sum equals to $\tilde{\gamma}_e(y_n)$, and can be evaluated recursively as follows,[1]

$$\tilde{\gamma}_s(y_n) = \begin{cases} \gamma_s(y_n) & s \in Leaves(T) \\ \alpha\gamma_s(y_n) + (1-\alpha)\tilde{\gamma}_{(x_{n-|s|},s)}(y_n) & \text{otherwise} \end{cases}, \quad (1)$$

For example, given that the input sequence is $\ldots, 0, 1, 1, 0$, then the probabilities of the mixtures of subtrees for the tree depicted on the left part of Fig. 1, for $y_n = b$ and given that $\alpha = 1/2$, are, $\tilde{\gamma}_{110}(b) = 0.4$, $\tilde{\gamma}_{10}(b) = 0.5 \cdot \gamma_{10}(b) + 0.5 \cdot 0.4 = 0.3$, $\tilde{\gamma}_0(b) = 0.5 \cdot \gamma_0(b) + 0.5 \cdot 0.3 = 0.25$, $\tilde{\gamma}_e(b) = 0.5 \cdot \gamma_e(b) + 0.5 \cdot 0.25 = 0.25$.

3 An Online Learning Algorithm

We now describe an efficient learning algorithm for a mixture of suffix tree transducers. The learning algorithm uses the recursive priors and the evidence to efficiently update the posterior weight of each possible subtree. In this section we assume that the output probability functions are known. Hence, we need to evaluate the following,

$$P(y_n|x_1, \ldots, x_n) = \sum_{T' \in Sub(T)} P(y_n|T')P(T'|(x_1, y_1), \ldots, (x_{n-1}, y_{n-1}))$$

$$\stackrel{def}{=} \sum_{T' \in Sub(T)} P(y_n|T')P_n(T') , \quad (2)$$

where $P_n(T')$ is the posterior weight of T'. Direct calculation of the above sum requires exponential time. However, using the idea of recursive calculation as in Equ. (1) we can efficiently calculate the prediction of the mixture. Similar to the definition of the recursive prior α, we define $q_n(s)$ to be the *posterior* weight of a node s compared to the mixture of all nodes below s. We can compute the prediction of the mixture of suffix tree transducers rooted at s by simply replacing the prior weight α with the posterior weight, $q_{n-1}(s)$, as follows,

$$\tilde{\gamma}_s(y_n) = \begin{cases} \gamma_s(y_n) & s \in Leaves(T) \\ q_{n-1}(s)\gamma_s(y_n) + (1-q_{n-1}(s))\tilde{\gamma}_{(x_{n-|s|},s)}(y_n) & \text{otherwise} \end{cases}, \quad (3)$$

In order to update $q_n(s)$ we introduce one more variable, denoted by $r_n(s)$. Setting $r_0(s) = \log(\alpha/(1-\alpha))$ for all s, $r_n(s)$ is updated as follows,

$$r_n(s) = r_{n-1}(s) + \log(\gamma_s(y_n)) - \log(\tilde{\gamma}_{x_{n-|s|}s}(y_n)) . \quad (4)$$

Therefore, $r_n(s)$ is the log-likelihood ratio between the prediction of s and the prediction of the mixture of all nodes below s in T. The new posterior weights $q_n(s)$ are calculated from $r_n(s)$,

$$q_n(s) = 1/(1 + e^{-r_n(s)}) . \quad (5)$$

In summary, for each new observation pair, we traverse the tree by following the path that corresponds to the input sequence $x_n x_{n-1} x_{n-2} \ldots$. The predictions of each sub-mixture are calculated using Equ. (3). Given these predictions the posterior weights of each sub-mixture are updated using Equ. (4) and Equ. (5). Finally, the probability of y_n induced by the whole mixture is the prediction propagated out of the root node, as stated by Lemma 3.1.

Lemma 3.1 $\sum_{T' \in Sub(T)} P(y_n|T')P_n(T') = \tilde{\gamma}_e(y_n)$.

Let $Loss_n(T)$ be the logarithmic loss (negative log-likelihood) of a suffix tree transducer T after n input-output pairs. That is, $Loss_n(T) = \sum_{i=1}^{n} -\log(P(y_i|T))$. Similarly, the loss

---
[1] A similar derivation still holds even if there is a different prior α_s at each node s of T. For the sake of simplicity we assume that α is constant.

of the mixture is defined to be, $Loss_n^{mix} = \sum_{i=1}^n -\log(\tilde{\gamma}_\mathbf{e}(y_i))$. The advantage of using a mixture of suffix tree transducers over a single suffix tree is due to the robustness of the solution, in the sense that the prediction of the mixture is almost as good as the prediction of the best suffix tree in the mixture.

Theorem 1 *Let T be a (possibly infinite) suffix tree transducer, and let $(x_1, y_1), \ldots, (x_n, y_n)$ be any possible sequence of input-output pairs. The loss of the mixture is at most, $Loss_n(T') - \log(P_0(T'))$, for each possible subtree T'. The running time of the algorithm is $D n$ where D is the maximal depth of T or n^2 when T is infinite.*

The proof is based on a technique introduced in [4]. Note that the additional loss is constant, hence the normalized loss per observation pair is, $P_0(T')/n$, which decreases like $O(\frac{1}{n})$.

Given a long sequence of input-output pairs or many short sequences, the structure of the suffix tree transducer is inferred as well. This is done by updating the output functions, as described in the next section, while *adding* new branches to the tree whenever the suffix of the input sequence does not appear in the current tree. The update of the weights, the parameters, and the structure ends when the maximal depth is reached, or when the beginning of the input sequence is encountered.

4 Parameter Estimation

In this section we describe how the output probability functions are estimated. Again, we devise an online scheme. Denote by $C_s^n(y)$ the number of times the output symbol y was observed out of the n times the node s was visited. A commonly used estimator smoothes each count by adding a constant ϵ as follows,

$$\gamma_s(y) \approx \hat{\gamma}_s^n(y) \stackrel{\text{def}}{=} (C_s^n(y) + \epsilon)/(n + \epsilon |\Sigma_{out}|) \ . \tag{6}$$

The special case of $\epsilon = \frac{1}{2}$ is termed Laplace's modified rule of succession or the add-$\frac{1}{2}$ estimator. In [9], Krichevsky and Trofimov proved that the loss of the add-$\frac{1}{2}$ estimator, when applied sequentially, has a bounded logarithmic loss compared to the best (maximum-likelihood) estimator calculated *after* observing the entire input-output sequence. The additional loss of the estimator after n observations is, $1/2(|\Sigma_{out}| - 1) \log(n) + |\Sigma_{out}| - 1$. When the output alphabet Σ_{out} is rather small, we approximate $\gamma_s(y)$ by $\hat{\gamma}_s(y)$ using Equ. (6) and increment the count of the corresponding symbol every time the node s is visited. We predict by replacing γ with its estimate $\hat{\gamma}$ in Equ. (3). The loss of the mixture with estimated output probability functions, compared to any subtree T' with *known* parameters, is now bounded as follows,

$$Loss_n^{mix} \leq Loss_n(T') - \log(P_0(T')) + 1/2 |T'| (|\Sigma_{out}| - 1) \log(n/|T'|) + |T'| (|\Sigma_{out}| - 1),$$

where $|T'|$ is the number of leaves in T'. This bound is obtained by combining the bound on the prediction of the mixture from Thm. 1 with the loss of the smoothed estimator while applying Jensen's inequality [3].

When $|\Sigma_{out}|$ is fairly large or the sample size if fairly small, the smoothing of the output probabilities is too crude. However, in many real problems, only a small subset of the output alphabet is observed in a given context (a node in the tree). For example, when mapping *phonemes* to *phones* [11], for a given sequence of input phonemes the phones that can be pronounced is limited to a few possibilities. Therefore, we would like to devise an estimation scheme that statistically depends on the *effective* local alphabet and not on the whole alphabet. Such an estimation scheme can be devised by employing again a mixture of models, one model for each possible subset Σ'_{out} of Σ_{out}. Although there are $2^{|\Sigma_{out}|}$ subsets of Σ_{out}, we next show that if the estimators depend only on the *size* of each subset then the whole mixture can be maintained in time *linear* in $|\Sigma_{out}|$.

Denote by $\hat{\gamma}_s^n(y| |\Sigma'_{out}| = i)$ the estimate of $\gamma_s(y)$ after n observations given that the alphabet Σ'_{out} is of size i. Using the add-$\frac{1}{2}$ estimator, $\hat{\gamma}_s^n(y| |\Sigma'_{out}| = i) = (C_s^n(y) + 1/2)/(n + i/2)$. Let $\Sigma_{out}^n(s)$ be the set of different output symbols observed at node s, i.e.

$$\Sigma_{out}^n(s) = \{\sigma \mid \sigma = y_{i_k}, s = (x_{i_k - |s| + 1}, \ldots, x_{i_k}), 1 \leq k \leq n\} \ ,$$

and define $\Sigma_{out}^0(s)$ to be the empty set. There are $\binom{|\Sigma_{out}| - |\Sigma_{out}^n(s)|}{i - |\Sigma_{out}^n(s)|}$ possible alphabets of size i. Thus, the prediction of the mixture of all possible subsets of Σ_{out} is,

$$\hat{\gamma}_s^n(y) = \sum_{j=|\Sigma_{out}^n(s)|}^{|\Sigma_{out}|} \binom{|\Sigma_{out}| - |\Sigma_{out}^n(s)|}{j - |\Sigma_{out}^n(s)|} w_j^n \, \hat{\gamma}_s^n(y|j) \ , \tag{7}$$

where w_i^n is the posterior probability of an alphabet of size i. Evaluation of this sum requires $O(|\Sigma_{out}|)$ operations (and not $O(2^{|\Sigma_{out}|})$). We can compute Equ. (7) in an online fashion as follows. Let,

$$\hat{\Gamma}_s^n(i) \stackrel{\text{def}}{=} \sum_{\Sigma_{out}^n(s) \subseteq \Sigma'_{out}, |\Sigma'_{out}|=i} w_i^0 \prod_{k=1}^n \hat{\gamma}_s^{k-1}(y_{i_k}|\Sigma'_{out})$$

$$= \binom{|\Sigma_{out}| - |\Sigma_{out}^n(s)|}{i - |\Sigma_{out}^n(s)|} w_i^0 \prod_{k=1}^n \hat{\gamma}_s^{k-1}(y_{i_k}|i) \ . \tag{8}$$

Without loss of generality, let us assume a uniform prior for the possible alphabet sizes. Then,

$$P_0(\Sigma'_{out}) = P_0(|\Sigma'_{out}| = i) \stackrel{\text{def}}{=} w_i^0 = 1/\left(|\Sigma_{out}| \binom{|\Sigma_{out}|}{i}\right) \ .$$

Thus, for all i $\hat{\Gamma}_s^0(i) = 1/|\Sigma_{out}|$. $\hat{\Gamma}_s^{n+1}(i)$ is updated from $\hat{\Gamma}_s^n(i)$ as follows,

$$\hat{\Gamma}_s^{n+1}(i) = \hat{\Gamma}_s^n(i) \times \begin{cases} 0 & \text{if } |\Sigma_{out}^{n+1}(s)| > i \\ \frac{C_s^n(y_{i_{n+1}}) + 1/2}{n + i/2} & \text{if } |\Sigma_{out}^{n+1}(s)| \leq i \text{ and } y_{i_{n+1}} \in \Sigma_{out}^n(s) \\ \frac{i - |\Sigma_{out}^n(s)|}{|\Sigma_{out}| - |\Sigma_{out}^n(s)|} \frac{1/2}{n + i/2} & \text{if } |\Sigma_{out}^{n+1}(s)| \leq i \text{ and } y_{i_{n+1}} \notin \Sigma_{out}^n(s) \end{cases}$$

Informally: If the number of different symbols observed so far exceeds a given size then all alphabets of this size are eliminated from the mixture by slashing their posterior probability to zero. Otherwise, if the next symbol was observed before, the output probability is the prediction of the $add\frac{1}{2}$ estimator. Lastly, if the next symbol is entirely new, we need to sum the predictions of all the alphabets of size i which agree on the first $|\Sigma_{out}^n(s)|$ and $y_{i_{n+1}}$ is one of their $i - |\Sigma_{out}^n(s)|$ (yet) unobserved symbols. Furthermore, we need to multiply by the apriori probability of observing $y_{i_{n+1}}$. Assuming a uniform prior over the unobserved symbols this probability equals to $1/(|\Sigma_{out}| - |\Sigma_{out}^n(s)|)$. Applying Bayes rule again, the prediction of the mixture of all possible subsets of the output alphabet is,

$$\hat{\gamma}_s^n(y_{i_{n+1}}) = \sum_{i=1}^{|\Sigma_{out}|} \hat{\Gamma}_s^{n+1}(i) \Big/ \sum_{i=1}^{|\Sigma_{out}|} \hat{\Gamma}_s^n(i) \ . \tag{9}$$

Applying twice the online mixture estimation technique, first for the structure and then for the parameters, yields an efficient and robust online algorithm. For a sample of size n, the time complexity of the algorithm is $D|\Sigma_{out}|n$ (or $|\Sigma_{out}|n^2$ if $\mathcal{T}$ is infinite). The predictions of the adaptive mixture is almost as good as *any* suffix tree transducer with *any* set of parameters. The logarithmic loss of the mixture depends on the number of *non-zero* parameters as follows,

$$Loss_n^{mix} \leq Loss_n(\mathcal{T}') - \log(P_0(\mathcal{T}')) + 1/2 \, l_{NZ} \log(n) + O(|\mathcal{T}'||\Sigma_{out}|) \ ,$$

where l_{NZ} is the number of non-zero parameters of the transducer $\mathcal{T}'$. If $l_{NZ} \ll |\mathcal{T}'||\Sigma_{out}|$ then the performance of the above scheme, when employing a mixture model for the parameters as well, is significantly better than using the add$\frac{1}{2}$ rule with the full alphabet.

5 Evaluation and Applications

In this section we briefly present evaluation results of the model and its learning algorithm. We also discuss and present results obtained from learning syntactic structure of noun phrases. We start with an evaluation of the estimation scheme for a multinomial source.

In order to check the convergence of a mixture model for a multinomial source, we simulated a source whose output symbols belong to an alphabet of size 10 and set the probabilities of observing any of the last five symbols to zero. Therefore, the actual alphabet is of size 5. The posterior probabilities for the sum of all possible subsets of Σ_{out} of size i ($1 \leq i \leq 10$) were calculated after each iteration. The results are plotted on the left part of Fig. 2. The very first observations rule out alphabets of size lower than 5 by slashing their posterior probability to zero. After few observations, the posterior probability is concentrated around the actual size, yielding an accurate online estimate of the multinomial source.

The simplicity of the learning algorithm and the online update scheme enable evaluation of the algorithm on *millions* of input-output pairs in few minutes. For example, the average update time for a suffix tree transducer of a maximal depth 10 when the output alphabet is of size 4 is about 0.2 millisecond on a Silicon Graphics workstation. A typical result is shown in Fig. 2 on the right. In the example, $\Sigma_{out} = \Sigma_{in} = \{1,2,3,4\}$. The description of the source is as follows. If $x_n \geq 3$ then y_n is uniformly distributed over Σ_{out}, otherwise ($x_n \leq 2$) $y_n = x_{n-5}$ with probability 0.9 and $y_{n-5} = 4 - x_{n-5}$ with probability 0.1. The input sequence $x_1, x_2, \ldots$ was created entirely at random. This source can be implemented by a sparse suffix tree transducer of maximal depth 5. Note that the actual size of the alphabet is only 2 at half of the leaves of the tree. We used a suffix tree transducer of maximal depth 20 to learn the source. The negative of the logarithm of the predictions (normalized per symbol) are shown for (a) the true source, (b) a mixture of suffix tree transducers and their parameters, (c) a mixture of only the possible suffix tree transducers (the parameters are estimated using the $add\frac{1}{2}$ scheme), and (d) a single (overestimated) model of depth 8. Clearly, the mixture model converge to the entropy of the source much faster than the single model. Moreover, employing twice the mixture estimation technique results in an even faster convergence.

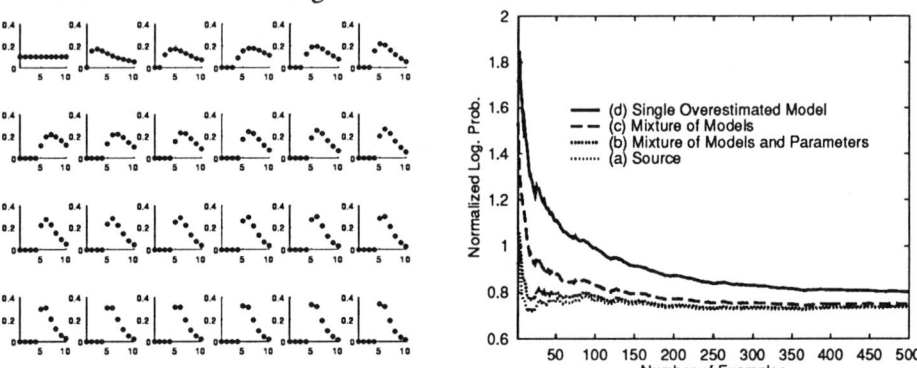

Figure 2: Left: Example of the convergence of the posterior probability of a mixture model for a multinomial source with large number of possible outcomes when the actual number of observed symbols is small. Right: performance comparison of the predictions of a single model, two mixture models and the true underlying transducer.

We are currently exploring the applicative possibilities of the algorithm. Here we briefly discuss and demonstrate how to induce an English noun phrase recognizer. Recognizing noun phrases is an important task in automatic natural text processing, for applications such as information retrieval, translation tools and data extraction from texts. A common practice is to recognize noun phrases by first analyzing the text with a part-of-speech tagger, which assigns the appropriate part-of-speech (verb, noun, adjective etc.) for each word in context. Then, noun phrases are identified by manually defined regular expression patterns that are matched against the part-of-speech sequences. We took an alternative route by building a suffix tree transducer based on a labeled data set from the UPENN tree-bank corpus. We defined Σ_{in} to be the set of possible part-of-speech tags and set $\Sigma_{out} = \{0, 1\}$, where the output symbol given its corresponding input symbol (the part-of-speech tag of the current word) is 1 *iff* the word is part of a noun phrase. We used over 250,000 marked tags and tested the performance on more than 37,000 tags. The test phase was performed by freezing the model structure, the mixture weights and the estimated parameters. The suffix tree transducer was of maximal depth 15 hence very long phrases can be statistically identified. By tresholding the output probability we classified the tags in the test data and found that less than 2.4% of the words were misclassified. A typical result is given in Table 1. We are currently investigating methods to incorporate linguistic knowledge into the model and its learning algorithm and compare the performance of the model with traditional techniques.

Sentence	Tom	Smith	,	group	chief	executive	of	U.K.	metals
POS tag	PNP	PNP	,	NN	NN	NN	IN	PNP	NNS
Class	1	1	0	1	1	1	0	1	1
Prediction	0.99	0.99	0.01	0.98	0.98	0.98	0.02	0.99	0.99
Sentence	and	industrial	materials	maker	,	will	become	chairman	.
POS tag	CC	JJ	NNS	NN	,	MD	VB	NN	.
Class	1	1	1	1	0	0	0	1	0
Prediction	0.67	0.96	0.99	0.96	0.03	0.03	0.01	0.87	0.01

Table 1: Extraction of noun phrases using a suffix tree transducer. In this typical example, two long noun phrases were identified correctly with high confidence.

Acknowledgments

Thanks to Y. Bengio, Y. Freund, F. Pereira, D. Ron, R. Schapire, and N. Tishby for helpful discussions. The work on syntactic structure induction is done in collaboration with I. Dagan and S. Engelson. This work was done while the author was at the Hebrew University of Jerusalem.

References

[1] Y. Bengio and P. Fransconi. An input output HMM architecture. In *NIPS-7*, 1994.

[2] N. Cesa-Bianchi, Y. Freund, D. Haussler, D.P. Helmbold, R.E. Schapire, and M. K. Warmuth. How to use expert advice. In *STOC-24*, 1993.

[3] T.M. Cover and J.A. Thomas. *Elements of information theory*. Wiley, 1991.

[4] A. DeSantis, G. Markowski, and M.N. Wegman. Learning probabilistic prediction functions. In *Proc. of the 1st Wksp. on Comp. Learning Theory*, pages 312–328, 1988.

[5] C.L. Giles, C.B. Miller, D. Chen, G.Z. Sun, H.H. Chen, and Y.C. Lee. Learning and extracting finite state automata with second-order recurrent neural networks. *Neural Computation*, 4:393–405, 1992.

[6] D. Haussler and A. Barron. How well do Bayes methods work for on-line prediction of $\{+1, -1\}$ values ? In *The 3rd NEC Symp. on Comput. and Cogn.*, 1993.

[7] D.P. Helmbold and R.E. Schapire. Predicting nearly as well as the best pruning of a decision tree. In *COLT-8*, 1995.

[8] R.A. Jacobs, M.I. Jordan, S.J. Nowlan, and G.E. Hinton. Adaptive mixture of local experts. *Neural Computation*, 3:79–87, 1991.

[9] R.E. Krichevsky and V.K. Trofimov. The performance of universal encoding. *IEEE Trans. on Inform. Theory*, 1981.

[10] Nick Littlestone and Manfred K. Warmuth. The weighted majority algorithm. *Information and Computation*, 108:212–261, 1994.

[11] M.D. Riley. A statistical model for generating pronounication networks. In *Proc. of IEEE Conf. on Acoustics, Speech and Signal Processing*, pages 737–740, 1991.

[12] D. Ron, Y. Singer, and N. Tishby. The power of amnesia. In *NIPS-6*, 1993.

[13] F.M.J. Willems, Y.M. Shtarkov, and T.J. Tjalkens. The context tree weighting method: Basic properties. *IEEE Trans. Inform. Theory*, 41(3):653–664, 1995.

REMAP: Recursive Estimation and Maximization of A Posteriori Probabilities - Application to Transition-Based Connectionist Speech Recognition

Yochai Konig, Hervé Bourlard,[*] and Nelson Morgan
{konig,bourlard,morgan}@icsi.berkeley.edu
International Computer Science Institute
1947 Center Street Berkeley, CA 94704, USA.

Abstract

In this paper, we introduce REMAP, an approach for the training and estimation of posterior probabilities using a recursive algorithm that is reminiscent of the EM-based Forward-Backward (Liporace 1982) algorithm for the estimation of sequence likelihoods. Although very general, the method is developed in the context of a statistical model for transition-based speech recognition using Artificial Neural Networks (ANN) to generate probabilities for Hidden Markov Models (HMMs). In the new approach, we use local conditional posterior probabilities of transitions to estimate global posterior probabilities of word sequences. Although we still use ANNs to estimate posterior probabilities, the network is trained with targets that are themselves estimates of local posterior probabilities. An initial experimental result shows a significant decrease in error-rate in comparison to a baseline system.

1 INTRODUCTION

The ultimate goal in speech recognition is to determine the sequence of words that has been uttered. Classical pattern recognition theory shows that the best possible system (in the sense of minimum probability of error) is the one that chooses the word sequence with the maximum a posteriori probability (conditioned on the

---

[*]Also affiliated with with Faculté Polytechnique de Mons, Mons, Belgium

evidence). If word sequence i is represented by the statistical model M_i, and the evidence (which, for the application reported here, is acoustical) is represented by a sequence $X = \{x_1, \ldots, x_n, \ldots, x_N\}$, then we wish to choose the sequence that corresponds to the largest $P(M_i|X)$. In (Bourlard & Morgan 1994), summarizing earlier work (such as (Bourlard & Wellekens 1989)), we showed that it was possible to compute the global a posteriori probability $P(M|X)$ of a discriminant form of Hidden Markov Model (Discriminant HMM), M, given a sequence of acoustic vectors X. In Discriminant HMMs, the global a posteriori probability $P(M|X)$ is computed as follows: if Γ represents all legal paths (state sequences $q_1, q_2, \ldots, q_N$) in M_i, N being the length of the sequence, then

$$P(M_i|X) = \sum_{\Gamma} P(M_i, q_1, q_2, \ldots, q_N|X)$$

in which q_n represents the specific state hypothesized at time n, from the set $\mathcal{Q} = \{q^1, \ldots, q^\ell, q^k, \ldots, q^K\}$ of all possible HMM states making up all possible models M_i. We can further decompose this into:

$$P(M_i, q_1, q_2, \ldots, q_N|X) = P(q_1, q_2, \ldots, q_N|X) P(M_i|q_1, q_2, \ldots, q_N, X)$$

Under the assumptions stated in (Bourlard & Morgan 1994) we can compute

$$P(q_1, q_2, \ldots, q_N|X) = \prod_{n=1}^{N} p(q_n|q_{n-1}, x_n)$$

The Discriminant HMM is thus described in terms of *conditional transition probabilities* $p(q_n^\ell|q_{n-1}^k, x_n)$, in which q_n^ℓ stands for the specific state q^ℓ of $\mathcal{Q}$ hypothesized at time n and can be schematically represented as in Figure 1.

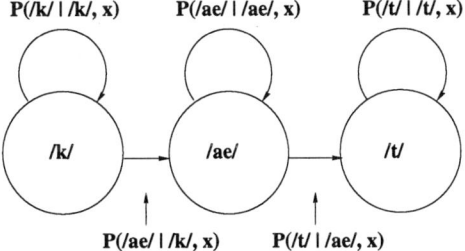

Figure 1: An example Discriminant HMM for the word "cat". The variable x refers to a specific acoustic observation x_n at time n.

Finally, given a state sequence we assume the following approximation:

$$P(M_i|q_1, q_2, \ldots, q_N, X) \approx P(M_i|q_1, q_2, \ldots, q_N)$$

We can estimate the right side of this last equation from a phonological model (in the case that a given state sequence can belong to two different models). All the required (local) conditional transition probabilities $p(q_n^\ell|q_{n-1}^k, x_n)$ can be estimated by the Multi-Layer Perceptron (MLP) shown in Figure 2.

Recent work at ICSI has provided us with further insight into the discriminant HMM, particularly in light of recent work on transition-based models (Konig & Morgan 1994; Morgan et al. 1994). This new perspective has motivated us to further develop the original Discriminant HMM theory. The new approach uses posterior probabilities at both local and global levels and is more discriminant in nature. In this paper, we introduce the Recursive Estimation-Maximization of A posteriori

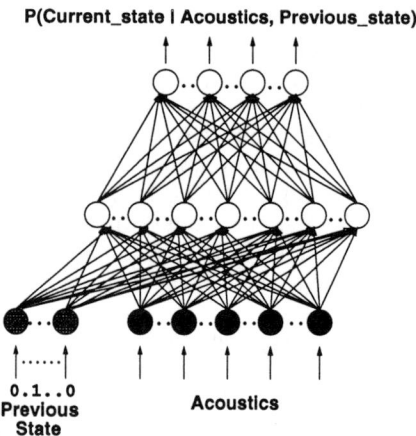

Figure 2: An MLP that estimates local conditional transition probabilities.

Probabilities (REMAP) training algorithm for hybrid HMM/MLP systems. The proposed algorithm models a probability distribution over all possible transitions (from all possible states and for all possible time frames n) rather than picking a single time point as a transition target. Furthermore, the algorithm incrementally increases the posterior probability of the correct model, while reducing the posterior probabilities of all other models. Thus, it brings the overall system closer to the optimal Bayes classifier.

A wide range of discriminant approaches to speech recognition have been studied by researchers (Katagiri *et al.* 1991; Bengio *et al.* 1992; Bourlard *et al.* 1994). A significant difficulty that has remained in applying these approaches to continuous speech recognition has been the requirement to run computationally intensive algorithms on all of the rival sentences. Since this is not generally feasible, compromises must always be made in practice. For instance, estimates for all rival sentences can be derived from a list of the "N-best" utterance hypotheses, or by using a fully connected word model composed of all phonemes.

2 REMAP TRAINING OF THE DISCRIMINANT HMM

2.1 MOTIVATIONS

The discriminant HMM/MLP theory as described above uses transition-based probabilities as the key building block for acoustic recognition. However, it is well known that estimating transitions accurately is a difficult problem (Glass 1988). Due to the inertia of the articulators, the boundaries between phones are blurred and overlapped in continuous speech. In our previous hybrid HMM/MLP system, targets were typically obtained by using a standard forced Viterbi alignment (segmentation). For a transition-based system as defined above, this procedure would thus yield rigid transition targets, which is not realistic.

Another problem related to the Viterbi-based training of the MLP presented in Figure 2 and used in Discriminant HMMs, is the lack of coverage of the input space during training. Indeed, during training (based on hard transitions), the MLP only processes inputs consisting of "correct" pairs of acoustic vectors and correct previous state, while in recognition the net should generalize to all possible combinations of acoustic vectors and previous states, since all possible models and transitions will be hypothesized for each acoustic input. For example, some hypothesized inputs may correspond to an impossible condition that has thus never been observed, such as the acoustics of the temporal center of a vowel in combination with a previous state that corresponds to a plosive. It is unfortunately possible that the interpolative capabilities of the network may not be sufficient to give these "impossible" pairs a sufficiently low probability during recognition.

One possible solution to these problems is to use a full MAP algorithm to find transition probabilities at each frame for all possible transitions by a forward-backward-like algorithm (Liporace 1982), taking all possible paths into account.

2.2 PROBLEM FORMULATION

As described above, global maximum a posteriori training of HMMs should find the optimal parameter set Θ maximizing

$$\prod_{j=1}^{J} P(M_j|X_j, \Theta) \tag{1}$$

in which M_j represents the Markov model associated with each training utterance X_j, with $j = 1, \ldots, J$.

Although in principle we could use a generalized back-propagation-like gradient procedure in Θ to maximize (1) (Bengio et al. 1992), an EM-like algorithm should have better convergence properties, and could preserve the statistical interpretation of the ANN outputs. In this case, training of the discriminant HMM by a global MAP criterion requires a solution to the following problem: given a trained MLP at iteration t providing a parameter set Θ^t and, consequently, estimates of $P(q_n^\ell|x_n, q_{n-1}^k, \Theta^t)$, how can we determine new MLP targets that:

1. will be smooth estimates of conditional transition probabilities $q_{n-1}^k \to q_n^\ell$, $\forall k, \ell \in [1, K]$ and $\forall n \in [1, N]$,

2. when training the MLP for iteration $t+1$, will lead to new estimates of Θ^{t+1} and $P(q_n^\ell|x_n, q_{n-1}^k, \Theta^{t+1})$ that are guaranteed to incrementally increase the global posterior probability $P(M_i|X, \Theta)$?

In (Bourlard et al. 1994), we prove that a re-estimate of MLP targets that guarantee convergence to a local maximum of (1) is given by[1]:

$$P^*(q_n^\ell|x_n, q_{n-1}^k, M) = P(q_n^\ell|X, q_{n-1}^k, \Theta^t, M) \tag{2}$$

where we have estimated the left-hand side using a mapping from the previous state and the local acoustic data to the current state, thus making the estimator realizable by an MLP with a local acoustic window.[2] Thus, we will want to estimate

---

[1] In most of the following, we consider only one particular training sequence X associated with one particular model M. It is, however, easy to see that all of our conclusions remain valid for the case of several training sequences X_j, $j = 1, \ldots, J$. A simple way to look at the problem is to consider all training sequences as a single training sequence obtained by concatenating all the X_j's with boundary conditions at every possible beginning and ending point.

[2] Note that, as done in our previous hybrid HMM/MLP systems, all conditional on x_n can be replaced by $X_{n-c}^{n+d} = \{x_{n-c}, \ldots, x_n, \ldots, x_{n+d}\}$ to take some acoustic context into account.

the transition probability conditioned on the *local* data (as MLP targets) by using the transition probability conditioned on *all* of the data.

In (Bourlard et al. 1994), we further prove that alternating MLP target estimation (the "estimation" step) and MLP training (the "maximization" step) is guaranteed to incrementally increase (1) over t.[3] The remaining problem is to find an efficient algorithm to express $P(q_n^\ell | X, q_{n-1}^k, M)$ in terms of $P(q_n^\ell | x_n, q_{n-1}^k)$ so that the next iteration targets can be found. We have developed several approaches to this estimation, some of which are described in (Bourlard et al. 1994). Currently, we are implementing this with an efficient recursion that estimates the sum of all possible paths in a model, for every possible transition at each possible time. From these values we can compute the desired targets (2) for network training by

$$P(q_n^\ell | X, M, q_{n-1}^k) = \frac{P(M, q_n^\ell, q_{n-1}^k | X)}{\sum_j P(M, q_n^j, q_{n-1}^k | X)} \qquad (3)$$

2.3 REMAP TRAINING ALGORITHM

The general scheme of the REMAP training of hybrid HMM/MLP systems can be summarized as follow:

1. Start from some initial net providing $P(q_n^\ell | x_n, q_{n-1}^k, \Theta^t)$, $t = 0$, $\forall$ possible (k, ℓ)-pairs[4].

2. Compute MLP targets $P(q_n^\ell | X_j, q_{n-1}^k, \Theta^t, M_j)$ according to (3), $\forall$ training sentences X_j associated with HMM M_j, $\forall$ possible (k, ℓ) state transition pairs in M_j and $\forall$ x_n, $n = 1, \ldots, N$ in X_j (see next point).

3. For every x_n in the training database, train the MLP to minimize the relative entropy between the outputs and targets. See (Bourlard et al. 1994) for more details. This provides us with a new set of parameters Θ^t, for $t = t + 1$.

4. Iterate from 2 until convergence.

This procedure is thus composed of two steps: an Estimation (E) step, corresponding to step 2 above, and a Maximization (M) step, corresponding to step 3 above. In this regards, it is reminiscent of the Estimation-Maximization (EM) algorithm as discussed in (Dempster et al. 1977). However, in the standard EM algorithm, the M step involves the actual maximization of the likelihood function. In a related approach, usually referred to as Generalized EM (GEM) algorithm, the M step does not actually maximize the likelihood but simply increases it (by using, e.g., a gradient procedure). Similarly, REMAP increases the global posterior function during the M step (in the direction of targets that actually maximize that global function), rather than actually maximizing it. Recently, a similar approach was suggested for mapping input sequences to output sequences (Bengio & Frasconi 1995).

---

[3] Note here that one "iteration" does not stand for one iteration of the MLP training but for one estimation-maximization iteration for which a complete MLP training will be required.

[4] This can be done, for instance, by training up such a net from a hand-labeled database like TIMIT or from some initial forward-backward estimator of equivalent local probabilities (usually referred to as "gamma" probabilities in the Baum-Welch procedure).

System	Error Rate
DHMM, pre-REMAP	14.9%
1 REMAP iteration	13.6%
2 REMAP iterations	13.2%

Table 1: Training and testing on continuous numbers, no syntax, no durational models.

3 EXPERIMENTS AND RESULTS

For testing our theory we chose the Numbers'93 corpus. It is a continuous speech database collected by CSLU at the Oregon Graduate Institute. It consists of numbers spoken naturally over telephone lines on the public-switched network (Cole et al. 1994). The Numbers'93 database consists of 2167 speech files of spoken numbers produced by 1132 callers. We used 877 of these utterances for training and 657 for cross-validation and testing (200 for cross-validation) saving the remaining utterances for final testing purposes. There are 36 words in the vocabulary, namely *zero, oh, 1, 2, 3,...,20, 30, 40, 50,...,100, 1000, a, and, dash, hyphen,* and *double*. All our nets have 214 inputs: 153 inputs for the acoustic features, and 61 to represent the previous state (one unit for every possible previous state, one state per phoneme in our case). The acoustic features are combined from 9 frames with 17 features each (RASTA-PLP8 + delta features + delta log gain) computed with an analysis window of 25 ms computed every 12.5 ms (overlapping windows) and with a sampling rate of 8 Khz. The nets have 200 hidden units and 61 outputs.

Our results are summarized in Table 1. The row entitled "DHMM, pre-REMAP" corresponds to a Discriminant HMM using the same training approach, with hard targets determined by the first system, and additional inputs to represent the previous state The improvement in the recognition rate as a result of REMAP iterations is significant at $p < 0.05$. However all the experiments were done using acoustic information alone. Using our (baseline) hybrid system under equal conditions, i.e., no duration information and no language information, we get 31.6% word error; adding the duration information back we get 12.4% word error. We are currently experimenting with enforcing minimum duration constraints in our framework.

4 CONCLUSIONS

In summary:

- We have a method for MAP training and estimation of sequences.

- This can be used in a new form of hybrid HMM/MLP. Note that recurrent nets or TDNNs could also be used. As with standard HMM/MLP hybrids, the network is used to estimate local posterior probabilities (though in this case they are conditional transition probabilities, that is, state probabilities conditioned on the acoustic data and the previous state). However, in the case of REMAP these nets are trained with probabilistic targets that are themselves estimates of local posterior probabilities.

- Initial experiments demonstrate a significant reduction in error rate for this process.

Acknowledgments

We would like to thank Kristine Ma and Su-Lin Wu for their help with the Numbers'93 database. We also thank OGI, in particular to Ron Cole, for providing the database. We gratefully acknowledge the support of the Office of Naval Research, URI No. N00014-92-J-1617 (via UCB), the European Commission via ESPRIT project 20077 (SPRACH), and ICSI and FPMs in general for supporting this work.

References

BENGIO, Y., & P. FRASCONI. 1995. An input output HMM architecture. In *Advances in Neural Information Processing Systems*, ed. by G. Tesauro, D. Touretzky, & T. Leen, volume 7. Cambridge: MIT press.

——, R. DE MORI, G. FLAMMIA, & R. KOMPE. 1992. Global optimization of a neural network-hidden Markov model hybrid. *IEEE trans. on Neural Networks* 3.252–258.

BOURLARD, H., Y. KONIG, & N. MORGAN. 1994. REMAP: Recursive estimation and maximization of a posteriori probabilities, application to transition-based connectionist speech recognition. Technical Report TR-94-064, International Computer Science Institute, Berkeley, CA.

——, & N. MORGAN. 1994. *Connectionist Speech Recognition - A Hybrid Approach*. Kluwer Academic Publishers.

——, & C. J. WELLEKENS. 1989. Links between Markov models and multilayer perceptrons. In *Advances in Neural Information Processing Systems 1*, ed. by D.J. Touretzky, 502–510, San Mateo. Morgan Kaufmann.

COLE, R.A., M. FANTY, & T. LANDER. 1994. Telephone speech corpus development at CSLU. In *Proceedings Int'l Conference on Spoken Language Processing*, Yokohama, Japan.

DEMPSTER, A. P., N. M. LAIRD, & D. B. RUBIN. 1977. Maximum likelihood from incomplete data via the *EM* algorithm. *Journal of the Royal Statistical Society, Series B* 34.1–38.

GLASS, J. R., 1988. *Finding Acoustic Regularities in Speech Applications to Phonetic Recognition*. M.I.T dissertation.

KATAGIRI, S., C.H. LEE, & JUANG B.H. 1991. New discriminative training algorithms based on the generalized probabilistic decent method. In *Proc. of the IEEE Workshop on Neural Netwroks for Signal Processing*, ed. by B.H. Juang, S.Y. Kung, & C.A. Kamm, 299–308.

KONIG, Y., & N. MORGAN. 1994. Modeling dynamics in connectionist speech recognition - the time index model. In *Proceedings Int'l Conference on Spoken Language Processing*, 1523–1526, Yokohama, Japan.

LIPORACE, L. A. 1982. Maximum likelihood estimation for multivariate observations of markov sources. *IEEE Trans. on Information Theory* IT-28.729–734.

MORGAN, N., H. BOURLARD, S. GREENBERG, & H. HERMANSKY. 1994. Stochastic perceptual auditory-event-based models for speech recognition. In *Proceedings Int'l Conference on Spoken Language Processing*, 1943–1946, Yokohama, Japan.

Recurrent Neural Networks for Missing or Asynchronous Data

Yoshua Bengio [*]
Dept. Informatique et
Recherche Opérationnelle
Université de Montréal
Montreal, Qc H3C-3J7
bengioy@iro.umontreal.ca

Francois Gingras
Dept. Informatique et
Recherche Opérationnelle
Université de Montréal
Montreal, Qc H3C-3J7
gingras@iro.umontreal.ca

Abstract

In this paper we propose recurrent neural networks with feedback into the input units for handling two types of data analysis problems. On the one hand, this scheme can be used for static data when some of the input variables are missing. On the other hand, it can also be used for sequential data, when some of the input variables are missing or are available at different frequencies. Unlike in the case of probabilistic models (e.g. Gaussian) of the missing variables, the network does not attempt to model the distribution of the missing variables given the observed variables. Instead it is a more "discriminant" approach that fills in the missing variables for the sole purpose of minimizing a learning criterion (e.g., to minimize an output error).

1 Introduction

Learning from examples implies discovering certain relations between variables of interest. The most general form of learning requires to essentially capture the joint distribution between these variables. However, for many specific problems, we are only interested in predicting the value of certain variables when the others (or some of the others) are given. A distinction is therefore made between input variables and output variables. Such a task requires less information (and less parameters, in the case of a parameterized model) than that of estimating the full joint distribution. For example in the case of classification problems, a traditional statistical approach is based on estimating the conditional distribution of the inputs for each class, as well as the class prior probabilities (thus yielding the full joint distribution of inputs and classes). A more discriminant approach concentrates on estimating the class boundaries (and therefore requires less parameters), as for example with a feedforward neural network trained to estimate the output class probabilities given the observed variables.

However, for many learning problems, only some of the input variables are given for each particular training case, and the missing variables differ from case to case. The simplest way to deal with this missing data problem consists in replacing the missing values by their *unconditional mean*. It can be used with "discriminant" training algorithms such as those used with feedforward neural networks. However, in some problems, one can obtain better results by taking advantage of the dependencies between the input variables. A simple idea therefore consists

---
[*] also, AT&T Bell Labs, Holmdel, NJ 07733

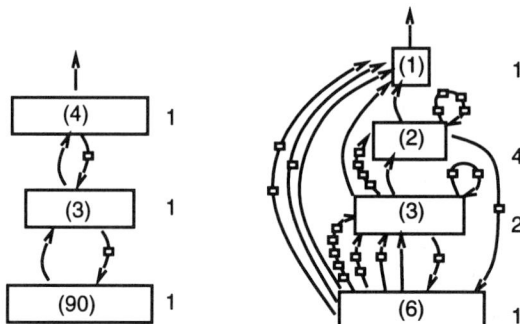

Figure 1: Architectures of the recurrent networks in the experiments. On the left a 90-3-4 architecture for static data with missing values, on the right a 6-3-2-1 architecture with multiple time-scales for asynchronous sequential data. Small squares represent a unit delay. The number of units in each layer is inside the rectangles. The time scale at which each layer operates is on the right of each rectangle.

in replacing the missing input variables by their *conditional* expected value, when the observed input variables are given. An even better scheme is to compute the expected output given the observed inputs, e.g. with a mixture of Gaussian. Unfortunately, this amounts to estimating the full joint distribution of all the variables. For example, with n_i inputs, capturing the possible effect of each observed variable on each missing variable would require $O(n_i^2)$ parameters (at least one parameter to capture some co-occurrence statistic on each pair of input variables). Many related approaches have been proposed to deal with missing inputs using a Gaussian (or Gaussian mixture) model (Ahmad and Tresp, 1993; Tresp, Ahmad and Neuneier, 1994; Ghahramani and Jordan, 1994). In the experiments presented here, the proposed recurrent network is compared with a Gaussian mixture model trained with EM to handle missing values (Ghahramani and Jordan, 1994).

The approach proposed in section 2 is more economical than the traditional Gaussian-based approaches for two reasons. Firstly, we take advantage of hidden units in a recurrent network, which might be less numerous than the inputs. The number of parameters depends on the product of the number of hidden units and the number of inputs. The hidden units only need to capture the dependencies between input variables which have some dependencies, *and* which are useful to reducing the output error. The second advantage is indeed that training is based on optimizing the desired criterion (e.g., reducing an output error), rather than predicting as well as possible the values of the missing inputs. The recurrent network is allowed to relax for a few iterations (typically as few as 4 or 5) in order to fill-in some values for the missing inputs and produce an output. In section 3 we present experimental results with this approach, comparing the results with those obtained with a feedforward network.

In section 4 we propose an extension of this scheme to sequential data. In this case, the network is not relaxing: inputs keep changing with time and the network maps an input sequence (with possibly missing values) to an output sequence. The main advantage of this extension is that it allows to deal with sequential data in which the variables occur at different frequencies. This type of problem is frequent for example with economic or financial data. An experiment with asynchronous data is presented in section 5.

2 Relaxing Recurrent Network for Missing Inputs

Networks with feedback such as those proposed in (Almeida, 1987; Pineda, 1989) can be applied to learning a static input/output mapping when some of the inputs are missing. In both cases, however, one has to wait for the network to relax either to a fixed point (assuming it does find one) or to a "stable distribution" (in the case of the Boltzmann machine). In the case of fixed-point recurrent networks, the training algorithm assumes that a fixed point has been reached. The gradient with respect to the weights is then computed in order to move the fixed point to a more desirable position. The approach we have preferred here avoids such an assumption.

Recurrent Neural Networks for Missing or Asynchronous Data 397

Instead it uses a more explicit optimization of the whole behavior of the network as it unfolds in time, fills-in the missing inputs and produces an output. The network is trained to minimize some function of its output by back-propagation through time.

Computation of Outputs Given Observed Inputs
Given: input vector $u = [u_1, u_2, \ldots, u_{n_i}]$
Result: output vector $y = [y_1, y_2, \ldots, y_{n_o}]$

1. Initialize for $t = 0$:
   For $i = 1 \ldots n_u$, $x_{0,i} \leftarrow 0$
   For $i = 1 \ldots n_i$, if u_i is missing then $x_{0,I(i)} \leftarrow E(i)$,
       Else $x_{0,I(i)} \leftarrow u_i$.
2. Loop over time:
   For $t = 1$ to T
      For $i = 1 \ldots n_u$
         If $i = I(k)$ is an input unit and u_k is not missing then
            $x_{t,i} \leftarrow u_k$
         Else
            $x_{t,i} \leftarrow (1-\gamma)x_{t-1,i} + \gamma f(\sum_{l \in S_i} w_l x_{t-d_l,p_l})$
            where S_i is a set of links from unit p_l to unit i,
            each with weight w_l and a discrete delay d_l
            (but terms for which $t - d_l < 0$ were not considered).
3. Collect outputs by averaging at the end of the sequence:
   $y_i \leftarrow \sum_{t=1}^{T} v_t \, x_{t,O(i)}$

Back-Propagation

The back-propagation computation requires an extra set of variables $\dot{x}_t$ and $\dot{w}$, which will contain respectively $\frac{\partial C}{\partial x_t}$ and $\frac{\partial C}{\partial w}$ after this computation.

Given: output gradient vector $\frac{\partial C}{\partial y}$
Result: input gradient $\frac{\partial C}{\partial u}$ and parameter gradient $\frac{\partial C}{\partial w}$.

1. Initialize unit gradients using outside gradient:
   Initialize $\dot{x}_{t,i} = 0$ for all t and i.
   For $i = 1 \ldots n_o$, initialize $\dot{x}_{t,O(i)} \leftarrow v_t \frac{\partial C}{\partial y_i}$
2. Backward loop over time:
   For $t = T$ to 1
      For $i = n_u \ldots 1$
         If $i = I(k)$ is an input unit and u_k is not missing then
            no backward propagation
         Else
            For $l \in S_i$
               If $t - d_l > 0$
                  $\dot{x}_{t-d_l,p_l} \leftarrow \dot{x}_{t-d_l,p_l} + (1-\gamma)\dot{x}_{t-d_l+1}$
                       $+ \gamma w_l \dot{x}_{t,i} f'(\sum_{l \in S_i} w_l x_{t-d_l,p_l})$
                  $\dot{w}_l \leftarrow \dot{w}_l + \gamma f'(\sum_{l \in S_i} w_l x_{t-d_l,p_l}) x_{t-d_l,p_l}$
3. Collect input gradients:
   For $i = 1 \ldots n_i$,
      If u_i is missing, then
         $\frac{\partial C}{\partial u_i} \leftarrow 0$
      Else
         $\frac{\partial C}{\partial u_i} \leftarrow \sum_t \dot{x}_{t,I(i)}$

The observed inputs are clamped for the whole duration of the sequence. The missing units corresponding to missing inputs are initialized to their unconditional expectation and their value is then updated using the feedback links for the rest of the sequence (just as if they were hidden units). To help stability of the network and prevent it from finding periodic solutions (in which the outputs have a correct output only periodically), output supervision is given for several time steps. A fixed vector v, with $v_t > 0$ and $\sum_t v_t = 1$ specifies a weighing scheme that distributes the responsibility for producing the correct output among different time steps. Its purpose is to encourage the network to develop stable dynamics which gradually converge toward the correct output (thus the weights v_t were chosen to gradually increase with t).

The neuron transfer function was a hyperbolic tangent in our experiments. The inertial term weighted by γ (in step 3 of the forward propagation algorithm below) was used to help the network find stable solutions. The parameter γ was fixed by hand. In the experiments described below, a value of 0.7 was used, but near values yielded similar results.

This module can therefore be combined within a hybrid system composed of several modules by propagating gradient through the combined system (as in (Bottou and Gallinari, 1991)). For example, as in Figure 2, there might be another module taking as input the recurrent network's output. In this case the recurrent network can be seen as a feature extractor that accepts data with missing values in input and computes a set of features that are never missing. In another example of hybrid system the non-missing values in input of the recurrent network are computed by another, upstream module (such as the preprocessing normalization used in our experiments), and the recurrent network would provide gradients to this upstream module (for example to better tune its normalization parameters).

3 Experiments with Static Data

A network with three layers (inputs, hidden, outputs) was trained to classify data with missing values from the *audiology* database. This database was made public thanks to Jergen and Quinlan, was used by (Bareiss and Porter, 1987), and was obtained from the UCI Repository of machine learning databases (`ftp.ics.uci.edu:pub/machine-learning-databases`). The original database has 226 patterns, with 69 attributes, and 24 classes. Unfortunately, most of the classes have only 1 exemplar. Hence we decided to cluster the classes into four groups. To do so, the average pattern for each of the 24 classes was computed, and the K-Means clustering algorithm was then applied on those 24 prototypical class "patterns", to yield the 4 "super-classes" used in our experiments. The multi-valued input symbolic attributes (with more than 2 possible values) where coded with a "one-out-of-n" scheme, using n inputs (all zeros except the one corresponding to the attribute value). Note that a missing value was represented with a special numeric value recognized by the neural network module. The inputs which were constant over the training set were then removed. The remaining 90 inputs were finally standardized (by computing mean and standard deviation) and transformed by a saturating non-linearity (a scaled hyperbolic tangent). The output class is coded with a "one-out-of-4" scheme, and the recognized class is the one for which the corresponding output has the largest value.

The architecture of the network is depicted in Figure 1 (left). The length of each relaxing sequence in the experiments was 5. Higher values would not bring any measurable improvements, whereas for shorter sequences performance would degrade. The number of hidden units was varied, with the best generalization performance obtained using 3 hidden units.

The recurrent network was compared with feedforward networks as well as with a mixture of Gaussians. For the feedforward networks, the missing input values were replaced by their unconditional expected value. They were trained to minimize the same criterion as the recurrent networks, i.e., the sum of squared differences between network output and desired output. Several feedforward neural networks with varying numbers of hidden units were trained. The best generalization was obtained with 15 hidden units. Experiments were also performed with no hidden units and two hidden layers (see Table 1). We found that the recurrent network not only generalized better but also learned much faster (although each pattern required 5 times more work because of the relaxation), as depicted in Figure 3.

The recurrent network was also compared with an approach based on a Gaussian and Gaussian mixture model of the data. We used the algorithm described in (Ghahramani and Jordan, 1994) for supervised leaning from incomplete data with the EM algorithm. The whole joint input/output distribution is modeled using a mixture model with Gaussians (for the inputs) and multinomial (outputs) components:

$$P(\mathbf{X} = \mathbf{x}, C = c) = \sum_j P(\omega_j) \frac{\mu_{jd}}{(2\pi)^{n/2}|\Sigma_j|^{1/2}} \exp\{-\frac{1}{2}(\mathbf{x} - \mu_j)'\Sigma_j^{-1}(\mathbf{x} - \mu_j)\}$$

where $\mathbf{x}$ is the input vector, c the output class, and $P(\omega_j)$ the prior probability of component j of the mixture. The μ_{jd} are the multinomial parameters; μ_j and Σ_j are the Gaussian mean vector

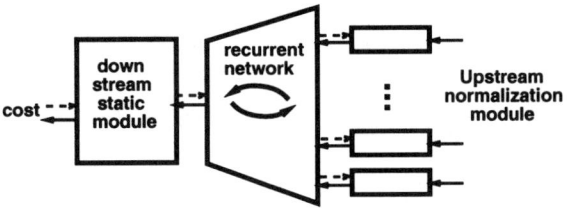

Figure 2: Example of hybrid modular system, using the recurrent network (middle) to extract features from patterns which may have missing values. It can be combined with upstream modules (e.g., a normalizing preprocessor, right) and downstream modules (e.g., a static classifier, left). Dotted arrows show the backward flow of gradients.

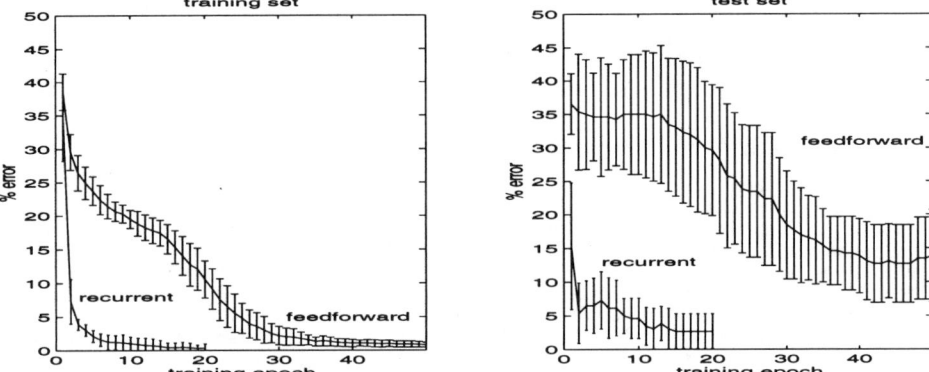

Figure 3: Evolution of training and test error for the recurrent network and for the best of the feedforward networks (90-15-4): average classification error w.r.t. training epoch, (with 1 standard deviation error bars, computed over 10 trials).

and covariance matrix for component j. Maximum likelihood training is applied as explained in (Ghahramani and Jordan, 1994), taking missing values into account (as additional missing variables of the EM algorithm).

For each architecture in Table 1, 10 training trials were run with a different subset of 200 training and 26 test patterns (and different initial weights for the neural networks). The recurrent network was clearly superior to the other architectures, probably for the reasons discussed in the conclusion. In addition, we have shown graphically the rate of convergence during training of the best feedforward network (90-15-4) as well as the best recurrent network (90-3-4), in Figure 3. Clearly, the recurrent network not only performs better at the end of training but also learns much faster.

4 Recurrent Network for Asynchronous Sequential Data

An important problem with many sequential data analysis problems such as those encountered in financial data sets is that different variables are known at different frequencies, at different times (phase), or are sometimes missing. For example, some variables are given daily, weekly, monthly, quarterly, or yearly. Furthermore, some variables may not even be given for some of the periods or the precise timing may change (for example the date at which a company reports financial performance my vary).

Therefore, we propose to extend the algorithm presented above for static data with missing values to the general case of sequential data with missing values or asynchronous variables. For time steps at which a low-frequency variable is not given, a missing value is assumed in input. Again, the feedback links from the hidden and output units to the input units allow the network

Table 1: Comparative performances of recurrent network, feedforward network, and Gaussian mixture density model on audiology data. The average percentage of classification error is shown after training, for both training and test sets, and the standard deviation in parenthesis, for 10 trials.

	Training set error	Test set error
90-3-4 Recurrent net	0.3(0.6)	2.7(2.6)
90-6-4 Recurrent net	0(0)	3.8(4)
90-25-4 Feedforward net	0.5(1.6)	15(7.3)
90-15-4 Feedforward net	0.8(0.4)	13.8(7)
90-10-6-4 Feedforward net	1(0.9)	16(5.3)
90-6-4 Feedforward net	6(4.9)	29(8.9)
90-2-4 Feedforward net	18.5(1)	27(10)
90-4 Feedforward net	22(1)	33(8)
1 Gaussian	35(1.6)	38(9.3)
4 Gaussians Mixture	36(1.5)	38(9.2)
8 Gaussians Mixture	36(2.1)	38(9.3)

to "complete" the missing data. The main differences with the static case are that the inputs and outputs vary with t (we use u_t and y_t at each time step instead of u and y). The training algorithm is otherwise the same.

5 Experiments with Asynchronous Data

To evaluate the algorithm, we have used a recurrent network with random weights, and feedback links on the input units to generate artificial data. The generating network has 6 inputs, 3 hidden and 1 outputs. The hidden layer is connected to the input layer (1 delay). The hidden layer receives inputs with delays 0 and 1 from the input layer and with delay 1 from itself. The output layer receives inputs from the hidden layer. At the initial time step as well as at 5% of the time steps (chosen randomly), the input units were clamped with random values to introduce some further variability. The missing values were then completed by the recurrent network. To generate asynchronous data, half of the inputs were then hidden with missing values 4 out of every 5 time steps. 100 training sequences and 50 test sequences were generated. The learning problem is therefore a sequence regression problem with missing and asynchronous input variables.

Preliminary comparative experiments show a clear advantage to completing the missing values (due to the the different frequencies of the input variables) with the recurrent network, as shown in Figure 4. The recognition recurrent network is shown on the right of Figure 1. It has multiple time scales (implemented with subsampling and oversampling, as in TDNNs (Lang, Waibel and Hinton, 1990) and reverse-TDNNs (Simard and LeCun, 1992)), to facilitate the learning of such asynchronous data. The static network is a time-delay neural network with 6 input, 8 hidden, and 1 output unit, and connections with delays 0, 2, and 4 from the input to hidden and hidden to output units. The "missing values" for slow-varying variables were replaced by the last observed value in the sequence. Experiments with 4 and 16 hidden units yielded similar results.

6 Conclusion

When there are dependencies between input variables, and the output prediction can be improved by taking them into account, we have seen that a recurrent network with input feedback can perform significantly better than a simpler approach that replaces missing values by their unconditional expectation. According to us, this explains the significant improvement brought by using the recurrent network instead of a feedforward network in the experiments.

On the other hand, the large number of input variables ($n_i = 90$, in the experiments) most likely explains the poor performance of the mixture of Gaussian model in comparison to both the static networks and the recurrent network. The Gaussian model requires estimating $O(n_i^2)$ parameters and inverting large covariance matrices.

The approach to handling missing values presented here can also be extended to sequential data with missing or asynchronous variables. As our experiments suggest, for such problems, using recurrence and multiple time scales yields better performance than static or time-delay networks for which the missing values are filled using a heuristic.

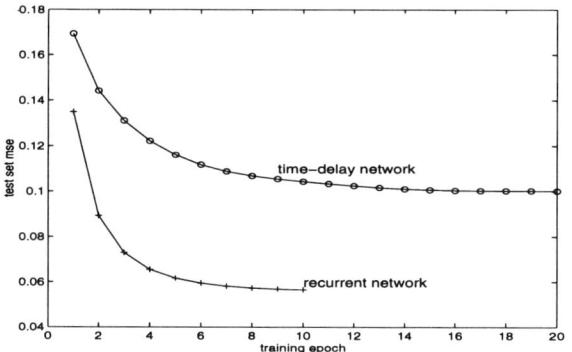

Figure 4: Test set mean squared error on the asynchronous data. Top: static network with time delays. Bottom: recurrent network with feedback to input values to complete missing data.

References

Ahmad, S. and Tresp, V. (1993). Some solutions to the missing feature problem in vision. In Hanson, S. J., Cowan, J. D., and Giles, C. L., editors, *Advances in Neural Information Processing Systems 5*, San Mateo, CA. Morgan Kaufman Publishers.

Almeida, L. (1987). A learning rule for asynchronous perceptrons with feedback in a combinatorial environment. In Caudill, M. and Butler, C., editors, *IEEE International Conference on Neural Networks*, volume 2, pages 609–618, San Diego 1987. IEEE, New York.

Bareiss, E. and Porter, B. (1987). Protos: An exemplar-based learning apprentice. In *Proceedings of the 4th International Workshop on Machine Learning*, pages 12–23, Irvine, CA. Morgan Kaufmann.

Bottou, L. and Gallinari, P. (1991). A framework for the cooperation of learning algorithms. In Lippman, R. P., Moody, R., and Touretzky, D. S., editors, *Advances in Neural Information Processing Systems 3*, pages 781–788, Denver, CO.

Ghahramani, Z. and Jordan, M. I. (1994). Supervised learning from incomplete data via an EM approach. In Cowan, J., Tesauro, G., and Alspector, J., editors, *Advances in Neural Information Processing Systems 6*, page , San Mateo, CA. Morgan Kaufmann.

Lang, K. J., Waibel, A. H., and Hinton, G. E. (1990). A time-delay neural network architecture for isolated word recognition. *Neural Networks*, 3:23–43.

Pineda, F. (1989). Recurrent back-propagation and the dynamical approach to adaptive neural computation. *Neural Computation*, 1:161–172.

Simard, P. and LeCun, Y. (1992). Reverse TDNN: An architecture for trajectory generation. In Moody, J., Hanson, S., and Lipmann, R., editors, *Advances in Neural Information Processing Systems 4*, pages 579–588, Denver, CO. Morgan Kaufmann, San Mateo.

Tresp, V., Ahmad, S., and Neuneier, R. (1994). Training neural networks with deficient data. In Cowan, J., Tesauro, G., and Alspector, J., editors, *Advances in Neural Information Processing Systems 6*, pages 128–135. Morgan Kaufman Publishers, San Mateo, CA.

Family Discovery

Stephen M. Omohundro
NEC Research Institute
4 Independence Way, Princeton, NJ 08540
om@research.nj.nec.com

Abstract

"Family discovery" is the task of learning the dimension and structure of a parameterized family of stochastic models. It is especially appropriate when the training examples are partitioned into "episodes" of samples drawn from a single parameter value. We present three family discovery algorithms based on surface learning and show that they significantly improve performance over two alternatives on a parameterized classification task.

1 INTRODUCTION

Human listeners improve their ability to recognize speech by identifying the accent of the speaker. "Might" in an American accent is similar to "mate" in an Australian accent. By first identifying the accent, discrimination between these two words is improved. We can imagine locating a speaker in a "space of accents" parameterized by features like pitch, vowel formants, "r"-strength, etc. This paper considers the task of learning such parameterized models from data.

Most speech recognition systems train hidden Markov models on labelled speech data. Speaker-dependent systems train on speech from a single speaker. Speaker-independent systems are usually similar, but are trained on speech from many different speakers in the hope that they will then recognize them all. This kind of training ignores speaker identity and is likely to result in confusion between pairs of words which are given the same pronunciation by speakers with different accents.

Speaker-independent recognition systems could more closely mimic the human approach by using a learning paradigm we call "family discovery". The system would be trained on speech data partitioned into "episodes" for each speaker. From this data, the system would construct a *parameterized family* of models representing dif-

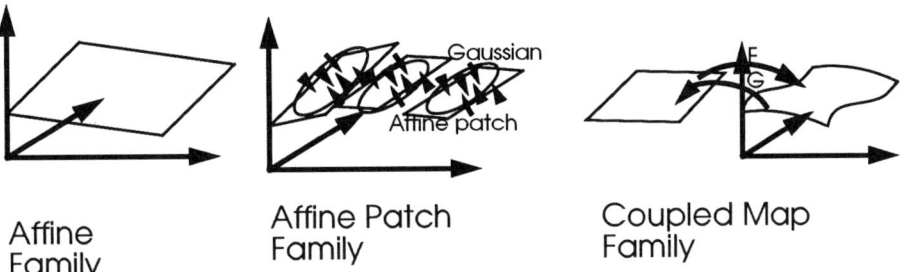

Figure 1: The structure of the three family discovery algorithms.

ferent accents. The learning algorithms presented in this paper could determine the dimension and structure of the parameterization. Given a sample of new speech, the best-fitting accent model would be used for recognition.

The same paradigm applies to many other recognition tasks. For example, an OCR system could learn a parameterized family of font models (Revow, et. al., 1994). Given new text, the system would identify the document's font parameters and use the corresponding character recognizer.

In general, we use "family discovery" to refer to the task of learning the dimension and structure of a parameterized family of stochastic models. The methods we present are equally applicable to parameterized density estimation, classification, regression, manifold learning, reinforcement learning, clustering, stochastic grammar learning, and other stochastic settings. Here we only discuss classification and primarily consider training examples which are explicitly partitioned into episodes.

This approach fits naturally into the neural network literature on "meta-learning" (Schmidhuber, 1995) and "network transfer" (Pratt, 1994). It may also be considered as a particular case of the "bias learning" framework proposed by Baxter at this conference (Baxter, 1996).

There are two primary alternatives to family discovery: 1) try to fit a single model to the data from all episodes or 2) use separate models for each episode. The first approach ignores the information that the different training sets came from distinct models. The second approach eliminates the possibility of inductive generalization from one set to another.

In Section 2, we present three algorithms for family discovery based on techniques for "surface learning" (Bregler and Omohundro, 1994 and 1995). As shown in Figure 1, the three alternative representations of the family are: 1) a single affine subspace of the parameter space, 2) a set of local affine patches smoothly blended together, and 3) a pair of coupled maps from the parameter space into the model space and back. In Section 3, we compare these three approaches to the two alternatives on a parameterized classification task.

2 THE FIVE ALGORITHMS

Let the space of all classifiers under consideration be parameterized by θ and assume that different values of θ correspond to different classifiers (ie. it is identifiable). For example, θ might represent the means, covariances, and class priors of a classifier with normal class-conditional densities. θ-space will typically have a much higher dimension than the parameterized family we are seeking. We write $p_\theta(x)$ for the total probability that the classifier θ assigns to a labelled or unlabelled example x.

The true models are drawn from a d-dimensional family parameterized by γ. Let the training set be partitioned into N episodes where episode i consists of N_i training examples t_{ij}, $1 \leq j \leq N_i$ drawn from a single underlying model with parameter θ_i^*. A family discovery learning algorithm uses this training data to estimate the underlying parameterized family.

From a parameterized family, we may define the projection operator P from θ-space to itself which takes each θ to the closest member of the family. Using this projection operator, we may define a "family prior" on θ-space which dies off exponentially with the square distance of a model from the family $m_P(\theta) \propto e^{-(\theta-P(\theta))^2}$. Each of the family discovery algorithms chooses a family so as to maximize the posterior probability of the training data with respect to this prior. If the data is very sparse, this MAP approximation to a full Bayesian solution can be supplemented by "Occam" terms (MacKay, 1995) or by using a Monte Carlo approximation.

The outer loop of each of the algorithms performs the optimization of the fit of the data by re-estimation in a manner similar to the Expectation Maximization (EM) approach (Jordan and Jacobs, 1994). First, the training data in each episode i is independently fit by a model θ_i. Then the dimension of the family is determined as described later and the family projection operator P is chosen to maximize the probability that the episode models θ_i came from that family $\prod_i m_P(\theta_i)$. The episode models θ_i are then re-estimated including the new prior probability m_P. These newly re-estimated models are influenced by the other episodes through m_P and so exhibit training set "transfer". The re-estimation loop is repeated until nothing changes.

The learned family can then be used to classify a set of N_{test} unlabelled test examples x_k, $1 \leq k \leq N_{test}$ drawn from a model θ_{test}^* in the family. First, the parameter θ_{test} is estimated by selecting the member of the family with the highest likelihood on the test samples. This model is then used to perform the classification. A good approximation to the best-fit family member is often to take the image of the best-fit model in the entire θ-space under the projection operator P.

In the next five sections, we describe the two alternative approaches and the three family discovery algorithms. They differ only in their choice of family representation as encoded in the projection operator P.

2.1 The Single Model Approach

The first alternative approach is to train a single model on all of the training data. It selects θ to maximize the total likelihood $L(\theta) = \prod_{i=1}^{N} \prod_{j=1}^{N_i} p_\theta(t_{ij})$. New test data is classified by this single selected model.

2.2 The Separate Models Approach

The second alternative approach fits separate models for each training episode. It chooses θ_i for $1 \leq i \leq N$ to maximize the episode likelihood $L_i(\theta_i) = \prod_{j=1}^{N_i} p_\theta(t_{ij})$. Given new test data, it determines which of the individual models θ_i fit best and classifies the data with it.

2.3 The Affine Algorithm

The affine model represents the underlying model family as an affine subspace of the model parameter space. The projection operator P_{affine} projects a parameter vector θ orthogonally onto the affine subspace. The subspace is determined by selecting the top principal vectors in a principal components analysis of the best-fit episode model parameters. As described in (Bregler & Omohundro, 1994) the dimension is chosen by looking for a gap in the principal values.

2.4 The Affine Patch Algorithm

The second family discovery algorithm is based on the "surface learning" procedure described in (Bregler and Omohundro, 1994). The family is represented by a collection of local affine patches which are blended together using Gaussian influence functions. The projection mapping P_{patch} is a smooth convex combination of projections onto the affine patches $P_{patch}(\theta) = \sum_{\alpha=1}^{m} I_\alpha(\theta) A_\alpha(\theta)$ where A_α is the projection operator for an affine patch and $I_\alpha(\theta) = \frac{G_\alpha(\theta)}{\sum_\alpha G_\alpha(\theta)}$ is a normalized Gaussian blending function.

The patches are initialized using k-means clustering on the episode models to choose k patch centers. A local principal components analysis is performed on the episode models which are closest to each center. The family dimension is determined by examining how the principal values scale as successive nearest neighbors are considered. Each patch may be thought of as a "pancake" lying in the surface. Dimensions which belong to the surface grow quickly as more neighbors are considered while dimensions across the surface grow only because of the curvature of the surface.

The Gaussian influence functions and the affine patches are then updated by the EM algorithm (Jordan and Jacobs, 1994). With the affine patches held fixed, the Gaussians G_α are refit to the errors each patch makes in approximating the episode models. Then with the Gaussians held fixed, the affine patches A_α are refit to the epsiode models weighted by the the corresponding Gaussian G_α. Similar patches may be merged together to form a more parsimonious model.

2.5 The Coupled Map Algorithm

The affine patch approach has the virtue that it can represent topologically complex families (eg. families representing physical objects might naturally be parameterized by the rotation group which is topologically a projective plane). It cannot, however, provide an explicit parameterization of the family which is useful in some applications (eg. optimization searches). The third family discovery algorithm therefore attempts to directly learn a parameterization of the model family.

Recall that the model parameters define θ-space, while the family parameters define γ-space. We represent a family by a mapping G from θ-space to γ-space together with a mapping F from γ-space back to θ-space. The projection operation is $P_{map}(\theta) = F(G(\theta))$. The map $G(\theta)$ defines the family parameter γ on the full θ-space.

This representation is similar to an "auto-associator" network in which we attempt to "encode" the best-fit episode parameters θ_i in the lower dimensional γ-space by the mapping G in such a way that they can be correctly reconstructed by the function F. Unfortunately, if we try to train F and G using back-propagation on the identity error function, we get no training data away from the family. There is no reason for G to project points away from the family to the closest family member. We can rectify this by training F and G iteratively. First an arbitrary G is chosen and F is trained to send the images $\gamma_i = G(\theta_i)$ back to θ_i. G is trained, however, on images under F corrupted by additive spherical Gaussian noise! This provides samples away from the family and on average the training signal sends each point in θ space to the closest family member.

To avoid iterative training, our experiments used a simpler approach. G was taken to be the affine projection operator defined by a global principal components analysis of the best-fit episode model parameters. Once G is defined, F is chosen to minimize the difference between $F(G(\theta_i))$ and θ_i for each best-fit episode parameter θ_i.

Any form of trainable nonlinear mapping could be used for F (eg. backprop neural networks or radial basis function networks). We represent F as a mixture of experts (Jordan and Jacobs, 1994) where each expert is an affine mapping and the mixture coefficients are Gaussians. The mapping is trained by the EM algorithm.

3 ALGORITHM COMPARISON

To compare these five algorithms, we consider a two-class classification task with unit-variance normal class-conditional distributions on a 5-dimensional feature space. The means of the class distributions are parameterized by a nonlinear two-parameter family:

$$m_1 = (\gamma_1 + \tfrac{1}{2}\cos\phi)\hat{e}_1 + (\gamma_2 + \tfrac{1}{2}\sin\phi)\hat{e}_2$$
$$m_2 = (\gamma_1 - \tfrac{1}{2}\cos\phi)\hat{e}_1 + (\gamma_2 - \tfrac{1}{2}\sin\phi)\hat{e}_2.$$

where $0 \leq \gamma_1, \gamma_2 \leq 10$ and $\phi = (\gamma_1 + \gamma_2)/3$. The class means are kept at a unit distance apart, ensuring significant class overlap over the whole family. The angle ϕ varies with the parameters so that the correct classification boundary changes orientation over the family. This choice of parameters introduces sufficient non-linearity in the task to distinguish the non-linear algorithms from the linear one.

Figure 1 shows the comparative performance of the 5 algorithms. The x-axis is the total number of training examples. Each set of examples consisted of approximately $N = \sqrt{x}$ episodes of approximately $N_i = \sqrt{x}$ examples each. The classifier parameters for an episode were drawn uniformly from the classifier family. The episode training examples were then sampled from the chosen classifier according to the classifier's distribution. Each of the 5 algorithms was then trained on these examples. The number of patches in the surface patch algorithm and the number of affine components in the surface map algorithm were both taken to be the square-root of

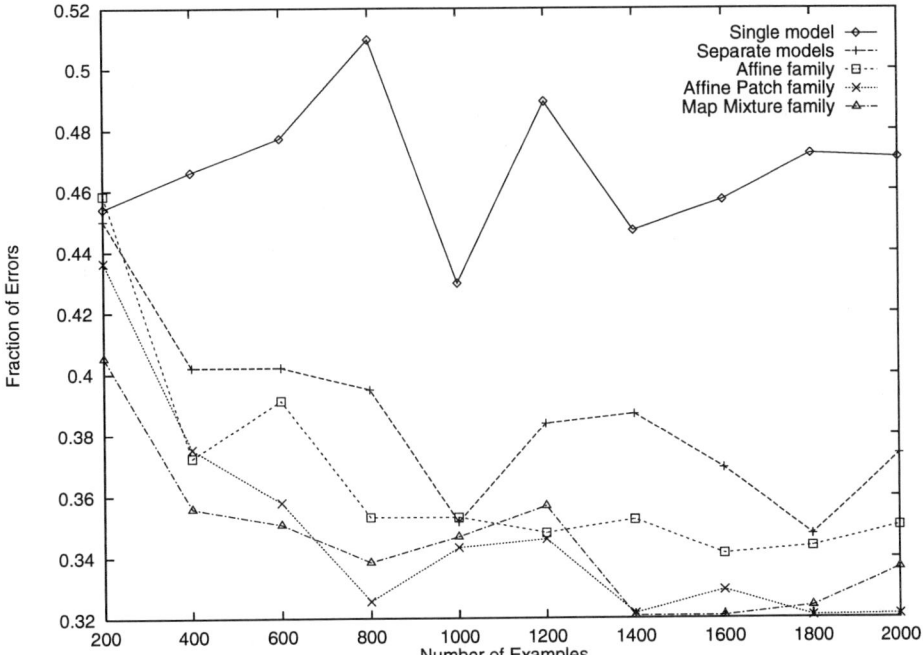

Figure 2: A comparison of the 5 family discovery algorithms on the classification task.

the number of training episodes.

The y-axis shows the percentage correct for each algorithm on an independent test set. Each test set consisted of 50 episodes of 50 examples each. The algorithms were presented with unlabelled data and their classification predictions were then compared with the correct classification label.

The results show significant improvement through the use of family discovery for this classification task. The single model approach performed significantly worse than any of the other approaches, especially for larger numbers of episodes (where the family discovery becomes possible). The separate model approach improves with the number of episodes, but is nearly always bested by the approaches which take explicit account of the underlying parameterized family. Because of the nonlinearity in this task, the simple affine model performs more poorly than the two nonlinear methods. It is simple to implement, however, and may well be the method of choice when the parameters aren't so nonlinear. From this data, there is not a clear winner between the surface patch and surface map approaches.

4 TRAINING SET DISCOVERY

Throughout this paper, we have assumed that the training set was partitioned into episodes by the teacher. Agents interacting with the world may not be given this explicit information. For example, a speech recognition system may not be told when it is conversing with a new speaker. Similarly, a character recognition system would probably not be given explicit information about font changes. Learners can sometimes use the data itself to detect these changes, however. In many situations there is a strong prior that successive events are likely to have come from a single model with only occasional model changes. The EM algorithm is often used for segmenting unlabelled speech. It may be used in a similar manner to find the training set episode boundaries. First, a clustering algorithm is used to partition the training examples into episodes. A parameterized family is then fit to these episodes. The data is then repartitioned according to the similarity of the induced family parameters and the process is repeated until it converges. A similar approach may be applied when the model parameters vary slowly with time rather than occasionally jumping discontinously.

Acknowledgements

I'd like to thank Chris Bregler for work on the affine patch approach to surface learning, Alexander Linden for suggesting coupled maps for surface learning, and Peter Blicher for discussions.

References

Baxter, J. (1995) Learning model bias. This volume.

Bregler, C. & Omohundro, S. (1994) Surface learning with applications to lipreading. In J. Cowan, G. Tesauro and J. Alspector (eds.), *Advances in Neural Information Processing Systems 6*, pp. 43-50. San Francisco, CA: Morgan Kaufmann Publishers.

Bregler, C. & Omohundro, S. (1995) Nonlinear image interpolation using manifold learning. In G. Tesauro, D. Touretzky and T. Leen (eds.), *Advances in Neural Information Processing Systems 7*. Cambridge, MA: MIT Press.

Bregler, C. & Omohundro, S. (1995) Nonlinear manifold learning for visual speech recognition. In W. Grimson (ed.), *Proceedings of the Fifth International Conference on Computer Vision*.

Jordan, M. & Jacobs, R. (1994) Hierarchical mixtures of experts and the EM algorithm. *Neural Computation*, **6**:181-214.

MacKay, D. (1995) Probable networks and plausible predictions - a review of practical Bayesian methods for supervised neural networks. *Network*, to appear.

Pratt, L. (1994) Experiments on the transfer of knowledge between neural networks. In S. Hanson, G. Drastal, and R. Rivest (eds.), *Computational Learning Theory and Natural Learning Systems, Constraints and Prospects*, pp. 523-560. Cambridge, MA: MIT Press.

Revow, M., Williams, C. and Hinton, G. (1994) Using generative models for handwritten digit recognition. Technical report, University of Toronto.

Schmidhuber, J. (1995) On learning how to learn learning strategies. Technical Report FKI-198-94, Fakultät für Informatik, Technische Universität München.

Discriminant Adaptive Nearest Neighbor Classification and Regression

Trevor Hastie
Department of Statistics
Sequoia Hall
Stanford University
California 94305
trevor@playfair.stanford.edu

Robert Tibshirani
Department of Statistics
University of Toronto
tibs@utstat.toronto.edu

Abstract

Nearest neighbor classification expects the class conditional probabilities to be locally constant, and suffers from bias in high dimensions We propose a locally adaptive form of nearest neighbor classification to try to finesse this curse of dimensionality. We use a local linear discriminant analysis to estimate an effective metric for computing neighborhoods. We determine the local decision boundaries from centroid information, and then shrink neighborhoods in directions orthogonal to these local decision boundaries, and elongate them parallel to the boundaries. Thereafter, any neighborhood-based classifier can be employed, using the modified neighborhoods. We also propose a method for global dimension reduction, that combines local dimension information. We indicate how these techniques can be extended to the regression problem.

1 Introduction

We consider a discrimination problem with J classes and N training observations. The training observations consist of predictor measurements $\mathbf{x} = (x_1, x_2, \ldots x_p)$ on p predictors and the known class memberships. Our goal is to predict the class membership of an observation with predictor vector $\mathbf{x}_0$

Nearest neighbor classification is a simple and appealing approach to this problem. We find the set of K nearest neighbors in the training set to $\mathbf{x}_0$ and then classify $\mathbf{x}_0$ as the most frequent class among the K neighbors.

Cover & Hart (1967) show that the one nearest neighbour rule has asymptotic error rate at most twice the Bayes rate. However in finite samples the curse of dimensionality can severely hurt the nearest neighbor rule. The relative radius of the nearest-neighbor sphere grows like $r^{1/p}$ where p is the dimension and r the radius for $p = 1$, resulting in severe bias at the target point $\mathbf{x}$. Figure 1 (left panel) illustrates the situation for a simple example. Nearest neighbor techniques are

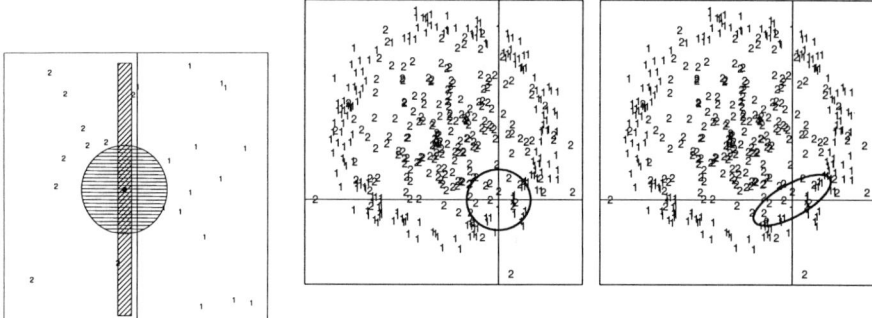

Figure 1: *In the left panel, the vertical strip denotes the NN region using only horizontal coordinate to find the nearest neighbor for the target point (solid dot). The sphere shows the NN region using both coordinates, and we see in this case it has extended into the class 1 region (and found the wrong class in this instance). The middle panel shows a spherical neighborhood containing 25 points, for a two class problem with a circular decision boundary. The right panel shows the ellipsoidal neighborhood found by the DANN procedure, also containing 25 points. The latter is elongated in a direction parallel to the true decision boundary (locally constant posterior probabilities), and flattened orthogonal to it.*

based on the assumption that locally the class posterior probabilities are constant. While that is clearly true in the vertical strip using only the vertical coordinate, using both this is no longer true. Figure 1 (middle and right panels) shows how we locally adapt the metric to overcome this problem, in a situation where the decision boundary is locally linear.

2 Discriminant adaptive nearest neighbors

Consider first a standard linear discriminant (LDA) classification procedure with K classes. Let $\mathbf{B}$ and $\mathbf{W}$ denote the between and within sum of squares matrices. In LDA the data are first sphered with respect to $\mathbf{W}$, then the target point is classified to the class of the closest centroid (with a correction for the class prior membership probabilities). Since only relative distances are relevant, any distances in the complement of the subspace spanned by the sphered centroids can be ignored. This complement corresponds to the null space of $\mathbf{B}$.

We propose to estimate $\mathbf{B}$ and $\mathbf{W}$ locally, and use them to form a local metric that approximately behaves like the LDA metric. One such candidate is

$$\begin{aligned} \Sigma &= \mathbf{W}^{-1}\mathbf{B}\mathbf{W}^{-1} \\ &= \mathbf{W}^{-1/2}(\mathbf{W}^{-1/2}\mathbf{B}\mathbf{W}^{-1/2})\mathbf{W}^{-1/2} \\ &= \mathbf{W}^{-1/2}\mathbf{B}^*\mathbf{W}^{-1/2}. \end{aligned} \quad (1)$$

where $\mathbf{B}^*$ is the between sum-of-squares in the sphered space. Consider the action of Σ as a metric for computing distances

$$(\mathbf{x} - \mathbf{x}_0)^T \Sigma (\mathbf{x} - \mathbf{x}_0) : \quad (2)$$

- it first spheres the space using $\mathbf{W}$;
- components of distance in the null space of $\mathbf{B}^*$ are ignored;
- other components are weighted according to the eigenvalues of $\mathbf{B}^*$ when there are more than 2 classes — directions in which the centroids are more spread out are weighted more than those in which they are close

Thus this metric would result in neighborhoods similar to the narrow strip in figure 1(left figure): infinitely long in the null space of $\mathbf{B}$, and then deformed appropriately in the centroid subspace according to how they are placed. It is dangerous to allow neighborhoods to extend infinitely in any direction, so we need to limit this stretching. Our proposal is

$$\begin{aligned}\Sigma &= \mathbf{W}^{-1/2}[\mathbf{W}^{-1/2}\mathbf{B}\mathbf{W}^{-1/2} + \epsilon\mathbf{I}]\mathbf{W}^{-1/2}\\ &= \mathbf{W}^{-1/2}[\mathbf{B}^* + \epsilon\mathbf{I}]\mathbf{W}^{-1/2}\end{aligned} \quad (3)$$

where ϵ is some small tuning parameter to be determined. The metric shrinks the neighborhood in directions in which the local class centroids differ, with the intention of ending up with a neighborhood in which the class centroids coincide (and hence nearest neighbor classification is appropriate). Given Σ we use perform K-nearest neighbor classification using the metric (2).

There are several details that we briefly describe here and in more detail in Hastie & Tibshirani (1994):

- $\mathbf{B}$ is defined to be the covariance of the class centroids, and $\mathbf{W}$ the pooled estimate of the common class covariance matrix. We estimate these locally using a *spherical*, compactly supported kernel (Cleveland 1979), where the bandwidth is determined by the distance of the K_M nearest neighbor.
- K_M above has to be supplied, as does the softening parameter ϵ. We somewhat arbitrarily use $K_M = \max(N/5, 50)$; so we use many more neighbors (50 or more) to determine the metric, and then typically $K = 1, \ldots, 5$ nearest neighbors in this metric to classify. We have found that the metric is relatively insensitive to different values of $0 < \epsilon < 5$, and typically use $\epsilon = 1$.
- Typically the data do not support the local calculation of $\mathbf{W}$ ($p(p+1)/2$ entries), and it can be argued that this is not necessary. We mostly resort to using the diagonal of $\mathbf{W}$ instead, or else use a global estimate.

Sections 4 and 5 illustrate the effectiveness of this approach on some simulated and real examples.

3 Dimension Reduction using Local Discriminant Information

The technique described above is entirely "memory based", in that we locally adapt a neighborhood about a query point at the time of classification. Here we describe a method for performing a global dimension reduction, by pooling the local dimension information over all points in the training set. In a nutshell we consider subspaces corresponding to *eigenvectors of the average local between sum-of-squares matrices*.

Consider first how linear discriminant analysis (LDA) works. After sphering the data, it concentrates in the space spanned by the class centroids $\bar{\mathbf{x}}_j$ or a reduced rank space that lies close to these centroids. If $\bar{\mathbf{x}}$ denote the overall centroid, this subspace is exactly a principal component hyperplane for the data points $\bar{\mathbf{x}}_j - \bar{\mathbf{x}}$, weighted by the class proportions, and is given by the eigen-decomposition of the between covariance $\mathbf{B}$.

Our idea to compute the deviations $\bar{\mathbf{x}}_j - \bar{\mathbf{x}}$ locally in a neighborhood around each of the N training points, and then do an overall principal components analysis for the $N \times J$ deviations. This amounts to an eigen-decomposition of the average between sum of squares matrix $\sum_{i=1}^{N} \mathbf{B}(i)/N$.

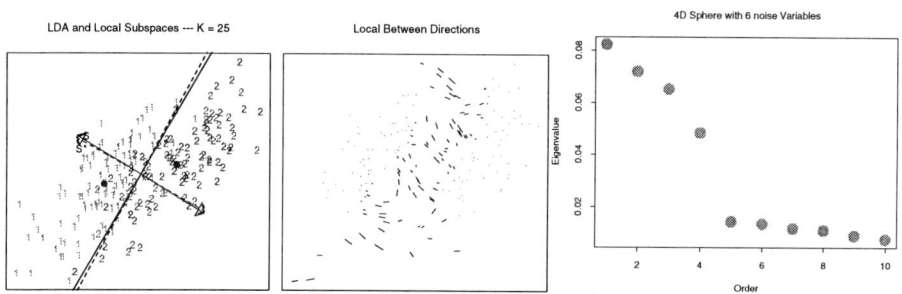

Figure 2: *[Left Panel] Two dimensional gaussian data with two classes and correlation 0.65. The solid lines are the LDA decision boundary and its equivalent subspace for classification, computed using both the between and (crucially) the within class covariance. The dashed lines were produced by the local procedure described in this section, without knowledge of the overall within covariance matrix. [Middle panel] Each line segment represents the local between information centered at that point. [Right panel] The eigenvalues of the average between matrix for the 4D sphere in 10D problem. Using these first four dimensions followed by our* DANN *nearest neighbor routine, we get better performance than 5NN in the real 4D subspace.*

Figure 2 (left two panels) demonstrates by a simple illustrative example that our subspace procedure can recover the correct LDA direction without making use of the within covariance matrix. Figure 2 (right panel) represents a two class problem with a 4-dimensional spherical decision boundary. The data for the two classes lie in concentric spheres in 4D, the one class lying inside the other with some overlap (a 4D version of the same 2D situation in figure 1.) In addition the are an extra 6 noise dimensions, and for future reference we denote such a model as the "4D spheres in 10D" problem. The decision boundary is a 4 dimensional sphere, although locally linear. The eigenvalues show a distinct change after 4 (the correct dimension), and using our DANN classifier in these four dimensions actually beats ordinary 5NN in the *known* 4D discriminant subspace.

4 Examples

Figure 3 summarizes the results of a number of simulated examples designed to test our procedures in both favorable and unfavorable situations. In all the situations DANN outperforms 5-NN. In the cases where 5NN is provided with the known lower-dimensional discriminant subspace, our subspace technique subDANN followed by DANN comes close to the optimal performance.

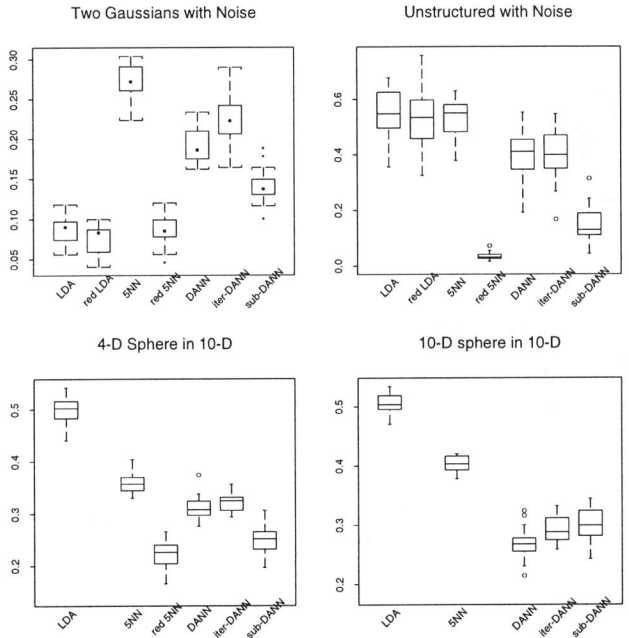

Figure 3: *Boxplots of error rates over 20 simulations. The top left panel has two gaussian distributions separated in two dimensions, with 14 noise dimensions. The notation* red-LDA *and* red-5NN *refers to these procedures in the known lower dimensional space.* iter-DANN *refers to an iterated version of* DANN *(which appears not to help), while* sub-DANN *refers to our global subspace approach, followed by* DANN. *The top right panel has 4 classes, each of which is a mixture of 3-gaussians in 2-D; in addition there are 8 noise variables. The lower two panels are versions of our sphere example.*

5 Image Classification Example

Here we consider an image classification problem. The data consist of 4 LANDSAT images in different spectral bands of a small area of the earths surface, and the goal is to classify into soil and vegetation types. Figure 4 shows the four spectral bands, two in the visible spectrum (red and green) and two in the infra red spectrum. These data are taken from the data archive of the STATLOG (Michie et al. 1994)[1]. The goal is to classify each pixel into one of 7 land types: *red soil, cotton, vegetation stubble, mixture, grey soil, damp grey soil, very damp grey soil*. We extract for each pixel its 8-neighbors, giving us $(8+1) \times 4 = 36$ features (the pixel intensities) per pixel to be classified. The data come scrambled, with 4435 training pixels and 2000 test pixels, each with their 36 features and the known classification. Included in figure 4 is the true classification, as well as that produced by linear discriminant analysis. The right panel compares DANN to all the procedures used in STATLOG, and we see the results are favorable.

---

[1]The authors thank C. Taylor and D. Spiegelhalter for making these images and data available

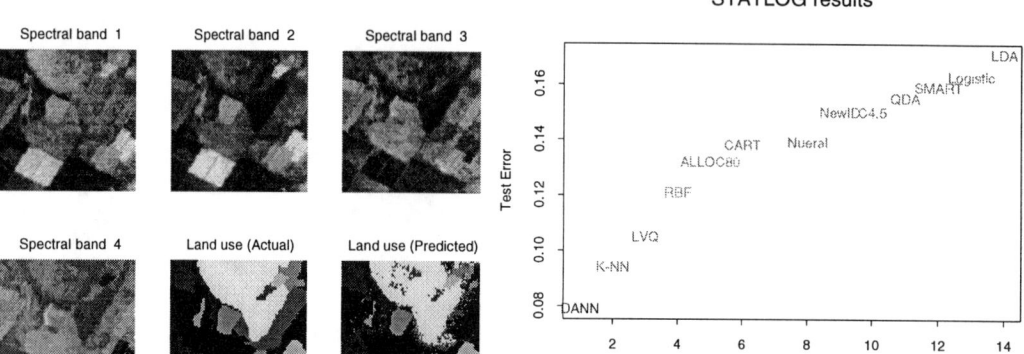

Figure 4: The first four images are the satellite images in the four spectral bands. The fifth image represents the known classification, and the final image is the classification map produced by linear discriminant analysis. The right panel shows the misclassification results of a variety of classification procedures on the satellite image test data (taken from Michie et al. (1994)). DANN is the overall winner.

6 Local Regression

Near neighbor techniques are used in the regression setting as well. Local polynomial regression (Cleveland 1979) is currently very popular, where, for example, locally weighted linear surfaces are fit in modest sized neighborhoods. Analogs of K-NN classification for small K are used less frequently. In this case the response variable is quantitative rather than a class label.

Duan & Li (1991) invented a technique called *sliced inverse regression*, a dimension reduction tool for situations where the regression function changes in a lower-dimensional space. They show that under symmetry conditions of the marginal distribution of X, the inverse regression curve $E(X|Y)$ is concentrated in the same lower-dimensional subspace. They estimate the curve by slicing Y into intervals, and computing conditional means of X in each interval, followed by a principal component analysis. There are obvious similarities with our DANN procedure, and the following generalizations of DANN are suggested for regression:

- locally we use the **B** matrix of the sliced means to form our DANN metric, and then perform local regression in the deformed neighborhoods.
- The local **B**(i) matrices can be pooled as in subDANN to extract global subspaces for regression. This has an apparent advantage over the Duan & Li (1991) approach: we only require symmetry locally, a condition that is locally encouraged by the convolution of the data with a spherical kernel[2]

7 Discussion

Short & Fukanaga (1980) proposed a technique close to ours for the two class problem. In our terminology they used our metric with $\mathbf{W} = \mathbf{I}$ and $\epsilon = 0$, with **B** determined locally in a neighborhood of size K_M. In effect this extends the

---

[2] We expect to be able to substantiate the claims in this section by the time of the NIPS995 meeting.

neighborhood infinitely in the null space of the local between class directions, but they restrict this neighborhood to the original K_M observations. This amounts to projecting the local data onto the line joining the two local centroids. In our experiments this approach tended to perform on average 10% worse than our metric, and we did not pursue it further. Short & Fukanaga (1981) extended this to $J > 2$ classes, but here their approach differs even more from ours. They computed a weighted average of the J local centroids from the overall average, and project the data onto it, a one dimensional projection. Myles & Hand (1990) recognized a shortfall of the Short and Fukanaga approach, since the averaging can cause cancellation, and proposed other metrics to avoid this, different from ours.

Friedman (1994) proposes a number of techniques for flexible metric nearest neighbor classification (and sparked our interest in the problem.) These techniques use a recursive partitioning style strategy to adaptively shrink and shape rectangular neighborhoods around the test point.

Acknowledgement

The authors thank Jerry Friedman whose research on this problem was a source of inspiration, and for many discussions. Trevor Hastie was supported by NSF DMS-9504495. Robert Tibshirani was supported by a Guggenheim fellowship, and a grant from the National Research Council of Canada.

References

Cleveland, W. (1979), 'Robust locally-weighted regression and smoothing scatterplots', *Journal of the American Statistical Society* **74**, 829–836.

Cover, T. & Hart, P. (1967), 'Nearest neighbor pattern classification', *Proc. IEEE Trans. Inform. Theory* pp. 21–27.

Duan, N. & Li, K.-C. (1991), 'Slicing regression: a link-free regression method', *Annals of Statistics* pp. 505–530.

Friedman, J. (1994), Flexible metric nearest neighbour classification, Technical report, Stanford University.

Hastie, T. & Tibshirani, R. (1994), Discriminant adaptive nearest neighbor classification, Technical report, Statistics Department, Stanford University.

Michie, D., Spigelhalter, D. & Taylor, C., eds (1994), *Machine Learning, Neural and Statistical Classification*, Ellis Horwood series in Artificial Intelligence, Ellis Horwood.

Myles, J. & Hand, D. J. (1990), 'The multi-class metric problem in nearest neighbour discrimination rules', *Pattern Recognition* **23**, 1291–1297.

Short, R. & Fukanaga, K. (1980), A new nearest neighbor distance measure, *in* 'Proc. 5th IEEE Int. Conf. on Pattern Recognition', pp. 81–86.

Short, R. & Fukanaga, K. (1981), 'The optimal distance measure for nearest neighbor classification', *IEEE transactions of Information Theory* **IT-27**, 622–627.

Clustering data through an analogy to the Potts model

Marcelo Blatt, Shai Wiseman and Eytan Domany
Department of Physics of Complex Systems,
The Weizmann Institute of Science, Rehovot 76100, Israel

Abstract

A new approach for clustering is proposed. This method is based on an analogy to a physical model; the ferromagnetic Potts model at thermal equilibrium is used as an analog computer for this hard optimization problem. We do not assume any structure of the underlying distribution of the data. Phase space of the Potts model is divided into three regions; ferromagnetic, super-paramagnetic and paramagnetic phases. The region of interest is that corresponding to the super-paramagnetic one, where domains of aligned spins appear. The range of temperatures where these structures are stable is indicated by a non-vanishing magnetic susceptibility. We use a very efficient Monte Carlo algorithm to measure the susceptibility and the spin spin correlation function. The values of the spin spin correlation function, at the super-paramagnetic phase, serve to identify the partition of the data points into clusters.

Many natural phenomena can be viewed as optimization processes, and the drive to understand and analyze them yielded powerful mathematical methods. Thus when wishing to solve a hard optimization problem, it may be advantageous to apply these methods through a physical analogy. Indeed, recently techniques from statistical physics have been adapted for solving hard optimization problems (see *e.g.* Yuille and Kosowsky, 1994). In this work we formulate the problem of clustering in terms of a ferromagnetic Potts spin model. Using the Monte Carlo method we estimate physical quantities such as the spin spin correlation function and the susceptibility, and deduce from them the number of clusters and cluster sizes.

Cluster analysis is an important technique in exploratory data analysis and is applied in a variety of engineering and scientific disciplines. The problem of *partitional clustering* can be formally stated as follows. With every one of $i = 1, 2, \ldots N$ patterns represented as a point $\vec{x}_i$ in a d-dimensional metric space, determine the partition of these N points into M groups, called *clusters*, such that points in a cluster are more similar to each other than to points in different clusters. The value of M also has to be determined.

The two main approaches to partitional clustering are called *parametric* and *non-parametric*. In parametric approaches some knowledge of the clusters' structure is assumed (*e.g.* each cluster can be represented by a center and a spread around it). This assumption is incorporated in a *global criterion*. The goal is to assign the data points so that the criterion is minimized. A typical example is *variance minimization* (Rose, Gurewitz, and Fox, 1993). On the other hand, in non-parametric approaches a *local criterion* is used to build clusters by utilizing local structure of the data. For example, clusters can be formed by identifying high-density regions in the data space or by assigning a point and its K-nearest neighbors to the same cluster. In recent years many parametric partitional clustering algorithms rooted in statistical physics were presented (see *e.g.* Buhmann and Kühnel , 1993). In the present work we use methods of statistical physics in non-parametric clustering.

Our aim is to use a physical problem as an analog to the clustering problem. The notion of clusters comes very naturally in Potts spin models (Wang and Swendsen, 1990) where clusters are closely related to ordered regions of spins. We place a Potts spin variable s_i at each point $\vec{x}_i$ (that represents one of the patterns), and introduce a short range ferromagnetic interaction J_{ij} between pairs of spins, whose strength decreases as the inter-spin distance $\|\vec{x}_i - \vec{x}_j\|$ increases. The system is governed by the Hamiltonian (energy function)

$$\mathcal{H} = - \sum_{<i,j>} J_{ij} \delta_{s_i, s_j} \qquad s_i = 1 \ldots q , \qquad (1)$$

where the notation $<i,j>$ stands for neighboring points i and j in a sense that is defined later. Then we study the ordering properties of this inhomogeneous Potts model.

As a concrete example, place a Potts spin at each of the data points of fig. 1.

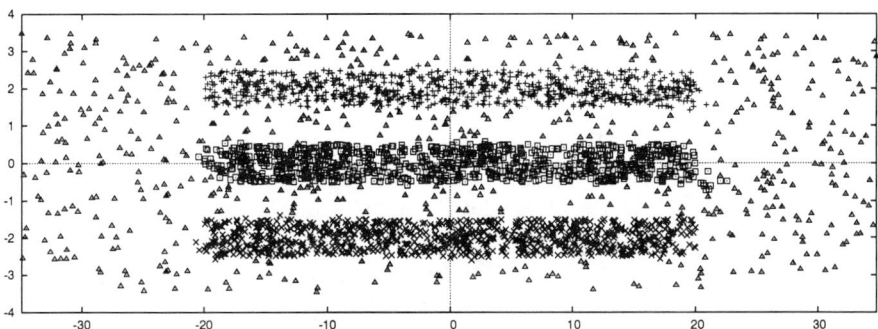

Figure 1: This data set is made of three rectangles, each consisting of 800 points uniformly distributed, and a uniform rectangular background of lower density, also consisting of 800 points. Points classified (with $T_{clus} = 0.08$ and $\theta = 0.5$) as belonging to the three largest clusters are marked by crosses, squares and x's. The fourth cluster is of size 2 and all others are single point clusters marked by triangles.

At high temperatures the system is in a disordered (paramagnetic) phase. As the temperature is lowered, larger and larger regions of high density of points (or spins) exhibit local ordering, until a phase transition occurs and spins in the three rectangular high density regions become completely aligned (*i.e.* within each region all s_i take the same value – super-paramagnetic phase).
The aligned regions define the clusters which we wish to identify. As the temperature

is further lowered, a pseudo-transition occurs and the system becomes completely ordered (ferromagnetic).

1 A mean field model

To support our main idea, we analyze an idealized set of points where the division into natural classes is distinct. The points are divided into M groups. The distance between any two points within the same group is d_1 while the distance between any two points belonging to different groups is $d_2 > d_1$ (d can be regarded as a similarity index). Following our main idea, we associate a Potts spin with each point and an interaction J_1 between points separated by distance d_1 and an J_2 between points separated by d_2, where $0 \leq J_2 < J_1$. Hence the Hamiltonian (1) becomes;

$$\mathcal{H} = -\frac{J_1}{N} \sum_\mu \sum_{i<j} \delta_{s_i^\mu, s_j^\mu} - \frac{J_2}{N} \sum_{\mu<\nu} \sum_{i,j} \delta_{s_i^\mu, s_j^\nu} \qquad s_i^\nu = 1, \ldots, q, \qquad (2)$$

where s_i^ν denotes the ith spin ($i = 1, \ldots, \frac{N}{M}$) of the νth group ($\nu = 1, \ldots, M$). From standard mean field theory for the Potts model (Wu, 1982) it is possible to show that the transition from the ferromagnetic phase to the paramagnetic phase is at $T_c = \frac{q-2}{2M(q-1)\log(q-1)} [J_1 + (M-1)J_2]$. The average spin spin correlation function, $\overline{\delta_{s_i, s_j}}$ at the paramagnetic phase is $\frac{1}{q}$ for all points $\vec{x}_i$ and $\vec{x}_j$; i.e. the spin value at each point is independent of the others. The ferromagnetic phase is further divided into two regions. At low temperatures, with high probability, all spins are aligned; that is $\overline{\delta_{s_i, s_j}} \approx 1$ for all i and j. At intermediate temperatures, between T^* and T_c, only spins of the same group ν are aligned with high probability; $\overline{\delta_{s_i^\nu, s_j^\nu}} \approx 1$, while spins belonging to different groups, μ and ν, are independent; $\overline{\delta_{s_i^\mu, s_j^\nu}} \approx \frac{1}{q}$.

The spin spin correlation function at the super-paramagnetic phase can be used to decide whether or not two spins belong to the same cluster. In contrast with the mere inter-point distance, the spin spin correlation function is sensitive to the collective behavior of the system and is therefore a suitable quantity for defining collective structures (clusters).

The transition temperature T^* may be calculated and shown to be proportional to J_2; $T^* = \alpha(N, M, q) J_2$. In figure 2 we present the phase diagram, in the ($\frac{T}{J_1}$, $\frac{J_2}{J_1}$) plane, for the case $M = 4$, $N = 1000$ and $q = 6$.

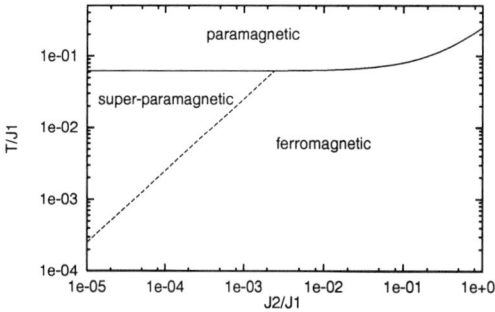

Figure 2: Phase diagram of the mean field Potts model (2) for the case $M = 4$, $N = 1000$ and $q = 6$. The critical temperature T_c is indicated by the solid line, and the transition temperature T^*, by the dashed line.

The phase diagram fig. 2 shows that the existence of natural classes can manifest itself in the thermodynamic properties of the proposed Potts model. Thus our approach is supported, provided that a correct choice of the interaction strengths is made.

2 Definition of local interaction

In order to minimize the intra-cluster interaction it is convenient to allow an interaction only between "neighbors". In common with other "local methods", we assume that there is a 'local length scale' $\sim a$, which is defined by the high density regions and is smaller than the typical distance between points in the low density regions. This property can be expressed in the ordering properties of the Potts system by choosing a short range interaction. Therefore we consider that each point interacts only with its neighbors with interaction strength

$$J_{ij} = J_{ji} = \frac{1}{\widehat{K}} \exp\left(-\frac{\|\vec{x}_i - \vec{x}_j\|^2}{2a^2}\right). \tag{3}$$

Two points, $\vec{x}_i$ and $\vec{x}_j$, are defined as neighbors if they have a mutual neighborhood value K; that is, if $\vec{x}_i$ is one of the K nearest neighbors of $\vec{x}_j$ and vice-versa. This definition ensures that J_{ij} is symmetric; the number of bonds of any site is less than K. We chose the "local length scale", a, to be the average of all distances $\|\vec{x}_i - \vec{x}_j\|$ between pairs i and j with a mutual neighborhood value K. $\widehat{K}$ is the average number of neighbors per site; i.e it is twice the number of non vanishing interactions, J_{ij} divided by the number of points N (This careful normalization of the interaction strength enables us to estimate the critical temperature T_c for any data sample).

3 Calculation of thermodynamic quantities

The ordering properties of the system are reflected by the susceptibility and the spin spin correlation function $\overline{\delta_{s_i,s_j}}$, where $\overline{\cdots}$ stands for a thermal average. These quantities can be estimated by averaging over the configurations generated by a Monte Carlo procedure. We use the Swendsen-Wang (Wang and Swendsen, 1990) Monte Carlo algorithm for the Potts model (1) not only because of its high efficiency, but also because it utilizes the SW clusters. As will be explained the SW clusters are strongly connected to the clusters we wish to identify. A layman's explanation of the method is as follows. The SW procedure stochastically identifies clusters of aligned spins, and then flips whole clusters simultaneously. Starting from a given spin configuration, SW go over all the bonds between neighboring points, and either "freeze" or delete them. A bond connecting two neighboring sites i and j, is deleted with probability $P_d^{i,j} = \exp(-\frac{J_{ij}}{T} \delta_{s_i,s_j})$ and frozen with probability $P_f^{i,j} = 1 - P_d^{i,j}$. Having gone over all the bonds, all spins which have a path of frozen bonds connecting them are identified as being in the same SW cluster. Note that, according to the definition of $P_d^{i,j}$, only spins of the same value can be frozen in the same SW cluster. Now a new spin configuration is generated by drawing, for each cluster, randomly a value $s = 1, \ldots q$, which is assigned to all its spins. This procedure defines one Monte Carlo step and needs to be iterated in order to obtain thermodynamic averages.

At temperatures where large regions of correlated spins occur, local methods (e.g. Metropolis), which flip one spin at a time, become very slow. The SW method overcomes this difficulty by flipping large clusters of aligned spins simultaneously. Hence the SW method exhibits much smaller autocorrelation times than local methods. The strong connection between the SW clusters and the ordering properties of the Potts spins is manifested in the relation

$$\overline{\delta_{s_i,s_j}} = \frac{(q-1)\,\overline{n_{ij}} + 1}{q}, \tag{4}$$

where $n_{ij} = 1$ whenever s_i and s_j belong to the same SW-cluster and $n_{ij} = 0$ otherwise. Thus, $\overline{n_{ij}}$ is the probability that s_i and s_j belong to the same SW-cluster. The r.h.s. of (4) has a smaller variance than its l.h.s., so that the probabilities $\overline{n_{ij}}$ provide an improved estimator of the spin spin correlation function.

4 Locating the super-paramagnetic phase

In order to locate the temperature range in which the system is in the super-paramagnetic phase we measure the susceptibility of the system which is proportional to the variance of the magnetization

$$\chi = \frac{N}{T}(\overline{m^2} - \overline{m}^2) \,. \tag{5}$$

The magnetization, m, is defined as

$$m = \frac{qN_{\max}/N - 1}{q - 1} \qquad N_{\max} = \max\{N_1, N_2, \ldots N_q\}\,, \tag{6}$$

where N_μ is the number of spins with the value μ.

In the ferromagnetic phase the fluctuations of the magnetization are negligible, so the susceptibility, χ, is small. As the temperature is raised, a sudden increase of the susceptibility occurs at the transition from the ferromagnetic to the super-paramagnetic phase. The susceptibility is non-vanishing only in the super-paramagnetic phase, which is the only phase where large fluctuations in the magnetization can occur. The point where the susceptibility vanishes again is an upper bound for the transition temperature from the super-paramagnetic to the paramagnetic phase.

5 The clustering procedure

Our method consists of two main steps. First we identify the range of temperatures where the clusters may be observed (that corresponding to the super-paramagnetic phase) and choose a temperature within this range. Secondly, the clusters are identified using the information contained in the spin spin correlation function at this temperature. The procedure is summarized here, leaving discussion concerning the choice of the parameters to a later stage.

(a) Assign to each point $\vec{x}_i$ a q-state Potts spin variable s_i. q was chosen equal to 20 in the example that we present in this work.

(b) Find all the pairs of points having mutual neighborhood value K. We set $K = 10$.

(c) Calculate the strength of the interactions using equation (3).

(d) Use the SW procedure with the Hamiltonian (1) to calculate the susceptibility χ for various temperatures. The transition temperature from the paramagnetic phase can be roughly estimated by $T_c \approx \frac{e^{-\frac{1}{2}}}{4\log(1+\sqrt{q})}$.

(e) Identify the range of temperatures of non-vanishing χ (the super-paramagnetic phase). Identify the temperature T_{max} where the susceptibility χ is maximal, and the temperature T_{vanish}, where χ vanishes at the high temperature side. The optimal temperature to identify the clusters lies between these two temperatures. As a rule of thumb we chose the "clustering temperature" $T_{clus} = \frac{T_{vanish}+T_{max}}{2}$ but the results depend only weakly on T_{clus}, as long as T_{clus} is in the super-paramagnetic range, $T_{max} < T_{clus} < T_{vanish}$.

(f) At the clustering temperature T_{clus}, estimate the spin spin correlation, $\overline{\delta_{s_i,s_j}}$, for all neighboring pairs of points $\vec{x}_i$ and $\vec{x}_j$, using (4).

(g) Clusters are identified according to a thresholding procedure. The spin spin correlation function $\overline{\delta_{s_i,s_j}}$ of points $\vec{x}_i$ and $\vec{x}_j$ is compared with a threshold, θ; if $\overline{\delta_{s_i,s_j}} > \theta$ they are defined as "friends". Then all mutual friends (including friends of friends, etc) are assigned to the same cluster. We chose $\theta = 0.5$.

In order to show how this algorithm works, let us consider the distribution of points presented in figure 1. Because of the overlap of the larger sparse rectangle with the smaller rectangles, and due to statistical fluctuations, the three dense rectangles actually contain 883, 874 and 863 points.
Going through steps (a) to (d) we obtained the susceptibility as a function of the temperature as presented in figure 3. The susceptibility χ is maximal at $T_{max} = 0.03$ and vanishes at $T_{vanish} = 0.13$. In figure 1 we present the clusters obtained according to steps (f) and (g) at $T_{clus} = 0.08$. The size of the largest clusters in descending order is 900, 894, 877, 2 and all the rest are composed of only one point. The three biggest clusters correspond to the clusters we are looking for, while the background is decomposed into clusters of size one.

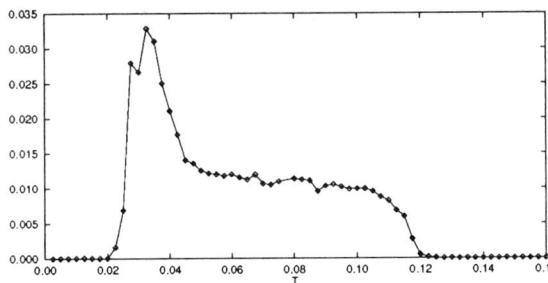

Figure 3: The susceptibility density $\frac{\chi T}{N}$ as a function of the temperature.

Let us discuss the effect of the parameters on the procedure. The number of Potts states, q, determines mainly the sharpness of the transition and the critical temperature. The higher q, the sharper the transition. On the other hand, it is necessary to perform more statistics (more SW sweeps) as the value of q increases. From our simulations, we conclude that the influence of q is very weak. The maximal number of neighbors, K, also affects the results very little; we obtained quite similar results for a wide range of K ($5 \leq K \leq 20$).
No dramatic changes were observed in the classification, when choosing clustering temperatures T_{clus} other than that suggested in (e). However this choice is clearly ad-hoc and a better choice should be found. Our method does not provide a natural way to choose a threshold θ for the spin spin correlation function. In practice though, the classification is not very sensitive to the value of θ, and values in the range $0.2 < \theta < 0.8$ yield similar results. The reason is that the frequency distribution of the values of the spin spin correlation function exhibits two peaks, one close to $\frac{1}{q}$ and the other close to 1, while for intermediate values it is very close to zero. In figure (4) we present the average size of the largest SW cluster as a function of the temperature, along with the size of the largest cluster obtained by the thresholding procedure (described in (7)) using three different threshold values $\theta = 0.2, 0.5, 0.9$. Note the agreement between the largest cluster size defined by the threshold $\theta = 0.5$ and the average size of the largest SW cluster for all temperatures (This agreement holds for the smaller clusters as well). It supports our thresholding procedure as a sensible one at all temperatures.

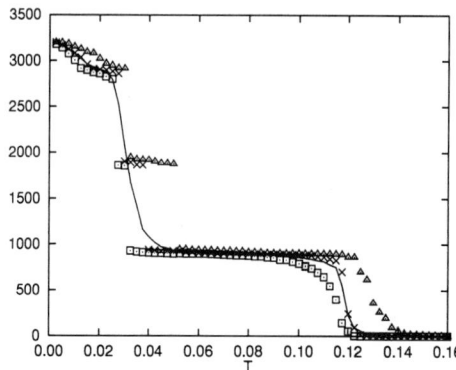

Figure 4: Average size of the largest SW cluster as a function of the temperature, is denoted by the solid line. The triangles, x's and squares denote the size of the largest cluster obtained with thresholds $\theta = 0.2$, 0.5 and 0.9 respectively.

6 Discussion

Other methods that were proposed previously, such as Fukunaga's (1990), can be formulated as a Metropolis relaxation of a ferromagnetic Potts model at $T = 0$. The clusters are then determined by the points having the same spin value at the local minima of the energy at which the relaxation process terminates. Clearly this procedure depends strongly on the initial conditions. There is a high probability of getting stuck in a metastable state that does not correspond to the desired answer. Such a $T = 0$ method does not provide any way to distinguish between "good" and "bad" metastable states. We applied Fukunaga's method on the data set of figure (1) using many different initial conditions. The right answer was never obtained. In all runs, domain walls that broke a cluster into two or more parts appeared.

Our method generalizes Fukunaga's method by introducing a finite temperature at which the division into clusters is stable. In addition, the SW dynamics are completely insensitive to the initial conditions and extremely efficient.

Work in progress shows that our method is especially suitable for hierarchical clustering. This is done by identifying clusters at several temperatures which are chosen according to features of the susceptibility curve. In particular our method is successful in dealing with "real life" problems such as the Iris data and Landsat data.

Acknowledgments

We thank I. Kanter for many useful discussions. This research has been supported by the US-Israel Bi-national Science Foundation (BSF), and the Germany-Israel Science Foundation (GIF).

References

J.M. Buhmann and H. Kühnel (1993); *Vector quantization with complexity costs*, IEEE Trans. Inf. Theory **39**, 1133.

K. Fukunaga (1990); *Introd. to statistical Pattern Recognition*, Academic Press.

K. Rose, E. Gurewitz, and G.C. Fox (1993); *Constrained clustering as an optimization method*, IEEE Trans on Patt. Anal. and Mach. Intel. **PAMI 15**, 785.

S. Wang and R.H. Swendsen (1990); *Cluster Monte Carlo alg.*, Physica **A 167**, 565.

F.Y. Wu (1982), *The Potts model*, Rev Mod Phys, **54**, 235.

A.L. Yuille and J.J. Kosowsky (1994); *Statistical algorithms that converge*, Neural Computation **6**, 341 (1994).

Generalized Learning Vector Quantization

Atsushi Sato & Keiji Yamada
Information Technology Research Laboratories,
NEC Corporation
1-1, Miyazaki 4-chome, Miyamae-ku,
Kawasaki, Kanagawa 216, Japan
E-mail: {asato, yamada}@pat.cl.nec.co.jp

Abstract

We propose a new learning method, "Generalized Learning Vector Quantization (GLVQ)," in which reference vectors are updated based on the steepest descent method in order to minimize the cost function. The cost function is determined so that the obtained learning rule satisfies the convergence condition. We prove that Kohonen's rule as used in LVQ does not satisfy the convergence condition and thus degrades recognition ability. Experimental results for printed Chinese character recognition reveal that GLVQ is superior to LVQ in recognition ability.

1 INTRODUCTION

Artificial neural network models have been applied to character recognition with good results for small-set characters such as alphanumerics (Le Cun et al., 1989) (Yamada et al., 1989). However, applying the models to large-set characters such as Japanese or Chinese characters is difficult because most of the models are based on Multi-Layer Perceptron (MLP) with the back propagation algorithm, which has a problem in regard to local minima as well as requiring a lot of calculation.

Classification methods based on pattern matching have commonly been used for large-set character recognition. Learning Vector Quantization (LVQ) has been studied to generate optimal reference vectors because of its simple and fast learning algorithm (Kohonen, 1989; 1995). However, one problem with LVQ is that reference vectors diverge and thus degrade recognition ability. Much work has been done on improving LVQ (Lee & Song, 1993) (Miyahara & Yoda, 1993) (Sato & Tsukumo, 1994), but the problem remains unsolved.

Recently, a generalization of the Simple Competitive Learning (SCL) has been under study (Pal et al., 1993) (Gonzalez et al., 1995), and one unsupervised learning rule has been derived based on the steepest descent method to minimize the cost function. Pal et al. call their model "Generalized Learning Vector Quantization," but it is not a generalization of Kohonen's LVQ.

In this paper, we propose a new learning method for supervised learning, in which reference vectors are updated based on the steepest descent method, to minimize the cost function. This is a generalization of Kohonen's LVQ, so we call it "Generalized Learning Vector Quantization (GLVQ)." The cost function is determined so that the obtained learning rule satisfies the convergence condition. We prove that Kohonen's rule as used in LVQ does not satisfy the convergence condition and thus degrades recognition ability. Preliminary experiments revealed that non-linearity in the cost function is very effective for improving recognition ability. Printed Chinese character recognition experiments were carried out, and we can show that the recognition ability of GLVQ is very high compared with LVQ.

2 REVIEW OF LVQ

Assume that a number of reference vectors w_k are placed in the input space. Usually, several reference vectors are assigned to each class. An input vector x is decided to belong to the same class to which the nearest reference vector belongs. Let $w_k(t)$ represent sequences of the w_k in the discrete-time domain. Heretofore, several LVQ algorithms have been proposed (Kohonen, 1995), but in this section, we will focus on LVQ2.1. Starting with properly defined initial values, the reference vectors are updated as follows by the LVQ2.1 algorithm:

$$w_i(t+1) = w_i(t) - \alpha(t)(x - w_i(t)), \quad (1)$$
$$w_j(t+1) = w_j(t) + \alpha(t)(x - w_j(t)), \quad (2)$$

where $0 < \alpha(t) < 1$, and $\alpha(t)$ may decrease monotonically with time. The two reference vectors w_i and w_j are the nearest to x; x and w_j belong to the same class, while x and w_i belong to different classes. Furthermore, x must fall into the "window," which is defined around the midplane of w_i and w_j. That is, if the following condition is satisfied, w_i and w_j are updated:

$$\min\left(\frac{d_i}{d_j}, \frac{d_j}{d_i}\right) > s, \quad (3)$$

where $d_i = |x - w_i|$, $d_j = |x - w_j|$. The LVQ2.1 algorithm is based on the idea of shifting the decision boundaries toward the Bayes limits with attractive and repulsive forces from x. However, no attention is given to what might happen to the location of the w_k, so the reference vectors diverge in the long run. LVQ3 has been proposed to ensure that the reference vectors continue approximating the class distributions, but it must be noted that if only one reference vector is assigned to each class, LVQ3 is the same as LVQ2.1, and the problem of reference vector divergence remains unsolved.

3 GENERALIZED LVQ

To ensure that the reference vectors continue approximating the class distributions, we propose a new learning method based on minimizing the cost function. Let w_1 be the nearest reference vector that belongs to the same class of x, and likewise let w_2 be the nearest reference vector that belongs to a different class from x. Let us consider the relative distance difference $\mu(x)$ defined as follows:

$$\mu(x) = \frac{d_1 - d_2}{d_1 + d_2}, \quad (4)$$

where d_1 and d_2 are the distances of x from w_1 and w_2, respectively. $\mu(x)$ ranges between -1 and $+1$, and if $\mu(x)$ is negative, x is classified correctly; otherwise, x is classified incorrectly. In order to improve error rates, $\mu(x)$ should decrease for all input vectors. Thus, a criterion for learning is formulated as the minimizing of a cost function S defined by

$$S = \sum_{i=1}^{N} f(\mu(x_i)), \tag{5}$$

where N is the number of input vectors for training, and $f(\mu)$ is a monotonically increasing function. To minimize S, w_1 and w_2 are updated based on the steepest descent method with a small positive constant α as follows:

$$w_i \leftarrow w_i - \alpha \frac{\partial S}{\partial w_i}, \quad i = 1, 2 \tag{6}$$

If squared Euclid distance, $d_i = |x - w_i|^2$, is used, we can obtain the following.

$$\frac{\partial S}{\partial w_1} = \frac{\partial S}{\partial \mu} \frac{\partial \mu}{\partial d_1} \frac{\partial d_1}{\partial w_1} = -\frac{\partial f}{\partial \mu} \frac{4 d_2}{(d_1 + d_2)^2} (x - w_1) \tag{7}$$

$$\frac{\partial S}{\partial w_2} = \frac{\partial S}{\partial \mu} \frac{\partial \mu}{\partial d_2} \frac{\partial d_2}{\partial w_2} = +\frac{\partial f}{\partial \mu} \frac{4 d_1}{(d_1 + d_2)^2} (x - w_2) \tag{8}$$

Therefore, the GLVQ's learning rule can be described as follows:

$$w_1 \leftarrow w_1 + \alpha \frac{\partial f}{\partial \mu} \frac{d_2}{(d_1 + d_2)^2} (x - w_1) \tag{9}$$

$$w_2 \leftarrow w_2 - \alpha \frac{\partial f}{\partial \mu} \frac{d_1}{(d_1 + d_2)^2} (x - w_2) \tag{10}$$

Let us discuss the meaning of $f(\mu)$. $\partial f/\partial \mu$ is a kind of gain factor for updating, and its value depends on x. In other words, $\partial f/\partial \mu$ is a weight for each x. To decrease the error rate, it is effective to update reference vectors mainly by input vectors around class boundaries, so that the decision boundaries are shifted toward the Bayes limits. Accordingly, $f(\mu)$ should be a *non-linear* monotonically increasing function, and it is considered that classification ability depends on the definition of $f(\mu)$. In this paper, $\partial f/\partial \mu = f(\mu, t)\{1 - f(\mu, t)\}$ was used in the experiments, where t is learning time and $f(\mu, t)$ is a sigmoid function of $1/(1 + e^{-\mu t})$. In this case, $\partial f/\partial \mu$ has a single peak at $\mu = 0$, and the peak width becomes narrower as t increases, so the input vectors that affect learning are gradually restricted to those around the decision boundaries.

Let us discuss the meaning of μ. w_1 and w_2 are updated by attractive and repulsive forces from x, respectively, as shown in Eqs. (9) and (10), and the quantities of updating, $|\Delta w_1|$ and $|\Delta w_2|$, depend on derivatives of μ. Reference vectors will converge to the equilibrium states defined by attractive and repulsive forces, so it is considered that convergence property depends on the definition of μ.

4 DISCUSSION

First, we show that the conventional LVQ algorithms can be derived based on the framework of GLVQ. If $\mu = d_1$ for $d_1 < d_2$, $\mu = -d_2$ for $d_1 > d_2$, and $f(\mu) = \mu$, the cost function is written as $S = \sum_{d_1 < d_2} d_1 - \sum_{d_1 > d_2} d_2$. Then, we can obtain the following:

$$w_1 \leftarrow w_1 + \alpha(x - w_1), \; w_2 \leftarrow w_2 \quad \text{for } d_1 < d_2 \tag{11}$$

$$w_2 \leftarrow w_2 - \alpha(x - w_2), \; w_1 \leftarrow w_1 \quad \text{for } d_1 > d_2 \tag{12}$$

This learning algorithm is the same as LVQ1. If $\mu = d_1 - d_2$ and $f(\mu) = \mu$ for $|\mu| < s$, $f(\mu) = \text{const}$ for $|\mu| > s$, the cost function is written as $S = \sum_{|\mu|<s}(d_1 - d_2) + C$. Then, we can obtain the following:

if $|\mu| < s$ (x falls into the window)

$$w_1 \leftarrow w_1 + \alpha(x - w_2) \quad (13)$$
$$w_2 \leftarrow w_2 - \alpha(x - w_2) \quad (14)$$

In this case, w_1 and w_2 are updated simultaneously, and this learning algorithm is the same as LVQ2.1. So it can be said that GLVQ is a generalized model that includes the conventional LVQs.

Next, we discuss the convergence condition. We can obtain other learning algorithms by defining a different cost function, but it must be noted that the convergence property depends on the definition of the cost function. The main difference between GLVQ and LVQ2.1 is the definition of μ; $\mu = (d_1 - d_2)/(d_1 + d_2)$ in GLVQ, $\mu = d_1 - d_2$ in LVQ2.1. Why do the reference vectors diverge in LVQ2.1, while they converge in GLVQ, as shown later? In order to clarify the convergence condition, let us consider the following learning rule:

$$w_1 \leftarrow w_1 + \alpha|x - w_2|^k(x - w_1) \quad (15)$$
$$w_2 \leftarrow w_2 - \alpha|x - w_1|^k(x - w_2) \quad (16)$$

Here, $|\Delta w_1|$ and $|\Delta w_2|$ are the quantities of updating by the attractive and the repulsive forces, respectively. The ratio of these two is calculated as follows:

$$\frac{|\Delta w_1|}{|\Delta w_2|} = \frac{\alpha|x - w_2|^k|x - w_1|}{\alpha|x - w_1|^k|x - w_2|} = \frac{|x - w_2|^{k-1}}{|x - w_1|^{k-1}} \quad (17)$$

If the initial values of reference vectors are properly defined, most x's will satisfy $|x - w_1| < |x - w_2|$. Therefore, if $k > 1$, the attractive force is greater than the repulsive force, and the reference vectors will converge, because the attractive forces come from x's that belong to the same class of w_1. In GLVQ, $k = 2$ as shown in Eqs. (9) and (10), and the vectors will converge, while they will diverge in LVQ2.1 because $k = 0$. According to the above discussion, we can use $d_i/(d_1 + d_2)$ or just d_i, instead of $d_i/(d_1 + d_2)^2$ in Eqs. (9) and (10). This correction does not affect the convergence condition. The essential problem in LVQ2.1 results from the drawback in Kohonen's rule with $k = 0$. In other words, the cost function used in LVQ is not determined so that the obtained learning rule satisfies the convergence condition.

5 EXPERIMENTS

5.1 PRELIMINARY EXPERIMENTS

The experimental results using Eqs. (15) and (16) with $\alpha = 0.001$, shown in Fig. 1, support the above discussion on the convergence condition. Two-dimensional input vectors with two classes shown in Fig. 1(a) were used in the experiments. The ideal decision boundary that minimizes the error rate is shown by the broken line. One reference vector was assigned to each class with initial values $(x, y) = (0.3, 0.5)$ for Class A and $(x, y) = (0.7, 0.5)$ for Class B. Figure 1(b) shows the distance between the two reference vectors during learning. The distance remains the same value for $k > 1$, while it increases with time for $k \leq 1$; that is, the reference vectors diverge.

Figure 2 shows the experimental results from GLVQ for linearly non-separable patterns compared with LVQ2.1. The input vectors shown in Fig. 2(a) were obtained by shifting all input vectors shown in Fig. 1(a) to the right by $|y - 0.5|$. The ideal

Generalized Learning Vector Quantization

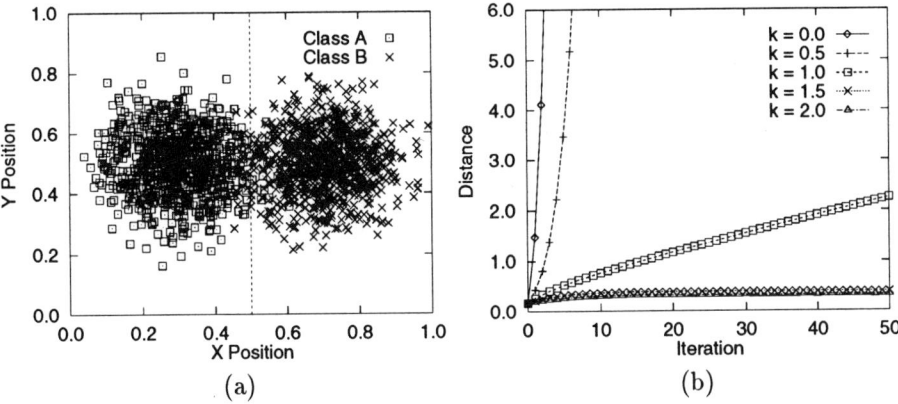

Figure 1: Experimental results that support the discussion on the convergence condition with one reference vector for each class. (a) Input vectors used in the experiments. The broken line shows the ideal decision boundary. (b) Distance between two reference vectors for each k value during learning. The distance remains the same value for $k > 1$, while it diverges for $k \leq 1$.

decision boundary that minimizes the error rate is shown by the broken line. Two reference vectors were assigned to each class with initial values $(x, y) = (0.3, 0.4)$ and $(0.3, 0.6)$ for Class A, and $(x, y) = (0.7, 0.4)$ and $(0.7, 0.6)$ for Class B. The gain factor α was 0.004 in GLVQ and LVQ2.1, and the window parameter s in LVQ2.1 was 0.8 in the experiments.

Figure 2(b) shows the number of error counts for all the input vectors during learning. GLVQ(NL) shows results by GLVQ with a non-linear function; that is, $\partial f/\partial \mu = f(\mu, t)\{1 - f(\mu, t)\}$. The number of error counts decreased with time to the minimum determined by the Bayes limit. GLVQ(L) shows results by GLVQ with a linear function; that is, $\partial f/\partial \mu = 1$. The number of error counts did not decrease to the minimum. This indicates that non-linearity of the cost function is very effective for improving recognition ability. Results using LVQ2.1 show that the number of error counts decreased in the beginning, but overall increased gradually with time. The degradation in the recognition ability results from the divergence of the reference vectors, as we have mentioned earlier.

5.2 CHARACTER RECOGNITION EXPERIMENTS

Printed Chinese character recognition experiments were carried out to examine the performance of GLVQ. Thirteen kinds of printed fonts with 500 classes were used in the experiments. The total number of characters was 13,000; half of which were used as training data, and the other half were used as test data. As input vectors, 256-dimensional orientation features were used (Hamanaka et al., 1993). Only one reference vector was assigned to each class, and their initial values were defined by averaging training data for each class.

Recognition results for test data are tabulated in Table 1 compared with other methods. TM is the template matching method using mean vectors. LVQ2 is the earlier version of LVQ2.1. The learning algorithm is the same as LVQ2.1 described in Section 2, but d_i must be less than d_j. The gain factor α was 0.05, and the window parameter s was 0.65 in the experiments. The experimental result by LVQ3 was

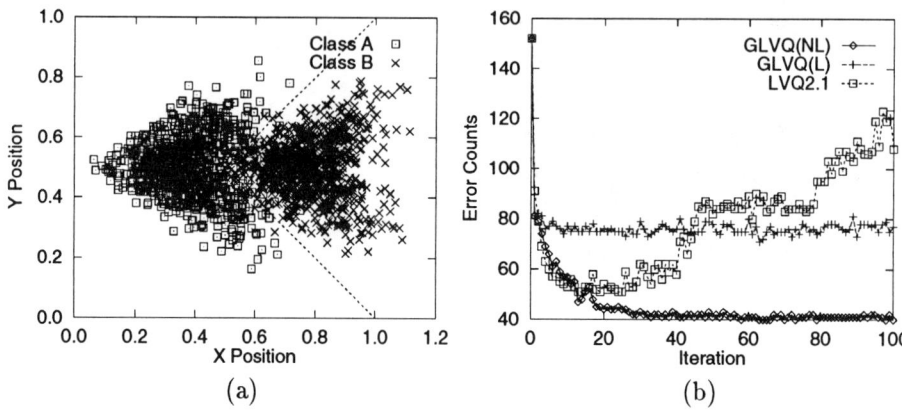

Figure 2: Experimental results for linearly non-separable patterns with two reference vectors for each class. (a) Input vectors used in the experiments. The broken line shows the ideal decision boundary. (b) The number of error counts during learning. GLVQ (NL) and GLVQ (L) denote the proposed method using a non-linear and linear function in the cost function, respectively. This shows that non-linearity of the cost function is very effective for improving classification ability.

Table 1: Experimental results for printed Chinese character recognition compared with other methods.

Methods	Error rates(%)
TM[1]	0.23
LVQ2[2]	0.18
LVQ2.1	0.11
IVQ[3]	0.08
GLVQ	0.05

[1] Template matching using mean vectors.
[2] The earlier version of LVQ2.1.
[3] Our previous model (Improved Vector Quantization).

the same as that by LVQ2.1, because only one reference vector was assigned to each class. IVQ (Improved Vector Quantization) is our previous model based on Kohonen's rule (Sato & Tsukumo, 1994).

The error rate was extremely low for GLVQ, and a recognition rate of 99.95% was obtained. Ambiguous results can be rejected by thresholding the value of $\mu(x)$. If input vectors with $\mu(x) \geq -0.02$ were rejected, a recognition rate of 100% would be obtained, with a rejection rate of 0.08% for this experiment.

6 CONCLUSION

We proposed the Generalized Learning Vector Quantization as a new learning method. We formulated the criterion for learning as the minimizing of the cost function, and obtained the learning rule based on the steepest descent method. GLVQ is a generalized method that includes LVQ. We discussed the convergence condition and showed that the convergence property depends on the definition of the cost function. We proved that the essential problem of the divergence of the reference vectors in LVQ2.1 results from a drawback of Kohonen's rule that does not satisfy the convergence condition. Preliminary experiments revealed that nonlinearity in the cost function is very effective for improving recognition ability. We carried out printed Chinese character recognition experiments and obtained a recognition rate of 99.95%. The experimental results revealed that GLVQ is superior to the conventional LVQ algorithms.

Acknowledgements

We are indebted to Mr. Jun Tsukumo and our colleagues in the Pattern Recognition Research Laboratory for their helpful cooperation.

References

Y. Le Cun, B. Bose, J. S. Denker, D. Henderson, R. E. Howard, W. Hubbard, and L. D. Jackel, "Handwritten Digit Recognition with a Back-Propagation Network," *Neural Information Processing Systems 2*, pp. 396–404 (1989).

K. Yamada, H. Kami, J. Tsukumo, and T. Temma, "Handwritten Numeral Recognition by Multi-Layered Neural Network with Improved Learning Algorithm," *Proc. of the International Joint Conference on Neural Networks 89*, Vol. 2, pp. 259–266 (1989).

T. Kohonen, *Self-Organization and Associative Memory*, 3rd ed., Springer-Verlag (1989).

T. Kohonen, "LVQ_PAK Version 3.1 — The Learning Vector Quantization Program Package," *LVQ Programming Team of the Helsinki University of Technology*, (1995).

S. W. Lee and H. H. Song, "Optimal Design of Reference Models Using Simulated Annealing Combined with an Improved LVQ3," *Proc. of the International Conference on Document Analysis and Recognition*, pp. 244–249 (1993).

K. Miyahara and F. Yoda, "Printed Japanese Character Recognition Based on Multiple Modified LVQ Neural Network," *Proc. of the International Conference on Document Analysis and Recognition*, pp. 250–253 (1993).

A. Sato and J. Tsukumo, "A Criterion for Training Reference Vectors and Improved Vector Quantization," *Proc. of the International Conference on Neural Networks*, Vol. 1, pp.161–166 (1994).

N. R. Pal, J. C. Bezdek, and E. C.-K. Tsao, "Generalized Clustering Networks and Kohonen's Self-organizing Scheme," *IEEE Trans. of Neural Networks*, Vol. 4, No. 4, pp. 549–557 (1993).

A. I. Gonzalez, M. Graña, and A. D'Anjou, "An Analysis of the GLVQ Algorithm," *IEEE Trans. of Neural Networks*, Vol. 6, No. 4, pp. 1012–1016 (1995).

M. Hamanaka, K. Yamada, and J. Tsukumo, "On-Line Japanese Character Recognition Experiments by an Off-Line Method Based on Normalization-Cooperated Feature Extraction," *Proc. of the International Conference on Document Analysis and Recognition*, pp. 204–207 (1993).

Stochastic Hillclimbing as a Baseline Method for Evaluating Genetic Algorithms

Ari Juels
Department of Computer Science
University of California at Berkeley*

Martin Wattenberg
Department of Mathematics
University of California at Berkeley[†]

Abstract

We investigate the effectiveness of stochastic hillclimbing as a baseline for evaluating the performance of genetic algorithms (GAs) as combinatorial function optimizers. In particular, we address two problems to which GAs have been applied in the literature: Koza's 11-multiplexer problem and the jobshop problem. We demonstrate that simple stochastic hillclimbing methods are able to achieve results comparable or superior to those obtained by the GAs designed to address these two problems. We further illustrate, in the case of the jobshop problem, how insights obtained in the formulation of a stochastic hillclimbing algorithm can lead to improvements in the encoding used by a GA.

1 Introduction

Genetic algorithms (GAs) are a class of randomized optimization heuristics based loosely on the biological paradigm of natural selection. Among other proposed applications, they have been widely advocated in recent years as a general method for obtaining approximate solutions to hard combinatorial optimization problems using a minimum of information about the mathematical structure of these problems. By means of a general "evolutionary" strategy, GAs aim to maximize an objective or *fitness* function $f : S \rightarrow \mathbf{R}$ over a combinatorial space S, i.e., to find some state $s \in S$ for which $f(s)$ is as large as possible. (The case in which f is to be minimized is clearly symmetrical.) For a detailed description of the algorithm see, for example, [7], which constitutes a standard text on the subject.

In this paper, we investigate the effectiveness of the GA in comparison with that of stochastic hillclimbing (SH), a probabilistic variant of hillclimbing. As the term

---

*Supported in part by NSF Grant CCR-9505448. E-mail: **juels@cs.berkeley.edu**
[†]E-mail: **wattenbe@math.berkeley.edu**

"hillclimbing" suggests, if we view an optimization problem as a "landscape" in which each point corresponds to a solution s and the "height" of the point corresponds to the fitness of the solution, $f(s)$, then hillclimbing aims to ascend to a peak by repeatedly moving to an adjacent state with a higher fitness.

A number of researchers in the GA community have already addressed the issue of how various versions of hillclimbing on the space of bitstrings, $\{0,1\}^n$, compare with GAs [1] [4] [9] [18] [15]. Our investigations in this paper differ in two important respects from these previous ones. First, we address more sophisticated problems than the majority of these studies, which make use of test functions developed for the purpose of exploring certain landscape characteristics. Second, we consider hillclimbing algorithms based on operators in some way "natural" to the combinatorial structures of the problems to which we are seeking solutions, very much as GA designers attempt to do. In one of the two problems in this paper, our SH algorithm employs an encoding exactly identical to that in the proposed GA. Consequently, the hillclimbing algorithms we consider operate on structures other than bitstrings.

Constraints in space have required the omission of a great deal of material found in the full version of this paper. This material includes the treatment of two additional problems: the NP-complete Maximum Cut Problem [11] and an NP-complete problem known as the multiprocessor document allocation problem (MDAP). Also in the full version of this paper is a substantially more thorough exposition of the material presented here. The reader is encouraged to refer to [10], available on the World Wide Web at http://www.cs.berkeley.edu/~juels/.

2 Stochastic Hillclimbing

The SH algorithm employed in this paper searches a discrete space S with the aim of finding a state whose fitness is as high (or as low) as possible. The algorithm does this by making successive improvements to some current state $\sigma \in S$. As is the case with genetic algorithms, the form of the states in S depends upon how the designer of the SH algorithm chooses to encode the solutions to the problems to be solved: as bitstrings, permutations, or in some other form. The local improvements effected by the SH algorithm are determined by the *neighborhood structure* and the fitness function f imposed on S in the design of the algorithm. We can consider the neighborhood structure as an undirected graph G on vertex set S. The algorithm attempts to improve its current state σ by making a transition to one of the neighbors of σ in G. In particular, the algorithm chooses a state τ according to some suitable probability distribution on the neighbors of σ. If the fitness of τ is as least as good as that of σ then τ becomes the new current state, otherwise σ is retained. This process is then repeated

3 GP and Jobshop

3.1 The Experiments

In this section, we compare the performance of SH algorithms with that of GAs proposed for two problems: the jobshop problem and Koza's 11-multiplexer problem. We gauge the performance of the GA and SH algorithms according to the fitness of the best solution achieved after a fixed number of function evaluations, rather than the running time of the algorithms. This is because evaluation of the fitness function generally constitutes the most substantial portion of the execution time of the optimization algorithm, and accords with standard practice in the GA community.

3.2 Genetic Programming

"Genetic programming" (GP) is a method of enabling a genetic algorithm to search a potentially infinite space of computer programs, rather than a space of fixed-length solutions to a combinatorial optimization problem. These programs take the form of Lisp symbolic expressions, called *S-expressions*. The S-expressions in GP correspond to programs which a user seeks to adapt to perform some pre-specified task. Details on GP, an increasingly common GA application, and on the 11-multiplexer problem which we address in this section, may be found, for example, in [13] [12] [14].

The boolean 11-multiplexer problem entails the generation of a program to perform the following task. A set of 11 distinct inputs is provided, with labels $a_0, a_1, a_2, d_0, d_1, \ldots, d_7$, where a stands for "address" and d for "data". Each input takes the value 0 or 1. The task is to output the value d_m, where $m = a_0 + 2a_1 + 4a_2$. In other words, for any 11-bit string, the input to the "address" variables is to be interpreted as an index to a specific "data" variable, which the program then yields as output. For example, on input $a_1 = 1, a_0 = a_2 = 0$, and $d_2 = 1, d_0 = d_1 = d_3 = \ldots = d_7 = 0$, a correct program will output a '1', since the input to the 'a' variables specifies address 2, and variable d_2 is given input 1.

The GA Koza's GP involves the use of a GA to generate an S-expression corresponding to a correct 11-multiplexer program. An S-expression comprises a tree of LISP *operators* and *operands*, operands being the set of data to be processed — the leaves of the tree — and operators being the functions applied to these data and internally in the tree. The nature of the operators and operands will depend on the problem at hand, since different problems will involve different sets of inputs and will require different functions to be applied to these inputs. For the 11-multiplexer problem in particular, where the goal is to create a specific boolean function, the operands are the input bits $a_0, a_1, a_2, d_0, d_1, \ldots, d_7$, and the operators are AND, OR, NOT, and IF. These operators behave as expected: the subtree (AND a_1 a_2), for instance, yields the value $a_1 \wedge a_2$. The subtree (IF a_1 d_4 d_3) yields the value d_4 if $a_1 = 0$ and d_3 if $a_1 = 1$ (and thus can be regarded as a "3-multiplexer"). NOT and OR work similarly. An S-expression constitutes a tree of such operators, with operands at the leaves. Given an assignment to the operands, this tree is evaluated from bottom to top in the obvious way, yielding a 0 or 1 output at the root.

Koza makes use of a "mating" operation in his GA which swaps subexpressions between two such S-expressions. The subexpressions to be swapped are chosen uniformly at random from the set of all subexpressions in the tree. For details on selection in this GA, see [13]. The fitness of an S-expression is computed by evaluating it on all 2048 possible inputs, and counting the number of correct outputs. Koza does not employ a mutation operator in his GA.

The SH Algorithm For this problem, the initial state in the SH algorithm is an S-expression consisting of a single operand chosen uniformly at random from $\{a_0, a_1, a_2, d_0, \ldots, d_7\}$. A transition in the search space involves the random replacement of an arbitrary node in the S-expression. In particular, to select a neighboring state, we chose a node uniformly at random from the current tree and replace it with a node selected randomly from the set of all possible operands and operators. With probability $\frac{1}{2}$ the replacement node is drawn uniformly at random from the set of operands $\{a_0, a_1, a_2, d_0, \ldots, d_7\}$, otherwise it is drawn uniformly at random from the set of operators, {AND, OR, NOT, IF}. In modifying the nodes of the S-expression in this way, we may change the number of inputs they require. By changing an AND node to a NOT node, for instance, we reduce the number of inputs taken by the node from 2 to 1. In order to accommodate such changes, we do the following. Where a replacement reduces the number of inputs taken by a node, we remove the required number of children from that node uniformly at random. Where, on the other hand, a replacement increases the number of inputs taken by a node, we add the required number of children chosen uniformly at random from the set of operands $\{a_0, a_1, a_2, d_0, \ldots, d_7\}$. A similar, though somewhat more involved approach of this kind, with additional experimentation using simulated annealing, may be found in [17].

Experimental Results In the implementation described in [14], Koza performs experiments with a GA on a pool of 4000 expressions. He records the results of 54 runs. These results are listed in the table below. The average number of function evaluations required to obtain a correct program is not given in [14]. In [12], however, where Koza performs a series of 21 runs with a slightly different selection scheme, he finds that the average number of function evaluations required to find a correct S-expression is 46,667.

In 100 runs of the SH algorithm, we found that the average time required to obtain a correct S-expression was 19,234.90 function evaluations, with a standard deviation of 5179.45. The minimum time to find a correct expression in these runs was 3733, and the maximum, 73,651. The average number of nodes in the correct S-expression found by the SH algorithm was 88.14; the low was 42, the high, 242, and the standard deviation, 29.16.

The following table compares the results presented in [14], indicated by the heading "GP", with those obtained using stochastic hillclimbing, indicated by "SH". We give the fraction of runs in which a correct program was found after a given number of function evaluations. (As this fraction was not provided for the 20000 iteration mark in [14], we omit the corresponding entry.)

$Function evaluations$	GP	SH
20000		61 %
40000	28 %	98 %
60000	78 %	99 %
80000	90 %	100 %

We observe that the performance of the SH is substantially better than that of the GA. It is interesting to note – perhaps partly in explanation of the SH algorithm's success on this problem – that the SH algorithm formulated here defines a neighborhood structure in which there are *no strict local minima*. Remarkably, this is true for any boolean formula. For details, as well as an elementary proof, see the full version of this paper [10].

3.3 Jobshop

Jobshop is a notoriously difficult NP-complete problem [6] that is hard to solve even for small instances. In this problem, a collection of J jobs are to be scheduled on M machines (or processors), each of which can process only one task at a time. Each job is a list of M tasks which must be performed in order. Each task must be performed on a specific machine, and no two tasks in a given job are assigned to the same machine. Every task has a fixed (integer) processing time. The problem is to schedule the jobs on the machines so that all jobs are completed in the shortest overall time. This time is referred to as the *makespan*.

Three instances formulated in [16] constitute a standard benchmark for this problem: a 6 job, 6 machine instance, a 10 job, 10 machine instance, and a 20 job, 5 machine instance. The 6x6 instance is now known to have an optimal makespan of 55. This is very easy to achieve. While the optimum value for the 10x10 problem is known to be 930, this is a difficult problem which remained unsolved for over 20 years [2]. A great deal of research has also been invested in the similarly challenging 20x5 problem, for which an optimal value of 1165 has been achieved, and a lower bound of 1164 [3].

A number of papers have considered the application of GAs to scheduling problems. We compare our results with those obtained in Fang et al. [5], one of the more recent of these articles.

The GA Fang et al. encode a jobshop schedule in the form of a string of integers, to which their GA applies a conventional crossover operator. This string contains JM integers $a_1, a_2, \ldots, a_{JM}$ in the range $1..J$. A circular list C of jobs, initialized to $(1, 2, \ldots, J)$ is maintained. For $i = 1, 2, \ldots, JM$, the first uncompleted task in the $(a_i \mod |C|)^{th}$ job in C is scheduled in the earliest plausible timeslot. A *plausible* timeslot is one which comes after the last scheduled task in the current job, and which is at least as long as the processing time of the task to be scheduled. When a job is complete, it is removed from C. Fang et al. also develop a highly specialized GA for this problem in which they use a scheme of increasing mutation rates and a technique known as GVOT (Gene-Variance based Operator Targeting). For the details see [5].

The SH Algorithm In our SH algorithm for this problem, a schedule is encoded in the form of an ordering $\sigma_1, \sigma_2, \ldots, \sigma_{JM}$ of JM markers. These markers have colors associated with them: there are exactly M markers of each color of $1, \ldots, J$. To construct a schedule, σ is read from left to right. Whenever a marker with color k is encountered, the next uncompleted task in job k is scheduled in the earliest plausible timeslot. Since there are exactly M markers of each color, and since every job contains exactly M tasks, this decoding of σ yields a complete schedule. Observe that since markers of the same color are interchangeable, many different ordering σ will correspond to the same scheduling of tasks.

To generate a neighbor of σ in this algorithm, a marker σ_i is selected uniformly at random and moved to a new position j chosen uniformly at random. To achieve this, it is necessary to shift the subsequence of markers between σ_i and σ_j (including σ_j) one position in the appropriate direction. If $i < j$, then $\sigma_{i+1}, \sigma_{i+2}, \ldots, \sigma_j$ are shifted one position to the left in σ. If $i > j$, then $\sigma_j, \sigma_{j+1}, \ldots, \sigma_{i-1}$ are shifted one position to the right. (If $i = j$, then the generated neighbor is of course identical to σ.) For an example, see the full version of this paper [10].

Fang et al. consider the makespan achieved after 300 iterations of their GVOT-based GA on a population of size 500. We compare this with an SH for which each experiment involves 150,000 iterations. In both cases therefore, a single execution of the algorithm involves a total of 150,000 function evaluations. Fang et al. present their average results over 10 trials, but do not indicate how they obtain their "best". We present the statistics resulting from 100 executions of the SH algorithm.

| | 10x10 Jobshop || 20x5 Jobshop ||
	GA	SH	GA	SH
Mean	977	966.96	1215	1202.40
SD		13.15		12.92
High		997		1288
Low	949	938	1189	1173
Best Known		930		1165

3.4 A New Jobshop GA

In this section, we reconsider the jobshop problem in an attempt to formulate a new GA encoding. We use the same encoding as in the SH algorithm described above: σ is an ordering $\sigma_1, \sigma_2, \ldots, \sigma_{JM}$ of the JM markers, which can be used to construct a schedule as before. We treated markers of the same color as effectively equivalent in the SH algorithm. Now, however, the label of a marker (a unique integer in $\{1, \ldots, JM\}$) will play a role.

The basic step in the crossover operator for this GA as applied to a pair (σ, τ) of orderings is as follows. A label i is chosen uniformly at random from the set $\{1, 2, \ldots, JM\}$. In σ, the marker with label i is moved to the position occupied by i in τ; conversely, the marker with label i in τ is moved to the position occupied by that marker in σ. In both cases, the necessary shifting is performed as before. Hence the idea is to move a single marker in σ (and in τ) to a new position as in the SH algorithm; instead of moving the marker to a random position, though, we move it to the position occupied by that marker in τ (and σ, respectively). The full crossover operator picks two labels $j \leq k$ uniformly at random from $\{1, 2, \ldots, JM\}$, and performs this basic operation first for label j, then $j+1$, and so forth, through k. The mutation operator in our GA performs exactly the same operation as that used to generate a neighbor in the SH algorithm. A marker σ_i is chosen uniformly at random and moved to a new position j, chosen uniformly at random. The usual shifting operation is then performed. Observe how closely the crossover and mutation operators in this GA for the jobshop problem are based on those in the corresponding SH algorithm.

Our GA includes, in order, the following phases: evaluation, elitist replacement, selection, crossover, and mutation. In the evaluation phase, the fitnesses of all members of the population are computed. Elitist replacement substitutes the fittest permutation from the evaluation phase of the previous iteration for the least fit permutation in the current population (except, of course, in the first iteration, in which there is no replacement). Because of its simplicity and its effectiveness in practice, we chose to use binary stochastic tournament selection (see [8] for details). The crossover step in our GA selects $\frac{P}{2}$ pairs uniformly at random without replacement from the population and applies the mating operator to each of these pairs independently with probability 0.6. The number of mutations performed on a given permutation in a single iteration is binomial with parameter $p = \frac{1}{n}$. The population in our GA is initialized by selecting every individual uniformly at random from S_n.

We execute this GA for 300 iterations on a population of size 500. Results of 100 experiments performed with this GA are indicated in the following table by "new GA". For comparison, we again give the results obtained by the GA of Fang et al. and the SH algorithm described in this paper.

	10x10 Jobshop			20x5 Jobshop		
	new GA	GA	SH	new GA	GA	SH
Mean	956.22	977	965.64	1193.21	1215	1204.89
SD	8.69		10.56	7.38		12.92
High	976		996	1211		1241
Low	937	949	949	1174	1189	1183
Best Known	930			1165		

4 Conclusion

As black-box algorithms, GAs are principally of interest in solving problems whose combinatorial structure is not understood well enough for more direct, problem-specific techniques to be applied. As we have seen in regard to the two problems presented in this paper, stochastic hillclimbing can offer a useful gauge of the performance of the GA. In some cases it shows that a GA-based approach may not be competitive with simpler methods; at others it offers insight into possible design decisions for the GA such as the choice of encoding and the formulation of mating and mutation operators. In light of the results presented in this paper, we hope that designers of black-box algorithms will be encouraged to experiment with stochastic hillclimbing in the initial stages of the development of their algorithms.

References

[1] D. Ackley. *A Connectionist Machine for Genetic Hillclimbing*. Kluwer Academic Publishers, 1987.

[2] D. Applegate and W. Cook. A computational study of the job-shop problem. *ORSA Journal of Computing*, 3(2), 1991.

[3] J. Carlier and E. Pinson. An algorithm for solving the jobshop problem. *Mngmnt. Sci.*, 35:(2):164–176, 1989.

[4] L. Davis. Bit-climbing, representational bias, and test suite design. In Belew and Booker, editors, *ICGA-4*, pages 18–23, 1991.

[5] H. Fang, P. Ross, and D. Corne. A promising GA approach to job-shop scheduling, rescheduling, and open-shop scheduling problems. In Forrest, editor, *ICGA-5*, 1993.

[6] M. Garey and D. Johnson. *Computers and Intractability*. W.H. Freeman and Co., 1979.

[7] D. Goldberg. *Genetic Algorithms in Search, Optimization, and Machine Learning*. Addison Wesley, 1989.

[8] D. Goldberg and K. Deb. A comparative analysis of selection schemes used in GAs. In *FOGA-2*, pages 69–93, 1991.

[9] K. De Jong. *An Analysis of the Behavior of a Class of Genetic Adaptive Systems*. PhD thesis, University of Michigan, 1975.

[10] A. Juels and M. Wattenberg. Stochastic hillclimbing as a baseline method for evaluating genetic algorithms. Technical Report CSD-94-834, UC Berkeley, CS Division, 1994.

[11] S. Khuri, T. Bäck, and J. Heitkötter. An evolutionary approach to combinatorial optimization problems. In *Procs. of CSC 1994*, 1994.

[12] J. Koza. *FOGA*, chapter A Hierarchical Approach to Learning the Boolean Multiplexer Function, pages 171–192. 1991.

[13] J. Koza. *Genetic Programming*. MIT Press, Cambridge, MA, 1991.

[14] J. Koza. The GP paradigm: Breeding computer programs. In Branko Souček and the IRIS Group, editors, *Dynamic, Genetic, and Chaotic Prog.*, pages 203–221. John Wiley and Sons, Inc., 1992.

[15] M. Mitchell, J. Holland, and S. Forrest. When will a GA outperform hill-climbing? In J.D. Cowen, G. Tesauro, and J. Alspector, editors, *Advances in Neural Inf. Processing Systems 6*, 1994.

[16] J. Muth and G. Thompson. *Industrial Scheduling*. Prentice Hall, 1963.

[17] U. O'Reilly and F. Oppacher. Program search with a hierarchical variable length representation: Genetic programing, simulated annealing and hill climbing. In *PPSN-3*, 1994.

[18] S. Wilson. GA-easy does not imply steepest-ascent optimizable. In Belew and Booker, editors, *ICGA-4*, pages 85–89, 1991.

Symplectic Nonlinear Component Analysis

Lucas C. Parra
Siemens Corporate Research
755 College Road East, Princeton, NJ 08540
lucas@scr.siemens.com

Abstract

Statistically independent features can be extracted by finding a factorial representation of a signal distribution. Principal Component Analysis (PCA) accomplishes this for linear correlated and Gaussian distributed signals. Independent Component Analysis (ICA), formalized by Comon (1994), extracts features in the case of linear statistical dependent but not necessarily Gaussian distributed signals. Nonlinear Component Analysis finally should find a factorial representation for nonlinear statistical dependent distributed signals. This paper proposes for this task a novel feed-forward, information conserving, nonlinear map - the explicit symplectic transformations. It also solves the problem of non-Gaussian output distributions by considering single coordinate higher order statistics.

1 Introduction

In previous papers Deco and Brauer (1994) and Parra, Deco, and Miesbach (1995) suggest volume conserving transformations and factorization as the key elements for a nonlinear version of Independent Component Analysis. As a general class of volume conserving transformations Parra et al. (1995) propose the symplectic transformation. It was defined by an implicit nonlinear equation, which leads to a complex relaxation procedure for the function recall. In this paper an explicit form of the symplectic map is proposed, overcoming thus the computational problems.

In order to correctly measure the factorization criterion for non-Gaussian output distributions, higher order statistics has to be considered. Comon (1994) includes in the linear case higher order cumulants of the output distribution. Deco and Brauer (1994) consider multi-variate, higher order moments and use them in the case of nonlinear volume conserving transformations. But the calculation of multi-coordinate higher moments is computational expensive.

The factorization criterion for statistical independence can be expressed in terms of minimal mutual information. Considering only volume conserving transformations allows to concentrate on single coordinate statistics, which leads to an important reduction of computational complexity. So far, this approach (Deco & Schürman, 1994; Parra et al., 1995) has been restricted to second order statistic. The present paper discusses the use of higher order cumulants for the estimation of the single coordinate output distributions. The single coordinate entropies measured by the proposed technique match the entropies of the sampled data more accurately. This leads in turns to better factorization results.

2 Statistical Independence

More general than decorrelation used in PCA the goal is to extract statistical independent features from a signal distribution $p(\mathbf{x})$. We look for a deterministic transformation on $\Re^n$: $\mathbf{y} = f(\mathbf{x})$ which generates a factorial representation $p(\mathbf{y}) = \prod_i p(y_i)$, or at least a representation where the individual coordinates $p(y_i)$ of the output variable $\mathbf{y}$ are "as factorial as possible". This can be accomplished by minimizing the mutual information $MI[p(\mathbf{y})]$.

$$0 \leq MI[p(\mathbf{y})] = \sum_{i=1}^{n} H[p(y_i)] - H[p(\mathbf{y})], \qquad (1)$$

since $MI[p(\mathbf{y})] = 0$ holds if $p(\mathbf{y})$ is factorial. The mutual information can be used as a measure of "independence". The entropies H in the definition (1) are defined as usual by $H[p(y)] = -\int_{-\infty}^{\infty} p(y) \ln p(y) \, dy$.

As in linear PCA we select volume conserving transformations, but now without restricting ourselves to linearity. In the noise-free case of reversible transformations volume conservation implies conservation of entropy from the input $\mathbf{x}$ to the output $\mathbf{y}$, i.e. $H[p(\mathbf{y})] = H[p(\mathbf{x})] = const$ (see Papoulis, 1991). The minimization of mutual information (1) reduces then to the minimization of the single coordinate output entropies $H[p(y_i)]$. This substantially simplifies the complexity of the problem, since no multi-coordinate statistics is required.

2.1 Measuring the Entropy with Cumulants

With an upper bound minimization criterion the task of measuring entropies can be avoided (Parra et al., 1995):

$$H[p(y_i)] \leq \frac{1}{2} \ln(2\pi e) + \frac{1}{2} \ln \sigma_i^2. \qquad (2)$$

Symplectic Nonlinear Component Analysis

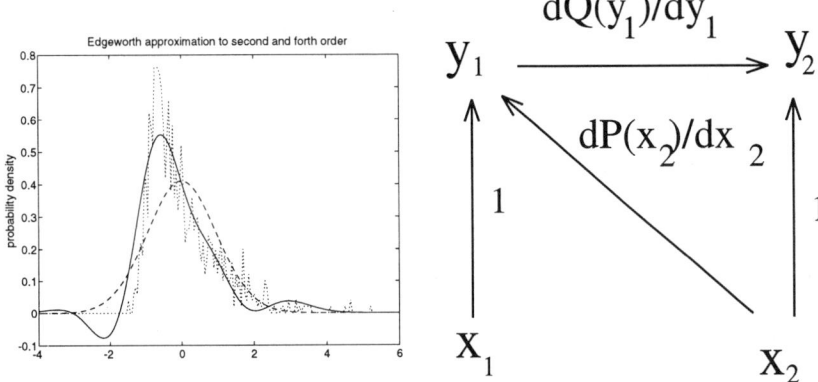

Figure 1: LEFT: Doted line: exponential distribution with additive Gaussian noise sampled with 1000 data points. (noise-variance/decay-constant = 0.2). Dashed line: Gaussian approximation equivalent to the Edgeworth approximation to second order. Solid line: Edgeworth approximation including terms up to fourth order. RIGHT: Structure of the volume conserving explicit symplectic map.

The minimization of the individual output coordinate entropies $H[p(y_i)]$ simplifies to the minimization of output variances σ_i. For the validity of that approach it is crucial that the map $\mathbf{y} = f(\mathbf{x})$ transforms the arbitrary input distribution $p(\mathbf{x})$ into a Gaussian output distribution. But volume conserving and continuous maps can not transform arbitrary distributions into Gaussians. To overcome this problem one includes statistics - higher than second order - to the optimization criterion.

Comon (1994) suggests to use the Edgeworth expansion of a probability distribution. This leads to an analytic expression of the entropy in terms of measurable higher order cumulants. Edgeworth expands the multiplicative correction to the best Gaussian approximation of the distribution in the orthonormal basis of Hermite polynomials $h_\alpha(y)$. The expansion coefficients are basically given by the cumulants c_α of distribution p(y). The Edgeworth expansions reads for a zero-mean distribution with variance σ^2, (see Kendall & Stuart, 1969)

$$p(y) = \frac{1}{\sqrt{2\pi}\sigma} e^{-\frac{y^2}{2\sigma^2}} f(y) \tag{3}$$

$$f(y) = 1 + \frac{c_3}{6\sigma^3} h_3(\tfrac{y}{\sigma}) + \frac{c_4}{24\sigma^4} h_4(\tfrac{y}{\sigma}) + \frac{c_5}{120\sigma^5} h_5(\tfrac{y}{\sigma}) + ...$$

Note, that by truncating this expansion at a certain order, we obtain an approximation $p_{app}(y)$, which is not strictly positive. Figure 1, left shows a sampled exponential distribution with additive Gaussian noise.

By cutting expansion (3) at fourth order, and further expanding the logarithm in definition of entropy up to sixth order, Comon (1994) approximates the entropy by,

$$H[p(y)_{app}] \approx \frac{1}{2}\ln(2\pi e) + \ln \sigma - \frac{1}{12}\frac{c_3^2}{\sigma^6} - \frac{1}{48}\frac{c_4^2}{\sigma^8} - \frac{7}{48}\frac{c_3^4}{\sigma^{12}} + \frac{1}{8}\frac{c_3^2}{\sigma^6}\frac{c_4}{\sigma^4} \quad (4)$$

We suggest to use this expression to minimize the single coordinate entropies in the definition of the mutual information (1).

2.2 Measuring the Entropy by Estimating an Approximation

Note that (4) could only be obtained by truncating the expansion (3). It is therefore limited to fourth order statistic, which might be not enough for a satisfactory approximation. Besides, the additional approximation of the logarithm is accurate only for small corrections to the best Gaussian approximation, *i.e.* for $f(y) \approx 1$. For distributions with non-Gaussian tails the correction terms might be rather large and even negative as noted above. We therefore suggest alternatively, to measure the entropy by estimating the logarithm of the approximated distribution $\ln p_{app}(y)$ with the given data points y_ν and using Edgeworth approximation (3) for $p_{app}(y)$,

$$H[p(y)] \approx -\frac{1}{N}\sum_{\nu=1}^{N}\ln p_{app}(y_\nu) = const + \ln \sigma - \frac{1}{N}\sum_{\nu=1}^{N}\ln f(y_\nu) \quad (5)$$

Furthermore, we suggest to correct the truncated expansion p_{app} by setting $f_{app}(y) \to 0$ for all $f_{app}(y) < 0$. For the entropy measurement (5) there is in principle no limitation to any specific order.

In table 1 the different measures of entropy are compared. The values in the row labeled 'partition' are measured by counting the numbers $n(i)$ of data points falling in equidistant intervals i of width Δy and summing $-p(i)\Delta y \ln p(i)$ over all intervals, with $p(i)\Delta y = n(i)/N$. This gives good results compared to the theoretical values only because of the relatively large sampling size. These values are presented here in order to have an reliable estimate for the case of the exponential distribution, where cumulant methods tend to fail.

The results for the exponential distribution show the difficulty of the measurement proposed by Comon, whereas the estimation measurement given by equation (5) is stable even when considering (for this case) unreliable 5th and 6th order cumulants. The results for the symmetric-triangular and uniform distribution demonstrate the insensibility of the Gaussian upper bound for the example of figure 2. A uniform squared distribution is rotated by an angle α. On the abscissa and ordinate a triangular or uniform distribution are observed for the different angles $\alpha = \Pi/4$ or $\alpha = 0$ respectively. The approximation of the single coordinate entropies with a Gaussian measure is in both cases the same. Whereas measurements including higher order statistics correctly detect minimal entropy (by fixed total information) for the uniform distribution at $\alpha = 0$.

3 Explicit Symplectic Transformation

Different ways of realizing a volume conserving transformation that guarantees $H[p(\mathbf{x})] = H[p(\mathbf{x})]$ have been proposed (Deco & Schürman, 1994; Parra et al.,

Measured entropy of sampled distributions	Gauss	uniform	triangular symmetric	exponential + Gauss noise
partition	$1.35 \pm .02$	$.024 \pm .006$	$.14 \pm .02$	$1.31 \pm .03$
Gaussian upper bound (2)	$1.415 \pm .02$	$.18 \pm .016$	$.18 \pm .02$	$1.53 \pm .04$
Comon, eq. (4)	$1.414 \pm .02$	$.14 \pm .015$	$.17 \pm .02$	3.0 ± 2.5
Estimate (5) - 4th order	$1.414 \pm .02$	$.13 \pm .015$	$.17 \pm .02$	$1.39 \pm .05$
Estimate (5) - 6th order	$1.414 \pm .02$	$.092 \pm .001$	$.16 \pm .02$	$1.3 \pm .5$
theoretical value	1.419	$.0$	$.153$	

Table 1: Entropy values for different distributions sampled with $N = 1000$ data points and the different estimation methods explained in the text. The standard deviations are obtained by multiple repetition of the experiment.

1995). A general class of volume conserving transformations are the symplectic maps (Abraham & Marsden, 1978). An interesting and for our purpose important fact is that any symplectic transformation can be expressed in terms of a scalar function. And in turn any scalar function defines a symplectic map. In (Parra et al., 1995) a non-reflecting symplectic transformation has been presented. But its implicit definition results in the need of solving a nonlinear equation for each data point. This leads to time consuming computations which limit in practice the applications to low dimensional problems ($n \leq 10$). In this work reflecting symplectic transformations with an explicit definition are used to define a "feed-forward" volume conserving maps. The input and output space is divided in two partitions $\mathbf{x} = (\mathbf{x}_1, \mathbf{x}_2)$ and $\mathbf{y} = (\mathbf{y}_1, \mathbf{y}_2)$, with $\mathbf{x}_1, \mathbf{x}_2, \mathbf{y}_1, \mathbf{y}_2 \in \Re^{n/2}$.

$$\mathbf{y}_1 = \mathbf{x}_1 - \frac{\partial P(\mathbf{x}_2)}{\partial \mathbf{x}_2} \quad , \quad \mathbf{y}_2 = \mathbf{x}_2 + \frac{\partial Q(\mathbf{y}_1)}{\partial \mathbf{y}_1}. \tag{6}$$

The structure of this symplectic map is represented in figure 1, right. Two scalar functions $P : \Re^{n/2} \mapsto \Re$ and $Q : \Re^{n/2} \mapsto \Re$ can be chosen arbitrarily. Note that for quadratic functions equation (6) represents a linear transformation. In order to have a general transformation we introduce for each of these scalar functions a 3-layer perceptron with nonlinear hidden units and a single linear output unit:

$$P(\mathbf{x}_2) = \mathbf{w}_2 \cdot g(W_2 \mathbf{x}_2) \quad , \quad Q(\mathbf{y}_1) = \mathbf{w}_1 \cdot g(W_1 \mathbf{y}_1). \tag{7}$$

The scalar functions P and Q are parameterized by the network parameters $\mathbf{w}_1, \mathbf{w}_2 \in R^m$ and $W_1, W_2 \in R^m \times R^{n/2}$. The hidden-unit, nonlinear activation function g applies to each component of the vectors $W_1 \mathbf{y}_1$ and $W_2 \mathbf{x}_2$ respectively. Because of the structure of equation (6) the output coordinates $\mathbf{y}_1$ depend only additively on the input coordinates $\mathbf{x}_1$. To obtain a more general nonlinear dependence a second symplectic layer has to be added.

To obtain factorial distributions the parameters of the map have to be trained. The approximations of the single coordinate entropies (4) or (5) are inserted in the mutual information optimization criterion (1). These approximations are expressed through moments in terms of the measured output data points. Therefore, the

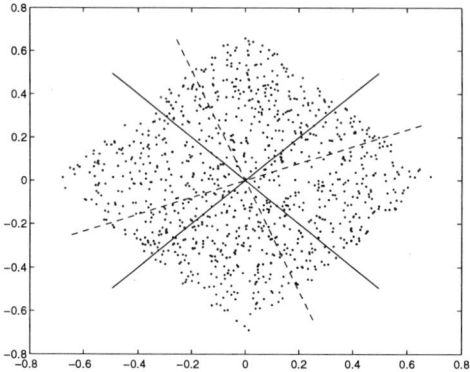

Figure 2: Sampled 2-dimensional squared uniform distribution rotated by $\pi/4$. Solid lines represent the directions found by any of the higher order techniques explained in the text. Dashed lines represent directions calculated by linear PCA. (This result is arbitrary and varies with noise).

gradient of these expressions with respect to parameters of the map can be computed in principle. For that matter different kinds of averages need to be computed. Even though, the computational complexity is not substantially increased compared with the efficient minimum variances criterion (2), the complexity of the algorithm increases considerably. Therefore, we applied an optimization algorithm that does not require any gradient information. The simple stochastic and parallel update algorithm ALOPEX (Unnikrishnan & Venugopal, 1994) was used.

4 Experiments

As explained above, finding the correct statistical independent directions of a rotated two dimensional uniform distribution causes problems for techniques which include only second order statistic. The statistical independent coordinates are simply the axes parallel to the edges of the distribution (see figure 2). A rotation *i.e.* a linear transformation suffices for this task. The covariance matrix of the data is diagonal for any rotation of the squared distribution and, hence, does not provide any information about the correct orientation of the square. It is well known, that PCA fails to find in the case of non-Gaussian distributions the statistical independent coordinates. Similarly the Gaussian upper bound technique (2) is not capable to minimize the mutual information in this case. Instead, with any one of the higher order criteria explained in the previous section one finds the appropriate coordinates for any linearly transformed multi-dimensional uniform distribution. This has been observed empirically for a series of setups. The symplectic map was restricted in this experiments to linearity by using square scalar functions.

The second example shows that the proposed technique in fact finds nonlinear relations between the input coordinates. An one-dimensional signal distributed according to the distribution of figure 1 was nonlinearly transformed into a two-

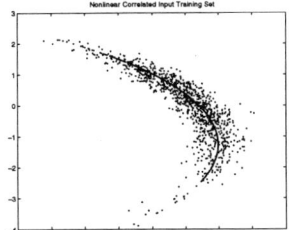 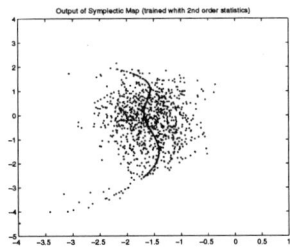 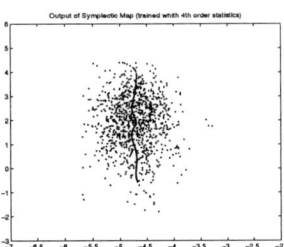

Figure 3: Symplectic map trained with 4th and 2nd order statistics corresponding to the equations (5) and (2) respectively. Left: input distribution. The line at the center of the distribution gives the nonlinear transformed noiseless signal distributed according to the distribution shown in figure 1. Center and Right: Output distribution of the symplectic map corresponding to the 4th order (right) and 2nd order (center) criterion.

dimensional signal and corrupted with additive noise, leading to the distribution shown in figure 3, left. The task of finding statistical independent coordinates has been tackled by an explicit symplectic transformation with $n = 2$ and $m = 6$. On figure 3 the different results for the optimization according to the Gaussian upper bound criterion (2) and the approximated entropy criterion (5) are shown. Obviously considering higher order statistics in fact improves the result by finding the better representation of the nonlinear dependency.

Reference

Abraham, R., & Marsden, J. (1978). *Foundations of Mechanics* The Benjamin-Cummings Publishing Company, Inc., London.

Comon, P. (1994). Independent component analysis, A new concept. *Signal Processing, 36*, 287–314.

Deco, G., & Brauer, W. (1994). Higher Order Statistical Decorrelation by Volume Concerving Nonlinear Maps. *Neural Networks, ?* submitted.

Deco, G., & Schürman, B. (1994). Learning Time Series Evolution by Unsupervised Extraction of Correlations. *Physical Review E, ?* submitted.

Kendall, M. G., & Stuart, A. (1969). *The Advanced Theory of Statistics* (3 edition)., Vol. 1. Charles Griffin and Company Limited, London.

Papoulis, A. (1991). *Probability, Random Variables, and Stochastic Processes.* Third Edition, McGraw-Hill, New York.

Parra, L., Deco, G., & Miesbach, S. (1995). Redundancy reduction with information-preserving nonlinear maps. *Network, 6*(1), 61–72.

Unnikrishnan, K., P., & Venugopal, K., P. (1994). Alopex: A Correlation-Based Learning Algorithm for Feedforward and Recurrent Neural Networks. *Neural Computation, 6*(3), 469–490.

A Unified Learning Scheme: Bayesian-Kullback Ying-Yang Machine

Lei Xu
1. Computer Science Dept., The Chinese University of HK, Hong Kong
2. National Machine Perception Lab, Peking University, Beijing

Abstract

A Bayesian-Kullback learning scheme, called Ying-Yang Machine, is proposed based on the two complement but equivalent Bayesian representations for joint density and their Kullback divergence. Not only the scheme unifies existing major supervised and unsupervised learnings, including the classical maximum likelihood or least square learning, the maximum information preservation, the EM & *em* algorithm and information geometry, the recent popular Helmholtz machine, as well as other learning methods with new variants and new results; but also the scheme provides a number of new learning models.

1 INTRODUCTION

Many different learning models have been developed in the literature. We may come to an age of searching a unified scheme for them. With a unified scheme, we may understand deeply the existing models and their relationships, which may cause cross-fertilization on them to obtain new results and variants; We may also be guided to develop new learning models, after we get better understanding on which cases we have already studied or missed, which deserve to be further explored.

Recently, a Bayesian-Kullback scheme, called the YING-YANG Machine, has been proposed as such an effort(Xu, 1995a). It bases on the Kullback divergence and two complement but equivalent Baysian representations for the joint distribution of the input space and the representation space, instead of merely using Kullback divergence for matching un-structuralized joint densities in information geometry type learnings (Amari, 1995a&b; Byrne, 1992; Csiszar, 1975). The two representations consist of four different components. The different combinations of choices of each component lead the YING-YANG Machine into different learning models. Thus, it acts as a general learning scheme for unifying the existing major unsupervised and supervised learnings. As shown in Xu(1995a), its one special case reduces to the EM algorithm (Dempster et al, 1977; Hathaway, 1986; Neal & Hinton, 1993) and the closely related *Information Geometry* theory and the *em* algorithm (Amari, 1995a&b), to MDL autoencoder with a "bits-back" argument by Hinton & Zemel (1994) and its alternative equivalent form that minimizes the bits of uncoded residual errors and the unused bits in the transmission channel's capacity (Xu, 1995d), as well as to *Multisets modeling* learning (Xu, 1995e)–a unified learning framework for clustering, PCA-type learnings and self-organizing map. It other special case reduces to maximum information preservation (Linsker, 1989; Atick & Redlich, 1990; Bell & Sejnowski, 1995). More interestingly its another special case reduces to Helmholtz machine (Dayan et al,1995; Hinton, 1995) with new understandings. Moreover, the YING-YANG machine includes also maximum likelihood or least square learning.

Furthermore, the *YING-YANG Machine* has also been extended to temporal patterns with a number of new models for signal modeling. Some of them are the extensions of Helmholtz machine or maximum information preservation learning to temporal processing. Some of them include and extend the Hidden Markov Model (HMM), AMAR and AR models (Xu, 1995b). In addition, it has also been shown in Xu(1995a&c, 1996a) that one special case of the YING-YANG machine can provide us three variants for clustering or VQ, particularly with criteria and an automatic procedure developed for solving how to select the number of clusters in clustering analysis or Gaussian mixtures — a classical problem that remains open for decades.

In this paper, we present a deep and systematical further study. Section 2 redescribes the unified scheme on a more precise and systematical basis via discussing the possible marital status of the two Bayesian representations for joint density. Section 3 summarizes and explains those existing models under the unified scheme, particularly we have clarified some confusion made in the previous papers (Xu, 1995a&b) on maximum information preservation learning. Section 4 proposed and summarizes a number of possible new models suggested by the unified scheme.

2 BAYESIAN-KULLBACK YING-YANG MACHINE

As argued in Xu (1995a), unsupervised and supervised learning problems can be summarized into the problem of estimating joint density $P(x, y)$ of patterns in the input space X and the representation space Y, as shown in Fig.1. Under the Bayesian framework, we have two representations for $P(x, y)$. One is $P_{M_1}(x, y) = P_{M_1}(y|x)P_{M_1}(x)$, implemented by a model M_1 called YANG/(male) part since it performs the task of transferring a pattern/(a real body) into a code/(a seed). The other is $P_{M_2}(x, y) = P_{M_2}(x|y)P_{M_2}(y)$, implemented by a model M_2 called YING part since it performs the task of generating a pattern/(a real body) from a code/(a seed). They are complement to each other and together implement an entire circle $x \to y \to x$. This compliments to the ancient chinese YING-YANG philosophy.

Here we have four components $P_{M_1}(x)$, $P_{M_1}(y|x)$, $P_{M_2}(x|y)$ and $P_{M_2}(y)$. The $P_{M_1}(x)$ can be fixed at some density estimate on input data, e.g., we have at least two choices–Parzen window estimate $P_h(x)$ or empirical estimate $P_0(x)$:

$$P_h(x) = \frac{1}{Nh^d} \sum_{i=1}^{N} K(\frac{x-x_i}{h}), \quad P_0(x) = \lim_{h \to 0} P_h(x) = \frac{1}{N} \sum_{i=1}^{N} \delta(x - x_i). \quad (1)$$

For $P_{M_1}(y|x)$, $P_{M_2}(x|y)$, each can have three choices: (1) from a *parametric* family specified by model M_1 or M_2; (2) free of model with $P_{M_1}(y|x) = P(y|x)$ or $P_{M_2}(x|y) = P(x|y)$; (3) broken channel $P_{M_1}(y|x) = P_{M_1}(y)$ or $P_{M_2}(x|y) = P_{M_2}(x)$. Finally, $P_{M_2}(y)$ with its y consistent to $P_{M_1}(y|x)$ can also being from a *parametric* family or free of model. Any combinations of the choices of the four components forms a potential YING-YANG pair. We at least have $2 \times 3 \times 3 \times 2 = 36$ pairs.

A YING-YANG pair has four types of marital status: (a) *marry*, i.e., YING and

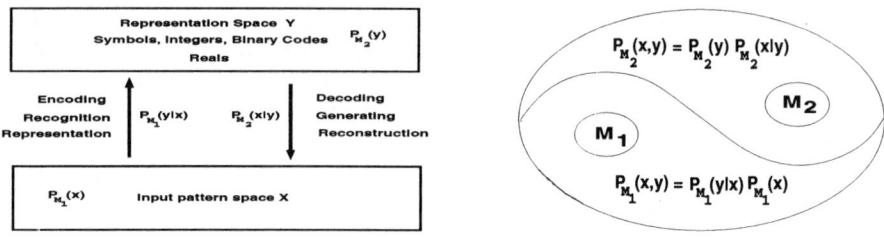

Figure 1   The joint spaces X, Y and the YING-YANG Machine

YANG match each other; (b) *divorce*, i.e., YING and YANG go away from each other; (c) YING chases YANG, YANG escapes; (d) YANG chases YING, but YING escapes. The four types can be described by a combination of minimization (chasing) and maximization (escaping) on one of the two Kullback divergences below:

$$K(M_1, M_2) = \int_{x,y} P_{M_1}(y|x) P_{M_1}(x) \log \frac{P_{M_1}(y|x) P_{M_1}(x)}{P_{M_2}(x|y) P_{M_2}(y)} dx dy \qquad (2a)$$

$$K(M_2, M_1) = \int_{x,y} P_{M_2}(x|y) P_{M_2}(y) \log \frac{P_{M_2}(x|y) P_{M_2}(y)}{P_{M_1}(y|x) P_{M_1}(x)} dx dy \qquad (2b)$$

Table 1 Mathematical description for marital status of a YING-YANG pair

$\min_{M_1,M_2} K(M_1, M_2)$ (a)	$\max_{M_1} \min_{M_2} K(M_1, M_2)$	$\max_{M_2} \min_{M_1} K(M_1, M_2)$
$\max_{M_1,M_2} K(M_1, M_2)$ (b)	$\min_{M_2} \max_{M_1} K(M_1, M_2)$	$\min_{M_1} \max_{M_2} K(M_1, M_2)$

We can replace $K(M_1, M_2)$ by $K(M_2, M_1)$ in the table. The 2nd & 3rd columns are for (c) (d) respectively, each has two cases depending on who starts the act and the two are usually not equivalent. Their results are undefined depending on initial condition for M_1, M_2, except of two special cases: (i) Free $P_{M_1}(y|x)$ and parametric $P_{M_2}(x|y)$, with $\min_{M_2} \max_{M_1} K$ being the same as (b) with broken $P_{M_1}(y|x)$, and with $\max_{M_2} \min_{M_1} K$ defined but useless. (ii) Free $P_{M_2}(x|y)$ and parametric $P_{M_1}(y|x)$, with $\min_{M_1} \max_{M_2} K$ the same as case (a) with broken $P_{M_2}(x|y)$, with $\min_{M_1} \max_{M_2} K$ defined but useless.

Therefore, we will focus on the status *marry* and *divorce*. Even so, not all of the above mentioned $2 \times 3 \times 3 \times 2 = 36$ YING-YANG pairs provide sensible learning models although $\min_{M_1,M_2} K$ and $\max_{M_1,M_2} K$ are always well defined. Fortunately, a quite number of them indeed lead us to useful learning models, as will be shown in the sequent sections.

We can implement $\min_{M_1,M_2} K(M_1, M_2)$ by the following *Alternative Minimization* (ALTMIN) procedure:
Step 1   Fix $M_2 = M_2^{old}$, to get $M_1^{new} = arg\ Min_{M_1}\ KL(M_1, M_2^{old})$
Step 2   Fix $M_1 = M_1^{old}$, to get $M_2^{new} = arg\ Min_{M_2}\ KL(M_1^{old}, M_2)$

The ALTMIN iteration will finally converge to a local minimum of $K(M_1, M_2)$. We can have a similar procedure for $\max_{M_1,M_2} K(M_1, M_2)$ via replacing Min by Max.

Since the above scheme bases on the two complement YING and YANG Bayesian representations and their Kullback divergence for their marital status, we call it *Bayesian-Kullback YING-YANG* learning scheme. Furthermore, under this scheme we call each obtained YING-YANG pair that is sensible for learning purpose as a *Bayesian-Kullback YING-YANG Machine* or *YING-YANG* machine shortly.

3   UNIFIED EXISTING LEARNINGS

Let $P_{M_1}(x) = P_0(x)$ by eq.(1) and put it into eq.(2), through certain mathematics we can get $K(M_1, M_2) = h_{M_1} - h_{\alpha M_1} - q_{M_{1,2}} + D$ with D independent of M_1, M_2 and $h_{M_1}, h_{\alpha M_1}, q_{M_{1,2}}$ given by Eqs.(E1)(E2)&(E4) in Tab.2 respectively. The larger is the h_{M_1}, the more discriminative or separable are the representations in Y for the input data set. The larger is the $h_{\alpha M_1}$, the more concentrated the representations in Y. The larger is the $q_{M_{1,2}}$, the better $P_{M_2}(x|y)$ fits the input data.

Therefore, $\min_{M_1,M_2} K(M_1, M_2)$ consists of (1) best fitting of $P_{M_2}(x|y)$ on input data via $\max q_{M_{1,2}}$, which is desirable, (2) producing more concentrated representations in Y to occupy less resource, which is also desirable and is the behind reason for solving the problem of selecting cluster number in clustering analysis Xu(1995a&c, 1996a), (3) but with the cost of less discriminative representations in Y for the input data. Inversely, $\max_{M_1,M_2} K(M_1, M_2)$ consists of (1) producing best discriminative or separable representation $P_{M_1}(y|x)$ in Y for the input data set, which is desirable, in the cost of (2) producing a more uniform representation in Y to fully occupy the resource, and (3) causing $P_{M_2}(x|y)$ away from fitting input data.

Shown in Table 2 are the unified existing unsupervised learnings. For the case H-f-W, we have $h_{M_1} = h$, $h_{\alpha M_1} = h_\alpha$, $q_{M_{1,2}} = q_{M_2}$, and $\min_{M_1} K(M_1, M_2)$ results in $P_{M_2}(y) = P_{M_1}(y) = \alpha_y$ and $P_{M_2}(x|y)P_{M_2}(y) = P_{M_2}(x)P_{M_1}(y|x)$ with $P_{M_2}(x) = \sum_{y=1}^{k} P_{M_2}(x|y)P_{M_2}(y)$. In turn, we get $K(M_1, M_2) = -L_{M_2} + D$ with L_{M_2} being the likelihood given by eq.(E5), i.e., we get maximum likelihood estimation on mixture model. In fact, the ALTMIN given in Tab.2 leads us to exactly the EM algorithm by Dempster et al(1977). Also, here $P_{M_1}(x,y)$, $P_{M_2}(x,y)$ is equivalent to the data submanifold $\mathcal{D}$ and model submanifold $\mathcal{M}$ in the *Information Geometry* theory (Amari, 1995a&b), with the ALTMIN being the *em* algorithm. As shown in Xu(95a), the cases also includes the MDL auto-encoder (Hinton & Zemel, 1994) and Multi-sets modeling (Xu, 1995e).

For the case *Single-M*, the $h_{M_1} - h_{\alpha M_1}$ is actually the information transmitted by the YANG part from x to y. In this case, its minimization produces a non-sensible model for learning. However, its maximization is exactly the Informax learning scheme (Linsker, 1989; Atick & Redlich, 1990; Bell & Sejnowski, 1995). Here, we clear up a confusion made in Xu(95a&b) where the minimization was mistakenly considered.

For the case *H-m-W*, the $h_{M_1} - h_{\alpha M_1} - q_{M_{1,2}}$ is just the $-F(d;\theta,Q)$ used by Dayan et al (1995) and Hinton et al (1995) for Helmholtz machine. We can set up the detailed correspondence that (i) here $P_{M_1}(y|x_i)$ is their Q_α; (ii) $\log P_{M_2}(x,y$ is their $-E_\alpha$; and (iii) their P_α is $P_{M_2}(y|x) = P_{M_2}(x|y)P_{M_2}(y)/\sum_y P_{M_2}(x|y)P_{M_2}(y)$. So, we get a new perspective for Helmholtz machine. Moreover, we know that $K(M_1, M_2)$ becomes a negative likelihood only when $P_{M_2}(x|y)P_{M_2}(y) = P_{M_2}(x)P_{M_1}(y|x)$, which is usually not true when the YANG and YING parts are both parametric. So Helmholtz machine is not equivalent to maximum likelihood learning in general with a gap depending on $P_{M_2}(x|y)P_{M_2}(y) - P_{M_2}(x)P_{M_1}(y|x)$. The equivalence is approximately acceptable only when the family of $P_{M_2}(x|y)$ or/and $P_{M_1}(y|x_i)$ is large enough or M_2, M_1 are both linear with gaussian density.

In Tab.4, the case *Single-M* under $K(M_2, M_1)$ is the classical maximum likelihood (ML) learning for supervised learning which includes the least square learning by back propagation (BP) for feedfarward net as a special case. Moreover, its counterpart for a backward net as inverse mapping is the case *Single-F* under $K(M_1, M_2)$.

4 NEW LEARNING MODELS

First, a number of variants for the above existing models are given in Table 2.

Second, a particular new model can be obtained from the case *H-m-W* by changing $\min_{M_1,M_2}$ into $\max_{M_1,M_2}$. That is, we have $\max_{M_1,M_2} [h_{M_1} - h_{\alpha M_1} - q_{M_{1,2}}]$, shortly

Table 2: BKC-YY Machine for Unsupervised Learning (Part I) : $K(M_1, M_2)$
Given Data $\{x_i\}_{i=1}^N$, Fix $P_{M_1}(x) = P_0(x)$ by eq.(1), and thus $K(M_1, M_2) = K_b + D$, with D irrelevant to M_1, M_2 and K_b given by the following formulae and table:

$$h = \frac{1}{N}\sum_{i,y}^{N,k} P(y|x_i)\log P(y|x_i), \qquad h_{M_1} = \frac{1}{N}\sum_{i,y} P_{M_1}(y|x_i)\log P_{M_1}(y|x_i), \tag{E1}$$

$$h_{\alpha M_1} = \sum_y \alpha_y^{M_1} \log \alpha_y^{M_1}, \qquad \alpha_y^{M_1} = \frac{1}{N}\sum_i P_{M_1}(y|x_i), \qquad h_\alpha = \sum_y \alpha_y \log \alpha_y, \tag{E2}$$

$$\alpha_y = \frac{1}{N}\sum_i P(y|x_i), \qquad P(y|x_i) = \alpha_y P_{M_2}(x_i|y)/\sum_y \alpha_y P_{M_2}(x_i|y), \tag{E3}$$

$$q_{M_{1,2}} = \frac{1}{N}\sum_{i,y} P_{M_1}(y|x_i)\log P_{M_2}(x_i|y), \qquad q_{M_2} = \frac{1}{N}\sum_{i,y} P(y|x_i)\log P_{M_2}(x_i|y), \tag{E4}$$

$$L_{M_2}^\alpha = \frac{1}{N}\sum_{i,y} \alpha_y \log P_{M_2}(x_i|y), \qquad L_{M_2} = \frac{1}{N}\sum_i \log \sum_y \alpha_y P_{M_2}(x_i|y) \tag{E5}$$

Marriage Status	H-f-W	Single-M	Single-F	H-m-W	W-f-H
Condition	$P_{M_1}(y\|x)$ free, i.e., $P_{M_1}(y\|x) = P(y\|x)$	$P_{M_2}(y) = P_{M_1}(y)$ $P_{M_2}(x\|y) = P_{M_2}(x) = P_0(x)$	$P_{M_1}(y\|x) = P_{M_1}(y)$	$P_{M_1}(y\|x)$ and $P_{M_2}(x\|y)$	Uniform $P_{M_2}(y)$, and free $P_{M_2}(x\|y) = \hat{P}(x\|y)$
K_b	$h - h_\alpha - q_{M_2}$ $= -L_{M_2}$ (min)	$h_{M_1} - h_{\alpha M_1}$ (max)	$-L_{M_2}^\alpha$ (min)	$[h_{M_1} - h_{\alpha M_1} - q_{M_{1,2}}]$ (min)	$h_{\alpha M_1}$ (min)
ALTMIN	S1: Fix M_2, get $P(y\|x_i)$ α_y by (E3), $\alpha_y^{M_1}$ by (E2) S2: get M_2 by max q_{M_2}.	Get M_1 by max $h_{M_1} - h_{\alpha M_1}$	Get M_2 by max $L_{M_2}^\alpha$.	S1: Fix M_2, get M_1 by min $[h_{M_1} - h_{\alpha M_1} - q_{M_{1,2}}]$ S2: Fix M_1, get M_2 by max $q_{M_{1,2}}$.	Get M_1 by min $h_{\alpha M_1}$
	Repeat S1, S2.	No Repeat	No Repeat	Repeat S1, S2.	No Repeat
Existing Equiv--lent models	1. ML on Mixtures & EM (Dem77) 2. Information geometry (Amari95) 3. MDL Auto-encoder (Hin94) 4. Multi-sets modeling (Xu94,95)	Informax, Maximum mutual Information (Lin89) (Ati90) (Bel95)	Duplicated models by ML learning on input data.	Helmholtz machine (Hin95) (Day95)	Related to PCA
New Results	1. For H-f-W type , we have: Three VQ variants when $P_{M_2}(x\|y)$ is Gaussian. Also, criteria for selecting the correct k for VQ or clustering (Xu95a&c). 2. For H-m-W type, we have: Robust PCA + criterion for determining subspace dimension (Xu, 95c).				
Variants	1. More smooth $P_{M_1}(x)$ given by Parzen window estimate. 2. Factorial coding $P_{M_2}(y) = \prod_i P_{M_2}(y_i)$ with binary $y = [y_1 \cdots, y_m]$. 3. Factorial coding $P_{M_1}(y\|x) = \prod_i P_{M_2}(y_i\|x)$ with binary $[y_1 \cdots, y_m]$. 4. Replace '$\sum_y \cdot$' in all the above items by '$\int_y \cdot dy$' for real y.				

Note: H–Husband, W–Wife, f–follows, M–Male, F–Female, m–matches. X-f-Y stands for X part is free. Single-X stands for the other part broken. H-m-W stands for both parts being parametric. '(min)' stands for min K_b and '(max)' stands for max K_b.

A Unified Learning Scheme: Bayesian-Kullback Ying-Yang Machine

Table 3: BKC-YY Machine for Unsupervised Learning (Part II) : $K(M_2, M_1)$
Given Data $\{x_i\}_{i=1}^N$, Fix $P_{M_1}(x) = P_0(x)$ by eq.(1), and thus $K(M_2, M_1) = K_b + D$, with D irrelevant to M_1, M_2 and K_b given by the following formulae and table:

$$h_{M_2} = \frac{1}{N}\sum_i P_{M_2}(x_i)\log P_{M_2}(x_i), \quad P_{M_2}(x) = \sum_y P_{M_2}(x|y)P_{M_2}(y), \quad (E6)$$

$$h_{\alpha M_2} = \sum_y \alpha_y^{M_2}\log\alpha_y^{M_2}, \quad \alpha_y^{M_2} = \frac{[\prod_i P_{M_1}(y|x_i)]^{1/N}}{\sum_y [\prod_i P_{M_1}(y|x_i)]^{1/N}}, \quad L_{\alpha M_1} = \sum_y \log\alpha_y^{M_1} \quad (E7)$$

$$L_{M_{1,2}} = \frac{1}{N}\sum_{i,y}\alpha_y^{M_2}\log P_{M_1}(y|x_i), \quad L_{M_1} = \frac{1}{N}\sum_{i,y}\alpha_y^{M_1}\log P_{M_1}(y|x_i), \quad (E8)$$

$$h_{M_2}^\alpha = \frac{1}{N}\sum_{i,y}\alpha_y P_{M_2}(x_i|y)\log P_{M_2}(x_i|y), \quad (E9)$$

$$q_{M_{2,1}} = \frac{1}{N}\sum_{i,y}\alpha_y^{M_1} P_{M_2}(x_i|y)\log P_{M_1}(y|x_i), \quad (E10)$$

$(\alpha_y^{M_1}, h_{\alpha M_1}, L_{M_1}$ given in Table 1)

Marriage Status	H-f-W	Single-M	Single-F	H-m-W	W-f-H	
Condition		The same as those in Table 1.				
K_b	h_{M_2} (max)	$[h_{\alpha M_2} - L_{M_{1,2}}]$ (min)	$[h_{\alpha M_1} - L_{M_1}]$ (if forcing $P_{M_1}(y) = P_{M_2}(y)$) (min)	$h_{M_2}^\alpha$ (max)	$[h_{M_2}^\alpha + h_{\alpha M_1} - q_{M_{2,1}}]$ (min)	$-L_{\alpha M_1}$ (min)
ALTMIN	Get M_2 by max h_{M_2}	S1: Fix M_1, get $\alpha_y^{M_2}$ by (E7). S2: update M_1 by max $L_{M_{1,2}}$	S1: Fix M_1, get $\alpha_y^{M_1}$ by (E2). in Tab.1 S2: update M_1 by max L_{M_1}	Get M_2 by max $h_{M_2}^\alpha$.	S1: Fix M_2, get M_1 by min $[h_{\alpha M_1} - q_{M_{2,1}}]$ S2: Fix M_1, get M_2 by min $h_{M_2}^\alpha - q_{M_{2,1}}$	Get M_1 by max $L_{\alpha M_1}$
	No Repeat	Repeat S1, S2	Repeat S1, S2	No Repeat	Repeat S1, S2	No Repeat
Existing models	no new !	no new !	no new !	no new !	no new !	no new !
Variants		Similar to those in Table 1.				

Table 4: BKC-YY Machine for Supervised Learning
Given Data $\{x_i, y_i\}_{i=1}^N$, Fix $P_{M_1}(x) = P_0(x)$ by eq.(1).

$$h_{M_1}^s = \frac{1}{N}\sum_i P_{M_1}(y_i|x_i)\log P_{M_1}(y_i|x_i), \quad h_{M_2}^s = \frac{1}{N}\sum_i P_{M_2}(x_i|y_i)\log P_{M_2}(x_i|y_i), \quad (E11)$$

$$q_{M_{1,2}}^s = \frac{1}{N}\sum_i P_{M_1}(y_i|x_i)\log P_{M_2}(x_i|y_i), \quad q_{M_{2,1}}^s = \frac{1}{N}\sum_i P_{M_2}(x_i|y_i)\log P_{M_1}(y_i|x_i), \quad (E12)$$

$$L_{M_1}^s = \frac{1}{N}\sum_i \log P_{M_1}(y_i|x_i), \quad L_{M_2}^s = \frac{1}{N}\sum_i \log P_{M_2}(x_i|y_i), \quad (E13)$$

	$K(M_1, M_2) = K_b + D$			$K(M_2, M_1) = K_b + D$		
Marriage Status	Single-M	Single-F	H-m-W	Single-M	Single-F	H-m-W
K_b	$h_{M_1}^s$ (max)	$-L_{M_2}^s$ (min)	$h_{M_1}^s - q_{M_{1,2}}^s$ (min)	$-L_{M_1}^s$ (min)	$h_{M_2}^s$ (max)	$h_{M_2}^s - q_{M_{2,1}}^s$ (min)
Feature	minimum entropy(ME) F-net	ML B-net	Mixed F-B net	ML F-net	minimum entropy B-net	Mixed B-F net
Existing models	no new !	BP on B-net	no new !	BP on F-net	no new !	no new !

denoted by H-m-W-Max. This model is a dual to the Helmholtz machine in order to focus on getting best discriminative or separable representations $P_{M_1}(y|x)$ in Y instead of best fitting of $P_{M_2}(x|y)$ on input data.

Third, by replacing $K(M_1, M_2)$ with $K(M_2, M_1)$, in Table 3 we can obtain new models that are the counterparts of those given in Table 2. For the case H-f-W, its $\max_{M_1,M_2}$ gives minimum entropy estimate on $P_{M_2}(x)$ instead of maximum likelihood estimate on $P_{M_2}(x)$ in Table 2. For the case Single-M, it will function similarly to the case Single-F in Table 2, but with minimum entropy on $P_{M_1}(y|x)$ in Table 2 replaced by maximum likelihood on $P_{M_1}(y|x)$ here. For the case H-m-W, the focus shifts from on getting best fitting of $P_{M_2}(x|y)$ on input data to on getting best discriminative representations $P_{M_1}(y|x)$ in Y, which is similar to the just mentioned H-m-W-Max, but with minimum entropy on $P_{M_1}(y|x)$ replaced by maximum likelihood on $P_{M_1}(y|x)$. The other two cases in Table 3 have been also changed similarly from those in Table 2.

Fourth, several new model have also been proposed in Table 4 for supervised learning. Instead of maximum likelihood, the new models suggest learning by minimum entropy or a mix of maximum likelihood and minimum entropy.

Finally, further studies on the other status in Table 1 are needed. Heuristically, we can also treat the case H-m-W by two separated steps. We first get M_1 by $\max[h_{M_1} - h_{\alpha M_1}]$, and then get M_2 by $\max q_{M_{1,2}}$; or we first get M_2 by $\min[h - h_\alpha - q_{M_2}]$ and then get M_1 by $\min[h_{M_1} - h_{\alpha M_1} - q_{M_{1,2}}]$. The two algorithms attempt to get both a good discriminative representation by $P_{M_1}(y|x)$ and a good fitting of $P_{M_2}(x|y)$ on input data. However whether they work well needs to be tested experimentally.

We are currently conducting experiments on comparison several of the above new models against their existing counterparts.

Acknowledgements *The work was Supported by the HK RGC Earmarked Grant CUHK250/94E.*

References

Amari, S(1995a) [Amari95] " Information geometry of the EM and em algorithms for neural networks", *Neural Networks 8*, to appear.
Amari, S(1995b), *Neural Computation 7*, pp13-18.
Atick, J.J. & Redlich, A.N. (1990) [Ati90], *Neural Computation* Vol.2, No.3, pp308-320.
Bell A. J. & Sejnowski, T. J.(1995) [Bel95], *Neural Computation* Vol.7, No.6, 1129-1159.
Byrne, W. (1992), *IEEE Trans. Neural Networks 3*, pp612-620.
Csiszar, I., (1975), *Annals of Probability 3*, pp146-158.
Dayan, P., Hinton, G. E., & Neal, R. N. (1995) [Day95], *Neural Computation* Vol.7, No.5, 889-904.
Dempster, A.P., Laird, N.M., & Rubin, D.B. (1977) [Dem77], *J. Royal Statist. Society, B39*, 1-38.
Hathaway, R.J.(1986), *Statistics & Probability Letters 4*, pp53-56.
Hinton, G. E., et al, (1995) [Hin95], *Science 268*, pp1158-1160.
Hinton, G. E. & Zemel, R.S. (1994) [Hin94], *Advances in NIPS 6*, pp3-10.
Linsker, R. (1989) [Lin89], *Advances in NIPS 1*, pp186-194.
Neal, R. N.& Hinton, G. E(1993), *A new view of the EM algorithm that justifies incremental and other variants*, preprint.
Xu, L. (1996), "How Many Clusters ? : A YING-YANG Machine Based Theory For A Classical Open Problem In Pattern Recognition", to appear on *Proc. IEEE ICNN96*.
Xu, L. (1995a), "YING-YANG Machine: a Bayesian-Kullback scheme for unified learnings and new results on vector quantization", Keynote talk, Proc. Intl Conf. on Neural Information Processing (ICONIP95), Oct 30 - Nov. 3, 1995, pp977-988.
Xu, L.(1995b), "YING-YANG Machine for Temporal Signals", Keynote talk, Proc IEEE intl Conf. Neural Networks & Signal Processing, Vol.I, pp644-651, Nanjing, 10-13, 1995.
Xu, L. (1995c), "New Advances on The YING-YANG Machine", Invited paper, Proc. of 1995 Intl. Symposium on Artificial Neural Networks, ppIS07-12, Dec. 18-20, Taiwan.
Xu, L. (1995d), "Cluster Number Selection, Adaptive EM Algorithms and Competitive Learnings", Invited paper, Proc. Intl Conf. on Neural Information Processing (ICONIP95), Oct 30 - Nov. 3, 1995, Vol.II, pp1499-1502.
Xu, L. (1995e), Invited paper, Proc. WCNN95, Vol.I, pp35-42. Also, Invited paper, Proc. IEEE ICNN 1994, ppI315-320.
Xu, L., & Jordan, M.I. (1993), *Proc. of WCNN'93*, Portland, OR, Vol. II, 431-434.

Universal Approximation and Learning of Trajectories Using Oscillators

Pierre Baldi[*]
Division of Biology
California Institute of Technology
Pasadena, CA 91125
pfbaldi@juliet.caltech.edu

Kurt Hornik
Technische Universität Wien
Wiedner Hauptstraße 8–10/1071
A-1040 Wien, Austria
Kurt.Hornik@tuwien.ac.at

Abstract

Natural and artificial neural circuits must be capable of traversing specific state space trajectories. A natural approach to this problem is to learn the relevant trajectories from examples. Unfortunately, gradient descent learning of complex trajectories in amorphous networks is unsuccessful. We suggest a possible approach where trajectories are realized by combining simple oscillators, in various modular ways. We contrast two regimes of fast and slow oscillations. In all cases, we show that banks of oscillators with bounded frequencies have universal approximation properties. Open questions are also discussed briefly.

1 INTRODUCTION: TRAJECTORY LEARNING

The design of artificial neural systems, in robotics applications and others, often leads to the problem of constructing a recurrent neural network capable of producing a particular trajectory, in the state space of its visible units. Throughout evolution, biological neural systems, such as central pattern generators, have also been faced with similar challenges. A natural approach to tackle this problem is to try to "learn" the desired trajectory, for instance through a process of trial and error and subsequent optimization. Unfortunately, gradient descent learning of complex trajectories in amorphous networks is unsuccessful. Here, we suggest a possible approach where trajectories are realized, in a modular and hierarchical fashion, by combining simple oscillators. In particular, we show that banks of oscillators have universal approximation properties.

---

[*]Also with the Jet Propulsion Laboratory, California Institute of Technology.

To begin with, we can restrict ourselves to the simple case of a network with one[1] visible linear unit and consider the problem of adjusting the network parameters in a way that the output unit activity $u(t)$ is equal to a target function $f(t)$, over an interval of time $[0, T]$. The hidden units of the network may be non-linear and satisfy, for instance, one of the usual neural network charging equations such as

$$\frac{du_i}{dt} = -\frac{u_i}{\tau_i} + \sum_j w_{ij} f_j u_j(t - \tau_{ij}), \tag{1}$$

where τ_i is the time constant of the unit, the τ_{ij} represent interaction delays, and the functions f_j are non-linear input/output functions, sigmoidal or other. In the next section, we briefly review three possible approaches for solving this problem, and some of their limitations. In particular, we suggest that complex trajectories can be synthesized by proper combination of simple oscillatory components.

2 THREE DIFFERENT APPROACHES TO TRAJECTORY LEARNING

2.1 GRADIENT DESCENT APPROACHES

One obvious approach is to use a form of gradient descent for recurrent networks (see [2] for a review), such as back-propagation through time, in order to modify any adjustable parameters of the networks (time constants, delays, synaptic weights and/or gains) to reduce a certain error measure, constructed by comparing the output $u(t)$ with its target $f(t)$. While conceptually simple, gradient descent applied to amorphous networks is not a successful approach, except on the most simple trajectories. Although intuitively clear, the exact reasons for this are not entirely understood, and overlap in part with the problems that can be encountered with gradient descent in simple feed-forward networks on regression or classification tasks.

There is an additional set of difficulties with gradient descent learning of fixed points or trajectories, that is specific to *recurrent* networks, and that has to do with the bifurcations of the system being considered. In the case of a recurrent[2] network, as the parameters are varied, the system may or may not undergo a series of bifurcations, i.e., of abrupt changes in the structure of its trajectories and, in particular, of its attractors (fixed points, limit cycles, ...). This in turn may translate into abrupt discontinuities, oscillations or non-convergence in the corresponding learning curve. At each bifurcation, the error function is usually discontinuous, and therefore the gradient is not defined. Learning can be disrupted in two ways: when unwanted abrupt changes occur in the flow of the dynamical system, or when desirable bifurcations are prevented from occurring. A classical example of the second type is the case of a neural network with very small initial weights being trained to oscillate, in a symmetric and stable fashion, around the origin. With small initial weights, the network in general converges to its unique fixed point at the origin, with a large error. If we slightly perturb the weights, remaining away from any bifurcation, the network continues to converge to its unique fixed point which now may be slightly displaced from the origin, and yield an even greater error, so that learning by gradient descent becomes impossible (the starting configuration of zero weights is a local minimum of the error function).

---

[1] All the results to be derived can be extended immediately to the case of higher-dimensional trajectories.

[2] In a feed-forward network, where the transfer functions of the units are continuous, the output is a continuous function of the parameters and therefore there are no bifurcations.

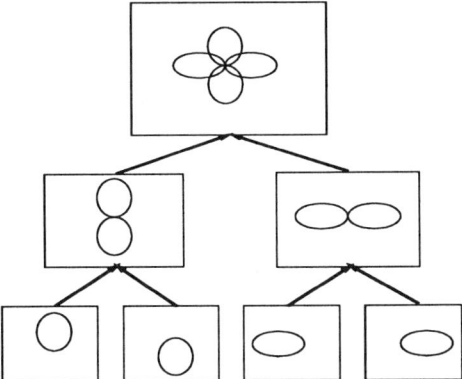

Figure 1: A schematic representation of a 3 layer oscillator network for double figure eight. Oscillators with period T in a given layer gate the corresponding oscillators, with period $T/2$, in the previous layer.

2.2 DYNAMICAL SYSTEM APPROACH

In the dynamical system approach, the function $f(t)$ is approximated in time, over $[0, T]$ by a sequence of points $y_0, y_1, \ldots$. These points are associated with the iterates of a dynamical system, i.e., $y_{n+1} = F(y_n) = F^n(y_0)$, for some function F. Thus the network implementation requires mainly a feed-forward circuit that computes the function F. It has a simple overall recursive structure where, at time n, the output $F(y_n)$ is calculated, and fed back into the input for the next iteration. While this approach is entirely general, it leaves open the problem of constructing the function F. Of course, F can be learned from examples in a usual feed-forward connectionist network. But, as usual, the complexity and architecture of such a network are difficult to determine in general. Another interesting issue in trajectory learning is how time is represented in the network, and whether some sort of clock is needed. Although occasionally in the literature certain authors have advocated the introduction of an input unit whose output is the time t, this explicit representation is clearly not a suitable representation, since the problem of trajectory learning reduces then entirely to a regression problem. The dynamical system approach relies on one basic clock to calculate F and recycle it to the input layer. In the next approach, an implicit representation of time is provided by the periods of the oscillators.

2.3 OSCILLATOR APPROACH

A different approach was suggested in [1] where, loosely speaking, complex trajectories are realized using weakly pre-structured networks, consisting of shallow hierarchical combinations of simple oscillatory modules. The oscillatory modules can consist, for instance, of simple oscillator rings of units satisfying Eq. 1, with two or three high-gain neurons, and an odd number of inhibitory connections ([3]).

To fix the ideas, consider the typical test problem of constructing a network capable of producing a trajectory associated with a double figure eight curve (i.e., a set of four loops joined at one point), see Fig. 1. In this example, the first level of the hierarchy could contain four oscillator rings, one for each loop of the target trajectory. The parameters in each one of these four modules can be adjusted, for instance by gradient descent, to match each of the loops in the target trajectory.

The second level of the pyramid should contain two control modules. Each of these modules controls a distinct pair of oscillator networks from the first level, so that each control network in the second level ends up producing a simple figure eight. Again, the control networks in level two can be oscillator rings and their parameters can be adjusted. In particular, after the learning process is completed, they should be operating in their high-gain regimes and have a period equal to the sum of the periods of the circuits each one controls.

Finally, the third layer consists of another oscillatory and adjustable module which controls the two modules in the second level, so as to produce a double figure eight. The third layer module must also end up operating in its high-gain regime with a period equal to four times the period of the oscillators in the first layer. In general, the final output trajectory is also a limit cycle because it is obtained by superposition of limit cycles in the various modules. If the various oscillators relax to their limit cycles independently of one another, it is essential to provide for adjustable delays between the various modules in order to get the proper phase adjustments. In this way, a sparse network with 20 units or so can be constructed that can successfully execute a double figure eight.

There are actually different possible neural network realizations depending on how the action of the control modules is implemented. For instance, if the control units are gating the connections between corresponding layers, this amounts to using higher order units in the network. If one high-gain oscillatory unit, with activity $c(t)$ always close to 0 or 1, gates the oscillatory activities of two units $u_1(t)$ and $u_2(t)$ in the previous layer, then the overall output can be written as

$$\text{out}(t) = c(t)u_1(t) + (1 - c(t))u_2(t). \tag{2}$$

The number of layers in the network then becomes a function of the order of the units one is willing to use. This approach could also be described in terms of a dynamic mixture of experts architecture, in its high gain regime. Alternatively, one could assume the existence of a fast weight dynamics on certain connections governed by a corresponding set of differential equations. Although we believe that oscillators with limit cycles present several attractive properties (stability, short transients, biological relevance, ...), one can conceivably use completely different circuits as building blocks in each module.

3 GENERALIZATION AND UNIVERSAL APPROXIMATION

We have just described an approach that combines a modular hierarchical architecture, together with some simple form of learning, enabling the synthesis of a neural circuit suitable for the production of a double figure eight trajectory. It is clear that the same approach can be extended to triple figure eight or, for that matter, to any trajectory curve consisting of an arbitrary number of simple loops with a common period and one common point. In fact it can be extended to any arbitrary trajectory. To see this, we can subdivide the time interval $[0, T]$ into n equal intervals of duration $\epsilon = T/n$. Given a certain level of required precision, we can always find n oscillator networks with period T (or a fraction of T) and visible trajectory $u_i(t)$, such that for each i, the i-th portion of the trajectory $u(t)$ with $i\epsilon \leq t \leq (i+1)\epsilon$ can be well approximated by a portion of $u_i(t)$, the trajectory of the i-th oscillator. The target trajectory can then be approximated as

$$u(t) \approx \sum_{i=1}^{n} c_i(t) u_i(t). \tag{3}$$

As usual, the control coefficient $c_i(t)$ must have also period T and be equal to 1 for $i\epsilon \leq t \leq (i+1)\epsilon$, and 0 otherwise. The control can be realized with one large high-gain oscillator, or as in the case described above, by a hierarchy of control oscillators arranged, for instance, as a binary tree of depth m if $n = 2^m$, with the corresponding multiple frequencies.

We can now turn to a slightly different oscillator approach, where trajectories are to be approximated with linear combinations of oscillators, with *constant* coefficients. What we would like to show again is that oscillators are universal approximators for trajectories. In a sense, this is already a well-known result of Fourier theory since, for instance, any reasonable function f with period T can be expanded in the form[3]

$$f(t) = \sum_{k=-\infty}^{\infty} \gamma_k e^{2\pi i \lambda_k t}, \qquad \lambda_k = k/T. \tag{4}$$

For sufficiently smooth target functions, without high frequencies in their spectrum, it is well known that the series in Eq. 4 can be truncated. Notice, however, that both Eqs. 3 and 4 require having component oscillators with relatively high frequencies, compared to the final trajectory. This is not implausible in biological motor control, where trajectories have typical time scales of a fraction of a second, and single control neurons operate in the millisecond range. A rather different situation arises if the component oscillators are "slow" with respect to the final product.

The Fourier representation requires in principle oscillations with arbitrarily large frequencies $(0, 1/T, 2/T, \ldots, n/T, \ldots)$. Most likely, relatively small variations in the parameters (for instance gains, delays and/or synaptic weights) of an oscillator circuit can only lead to relatively small but continuous variations of the overall frequency. For instance, in [3] it is shown that the period T of an oscillator ring with n units obeying Eq. 1 must satisfy

$$2 \left(\sum_i \tau_{ii-1} + \ln 2 \sum_i \tau_i \right) \leq T \leq 2 \left(\sum_i \tau_{ii-1} + \sum_i \tau_i \right).$$

Thus, we need to show that a decomposition similar in flavor to Eq. 4 is possible, but using oscillators with frequencies in a bounded interval. Notice that by varying the parameters of a basic oscillator, any frequency in the allowable frequency range can be realized, see [3]. Such a linear combination is slightly different in spirit from Eq. 2, since the coefficients are independent of time, and can be seen as a soft mixture of experts. We have the following result.

Theorem 1 *Let $a < b$ be two arbitrary real numbers and let f be a continuous function on $[0,T]$. Then for any error level $\epsilon > 0$, there exist n and a function g_n of the form*

$$g_n(t) = \sum_{k=1}^{n} \alpha_k e^{2\pi i \lambda_k t}, \qquad a \leq \lambda_1, \ldots, \lambda_n \leq b$$

such that the uniform distance $\|f - g_n\|_\infty$ is less than ϵ.

In fact, it is not even necessary to vary the frequencies λ over a continuous band $[a, b]$. We have the following.

Theorem 2 *Let $\{\lambda_k\}$ be an infinite sequence with a finite accumulation point, and let f be a continuous function on $[0, T]$. Then for any error level $\epsilon > 0$, there exist n and a function $g_n(t) = \sum_{k=1}^{n} \alpha_k e^{2\pi i \lambda_k t}$ such that $\|f - g_n\|_\infty < \epsilon$.*

---

[3] In what follows, we use the complex form for notational convenience.

Thus, we may even fix the oscillator frequencies as e.g. $\lambda_k = 1/k$ without losing universal approximation capabilities. Similar statements can be made about mean-square approximation or, more generally, approximation in p-norm $L^p(\mu)$, where $1 \leq p < \infty$ and μ is a finite measure on $[0, T]$:

Theorem 3 *For all p and f in $L^p(\mu)$ and for all $\epsilon > 0$, we can always find n and g_n as above such that $\|f - g_n\|_{L^p(\mu)} < \epsilon$.*

The proof of these results is surprisingly simple. Following the proofs in [4], if one of the above statements was not true, there would exist a nonzero, signed finite measure σ with support in $[0, T]$ such that $\int_{[0,T]} e^{2\pi i \lambda t} d\sigma(t) = 0$ for all "allowed" frequencies λ. Now the function $z \mapsto \int_{[0,T]} e^{2\pi i z t} d\sigma(t)$ is clearly analytic on the whole complex plane. Hence, by a well-known result from complex variables, if it vanishes along an infinite sequence with a finite accumulation point, it is identically zero. But then in particular the Fourier transform of σ vanishes, which in turn implies that σ is identically zero by the uniqueness theorem on Fourier transforms, contradicting the initial assumption.

Notice that the above results do not imply that f can exactly be represented as e.g. $f(t) = \int_a^b e^{2\pi i \lambda t} d\nu(\lambda)$ for some signed finite measure ν—such functions are not only band-limited, but also extremely smooth (they have an analytic extension to the whole complex plane).

Hence, one might even conjecture that the above approximations are rather poor in the sense that unrealistically many terms are needed for the approximation. However, this is not true—one can easily show that the *rates of approximation cannot be worse that those for approximation with polynomials*. Let us briefly sketch the argument, because it also shows how bounded-frequency oscillators could be constructed.

Following an idea essentially due to Stinchcombe & White [5], let, more generally, g be an analytic function in a neighborhood of the real line for which no derivative vanishes at the origin (above, we had $g(t) = e^{2\pi i t}$). Pick a nonnegative integer n and a polynomial p of degree not greater than $n - 1$ arbitrarily. Let us show that for any $\epsilon > 0$, we can always find a g_n of the form $g_n(t) = \sum_{k=1}^n \alpha_k g(\lambda_k t)$ with λ_k arbitrarily small such that $\|p - g_n\|_\infty < \epsilon$. To do so, note that we can write

$$g(\lambda t) = \sum_{l=0}^{n-1} \beta_l (\lambda t)^l + r_n(\lambda t), \qquad p(t) = \sum_{l=0}^{n-1} \delta_l t^l,$$

where $r_n(\lambda t)$ is of the order of λ^n, as $\lambda \to 0$, uniformly for t in $[0, T]$. Hence,

$$\sum_{k=1}^n \alpha_k g(\lambda_k t) = \sum_{k=1}^n \alpha_k \left(\sum_{l=0}^{n-1} \beta_l (\lambda_k t)^l + r_n(\lambda_k t) \right)$$

$$= \sum_{l=0}^{n-1} \left(\sum_{k=1}^n \alpha_k \lambda_k^l \right) \beta_l t^l + \sum_{k=1}^n \alpha_k r_n(\lambda_k t).$$

Now fix n distinct numbers $\ell_1, \ldots, \ell_n$, let $\lambda_k = \lambda_k(\rho) = \rho \ell_k$, and choose the $\alpha_k = \alpha_k(\rho)$ such that $\sum_{k=1}^n \alpha_k(\rho) \lambda_k(\rho)^l = \delta_l / \beta_l$ for $l = 0, \ldots, n-1$. (This is possible because, by assumption, all β_l are non-zero.) It is readily seen that $\alpha_k(\rho)$ is of the order of ρ^{1-n} as $\rho \to 0$ (in fact, the j-th row of the inverse of the coefficient matrix of the linear system is given by the coefficients of the polynomial $\prod_{k \neq j} (\lambda - \lambda_k)/(\lambda_j - \lambda_k)$). Hence, as $\rho \to 0$, the remainder term $\sum_{k=1}^n \alpha_k(\rho) r_n(\lambda_k(\rho) t)$ is of the order of ρ, and thus $\sum_{k=1}^n \alpha_k(\rho) g(\lambda_k(\rho) t) \to \sum_{l=0}^{n-1} \delta_l t^l = p(t)$ uniformly on $[0, T]$.

Note that using the above method, the coefficients in the approximation grow quite rapidly when the approximation error tends to 0. In some sense, this was to be expected from the observation that the classes of small-band-limited functions are rather "small". There is a fundamental tradeoff between the size of the frequencies, and the size of the mixing coefficients. How exactly the coefficients scale with the width of the allowed frequency band is currently being investigated.

4 CONCLUSION

The modular oscillator approach leads to trajectory architectures which are more structured than fully interconnected networks, with a general feed-forward flow of information and sparse recurrent connections to achieve dynamical effects. The sparsity of units and connections are attractive features for hardware design; and so is also the modular organization and the fact that learning is much more circumscribed than in fully interconnected systems. We have shown in different ways that such architectures have universal approximation properties. In these architectures, however, some form of learning remains essential, for instance to fine tune each one of the modules. This, in itself, is a much easier task than the one a fully interconnected and random network would have been faced with. It can be solved by gradient or random descent or other methods. Yet, fundamental open problems remain in the overall organization of learning across modules, and in the origin of the decomposition. In particular, can the modular architecture be the outcome of a simple internal organizational process rather than an external imposition and how should learning be coordinated in time and across modules (other than the obvious: modules in the first level learn first, modules in the second level second, ...)? How successful is a global gradient descent strategy applied across modules? How can the same modular architecture be used for different trajectories, with short switching times between trajectories and proper phases along each trajectory?

Acknowledgments

The work of PB is in part supported by grants from the ONR and the AFOSR.

References

[1] Pierre Baldi. A modular hierarchical approach to learning. In *Proceedings of the 2nd International Conference on Fuzzy Logic and Neural Networks*, volume II, pages 985–988, IIzuka, Japan, 1992.

[2] Pierre F. Baldi. Gradient descent learning algorithm overview: a general dynamic systems perspective. *IEEE Transactions on Neural Networks*, 6(1):182–195, January 1995.

[3] Pierre F. Baldi and Amir F. Atiya. How delays affect neural dynamics and learning. *IEEE Transactions on Neural Networks*, 5(4):612–621, July 1994.

[4] Kurt Hornik. Some new results on neural network approximation. *Neural Networks*, 6:1069–1072, 1993.

[5] Maxwell B. Stinchcombe and Halbert White. Approximating and learning unknown mappings using multilayer feedforward networks with bounded weights. In *International Joint Conference on Neural Networks*, volume III, pages 7–16, Washington, 1990. Lawrence Earlbaum, Hillsdale.

A Smoothing Regularizer for Recurrent Neural Networks

Lizhong Wu and John Moody
Oregon Graduate Institute, Computer Science Dept., Portland, OR 97291-1000

Abstract

We derive a smoothing regularizer for recurrent network models by requiring robustness in prediction performance to perturbations of the training data. The regularizer can be viewed as a generalization of the first order Tikhonov stabilizer to dynamic models. The closed-form expression of the regularizer covers both time-lagged and simultaneous recurrent nets, with feedforward nets and one-layer linear nets as special cases. We have successfully tested this regularizer in a number of case studies and found that it performs better than standard quadratic weight decay.

1 Introduction

One technique for preventing a neural network from overfitting noisy data is to add a regularizer to the error function being minimized. Regularizers typically smooth the fit to noisy data. Well-established techniques include ridge regression, see (Hoerl & Kennard 1970), and more generally spline smoothing functions or Tikhonov stabilizers that penalize the mth-order squared derivatives of the function being fit, as in (Tikhonov & Arsenin 1977), (Eubank 1988), (Hastie & Tibshirani 1990) and (Wahba 1990). These methods have recently been extended to networks of radial basis functions (Girosi, Jones & Poggio 1995), and several heuristic approaches have been developed for sigmoidal neural networks, for example, quadratic weight decay (Plaut, Nowlan & Hinton 1986), weight elimination (Scalettar & Zee 1988),(Chauvin 1990),(Weigend, Rumelhart & Huberman 1990) and soft weight sharing (Nowlan & Hinton 1992).[1] All previous studies on regularization have concentrated on feedforward neural networks. To our knowledge, recurrent learning with regularization has not been reported before.

---

[1]Two additional papers related to ours, but dealing only with feed forward networks, came to our attention or were written after our work was completed. These are (Bishop 1995) and (Leen 1995). Also, Moody & Rögnvaldsson (1995) have recently proposed several new classes of smoothing regularizers for feedforward nets.

A Smoothing Regularizer for Recurrent Neural Networks

In Section 2 of this paper, we develop a smoothing regularizer for general dynamic models which is derived by considering perturbations of the training data. We present a closed-form expression for our regularizer for two layer feedforward and recurrent neural networks, with standard weight decay being a special case. In Section 3, we evaluate our regularizer's performance on predicting the U.S. Index of Industrial Production. The advantage of our regularizer is demonstrated by comparing to standard weight decay in both feedforward and recurrent modeling. Finally, we conclude our paper in Section 4.

2 Smoothing Regularization

2.1 Prediction Error for Perturbed Data Sets

Consider a training data set $\{P : Z(t), X(t)\}$, where the targets $Z(t)$ are assumed to be generated by an unknown dynamical system $F^*(I(t))$ and an unobserved noise process:

$$Z(t) = F^*(I(t)) + \varepsilon^*(t) \quad \text{with} \quad I(t) = \{X(s), s = 1, 2, \cdots, t\} . \tag{1}$$

Here, $I(t)$ is the information set containing both current and past inputs $X(s)$, and the $\varepsilon^*(t)$ are independent random noise variables with zero mean and variance σ^{*2}. Consider next a dynamic network model $\hat{Z}(t) = F(\Phi, I(t))$ to be trained on data set P, where Φ represents a set of network parameters, and $F(\ )$ is a network transfer function which is assumed to be nonlinear and dynamic. We assume that $F(\ )$ has good approximation capabilities, such that $F(\Phi_P, I(t)) \approx F^*(I(t))$ for learnable parameters Φ_P.

Our goal is to derive a smoothing regularizer for a network trained on the actual data set P that in effect optimizes the expected network performance (prediction risk) on perturbed test data sets of form $\{Q : \tilde{Z}(t), \tilde{X}(t)\}$. The elements of Q are related to the elements of P via small random perturbations $\varepsilon_z(t)$ and $\varepsilon_x(t)$, so that

$$\tilde{Z}(t) = Z(t) + \varepsilon_z(t), \tag{2}$$
$$\tilde{X}(t) = X(t) + \varepsilon_x(t). \tag{3}$$

The $\varepsilon_z(t)$ and $\varepsilon_x(t)$ have zero mean and variances σ_z^2 and σ_x^2 respectively. The training and test errors for the data sets P and Q are

$$D_P = \frac{1}{N}\sum_{t=1}^{N}[Z(t) - F(\Phi_P, I(t))]^2 \tag{4}$$

$$D_Q = \frac{1}{N}\sum_{t=1}^{N}[\tilde{Z}(t) - F(\Phi_P, \tilde{I}(t))]^2 , \tag{5}$$

where Φ_P denotes the network parameters obtained by training on data set P, and $\tilde{I}(t) = \{\tilde{X}(s), s = 1, 2, \cdots, t\}$ is the perturbed information set of Q. With this notation, our goal is to minimize the expected value of D_Q, while training on D_P.

Consider the prediction error for the perturbed data point at time t:

$$d(t) = [\tilde{Z}(t) - F(\Phi_P, \tilde{I}(t))]^2 . \tag{6}$$

With Eqn (2), we obtain

$$\begin{aligned}d(t) &= [Z(t) + \varepsilon_z(t) - F(\Phi_P, I(t)) + F(\Phi_P, I(t)) - F(\Phi_P, \tilde{I}(t))]^2, \\ &= [Z(t) - F(\Phi_P, I(t))]^2 + [F(\Phi_P, I(t)) - F(\Phi_P, \tilde{I}(t))]^2 + [\varepsilon_z(t)]^2 \\ &\quad + 2[Z(t) - F(\Phi_P, I(t))][F(\Phi_P, I(t)) - F(\Phi_P, \tilde{I}(t))] \\ &\quad + 2\varepsilon_z(t)[Z(t) - F(\Phi_P, \tilde{I}(t))]. \end{aligned} \tag{7}$$

Assuming that $\varepsilon_z(t)$ is uncorrelated with $[Z(t) - F(\Phi_P, \tilde{I}(t))]$ and averaging over the exemplars of data sets P and Q, Eqn(7) becomes

$$D_Q = D_P + \frac{1}{N}\sum_{t=1}^{N}[F(\Phi_P, I(t)) - F(\Phi_P, \tilde{I}(t))]^2 + \frac{1}{N}\sum_{t=1}^{N}[\varepsilon_z(t)]^2$$
$$+ \frac{2}{N}\sum_{t=1}^{N}[Z(t) - F(\Phi_P, I(t))][F(\Phi_P, I(t)) - F(\Phi_P, \tilde{I}(t))]. \quad (8)$$

The third term, $\sum_{t=1}^{N}[\varepsilon_z(t)]^2$, in Eqn(8) is independent of the weights, so it can be neglected during the learning process. The fourth term in Eqn(8) is the cross-covariance between $[Z(t) - F(\Phi_P, I(t))]$ and $[F(\Phi_P, I(t)) - F(\Phi_P, \tilde{I}(t))]$. Using the inequality $2ab \leq a^2 + b^2$, we can see that minimizing the first term D_P and the second term $\frac{1}{N}\sum_{t=1}^{N}[F(\Phi_P, I(t)) - F(\Phi_P, \tilde{I}(t))]^2$ in Eqn (8) during training will automatically decrease the effect of the cross-covariance term. Therefore, we exclude the cross-covariance term from the training criterion.

The above analysis shows that the expected test error D_Q can be minimized by minimizing the objective function D:

$$D = \frac{1}{N}\sum_{t=1}^{N}[Z(t) - F(\Phi, I(t))]^2 + \frac{1}{N}\sum_{t=1}^{N}[F(\Phi_P, I(t)) - F(\Phi_P, \tilde{I}(t))]^2. \quad (9)$$

In Eqn (9), the second term is the time average of the squared disturbance $\|\tilde{\hat{Z}}(t) - \hat{Z}(t)\|^2$ of the trained network output due to the input perturbation $\|\tilde{I}(t) - I(t)\|^2$. Minimizing this term demands that small changes in the input variables yield correspondingly small changes in the output. This is the standard smoothness prior, namely that if nothing else is known about the function to be approximated, a good option is to assume a high degree of smoothness. Without knowing the correct functional form of the dynamical system F^* or using such prior assumptions, the data fitting problem is ill-posed. In (Wu & Moody 1996), we have shown that the second term in Eqn (9) is a dynamic generalization of the first order Tikhonov stabilizer.

2.2 Form of the Proposed Smoothing Regularizer

Consider a general, two layer, nonlinear, dynamic network with recurrent connections on the internal layer [2] as described by

$$Y(t) = \mathbf{f}\left(WY(t-\tau) + VX(t)\right), \hat{Z}(t) = UY(t) \quad (10)$$

where $X(t)$, $Y(t)$ and $\hat{Z}(t)$ are respectively the network input vector, the hidden output vector and the network output; $\Phi = \{U, V, W\}$ is the output, input and recurrent connections of the network; $\mathbf{f}(\ )$ is the vector-valued nonlinear transfer function of the hidden units; and τ is a time delay in the feedback connections of hidden layer which is pre-defined by a user and will not be changed during learning. τ can be zero, a fraction, or an integer, but we are interested in the cases with a small τ.[3]

---
[2] Our derivation can easily be extended to other network structures.
[3] When the time delay τ exceeds some critical value, a recurrent network becomes unstable and lies in oscillatory modes. See, for example, (Marcus & Westervelt 1989).

When $\tau = 1$, our model is a recurrent network as described by (Elman 1990) and (Rumelhart, Hinton & Williams 1986) (see Figure 17 on page 355). When τ is equal to some fraction smaller than one, the network evolves $\frac{1}{\tau}$ times within each input time interval. When τ decreases and approaches zero, our model is the same as the network studied by (Pineda 1989), and earlier, widely-studied *additive networks*. In (Pineda 1989), τ was referred to as the *network relaxation time scale*. (Werbos 1992) distinguished the recurrent networks with zero τ and non-zero τ by calling them *simultaneous recurrent networks* and *time-lagged recurrent networks* respectively.

We have found that minimizing the second term of Eqn(9) can be obtained by smoothing the output response to an input perturbation at every time step. This yields, see (Wu & Moody 1996):

$$\|\tilde{\hat{Z}}(t) - \hat{Z}(t)\|^2 \leq \rho_\tau^2(\Phi_P) \|\tilde{X}(t) - X(t)\|^2 \text{ for } t = 1, 2, \ldots, N. \quad (11)$$

We call $\rho_\tau^2(\Phi_P)$ the *output sensitivity* of the trained network Φ_P to an input perturbation. $\rho_\tau^2(\Phi_P)$ is determined by the network parameters only and is independent of the time variable t.

We obtain our new regularizer by training directly on the expected prediction error for perturbed data sets Q. Based on the analysis leading to Eqns (9) and (11), the training criterion thus becomes

$$D = \frac{1}{N} \sum_{t=1}^{N} [Z(t) - F(\Phi, I(t))]^2 + \lambda \rho_\tau^2(\Phi) . \quad (12)$$

The coefficient λ in Eqn(12) is a regularization parameter that measures the degree of input perturbation $\|\tilde{I}(t) - I(t)\|^2$. The algebraic form for $\rho_\tau(\Phi)$ as derived in (Wu & Moody 1996) is:

$$\rho_\tau(\Phi) = \frac{\gamma \|U\| \|V\|}{1 - \gamma \|W\|} \left\{ 1 - \exp\left(\frac{\gamma \|W\| - 1}{\tau} \right) \right\} , \quad (13)$$

for time-lagged recurrent networks ($\tau > 0$). Here, $\|\ \|$ denotes the Euclidean matrix norm. The factor γ depends upon the maximal value of the first derivatives of the activation functions of the hidden units and is given by:

$$\gamma = \max_{t,j} | f_j'(o_j(t)) | , \quad (14)$$

where j is the index of hidden units and $o_j(t)$ is the input to the jth unit. In general, $\gamma \leq 1$. [4] To insure stability and that the effects of small input perturbations are damped out, it is required, see (Wu & Moody 1996), that

$$\gamma \|W\| < 1 . \quad (15)$$

The regularizer Eqn(13) can be deduced for the simultaneous recurrent networks in the limit $\tau \mapsto 0$ by:

$$\rho(\Phi) \equiv \rho_0(\Phi) = \frac{\gamma \|U\| \|V\|}{1 - \gamma \|W\|} . \quad (16)$$

If the network is feedforward, $W = 0$ and $\tau = 0$, Eqns (13) and (16) become

$$\rho(\Phi) = \gamma \|U\| \|V\| . \quad (17)$$

Moreover, if there is no hidden layer and the inputs are directly connected to the outputs via U, the network is an ordinary linear model, and we obtain

$$\rho(\Phi) = \|U\| , \quad (18)$$

---

[4] For instance, $f'(x) = [1 - f(x)]f(x)$ if $f(x) = \frac{1}{1+e^{-x}}$. Then, $\gamma = \max | f'(x) | = \frac{1}{4}$.

which is standard quadratic weight decay (Plaut et al. 1986) as is used in ridge regression (Hoerl & Kennard 1970).

The regularizer (Eqn(17) for feedforward networks and Eqn (13) for recurrent networks) was obtained by requiring smoothness of the network output to perturbations of data. We therefore refer to it as a smoothing regularizer. Several approaches can be applied to estimate the regularization parameter λ, as in (Eubank 1988), (Hastie & Tibshirani 1990) and (Wahba 1990). We will not discuss this subject in this paper.

In the next section, we evaluate the new regularizer for the task of predicting the U.S. Index of Industrial Production. Additional empirical tests can be found in (Wu & Moody 1996).

3 Predicting the U.S. Index of Industrial Production

The Index of Industrial Production (IP) is one of the key measures of economic activity. It is computed and published monthly. Our task is to predict the one-month rate of change of the index from January 1980 to December 1989 for models trained from January 1950 to December 1979. The exogenous inputs we have used include 8 time series such as the index of leading indicators, housing starts, the money supply M2, the *S&P* 500 Index. These 8 series are also recorded monthly. In previous studies by (Moody, Levin & Rehfuss 1993), with the same defined training and test data sets, the normalized prediction errors of the one month rate of change were 0.81 with the **neuz** neural network simulator, and 0.75 with the **proj** neural network simulator.

We have simulated feedforward and recurrent neural network models. Both models consist of two layers. There are 9 input units in the recurrent model, which receive the 8 exogenous series and the previous month IP index change. We set the time-delayed length in the recurrent connections $\tau = 1$. The feedforward model is constructed with 36 input units, which receive 4 time-delayed versions of each input series. The time-delay lengths are 1, 3, 6 and 12, respectively. The activation functions of hidden units in both feedforward and recurrent models are *tanh* functions. The number of hidden units varies from 2 to 6. Each model has one linear output unit.

We have divided the data from January 1950 to December 1979 into four non-overlapping sub-sets. One sub-set consists of 70% of the original data and each of the other three subsets consists of 10% of the original data. The larger sub-set is used as training data and the three smaller sub-sets are used as validation data. These three validation data sets are respectively used for determination of early stopped training, selecting the regularization parameter and selecting the number of hidden units.

We have formed 10 random training-validation partitions. For each training-validation partition, three networks with different initial weight parameters are trained. Therefore, our prediction committee is formed by 30 networks.

The committee error is the average of the errors of all committee members. All networks in the committee are trained simultaneously and stopped at the same time based on the committee error of a validation set. The value of the regularization parameter and the number of hidden units are determined by minimizing the committee error on separate validation sets.

Table 1 compares the out-of-sample performance of recurrent networks and feedfor-

Table 1: Normalized prediction errors for the one-month rate of return on the U.S. Index of Industrial Production (Jan. 1980 - Dec. 1989). Each result is based on 30 networks.

Model	Regularizer	Mean ± Std	Median	Max	Min	Committee
Recurrent Networks	Smoothing	0.646±0.008	0.647	0.657	0.632	0.639
	Weight Decay	0.734±0.018	0.737	0.767	0.704	0.734
Feedforward Networks	Smoothing	0.700±0.023	0.707	0.729	0.654	0.693
	Weight Decay	0.745±0.043	0.748	0.805	0.676	0.731

ward networks trained with our smoothing regularizer to that of networks trained with standard weight decay. The results are based on 30 networks. As shown, the smoothing regularizer again outperforms standard weight decay with 95% confidence (in t-distribution hypothesis) in both cases of recurrent networks and feedforward networks. We also list the median, maximal and minimal prediction errors over 30 predictors. The last column gives the committee results, which are based on the simple average of 30 network predictions. We see that the median, maximal and minimal values and the committee results obtained with the smoothing regularizer are all smaller than those obtained with standard weight decay, in both recurrent and feedforward network models.

4 Concluding Remarks

Regularization in learning can prevent a network from overtraining. Several techniques have been developed in recent years, but all these are specialized for feedforward networks. To our best knowledge, a regularizer for a recurrent network has not been reported previously.

We have developed a smoothing regularizer for recurrent neural networks that captures the dependencies of input, output, and feedback weight values on each other. The regularizer covers both simultaneous and time-lagged recurrent networks, with feedforward networks and single layer, linear networks as special cases. Our smoothing regularizer for linear networks has the same form as standard weight decay. The regularizer developed depends on only the network parameters, and can easily be used. A more detailed description of this work appears in (Wu & Moody 1996).

References

Bishop, C. (1995), 'Training with noise is equivalent to Tikhonov regularization', *Neural Computation* **7**(1), 108–116.

Chauvin, Y. (1990), Dynamic behavior of constrained back-propagation networks, *in* D. Touretzky, ed., 'Advances in Neural Information Processing Systems 2', Morgan Kaufmann Publishers, San Francisco, CA, pp. 642–649.

Elman, J. (1990), 'Finding structure in time', *Cognition Science* **14**, 179–211.

Eubank, R. L. (1988), *Spline Smoothing and Nonparametric Regression*, Marcel Dekker, Inc.

Girosi, F., Jones, M. & Poggio, T. (1995), 'Regularization theory and neural networks architectures', *Neural Computation* **7**, 219–269.

Hastie, T. J. & Tibshirani, R. J. (1990), *Generalized Additive Models*, Vol. 43 of *Monographs on Statistics and Applied Probability*, Chapman and Hall.

Hoerl, A. & Kennard, R. (1970), 'Ridge regression: biased estimation for nonorthogonal problems', *Technometrics* **12**, 55–67.

Leen, T. (1995), 'From data distributions to regularization in invariant learning', *Neural Computation* **7**(5), 974–981.

Marcus, C. & Westervelt, R. (1989), Dynamics of analog neural networks with time delay, *in* D. Touretzky, ed., 'Advances in Neural Information Processing Systems 1', Morgan Kaufmann Publishers, San Francisco, CA.

Moody, J. & Rögnvaldsson, T. (1995), Smoothing regularizers for feed-forward neural networks, Oregon Graduate Institute Computer Science Dept. Technical Report, submitted for publication, 1995.

Moody, J., Levin, U. & Rehfuss, S. (1993), 'Predicting the U.S. index of industrial production', *In proceedings of the 1993 Parallel Applications in Statistics and Economics Conference, Zeist, The Netherlands. Special issue of* Neural Network World **3**(6), 791–794.

Nowlan, S. & Hinton, G. (1992), 'Simplifying neural networks by soft weight-sharing', *Neural Computation* **4**(4), 473–493.

Pineda, F. (1989), 'Recurrent backpropagation and the dynamical approach to adaptive neural computation', *Neural Computation* **1**(2), 161–172.

Plaut, D., Nowlan, S. & Hinton, G. (1986), Experiments on learning by back propagation, Technical Report CMU-CS-86-126, Carnegie-Mellon University.

Rumelhart, D., Hinton, G. & Williams, R. (1986), Learning internal representations by error propagation, *in* D. Rumelhart & J. McClelland, eds, 'Parallel Distributed Processing: Exploration in the microstructure of cognition', MIT Press, Cambridge, MA, chapter 8, pp. 319–362.

Scalettar, R. & Zee, A. (1988), Emergence of grandmother memory in feed forward networks: learning with noise and forgetfulness, *in* D. Waltz & J. Feldman, eds, 'Connectionist Models and Their Implications: Readings from Cognitive Science', Ablex Pub. Corp.

Tikhonov, A. N. & Arsenin, V. I. (1977), *Solutions of Ill-posed Problems*, Winston ; New York : distributed solely by Halsted Press. Scripta series in mathematics. Translation editor, Fritz John.

Wahba, G. (1990), *Spline models for observational data*, CBMS-NSF Regional Conference Series in Applied Mathematics.

Weigend, A., Rumelhart, D. & Huberman, B. (1990), Back-propagation, weight-elimination and time series prediction, *in* T. Sejnowski, G. Hinton & D. Touretzky, eds, 'Proceedings of the connectionist models summer school', Morgan Kaufmann Publishers, San Mateo, CA, pp. 105–116.

Werbos, P. (1992), Neurocontrol and supervised learning: An overview and evaluation, *in* D. White & D. Sofge, eds, 'Handbook of Intelligent Control', Van Nostrand Reinhold, New York.

Wu, L. & Moody, J. (1996), 'A smoothing regularizer for feedforward and recurrent neural networks', *Neural Computation* **8**(3), 463–491.

EM Optimization of Latent-Variable Density Models

Christopher M Bishop, Markus Svensén and Christopher K I Williams
Neural Computing Research Group
Aston University, Birmingham, B4 7ET, UK
c.m.bishop@aston.ac.uk svensjfm@aston.ac.uk c.k.i.williams@aston.ac.uk

Abstract

There is currently considerable interest in developing general non-linear density models based on latent, or hidden, variables. Such models have the ability to discover the presence of a relatively small number of underlying 'causes' which, acting in combination, give rise to the apparent complexity of the observed data set. Unfortunately, to train such models generally requires large computational effort. In this paper we introduce a novel latent variable algorithm which retains the general non-linear capabilities of previous models but which uses a training procedure based on the EM algorithm. We demonstrate the performance of the model on a toy problem and on data from flow diagnostics for a multi-phase oil pipeline.

1 INTRODUCTION

Many conventional approaches to density estimation, such as mixture models, rely on linear superpositions of basis functions to represent the data density. Such approaches are unable to discover structure within the data whereby a relatively small number of 'causes' act in combination to account for apparent complexity in the data. There is therefore considerable interest in *latent variable* models in which the density function is expressed in terms of of hidden variables. These include density networks (MacKay, 1995) and Helmholtz machines (Dayan *et al.*, 1995). Much of this work has been concerned with predicting binary variables. In this paper we focus on continuous data.

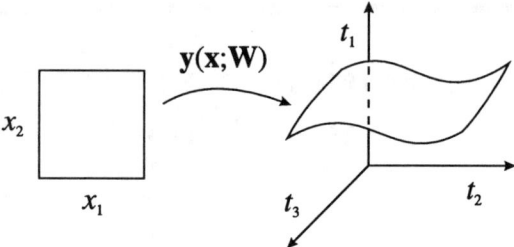

Figure 1: The latent variable density model constructs a distribution function in t-space in terms of a non-linear mapping $\mathbf{y}(\mathbf{x};\mathbf{W})$ from a latent variable x-space.

2 THE LATENT VARIABLE MODEL

Suppose we wish to model the distribution of data which lives in a D-dimensional space $\mathbf{t} = (t_1, \ldots, t_D)$. We first introduce a transformation from the hidden variable space $\mathbf{x} = (x_1, \ldots, x_L)$ to the data space, governed by a non-linear function $\mathbf{y}(\mathbf{x};\mathbf{W})$ which is parametrized by a matrix of weight parameters $\mathbf{W}$. Typically we are interested in the situation in which the dimensionality L of the latent variable space is less than the dimensionality D of the data space, since we wish to capture the fact that the data itself has an intrinsic dimensionality which is less than D. The transformation $\mathbf{y}(\mathbf{x};\mathbf{W})$ then maps the hidden variable space into an L-dimensional non-Euclidean subspace embedded within the data space. This is illustrated schematically for the case of $L = 2$ and $D = 3$ in Figure 1.

If we define a probability distribution $p(\mathbf{x})$ on the latent variable space, this will induce a corresponding distribution $p(\mathbf{y})$ in the data space. We shall refer to $p(\mathbf{x})$ as the prior distribution of $\mathbf{x}$ for reasons which will become clear shortly. Since $L < D$, the distribution in t-space would be confined to a manifold of dimension L and hence would be singular. Since in reality data will only approximately live on a lower-dimensional space, it is appropriate to include a noise model for the $\mathbf{t}$ vector. We therefore define the distribution of $\mathbf{t}$, for given $\mathbf{x}$ and $\mathbf{W}$, given by a spherical Gaussian centred on $\mathbf{y}(\mathbf{x};\mathbf{W})$ having variance β^{-1} so that

$$p(\mathbf{t}|\mathbf{x},\mathbf{W}) = \left(\frac{\beta}{2\pi}\right)^{D/2} \exp\left\{-\frac{\beta}{2}\sum_{k=1}^{D}\{y_k(\mathbf{x};\mathbf{W}) - t_k\}^2\right\}. \tag{1}$$

The distribution in t-space, for a given value of the weight matrix $\mathbf{W}$, is then obtained by integration over the x-distribution

$$p(\mathbf{t}|\mathbf{W}) = \int p(\mathbf{t}|\mathbf{x},\mathbf{W}) p(\mathbf{x}) \, d\mathbf{x}. \tag{2}$$

For a given data set $\mathcal{D} = (\mathbf{t}^1, \ldots, \mathbf{t}^N)$ of N data points, we can determine the weight matrix $\mathbf{W}$ using maximum likelihood. For convenience we introduce an error function given by the negative log likelihood:

$$E(\mathbf{W}) = -\ln \prod_{n=1}^{N} p(\mathbf{t}^n|\mathbf{W}) = -\sum_{n=1}^{N} \ln\left\{\int p(\mathbf{t}^n|\mathbf{x}^n,\mathbf{W}) p(\mathbf{x}^n) \, d\mathbf{x}^n\right\}. \tag{3}$$

EM Optimization of Latent-Variable Density Models

In principle we can now seek the maximum likelihood solution for the weight matrix, once we have specified the prior distribution $p(\mathbf{x})$ and the functional form of the mapping $\mathbf{y}(\mathbf{x}; \mathbf{W})$, by minimizing $E(\mathbf{W})$. However, the integrals over $\mathbf{x}$ occuring in (3), and in the corresponding expression for ∇E, will, in general, be analytically intractable. MacKay (1995) uses Monte Carlo techniques to evaluate these integrals and conjugate gradients to find the weights. This is computationally very intensive, however, since a Monte Carlo integration must be performed every time the conjugate gradient algorithm requests a value for $E(\mathbf{W})$ or $\nabla E(\mathbf{W})$. We now show how, by a suitable choice of model, it is possible to find an EM algorithm for determining the weights.

2.1 EM ALGORITHM

There are three key steps to finding a tractable EM algorithm for evaluating the weights. The first is to use a generalized linear network model for the mapping function $\mathbf{y}(\mathbf{x}; \mathbf{W})$. Thus we write

$$\mathbf{y}(\mathbf{x}; \mathbf{W}) = \mathbf{W}\boldsymbol{\phi}(\mathbf{x}) \tag{4}$$

where the elements of $\boldsymbol{\phi}(\mathbf{x})$ consist of M fixed basis functions $\phi_j(\mathbf{x})$, and $\mathbf{W}$ is a $D \times M$ matrix with elements w_{kj}. Generalized linear networks possess the same universal approximation capabilities as multi-layer adaptive networks. The price which has to be paid, however, is that the number of basis functions must typically grow exponentially with the dimensionality L of the input space. In the present context this is not a serious problem since the dimensionality is governed by the latent variable space and will typically be small. In fact we are particularly interested in visualization applications, for which $L = 2$.

The second important step is to use a simple Monte Carlo approximation for the integrals over $\mathbf{x}$. In general, for a function $Q(\mathbf{x})$ we can write

$$\int Q(\mathbf{x})p(\mathbf{x})\, d\mathbf{x} \simeq \frac{1}{K}\sum_{i=1}^{K} Q(\mathbf{x}^i) \tag{5}$$

where $\mathbf{x}^i$ represents a sample drawn from the distribution $p(\mathbf{x})$. If we apply this to (3) we obtain

$$E(\mathbf{W}) = -\sum_{n=1}^{N}\ln\left\{\frac{1}{K}\sum_{i=1}^{K}p(\mathbf{t}^n|\mathbf{x}^{ni}, \mathbf{W})\right\} \tag{6}$$

The third key step to choose the sample of points $\{\mathbf{x}^{ni}\}$ to be the same for each term in the summation over n. Thus we can drop the index n on $\mathbf{x}^{ni}$ to give

$$E(\mathbf{W}) = -\sum_{n=1}^{N}\ln\left\{\frac{1}{K}\sum_{i=1}^{K}p(\mathbf{t}^n|\mathbf{x}^i, \mathbf{W})\right\} \tag{7}$$

We now note that (7) represents the negative log likelihood under a distribution consisting of a mixture of K kernel functions. This allows us to apply the EM algorithm to find the maximum likelihood solution for the weights. Furthermore, as a consequence of our choice (4) for the non-linear mapping function, it will turn out that the M-step can be performed explicitly, leading to a solution in terms of a set of linear equations. We note that this model corresponds to a *constrained* Gaussian mixture distribution of the kind discussed in Hinton et al. (1992).

We can formulate the EM algorithm for this system as follows. Setting the derivatives of (7) with respect to w_{kj} to zero we obtain

$$\sum_{n=1}^{N}\sum_{i=1}^{K} R_{in}(\mathbf{W})\left\{\sum_{r=1}^{M} w_{kr}\phi_r(\mathbf{x}^i) - t_k^n\right\}\phi_j(\mathbf{x}^i) = 0 \qquad (8)$$

where we have used Bayes' theorem to introduce the posterior probabilities, or *responsibilities*, for the mixture components given by

$$R_{in}(\mathbf{W}) = \frac{p(\mathbf{t}^n|\mathbf{x}^i,\mathbf{W})}{\sum_{i'=1}^{K} p(\mathbf{t}^n|\mathbf{x}^{i'},\mathbf{W})}. \qquad (9)$$

Similarly, maximizing with respect to β we obtain

$$\frac{1}{\beta} = \frac{1}{ND}\sum_{i=1}^{K}\sum_{n=1}^{N} R_{ni}(\mathbf{W})\|\mathbf{y}(\mathbf{x}^n;\mathbf{W}) - \mathbf{t}^n\|^2. \qquad (10)$$

The EM algorithm is obtained by supposing that, at some point in the algorithm, the current weight matrix is given by $\mathbf{W}^{\text{old}}$ and the current value of β is β^{old}. Then we can evaluate the responsibilities using these values for $\mathbf{W}$ and β (the E-step), and then solve (8) for the weights to give $\mathbf{W}^{\text{new}}$ and subsequently solve (10) to give β^{new} (the M-step). The two steps are repeated until a suitable convergence criterion is reached. In practice the algorithm converges after a relatively small number of iterations.

A more formal justification for the EM algorithm can be given by introducing auxiliary variables to label which component is responsible for generating each data point, and then computing the expectation with respect to the distribution of these variables. Application of Jensen's inequality then shows that, at each iteration of the algorithm, the error function will decrease unless it is already at a (local) minimum, as discussed for example in Bishop (1995).

If desired, a regularization term can be added to the error function to control the complexity of the model $\mathbf{y}(\mathbf{x};\mathbf{W})$. From a Bayesian viewpoint, this corresponds to a prior distribution over weights. For a regularizer which is a quadratic function of the weight parameters, this leads to a straightforward modification to the weight update equations. It is convenient to write the condition (8) in matrix notation as

$$(\mathbf{\Phi}^{\mathrm{T}}\mathbf{G}^{\text{old}}\mathbf{\Phi} + \lambda\mathbf{I})(\mathbf{W}^{\text{new}})^{\mathrm{T}} = \mathbf{\Phi}^{\mathrm{T}}\mathbf{T}^{\text{old}} \qquad (11)$$

where we have included a regularization term with coefficient λ, and $\mathbf{I}$ denotes the unit matrix. In (11) $\mathbf{\Phi}$ is a $K \times M$ matrix with elements $\Phi_{ij} = \phi_j(\mathbf{x}^i)$, $\mathbf{T}$ is a $K \times D$ matrix, and $\mathbf{G}$ is a $K \times K$ diagonal matrix, with elements

$$T_{ik} = \sum_{n=1}^{N} R_{in}(\mathbf{W})t_k^n \qquad G_{ii} = \sum_{n=1}^{N} R_{in}(\mathbf{W}). \qquad (12)$$

We can now solve (11) for $\mathbf{W}^{\text{new}}$ using standard linear matrix inversion techniques, based on singular value decomposition to allow for possible ill-conditioning. Note that the matrix $\mathbf{\Phi}$ is constant throughout the algorithm, and so need only be evaluated once at the start.

EM Optimization of Latent-Variable Density Models

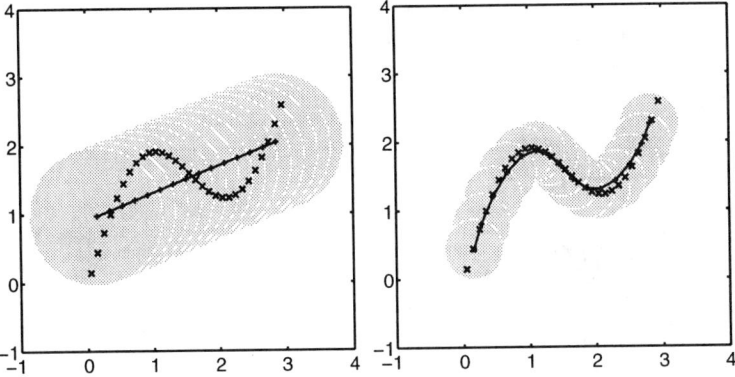

Figure 2: Results from a toy problem involving data ('×') generated from a 1-dimensional curve embedded in 2 dimensions, together with the projected sample points ('+') and their Gaussian noise distributions (filled circles). The initial configuration, determined by principal component analysis, is shown on the left, and an intermediate configuration, obtained after 4 iterations of EM, is shown on the right.

3 RESULTS

We now present results from the application of this algorithm first to a toy problem involving data in three dimensions, and then to a more realistic problem involving 12-dimensional data arising from diagnostic measurements of oil flows along multi-phase pipelines.

For simplicity we choose the distribution $p(\mathbf{x})$ to be uniform over the unit square. The basis functions $\phi_j(\mathbf{x})$ are taken to be spherically symmetric Gaussian functions whose centres are distributed on a uniform grid in $\mathbf{x}$-space, with a common width parameter chosen so that the standard deviation is equal to the separation of neighbouring basis functions. For both problems the weights in the network were initialized by performing principal components analysis on the data and then finding the least-squares solution for the weights which best approximates the linear transformation which maps latent space to target space while generating the correct mean and variance in target space.

As a simple demonstration of this algorithm, we consider data generated from a one-dimensional distribution embedded in two dimensions, as shown in Figure 2.

3.1 OIL FLOW DATA

Our second example arises in the problem of determining the fraction of oil in a multi-phase pipeline carrying a mixture of oil, water and gas (Bishop and James, 1993). Each data point consists of 12 measurements taken from dual-energy gamma densitometers measuring the attenuation of gamma beams passing through the pipe. Synthetically generated data is used which models accurately the attenuation processes in the pipe, as well as the presence of noise (arising from photon statistics). The three phases in the pipe (oil, water and gas) can belong to one of three different geometrical configurations, corresponding to stratified, homogeneous, and annular flows, and the data set consists of 1000 points distributed equally between the 3

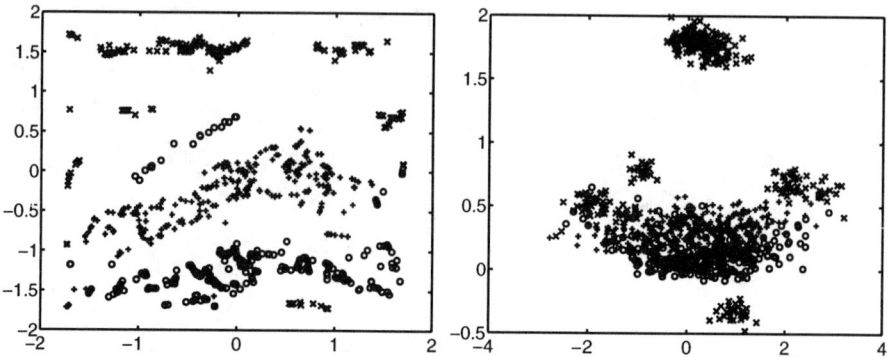

Figure 3: The left plot shows the posterior-mean projection of the oil data in the latent space of the non-linear model. The plot on the right shows the same data set projected onto the first two principal components. In both plots, crosses, circles and plus-signs represent the stratified, annular and homogeneous configurations respectively.

classes. We take the latent variable space to be two-dimensional. This is appropriate for this problem as we know that, locally, the data must have an intrinsic dimensionality of two (neglecting noise on the data) since, for any given geometrical configuration of the three phases, there are two degrees of freedom corresponding to the fractions of oil and water in the pipe (the fraction of gas being redundant since the three fractions must sum to one). It also allows us to use the latent variable model to visualize the data by projection onto x-space.

For the purposes of visualization, we note that a data point t^n induces a posterior distribution $p(x|t^n, W^*)$ in x-space, where W^* denotes the value of the weight matrix for the trained network. This provides considerably more information in the visualization space than many simple techniques (which generally project each data point onto a single point in the visualization space). For example, the posterior distribution may be multi-modal, indicating that there is more than one region of x-space which can claim significant responsibility for generating the data point. However, it is often convenient to project each data point down to a unique point in x-space. This can be done by finding the mean of the posterior distribution, which itself can be evaluated by a simple Monte Carlo integration using quantities already calculated in the evaluation of W^*.

Figure 3 shows the oil data visualized in the latent-variable space in which, for each data point, we have plotted the posterior mean vector. Again the points have been labelled according to their multi-phase configuration. We have compared these results with those from a number of conventional techniques including *factor analysis* and *principal component analysis*. Note that factor analysis is precisely the model which results if a linear mapping is assumed for $y(x; W)$, a Gaussian distribution $p(x)$ is chosen in the latent space, and the noise distribution in data space is taken to be Gaussian with a diagonal covariance matrix. Of these techniques, principal component analysis gave the best class separation (assessed subjectively) and is illustrated in Figure 3. Comparison with the results from the non-linear model clearly shows that the latter gives much better separation of the three classes, as a consequence of the non-linearity permitted by the latent variable mapping.

4 DISCUSSION

There are interesting relationships between the model discussed here and a number of well-known algorithms for unsupervised learning. We have already commented that factor analysis is a special case of this model, involving a linear mapping from latent space to data space. The Kohonen topographic map algorithm (Kohonen, 1995) can be regarded as an approximation to a latent variable density model of the kind outlined here. Finally, there are interesting similarities to a 'soft' version of the 'principal curves' algorithm (Tibshirani, 1992).

The model we have described can readily be extended to deal with the problem of missing data, provided we assume that the missing data is *ignorable* and *missing at random* (Little and Rubin, 1987). This involves maximizing the likelihood function in which the missing values have been integrated out. For the model discussed here, the integrations can be performed analytically, leading to a modified form of the EM algorithm.

Currently we are extending the model to allow for mixed continuous and categorical variables. We are also exploring Bayesian approaches, based on Markov chain Monte Carlo, to replace the maximum likelihood procedure.

Acknowledgements

This work was partially supported by EPSRC grant GR/J75425: *Novel Developments in Learning Theory*. Markus Svensén would like to thank the staff of the SANS group in Stockholm for their hospitality during part of this project.

References

Bishop, C. M. (1995). *Neural Networks for Pattern Recognition*. Oxford University Press.

Bishop, C. M. and G. D. James (1993). Analysis of multiphase flows using dual-energy gamma densitometry and neural networks. *Nuclear Instruments and Methods in Physics Research* **A327**, 580–593.

Dayan, P., G. E. Hinton, R. M. Neal, and R. S. Zemel (1995). The Helmholtz machine. *Neural Computation* **7** (5), 889–904.

Hinton, G. E., C. K. I. Williams, and M. D. Revow (1992). Adaptive elastic models for hand-printed character recognition. In J. E. Moody, S. J. Hanson, and R. P. Lippmann (Eds.), *Advances in Neural Information Processing Systems 4*. Morgan Kauffmann.

Kohonen, T. (1995). *Self-Organizing Maps*. Berlin: Springer-Verlag.

Little, R. J. A. and D. B. Rubin (1987). *Statistical Analysis with Missing Data*. New York: John Wiley.

MacKay, D. J. C. (1995). Bayesian neural networks and density networks. *Nuclear Instruments and Methods in Physics Research, A* **354** (1), 73–80.

Tibshirani, R. (1992). Principal curves revisited. *Statistics and Computing* **2**, 183–190.

Factorial Hidden Markov Models

Zoubin Ghahramani
zoubin@psyche.mit.edu
Department of Computer Science
University of Toronto
Toronto, ON M5S 1A4
Canada

Michael I. Jordan
jordan@psyche.mit.edu
Department of Brain & Cognitive Sciences
Massachusetts Institute of Technology
Cambridge, MA 02139
USA

Abstract

We present a framework for learning in hidden Markov models with distributed state representations. Within this framework, we derive a learning algorithm based on the Expectation–Maximization (EM) procedure for maximum likelihood estimation. Analogous to the standard Baum-Welch update rules, the M-step of our algorithm is exact and can be solved analytically. However, due to the combinatorial nature of the hidden state representation, the exact E-step is intractable. A simple and tractable mean field approximation is derived. Empirical results on a set of problems suggest that both the mean field approximation and Gibbs sampling are viable alternatives to the computationally expensive exact algorithm.

1 Introduction

A problem of fundamental interest to machine learning is time series modeling. Due to the simplicity and efficiency of its parameter estimation algorithm, the hidden Markov model (HMM) has emerged as one of the basic statistical tools for modeling discrete time series, finding widespread application in the areas of speech recognition (Rabiner and Juang, 1986) and computational molecular biology (Baldi et al., 1994). An HMM is essentially a mixture model, encoding information about the history of a time series in the value of a single multinomial variable (the hidden state). This multinomial assumption allows an efficient parameter estimation algorithm to be derived (the Baum-Welch algorithm). However, it also severely limits the representational capacity of HMMs. For example, to represent 30 bits of information about the history of a time sequence, an HMM would need 2^{30} distinct states. On the other hand an HMM with a *distributed* state representation could achieve the same task with 30 binary units (Williams and Hinton, 1991). This paper addresses the problem of deriving efficient learning algorithms for hidden Markov models with distributed state representations.

The need for distributed state representations in HMMs can be motivated in two ways. First, such representations allow the state space to be decomposed into features that naturally decouple the dynamics of a single process generating the time series. Second, distributed state representations simplify the task of modeling time series generated by the interaction of multiple independent processes. For example, a speech signal generated by the superposition of multiple simultaneous speakers can be potentially modeled with such an architecture.

Williams and Hinton (1991) first formulated the problem of learning in HMMs with distributed state representation and proposed a solution based on deterministic Boltzmann learning. The approach presented in this paper is similar to Williams and Hinton's in that it is also based on a statistical mechanical formulation of hidden Markov models. However, our learning algorithm is quite different in that it makes use of the special structure of HMMs with distributed state representation, resulting in a more efficient learning procedure. Anticipating the results in section 2, this learning algorithm both obviates the need for the two-phase procedure of Boltzmann machines, and has an exact M-step. A different approach comes from Saul and Jordan (1995), who derived a set of rules for computing the gradients required for learning in HMMs with distributed state spaces. However, their methods can only be applied to a limited class of architectures.

2 Factorial hidden Markov models

Hidden Markov models are a generalization of mixture models. At any time step, the probability density over the observables defined by an HMM is a mixture of the densities defined by each state in the underlying Markov model. Temporal dependencies are introduced by specifying that the prior probability of the state at time t depends on the state at time $t-1$ through a transition matrix, P (Figure 1a).

Another generalization of mixture models, the cooperative vector quantizer (CVQ; Hinton and Zemel, 1994), provides a natural formalism for distributed state representations in HMMs. Whereas in simple mixture models each data point must be accounted for by a single mixture component, in CVQs each data point is accounted for by the combination of contributions from many mixture components, one from each separate vector quantizer. The total probability density modeled by a CVQ is also a mixture model; however this mixture density is assumed to factorize into a product of densities, each density associated with one of the vector quantizers. Thus, the CVQ is a mixture model with distributed representations for the mixture components.

Factorial hidden Markov models[1] combine the state transition structure of HMMs with the distributed representations of CVQs (Figure 1b). Each of the d underlying Markov models has a discrete state $\mathbf{s}_i^t$ at time t and transition probability matrix P_i. As in the CVQ, the states are mutually exclusive within each vector quantizer and we assume real-valued outputs. The sequence of observable output vectors is generated from a normal distribution with mean given by the weighted combination of the states of the underlying Markov models:

$$\mathbf{y}^t \sim N\left(\sum_{i=1}^d W_i \mathbf{s}_i^t, C\right),$$

where C is a common covariance matrix. The k-valued states $\mathbf{s}_i$ are represented as

---

[1]We refer to HMMs with distributed state as *factorial* HMMs as the features of the distributed state factorize the total state representation.

discrete column vectors with a 1 in one position and 0 everywhere else; the mean of the observable is therefore a combination of columns from each of the W_i matrices.

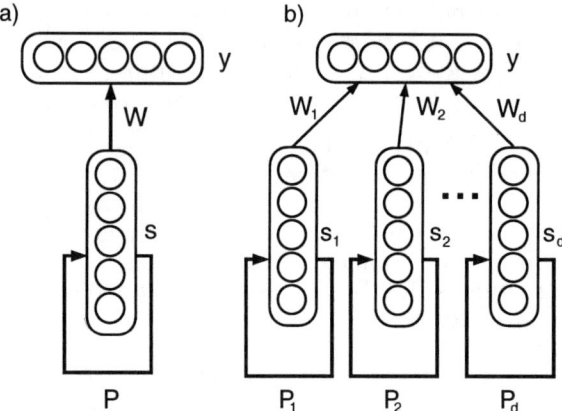

Figure 1. a) Hidden Markov model. b) Factorial hidden Markov model.

We capture the above probability model by defining the energy of a sequence of T states and observations, $\{(\mathbf{s}^t, \mathbf{y}^t)\}_{t=1}^T$, which we abbreviate to $\{\mathbf{s}, \mathbf{y}\}$, as:

$$\mathcal{H}(\{\mathbf{s},\mathbf{y}\}) = \frac{1}{2}\sum_{t=1}^T \left[\mathbf{y}^t - \sum_{i=1}^d W_i \mathbf{s}_i^t\right]' C^{-1}\left[\mathbf{y}^t - \sum_{i=1}^d W_i \mathbf{s}_i^t\right] - \sum_{t=1}^T\sum_{i=1}^d \mathbf{s}_i^{t'} A_i \mathbf{s}_i^{t-1}, \quad (1)$$

where $[A_i]_{jl} = \log P(s_{ij}^t|s_{il}^{t-1})$ such that $\sum_{j=1}^k e^{[A_i]_{jl}} = 1$, and $'$ denotes matrix transpose. Priors for the initial state, $\mathbf{s}^1$, are introduced by setting the second term in (1) to $-\sum_{i=1}^d \mathbf{s}_i^{1'} \log \boldsymbol{\pi}_i$. The probability model is defined from this energy by the Boltzmann distribution

$$P(\{\mathbf{s},\mathbf{y}\}) = \frac{1}{Z}\exp\{-\mathcal{H}(\{\mathbf{s},\mathbf{y}\})\}. \quad (2)$$

Note that like in the CVQ (Ghahramani, 1995), the unclamped partition function

$$Z = \int d\{\mathbf{y}\} \sum_{\{\mathbf{s}\}} \exp\{-\mathcal{H}(\{\mathbf{s},\mathbf{y}\})\},$$

evaluates to a constant, independent of the parameters. This can be shown by first integrating the Gaussian variables, removing all dependency on $\{\mathbf{y}\}$, and then summing over the states using the constraint on $e^{[A_i]_{jl}}$.

The EM algorithm for Factorial HMMs

As in HMMs, the parameters of a factorial HMM can be estimated via the EM (Baum-Welch) algorithm. This procedure iterates between assuming the current parameters to compute probabilities over the hidden states (E-step), and using these probabilities to maximize the expected log likelihood of the parameters (M-step).

Using the likelihood (2), the expected log likelihood of the parameters is

$$Q(\phi^{\text{new}}|\phi) = \langle -\mathcal{H}(\{\mathbf{s},\mathbf{y}\}) - \log Z \rangle_c, \quad (3)$$

Factorial Hidden Markov Models

where $\phi = \{W_i, P_i, C\}_{i=1}^{d}$ denotes the current parameters, and $\langle \cdot \rangle_c$ denotes expectation given the clamped observation sequence and ϕ. Given the observation sequence, the only random variables are the hidden states. Expanding equation (3) and limiting the expectation to these random variables we find that the statistics that need to be computed for the E-step are $\langle s_i^t \rangle_c$, $\langle s_i^t s_j^{t'} \rangle_c$, and $\langle s_i^t s_i^{t-1'} \rangle_c$. Note that in standard HMM notation (Rabiner and Juang, 1986), $\langle s_i^t \rangle_c$ corresponds to γ_t and $\langle s_i^t s_i^{t-1'} \rangle_c$ corresponds to ξ_t, whereas $\langle s_i^t s_j^{t'} \rangle_c$ has no analogue when there is only a single underlying Markov model. The M-step uses these expectations to maximize Q with respect to the parameters.

The constant partition function allowed us to drop the second term in (3). Therefore, unlike the Boltzmann machine, the expected log likelihood does not depend on statistics collected in an unclamped phase of learning, resulting in much faster learning than the traditional Boltzmann machine (Neal, 1992).

M-step

Setting the derivatives of Q with respect to the output weights to zero, we obtain a linear system of equations for W:

$$W^{\text{new}} = \left[\sum_{N,t} \langle ss' \rangle_c \right]^{\dagger} \left[\sum_{N,t} \langle s \rangle_c y' \right],$$

where s and W are the vector and matrix of concatenated s_i and W_i, respectively, $\sum_N$ denotes summation over a data set of N sequences, and $\dagger$ is the Moore-Penrose pseudo-inverse. To estimate the log transition probabilities we solve $\partial Q / \partial [A_i]_{jl} = 0$ subject to the constraint $\sum_j e^{[A_i]_{jl}} = 1$, obtaining

$$[A_i]_{jl}^{\text{new}} = \log \left(\frac{\sum_{N,t} \langle s_{ij}^t s_{il}^{t-1} \rangle_c}{\sum_{N,t,j} \langle s_{ij}^t s_{il}^{t-1} \rangle_c} \right). \tag{4}$$

The covariance matrix can be similarly estimated:

$$C^{\text{new}} = \sum_{N,t} yy' - \sum_{N,t} y \langle s \rangle_c' \langle ss' \rangle_c^{\dagger} \langle s \rangle_c y'.$$

The M-step equations can therefore be solved analytically; furthermore, for a single underlying Markov chain, they reduce to the traditional Baum-Welch re-estimation equations.

E-step

Unfortunately, as in the simpler CVQ, the exact E-step for factorial HMMs is computationally intractable. For example, the expectation of the jth unit in vector i at time step t, given $\{y\}$, is:

$$\langle s_{ij}^t \rangle_c = P(s_{ij}^t = 1 | \{y\}, \phi)$$

$$= \sum_{j_1, \ldots, j_h \neq i, \ldots, j_d}^{k} P(s_{1j_1}^t = 1, \ldots, s_{ij}^t = 1, \ldots, s_{d,j_d}^t = 1 | \{y\}, \phi)$$

Although the Markov property can be used to obtain a forward-backward–like factorization of this expectation across time steps, the sum over all possible configurations of the other hidden units *within* each time step is unavoidable. For a data set of N sequences of length T, the full E-step calculated through the forward-backward procedure has time complexity $\mathcal{O}(NTk^{2d})$. Although more careful bookkeeping can reduce the complexity to $\mathcal{O}(NTdk^{d+1})$, the exponential time cannot be avoided. This intractability of the exact E-step is due inherently to the cooperative nature of the model—the setting of one vector only determines the mean of the observable if all the other vectors are fixed.

Rather than summing over all possible hidden state patterns to compute the exact expectations, a natural approach is to approximate them through a Monte Carlo method such as Gibbs sampling. The procedure starts with a clamped observable sequence $\{\mathbf{y}\}$ and a random setting of the hidden states $\{\mathbf{s}_j^t\}$. At each time step, each state vector is updated stochastically according to its probability distribution conditioned on the setting of all the other state vectors: $\mathbf{s}_i^t \sim P(\mathbf{s}_i^t | \{\mathbf{y}\}, \{\mathbf{s}_j^\tau : j \neq i \text{ or } \tau \neq t\}, \phi)$. These conditional distributions are straightforward to compute and a full pass of Gibbs sampling requires $\mathcal{O}(NTkd)$ operations. The first and second-order statistics needed to estimate $\langle \mathbf{s}_i^t \rangle_c$, $\langle \mathbf{s}_i^t \mathbf{s}_j^{t'} \rangle_c$ and $\langle \mathbf{s}_i^t \mathbf{s}_i^{t-1'} \rangle_c$ are collected using the s_{ij}^t's visited and the probabilities estimated during this sampling process.

Mean field approximation

A different approach to computing the expectations in an intractable system is given by mean field theory. A mean field approximation for factorial HMMs can be obtained by defining the energy function

$$\tilde{\mathcal{H}}(\{\mathbf{s},\mathbf{y}\}) = \frac{1}{2}\sum_t [\mathbf{y}^t - \boldsymbol{\mu}^t]' C^{-1} [\mathbf{y}^t - \boldsymbol{\mu}^t] - \sum_{t,i} \mathbf{s}_i^{t'} \log \mathbf{m}_i^t.$$

which results in a completely factorized approximation to probability density (2):

$$\tilde{P}(\{\mathbf{s},\mathbf{y}\}) \propto \prod_t \exp\{-\frac{1}{2}[\mathbf{y}^t - \boldsymbol{\mu}^t]' C^{-1} [\mathbf{y}^t - \boldsymbol{\mu}^t]\} \prod_{t,i,j} (m_{ij}^t)^{s_{ij}^t} \qquad (5)$$

In this approximation, the observables are independently Gaussian distributed with mean $\boldsymbol{\mu}^t$ and each hidden state vector is multinomially distributed with mean $\mathbf{m}_i^t$. This approximation is made as tight as possible by chosing the mean field parameters $\boldsymbol{\mu}^t$ and $\mathbf{m}_i^t$ that minimize the Kullback-Liebler divergence

$$\mathcal{KL}(\tilde{P}\|P) \equiv \langle \log P \rangle_{\tilde{P}} - \langle \log \tilde{P} \rangle_{\tilde{P}}$$

where $\langle \cdot \rangle_{\tilde{P}}$ denotes expectation over the mean field distribution (5). With the observables clamped, $\boldsymbol{\mu}^t$ can be set equal to the observable $\mathbf{y}^t$. Minimizing $\mathcal{KL}(\tilde{P}\|P)$ with respect to the mean field parameters for the states results in a fixed-point equation which can be iterated until convergence:

$$\mathbf{m}_i^{t\ \text{new}} = \sigma\{W_i'C^{-1}[\mathbf{y}^t - \hat{\mathbf{y}}^t] + W_i'C^{-1}W_i\mathbf{m}_i^t - \frac{1}{2}\text{diag}\{W_i'C^{-1}W_i\} - 1 \quad (6)$$
$$+ A_i \mathbf{m}_i^{t-1} + A_i' \mathbf{m}_i^{t+1}\}$$

where $\hat{\mathbf{y}}^t \equiv \sum_i W_i \mathbf{m}_i^t$ and $\sigma\{\cdot\}$ is the softmax exponential, normalized over each hidden state vector. The first term is the projection of the error in the observable onto the weights of state vector i—the more a hidden unit can reduce this error, the larger its mean field parameter. The next three terms arise from the fact that $\langle s_{ij}^2 \rangle_{\tilde{P}}$ is equal to m_{ij} and not m_{ij}^2. The last two terms introduce dependencies forward and backward in time. Each state vector is asynchronously updated using (6), at a time cost of $\mathcal{O}(NTkd)$ per iteration. Convergence is diagnosed by monitoring the $\mathcal{KL}$ divergence in the mean field distribution between successive time steps; in practice convergence is very rapid (about 2 to 10 iterations of (6)).

Table 1: Comparison of factorial HMM on four problems of varying size

d	k	Alg	#	Train	Test	Cycles	Time/Cycle
3	2	HMM	5	649 ± 8	358 ± 81	33 ± 19	1.1 s
		Exact		877 ± 0	768 ± 0	22 ± 6	3.0 s
		Gibbs		710 ± 152	627 ± 129	28 ± 11	6.0 s
		MF		755 ± 168	670 ± 137	32 ± 22	1.2 s
3	3	HMM	5	670 ± 26	-782 ± 128	23 ± 10	3.6 s
		Exact		568 ± 164	276 ± 62	35 ± 12	5.2 s
		Gibbs		564 ± 160	305 ± 51	45 ± 16	9.2 s
		MF		495 ± 83	326 ± 62	38 ± 22	1.6 s
5	2	HMM	5	588 ± 37	-2634 ± 566	18 ± 1	5.2 s
		Exact		223 ± 76	159 ± 80	31 ± 17	6.9 s
		Gibbs		123 ± 103	73 ± 95	40 ± 5	12.7 s
		MF		292 ± 101	237 ± 103	54 ± 29	2.2 s
5	3	HMM	3	1671,1678,1690	$-\infty,-\infty,-\infty$	14,14,12	90.0 s
		Exact		-55,-354,-295	-123,-378,-402	90,100,100	51.0 s
		Gibbs		-123,-160,-194	-202,-237,-307	100,73,100	14.2 s
		MF		-287,-286,-296	-364,-370,-365	100,100,100	4.7 s

Table 1. Data was generated from a factorial HMM with d underlying Markov models of k states each. The training set was 10 sequences of length 20 where the observable was a 4-dimensional vector; the test set was 20 such sequences. HMM indicates a hidden Markov model with k^d states; the other algorithms are factorial HMMs with d underlying k-state models. Gibbs sampling used 10 samples of each state. The algorithms were run until convergence, as monitored by relative change in the likelihood, or a maximum of 100 cycles. The # column indicates number of runs. The Train and Test columns show the log likelihood ± one standard deviation on the two data sets. The last column indicates approximate time per cycle on a Silicon Graphics R4400 processor running Matlab.

3 Empirical Results

We compared three EM algorithms for learning in factorial HMMs—using Gibbs sampling, mean field approximation, and the exact (exponential) E step—on the basis of performance and speed on randomly generated problems. Problems were generated from a factorial HMM structure, the parameters of which were sampled from a uniform $[0, 1]$ distribution, and appropriately normalized to satisfy the sum-to-one constraints of the transition matrices and priors. Also included in the comparison was a traditional HMM with as many states (k^d) as the factorial HMM.

Table 1 summarizes the results. Even for moderately large state spaces ($d \geq 3$ and $k \geq 3$) the standard HMM with k^d states suffers from severe overfitting. Furthermore, both the standard HMM and the exact E-step factorial HMM are extremely slow on the larger problems. The Gibbs sampling and mean field approximations offer roughly comparable performance at a great increase in speed.

4 Discussion

The basic contribution of this paper is a learning algorithm for hidden Markov models with distributed state representations. The standard Baum-Welch procedure is intractable for such architectures as the size of the state space generated from the cross product of d k-valued features is $\mathcal{O}(k^d)$, and the time complexity of Baum-Welch is quadratic in this size. More importantly, unless special constraints are applied to this cross-product HMM architecture, the number of parameters also grows as $\mathcal{O}(k^{2d})$, which can result in severe overfitting.

The architecture for factorial HMMs presented in this paper did not include any coupling between the underlying Markov chains. It is possible to extend the algorithm presented to architectures which incorporate such couplings. However, these couplings must be introduced with caution as they may result either in an exponential growth in parameters or in a loss of the constant partition function property.

The learning algorithm derived in this paper assumed real-valued observables. The algorithm can also be derived for HMMs with discrete observables, an architecture closely related to sigmoid belief networks (Neal, 1992). However, the nonlinearities induced by discrete observables make both the E-step and M-step of the algorithm more difficult.

In conclusion, we have presented Gibbs sampling and mean field learning algorithms for factorial hidden Markov models. Such models incorporate the time series modeling capabilities of hidden Markov models and the advantages of distributed representations for the state space. Future work will concentrate on a more efficient mean field approximation in which the forward-backward algorithm is used to compute the E-step exactly within each Markov chain, and mean field theory is used to handle interactions between chains (Saul and Jordan, 1996).

Acknowledgements

This project was supported in part by a grant from the McDonnell-Pew Foundation, by a grant from ATR Human Information Processing Research Laboratories, by a grant from Siemens Corporation, and by grant N00014-94-1-0777 from the Office of Naval Research.

References

Baldi, P., Chauvin, Y., Hunkapiller, T., and McClure, M. (1994). Hidden Markov models of biological primary sequence information. *Proc. Nat. Acad. Sci. (USA)*, 91(3):1059–1063.

Ghahramani, Z. (1995). Factorial learning and the *EM* algorithm. In Tesauro, G., Touretzky, D., and Leen, T., editors, *Advances in Neural Information Processing Systems 7*. MIT Press, Cambridge, MA.

Hinton, G. and Zemel, R. (1994). Autoencoders, minimum description length, and Helmholtz free energy. In Cowan, J., Tesauro, G., and Alspector, J., editors, *Advances in Neural Information Processing Systems 6*. Morgan Kaufmanm Publishers, San Francisco, CA.

Neal, R. (1992). Connectionist learning of belief networks. *Artificial Intelligence*, 56:71–113.

Rabiner, L. and Juang, B. (1986). An Introduction to hidden Markov models. *IEEE Acoustics, Speech & Signal Processing Magazine*, 3:4–16.

Saul, L. and Jordan, M. (1995). Boltzmann chains and hidden Markov models. In Tesauro, G., Touretzky, D., and Leen, T., editors, *Advances in Neural Information Processing Systems 7*. MIT Press, Cambridge, MA.

Saul, L. and Jordan, M. (1996). Exploiting tractable substructures in Intractable networks. In Touretzky, D., Mozer, M., and Hasselmo, M., editors, *Advances in Neural Information Processing Systems 8*. MIT Press.

Williams, C. and Hinton, G. (1991). Mean field networks that learn to discriminate temporally distorted strings. In Touretzky, D., Elman, J., Sejnowski, T., and Hinton, G., editors, *Connectionist Models: Proceedings of the 1990 Summer School*, pages 18–22. Morgan Kaufmann Publishers, Man Mateo, CA.

Boosting Decision Trees

Harris Drucker
AT&T Bell Laboratories
Holmdel, New Jersey 07733

Corinna Cortes
AT&T Bell Laboratories
Murray Hill, New Jersey 07974

Abstract

A new boosting algorithm of Freund and Schapire is used to improve the performance of decision trees which are constructed using the information ratio criterion of Quinlan's C4.5 algorithm. This boosting algorithm iteratively constructs a series of decision trees, each decision tree being trained and pruned on examples that have been filtered by previously trained trees. Examples that have been incorrectly classified by the previous trees in the ensemble are resampled with higher probability to give a new probability distribution for the next tree in the ensemble to train on. Results from optical character recognition (OCR), and knowledge discovery and data mining problems show that in comparison to single trees, or to trees trained independently, or to trees trained on subsets of the feature space, the boosting ensemble is much better.

1 INTRODUCTION

A new boosting algorithm termed **AdaBoost** by their inventors (Freund and Schapire, 1995) has advantages over the original boosting algorithm (Schapire, 1990) and a second version (Freund, 1990). The implications of a boosting algorithm is that one can take a series of learning machines (termed weak learners) each having a poor error rate (but no worse than $.5-\gamma$, where γ is some small positive number) and combine them to give an ensemble that has very good performance (termed a strong learner). The first practical implementation of boosting was in OCR (Drucker, 1993, 1994) using neural networks as the weak learners. In a series of comparisons (Bottou, 1994) boosting was shown to be superior to other techniques on a large OCR problem.

The general configuration of **AdaBoost** is shown in Figure 1. Each box is a decision tree built using Quinlans C4.5 algorithm (Quinlan, 1993) The key idea is that each weak learner is trained sequentially. The first weak learner is trained on a set of patterns picked randomly (with replacement) from a training set. After training and pruning, the training patterns are passed through this first decision tree. In the two class case the hypothesis h_1 is either class 0 or class 1. Some of the patterns will be in error. The training set for the

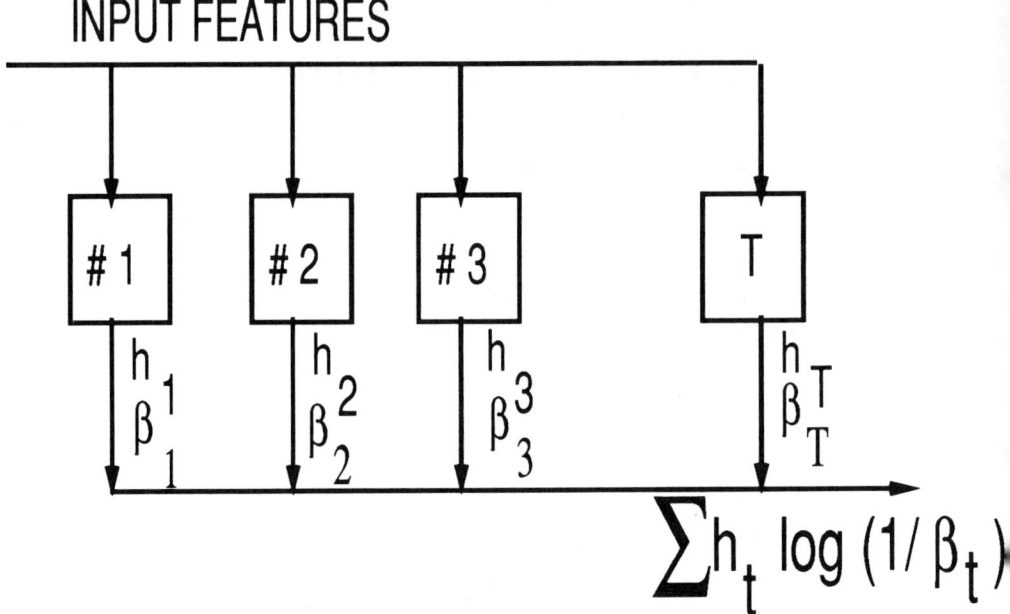

FIGURE 1. BOOSTING ENSEMBLE

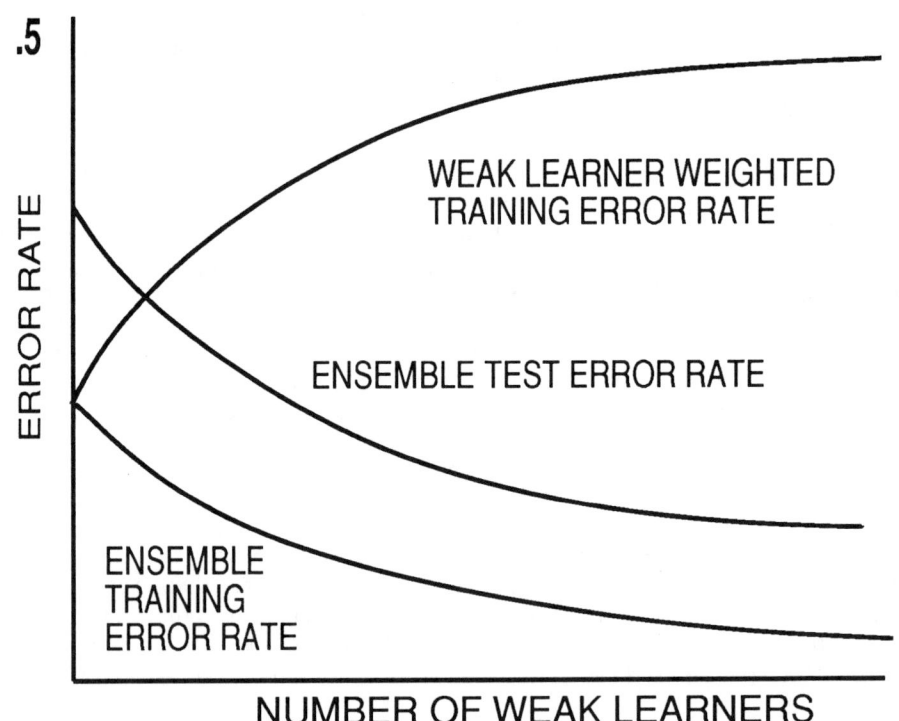

FIGURE 2. INDIVIDUAL WEAK LEARNER ERROR RATE AND ENSEMBLE TRAINING AND TEST ERROR RATES

Boosting Decision Trees

second weak learner will consist of patterns picked from the training set with higher probability assigned to those patterns the first weak learner classifies incorrectly. Since patterns are picked with replacement, difficult patterns are more likely to occur multiple times in the training set. Thus as we proceed to build each member of the ensemble, patterns which are more difficult to classify correctly appear more and more likely. The training error rate of an *individual* weak learner tends to grow as we increase the number of weak learners because each weak learner is asked to classify progressively more difficult patterns. However the boosting algorithm shows us that the *ensemble* training and test error rate decrease as we increase the number of weak learners. The ensemble output is determined by weighting the hypotheses with the log of $(1/\beta_i)$ where β is proportional to the weak learner error rate. If the weak learner has good error rate performance, it will contribute significantly to the output, because then $1/\beta$ will be large.

Figure 2 shows the general shape of the curves we would expect. Say we have constructed N weak learners where N is a large number (right hand side of the graph). The N'th weak learner (top curve) will have a training error rate that approaches .5 because it is trained on difficult patterns and can do only sightly better than guessing. The bottom two curves show the test and training error rates of the ensemble using **all** N weak learners. which decrease as weak learners are added to the ensemble.

2 BOOSTING

Boosting arises from the PAC (probably approximately correct) learning model which has as one of its primary interests the efficiency of learning. Schapire was the first one to show that a series of weak learners could be converted to a strong learner. The detailed algorithm is show in Figure 3. Let us call the set of N_1 distinct examples the **original** training set. We distinguish the original training set from what we will call the **filtered** training set which consists of N_1 examples picked with replacement from the original training set. Basically each of N_1 original examples is assigned a weight which is proportional to the probability that the example will appear in the filtered training set (these weights have nothing to do with the weights usually associated with neural networks). Initially all examples are assigned a weight of unity so that all the examples are equally likely to show up in the initial set of training examples. However, the weights are altered at each state of boosting (Step 5 of Figure 3) and if the weights are high we may have multiple copies of some of the original examples appearing in the filtered training set. In step three of this algorithm, we calculate what is called the weighted training error and this is the error rate over all the **original** N_1 training examples weighted by their current respective probabilities. The algorithms terminates if this error rate is .5 (no better than guessing) or zero (then the weights of step 5 do not change). Although not called for in the original C4.5 algorithm, we also have an original set of pruning examples which also are assigned weights to form a filtered pruning set and used to prune the classification trees constructed using the filtered training set. It is known (Mingers, 1989a) that reducing the size of the tree (pruning) improves generalization.

3 DECISION TREES

For our implementation of decision trees, we have a set of features (attributes) that specifies an example along with their classification (we discuss the two-class problem primarily). We pick a feature that based on some criterion, best splits the examples into two subsets. Each of these two subsets will usually not contain examples of just one class, so we recursively divide the subsets until the final subsets each contain examples of just one class. Thus, each internal node specifies a feature and a value for that feature that determines whether one should take the left or right branch emanating from that node. At terminal nodes, we make the final decision, class 0 or 1. Thus, in decision trees one starts at a root node and progressively traverses the tree from the root node to one of the

Inputs: N_1 training patterns, N_2 pruning patterns, N_3 test patterns

Initialize the weight vector of the N_1 training patterns: $w_i^1 = 1$ for $i=1,...,N_1$
Initialize the weight vector of the N_2 pruning patterns: $s_i^1 = 1$ for $i=1,...,N_2$
Initialize the number of trees in the ensemble to $t = 1$

Do Until weighted training error rate is 0 or .5 or ensemble test error rate asymptotes

1. For the training set and pruning sets

$$p^t = \frac{w^t}{\sum_{i=1}^{N_1} w_i^t} \qquad r^t = \frac{s^t}{\sum_{i=1}^{N_2} s_i^t}$$

Pick N_1 samples from original training set with probability p(i) to form filtered training set.
Pick N_2 samples from original pruning set with probability r(i) to form filtered pruning set.

2. Train tree t using filtered training set and prune using filtered pruning set

3. Pass the N_1 original training examples through the pruned tree whose output $h_t(i)$ is either 0 or 1 and classification c(i) is either 0 or 1. Calculate the weighted training error rate: $\varepsilon_t = \sum_{i=1}^{N_1} p_i^t | h_t(i) - c(i) |$

4. Set $\beta_t = \dfrac{\varepsilon_t}{1 - \varepsilon_t}$

5. Set the new training weight vector to be

$$w_i^{t+1} = w_i^t \{\beta_t ** (1-|h_t(i) - c(i)|)\} \qquad i = 1,...,N_1$$

Pass the N_2 original pruning patterns through the pruned tree and calculate new pruning weight vector:

$$s_i^{t+1} = s_i^t \{\beta_t ** (1-|h_t(i) - c(i)|)\} \qquad i = 1,...,N_2$$

6. For each tree t in the ensemble (total trees T), pass the j'th test pattern through and obtain $h_t(j)$ for each t. The final hypothesis $h_f(j)$ for this pattern:

$$h_f(j) = \begin{cases} 1, & \sum_{t=1}^{T} (\log \frac{1}{\beta_t}) h_t(j) \geq \frac{1}{2} \sum_{t=1}^{T} \log \frac{1}{\beta_t} \\ 0, & \text{otherwise} \end{cases}$$

Do for each test pattern and calculate the ensemble test error rate:

7. $t = t + 1$

End_Until

Figure 3: Boosting Algorithm

terminal nodes where a final decision is made. CART (Breiman, 1984) and C4.5 (Quinlan 1993) are perhaps the two most popular tree building algorithms. Here, C4.5 is used. The attraction of trees is that the simplest decision tree can be respecified as a series of rules and for certain potential users this is more appealing than a nonlinear "black box" such as a neural network. That is not to say that one can not design trees where the decision at each node depends on some nonlinear combination of features, but this will not be our implementation.

Other attractions of decision trees are speed of learning and evaluation. Whether trees are more accurate than other techniques depends on the application domain and the effectiveness of the particular implementation. In OCR, our neural networks are more accurate than trees but the penalty is in training and evaluation times. In other applications which we will discuss later a boosting network of trees is more accurate. As an initial example of the power of boosting, we will use trees for OCR of hand written digits. The main rationale for using OCR applications to evaluate **AdaBoost** is that we have experience in the use of a competing technology (neural networks) and we have from the National Institute of Standards and Technology (NIST) a large database of 120,000 digits, large enough so we can run multiple experiments. However, we will not claim that trees for OCR have the best error performance.

Once the tree is constructed, it is pruned to give hopefully better generalization performance than if the original tree was used. C4.5 uses the original training set for what is called "pessimistic pruning" justified by the fact that there may not be enough extra examples to form a set of pruning examples. However, we prefer to use an independent set of examples to prune this tree. In our case, we have (for each tree in the ensemble) an independent filtered pruning set of examples whose statistical distribution is similar to that of the filtered training set. Since the filtering imposed by the previous members of the ensemble can severely distort the original training distribution, we trust this technique more than pessimistic pruning. In pruning (Mingers, 1989), we pass the pruning set though the tree recording at each node (including non-terminal nodes) how many errors there would be if the tree was terminated there. Then, for each node (except for terminal nodes), we examine the subtree of that node. We then calculate the number of errors that would be obtained if that node would be made a terminal node and compare it to the number of errors at the terminal nodes of that subtree. If the number of errors at the root node of this subtree is less than or equal to that of the subtree, we replace the subtree with that node and make it a terminal node. Pruning tends to substantially reduce the size of the tree, even if the error rates are not substantially decreased.

4 EXPERIMENTS

In order to run enough experiments to claim statistical validity we needed a large supply of data and few enough features that the information ratio could be determined in a reasonable amount of time. Thus we used the 120,000 examples in a NIST database of digits subsampled to give us a 10x10 pixel array (100 features) where the features are continuous values. We do not claim that OCR is best done by using classification trees and certainly not in 100-dimensional space. We used 10,000 training examples, 2000 pruning examples and 2000 test examples for a total of 14,000 examples.

We also wanted to test our techniques on a wide range of problems, from easy to hard. Therefore, to make the problem reasonably difficult, we assigned class 0 to all digits from 0 to 4 (inclusive) and assigned class 1 to the remainder of the digits. To vary the difficulty of the problem, we prefiltered the data to form data sets of difficulty f. Think of f as the fraction of hard examples generated by passing the 120,000 examples through a poorly trained neural network and accepting the misclassified examples with probability f and the correctly classified examples with probability $1-f$. Thus $f = .9$ means that the training set consists of 10,000 examples that if passed through this neural network would have an error rate of .9. Table I compares the boosting performance with single tree performance. Also indicated is the average number of trees required to reach that performance. Overtraining never seems to be a problem for these weak learners, that is, as one increases the number of trees, the ensemble test error rate asymptotes and never increases.

Table 1. For fraction f of difficult examples, the error rate for a single tree and a boosting ensemble and the number of trees required to reach the error rate for that ensemble.

f	single tree	boosting trees	number of trees
.1	12%	3.5%	25
.3	13	4.5	28
.5	16	7.1	31
.7	21	7.7	60
.9	23	8.1	72

We wanted to compare the boosting ensemble to other techniques for constructing ensembles using 14,000 examples, holding out 2000 for testing. The problem with decision trees is that invariably, even if the training data is different (but drawn from the same distribution), the features chosen for the first few nodes are usually the same (at least for the OCR data). Thus, different decision surfaces are not created. In order to create different decision regions for each tree, we can force each decision tree to consider another attribute as the root node, perhaps choosing that attribute from the first few attributes with largest information ratio. This is similar to what Kwok and Carter (1990) have suggested but we have many more trees and their interactive approach did not look feasible here. Another technique suggested by T.K. Ho (1992) is to construct independent trees on the same 10,000 examples but randomly striking out the use of fifty of the 100 possible features. Thus, for each tree, we randomly pick 50 features to construct the tree. When we use up to ten trees, the results using Ho's technique gives similar results to that of boosting but the asymptotic performance is far better for boosting. After we had performed these experiments, we learned of a technique termed "bagging" (Breiman, 1994) and we have yet to resolve the issue of whether bagging or boosting is better.

5 CONCLUSIONS

Based on preliminary evidence, it appears that for these applications a new boosting algorithm using trees as weak learners gives far superior performance to single trees and any other technique for constructing ensemble of trees. For boosting to work on any problem, one must find a weak learner that gives an error rate of less than 0.5 on the filtered training set. An important aspect of the building process is to prune based on a separate pruning set rather than pruning based on a training set. We have also tried this technique on knowledge discovery and data mining problems and the results are better than single neural networks.

References

L. Bottou, C. Cortes, J.S. Denker, H. Drucker, I. Guyon, L.D. Jackel, Y. LeCun, U.A. Muller, E. Sackinger, P. Simard, and V. Vapnik (1994), "Comparison of Classifier Methods: A Case Study in Handwritten Digit Recognition", 1994 International Conference on Pattern Recognition, Jerusalem.

L. Breiman, J. Friedman, R.A. Olshen, and C.J. Stone (1984), *Classification and Regression Trees*, Chapman and Hall.

L. Breiman, "Bagging Predictors", Technical Report No. 421, Department of Statistics University of California, Berkeley, California 94720, September 1994.

H. Drucker (1994), C. Cortes, LD Jackel, Y. LeCun "Boosting and Other Ensemble Methods", *Neural Computation*, vol 6, no. 6, pp. 1287-1299.

H. Drucker, R.E. Schapire, and P. Simard (1993) "Boosting Performance in Neural Networks", *International Journal of Pattern Recognition and Artificial Intelligence*, Vol 7. No 4, pp. 705-719.

Y. Freund (1990), "Boosting a Weak Learning Algorithm by Majority", *Proceedings of the Third Workshop on Computational Learning Theory*, Morgan-Kaufmann, 202-216.

Y. Freund and R.E. Schapire (1995), "A decision-theoretic generalization of on-line learning and an application to boosting", *Proceeding of the Second European Conference on Computational Learning*.

T.K. Ho (1992), *A theory of Multiple Classifier Systems and Its Applications to Visual Word Recognition*, Doctoral Dissertation, Department of Computer Science, SUNY at Buffalo.

S.W. Kwok and C. Carter (1990), "Multiple Decision Trees", *Uncertainty in Artificial Intelligence 4*, R.D. Shachter, T.S. Levitt, L.N. Kanal, J.F Lemmer (eds) Elsevier Science Publishers.

J.R. Quinlan (1993), *C4.5: Programs For Machine Learning*, Morgan Kauffman.

J. Mingers (1989), "An Empirical Comparison of Pruning Methods for Decision Tree Induction", *Machine Learning*, 4:227-243.

R.E. Schapire (1990), The strength of weak learnability, *Machine Learning*, 5(2):197-227.

Exploiting Tractable Substructures in Intractable Networks

Lawrence K. Saul and Michael I. Jordan
{lksaul,jordan}@psyche.mit.edu
Center for Biological and Computational Learning
Massachusetts Institute of Technology
79 Amherst Street, E10-243
Cambridge, MA 02139

Abstract

We develop a refined mean field approximation for inference and learning in probabilistic neural networks. Our mean field theory, unlike most, does not assume that the units behave as independent degrees of freedom; instead, it exploits in a principled way the existence of large substructures that are computationally tractable. To illustrate the advantages of this framework, we show how to incorporate weak higher order interactions into a first-order hidden Markov model, treating the corrections (but not the first order structure) within mean field theory.

1 INTRODUCTION

Learning the parameters in a probabilistic neural network may be viewed as a problem in statistical estimation. In networks with sparse connectivity (e.g. trees and chains), there exist efficient algorithms for the exact probabilistic calculations that support inference and learning. In general, however, these calculations are intractable, and approximations are required.

Mean field theory provides a framework for approximation in probabilistic neural networks (Peterson & Anderson, 1987). Most applications of mean field theory, however, have made a rather drastic probabilistic assumption—namely, that the units in the network behave as independent degrees of freedom. In this paper we show how to go beyond this assumption. We describe a self-consistent approximation in which tractable substructures are handled by exact computations and only the remaining, intractable parts of the network are handled within mean field theory. For simplicity we focus on networks with binary units; the extension to discrete-valued (Potts) units is straightforward.

We apply these ideas to hidden Markov modeling (Rabiner & Juang, 1991). The first order probabilistic structure of hidden Markov models (HMMs) leads to networks with chained architectures for which efficient, exact algorithms are available. More elaborate networks are obtained by introducing couplings between multiple HMMs (Williams & Hinton, 1990) and/or long-range couplings within a single HMM (Stolorz, 1994). Both sorts of extensions have interesting applications; in speech, for example, multiple HMMs can provide a distributed representation of the articulatory state, while long-range couplings can model the effects of coarticulation. In general, however, such extensions lead to networks for which exact probabilistic calculations are not feasible. One would like to develop a mean field approximation for these networks that exploits the tractability of first-order HMMs. This is possible within the more sophisticated mean field theory described here.

2 MEAN FIELD THEORY

We briefly review the basic methodology of mean field theory for networks of binary (± 1) stochastic units (Parisi, 1988). For each configuration $\{S\} = \{S_1, S_2, \ldots, S_N\}$, we define an energy $E\{S\}$ and a probability $P\{S\}$ via the Boltzmann distribution:

$$P\{S\} = \frac{e^{-\beta E\{S\}}}{Z}, \tag{1}$$

where β is the inverse temperature and Z is the partition function. When it is intractable to compute averages over $P\{S\}$, we are motivated to look for an approximating distribution $Q\{S\}$. Mean field theory posits a particular parametrized form for $Q\{S\}$, then chooses parameters to minimize the Kullback-Liebler (KL) divergence:

$$\mathrm{KL}(Q\|P) = \sum_{\{S\}} Q\{S\} \ln\left[\frac{Q\{S\}}{P\{S\}}\right]. \tag{2}$$

Why are mean field approximations valuable for learning? Suppose that $P\{S\}$ represents the posterior distribution over hidden variables, as in the E-step of an EM algorithm (Dempster, Laird, & Rubin, 1977). Then we obtain a mean field approximation to this E-step by replacing the statistics of $P\{S\}$ (which may be quite difficult to compute) with those of $Q\{S\}$ (which may be much simpler). If, in addition, Z represents the likelihood of observed data (as is the case for the example of section 3), then the mean field approximation yields a lower bound on the log-likelihood. This can be seen by noting that for any approximating distribution $Q\{S\}$, we can form the lower bound:

$$\ln Z = \ln \sum_{\{S\}} e^{-\beta E\{S\}} \tag{3}$$

$$= \ln \sum_{\{S\}} Q\{S\} \cdot \left[\frac{e^{-\beta E\{S\}}}{Q\{S\}}\right] \tag{4}$$

$$\geq \sum_{\{S\}} Q\{S\} [-\beta E\{S\} - \ln Q\{S\}], \tag{5}$$

where the last line follows from Jensen's inequality. The difference between the left and right-hand side of eq. (5) is exactly $\mathrm{KL}(Q\|P)$; thus the better the approximation to $P\{S\}$, the tighter the bound on $\ln Z$. Once a lower bound is available, a learning procedure can maximize the lower bound. This is useful when the true likelihood itself cannot be efficiently computed.

2.1 Complete Factorizability

The simplest mean field theory involves assuming marginal independence for the units S_i. Consider, for example, a quadratic energy function

$$-\beta E\{S\} = \sum_{i<j} J_{ij} S_i S_j + \sum_i h_i S_i, \qquad (6)$$

and the factorized approximation:

$$Q\{S\} = \prod_i \left(\frac{1 + m_i S_i}{2}\right). \qquad (7)$$

The expectations under this mean field approximation are $\langle S_i \rangle = m_i$ and $\langle S_i S_j \rangle = m_i m_j$ for $i \neq j$. The best approximation of this form is found by minimizing the KL-divergence,

$$\begin{aligned}\mathrm{KL}(Q\|P) &= \sum_i \left[\left(\frac{1+m_i}{2}\right)\ln\left(\frac{1+m_i}{2}\right) + \left(\frac{1-m_i}{2}\right)\ln\left(\frac{1-m_i}{2}\right)\right] \qquad (8)\\ &\quad - \sum_{i<j} J_{ij} m_i m_j - \sum_i h_i m_i + \ln Z,\end{aligned}$$

with respect to the mean field parameters m_i. Setting the gradients of eq. (8) equal to zero, we obtain the (classical) mean field equations:

$$\tanh^{-1}(m_i) = \sum_j J_{ij} m_j + h_i. \qquad (9)$$

2.2 Partial Factorizability

We now consider a more structured model in which the network consists of interacting modules that, taken in isolation, define tractable substructures. One example of this would be a network of weakly coupled HMMs, in which each HMM, taken by itself, defines a chain-like substructure that supports efficient probabilistic calculations. We denote the interactions between these modules by parameters $K_{ij}^{\mu\nu}$, where the superscripts μ and ν range over modules and the subscripts i and j index units within modules. An appropriate energy function for this network is:

$$-\beta E\{S\} = \sum_\mu \left\{\sum_{i<j} J_{ij}^\mu S_i^\mu S_j^\mu + \sum_i h_i^\mu S_i^\mu\right\} + \sum_{\substack{\mu<\nu \\ ij}} K_{ij}^{\mu\nu} S_i^\mu S_j^\nu. \qquad (10)$$

The first term in this energy function contains the intra-modular interactions; the last term, the inter-modular ones.

We now consider a mean field approximation that maintains the first sum over modules but dispenses with the inter-modular corrections:

$$Q\{S\} = \frac{1}{Z_Q} \exp\left\{\sum_\mu \left[\sum_{i<j} J_{ij}^\mu S_i^\mu S_j^\mu + \sum_i H_i^\mu S_i^\mu\right]\right\} \qquad (11)$$

The parameters of this mean field approximation are H_i^μ; they will be chosen to provide a self-consistent model of the inter-modular interactions. We easily obtain the following expectations under the mean field approximation, where $\mu \neq \nu$:

$$\langle S_i^\mu S_j^\omega \rangle = \delta_{\mu\omega} \langle S_i^\omega S_j^\omega \rangle + (1 - \delta_{\mu\omega}) \langle S_i^\mu \rangle \langle S_j^\omega \rangle, \qquad (12)$$

$$\begin{aligned}\langle S_i^\mu S_j^\nu S_k^\omega \rangle &= \delta_{\mu\omega} \langle S_i^\omega S_k^\omega \rangle \langle S_j^\nu \rangle + \delta_{\nu\omega} \langle S_j^\omega S_k^\omega \rangle \langle S_i^\mu \rangle + \\ &\quad (1 - \delta_{\nu\omega})(1 - \delta_{\omega\mu}) \langle S_i^\mu \rangle \langle S_j^\nu \rangle \langle S_k^\omega \rangle.\end{aligned} \qquad (13)$$

Note that units in the same module are statistically correlated and that these correlations are assumed to be taken into account in calculating the expectations. We assume that an efficient algorithm is available for handling these intra-modular correlations. For example, if the factorized modules are chains (e.g. obtained from a coupled set of HMMs), then computing these expectations requires a forward-backward pass through each chain.

The best approximation of the form, eq. (11), is found by minimizing the KL-divergence,

$$\mathrm{KL}(Q||P) = \ln(Z/Z_Q) + \sum_{\mu i}(H_i^\mu - h_i^\mu)\langle S_i^\mu \rangle - \sum_{\substack{\mu < \nu \\ ij}} K_{ij}^{\mu\nu}\langle S_i^\mu S_j^\nu \rangle, \quad (14)$$

with respect to the mean field parameters H_k^ω. To compute the appropriate gradients, we use the fact that derivatives of expectations under a Boltzmann distribution (e.g. $\partial \langle S_i^\mu \rangle / \partial H_k^\omega$) yield cumulants (e.g. $\langle S_i^\mu S_k^\omega \rangle - \langle S_i^\mu \rangle \langle S_k^\omega \rangle$). The conditions for stationarity are then:

$$0 = \sum_{\mu i}(H_i^\mu - h_i^\mu)[\langle S_i^\mu S_k^\omega \rangle - \langle S_i^\mu \rangle \langle S_k^\omega \rangle] - \sum_{\substack{\mu < \nu \\ ij}} K_{ij}^{\mu\nu}[\langle S_i^\mu S_j^\nu S_k^\omega \rangle - \langle S_i^\mu S_j^\nu \rangle \langle S_k^\omega \rangle]. \quad (15)$$

Substituting the expectations from eqs. (12) and (13), we find that $KL(Q||P)$ is minimized when

$$0 = \sum_i \left\{ H_i^\omega - h_i^\omega - \sum_{\nu \neq \omega} \sum_j K_{ij}^{\omega\nu}\langle S_j^\nu \rangle \right\} [\langle S_i^\omega S_k^\omega \rangle - \langle S_i^\omega \rangle \langle S_k^\omega \rangle]. \quad (16)$$

The resulting mean field equations are:

$$H_i^\omega = \sum_{\nu \neq \omega} \sum_j K_{ij}^{\omega\nu}\langle S_j^\nu \rangle + h_i^\omega. \quad (17)$$

These equations may be solved by iteration, in which the (assumed) tractable algorithms for averaging over $Q\{S\}$ are invoked as subroutines to compute the expectations $\langle S_j^\nu \rangle$ on the right hand side. Because these expectations depend on H_i^ν, these equations may be viewed as a self-consistent model of the inter-modular interactions. Note that the mean field parameter H_i^ω plays a role analogous to $\tanh^{-1}(m_i)$ in eq. (9) of the fully factorized case.

2.3 Inducing Partial Factorizability

Many interesting networks do not have strictly modular architectures and can only be approximately decomposed into tractable core structures. Techniques are needed in such cases to induce partial factorizability. Suppose for example that we are given an energy function

$$-\beta E\{S\} = \sum_{i<j} J_{ij} S_i S_j + \sum_i h_i S_i + \sum_{i<j} K_{ij} S_i S_j \quad (18)$$

for which the first two terms represent tractable interactions and the last term, intractable ones. Thus the weights J_{ij} by themselves define a tractable skeleton network, but the weights K_{ij} spoil this tractability. Mimicking the steps of the previous section, we obtain the mean field equations:

$$0 = \sum_i (\langle S_i S_k \rangle - \langle S_i \rangle \langle S_k \rangle) [H_i - h_i] - \sum_{i<j} K_{ij}[\langle S_i S_j S_k \rangle - \langle S_i S_j \rangle \langle S_k \rangle]. \quad (19)$$

In this case, however, the weights K_{ij} couple units in the same core structure. Because these units are not assumed to be independent, the triple correlator $\langle S_i S_j S_k \rangle$ does not factorize, and we no longer obtain the decoupled update rules of eq. (17). Rather, for these mean field equations, each iteration requires computing triple correlators and solving a large set of coupled linear equations.

To avoid this heavy computational load, we instead manipulate the energy function into one that can be partially factorized. This is done by introducing extra hidden variables $W_{ij} = \pm 1$ on the intractable links of the network. In particular, consider the energy function

$$-\beta E\{S, W\} = \sum_{i<j} J_{ij} S_i S_j + \sum_i h_i S_i + \sum_{i<j} \left[K_{ij}^{(1)} S_i + K_{ij}^{(2)} S_j \right] W_{ij}. \quad (20)$$

The hidden variables W_{ij} in eq. (20) serve to decouple the units connected by the intractable weights K_{ij}. However, we can always choose the new interactions, $K_{ij}^{(1)}$ and $K_{ij}^{(2)}$, so that

$$e^{-\beta E\{S\}} = \sum_{\{W\}} e^{-\beta E\{S, W\}}. \quad (21)$$

Eq. (21) states that the marginal distribution over $\{S\}$ in the new network is identical to the joint distribution over $\{S\}$ in the original one. Summing both sides of eq. (21) over $\{S\}$, it follows that both networks have the same partition function.

The form of the energy function in eq. (20) suggests the mean field approximation:

$$Q\{S, W\} = \frac{1}{Z_Q} \exp \left\{ \sum_{i<j} J_{ij} S_i S_j + \sum_i H_i S_i + \sum_{i<j} H_{ij} W_{ij} \right\}, \quad (22)$$

where the mean field parameters H_i have been augmented by a set of additional mean field parameters H_{ij} that account for the extra hidden variables. In this expression, the variables S_i and W_{ij} act as decoupled degrees of freedom and the methods of the preceding section can be applied directly. We consider an example of this reduction in the following section.

3 EXAMPLE

Consider a continuous-output HMM in which the probability of an output $\vec{X}_t$ at time t is dependent not only on the state at time t, but also on the state at time $t + \Delta$. Such a context-sensitive HMM may serve as a flexible model of anticipatory coarticulatory effects in speech, with $\Delta \approx 50$ms representing a mean phoneme lifetime. Incorporating these interactions into the basic HMM probability model, we obtain the following joint probability on states and outputs:

$$P\{S, \vec{X}\} = \prod_{t=1}^{T-1} a_{S_t S_{t+1}} \prod_{t=1}^{T-\Delta} \frac{1}{(2\pi)^{D/2}} \exp \left\{ -\frac{1}{2} \left[\vec{X}_t - \vec{U}_{S_t} - \vec{V}_{S_{t+\Delta}} \right]^2 \right\}. \quad (23)$$

Denoting the likelihood of an output sequence by Z, we have

$$Z = P\{\vec{X}\} = \sum_{\{S\}} P\{S, \vec{X}\}. \quad (24)$$

We can represent this probability model using energies rather than transition probabilities (Luttrell, 1989; Saul and Jordan, 1995). For the special case of binary states, this is done by choosing weights J, K, and h_t related to the parameters of the HMM and the output sequence as follows[1]:

$$J = \frac{1}{4} \ln\left[\frac{a_{++}a_{--}}{a_{+-}a_{-+}}\right], \qquad K = -\frac{1}{4}(\vec{U}_+ - \vec{U}_-) \cdot (\vec{V}_+ - \vec{V}_-), \qquad (25)$$

$$h_t = \frac{1}{2}\ln\left[\frac{a_{++}}{a_{--}}\right] + \frac{1}{2}\left[\vec{X}_t - \frac{\vec{U}_+ + \vec{U}_- + \vec{V}_+ + \vec{V}_-}{2}\right] \cdot \left[\vec{U}_+ + \vec{V}_+ - \vec{U}_- - \vec{V}_-\right] (26)$$

Here, a_{++} is the probability of transitioning from the ON state to the ON state (and similarly for the other a parameters), while $\vec{U}_+$ and $\vec{V}_+$ are the mean outputs associated with the ON state at time steps t and $t + \Delta$ (and similarly for $\vec{U}_-$ and $\vec{V}_-$). Given these definitions, we obtain an equivalent expression for the likelihood:

$$Z = \sum_{\{S\}} \exp\left\{-\varepsilon_0 + \sum_{t=1}^{T-1} JS_tS_{t+1} + \sum_{t=1}^{T} h_tS_t + \sum_{t=1}^{T-\Delta} KS_tS_{t+\Delta}\right\}, \qquad (27)$$

where ε_0 is a placeholder for the terms in $\ln P\{S, \vec{X}\}$ that do not depend on $\{S\}$. We can interpret Z as the partition function for the chained network of T binary units that represents the HMM unfolded in time. The nearest neighbor connectivity of this network reflects the first order structure of the HMM; the long-range connectivity reflects the higher order interactions that model sensitivity to context.

The exact likelihood can in principle be computed by summing over the hidden states in eq. (27), but the required forward-backward algorithm scales much worse than the case of first-order HMMs. Because the likelihood can be identified as a partition function, however, we can obtain a lower bound on its value from mean field theory. To exploit the tractable first order structure of the HMM, we induce a partially factorizable network by introducing extra link variables on the long-range connections, as described in section 2.3. The resulting mean field approximation uses the chained structure as its backbone and should be accurate if the higher order effects in the data are weak compared to the basic first-order structure.

The above scenario was tested in numerical simulations. In actuality, we implemented a generalization of the model in eq. (23): our HMM had non-binary hidden states and a coarticulation model that incorporated both left and right context. This network was trained on several artificial data sets according to the following procedure. First, we fixed the "context" weights to zero and used the Baum-Welch algorithm to estimate the first order structure of the HMM. Then, we lifted the zero constraints and re-estimated the parameters of the HMM by a mean field EM algorithm. In the E-step of this algorithm, the true posterior $P\{S|\vec{X}\}$ was approximated by the distribution $Q\{S|\vec{X}\}$ obtained by solving the mean field equations; in the M-step, the parameters of the HMM were updated to match the statistics of $Q\{S|\vec{X}\}$. Figure 1 shows the type of structure captured by a typical network.

4 CONCLUSIONS

Endowing networks with probabilistic semantics provides a unified framework for incorporating prior knowledge, handling missing data, and performing inferences under uncertainty. Probabilistic calculations, however, can quickly become intractable, so it is important to develop techniques that both approximate probability distributions in a flexible manner and make use of exact techniques wherever possible. In

---

[1]There are boundary corrections to h_t (not shown) for $t = 1$ and $t > T - \Delta$.

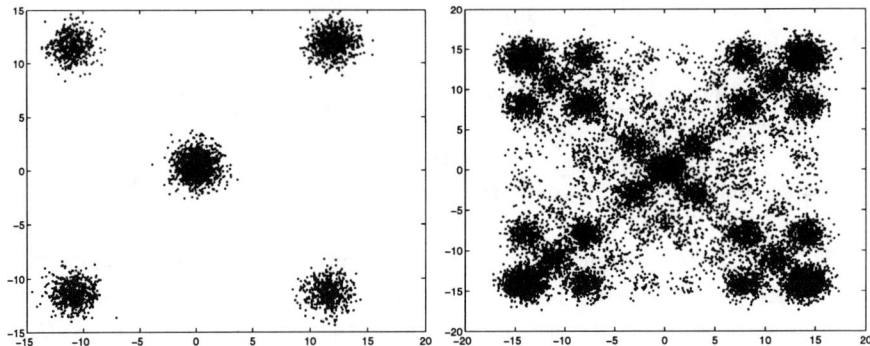

Figure 1: 2D output vectors $\{\vec{X}_t\}$ sampled from a first-order HMM and a context-sensitive HMM, each with $n = 5$ hidden states. The latter's coarticulation model used left and right context, coupling $\vec{X}_t$ to the hidden states at times t and $t \pm 5$. At left: the five main clusters reveal the basic first-order structure. At right: weak modulations reveal the effects of context.

this paper we have developed a mean field approximation that meets both these objectives. As an example, we have applied our methods to context-sensitive HMMs, but the methods are general and can be applied more widely.

Acknowledgements

The authors acknowledge support from NSF grant CDA-9404932, ONR grant N00014-94-1-0777, ATR Research Laboratories, and Siemens Corporation.

References

A. Dempster, N. Laird, and D. Rubin. (1977) Maximum likelihood from incomplete data via the EM algorithm. *J. Roy. Stat. Soc.* **B39**:1-38.

B. H. Juang and L. R. Rabiner. (1991) Hidden Markov models for speech recognition, *Technometrics* **33**: 251-272.

S. Luttrell. (1989) The Gibbs machine applied to hidden Markov model problems. *Royal Signals and Radar Establishment: SP Research Note* **99**.

G. Parisi. (1988) *Statistical field theory.* Addison-Wesley: Redwood City, CA.

C. Peterson and J. R. Anderson. (1987) A mean field theory learning algorithm for neural networks. *Complex Systems* **1**:995-1019.

L. Saul and M. Jordan. (1994) Learning in Boltzmann trees. *Neural Comp.* **6**: 1174-1184.

L. Saul and M. Jordan. (1995) Boltzmann chains and hidden Markov models. In G. Tesauro, D. Touretzky, and T. Leen, eds. *Advances in Neural Information Processing Systems* **7**. MIT Press: Cambridge, MA.

P. Stolorz. (1994) Recursive approaches to the statistical physics of lattice proteins. In L. Hunter, ed. *Proc. 27th Hawaii Intl. Conf. on System Sciences* **V**: 316-325.

C. Williams and G. E. Hinton. (1990) Mean field networks that learn to discriminate temporally distorted strings. *Proc. Connectionist Models Summer School*: 18-22.

Hierarchical Recurrent Neural Networks for Long-Term Dependencies

Salah El Hihi
Dept. Informatique et
Recherche Opérationnelle
Université de Montréal
Montreal, Qc H3C-3J7
elhihi@iro.umontreal.ca

Yoshua Bengio *
Dept. Informatique et
Recherche Opérationnelle
Université de Montréal
Montreal, Qc H3C-3J7
bengioy@iro.umontreal.ca

Abstract

We have already shown that extracting long-term dependencies from sequential data is difficult, both for deterministic dynamical systems such as recurrent networks, and probabilistic models such as hidden Markov models (HMMs) or input/output hidden Markov models (IOHMMs). In practice, to avoid this problem, researchers have used domain specific a-priori knowledge to give meaning to the hidden or state variables representing past context. In this paper, we propose to use a more general type of a-priori knowledge, namely that the temporal dependencies are structured hierarchically. This implies that long-term dependencies are represented by variables with a long time scale. This principle is applied to a recurrent network which includes delays and multiple time scales. Experiments confirm the advantages of such structures. A similar approach is proposed for HMMs and IOHMMs.

1 Introduction

Learning from examples basically amounts to identifying the relations between random variables of interest. Several learning problems involve *sequential data*, in which the variables are ordered (e.g., time series). Many learning algorithms take advantage of this sequential structure by assuming some kind of homogeneity or continuity of the model over time, e.g., by sharing parameters for different times, as in Time-Delay Neural Networks (TDNNs) (Lang, Waibel and Hinton, 1990), recurrent neural networks (Rumelhart, Hinton and Williams, 1986), or hidden Markov models (Rabiner and Juang, 1986). This general a-priori assumption considerably simplifies the learning problem.

In previous papers (Bengio, Simard and Frasconi, 1994; Bengio and Frasconi, 1995a), we have shown for recurrent networks and Markovian models that, even with this assumption, dependencies that span longer intervals are significantly harder to learn. In all of the systems we have considered for learning from sequential data, some form of representation of context (or state) is required (to summarize all "useful" past information). The "hard learning" problem is to *learn to represent context*, which involves performing the proper

---
*also, AT&T Bell Labs, Holmdel, NJ 07733

credit assignment through time. Indeed, in practice, recurrent networks (e.g., injecting prior knowledge for grammar inference (Giles and Omlin, 1992; Frasconi et al., 1993)) and HMMs (e.g., for speech recognition (Levinson, Rabiner and Sondhi, 1983; Rabiner and Juang, 1986)) work quite well when the representation of context (the meaning of the state variable) is decided a-priori. The hidden variable is not any more completely hidden. Learning becomes much easier. Unfortunately, this requires a very precise knowledge of the appropriate state variables, which is not available in many applications.

We have seen that the successes of TDNNs, recurrent networks and HMMs are based on a general assumption on the sequential nature of the data. In this paper, we propose another, simple, a-priori assumption on the sequences to be analyzed: the temporal dependencies have a hierarchical structure. This implies that dependencies spanning long intervals are "robust" to small local changes in the timing of events, whereas dependencies spanning short intervals are allowed to be more sensitive to the precise timing of events. This yields a multi-resolution representation of state information. This general idea is not new and can be found in various approaches to learning and artificial intelligence. For example, in convolutional neural networks, both for sequential data with TDNNs (Lang, Waibel and Hinton, 1990), and for 2-dimensional data with MLCNNs (LeCun et al., 1989; Bengio, LeCun and Henderson, 1994), the network is organized in layers representing features of increasing temporal or spatial coarseness. Similarly, mostly as a tool for analyzing and preprocessing sequential or spatial data, wavelet transforms (Daubechies, 1990) also represent such information at multiple resolutions. Multi-scale representations have also been proposed to improve reinforcement learning systems (Singh, 1992; Dayan and Hinton, 1993; Sutton, 1995) and path planning systems. However, with these algorithms, one generally assumes that the state of the system is observed, whereas, in this paper we concentrate on the difficulty of learning what the state variable should represent. A related idea using a hierarchical structure was presented in (Schmidhuber, 1992).

On the HMM side, several researchers (Brugnara et al., 1992; Suaudeau, 1994) have attempted to improve HMMs for speech recognition to better model the different types of variables, intrinsically varying at different time scales in speech. In those papers, the focus was on setting an a-priori representation, not on learning how to represent context.

In section 2, we attempt to draw a common conclusion from the analyses performed on recurrent networks and HMMs to learn to represent long-term dependencies. This will justify the proposed approach, presented in section 3. In section 4 a specific hierarchical model is proposed for recurrent networks, using different time scales for different layers of the network. Experiments performed with this model are described in section 4. Finally, we discuss a similar scheme for HMMs and IOHMMs in section 5.

2 Too Many Products

In this section, we take another look at the analyses of (Bengio, Simard and Frasconi, 1994) and (Bengio and Frasconi, 1995a), for recurrent networks and HMMs respectively. The objective is to draw a parallel between the problems encountered with the two approaches, in order to guide us towards some form of solution, and justify the proposals made here. First, let us consider the deterministic dynamical systems (Bengio, Simard and Frasconi, 1994) (such as recurrent networks), which map an input sequence $u_1, \ldots, u_T$ to an output sequence $\hat{y}_1, \ldots, \hat{y}_T$. The state or context information is represented at each time t by a variable x_t, for example the activities of all the hidden units of a recurrent network:

$$x_t = f(x_{t-1}, u_t) \qquad (1)$$

where u_t is the system input at time t and f is a differentiable function (such as $\tanh(W x_{t-1} + u_t)$). When the sequence of inputs $u_1, u_2, \ldots, u_T$ is given, we can write $x_t = f_t(x_{t-1}) = f_t(f_{t-1}(\ldots f_1(x_0))\ldots)$. A learning criterion C_t yields gradients on outputs, and therefore on the state variables x_t. Since parameters are shared across time, learning using a gradient-based algorithm depends on the influence of parameters W on C_t through all time steps before t:

$$\frac{\partial C_t}{\partial W} = \sum_\tau \frac{\partial C_t}{\partial x_t} \frac{\partial x_t}{\partial x_\tau} \frac{\partial x_\tau}{\partial W} \qquad (2)$$

The Jacobian matrix of derivatives $\frac{\partial x_t}{\partial x_\tau}$ can further be factored as follows:

$$\frac{\partial x_t}{\partial x_\tau} = \frac{\partial x_t}{\partial x_{t-1}} \frac{\partial x_{t-1}}{\partial x_{t-2}} \cdots \frac{\partial x_{\tau+1}}{\partial x_\tau} = f'_t f'_{t-1} \cdots f'_{\tau+1} \qquad (3)$$

Our earlier analysis (Bengio, Simard and Frasconi, 1994) shows that the difficulty revolves around the matrix product in equation 3. In order to reliably "store" information in the dynamics of the network, the state variable x_t must remain in regions where $|f'_t| < 1$ (i.e., near enough to a stable attractor representing the stored information). However, the above products then rapidly converge to 0 when $t - \tau$ increases. Consequently, the sum in 2 is dominated by terms corresponding to short-term dependencies ($t - \tau$ is small).

Let us now consider the case of Markovian models (including HMMs and IOHMMs (Bengio and Frasconi, 1995b)). These are probabilistic models, either of an "output" sequence $P(y_1 \ldots y_T)$ (HMMs) or of an output sequence given an input sequence $P(y_1 \ldots y_T | u_1 \ldots u_T)$ (IOHMMs). Introducing a discrete state variable x_t and using Markovian assumptions of independence this probability can be factored in terms of transition probabilities $P(x_t|x_{t-1})$ (or $P(x_t|x_{t-1}, u_t)$) and output probabilities $P(y_t|x_t)$ (or $P(y_t|x_t, u_t)$). According to the model, the distribution of the state x_t at time t given the state x_τ at an earlier time τ is given by the matrix

$$P(x_t|x_\tau) = P(x_t|x_{t-1})P(x_{t-1}|x_{t-2})\ldots P(x_{\tau+1}|x_\tau) \qquad (4)$$

where each of the factors is a matrix of transition probabilities (conditioned on inputs in the case of IOHMMs). Our earlier analysis (Bengio and Frasconi, 1995a) shows that the difficulty in representing and learning to represent context (i.e., learning what x_t should represent) revolves around equation 4. The matrices in the above equations have one eigenvalue equal to 1 (because of the normalization constraint) and the others ≤ 1. In the case in which all eigenvalues are 1 the matrices have only 1's and 0's, i.e, we obtain deterministic dynamics for IOHMMs or pure cycles for HMMs (which cannot be used to model most interesting sequences). Otherwise the above product converges to a lower rank matrix (some or most of the eigenvalues converge toward 0). Consequently, $P(x_t|x_\tau)$ becomes more and more independent of x_τ as $t-\tau$ increases. Therefore, **both** representing **and** learning context becomes more difficult as the span of dependencies increases or when the Markov model is more non-deterministic (transition probabilities not close to 0 or 1).

Clearly, a common trait of both analyses lies in taking *too many products, too many time steps, or too many transformations* to relate the state variable at time τ with the state variable at time $t > \tau$, as in equations 3 and 4. Therefore the idea presented in the next section is centered on allowing *several paths* between x_τ and x_t, some with few "transformations" and some with many transformations. At least through those with few transformations, we expect context information (forward), and credit assignment (backward) to propagate more easily over longer time spans than through "paths" involving many transformations.

3 Hierarchical Sequential Models

Inspired by the above analysis we introduce an assumption about the sequential data to be modeled, although it will be a very simple and general a-priori on the structure of the data. Basically, we will assume that the sequential structure of data can be described *hierarchically*: long-term dependencies (e.g., between two events remote from each other in time) do not depend on a precise time scale (i.e., on the precise timing of these events). Consequently, in order to represent a context variable taking these long-term dependencies into account, we will be able to use a coarse time scale (or a slowly changing state variable).

Therefore, instead of a single homogeneous state variable, we will introduce several levels of state variables, each "working" at a different time scale. To implement in a discrete-time system such a multi-resolution representation of context, two basic approaches can be considered. Either the higher level state variables change value less often or they are constrained to change more slowly at each time step. In our experiments, we have considered input and output variables both at the shortest time scale (highest frequency), but one of the potential advantages of the approach presented here is that it becomes very

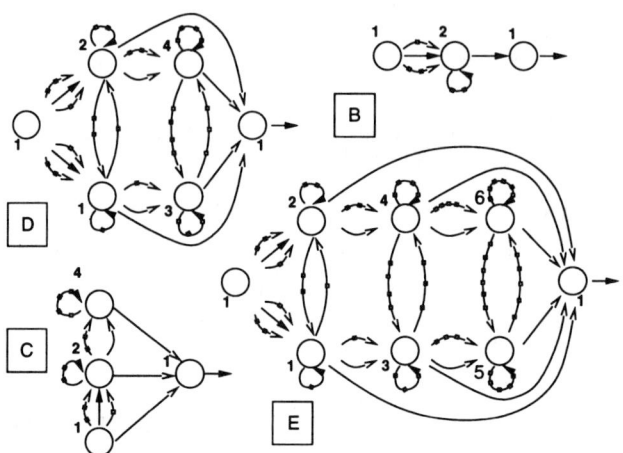

Figure 1: Four multi-resolution recurrent architectures used in the experiments. Small squares represent a discrete delay, and numbers near each neuron represent its time scale. The architectures **B** to **E** have respectively 2, 3, 4, and 6 time scales.

simple to incorporate input and output variables that operate at different time scales. For example, in speech recognition and synthesis, the variable of interest is not only the speech signal itself (fast) but also slower-varying variables such as prosodic (average energy, pitch, etc...) and phonemic (place of articulation, phoneme duration) variables. Another example is in the application of learning algorithms to financial and economic forecasting and decision taking. Some of the variables of interest are given daily, others weekly, monthly, etc...

4 Hierarchical Recurrent Neural Network: Experiments

As in TDNNs (Lang, Waibel and Hinton, 1990) and reverse-TDNNs (Simard and LeCun, 1992), we will use discrete time delays and subsampling (or oversampling) in order to implement the multiple time scales. In the time-unfolded network, paths going through the recurrences in the slow varying units (long time scale) will carry context farther, while paths going through faster varying units (short time scale) will respond faster to changes in input or desired changes in output. Examples of such multi-resolution recurrent neural networks are shown in Figure 1. Two sets of simple experiments were performed to validate some of the ideas presented in this paper. In both cases, we compare a hierarchical recurrent network with a single-scale fully-connected recurrent network.

In the first set of experiments, we want to evaluate the performance of a hierarchical recurrent network on a problem already used for studying the difficulty in learning long-term dependencies (Bengio, Simard and Frasconi, 1994; Bengio and Frasconi, 1994). In this 2-class problem, the network has to detect a pattern at the beginning of the sequence, keeping a bit of information in "memory" (while the inputs are noisy) until the end of the sequence (supervision is only a the end of the sequence). As in (Bengio, Simard and Frasconi, 1994; Bengio and Frasconi, 1994) only the first 3 time steps contain information about the class (a 3-number pattern was randomly chosen for each class within $[-1,1]^3$). The length of the sequences is varied to evaluate the effect of the span of input/output dependencies. Uniformly distributed noisy inputs between -.1 and .1 are added to the initial patterns as well as to the remainder of the sequence. For each sequence length, 10 trials were run with different initial weights and noise patterns, with 30 training sequences. Experiments were performed with sequence of lengths 10, 20, 40 and 100.

Several recurrent network architectures were compared. All were trained with the same algorithm (back-propagation through time) to minimize the sum of squared differences between the final output and a desired value. The simplest architecture (**A**) is similar to architecture **B** in Figure 1 but it is not hierarchical: it has a single time scale. Like the

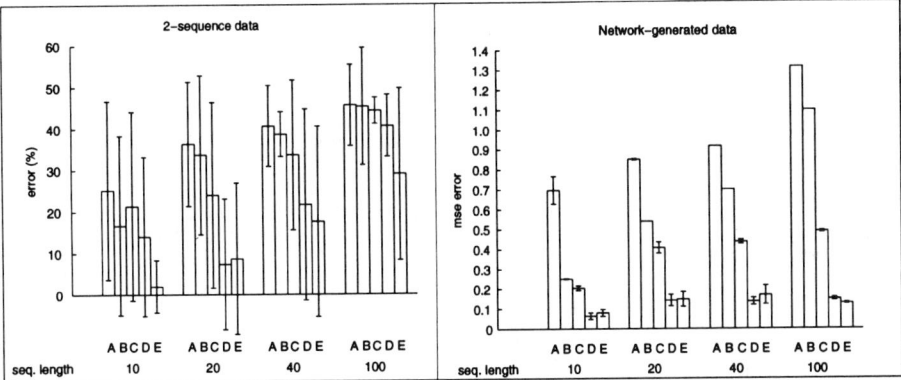

Figure 2: Average classification error after training for 2-sequence problem (left, classification error) and network-generated data (right, mean squared error), for varying sequence lengths and architectures. Each set of 5 consecutive bars represents the performance of 5 architectures **A** to **E**, with respectively 1, 2, 3, 4 and 6 time scales (the architectures **B** to **E** are shown in Figure 1). Error bars show the standard deviation over 10 trials.

other networks, it has however a theoretically "sufficient" architecture, i.e., there exists a set of weights for which it classifies perfectly the training sequences. Four of the five architectures that we compared are shown in Figure 1, with an increasing number of levels in the hierarchy. The performance of these four architectures (**B** to **E**) as well as the architecture with a single time-scale (**A**) are compared in Figure 2 (left, for the 2-sequence problem). Clearly, adding more levels to the hierarchy has significantly helped to reduce the difficulty in learning long-term dependencies.

In a second set of experiments, a hierarchical recurrent network with 4 time scales was initialized with random (but large) weights and used to generate a data set. To generate the inputs as well as the outputs, the network has feedback links from hidden to input units. At the initial time step as well as at 5% of the time steps (chosen randomly), the input was clamped with random values to introduce some further variability. It is a regression task, and the mean squared error is shown on Figure 2. Because of the network structure, we expect the data to contain long-term dependencies that can be modeled with a hierarchical structure. 100 training sequences of length 10, 20, 40 and 100 were generated by this network. The same 5 network architectures as in the previous experiments were compared (see Figure 1 for architectures **B** to **E**), with 10 training trials per network and per sequence length. The results are summarized in Figure 2 (right). More high-level hierarchical structure appears to have improved performance for long-term dependencies. The fact that the simpler 1-level network does not achieve a good performance suggests that there were some difficult long-term dependencies in the the artificially generated data set. It is interesting to compare those results with those reported in (Lin et al., 1995) which show that using longer delays in certain recurrent connections helps learning longer-term dependencies. In both cases we find that introducing longer time scales allows to learn dependencies whose span is proportionally longer.

5 Hierarchical HMMs

How do we represent multiple time scales with a HMM? Some solutions have already been proposed in the speech recognition literature, motivated by the obvious presence of different time scales in the speech phenomena. In (Brugnara et al., 1992) two Markov chains are coupled in a "master/slave" configuration. For the "master" HMM, the observations are slowly varying features (such as the signal energy), whereas for the "slave" HMM the observations are the speech spectra themselves. The two chains are synchronous and operate at the same time scale, therefore the problem of diffusion of credit in HMMs would probably also make difficult the learning of long-term dependencies. Note on the other hand that in most applications of HMMs to speech recognition the meaning of states is fixed a-priori rather than learned from the data (see (Bengio and Frasconi, 1995a) for a discussion). In a more recent contribution, Nelly Suaudeau (Suaudeau, 1994) proposes a "two-level HMM" in which the higher level HMM represents "segmental" variables (such as phoneme duration). The two levels operate at different scales: the higher level state variable represents the phonetic identity and models the distributions of the average energy and the duration within each phoneme. Again, this work is not geared towards learning a representation of context, but rather, given the traditional (phoneme-based) representation of context in speech recognition, towards building a better model of the distribution of "slow" segmental variables such as phoneme duration and energy. Another promising approach was recently proposed in (Saul and Jordan, 1995). Using decimation techniques from statistical mechanics, a polynomial-time algorithm is derived for parallel Boltzmann chains (which are similar to parallel HMMs), which can operate at different time scales.

The ideas presented here point toward a HMM or IOHMM in which the (hidden) state variable x_t is represented by the Cartesian product of several state variables x_t^s, each "working" at a different time scale: $x_t = (x_t^1, x_t^2, \ldots, x_t^L)$. To take advantage of the decomposition, we propose to consider that the state distributions at the different levels are conditionally independent (given the state at the previous time step and at the current and previous levels). Transition probabilities are therefore factored as followed:

$$P(x_t|x_{t-1}) = \prod_s P(x_t^s|x_{t-1}^s, x_{t-1}^{s-1}) \quad (5)$$

To force the state variable at a each level to effectively work at a given time scale, self-transition probabilities are constrained as follows (using above independence assumptions):

$$P(x_t^s=j_s|x_{t-1}^1=j_1,\ldots,x_{t-1}^s=j_s,\ldots,x_{t-1}^L=j_S) = P(x_t^s=j_s|x_{t-1}^s=j_s, x_{t-1}^{s-1}=j_{s-1}) = w_s$$

6 Conclusion

Motivated by the analysis of the problem of learning long-term dependencies in sequential data, i.e., of learning to represent context, we have proposed to use a very general assumption on the structure of sequential data to reduce the difficulty of these learning tasks. Following numerous previous work in artificial intelligence we are assuming that context can be represented with a hierarchical structure. More precisely, here, it means that long-term dependencies are insensitive to small timing variations, i.e., they can be represented with a coarse temporal scale. This scheme allows context information and credit information to be respectively propagated forward and backward more easily.

Following this intuitive idea, we have proposed to use *hierarchical recurrent networks* for sequence processing. These networks use multiple-time scales to achieve a multi-resolution representation of context. Series of experiments on artificial data have confirmed the advantages of imposing such structures on the network architecture. Finally we have proposed a similar application of this concept to hidden Markov models (for density estimation) and input/output hidden Markov models (for classification and regression).

References

Bengio, Y. and Frasconi, P. (1994). Credit assignment through time: Alternatives to backpropagation. In Cowan, J., Tesauro, G., and Alspector, J., editors, *Advances in Neural Information Processing Systems 6*. Morgan Kaufmann.

Bengio, Y. and Frasconi, P. (1995a). Diffusion of context and credit information in markovian models. *Journal of Artificial Intelligence Research*, 3:223–244.

Bengio, Y. and Frasconi, P. (1995b). An input/output HMM architecture. In Tesauro, G., Touretzky, D., and Leen, T., editors, *Advances in Neural Information Processing Systems 7*, pages 427–434. MIT Press, Cambridge, MA.

Bengio, Y., LeCun, Y., and Henderson, D. (1994). Globally trained handwritten word recognizer using spatial representation, space displacement neural networks and hidden Markov models. In Cowan, J., Tesauro, G., and Alspector, J., editors, *Advances in Neural Information Processing Systems 6*, pages 937–944.

Bengio, Y., Simard, P., and Frasconi, P. (1994). Learning long-term dependencies with gradient descent is difficult. *IEEE Transactions on Neural Networks*, 5(2):157–166.

Brugnara, F., DeMori, R., Giuliani, D., and Omologo, M. (1992). A family of parallel hidden markov models. In *International Conference on Acoustics, Speech and Signal Processing*, pages 377–370, New York, NY, USA. IEEE.

Daubechies, I. (1990). The wavelet transform, time-frequency localization and signal analysis. *IEEE Transaction on Information Theory*, 36(5):961–1005.

Dayan, P. and Hinton, G. (1993). Feudal reinforcement learning. In Hanson, S. J., Cowan, J. D., and Giles, C. L., editors, *Advances in Neural Information Processing Systems 5*, San Mateo, CA. Morgan Kaufmann.

Frasconi, P., Gori, M., Maggini, M., and Soda, G. (1993). Unified integration of explicit rules and learning by example in recurrent networks. *IEEE Transactions on Knowledge and Data Engineering*. (in press).

Giles, C. L. and Omlin, C. W. (1992). Inserting rules into recurrent neural networks. In Kung, Fallside, Sorenson, and Kamm, editors, *Neural Networks for Signal Processing II, Proceedings of the 1992 IEEE workshop*, pages 13–22. IEEE Press.

Lang, K. J., Waibel, A. H., and Hinton, G. E. (1990). A time-delay neural network architecture for isolated word recognition. *Neural Networks*, 3:23–43.

LeCun, Y., Boser, B., Denker, J., Henderson, D., Howard, R., Hubbard, W., and Jackel, L. (1989). Backpropagation applied to handwritten zip code recognition. *Neural Computation*, 1:541–551.

Levinson, S., Rabiner, L., and Sondhi, M. (1983). An introduction to the application of the theory of probabilistic functions of a Markov process to automatic speech recognition. *Bell System Technical Journal*, 64(4):1035–1074.

Lin, T., Horne, B., Tino, P., and Giles, C. (1995). Learning long-term dependencies is not as difficult with NARX recurrent neural networks. Technical Report UMICAS-TR-95-78, Institute for Advanced Computer Studies, University of Mariland.

Rabiner, L. and Juang, B. (1986). An introduction to hidden Markov models. *IEEE ASSP Magazine*, pages 257–285.

Rumelhart, D., Hinton, G., and Williams, R. (1986). Learning internal representations by error propagation. In Rumelhart, D. and McClelland, J., editors, *Parallel Distributed Processing*, volume 1, chapter 8, pages 318–362. MIT Press, Cambridge.

Saul, L. and Jordan, M. (1995). Boltzmann chains and hidden markov models. In Tesauro, G., Touretzky, D., and Leen, T., editors, *Advances in Neural Information Processing Systems 7*, pages 435–442. MIT Press, Cambridge, MA.

Schmidhuber, J. (1992). Learning complex, extended sequences using the principle of history compression. *Neural Computation*, 4(2):234–242.

Simard, P. and LeCun, Y. (1992). Reverse TDNN: An architecture for trajectory generation. In Moody, J., Hanson, S., and Lipmann, R., editors, *Advances in Neural Information Processing Systems 4*, pages 579–588, Denver, CO. Morgan Kaufmann, San Mateo.

Singh, S. (1992). Reinforcement learning with a hierarchy of abstract models. In *Proceedings of the 10th National Conference on Artificial Intelligence*, pages 202–207. MIT/AAAI Press.

Suaudeau, N. (1994). *Un modèle probabiliste pour intégrer la dimension temporelle dans un système de reconnaissance automatique de la parole*. PhD thesis, Université de Rennes I, France.

Sutton, R. (1995). TD models: modeling the world at a mixture of time scales. In *Proceedings of the 12th International Conference on Machine Learning*. Morgan Kaufmann.

Discovering Structure in Continuous Variables Using Bayesian Networks

Reimar Hofmann and Volker Tresp[*]
Siemens AG, Central Research
Otto-Hahn-Ring 6
81730 München, Germany

Abstract

We study Bayesian networks for continuous variables using nonlinear conditional density estimators. We demonstrate that useful structures can be extracted from a data set in a self-organized way and we present sampling techniques for belief update based on Markov blanket conditional density models.

1 Introduction

One of the strongest types of information that can be learned about an unknown process is the discovery of dependencies and —even more important— of independencies. A superior example is medical epidemiology where the goal is to find the causes of a disease and exclude factors which are irrelevant. Whereas complete independence between two variables in a domain might be rare in reality (which would mean that the joint probability density of variables A and B can be factored: $p(A, B) = p(A)p(B)$), conditional independence is more common and is often a result from true or apparent causality: consider the case that A is the cause of B and B is the cause of C, then $p(C|A, B) = p(C|B)$ and A and C are independent under the condition that B is known. Precisely this notion of cause and effect and the resulting independence between variables is represented explicitly in Bayesian networks. Pearl (1988) has convincingly argued that causal thinking leads to clear knowledge representation in form of conditional probabilities and to efficient local belief propagating rules.

Bayesian networks form a complete probabilistic model in the sense that they represent the joint probability distribution of all variables involved. Two of the powerful

---

[*]Reimar.Hofmann@zfe.siemens.de Volker.Tresp@zfe.siemens.de

features of Bayesian networks are that any variable can be predicted from any subset of known other variables and that Bayesian networks make explicit statements about the certainty of the estimate of the state of a variable. Both aspects are particularly important for medical or fault diagnosis systems. More recently, learning of structure and of parameters in Bayesian networks has been addressed allowing for the discovery of structure between variables (Buntine, 1994, Heckerman, 1995).

Most of the research on Bayesian networks has focused on systems with discrete variables, linear Gaussian models or combinations of both. Except for linear models, continuous variables pose a problem for Bayesian networks. In Pearl's words (Pearl, 1988): "representing each [continuous] quantity by an estimated magnitude and a range of uncertainty, we quickly produce a computational mess. [Continuous variables] actually impose a computational tyranny of their own." In this paper we present approaches to applying the concept of Bayesian networks towards arbitrary nonlinear relations between continuous variables. Because they are fast learners we use Parzen windows based conditional density estimators for modeling local dependencies. We demonstrate how a parsimonious Bayesian network can be extracted out of a data set using unsupervised self-organized learning. For belief update we use local Markov blanket conditional density models which —in combination with Gibbs sampling— allow relatively efficient sampling from the conditional density of an unknown variable.

2 Bayesian Networks

This brief introduction of Bayesian networks follows closely Heckerman, 1995. Considering a joint probability density[1] $p(x)$ over a set of variables $\{x_1, \ldots, x_N\}$ we can decompose using the chain rule of probability

$$p(x) = \prod_{i=1}^{N} p(x_i | x_1, \ldots, x_{i-1}). \tag{1}$$

For each variable x_i, let the parents of x_i denoted by $\mathcal{P}_i \subseteq \{x_1, \ldots, x_{i-1}\}$ be a set of variables[2] that renders x_i and $\{x_1, \ldots, x_{i-1}\}$ independent, that is

$$p(x_i | x_1, \ldots, x_{i-1}) = p(x_i | \mathcal{P}_i). \tag{2}$$

Note, that $\mathcal{P}_i$ does not need to include all elements of $\{x_1, \ldots, x_{i-1}\}$ which indicates conditional independence between those variables not included in $\mathcal{P}_i$ and x_i given that the variables in $\mathcal{P}_i$ are known. The dependencies between the variables are often depicted as directed acyclic[3] graphs (DAGs) with directed arcs from the members of $\mathcal{P}_i$ (the parents) to x_i (the child). Bayesian networks are a natural description of dependencies between variables if they depict causal relationships between variables. Bayesian networks are commonly used as a representation of the knowledge of domain experts. Experts both define the structure of the Bayesian network and the local conditional probabilities. Recently there has been great

---

[1] For simplicity of notation we will only treat the continuous case. Handling mixtures of continuous and discrete variables does not impose any additional difficulties.
[2] Usually the smallest set will be used. Note that in $\mathcal{P}_i$ is defined with respect to a given ordering of the variables.
[3] i.e. not containing any *directed* loops.

emphasis on learning structure and parameters in Bayesian networks (Heckerman, 1995). Most of previous work concentrated on models with only discrete variables or on linear models of continuous variables where the probability distribution of all continuous given all discrete variables is a multidimensional Gaussian. In this paper we use these ideas in context with continuous variables and nonlinear dependencies.

3 Learning Structure and Parameters in Nonlinear Continuous Bayesian Networks

Many of the structures developed in the neural network community can be used to model the conditional density distribution of continuous variables $p(x_i|\mathcal{P}_i)$. Under the usual signal-plus independent Gaussian noise model a feedforward neural network $NN(.)$ is a conditional density model such that $p(x_i|\mathcal{P}_i) = G(x_i; NN(\mathcal{P}_i), \sigma^2)$, where $G(x; c, \sigma^2)$ is our notation for a normal density centered at c and with variance σ^2. More complex conditional densities can, for example, be modeled by mixtures of experts or by Parzen windows based density estimators which we used in our experiments (Section 5). We will use $p^M(x_i|\mathcal{P}_i)$ for a generic conditional probability model. The joint probability model is then

$$p^M(x) = \prod_{i=1}^{N} p^M(x_i|\mathcal{P}_i). \qquad (3)$$

following Equations 1 and 2. Learning Bayesian networks is usually decomposed into the problems of learning structure (that is the arcs in the network) and of learning the conditional density models $P^M(x_i|\mathcal{P}_i)$ given the structure[4]. First assume the structure of the network is given. If the data set only contains complete data, we can train conditional density models $P^M(x_i|\mathcal{P}_i)$ independently of each other since the log-likelihood of the model decomposes conveniently into the individual likelihoods of the models for the conditional probabilities. Next, consider two competing network structures. We are basically faced with the well-known bias-variance dilemma: if we choose a network with too many arcs, we introduce large parameter variance and if we remove too many arcs we introduce bias. Here, the problem is even more complex since we also have the freedom to reverse arcs. In our experiments we evaluate different network structures based on the model likelihood using leave-one-out cross-validation which defines our scoring function for different network structures. More explicitly, the score for network structure S is $Score = \log(p(S)) + L^{cv}$, where $p(S)$ is a prior over the network structures and $L^{cv} = \sum_{k=1}^{D} \log(p^M(x^k|S, X - \{x^k\}))$ is the leave-one-out cross-validation log-likelihood (later referred to as cv-log-likelihood). $X = \{x^k\}_{k=1}^{D}$ is the set of training samples, and $p^M(x^k|S, X - \{x^k\})$ is the probability density of sample x_k given the structure S and all other samples. Each of the terms $p^M(x^k|S, X - \{x^k\})$ can be computed from local densities using Equation 3.

Even for small networks it is computationally impossible to calculate the score for all possible network structures and the search for the global optimal network structure

---

[4] Differing from Heckerman we do not follow a fully Bayesian approach in which priors are defined on parameters and structure; a fully Bayesian approach is elegant if the occurring integrals can be solved in closed form which is not the case for general nonlinear models or if data are incomplete.

4 Prior Models

In a Bayesian framework it is useful to provide means for exploiting prior knowledge, typically introducing a bias for simple structures. Biasing models towards simple structures is also useful if the model selection criteria is based on cross-validation, as in our case, because of the variance in this score. In the experiments we added a penalty per arc to the log-likelihood i.e. $\log p(S) \propto -\alpha N_A$ where N_A is the number of arcs and the parameter α determines the weight of the penalty. Given more specific knowledge in form of a structure defined by a domain expert we can alternatively penalize the deviation in the arc structure (Heckerman, 1995). Furthermore, prior knowledge can be introduced in form of a set of artificial training data. These can be treated identical to real data and loosely correspond to the concept of a conjugate prior.

5 Experiment

In the experiment we used Parzen windows based conditional density estimators to model the conditional densities $p^M(x_i|\mathcal{P}_i)$ from Equation 2, i.e.

$$p^M(x_i|\mathcal{P}_i) = \frac{\sum_{k=1}^{D} G((x_i, \mathcal{P}_i); (x_i^k, \mathcal{P}_i^k), \sigma_i^2)}{\sum_{k=1}^{D} G(\mathcal{P}_i; \mathcal{P}_i^k, \sigma_i^2)}, \quad (4)$$

where $\{x^j\}_{j=1}^{D}$ is the training set. The Gaussians in the nominator are centered at $(x_i^k, \mathcal{P}_i^k)$ which is the location of the k-th sample in the joint input/output (or parent/child) space and the Gaussians in the denominator are centered at $(\mathcal{P}_i^k)$ which is the location of the k-th sample in the input (or parent) space. For each conditional model, σ_i was optimized using leave-one-out cross validation[5].

The unsupervised structure optimization procedure starts with a complete Bayesian model corresponding to Equation 1, i.e. a model where there is an arc between any pair of variables[6]. Next, we tentatively try all possible arc direction changes, arc removals and arc additions which do not produce directed loops and evaluate the change in score. After evaluating all legal single modifications, we accept the change which improves the score the most. The procedure stops if every arc change decreases the score. This greedy strategy can get stuck in local minima which could in principle be avoided if changes which result in worse performance are also accepted with a nonzero probability [7] (such as in annealing strategies, Heckerman, 1995). Calculating the new score at each step requires only local computation. The removal or addition of an arc corresponds to a simple removal or addition of the corresponding dimension in the Gaussians of the local density model. However,

---

[5] Note that if we maintained a *global* σ for all density estimators, we would maintain likelihood equivalence which means that each network displaying the same independence model gets the same score on any test set.

[6] The order of nodes determining the direction of initial arcs is random.

[7] In our experiments we treated very small changes in score as if they were exactly zero thus allowing small decreases in score.

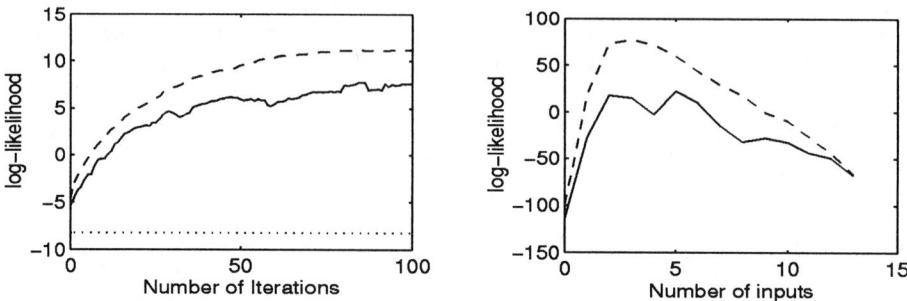

Figure 1: Left: evolution of the cv-log-likelihood (dashed) and of the log-likelihood on the test set (continuous) during structure optimization. The curves are averages over 20 runs with different partitions of training and test sets and the likelihoods are normalized with respect to the number of cv- or test-samples, respectively. The penalty per arc was $\alpha = 0.1$. The dotted line shows the Parzen joint density model commonly used in statistics, i.e. assuming no independencies and using the same width for all Gaussians in all conditional density models. Right: log-likelihood of the local conditional Parzen model for variable 3 ($p^M(x_3|\mathcal{P}_3)$) on the test set (continuous) and the corresponding cv-log-likelihood (dashed) as a function of the number of parents (inputs).

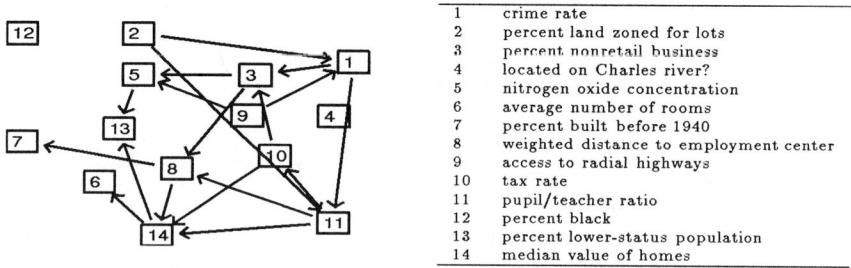

1	crime rate
2	percent land zoned for lots
3	percent nonretail business
4	located on Charles river?
5	nitrogen oxide concentration
6	average number of rooms
7	percent built before 1940
8	weighted distance to employment center
9	access to radial highways
10	tax rate
11	pupil/teacher ratio
12	percent black
13	percent lower-status population
14	median value of homes

Figure 2: Final structure of a run on the full data set.

after each such operation the widths of the Gaussians σ_i in the affected local models have to be optimized. An arc reversal is simply the execution of an arc removal followed by an arc addition.

In our experiment, we used the Boston housing data set, which contains 506 samples. Each sample consists of the housing price and 14 variables which supposedly influence the housing price in a Boston neighborhood (Figure 2). Figure 1 (left) shows an experiment where one third of the samples was reserved as a test set to monitor the process. Since the algorithm never sees the test data the increase in likelihood of the model on the test data is an unbiased estimator for how much the model has improved by the extraction of structure from the data. The large increase in the log-likelihood can be understood by studying Figure 1 (right). Here we picked a single variable (node 3) and formed a density model to predict this variable from the remaining 13 variables. Then we removed input variables in the order of their significance. After the removal of a variable, σ_3 is optimized. Note that the cv-log-likelihood increases until only three input variables are left due to the fact that irrelevant variables or variables which are well represented by the remaining input variables are removed. The log-likelihood of the fully connected initial model is therefore low (Figure 1 left).

We did a second set of 15 runs with no test set. The scores of the final structures had a standard deviation of only 0.4. However, comparing the final structures in terms of undirected arcs[8] the difference was 18% on average. The structure from one of these runs is depicted in Figure 2 (right). In comparison to the initial complete structure with 91 arcs, only 18 arcs are left and 8 arcs have changed direction.

One of the advantages of Bayesian networks is that they can be easily interpreted. The goal of the original Boston housing data experiment was to examine whether the nitrogen oxide concentration (5) influences the housing price (14). Under the structure extracted by the algorithm, 5 and 14 are dependent given all other variables because they have a common child, 13. However, if all variables except 13 are known then they are independent. Another interesting question is what the relevant quantities are for predicting the housing price, i.e. which variables have to be known to render the housing price independent from all other variables. These are the parents, children, and children's parents of variable 14, that is variables 8, 10, 11, 6, 13 and 5. It is well known that in Bayesian networks, different constellations of directions of arcs may induce the same independencies, i.e. that the direction of arcs is not uniquely determined. It can therefore not be expected that the arcs actually reflect the direction of causality.

6 Missing Data and Markov Blanket Conditional Density Model

Bayesian networks are typically used in applications where variables might be missing. Given partial information (i. e. the states of a subset of the variables) the goal is to update the beliefs (i. e. the probabilities) of all unknown variables. Whereas there are powerful local update rules for networks of discrete variables without (undirected) loops, the belief update in networks with loops is in general NP-hard. A generally applicable update rule for the unknown variables in networks of discrete or continuous variables is Gibbs sampling. Gibbs sampling can be roughly described as follows: for all variables whose state is known, fix their states to the known values. For all unknown variables choose some initial states. Then pick a variable x_i which is not known and update its value following the probability distribution

$$p(x_i|\{x_1,\ldots,x_N\} \setminus \{x_i\}) \propto p(x_i|\mathcal{P}_i) \prod_{x_i \in \mathcal{P}_j} p(x_j|\mathcal{P}_j). \tag{5}$$

Do this repeatedly for all unknown variables. Discard the first samples. Then, the samples which are generated are drawn from the probability distribution of the unknown variables given the known variables. Using these samples it is easy to calculate the expected value of any of the unknown variables, estimate variances, covariances and other statistical measures such as the mutual information between variables.

---

[8] Since the direction of arcs is not unique we used the difference in undirected arcs to compare two structures. We used the number of arcs present in one and only one of the structures normalized with respect to the number of arcs in a fully connected network.

Gibbs sampling requires sampling from the univariate probability distribution in Equation 5 which is not straightforward in our model since the conditional density does not have a convenient form. Therefore, sampling techniques such as importance sampling have to be used. In our case they typically produce many rejected samples and are therefore inefficient. An alternative is sampling based on *Markov blanket conditional density models*. The Markov blanket of x_i, $\mathcal{M}_i$ is the smallest set of variables such that $p(x_i|\{x_1,\ldots,x_N\} \setminus x_i) = p(x_i|\mathcal{M}_i)$ (given a Bayesian network, the Markov blanket of a variable consists of its parents, its children and its children's parents.). The idea is to form a conditional density model $p^M(x_i|\mathcal{M}_i) \approx p(x_i|\mathcal{M}_i)$ for each variable in the network instead of computing it according to Equation 5. Sampling from this model is simple using conditional Parzen models: the conditional density is a mixture of Gaussians from which we can sample without rejection[9]. Markov blanket conditional density models are also interesting if we are only interested in always predicting one particular variable, as in most neural network applications. Assuming that a signal-plus-noise model is a reasonably good model for the conditional density, we can train an ordinary neural network to predict the variable of interest. In addition, we train a model for each input variable predicting it from the remaining variables. In addition to having obtained a model for the complete data case, we can now also handle missing inputs and do backward inference using Gibbs sampling.

7 Conclusions

We demonstrated that Bayesian models of local conditional density estimators form promising nonlinear dependency models for continuous variables. The conditional density models can be trained locally if training data are complete. In this paper we focused on the self-organized extraction of structure. Bayesian networks can also serve as a framework for a modular construction of large systems out of smaller conditional density models. The Bayesian framework provides consistent update rules for the probabilities i.e. communication between modules. Finally, consider input pruning or variable selection in neural networks. Note, that our pruning strategy in Figure 1 can be considered a form of variable selection by not only removing variables which are statistically independent of the output variable but also removing variables which are represented well by the remaining variables. This way we obtain more compact models. If input values are missing then the indirect influence of the pruned variables on the output will be recovered by the sampling mechanism.

References

Buntine, W. (1994). Operations for learning with graphical models. *Journal of Artificial Intelligence Research* 2:159-225.

Heckerman, D. (1995). A tutorial on learning Bayesian networks. Microsoft Research, TR. MSR-TR-95-06, 1995.

Pearl, J. (1988). *Probabilistic Reasoning in Intelligent Systems*. San Mateo, CA: Morgan Kaufmann.

---

[9]There are, however, several open issues concerning consistency between the conditional models.

Using Pairs of Data-Points to Define Splits for Decision Trees

Geoffrey E. Hinton
Department of Computer Science
University of Toronto
Toronto, Ontario, M5S 1A4, Canada
hinton@cs.toronto.edu

Michael Revow
Department of Computer Science
University of Toronto
Toronto, Ontario, M5S 1A4, Canada
revow@cs.toronto.edu

Abstract

Conventional binary classification trees such as CART either split the data using axis-aligned hyperplanes or they perform a computationally expensive search in the continuous space of hyperplanes with unrestricted orientations. We show that the limitations of the former can be overcome without resorting to the latter. For every pair of training data-points, there is one hyperplane that is orthogonal to the line joining the data-points and bisects this line. Such hyperplanes are plausible candidates for splits. In a comparison on a suite of 12 datasets we found that this method of generating candidate splits outperformed the standard methods, particularly when the training sets were small.

1 Introduction

Binary decision trees come in many flavours, but they all rely on splitting the set of k-dimensional data-points at each internal node into two disjoint sets. Each split is usually performed by projecting the data onto some direction in the k-dimensional space and then thresholding the scalar value of the projection. There are two commonly used methods of picking a projection direction. The simplest method is to restrict the allowable directions to the k axes defined by the data. This is the default method used in CART [1]. If this set of directions is too restrictive, the usual alternative is to search general directions in the full k-dimensional space or general directions in a space defined by a subset of the k axes.

Projections onto one of the k axes defined by the the data have many advantages over projections onto a more general direction:

1. It is very efficient to perform the projection for each of the data-points. We simply ignore the values of the data-point on the other axes.

2. For N data-points, it is feasible to consider all possible axis-aligned projections and thresholds because there are only k possible projections and for each of these there are at most $N-1$ threshold values that yield different splits. Selecting from a fixed set of projections and thresholds is simpler than searching the k-dimensional continuous space of hyperplanes that correspond to unrestricted projections and thresholds.

3. Since a split is selected from only about Nk candidates, it takes only about $\log_2 N + \log_2 k$ bits to define the split. So it should be possible to use many more of these axis-aligned splits before overfitting occurs than if we use more general hyperplanes. If the data-points are in general position, each subset of size k defines a different hyperplane so there are $N!/k!(N-k)!$ distinctly different hyperplanes and if $k << N$ it takes approximately $k \log_2 N$ bits to specify one of them.

For some datasets, the restriction to axis-aligned projections is too limiting. This is especially true for high-dimensional data, like images, in which there are strong correlations between the intensities of neighbouring pixels. In such cases, many axis-aligned boundaries may be required to approximate a planar boundary that is not axis-aligned, so it is natural to consider unrestricted projections and some versions of the CART program allow this. Unfortunately this greatly increases the computational burden and the search may get trapped in local minima. Also significant care must be exercised to avoid overfitting. There is, however, an intermediate approach which allows the projections to be non-axis-aligned but preserves all three of the attractive properties of axis-aligned projections: It is trivial to decide which side of the resulting hyperplane a given data-point lies on; the hyperplanes can be selected from a modest-sized set of sensible candidates; and hence many splits can be used before overfitting occurs because only a few bits are required to specify each split.

2   Using two data-points to define a projection

Each pair of data-points defines a direction in the data space. This direction is a plausible candidate for a projection to be used in splitting the data, especially if it is a classification task and the two data-points are in different classes. For each such direction, we could consider all of the $N-1$ possible thresholds that would give different splits, or, to save time and reduce complexity, we could only consider the threshold value that is halfway between the two data-points that define the projection. If we use this threshold value, each pair of data-points defines exactly one hyperplane and we call the two data-points the "poles" of this hyperplane.

For a general k-dimensional hyperplane it requires $O(k)$ operations to decide whether a data-point, C, is on one side or the other. But we can save a factor of k by using hyperplanes defined by pairs of data-points. If we already know the distances of C from each of the two poles, A, B then we only need to compare

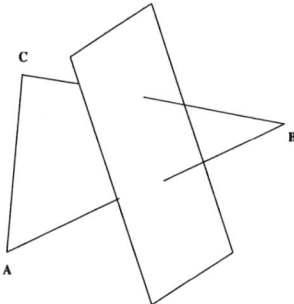

Figure 1: A hyperplane orthogonal to the line joining points A and B. We can quickly determine on which side a test point, C, lies by comparing the distances AC and BC.

these two distances (see figure 1).[1] So if we are willing to do $O(kN^2)$ operations to compute all the pairwise distances between the data-points, we can then decide in constant time which side of the hyperplane a point lies on.

As we are building the decision tree, we need to compute the gain in performance from using each possible split at each existing terminal node. Since all the terminal nodes combined contain N data-points and there are $N(N-1)/2$ possible splits[2] this takes time $O(N^3)$ instead of $O(kN^3)$. So the work in computing all the pairwise distances is trivial compared with the savings.

Using the Minimum Description Length framework, it is clear that pole-pair splits can be described very cheaply, so a lot of them can be used before overfitting occurs. When applying MDL to a supervised learning task we can assume that the receiver gets to see the input vectors for free. It is only the output vectors that need to be communicated. So if splits are selected from a set of $N(N-1)/2$ possibilities that is determined by the input vectors, it takes only about $2\log_2 N$ bits to communicate a split to a receiver. Even if we allow all $N-1$ possible threshold values along the projection defined by two data-points, it takes only about $3\log_2 N$ bits. So the number of these splits that can be used before overfitting occurs should be greater by a factor of about $k/2$ or $k/3$ than for general hyperplanes. Assuming that $k << N$, the same line of argument suggests that even more axis-aligned planes can be used, but only by a factor of about 2 or 3.

To summarize, the hyperplanes planes defined by pairs of data-points are computationally convenient and seem like natural candidates for good splits. They overcome the major weakness of axis-aligned splits and, because they can be specified in a modest number of bits, they may be more effective than fully general hyperplanes when the training set is small.

---

[1] If the threshold value is not midway between the poles, we can still save a factor of k but we need to compute $(d_{AC}^2 - d_{BC}^2)/2d_{AB}$ instead of just the sign of this expression.

[2] Since we only consider splits in which the poles are in different classes, this number ignores a factor that is independent of N.

3 Building the decision tree

We want to compare the "pole-pair" method of generating candidate hyperplanes with the standard axis-aligned method and the method that uses unrestricted hyperplanes. We can see no reason to expect strong interactions between the method of building the tree and the method of generating the candidate hyperplanes, but to minimize confounding effects we always use exactly the same method of building the decision tree.

We faithfully followed the method described in [1], except for a small modification where the code that was kindly supplied by Leo Breiman used a slightly different method for determining the amount of pruning.

Training a decision tree involves two distinct stages. In the first stage, nodes are repeatedly split until each terminal node is "pure" which means that all of its datapoints belong to the same class. The pure tree therefore fits the training data perfectly. A node is split by considering all candidate decision planes and choosing the one that maximizes the decrease in impurity. Breiman *et. al* recommend using the *Gini* index to measure impurity.[3] If $p(j|t)$ is the probability of class j at node t, then the Gini index is $1 - \sum_j p^2(j|t)$.

Clearly the tree obtained at the end of the first stage will overfit the data and so in the second stage the tree is pruned by recombining nodes. For a tree, T_i, with $|T_i|$ terminal nodes we consider the regularized cost:

$$C = E + \alpha |T_i| \qquad (1)$$

where E is the classification error and α is a pruning parameter. In "weakest-link" pruning the terminal nodes are eliminated in the order which keeps (1) minimal as α increases. This leads to a particular sequence, $T = \{T_1, T_2, ...T_k\}$ of subtrees, in which $|T_1| > |T_2|... > |T_k|$. We call this the "main" sequence of subtrees because they are trained on *all* of the training data.

The last remaining issue to be resolved is which tree in the main sequence to use. The simplest method is to use a separate validation set and choose the tree size that gives best classification on it. Unfortunately, many of the datasets we used were too small to hold back a reserved validation set. So we always used 10-fold cross validation to pick the size of the tree. We first grew 10 different subsidiary trees until their terminal nodes were pure, using 9/10 of the data for training each of them. Then we pruned back each of these pure subsidiary trees, as above, producing 10 sequences of subsidiary subtrees. These subsidiary sequences could then be used for estimating the performance of each subtree in the main sequence. For each of the main subtrees, T_i, we found the largest tree in each subsidiary sequence that was no larger than T_i and estimated the performance of T_i to be the average of the performance achieved by each subsidiary subtree on the 1/10 of the data that was not used for training that subsidiary tree. We then chose the T_i that achieved the best performance estimate and used it on the test set[4]. Results are expressed as

---

[3]Impurity is not an information measure but, like an information measure, it is minimized when all the nodes are pure and maximized when all classes at each node have equal probability.

[4]This differs from the conventional application of cross validation, where it is used to

	IR	TR	LV	DB	BC	GL	VW	WN	VH	WV	IS	SN
Size (N)	150	215	345	768	683	163	990	178	846	2100	351	208
Classes (c)	3	3	2	2	2	2	11	3	4	3	2	2
Attributes (k)	4	5	6	8	9	9	10	13	18	21	34	60

Table 1: Summary of the datasets used.

the ratio of the test error rate to the baseline rate, which is the error rate of a tree with only a single terminal node.

4 The Datasets

Eleven datasets were selected from the database of machine learning tasks maintained by the University of California at Irvine (see the appendix for a list of the datasets used). Except as noted in the appendix, the datasets were used exactly in the form of the distribution as of June 1993. All datasets have only continuous attributes and there are no missing values.[5] The synthetic "waves" example [1] was added as a twelfth dataset.

Table 1 gives a brief description of the datasets. Datasets are identified by a two letter abbreviation along the top. The rows in the table give the total number of instances, number of classes and number of attributes for each dataset.

A few datasets in the original distribution have designated training and testing subsets while others do not. To ensure regularity among datasets, we pooled all usable examples in a given dataset, randomized the order in the pool and then divided the pool into training and testing sets. Two divisions were considered. The *large* training division had $\frac{2}{3}$ of the pooled examples allocated to the training set and $\frac{1}{3}$ to the test set. The *small* training division had $\frac{1}{3}$ of the data in the training set and $\frac{2}{3}$ in the test set.

5 Results

Table 2 gives the error rates for both the *large* and *small* divisions of the data, expressed as a percentage of the error rate obtained by guessing the dominant class.

In both the *small* and *large* training divisions of the datasets, the pole-pair method had lower error rates than axis-aligned or linear cart in the majority of datasets tested. While these results are interesting, they do not provide any measure of confidence that one method performs better or worse than another. Since all methods were trained and tested on the same data, we can perform a two-tailed *McNemar test* [2] on the predictions for pairs of methods. The resulting P-values are given in table 3. On most of the tasks, the pole-pair method is significantly better than at least one of the standard methods for at least one of the training set sizes and there are only 2 tasks for which either of the other methods is significantly better on either training set size.

---

determine the best value of α rather than the tree size

[5]In the BC dataset we removed the case identification number attribute and had to delete 16 cases with missing values.

Database	Small Train			Large Train		
	cart	linear	pole	cart	linear	pole
IR	14.3	14.3	4.3	5.6	5.6	5.6
TR	36.6	26.8	14.6	33.3	33.3	20.8
LV	88.9	100.0	100.0	108.7	87.0	97.8
DB	85.8	82.2	87.0	69.7	69.7	59.6
BC	12.8	14.1	8.3	15.7	12.0	9.6
GL	62.5	81.3	89.6	46.4	46.4	35.7
VW	31.8	37.7	30.0	21.4	26.2	19.2
WN	17.8	13.7	11.0	14.7	11.8	14.7
VH	42.5	46.5	44.2	36.2	43.9	40.7
WV	28.9	25.8	24.3	30.6	24.8	26.6
IS	44.0	31.0	41.7	21.4	23.8	42.9
SN	65.2	71.2	48.5	48.4	45.2	48.4

Table 2: Relative error rates expressed as a percentage of the baseline rate on the small and large training sets.

6 Discussion

We only considered hyperplanes whose poles were in different classes, since these seemed more plausible candidates. An alternative strategy is to disregard class membership, and consider *all* possible pole-pairs. Another variant of the method arises depending on whether the inputs are scaled. We transformed all inputs so that the training data has zero mean and unit variance. However, using unscaled inputs and/or allowing both poles to have the same class makes little difference to the overall advantage of the pole-pair method.

To summarize, we have demonstrated that the pole-pair method is a simple, effective method for generating projection directions at binary tree nodes. The same idea of minimizing complexity by selecting among a sensible fixed set of possibilities rather than searching a continuous space can also be applied to the choice of input-to-hidden weights in a neural network.

A Databases used in the study

IR - Iris plant database.
TR - Thyroid gland data.
LV - BUPA liver disorders.
DB - Pima Indians Diabetes.
BC - Breast cancer database from the University of Wisconsin Hospitals.
GL - Glass identification database. In these experiments we only considered the classification into float/nonfloat processed glass, ignoring other types of glass.
VW - Vowel recognition.
WN - Wine recognition.
VH - Vehicle silhouettes.
WV - Waveform example, the synthetic example from [1].
IS - Johns Hopkins University Ionosphere database.
SN - Sonar - mines versus rocks discrimination. We did not control for aspect-angle.

Small Training - Large Test

	IR	TR	LV	DB	BC	GL	VW	WN	VH	WV	IS	SN
Axis-<u>Pole</u>	.02	.02	.18	.46	.06	.02	.24	.15	.33	<u>.00</u>	.44	.07
Linear-<u>Pole</u>	.02	.13	1.0	.26	.02	.30	<u>.00</u>	.41	.27	.17	.09	.02
<u>Axis</u>-Linear	1.0	.06	.18	.30	.40	.00	.00	.31	.08	<u>.03</u>	.02	.32

Large Training - Small Test

	IR	TR	LV	DB	BC	GL	VW	WN	VH	WV	IS	SN
Axis-<u>Pole</u>	.75	.23	.29	<u>.04</u>	.11	.29	.26	.69	.14	.08	.02	.60
Linear-<u>Pole</u>	.75	.23	.26	<u>.04</u>	.25	.30	<u>.01</u>	.50	.25	.26	.05	.50
<u>Axis</u>-Linear	1.0	1.0	.07	1.0	.29	.69	.06	.50	.03	<u>.01</u>	.50	.50

Table 3: P-Values using a two-tailed *McNemar* test on the *small* (top) and *large* (bottom) training sets. Each row gives P-values when the methods in the left most column are compared. A significant difference at the $P = 0.05$ level is indicated with a line above (below) the P-value depending on whether the first (second) mentioned method in the first column had superior performance. For example, in the top most row, the pole-pair method was significantly better than the axis-aligned method on the TR dataset.

Acknowledgments

We thank Leo Breiman for kindly making his CART code available to us. This research was funded by the Institute for Robotics and Intelligent Systems and by NSERC. Hinton is a fellow of the Canadian Institute for Advanced Research.

References

[1] L. Breiman, J. H. Freidman, R. A. Olshen, and C. J. Stone. *Classification and regression trees*. Wadsworth international Group, Belmont, California, 1984.

[2] J. L. Fleiss. *Statistical methods for rates and proportions*. Second edition. Wiley, 1981.

Gaussian Processes for Regression

Christopher K. I. Williams
Neural Computing Research Group
Aston University
Birmingham B4 7ET, UK
c.k.i.williams@aston.ac.uk

Carl Edward Rasmussen
Department of Computer Science
University of Toronto
Toronto, ONT, M5S 1A4, Canada
carl@cs.toronto.edu

Abstract

The Bayesian analysis of neural networks is difficult because a simple prior over weights implies a complex prior distribution over functions. In this paper we investigate the use of Gaussian process priors over functions, which permit the predictive Bayesian analysis for fixed values of hyperparameters to be carried out exactly using matrix operations. Two methods, using optimization and averaging (via Hybrid Monte Carlo) over hyperparameters have been tested on a number of challenging problems and have produced excellent results.

1 INTRODUCTION

In the Bayesian approach to neural networks a prior distribution over the weights induces a prior distribution over functions. This prior is combined with a noise model, which specifies the probability of observing the targets t given function values y, to yield a posterior over functions which can then be used for predictions. For neural networks the prior over functions has a complex form which means that implementations must either make approximations (e.g. MacKay, 1992) or use Monte Carlo approaches to evaluating integrals (Neal, 1993).

As Neal (1995) has argued, there is no reason to believe that, for real-world problems, neural network models should be limited to nets containing only a "small" number of hidden units. He has shown that it is sensible to consider a limit where the number of hidden units in a net tends to infinity, and that good predictions can be obtained from such models using the Bayesian machinery. He has also shown that a large class of neural network models will converge to a Gaussian process prior over functions in the limit of an infinite number of hidden units.

In this paper we use Gaussian processes specified parametrically for regression problems. The advantage of the Gaussian process formulation is that the combination of

Gaussian Processes for Regression

the prior and noise models can be carried out exactly using matrix operations. We also show how the *hyperparameters* which control the form of the Gaussian process can be estimated from the data, using either a maximum likelihood or Bayesian approach, and that this leads to a form of "Automatic Relevance Determination" (Mackay 1993; Neal 1995).

2 PREDICTION WITH GAUSSIAN PROCESSES

A stochastic process is a collection of random variables $\{Y(\boldsymbol{x})|\boldsymbol{x} \in X\}$ indexed by a set X. In our case X will be the input space with dimension d, the number of inputs. The stochastic process is specified by giving the probability distribution for every finite subset of variables $Y(\boldsymbol{x}^{(1)}), \ldots, Y(\boldsymbol{x}^{(k)})$ in a consistent manner. A Gaussian process is a stochastic process which can be fully specified by its mean function $\mu(\boldsymbol{x}) = E[Y(\boldsymbol{x})]$ and its covariance function $C(\boldsymbol{x}, \boldsymbol{x}') = E[(Y(\boldsymbol{x}) - \mu(\boldsymbol{x}))(Y(\boldsymbol{x}') - \mu(\boldsymbol{x}'))]$; any finite set of points will have a joint multivariate Gaussian distribution. Below we consider Gaussian processes which have $\mu(\boldsymbol{x}) \equiv 0$.

In section 2.1 we will show how to parameterise covariances using hyperparameters; for now we consider the form of the covariance C as given. The training data consists of n pairs of inputs and targets $\{(\boldsymbol{x}^{(i)}, t^{(i)}), i = 1 \ldots n\}$. The input vector for a test case is denoted $\boldsymbol{x}$ (with no superscript). The inputs are d-dimensional $x_1, \ldots, x_d$ and the targets are scalar.

The predictive distribution for a test case $\boldsymbol{x}$ is obtained from the $n+1$ dimensional joint Gaussian distribution for the outputs of the n training cases and the test case, by conditioning on the observed targets in the training set. This procedure is illustrated in Figure 1, for the case where there is one training point and one test point. In general, the predictive distribution is Gaussian with mean and variance

$$\hat{y}(\boldsymbol{x}) = \boldsymbol{k}^T(\boldsymbol{x}) K^{-1} \boldsymbol{t} \qquad (1)$$

$$\sigma_{\hat{y}}^2(\boldsymbol{x}) = C(\boldsymbol{x}, \boldsymbol{x}) - \boldsymbol{k}^T(\boldsymbol{x}) K^{-1} \boldsymbol{k}(\boldsymbol{x}), \qquad (2)$$

where $\boldsymbol{k}(\boldsymbol{x}) = (C(\boldsymbol{x}, \boldsymbol{x}^{(1)}), \ldots, C(\boldsymbol{x}, \boldsymbol{x}^{(n)}))^T$, K is the covariance matrix for the training cases $K_{ij} = C(\boldsymbol{x}^{(i)}, \boldsymbol{x}^{(j)})$, and $\boldsymbol{t} = (t^{(1)}, \ldots, t^{(n)})^T$.

The matrix inversion step in equations (1) and (2) implies that the algorithm has $O(n^3)$ time complexity (if standard methods of matrix inversion are employed); for a few hundred data points this is certainly feasible on workstation computers, although for larger problems some iterative methods or approximations may be needed.

2.1 PARAMETERIZING THE COVARIANCE FUNCTION

There are many choices of covariance functions which may be reasonable. Formally, we are required to specify functions which will generate a non-negative definite covariance matrix for any set of points $(\boldsymbol{x}^{(1)}, \ldots, \boldsymbol{x}^{(k)})$. From a modelling point of view we wish to specify covariances so that points with nearby inputs will give rise to similar predictions. We find that the following covariance function works well:

$$C(\boldsymbol{x}^{(i)}, \boldsymbol{x}^{(j)}) = v_0 \exp\{-\frac{1}{2} \sum_{l=1}^{d} w_l (x_l^{(i)} - x_l^{(j)})^2\} \qquad (3)$$

$$+ a_0 + a_1 \sum_{l=1}^{d} x_l^{(i)} x_l^{(j)} + v_1 \delta(i, j),$$

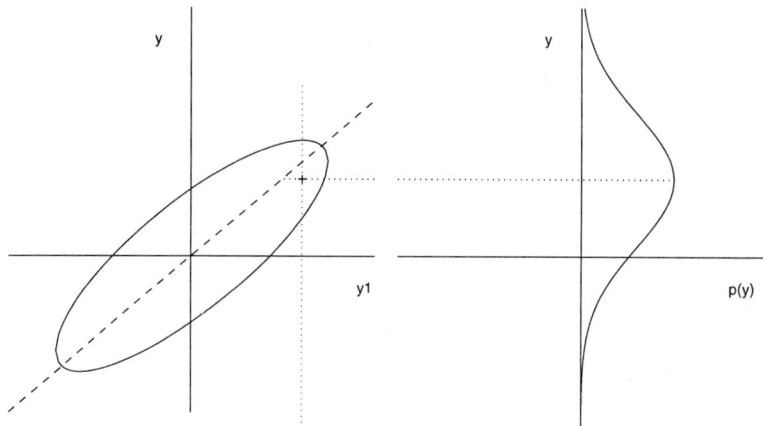

Figure 1: An illustration of prediction using a Gaussian process. There is one training case $(x^{(1)}, t^{(1)})$ and one test case for which we wish to predict y. The ellipse in the left-hand plot is the one standard deviation contour plot of the joint distribution of y_1 and y. The dotted line represents an observation $y_1 = t^{(1)}$. In the right-hand plot we see the distribution of the output for the test case, obtained by conditioning on the observed target. The y axes have the same scale in both plots.

where $\theta = \log(v_0, v_1, w_1, \ldots, w_d, a_0, a_1)$ plays the role of hyperparameters[1]. We define the hyperparameters to be the log of the variables in equation (4) since these are positive scale-parameters.

The covariance function is made up of three parts; the first term, a linear regression term (involving a_0 and a_1) and a noise term $v_1 \delta(i,j)$. The first term expresses the idea that cases with nearby inputs will have highly correlated outputs; the w_l parameters allow a different distance measure for each input dimension. For irrelevant inputs, the corresponding w_l will become small, and the model will ignore that input. This is closely related to the Automatic Relevance Determination (ARD) idea of MacKay and Neal (MacKay, 1993; Neal 1995). The v_0 variable gives the overall scale of the local correlations. This covariance function is valid for all input dimensionalities as compared to splines, where the integrated squared mth derivative is only a valid regularizer for $2m > d$ (see Wahba, 1990). a_0 and a_1 are variables controlling the scale the of bias and linear contributions to the covariance. The last term accounts for the noise on the data; v_1 is the variance of the noise.

Given a covariance function, the log likelihood of the training data is given by

$$l = -\frac{1}{2}\log \det K - \frac{1}{2}t^T K^{-1} t - \frac{n}{2}\log 2\pi. \qquad (4)$$

In section 3 we will discuss how the hyperparameters in C can be adapted, in response to the training data.

2.2 RELATIONSHIP TO PREVIOUS WORK

The Gaussian process view provides a unifying framework for many regression methods. ARMA models used in time series analysis and spline smoothing (e.g. Wahba, 1990 and earlier references therein) correspond to Gaussian process prediction with

---

[1] We call θ the hyperparameters as they correspond closely to hyperparameters in neural networks; in effect the weights have been integrated out exactly.

a particular choice of covariance function[2]. Gaussian processes have also been used in the geostatistics field (e.g. Cressie, 1993), and are known there as "kriging", but this literature has concentrated on the case where the input space is two or three dimensional, rather than considering more general input spaces.

This work is similar to Regularization Networks (Poggio and Girosi, 1990; Girosi, Jones and Poggio, 1995), except that their derivation uses a smoothness functional rather than the equivalent covariance function. Poggio *et al* suggested that the hyperparameters be set by cross-validation. The main contributions of this paper are to emphasize that a maximum likelihood solution for θ is possible, to recognize the connections to ARD and to use the Hybrid Monte Carlo method in the Bayesian treatment (see section 3).

3 TRAINING A GAUSSIAN PROCESS

The partial derivative of the log likelihood of the training data l with respect to all the hyperparameters can be computed using matrix operations, and takes time $O(n^3)$. In this section we present two methods which can be used to adapt the hyperparameters using these derivatives.

3.1 MAXIMUM LIKELIHOOD

In a maximum likelihood framework, we adjust the hyperparameters so as to maximize that likelihood of the training data. We initialize the hyperparameters to random values (in a reasonable range) and then use an iterative method, for example conjugate gradient, to search for optimal values of the hyperparameters. Since there are only a small number of hyperparameters ($d+4$) a relatively small number of iterations are usually sufficient for convergence. However, we have found that this approach is sometimes susceptible to local minima, so it is advisable to try a number of random starting positions in hyperparameter space.

3.2 INTEGRATION VIA HYBRID MONTE CARLO

According to the Bayesian formalism, we should start with a prior distribution $P(\theta)$ over the hyperparameters which is modified using the training data D to produce a posterior distribution $P(\theta|D)$. To make predictions we then integrate over the posterior; for example, the predicted mean $\overline{y}(x)$ for test input x is given by

$$\overline{y}(x) = \int \hat{y}_\theta(x) P(\theta|D) d\theta \qquad (5)$$

where $\hat{y}_\theta(x)$ is the predicted mean (as given by equation 1) for a particular value of θ. It is not feasible to do this integration analytically, but the Markov chain Monte Carlo method of Hybrid Monte Carlo (HMC) (Duane *et al*, 1987) seems promising for this application. We assign broad Gaussians priors to the hyperparameters, and use Hybrid Monte Carlo to give us samples from the posterior.

HMC works by creating a fictitious dynamical system in which the hyperparameters are regarded as position variables, and augmenting these with momentum variables p. The purpose of the dynamical system is to give the hyperparameters "inertia" so that random-walk behaviour in θ-space can be avoided. The total energy, H, of the system is the sum of the kinetic energy, K, (a function of the momenta) and the potential energy, E. The potential energy is defined such that $p(\theta|D) \propto \exp(-E)$. We sample from the joint distribution for θ and p given by $p(\theta, p) \propto \exp(-E -$

---

[2] Technically splines require generalized covariance functions.

K); the marginal of this distribution for θ is the required posterior. A sample of hyperparameters from the posterior can therefore be obtained by simply ignoring the momenta.

Sampling from the joint distribution is achieved by two steps: (i) finding new points in phase space with near-identical energies H by simulating the dynamical system using a discretised approximation to Hamiltonian dynamics, and (ii) changing the energy H by doing Gibbs sampling for the momentum variables.

Hamiltonian Dynamics

Hamilton's first order differential equations for H are approximated by a discrete step (specifically using the *leapfrog* method). The derivatives of the likelihood (equation 4) enter through the derivative of the potential energy. This proposed state is then accepted or rejected using the Metropolis rule depending on the final energy H^* (which is not necessarily equal to the initial energy H because of the discretization). The same step size ε is used for all hyperparameters, and should be as large as possible while keeping the rejection rate low.

Gibbs Sampling for Momentum Variables

The momentum variables are updated using a modified version of Gibbs sampling, thereby allowing the energy H to change. A "persistence" of 0.95 is used; the new value of the momentum is a weighted sum of the previous value (with weight 0.95) and the value obtained by Gibbs sampling (weight $(1 - 0.95^2)^{1/2}$). With this form of persistence, the momenta change approximately twenty times more slowly, thus increasing the "inertia" of the hyperparameters, so as to further help in avoiding random walks. Larger values of the persistence will further increase the inertia, but reduce the rate of exploration of H.

Practical Details

The priors over hyperparameters are set to be Gaussian with a mean of -3 and a standard deviation of 3. In all our simulations a step size $\varepsilon = 0.05$ produced a very low rejection rate ($< 1\%$). The hyperparameters corresponding to v_1 and to the w_l's were initialised to -2 and the rest to 0.

To apply the method we first rescale the inputs and outputs so that they have mean of zero and a variance of one on the training set. The sampling procedure is run for the desired amount of time, saving the values of the hyperparameters 200 times during the last two-thirds of the run. The first third of the run is discarded; this "burn-in" is intended to give the hyperparameters time to come close to their equilibrium distribution. The predictive distribution is then a mixture of 200 Gaussians. For a squared error loss, we use the mean of this distribution as a point estimate. The width of the predictive distribution tells us the uncertainty of the prediction.

4 EXPERIMENTAL RESULTS

We report the results of prediction with Gaussian process on (i) a modified version of MacKay's robot arm problem and (ii) five real-world data sets.

4.1 THE ROBOT ARM PROBLEM

We consider a version of MacKay's robot arm problem introduced by Neal (1995). The standard robot arm problem is concerned with the mappings

$$y_1 = r_1 \cos x_1 + r_2 \cos(x_1 + x_2) \qquad y_2 = r_1 \sin x_1 + r_2 \sin(x_1 + x_2) \qquad (6)$$

Method	No. of inputs	sum squared test error
Gaussian process	2	1.126
Gaussian process	6	1.138
MacKay	2	1.146
Neal	2	1.094
Neal	6	1.098

Table 1: Results on the robot arm task. The bottom three lines of data were obtained from Neal (1995). The MacKay result is the test error for the net with highest "evidence".

The data was generated by picking x_1 uniformly from [-1.932, -0.453] and [0.453, 1.932] and picking x_2 uniformly from [0.534, 3.142]. Neal added four further inputs, two of which were copies of x_1 and x_2 corrupted by additive Gaussian noise of standard deviation 0.02, and two further irrelevant Gaussian-noise inputs with zero mean and unit variance. Independent zero-mean Gaussian noise of variance 0.0025 was then added to the outputs y_1 and y_2. We used the same datasets as Neal and MacKay, with 200 examples in the training set and 200 in the test set.

The theory described in section 2 deals only with the prediction of a scalar quantity Y, so predictors were constructed for the two outputs separately, although a joint prediction is possible within the Gaussian process framework (see co-kriging, §3.2.3 in Cressie, 1993).

Two experiments were conducted, the first using only the two "true" inputs, and the second one using all six inputs. In this section we report results using maximum likelihood training; similar results were obtained with HMC. The $\log(v)$'s and $\log(w)$'s were all initialized to values chosen uniformly from [-3.0, 0.0], and were adapted separately for the prediction of y_1 and y_2 (in these early experiments the linear regression terms in the covariance function involving a_0 and a_1 were not present). The conjugate gradient search algorithm was allowed to run for 100 iterations, by which time the likelihood was changing very slowly. Results are reported for the run which gave the highest likelihood of the training data, although in fact all runs performed very similarly. The results are shown in Table 1 and are encouraging, as they indicate that the Gaussian process approach is giving very similar performance to two well-respected techniques. All of the methods obtain a level of performance which is quite close to the theoretical minimum error level of 1.0. It is interesting to look at the values of the w's obtained after the optimization; for the y_2 task the values were 0.243, 0.237, 0.0639, 7.0×10^{-4}, 2.32×10^{-6}, 1.70×10^{-6}, and v_0 and v_1 were 7.5278 and 0.0022 respectively. The w values show nicely that the first two inputs are the most important, followed by the corrupted inputs and then the irrelevant inputs. During training the irrelevant inputs are detected quite quickly, but the w's for the corrupted inputs shrink more slowly, implying that the input noise has relatively little effect on the likelihood.

4.2 FIVE REAL-WORLD PROBLEMS

Gaussian Processes as described above were compared to several other regression algorithms on five real-world data sets in (Rasmussen, 1996; in this volume). The data sets had between 80 and 256 training examples, and the input dimension ranged from 6 to 16. The length of the HMC sampling for the Gaussian processes was from 7.5 minutes for the smallest training set size up to 1 hour for the largest ones on a R4400 machine. The results rank the methods in the order (lowest error first) a full-blown Bayesian treatment of neural networks using HMC, Gaussian processes, ensembles of neural networks trained using cross validation and weight decay, the Evidence framework for neural networks (MacKay, 1992), and MARS. We are currently working on assessing the statistical significance of this ordering.

5 DISCUSSION

We have presented the method of regression with Gaussian processes, and shown that it performs well on a suite of real-world problems.

We have also conducted some experiments on the approximation of neural nets (with a finite number of hidden units) by Gaussian processes, although space limitations do not allow these to be described here. Some other directions currently under investigation include (i) the use of Gaussian processes for classification problems by softmaxing the outputs of k regression surfaces (for a k-class classification problem), (ii) using non-stationary covariance functions, so that $C(\boldsymbol{x}, \boldsymbol{x}') \neq C(|\boldsymbol{x} - \boldsymbol{x}'|)$ and (iii) using a covariance function containing a sum of two or more terms of the form given in line 1 of equation 3.

We hope to make our code for Gaussian process prediction publically available in the near future. Check http://www.cs.utoronto.ca/neuron/delve/delve.html for details.

Acknowledgements

We thank Radford Neal for many useful discussions, David MacKay for generously providing the robot arm data used in this paper, and Chris Bishop, Peter Dayan, Radford Neal and Huaiyu Zhu for comments on earlier drafts. CW was partially supported by EPSRC grant GR/J75425.

References

Cressie, N. A. C. (1993). *Statistics for Spatial Data*. Wiley.

Duane, S., Kennedy, A. D., Pendleton, B. J., and Roweth, D. (1987). Hybrid Monte Carlo. *Physics Letters B*, 195:216–222.

Girosi, F., Jones, M., and Poggio, T. (1995). Regularization Theory and Neural Networks Architectures. *Neural Computation*, 7(2):219–269.

MacKay, D. J. C. (1992). A Practical Bayesian Framework for Backpropagation Networks. *Neural Computation*, 4(3):448–472.

MacKay, D. J. C. (1993). Bayesian Methods for Backpropagation Networks. In van Hemmen, J. L., Domany, E., and Schulten, K., editors, *Models of Neural Networks II*. Springer.

Neal, R. M. (1993). Bayesian Learning via Stochastic Dynamics. In Hanson, S. J., Cowan, J. D., and Giles, C. L., editors, *Neural Information Processing Systems, Vol. 5*, pages 475–482. Morgan Kaufmann, San Mateo, CA.

Neal, R. M. (1995). *Bayesian Learning for Neural Networks*. PhD thesis, Dept. of Computer Science, University of Toronto.

Poggio, T. and Girosi, F. (1990). Networks for approximation and learning. *Proceedings of IEEE*, 78:1481–1497.

Rasmussen, C. E. (1996). A Practical Monte Carlo Implementation of Bayesian Learning. In Touretzky, D. S., Mozer, M. C., and Hasselmo, M. E., editors, *Advances in Neural Information Processing Systems 8*. MIT Press.

Wahba, G. (1990). *Spline Models for Observational Data*. Society for Industrial and Applied Mathematics. CBMS-NSF Regional Conference series in applied mathematics.

Pruning with generalization based weight saliencies: γOBD, γOBS

Morten With Pedersen
Lars Kai Hansen
Jan Larsen
CONNECT, Electronics Institute
Technical University of Denmark B349
DK-2800 Lyngby, DENMARK
emails: with,lkhansen,jlarsen@ei.dtu.dk

Abstract

The purpose of most architecture optimization schemes is to improve generalization. In this presentation we suggest to estimate the weight saliency as the associated change in generalization error if the weight is pruned. We detail the implementation of both an $O(N)$-storage scheme extending OBD, as well as an $O(N^2)$ scheme extending OBS. We illustrate the viability of the approach on prediction of a chaotic time series.

1 BACKGROUND

Optimization of feed-forward neural networks by pruning is a well-established tool, used in many practical applications. By careful fine tuning of the network architecture we may improve generalization, decrease the amount of computation, and facilitate interpretation.

The two most widely used schemes for pruning of feed-forward nets are: Optimal Brain Damage (OBD) due to (LeCun et al., 90) and the Optimal Brain Surgeon (OBS) (Hassibi et al., 93). Both schemes are based on weight ranking according to *saliency* defined as the change in *training error* when the particular weight is pruned. In OBD the saliency is estimated as the direct change in training error, i.e., without retraining of the remaining weights, while the OBS scheme includes retraining in a local quadratic approximation. The *rationale* of both methods is that if the least significant weights (according to training error) are deleted, we gracefully relieve the danger of overfitting. However, in both cases one clearly needs a *stop criterion*. As both schemes aim at minimal generalization error an estimator for this quantity is needed. The most obvious candidate estimate is a *test error* estimated on a validation set. Validation sets, unfortunately, are notoriously very noisy (see, e.g., the discussion in Weigend et al., 1990). Hence, an attractive alternative is to estimate the test error by statistical means, e.g., Akaike's FPE (Akaike, 69). For regression type problems such a pruning stop criterion was suggested in (Svarer et al., 93).

However, why not let the saliency itself reflect the possible improvement in test error? This is the idea that we explore in this contribution.

2 GENERALIZATION IN REGULARIZED NEURAL NETWORKS

The basic asymptotic estimate of the generalization error was derived by Akaike (Akaike, 1969); the so-called Final Prediction Error (FPE). The use of FPE-theory for neural net learning has been pioneered by Moody (see e.g. (Moody, 91)), who derived estimators for the average generalization error in regularized networks.

Our network is a feed-forward architecture with n_I input units, n_H hidden sigmoid units and a single linear output unit, appropriate for scalar function approximation. The initial network is fully connected between layers and implements a non-linear mapping from input space $\mathbf{x}(k)$ to the real axis: $\hat{y}(k) = F_\mathbf{u}(\mathbf{x}(k))$, where $\mathbf{u} = [\mathbf{w}, \mathbf{W}]$ is the N-dimensional weight vector and $\hat{y}(k)$ is the prediction of the target output $y(k)$. The particular family of non-linear mappings considered can be written as:

$$F_\mathbf{u}(\mathbf{x}(k)) = \sum_{j=1}^{n_H} W_j \tanh\left(\sum_{i=1}^{n_I} w_{ji} x_i(k) + w_{j0}\right) + W_0, \tag{1}$$

W_j are the hidden-to-output weights while w_{ij} connect the input and hidden units.

We use the sum of squared errors to measure the network performance

$$E_{\text{train}} = \frac{1}{p} \sum_{k=1}^{p} [y(k) - F_\mathbf{u}(\mathbf{x}(k))]^2, \tag{2}$$

where p is the number of training examples. To ensure numerical stability and to assist the pruning procedure we augment the cost function with a regularization term.[1] The resulting cost function reads

$$E = E_{\text{train}} + \frac{1}{2}\mathbf{u}^T \mathbf{R} \mathbf{u} \tag{3}$$

The main source of uncertainty in learning is the shortage of training data. Fitting the network from a finite set of noisy examples means that the noise in these particular examples will be fitted as well and when presented with a new test example the network will make an error which is larger than the error of the "optimal network" trained on an infinite training set. By careful control of the fitting capabilities, e.g., by pruning, such overfitting may be reduced.

The generalization error is defined as the average squared error on an example from the example distribution function $P(\mathbf{x}, y)$. The examples are modeled by a *teacher* network with weights $\mathbf{u}^*$, degraded by additive noise: $y(k) = F_{\mathbf{u}^*}(\mathbf{x}(k)) + \nu(k)$. The noise samples $\nu(k)$ are independent identically distributed variables with finite, but unknown variance σ^2. Further, we assume that the noise terms are independent of the corresponding inputs. The quantity of interest for model optimization is the training set average of the generalization error, viz., the average over an ensemble

---

[1] $\mathbf{R}$ will be a positive definite diagonal matrix.

of networks in which each network is provided with its individual training set. This averaged generalization error is estimated by

$$\widehat{E}_{\text{test}} = \left(1 + \frac{N_{\text{eff}}}{p}\right)\sigma^2 + O\left((1/p)^2\right), \tag{4}$$

with the effective number of parameters being $N_{\text{eff}} = \text{tr}(\mathbf{HJ}^{-1}\mathbf{HJ}^{-1})$ (Larsen and Hansen, 94). The Hessian, $\mathbf{H}$, is the second derivative matrix of the training error with respect to the weights and thresholds, while $\mathbf{J}$ is the regularized Hessian: $\mathbf{J} = \mathbf{H} + \mathbf{R}$. An asymptotically unbiased estimator of the noise level is provided by: $\sigma^2 = E_{\text{train}}/(1 - N_{\text{eff}}/p)$. Inserting, we get

$$\widehat{E}_{\text{test}} = \frac{p + N_{\text{eff}}}{p - N_{\text{eff}}} E_{\text{train}} \approx \left(1 + \frac{2N_{\text{eff}}}{p}\right) E_{\text{train}}. \tag{5}$$

While OBD and OBS are based on estimates of the change in E_{train} we see that in order to obtain saliencies that estimate the change in generalization we must generally take the prefactor into account. We note that if the network is *not* regularized $N_{\text{eff}} = \text{tr}(\mathbf{HJ}^{-1}\mathbf{HJ}^{-1}) = \text{tr}(\mathbf{1}) = N$, in which case the prefactor is only a function of the total number of weights. In this case ranking according to training error saliency is equivalent to ranking according to generalization error.

However, in the generic case of a regularized network this is no more true ($N_{\text{eff}} < N$), and we need to evaluate the change in the prefactor, i.e., in the effective number of parameters, associated with pruning a weight. Denoting the generalization based saliency of weight u_l as $E_{\text{test},l}$, we find

$$\delta E_{\text{test},l} \approx \delta E_{\text{train},l} - \frac{2\left(N_{\text{eff}} - N_{\text{eff},l}\right)}{p} E_{\text{train}} \tag{6}$$

Where the number of parameters after pruning of weight l is $N_{\text{eff},l}$, and $\delta E_{\text{train},l}$ is the training error based saliency.

To proceed we outline two implementations, the major difference being the computational complexity involved. In the first, which is an elaboration on the OBD scheme, the storage complexity is proportional to the number of weights and thresholds (N), while in the second scheme the complexity scales with N^2, and is a generalization of the OBS. To emphasize that we use the generalization error for ranking of weights we use the prefix γ: γOBD and γOBS.

3 γOBD: AN $O(N)$ IMPLEMENTATION

Our $O(N)$ simulator is based on *batch mode*, second order pseudo-Gauss Newton optimization which is described in (Svarer et al., 93). The scheme, being based on the diagonal approximation for the Hessian, requires storage of a number of variables scaling linearly with the number of parameters N. As in (Le Cun et al., 90) we approximate the second derivative matrix by the positive semi-definite expression:

$$\frac{\partial^2 E_{\text{train}}}{\partial u_j^2} \approx \frac{2}{p}\sum_{k=1}^{p}\left(\frac{\partial F_{\mathbf{u}}(\mathbf{x}(k))}{\partial u_j}\right)^2. \tag{7}$$

In the diagonal approximation we find

$$N_{\text{eff}} = \sum_{j=1}^{N}\left(\frac{\lambda_j}{\lambda_j + \alpha_j/p}\right)^2, \tag{8}$$

where $\lambda_j \equiv \partial^2 E_{\text{train}}/\partial u_j^2$. Further, α_j/p are the weight decay parameters (diagonal elements of the regularization matrix $\mathbf{R}$).

The OBD method proposed by (Le Cun et al., 90) was successfully applied to reduce large networks for recognition of handwritten digits. The basic idea is to estimate the increase in the *training error* when deleting weights. Expanding the training error to second order in the pruned weight magnitude it is found that

$$\delta E_{\text{train},l} = \left(\frac{\alpha_l}{p} + \frac{1}{2}\frac{\partial^2 E_{\text{train}}}{\partial u_l^2}\right) u_l^2. \tag{9}$$

This estimate takes into account that the weight decay terms force the weights to depart from the minimum of the training set error. The first derivative of the training error is non-zero, hence, the first term in (9). Computationally, we note that the diagonal Hessian terms are reused from the pseudo Gauss-Newton training scheme.

Using (6) and the diagonal form of N_{eff}, we find the following approximative expression for generalization saliency (γOBD):

$$\delta E_{\text{test},l} \approx \delta E_{\text{train},l} - \frac{2}{p}\left(\frac{\lambda_l}{\lambda_l + \alpha_l/p}\right)^2 E_{\text{train}} \tag{10}$$

From this expression we learn that of two weights inducing similar changes in training error we should delete the one which has the largest ratio of training error curvature (λ) to weight decay, i.e., the weight which has been *least* influenced by weight decay. However, from a computational point of view we also want to reduce the number of parameters as far as possible; so we might in fact accept to delete weights with small positive generalization saliency (in particular considering the amount of approximation involved in the estimates).

4 γOBS: AN $O(N^2)$ IMPLEMENTATION

In the Optimal Brain Surgeon (Hassibi et al., 92) the increase in training error is estimated including the effects of quadratic retraining. This allows for pruning of more general degrees of freedom, e.g., situations where the training error induces linear constraints among two or more weights. The price to be paid is that we need to operate with the full $N \times N$ Hessian matrix of second derivatives. The $O(N^2)$ simulator, hence, is based on full Gauss Newton optimization. When eliminating the l'th weight retraining is determined by

$$\delta \mathbf{u}_l = -\frac{u_l}{(\mathbf{J}^{-1})_{ll}}\mathbf{J}^{-1}\mathbf{e}_l \tag{11}$$

where $\mathbf{e}_l$ is the l'th unit vector. We need to modify the OBS saliencies when working from a weight decay regularized cost function. The modified saliencies were given in (Hansen and With, 94)[2]

$$\delta E_{train,l} = \frac{1}{2}\frac{u_l^2}{(\mathbf{J}^{-1})_{ll}} + \frac{\alpha}{p}\left(\frac{u_l(\mathbf{e}_l^T \mathbf{J}^{-1}\mathbf{u})}{(\mathbf{J}^{-1})_{ll}} - \frac{1}{2}\frac{u_l^2(\mathbf{J}^{-2})_{ll}}{((\mathbf{J}^{-1})_{ll})^2}\right) \tag{12}$$

Whether using the generalization based γOBS or standard OBS, we want to point to an important aspect of OBS that seems not to be generally appreciated, namely the

---

[2]The expression is for the case of all weight decays being equal, see (Hansen and With, 94) for the general expression.

problem of "nuisance" parameters (White, 89), (Larsen, 93). When eliminating an output weight u_o, all the weights to the corresponding hidden unit are in effect also pruned away. Such a situation is well-known in the statistics literature on model selection where such "ghost" input weights are known as nuisance parameters. It is important to remove these parameters from the network function before estimating the saliency $\delta E_{train,o}$ and the resulting effective number of parameters N_{eff}, as they would otherwise give "spurious" contributions to these estimates. Applying OBS without taking this fact into consideration often results in sudden jumps in the level of the network error due to pruning of an important weight based on a corrupted saliency estimate. Removing the superfluous weights from the weight vector $\mathbf{u}$ and the corresponding rows and columns in $\mathbf{J}$ to form the reduced (regularized) Hessian $\mathbf{J}_1$ is straightforward, but it is computationally expensive to invert each of the resulting (sub-)matrices $\mathbf{J}_1$ for use in (11) and (12). This cost can be considerably reduced by rearranging the rows and columns of $\mathbf{J}$ as

$$\mathbf{J} = \begin{bmatrix} \mathbf{J}_1 & \mathbf{J}_2 \\ \mathbf{J}_3 & \mathbf{J}_4 \end{bmatrix} \rightarrow \mathbf{J}^{-1} = \begin{bmatrix} (\mathbf{J}^{-1})_1 & (\mathbf{J}^{-1})_2 \\ (\mathbf{J}^{-1})_3 & (\mathbf{J}^{-1})_4 \end{bmatrix} \qquad (13)$$

where $\mathbf{J}_2$, $\mathbf{J}_3$ and $\mathbf{J}_4$ are the rows and columns corresponding to the nuisance parameters. Using a standard lemma for partitioned matrices, we obtain

$$(\mathbf{J}_1)^{-1} = (\mathbf{J}^{-1})_1 - (\mathbf{J}^{-1})_2[(\mathbf{J}^{-1})_4]^{-1}(\mathbf{J}^{-1})_3 \qquad (14)$$

which only calls for inversion of the (small) submatrix $(\mathbf{J}^{-1})_4$. In (Hassibi et al., 93) it was argued that one might save on computation by using an iterative scheme for calculation of the inverse Hessian $\mathbf{J}^{-1}$. However, since standard matrix inversion is an $O(N^3)$ operation while the iterative scheme scales as $O(pN^2)$, a detailed count shows that that it is only beneficial to use the iterative scheme in the atypical case $N > p/2$.

5 EXPERIMENT

We will illustrate the viability of the proposed methods on a standard problem of nonlinear dynamics viz. the Mackey-Glass chaotic time series. The series is generated by integration of the differential equation

$$\frac{dz(t)}{dt} = -bz(t) + a\frac{z(t-\tau)}{1 + z(t-\tau)^{10}} \qquad (15)$$

where the constants are $a = 0.2$, $b = 0.1$ and $\tau = 17$. The series is resampled with sampling period 1 according to standard practice. The network configuration is $n_I = 6$, $n_H = 10$ and we train to implement a six step ahead prediction. That is, $\mathbf{x}(k) = [z(k-6), z(k-12), \cdots, z(k-6n_I)]$ and $y(k) = z(k)$. In Fig. 1 we show pruning scenarios based on the two different implementations. The training errors, test errors and FPE errors are plotted for a training set size of 250 examples, the test set comprises 8500 examples. In the left panel we show the results of pruning according to γOBD and similarly in the right panel we show the results of pruning as it occurred using γOBS. In this example we do not find significant improvement in performance by use of γOBS.

To illustrate the ability of the estimators for predicting the effects of pruning on the test error we plot in figure 2 the estimated test errors versus the actual test errors after pruning. In the OBD case this means the test error resulting from pruning the parameters without retraining, while in the OBS case it means the test error following pruning and retraining in the quadratic approximation. We note that the γOBD estimates of the test error approximately equal the actual

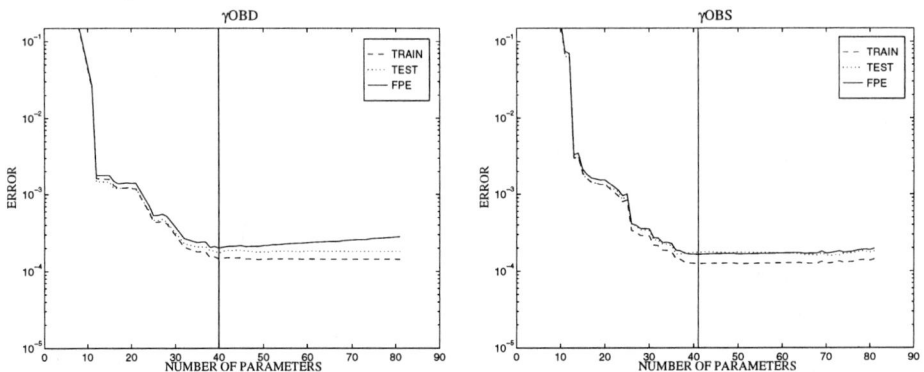

Figure 1: The evolution of training and test errors during pruning for the Mackey-Glass time series for a training set of size 250. In the left panel is shown pruning by γOBD, while in the right we show pruning by γOBS. The vertical solid line indicates the network for which the *estimated* test error is minimal.

test error, offset by a constant corresponding to the FPE-offset in the left panel of figure 1. The most important feature of this plot is that ranking according to the estimated test error is consistent with ranking according to the actual test error. In the right panel of figure 2, however, we see that γOBS highly underestimates the actual errors resulting from the quadratic retraining. It is not clear how the ranking inconsistencies affect the overall performance of γOBS. The weight selected for pruning (indicated by a circle) is clearly not the optimal according to the actual test error. However, as depicted in the figure, after full Gauss-Newton retraining for 20 epochs the measured actual test error is comparable to the estimated value (retraining is indicated by the arrow). Hence, one may say that γOBS "recovers" after retraining, while the initial estimate based on quadratic retraining is rather poor.

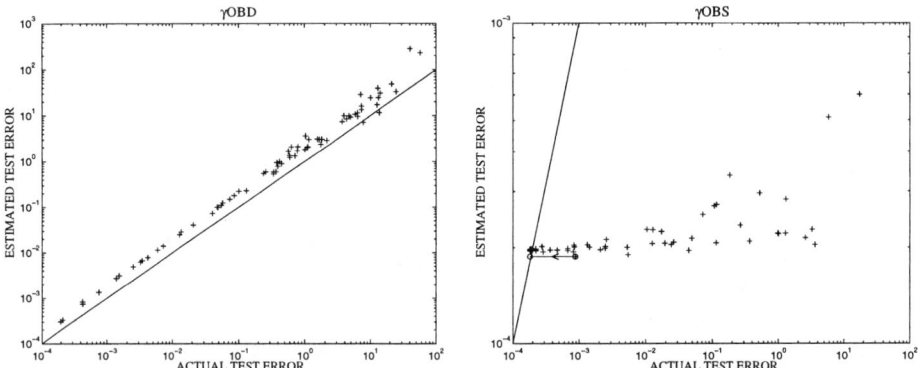

Figure 2: Left panel: Estimated test errors for fully connected network using γOBD and the actual test errors computed by actual deletion of the weight and computing the test error on the 8500 members test set. Right panel: Errors for fully connected network using γOBS. The weight selected for pruning is indicated by a circle, the result of further retraining is indicated by an arrow.

6 CONCLUSION

Since a main objective of pruning algorithms is to improve generalization we suggest that weight saliencies are estimated from the test error rather than the training error. We have shown how this might be carried out for scalar function approximation, in which case we have a rather simple test error estimate (based on Akaike's FPE). We provided implementation details for a scheme of linear complexity, γOBD, which is the generalization of OBD and a scheme of quadratic complexity γOBS which is the generalization of OBS. Furthermore, we provided a way to significantly reduce the computational overhead involved in the handling of nuisance parameters. An application within time series prediction showed the viability of the suggested approach.

Acknowledgements

We thank Peter Magnus Nørgaard for valuable discussions. This research is supported by the Danish Natural Science and Technical Research Councils through the Computational Neural Network Center (CONNECT). JL acknowledge the Radioparts Foundation for financial support.

References

H. Akaike: *Fitting Autoregressive Models for Prediction.* Ann. Inst. Stat. Mat. **21**, 243–247, (1969).

Y. Le Cun, J.S. Denker, and S.A. Solla: *Optimal Brain Damage.* In Advances in Neural Information Processing Systems 2, Morgan Kaufman, 598–605, (1990).

L.K. Hansen and M. With Petersen: *Controlled Growth of Cascade Correlation Nets.* Proceedings of ICANN'94 International Conference on Neural Networks, Sorrento, Italy, 1994. Eds. M. Marinaro and P.G. Morasso, 797–800, (1994).

B. Hassibi, D. G. Stork, and G. J. Wolff: *Optimal Brain Surgeon and General Network Pruning*, in Proceedings of the 1993 IEEE International Conference on Neural Networks, San Francisco (Eds. E.H. Ruspini et al.) 293–299, (1993).

J. Larsen: *Design of Neural Network Filters.* Ph.D. Thesis, Electronics Institute, Technical University of Denmark, (1993).

J. Larsen and L.K. Hansen: *Generalization Performance of Regularized Neural Network Models.* "Neural Networks for Signal Processing IV" Proceedings of the IEEE Workshop, Eds. J. Vlontzos et al., IEEE Service Center, Piscataway NJ, 42–51, (1994).

J.E. Moody: *Note on Generalization, Regularization and Architecture Selection in Nonlinear Systems.* In Neural Networks For Signal Processing; Proceedings of the 1991 IEEE-SP Workshop, (Eds. B.H. Juang, S.Y. Kung, and C. Kamm), IEEE Service Center, 1–10, (1991).

C. Svarer, L.K. Hansen, and J. Larsen: *On Design and Evaluation of Tapped Delay Line Networks*, In Proceedings of the 1993 IEEE International Conference on Neural Networks, San Francisco, (Eds. E.H. Ruspini et al.) 46–51, (1993).

A.S. Weigend, B.A. Huberman, and D.E. Rumelhart: *Prediction the future: A Connectionist Approach.* Int. J. of Neural Systems **3**, 193-209, (1990).

H. White: *Learning in Artificial Neural Networks: A Statistical Perspective.* Neural Computation **1**, 425–464, (1989).

Fast Learning by Bounding Likelihoods in Sigmoid Type Belief Networks

Tommi Jaakkola
tommi@psyche.mit.edu

Lawrence K. Saul
lksaul@psyche.mit.edu

Michael I. Jordan
jordan@psyche.mit.edu

Department of Brain and Cognitive Sciences
Massachusetts Institute of Technology
Cambridge, MA 02139

Abstract

Sigmoid type belief networks, a class of probabilistic neural networks, provide a natural framework for compactly representing probabilistic information in a variety of unsupervised and supervised learning problems. Often the parameters used in these networks need to be learned from examples. Unfortunately, estimating the parameters via exact probabilistic calculations (i.e, the EM-algorithm) is intractable even for networks with fairly small numbers of hidden units. We propose to avoid the infeasibility of the E step by bounding likelihoods instead of computing them exactly. We introduce extended and complementary representations for these networks and show that the estimation of the network parameters can be made fast (reduced to quadratic optimization) by performing the estimation in either of the alternative domains. The complementary networks can be used for continuous density estimation as well.

1 Introduction

The appeal of probabilistic networks for knowledge representation, inference, and learning (Pearl, 1988) derives both from the sound Bayesian framework and from the explicit representation of dependencies among the network variables which allows ready incorporation of prior information into the design of the network. The Bayesian formalism permits full propagation of probabilistic information across the network regardless of which variables in the network are instantiated. In this sense these networks can be "inverted" probabilistically.

This inversion, however, relies heavily on the use of look-up table representations of conditional probabilities or representations equivalent to them for modeling dependencies between the variables. For sparse dependency structures such as trees or chains this poses no difficulty. In more realistic cases of reasonably interdependent variables the exact algorithms developed for these belief networks (Lauritzen & Spiegelhalter, 1988) become infeasible due to the exponential growth in the size of the conditional probability tables needed to store the exact dependencies. Therefore the use of compact representations to model probabilistic interactions is unavoidable in large problems. As belief network models move away from tables, however, the representations can be harder to assess from expert knowledge and the important role of learning is further emphasized.

Compact representations of interactions between simple units have long been emphasized in neural networks. Lacking a thorough probabilistic interpretation, however, classical feed-forward neural networks cannot be inverted in the above sense; e.g. given the output pattern of a feed-forward neural network it is not feasible to compute a probability distribution over the possible input patterns that would have resulted in the observed output. On the other hand, stochastic neural networks such as Boltzman machines admit probabilistic interpretations and therefore, at least in principle, can be inverted and used as a basis for inference and learning in the presence of uncertainty.

Sigmoid belief networks (Neal, 1992) form a subclass of probabilistic neural networks where the activation function has a sigmoidal form – usually the logistic function. Neal (1992) proposed a learning algorithm for these networks which can be viewed as an improvement of the algorithm for Boltzmann machines. Recently Hinton et al. (1995) introduced the wake-sleep algorithm for layered bi-directional probabilistic networks. This algorithm relies on forward sampling and has an appealing coding theoretic motivation. The Helmholtz machine (Dayan et al., 1995), on the other hand, can be seen as an alternative technique for these architectures that avoids Gibbs sampling altogether. Dayan et al. also introduced the important idea of bounding likelihoods instead of computing them exactly. Saul et al. (1995) subsequently derived rigorous mean field bounds for the likelihoods. In this paper we introduce the idea of alternative – extended and complementary – representations of these networks by reinterpreting the nonlinearities in the activation function. We show that deriving likelihood bounds in the new representational domains leads to efficient (quadratic) estimation procedures for the network parameters.

2   The probability representations

Belief networks represent the joint probability of a set of variables $\{S\}$ as a product of conditional probabilities given by

$$P(S_1,\ldots,S_n) = \prod_{k=1}^{n} P(S_k|pa[k]), \quad (1)$$

where the notation $pa[k]$, "parents of S_k", refers to all the variables that directly influence the probability of S_k taking on a particular value (for equivalent representations, see Lauritzen et al. 1988). The fact that the joint probability can be written in the above form implies that there are no "cycles" in the network; i.e. there exists an ordering of the variables in the network such that no variable directly influences any preceding variables.

In this paper we consider sigmoid belief networks where the variables S are binary

(0/1), the conditional probabilities have the form

$$P(S_i|\text{pa}[i]) = g\left((2S_i - 1)\sum_j W_{ij} S_j\right) \qquad (2)$$

and the weights W_{ij} are zero unless S_j is a parent of S_i, thus preserving the feed-forward directionality of the network. For notational convenience we have assumed the existence of a bias variable whose value is clamped to one. The activation function $g(\cdot)$ is chosen to be the cumulative Gaussian distribution function given by

$$g(x) = \frac{1}{\sqrt{2\pi}}\int_{-\infty}^{x} e^{-\frac{1}{2}z^2}dz = \frac{1}{\sqrt{2\pi}}\int_{0}^{\infty} e^{-\frac{1}{2}(z-x)^2}dz \qquad (3)$$

Although very similar to the standard logistic function, this activation function derives a number of advantages from its integral representation. In particular, we may reinterpret the integration as a marginalization and thereby obtain alternative representations for the network. We consider two such representations.

We derive an *extended* representation by making explicit the nonlinearities in the activation function. More precisely,

$$\begin{aligned}
P(S_i|\text{pa}[i]) &= g\left((2S_i - 1)\sum_j W_{ij} S_j\right) \\
&= \int_0^\infty \frac{1}{\sqrt{2\pi}} e^{-\frac{1}{2}[Z_i - (2S_i - 1)\sum_j W_{ij} S_j]^2} dZ_i \\
&\stackrel{def}{=} \int_0^\infty P(S_i, Z_i|\text{pa}[i]) dZ_i \qquad (4)
\end{aligned}$$

This suggests defining the extended network in terms of the new conditional probabilities $P(S_i, Z_i|\text{pa}[i])$. By construction then the original binary network is obtained by marginalizing over the extra variables Z. In this sense the extended network is (marginally) equivalent to the binary network.

We distinguish a *complementary* representation from the extended one by writing the probabilities entirely in terms of continuous variables[1]. Such a representation can be obtained from the extended network by a simple transformation of variables. The new continuous variables are defined by $\tilde{Z}_i = (2S_i - 1)Z_i$, or, equivalently, by $Z_i = |\tilde{Z}_i|$ and $S_i = \theta(\tilde{Z}_i)$ where $\theta(\cdot)$ is the step function. Performing this transformation yields

$$P(\tilde{Z}_i|\text{pa}[i]) = \frac{1}{\sqrt{2\pi}} e^{-\frac{1}{2}[\tilde{Z}_i - \sum_j W_{ij}\theta(\tilde{Z}_j)]^2} \qquad (5)$$

which defines a network of conditionally Gaussian variables. The original network in this case can be recovered by conditional marginalization over $\tilde{Z}$ where the conditioning variables are $\theta(\tilde{Z})$.

Figure 1 below summarizes the relationships between the different representations. As will become clear later, working with the alternative representations instead of the original binary representation can lead to more flexible and efficient (least-squares) parameter estimation.

3 The learning problem

We consider the problem of learning the parameters of the network from instantiations of variables contained in a training set. Such instantiations, however, need not

---

[1] While the binary variables are the outputs of each unit the continuous variables pertain to the inputs – hence the name complementary.

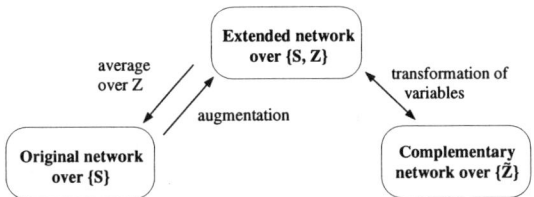

Figure 1: The relationship between the alternative representations.

be complete; there may be variables that have no value assignments in the training set as well as variables that are always instantiated. The tacit division between hidden (H) and visible (V) variables therefore depends on the particular training example considered and is not an intrinsic property of the network.

To learn from these instantiations we adopt the principle of maximum likelihood to estimate the weights in the network. In essence, this is a density estimation problem where the weights are chosen so as to match the probabilistic behavior of the network with the observed activities in the training set. Central to this estimation is the ability to compute likelihoods (or log-likelihoods) for any (partial) configuration of variables appearing in the training set. In other words, if we let X^V be the configuration of visible or instantiated variables[2] and X^H denote the hidden or uninstantiated variables, we need to compute marginal probabilities of the form

$$\log P(X^V) = \log \sum_{X^H} P(X^V, X^H) \qquad (6)$$

If the training samples are independent, then these log marginals can be added to give the overall log-likelihood of the training set

$$\log P(\text{training set}) = \sum_t \log P(X^{V_t}) \qquad (7)$$

Unfortunately, computing each of these marginal probabilities involves summing (integrating) over an exponential number of different configurations assumed by the hidden variables in the network. This renders the sum (integration) intractable in all but few special cases (e.g. trees and chains). It is possible, however, to instead find a manageable lower bound on the log-likelihood and optimize the weights in the network so as to maximize this bound.

To obtain such a lower bound we resort to Jensen's inequality:

$$\begin{aligned}\log P(X^V) &= \log \sum_{X^H} P(X^H, X^V) = \log \sum_{X^H} Q(X^H) \frac{P(X^H, X^V)}{Q(X^H)} \\ &\geq \sum_{X^H} Q(X^H) \log \frac{P(X^H, X^V)}{Q(X^H)}\end{aligned} \qquad (8)$$

Although this bound holds for all distributions $Q(X)$ over the hidden variables, the accuracy of the bound is determined by how closely Q approximates the posterior distribution $P(X^H|X^V)$ in terms of the Kullback-Leibler divergence; if the approximation is perfect the divergence is zero and the inequality is satisfied with equality. Suitable choices for Q can make the bound both accurate and easy to compute. The feasibility of finding such Q, however, is highly dependent on the choice of the representation for the network.

---

[2] To postpone the issue of representation we use X to denote S, $\{S, Z\}$, or $\tilde{Z}$ depending on the particular representation chosen.

4 Likelihood bounds in different representations

To complete the derivation of the likelihood bound (equation 8) we need to fix the representation for the network. Which representation to select, however, affects the quality and accuracy of the bound. In addition, the accompanying bound of the chosen representation implies bounds in the other two representational domains as they all code the same distributions over the observables. In this section we illustrate these points by deriving bounds in the complementary and extended representations and discuss the corresponding bounds in the original binary domain.

Now, to obtain a lower bound we need to specify the approximate posterior Q. In the complementary representation the conditional probabilities are Gaussians and therefore a reasonable approximation (mean field) is found by choosing the posterior approximation from the family of factorized Gaussians:

$$Q(\tilde{Z}) = \prod_i \frac{1}{\sqrt{2\pi}} e^{-(\tilde{Z}_i - h_i)^2/2} \qquad (9)$$

Substituting this into equation 8 we obtain the bound

$$\log P(S^*) \geq -\frac{1}{2} \sum_i (h_i - \Sigma_j J_{ij} g(h_j))^2 - \frac{1}{2} \sum_{ij} J_{ij}^2 g(h_j) g(-h_j) \qquad (10)$$

The means h_i for the hidden variables are adjustable parameters that can be tuned to make the bound as tight as possible. For the instantiated variables we need to enforce the constraints $g(h_i) = S_i^*$ to respect the instantiation. These can be satisfied very accurately by setting $h_i = 4(2S_i^* - 1)$. A very convenient property of this bound and the complementary representation in general is the quadratic weight dependence – a property very conducive to fast learning. Finally, we note that the complementary representation transforms the binary estimation problem into a continuous density estimation problem.

We now turn to the interpretation of the above bound in the binary domain. The same bound can be obtained by first fixing the inputs to all the units to be the means h_i and then computing the negative total mean squared error between the fixed inputs and the corresponding probabilistic inputs propagated from the parents. The fact that this procedure in fact gives a lower bound on the log-likelihood would be more difficult to justify by working with the binary representation alone.

In the extended representation the probability distribution for Z_i is a truncated Gaussian given S_i and its parents. We therefore propose the partially factorized posterior approximation:

$$Q(S, Z) = \prod_i Q(Z_i|S_i) Q(S_i) \qquad (11)$$

where $Q(Z_i|S_i)$ is a truncated Gaussian:

$$Q(Z_i|S_i) = \frac{1}{g((2S_i-1)h_i)} \frac{1}{\sqrt{2\pi}} e^{-\frac{1}{2}(Z_i - (2S_i-1)h_i)^2} \qquad (12)$$

As in the complementary domain the resulting bound depends quadratically on the weights. Instead of writing out the bound here, however, it is more informative to see its derivation in the binary domain.

A factorized posterior approximation (mean field) $Q(S) = \prod_i q_i^{S_i}(1-q_i)^{1-S_i}$ for the binary network yields a bound

$$\log P(S^*) \geq \sum_i \left\{ \langle S_i \log g(\sum_j J_{ij} S_j) \rangle + \langle (1-S_i) \log(1 - g(\sum_j J_{ij} S_j)) \rangle \right\}$$

$$-\sum_i [q_i \log q_i + (1-q_i)\log(1-q_i)] \qquad (13)$$

where the averages $\langle \cdot \rangle$ are with respect to the Q distribution. These averages, however, do not conform to analytical expressions. The tractable posterior approximation in the extended domain avoids the problem by implicitly making the following Legendre transformation:

$$\log g(x) = [\frac{1}{2}x^2 + \log g(x)] - \frac{1}{2}x^2 \geq \lambda x - G(\lambda) - \frac{1}{2}x^2 \qquad (14)$$

which holds since $x^2/2 + \log g(x)$ is a convex function. Inserting this back into the relevant parts of equation 13 and performing the averages gives

$$\log P(S^*) \geq \sum_i \Big\{ [q_i \lambda_i - (1-q_i)\bar{\lambda}_i] \sum_j J_{ij} q_j - q_i G(\lambda_i) - (1-q_i) G(\bar{\lambda}_i) \Big\}$$

$$-\frac{1}{2}(\sum_j J_{ij} q_j)^2 - \frac{1}{2}\sum_{ij} J_{ij}^2 q_j (1-q_j)$$

$$-\sum_i [q_i \log q_i + (1-q_i)\log(1-q_i)] \qquad (15)$$

which is quadratic in the weights as expected. The mean activities q for the hidden variables and the parameters λ can be optimized to make the bound tight. For the instantiated variables we set $q_i = S_i^*$.

5 Numerical experiments

To test these techniques in practice we applied the complementary network to the problem of detecting motor failures from spectra obtained during motor operation (see Petsche et al. 1995). We cast the problem as a continuous density estimation problem. The training set consisted of 800 out of 1283 FFT spectra each with 319 components measured from an electric motor in a good operating condition but under varying loads. The test set included the remaining 483 FFTs from the same motor in a good condition in addition to three sets of 1340 FFTs each measured when a particular fault was present. The goal was to use the likelihood of a test FFT with respect to the estimated density to determine whether there was a fault present in the motor.

We used a layered $6 \rightarrow 20 \rightarrow 319$ generative model to estimate the training set density. The resulting classification error rates on the test set are shown in figure 2 as a function of the threshold likelihood. The achieved error rates are comparable to those of Petsche et al. (1995).

6 Conclusions

Network models that admit probabilistic formulations derive a number of advantages from probability theory. Moving away from explicit representations of dependencies, however, can make these properties harder to exploit in practice. We showed that an efficient estimation procedure can be derived for sigmoid belief networks, where standard methods are intractable in all but a few special cases (e.g. trees and chains). The efficiency of our approach derived from the combination of two ideas. First, we avoided the intractability of computing likelihoods in these networks by computing lower bounds instead. Second, we introduced new representations for these networks and showed how the lower bounds in the new representational domains transform the parameter estimation problem into

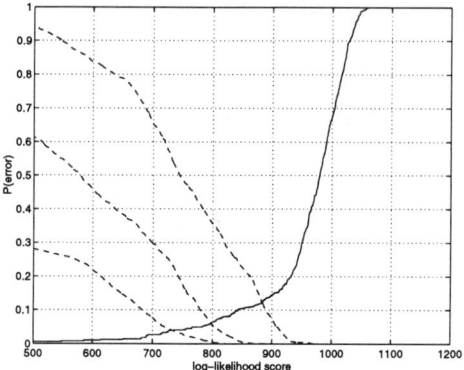

Figure 2: The probability of error curves for missing a fault (dashed lines) and misclassifying a good motor (solid line) as a function of the likelihood threshold.

quadratic optimization.

Acknowledgments

The authors wish to thank Peter Dayan for helpful comments. This project was supported in part by NSF grant CDA-9404932, by a grant from the McDonnell-Pew Foundation, by a grant from ATR Human Information Processing Research Laboratories, by a grant from Siemens Corporation, and by grant N00014-94-1-0777 from the Office of Naval Research. Michael I. Jordan is a NSF Presidential Young Investigator.

References

P. Dayan, G. Hinton, R. Neal, and R. Zemel (1995). The helmholtz machine. *Neural Computation* **7**: 889-904.

A. Dempster, N. Laird, and D. Rubin. Maximum likelihood from incomplete data via the EM algorithm (1977). *J. Roy. Statist. Soc. B* **39**:1-38.

G. Hinton, P. Dayan, B. Frey, and R. Neal (1995). The wake-sleep algorithm for unsupervised neural networks. *Science* **268**: 1158-1161.

S. L. Lauritzen and D. J. Spiegelhalter (1988). Local computations with probabilities on graphical structures and their application to expert systems. *J. Roy. Statist. Soc. B* **50**:154-227.

R. Neal. Connectionist learning of belief networks (1992). *Artificial Intelligence* **56**: 71-113.

J. Pearl (1988). *Probabilistic Reasoning in Intelligent Systems*. Morgan Kaufmann: San Mateo.

T. Petsche, A. Marcantonio, C. Darken, S. J. Hanson, G. M. Kuhn, I. Santoso (1995). A neural network autoassociator for induction motor failure prediction. In *Advances in Neural Information Processing Systems 8*. MIT Press.

L. K. Saul, T. Jaakkola, and M. I. Jordan (1995). Mean field theory for sigmoid belief networks. *M.I.T. Computational Cognitive Science Technical Report* **9501**.

Generating Accurate and Diverse Members of a Neural-Network Ensemble

David W. Opitz
Computer Science Department
University of Minnesota
Duluth, MN 55812
opitz@d.umn.edu

Jude W. Shavlik
Computer Sciences Department
University of Wisconsin
Madison, WI 53706
shavlik@cs.wisc.edu

Abstract

Neural-network ensembles have been shown to be very accurate classification techniques. Previous work has shown that an effective ensemble should consist of networks that are not only highly correct, but ones that make their errors on different parts of the input space as well. Most existing techniques, however, only indirectly address the problem of creating such a set of networks. In this paper we present a technique called ADDEMUP that uses genetic algorithms to directly search for an accurate and diverse set of trained networks. ADDEMUP works by first creating an initial population, then uses genetic operators to continually create new networks, keeping the set of networks that are as accurate as possible while disagreeing with each other as much as possible. Experiments on three DNA problems show that ADDEMUP is able to generate a set of trained networks that is more accurate than several existing approaches. Experiments also show that ADDEMUP is able to effectively incorporate prior knowledge, if available, to improve the quality of its ensemble.

1 Introduction

Many researchers have shown that simply combining the output of many classifiers can generate more accurate predictions than that of any of the individual classifiers (Clemen, 1989; Wolpert, 1992). In particular, combining separately trained neural networks (commonly referred to as a neural-network *ensemble*) has been demonstrated to be particularly successful (Alpaydin, 1993; Drucker et al., 1994; Hansen and Salamon, 1990; Hashem et al., 1994; Krogh and Vedelsby, 1995; Maclin and Shavlik, 1995; Perrone, 1992). Both theoretical (Hansen and Salamon, 1990; Krogh and Vedelsby, 1995) and empirical (Hashem et al., 1994;

Maclin and Shavlik, 1995) work has shown that a good ensemble is one where the individual networks are both accurate and make their errors on different parts of the input space; however, most previous work has either focussed on combining the output of multiple trained networks or only indirectly addressed how we should generate a good set of networks. We present an algorithm, ADDEMUP (Accurate anD Diverse Ensemble-Maker giving United Predictions), that uses genetic algorithms to *generate* a population of neural networks that are highly accurate, while at the same time having minimal overlap on where they make their error.

Traditional ensemble techniques generate their networks by randomly trying different topologies, initial weight settings, parameters settings, or use only a part of the training set in the hopes of producing networks that disagree on where they make their errors (we henceforth refer to *diversity* as the measure of this disagreement). We propose instead to actively *search* for a good set of networks. The key idea behind our approach is to consider many networks and keep a subset of the networks that minimizes our objective function consisting of both an accuracy and a diversity term. In many domains we care more about generalization performance than we do about generating a solution quickly. This, coupled with the fact that computing power is rapidly growing, motivates us to effectively utilize available CPU cycles by continually considering networks to possibly place in our ensemble.

ADDEMUP proceeds by first creating an initial set of networks, then continually produces new individuals by using the genetic operators of crossover and mutation. It defines the overall fitness of an individual to be a combination of accuracy and diversity. Thus ADDEMUP keeps as its population a set of highly fit individuals that will be highly accurate, while making their mistakes in a different part of the input space. Also, it actively tries to generate good candidates by emphasizing the current population's erroneous examples during backpropagation training. Experiments reported herein demonstrate that ADDEMUP is able to generate an effective set of networks for an ensemble.

2 The Importance of an Accurate and Diverse Ensemble

Figure 1 illustrates the basic framework of a neural-network ensemble. Each network in the ensemble (network 1 through network N in this case) is first trained using the training instances. Then, for each example, the predicted output of each of these networks (o_i in Figure 1) is combined to produce the output of the ensemble ($\hat{o}$ in Figure 1). Many researchers (Alpaydin, 1993; Hashem et al., 1994; Krogh and Vedelsby, 1995; Mani, 1991) have demonstrated the effectiveness of combining schemes that are simply the weighted average of the networks (i.e., $\hat{o} = \sum_{i \in N} w_i \cdot o_i$ and $\sum_{i \in N} w_i = 1$), and this is the type of ensemble we focus on in this paper.

Hansen and Salamon (1990) proved that for a neural-network ensemble, if the average error rate for a pattern is less than 50% and the networks in the ensemble are independent in the production of their errors, the expected error for that pattern can be reduced to zero as the number of networks combined goes to infinity; however, such assumptions rarely hold in practice. Krogh and Vedelsby (1995) later proved that if diversity[1] D_i of network i is measured by:

$$D_i = \sum_x [o_i(x) - \hat{o}(x)]^2, \qquad (1)$$

then the ensemble generalization error ($\hat{E}$) consists of two distinct portions:

$$\hat{E} = \bar{E} - \bar{D}, \qquad (2)$$

---

[1] Krogh and Vedelsby referred to this term as *ambiguity*.

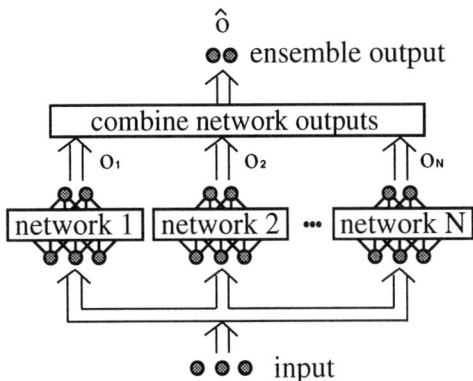

Figure 1: A neural-network ensemble.

where $\bar{D} = \sum_i w_i \cdot D_i$ and $\bar{E} = \sum_i w_i \cdot E_i$ (E_i is the error rate of network i and the w_i's sum to 1). What the equation shows then, is that we want our ensemble to consist of highly correct networks that disagree as much as possible. *Creating such a set of networks is the focus of this paper.*

3 The ADDEMUP Algorithm

Table 1 summarizes our new algorithm, ADDEMUP, that uses genetic algorithms to generate a set of neural networks that are accurate and diverse in their classifications. (Although ADDEMUP currently uses neural networks, it could be easily extended to incorporate other types of learning algorithms as well.) ADDEMUP starts by creating and training its initial population of networks. It then creates new networks by using standard genetic operators, such as crossover and mutation. ADDEMUP trains these new individuals, emphasizing examples that are misclassified by the current population, as explained below. ADDEMUP adds these new networks to the population then scores each population members with the fitness function:

$$Fitness_i = Accuracy_i + \lambda\ Diversity_i = (1 - E_i) + \lambda\ D_i, \qquad (3)$$

where λ defines the tradeoff between accuracy and diversity. Finally, ADDEMUP prunes the population to the N most-fit members, which it defines to be its current ensemble, then repeats this process.

We define our accuracy term, $1 - E_i$, to be network i's validation-set accuracy (or training-set accuracy if a validation set is not used), and we use Equation 1 over this validation set to calculate our diversity term D_i. We then separately normalize each term so that the values range from 0 to 1. Normalizing both terms allows λ to have the same meaning across domains. Since it is not always clear at what value one should set λ, we have therefore developed some rules for automatically setting λ. First, we never change λ if the ensemble error $\hat{E}$ is decreasing while we consider new networks; otherwise we change λ if one of following two things happen: (1) population error $\bar{E}$ is not increasing and the population diversity $\bar{D}$ is decreasing; diversity seems to be under-emphasized and we increase λ, or (2) $\bar{E}$ is increasing and $\bar{D}$ is not decreasing; diversity seems to be over-emphasized and we decrease λ. (We started λ at 0.1 for the results in this paper.)

A useful network to add to an ensemble is one that correctly classifies as many examples as possible while making its mistakes primarily on examples that most

Table 1: The ADDEMUP algorithm.

GOAL: Genetically create an accurate and diverse ensemble of networks.
1. Create and train the initial population of networks.
2. Until a stopping criterion is reached:
    (a) Use genetic operators to create new networks.
    (b) Train the new networks using Equation 4 and add them to the population.
    (c) Measure the diversity of each network with respect to the current population (see Equation 1).
    (d) Normalize the accuracy scores and the diversity scores of the individual networks.
    (e) Calculate the fitness of each population member (see Equation 3).
    (f) Prune the population to the N fittest networks.
    (g) Adjust λ (see the text for an explanation).
    (h) Report the current population of networks as the ensemble. Combine the output of the networks according to Equation 5.

---

of the current population members correctly classify. We address this during backpropagation training by multiplying the usual cost function by a term that measures the combined population error on that example:

$$Cost = \sum_{k \in T} \left| \frac{t(k) - \hat{o}(k)}{\hat{E}} \right|^{\frac{\lambda}{\lambda+1}} [t(k) - a(k)]^2, \qquad (4)$$

where $t(k)$ is the target and $a(k)$ is the network activation for example k in the training set T. Notice that since our network is not yet a member of the ensemble, $\hat{o}(k)$ and $\hat{E}$ are not dependent on our network; our new term is thus a constant when calculating the derivatives during backpropagation. We normalize $t(k) - \hat{o}(k)$ by the ensemble error $\hat{E}$ so that the *average* value of our new term is around 1 regardless of the correctness of the ensemble. This is especially important with highly accurate populations, since $t_k - \hat{o}(k)$ will be close to 0 for most examples, and the network would only get trained on a few examples. The exponent $\frac{\lambda}{\lambda+1}$ represents the ratio of importance of the diversity term in the fitness function. For instance, if λ is close to 0, diversity is not considered important and the network is trained with the usual cost function; however, if λ is large, diversity is considered important and our new term in the cost function takes on more importance.

We combine the predictions of the networks by taking a weighted sum of the output of each network, where each weight is based on the validation-set accuracy of the network. Thus we define our weights for combining the networks as follows:

$$w_i = \frac{1 - E_i}{\sum_k (1 - E_k)} \qquad (5)$$

While simply averaging the outputs generates a good composite model (Clemen, 1989), we include the predicted accuracy in our weights since one should believe accurate models more than inaccurate ones.

4 Experimental Study

The genetic algorithm we use for generating new network topologies is the REGENT algorithm (Opitz and Shavlik, 1994). REGENT uses genetic algorithms to search through the space of *knowledge-based neural network* (KNN) topologies. KNNs are networks whose topologies are determined as a result of the direct mapping of a set of background rules that represent what we currently know about our task. KBANN (Towell and Shavlik, 1994), for instance, translates a set of propositional rules into a neural network, then refines the resulting network's weights using backpropagation. Trained KNNs, such as KBANN's networks, have been shown to frequently generalize better than many other inductive-learning techniques such as standard neural networks (Opitz, 1995; Towell and Shavlik, 1994). Using KNNs allows us to have highly correct networks in our ensemble; however, since each network in our ensemble is initialized with the same set of domain-specific rules, we do not expect there to be much disagreement among the networks. An alternative we consider in our experiments is to randomly generate our initial population of network topologies, since domain-specific rules are sometimes not available.

We ran ADDEMUP on NYNEX's MAX problem set and on three problems from the Human Genome Project that aid in locating genes in DNA sequences (recognizing *promoters, splice-junctions,* and *ribosome-binding sites - RBS*). Each of these domains is accompanied by a set of approximately correct rules describing what is currently known about the task (see Opitz, 1995 or Opitz and Shavlik, 1994 for more details). Our experiments measure the test-set error of ADDEMUP on these tasks. Each ensemble consists of 20 networks, and the REGENT and ADDEMUP algorithms considered 250 networks during their genetic search.

Table 2a presents the results from the case where the learners randomly create the topology of their networks (i.e., they do not use the domain-specific knowledge). Table 2a's first row, `best-network`, results from a single-layer neural network where, for each fold, we trained 20 networks containing between 0 and 100 (uniformly) hidden nodes and used a validation set to choose the best network. The next row, `bagging`, contains the results of running Breiman's (1994) *bagging* algorithm on standard, single-hidden-layer networks, where the number of hidden nodes is randomly set between 0 and 100 for each network.[2] Bagging is a "bootstrap" ensemble method that trains each network in the ensemble with a different partition of the training set. It generates each partition by randomly drawing, with replacement, N examples from the training set, where N is the size of the training set. Breiman (1994) showed that bagging is effective on "unstable" learning algorithms, such as neural networks, where small changes in the training set result in large changes in predictions. The bottom row of Table 2a, ADDEMUP, contains the results of a run of ADDEMUP where its initial population (of size 20) is randomly generated. The results show that on these domains combining the output of multiple trained networks generalizes better than trying to pick the single-best network.

While the top table shows the power of neural-network ensembles, Table 2b demonstrates ADDEMUP's ability to utilize prior knowledge. The first row of Table 2b contains the generalization results of the KBANN algorithm, while the next row, KBANN-bagging, contains the results of the ensemble where each individual network in the ensemble is the KBANN network trained on a different partition of the training set. Even though each of these networks start with the same topology and

---

[2] We also tried other ensemble approaches, such as randomly creating varying multi-layer network topologies and initial weight settings, but bagging did significantly better on all datasets (by 15-25% on all three DNA domains).

Table 2: Test-set error from a ten-fold cross validation. Table (a) shows the results from running three learners without the domain-specific knowledge; Table (b) shows the results of running three learners with this knowledge. Pairwise, one-tailed t-tests indicate that ADDEMUP in Table (b) differs from the other algorithms in both tables at the 95% confidence level, except with REGENT in the splice-junction domain.

Standard neural networks (no domain-specific knowledge used)				
	Promoters	Splice Junction	RBS	MAX
best-network	6.6%	7.8%	10.7%	37.0%
bagging	4.6%	4.5%	9.5%	35.7%
ADDEMUP	4.6%	4.9%	9.0%	34.9%

(a)

Knowledge-based neural networks (domain-specific knowledge used)				
	Promoters	Splice Junction	RBS	MAX
KBANN	6.2%	5.3%	9.4%	35.8%
KBANN-bagging	4.2%	4.5%	8.5%	35.6%
REGENT-combined	3.9%	3.9%	8.2%	35.6%
ADDEMUP	2.9%	3.6%	7.5%	34.7%

(b)

"large" initial weight settings (i.e., the weights resulting from the domain-specific knowledge), small changes in the training set still produce significant changes in predictions. Also notice that on all datasets, KBANN-bagging is as good as or better than running bagging on randomly generated networks (i.e., bagging in Table 2a).

The next row, REGENT-combined, contains the results of simply combining, using Equation 5, the networks in REGENT's final population. ADDEMUP, the final row of Table 2b, mainly differs from REGENT-combined in two ways: (a) its fitness function (i.e., Equation 3) takes into account diversity rather than just network accuracy, and (b) it trains new networks by emphasizing the erroneous examples of the current ensemble. Therefore, comparing ADDEMUP with REGENT-combined helps directly test ADDEMUP's diversity-achieving heuristics, though additional results reported in Opitz (1995) show ADDEMUP gets *most* of its improvement from its fitness function. There are two main reasons why we think the results of ADDEMUP in Table 2b are especially encouraging: (a) by comparing ADDEMUP with REGENT-combined, we explicitly test the quality of our heuristics and demonstrate their effectiveness, and (b) ADDEMUP is able to effectively utilize background knowledge to decrease the error of the individual networks in its ensemble, while still being able to create enough diversity among them so as to improve the overall quality of the ensemble.

5 Conclusions

Previous work with neural-network ensembles have shown them to be an effective technique if the classifiers in the ensemble are both highly correct and disagree with each other as much as possible. Our new algorithm, ADDEMUP, uses genetic algorithms to search for a correct and diverse population of neural networks to be used in the ensemble. It does this by collecting the set of networks that best fits an objective function that measures both the accuracy of the network and the disagreement of that network with respect to the other members of the set. ADDEMUP tries to actively generate quality networks during its search by emphasizing the current ensemble's erroneous examples during backpropagation training.

Experiments demonstrate that our method is able to find an effective set of networks for our ensemble. Experiments also show that ADDEMUP is able to effectively incorporate prior knowledge, if available, to improve the quality of this ensemble. In fact, when using domain-specific rules, our algorithm showed statistically significant improvements over (a) the single best network seen during the search, (b) a previously proposed ensemble method called bagging (Breiman, 1994), and (c) a similar algorithm whose objective function is simply the validation-set correctness of the network. In summary, ADDEMUP is successful in generating a set of neural networks that work well together in producing an accurate prediction.

Acknowledgements

This work was supported by Office of Naval Research grant N00014-93-1-0998.

References

Alpaydin, E. (1993). Multiple networks for function learning. In *Proceedings of the 1993 IEEE International Conference on Neural Networks*, vol I, pages 27–32, San Fransisco.

Breiman, L. (1994). Bagging predictors. Technical Report 421, Department of Statistics, University of California, Berkeley.

Clemen, R. (1989). Combining forecasts: A review and annotated bibliography. *International Journal of Forecasting*, 5:559–583.

Drucker, H., Cortes, C., Jackel, L., LeCun, Y., and Vapnik, V. (1994). Boosting and other machine learning algorithms. In *Proceedings of the Eleventh International Conference on Machine Learning*, pages 53–61, New Brunswick, NJ. Morgan Kaufmann.

Hansen, L. and Salamon, P. (1990). Neural network ensembles. *IEEE Transactions on Pattern Analysis and Machine Intelligence*, 12:993–1001.

Hashem, S., Schmeiser, B., and Yih, Y. (1994). Optimal linear combinations of neural networks: An overview. In *Proceedings of the 1994 IEEE International Conference on Neural Networks*, Orlando, FL.

Krogh, A. and Vedelsby, J. (1995). Neural network ensembles, cross validation, and active learning. In Tesauro, G., Touretzky, D., and Leen, T., editors, *Advances in Neural Information Processing Systems*, vol 7, Cambridge, MA. MIT Press.

Maclin, R. and Shavlik, J. (1995). Combining the predictions of multiple classifiers: Using competitive learning to initialize neural networks. In *Proceedings of the Fourteenth International Joint Conference on Artificial Intelligence*, Montreal, Canada.

Mani, G. (1991). Lowering variance of decisions by using artificial neural network portfolios. *Neural Computation*, 3:484–486.

Opitz, D. (1995). *An Anytime Approach to Connectionist Theory Refinement: Refining the Topologies of Knowledge-Based Neural Networks*. PhD thesis, Computer Sciences Department, University of Wisconsin, Madison, WI.

Opitz, D. and Shavlik, J. (1994). Using genetic search to refine knowledge-based neural networks. In *Proceedings of the Eleventh International Conference on Machine Learning*, pages 208–216, New Brunswick, NJ. Morgan Kaufmann.

Perrone, M. (1992). A soft-competitive splitting rule for adaptive tree-structured neural networks. In *Proceedings of the International Joint Conference on Neural Networks*, pages 689–693, Baltimore, MD.

Towell, G. and Shavlik, J. (1994). Knowledge-based artificial neural networks. *Artificial Intelligence*, 70(1,2):119–165.

Wolpert, D. (1992). Stacked generalization. *Neural Networks*, 5:241–259.

Improved Gaussian Mixture Density Estimates Using Bayesian Penalty Terms and Network Averaging

Dirk Ormoneit
Institut für Informatik (H2)
Technische Universität München
80290 München, Germany
ormoneit@informatik.tu-muenchen.de

Volker Tresp
Siemens AG
Central Research
81730 München, Germany
Volker.Tresp@zfe.siemens.de

Abstract

We compare two regularization methods which can be used to improve the generalization capabilities of Gaussian mixture density estimates. The first method uses a Bayesian prior on the parameter space. We derive EM (Expectation Maximization) update rules which maximize the a posterior parameter probability. In the second approach we apply ensemble averaging to density estimation. This includes Breiman's "bagging", which recently has been found to produce impressive results for classification networks.

1 Introduction

Gaussian mixture models have recently attracted wide attention in the neural network community. Important examples of their application include the training of radial basis function classifiers, learning from patterns with missing features, and active learning. The appeal of Gaussian mixtures is based to a high degree on the applicability of the EM (Expectation Maximization) learning algorithm, which may be implemented as a fast neural network learning rule ([Now91], [Orm93]). Severe problems arise, however, due to singularities and local maxima in the log-likelihood function. Particularly in high-dimensional spaces these problems frequently cause the computed density estimates to possess only relatively limited generalization capabilities in terms of predicting the densities of new data points. As shown in this paper, considerably better generalization can be achieved using regularization.

We will compare two regularization methods. The first one uses a Bayesian prior on the parameters. By using conjugate priors we can derive EM learning rules for finding the MAP (maximum a posteriori probability) parameter estimate. The second approach consists of averaging the outputs of ensembles of Gaussian mixture density estimators trained on identical or resampled data sets. The latter is a form of "bagging" which was introduced by Breiman ([Bre94]) and which has recently been found to produce impressive results for classification networks. By using the regularized density estimators in a Bayes classifier ([THA93], [HT94], [KL95]), we demonstrate that both methods lead to density estimates which are superior to the unregularized Gaussian mixture estimate.

2 Gaussian Mixtures and the EM Algorithm

Consider the problem of estimating the probability density of a continuous random vector $x \in \mathcal{R}^d$ based on a set $x^* = \{x^k | 1 \leq k \leq m\}$ of iid. realizations of x. As a density model we choose the class of Gaussian mixtures $p(x|\Theta) = \sum_{i=1}^{n} \kappa_i p(x|i, \mu_i, \Sigma_i)$, where the restrictions $\kappa_i \geq 0$ and $\sum_{i=1}^{n} \kappa_i = 1$ apply. Θ denotes the parameter vector $(\kappa_i, \mu_i, \Sigma_i)_{i=1}^n$. The $p(x|i, \mu_i, \Sigma_i)$ are multivariate normal densities:

$$p(x|i, \mu_i, \Sigma_i) = (2\pi)^{-\frac{d}{2}} |\Sigma_i|^{-1/2} \exp\left[-1/2(x - \mu_i)^t \Sigma_i^{-1}(x - \mu_i)\right].$$

The Gaussian mixture model is well suited to approximate a wide class of continuous probability densities. Based on the model and given the data x^*, we may formulate the log-likelihood as

$$l(\Theta) = \log\left[\prod_{k=1}^{m} p(x^k|\Theta)\right] = \sum_{k=1}^{m} \log \sum_{i=1}^{n} \kappa_i p(x^k|i, \mu_i, \Sigma_i).$$

Maximum likelihood parameter estimates $\hat{\Theta}$ may efficiently be computed with the EM (Expectation Maximization) algorithm ([DLR77]). It consists of the iterative application of the following two steps:

1. In the E-step, based on the current parameter estimates, the posterior probability that unit i is responsible for the generation of pattern x^k is estimated as

$$h_i^k = \frac{\kappa_i p(x^k|i, \mu_i, \Sigma_i)}{\sum_{i'=1}^{n} \kappa_{i'} p(x^k|i', \mu_{i'}, \Sigma_{i'})}. \tag{1}$$

2. In the M-step, we obtain new parameter estimates (denoted by the prime):

$$\kappa_i' = \frac{1}{m} \sum_{k=1}^{m} h_i^k \quad (2) \qquad \mu_i' = \frac{\sum_{k=1}^{m} h_i^k x^k}{\sum_{l=1}^{m} h_i^l} \tag{3}$$

$$\Sigma_i' = \frac{\sum_{k=1}^{m} h_i^k (x^k - \mu_i')(x^k - \mu_i')^t}{\sum_{l=1}^{m} h_i^l}. \tag{4}$$

Note that κ_i' is a scalar, whereas μ_i' denotes a d-dimensional vector and Σ_i' is a $d \times d$ matrix.

It is well known that training neural networks as predictors using the maximum likelihood parameter estimate leads to overfitting. The problem of overfitting is even more severe in density estimation due to singularities in the log-likelihood function. Obviously, the model likelihood becomes infinite in a trivial way if we concentrate all the probability mass on one or several samples of the training set.

In a Gaussian mixture this is just the case if the center of a unit coincides with one of the data points and Σ approaches the zero matrix. Figure 1 compares the true and the estimated probability density in a toy problem. As may be seen, the contraction of the Gaussians results in (possibly infinitely) high peaks in the Gaussian mixture density estimate. A simple way to achieve numerical stability is to artificially enforce a lower bound on the diagonal elements of Σ. This is a very rude way of regularization, however, and usually results in low generalization capabilities. The problem becomes even more severe in high-dimensional spaces. To yield reasonable approximations, we will apply two methods of regularization, which will be discussed in the following two sections.

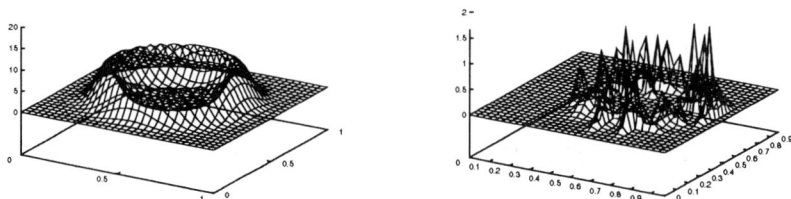

Figure 1: *True density (left) and unregularized density estimation (right).*

3 Bayesian Regularization

In this section we propose a Bayesian prior distribution on the Gaussian mixture parameters, which leads to a numerically stable version of the EM algorithm. We first select a family of prior distributions on the parameters which is *conjugate**. Selecting a conjugate prior has a number of advantages. In particular, we obtain analytic solutions for the posterior density and the predictive density. In our case, the posterior density is a complex mixture of densities[†]. It is possible, however, to derive EM-update rules to obtain the MAP parameter estimates.

A conjugate prior of a single multivariate normal density is a product of a normal density $N(\mu_i|\hat{\mu}, \eta^{-1}\Sigma_i)$ and a Wishart density $Wi(\Sigma_i^{-1}|\alpha, \beta)$ ([Bun94]). A proper conjugate prior for the the mixture weightings $\kappa = (\kappa_1, ..., \kappa_n)$ is a Dirichlet density $D(\kappa|\gamma)$[‡]. Consequently, the prior of the overall Gaussian mixture is the product $D(\kappa|\gamma) \prod_{i=1}^{n} N(\mu_i|\hat{\mu}, \eta^{-1}\Sigma_i) Wi(\Sigma_i^{-1}|\alpha, \beta)$. Our goal is to find the MAP parameter estimate, that is parameters which assume the maximum of the log-posterior

$$l_p(\Theta) = \sum_{k=1}^{m} \log \sum_{i=1}^{n} \kappa_i p(x^k|i, \mu_i, \Sigma_i) + \log D(\kappa|\gamma)$$
$$+ \sum_{i=1}^{n} [\log N(\mu_i|\hat{\mu}, \eta^{-1}\Sigma_i) + \log Wi(\Sigma_i^{-1}|\alpha, \beta)].$$

As in the unregularized case, we may use the EM-algorithm to find a local maximum

---

*A family F of probability distributions on Θ is said to be *conjugate* if, for every $\pi \in F$, the posterior $\pi(\Theta|x)$ also belongs to F ([Rob94]).

[†]The posterior distribution can be written as a sum of n^m simple terms.

[‡]Those densities are defined as follows (b and c are normalizing constants):

$$D(\kappa|\gamma) = b \prod_{i=1}^{n} \kappa_i^{\gamma_i - 1}, \text{ with } \kappa_i \geq 0 \text{ and } \sum_{i=1}^{n} \kappa_i = 1$$
$$N(\mu_i|\hat{\mu}, \eta^{-1}\Sigma_i) = (2\pi)^{-\frac{d}{2}} |\eta^{-1}\Sigma_i|^{-1/2} \exp\left[-\frac{\eta}{2}(\mu_i - \hat{\mu})^t \Sigma_i^{-1}(\mu_i - \hat{\mu})\right]$$
$$Wi(\Sigma_i^{-1}|\alpha, \beta) = c|\Sigma_i^{-1}|^{\alpha - (d+1)/2} \exp\left[-tr(\beta\Sigma_i^{-1})\right].$$

of $l_p(\Theta)$. The E-step is identical to (1). The M-step becomes

$$\kappa_i' = \frac{\sum_{k=1}^{m} h_i^k + \gamma_i - 1}{m + \sum_{i=1}^{n} \gamma_i - n} \quad (5) \qquad \mu_i' = \frac{\sum_{k=1}^{m} h_i^k x^k + \eta \hat{\mu}}{\sum_{l=1}^{m} h_i^l + \eta} \quad (6)$$

$$\Sigma_i' = \frac{\sum_{k=1}^{m} h_i^k (x^k - \mu_i')(x^k - \mu_i')^t + \eta(\mu_i' - \hat{\mu})(\mu_i' - \hat{\mu})^t + 2\beta}{\sum_{l=1}^{m} h_i^l + 2\alpha - d}. \quad (7)$$

As typical for conjugate priors, prior knowledge corresponds to a set of artificial training data which is also reflected in the EM-update equations. In our experiments, we focus on a prior on the variances which is implemented by $\beta \neq 0$, where 0 denotes the $d \times d$ zero matrix. All other parameters we set to "neutral" values:

$$\gamma_i = 1 \ \forall i : 1 \leq i \leq n, \quad \alpha = (d+1)/2, \quad \eta = 0, \quad \beta = \bar{\beta} I^d$$

I^d is the $d \times d$ unity matrix. The choice of α introduces a bias which favors large variances[§]. The effect of various values of the scalar $\bar{\beta}$ on the density estimate is illustrated in figure 2. Note that if $\bar{\beta}$ is chosen too small, overfitting still occurs. If it is chosen to large, on the other hand, the model is too constraint to recognize the underlying structure.

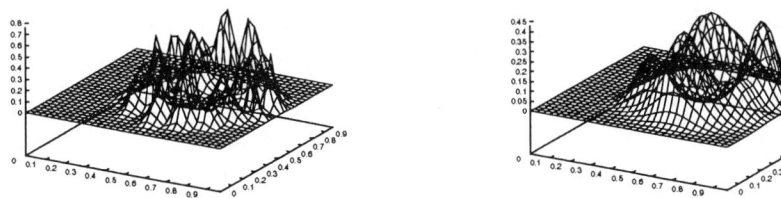

Figure 2: *Regularized density estimates (left: $\bar{\beta} = 0.05$, right: $\bar{\beta} = 0.1$).*

Typically, the optimal value for $\bar{\beta}$ is not known a priori. The simplest procedure consists of using that $\bar{\beta}$ which leads to the best performance on a validation set, analogous to the determination of the optimal weight decay parameter in neural network training. Alternatively, $\bar{\beta}$ might be determined according to appropriate Bayesian methods ([Mac91]). Either way, only few additional computations are required for this method if compared with standard EM.

4 Averaging Gaussian Mixtures

In this section we discuss the averaging of several Gaussian mixtures to yield improved probability density estimation. The averaging over neural network ensembles has been applied previously to regression and classification tasks ([PC93]).

There are several different variants on the simple averaging idea. First, one may train all networks on the complete set of training data. The only source of disagreement between the individual predictions consists in different local solutions found by the likelihood maximization procedure due to different starting points. Disagreement is essential to yield an improvement by averaging, however, so that this proceeding only seems advantageous in cases where the relation between training data and weights is extremely non-deterministic in the sense that in training,

---

[§]If λ is distributed according to $Wi(\lambda|\alpha, \beta)$, then $E[\lambda^{-1}] = (\alpha - (d+1)/2)^{-1}\beta$. In our case λ is Σ_i^{-1}, so that $E[\Sigma_i] \to \infty \cdot \beta$ for $\alpha \to (d+1)/2$.

different solutions are found from different random starting points. A straightforward way to increase the disagreement is to train each network on a resampled version of the original data set. If we resample the data *without replacement*, the size of each training set is reduced, in our experiments to 70% of the original. The averaging of neural network predictions based on resampling *with replacement* has recently been proposed under the notation "bagging" by Breiman ([Bre94]), who has achieved dramatically improved results in several classification tasks. He also notes, however, that an actual improvement of the prediction can only result if the estimation procedure is relatively unstable. As discussed, this is particularly the case for Gaussian mixture training. We therefore expect bagging to be well suited for our task.

5 Experiments and Results

To assess the practical advantage resulting from regularization, we used the density estimates to construct classifiers and compared the resulting prediction accuracies using a toy problem and a real-world problem. The reason is that the generalization error of density estimates in terms of the likelihood based on the test data is rather unintuitive whereas performance on a classification problem provides a good impression of the degree of improvement. Assume we have a set of N labeled data $z^* = \{(x^k, l^k) | k = 1, ..., N\}$, where $l_k \in \Upsilon = \{1, ..., C\}$ denotes the class label of each input x^k. A classifier of new inputs x is yielded by choosing the class l with the maximum posterior class-probability $p(l|x)$. The posterior probabilities may be derived from the class-conditional data likelihood $p(x|l)$ via Bayes theorem: $p(l|x) = p(x|l)p(l)/p(x) \propto p(x|l)p(l)$. The resulting partitions of the input space are optimal for the true $p(l|x)$. A viable way to approximate the posterior $p(l|x)$ is to estimate $p(x|l)$ and $p(l)$ from the sample data.

5.1 Toy Problem

In the toy classification problem the task is to discriminate the two classes of circulatory arranged data shown in figure 3. We generated 200 data points for each class and subdivided them into two sets of 100 data points. The first was used for training, the second to test the generalization performance. As a network architecture we chose a Gaussian mixture with 20 units. Table 1 summarizes the results, beginning with the unregularized Gaussian mixture which is followed by the averaging and the Bayesian penalty approaches. The three rows for averaging correspond to the results yielded without applying resampling (local max.), with resampling with-

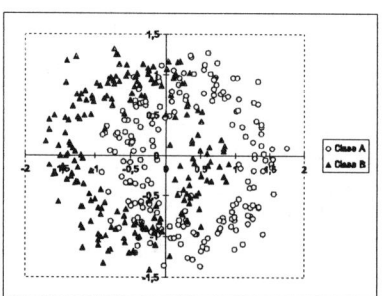

Figure 3: *Toy Classification Task.*

out replacement (70% subsets), and with resampling with replacement (bagging). The performances on training and test set are measured in terms of the model log-likelihood. Larger values indicate a better performance. We report separate results for class A and B, since the densities of both were estimated separately. The final column shows the prediction accuracy in terms of the percentage of correctly classified data in the test set. We report the average results from 20 experiments. The numbers in brackets denote the standard deviations σ of the results. Multiplying σ with $\tau_{19;95\%}/\sqrt{20} = 0.4680$ yields 95% confidence intervals. The best result in each category is underlined.

| Algorithm | Log-Likelihood | | | | Accuracy |
| | Training | | Test | | |
	A	B	A	B	
unreg.	-120.8 (13.3)	-120.4 (10.8)	-224.9 (32.6)	-241.9 (34.1)	80.6% (2.8)
Averaging:					
local max.	-115.6 (6.0)	-112.6 (6.6)	-200.9 (13.9)	-209.1 (16.3)	81.8% (3.1)
70% subset	-106.8 (5.8)	-105.1 (6.7)	-188.8 (9.5)	-196.4 (11.3)	83.2% (2.9)
bagging	<u>-83.8</u> (4.9)	<u>-83.1</u> (7.1)	-194.2 (7.3)	-200.1 (11.3)	82.6% (3.4)
Penalty:					
$\bar{\beta} = 0.01$	-149.3 (18.5)	-146.5 (5.9)	-186.2 (13.9)	-182.9 (11.6)	83.1% (2.9)
$\bar{\beta} = 0.02$	-156.0 (16.5)	-153.0 (4.8)	<u>-177.1</u> (11.8)	-174.9 (7.0)	<u>84.4%</u> (6.3)
$\bar{\beta} = 0.05$	-173.9 (24.3)	-167.0 (15.8)	-182.0 (20.1)	<u>-173.9</u> (14.3)	81.5% (5.9)
$\bar{\beta} = 0.1$	-183.0 (21.9)	-181.9 (21.1)	-184.6 (21.0)	-182.5 (21.1)	78.5% (5.1)

Table 1: Performances in the toy classification problem.

As expected, all regularization methods outperform the maximum likelihood approach in terms of correct classification. The performance of the Bayesian regularization is hereby very sensitive to the appropriate choice of the regularization parameter $\bar{\beta}$. Optimality of $\bar{\beta}$ with respect to the density prediction and optimality with respect to prediction accuracy on the test set roughly coincide (for $\bar{\beta} = 0.02$). Averaging is inferior to the Bayesian approach if an optimal $\bar{\beta}$ is chosen.

5.2 BUPA Liver Disorder Classification

As a second task we applied our methods to a real-world decision problem from the medical environment. The problem is to detect liver disorders which might arise from excessive alcohol consumption. Available information consists of five blood tests as well as a measure of the patients' daily alcohol consumption. We subdivided the 345 available samples into a training set of 200 and a test set of 145 samples. Due to the relatively few data we did not try to determine the optimal regularization parameter using a validation process and will report results on the test set for different parameter values.

Algorithm	Accuracy
unregularized	64.8 %
Bayesian penalty ($\bar{\beta} = 0.05$)	65.5 %
Bayesian penalty ($\bar{\beta} = 0.10$)	66.9 %
Bayesian penalty ($\bar{\beta} = 0.20$)	61.4 %
averaging (local maxima)	65.5 %
averaging (70 % subset)	<u>72.4 %</u>
averaging (bagging)	71.0 %

Table 2: Performances in the liver disorder classification problem.

The results of our experiments are shown in table 2. Again, both regularization methods led to an improvement in prediction accuracy. In contrast to the toy problem, the averaged predictor was superior to the Bayesian approach here. Note that the resampling led to an improvement of more than five percent points compared to unresampled averaging.

6 Conclusion

We proposed a Bayesian and an averaging approach to regularize Gaussian mixture density estimates. In comparison with the maximum likelihood solution both approaches led to considerably improved results as demonstrated using a toy problem and a real-world classification task. Interestingly, none of the methods outperformed the other in both tasks. This might be explained with the fact that Gaussian mixture density estimates are particularly unstable in high-dimensional spaces with relatively few data. The benefit of averaging might thus be greater in this case. Averaging proved to be particularly effective if applied in connection with resampling of the training data, which agrees with results in regression and classification tasks. If compared to Bayesian regularization, averaging is computationally expensive. On the other hand, Baysian approaches typically require the determination of hyper parameters (in our case $\bar{\beta}$), which is not the case for averaging approaches.

References

[Bre94] L. Breiman. Bagging predictors. Technical report, UC Berkeley, 1994.

[Bun94] W. Buntine. Operations for learning with graphical models. *Journal of Artificial Intelligence Research*, 2:159–225, 1994.

[DLR77] A. P. Dempster, N. M. Laird, and D. B. Rubin. Maximum likelihood from incomplete data via the EM algorithm. *J. Royal Statistical Society B*, 1977.

[HT94] T. Hastie and R. Tibshirani. Discriminant analysis by gaussian mixtures. Technical report, AT&T Bell Labs and University of Toronto, 1994.

[KL95] N. Kambhatla and T. K. Leen. Classifying with gaussian mixtures and clusters. In *Advances in Neural Information Processing Systems 7*. Morgan Kaufman, 1995.

[Mac91] D. MacKay. *Bayesian Modelling and Neural Networks*. PhD thesis, California Institute of Technology, Pasadena, 1991.

[Now91] S. J. Nowlan. *Soft Competitive Adaption: Neural Network Learning Algorithms based on Fitting Statistical Mixtures*. PhD thesis, School of Computer Science, Carnegie Mellon University, Pittsburgh, 1991.

[Orm93] D. Ormoneit. Estimation of probability densities using neural networks. Master's thesis, Technische Universität München, 1993.

[PC93] M. P. Perrone and L. N. Cooper. When networks disagree: Ensemble methods for hybrid Neural networks. In *Neural Networks for Speech and Image Processing*. Chapman Hall, 1993.

[Rob94] C. P. Robert. *The Bayesian Choice*. Springer-Verlag, 1994.

[THA93] V. Tresp, J. Hollatz, and S. Ahmad. Network structuring and training using rule-based knowledge. In *Advances in Neural Information Processing Systems 5*. Morgan Kaufman, 1993.

Explorations with the Dynamic Wave Model

Thomas P. Rebotier
Department of Cognitive Science
UCSD, 9500 Gilman Dr
LA JOLLA CA 92093-0515
rebotier@cogsci.ucsd.edu

Jeffrey L. Elman
Department of Cognitive Science
UCSD, 9500 Gilman Dr
LA JOLLA CA 92093-0515
elman@cogsci.ucsd.edu

Abstract

Following Shrager and Johnson (1995) we study growth of logical function complexity in a network swept by two overlapping waves: one of pruning, and the other of Hebbian reinforcement of connections. Results indicate a significant spatial gradient in the appearance of both linearly separable and non linearly separable functions of the two inputs of the network; the n.l.s. cells are much sparser and their slope of appearance is sensitive to parameters in a highly non-linear way.

1 INTRODUCTION

Both the complexity of the brain (and concomittant difficulty encoding that complexity through any direct genetic mapping), as well as the apparently high degree of cortical plasticity suggest that a great deal of cortical structure is emergent rather than pre-specified. Several neural models have explored the emergence of complexity. Von der Marlsburg (1973) studied the grouping of orientation selectivity by competitive Hebbian synaptic modification. Linsker (1986.a, 1986.b and 1986.c) showed how spatial selection cells (off-center on-surround), orientation selective cells, and finally orientation columns, emerge in successive layers from random input by simple, Hebbian-like learning rules. Miller (1992, 1994) studied the emergence of orientation selective columns from activity dependant competition between on-center and off-center inputs.

Kerzsberg, Changeux and Dehaene (1992) studied a model with a dual-aspect learning mechanism: Hebbian reinforcement of the connection strengths in case of correlated activity, and gradual pruning of immature connections. Cells in this model were organized on a 2D grid, connected to each other according to a probability exponentially decreasing with distance, and received inputs from two different sources,

A and B, which might or might not be correlated. The analysis of the network revealed 17 different kinds of cells: those whose output after several cycles depended on the network's initial state, and the 16 possible logical functions of two inputs. Kerzsberg et al. found that learning and pruning created different patches of cells implementing common logical functions, with strong excitation within the patches and inhibition between patches.

Shrager and Johnson (1995) extended that work by giving the network structure in space (structuring the inputs in intricated stripes) or in time, by having a Hebbian learning occur in a spatiotemporal wave that passed through the network rather than occurring everywhere simultaneously. Their motivation was to see if these learning conditions might create a cascade of increasingly complex functions. The approach was also motivated by developmental findings in humans and monkeys suggesting a move of the peak of maximal plasticity from the primary sensory and motor areas towards parietal and then frontal regions. Shrager and Johnson classified the logical functions into three groups: the constants (order 0), those that depend on one input only (order 1), those that depend on both inputs (order 2). They found that a slow wave favored the growth of order 2 cells, whereas a fast wave favored order 1 cells. However, they only varied the connection reinforcement (the growth Trophic Factor), so that the still diffuse pruning affected the rightmost connections before they could stabilize, resulting in an overall decrease which had to be compensated for in the analysis.

In this work, we followed Shrager and Johnson in their study of the effect of a dynamic wave of learning. We present three novel features. Firstly, both the growth trophic factor (hereafter, TF) and the probability of pruning (by analogy, "death factor", DF) travel in gaussian-shaped waves. Second, we classify the cells in 4, not 3, orders: order 3 is made of the non-linearly separable logical functions, whereas the order 2 is now restricted to linearly separable logical functions of both inputs. Third, we use an overall measure of network performance: the slope of appearance of units of a given order. The density is neglected as a measure not related to the specific effects we are looking for, namely, spatial changes in complexity. Thus, each run of our network can be analyzed using 4 values: the slopes for units of order 0, 1, 2 and 3 (See Table 1.). This extreme summarization of functional information allows us to explore systematically many parameters and to study their influence over how complexity grows in space.

Table 1: Orders of logical complexity

ORDER	FUNCTIONS
0	True False
1	A !A B !B
2	A.B !A.B A.!B !A.!B AvB !AvB Av!B !Av!B
3	A xor B, A==B

2 METHODS

Our basic network consisted of 4 columns of 50 units (one simulation verified the scaling up of results, see section 3.2). Internal connections had a gaussian bandwidth and did not wrap around. All initial connections were of weight 1, so that the connectivity weights given as parameters specified a number of labile connections. Early investigations were made with a set of manually chosen parameters ("MAN-

UAL"). Afterwards, two sets of parameters were determined by a Genetic Algorithm (see Goldberg 1989): the first, "SYM", by maximizing the slope of appearance of order 3 units only, the second, "ASY", byoptimizing jointly the appearance of order 2 and order 3 units ("ASY"). The "SYM" network keeps a symmetrical rate of presentation between inputs A and B. In contrast, the "ASY" net presents input B much more often than input A. Parameters are specified in Table 1 and, are in "natural" units: bandwidths and distances are in "cells apart", trophic factor is homogenous to a weight, pruning is a total probability. Initial values and pruning necessited random number generation. We used a linear congruence generator (see p284 in Press 1988), so that given the same seed, two different machines could produce exactly the same run. All the points of each Figure are means of several (usually 40) runs with different random seeds and share the same series of random seeds.

Table 2: Default parameters

MAN.	SYM.	ASY.	name	description
8.5	6.20	12	Wae	mean ini. weight of A excitatory connections
6.5	5.2	9.7	Wai	mean ini. weight of A inhibitory connections
8.5	8.5	13.4	Wbe	mean ini. weight of B excitatory connections
6.5	6.5	14.1	Wbi	mean ini. weight of B inhibitory connections
5.0	6.5	9.9	Wne	m.ini. density of internal excitatory connections
3.5	1.24	12.4	Wni	m.ini. density of internal inhibitory connections
0.2	0.20	0.28	DW	relative variation in initial weights
7.0	1.26	0.65	Bne	bandwidth of internal excitatory connections
7.0	2.86	0.03	Bni	bandwidth of internal inhibitory connections
0.7	0.68	0.98	Cdw	celerity of dynamic wave
1.5	3.0	-3.2	Ddw	distance between the peaks of both waves
9.87	17.6	16.4	Wtf	base level of TF (=highest available weight)
0.6	0.6	0.6	Btf	bandwidth of TF dynamic wave
3.5	1.87	3.3	Tst	Threshold of stabilisation (pruning stop)
0.6	0.64	0.5	Bdf	bandwidth of DF dynamic wave
0.65	0.62	0.12	Pdf	base level of DF (total proba. of degeneration)
0.5	0.5	0.06	Pa	probability of A alone in the stimulus set
0.5	0.5	0.81	Pb	probability of B alone in the stimulus set
0.00	0.00	0.00	Pab	probability of simultaneous s A and B

3 RESULTS

3.1 RESULTS FORMAT

All Figures have the same format and summarize 40 runs per point unless otherwise specified. The top graph presents the mean slope of appearance of all 4 orders of complexity (see Table 1) on the y axis, as a function of different values of the experimentally manipulated parameter, on the x axis. The bottom left graph shows the mean slope for order 2, surrounded by a gray area one standard deviation below and above. The bottom right graph shows the mean slope for order 3, also with a 1-s.d. surrounding area. The slopes have not been normalized, and come from networks whose columns are 50 units high, so that a slope of 1.0 indicates that the number of such units increase in average by one unit per columns, ie, by 3 units across a 4-column network. Because there were very few if any "undefined" units, the slopes approximately sum to zero. Standard deviations are obtained pointwise, which gives a very conservative estimate of reliability.

3.2 OVERALL ASPECT OF THE NETS

Very few order 3 units were appearing. The mean slope with the "SYM" and "ASY" netwts was about 0.3 unit/column. As in Kertzsberg et al., units with identical function tended to appear in blocks. The "SYM" nets tend to have a general overlay of order 2 units, with sparse units of other orders appearing in the rightmost columns. The "ASY" nets manifest sharp transitions between order 0 columns to the left and order 2 columns to the right, with sparse order 3 units almost exclusively in the rightmost column.

3.3 CHANGE IN NETWORK WIDTH

Figure 1 presents the results of 4000 runs for each of 4 networks with identical parameters ("SYM") except for the number of columns, which varied from 4 to 10. This Figure allows to see how the other results of this paper scale when wider networks are being used. All slopes decrease in a nearly hyperbolic manner. Since the mean network of width N is embedded as the beginning of the mean network of width N+P, this suggests that the effects of the growth reach a ceiling between width 4 and 6, and that the lesser slopes of networks of width 6, 8 and 10 is due to averaging between high slope in the first 4 columns and little afterwards. All parameter sets gave similar results. In essence, this justifies our using only 4 columns for this study.

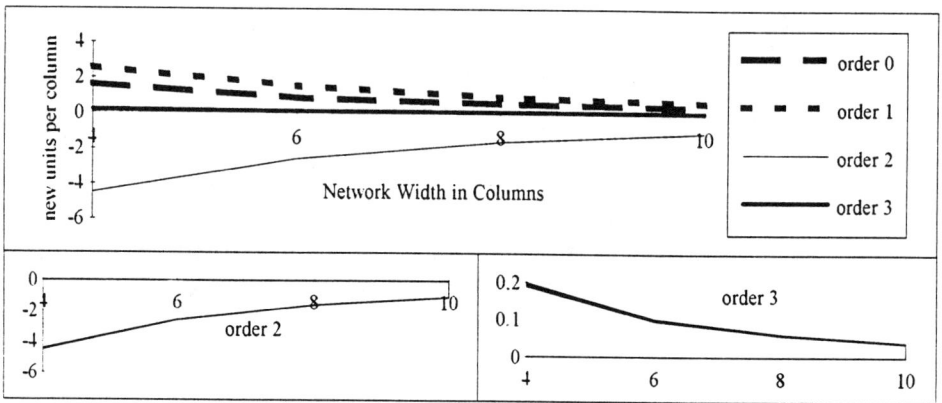

Figure 1: Scaling of the effects with network width.

3.4 CONFIRMATION OF SHRAGER AND JOHNSON'S RESULTS

Although our focus on order 3 units, especially XOR, led us to choose anti-correlated inputs (A and B never simultaneously present, Pab=0), we ran an exploration along the simultaneity axis which allowed to confirm Shrager and Johnson's findings of increase in order 2 units when Pab=0.5. Figure 2 presents the results of varying Pab from 0 to 1. There is a regular increase of the order 2 slope with Pab, and that the value which Shrager and Johnson used (0.5) yields indeed a positive slope more than 3 s.d.'s above zero. The speed of the dynamic wave of trophic factor, which was an important determinant of the emergence of complexity in Shrager and Jonshon's study, had no remarkable influence in ours.

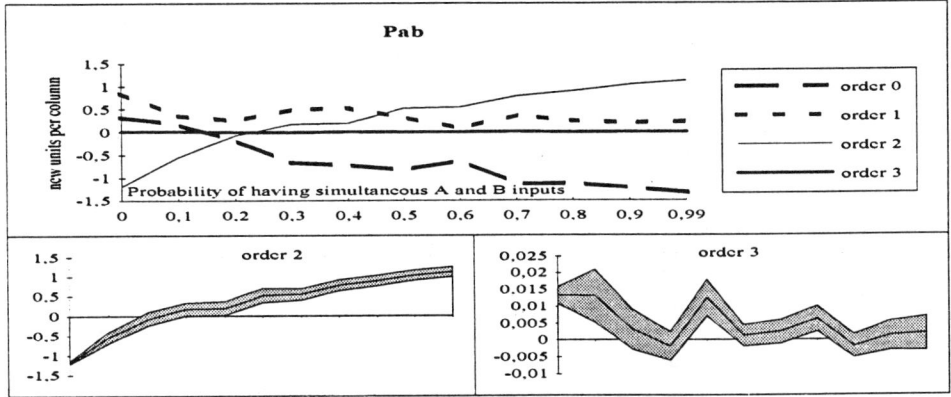

Figure 2: Influence of Simultaneity of Appearance of A and B

3.5 DENSITY OF TROPHIC FACTOR

The total amount of trophic factor distributed by the TF wave over a connection that does not die prematurely is one of the two factors of development, the other being pruning. A trophic factor of 1 means that the connection can at best double its strength (but will do so only if both neurons are in synchrony all the time). We explored amounts of trophic fators from 0 to 20 by increments of 2, with both the "SYM" and the "ASY" default parameter sets. The results show that for low levels of trophic factor (for 0 to 6) there is a linear increase of all effects with the TF level (see Figure 3 for "SYM"; in "ASY" both order 2 and order 3 slopes are positive and have the same linear-with-ceiling shape).

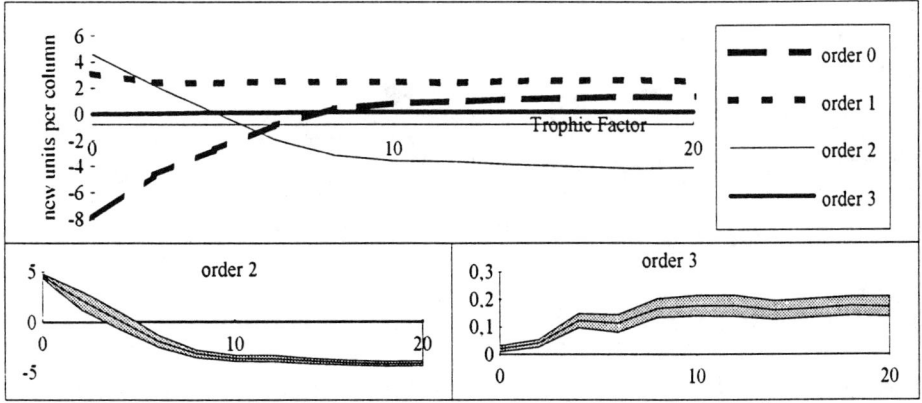

Figure 3: Influence of Trophic Factor density for "SYM"

3.6 PROBABILITY OF PRUNING

Pruning is determined by a probability of connection death, which has been varied from 0 to 0.99 (See Figures 4 and 5). In the "ASY" network, pruning has only a small negative effect on the slope of appearance of order 2 units, but it weights heavily against appearance of order 3 units. In the "SYM" network, pruning causes a stronger slope of disappearance for order 2 units, but its influence on order 3 units is non-linear, with an inverse U shape. The ascending part of that curve suggests that order 3 units appear by pruning of order 2 units. However, there is a need for blocks of order 2 units around the blocks of order 3 units, which accounts for the second part of the inverted U curve.

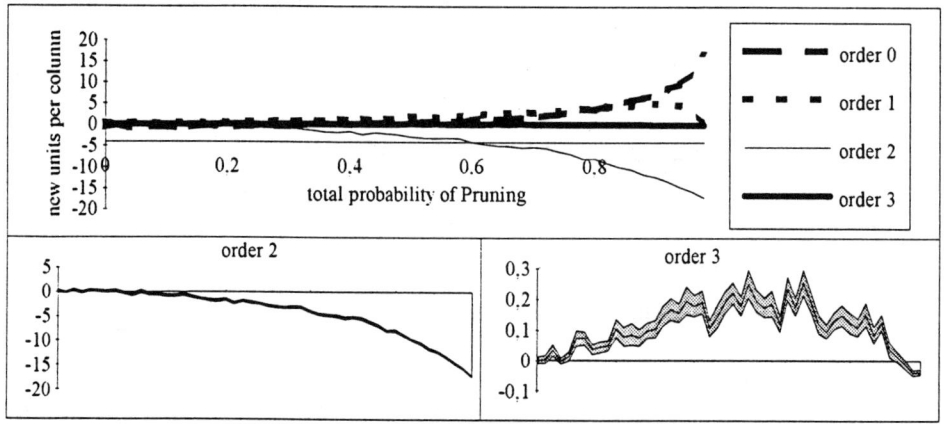

Figure 4: Influence of Pruning probability for "SYM"

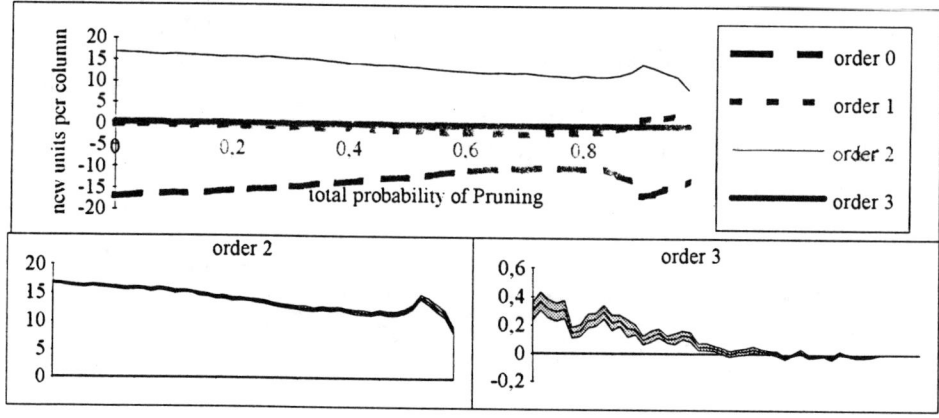

Figure 5: Influence of Pruning probability for "ASY"

4 CONCLUSION

There are two results of primary interest in these simulations. First, we find that, with several different parameter settings, non-linearly separable functions appear almost systematically in the right half of the network. This is the region of "late-learning" columns. The finding that a network trained under a Hebbian learning regime might learn the XOR function is unanticipated, since Hebbian learning in the general case will not learn uncorrelated patterns. Given the biological plausibility of Hebbian learning, it would be useful to discover a scheme by which such function coud be learned. The result obtained here suggests one such plausible scheme. The "high-order" XOR function can be composed of two lower-order functions (e.g., AND and OR; NAND and NOR). The effect of forcing learning to follow a spatiotemporal gradient is that early learning units extract low-order features from the input. These early learning units then provide an additional source of input to late-learning units, which learn the XOR funtion.

The second result is that this learning scheme suggests one account by which brain organization might be produced, not through explicit assignment of function to different spatial regions, but as an emergent result of a developmental process. Thus, the current findings support Shager and Johnson's hypothesis that a dynamical wave model might lead to such organization. The question we are currently pursuing is whether complex inputs (e.g., inputs with spatial structure) might be decomposed in a similar manner, with early learning regions extracting simpler features, and later learning regions extracting higher order, more abstract features.

Acknowledgements

We want to thank Jeff Shrager and Mark Johnson for their help and cooperation. This work was supported by a contract to the second author from the Office of Naval Research, contract N00014-93-1-0194.

References

Goldberg DE, 1989, "Genetic Algorithms", Addison-Wesley

Kerzsberg M, Dehaene S, and Changeux JP, 1992, "Stabilization of complex input-output functions in neural clusters formed by synapse selection", Neural Networks, 5:403-413

Linsker R, 1986.a, "From basic network principles to neural architecture: emergence of spatial-opponent cells", Proceedings of the National Academy of Science USA, 83:7508-7512

Linsker R, 1986.b, "From basic network principles to neural architecture: emergence of orientation-selective cells", Proceedins of the National Academy of Science USA, 83:8390-8394

Linsker R, 1986.c, "From basic network principles to neural architecture: emergence of orientation columns", Proceedings of the National Academy of Science USA, 83:8779-8783

Miller KD, 1992, "Development of orientation columns via competition between on and off-center inputs", NeuroReport 3:73-76

Miller KD, 1994, "A model for the development of simple cell receptive fields and the ordered arrangement of orientation columns through activity-dependant competition between on and off-center inputs", the Journal of Neuroscience, 14:409-441

Press WH, 1988, "Numerical recipes in C: the art of scientific computing", Cambridge University Press, Cambridge, MASS

Shrager J and Johnson MH, 1995, "Modeling the development of cortical function", in Kovacks I and Julesz B, Eds., "Maturational Windows ans Cortical Plasticity" (working title), The Santa Fe Institute Press, Santa Fe, NM

von der Marlsburg C, 1973, "Self-organisation of orientation sensitive cells in the striate cortex", Kybernetic, 14:85-100

The Capacity of a Bump

Gary William Flake*
Institute for Advance Computer Studies
University of Maryland
College Park, MD 20742

Abstract

Recently, several researchers have reported encouraging experimental results when using Gaussian or bump-like activation functions in multilayer perceptrons. Networks of this type usually require fewer hidden layers and units and often learn much faster than typical sigmoidal networks. To explain these results we consider a *hyper-ridge* network, which is a simple perceptron with no hidden units and a ridge activation function. If we are interested in partitioning p points in d dimensions into two classes then in the limit as d approaches infinity the capacity of a hyper-ridge and a perceptron is identical. However, we show that for $p \gg d$, which is the usual case in practice, the ratio of hyper-ridge to perceptron dichotomies approaches $p/2(d+1)$.

1 Introduction

A *hyper-ridge* network is a simple perceptron with no hidden units and a ridge activation function. With one output this is conveniently described as $y = g(h) = g(\mathbf{w} \cdot \mathbf{x} - b)$ where $g(h) = \text{sgn}(1 - h^2)$. Instead of dividing an input-space into two classes with a single hyperplane, a hyper-ridge network uses two parallel hyperplanes. All points in the interior of the hyperplanes form one class, while all exterior points form another. For more information on hyper-ridges, learning algorithms, and convergence issues the curious reader should consult [3].

We wouldn't go so far as to suggest that anyone actually use a hyper-ridge for a real-world problem, but it is interesting to note that a hyper-ridge can represent linear inseparable mappings such as XOR, NEGATE, SYMMETRY, and COUNT(m) [2, 3]. Moreover, hyper-ridges are very similar to multilayer perceptrons with bump-like activation functions, such as a Gaussian, in the way the input space is partitioned. Several researchers [6, 2, 3, 5] have independently found that Gaussian units offer many advantages over sigmoidal units.

---

*Current address: Adaptive Information and Signal Processing Department, Siemens Corporate Research, 755 College Road East, Princeton, NJ 08540. Email: flake@scr.siemens.com

The Capacity of a Bump

In this paper we derive the capacity of a hyper-ridge network. Our first result is that hyper-ridges and simple perceptrons are equivalent in the limit as the input dimension size approaches infinity. However, when the number of patterns is far greater than the input dimension (as is the usual case) the ratio of hyper-ridge to perceptron dichotomies approaches $p/2(d+1)$, giving some evidence that bump-like activation functions offer an advantage over the more traditional sigmoid.

The rest of this paper is divided into three more sections. In Section 2 we derive the number of dichotomies for a hyper-ridge network. The capacities for hyper-ridges and simple perceptrons are compared in Section 3. Finally, in Section 4 we give our conclusions.

2 The Representation Power of a Hyper-Ridge

Suppose we have p patterns in the pattern-space, $\Re^d$, where d is the number of inputs of our neural network. A *dichotomy* is a classification of all of the points into two distinct sets. Clearly, there are at most 2^p dichotomies that exist. We are concerned with the number of dichotomies that a single hyper-ridge node can represent. Let the number of dichotomies of p patterns in d dimensions be denoted as $D(p, d)$.

For the case of $D(1, d)$, when $p = 1$ there are always two and only two dichotomies since one can trivially include the single point or no points. Thus, $D(1, d) = 2$.

For the case of $D(p, 1)$, all of the points are constrained to fall on a line. From this set pick two points, say x_a and x_b. It is always possible to place a ridge function such that all points between x_a and x_b (inclusive of the end points) are included in one set, and all other points are excluded. Thus, there are p dichotomies consisting of a single point, $p-1$ dichotomies consisting of two points, $p-2$ dichotomies consisting of three points, and so on. No other dichotomies besides the empty set are possible. The number of possible hyper-ridge dichotomies in one dimension can now be expressed as

$$D(p, 1) = \sum_{i=1}^{p} i + 1 = \frac{1}{2}p(p+1) + 1, \tag{1}$$

with the extra dichotomy coming from the empty set.

To derive the general form of the recurrence relationship, we would have to resort to techniques similar to those used by Cover [1], Nilsson [7], and Gardner [4]. Because of space considerations, we do not give the full derivation of the general form of the recurrence relationship in this paper, but instead cite the complete derivation given in [3]. The short version of the story is that the general form of the recurrence relationship for hyper-ridge dichotomies is identical to the equivalent expression for simple perceptrons:

$$D(p, d) = D(p-1, d) + D(p-1, d-1). \tag{2}$$

All differences between the capacity of hyper-ridges and simple perceptrons are, therefore, a consequence of the different base cases for the recurrence expression.

To get Equation 2 into closed form, we first expand $D(p, d)$ a total of p times, yielding

$$D(p, d) = \sum_{i=0}^{p-1} \binom{p-1}{i} D(1, d-i). \tag{3}$$

For Equation 3 it is possible for the second term of $D(1, d-1)$ to become zero or negative. Taking the two identities $D(p, 0) = p + 1$ and $D(p, -1) = 1$ are the only choices that are consistent with the recurrent relationship expressed in Equation 2. With this in mind, there are three separate cases that we need to be concerned with: $p < d+2$, $p = d+2$, and

$p > d + 2$. When $p < d + 2$

$$D(p, d) = \sum_{i=0}^{p-1} \binom{p-1}{i} D(1, d-i) = 2 \sum_{i=0}^{p-1} \binom{p-1}{i} = 2^p, \qquad (4)$$

since all of the second terms in $D(1, d - i)$ are always greater or equal to zero. When $p = d + 2$, the last term in $D(1, d - i)$, in the summation, will be equal to -1. Thus we can expand Equation 3 in this case to

$$\begin{aligned} D(p, d) &= \sum_{i=0}^{p-1} \binom{p-1}{i} D(1, d-i) = \sum_{i=0}^{p-1} \binom{p-1}{i} D(1, p-2-i) \\ &= \sum_{i=0}^{p-2} \binom{p-1}{i} D(1, p-2-i) + 1 = 2 \sum_{i=0}^{p-2} \binom{p-1}{i} + 1 \\ &= 2(2^{p-1} - 1) + 1 = 2^p - 1. \qquad (5) \end{aligned}$$

Finally, when $p > d + 2$, some of the last terms in $D(1, d - i)$ are always negative. We can disregard all $d - i < -1$, taking $D(1, d - i)$ equal to zero in these cases (which is consistent with the recurrence relationship),

$$\begin{aligned} D(p, d) &= \sum_{i=0}^{p-1} \binom{p-1}{i} D(1, d-i) = \sum_{i=0}^{d+1} \binom{p-1}{i} D(1, d-i) \\ &= \sum_{i=0}^{d} \binom{p-1}{i} D(1, d-i) + \binom{p-1}{d+1} = 2 \sum_{i=0}^{d} \binom{p-1}{i} + \binom{p-1}{d+1}. \qquad (6) \end{aligned}$$

Combining Equations 4, 5, and 6 gives

$$D(p, d) = \begin{cases} 2 \sum_{i=0}^{d} \binom{p-1}{i} + \binom{p-1}{d+1} & \text{for } p > d + 2 \\ 2^p - 1 & \text{for } p = d + 2 \\ 2^p & \text{for } p < d + 2 \end{cases}. \qquad (7)$$

3 Comparing Representation Power

Cover [1], Nilsson [7], and Gardner [4] have all shown that $D(p, d)$ for simple perceptrons obeys the rule

$$D(p, d) = \begin{cases} 2 \sum_{i=0}^{d} \binom{p-1}{i} & \text{for } p > d + 2 \\ 2^p - 2 & \text{for } p = d + 2 \\ 2^p & \text{for } p < d + 2 \end{cases}. \qquad (8)$$

The interesting case is when $p > d + 2$, since that is where Equations 7 and 8 differ the most. Moreover, problems are more difficult when the number of training patterns greatly exceeds the number of trainable weights in a neural network.

Let $D_h(p, d)$ and $D_p(p, d)$ denote the number of dichotomies possible for hyper-ridge networks and simple perceptrons, respectively. Additionally, Let C_h, and C_p denote the

The Capacity of a Bump

respective capacities. We should expect both $D_h(p,d)/2^p$ and $D_p(p,d)/2^p$ to be at or around 1 for small values of $p/(d+1)$. At some point, for large $p/(d+1)$, the 2^p term should dominate, making the ratio go to zero. The capacity of a network can loosely be defined as the value $p/(d+1)$ such that $D(p,d)/2^p = \frac{1}{2}$. This is more rigorously defined as

$$C = \left\{ c : \lim_{d \to \infty} \frac{D(c(d+1), d)}{2^{c(d+1)}} = \frac{1}{2} \right\},$$

which is the point in which the transition occurs in the limit as the input dimension goes to infinity.

Figures 1, 2, and 3 illustrate and compare C_p and C_h at different stages. In Figure 1 the capacities are illustrated for perceptrons and hyper-ridges, respectively, by plotting $D(p,d)/2^p$ versus $p/(d+1)$ for various values of d. On par with our intuition, the ratio $D(p,d)/2^p$ equals 1 for small values of $p/(d+1)$ but decreases to zero as $p(d+1)$ increases. Figure 2 and the left diagram of Figure 3 plot $D(p,d)/2^p$ versus $p/(d+1)$ for perceptron and hyper-ridges, side by side, with values of $d = 5, 20$, and 100. As d increases, the two curves become more similar. This fact is further illustrated in the right diagram of Figure 3 where the plot is of $D_h(p,d)/D_p(p,d)$ versus p for various values of d. The ratio clearly approaches 1 as d increases, but there is significant difference for smaller values of d.

The differences between D_p and D_h can be more explicitly quantified by noting that

$$D_h(p,d) = D_p(p,d) + \binom{p-1}{d+1}$$

for $p > d+2$. This difference clearly shows up in in the plots comparing the two capacities. We will now show that the capacities are identical in the limit as d approaches infinity. To do this, we will prove that the capacity curves for both hyper-ridges and perceptrons crosses $\frac{1}{2}$ at $p/(d+1) = 2$. This fact is already widely known for perceptrons. Because of space limitations we will handwave our way through lemma and corollary proofs. The curious reader should consult [3] for the complete proofs.

Lemma 3.1

$$\lim_{n \to \infty} \frac{1}{2^{2n}} \binom{2n}{n} = 0.$$

Short Proof Since n approaches infinity, we can use Stirling's formula as an approximation of the factorials.

□

Corollary 3.2 For all positive integer constants, a, b, and c,

$$\lim_{n \to \infty} \frac{1}{2^{2n+a}} \binom{2n+b}{n+c} = 0.$$

Short Proof When adding the constants b and c to the combination, the whole combination can always be represented as $\text{comb}(2n, n) \cdot \gamma$, where γ is some multiplicative constant. Such a constant can always be factored out of the limit. Additionally, large values of a only increase the growth rate of the denominator.

□

Lemma 3.3 For $p/(d+1) = 2$, $\lim_{d \to \infty} D_p(p,d)/2^p = \frac{1}{2}$.

Short Proof Consult any of Cover [1], Nilsson [7], or Gardner [4] for full proof.

□

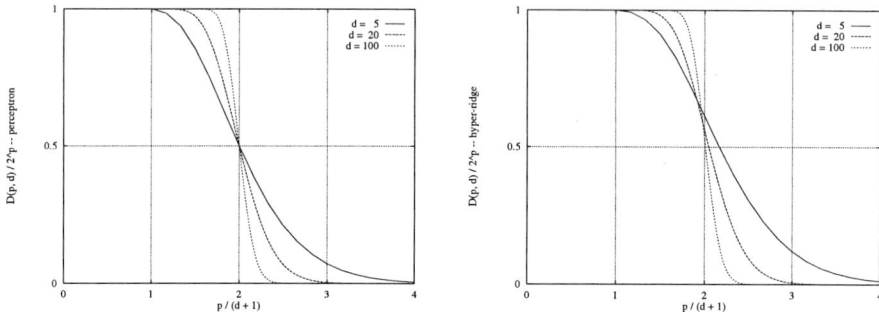

Figure 1: On the left, $D_p(p, d)/2^p$ versus $p/(d+1)$, and on the right, $D_h(p, d)/2^p$ versus $p/(d+1)$ for various values of d. Notice that for perceptrons the curve always passes through $\frac{1}{2}$ at $p/(d+1) = 2$. For hyper-ridges, the point where the curve passes through $\frac{1}{2}$ decreases as d increases.

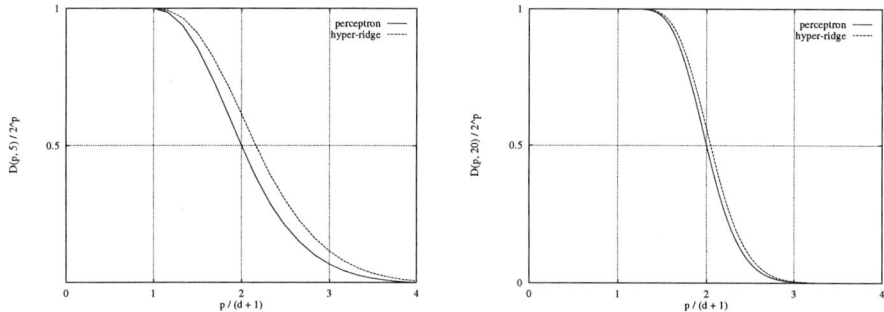

Figure 2: On the left, capacity comparison for $d = 5$. There is considerable difference for small values of d, especially when one considers that the capacities are normalized by 2^p. On the right, comparison for $d = 20$. The difference between the two capacities is much more subtle now that d is fairly large.

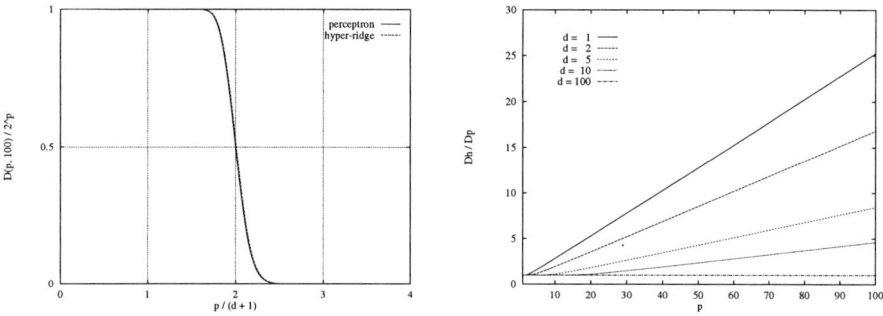

Figure 3: On the left, capacity comparison for $d = 100$. For this value of d, the capacities are visibly indistinguishable. On the right, $D_h(p, d)/D_p(p, d)$ versus p for various values of d. For small values of d the capacity of a hyper-ridge is much greater than a perceptron. As d grows, the ratio asymptotically approaches 1.

The Capacity of a Bump

Theorem 3.4 *For $p/(d+1) = 2$,*
$$\lim_{d \to \infty} \frac{D_h(p, d)}{2^p} = \frac{1}{2}.$$

Proof Taking advantage of the relationship between perceptron dichotomies and hyper-ridge dichotomies allows us to expand $D_h(p, d)$,
$$\lim_{d \to \infty} \frac{D_h(p, d)}{2^p} = \lim_{d \to \infty} \frac{D_p(p, d)}{2^p} + \lim_{d \to \infty} \binom{p-1}{d+1}.$$

By Lemma 3.3, and substituting $2(d + 1)$ for p, we get:
$$\frac{1}{2} + \lim_{d \to \infty} \binom{2d+1}{d+1}.$$

Finally, by Corollary 3.2 the right limit vanishes leaving us with $\frac{1}{2}$. □

Superficially, Theorem 3.4 would seem to indicate that there is no difference between the representation power of a perceptron and a hyper-ridge network. However, since this result is only valid in the limit as the number of inputs goes to infinity, it would be interesting to know the exact relationship between $D_p(d, p)$ and $D_h(d, p)$ for finite values of d.

In the right diagram of Figure 3 values of $D_p(d, p)/D_h(d, p)$ are plotted against various values of p. The figure is slightly misleading since the ratio appears to be linear in p, when, in fact, the ratio is only approximately linear in p. If we normalize the ratio by $\frac{1}{p}$ and recompute the ratio in the limit as p approaches infinity the ratio becomes linear in d. Theorem 3.5 establishes this rigorously.

Theorem 3.5
$$\lim_{p \to \infty} \frac{1}{p} \frac{D_h(d, p)}{D_p(d, p)} = \frac{1}{2(d+1)}.$$

Proof First, note that we can simplify the left hand side of the expression to
$$\lim_{p \to \infty} \frac{1}{p} \frac{D_h(d, p)}{D_p(d, p)} = \lim_{p \to \infty} \frac{1}{p} \frac{D_p(d, p) + \binom{p-1}{d+1}}{D_p(d, p)} = \lim_{p \to \infty} \frac{1}{p} \frac{\binom{p-1}{d+1}}{D_p(d, p)} \quad (9)$$

In the next step, we will invert Equation 9, making it easier to work with. We need to show that the new expression is equal to $2(d + 1)$.

$$\lim_{p \to \infty} p \frac{D_p(d, p)}{\binom{p-1}{d+1}} = \lim_{p \to \infty} 2p \frac{\sum_{i=0}^{d} \binom{p-1}{i}}{\binom{p-1}{d+1}} =$$

$$\lim_{p \to \infty} 2p \sum_{i=0}^{d} \frac{(p-1)!}{i!(p-i-1)!} \frac{(d+1)!(p-d-2)!}{(p-1)!} = \lim_{p \to \infty} 2p \sum_{i=0}^{d} \frac{(d+1)!(p-d-2)!}{i!(p-i-1)!} =$$

$$\lim_{p \to \infty} \frac{p}{(p-1-d)} 2(d+1) \sum_{i=0}^{d} \frac{d!(p-d-1)!}{i!(p-i-1)!} = \lim_{p \to \infty} 2(d+1) \sum_{i=0}^{d} \frac{d!(p-d-1)!}{i!(p-i-1)!} \quad (10)$$

In Equation 10, the summation can be reduced to 1 since
$$\lim_{p \to \infty} \frac{d!(p-d-1)!}{i!(p-i-1)!} = \begin{cases} 0 & \text{when } 0 \le i < d \\ 1 & \text{when } i = d \end{cases}.$$

Thus, Equation 10 is equal to $2(d + 1)$, which proves the theorem.
□

Theorem 3.5 is valid only in the case when $p \gg d$, which is typically true in interesting classification problems. The result of the theorem gives us a good estimate of how many more dichotomies are computable with a hyper-ridge network when compared to a simple perceptron. When $p \gg d$ the equation

$$\frac{D_h(d, p)}{D_p(d, p)} \simeq \frac{p}{2(d + 1)} \qquad (11)$$

is an accurate estimate of the difference between the capacities of the two architectures. For example, taking $d = 4$ and $p = 60$ and applying the values to Equation 11 yields the ratio of 6, which should be interpreted as meaning that one could store six times the number of mappings in a hyper-ridge network than one could in a simple perceptron. Moreover, Equation 11 is in agreement with the right diagram of Figure 3 for all values of $p \gg d$.

4 Conclusion

An interesting footnote to this work is that the VC dimension [8] of a hyper-ridge network is identical to a simple perceptron, namely d. However, the real difference between perceptrons and hyper-ridges is more noticeable in practice, especially when one considers that linear inseparable problems are representable by hyper-ridges.

We also know that there is no such thing as a free lunch and that generalization is sure to suffer in just the cases when representation power is increased. Yet given all of the comparisons between MLPs and radial basis functions (RBFs) we find it encouraging that there may be a class of approximators that is a compromise between the local nature of RBFs and the global structure of MLPs.

References

[1] T.M. Cover. Geometrical and statistical properties of systems of linear inequalities with applications in pattern recognition. *IEEE Transactions on Electronic Computers*, 14:326–334, 1965.

[2] M.R.W. Dawson and D.P. Schopflocher. Modifying the generalized delta rule to train networks of non-monotonic processors for pattern classification. *Connection Science*, 4(1), 1992.

[3] G. W. Flake. *Nonmonotonic Activation Functions in Multilayer Perceptrons*. PhD thesis, University of Maryland, College Park, MD, December 1993.

[4] E. Gardner. Maximum storage capacity in neural networks. *Europhysics Letters*, 4:481–485, 1987.

[5] F. Girosi, M. Jones, and T. Poggio. Priors, stabilizers and basis functions: from regularization to radial, tensor and additive splines. Technical Report A.I. Memo No. 1430, C.B.C.L. Paper No. 75, MIT AI Laboratory, 1993.

[6] E. Hartman and J. D. Keeler. Predicting the future: Advanges of semilocal units. *Neural Computation*, 3:566–578, 1991.

[7] N.J. Nilsson. *Learning Machines: Foundations of Trainable Pattern Classifying Systems*. McGraw-Hill, New York, 1965.

[8] V.N. Vapnik and A.Y. Chervonenkis. On the uniform convergence of relative frequencies of events to their probabilities. *Theory of Probability and Its Applications*, 16:264–280, 1971.

Tempering Backpropagation Networks: Not All Weights are Created Equal

Nicol N. Schraudolph
EVOTEC BioSystems GmbH
Grandweg 64
22529 Hamburg, Germany
nici@evotec.de

Terrence J. Sejnowski
Computational Neurobiology Lab
The Salk Institute for Biol. Studies
San Diego, CA 92186-5800, USA
terry@salk.edu

Abstract

Backpropagation learning algorithms typically collapse the network's structure into a single vector of weight parameters to be optimized. We suggest that their performance may be improved by utilizing the structural information instead of discarding it, and introduce a framework for "tempering" each weight accordingly.

In the tempering model, activation and error signals are treated as approximately independent random variables. The characteristic scale of weight changes is then matched to that of the residuals, allowing structural properties such as a node's fan-in and fan-out to affect the local learning rate and backpropagated error. The model also permits calculation of an upper bound on the global learning rate for batch updates, which in turn leads to different update rules for bias *vs.* non-bias weights.

This approach yields hitherto unparalleled performance on the family relations benchmark, a deep multi-layer network: for both batch learning with momentum and the *delta-bar-delta* algorithm, convergence at the optimal learning rate is sped up by more than an order of magnitude.

1 Introduction

Although neural networks are structured graphs, learning algorithms typically view them as a single vector of parameters to be optimized. All information about a network's architecture is thus discarded in favor of the presumption of an *isotropic* weight space — the notion that *a priori* all weights in the network are created equal. This serves to decouple the learning process from network design and makes a large body of function optimization techniques directly applicable to backpropagation learning.

But what if the discarded structural information holds valuable clues for efficient weight optimization? Adaptive step size and second-order gradient techniques (Battiti, 1992) may recover some of it, at considerable computational expense. *Ad hoc* attempts to incorporate structural information such as the fan-in (Plaut et al., 1986) into local learning rates have become a familiar part of backpropagation lore; here we derive a more comprehensive framework — which we call *tempering* — and demonstrate its effectiveness.

Tempering is based on modeling the activities and error signals in a backpropagation network as independent random variables. This allows us to calculate activity- and weight-invariant upper bounds on the effect of synchronous weight updates on a node's activity. We then derive appropriate local step size parameters by relating this maximal change in a node's activity to the characteristic scale of its residual through a global learning rate.

Our subsequent derivation of an upper bound on the global learning rate for batch learning suggests that the d.c. component of the error signal be given special treatment. Our experiments show that the resulting method of *error shunting* allows the global learning rate to approach its predicted maximum, for highly efficient learning performance.

2 Local Learning Rates

Consider a neural network with feedforward activation given by

$$x_j = f_j(y_j), \quad y_j = \sum_{i \in A_j} x_i w_{ij}, \tag{1}$$

where A_j denotes the set of *anterior* nodes feeding directly into node j, and f_j is a nonlinear (typically sigmoid) activation function. We imply that nodes are activated in the appropriate sequence, and that some have their values clamped so as to represent external inputs.

With a local learning rate of η_j for node j, gradient descent in an objective function E produces the weight update

$$\Delta w_{ij} = \eta_j \delta_j x_i, \quad \text{where} \quad \delta_j \equiv \frac{\partial E}{\partial y_j}. \tag{2}$$

Linearizing f_j around y_j approximates the resultant change in activation x_j as

$$\Delta x_j \approx f'_j(y_j) \sum_{i \in A_j} x_i \Delta w_{ij} = \eta_j \delta_j f'_j(y_j) \sum_{i \in A_j} x_i^2. \tag{3}$$

Our goal is to put the scale of Δx_j in relation to that of the error signal δ_j. Specifically, when averaged over many training samples, we want the change in output activity of each node in response to each pattern limited to a certain proportion — given by the global learning rate η — of its residual. We achieve this by relating the *variation* of Δx_j over the training set to that of the error signal:

$$(\forall j) \quad \langle \Delta x_j^2 \rangle \leq \eta^2 \langle \delta_j^2 \rangle, \tag{4}$$

where $\langle \cdot \rangle$ denotes averaging over training samples. Formally, this approach may be interpreted as a diagonal approximation of the inverse Fischer information matrix (Amari, 1995). We implement (4) by deriving an upper bound for the left-hand side which is then equated with the right-hand side. Replacing the activity-dependent slope of f_j by its maximum value

$$s(f_j) \equiv \max_u |f'_j(u)| \tag{5}$$

and assuming that there are no correlations[1] between inputs x_i and error δ_j, we obtain

$$\langle \Delta x_j^2 \rangle \leq \eta_j^2 s(f_j)^2 \langle \delta_j^2 \rangle \xi_j \tag{6}$$

---

[1] Note that such correlations are minimized by the local weight update.

from (3), provided that

$$\xi_j \geq \xi_j^* \equiv \left\langle \left[\sum_{i \in A_j} x_i^2\right]^2 \right\rangle. \tag{7}$$

We can now satisfy (4) by setting the local learning rate to

$$\eta_j \equiv \frac{\eta}{s(f_j)\sqrt{\xi_j}}. \tag{8}$$

There are several approaches to computing an upper bound ξ_j on the total squared input power ξ_j^*. One option would be to calculate the latter empirically during training, though this raises sampling and stability issues. For external inputs we may precompute ξ_j^* or derive an upper bound based on prior knowledge of the training data. For inputs from other nodes in the network we assume independence and derive ξ_j from the range of their activation functions:

$$\xi_j = \sum_{i \in A_j} p(f_i)^2, \quad \text{where} \quad p(f_i) \equiv \max_u f_i(u)^2. \tag{9}$$

Note that when all nodes use the same activation function f, we obtain the well-known $\sqrt{fan\text{-}in}$ heuristic (Plaut et al., 1986) as a special case of (8).

3 Error Backpropagation

In deriving local learning rates above we have tacitly used the error signal as a stand-in for the residual proper, *i.e.* the distance to the target. For output nodes we can scale the error to never exceed the residual:

$$\delta_j = \frac{1}{\phi_j} \frac{\partial E}{\partial y_j}, \quad \text{where} \quad \phi_j \equiv \max_{y_j} \left| f_j'(y_j) \frac{\partial^2 E}{\partial f_j(y_j)^2} \right|. \tag{10}$$

Note that for the conventional quadratic error this simplifies to $\phi_j = s(f_j)$. What about the remainder of the network? Unlike (Krogh et al., 1990), we do not wish to prescribe definite targets (and hence residuals) for hidden nodes. Instead we shall use our bounds and independence arguments to scale backpropagated error signals to roughly appropriate magnitude. For this purpose we introduce an attenuation coefficient a_i into the error backpropagation equation:

$$\delta_i = a_i f_i'(y_i) \sum_{j \in P_i} w_{ij} \delta_j, \tag{11}$$

where P_i denotes the set of *posterior* nodes fed directly from node i. We posit that the appropriate variation for δ_i be no more than the weighted average of the variation of backpropagated errors:

$$\langle \delta_i^2 \rangle \leq \frac{1}{|P_i|} \sum_{j \in P_i} w_{ij}^2 \langle \delta_j^2 \rangle \tag{12}$$

whereas, assuming independence between the δ_j and replacing the slope of f_i by its maximum value, (11) gives us

$$\langle \delta_i^2 \rangle \leq a_i^2 s(f_i)^2 \sum_{j \in P_i} w_{ij}^2 \langle \delta_j^2 \rangle. \tag{13}$$

Again we equate the right-hand sides of both inequalities to satisfy (12), yielding

$$a_i \equiv \frac{1}{s(f_i)\sqrt{|P_i|}}. \tag{14}$$

Note that the incorporation of the weights into (12) is *ad hoc*, as we have no *a priori* reason to scale a node's step size in proportion to the size of its vector of outgoing weights. We have chosen (12) simply because it produces a weight-invariant value for the attenuation coefficient. The scale of the backpropagated error could be controlled more rigorously, at the expense of having to recalculate a_i after each weight update.

4 Global Learning Rate

We now derive the appropriate global learning rate for the batch weight update

$$\widehat{\Delta} w_{ij} \equiv \eta_j \sum_{t \in T} \delta_j(t) \, x_i(t) \qquad (15)$$

over a non-redundant training sample T. Assuming independent and zero-mean residuals, we then have

$$\widehat{\Delta} x_j^2 = |T| \langle \Delta x_j^2 \rangle \leq |T| \eta^2 \langle \delta_j^2 \rangle \qquad (16)$$

by virtue of (4). Under these conditions we can ensure

$$\widehat{\Delta} x_j^2 \leq \langle \delta_j^2 \rangle , \qquad (17)$$

i.e. that the variation of the batch weight update does not exceed that of the residual, by using a global learning rate of

$$\eta \leq \eta^* \equiv 1/\sqrt{|T|}. \qquad (18)$$

Even when redundancy in the training set forces us to use a lower rate, knowing the upper bound η^* effectively allows an educated guess at η, saving considerable time in practice.

5 Error Shunting

It remains to deal with the assumption made above that the residuals be zero-mean, *i.e.* that $\langle \delta_j \rangle = 0$. Any d.c. component in the error requires a learning rate inversely proportional to the batch size — far below η^*, the rate permissible for zero-mean residuals. This suggests handling the d.c. component of error signals separately. This is the proper job of the bias weight, so we update it accordingly:

$$\widehat{\Delta} w_{oj} = \langle \delta_j \rangle / s(f_j). \qquad (19)$$

In order to allow learning at rates close to η^* for all other weights, their error signals are then centered by subtracting the mean:

$$(\forall i \neq 0) \quad \widehat{\Delta} w_{ij} = \eta_j \sum_{t \in T} (\delta_j(t) - \langle \delta_j \rangle) \, x_i(t) \qquad (20)$$

$$= \eta_j \left(\sum_{t \in T} \delta_j(t) \, x_i(t) - \langle x_i \rangle \sum_{t \in T} \delta_j(t) \right) . \qquad (21)$$

Note that both sums in (21) must be collected in batch implementations of backpropagation anyway — the only additional statistic required is the average input activity $\langle x_i \rangle$. Indeed for batch update centering errors is equivalent to centering inputs, which is known to assist learning by removing a large eigenvalue of the Hessian (LeCun et al., 1991). We expect online implementations to perform best when *both* input and error signals are centered so as to improve the stochastic approximation.

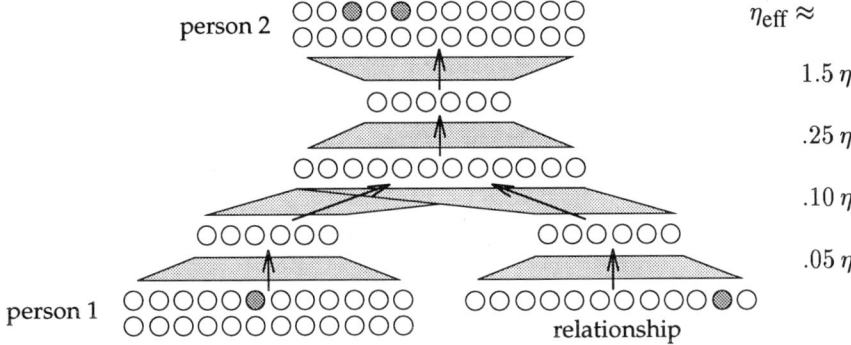

Figure 1: Backpropagation network for learning family relations (Hinton, 1986).

6 Experimental Setup

We tested these ideas on the family relations task (Hinton, 1986): a backpropagation network is given examples of a family member and relationship as input, and must indicate on its output which family members fit the relational description according to an underlying family tree. Its architecture (Figure 1) consists of a central *association* layer of hidden units surrounded by three *encoding* layers that act as informational bottlenecks, forcing the network to make the deep structure of the data explicit.

The input is presented to the network in a canonical local encoding: for any given training example, exactly one input in each of the two input layers is active. On account of the always active bias input, the squared input power for tempering at these layers is thus $\xi^* = 4$. Since the output uses the same local code, only one or two targets at a time will be active; we therefore do not attenuate error signals in the immediately preceding layer. We use cross-entropy error and the logistic squashing function $(1 + e^{-y})^{-1}$ at the output (giving $\phi = 1$) but prefer the hyperbolic tangent for hidden units, with $p(\tanh) = s(\tanh) = 1$.

To illustrate the impact of tempering on this architecture we translate the combined effect of local learning rate and error attenuation into an *effective* learning rate[2] for each layer, shown on the right in Figure 1. We observe that effective learning rates are largest near the output and decrease towards the input due to error attenuation. Contrary to textbook opinion (LeCun, 1993; Haykin, 1994, page 162) we find that such unequal step sizes are in fact the key to efficient learning here. We suspect that the logistic squashing function may owe its popularity largely to the error attenuation side-effect inherent in its maximum slope of $1/4$.

We expect tempering to be applicable to a variety of backpropagation learning algorithms; here we present first results for batch learning with momentum and the *delta-bar-delta* rule (Jacobs, 1988). Both algorithms were tested under three conditions: conventional, tempered (as described in Sections 2 and 3), and tempered with error shunting. All experiments were performed with a customized simulator based on Xerion 3.1.[3]

For each condition the global learning rate η was empirically optimized (to single-digit precision) for fastest reliable learning performance, as measured by the sum of empirical mean and standard deviation of epochs required to reach a given low value of the cost function. All other parameters were held invariant across experiments; their values (shown in Table 1) were chosen in advance so as not to bias the results.

---

[2]This is possible only for strictly layered networks, *i.e.* those with no shortcut (or "skip-through") connections between topologically non-adjacent layers.

[3]At the time of writing, the Xerion neural network simulator and its successor UTS are available by anonymous file transfer from ai.toronto.edu, directory pub/xerion.

Parameter	Value	Parameter	Value
training set size (= epoch)	100	zero-error radius around target	0.2
momentum parameter	0.9	acceptable error & weight cost	1.0
uniform initial weight range	±0.3	delta-bar-delta gain increment	0.1
weight decay rate per epoch	10^{-4}	delta-bar-delta gain decrement	0.9

Table 1: Invariant parameter settings for our experiments.

7 Experimental Results

Table 2 lists the empirical mean and standard deviation (over ten restarts) of the number of epochs required to learn the family relations task under each condition, and the optimal learning rate that produced this performance. Training times for conventional backpropagation are quite long; this is typical for deep multi-layer networks. For comparison, Hinton reports around 1,500 epochs on this problem when both learning rate and momentum have been optimized (personal communication). Much faster convergence — though to a far looser criterion — has recently been observed for online algorithms (O'Reilly, 1996).

Tempering, on the other hand, is seen here to speed up two batch learning methods by almost an order of magnitude. It reduces not only the average training time but also its coefficient of variation, indicating a more reliable optimization process. Note that tempering makes simple batch learning with momentum run about twice as fast as the delta-bar-delta algorithm. This is remarkable since delta-bar-delta uses online measurements to continually adapt the learning rate for each individual weight, whereas tempering merely prescales it based on the network's architecture. We take this as evidence that tempering establishes appropriate local step sizes upfront that delta-bar-delta must discover empirically.

This suggests that by using tempering to set the initial (equilibrium) learning rates for delta-bar-delta, it may be possible to reap the benefits of both prescaling and adaptive step size control. Indeed Table 2 confirms that the respective speedups due to tempering and delta-bar-delta multiply when the two approaches are combined in this fashion. Finally, the addition of error shunting increases learning speed yet further by allowing the global learning rate to be brought close to the maximum of $\eta^* = 0.1$ that we would predict from (18).

8 Discussion

In our experiments we have found tempering to dramatically improve speed and reliability of learning. More network architectures, data sets and learning algorithms will have to be "tempered" to explore the general applicability and limitations of this approach; we also hope to extend it to recurrent networks and online learning. Error shunting has proven useful in facilitating of near-maximal global learning rates for rapid optimization.

Algorithm	batch & momentum		delta-bar-delta	
Condition	$\eta =$ mean	st.d.	$\eta =$ mean	st.d.
conventional	$3 \cdot 10^{-3}$ 2438 ± 1153		$3 \cdot 10^{-4}$ 696 ± 218	
with tempering	$1 \cdot 10^{-2}$ 339 ± 95.0		$3 \cdot 10^{-2}$ 89.6 ± 11.8	
tempering & shunting	$4 \cdot 10^{-2}$ 142 ± 27.1		$9 \cdot 10^{-2}$ 61.7 ± 8.1	

Table 2: Epochs required to learn the family relations task.

Although other schemes may speed up backpropagation by comparable amounts, our approach has some unique advantages. It is computationally cheap to implement: local learning and error attenuation rates are invariant with respect to network weights and activities and thus need to be recalculated only when the network architecture is changed.

More importantly, even advanced gradient descent methods typically retain the isotropic weight space assumption that we improve upon; one would therefore expect them to benefit from tempering as much as delta-bar-delta did in the experiments reported here. For instance, tempering could be used to set non-isotropic model-trust regions for conjugate and second-order gradient descent algorithms.

Finally, by restricting ourselves to fixed learning rates and attenuation factors for now we have arrived at a simplified method that is likely to leave room for further improvement. Possible refinements include taking weight vector size into account when attenuating error signals, or measuring quantities such as $\langle \delta^2 \rangle$ online instead of relying on invariant upper bounds. How such adaptive tempering schemes will compare to and interact with existing techniques for efficient backpropagation learning remains to be explored.

Acknowledgements

We would like to thank Peter Dayan, Rich Zemel and Jenny Orr for being instrumental in discussions that helped shape this work. Geoff Hinton not only offered invaluable comments, but is the source of both our simulator and benchmark problem. N. Schraudolph received financial support from the McDonnell-Pew Center for Cognitive Neuroscience in San Diego, and the Robert Bosch Stiftung GmbH.

References

Amari, S.-I. (1995). Learning and statistical inference. In Arbib, M. A., editor, *The Handbook of Brain Theory and Neural Networks*, pages 522–526. MIT Press, Cambridge.

Battiti, T. (1992). First- and second-order methods for learning: Between steepest descent and Newton's method. *Neural Computation*, 4(2):141–166.

Haykin, S. (1994). *Neural Networks: A Comprehensive Foundation*. Macmillan, New York.

Hinton, G. (1986). Learning distributed representations of concepts. In *Proceedings of the Eighth Annual Conference of the Cognitive Science Society*, pages 1–12, Amherst 1986. Lawrence Erlbaum, Hillsdale.

Jacobs, R. (1988). Increased rates of convergence through learning rate adaptation. *Neural Networks*, 1:295–307.

Krogh, A., Thorbergsson, G., and Hertz, J. A. (1990). A cost function for internal representations. In Touretzky, D. S., editor, *Advances in Neural Information Processing Systems*, volume 2, pages 733–740, Denver, CO, 1989. Morgan Kaufmann, San Mateo.

LeCun, Y. (1993). Efficient learning & second-order methods. Tutorial given at the NIPS Conference, Denver, CO.

LeCun, Y., Kanter, I., and Solla, S. A. (1991). Second order properties of error surfaces: Learning time and generalization. In Lippmann, R. P., Moody, J. E., and Touretzky, D. S., editors, *Advances in Neural Information Processing Systems*, volume 3, pages 918–924, Denver, CO, 1990. Morgan Kaufmann, San Mateo.

O'Reilly, R. C. (1996). Biologically plausible error-driven learning using local activation differences: The generalized recirculation algorithm. *Neural Computation*, 8.

Plaut, D., Nowlan, S., and Hinton, G. (1986). Experiments on learning by back propagation. Technical Report CMU–CS–86–126, Department of Computer Science, Carnegie Mellon University, Pittsburgh, PA.

Investment Learning with Hierarchical PSOMs

Jörg Walter and **Helge Ritter**
Department of Information Science
University of Bielefeld, D-33615 Bielefeld, Germany
Email: {walter,helge}@techfak.uni-bielefeld.de

Abstract

We propose a hierarchical scheme for rapid learning of context dependent "skills" that is based on the recently introduced *"Parameterized Self-Organizing Map"* ("PSOM"). The underlying idea is to first invest some learning effort to *specialize the system into a rapid learner* for a more restricted range of contexts.

The specialization is carried out by a prior "investment learning stage", during which the system acquires a set of basis mappings or "skills" for a set of prototypical contexts. Adaptation of a "skill" to a new context can then be achieved by interpolating in the space of the basis mappings and thus can be extremely rapid.

We demonstrate the potential of this approach for the task of a 3D visuo-motor map for a Puma robot and two cameras. This includes the forward and backward robot kinematics in 3D end effector coordinates, the 2D+2D retina coordinates and also the 6D joint angles. After the *investment phase* the transformation can be learned for a new camera set-up with a *single* observation.

1 Introduction

Most current applications of neural network learning algorithms suffer from a large number of required training examples. This may not be a problem when data are abundant, but in many application domains, for example in robotics, training examples are costly and the benefits of learning can only be exploited when significant progress can be made within a very small number of learning examples.

In the present contribution, we propose in section 3 a hierarchically structured learning approach which can be applied to many learning tasks that require system identification from a limited set of observations. The idea builds on the recently introduced *"Parameterized Self-Organizing Maps"* ("PSOMs"), whose strength is learning maps from a very small number of training examples [8, 10, 11].

In [8], the feasibility of the approach was demonstrated in the domain of robotics, among them, the learning of the inverse kinematics transform of a full 6-degree of freedom (DOF) Puma robot. In [10], two improvements were introduced, both achieve a significant increase in mapping accuracy and computational efficiency. In the next section, we give a short summary of the PSOM algorithm; it is decribed in more detail in [11] which also presents applications in the domain of visual learning.

2 The PSOM Algorithm

A *Parameterized Self-Organizing Map* is a parametrized, m-dimensional hyper-surface $M = \{\mathbf{w}(\mathbf{s}) \in X \subseteq \mathbb{R}^d | \mathbf{s} \in S \subseteq \mathbb{R}^m\}$ that is embedded in some higher-dimensional vector space X. M is used in a very similar way as the standard discrete self-organizing map: given a distance measure $dist(\mathbf{x}, \mathbf{x}')$ and an input vector $\mathbf{x}$, a best-match location $\mathbf{s}^*(\mathbf{x})$ is determined by minimizing

$$\mathbf{s}^* := \underset{\mathbf{s} \in S}{\mathrm{argmin}}\ dist(\mathbf{x}, \mathbf{w}(\mathbf{s})) \qquad (1)$$

The associated "best-match vector" $\mathbf{w}(\mathbf{s}^*)$ provides the best approximation of input $\mathbf{x}$ in the manifold M. If we require $dist(\cdot)$ to vary only in a subspace X^{in} of X (i.e., $dist(\mathbf{x}, \mathbf{x}') = dist(\mathbf{Px}, \mathbf{Px}')$, where the diagonal matrix $\mathbf{P}$ projects into X^{in}), $\mathbf{s}^*(\mathbf{x})$ actually will only depend on $\mathbf{Px}$. The projection $(\mathbf{1}-\mathbf{P})\mathbf{w}(\mathbf{s}^*(\mathbf{x})) \in X^{out}$ of $\mathbf{w}(\mathbf{s}^*(\mathbf{x}))$ lies in the orthogonal subspace X^{out} can be viewed as a (non-linear) *associative completion of a fragmentary input $\mathbf{x}$ of which only the part $\mathbf{Px}$ is reliable*. It is this associative mapping that we will exploit in applications of the PSOM.

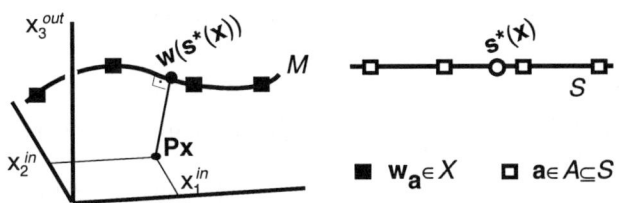

Figure 1: Best-match $\mathbf{s}^*$ and associative completion $\mathbf{w}(\mathbf{s}^*(\mathbf{x}))$ of input x_1, x_2 ($\mathbf{Px}$) given in the input subspace X^{in}. Here in this simple case, the $m = 1$ dimensional manifold M is constructed to pass through four data vectors (square marked). The *left* side shows the $d = 3$ dimensional embedding space $X = X^{in} \times X^{out}$ and the *right* side depicts the best match parameter $\mathbf{s}^*(\mathbf{x})$ parameter manifold S together with the "hyper-lattice" $\mathbf{A}$ of parameter values (indicated by white squares) belonging to the data vectors.

M is constructed as a manifold that passes through a given set D of data examples (Fig. 1 depicts the situation schematically). To this end, we assign to each data sample a point $\mathbf{a} \in S$ and denote the associated data sample by $\mathbf{w_a}$. The set $\mathbf{A}$ of the assigned parameter values $\mathbf{a}$ should provide a good discrete "model" of the topology of our data set (Fig. 1 right). The assignment between data vectors and points $\mathbf{a}$ must be made in a topology preserving fashion to ensure good interpolation by the manifold M that is obtained by the following steps.

For each point $\mathbf{a} \in \mathbf{A}$, we construct a "basis function" $H(\cdot, \mathbf{a}; \mathbf{A})$ or simplified[1] $H(\cdot, \mathbf{a})$: $S \mapsto \mathbb{R}$ that obeys (i) $H(\mathbf{a}_i, \mathbf{a}_j) = 1$ for $i = j$ and vanishes at all other points of $\mathbf{A}$ $i \neq j$ (orthonormality condition,) and (ii) $\sum_{\mathbf{a} \in \mathbf{A}} H(\mathbf{a}, \mathbf{s}) = 1$ for $\forall \mathbf{s}$ ("partition of unity" condition.) We will mainly be concerned with the case of $\mathbf{A}$ being a m-dimensional rectangular hyper-lattice; in this case, the functions $H(\cdot, \mathbf{a})$ can be constructed as products of Lagrange interpolation polynomials, see [11]. Then,

$$\mathbf{w}(\mathbf{s}) = \sum_{\mathbf{a} \in \mathbf{A}} H(\mathbf{s}, \mathbf{a}) \, \mathbf{w}_\mathbf{a}. \tag{2}$$

defines a manifold M that passes through all data examples. Minimizing $dist(\cdot)$ in Eq. 1 can be done by some iterative procedure, such as gradient descent or – preferably – the Levenberg-Marquardt algorithm [11]. This makes M into the attractor manifold of a (discrete time) dynamical system. Since M contains the data set D, any at least m-dimensional "fragment" of a data example $\mathbf{x} = \mathbf{w} \in D$ will be attracted to the correct completion $\mathbf{w}$. Inputs $\mathbf{x} \notin D$ will be attracted to some approximating manifold point.

This approach is in many ways the continuous analog of the standard discrete self-organizing map. Particularly attractive features are (i) that the construction of the map manifold is direct from a *small set* of training vectors, without any need for time consuming adaptation sequences, (ii) the capability of associative completion, which allows to freely redefine variables as inputs or outputs (by changing $dist(\cdot)$ on demand, e.g. one can reverse the mapping direction), and (iii) the possibility of having *attractor manifolds* instead of just attractor points.

3 Hierarchical PSOMs: Structuring Learning

Rapid learning requires that the structure of the learner is well matched to his task. However, if one does not want to pre-structure the learner by hand, learning again seems to be the only way to achieve the necessary pre-structuring. This leads to the idea of *structuring learning itself* and motivates to *split* learning into two stages:
(i) The earlier stage is considered as an *"investment stage"* that may be slow and that may require a larger number of examples. It has the task to pre-structure the system in such a way that in the later stage,
(ii) the now specialized system can learn *fast* and with extremely few examples.

To be concrete, we consider specialized mappings or "skills", which are dependent on the state of the system or system environment. Pre-structuring the system is achieved by learning a set of basis mappings, each in a prototypical system context or environment state ("investment phase".) This imposes a strong need for an efficient learning tool – efficient in particular with respect to the number of required training data points.

The PSOM networks appears as a very attractive solution: Fig. 2 shows a hierarchical arrangement of two PSOM. The task of mapping from input to output spaces is learned – and performed, by the "Transformation-PSOM" ("T-PSOM").

During the first learning stage, the *investment learning* phase the T-PSOM is used to learn a set of basis mappings $T_j : \vec{x}_1 \leftrightarrow \vec{x}_2$ or context dependent "skills" is constructed in the "T-PSOM", each of which gets encoded as a internal parameter or "weight" set ω_j. The

---

[1] In contrast to kernel methods, the basis functions may depend on the relative position to all other knots. However, we drop in our notation the dependency $H(\mathbf{a}, \mathbf{s}) = H(\mathbf{a}, \mathbf{s}; \mathbf{A})$ on the latter.

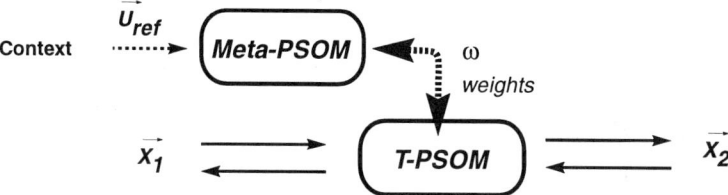

Figure 2: The transforming "T-PSOM" maps between input and output spaces (changing direction on demand). In a particular environmental context, the correct transformation is learned, and encoded in the internal parameter or weight set ω. Together with an characteristic environment observation $\vec{u}_{\mathrm{ref}}$, the weight set ω is employed as a training vector for the second level "Meta-PSOM". After learning a structured set of mappings, the Meta-PSOM is able to generalizing the mapping for a new environment. When encountering any change, the environment observation $\vec{u}_{\mathrm{ref}}$ gives input to the Meta-PSOM and determines the new weight set ω for the basis T-PSOM.

second level PSOM ("Meta-PSOM") is responsible for learning the association between the weight sets ω_j of the first level T-PSOM and their situational contexts.
The system context is characterized by a suitable environment observation, denoted $\vec{u}_{ref}$, see Fig. 2.
The context situations are chosen such that the associated basis mappings capture already a significant amount of the underlying model structure, while still being sufficiently general to capture the variations with respect to which system environment identification is desired. For the training of the second level Meta-PSOM each constructed T-PSOM weight set ω_j serves together with its associated environment observation $\vec{u}_{ref,j}$ as a high dimensional training data vector.

Rapid learning is the return on invested effort in the longer pre-training phase. As a result, the task of learning the "skill" associated with an unknown system context now takes the form of an *immediate* Meta-PSOM → T-PSOM mapping: the Meta-PSOM maps the new system context observation $\vec{u}_{ref,new}$ into the parameter set ω_{new} for the T-PSOM. Equipped with ω_{new}, the T-PSOM provides the desired mapping T_{new}.

4 Rapid Learning of a Stereo Visuo-motor Map

In the following, we demonstrate the potential of the investment learning approach with the task of fast learning of 3D visuo-motor maps for a robot manipulator seen by a pair of movable cameras. Thus, in this demonstration, each situated context is given by a particular camera arrangement, and the assicuated "skill" is the mapping between camera and robot coordinates.
The Puma robot is positioned behind a table and the entire scene is displayed on two windows on a computer monitor. By mouse-pointing, a user can, for example, select on the monitor one point and the position on a line appearing in the other window, to indicate a good position for the robot end effector, see Fig. 3. This requires to compute the transformation T between pixel coordinates $\vec{u} = (\vec{u}^L, \vec{u}^R)$ on the monitor images and corresponding world coordinates $\vec{x}$ in the robot reference frame – or alternatively – the corresponding six robot joint angles $\vec{\theta}$ (6 DOF). Here we demonstrate an integrated solution, offering both solutions with the same network.

The T-PSOM learns each individual basis mapping T_j by visiting a rectangular grid set of end effector positions ξ_i (here a 3×3×3 grid in $\vec{x}$ of size $40 \times 40 \times 30\,\mathrm{cm}^3$) jointly with

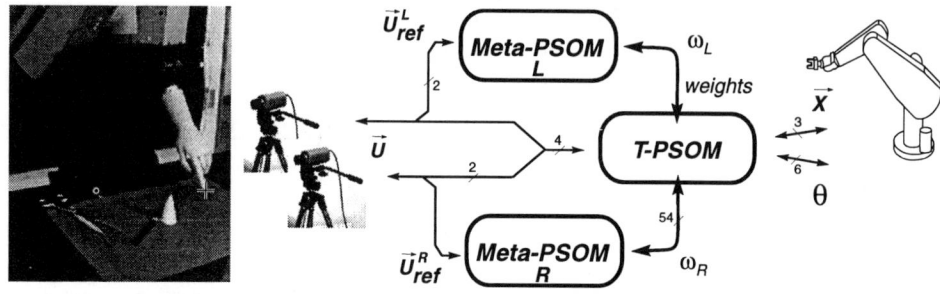

Figure 3: Rapid learning of the 3D visuo-motor coordination for two cameras. The basis T-PSOM ($m = 3$) is capable of mapping to and from three coordinate systems: Cartesian robot world coordinates, the robot joint angles (6-DOF), and the location of the end-effector in coordinates of the two camera retinas. Since the left and right camera can be relocated independently, the weight set of T-PSOM is split, and parts ω_L, ω_R are learned in two separate Meta-PSOMs ("L" and "R").

the joint angle tuple $\vec{\theta}_j$ and the location in camera retina coordinates (2D in each camera) $\vec{u}_j^L, \vec{u}_j^R$. Thus the training vectors $\mathbf{w}_{\mathbf{a}_i}$ for the construction of the T-PSOM are the tuples $(\vec{x}_i, \vec{\theta}_i, \vec{u}_i^L, \vec{u}_i^R)$.

However, each T_j solves the mapping task only for the current camera arrangement, for which T_j was learned. Thus there is not yet any particular advantage to other, specialized methods for camera calibration [1]. The important point is, that we now will employ the Meta-PSOM to *interpolate* in the space of the mappings $\{T_j\}$.

To keep the number of prototype mappings manageable, we reduce some DOFs of the cameras by calling for fixed focal length, camera tripod height, and twist joint. To constrain the elevation and azimuth viewing angle, we require one land mark ξ_{fix} to remain visible in a constant image position. This leaves two free parameters per camera, that can now be determined by *one* extra observation of a chosen auxiliary world reference point ξ_{ref}. We denote the camera image coordinates of ξ_{ref} by $\vec{u}_{ref} = (\vec{u}_{ref}^L, \vec{u}_{ref}^R)$. By reuse of the cameras as "environment sensor", $\vec{u}_{ref}$ now implicitly encodes the two camera positions.

In the investing pre-training phase, nine mappings T_j are learned by the T-PSOM, each camera visiting a 3×3 grid, sharing the set of visited robot positions ξ_i. As Fig. 2 suggests, normally the entire weight set ω serves as part of the training vector to the Meta-PSOM. Here the problem becomes factorized since the left and right camera change tripod place independently: the weight set of the T-PSOM is split, and the two parts can be learned in separate Meta-PSOMs. Each training vector $\mathbf{w}_{\mathbf{a}_j}$ for the left camera Meta-PSOM consists of the context observation $\vec{u}_{ref}^L$ and the T-PSOM weight set part $\omega_L = (\vec{u}_1^L, \ldots, \vec{u}_{27}^L)$ (analogous the right camera Meta-PSOM.)

This enables in the following phase the *rapid learning*, for new, unknown camera places. On the basis of *one single* observation $\vec{u}_{ref}$, the desired transformation T is constructed. As visualized in Fig. 3, $\vec{u}_{ref}$ serves as the input to the second level Meta-PSOMs. Their outputs are interpolations between previously learned weight sets and they project directly into the weight set of the basis level T-PSOM.

The resulting T-PSOM can map in various directions. This is achieved by specifying a suitable distance function $dist(\cdot)$ via the projection matrix $\mathbf{P}$, e.g.:

$$\vec{x}(\vec{u}) = F_{T-PSOM}^{u \mapsto x}(\vec{u};\ \omega_L(\vec{u}_{ref}^L), \omega_R(\vec{u}_{ref}^R)) \qquad (3)$$

$$\vec{\theta}(\vec{u}) = F^{u \mapsto \theta}_{T-PSOM}(\vec{u};\ \omega_L(\vec{u}^L_{ref}), \omega_R(\vec{u}^R_{ref})) \qquad (4)$$

$$\vec{u}(\vec{x}) = F^{x \mapsto u}_{T-PSOM}(\vec{x};\ \omega_L(\vec{u}^L_{ref}), \omega_R(\vec{u}^R_{ref})) \qquad (5)$$

$$\omega_L(\vec{u}^L_{ref}) = F^{u \mapsto \omega}_{Meta-PSOM,L}(\vec{u}^L_{ref};\ \Omega_L);\ \text{analog}\ \omega_R(\vec{u}^R_{ref}) \qquad (6)$$

Table 1 shows experimental results averaged over 100 random locations ξ (from within the range of the training set) seen in 10 different camera set-ups, from within the 3×3 square grid of the training positions, located in a normal distance of about 125 cm (center to work space center, $1\,\text{m}^2$, total range of about 55–210 cm), covering a disparity angle range of 25°–150°. For identification of the positions ξ in image coordinates, a tiny light source was installed at the manipulator tip and a simple procedure automated the finding of $\vec{u}$ with about ±0.8 pixel accuracy. For the achieved precision it is important to share the same set of robot positions ξ_i, and that the sets are topologically ordered, here as a 3×3×3 goal position grid (i) and two 3×3 camera location (j) grids.

Mapping Direction	Direct trained T-PSOM		T-PSOM with Meta-PSOM	
pixel $\vec{u} \mapsto \vec{x}_{robot}$ $\Rightarrow$ Cartesian error $\Delta \vec{x}$	1.4 mm	0.008	4.4 mm	0.025
Cartesian $\vec{x} \mapsto \vec{u}$ $\Rightarrow$ pixel error	1.2 pix	0.010	3.3 pix	0.025
pixel $\vec{u} \mapsto \vec{\theta}_{robot}$ $\Rightarrow$ Cartesian error $\Delta \vec{x}$	3.8 mm	0.023	5.4 mm	0.030

Table 1: Mean Euclidean deviation (mm or pixel) and normalized root mean square error (NRMS) for 1000 points total in comparison of a direct trained T-PSOM and the described hierarchical Meta-PSOM network, in the rapid learning mode after *one single* observation.

5 Discussion and Conclusion

A crucial question is how to structure systems, such that learning can be efficient. In the present paper, we demonstrated a hierarchical approach that is motivated by a *decomposition of the learning phase into two different stages:* A longer, initial learning phase "invests" effort into a gradual and domain-specific specialization of the system. This *investment learning* does not yet produce the final solution, but instead pre-structures the system such that the subsequently final specialization to a particular solution (within the chosen domain) can be achieved extremely rapidly.

To implement this approach, we used a hierarchical architecture of mappings. While in principle various kinds of network types could be used for this mappings, a practically feasible solution must be based on a network type that allows to construct the required basis mappings from rather small number of training examples. In addition, since we use interpolation in weight space, similar mappings should give rise to similar weight sets to make interpolation meaningful. PSOM meat this requirements very well, since they allow a direct non-iterative construction of smooth mappings from rather small data sets. They achieve this be generalizing the discrete self-organizing map [3, 9] into a continuous map manifold such that interpolation for new data points can benefit from topology information that is not available to most other methods.

While PSOMs resemble local models [4, 5, 6] in that there is no interference between different training points, their use of a orthogonal set of basis functions to construct the map manifold put them in a intermediate position between the extremes of local and of fully distributed models.

A further very useful property in the present context is the ability of PSOMs to work as an attractor network with a continuous attractor manifold. Thus a PSOM needs no fixed designation of variables as inputs and outputs; Instead the projection matrix **P** can be used to freely partition the full set of variables into input and output values. Values of the latter are obtained by a process of associative completion.

Technically, the investment learning phase is realized by learning a set of *prototypical basis mappings* represented as weight sets of a T-PSOM that attempt to cover the range of tasks in the given domain. The capability for subsequent rapid specialization within the domain is then provided by an additional mapping that maps a situational context into a suitable combination of the previously learned prototypical basis mappings. The construction of this mapping again is solved with a PSOM ("Meta"-PSOM) that *interpolates in the space of prototypical basis mappings* that were constructed during the "investment phase".

We demonstrated the potential of this approach with the task of 3D visuo-motor mapping, learn-able with a single observation after repositioning a pair of cameras.
The achieved accuracy of 4.4 mm after learning by a single observation, compares very well with the distance range 0.5–2.1 m of traversed positions. As further data becomes available, the T-PSOM can certainly be fine-tuned to improve the performance to the level of the directly trained T-PSOM.

The presented arrangement of a basis T-PSOM and two Meta-PSOMs demonstrates further the possibility to split hierarchical learning in independently changing domain sets. When the number of involved free context parameters is growing, this factorization is increasingly crucial to keep the number of pre-trained prototype mappings manageable.

References

[1] K. Fu, R. Gonzalez and C. Lee. *Robotics : Control, Sensing, Vision, and Intelligence.* McGraw-Hill, 1987

[2] F. Girosi and T. Poggio. Networks and the best approximation property. *Biol. Cybern.*, 63(3):169–176, 1990.

[3] T. Kohonen. *Self-Organization and Associative Memory.* Springer, Heidelberg, 1984.

[4] J. Moody and C. Darken. Fast learning in networks of locally-tuned processing units. *Neural Computation*, 1:281–294, 1989.

[5] S. Omohundro. Bumptrees for efficient function, constraint, and classification learning. In *NIPS*3*, pages 693–699. Morgan Kaufman Publishers, 1991.

[6] J. Platt. A resource-allocating network for function interpolation. *Neural Computation*, 3:213–255, 1991

[7] M. Powell. *Radial basis functions for multivariable interpolation: A review*, pages 143–167. Clarendon Press, Oxford, 1987.

[8] H. Ritter. Parametrized self-organizing maps. In S. Gielen and B. Kappen, editors, *ICANN'93-Proceedings, Amsterdam*, pages 568–575. Springer Verlag, Berlin, 1993.

[9] H. Ritter, T. Martinetz, and K. Schulten. *Neural Computation and Self-organizing Maps.* Addison Wesley, 1992.

[10] J. Walter and H. Ritter. Local PSOMs and Chebyshev PSOMs – improving the parametrised self-organizing maps. In *Proc. ICANN, Paris*, volume 1, pages 95–102, October 1995.

[11] J. Walter and H. Ritter. Rapid learning with parametrized self-organizing maps. *Neurocomputing, Special Issue*, (in press), 1996.

Learning long–term dependencies is not as difficult with NARX networks

Tsungnan Lin[*]
Department of Electrical Engineering
Princeton University
Princeton, NJ 08540

Bill G. Horne
NEC Research Institute
4 Independence Way
Princeton, NJ 08540

Peter Tiño
Dept. of Computer Science and Engineering
Slovak Technical University
Ilkovicova 3, 812 19 Bratislava, Slovakia

C. Lee Giles[†]
NEC Research Institute
4 Independence Way
Princeton, NJ 08540

Abstract

It has recently been shown that gradient descent learning algorithms for recurrent neural networks can perform poorly on tasks that involve long–term dependencies. In this paper we explore this problem for a class of architectures called NARX networks, which have powerful representational capabilities. Previous work reported that gradient descent learning is more effective in NARX networks than in recurrent networks with "hidden states". We show that although NARX networks do not circumvent the problem of long–term dependencies, they can greatly improve performance on such problems. We present some experimental results that show that NARX networks can often retain information for two to three times as long as conventional recurrent networks.

1 Introduction

Recurrent Neural Networks (RNNs) are capable of representing arbitrary nonlinear dynamical systems [19, 20]. However, learning simple behavior can be quite

---
[*]Also with NEC Research Institute.
[†]Also with UMIACS, University of Maryland, College Park, MD 20742

difficult using gradient descent. For example, even though these systems are Turing equivalent, it has been difficult to get them to successfully learn small finite state machines from example strings encoded as temporal sequences. Recently, it has been demonstrated that at least part of this difficulty can be attributed to *long–term dependencies*, i.e. when the desired output at time T depends on inputs presented at times $t \ll T$. In [13] it was reported that RNNs were able to learn short term musical structure using gradient based methods, but had difficulty capturing global behavior. These ideas were recently formalized in [2], which showed that if a system is to robustly latch information, then the fraction of the gradient due to information n time steps in the past approaches zero as n becomes large.

Several approaches have been suggested to circumvent this problem. For example, gradient–based methods can be abandoned in favor of alternative optimization methods [2, 15]. However, the algorithms investigated so far either perform just as poorly on problems involving long–term dependencies, or, when they are better, require far more computational resources [2]. Another possibility is to modify conventional gradient descent by more heavily weighing the fraction of the gradient due to information far in the past, but there is no guarantee that such a modified algorithm would converge to a minima of the error surface being searched [2]. Another suggestion has been to alter the input data so that it represents a reduced description that makes global features more explicit and more readily detectable [7, 13, 16, 17]. However, this approach may fail if short term dependencies are equally as important. Finally, it has been suggested that a network architecture that operates on multiple time scales might be useful [5, 6].

In this paper, we also propose an architectural approach to deal with long–term dependencies [11]. We focus on a class of architectures based upon Nonlinear AutoRegressive models with eXogenous inputs (NARX models), and are therefore called *NARX networks* [3, 14]. This is a powerful class of models which has recently been shown to be computationally equivalent to Turing machines [18]. Furthermore, previous work has shown that gradient descent learning is more effective in NARX networks than in recurrent network architectures with "hidden states" when applied to problems including grammatical inference and nonlinear system identification [8]. Typically, these networks converge much faster and generalize better than other networks. The results in this paper give an explanation of this phenomenon.

2 Vanishing gradients and long–term dependencies

Bengio *et al.* [2] have analytically explained why learning problems with long–term dependencies is difficult. They argue that for many practical applications the goal of the network must be to *robustly latch information*, i.e. the network must be able to store information for a long period of time in the presence of noise. More specifically, they argue that latching of information is accomplished when the states of the network stay within the vicinity of a hyperbolic attractor, and robustness to noise is accomplished if the states of the network are contained in the *reduced attracting set* of that attractor, i.e. those set of points at which the eigenvalues of the Jacobian are contained within the unit circle.

In algorithms such as Backpropagation Through Time (BPTT), the gradient of the cost function function C is written assuming that the weights at different time

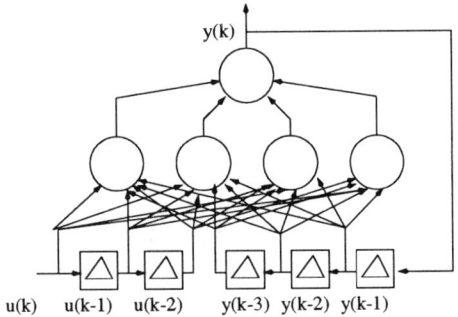

Figure 1: NARX network.

indices are independent and computing the partial gradient with respect to these weights. The total gradient is then equal to the sum of these partial gradients.

It can be easily shown that the weight updates are proportional to

$$\nabla_{\mathbf{w}} C = \sum_p (\mathbf{y}_p(T) - \mathbf{d}_p) \nabla_{\mathbf{x}(T)} \mathbf{y}_p(T) \left[\sum_{\tau=1}^{T} J_{\mathbf{x}}(T, T - \tau) \nabla_{\mathbf{w}(\tau)} \mathbf{x}(\tau) \right],$$

where $\mathbf{y}_p(T)$ and $\mathbf{d}_p$ are the actual and desired (or target) output for the pth pattern[1], $\mathbf{x}(t)$ is the state vector of the network at time t and $J_{\mathbf{x}}(T, T - \tau) = \nabla_{\mathbf{x}(\tau)} \mathbf{x}(T)$ denotes the Jacobian of the network expanded over $T - \tau$ time steps.

In [2], it was shown that if the network robustly latches information, then $J_{\mathbf{x}}(T, n)$ is an exponentially decreasing function of n, so that $\lim_{n \to \infty} J_{\mathbf{x}}(T, n) = 0$. This implies that the portion of $\nabla_{\mathbf{w}} C$ due to information at times $\tau \ll T$ is insignificant compared to the portion at times near T. This vanishing gradient is the essential reason why gradient descent methods are not sufficiently powerful to discover a relationship between target outputs and inputs that occur at a much earlier time.

3 NARX networks

An important class of discrete–time nonlinear systems is the *Nonlinear AutoRegressive with eXogenous inputs* (NARX) model [3, 10, 12, 21]:

$$y(t) = f\left(u(t - D_u), \ldots, u(t-1), u(t), y(t - D_y), \ldots, y(t-1)\right),$$

where $u(t)$ and $y(t)$ represent input and output of the network at time t, D_u and D_y are the input and output order, and f is a nonlinear function. When the function f can be approximated by a Multilayer Perceptron, the resulting system is called a *NARX network* [3, 14].

In this paper we shall consider NARX networks with zero input order and a one dimensional output. However there is no reason why our results could not be extended to networks with higher input orders. Since the states of a discrete–time

---

[1] We deal only with problems in which the target output is presented at the *end* of the sequence.

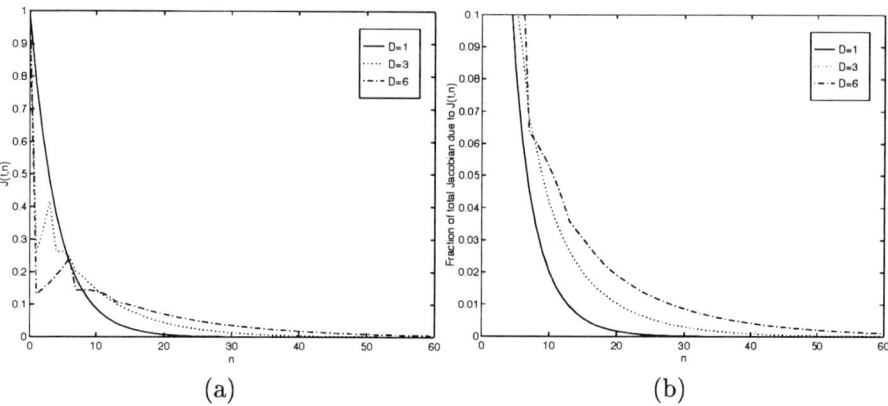

Figure 2: Results for the latching problem. (a) Plots of $J(t,n)$ as a function of n. (b) Plots of the ratio $\frac{J(t,n)}{\sum_{\tau=1}^{n} J(t,\tau)}$ as a function of n.

dynamical system can always be associated with the unit–delay elements in the realization of the system, we can then describe such a network in a state space form

$$x_i(t+1) = \begin{cases} \Psi\left(u(t), \mathbf{x}(t)\right) & i = 1 \\ x_{i-1}(t) & i = 2, \ldots, D \end{cases} \quad (1)$$

with $y(t) = x_1(t+1)$.

If the Jacobian of this system has all of its eigenvalues inside the unit circle at each time step, then the states of the network will be in the reduced attracting set of some hyperbolic attractor, and thus the system will be robustly latched at that time. As with any other RNN, this implies that $\lim_{n \to \infty} J_{\mathbf{x}}(t,n) = 0$. Thus, NARX networks will also suffer from vanishing gradients and the long–term dependencies problem. However, we find in the simulation results that follow that NARX networks are often much better at discovering long–term dependencies than conventional RNNs.

An intuitive reason why output delays can help long–term dependencies can be found by considering how gradients are calculated using the Backpropagation Through Time algorithm. BPTT involves two phases: unfolding the network in time and backpropagating the error through the unfolded network. When a NARX network is unfolded in time, the output delays will appear as jump–ahead connections in the unfolded network. Intuitively, these jump–ahead connections provide a shorter path for propagating gradient information, thus reducing the sensitivity of the network to long–term dependencies. However, this intuitive reasoning is only valid if the total gradient through these jump–ahead pathways is greater than the gradient through the layer–to–layer pathways.

It is possible to derive analytical results for some simple toy problems to show that NARX networks are indeed less sensitive to long–term dependencies. Here we give one such example, which is based upon the latching problem described in [2]. Consider the one node autonomous recurrent network described by, $x(t) = \tanh(wx(t-1))$ where $w = 1.25$, which has two stable fixed points at ± 0.710 and one unstable fixed point at zero. The one node, autonomous NARX network $x(t) = \tanh\left(\sum_{\tau=1}^{D} w_\tau x(t-\tau)\right)$ has the same fixed points as long as $\sum_{i=1}^{D} w_i = w$.

Assume the state of the network has reached equilibrium at the positive stable fixed point and there are no external inputs. For simplicity, we only consider the Jacobian $J(t,n) = \frac{\partial x(t)}{\partial x(t-n)}$, which will be a component of the gradient $\nabla_\mathbf{w} C$. Figure 2a shows plots of $J(t,n)$ with respect to n for $D = 1$, $D = 3$ and $D = 6$ with $w_i = w/D$. These plots show that the effect of output delays is to flatten out the curves and place more emphasis on the gradient due to terms farther in the past. Note that the gradient contribution due to short term dependencies is deemphasized. In Figure 2b we show plots of the ratio $\frac{J(t,n)}{\sum_{\tau=1}^{n} J(t,\tau)}$, which illustrates the percentage of the total gradient that can be attributed to information n time steps in the past. These plots show that this percentage is larger for the network with output delays, and thus one would expect that these networks would be able to more effectively deal with long–term dependencies.

4 Experimental results

4.1 The latching problem

We explored a slight modification on the latching problem described in [2], which is a minimal task designed as a test that must necessarily be passed in order for a network to robustly latch information. In this task there are three inputs $u_1(t)$, $u_2(t)$, and a noise input $e(t)$, and a single output $y(t)$. Both $u_1(t)$ and $u_2(t)$ are zero for all times $t > 1$. At time $t = 1$, $u_1(1) = 1$ and $u_2(1) = 0$ for samples from class 1, and $u_1(1) = 0$ and $u_2(1) = 1$ for samples from class 2. The noise input $e(t)$ is drawn uniformly from $[-b, b]$ when $L < t \leq T$, otherwise $e(t) = 0$ when $t \leq L$. This network used to solve this problem is a NARX network consisting of a single neuron,

$$x(t) = \tanh\left(\sum_{\tau=1}^{D} w_\tau x(t-\tau) + \sum_{i=1}^{3} h_i^1 u_1(t-i+1) + \sum_{i=1}^{3} h_i^2 u_2(t-i+1) + e(t)\right)$$

where the parameters h_i^j are adjustable and the recurrent weights w_τ are fixed [2].

We fixed the recurrent feedback weight to $w_\tau = 1.25/D$, which gives the autonomous network two stable fixed points at ± 0.710, as described in Section 3. It can be shown [4] that the network is robust to perturbations in the range $[-0.155, 0.155]$. Thus, the uniform noise in $e(t)$ was restricted to this range.

For each simulation, we generated 30 strings from each class, each with a different $e(t)$. The initial values of h_i^j for each simulation were also chosen from the same distribution that defines $e(t)$. For strings from class one, a target value of 0.8 was chosen, for class two -0.8 was chosen. The network was run using a simple BPTT algorithm with a learning rate of 0.1 for a maximum of 100 epochs. (We found that the network converged to some solution consistently within a few dozen epochs.) If the simulation exceeded 100 epochs and did not correctly classify all strings then the simulation was ruled a failure. We varied T from 10 to 200 in increments of 2. For each value of T, we ran 50 simulations. Figure 3a shows a plot of the percentage of those runs that were successful for each case. It is clear from these plots that

---

[2] Although this description may appear different from the one in [2], it can be shown that they are actually identical experiments for $D = 1$.

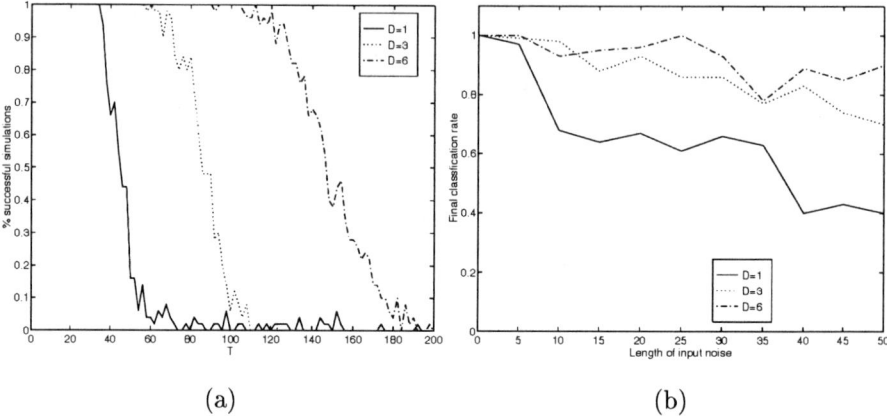

Figure 3: (a) Plots of percentage of successful simulations as a function of T, the length of the input strings. (b) Plots of the final classification rate with respect to different length input strings.

the NARX networks become increasingly less sensitive to long–term dependencies as the output order is increased.

4.2 The parity problem

In the parity problem, the task is to classify sequences depending on whether or not the number of 1s in the input string is odd. We generated 20 strings of different lengths from 3 to 5 and added uniformly distributed noise in the range $[-0.2, 0.2]$ at the end of each string. The length of input noise varied from 0 to 50. We arbitrarily chose 0.7 and -0.7 to represent the symbol "1" and "0". The target is only given at the end of each string. Three different networks with different number of output delays were run on this problem in order to evaluate the capability of the network to learn long–term dependencies. In order to make the networks comparable, we chose networks in which the number of weights was roughly equal. For networks with one to three delays, 5, 4 and 3 hidden neurons were chosen respectively, giving 21, 21, and 19 trainable weights. Initial weight values were randomly generated between -0.5 and 0.5 for 10 trials.

Fig. 3b shows the average classification rate with respect to different length of input noise. When the length of the noise is less than 5, all three of the networks can learn all the sequences with the classification rate near to 100%. When the length increases to between 10 and 35, the classification rate of networks with one feedback delay drops quickly to about 60% while the rate of those networks with two or three feedback delays still remains about 80%.

5 Conclusion

In this paper we considered an architectural approach to dealing with the problem of learning long–term dependencies. We explored the ability of a class of architectures called NARX networks to solve such problems. This has been observed previously, in the sense that gradient descent learning appeared to be more effective in NARX networks than in RNNs [8]. We presented an analytical example that showed that the gradients do not vanish as quickly in NARX networks as they do in networks without multiple delays when the network is operating at a fixed point. We also presented two experimental problems which show that NARX networks can outperform networks with single delays on some simple problems involving long–term dependencies.

We speculate that similar results could be obtained for other networks. In particular we hypothesize that any network that uses tapped delay feedback [1, 9] would demonstrate improved performance on problems involving long–term dependencies.

Acknowledgements

We would like to thank A. Back and Y. Bengio for many useful suggestions.

References

[1] A.D. Back and A.C. Tsoi. FIR and IIR synapses, a new neural network architecture for time series modeling. *Neural Computation*, 3(3):375–385, 1991.

[2] Y. Bengio, P. Simard, and P. Frasconi. Learning long-term dependencies with gradient is difficult. *IEEE Trans. on Neural Networks*, 5(2):157–166, 1994.

[3] S. Chen, S.A. Billings, and P.M. Grant. Non-linear system identification using neural networks. *International Journal of Control*, 51(6):1191–1214, 1990.

[4] P. Frasconi, M. Gori, M. Maggini, and G. Soda. Unified integration of explicit knowledge and learning by example in recurrent networks. *IEEE Trans. on Know. and Data Eng.*,7(2):340-346, 1995.

[5] M. Gori, M. Maggini, and G. Soda. Scheduling of modular architectures for inductive inference of regular grammars. In *ECAI'94 Work. on Comb. Sym. and Connectionist Proc.*, pages 78–87.

[6] S. El Hihi and Y. Bengio. Hierarchical recurrent neural networks for long-term dependencies. In *NIPS 8*, 1996. (In this Proceedings.)

[7] S. Hochreiter and J. Schmidhuber. Long short term memory. Technical Report FKI-207-95, Technische Universität München, 1995.

[8] B.G. Horne and C.L. Giles. An experimental comparison of recurrent neural networks. In *NIPS 7*, pages 697-704, 1995.

[9] R.R. Leighton and B.C. Conrath. The autoregressive backpropagation algorithm. In *Proceedings of the International Joint Conference on Neural Networks*, volume 2, pages 369–377, July 1991.

[10] I.J. Leontaritis and S.A. Billings. Input–output parametric models for non–linear systems: Part I: deterministic non–linear systems. *International Journal of Control*, 41(2):303–328, 1985.

[11] T.N. Lin, B.G. Horne, P.Tino and C.L. Giles. Learning long-term dependencies is not as difficult with NARX recurrent neural networks. Technical Report UMIACS-TR-95-78 and CS-TR-3500, Univ. Of Maryland, 1995.

[12] L. Ljung. *System identification: Theory for the user*. Prentice-Hall, 1987.

[13] M. C. Mozer. Induction of multiscale temporal structure. In J.E. Moody, S. J. Hanson, and R.P. Lippmann, editors, *NIPS 4*, pages 275–282, 1992.

[14] K.S. Narendra and K. Parthasarathy. Identification and control of dynamical systems using neural networks. *IEEE Trans. on Neural Networks*, 1:4–27, March 1990.

[15] G.V. Puskorius and L.A. Feldkamp. Recurrent network training with the decoupled extended Kalman filter. In *Proc. 1992 SPIE Conf. on the Sci. of ANN*, Orlando, Florida, April 1992.

[16] J. Schmidhuber. Learning complex, extended sequences using the principle of history compression. In *Neural Computation*, 4(2):234-242, 1992.

[17] J. Schmidhuber. Learning unambiguous reduced sequence descriptions. In *NIPS 4*, pages 291–298, 1992.

[18] H.T. Siegelmann, B.G. Horne, and C.L. Giles. Computational capabilities of NARX neural networks. In *IEEE Trans. on Systems, Man and Cybernetics*, 1996. Accepted.

[19] H.T. Siegelmann and E.D. Sontag. On the computational power of neural networks. *Journal of Computer and System Science*, 50(1):132–150, 1995.

[20] E.D. Sontag. Systems combining linearity and saturations and relations to neural networks. Technical Report SYCON-92-01, Rutgers Center for Systems and Control, 1992.

[21] H. Su, T. McAvoy, and P. Werbos. Long–term predictions of chemical processes using recurrent neural networks: A parallel training approach. *Ind. Eng. Chem. Res.*, 31:1338, 1992.

Constructive Algorithms for Hierarchical Mixtures of Experts

S.R.Waterhouse   A.J.Robinson
Cambridge University Engineering Department,
Trumpington St., Cambridge, CB2 1PZ, England.
Tel: [+44] 1223 332754, Fax: [+44] 1223 332662,
Email: srw1001, ajr @eng.cam.ac.uk

Abstract

We present two additions to the hierarchical mixture of experts (HME) architecture. By applying a likelihood splitting criteria to each expert in the HME we "grow" the tree adaptively during training. Secondly, by considering only the most probable path through the tree we may "prune" branches away, either temporarily, or permanently if they become redundant. We demonstrate results for the growing and path pruning algorithms which show significant speed ups and more efficient use of parameters over the standard fixed structure in discriminating between two interlocking spirals and classifying 8-bit parity patterns.

INTRODUCTION

The HME (Jordan & Jacobs 1994) is a tree structured network whose terminal nodes are simple function approximators in the case of regression or classifiers in the case of classification. The outputs of the terminal nodes or experts are recursively combined upwards towards the root node, to form the overall output of the network, by "gates" which are situated at the non-terminal nodes.

The HME has clear similarities with tree based statistical methods such as Classification and Regression Trees (CART) (Breiman, Friedman, Olshen & Stone 1984). We may consider the gate as replacing the set of "questions" which are asked at each branch of CART. From this analogy, we may consider the application of the splitting rules used to build CART. We start with a simple tree consisting of two experts and one gate. After partially training this simple tree we apply the splitting criterion to each terminal node. This evaluates the log-likelihood increase by splitting each expert into two experts and a gate. The split which yields the best increase in log-likelihood is then added permanently to the tree. This process of training followed by growing continues until the desired modelling power is reached.

Constructive Algorithms for Hierarchical Mixtures of Experts

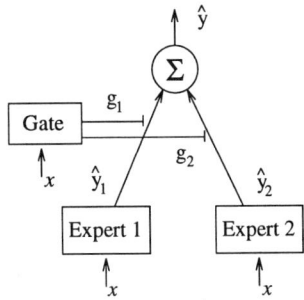

Figure 1: A simple mixture of experts.

This approach is reminiscent of Cascade Correlation (Fahlman & Lebiere 1990) in which new hidden nodes are added to a multi-layer perceptron and trained while the rest of the network is kept fixed.

The HME also has similarities with model merging techniques such as stacked regression (Wolpert 1993), in which explicit partitions of the training set are combined. However the HME differs from model merging in that each expert considers the whole input space in forming its output. Whilst this allows the network more flexibility since each gate may implicitly partition the whole input space in a "soft" manner, it leads to unnecessarily long computation in the case of near optimally trained models. At any one time only a few paths through a large network may have high probability. In order to overcome this drawback, we introduce the idea of "path pruning" which considers only those paths from the root node which have probability greater than a certain threshold.

CLASSIFICATION USING HIERARCHICAL MIXTURES OF EXPERTS

The mixture of experts, shown in Figure 1, consists of a set of "experts" which perform local function approximation. The expert outputs are combined by a gate to form the overall output. In the hierarchical case, the experts are themselves mixtures of further experts, thus extending the architecture in a tree structured fashion. Each terminal node or "expert" may take on a variety of forms, depending on the application. In the case of multi-way classification, each expert outputs a vector $\hat{y}_j$ in which element m is the conditional probability of class m ($m = 1 \ldots M$) which is computed using the softmax function:

$$P(c_m|x^{(n)}, w_j) = \exp(w_{m,j}^T x^{(n)}) \Big/ \sum_{k=1}^{K} \exp(w_{m,k}^T x^{(n)})$$

where $w_j = [w_{1j}\ w_{2j}\ \ldots\ w_{Mj}]$ is the parameter matrix for expert j and c_i denotes class i.

The outputs of the experts are combined using a "gate" which sits at the non-terminal nodes. The gate outputs are estimates of the conditional probability of selecting the daughters of the non-terminal node given the input and the path taken to that node from the root node. This is once again computed using the softmax function:

$$P(z_j|x^{(n)}, \xi) = \exp(\xi_j^T x^{(n)}) \Big/ \sum_{i=1}^{J} \exp(\xi_i^T x^{(n)})$$

where $\xi = [\xi_1\ \xi_2\ \ldots\ \xi_J]$ is the parameter matrix for the gate, and z_j denotes expert j.

The overall output is given by a probabilistic mixture in which the gate outputs are the mixture weights and the expert outputs are the mixture components. The probability of class m is then given by:

$$P(c_m|\boldsymbol{x}^{(n)}, \Theta) = \sum_{i=1}^{J} P(z_i|\boldsymbol{x}^{(n)}, \xi) P(c_m|\boldsymbol{x}^{(n)}, \mathbf{w}_i).$$

A straightforward extension of this model also gives us the conditional probability $h_j^{(n)}$ of selecting expert j given input $\boldsymbol{x}^{(n)}$ and correct class c_k,

$$h_j^{(n)} \equiv P(z_j|c_k, \boldsymbol{x}^{(n)}, \mathbf{w}_j) = P(z_j|\boldsymbol{x}^{(n)}, \xi) P(c_k|\boldsymbol{x}^{(n)}, \mathbf{w}_j) \bigg/ \sum_{i=1}^{J} P(z_i|\boldsymbol{x}^{(n)}, \xi) P(c_k|\boldsymbol{x}^{(n)}, \mathbf{w}_i)$$

In order to train the HME to perform classification we maximise the log likelihood $L = \sum_{n=1}^{N} \sum_{m=1}^{M} t_m^{(n)} \log P(c_m|\boldsymbol{x}^{(n)}, \Theta)$, where the variable $t_m^{(n)}$ is one if m is the correct class at exemplar (n) and zero otherwise. This is done via the expectation maximisation (EM) algorithm of Dempster, Laird & Rubin (1977), as described by Jordan & Jacobs (1994).

TREE GROWING

The standard HME differs from most tree based statistical models in that its architecture is fixed. By relaxing this constraint and allowing the tree to grow, we achieve a greater degree of flexibility in the network. Following the work on CART we start with a simple tree, for instance with two experts and one gate which we train for a small number of cycles. Given this semi-trained network, we then make a set of candidate splits $\{S_i\}$ of terminal nodes $\{z_i\}$. Each split involves replacing an expert z_i with a pair of new experts $\{z_{ij}\}_{j=1}^{2}$ and a gate, as shown in Figure 2.

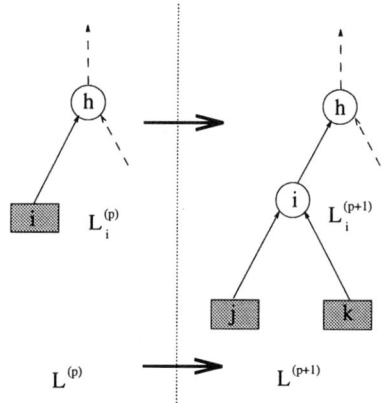

Figure 2: Making a candidate split of a terminal node.

We wish to select eventually only the "best" split $\tilde{S}$ out of these candidate splits. Let us define the best split as being that which maximises the increase in overall log-likelihood due to the split, $\Delta L = L^{(p+1)} - L^{(p)}$ where $L^{(p)}$ is the likelihood at the pth generation of the tree. If we make the constraint that all the parameters of the tree remain fixed apart from the parameters of the new split whenever a candidate split is made, then the maximisation is simplified into a dependency on the increases in the local likelihoods $\{L_i\}$ of the nodes $\{z_i\}$. We thus constrain the tree growing process to be localised such that we find the node which gains the most by being split.

$$\max_{i} \Delta L(S_i) \equiv \max_{i} \Delta L_i = \max_{i}(L_i^{(p+1)} - L_i^{(p)})$$

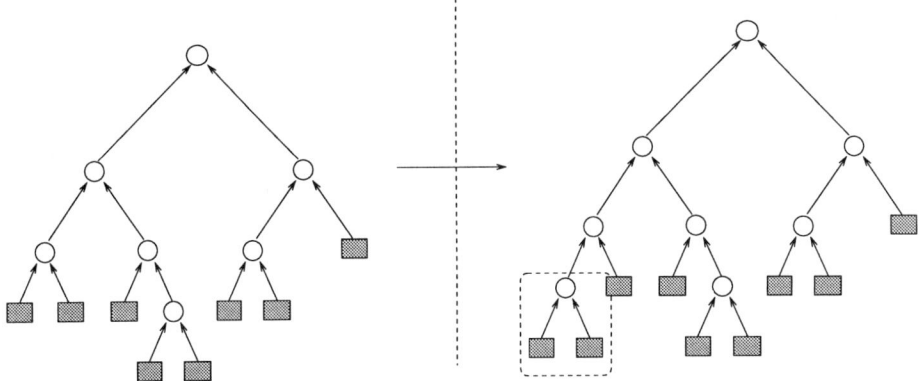

Figure 3: Growing the HME. This figure shows the addition of a pair of experts to the partially grown tree.

where
$$L_i^{(p)} = \sum_n \sum_m t_m^{(n)} \log P(c_m | \boldsymbol{x}^{(n)}, z_i, \mathbf{w}_i)$$
$$L_i^{(p+1)} = \sum_n \sum_m t_m^{(n)} \log \sum_j P(z_{ij} | \boldsymbol{x}^{(n)}, \xi_j, z_i) P(c_m | \boldsymbol{x}^{(n)}, z_{ij}, \mathbf{w}_{ij})$$

This splitting rule is similar in form to the CART splitting criterion which uses maximisation of the entropy of the node split, equivalent to our local increase in log-likelihood.

The final growing algorithm starts with a tree of generation p and firstly fixes the parameters of all non-terminal nodes. All terminal nodes are then split into two experts and a gate. A split is only made if the sum of posterior probabilities $\sum_n h_i^{(n)}$, as described (1), at the node is greater than a small threshold. This prevents splits being made on nodes which have very little data assigned to them. In order to break symmetry, the new experts of a split are initialised by adding small random noise to the original expert parameters. The gate parameters are set to small random weights. For each node i, we then evaluate ΔL_i by training the tree using the standard EM method. Since all non-terminal node parameters are fixed the only changes to the log-likelihood are due the new splits. Since the parameters of each split are thus independent of one another, all splits can be trained at once, removing the need to train multiple trees separately.

After each split has been evaluated, the best split is chosen. This split is kept and all other splits are discarded. The original tree structure is then recovered except for the additional winning split, as shown in Figure 3. The new tree, of generation $p+1$ is then trained as usual using EM. At present the decision on when to add a new split to the tree is fairly straightforward: a candidate split is made after training the fixed tree for a set number of iterations. An alternative scheme we have investigated is to make a split when the overall log-likelihood of the fixed tree has not increased for a set number of cycles. In addition, splits are rejected if they add too little to the local log-likelihood.

Although we have not discussed the issue of over-fitting in this paper, a number of techniques to prevent over-fitting can be used in the HME. The most simple technique, akin to those used in CART, involves growing a large tree and successively removing nodes from the tree until the performance on a cross validation set reaches an optimum. Alternatively the Bayesian techniques of Waterhouse, MacKay & Robinson (1995) could be applied.

Tree growing simulations

This algorithm was used to solve the 8-bit parity classification task. We compared the growing algorithm to a fixed HME with depth of 4 and binary branches. As can be seen in Figures 4(a) and (b), the factorisation enabled by the growing algorithm significantly speeds up computation over the standard fixed structure. The final tree shape obtained is shown in Figure 4(c). We showed in an earlier paper (Waterhouse & Robinson 1994) that the XOR problem may be solved using at least 2 experts and a gate. The 8 bit parity problem is therefore being solved by a series of XOR classifiers, each gated by its parent node, which is an intuitively appealing form with an efficient use of parameters.

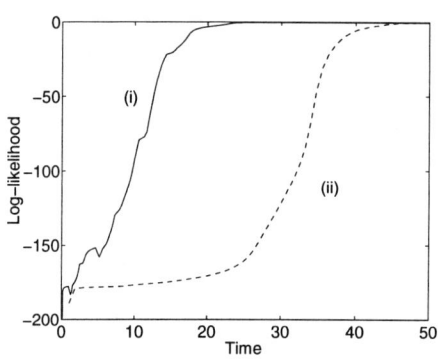

(a) Evolution of log-likelihood vs. time in CPU seconds.

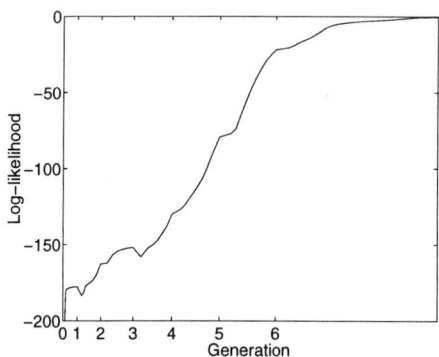

(b) Evolution of log-likelihood for (i) vs generations of tree.

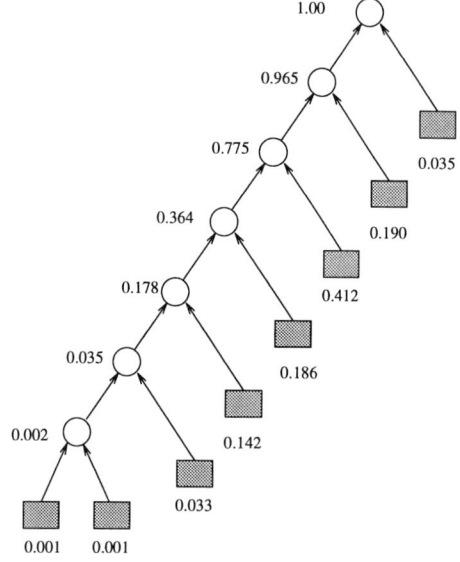

(c) Final tree structure obtained from (i), showing utilisation U_i of each node where $U_i = \sum_n P(z_i, R_i | x^{(n)}) / N$, and R_i is the path taken from the root node to node i.

Figure 4: HME GROWING ON THE 8 BIT PARITY PROBLEM; (i) growing HME with 6 generations; (ii) 4 deep binary branching HME (no growing).

PATH PRUNING

If we consider the HME to be a good model for the data generation process, the case for path pruning becomes clear. In a tree with sufficient depth to model the underlying sub-processes producing each data point, we would expect the activation of each expert to tend to binary values such that only one expert is selected at each time exemplar.

The path pruning scheme is depicted in Figure 5. The pruning scheme utilises the "activation" of each node at each exemplar. The activation is defined as the product of node probabilities along a path from the root node to the current node, $J_i^{(n)} = \sum_i \log P(z_i|R_i, x^{(n)})$, where R_i is the path taken to node i from the root node. If $J_l^{(n)}$ for node l at exemplar n falls below a threshold value, f_l, then we ignore the subtree S_l and we backtrack up to the parent node of l. During training this involves not accumulating the statistics of the subtree S_l; during evaluation it involves setting the output of subtree S_l to zero. In addition to this path pruning scheme we can use the activation of the nodes to do more permanent pruning. If the overall utilisation $U_i = \sum_n P(z_i, R_i|x^{(n)})/N$ of a node falls below a small threshold, then a node is pruned completely from the tree. The sister subtrees of the removed node then subsume their parent nodes. This process is used solely to improve computational efficiency in this paper, although conceivably it could be used as a regularisation method, akin to the brain surgery techniques of Cun, Denker & Solla (1990). In such a scheme, however, a more useful measure of node utilisation would be the *effective* number of parameters (Moody 1992).

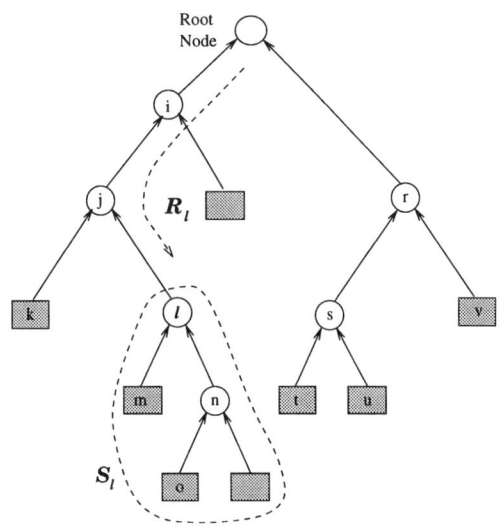

Figure 5: Path pruning in the HME.

Path pruning simulations

Figure 6 shows the application of the pruning algorithm to the task of discriminating between two interlocking spirals. With no pruning the solution to the two-spirals takes over 4,000 CPU seconds, whereas with pruning the solution is achieved in 155 CPU seconds.

One problem which we encountered when implementing this algorithm was in computing updates for the parameters of the tree in the case of high pruning thresholds. If a node is visited too few times during a training pass, it will sometimes have too little data to form reliable statistics and thus the new parameter values may be unreliable and lead to instability. This is particularly likely when the gates are saturated. To avoid this saturation we use a simplified version of the regularisation scheme described in Waterhouse et al. (1995).

CONCLUSIONS

We have presented two extensions to the standard HME architecture. By pruning branches either during training or evaluation we may significantly reduce the computational requirements of the HME. By applying tree growing we allow greater flexibility in the HME which results in faster training and more efficient use of parameters.

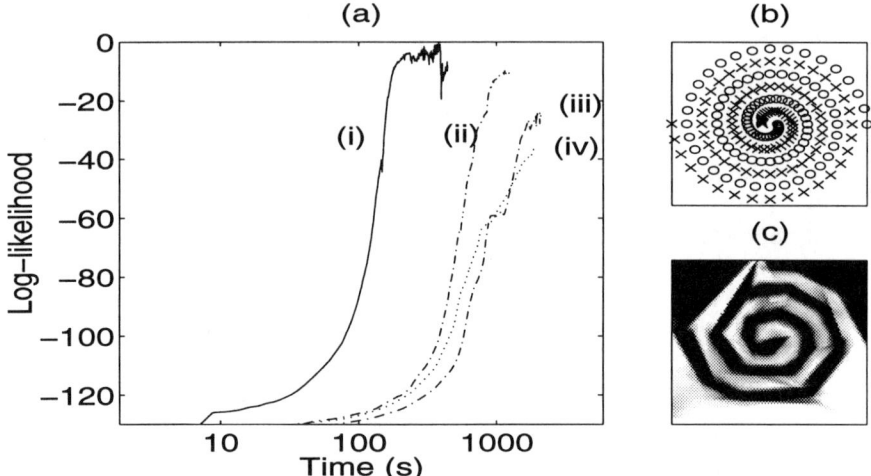

Figure 6: The effect of pruning on the two spirals classification problem by a 8 deep binary branching hme:(a) Log-likelihood vs. Time (CPU seconds), with log pruning thresholds for experts and gates f: (i) $f = -5.6$,(ii) $f = -10$,(iii) $f = -15$,(iv) no pruning, (b) training set for two-spirals task; the two classes are indicated by crosses and circles, (c) Solution to two spirals problem.

References

Breiman, L., Friedman, J., Olshen, R. & Stone, C. J. (1984), *Classification and Regression Trees*, Wadswoth and Brooks/Cole.

Cun, Y. L., Denker, J. S. & Solla, S. A. (1990), Optimal brain damage, *in* D. S. Touretzky, ed., 'Advances in Neural Information Processing Systems 2', Morgan Kaufmann, pp. 598–605.

Dempster, A. P., Laird, N. M. & Rubin, D. B. (1977), 'Maximum likelihood from incomplete data via the EM algorithm', *Journal of the Royal Statistical Society, Series B* **39**, 1–38.

Fahlman, S. E. & Lebiere, C. (1990), The Cascade-Correlation learning architecture, Technical Report CMU-CS-90-100, School of Computer Science, Carnegie Mellon University, Pittsburgh, PA 15213.

Jordan, M. I. & Jacobs, R. A. (1994), 'Hierarchical Mixtures of Experts and the EM algorithm', *Neural Computation* **6**, 181–214.

Moody, J. E. (1992), The *effective* number of parameters: An analysis of generalization and regularization in nonlinear learning systems, *in* J. E. Moody, S. J. Hanson & R. P. Lippmann, eds, 'Advances in Neural Information Processing Systems 4', Morgan Kaufmann, San Mateo, California, pp. 847–854.

Waterhouse, S. R. & Robinson, A. J. (1994), Classification using hierarchical mixtures of experts, *in* 'IEEE Workshop on Neural Networks for Signal Processing', pp. 177–186.

Waterhouse, S. R., MacKay, D. J. C. & Robinson, A. J. (1995), Bayesian methods for mixtures of experts, *in* M. C. M. D. S. Touretzky & M. E. Hasselmo, eds, 'Advances in Neural Information Processing Systems 8', MIT Press.

Wolpert, D. H. (1993), Stacked generalization, Technical Report LA-UR-90-3460, The Santa Fe Institute, 1660 Old Pecos Trail, Suite A, Santa Fe, NM, 87501.

An Information-theoretic Learning Algorithm for Neural Network Classification

David J. Miller
Department of Electrical Engineering
The Pennsylvania State University
State College, Pa. 16802

Ajit Rao, Kenneth Rose, and Allen Gersho
Department of Electrical and Computer Engineering
University of California
Santa Barbara, Ca. 93106

Abstract

A new learning algorithm is developed for the design of statistical classifiers minimizing the rate of misclassification. The method, which is based on ideas from information theory and analogies to statistical physics, assigns data to classes *in probability*. The distributions are chosen to minimize the expected classification error while simultaneously enforcing the classifier's structure and a level of "randomness" measured by Shannon's entropy. Achievement of the classifier structure is *quantified* by an associated cost. The constrained optimization problem is equivalent to the minimization of a Helmholtz free energy, and the resulting optimization method is a basic extension of the deterministic annealing algorithm that explicitly enforces structural constraints on assignments while reducing the entropy and expected cost with temperature. In the limit of low temperature, the error rate is minimized directly and a hard classifier with the requisite structure is obtained. This learning algorithm can be used to design a variety of classifier structures. The approach is compared with standard methods for radial basis function design and is demonstrated to substantially outperform other design methods on several benchmark examples, while often retaining design complexity comparable to, or only moderately greater than that of strict descent-based methods.

1 Introduction

The problem of designing a statistical classifier to minimize the probability of misclassification or a more general risk measure has been a topic of continuing interest since the 1950s. Recently, with the increase in power of serial and parallel computing resources, a number of complex neural network classifier structures have been proposed, along with associated learning algorithms to design them. While these structures offer great potential for classification, this potential cannot be fully realized without effective learning procedures well-matched to the minimum classification-error objective. Methods such as back propagation which approximate class targets in a squared error sense do not directly minimize the probability of error. Rather, it has been shown that these approaches design networks to approximate the class a posteriori probabilities. The probability estimates can then be used to form a decision rule. While large networks can in principle accurately approximate the Bayes discriminant, in practice the network size must be constrained to avoid overfitting the (finite) training set. Thus, discriminative learning techniques, e.g. (Juang and Katagiri, 1992), which seek to directly minimize classification error may achieve better results. However, these methods may still be susceptible to finding shallow local minima far from the global minimum.

As an alternative to strict descent-based procedures, we propose a new deterministic learning algorithm for statistical classifier design with a demonstrated potential for avoiding local optima of the cost. Several deterministic, annealing-based techniques have been proposed for avoiding nonglobal optima in computer vision and image processing (Yuille, 1990), (Geiger and Girosi,1991), in combinatorial optimization, and elsewhere. Our approach is derived based on ideas from information theory and statistical physics, and builds on the probabilistic framework of the deterministic annealing (DA) approach to clustering and related problems (Rose et al., 1990,1992,1993). In the DA approach for data clustering, the probability distributions are chosen to minimize the expected clustering cost, given a constraint on the level of randomness, as measured by Shannon's entropy [1].

In this work, the DA approach is extended in a novel way, most significantly *to incorporate structural constraints on data assignments*, but also to minimize the probability of error as the cost. While the general approach we suggest is likely applicable to problems of structured vector quantization and regression as well, we focus on the classification problem here. Most design methods have been developed for specific classifier structures. In this work, we will develop a general approach but only demonstrate results for RBF classifiers. The design of nearest prototype and MLP classifiers is considered in (Miller et al., 1995a,b). Our method provides substantial performance gains over conventional designs for all of these structures, while retaining design complexity in many cases comparable to the strict descent methods. Our approach often designs small networks to achieve training set performance that can only be obtained by a much larger network designed in a conventional way. The design of smaller networks may translate to superior performance outside the training set.

---

[1] Note that in (Rose et al., 1990,1992,1993), the DA method was formally derived using the maximum entropy principle. Here we emphasize the alternative, but mathematically equivalent description that the chosen distributions minimize the expected cost given constrained entropy. This formulation may have more intuitive appeal for the optimization problem at hand.

2 Classifier Design Formulation

2.1 Problem Statement

Let $\mathcal{T} = \{(\mathbf{x}, c)\}$ be a training set of N labelled vectors, where $\mathbf{x} \in \mathcal{R}^n$ is a feature vector and $c \in \mathcal{I}$ is its class label from an index set $\mathcal{I}$. A classifier is a mapping $C : \mathcal{R}^n \to \mathcal{I}$, which assigns a class label in $\mathcal{I}$ to each vector in $\mathcal{R}^n$. Typically, the classifier is represented by a set of model parameters Λ. The classifier specifies a partitioning of the feature space into regions $R_j \equiv \{\mathbf{x} \in \mathcal{R}^n : C(\mathbf{x}) = j\}$, where $\bigcup_j R_j \equiv \mathcal{R}^n$ and $\bigcap_j R_j \equiv \emptyset$. It also induces a partitioning of the training set into sets $\mathcal{T}_j \subset \mathcal{T}$, where $\mathcal{T}_j \equiv \{\{\mathbf{x}, c\} : \mathbf{x} \in R_j, (\mathbf{x}, c) \in \mathcal{T}\}$. A training pair $(\mathbf{x}, c) \in \mathcal{T}$ is *misclassified* if $C(\mathbf{x}) \neq c$. The performance measure of primary interest is the empirical error fraction P_e of the classifier, i.e. the fraction of the training set (for generalization purposes, the fraction of the test set) which is misclassified:

$$P_e = \frac{1}{N} \sum_{(\mathbf{x},c) \in \mathcal{T}} \delta(c, C(\mathbf{x})) = \frac{1}{N} \sum_{j \in \mathcal{I}} \sum_{(\mathbf{x},c) \in \mathcal{T}_j} \delta(c, j), \quad (1)$$

where $\delta(c, j) = 1$ if $c \neq j$ and 0 otherwise. In this work, we will assume that the classifier produces an output $F_j(\mathbf{x})$ associated with each class, and uses a "winner-take-all" classification rule:

$$R_j \equiv \{\mathbf{x} \in \mathcal{R}^n : F_j(\mathbf{x}) \geq F_k(\mathbf{x}) \; \forall k \in \mathcal{I}\}. \quad (2)$$

This rule is consistent with MLP and RBF-based classification.

2.2 Randomized Classifier Partition

As in the original DA approach for clustering (Rose et al., 1990,1992), we cast the optimization problem in a framework in which data are assigned to classes *in probability*. Accordingly, we define the *probabilities of association* between a feature $\mathbf{x}$ and the class regions, i.e. $\{P[\mathbf{x} \in R_j]\}$. As our design method, which optimizes over these probabilities, must ultimately form a classifier that makes "hard" decisions based on a specified network model, the distributions must be chosen to be consistent with the decision rule of the model. In other words, we need to introduce randomness into the classifier's partition. Clearly, there are many ways one could define probability distributions which are consistent with the hard partition at some limit. We use an information-theoretic approach. We measure the randomness or uncertainty by Shannon's entropy, and determine the distribution for a given level of entropy. At the limit of zero entropy we should recover a hard partition. For now, suppose that the values of the model parameters Λ have been fixed. We can then write an objective function whose maximization determines the hard partition for a given Λ:

$$F_h = \frac{1}{N} \sum_{j \in \mathcal{I}} \sum_{(\mathbf{x},c) \in \mathcal{T}_j} F_j(\mathbf{x}). \quad (3)$$

Note specifically that maximizing (3) over all possible partitions captures the decision rule of (2). The probabilistic generalization of (3) is

$$F = \frac{1}{N} \sum_{(\mathbf{x},c) \in \mathcal{T}} \sum_j P[\mathbf{x} \in R_j] F_j(\mathbf{x}), \quad (4)$$

where the (randomized) partition is now represented by association probabilities, and the corresponding entropy is

$$H = -\frac{1}{N} \sum_{(\mathbf{x},c) \in \mathcal{T}} \sum_j P[\mathbf{x} \in R_j] \log P[\mathbf{x} \in R_j]. \quad (5)$$

We determine the distribution at a given level of randomness as the one which maximizes F while maintaining H at a prescribed level $\hat{H}$:

$$\max_{\{P[\mathbf{x} \in R_j]\}} F \text{ subject to } H = \hat{H}. \tag{6}$$

The result is the *best* probabilistic partition, in the sense of F, *at the specified level of randomness*. For $\hat{H} = 0$ we get back the hard partition maximizing (3). At any $\hat{H}$, the solution of (6) is the Gibbs distribution

$$P[\mathbf{x} \in R_j] \equiv P_{j|x}(\Lambda) = \frac{e^{\gamma F_j(\mathbf{X})}}{\sum_k e^{\gamma F_k(\mathbf{X})}}, \tag{7}$$

where γ is the Lagrange multiplier. For $\gamma \to 0$, the associations become increasingly uniform, while for $\gamma \to \infty$, they revert to hard classifications, equivalent to application of the rule in (2). Note that the probabilities depend on Λ through the network outputs. Here we have emphasized this dependence through our choice of concise notation.

2.3 Information-Theoretic Classifier Design

Until now we have formulated a controlled way of introducing randomness into the classifier's partition while enforcing its structural constraint. However, the derivation assumed that the model parameters were given, and thus produced only the *form* of the distribution $P_{j|x}(\Lambda)$, without actually prescribing how to choose the values of its parameter set. Moreover the derivation did not consider the ultimate goal of minimizing the probability of error. Here we remedy both shortcomings.

The method we suggest gradually enforces formation of a hard classifier minimizing the probability of error. We start with a highly random classifier and a high expected misclassification cost. We then gradually reduce both the randomness and the cost in a deterministic learning process which enforces formation of a hard classifier with the requisite structure. As before, we need to introduce randomness into the partition while enforcing the classifier's structure, only now we are also interested in minimizing the expected misclassification cost. While satisfying these multiple objectives may appear to be a formidable task, the problem is greatly simplified by restricting the choice of random classifiers to the set of distributions $\{P_{j|x}(\Lambda)\}$ as given in (7) – these random classifiers naturally enforce the structural constraint through γ. Thus, from the parametrized set $\{P_{j|x}(\Lambda)\}$, we seek that distribution which minimizes the average misclassification cost while constraining the entropy:

$$\min_{\gamma,\Lambda} <P_e> \equiv \min_{\gamma,\Lambda} \frac{1}{N} \sum_{(\mathbf{X},c) \in \mathcal{T}} \sum_j P_{j|x}(\Lambda) \delta(c, j), \tag{8}$$

subject to

$$H = \hat{H}.$$

The solution yields the *best* random classifier in the sense of minimum $<P_e>$ for a given $\hat{H}$. At the limit of zero entropy, we should get the best *hard* classifier in the sense of P_e with the desired structure, i.e. satisfying (2).

The constrained minimization (8) is equivalent to the unconstrained minimization of the Lagrangian:

$$\min_{\Lambda,\gamma} L \equiv \min_{\Lambda,\gamma} \beta <P_e> -H, \tag{9}$$

where β is the Lagrange multiplier associated with (8). For $\beta = 0$, the sole objective is entropy maximization, which is achieved by the uniform distribution. This solution, which is the global minimum for L at $\beta = 0$, can be obtained by choosing $\gamma = 0$. At the other end of the spectrum, for $\beta \to \infty$, the sole objective is to minimize $<P_e>$, and is achieved by choosing a non-random (hard) classifier (hence minimizing P_e). The hard solution satisfies the classification rule (2) and is obtained for $\gamma \to \infty$.

Motivation for minimizing the Lagrangian can be obtained from a physical perspective by noting that L is the Helmholtz free energy of a simulated system, with $<P_e>$ the "energy", H the system entropy, and $\frac{1}{\beta}$ the "temperature". Thus, from this physical view we can suggest a deterministic annealing (DA) process which involves minimizing L starting at the global minimum for $\beta = 0$ (high temperature) and tracking the solution while increasing β towards infinity (zero temperature). In this way, we obtain a sequence of solutions of decreasing entropy and average misclassification cost. Each such solution is the best random classifier in the sense of $<P_e>$ for a given level of randomness. The annealing process is useful for avoiding local optima of the cost $<P_e>$, and minimizes $<P_e>$ directly at low temperature. While this annealing process ostensibly involves the quantities H and $<P_e>$, the restriction to $\{P_{j|x}(\Lambda)\}$ from (7) ensures that the process also enforces the structural constraint on the classifier in a controlled way. *Note in particular that γ has not lost its interpretation as a Lagrange multiplier determining F.* Thus, $\gamma = 0$ means that F is unconstrained – we are free to choose the uniform distribution. Similarly, sending $\gamma \to \infty$ requires maximizing F – hence the hard solution. Since γ is chosen to minimize L, this parameter effectively determines the level of F – the level of structural constraint – *consistent with H and $<P_e>$ for a given β*. As β is increased, the entropy constraint is relaxed, allowing greater satisfaction of *both* the minimum $<P_e>$ and maximum F objectives. Thus, annealing in β gradually enforces both the structural constraint (via γ) and the minimum $<P_e>$ objective [2].

Our formulation clearly identifies what distinguishes the annealing approach from direct descent procedures. Note that a descent method could be obtained by simply neglecting the constraint on the entropy, instead choosing to directly minimize $<P_e>$ over the parameter set. This minimization will directly lead to a hard classifier, and is akin to the method described in (Juang and Katagiri, 1992) as well as other related approaches which attempt to directly minimize a smoothed probability of error cost. However, as we will experimentally verify through simulations, our annealing approach outperforms design based on directly minimizing $<P_e>$.

For conciseness, we will not derive necessary optimality conditions for minimizing the Lagrangian at a give temperature, nor will we specialize the formulation for individual classification structures here. The reader is referred to (Miller et al., 1995a) for these details.

3 Experimental Comparisons

We demonstrate the performance of our design approach in comparison with other methods for the normalized RBF structure (Moody and Darken, 1989). For the DA method, steepest descent was used to minimize L at a sequence of exponentially increasing β, given by $\beta(n + 1) = \alpha\beta(n)$, for α between 1.05 and 1.1. We have found that much of the optimization occurs at or near a critical temperature in the

---

[2] While not shown here, the method does converge directly for $\beta \to \infty$, and at this limit enforces the classifier's structure.

Method	DA		TR-RBF				MD-RBF		∇P_e
M	4	30	4	10	30	50	10	50	10
P_e (train)	0.11	0.028	0.33	0.162	0.145	0.129	0.3	0.19	0.18
P_e (test)	0.13	0.167	0.35	0.165	0.168	0.179	0.37	0.18	0.20

Table 1: A comparison of DA with known design techniques for RBF classification on the 40-dimensional noisy waveform data from (Breiman et al., 1980).

solution process. Beyond this critical temperature, the annealing process can often be "quenched" to zero temperature by sending $\gamma \to \infty$ without incurring significant performance loss. Quenching the process often makes the design complexity of our method comparable to that of descent-based methods such as back propagation or gradient descent on $< P_e >$.

We have compared our RBF design approach with the method in (Moody and Darken, 1989) (MD-RBF), with a method described in (Tarassenko and Roberts,1994) (TR-RBF), with the approach in (Musavi et al., 1992), and with steepest descent on $< P_e >$ (G-RBF). MD-RBF combines unsupervised learning of receptive field parameters with supervised learning of the weights from the receptive fields so as to minimize the squared distance to target class outputs. The primary advantage of this approach is its modest design complexity. However, the receptive fields are not optimized in a supervised fashion, which can cause performance degradation. TR-RBF optimizes all of the RBF parameters to approximate target class outputs. This design is more complex than MD-RBF and achieves better performance for a given model size. However, as aforementioned, the TR-RBF design objective is not equivalent to minimizing P_e, but rather to approximating the Bayes-optimal discriminant. While direct descent on $< P_e >$ may minimize the "right" objective, problems of local optima may be quite severe. In fact, we have found that the performance of all of these methods can be quite poor without a judicious initialization. For all of these methods, we have employed the unsupervised learning phase described in (Moody and Darken, 1989) (based on Isodata clustering and variance estimation) as model initialization. Then, steepest descent was performed on the respective cost surface. We have found that the complexity of our design is typically 1-5 times that of TR-RBF or G-RBF (though occasionally our design is actually faster than G-RBF). Accordingly, we have chosen the best results based on five random initializations for these techniques, and compared with the single DA design run.

One example reported here is the 40D "noisy" waveform data used in (Breiman et al., 1980) (obtained from the UC-Irvine machine learning database repository.). We split the 5000 vectors into equal size training and test sets. Our results in Table I demonstrate quite substantial performance gains over all the other methods, and performance quite close to the estimated Bayes rate of 14%. Note in particular that the other methods perform quite poorly for a small number of receptive fields (M), and need to increase M to achieve training set performance comparable to our approach. However, performance on the test set does not necessarily improve, and may degrade for increasing M.

To further justify this claim, we compared our design with results reported in (Musavi et al., 1992), for the two and eight dimensional mixture examples. For the 2D example, our method achieved $P_{e_{train}} = 6.0\%$ for a 400 point training set and $P_{e_{test}} = 6.1\%$ on a 20,000 point test set, using $M = 3$ units (These results are near-optimal, based on the Bayes rate.). By contrast, the method of Musavi et al. used 86 receptive fields and achieved $P_{e_{test}} = 9.26\%$. For the 8D example and $M = 5$, our method achieved $P_{e_{train}} = 8\%$ and $P_{e_{test}} = 9.4\%$ (again near-optimal), while the method in (Musavui et al., 1992) achieved $P_{e_{test}} = 12.0\%$ using $M = 128$.

In summary, we have proposed a new, information-theoretic learning algorithm for classifier design, demonstrated to outperform other design methods, and with general applicability to a variety of structures. Future work may investigate important applications, such as recognition problems for speech and images. Moreover, our extension of DA to incorporate structure is likely applicable to structured vector quantizer design and to regression modelling. These problems will be considered in future work.

Acknowledgements

This work was supported in part by the National Science Foundation under grant no. NCR-9314335, the University of California MICRO program, DSP Group, Inc. Echo Speech Corporation, Moseley Associates, National Semiconductor Corp., Qualcomm, Inc., Rockwell International Corporation, Speech Technology Labs, and Texas Instruments, Inc.

References

L. Breiman, J. H. Friedman, R. A. Olshen, and C. J. Stone. *Classification and Regression Trees*. The Wadsworth Statistics/Probability Series, Belmont,CA., 1980.

D. Geiger and F. Girosi. Parallel and deterministic algorithms from MRFs: Surface reconstruction. *IEEE Trans. on Patt. Anal. and Mach. Intell.*, 13:401–412, 1991.

B.-H. Juang and S. Katagiri. Discriminative learning for minimum error classification. *IEEE Trans. on Sig. Proc.*, 40:3043–3054, 1992.

D. Miller, A. Rao, K. Rose, and A. Gersho. A global optimization technique for statistical classifier design. (Submitted for publication.), 1995.

D. Miller, A. Rao, K. Rose, and A. Gersho. A maximum entropy framework for optimal statistical classification. In *IEEE Workshop on Neural Networks for Signal Processing.*), 1995.

J. Moody and C. J. Darken. Fast learning in locally-tuned processing units. *Neural Comp.*, 1:281–294, 1989.

M. T. Musavi, W. Ahmed, K. H. Chan, K. B. Faris, and D. M. Hummels. On the training of radial basis function classifiers. *Neural Networks*, 5:595–604, 1992.

K. Rose, E. Gurewitz, and G. C. Fox. Statistical mechanics and phase transitions in clustering. *Phys. Rev. Lett.*, 65:945–948, 1990.

K. Rose, E. Gurewitz, and G. C. Fox. Vector quantization by deterministic annealing. *IEEE Trans. on Inform. Theory*, 38:1249–1258, 1992.

K. Rose, E. Gurewitz, and G. C. Fox. Constrained clustering as an optimization method. *IEEE Trans. on Patt. Anal. and Mach. Intell.*, 15:785–794, 1993.

L. Tarassenko and S. Roberts. Supervised and unsupervised learning in radial basis function classifiers. *IEE Proc.-Vis. Image Sig. Proc.*, 141:210–216, 1994.

A. L. Yuille. Generalized deformable models, statistical physics, and matching problems. *Neural Comp.*, 2:1–24, 1990.

A Practical Monte Carlo Implementation of Bayesian Learning

Carl Edward Rasmussen
Department of Computer Science
University of Toronto
Toronto, Ontario, M5S 1A4, Canada
carl@cs.toronto.edu

Abstract

A practical method for Bayesian training of feed-forward neural networks using sophisticated Monte Carlo methods is presented and evaluated. In reasonably small amounts of computer time this approach outperforms other state-of-the-art methods on 5 data-limited tasks from real world domains.

1 INTRODUCTION

Bayesian learning uses a prior on model parameters, combines this with information from a training set, and then integrates over the resulting posterior to make predictions. With this approach, we can use large networks without fear of overfitting, allowing us to capture more structure in the data, thus improving prediction accuracy and eliminating the tedious search (often performed using cross validation) for the model complexity that optimises the bias/variance tradeoff. In this approach the size of the model is limited only by computational considerations.

The application of Bayesian learning to neural networks has been pioneered by MacKay (1992), who uses a Gaussian approximation to the posterior weight distribution. However, the Gaussian approximation is poor because of multiple modes in the posterior. Even locally around a mode the accuracy of the Gaussian approximation is questionable, especially when the model is large compared to the amount of training data.

Here I present and test a Monte Carlo method (Neal, 1995) which avoids the Gaussian approximation. The implementation is complicated, but the user is not required to have extensive knowledge about the algorithm. Thus, the implementation represents a practical tool for learning in neural nets.

A Practical Monte Carlo Implementation of Bayesian Learning

1.1 THE PREDICTION TASK

The training data consists of n examples in the form of inputs $\mathbf{x} = \{x^{(i)}\}$ and corresponding outputs $\mathbf{y} = \{y^{(i)}\}$ where $i = 1\ldots n$. For simplicity we consider only real-valued scalar outputs. The network is parametrised by weights $\mathbf{w}$, and hyperparameters $\mathbf{h}$ that control the distributions for weights, playing a role similar to that of conventional weight decay. Weights and hyperparameters are collectively termed θ, and the network function is written as $F_\theta(x)$, although the function value is only indirectly dependent on the hyperparameters (through the weights).

Bayes' rule gives the posterior distribution for the parameters in terms of the likelihood, $p(\mathbf{y}|\mathbf{x},\theta)$, and prior, $p(\theta)$:

$$p(\theta|\mathbf{x},\mathbf{y}) = \frac{p(\theta)p(\mathbf{y}|\mathbf{x},\theta)}{p(\mathbf{y}|\mathbf{x})}.$$

To minimize the expected squared error on an unseen test case with input $\mathbf{x}^{(n+1)}$, we use the mean prediction

$$\hat{y}^{(n+1)} = \int F_\theta(x^{(n+1)}) p(\theta|\mathbf{x},\mathbf{y}) d^k\theta. \tag{1}$$

2 MONTE CARLO SAMPLING

The following implementation is due to Neal (1995). The network weights are updated using the *hybrid Monte Carlo* method (Duane et al. 1987). This method combines the Metropolis algorithm with dynamical simulation. This helps to avoid the random walk behavior of simple forms of Metropolis, which is essential if we wish to explore weight space efficiently. The hyperparameters are updated using Gibbs sampling.

2.1 NETWORK SPECIFICATION

The networks used here are always of the same form: a single linear output unit, a single hidden layer of tanh units and a task dependent number of input units. All layers are fully connected in a feed forward manner (including direct connections from input to output). The output and hidden units have biases.

The network priors are specified in a hierarchical manner in terms of hyperparameters; weights of different kinds are divided into groups, each group having it's own prior. The output-bias is given a zero-mean Gaussian prior with a std. dev. of $\sigma = 1000$, so it is effectively unconstrained.

The hidden-biases are given a two layer prior: the bias b is given a zero-mean Gaussian prior $b \sim \mathcal{N}(0,\sigma^2)$; the value of σ is specified in terms of *precision* $\tau = \sigma^{-2}$, which is given a Gamma prior with mean $\mu = 400$ (corresponding to $\sigma = 0.05$) and shape parameter $\alpha = 0.5$; the Gamma density is given by $p(\tau) \sim \text{Gamma}(\mu,\alpha) \propto \tau^{\alpha/2-1}\exp(-\tau\alpha/2\mu)$. Note that this type of prior introduces a dependency between the biases for different hidden units through the common τ. The prior for the hidden-to-output weights is identical to the prior for the hidden-biases, except that the variance of these weights under the prior is scaled down by the square root of the number of hidden units, such that the network output magnitude becomes independent of the number of hidden units. The noise variance is also given a Gamma prior with these parameters.

The input-to-hidden weights are given a three layer prior: again each weight is given a zero-mean Gaussian prior $w \sim \mathcal{N}(0, \sigma^2)$; the corresponding precision for the weights out of input unit i is given a Gamma prior with a mean μ and a shape parameter $\alpha_1 = 0.5$: $\tau_i \sim \text{Gamma}(\mu, \alpha_1)$. The mean μ is determined on the top level by a Gamma distribution with mean and shape parameter $\alpha_0 = 1$: $\mu_i \sim \text{Gamma}(400, \alpha_0)$. The direct input-to-output connections are also given this prior.

The above-mentioned 3 layer prior incorporates the idea of Automatic Relevance Determination (ARD), due to MacKay and Neal, and discussed in Neal (1995). The hyperparameters, τ_i, associated with individual inputs can adapt according to the relevance of the input; for an unimportant input, τ_i can grow very large (governed by the top level prior), thus forcing σ_i and the associated weights to vanish.

2.2 MONTE CARLO SPECIFICATION

Sampling from the posterior weight distribution is performed by iteratively updating the values of the network weights and hyperparameters. Each iteration involves two components: weight updates and hyperparameter updates. A cursory description of these steps follows.

2.2.1 Weight Updates

Weight updates are done using the hybrid Monte Carlo method. A fictitious dynamical system is generated by interpreting weights as positions, and augmenting the weights **w** with momentum variables **p**. The purpose of the dynamical system is to give the weights "inertia" so that slow random walk behaviour can be avoided during exploration of weight space. The total energy, H, of the system is the sum of the kinetic energy, K, (a function of the momenta) and the potential energy, E. The potential energy is defined such that $p(\mathbf{w}) \propto \exp(-E)$. We sample from the joint distribution for **w** and **p** given by $p(\mathbf{w}, \mathbf{p}) \propto \exp(-E - K)$, under which the marginal distribution for **w** is given by the posterior. A sample of weights from the posterior can therefore be obtained by simply ignoring the momenta.

Sampling from the joint distribution is achieved by two steps: 1) finding new points in phase space with near-identical energies H by simulating the dynamical system using a discretised approximation to Hamiltonian dynamics, and 2) changing the energy H by doing Gibbs sampling for the momentum variables.

Hamiltonian Dynamics. Hamilton's first order differential equations for H are approximated by a series of discrete first order steps (specifically by the *leapfrog* method). The first derivatives of the network error function enter through the derivative of the potential energy, and are computed using backpropagation. In the original version of the hybrid Monte Carlo method the final position is then accepted or rejected depending on the final energy H^* (which is not necessarily equal to the initial energy H because of the discretisation). Here we use a modified version that uses an average over a window of states instead. The step size of the discrete dynamics should be as large as possible while keeping the rejection rate low. The step sizes are set individually using several heuristic approximations, and scaled by an overall parameter ε. We use $L = 200$ iterations, a window size of 20 and a step size of $\varepsilon = 0.2$ for all simulations.

Gibbs Sampling for Momentum Variables. The momentum variables are updated using a modified version of Gibbs sampling, allowing the energy H to change. A "persistence" of 0.95 is used; the new value of the momentum is a weighted sum of the previous value (weight 0.95) and the value obtained by Gibbs sampling (weight $(1 - 0.95^2)^{1/2}$). With this form of persistence, the momenta changes approx. 20 times more slowly, thus increasing the "inertia" of the weights, so as to further help in avoiding random walks. Larger values of the persistence will further increase the weight inertia, but reduce the rate of exploration of H. The advantage of increasing the weight inertia in this way rather than by increasing L is that the hyperparameters are updated at shorter intervals, allowing them to adapt to the rapidly changing weights.

2.2.2 Hyperparameter Updates

The hyperparameters are updated using Gibbs sampling. The conditional distributions for the hyperparameters given the weights are of the Gamma form, for which efficient generators exist, except for the top-level hyperparameter in the case of the 3 layer priors used for the weights from the inputs; in this case the conditional distribution is more complicated and a form of rejection sampling is employed.

2.3 NETWORK TRAINING AND PREDICTION

The network training consists of two levels of initialisation before sampling for networks used for prediction. At the first level of initialisation the hyperparameters (variance of the Gaussians) are kept constant at 1, allowing the weights to grow during 1000 leapfrog iterations. Neglecting this phase can cause the network to get caught for a long time in a state where weights and hyperparameters are both very small.

The scheme described above is then invoked and run for as long as desired, eventually producing networks from the posterior distribution. The initial 1/3 of these nets are discarded, since the algorithm may need time to reach regions of high posterior probability. Networks sampled during the remainder of the run are saved for making predictions.

The predictions are made using an average of the networks sampled from the posterior as an approximation to the integral in eq. (1). Since the output unit is linear the final prediction can be seen as coming from a huge (fully connected) ensemble net with appropriately scaled output weights. All the results reported here were for ensemble nets with 4000 hidden units. The size of the individual nets is given by the rule that we want at least as many network parameters as we have training examples (with a lower limit of 4 hidden units). We hope thereby to be well out of the underfitting region. Using even larger nets would probably not gain us much (in the face of the limited training data) and is avoided for computational reasons.

All runs used the parameter values given above. The only check that is necessary is that the rejection rate stays low, say below 5%; if not, the step size should be lowered. In all runs reported here, $\varepsilon = 0.2$ was adequate. The parameters concerning the Monte Carlo method and the network priors were all selected based on intuition and on experience with toy problems. Thus no parameters need to be set by the user.

3 TESTS

The performance of the algorithm was evaluated by comparing it to other state-of-the-art methods on 5 real-world regression tasks. All 5 data sets have previously been studied using a 10-way cross-validation scheme (Quinlan 1993). The tasks in these domains is to predict price or performance of an object from various discrete and real-valued attributes. For each domain the data is split into two sets of roughly equal size, one for training and one for testing. The training data is further subdivided into full-, half-, quarter- and eighth-sized subsets, 15 subsets in total. Networks are trained on each of these partitions, and evaluated on the large common test set. On the small training sets, the average performance and one std. dev. error bars on this estimate are computed.

3.1 ALGORITHMS

The Monte Carlo method was compared to four other algorithms. For the three neural network methods nets with a single hidden layer and direct input-output connections were used. The Monte Carlo method was run for 1 hour on each of the small training sets, and 2, 4 and 8 hours respectively on the larger training sets. All simulations were done on a 200 MHz MIPS R4400 processor. The Gaussian Process method is described in a companion paper (Williams & Rasmussen 1996).

The Evidence method (MacKay 1992) was used for a network with separate hyperparameters for the direct connections, the weights from individual inputs (ARD), hidden biases, and output biases. Nets were trained using a conjugate gradient method, allowing 10000 gradient evaluations (batch) before each of 6 updates of the hyperparameters. The network Hessian was computed analytically. The value of the evidence was computed without compensating for network symmetries, since this can lead to a vastly over-estimated evidence for big networks where the posterior Gaussians from different modes overlap. A large number of nets were trained for each task, with the number of hidden units computed from the results of previous nets by the following heuristics: The min and max number of hidden units in the 20% nets with the highest evidences were found. The new architecture is picked from a Gaussian (truncated at 0) with mean (max − min)/2 and std. dev. 2 + max − min, which is thought to give a reasonable trade-off between exploration and exploitation. This procedure is run for 1 hour of cpu time or until more than 1000 nets have been trained. The final predictions are made from an ensemble of the 20% (but a maximum of 100) nets with the highest evidence.

An ensemble method using cross-validation to search over a 2-dimensional grid for the number of hidden units and the value of a single weight decay parameter has been included, as an attempt to have a thorough version of "common practise". The weight decay parameter takes on the values 0, 0.01, 0.04, 0.16, 0.64 and 2.56. Up to 6 sizes of nets are used, from 0 hidden units (a linear model) up to a number that gives as many weights as training examples. Networks are trained with a conjugent gradient method for 10000 epochs on each of these up to 36 networks, and performance was monitored on a validation set containing 1/3 of the examples, selected at random. This was repeated 5 times with different random validation sets, and the architecture and weight decay that did best on average was selected. The predictions are made from an ensemble of 10 nets with this architecture, trained on the full training set. This algorithm took several hours of cpu time for the largest training sets.

The Multivariate Adaptive Regression Splines (MARS) method (Friedman 1991) was included as a non-neural network approach. It is possible to vary the maximum number of variables allowed to interact in the additive components of the model. It is common to allow either pairwise or full interactions. I do not have sufficient experience with MARS to make this choice. Therefore, I tried both options and reported for each partition on each domain the best performance based on the test error, so results as good as the ones reported here might not be obtainable in practise. All other parameters of MARS were left at their default values. MARS always required less than 1 minute of cpu time.

A Practical Monte Carlo Implementation of Bayesian Learning

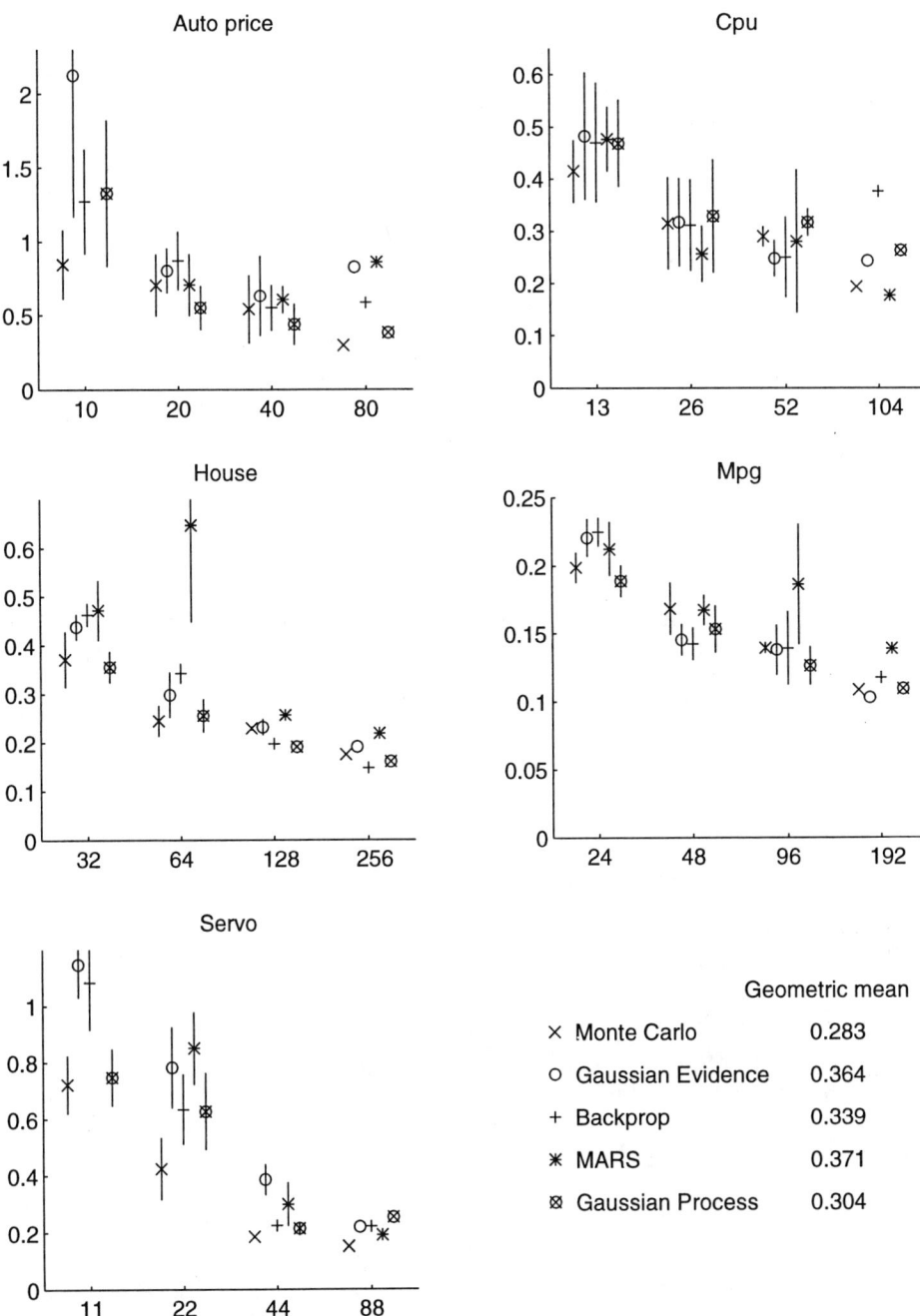

Figure 1: Squared error on test cases for the five algorithms applied to the five problems. Errors are normalized with respect to the variance on the test cases. The x-axis gives the number of training examples; four different set sizes were used on each domain. The error bars give one std. dev. for the distribution of the *mean* over training sets. No error bar is given for the largest size, for which only a single training set was available. Some of the large error bars are cut of at the top. MARS was unable to run on the smallest partitions from the `Auto price` and the `servo` domains; in these cases the means of the four other methods were used in the reported geometric mean for MARS.

Table 1: Data Sets

domain	# training cases	# test cases	# binary inputs	# real inputs
Auto Price	80	79	0	16
Cpu	104	105	0	6
House	256	250	1	12
Mpg	192	200	6	3
Servo	88	79	10	2

3.2 PERFORMANCE

The test results are presented in fig. 1. On the **servo** domain the Monte Carlo method is uniformly better than all other methods, although the difference should probably not always be considered statistically significant. The Monte Carlo method generally does well for the smallest training sets. Note that no single method does well on all these tasks. The Monte Carlo method is never vastly out-performed by the other methods.

The geometric mean of the performances over all 5 domains for the the 4 different training set sizes is computed. Assuming a Gaussian distribution of prediction errors, the log of the error variance can (apart from normalising constants) be interpreted as the amount of information unexplained by the models. Thus, the log of the geometric means in fig. 1 give the average information unexplained by the models. According to this measure the Monte Carlo method does best, closely followed by the Gaussian Process method. Note that MARS is the worst, even though the decision between pairwise and full interactions were made on the basis of the test errors.

4 CONCLUSIONS

I have outlined a black-box Monte Carlo implementation of Bayesian learning in neural networks, and shown that it has an excellent performance. These results suggest that Monte Carlo based Bayesian methods are serious competitors for practical prediction tasks on data limited domains.

Acknowledgements

I am grateful to Radford Neal for his generosity with insight and software. This research was funded by a grant to G. Hinton from the Institute for Robotics and Intelligent Systems.

References

S. Duane, A. D. Kennedy, B. J. Pendleton & D. Roweth (1987) "Hybrid Monte Carlo", *Physics Letters B*, vol. 195, pp. 216–222.

J. H. Friedman (1991) "Multivariate adaptive regression splines" (with discussion), *Annals of Statistics*, 19, 1-141 (March). Source: http://lib.stat.cmu.edu/general/mars3.5.

D. J. C. MacKay (1992) "A practical Bayesian framework for backpropagation networks", *Neural Computation*, vol. 4, pp. 448–472.

R. M. Neal (1995) *Bayesian Learning for Neural Networks*, PhD thesis, Dept. of Computer Science, University of Toronto, ftp: pub/radford/thesis.ps.Z from ftp.cs.toronto.edu.

J. R. Quinlan (1993) "Combining instance-based and model-based learning", *Proc. ML'93* (ed P.E. Utgoff), San Mateo: Morgan Kaufmann.

C. K. I. Williams & C. E. Rasmussen (1996). "Regression with Gaussian processes", *NIPS 8*, editors D. Touretzky, M. Mozer and M. Hesselmo. (this volume).

From Isolation to Cooperation:
An Alternative View of a System of Experts

Stefan Schaal[‡*]
sschaal@cc.gatech.edu
http://www.cc.gatech.edu/fac/Stefan.Schaal

Christopher C. Atkeson[‡]
cga@cc.gatech.edu
http://www.cc.gatech.edu/fac/Chris.Atkeson

[‡]College of Computing, Georgia Tech, 801 Atlantic Drive, Atlanta, GA 30332-0280
[*]ATR Human Information Processing, 2-2 Hikaridai, Seiko-cho, Soraku-gun, 619-02 Kyoto

Abstract

We introduce a constructive, incremental learning system for regression problems that models data by means of locally linear experts. In contrast to other approaches, the experts are trained independently and do not compete for data during learning. Only when a prediction for a query is required do the experts cooperate by blending their individual predictions. Each expert is trained by minimizing a penalized local cross validation error using second order methods. In this way, an expert is able to find a local distance metric by adjusting the size and shape of the receptive field in which its predictions are valid, and also to detect relevant input features by adjusting its bias on the importance of individual input dimensions. We derive asymptotic results for our method. In a variety of simulations the properties of the algorithm are demonstrated with respect to interference, learning speed, prediction accuracy, feature detection, and task oriented incremental learning.

1. INTRODUCTION

Distributing a learning task among a set of experts has become a popular method in computational learning. One approach is to employ several experts, each with a *global* domain of expertise (e.g., Wolpert, 1990). When an output for a given input is to be predicted, every expert gives a prediction together with a confidence measure. The individual predictions are combined into a single result, for instance, based on a confidence weighted average. Another approach—the approach pursued in this paper—of employing experts is to create experts with *local* domains of expertise. In contrast to the global experts, the local experts have little overlap or no overlap at all. To assign a local domain of expertise to each expert, it is necessary to learn an expert selection system in addition to the experts themselves. This classifier determines which expert models are used in which part of the input space. For incremental learning, competitive learning methods are usually applied. Here the experts compete for data such that they change their domains of expertise until a stable configuration is achieved (e.g., Jacobs, Jordan, Nowlan, & Hinton, 1991). The advantage of local experts is that they can have simple parameterizations, such as locally constant or locally linear models. This offers benefits in terms of analyzability, learning speed, and robustness (e.g., Jordan & Jacobs, 1994). For simple experts, however, a large number of experts is necessary to model a function. As a result, the expert selection system has to be more complicated and, thus, has a higher risk of getting stuck in local minima and/or of learning rather slowly. In incremental learning, another potential danger arises when the input distribution of the data changes. The expert selection system usually makes either implicit or explicit prior assumptions about the input data distribution. For example, in the classical mixture model (McLachlan & Basford, 1988) which was employed in several local expert approaches, the prior probabilities of each mixture model can be interpreted as the fraction of data points each expert expects to experience. Therefore, a change in input distribution will cause *all* experts to change their domains of expertise in order to fulfill these prior assumptions. This can lead to catastrophic interference.

In order to avoid these problems and to cope with the interference problems during incremental learning due to changes in input distribution, we suggest eliminating the competition among experts and instead isolating them during learning. Whenever some new data is experienced which is not accounted for by one of the current experts, a new expert is created. Since the experts do not compete for data with their peers, there is no reason for them to change the location of their domains of expertise. However, when it comes to making a prediction at a query point, all the experts cooperate by giving a prediction of the output together with a confidence measure. A blending of all the predictions of all experts results in the final prediction. It should be noted that these local experts combine properties of both the global and local experts mentioned previously. They act like global experts by learning independently of each other and by blending their predictions, but they act like local experts by confining themselves to a local domain of expertise, i.e., their confidence measures are large only in a local region.

The topic of data fitting with structurally simple local models (or experts) has received a great deal of attention in nonparametric statistics (e.g., Nadaraya, 1964; Cleveland, 1979; Scott, 1992, Hastie & Tibshirani, 1990). In this paper, we will demonstrate how a nonparametric approach can be applied to obtain the isolated expert network (Section 2.1), how its asymptotic properties can be analyzed (Section 2.2), and what characteristics such a learning system possesses in terms of the avoidance of interference, feature detection, dimensionality reduction, and incremental learning of motor control tasks (Section 3).

2. RECEPTIVE FIELD WEIGHTED REGRESSION

This paper focuses on regression problems, i.e., the learning of a map from $\Re^n \to \Re^m$. Each expert in our learning method, Receptive Field Weighted Regression (RFWR), consists of two elements, a locally linear model to represent the local functional relationship, and a receptive field which determines the region in input space in which the expert's knowledge is valid. As a result, a given data set will be modeled by piecewise linear elements, blended together. For 1000 noisy data points drawn from the unit interval of the function $z = \max[\exp(-10x^2), \exp(-50y^2), 1.25\exp(-5(x^2 + y^2))]$, Figure 1 illustrates an example of function fitting with RFWR. This function consists of a narrow and a wide ridge which are perpendicular to each other, and a Gaussian bump at the origin. Figure 1b shows the receptive fields which the system created during the learning process. Each experts' location is at the center of its receptive field, marked by a $\oplus$ in Figure 1b. The recep-

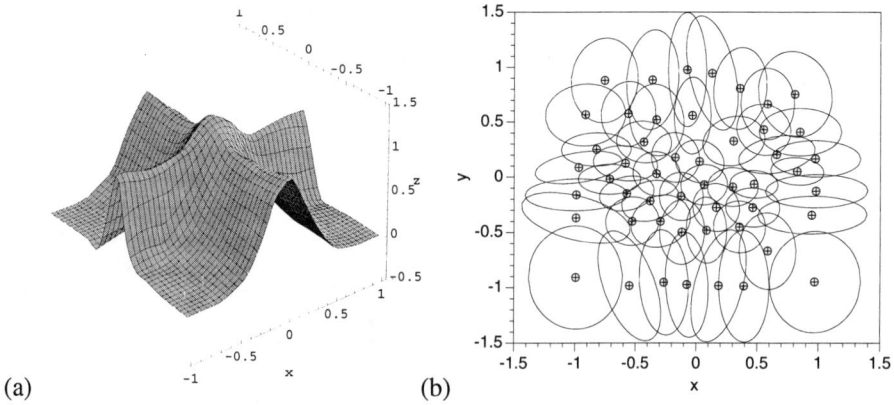

Figure 1: (a) result of function approximation with RFWR, (b) contour lines of 0.1 iso-activation of each expert in input space (the experts' centers are marked by small circles).

tive fields are modeled by Gaussian functions, and their 0.1 iso-activation lines are shown in Figure 1b as well. As can be seen, each expert focuses on a certain region of the input space, and the shape and orientation of this region reflects the function's complexity, or more precisely, the function's curvature, in this region. It should be noticed that there is a certain amount of overlap among the experts, and that the placement of experts occurred on a greedy basis during learning and is not globally optimal. The approximation result (Figure 1a) is a faithful reconstruction of the real function (MSE = 0.0025 on a test set, 30 epochs training, about 1 minute of computation on a SPARC10). As a baseline comparison, a similar result with a sigmoidal 3-layer neural network required about 100 hidden units and 10000 epochs of annealed standard backpropagation (about 4 hours on a SPARC10).

2.1 THE ALGORITHM

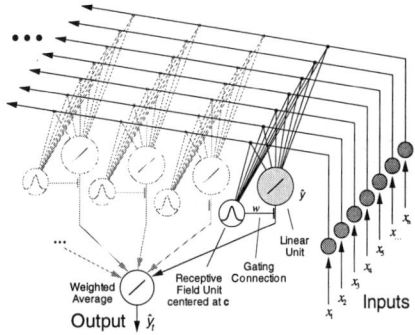

Figure 2: The RFWR network

RFWR can be sketched in network form as shown in Figure 2. All inputs connect to all expert networks, and new experts can be added as needed. Each expert is an independent entity. It consists of a two layer linear subnet and a receptive field subnet. The receptive field subnet has a single unit with a bell-shaped activation profile, centered at the fixed location $\mathbf{c}$ in input space. The maximal output of this unit is "1" at the center, and it decays to zero as a function of the distance from the center. For analytical convenience, we choose this unit to be Gaussian:

$$w = \exp\left(-\frac{1}{2}(\mathbf{x}-\mathbf{c})^T \mathbf{D}(\mathbf{x}-\mathbf{c})\right), \quad \text{where } \mathbf{D} = \mathbf{M}^T\mathbf{M} \tag{1}$$

$\mathbf{x}$ is the input vector, and $\mathbf{D}$ the distance metric, a positive definite matrix that is generated from the upper triangular matrix $\mathbf{M}$. The output of the linear subnet is:

$$\hat{y} = \mathbf{x}^T\mathbf{b} + b_0 = \tilde{\mathbf{x}}^T\boldsymbol{\beta} \tag{2}$$

The connection strengths $\mathbf{b}$ of the linear subnet and its bias b_0 will be denoted by the d-dimensional vector β from now on, and the tilde sign will indicate that a vector has been augmented by a constant "1", e.g., $\tilde{\mathbf{x}} = (\mathbf{x}^T, 1)^T$. In generating the total output, the receptive field units act as a gating component on the output, such that the total prediction is:

$$\hat{y}_t = \left(\sum_k w_k \hat{y}_k\right) \bigg/ \left(\sum_k w_k\right) \tag{3}$$

The parameters β and $\mathbf{M}$ are the primary quantities which have to be adjusted in the learning process: β forms the locally linear model, while $\mathbf{M}$ determines the shape and orientation of the receptive fields. Learning is achieved by incrementally minimizing the cost function:

$$J = \left(\sum_i w_i (y_i - \hat{y}_{i,-i})^2\right) \bigg/ \left(\sum_i w_i\right) + \gamma \sum_{n,m} D_{nm}^2 \tag{4}$$

The first term of this function is the weighted mean squared cross validation error over all experienced data points, a local cross validation measure (Schaal & Atkeson, 1994). The second term is a regularization or penalty term. Local cross validation by itself is consistent, i.e., with an increasing amount of data, the size of the receptive field of an expert would shrink to zero. This would require the creation of an ever increasing number of experts during the course of learning. The penalty term introduces some non-vanishing bias in each expert such that its receptive field size does not shrink to zero. By penalizing the squared coefficients of $\mathbf{D}$, we are essentially penalizing the second derivatives of the function at the site of the expert. This is similar to the approaches taken in spline fitting (deBoor, 1978) and acts as a low-pass filter: the higher the second derivatives, the more smoothing (and thus bias) will be introduced. This will be analyzed further in Section 2.2.

The update equations for the linear subnet are the standard weighted recursive least squares equation with forgetting factor λ (Ljung & Söderström, 1986):

$$\beta^{n+1} = \beta^n + w\mathbf{P}^{n+1}\tilde{\mathbf{x}}e_{cv}, \text{ where } \mathbf{P}^{n+1} = \frac{1}{\lambda}\left(\mathbf{P}^n - \frac{\mathbf{P}^n\tilde{\mathbf{x}}\tilde{\mathbf{x}}^T\mathbf{P}^n}{\lambda/w + \tilde{\mathbf{x}}^T\mathbf{P}^n\tilde{\mathbf{x}}}\right) \text{ and } e_{cv} = \left(y - \tilde{\mathbf{x}}^T\beta^n\right) \quad (5)$$

This is a Newton method, and it requires maintaining the matrix $\mathbf{P}$, which is size $0.5d \times (d+1)$. The update of the receptive field subnet is a gradient descent in J:

$$\mathbf{M}^{n+1} = \mathbf{M}^n - \alpha\,\partial J/\partial \mathbf{M} \quad (6)$$

Due to space limitations, the derivation of the derivative in (6) will not be explained here. The major ingredient is to take this derivative as in a batch update, and then to reformulate the result as an iterative scheme. The derivatives in batch mode can be calculated exactly due to the Sherman-Morrison-Woodbury theorem (Belsley, Kuh, & Welsch, 1980; Atkeson, 1992). The derivative for the incremental update is a very good approximation to the batch update and realizes incremental local cross validation.

A new expert is initialized with a default $\mathbf{M}_{def}$ and all other variables set to zero, except the matrix $\mathbf{P}$. $\mathbf{P}$ is initialized as a diagonal matrix with elements $1/r_i^2$, where the r_i are usually small quantities, e.g., 0.01. The r_i are ridge regression parameters. From a probabilistic view, they are Bayesian priors that the β vector is the zero vector. From an algorithmic view, they are fake data points of the form $[\mathbf{x} = (0,...,r_i^2,0,...)^T, y = 0]$ (Atkeson, Moore, & Schaal, submitted). Using the update rule (5), the influence of the ridge regression parameters would fade away due to the forgetting factor λ. However, it is useful to make the ridge regression parameters adjustable. As in (6), r_i can be updated by gradient descent:

$$r_i^{n+1} = r_i^n - \alpha\,\partial J/\partial r_i \quad (7)$$

There are d ridge regression parameters, one for each diagonal element of the $\mathbf{P}$ matrix. In order to add in the update of the ridge parameters as well as to compensate for the forgetting factor, an iterative procedure based on (5) can be devised which we omit here. The computational complexity of this update is much reduced in comparison to (5) since many computations involve multiplications by zero.

```
Initialize the RFWR network with no expert;
For every new training sample (x,y):
  a)    For k=1 to #experts:
          – calculate the activation from (1)
          – update the expert's parameters according to (5), (6), and (7)
        end;
  b)    If no expert was activated by more than w_gen:
          – create a new expert with c=x
        end;
  c)    If two experts are activated more than w_prune:
          – erase the expert with the smaller receptive field
        end;
  d)    calculate the mean, err_mean, and standard deviation err_std of the
        incrementally accumulated error err_k of all experts;
  e)    For k=1 to #experts:
          If (|err_k – err_mean| > θ err_std) reinitialize expert k with M = 2 * M_def
        end;
end;
```

In sum, a RFWR expert consists of three sets of parameters, one for the locally linear model, one for the size and shape of the receptive fields, and one for the bias. The linear model parameters are updated by a Newton method, while the other parameters are updated by gradient descent. In our implementations, we actually use second order gradient descent based on Sutton (1992), since, with minor extra effort, we can obtain estimates of the second derivatives of the cost function with respect to all parameters. Finally, the logic of RFWR becomes as shown in the pseudo-code above. Point c) and e) of the algorithm introduce a pruning facility. Pruning takes place either when two experts overlap too much, or when an expert has an exceptionally large mean squared error. The latter method corresponds to a simple form of outlier detection. Local optimization of a distance metric always has a minimum for a very large receptive field size. In our case, this would mean that an expert favors global instead of locally linear regression. Such an expert will accumulate a very large error which can easily be detected

2.2 ASYMPTOTIC BIAS AND PENALTY SELECTION

The penalty term in the cost function (4) introduces bias. In order to assess the asymptotic value of this bias, the real function $f(\mathbf{x})$, which is to be learned, is assumed to be represented as a Taylor series expansion at the center of an expert's receptive field. Without loss of generality, the center is assumed to be at the origin in input space. We furthermore assume that the size and shape of the receptive field are such that terms higher than $O(2)$ are negligible. Thus, the cost (4) can be written as:

$$J \approx \left(\int_{-\infty}^{+\infty} w \left(f_o + \mathbf{f}^T \mathbf{x} + \frac{1}{2} \mathbf{x}^T \mathbf{F} \mathbf{x} - b_o - \mathbf{b}^T \mathbf{x} \right)^2 d\mathbf{x} \right) \bigg/ \left(\int_{-\infty}^{+\infty} w \, d\mathbf{x} \right) + \gamma \sum_{n,m} D_{nm} \qquad (8)$$

where f_o, $\mathbf{f}$, and $\mathbf{F}$ denote the constant, linear, and quadratic terms of the Taylor series expansion, respectively. Inserting Equation (1), the integrals can be solved analytically after the input space is rotated by an orthonormal matrix transforming $\mathbf{F}$ to the diagonal matrix $\mathbf{F}'$. Subsequently, b_o, $\mathbf{b}$, and $\mathbf{D}$ can be determined such that J is minimized:

$$b_0^* = f_o + bias = f_o + \frac{\gamma^{0.25}}{2^{0.75}} \sum_n \left(sgn(F'_{nn}) \sqrt{|F'_{nn}|} \right), \quad \mathbf{b}^* = \mathbf{f}, \quad D'^*_{nn} = \frac{\sqrt{|F'_{nn}|}}{(2\gamma)^2} \qquad (9)$$

This states that the linear model will asymptotically acquire the correct locally linear model, while the constant term will have bias proportional to the square root of the sum of the eigenvalues of $\mathbf{F}$, i.e., the F'_{nn}. The distance metric $\mathbf{D}$, whose diagonalized counterpart is $\mathbf{D}'$, will be a scaled image of the Hessian $\mathbf{F}$ with an additional square root distortion. Thus, the penalty term accomplishes the intended task: it introduces more smoothing the higher the curvature at an expert's location is, and it prevents the receptive field of an expert shrinking to zero size (which would obviously happen for $\gamma \to 0$). Additionally, Equation (9) shows how to determine γ for a given learning problem from an estimate of the eigenvalues and a permissible bias. Finally, it is possible to derive estimates of the bias and the mean squared error of each expert from the current distance metric $\mathbf{D}$:

$$bias_{est} = \sqrt{0.5\gamma \sum_n [eigenvalues(D)]_n} \; ; \quad err^2_{est} = \gamma \sum_{n,m} D^2_{nm} \qquad (10)$$

The latter term was incorporated in the mean squared error, err, in Section 2.1. Empirical evaluations (not shown here) verified the validity of these asymptotic results.

3. SIMULATION RESULTS

This section will demonstrate some of the properties of RFWR. In all simulations, the threshold parameters of the algorithm were set to $\theta = 3.5$, $w_{prune} = 0.9$, and $w_{min} = 0.1$. These quantities determine the overlap of the experts as well as the outlier removal threshold; the results below are not affected by moderate changes in these parameters.

3.1 AVOIDING INTERFERENCE

In order to test RFWR's sensitivity with respect to changes in input data distribution, the data of the example of Figure 1 was partitioned into three separate training sets $T_1 = \{(x,y,z) | -1.0 < x < -0.2\}$, $T_2 = \{(x,y,z) | -0.4 < x < 0.4\}$, $T_3 = \{(x,y,z) | 0.2 < x < 1.0\}$. These data sets correspond to three overlapping stripes of data, each having about 400 uniformly distributed samples. From scratch, a RFWR network was trained first on T_1 for 20 epochs, then on T_2 for 20 epochs, and finally on T_3 for 20 epochs. The penalty was chosen as in the example of Figure 1 to be $\gamma = 1.e - 7$, which corresponds to an asymptotic bias of

0.1 at the sharp ridge of the function. The default distance metric **D** was 50***I**, where **I** is the identity matrix. Figure 3 shows the results of this experiment. Very little interference can be found. The MSE on the test set increased from 0.0025 (of the original experiment of Figure 1) to 0.003, which is still an excellent reconstruction of the real function.

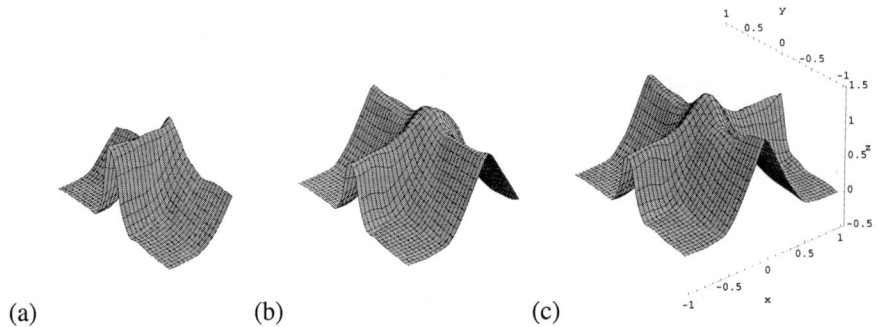

(a)   (b)   (c)

Figure 3: Reconstructed function after training on (a) T_1, (b) then T_2, (c) and finally T_3.

3.2 LOCAL FEATURE DETECTION

The examples of RFWR given so far did not require ridge regression parameters. Their importance, however, becomes obvious when dealing with locally rank deficient data or with irrelevant input dimensions. A learning system should be able to recognize irrelevant input dimensions. It is important to note that this cannot be accomplished by a distance metric. The distance metric is only able to decide to what spatial extent averaging over data in a certain dimension should be performed. However, the distance metric has no means to exclude an input dimension. In contrast, bias learning with ridge regression parameters is able to exclude input dimensions. To demonstrate this, we added 8 purely noisy inputs (N(0,0.3)) to the data drawn from the function of Figure 1. After 30 epochs of training on a 10000 data point training set, we analyzed histograms of the order of magnitude of the ridge regression parameters in all 10+bias input dimensions over all the 79 experts that had been generated by the learning algorithm. All experts recognized that the input dimensions 3 to 8 did not contain relevant information, and correctly increased the corresponding ridge parameters to large values. The effect of a large ridge regression parameter is that the associated regression coefficient becomes zero. In contrast, the ridge parameters of the inputs 1, 2, and the bias input remained very small. The MSE on the test set was 0.0026, basically identical to the experiment with the original training set.

3.3 LEARNING AN INVERSE DYNAMICS MODEL OF A ROBOT ARM

Robot learning is one of the domains where incremental learning plays an important role. A real movement system experiences data at a high rate, and it should incorporate this data immediately to improve its performance. As learning is task oriented, input distributions will also be task oriented and interference problems can easily arise. Additionally, a real movement system does not sample data from a training set but rather has to move in order to receive new data. Thus, training data is always temporally correlated, and learning must be able to cope with this. An example of such a learning task is given in Figure 4 where a simulated 2 DOF robot arm has to learn to draw the figure "8" in two different regions of the work space at a moderate speed (1.5 sec duration). In this example, we assume that the correct movement plan exists, but that the inverse dynamics model which is to be used to control this movement has not been acquired. The robot is first trained for 10 minutes (real movement time) in the region of the lower target trajectory where it performs a variety of rhythmic movements under simple PID control. The initial performance of this controller is shown in the bottom part of Figure 4a. This training enables the robot to learn the locally appropriate inverse dynamics model, a $\Re^6 \rightarrow \Re^2$ continuous mapping. Subsequent per-

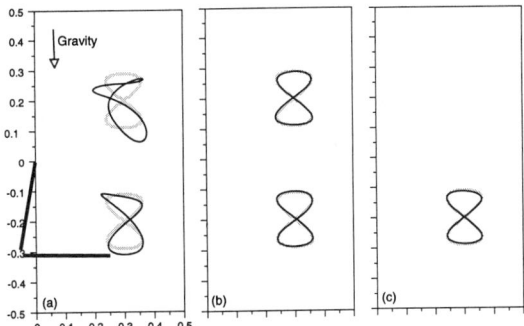

Figure 4: Learning to draw the figure "8" with a 2-joint arm: (a) Performance of a PID controller before learning (the dimmed lines denote the desired trajectories, the solid lines the actual performance); (b) Performance after learning using a PD controller with feedforward commands from the learned inverse model; (c) Performance of the learned controller after training on the upper "8" of (b) (see text for more explanations).

formance using this inverse model for control is depicted in the bottom part of Figure 4b. Afterwards, the same training takes place in the region of the upper target trajectory in order to acquire the inverse model in this part of the world. The figure "8" can then equally well be drawn there (upper part of Figure 4a,b). Switching back to the bottom part of the work space (Figure 4c), the first task can still be performed as before. No interference is recognizable. Thus, the robot could learn fast and reliably to fulfill the two tasks. It is important to note that the data generated by the training movements did not always have locally full rank. All the parameters of RFWR were necessary to acquire the local inverse model appropriately. A total of 39 locally linear experts were generated.

4. DISCUSSION

We have introduced an incremental learning algorithm, RFWR, which constructs a network of isolated experts for supervised learning of regression tasks. Each expert determines a locally linear model, a local distance metric, and local bias parameters by incrementally minimizing a penalized local cross validation error. Our algorithm differs from other local learning techniques by entirely avoiding competition among the experts, and by being based on nonparametric instead of parametric statistics. The resulting properties of RFWR are a) avoidance of interference in the case of changing input distributions, b) fast incremental learning by means of Newton and second order gradient descent methods, c) analyzable asymptotic properties which facilitate the selection of the fit parameters, and d) local feature detection and dimensionality reduction. The isolated experts are also ideally suited for parallel implementations. Future work will investigate computationally less costly delta-rule implementations of RFWR, and how well RFWR scales in higher dimensions.

5. REFERENCES

Atkeson, C. G., Moore, A. W., & Schaal, S. (submitted). "Locally weighted learning." *Artificial Intelligence Review*.

Atkeson, C. G. (1992). "Memory-based approaches to approximating continuous functions." In: Casdagli, M., & Eubank, S. (Eds.), *Nonlinear Modeling and Forecasting*, pp.503-521. Addison Wesley.

Belsley, D. A., Kuh, E., & Welsch, R. E. (1980). *Regression diagnostics: Identifying influential data and sources of collinearity*. New York: Wiley.

Cleveland, W. S. (1979). "Robust locally weighted regression and smoothing scatterplots." *J. American Stat. Association*, 74, pp.829-836.

de Boor, C. (1978). *A practical guide to splines*. New York: Springer.

Hastie, T. J., & Tibshirani, R. J. (1990). *Generalized additive models*. London: Chapman and Hall.

Jacobs, R. A., Jordan, M. I., Nowlan, S. J., & Hinton, G. E. (1991). "Adaptive mixtures of local experts." *Neural Computation*, 3, pp.79-87.

Jordan, M. I., & Jacobs, R. (1994). "Hierarchical mixtures of experts and the EM algorithm." *Neural Computation*, 6, pp.79-87.

Ljung, L., & S_derstr_m, T. (1986). *Theory and practice of recursive identification*. Cambridge, MIT Press.

McLachlan, G. J., & Basford, K. E. (1988). *Mixture models*. New York: Marcel Dekker.

Nadaraya, E. A. (1964). "On estimating regression." *Theor. Prob. Appl.*, 9, pp.141-142.

Schaal, S., & Atkeson, C. G. (1994b). "Assessing the quality of learned local models." In: Cowan, J. , Tesauro, G., & Alspector, J. (Eds.), *Advances in Neural Information Processing Systems 6*. Morgan Kaufmann.

Scott, D. W. (1992). *Multivariate Density Estimation*. New York: Wiley.

Sutton, R. S. (1992). "Gain adaptation beats least squares." In: *Proc. of 7th Yale Workshop on Adaptive and Learning Systems*, New Haven, CT.

Wolpert, D. H. (1990). "Stacked genealization." Los Alamos Technical Report LA-UR-90-3460.

Finite State Automata that Recurrent Cascade-Correlation Cannot Represent

Stefan C. Kremer
Department of Computing Science
University of Alberta
Edmonton, Alberta, CANADA T6H 5B5

Abstract

This paper relates the computational power of Fahlman's Recurrent Cascade Correlation (RCC) architecture to that of finite state automata (FSA). While some recurrent networks are FSA equivalent, RCC is not. The paper presents a theoretical analysis of the RCC architecture in the form of a proof describing a large class of FSA which cannot be realized by RCC.

1 INTRODUCTION

Recurrent networks can be considered to be defined by two components: a network architecture, and a learning rule. The former describes how a network with a given set of weights and topology computes its output values, while the latter describes how the weights (and possibly topology) of the network are updated to fit a specific problem. It is possible to evaluate the computational power of a network architecture by analyzing the types of computations a network could perform assuming appropriate connection weights (and topology). This type of analysis provides an upper bound on what a network can be expected to learn, since no system can learn what it cannot represent.

Many recurrent network architectures have been proven to be finite state automaton or even Turing machine equivalent (see for example [Alon, 1991], [Goudreau, 1994], [Kremer, 1995], and [Siegelmann, 1992]). The existence of such equivalence proofs naturally gives confidence in the use of the given architectures.

This paper relates the computational power of Fahlman's Recurrent Cascade Correlation architecture [Fahlman, 1991] to that of finite state automata. It is organized as follows: Section 2 reviews the RCC architecture as proposed by Fahlman. Section 3 describes finite state automata in general and presents some specific automata which will play an important role in the discussions which follow. Section 4 describes previous work by other authors evaluating RCC's computational power. Section 5 expands upon the previous work, and presents a new class of automata which cannot be represented by RCC. Section 6 further expands the result of the previous section to identify an infinite number of other unrealizable classes of automata. Section 7 contains some concluding remarks.

2 THE RCC ARCHITECTURE

The RCC architecture consists of three types of units: input units, hidden units and output units. After training, a RCC network performs the following computation: First, the activation values of the hidden units are initialized to zero. Second, the input unit activation values are initialized based upon the input signal to the network. Third, each hidden unit computes its new activation value. Fourth, the output units compute their new activations. Then, steps two through four are repeated for each new input signal.

The third step of the computation, computing the activation value of a hidden unit, is accomplished according to the formula:

$$a_j(t+1) = \sigma\left(\sum_{i=1}^{j-1} W_{ij} a_i(t+1) + W_{jj} a_j(t)\right).$$

Here, $a_i(t)$ represents the activation value of unit i at time t, $\sigma(\bullet)$ represents a sigmoid squashing function with finite range (usually from 0 to 1), and W_{ij} represents the weight of the connection from unit i to unit j. That is, each unit computes its activation value by multiplying the new activations of all lowered numbered units and its own previous activation by a set of weights, summing these products, and passing the sum through a logistic activation function. The recurrent weight W_{jj} from a unit to itself functions as a sort of memory by transmitting a modulated version of the unit's old activation value.

The output units of the RCC architecture can be viewed as special cases of hidden units which have weights of value zero for all connections originating from other output units. This interpretation implies that any restrictions on the computational powers of general hidden units will also apply to the output units. For this reason, we shall concern ourselves exclusively with hidden units in the discussions which follow.

Finally, it should be noted that since this paper is about the representational power of the RCC architecture, its associated learning rule will not be discussed here. The reader wishing to know more about the learning rule, or requiring a more detailed description of the operation of the RCC architecture, is referred to [Fahlman, 1991].

3 FINITE STATE AUTOMATA

A Finite State Automaton (FSA) [Hopcroft, 1979] is a formal computing machine defined by a 5-tuple $M=(Q,\Sigma,\delta,q_0,F)$, where Q represents a finite set of states, Σ a finite input alphabet, δ a state transition function mapping $Q \times \Sigma$ to Q, $q_0 \in Q$ the initial state, and $F \subset Q$ a set of final or accepting states. FSA accept or reject strings of input symbols according to the following computation: First, the FSA's current state is initialized to q_0. Second, the next inut symbol of the str ing, selected from Σ, is presented to the automaton by the outside world. Third, the transition function, δ, is used to compute the FSA's new state based upon the input symbol, and the FSA's previous state. Fourth, the acceptability of the string is computed by comparing the current FSA state to the set of valid final states, F. If the current state is a member of F then the automaton is said to accept the string of input symbols presented so far. Steps two through four are repeated for each input symbol presented by the outside world. Note that the steps of this computation mirror the steps of an RCC network's computation as described above.

It is often useful to describe specific automata by means of a *transition diagram* [Hopcroft, 1979]. Figure 1 depicts the transition diagrams of five FSA. In each case, the states, Q, are depicted by circles, while the transitions defined by δ are represented as arrows from the old state to the new state labelled with the appropriate input symbol. The arrow labelled "Start" indicates the initial state, q_0; and final accepting states are indicated by double circles.

We now define some terms describing particular FSA which we will require for the following proof. The first concerns input signals which oscillate. Intuitively, the input signal to a FSA oscillates if every p^{th} symbol is repeated for $p>1$. More formally, a sequence of input symbols, $s(t)$, $s(t+1)$, $s(t+2)$, ..., oscillates with a period of p if and only if p is the minimum value such that: $\forall t \; s(t)=s(t+p)$.

Our second definition concerns oscillations of a FSA's internal state, when the machine is presented a certain sequence of input signals. Intuitively, a FSA's internal state can oscillate in response to a given input sequence if there is some starting state for which every subsequent ω^{th} state is repeated. Formally, a FSA's state can oscillate with a period of ω in response to a sequence of input symbols, $s(t)$, $s(t+1)$, $s(t+2)$, ..., if and only if ω is the minimum value for which:

$$\exists q_0 \text{ s.t. } \forall t \; \delta(q_0, s(t)) = \delta(\ldots \delta(\delta(\delta(q_0, s(t)), s(t+1)), s(t+2)), \ldots , s(t+\omega))$$

The recursive nature of this formulation is based on the fact a FSA's state depends on its previous state, which in turn depends on the state before, etc..

We can now apply these two definitions to the FSA displayed in Figure 1. The automaton labelled "a)" has a state which oscillates with a period of $\omega=2$ in response to any sequence consisting of 0s and 1s (e.g. "00000...", "11111....", "010101...", etc.). Thus, we can say that it has a state cycle of period $\omega=2$ (i.e. $q_0q_1q_0q_1...$), when its input cycles with a period of $p=1$ (i.e. "0000..."). Similarly, when automaton b)'s input cycles with period $p=1$ (i.e. "000000..."), its state will cycle with period $\omega=3$ (i.e. $q_0q_1q_2q_0q_1q_2...$).

For automaton c), things are somewhat more complicated. When the input is the sequence "0000...", the state sequence will either be $q_0q_0q_0q_0...$ or $q_1q_1q_1q_1...$ depending on the initial state. On the other hand, when the input is the sequence "1111...", the state sequence will alternate between q_0 and q_1. Thus, we say that automaton c) has a state cycle of $\omega=2$ when its input cycles with period $p=1$. But, this automaton can also have larger state cycles. For example, when the input oscillates with a period $p=2$ (i.e. "01010101..."), then the state of the automaton will oscillate with a period $\omega=4$ (i.e. $q_0q_0q_1q_1q_0q_0q_1q_1...$). Thus, we can also say that automaton c) has a state cycle of $\omega=4$ when its input cycles with period $p=2$.

The remaining automata also have state cycles for various input cycles, but will not be discussed in detail. The importance of the relationship between input period (p) and the state period (ω) will become clear shortly.

4 PREVIOUS RESULTS CONCERNING THE COMPUTATIONAL POWER OF RCC

The first investigation into the computational powers of RCC was performed by Giles et. al. [Giles, 1995]. These authors proved that the RCC architecture, regardless of connection weights and number of hidden units, is incapable of representing any FSA which "for the same input has an output period greater than 2" (p. 7). Using our oscillation definitions above, we can re-express this result as: if a FSA's input oscillates with a period of $p=1$ (i.e. input is constant), then its state can oscillate with a period of at most $\omega=2$. As already noted, Figure 1b) represents a FSA whose state oscillates with a period of $\omega=3$ in response to an input which oscillates with a period of $p=1$. Thus, Giles et. al.'s theorem proves that the automaton in Figure 1b) cannot be implemented (and hence learned) by a RCC network.

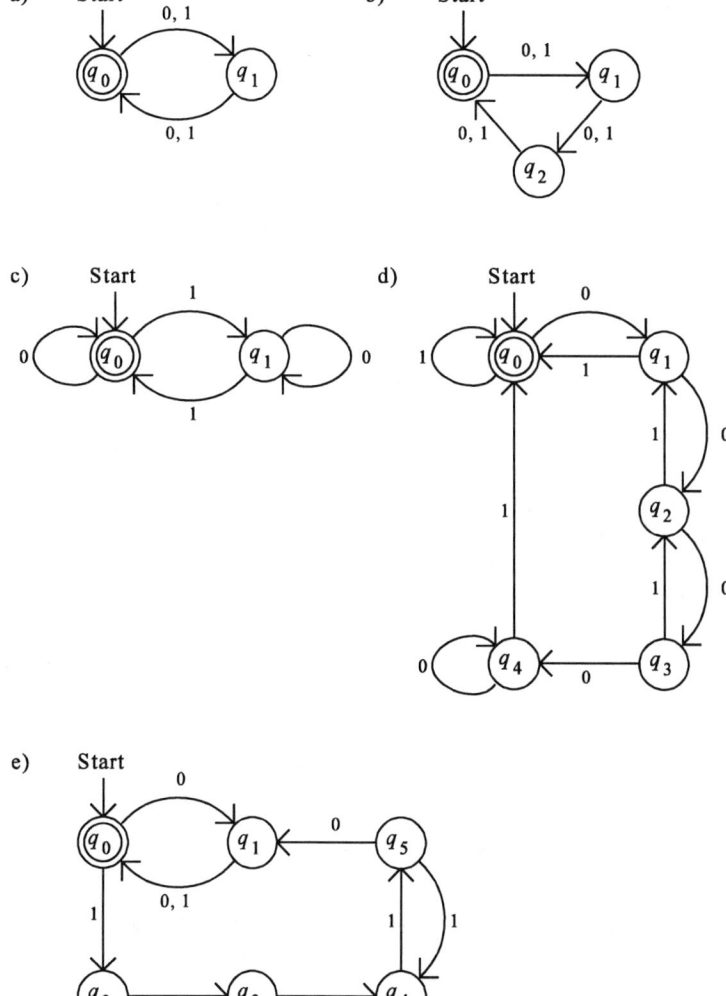

Figure 1: Finite State Automata.

Giles et. al. also examined the automata depicted in Figures 1a) and 1c). However, unlike the formal result concerning FSA b), the authors' conclusions about these two automata were of an empirical nature. In particular, the authors noted that while automata which oscillated with a period of 2 under constant input (i.e. Figure 1a)) were realizable, the automaton of 1c) appeared not be be realizable by RCC. Giles et. al. could not account for this last observation by a formal proof.

5 AUTOMATA WITH CYCLES UNDER ALTERNATING INPUT

We now turn our attention to the question: why is a RCC network unable to learn the automaton of 1c)? We answer this question by considering what would happen if 1c) were realizable. In particular, suppose that the input units of a RCC network which implements automaton 1c) are replaced by the hidden units of a RCC network implementing 1a). In this situation, the hidden units of 1a) will oscillate with a period of 2 under constant input. But if the inputs to 1c) oscillate with a period of 2, then the state of 1c) will oscillate with a period of 4. Thus, the combined network's state would oscillate with a period of four under constant input. Furthermore, the cascaded connectivity scheme of the RCC architecture implies that a network constructed by treating one network's hidden units as the input units of another, would not violate any of the connectivity constraints of RCC. In other words, if RCC could implement the automaton of 1c), then it would also be able to implement a network which oscillates with a period of 4 under constant input. Since Giles et. al. proved that the latter cannot be the case, it must also be the case that RCC cannot implement the automaton of 1c).

The line of reasoning used here to prove that the FSA of Figure 1c) is unrealizable can also be applied to many other automata. In fact, any automaton whose state oscillates with a period of more than 2 under input which oscillates with a period 2, could be used to construct one of the automata proven to be illegal by Giles. This implies that RCC cannot implement any automaton whose state oscillates with a period of greater than $\omega=2$ when its input oscillates with a period of $p=2$.

6 AUTOMATA WITH CYCLES UNDER OSCILLATING INPUT

Giles et. al.'s theorem can be viewed as defining a class of automata which cannot be implemented by the RCC architecture. The proof in Section 5 adds another class of automata which also cannot be realized. More precisely, the two proofs concern inputs which oscillate with periods of one and two respectively. It is natural to ask whether further proofs for state cycles can be developed when the input oscillates with a period of greater than two. We now present the central theorem of this paper, a unified definition of unrealizable automata:

Theorem: If the input signal to a RCC network oscillates with a period, p, then the network can represent only those FSA whose outputs form cycles of length ω, where $p \bmod \omega = 0$ if p is even and $2p \bmod \omega = 0$ if p is odd.

To prove this theorem we will first need to prove a simpler one relating the rate of oscillation of the input signal to one node in an RCC network to the rate of oscillation of that node's output signal. By "the input signal to one node" we mean the weighted sum of all activations of all connected nodes (i.e. all input nodes, and all lower numbered hidden nodes), but not the recurrent signal. I.e.:

$$\lambda(t+1) = \sum_{i=1}^{j-1} W_{ij} a_i(t+1) .$$

Using this definition, it is possible to rewrite the equation to compute the activation of node j (given in Section 2) as:

$$a_j(t+1) = \sigma(\lambda(t+1) + W_{jj} a_j(t)) .$$

But if we assume that the input signal oscillates with a period of p, then every value of $\lambda(t+1)$ can be replaced by one of a finite number of input signals ($\lambda_0, \lambda_1, \lambda_2, \ldots \lambda_{p-1}$). In other words, $\lambda(t+1) = \lambda_{t \bmod p}$. Using this substitution, it is possible to repeatedly expand the addend of the previous equation to derive the formula:

$$a_j(t+1) = \sigma(\lambda_{t \bmod p} + W_{jj} \cdot \\ \sigma(\lambda_{(t-1) \bmod p} + W_{jj} \cdot \\ \sigma(\lambda_{(t-2) \bmod p} + W_{jj} \cdot \ldots \sigma(\lambda_{(t-p+1) \bmod p} + W_{jj} \cdot a_j(t-p+1)) \ldots)))$$

The unravelling of the recursive equation now allows us to examine the relationship between $a_j(t+1)$ and $a_j(t-p+1)$. Specifically, we note that if $W_{jj} > 0$ or if p is even then $a_j(t+1) = f(a_j(t-p+1))$ implies that f is a monotonically increasing function. Furthermore, since σ is a function with finite range, f must also have finite range.

It is well known that for any monotonically increasing function with finite range, f, the sequence, $f(x)$, $f(f(x))$, $f(f(f(x)))$, ..., is guaranteed to monotonically approach a fixed point (where $f(x)=x$). This implies that the sequence, $a_j(t+1)$, $a_j(t+p+1)$, $a_j(t+2p+1)$, ..., must also monotonically approach a fixed point (where $a_j(t+1) = a_j(t-p+1)$). In other words, the sequence does **not** oscillate. Since every p^{th} value of $a_j(t)$ approaches a fixed point, the sequence $a_j(t)$, $a_j(t+1)$, $a_j(t+2)$, ... can have a period of at most p, and must have a period which divides p evenly. We state this as our first lemma:

Lemma 1: If $\lambda(t)$ oscillates with even period, p, or if $W_{jj} > 0$, then state unit j's activation value must oscillate with a period ω, where $p \bmod \omega = 0$.

We must now consider the case where $W_{jj} < 0$ and p is odd. In this case, $a_j(t+1) = f(a_j(t-p+1))$ implies that f is a monotonically decreasing function. But, in this situation the function $f^2(x) = f(f(x))$ must be monotonically increasing with finite range. This implies that the sequence: $a_j(t+1)$, $a_j(t+2p+1)$, $a_j(t+4p+1)$, ..., must monotonically approach a fixed point (where $a_j(t+1) = a_j(t-2p+1)$). This in turn implies that the sequence $a_j(t)$, $a_j(t+1)$, $a_j(t+2)$, ..., can have a period of at most $2p$, and must have a period which divides $2p$ evenly. Once again, we state this result in a lemma:

Lemma 2: If $\lambda(t)$ oscillates with odd period p, and if $W_{jj} < 0$, then state unit j must oscillate with a period ω, where $2p \bmod \omega = 0$.

Lemmas 1 and 2 relate the rate of oscillation of the weighted sum of input signals and lower numbered unit activations, $\lambda(t)$ to that of unit j. However, the theorem which we wish to prove relates the rate of oscillation of **only** the RCC network's input signal to the **entire** hidden unit activations. To prove the theorem, we use a proof by induction on the unit number, i:

Basis: Node $i=1$ is connected only to the network inputs. Therefore, if the input signal oscillates with period p, then node i can only oscillate with period ω, where $p \bmod \omega = 0$ if p is even and $2p \bmod \omega = 0$ if p is odd. (This follows from Lemmas 1 and 2).

Assumption: If the input signal to the network oscillates with period p, then node i can only oscillate with period ω, where $p \bmod \omega = 0$ if p is even and $2p \bmod \omega = 0$ if p is odd.

Proof: If the Assumption holds for all nodes i, then Lemmas 1 and 2 imply that it must also hold for node $i+1$. □

This proves the theorem:

Theorem: If the input signal to a RCC network oscillates with a period, p, then the network can represent only those FSA whose outputs form cycles of length ω, where $p \bmod \omega = 0$ if p is even and $2p \bmod \omega = 0$ if p is odd.

7 CONCLUSIONS

It is interesting to note that both Giles et. al.'s original proof and the constructive proof by contradiction described in Section 5 are special cases of the theorem. Specifically, Giles et. al.'s original proof concerns input cycles of length $p=1$. Applying the theorem of Section 6 proves that an RCC network can only represent those FSA whose state transitions form cycles of length ω, where $2(1) \bmod \omega = 0$, implying that state cannot oscillate with a period of greater than 2. This is exactly what Giles et. al concluded, and proves that (among others) the automaton of Figure 1b) cannot be implemented by RCC.

Similarly, the proof of Section 5 concerns input cycles of length $p=2$. Applying our theorem proves that an RCC network can only represent those machines whose state transitions form cycles of length ω, where $(2) \bmod \omega = 0$. This again implies that state cannot oscillate with a period greater than 2, which is exactly what was proven in Section 5. This proves that the automaton of Figure 1c) (among others) cannot be implemented by RCC.

In addition to unifying both the results of Giles et. al. and Section 5, the theorem of Section 6 also accounts for many other FSA which are not representable by RCC. In fact, the theorem identifies an infinite number of other classes of non-representable FSA (for $p=3, p=4, p=5, \ldots$). Each class itself of course contains an infinite number of machines. Careful examination of the automaton illustrated in Figure 1d) reveals that it contains a state cycle of length 9 ($q_0 q_1 q_2 q_1 q_2 q_3 q_2 q_3 q_4 q_0 q_1 q_2 q_1 q_2 q_3 q_2 q_3 q_4 \ldots$) in response to an input cycle of length 3 ("001001..."). Since this is not one of the allowable input/state cycle relationships defined by the theorem, it can be concluded that the automaton of Figure 1d) (among others) cannot be represented by RCC.

Finally, it should be noted that it remains unknown if the classes identified by this paper's theorem represent the complete extent of RCC's computational limitations. Consider for example the automaton of Figure 1e). This device has no input/state cycles which violate the theorem, thus we cannot conclude that it is unrepresentable by RCC. Of course, the issue of whether or not this particular automaton is representable is of little interest. However, the class of automata to which the theorem does not apply, which includes automaton 1e), requires further investigation. Perhaps all automata in this class are representable; perhaps there are other subclasses (not identified by the theorem) which RCC cannot represent. This issue will be addressed in future work.

References

N. Alon, A. Dewdney, and T. Ott, Efficient simulation of finite automata by neural nets, *Journal of the Association for Computing Machinery*, 38 (2) (1991) 495-514.

S. Fahlman, The recurrent cascade-correlation architecture, in: R. Lippmann, J. Moody and D. Touretzky, Eds., *Advances in Neural Information Processing Systems 3* (Morgan Kaufmann, San Mateo, CA, 1991) 190-196.

C.L. Giles, D. Chen, G.Z. Sun, H.H. Chen, Y.C. Lee, and M.W. Goudreau, Constructive Learning of Recurrent Neural Networks: Limitations of Recurrent Cascade Correlation and a Simple Solution, *IEEE Transactions on Neural Networks*, 6 (4) (1995) 829-836.

M. Goudreau, C. Giles, S. Chakradhar, and D. Chen, First-order v.s. second-order single layer recurrent neural networks, *IEEE Transactions on Neural Networks*, 5 (3) (1994) 511-513.

J.E. Hopcroft and J.D. Ullman, *Introduction to Automata Theory, Languages and Computation* (Addison-Wesley, Reading, MA, 1979).

S.C. Kremer, On the Computational Power of Elman-style Recurrent Networks, *IEEE Transactions on Neural Networks*, 6 (4) (1995) 1000-1004.

H.T. Siegelmann and E.D. Sontag, On the Computational Power of Neural Nets, in: *Proceedings of the Fifth ACM Workshop on Computational Learning Theory*, (ACM, New York, NY, 1992) 440-449.

SPERT-II: A Vector Microprocessor System and its Application to Large Problems in Backpropagation Training

John Wawrzynek, Krste Asanović, & Brian Kingsbury
University of California at Berkeley
Department of Electrical Engineering and Computer Sciences
Berkeley, CA 94720-1776
{johnw,krste,bedk}@cs.berkeley.edu

James Beck, David Johnson, & Nelson Morgan
International Computer Science Institute
1947 Center Street, Suite 600
Berkeley, CA 94704-1105
{beck,davidj,morgan}@icsi.berkeley.edu

Abstract

We report on our development of a high-performance system for neural network and other signal processing applications. We have designed and implemented a vector microprocessor and packaged it as an attached processor for a conventional workstation. We present performance comparisons with commercial workstations on neural network backpropagation training. The SPERT-II system demonstrates significant speedups over extensively hand-optimization code running on the workstations.

1 Introduction

We are working on pattern recognition problems using neural networks with a large number of parameters. Because of the large computational requirements of our area of research, we set out to design an integrated circuit that would serve as a good building block for our systems. Initially we considered designing extremely specialized chips, as this would maximize performance for a particular algorithm. However, the algorithms we use undergo considerable change as our research progresses. Still, we needed to provide some specialization if our design was to offer significant improvement over commercial workstation systems. Competing with workstations is a challenge to anyone designing custom programmable processors, but as will be shown in this paper, one can still provide a performance advantage by focusing on one general class of computation.

Our solution was to design a vector microprocessor, T0, optimized for fixed-point computations, and to package this as an inexpensive workstation accelerator board. In this manner, we gain a considerable performance/cost advantage for neural network and other signal processing algorithms, while leveraging the commercial workstation environment for software development and I/O services.

In this paper, we focus on the neural network applications of the SPERT-II system. We are also investigating other applications in the areas of human-machine interface and multimedia processing, as we believe vector microprocessors show promise in providing the flexible, cost-effective, high-performance computing required.

Section 2 discusses the design of the hardware, followed in Section 3 by a discussion of the software environment we are developing and a discussion of related systems in Section 4. In Section 5 we discuss how we map a backpropagation training task to the system and in Section 6 we compare the resulting performance with two commercial workstation systems.

2 SPERT-II System

SPERT-II is a double slot SBus card for use in Sun compatible workstations and is shown in Figure 1. The board contains a T0 vector microprocessor and its memory, a Xilinx FPGA device for interfacing with the host, and various system support devices.

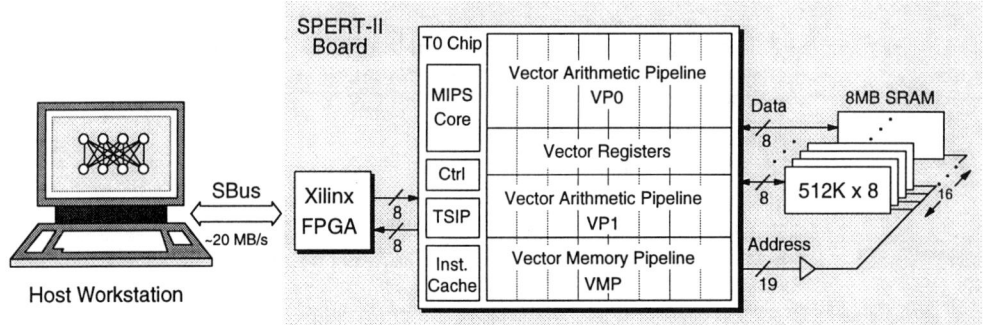

Figure 1: SPERT-II System Organization

2.1 The T0 vector microprocessor

Development of the T0 vector microprocessor follows our earlier work on the original SPERT VLIW/SIMD neuro-microprocessor (Wawrzynek, 1993). The most significant change we have made to the architecture is to move to a vector instruction set architecture (ISA), based on the industry standard MIPS RISC scalar ISA (Kane, 1992) extended with vector coprocessor instructions. The resulting ISA, which we call Torrent, offers important advantages over our previous design. We gain access to existing software tools for the MIPS architecture, including optimizing C compilers, assemblers, linkers, and debuggers. VLIW machines expose details of the hardware implementation at the instruction set level, and so must change instruction sets when scaling to higher degrees of on-chip parallelism. In contrast, vector ISAs provide a simple abstraction of regular data parallelism that enables different hardware implementations to make different trade-offs between cost and performance while remaining software compatible. Compared with the VLIW/SIMD design, the vector ISA reduces requirements on instruction cache space and fetch bandwidth. It also makes it easier to write optimized library routines in assembly language, and these library routines will still run well on future devices with greater on-chip parallelism.

In the design of the T0 vector microprocessor, the main technique we employ to improve cost-performance over a commercial general purpose processor is to integrate multiple fixed-point datapaths with a high-bandwidth memory system. Fast digital arithmetic units, multipliers in particular, require chip area proportional to the *square* of the number of operand bits. In modern microprocessors and digital signal processors a single floating-point unit takes up a significant portion of the chip area. High-precision arithmetic units also requires high memory bandwidth to move large operands. However, for a wide class of problems, full-precision floating-point, or even high-precision fixed-point arithmetic, is not needed. Studies by ourselves and others have shown that for error back-propagation training of neural networks, 16-bit weights and 8-bit activation values provide similar training performance to IEEE single-precision floating-point (Asanović, 1991).

However, fast fixed-point multiply-adds alone are not sufficient to increase performance on a wide range of problems. Other components of a complete application may dominate total compute time if only multiply-add operations are accelerated. Our processor integrates a fast general-purpose RISC core, and includes general purpose operations in its vector instruction set to obtain a balanced design.

The T0 processor is a complete single chip implementation of the Torrent architecture. It was fabricated in Hewlett-Packard's CMOS26B process using $1.0\,\mu m$ scalable CMOS design rules and two layers of metal. The die measures 16.75mm $\times$ 16.75mm, and contains 730,701 transistors. T0 runs at an internal clock rate of 40MHz.

The main components of T0 are the MIPS-II compatible RISC CPU with an on-chip instruction cache, a vector unit coprocessor, a 128-bit wide external memory interface, and an 8-bit wide serial host interface (TSIP) and control unit. The external memory interface supports up to 4 GB of memory over a 128-bit wide data bus. The current SPERT-II board uses 16, 4 Mb SRAM parts to provide 8 MB of main memory.

At the core of the T0 processor is a MIPS-II compatible 32-bit integer RISC processor with a 1 KB instruction cache. The system coprocessor provides a 32-bit counter/timer and registers for host synchronization and exception handling.

The vector unit contains a vector register file with 16 vector registers, each holding 32 elements of 32 bits each, and three vector functional units, VP0, VP1, and VMP. VP0 and VP1 are vector arithmetic functional units. With the exception of multiplies, that must execute in VP0, either pipeline can execute any arithmetic operation. The multipliers perform 16-bit $\times$ 16-bit multiplies producing 32-bit results. All other arithmetic, logical and shift functions operate on 32 bits. VMP is the vector memory unit, and it handles all vector load/store operations, scalar load/store operations, and the vector insert/extract operations.

All three vector functional units are composed of 8 parallel pipelines, and so can each produce up to 8 results per cycle. The T0 memory interface has a single memory address port, therefore non-unit stride and indexed memory operations are limited to a rate of one element per cycle.

The elements of a vector register are striped across all 8 pipelines. With the maximum vector length of 32, a vector functional unit can accept a new instruction every 4 cycles. T0 can saturate all three vector functional units by issuing one instruction per cycle to each, leaving a single issue slot every 4 cycles for the scalar unit. In this manner, T0 can sustain up to 24 operations per cycle. Several important library routines, such as matrix-vector and matrix-matrix multiplies, have been written which achieve this level of performance. All vector pipeline hazards are fully interlocked in hardware, and so instruction scheduling is only required to improve performance, not to ensure correctness.

3 SPERT-II Software Environment

The primary design goal for the SPERT-II software environment was that it should appear as similar as possible to a conventional workstation environment. This should ease the task of porting existing workstation applications, as well as provide a comfortable environment for developing new code.

The Torrent instruction set architecture is based on the MIPS-II instruction set, with extra coprocessor instructions added to access the vector unit functionality. This compatibility allows us to base our software environment on the GNU tools which already include support for MIPS based machines. We have ported the gcc C/C++ compiler, modified the gdb symbolic debugger to debug T0 programs remotely from the host, enhanced the gas assembler to understand the new vector instructions and to schedule code to avoid interlocks, and we also employ the GNU linker and other library management utilities.

Currently, the only access to the vector unit we provide is either through library routines or directly via the scheduling assembler. We have developed an extensive set of optimized vector library routines including fixed-point matrix and vector operations, function approximation through linear interpolation, and IEEE single precision floating-point emulation. The majority of the routines are written in Torrent assembler, although a parallel set of functions have been written in ANSI C to allow program development and execution on workstations. Finally, there is a standard C library containing the usual utility, I/O and scalar math routines.

After compilation and linking, a T0 executable is run on the SPERT-II board by invoking a "server" program on the host. The server loads a small operating system "kernel" into T0 memory followed by the T0 executable. While the T0 application runs, the server services I/O requests on behalf of the T0 process.

4 Related Systems

Several programmable digital neurocomputers have been constructed, most notably systems based on the CNAPS chip from Adaptive Solutions (Hammerstrom, 1990) and the SYNAPSE-1, based on the MA-16 chip from Siemens (Ramacher, 1991).

The Adaptive Solutions CNAPS-1064 chip contains a SIMD array with 64 16-bit processing elements (PEs) per chip. Systems require an external microcode sequencer. The PEs have 16-bit datapaths with a single 32-bit accumulator, and are less flexible than the T0 datapaths. This chip provides on-chip memory for 128K 16-bit weights, distributed among the individual PEs. Off-chip memory bandwidth is limited by an 8-bit port. In contrast, T0 integrates an on-chip CPU that acts as controller, and provides fast access to a external memory equally accessible by all datapaths thereby increasing the range of applications that can be run efficiently.

Like SPERT-II, the SYNAPSE-1 leverages commercial memory parts. It features an array of MA-16 chips connected to interleaved DRAM memory banks. The MA-16 chips require extensive external circuitry, including 68040 CPUs with attached arithmetic pipelines, to execute computations not supported by the MA-16 itself. The SYNAPSE-1 system is a complex and expensive multi-board design, containing several different control streams that must be carefully orchestrated to run an application. However, for some applications the MA-16 could potentially provide greater throughput than T0 as the former's more specialized architecture permits more multiply–add units on each chip.

5 Mapping Backpropagation to T0

One artificial neural network (ANN) training task that we have done is taken from a speaker-independent continuous speech recognition system. The ANN is a simple feed-forward multi-layer perceptron (MLP) with three layers. Typical MLPs have between 100–400 input units. The input layer is fully connected to a hidden layer of 100–4000 hidden units. The hidden layer is fully connected to an output layer that contains one output per phoneme, typically 56–61. The hidden units incorporate a standard sigmoid activation function. The output units compute a "soft-max" activation function. All training is "on-line", with the weight matrices updated after each pattern presentation.

All of the compute-intensive sections can be readily vectorized on T0.

Three operations are performed on the weight matrices: forward propagation, error back-propagation, and weight update. These operations are available as three standard linear algebra routines in the T0 library: vector-matrix multiply, matrix-vector multiply, and scaled outer-product accumulation, respectively.

T0 can sustain one multiply-add per cycle in each of the 8 datapath slices, and can support this with one 16-bit memory access per cycle to each datapath slice provided that vector accesses have unit stride. The loops for the matrix operations are rearranged to perform only unit-stride memory accesses, and memory bandwidth requirements are further reduced by tiling matrix accesses and reusing operands from the vector registers whenever possible.

There are a number of other operations required while handling input and output vectors and activation values. While these require only $O(n)$ computation versus the $O(n^2)$ requirements of the matrix operations, they would present a significant overhead on smaller networks if not vectorized.

The sigmoid activation function is implemented using a library piecewise-linear function approximation routine. The function approximation routine makes use of the vector indexed load operations to perform the table lookups. Although T0 can only execute vector indexed operations at the rate of one element transfer per cycle, the table lookup routine can simultaneously perform all the arithmetic operations for index calculation and linear interpolation in the vector arithmetic units, achieving a rate of one 16-bit sigmoid result every 2 cycles. Similarly, a table based vector `logadd` routine is used to implement the soft-max function, also producing one result every 2 cycles.

To simplify software porting, the MLP code uses standard IEEE single-precision floating-point for input and output values. Vector library routines convert formats to the internal fixed-point representation. These conversion routines operate at the rate of up to 1 conversion every 2 cycles.

6 Performance Evaluation

We chose two commercial RISC workstations against which to compare the performance of the SPERT-II system. The first is a SPARCstation-20/61 containing a single 60 MHz SuperSPARC+ processor with a peak performance of 60 MFLOPS, 1 MB of second level cache, and 128 MB of DRAM main memory. The SPARCstation-20/61 is representative of a current mid-range workstation. The second is an IBM RS/6000-590, containing the RIOS-2 chipset running at 72 MHz with a peak performance of 266 MFLOPS, 256 KB of primary cache, and 768 MB of DRAM main memory. The RS/6000 is representative of a current high-end workstation.

The workstation version of the code performs all input and output and all computation using IEEE single precision floating-point arithmetic. The matrix and vector operations within the backprop algorithm have been extensively hand optimized, using manual loop unrolling together with register and cache blocking.

The SPERT-II numbers are obtained for a single T0 processor running at 40 MHz with 8 MB of SRAM main memory. The SPERT-II version of the application maintains the same interface, with input and output in IEEE single precision floating-point format, but performs all MLP computation using saturating fixed-point arithmetic with 16-bit weights, 16-bit activation values, and 32-bit intermediate results. The SPERT-II timings below include the time for conversion between floating-point and fixed-point for input and output.

Figure 2 shows the performance of the three systems for a set of three-layer networks on both backpropagation training and forward propagation. For ease of presentation we use networks with the same number of units per layer. Table 1 presents performance results for two speech network architectures. The general trend we observe in these evaluations is that for small networks the three hardware systems exhibit similar performance, while for larger network sizes the SPERT-II system demonstrates a significant performance advantage. For large networks the SPERT-II system demonstrates roughly 20–30 times the performance of a SPARC20 workstation and 4–6 times the performance of the IBM RS/6000-590 workstation.

Acknowledgements

Thanks to Jerry Feldman for his contribution to the design of the SPERT-II system, Bertrand Irrisou for his work on the T0 chip, John Hauser for Torrent libraries, and John Lazzaro for his advice on chip and system building. Primary support for this work was from the ONR, URI Grant N00014-92-J-1617 and ARPA contract number N0001493-C0249. Additional support was provided by the NSF and ICSI.

SPERT-II: A Vector Microprocessor System

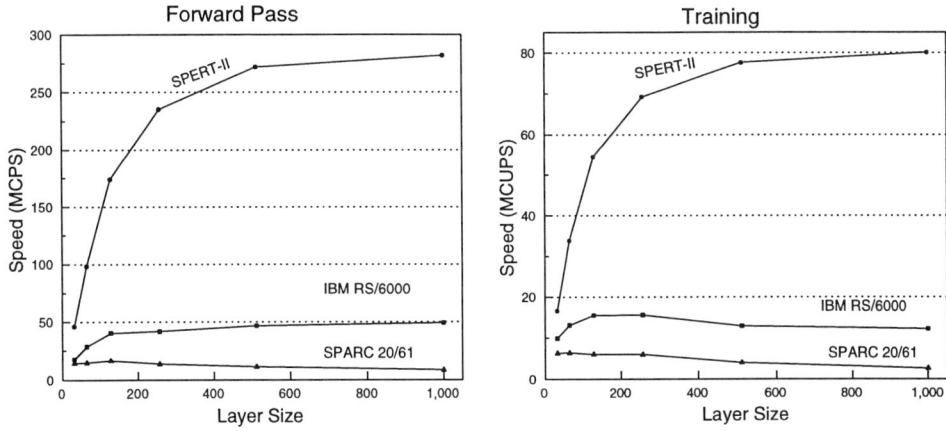

Figure 2: Performance Evaluation Results (all layers the same size).

Table 1: Performance Evaluation for Selected Net Sizes.

net type	net size (in × hidden × out)	SPERT-II	SPARC20	IBM RS/6000-590
Forward Pass (MCPS)				
small speech net	153 × 200 × 56	181	17.6	43.0
large speech net	342 × 4000 × 61	276	11.3	45.1
Training (MCUPS)				
small speech net	153 × 200 × 56	55.8	7.00	16.7
large speech net	342 × 4000 × 61	78.7	4.18	17.2

References

Krste Asanović and Nelson Morgan. Experimental Determination of Precision Requirements for Back-Propagation Training of Artificial Neural Networks. In *Proc. 2nd Intl. Conf. on Microelectronics for Neural Networks*, Munich, Oct. 1991.

D. Hammerstrom. A VLSI architecture for High-Performance, Low-Cost, On-Chip Learning. In *Proc. Intl. Joint Conf. on Neural Networks*, pages II–537–543, 1990.

G. Kane, and Heinrich, J. *MIPS RISC Architecture*. Prentice Hall, 1992.

U. Ramacher, J. Beichter, W. Raab, J. Anlauf, N. Bruls, M. Hachmann, and M. Wesseling. Design of a 1st Generation Neurocomputer. In *VLSI Design of Neural Networks*. Kluwer Academic, 1991.

J. Wawrzynek, K. Asanović, and N. Morgan. The Design of a Neuro-Microprocessor. *IEEE Journal on Neural Networks*, 4(3), 1993.

Softassign versus Softmax: Benchmarks in Combinatorial Optimization

Steven Gold
Department of Computer Science
Yale University
New Haven, CT 06520-8285

Anand Rangarajan
Dept. of Diagnostic Radiology
Yale University
New Haven, CT 06520-8042

Abstract

A new technique, termed *softassign*, is applied for the first time to two classic combinatorial optimization problems, the traveling salesman problem and graph partitioning. Softassign, which has emerged from the recurrent neural network/statistical physics framework, enforces two-way (assignment) constraints without the use of penalty terms in the energy functions. The softassign can also be generalized from two-way winner-take-all constraints to multiple membership constraints which are required for graph partitioning. The softassign technique is compared to the softmax (Potts glass). Within the statistical physics framework, softmax and a penalty term has been a widely used method for enforcing the two-way constraints common within many combinatorial optimization problems. The benchmarks present evidence that softassign has clear advantages in accuracy, speed, parallelizability and algorithmic simplicity over softmax and a penalty term in optimization problems with two-way constraints.

1 Introduction

In a series of papers in the early to mid 1980's, Hopfield and Tank introduced techniques which allowed one to solve combinatorial optimization problems with recurrent neural networks [Hopfield and Tank, 1985]. As researchers attempted to reproduce the original traveling salesman problem results of Hopfield and Tank, problems emerged, especially in terms of the quality of the solutions obtained. More recently however, a number of techniques from statistical physics have been adopted to mitigate these problems. These include deterministic annealing which convexifies the energy function in order help avoid some local minima and the Potts glass approximation which results in a hard enforcement of a one-way (one set of) winner-take-all (WTA) constraint via the softmax. In the late 80's, armed with these techniques optimization problems like the traveling salesman problem (TSP) [Peterson and Soderberg, 1989] and graph partitioning [Peterson and Soderberg, 1989, Van den Bout and Miller III, 1990] were reexamined and much better results compared to the original Hopfield-Tank dynamics were obtained.

However, when the problem calls for two-way interlocking WTA constraints, as do TSP and graph partitioning, the resulting energy function must still include a penalty term when the softmax is employed in order to enforce the second set of WTA constraints. Such penalty terms may introduce spurious local minima in the energy function and involve free parameters which are hard to set. A new technique, termed *softassign*, eliminates the need for all such penalty terms. The first use of the softassign was in an algorithm for the assignment problem [Kosowsky and Yuille, 1994]. It has since been applied to much more difficult optimization problems, including parametric assignment problems—point matching [Gold et al., 1994, Gold et al., 1995, Gold et al., 1996] and quadratic assignment problems—graph matching [Gold et al., 1996, Gold and Rangarajan, 1996, Gold, 1995].

Here, we for the first time apply the softassign to two classic combinatorial optimization problems, TSP and graph partitioning. Moreover, we show that the softassign can be generalized from two-way winner-take-all constraints to multiple membership constraints, which are required for graph partitioning (as described below). We then run benchmarks against the older softmax (Potts glass) methods and demonstrate advantages in terms of accuracy, speed, parallelizability, and simplicity of implementation.

It must be emphasized there are other conventional techniques, for solving some combinatorial optimization problems such as TSP, which remain superior to this method in certain ways [Lawler et al., 1985]. (We think for some problems—specifically the type of pattern matching problems essential for cognition [Gold, 1995]—this technique is superior to conventional methods.) Even within neural networks, elastic net methods may still be better in certain cases. However, the elastic net uses only a one-way constraint in TSP. The main goal of this paper is to provide evidence, that when minimizing energy functions within the neural network framework, which have two-way constraints, the softassign should be the technique of choice. We therefore compare it to the current dominant technique, softmax with a penalty term.

2 Optimizing With Softassign

2.1 The Traveling Salesman Problem

The traveling salesman problem may be defined in the following way. Given a set of intercity distances $\{\delta_{ab}\}$ which may take values in R^+, find the permutation matrix M such that the following objective function is minimized.

$$E_1(M) = \frac{1}{2} \sum_{a=1}^{N} \sum_{b=1}^{N} \sum_{i=1}^{N} \delta_{ab} M_{ai} M_{b(i\oplus 1)} \qquad (1)$$

subject to $\forall a \sum_{i=1}^{N} M_{ai} = 1$, $\forall i \sum_{a=1}^{N} M_{ai} = 1$, $\forall ai\ M_{ai} \in \{0,1\}$.

In the above objective δ_{ab} represents the distance between cities a and b. M is a permutation matrix whose rows represent cities, and whose columns represent the day (or order) the city was visited and N is the number of cities. (The notation $i \oplus 1$

is used to indicate that subscripts are defined modulo N, i.e. $M_{a(N+1)} = M_{a1}$.) So if $M_{ai} = 1$ it indicates that city a was visited on day i.

Then, following [Peterson and Soderberg, 1989, Yuille and Kosowsky, 1994] we employ Lagrange multipliers and an $x \log x$ barrier function to enforce the constraints, as well as a γ term for stability, resulting in the following objective:

$$E_2(M, \mu, \nu) = \frac{1}{2} \sum_{a=1}^{N} \sum_{b=1}^{N} \sum_{i=1}^{N} \delta_{ab} M_{ai} M_{b(i\oplus 1)} - \frac{\gamma}{2} \sum_{a=1}^{N} \sum_{i=1}^{N} M_{ai}^2$$
$$+ \frac{1}{\beta} \sum_{a=1}^{N} \sum_{i=1}^{N} M_{ai}(\log M_{ai} - 1) + \sum_{a=1}^{N} \mu_a(\sum_{i=1}^{N} M_{ai} - 1) + \sum_{i=1}^{N} \nu_i(\sum_{a=1}^{N} M_{ai} - 1) \quad (2)$$

In the above we are looking for a saddle point by minimizing with respect to M and maximizing with respect to μ and ν, the Lagrange multipliers.

2.2 The Softassign

In the above formulation of TSP we have two-way interlocking WTA constraints. $\{M_{ai}\}$ must be a permutation matrix to ensure that a valid tour—one in which each city is visited once and only once—is described. A permutation matrix means all the rows and columns must add to one (and the elements must be zero or one) and therefore requires two-way WTA constraints—a set of WTA constraints on the rows and a set of WTA constraints on the columns. This set of two-way constraints may also be considered assignment constraints, since each city must be assigned to one and only one day (the row constraint) and each day must be assigned to one and only one city (the column constraint).

These assignment constraints can be satisfied using a result from [Sinkhorn, 1964]. In [Sinkhorn, 1964] it is proven that any square matrix whose elements are all positive will converge to a doubly stochastic matrix just by the iterative process of alternatively normalizing the rows and columns. (A doubly stochastic matrix is a matrix whose elements are all positive and whose rows and columns all add up to one—it may roughly be thought of as the continuous analog of a permutation matrix).

The softassign simply employs Sinkhorn's technique within a deterministic annealing context. Figure 1 depicts the contrast between the softassign and the softmax. In the softmax, a one-way WTA constraint is strictly enforced by normalizing over a vector.

[Kosowsky and Yuille, 1994] used the softassign to solve the assignment problem, i.e. minimize: $-\sum_{a=1}^{A} \sum_{i=1}^{I} M_{ai} Q_{ai}$. For the special case of the quadratic assignment problem, being solved here, by setting $Q_{ai} = -\frac{\partial \tilde{E}_2}{\partial M_{ai}}$, and using the values of M from the previous iteration, we can at each iteration produce a new assignment problem for which the softassign then returns a doubly stochastic matrix. As the temperature is lowered a series of assignment problems are generated, along with the corresponding doubly stochastic matrices returned by each softassign, until a permutation matrix is reached.

The update with the partial derivative in the preceding may be derived using a Taylor series expansion. See [Gold and Rangarajan, 1996, Gold, 1995] for details.

The algorithm dynamics then become:

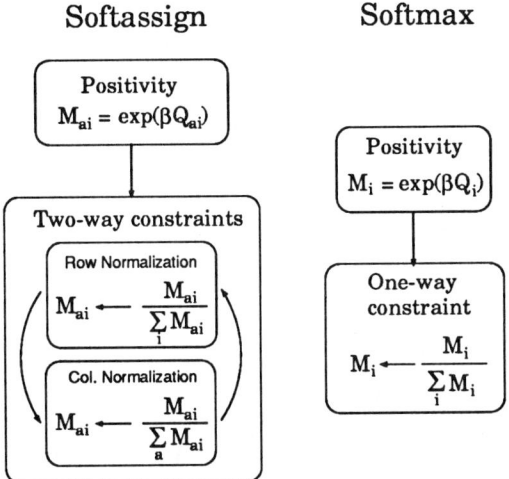

Figure 1: Softassign and softmax. This paper compares these two techniques.

$$Q_{ai} = -\frac{\partial \hat{E}_2}{\partial M_{ai}} \qquad (3)$$

$$M_{ai} = Softassign_{ai}(Q) \qquad (4)$$

$\hat{E}_2$ is E_2 without the β, μ or ν terms of (2), therefore no penalty terms are now included. The above dynamics are iterated as β, the inverse temperature, is gradually increased.

These dynamics may be obtained by evaluating the saddle points of the objective in (2). Sinkhorn's method finds the saddle points for the Lagrange parameters.

2.3 Graph Partitioning

The graph partitioning problem maybe defined in the following way. Given an unweighted graph G, find the membership matrix M such that the following objective function is minimized.

$$E_3(M) = -\sum_{a=1}^{A}\sum_{i=1}^{I}\sum_{j=1}^{I} G_{ij} M_{ai} M_{aj} \qquad (5)$$

subject to $\forall a \sum_{i=1}^{I} M_{ai} = I/A$, $\forall i \sum_{a=1}^{A} M_{ai} = 1$, $\forall ai\, M_{ai} \in \{0,1\}$ where graph G has I nodes which should be equally partitioned into A bins.

$\{G_{ij}\}$ is the adjacency matrix of the graph, whose elements must be 0 or 1. M is a membership matrix such that $M_{ai} = 1$ indicates that node i is in bin a. The permutation matrix constraint present in TSP is modified to the membership constraint. Node i is a member of only bin a and the number of members in each bin is fixed at I/A. When the above objective is at a minimum, then graph G will be partitioned into A equal sized bins, such that the cutsize is minimum for all possible partitionings of G into A equal sized bins. We assume I/A is an integer.

Then following the treatment for TSP, we derive the following objective:

$$E_4(M,\mu,\nu) = -\sum_{a=1}^{A}\sum_{i=1}^{I}\sum_{j=1}^{I} G_{ij} M_{ai} M_{aj} - \frac{\gamma}{2}\sum_{a=1}^{A}\sum_{i=1}^{I} M_{ai}^2$$
$$+\frac{1}{\beta}\sum_{a=1}^{A}\sum_{i=1}^{I} M_{ai}(\log M_{ai} - 1) + \sum_{a=1}^{A}\mu_a(\sum_{i=1}^{I} M_{ai} - I/A) + \sum_{i=1}^{I}\nu_i(\sum_{a=1}^{A} M_{ai} - 1) \quad (6)$$

which is minimized with a similar algorithm employing the softassign. Note however now in the softassign the columns are normalized to I/A instead of 1.

3 Experimental Results

Experiments on Euclidean TSP and graph partitioning were conducted. For each problem three different algorithms were run. One used the softassign described above. The second used the Potts glass dynamics employing synchronous update as described in [Peterson and Soderberg, 1989]. The third used the Potts glass dynamics employing serial update as described in [Peterson and Soderberg, 1989]. Originally the intention was to employ just the synchronous updating version of the Potts glass dynamics, since that is the dynamics used in the algorithms employing softassign and is the method that is massively parallelizable. We believe massive parallelism to be such a critical feature of the neural network architecture [Rumelhart and McClelland, 1986] that any algorithm that does not have this feature loses much of the power of the neural network paradigm. Unfortunately the synchronous updating algorithms just worked so poorly that we also ran the serial versions in order to get a more extensive comparison. Note that the results reported in [Peterson and Soderberg, 1989] were all with the serial versions.

3.1 Euclidean TSP Experiments

Figure 2 shows the results of the Euclidean TSP experiments. 500 different 100-city tours from points uniformly generated in the 2D unit square were used as input. The asymptotic expected length of an optimal tour for cities distributed in the unit square is given by $L(n) = K\sqrt{n}$ where n is the number of cities and $0.765 \leq K \leq 0.765 + \frac{4}{n}$ [Lawler et al., 1985]. This gives the interval $[7.65, 8.05]$ for the 100 city TSP. 95% of the tour lengths fall in the interval $[8, 11]$ when using the softassign approach. Note the large difference in performance between the softassign and the Potts glass algorithms. The serial Potts glass algorithm ran about 5 times slower than the softassign version. Also as noted previously the serial version is not massively parallelizable. The synchronous Potts glass ran about 2 times slower. Also note the softassign algorithm is much simpler to implement—fewer parameters to tune.

3.2 Graph Partitioning Experiments

Figure 3 shows the results of the graph partitioning experiments. 2000 different randomly generated 100 node graphs with 10% connectivity were used as input. These graphs were partitioned into four bins. The softassign performs better than the Potts glass algorithms, however here the difference is more modest than in the TSP experiments. However the serial Potts glass algorithm again ran about 5 times slower then the softassign version and as noted previously the serial version is not massively parallelizable. The synchronous Potts glass ran about 2 times slower.

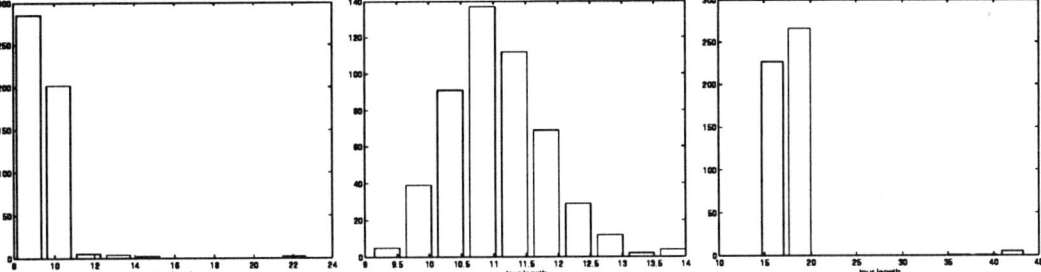

Figure 2: 100 City Euclidean TSP. 500 experiments. Left: **Softassign.**. Middle: **Softmax (serial update)**. Right: **Softmax (synchronous update)**.

Also again note the softassign algorithm was much simpler to implement—fewer parameters to tune.

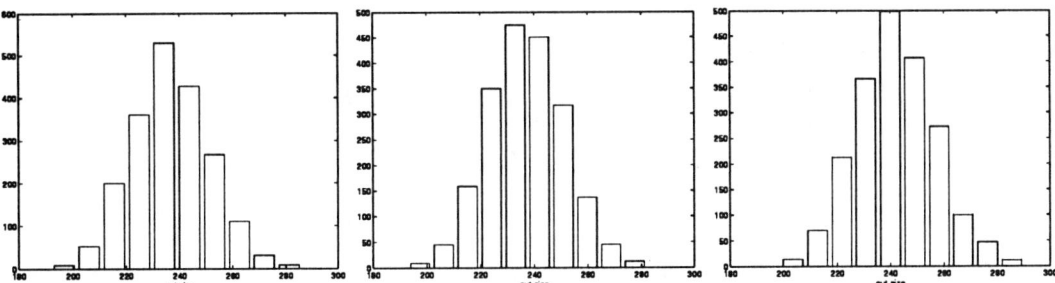

Figure 3: 100 node Graph Partitioning, 4 bins. 2000 experiments. Left: **Softassign.**. Middle: **Softmax (serial update)**. Right: **Softmax (synchronous update)**.

A relatively simple version of graph partitioning was run. It is likely that as the number of bins are increased the results on graph partitioning will come to resemble more closely the TSP results, since when the number of bins equal the number of nodes, the TSP can be considered a special case of graph partitioning (there are some additional restrictions). However even in this simple case the softassign has clear advantages over the softmax and penalty term.

4 Conclusion

For the first time, two classic combinatorial optimization problems, TSP and graph partitioning, are solved using a new technique for constraint satisfaction, the softassign. The softassign, which has recently emerged from the statistical physics/neural networks framework, enforces a two-way (assignment) constraint, without penalty terms in the energy function. We also show that the softassign can be generalized from two-way winner-take-all constraints to multiple membership constraints, which are required for graph partitioning. Benchmarks against the Potts glass methods, using softmax and a penalty term, clearly demonstrate its advantages in terms of accuracy, speed, parallelizability and simplicity of implementation. Within the neural network/statistical physics framework, softassign should be considered the technique of choice for enforcing two-way constraints in energy functions.

References

[Gold, 1995] Gold, S. (1995). *Matching and Learning Structural and Spatial Representations with Neural Networks*. PhD thesis, Yale University.

[Gold et al., 1995] Gold, S., Lu, C. P., Rangarajan, A., Pappu, S., and Mjolsness, E. (1995). New algorithms for 2-D and 3-D point matching: pose estimation and correspondence. In Tesauro, G., Touretzky, D. S., and Leen, T. K., editors, *Advances in Neural Information Processing Systems 7*, pages 957–964. MIT Press, Cambridge, MA.

[Gold et al., 1994] Gold, S., Mjolsness, E., and Rangarajan, A. (1994). Clustering with a domain specific distance measure. In Cowan, J., Tesauro, G., and Alspector, J., editors, *Advances in Neural Information Processing Systems 6*, pages 96–103. Morgan Kaufmann, San Francisco, CA.

[Gold and Rangarajan, 1996] Gold, S. and Rangarajan, A. (1996). A graduated assignment algorithm for graph matching. *IEEE Transactions on Pattern Analysis and Machine Intelligence*, (in press).

[Gold et al., 1996] Gold, S., Rangarajan, A., and Mjolsness, E. (1996). Learning with preknowledge: clustering with point and graph matching distance measures. *Neural Computation*, (in press).

[Hopfield and Tank, 1985] Hopfield, J. J. and Tank, D. (1985). 'Neural' computation of decisions in optimization problems. *Biological Cybernetics*, 52:141–152.

[Kosowsky and Yuille, 1994] Kosowsky, J. J. and Yuille, A. L. (1994). The invisible hand algorithm: Solving the assignment problem with statistical physics. *Neural Networks*, 7(3):477–490.

[Lawler et al., 1985] Lawler, E. L., Lenstra, J. K., Kan, A. H. G. R., and Shmoys, D. B., editors (1985). *The Traveling Salesman Problem*. John Wiley and Sons, Chichester.

[Peterson and Soderberg, 1989] Peterson, C. and Soderberg, B. (1989). A new method for mapping optimization problems onto neural networks. *Intl. Journal of Neural Systems*, 1(1):3–22.

[Rumelhart and McClelland, 1986] Rumelhart, D. and McClelland, J. L. (1986). *Parallel Distributed Processing*, volume 1. MIT Press, Cambridge, MA.

[Sinkhorn, 1964] Sinkhorn, R. (1964). A relationship between arbitrary positive matrices and doubly stochastic matrices. *Ann. Math. Statist.*, 35:876–879.

[Van den Bout and Miller III, 1990] Van den Bout, D. E. and Miller III, T. K. (1990). Graph partitioning using annealed networks. *IEEE Trans. Neural Networks*, 1(2):192–203.

[Yuille and Kosowsky, 1994] Yuille, A. L. and Kosowsky, J. J. (1994). Statistical physics algorithms that converge. *Neural Computation*, 6(3):341–356.

A Multiscale Attentional Framework for Relaxation Neural Networks

Dimitris I. Tsioutsias
Dept. of Electrical Engineering
Yale University
New Haven, CT 06520-8285
tsioutsias@cs.yale.edu

Eric Mjolsness
Dept. of Computer Science & Engineering
University of California, San Diego
La Jolla, CA 92093-0114
emj@cs.ucsd.edu

Abstract

We investigate the optimization of neural networks governed by general objective functions. Practical formulations of such objectives are notoriously difficult to solve; a common problem is the poor local extrema that result by any of the applied methods. In this paper, a novel framework is introduced for the solution of large-scale optimization problems. It assumes little about the objective function and can be applied to general nonlinear, non-convex functions; objectives in thousand of variables are thus efficiently minimized by a combination of techniques - deterministic annealing, multiscale optimization, attention mechanisms and trust region optimization methods.

1 INTRODUCTION

Many practical problems in computer vision, pattern recognition, robotics and other areas can be described in terms of constrained optimization. In the past decade, researchers have proposed means of solving such problems with the use of neural networks [Hopfield & Tank, 1985; Koch et al., 1986], which are thus derived as relaxation dynamics for the objective functions codifying the optimization task.

One disturbing aspect of the approach soon became obvious, namely the apparent inability of the methods to scale up to practical problems, the principal reason being the rapid increase in the number of local minima present in the objectives as the dimension of the problem increases. Moreover most objectives, $E(v)$, are highly nonlinear, non-convex functions of v, and simple techniques (e.g. steepest descent) will, in general, locate the first minimum from the starting point.

In this work, we propose a framework for solving large-scale instances of such optimization problems. We discuss several techniques which assist in avoiding spurious minima and whose combined result is an objective function solution that is computationally efficient, while at the same time being globally convergent. In section 2.1 we discuss the use of deterministic annealing as a means of avoiding getting trapped into local minima. Section 2.2 describes multiscale representations of the original objective in reduced spatial domains. In section 2.3 we present a scheme for reducing the computational requirements of the optimization method used, by means of a *focus of attention* mechanism. Then, in section 2.4 we introduce a trust region method for the relaxation phase of the framework, which uses second order information (i.e. curvature) of the objective function. In section 3 we present experimental results on the application of our framework to a 2-D region segmentation objective with discontinuities. Finally, section 4 summarizes our presentation.

2 THEORETICAL FRAMEWORK

Our optimization framework takes the form of a list of nested loops indicating the order of conceptual (and computational) phases that occur: from the outer to the inner loop we make use of deterministic annealing, a multiscale representation, an attentional mechanism and a trust region optimization method.

2.1 ANNEALING NETS

The usefulness of statistical mechanics for designing optimization procedures has recently been established; prime examples are simulated annealing and its various mean field theory approximations [Hopfield & Tank, 1985; Durbin & Willshaw, 1987]. The success of such methods is primarily due to *entropic* terms included in the objective (i.e. *syntactic* terms), but the price to pay is their highly nonlinear form. Interestingly, those terms can effectively be convexified by the use of a "temperature" parameter, T, allowing for a reduction in the number of minima and the ability to *track* the solution through "temperature".

2.2 MULTISCALE REPRESENTATION

To solve large-scale problems in thousands of variables, we need to speed up the convergence of the method while still retaining *valid* state-space trajectories. To accomplish this we introduce smaller, approximate versions of the problem at coarser spatial scales [Mjolsness et al., 1991]; the nonlinearity of the original objective is maintained at all scales, as opposed to other approaches where the objectives and their derivatives are either approximated by the use of finite difference methods, or solved for by multigrid techniques where a quadratic objective is still assumed. Consequently, the multiscale representation exploits the effective *smoothness* in the objectives: by alternating relaxation phases between coarser and finer scales, we use the former to *identify* extrema and the latter to *localise* them.

2.3 FOCUS OF ATTENTION

To further reduce the computational requirements of large-scale optimization (and indirectly control its temporal behavior), we use a *focus of attention* (*FoA*) mechanism [Mjolsness & Miranker, 1993], reminiscent of the *spotlight* hypothesis argued to exist in early vision systems [Koch & Ullman, 1985; Olshausen et al., 1993]. The effect of a *FoA* is to support efficient, responsive analysis: it allows resources to be *focused* on selected areas of a computation and can rapidly redirect them as the task requirements evolve.

Specifically, the *FoA* becomes a characteristic function, $\pi(\chi)$, determining which of the N neurons are active and which are clamped during relaxation, by use of a discrete-valued vector, χ, and by the rule: $\pi_i(\chi) = 1$ if neuron v_i is in the *FoA*, and zero otherwise. Moreover, a limited number, n, of neurons v_i are active at any given instant: $\sum_i \pi_i(\chi) = n$, with $n \ll N$ and n chosen as an optimal *FoA* size. To tie the attentional mechanism to the multiscale representation, we introduce a partition of the neurons v_i into blocks indexed by a (corresponding to coarse-scale block-neurons), via a sparse rectangular matrix $B_{ia} \in \{0,1\}$ such that $\sum_a B_{ia} = 1, \forall i$, with $i = 1, \ldots, N$, $a = 1, \ldots, K$ and $K \ll N$. Then $\pi_i(\chi) = \sum_a B_{ia} \chi_a$, and we use each component of χ for switching a different block of the partition; thus, a neuron v_i is in the *FoA* iff its coarse scale block a is in the *FoA*, as indicated by χ_a. As a result, our *FoA* need not necessarily have a single region of activity: it may well have a distributed activity pattern as determined by the partitions B_{ia}.[1]

Clocked objective function notation [Mjolsness & Miranker, 1993] makes the task more apparent: during the active-χ phase the *FoA* is computed for the next active-v phase, determining the subset of neurons v_i on which optimization is to be carried out. We introduce the quantity $E_{;i}[v] \equiv \frac{\partial E}{\partial v_i} \frac{dv_i}{d\tau_i}$ (τ_i is a time axis for v_i) [Mjolsness & Miranker, 1993] as an estimate of the *predicted* ΔE arising from each v_i if it joins the *FoA*. For Hopfield/Grossberg dynamics this measure becomes:

$$E_{;i}[v] = -g'_i(g_i^{-1}(v_i)) \left(\frac{\partial E}{\partial v_i}\right)^2 \equiv -g'_i(u_i)(E_{,i})^2 \qquad (1)$$

with $E_{,i} \stackrel{def}{=} \nabla_i E$, and g_i the transfer function for neuron v_i (e.g. a sigmoid function). Eq. (1) is used here analogously to *saliency measures* introduced into neurophysiological work [Koch & Ullman, 1985]; we propose it as a global measure of conspicuousness. As a result, attention becomes a k-winner-take-all ($kWTA$) network:

$$E_{block}^{(l)} = [\sum_a \chi_a^{(l)} \sum_i B_{ia}^{(l)} E_{;i}(\bar{v}^{(l)}) + kWTA(\chi^{(l)})] \oplus E(v^{(l)}\{\sum_a B_{ia}^{(l)} \chi_a^{(l)}\}), \qquad (2)$$

where l refers to the scale for which the *FoA* is being determined ($l = 1, \ldots, L$), $\oplus$ conforms with the clocked objective notation, and the last summand corresponds to the subspace on which optimization is to be performed, as determined by the current *FoA*.[2] Periodically, an analogous *FoA* through spatial scales is run, allowing re-direction of system resources to the scale which seems to be having the largest combined benefit and cost effect on the optimization [Tsioutsias & Mjolsness, 1995]. The combined effect of multiscale optimization and *FoA* is depicted schematically in Fig. 1: reduced-dimension functionals are created and a *FoA beam* "shines" through scales picking the neurons to work on.

---

[1] Preferably, B_{ia} will be chosen to minimize the number of inter-block connections.
[2] Before computing a new *FoA* we update the neighbors of all neurons that were included in the last focus; this has a similar effect to an implicit *spreading of activation*.

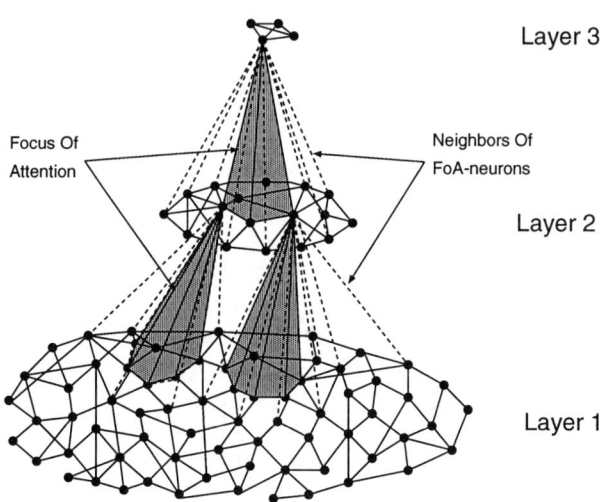

Figure 1: Multiscale Attentional Neural Nets: *FoA* on a layer (e.g. $L=1$) competes with another *FoA* (e.g. $L=2$) to determine both preferable scale and subspace.

2.4 OPTIMIZATION PHASE

To overcome the problems generally associated with the steepest descent method, other techniques have been devised. Newton's method, although successful in small to medium-sized problems, does not scale well in large non-convex instances and is computationally intensive. Quasi-Newton methods are efficient to compute, have quadratic termination but are not globally convergent for general nonlinear, non-convex functions. A method that guarantees global convergence is the trust region method [Conn et al., 1993]. The idea is summarized as follows: Newton's method suffers from non-positive definite Hessians; in such a case, the underlying function $m^{(k)}(\boldsymbol{\delta})$ obtained from the 2nd order Taylor expansion of $E(\boldsymbol{v}_k + \boldsymbol{\delta})$ does not have a minimum and the method is not defined, or equivalently, the region around the current point $\boldsymbol{v}_k$ in which the Taylor series is adequate does not include a minimizing point of $m^{(k)}(\boldsymbol{\delta})$. To resolve this, we can define a neighborhood Ω_k of $\boldsymbol{v}_k$ such that $m^{(k)}(\boldsymbol{\delta})$ agrees with $E(\boldsymbol{v}_k + \boldsymbol{\delta})$ in some sense; then, we pick $\boldsymbol{v}_{k+1} = \boldsymbol{v}_k + \boldsymbol{\delta}_k$, where $\boldsymbol{\delta}_k$ minimizes $m^{(k)}(\boldsymbol{\delta})$, $\forall (\boldsymbol{v}_k + \boldsymbol{\delta}) \in \Omega_k$. Thus, we seek a solution to the resulting subproblem:

$$\min_{\boldsymbol{\delta}} m^{(k)}(\boldsymbol{\delta}) \quad s.t. \quad \|\boldsymbol{\delta}\|_p \leq \Delta_k \tag{3}$$

where $\|\cdot\|_p$ is any kind of norm (for instance, the L_2 norm leads to the Levenberg-Marquardt methods), and Δ_k is the radius of Ω_k, adaptively modified based on an *accuracy ratio* $r_k = (\Delta E^{(k)}/\Delta m^{(k)}) \equiv (E^{(k)} - E(\boldsymbol{v}_k + \boldsymbol{\delta}_k))/(m^{(k)}(0) - m^{(k)}(\boldsymbol{\delta}_k))$; $\Delta E^{(k)}$ is the "actual reduction" in $E^{(k)}$ when step $\boldsymbol{\delta}_k$ is taken, and $\Delta m^{(k)}$ the "predicted reduction". The closer r_k is to unity, the better the agreement between the local quadratic model of $E^{(k)}$ and the objective itself is, and Δ_k is modified adaptively to reflect this [Conn et al., 1993].

We need to make some brief points here (a complete discussion will be given elsewhere [Tsioutsias & Mjolsness, 1995]):

- At each spatial scale of our multiscale representation, we optimize the corresponding objective by applying a trust region method. To obtain sufficient relaxation progress as we move through scales we have to maintain meaningful region sizes, Δ_k; to that end we use a criterion based on the curvature of the functionals along a searching direction.

- The dominant relaxation computation within the algorithm is the solution of eq. (3). We have chosen to solve this subproblem with a preconditioned conjugate gradient method (PCG) that uses a truncated Newton step to speed up the computation; steps are accepted when a sufficiently good approximation to the quasi-Newton step is found.[3] In our case, the norm in eq. (3) becomes the *elliptical* norm $\|\delta\|_C = \delta^t C \delta$, where a diagonal preconditioner to the Hessian is used as the scaling matrix C.

- If the neuronal connectivity pattern of the original objective is sparse (as happens for most practical combinatorial optimization problems), the pattern of the resulting Hessian can readily be represented by sparse static data structures,[4] as we have done within our framework. Moreover, the partition matrices, B_{ia}, introduce a moderate fill-in in the coarser objectives and the sparsity of the corresponding Hessians is again taken into account.

3 EXPERIMENTS

We have applied our proposed optimization framework to a spatially structured objective from low-level vision, namely smooth 2-D region segmentation with the inclusion of discontinuity detection processes:

$$E[\boldsymbol{f}, \boldsymbol{l}^v, \boldsymbol{l}^h] = A\sum_{ij}(1 - l_{ij}^v)(f_{i+1,j} - f_{ij})^2 + A\sum_{ij}(1 - l_{ij}^h)(f_{i,j+1} - f_{ij})^2$$
$$+ B\sum_{ij}(f_{ij} - d_{ij})^2 + C\sum_{ij}(l_{ij}^v + l_{ij}^h) + T\sum_{ij}(\phi(l_{ij}^v) + \phi(l_{ij}^h)) \quad (4)$$

where $\boldsymbol{d}$ is the set of image intensities, $\boldsymbol{f}$ is the real-valued smooth surface to be fit to the data, $\boldsymbol{l}^v$ and $\boldsymbol{l}^h$ are the discrete-valued *line processes* indicating a non-zero value in the intensity gradient, and $\phi(x) = -(2g_0)^{-1}[\ln x + \ln(1-x)]$ is a *barrier function* restricting each variable into (0,1) by infinite barriers at the borders. Eq. (4) is a mixed-nonlinear objective involving both continuous and binary variables; our framework optimizes vectors $\boldsymbol{f}, \boldsymbol{l}^h$ and $\boldsymbol{l}^v$ *simultaneously* at any given scale as continuous variables, instead of earlier two-step, alternate continuous/discrete-phase approaches [Terzopoulos, 1986].

We have tested our method on gradually increasing objectives, from a "small" size of N=12,288 variables for a 64x64 image, up to a large size of N=786,432 variables for a 512x512 image; the results seem to coincide with our theoretical expectations: a significant reduction in computational cost was observed and consistent convergence towards the optimum of the objective was found for various numbers of coarse scales and FoA sizes. The dimension of the objective at any scale l was chosen via a *power law*: $N^{(L-l+1)/L}$, where L is the total number of scales and N the size of

---

[3] The algorithm can also handle directions of negative curvature.
[4] This property becomes important in a neural net implementation.

the original objective.

The effect of our multiscale optimization with and without a *FoA* is shown in Fig. 2 for the 128x128 and the 512x512 nets, where $E(\boldsymbol{v}^*)$ is the best final configuration with a one-level no-*FoA* net, and *cumulative cost* is an accumulated measure in the number of connection updates at each scale; a consistent scale-up in computational efficiency can be noted when $L > 1$, while the cost measure also reflects the relative total wall-clock times needed for convergence. Fig. 3 shows part of a comparative study we made for saliency measures alternative to eq. (1) (e.g. $g'_i|E_{,i}|$), in order to investigate the validity of eq. (1) as a *predictor* of ΔE: the more prominent "linearity" in the left scatterplot seems to justify our choice of saliency.

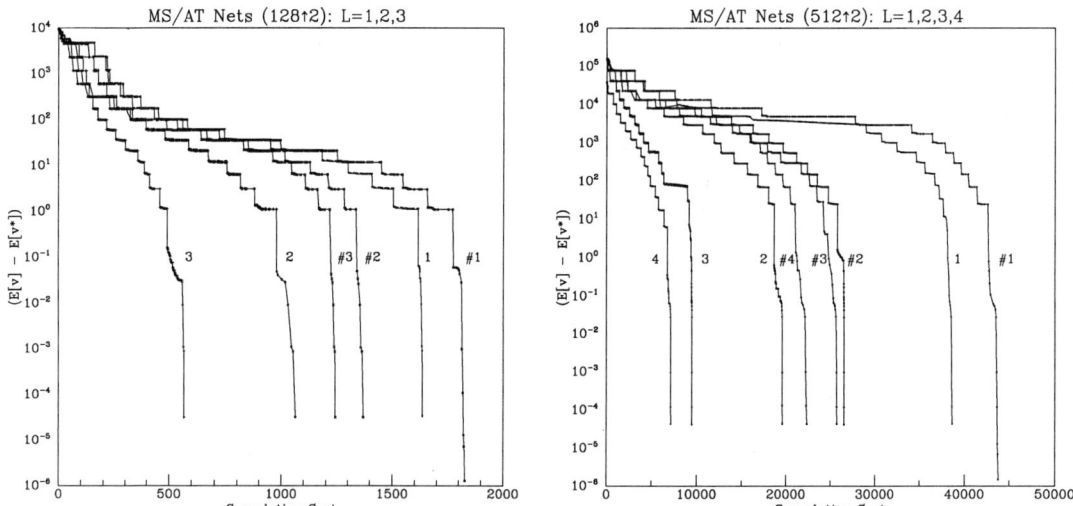

Figure 2: Multiscale Optimization (curves labeled by number of scales used): #-numbered curves correspond to nets without a *FoA*, simply-numbered ones to nets with a *FoA* used at all scales. The lowest costs result from the combined use of multiscale optimization and *FoA*.

4 CONCLUSION

We have presented a framework for the optimization of large-scale objective functions using neural networks that incorporate a multiscale attentional mechanism. Our method allows for a continuous adaptation of the system resources to the computational requirements of the relaxation problem through the combined use of several techniques. The framework was applied to a 2-D image segmentation objective with discontinuities; formulations of this problem with tens to hundreds of thousands of variables were then successfully solved.

Acknowledgements

This work was supported partly by AFOSR-F49620-92-J-0465 and the *Yale Center of Theoretical and Applied Neuroscience*.

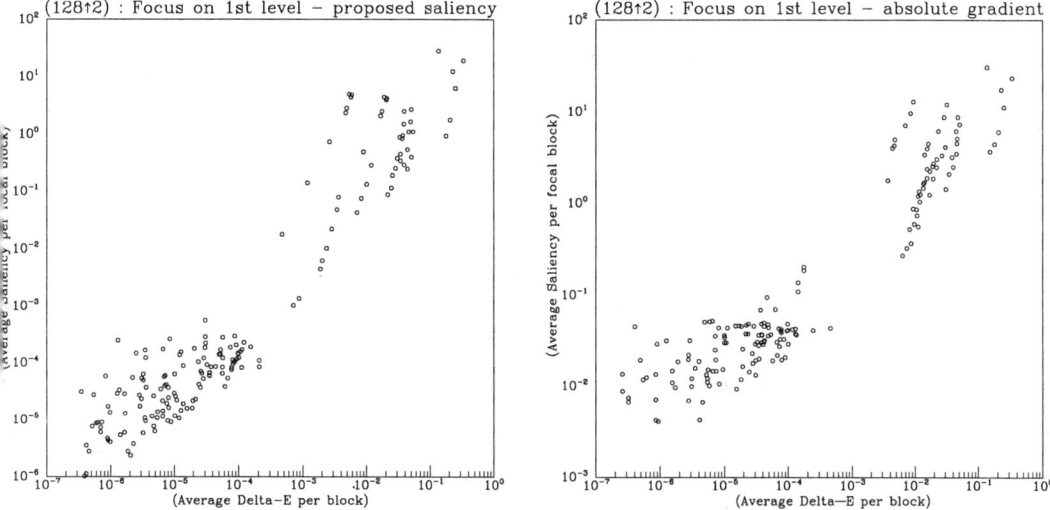

Figure 3: Saliency Comparison: (*left*), saliency as in eq. (1); (*right*), the absolute gradient was used instead.

References

A. Conn, N. Gould, A. Sartanaer, & Ph. Toint. (1993) Global Convergence of a Class of Trust Region Algorithms for Optimization Using Inexact Projections on Convex Constraints. *SIAM J. of Optimization*, **3**(1):164-221.

R. Durbin & D. Willshaw. (1987) An Analogue Approach to the TSP Problem Using an Elastic Net Method. *Nature*, **326**:689-691.

J. Hopfield & D. W. Tank. (1985) Neural Computation of Decisions in Optimization Problems. *Biol. Cybernet.*, **52**:141-152.

C. Koch, J. Marroquin & A. Yuille. (1986) Analog 'Neuronal' Networks in Early Vision. *Proc. of the National Academy of Sciences USA*, **83**:4263-4267.

C. Koch, & S. Ullman. (1985) Shifts in Selective Visual Attention: Towards the Underlying Neural Circuitry. *Human Neurobiology*, **4**:219-227.

E. Mjolsness, C. Garrett, & W. Miranker. (1991) Multiscale Optimization in Neural Nets. *IEEE Trans. on Neural Networks*, **2**(2):263-274.

E. Mjolsness & W. Miranker. (1993) Greedy Lagrangians for Neural Networks: Three Levels of Optimization in Relaxation Dynamics. *YALEU/DCS/TR-945*. (URL file://cs.ucsd.edu/pub/emj/papers/yale-TR-945.ps.Z)

B. Olshausen, C. Anderson, & D. Van Essen. (1993) A Neurobiological Model of Visual Attention and Invariant Pattern Recognition Based on Dynamic Routing of Information. *The Journal of Neuroscience*, **13**(11):4700-4719.

D. Terzopoulos. (1986) Regularization of Inverse Visual Problems Involving Discontinuities. *IEEE Trans. PAMI*, **8**:419-429.

D. I. Tsioutsias & E. Mjolsness. (1995) Global Optimization in Neural Nets: A Novel Relaxation Framework. To appear as a *UCSD-CSE-TR*, Dec. 1995.

Is Learning The n-th Thing Any Easier Than Learning The First?

Sebastian Thrun[1]

Computer Science Department
Carnegie Mellon University
Pittsburgh, PA 15213-3891
World Wide Web: http://www.cs.cmu.edu/~thrun

Abstract

This paper investigates learning in a lifelong context. Lifelong learning addresses situations in which a learner faces a whole stream of learning tasks. Such scenarios provide the opportunity to transfer knowledge across multiple learning tasks, in order to generalize more accurately from less training data. In this paper, several different approaches to lifelong learning are described, and applied in an object recognition domain. It is shown that across the board, lifelong learning approaches generalize consistently more accurately from less training data, by their ability to transfer knowledge across learning tasks.

1 Introduction

Supervised learning is concerned with approximating an unknown function based on examples. Virtually all current approaches to supervised learning assume that one is given a set of input-output examples, denoted by X, which characterize an unknown function, denoted by f. The target function f is drawn from a class of functions, F, and the learner is given a space of hypotheses, denoted by H, and an order (preference/prior) with which it considers them during learning. For example, H might be the space of functions represented by an artificial neural network with different weight vectors.

While this formulation establishes a rigid framework for research in machine learning, it dismisses important aspects that are essential for human learning. Psychological studies have shown that humans often employ more than just the training data for generalization. They are often able to generalize correctly even from a single training example [2, 10]. One of the key aspects of the learning problem faced by humans, which differs from the vast majority of problems studied in the field of neural network learning, is the fact that humans encounter a whole stream of learning problems over their entire lifetime. When faced with a new thing to learn, humans can usually exploit an enormous amount of training data and

---

[1]also affiliated with: Institut für Informatik III, Universität Bonn, Römerstr. 164, Germany

experiences that stem from other, related learning tasks. For example, when learning to drive a car, years of learning experience with basic motor skills, typical traffic patterns, logical reasoning, language and much more precede and influence this learning task. The transfer of knowledge across learning tasks seems to play an essential role for generalizing accurately, particularly when training data is scarce.

A framework for the study of the transfer of knowledge is the *lifelong learning framework*. In this framework, it is assumed that a learner faces a whole collection of learning problems over its entire lifetime. Such a scenario opens the opportunity for synergy. When facing its n-th learning task, a learner can re-use knowledge gathered in its previous $n - 1$ learning tasks to boost the generalization accuracy.

In this paper we will be interested in the most simple version of the lifelong learning problem, in which the learner faces a family of *concept learning tasks*. More specifically, the functions to be learned over the lifetime of the learner, denoted by $f_1, f_2, f_3, \ldots \in F$, are all of the type $f : I \longrightarrow \{0, 1\}$ and sampled from F. Each function $f \in \{f_1, f_2, f_3, \ldots\}$ is an indicator function that defines a particular concept: a pattern $x \in I$ is member of this concept if and only if $f(x) = 1$. When learning the n-th indicator function, f_n, the training set X contains examples of the type $\langle x, f_n(x) \rangle$ (which may be distorted by noise). In addition to the training set, the learner is also given $n - 1$ sets of examples of other concept functions, denoted by X_k ($k = 1, \ldots, n - 1$). Each X_k contains training examples that characterize f_k. Since this additional data is desired to support learning f_n, X_k is called a *support set* for the training set X.

An example of the above is the recognition of faces [5, 7]. When learning to recognize the n-th person, say f_{Bob}, the learner is given a set of positive and negative example of face images of this person. In lifelong learning, it may also exploit training information stemming from other persons, such as $f \in \{f_{\text{Rich}}, f_{\text{Mike}}, f_{\text{Dave}}, \ldots\}$. The support sets usually cannot be used directly as training patterns when learning a new concept, since they describe different concepts (hence have different class labels). However, certain features (like the shape of the eyes) are more important than others (like the facial expression, or the location of the face within the image). Once the invariances of the domain are learned, they can be transferred to new learning tasks (new people) and hence improve generalization.

To illustrate the potential importance of related learning tasks in lifelong learning, this paper does not present just one particular approach to the transfer of knowledge. Instead, it describes several, all of which extend conventional memory-based or neural network algorithms. These approaches are compared with more traditional learning algorithms, *i.e.*, those that do not transfer knowledge. The goal of this research is to demonstrate that, independent of a particular learning approach, more complex functions can be learned from less training data if learning is embedded into a lifelong context.

2 Memory-Based Learning Approaches

Memory-based algorithms memorize all training examples explicitly and interpolate them at query-time. We will first sketch two simple, well-known approaches to memory-based learning, then propose extensions that take the support sets into account.

2.1 Nearest Neighbor and Shepard's Method

Probably the most widely used memory-based learning algorithm is K-*nearest neighbor* (*KNN*) [15]. Suppose x is a query pattern, for which we would like to know the output y. KNN searches the set of training examples X for those K examples $\langle x_i, y_i \rangle \in X$ whose input patterns x_i are nearest to x (according to some distance metric, *e.g.*, the Euclidian distance). It then returns the mean output value $\frac{1}{K} \sum y_i$ of these nearest neighbors.

Another commonly used method, which is due to Shepard [13], averages the output values of *all* training examples but weights each example according to the inverse distance to the query point x.

$$s(x) := \left(\sum_{\langle x_i, y_i \rangle \in X} \frac{y_i}{\|x - x_i\| + \varepsilon} \right) \cdot \left(\sum_{\langle x_i, y_i \rangle \in X} \frac{1}{\|x - x_i\| + \varepsilon} \right)^{-1} \quad (1)$$

Here $\varepsilon > 0$ is a small constant that prevents division by zero. Plain memory-based learning uses exclusively the training set X for learning. There is no obvious way to incorporate the support sets, since they carry the wrong class labels.

2.2 Learning A New Representation

The first modification of memory-based learning proposed in this paper employs the support sets to learn a *new representation* of the data. More specifically, the support sets are employed to learn a function, denoted by $g : I \longrightarrow I'$, which maps input patterns in I to a new space, I'. This new space I' forms the input space for a memory-based algorithm.

Obviously, the key property of a good data representations is that multiple examples of a single concept should have a similar representation, whereas the representation of an example and a counterexample of a concept should be more different. This property can directly be transformed into an energy function for g:

$$E := \sum_{k=1}^{n-1} \sum_{\langle x, y=1 \rangle \in X_k} \left(\sum_{\langle x', y'=1 \rangle \in X_k} \|g(x) - g(x')\| - \sum_{\langle x', y'=0 \rangle \in X_k} \|g(x) - g(x')\| \right) \quad (2)$$

Adjusting g to minimize E forces the distance between pairs of examples of the same concept to be small, and the distance between an example and a counterexample of a concept to be large. In our implementation, g is realized by a neural network and trained using the Back-Propagation algorithm [12].

Notice that the new representation, g, is obtained through the support sets. Assuming that the learned representation is appropriate for new learning tasks, standard memory-based learning can be applied using this new representation when learning the n-th concept.

2.3 Learning A Distance Function

An alternative way for exploiting support sets to improve memory-based learning is to learn a distance function [3, 9]. This approach learns a function $d : I \times I \longrightarrow [0, 1]$ which accepts two input patterns, say x and x', and outputs whether x and x' are members of the same concept, regardless what the concept is. Training examples for d are

$$\langle (x, x'), 1 \rangle \quad \text{if } y = y' = 1$$
$$\langle (x, x'), 0 \rangle \quad \text{if } (y=1 \wedge y'=0) \text{ or } (y=0 \wedge y'=1) \ .$$

They are derived from pairs of examples $\langle x, y \rangle, \langle x', y' \rangle \in X_k$ taken from a single support set X_k ($k = 1, \ldots, n-1$). In our implementation, d is an artificial neural network trained with Back-Propagation. Notice that the training examples for d lack information concerning the concept for which they were originally derived. Hence, all support sets can be used to train d. After training, d can be interpreted as the probability that two patterns $x, x' \in I$ are examples of the same concept.

Once trained, d can be used as a *generalized distance function* for a memory-based approach. Suppose one is given a training set X and a query point $x \in I$. Then, for each positive example $\langle x', y' = 1 \rangle \in X$, $d(x, x')$ can be interpreted as the probability that x is a member of the target concept. Votes from multiple positive examples $\langle x_1, 1 \rangle, \langle x_2, 1 \rangle, \ldots \in X$ are combined using Bayes' rule, yielding

$$Prob(f_n(x) = 1) := 1 - \left(1 + \prod_{\langle x', y'=1 \rangle \in X_k} \frac{d(x, x')}{1 - d(x, x')} \right)^{-1} \quad (3)$$

Notice that d is not a distance metric. It generalizes the notion of a distance metric, because the triangle inequality needs not hold, and because an example of the target concept x' can provide evidence that x is *not* a member of that concept (if $d(x, x') < 0.5$).

3 Neural Network Approaches

To make our comparison more complete, we will now briefly describe approaches that rely exclusively on artificial neural networks for learning f_n.

3.1 Back-Propagation

Standard Back-Propagation can be used to learn the indicator function f_n, using X as training set. This approach does not employ the support sets, hence is unable to transfer knowledge across learning tasks.

3.2 Learning With Hints

Learning with hints [1, 4, 6, 16] constructs a neural network with n output units, one for each function f_k ($k = 1, 2, \ldots, n$). This network is then trained to simultaneously minimize the error on both the support sets $\{X_k\}$ and the training set X. By doing so, the internal representation of this network is not only determined by X but also shaped through the support sets $\{X_k\}$. If similar internal representations are required for all functions f_k ($k = 1, 2, \ldots, n$), the support sets provide additional training examples for the internal representation.

3.3 Explanation-Based Neural Network Learning

The last method described here uses the *explanation-based neural network learning algorithm* (EBNN), which was originally proposed in the context of reinforcement learning [8, 17]. EBNN trains an artificial neural network, denoted by $h : I \longrightarrow [0, 1]$, just like Back-Propagation. However, in addition to the target values given by the training set X, EBNN estimates the *slopes* (tangents) of the target function f_n for each example in X. More specifically, training examples in EBNN are of the sort $\langle x, f_n(x), \nabla_x f_n(x) \rangle$, which are fit using the Tangent-Prop algorithm [14]. The input x and target value $f_n(x)$ are taken from the training set X. The third term, the slope $\nabla_x f_n(x)$, is estimated using the learned distance function d described above. Suppose $\langle x', y' = 1 \rangle \in X$ is a (positive) training example. Then, the function $d_{x'} : I \longrightarrow [0, 1]$ with $d_{x'}(z) := d(z, x')$ maps a single input pattern to $[0, 1]$, and is an approximation to f_n. Since $d(z, x')$ is represented by a neural network and neural networks are differentiable, the gradient $\partial d_{x'}(z)/\partial z$ is an estimate of the slope of f_n at z. Setting $z := x$ yields the desired estimate of $\nabla_x f_n(x)$. As stated above, both the target value $f_n(x)$ and the slope vector $\nabla_x f_n(x)$ are fit using the Tangent-Prop algorithm for each training example $x \in X$.

The slope $\nabla_x f_n$ provides additional information about the target function f_n. Since d is learned using the support sets, EBNN approach transfers knowledge from the support sets to the new learning task. EBNN relies on the assumption that d is accurate enough to yield helpful sensitivity information. However, since EBNN fits both training patterns (values) and slopes, misleading slopes can be overridden by training examples. See [17] for a more detailed description of EBNN and further references.

4 Experimental Results

All approaches were tested using a database of color camera images of different objects (see Fig. 3.3). Each of the object in the database has a distinct color or size. The n-th

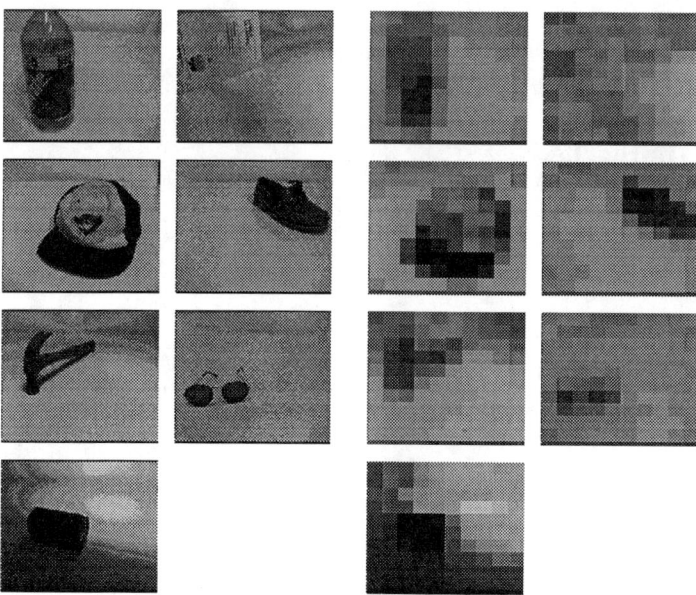

Figure 1: The support sets were compiled out of a hundred images of a *bottle*, a *hat*, a *hammer*, a *coke can*, and a *book*. The n-th learning tasks involves distinguishing the *shoe* from the *sunglasses*. Images were subsampled to a 100×100 pixel matrix (each pixel has a color, saturation, and a brightness value), shown on the right side.

learning task was the recognition of one of these objects, namely the *shoe*. The previous $n-1$ learning tasks correspond to the recognition of five other objects, namely the *bottle*, the *hat*, the *hammer*, the *coke can*, and the *book*. To ensure that the latter images could not be used simply as additional training data for f_n, the only counterexamples of the *shoe* was the seventh object, the *sunglasses*. Hence, the training set for f_n contained images of the *shoe* and the *sunglasses*, and the support sets contained images of the other five objects. The object recognition domain is a good testbed for the transfer of knowledge in lifelong learning. This is because finding a good approximation to f_n involves recognizing the target object invariant of rotation, translation, scaling in size, change of lighting and so on. Since these invariances are common to all object recognition tasks, images showing other objects can provide additional information and boost the generalization accuracy.

Transfer of knowledge is most important when training data is scarce. Hence, in an initial experiment we tested all methods using a single image of the *shoe* and the *sunglasses* only. Those methods that are able to transfer knowledge were also provided 100 images of each of the other five objects. The results are intriguing. The generalization accuracies

KNN	Shepard	repr. g+Shep.	distance d	Back-Prop	hints	EBNN
60.4%	60.4%	**74.4%**	**75.2%**	59.7%	**62.1%**	**74.8%**
±8.3%	±8.3%	**±18.5%**	**±18.9%**	±9.0%	**±10.2%**	**±11.1%**

illustrate that all approaches that transfer knowledge (printed in bold font) generalize significantly better than those that do not. With the exception of the hint learning technique, the approaches can be grouped into two categories: Those which generalize approximately 60% of the testing set correctly, and those which achieve approximately 75% generalization accuracy. The former group contains the standard supervised learning algorithms, and the latter contains the "new" algorithms proposed here, which are capable of transferring knowledge. The differences within each group are statistically not significant, while the differences between them are (at the 95% level). Notice that random guessing classifies 50% of the testing examples correctly.

These results suggest that the generalization accuracy merely depends on the particular choice of the learning algorithm (memory-based vs. neural networks). Instead, the main factor determining the generalization accuracy is the fact whether or not knowledge is transferred from past learning tasks.

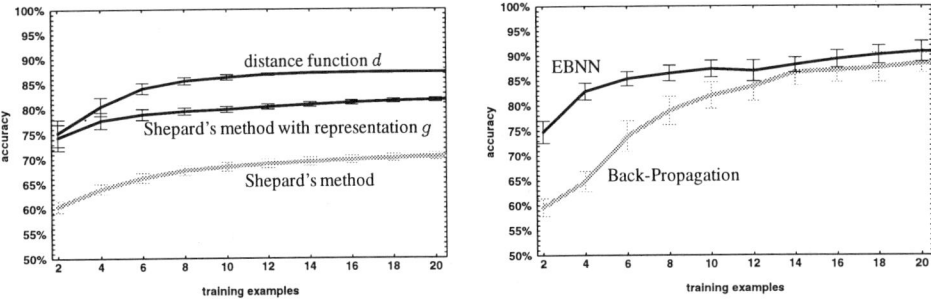

Figure 2: Generalization accuracy as a function of training examples, measured on an independent test set and averaged over 100 experiments. 95%-confidence bars are also displayed.

What happens as more training data arrives? Fig. 2 shows generalization curves with increasing numbers of training examples for some of these methods. As the number of training examples increases, prior knowledge becomes less important. After presenting 20 training examples, the results

KNN	Shepard	repr. g+Shep.	distance d	Back-Prop	hints	EBNN
81.0%	70.5%	**81.7%**	**87.3%**	88.4%	n.avail.	**90.8%**
±3.4%	±4.9%	**±2.7%**	**±0.9%**	±2.5%		**±2.7%**

illustrate that some of the standard methods (especially Back-Propagation) generalize about as accurately as those methods that exploit support sets. Here the differences in the underlying learning mechanisms becomes more dominant. However, when comparing lifelong learning methods with their corresponding standard approaches, the latter ones are still inferior: Back-Propagation (88.4%) is outperformed by EBNN (90.8%), and Shepard's method (70.5%) generalizes less accurately when the representation is learned (81.7%) or when the distance function is learned (87.3%). All these differences are significant at the 95% confidence level.

5 Discussion

The experimental results reported in this paper provide evidence that learning becomes easier when embedded in a lifelong learning context. By transferring knowledge across related learning tasks, a learner can become "more experienced" and generalize better. To test this conjecture in a more systematic way, a variety of learning approaches were evaluated and compared with methods that are unable to transfer knowledge. It is consistently found that lifelong learning algorithms generalize significantly more accurately, particularly when training data is scarce.

Notice that these results are well in tune with other results obtained by the author. One of the approaches here, EBNN, has extensively been studied in the context of robot perception [11], reinforcement learning for robot control, and chess [17]. In all these domains, it has consistently been found to generalize better from less training data by transferring knowledge from previous learning tasks. The results are also consistent with observations made about human learning [2, 10], namely that previously learned knowledge plays an important role in generalization, particularly when training data is scarce. [18] extends these techniques to situations where most support sets are not related.w

However, lifelong learning rests on the assumption that more than a single task is to be learned, and that learning tasks are appropriately related. Lifelong learning algorithms are particularly well-suited in domains where the costs of collecting training data is the dominating factor in learning, since these costs can be amortized over several learning tasks. Such domains include, for example, autonomous service robots which are to learn and improve over their entire lifetime. They include personal software assistants which have to perform various tasks for various users. Pattern recognition, speech recognition, time series prediction, and database mining might be other, potential application domains for the techniques presented here.

References

[1] Y. S. Abu-Mostafa. Learning from hints in neural networks. *Journal of Complexity*, 6:192–198, 1990.

[2] W.-K. Ahn and W. F. Brewer. Psychological studies of explanation-based learning. In G. DeJong, editor, *Investigating Explanation-Based Learning*. Kluwer Academic Publishers, Boston/Dordrecht/London, 1993.

[3] C. A. Atkeson. Using locally weighted regression for robot learning. In *Proceedings of the 1991 IEEE International Conference on Robotics and Automation*, pages 958–962, Sacramento, CA, April 1991.

[4] J. Baxter. Learning internal representations. In *Proceedings of the Conference on Computation Learning Theory*, 1995.

[5] D. Beymer and T. Poggio. Face recognition from one model view. In *Proceedings of the International Conference on Computer Vision*, 1995.

[6] R. Caruana. Multitask learning: A knowledge-based of source of inductive bias. In P. E. Utgoff, editor, *Proceedings of the Tenth International Conference on Machine Learning*, pages 41–48, San Mateo, CA, 1993. Morgan Kaufmann.

[7] M. Lando and S. Edelman. Generalizing from a single view in face recognition. Technical Report CS-TR 95-02, Department of Applied Mathematics and Computer Science, The Weizmann Institute of Science, Rehovot 76100, Israel, January 1995.

[8] T. M. Mitchell and S. Thrun. Explanation-based neural network learning for robot control. In S. J. Hanson, J. Cowan, and C. L. Giles, editors, *Advances in Neural Information Processing Systems 5*, pages 287–294, San Mateo, CA, 1993. Morgan Kaufmann.

[9] A. W. Moore, D. J. Hill, and M. P. Johnson. An Empirical Investigation of Brute Force to choose Features, Smoothers and Function Approximators. In S. Hanson, S. Judd, and T. Petsche, editors, *Computational Learning Theory and Natural Learning Systems, Volume 3*. MIT Press, 1992.

[10] Y. Moses, S. Ullman, and S. Edelman. Generalization across changes in illumination and viewing position in upright and inverted faces. Technical Report CS-TR 93-14, Department of Applied Mathematics and Computer Science, The Weizmann Institute of Science, Rehovot 76100, Israel, 1993.

[11] J. O'Sullivan, T. M. Mitchell, and S. Thrun. Explanation-based neural network learning from mobile robot perception. In K. Ikeuchi and M. Veloso, editors, *Symbolic Visual Learning*. Oxford University Press, 1995.

[12] D. E. Rumelhart, G. E. Hinton, and R. J. Williams. Learning internal representations by error propagation. In D. E. Rumelhart and J. L. McClelland, editors, *Parallel Distributed Processing. Vol. I + II*. MIT Press, 1986.

[13] D. Shepard. A two-dimensional interpolation function for irregularly spaced data. In *23rd National Conference ACM*, pages 517–523, 1968.

[14] P. Simard, B. Victorri, Y. LeCun, and J. Denker. Tangent prop – a formalism for specifying selected invariances in an adaptive network. In J. E. Moody, S. J. Hanson, and R. P. Lippmann, editors, *Advances in Neural Information Processing Systems 4*, pages 895–903, San Mateo, CA, 1992. Morgan Kaufmann.

[15] C. Stanfill and D. Waltz. Towards memory-based reasoning. *Communications of the ACM*, 29(12):1213–1228, December 1986.

[16] S. C. Suddarth and A. Holden. Symbolic neural systems and the use of hints for developing complex systems. *International Journal of Machine Studies*, 35, 1991.

[17] S. Thrun. *Explanation-Based Neural Network Learning: A Lifelong Learning Approach*. Kluwer Academic Publishers, Boston, MA, 1996. to appear.

[18] S. Thrun and J. O'Sullivan. Clustering learning tasks and the selective cross-task transfer of knowledge. Technical Report CMU-CS-95-209, Carnegie Mellon University, School of Computer Science, Pittsburgh, PA 15213, November 1995.

Using Unlabeled Data for Supervised Learning

Geoffrey Towell
Siemens Corporate Research
755 College Road East
Princeton, NJ 08540

Abstract

Many classification problems have the property that the only costly part of obtaining examples is the class label. This paper suggests a simple method for using distribution information contained in unlabeled examples to augment labeled examples in a supervised training framework. Empirical tests show that the technique described in this paper can significantly improve the accuracy of a supervised learner when the learner is well below its asymptotic accuracy level.

1 INTRODUCTION

Supervised learning problems often have the following property: unlabeled examples have little or no cost while class labels have a high cost. For example, it is trivial to record hours of heartbeats from hundreds of patients. However, it is expensive to hire cardiologists to label each of the recorded beats. One response to the expense of class labels is to squeeze the most information possible out of each labeled example. Regularization and cross-validation both have this goal. A second response is to start with a small set of labeled examples and request labels of only those currently unlabeled examples that are expected to provide a significant improvement in the behavior of the classifier (Lewis & Catlett, 1994; Freund et al., 1993).

A third response is to tap into a largely ignored potential source of information; namely, unlabeled examples. This response is supported by the theoretical work of Castelli and Cover (1995) which suggests that unlabeled examples have value in learning classification problems. The algorithm described in this paper, referred to as SULU (*Supervised learning Using Labeled and Unlabeled examples*), takes this third path by using distribution information from unlabeled examples during supervised learning. Roughly, SULU uses the centroid of labeled and unlabeled examples in the neighborhood of a labeled example as a new training example. In this way, SULU extracts information about the local variability of the input from unlabeled data. SULU is described in Section 2.

In its use of unlabeled examples to alter labeled examples, SULU is reminiscent of techniques for adding noise to networks during training (Hanson, 1990; Matsuoka, 1992). SULU is also reminiscent of instantiations of the EM algorithm that attempt to fill in missing parts of examples (Ghahramani & Jordan, 1994). The similarity of SULU to these, and other, works is explored in Section 3.

SULU is intended to work on classification problems for which there is insufficient labeled training data to allow a learner to approach its asymptotic accuracy level. To explore this problem, the experiments described in Section 4 focus on the early parts of the learning curves of six datasets (described in Section 4.1). The results show that SULU consistently, and statistically significantly, improves classification accuracy over systems trained with only the labeled data. Moreover, SULU is consistently more accurate than an implementation of the EM-algorithm that was specialized for the task of filling in missing class labels. From these results, it is reasonable to conclude that SULU is able to use the distribution information in unlabeled examples to improve classification accuracy.

2 THE ALGORITHM

SULU uses standard neural-network supervised training techniques except that it occasionally replaces a labeled example with a synthetic example. in addition, the criterion to stop training is slightly modified to require that the network correctly classify almost every labeled example and a majority of the synthetic examples. For instance, the experiments reported in Section 4 generate synthetic examples 50% of the time; the stopping criterion requires that 80% of the examples seen in a single epoch are classified correctly. The **main** function in Table 1 provides psuedocode for this process.

The **synthesize** function in Table 1 describes the process through which an example is synthesized. Given a labeled example to use as a seed, **synthesize** collects neighboring examples and returns an example that is the centroid of the collected examples with the label of the starting point. **synthesize** collects neighboring examples until reaching one of the following three stopping points. First, the maximum number of points is reached; the goal of SULU is to get information about the local variance around known points, this criterion guarantees locality. Second, the next closest example to the seed is a labeled example with a different label; this criterion prevents the inclusion of obviously incorrect information in synthetic examples. Third, the next closest example to the seed is an unlabeled example and the closest labeled example to that unlabeled example has a different label from the seed; this criterion is intended to detect borders between classification areas in example space.

The call to **synthesize** from **main** effectively samples with replacement from a space defined by a labeled example and its neighbors. As such, there are many ways in which **main** and **synthesize** could be written. The principle consideration in this implementation is memory; the space around the labeled examples can be huge.

Table 1: Pseudocode for SULU

```
RANDOM(min,max):
  return a uniformly distributed random integer between min and max, inclusive

MAIN(B,M):
  /* B - in [0..100], controls the rate of example synthesis */
  /* M - controls neighborhood size during synthesis         */
  Let: E   /* a set of labeled examples   */
       U   /* a set of unlabeled examples */
       N   /* an appropriate neural network */
  Repeat
    Permute E
    Foreach e in E
      if random(0,100) > B then
        e <- SYNTHESIZE(e,E,U,random(2,M))
      TRAIN N using e
    Until a stopping criterion is reached

SYNTHESIZE(e,E,U,m):
  Let: C   /* will hold a collection of examples */
  For i from 1 to m
    c <- ith nearest neighbor of e in E union U
    if ((c is labeled) and (label of c not equal to label of e)) then STOP
    if c is not labeled
      cc <- nearest neighbor of c in E
      if label of cc not equal to label of e then STOP
    add c to C
  return an example whose input is the centroid of the
    inputs of the examples in C and has the class label of e.
```

3 RELATED WORK

SULU is similar to two methods of exploring the input space beyond the boundaries of the labeled examples; example generation and noise addition. Example generation commonly uses a model of how a space deforms and an example of the space to generate new examples. For instance, in training a vehicle to turn, Pomerleau (1993) used information about how the scene shifts when a car is turned to generate examples of turns. The major problem with example generation is that deformation models are uncommon.

By contrast to example generation, noise addition is a model-free procedure. In general, the idea is to add a small amount of noise to either inputs (Matsuoka, 1992), link weights (Hanson, 1990), or hidden units (Judd & Munro, 1993). For example, Hanson (1990) replaces link weights with a Gaussian. During a forward pass, the Gaussian is sampled to determine the link weight. Training affects both the mean and the variance of the Gaussian. In so doing, Hanson's method uses distribution information in the labeled examples to estimate the global variance of each input dimension. By contrast, SULU uses both labeled and unlabeled examples to make local variance estimates. (Experiments, results not shown, with Hanson's method indicate that it cannot improve classification results as much as SULU.)

Finally, there has been some other work on using unclassified examples during training. de Sa (1994) uses the co-occurrence of inputs in multiple sensor modalities to substitute for missing class information. However, sensor data from multiple modalities is often not available. Another approach is to use the EM algorithm (Ghahramani & Jordan, 1994) which iteratively guesses the value of missing information (both input and output) and builds structures to predict the missing information. Unlike SULU, EM uses global information in this process so it may not perform well on highly disjunctive problems. Also SULU may have an advantage over EM in domains in which only the class label is missing as that is SULU's specific focus.

4 EXPERIMENTS

The experiments reported in this section explore the behavior of SULU on six datasets. Each of the datasets has been used previously so they are only briefly described in the first subsection. The results of the experiments reported in the last part of this section show that SULU significantly and consistently improves classification results.

4.1 DATASETS

The first two datasets are from molecular biology. Each take a DNA sequence and encode it using four bits per nucleotide. The first problem, promoter recognition (Opitz & Shavlik, 1994), is: given a sequence of 57 DNA nucleotides, determine if a promoter begins at a particular position in the sequence. Following Opitz and Shavlik, the experiments in this paper use 234 promoters and 702 nonpromoters. The second molecular biology problem, splice-junction determination (Towell & Shavlik, 1994), is: given a sequence of 60 DNA nucleotides, determine if there is a splice-junction (and the type of the junction) at the middle of the sequence. The data consist of 243 examples of one junction type (acceptors), 228 examples of the other junction type (donors) and 536 examples of non-junctions. For both of these problems, the best randomly initialized neural networks have a small number of hidden units in a single layer (Towell & Shavlik, 1994).

The remaining four datasets are word sense disambiguation problems (i.e. determine the intended meaning of the word "pen" in the sentence "the box is in the pen"). The problems are to learn to distinguish between six noun senses of "line" or four verb senses of "serve" using either topical or local encodings (Leacock et al., 1993) of a context around the target word. The line dataset contains 349 examples of each sense. Topical encoding, retaining all words that occur more than twice, requires 5700 position vectors. Local encoding, using three words on either side of line, requires 4500 position vectors. The serve dataset contains 350 examples of each sense. Under the same conditions as line, topical encoding requires 4400 position vectors while local encoding requires 4500 position vectors. The best neural networks for these problems have no hidden units (Leacock et al., 1993).

4.2 METHODOLOGY

The following methodology was used to test SULU on each dataset. First, the data was split into three sets, 25 percent was set aside to be used for assessing generalization, 50 percent had the class labels stripped off, and the remaining 25 percent was to be used for training. To create learning curves, the training set was

Table 2: Endpoints of the learnings curves for standard neural networks and the best result for each of the six datasets.

Training Set size	Promoter	Splice Junction	Serve Local	Serve Topical	Line Local	Line Topical
smallest	74.7	66.4	53.9	41.8	38.7	40.6
largest	90.3	85.4	71.7	63.0	58.8	63.3
asymptotic	95.8	94.4	83.1	75.5	70.1	79.2

further subdivided into sets containing 5, 10, 15, 20 and 25 percent of the data such that smaller sets were always subsets of larger sets. Then, a single neural network was created and copied 25 times. At each training set size, a new copy of the network was trained under each of the following conditions: 1) using SULU, 2) using SULU but supplying only the labeled training examples to synthesize, 3) standard network training, 4) using a variant of the EM algorithm that has been specialized to the task of filling in missing class labels, and 5) using standard network training but with the 50% unlabeled prior to stripping the labels. This procedure was repeated eleven times to average out the effects of example selection and network initialization.

When SULU was used, synthetic examples replaced labeled examples 50 percent of the time. Networks using the full SULU (case 1) were trained until 80 percent of the examples in a single epoch were correctly classified. All other networks were trained until at least 99.5% of the examples were correctly classified. Stopping criteria intended to prevent overfitting were investigated, but not used because they never improved generalization.

4.3 RESULTS & DISCUSSION

Figure 1 and Table 2 summarize the results of these experiments. The graphs in Figure 1 show the efficacy of each algorithm. Except for the largest training set on the splice junction problem, SULU always results in a statistically significant improvement over the standard neural network with at least 97.5 percent confidence (according to a one-tailed paired-sample t-test). Interestingly, SULU's improvement is consistently between $\frac{1}{4}$ and $\frac{1}{2}$ of that achieved by labeling the unlabeled examples. This result contrasts Castelli and Cover's (1995) analysis which suggests that labeled examples are exponentially more valuable than unlabeled examples.

In addition, SULU is consistently and significantly superior to the instantiation of the EM-algorithm when there are very few labeled samples. As the number of labeled samples increases the advantage of SULU decreases. At the largest training set sizes tested, the two systems are roughly equally effective.

A possible criticism of SULU is that it does not actually need the unlabeled examples; the procedure may be as effective using only the labeled training data. This hypothesis is incorrect, As shown in Figure 1, SULU when given no unlabeled examples is consistently and significantly inferior ti SULU when given a large number of unlabeled examples. In addition, SULU with no unlabeled examples is consistently, although not always significantly, inferior to a standard neural network.

The failure of SULU with only labeled examples points to a significant weakness

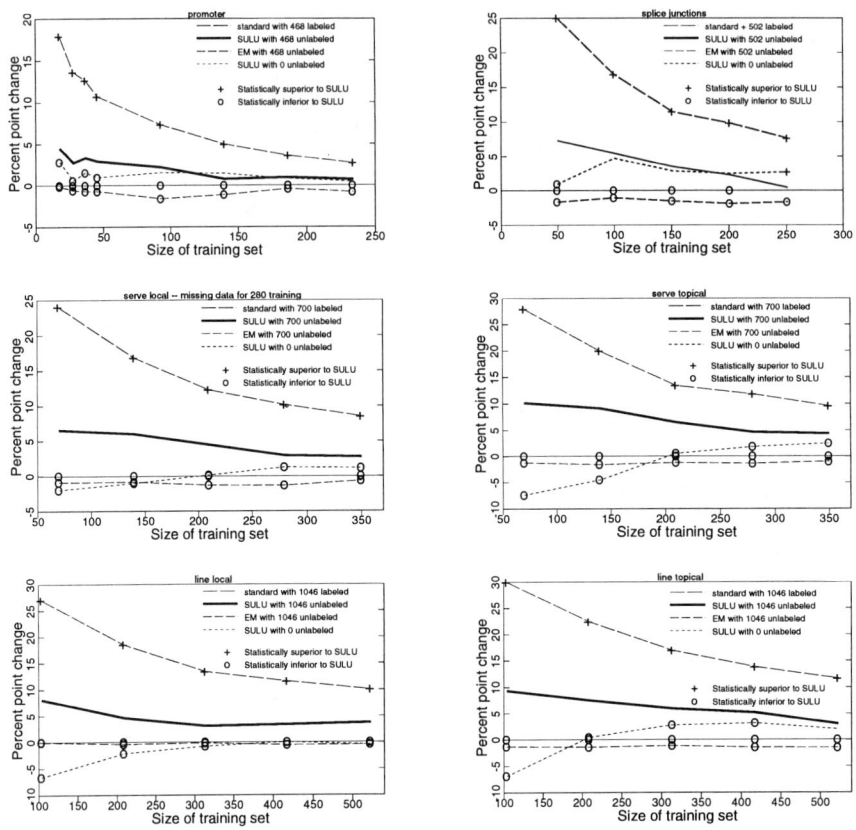

Figure 1: The effect of five training procedures on each of six learning problems. In each of the above graphs, the effect of standard neural learning has been subtracted from all results to suppress the increase in accuracy that results simply from an increase in the number of labeled training examples. Observations marked by a 'o' or a '+' respectively indicate that the point is statistically significantly inferior or superior to a network trained using SULU.

in its current implementation. Specifically, SULU finds the nearest neighbors of an example using a simple mismatch counting procedure. Tests of this procedure as an independent classification technique (results not shown) indicate that it is consistently much worse than any of the methods plotted in in Figure 1. Hence, its use imparts a downward bias to the generalization results.

A second indication of room for improvement in SULU is the difference in generalization between SULU and a network trained using data in which the unlabeled examples provided to SULU have labels (case 5 above). On every dataset, the gain from labeling the examples is statistically significant. The accuracy of a network trained with all labeled examples is an upper bound for SULU, and one that is likely not reachable. However, the distance between the upper bound and SULU's current performance indicate that there is room for improvement.

5 CONCLUSIONS

This paper has presented the SULU algorithm that combines aspects of nearest neighbor classification with neural networks to learn using both labeled and unlabeled examples. The algorithm uses the labeled and unlabeled examples to construct synthetic examples that capture information about the local characteristics of the example space. In so doing, the range of examples seen by the neural network during its supervised learning is greatly expanded which results in improved generalization. Results of experiments on six real-work datasets indicate that SULU can significantly improve generalization when when there is little labeled data. Moreover, the results indicate that SULU is consistently more effective at using unlabeled examples than the EM-algorithm when there is very little labeled data. The results suggest that SULU will be effective given the following conditions: 1) there is little labeled training data, 2) unlabeled training data is essentially free, 3) the accuracy of the classifier when trained with all of the available data is below the level which is expected to be achievable. On problems with all of these properties SULU may significantly improve the generalization accuracy of inductive classifiers.

References

Castelli, V. & Cover, T. (1995). *The relative value of labeled and unlabeled samples in pattern recognition with an unknown mixing parameter.* (Technical Report 86), Department of Statistics: Stanford University.

de Sa, V. (1994). Learning classification with unlabeled data. *Advances in Neural Information Processing Systems, 6.*

Freund, Y., Seung, H. S., Shamit, E., & Tishby, N. (1993). Information, prediction and query by committee. *Advances in Neural Information Processing Systems, 5.*

Ghahramani, Z. & Jordan, M. I. (1994). Supervised learning from incomplete data via an EM approach. *Advances in Neural Information Processing Systems, 6.*

Hanson, S. J. (1990). A stochastic version of the delta rule. *Physica D*, 42, 265–272.

Judd, J. S. & Munro, P. W. (1993). Nets with unreliable hidden units learn error-correcting codes. *Advances in Neural Information Processing Systems, 5.*

Leacock, C., Towell, G., & Voorhees, E. M. (1993). Towards building contextual representations of word senses using statistical models. *Proceedings of SIGLEX Workshop: Acquisition of Lexical Knowledge from Text.* Association for Computational Linguistics.

Lewis, D. D. & Catlett, J. (1994). Heterogeneous uncertainty sampling for supervised learning. *Eleventh International Machine Learning Conference.*

Matsuoka, K. (1992). Noise injection into inputs in back-propagation learning. *IEEE Transactions on Systems, Man and Cybernetics*, 22, 436–440.

Opitz, D. W. & Shavlik, J. W. (1994). Using genetic search to refine knowledge-based neural networks. *Eleventh International Machine Learning Conference.*

Pomerleau, D. A. (1993). *Neural Network Perception for Mobile Robot Guidance.* Boston: Kluwer.

Towell, G. G. & Shavlik, J. W. (1994). Knowledge-based artificial neural networks. *Artificial Intelligence*, 70, 119–165.

Learning Sparse Perceptrons

Jeffrey C. Jackson
Mathematics & Computer Science Dept.
Duquesne University
600 Forbes Ave
Pittsburgh, PA 15282
jackson@mathcs.duq.edu

Mark W. Craven
Computer Sciences Dept.
University of Wisconsin-Madison
1210 West Dayton St.
Madison, WI 53706
craven@cs.wisc.edu

Abstract

We introduce a new algorithm designed to learn *sparse perceptrons* over input representations which include high-order features. Our algorithm, which is based on a hypothesis-boosting method, is able to PAC-learn a relatively natural class of target concepts. Moreover, the algorithm appears to work well in practice: on a set of three problem domains, the algorithm produces classifiers that utilize small numbers of features yet exhibit good generalization performance. Perhaps most importantly, our algorithm generates concept descriptions that are easy for humans to understand.

1 Introduction

Multi-layer perceptron (MLP) learning is a powerful method for tasks such as concept classification. However, in many applications, such as those that may involve scientific discovery, it is crucial to be able to *explain* predictions. Multi-layer perceptrons are limited in this regard, since their representations are notoriously difficult for humans to understand. We present an approach to learning understandable, yet accurate, classifiers. Specifically, our algorithm constructs *sparse perceptrons*, i.e., single-layer perceptrons that have relatively few non-zero weights. Our algorithm for learning sparse perceptrons is based on a new *hypothesis boosting* algorithm (Freund & Schapire, 1995). Although our algorithm was initially developed from a learning-theoretic point of view and retains certain theoretical guarantees (it PAC-learns the class of sparse perceptrons), it also works well in practice. Our experiments in a number of real-world domains indicate that our algorithm produces perceptrons that are relatively comprehensible, and that exhibit generalization performance comparable to that of backprop-trained MLP's (Rumelhart et al., 1986) and better than decision trees learned using C4.5 (Quinlan, 1993).

We contend that sparse perceptrons, unlike MLP's, are comprehensible because they have relatively few parameters, and each parameter describes a simple (i.e. linear) relationship. As evidence that sparse perceptrons are comprehensible, consider that such linear functions are commonly used to express domain knowledge in fields such as medicine (Spackman, 1988) and molecular biology (Stormo, 1987).

2 Sparse Perceptrons

A *perceptron* is a weighted threshold over the set of input features and over higher-order features consisting of functions operating on only a limited number of the input features. Informally, a *sparse* perceptron is any perceptron that has relatively few non-zero weights. For our later theoretical results we will need a more precise definition of sparseness which we develop now. Consider a Boolean function $f : \{0,1\}^n \to \{-1,+1\}$. Let C_k be the set of all conjunctions of at most k of the inputs to f. C_k includes the "conjunction" of 0 inputs, which we take as the identically 1 function. All of the functions in C_k map to $\{-1,+1\}$, and every conjunction in C_k occurs in both a positive sense ($+1$ represents true) and a negated sense (-1 represents true). Then the function f is a k-perceptron if there is some integer s such that $f(x) = \text{sign}(\sum_{i=1}^{s} h_i(x))$, where for all i, $h_i \in C_k$, and $\text{sign}(y)$ is undefined if $y = 0$ and is $y/|y|$ otherwise. Note that while we have not explicitly shown any weights in our definition of a k-perceptron f, integer weights are implicitly present in that we allow a particular $h_i \in C_k$ to appear more than once in the sum defining f. In fact, it is often convenient to think of a k-perceptron as a simple linear discriminant function with integer weights defined over a feature space with $O(n^k)$ features, one feature for each element of C_k.

We call a given collection of s conjunctions $h_i \in C_k$ a k-perceptron *representation* of the corresponding function f, and we call s the *size* of the representation. We define the *size* of a given k-perceptron function f as the minimal size of any k-perceptron representation of f. An s-sparse k-perceptron is a k-perceptron f such that the size of f is at most s. We denote by $\mathcal{P}_k^n$ the set of Boolean functions over $\{0,1\}^n$ which can be represented as k-perceptrons, and we define $\mathcal{P}_k = \cup_n \mathcal{P}_k^n$. The subclass of s-sparse k-perceptrons is denoted by $\mathcal{P}_{k,s}$. We are also interested in the class $\mathcal{P}_{k,r}^R$ of k-perceptrons with real-valued weights, at most r of which are non-zero.

3 The Learning Algorithm

In this section we develop our learning algorithm and prove certain performance guarantees. Our algorithm is based on a recent "hypothesis boosting" algorithm that we describe after reviewing some basic learning-theory terminology.

3.1 PAC Learning and Hypothesis Boosting

Following Valiant (1984), we say that a function class $\mathcal{F}$ (such as $\mathcal{P}_k$ for fixed k) is *(strongly) PAC-learnable* if there is an algorithm $\mathcal{A}$ and a polynomial function p_1 such that for any positive ϵ and δ, any $f \in \mathcal{F}$ (the *target function*), and any probability distribution D over the domain of f, with probability at least $1 - \delta$, algorithm $\mathcal{A}(EX(f,D), \epsilon, \delta)$ produces a function h (the *hypothesis*) such that $\Pr[\Pr_D[f(x) \neq h(x)] > \epsilon] < \delta$. The outermost probability is over the random choices made by the EX oracle and any random choices made by $\mathcal{A}$. Here $EX(f,D)$ denotes an oracle that, when queried, chooses a vector of input values x with probability D and returns the pair $\langle x, f(x) \rangle$ to $\mathcal{A}$. The learning algorithm $\mathcal{A}$ must run in time $p_1(n, s, \epsilon^{-1}, \delta^{-1})$, where n is the length of the input vector to f and s is the size of

AdaBoost
Input: training set S of m examples of function f, weak learning algorithm WL that is $(\frac{1}{2} - \gamma)$-approximate, γ
Algorithm:

1. $T \leftarrow \frac{1}{2\gamma^2} \ln(m)$
2. for all $x \in S$, $w(x) \leftarrow 1/m$
3. **for** $i = 1$ to T **do**
4.   for all $x \in S$, $D_i(x) \leftarrow w(x)/\sum_{j=1}^{m} w(x)$.
5.   invoke WL on S and distribution D_i, producing weak hypothesis h_i
6. $\epsilon_i \leftarrow \sum_{x.h_i(x) \neq f(x)} D_i(x)$
7. $\beta_i \leftarrow \epsilon_i/(1 - \epsilon_i)$
8.   for all $x \in S$, if $h(x) = f(x)$ then $w(x) \leftarrow w(x) \cdot \beta_i$
9. **enddo**

Output: $h(x) \equiv sign\left(\sum_{i=1}^{T} -\ln(\beta_i) \cdot h_i(x)\right)$

Figure 1: The AdaBoost algorithm.

f; the algorithm is charged one unit of time for each call to EX. We sometimes call the function h output by $\mathcal{A}$ an ϵ-*approximator* (or *strong approximator*) to f with respect to D. If $\mathcal{F}$ is PAC-learnable by an algorithm $\mathcal{A}$ that outputs only hypotheses in class $\mathcal{H}$ then we say that $\mathcal{F}$ is *PAC-learnable by* $\mathcal{H}$. If $\mathcal{F}$ is PAC-learnable for $\epsilon = 1/2 - 1/p_2(n,s)$, where p_2 is a polynomial function, then $\mathcal{F}$ is *weakly PAC-learnable*, and the output hypothesis h in this case is called a *weak approximator*.

Our algorithm for finding sparse perceptrons is, as indicated earlier, based on the notion of hypothesis boosting. The specific boosting algorithm we use (Figure 1) is a version of the recent AdaBoost algorithm (Freund & Schapire, 1995). In the next section we apply AdaBoost to "boost" a weak learning algorithm for $\mathcal{P}_{k,s}$ into a strong learner for $\mathcal{P}_{k,s}$. AdaBoost is given a set S of m examples of a function $f : \{0,1\}^n \rightarrow \{-1,+1\}$ and a weak learning algorithm WL which takes $\epsilon = \frac{1}{2} - \gamma$ for a given γ (γ must be bounded by an inverse polynomial in n and s). AdaBoost runs for $T = \ln(m)/(2\gamma^2)$ stages. At each stage it creates a probability distribution D_i over the training set and invokes WL to find a weak hypothesis h_i with respect to D_i (note that an example oracle $EX(f, D_i)$ can be simulated given D_i and S). At the end of the T stages a final hypothesis h is output; this is just a weighted threshold over the weak hypotheses $\{h_i \mid 1 \leq i \leq T\}$. If the weak learner succeeds in producing a $(\frac{1}{2} - \gamma)$-approximator at each stage then AdaBoost's final hypothesis is guaranteed to be consistent with the training set (Freund & Schapire, 1995).

3.2 PAC-Learning Sparse k-Perceptrons

We now show that sparse k-perceptrons are PAC learnable by real-weighted k-perceptrons having relatively few nonzero weights. Specifically, ignoring log factors, $\mathcal{P}_{k,s}$ is learnable by $\mathcal{P}^R_{k,O(s^2)}$ for any constant k. We first show that, given a training set for any $f \in \mathcal{P}_{k,s}$, we can efficiently find a consistent $h \in \mathcal{P}^R_{k,O(s^2)}$. This *consistency algorithm* is the basis of the algorithm we later apply to empirical learning problems. We then show how to turn the consistency algorithm into a PAC learning algorithm. Our proof is implicit in somewhat more general work by Freund (1993), although he did not actually present a learning algorithm for this class or analyze the sample size needed to ensure ϵ-approximation, as we do. Following Freund, we begin our development with the following lemma (Goldmann et al., 1992):

Lemma 1 (Goldmann Hastad Razborov) *For $f : \{0,1\}^n \to \{-1,+1\}$ and H, any set of functions with the same domain and range, if f can be represented as $f(x) = \text{sign}(\sum_{i=1}^{s} h_i(x))$, where $h_i \in H$, then for any probability distribution D over $\{0,1\}^n$ there is some h_i such that $\Pr_D[f(x) \neq h_i(x)] \leq \frac{1}{2} - \frac{1}{2s}$.*

If we specialize this lemma by taking $H = C_k$ (recall that C_k is the set of conjunctions of at most k input features of f) then this implies that for any $f \in \mathcal{P}_{k,s}$ and any probability distribution D over the input features of f there is some $h_i \in C_k$ that weakly approximates f with respect to D. Therefore, given a training set S and distribution D that has nonzero weight only on instances in S, the following simple algorithm is a weak learning algorithm for $\mathcal{P}_k$: exhaustively test each of the $O(n^k)$ possible conjunctions of at most k features until we find a conjunction that $(\frac{1}{2} - \frac{1}{2s})$-approximates f with respect to D (we can efficiently compute the approximation of a conjunction h_i by summing the values of D over those inputs where h_i and f agree). Any such conjunction can be returned as the weak hypothesis. The above lemma proves that if f is a k-perceptron then this exhaustive search must succeed at finding such a hypothesis. Therefore, given a training set of m examples of any s-sparse k-perceptron f, AdaBoost run with the above weak learner will, after $2s^2 \ln(m)$ stages, produce a hypothesis consistent with the training set. Because each stage adds one weak hypothesis to the output hypothesis, the final hypothesis will be a real-weighted k-perceptron with at most $2s^2 \ln(m)$ nonzero weights.

We can convert this consistency algorithm to a PAC learning algorithm as follows. First, given a finite set of functions $\mathcal{F}$, it is straightforward to show the following (see, e.g., Haussler, 1988):

Lemma 2 *Let $\mathcal{F}$ be a finite set of functions over a domain X. For any function f over X, any probability distribution D over X, and any positive ϵ and δ, given a set S of m examples drawn consecutively from $EX(f, D)$, where $m \geq \epsilon^{-1}(\ln \delta^{-1} + \ln |\mathcal{F}|)$, then $\Pr[\exists h \in \mathcal{F} \mid \forall x \in S \; f(x) = h(x) \; \& \; \Pr_D[f(x) \neq h(x)] > \epsilon] < \delta$, where the outer probability is over the random choices made by $EX(f, D)$.*

The consistency algorithm above finds a consistent hypothesis in $\mathcal{P}_{k,r}^{\text{R}}$, where $r = 2s^2 \ln(m)$. Also, based on a result of Bruck (1990), it can be shown that $\ln |\mathcal{P}_{k,r}^{\text{R}}| = O(r^2 + kr \log n)$. Therefore, ignoring log factors, a randomly-generated training set of size $\Omega(ks^4/\epsilon)$ is sufficient to guarantee that, with high probability, our algorithm will produce an ϵ-approximator for any s-sparse k-perceptron target. In other words, the following is a PAC algorithm for $\mathcal{P}_{k,s}$: compute sufficiently large (but polynomial in the PAC parameters) m, draw m examples from $EX(f, D)$ to create a training set, and run the consistency algorithm on this training set.

So far we have shown that sparse k-perceptrons are learnable by sparse perceptron hypotheses (with potentially polynomially-many more weights). In practice, of course, we expect that many real-world classification tasks cannot be performed exactly by sparse perceptrons. In fact, it can be shown that for certain (reasonable) definitions of "noisy" sparse perceptrons (loosely, functions that are approximated reasonably well by sparse perceptrons), the class of noisy sparse k-perceptrons is still PAC-learnable. This claim is based on results of Aslam and Decatur (1993), who present a noise-tolerant boosting algorithm. In fact, several different boosting algorithms could be used to learn $\mathcal{P}_{k,s}$ (e.g., Freund, 1993). We have chosen to use AdaBoost because it seems to offer significant practical advantages, particularly in terms of efficiency. Also, our empirical results to date indicate that our algorithm works very well on difficult (presumably "noisy") real-world problems. However, one potential advantage of basing the algorithm on one of these earlier boosters instead of AdaBoost is that the algorithm would then produce a perceptron with integer weights while still maintaining the sparseness guarantee of the AdaBoost-based algorithm.

3.3 Practical Considerations

We turn now to the practical details of our algorithm, which is based on the consistency algorithm above. First, it should be noted that the theory developed above works over *discrete* input domains (Boolean or nominal-valued features). Thus, in this paper, we consider only tasks with discrete input features. Also, because the algorithm uses exhaustive search over all conjunctions of size k, learning time depends exponentially on the choice of k. In this study we to use $k = 2$ throughout, since this choice results in reasonable learning times.

Another implementation concern involves deciding when the learning algorithm should terminate. The consistency algorithm uses the size of the target function in calculating the number of boosting stages. Of course, such size information is not available in real-world applications, and in fact, the target function may not be exactly representable as a sparse perceptron. In practice, we use cross validation to determine an appropriate termination point. To facilitate comprehensibility, we also limit the number of boosting stages to at most the number of weights that would occur in an ordinary perceptron for the task. For similar reasons, we also modify the criteria used to select the weak hypothesis at each stage so that simple features are preferred over conjunctive features. In particular, given distribution D at some stage j, for each $h_i \in C_k$ we compute a correlation $E_D[f \cdot h_i]$. We then multiply each high-order feature's correlation by $\frac{1}{k}$. The h_i with the largest resulting correlation serves as the weak hypothesis for stage j.

4 Empirical Evaluation

In our experiments, we are interested in assessing both the generalization ability and the complexity of the hypotheses produced by our algorithm. We compare our algorithm to ordinary perceptrons trained using backpropagation (Rumelhart et al., 1986), multi-layer perceptrons trained using backpropagation, and decision trees induced using the C4.5 system (Quinlan, 1993). We use C4.5 in our experiments as a representative of "symbolic" learning algorithms. Symbolic algorithms are widely believed to learn hypotheses that are more comprehensible than neural networks. Additionally, to test the hypothesis that the performance of our algorithm can be explained solely by its use of second-order features, we train ordinary perceptrons using feature sets that include all pairwise conjunctions, as well as the ordinary features. To test the hypothesis that the performance of our algorithm can be explained by its use of relatively few weights, we consider ordinary perceptrons which have been pruned using a variant of the Optimal Brain Damage (OBD) algorithm (Le Cun et al., 1989). In our version of OBD, we train a perceptron until the stopping criteria are met, prune the weight with the smallest salience, and then iterate the process. We use a validation set to decide when to stop pruning weights. For each training set, we use cross-validation to select the number of hidden units (5, 10, 20, 40 or 80) for the MLP's, and the pruning confidence level for the C4.5 trees. We use a validation set to decide when to stop training for the MLP's.

We evaluate our algorithm using three real-world domains: the voting data set from the UC-Irvine database; a promoter data set which is a more complex superset of

Table 1: Test-set accuracy.

domain	boosting	C4.5	perceptrons			
			multi-layer	ordinary	2nd-order	pruned
voting	91.5%	89.2% *	92.2%	90.8%	89.2% *	87.6% *
promoter	92.7	84.4 *	90.6	90.0 *	88.7 *	88.2 *
coding	72.9	62.6 *	71.6 *	70.7 *	69.8 *	70.3 *

Table 2: Hypothesis complexity (# weights).

domain	boosting	perceptrons			
		multi-layer	ordinary	2nd-order	pruned
voting	12	651	30	450	12
promoters	41	2267	228	25764	59
protein coding	52	4270	60	1740	37

UC-Irvine one; and a data set in which the task is to recognize protein-coding regions in DNA (Craven & Shavlik, 1993). We remove the physician-fee-freeze feature from the voting data set to make the problem more difficult. We conduct our experiments using a 10-fold cross validation methodology, except for in the protein-coding domain. Because of certain domain-specific characteristics of this data set, we use 4-fold cross-validation for our experiments with it.

Table 1 reports test-set accuracy for each method on all three domains. We measure the statistical significance of accuracy differences using a paired, two-tailed t-test. The symbol '*' marks results in cases where another algorithm is less accurate than our boosting algorithm at the $p \leq 0.05$ level of significance. No other algorithm is significantly better than our boosting method in any of the domains. From these results we conclude that (1) our algorithm exhibits good generalization performance on number of interesting real-world problems, and (2) the generalization performance of our algorithm is not explained solely by its use of second-order features, nor is it solely explained by the sparseness of the perceptrons it produces. An interesting open question is whether perceptrons trained with both pruning and second-order features are able to match the accuracy of our algorithm; we plan to investigate this question in future work.

Table 2 reports the average number of weights for all of the perceptrons. For all three problems, our algorithm produces perceptrons with fewer weights than the MLP's, the ordinary perceptrons, and the perceptrons with second-order features. The sizes of the OBD-pruned perceptrons and those produced by our algorithm are comparable for all three domains. Recall, however, that for all three tasks, the perceptrons learned by our algorithm had significantly better generalization performance than their similar-sized OBD-pruned counterparts. We contend that the sizes of the perceptrons produced by our algorithm are within the bounds of what humans can readily understand. In the biological literature, for example, linear discriminant functions are frequently used to communicate domain knowledge about sequences of interest. These functions frequently involve more weights than the perceptrons produced by our algorithm. We conclude, therefore, that our algorithm produces hypotheses that are not only accurate, but also comprehensible.

We believe that the results on the protein-coding domain are especially interesting. The input representation for this problem consists of 15 nominal features representing 15 consecutive *bases* in a DNA sequence. In the regions of DNA that encode proteins (the positive examples in our task), non-overlapping triplets of consecutive bases represent meaningful "words" called *codons*. In previous work (Craven & Shavlik, 1993), it has been found that a feature set that explicitly represents codons results in better generalization than a representation of just bases. However, we used the bases representation in our experiments in order to investigate the ability of our algorithm to select the "right" second-order features. Interestingly, nearly all of the second-order features included in our sparse perceptrons represent conjunctions of bases that are in the same codon. This result suggests that our algorithm is especially good at selecting relevant features from large feature sets.

5 Future Work

Our present algorithm has a number of limitations which we plan to address. Two areas of current research are generalizing the algorithm for application to problems with real-valued features and developing methods for automatically suggesting high-order features to be included in our algorithm's feature set.

Acknowledgements

Mark Craven was partially supported by ONR grant N00014-93-1-0998. Jeff Jackson was partially supported by NSF grant CCR-9119319.

References

Aslam, J. A. & Decatur, S. E. (1993). General bounds on statistical query learning and PAC learning with noise via hypothesis boosting. In *Proc. of the 34th Annual Annual Symposium on Foundations of Computer Science*, (pp. 282–291).

Bruck, J. (1990). Harmonic analysis of polynomial threshold functions. *SIAM Journal of Discrete Mathematics*, 3(2):168–177.

Craven, M. W. & Shavlik, J. W. (1993). Learning to represent codons: A challenge problem for constructive induction. In *Proc. of the 13th International Joint Conf. on Artificial Intelligence*, (pp. 1319–1324), Chambery, France.

Freund, Y. (1993). *Data Filtering and Distribution Modeling Algorithms for Machine Learning*. PhD thesis, University of California at Santa Cruz.

Freund, Y. & Schapire, R. E. (1995). A decision-theoretic generalization of on-line learning and an application to boosting. In *Proc. of the 2nd Annual European Conf. on Computational Learning Theory*.

Goldmann, M., Hastad, J., & Razborov, A. (1992). Majority gates vs. general weighted threshold gates. In *Proc. of the 7th IEEE Conf. on Structure in Complexity Theory*.

Haussler, D. (1988). Quantifying inductive bias: AI learning algorithms and Valiant's learning framework. *Artificial Intelligence*, (pp. 177–221).

Le Cun, Y., Denker, J. S., & Solla, S. A. (1989). Optimal brain damage. In Touretzky, D., editor, *Advances in Neural Information Processing Systems (volume 2)*.

Quinlan, J. R. (1993). *C4.5: Programs for Machine Learning*. Morgan Kaufmann.

Rumelhart, D., Hinton, G., & Williams, R. (1986). Learning internal representations by error propagation. In Rumelhart, D. & McClelland, J., editors, *Parallel Distributed Processing: Explorations in the microstructure of cognition. Volume 1*. MIT Press.

Spackman, K. A. (1988). Learning categorical decision criteria. In *Proc. of the 5th International Conf. on Machine Learning*, (pp. 36–46), Ann Arbor, MI.

Stormo, G. (1987). Identifying coding sequences. In Bishop, M. J. & Rawlings, C. J., editors, *Nucleic Acid and Protein Sequence Analysis: A Practical Approach*. IRL Press.

Valiant, L. G. (1984). A theory of the learnable. *Comm. of the ACM*, 27(11):1134–1142.

Does the Wake-sleep Algorithm Produce Good Density Estimators?

Brendan J. Frey, Geoffrey E. Hinton
Department of Computer Science
University of Toronto
Toronto, ON M5S 1A4, Canada
{frey, hinton}@cs.toronto.edu

Peter Dayan
Department of Brain and Cognitive Sciences
Massachusetts Institute of Technology
Cambridge, MA 02139, USA
dayan@ai.mit.edu

Abstract

The wake-sleep algorithm (Hinton, Dayan, Frey and Neal 1995) is a relatively efficient method of fitting a multilayer stochastic generative model to high-dimensional data. In addition to the top-down connections in the generative model, it makes use of bottom-up connections for approximating the probability distribution over the hidden units given the data, and it trains these bottom-up connections using a simple delta rule. We use a variety of synthetic and real data sets to compare the performance of the wake-sleep algorithm with Monte Carlo and mean field methods for fitting the same generative model and also compare it with other models that are less powerful but easier to fit.

1 INTRODUCTION

Neural networks are often used as bottom-up recognition devices that transform input vectors into representations of those vectors in one or more hidden layers. But multilayer networks of stochastic neurons can also be used as top-down generative models that produce patterns with complicated correlational structure in the bottom visible layer. In this paper we consider generative models composed of layers of stochastic binary logistic units. Given a generative model parameterized by top-down weights, there is an obvious way to perform unsupervised learning. The generative weights are adjusted to maximize the probability that the visible vectors generated by the model would match the observed data. Unfortunately, to compute the derivatives of the log probability of a visible vector, d, with respect to the generative weights, θ, it is necessary to consider all possible ways in which d could be generated. For each possible binary representation α in the hidden units the derivative needs to be weighted by the posterior probability of α given d and θ:

$$P(\alpha|d, \theta) = P(\alpha|\theta)P(d|\alpha, \theta) / \sum_{\beta} P(\beta|\theta)P(d|\beta, \theta). \qquad (1)$$

It is intractable to compute $P(\alpha|d, \theta)$, so instead of minimizing $-\log P(d|\theta)$, we minimize an easily computed upper bound on this quantity that depends on some additional parameters, ϕ:

$$-\log P(d|\theta) \leq F(d|\theta, \phi) = -\sum_\alpha Q(\alpha|d, \phi)\log P(\alpha, d|\theta) + \sum_\alpha Q(\alpha|d, \phi)\log Q(\alpha|d, \phi). \quad (2)$$

$F(d|\theta, \phi)$ is a Helmholtz free energy and is equal to $-\log P(d|\theta)$ when the distribution $Q(\bullet|d, \phi)$ is the same as the posterior distribution $P(\bullet|d, \theta)$. Otherwise, $F(d|\theta, \phi)$ exceeds $-\log P(d|\theta)$ by the asymmetric divergence:

$$D = \sum_\alpha Q(\alpha|d, \phi)\log(Q(\alpha|d, \phi)/P(\alpha|d, \theta)). \quad (3)$$

We restrict $Q(\bullet|d, \phi)$ to be a product distribution within each layer that is conditional on the binary states in the layer below and we can therefore compute it efficiently using a bottom-up recognition network. We call a model that uses bottom-up connections to minimize the bound in equation 2 in this way a *Helmholtz machine* (Dayan, Hinton, Neal and Zemel 1995). The recognition weights ϕ take the binary activities in one layer and stochastically produce binary activities in the layer above using a logistic function. So, for a given visible vector, the recognition weights may produce many different representations in the hidden layers, but we can get an unbiased sample from the distribution $Q(\bullet|d, \phi)$ in a single bottom-up pass through the recognition network.

The highly restricted form of $Q(\bullet|d, \phi)$ means that even if we use the optimal recognition weights, the gap between $F(d|\theta, \phi)$ and $-\log P(d|\theta)$ is large for some generative models. However, when $F(d|\theta, \phi)$ is minimized with respect to the generative weights, these models will generally be avoided.

$F(d|\theta, \phi)$ can be viewed as the expected number of bits required to communicate a visible vector to a receiver. First we use the recognition model to get a sample from the distribution $Q(\bullet|d, \phi)$. Then, starting at the top layer, we communicate the activities in each layer using the top-down expectations generated from the already communicated activities in the layer above. It can be shown that the number of bits required for communicating the state of each binary unit is $s_k \log(q_k/p_k) + (1-s_k)\log[(1-q_k)/(1-p_k)]$, where p_k is the top-down probability that s_k is on and q_k is the bottom-up probability that s_k is on.

There is a very simple on-line algorithm that minimizes $F(d|\theta, \phi)$ with respect to the generative weights. We simply use the recognition network to generate a sample from the distribution $Q(\bullet|d, \phi)$ and then we increment each top-down weight θ_{kj} by $\varepsilon s_k(s_j - p_j)$, where θ_{kj} connects unit k to unit j. It is much more difficult to exactly follow the gradient of $F(d|\theta, \phi)$ with respect to the recognition weights, but there is a simple approximate method (Hinton, Dayan, Frey and Neal 1995). We generate a stochastic sample from the generative model and then we increment each bottom-up weight ϕ_{ij} by $\varepsilon s_i(s_j - q_j)$ to increase the log probability that the recognition weights would produce the correct activities in the layer above. This way of fitting a Helmholtz machine is called the "wake-sleep" algorithm and the purpose of this paper is to assess how effective it is at performing high-dimensional density estimation on a variety of synthetically constructed data sets and two real-world ones. We compare it with other methods of fitting the same type of generative model and also with simpler models for which there are efficient fitting algorithms.

2 COMPETITORS

We compare the wake-sleep algorithm with six other density estimation methods. All data units are binary and can take on values $d_k = 1$ (on) and $d_k = 0$ (off).

Gzip. Gzip (Gailly, 1993) is a practical compression method based on Lempel-Ziv coding. This sequential data compression technique encodes future segments of data by transmitting codewords that consist of a pointer into a buffer of recent past output together with the length of the segment being coded. Gzip's performance is measured by subtracting the length of the compressed training set from the length of the compressed training set plus a subset of the test set. Taking all disjoint test subsets into account gives an overall test set code cost. Since we are interested in estimating the expected performance on *one* test case, to get a tight lower bound on gzip's performance, the subset size should be kept as small as possible in order to prevent gzip from using early test data to compress later test data.

Base Rate Model. Each visible unit k is assumed to be independent of the others with a probability p_k of being on. The probability of vector d is $p(d) = \prod_k p_k^{d_k} (1-p_k)^{1-d_k}$. The arithmetic mean of unit k's activity is used to estimate p_k, except in order to avoid serious overfitting, one extra on and one extra off case are included in the estimate.

Binary Mixture Model. This method is a hierarchical extension of the base rate model which uses more than one set of base rates. Each set is called a component. Component j has probability π_j and awards each visible unit k a probability p_{jk} of being on. The net probability of d is $p(d) = \sum_j \pi_j \prod_k p_{jk}^{d_k} (1-p_{jk})^{1-d_k}$. For a given training datum, we consider the component identity to be a missing value which must be filled in before the parameters can be adjusted. To accomplish this, we use the expectation maximization algorithm (Dempster, Laird and Rubin 1977) to maximize the log-likelihood of the training set, using the same method as above to avoid serious overfitting.

Gibbs Machine (GM). This machine uses the same generative model as the Helmholtz machine, but employs a Monte Carlo method called Gibbs sampling to find the posterior in equation 1 (Neal, 1992). Unlike the Helmholtz machine it does not require a separate recognition model and with sufficiently prolonged sampling it inverts the generative model perfectly. Each hidden unit is sampled in fixed order from a probability distribution conditional on the states of the other hidden and visible units. To reduce the time required to approach equilibrium, the network is annealed during sampling.

Mean Field Method (MF). Instead of using a separate recognition model to approximate the posterior in equation 1, we can assume that the distribution over hidden units is factorial for a given visible vector. Obtaining a good approximation to the posterior is then a matter of minimizing free energy with respect to the mean activities. In our experiments, we use the on-line mean field learning algorithm due to Saul, Jaakkola, and Jordan (1996).

Fully Visible Belief Network (FVBN). This method is a special case of the Helmholtz machine where the top-down network is fully connected and there are no hidden units. No recognition model is needed since there is no posterior to be approximated.

3 DATA SETS

The performances of these methods were compared on five synthetic data sets and two real ones. The synthetic data sets had matched complexities: the generative models that produced them had 100 visible units and between 1000 and 2500 parameters. A data set with 100,000 examples was generated from each model and then partitioned into 10,000 for training, 10,000 for validation and 80,000 for testing. For tractable cases, each data set entropy was approximated by the negative log-likelihood of the training set under its generative model. These entropies are approximate lower bounds on the performance.

The first synthetic data set was generated by a mixture model with 20 components. Each component is a vector of 100 base rates for the 100 visible units. To make the data more realistic, we arranged for there to be many different components whose base rates are all extreme (near 0 or 1) — representing well-defined clusters — and a few components with most base rates near 0.5 — representing much broader clusters. For component j, we selected base rate p_{jk} from a beta distribution with mean μ_j and variance $\mu_j(1-\mu_j)/40$ (we chose this variance to keep the entropy of visible units low for μ_j near 0 or 1, representing well-defined clusters). Then, as often as not we randomly replaced each p_{jk} with $1-p_{jk}$ to make each component different (without doing this, all components would favor all units off). In order to obtain many well-defined clusters, the component means μ_j were themselves sampled from a beta distribution with mean 0.1 and variance 0.02.

The next two synthetic data sets were produced using sigmoidal belief networks (Neal 1992) which are just the generative parts of binary stochastic Helmholtz machines. These networks had full connectivity between layers, one with a $20 \Rightarrow 100$ architecture and one with a $5 \Rightarrow 10 \Rightarrow 15 \Rightarrow 20 \Rightarrow 100$ architecture. The biases were set to 0 and the weights were sampled uniformly from [-2,2), a range chosen to keep the networks from being deterministic.

The final two synthetic data sets were produced using Markov random fields. These networks had full bidirectional connections between layers. One had a $10 \Leftrightarrow 20 \Leftrightarrow 100$ architecture, and the other was a concatenation of ten independent $10 \Leftrightarrow 10$ fields. The biases were set to 0 and the weights were sampled from the set $\{-4, 0, 4\}$ with probabilities $\{0.4, 0.4, 0.2\}$. To find data sets with high-order structure, versions of these networks were sampled until data sets were found for which the base rate method performed badly.

We also compiled two versions of a data set to which the wake-sleep algorithm has previously been applied (Hinton *et al.* 1995). These data consist of normalized and quantized 8x8 binary images of handwritten digits made available by the US Postal Service Office of Advanced Technology. The first version consists of a total of 13,000 images partitioned as 6000 for training, 2000 for validation and 5000 for testing. The second version consists of *pairs* of 8x8 images (*ie.* 128 visible units) made by concatenating vectors from each of the above data sets with those from a random reordering of the respective data set.

4 TRAINING DETAILS

The exact log-likelihoods for the base rate and mixture models can be computed, because these methods have no or few hidden variables. For the other methods, computing the exact log-likelihood is usually intractable. However, these methods provide an approximate upper bound on the negative log-likelihood in the form of a coding cost or Helmholtz free energy, and results are therefore presented as coding costs in bits.

Because gzip performed poorly on the synthetic tasks, we did not break up the test and validation sets into subsets. On the digit tasks, we broke the validation and test sets up to make subsets of 100 visible vectors. Since the "-9" gzip option did not improve performance significantly, we used the default configuration.

To obtain fair results, we tried to automate the model selection process subject to the constraint of obtaining results in a reasonable amount of time. For the mixture model, the Gibbs machine, the mean field method, and the Helmholtz machine, a single learning run was performed with each of four different architectures using performance on a validation set to avoid wasted effort. Performance on the validation set was computed every five epochs, and if two successive validation performances were not better than the previous one by more than 0.2%, learning was terminated. The network corresponding to the best validation performance was selected for test set analysis. Although it would be desirable to explore a wide range of architectures, it would be computationally ruinous. The architectures used are given in tables 3 and 4 in the appendix.

The Gibbs machine was annealed from an initial temperature of 5.0. Between each sweep of the network, during which each hidden unit was sampled once, the temperature was multiplied by 0.9227 so that after 20 sweeps the temperature was 1.0. Then, the generative weights were updated using the delta rule. To bound the datum probability, the network is annealed as above and then 40 sweeps at unity temperature are performed while summing the probability over one-nearest-neighbor configurations, checking for overlap.

A learning rate of 0.01 was used for the Gibbs machine, the mean field method, the Helmholtz machine, and the fully visible belief network. For each of these methods, this value was found to be roughly the largest possible learning rate that safely avoided oscillations.

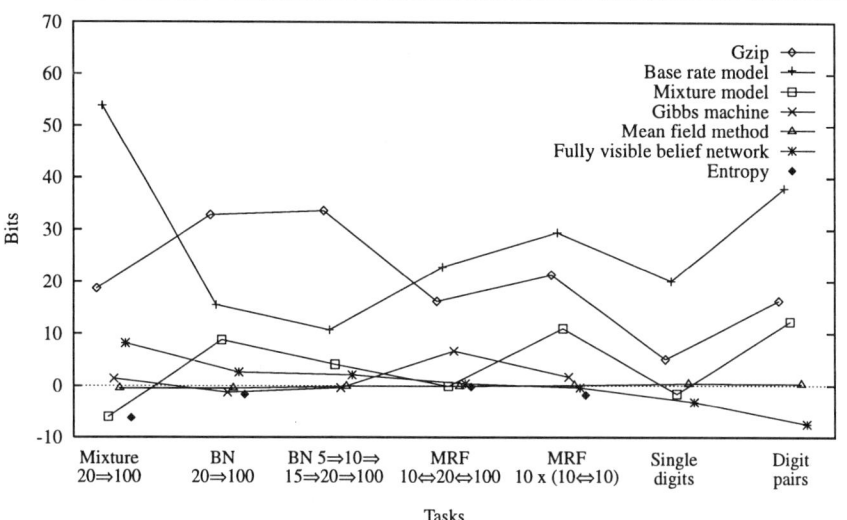

Figure 1. Compression performance relative to the Helmholtz machine. Lines connecting the data points are for visualization only, since there is no meaningful interpolant.

5 RESULTS

The learning times and the validation performances are given in tables 3 and 4 of the appendix. Test set appraisals and total learning times are given in table 1 for the synthetic tasks and in table 2 for the digit tasks. Because there were relatively many training cases in each simulation, the validation procedure serves to provide timing information more than to prevent overfitting. Gzip and the base rate model were very fast, followed by the fully visible belief network, the mixture model, the Helmholtz machine, the mean field method, and finally the Gibbs machine. Test set appraisals are summarized by compression performance relative to the Helmholtz machine in figure 1 above. Greater compression sizes correspond to lower test set likelihoods and imply worse density estimation. When available, the data set entropies indicate how close to optimum each method comes.

The Helmholtz machine yields a much lower cost compared to gzip and base rates on all tasks. Compared to the mixture model, it gives a lower cost on both BN tasks and the MRF 10 x (10⇔10) task. The latter case shows that the Helmholtz machine was able to take advantage of the independence of the ten concatenated input segments, whereas the mixture method was not. Simply to *represent* a problem where there are only two distinct clusters present in each of the ten segments, the mixture model would require 2^{10} components. Results on the two BN tasks indicate the Helmholtz machine is better able to model multiple simultaneous causes than the mixture method, which requires that only one component (cause) is active at a time. On the other hand, compared to the mixture model, the Helmholtz machine performs poorly on the Mixture 20⇒100 task. It is not able to learn that only one cause should be active at a time. This problem can be avoided by hard-wiring softmax groups into the Helmholtz machine. On the five synthetic tasks, the Helmholtz machine performs about the same as or better than the Gibbs machine, and runs two orders of magnitude faster. (The Gibbs machine was too slow to run on the digit tasks.) While the quality of density estimation produced by the mean field method is indistinguishable from the Helmholtz machine, the latter runs an order of magnitude faster than the mean field algorithm we used. The fully visible belief network performs significantly better than the Helmholtz machine on the two digit tasks and significantly worse on two of the synthetic tasks. It is trained roughly two orders of magnitude faster than the Helmholtz machine.

Table 1. Test set cost (bits) and total training time (*hrs*) for the synthetic tasks.

	Model used to produce synthetic data								
	Mixture 20⇒100		BN 20⇒100		BN 5⇒10⇒ 15⇒20⇒100		MRF 10⇔20⇔100		MRF 10 x (10⇔10)
Entropy	36.5		63.5		unknown		19.2		36.8
gzip	61.4	0	98.0	0	92.1	0	35.6	0	59.9	0
Base rates	96.6	0	80.7	0	69.2	0	42.2	0	68.1	0
Mixture	36.7	0	74.0	0	62.6	1	19.3	1	49.6	1
GM	44.1	131	63.9	240	58.1	251	26.1	195	40.3	145
MF	42.2	68	64.7	80	58.4	68	19.3	75	38.7	89
HM	42.7	8	65.2	3	58.5	4	19.4	2	38.6	4
FVBN	50.9	0	67.8	0	60.6	0	19.8	0	38.2	0

Table 2. Test set cost (bits) and training time (*hrs*) for the digit tasks.

Method	Single digits		Method	Digit pairs	
gzip	44.3	0	gzip	89.2	0
Base rates	59.2	0	Base rates	118.4	0
Mixture	37.5	0	Mixture	92.7	1
MF	39.5	38	MF	80.7	104
HM	39.1	2	HM	80.4	7
FVBN	35.9	0	FVBN	72.9	0

6 CONCLUSIONS

If we were given a new data set and asked to leave our research biases aside and do efficient density estimation, how would we proceed? Evidently it would not be worth trying gzip and the base rate model. We'd first try the fully visible belief network and the mixture model, since these are fast and sometimes give good estimates. Hoping to extract extra higher-order structure, we would then proceed to use the Helmholtz machine or the mean field method (keeping in mind that our implementation of the Helmholtz machine is considerably faster than Saul *et al.*'s implementation of the mean field method). Because it is so slow, we would avoid using the Gibbs machine unless the data set was very small.

Acknowledgments

We greatly appreciate the mean field software provided by Tommi Jaakkola and Lawrence Saul. We thank members of the Neural Network Research Group at the University of Toronto for helpful advice. The financial support from ITRC, IRIS, and NSERC is appreciated.

References

Dayan, P., Hinton, G. E., Neal, R. M., and Zemel, R. S. 1995. The Helmholtz machine. *Neural Computation* 7, 889-904.

Dempster, A. P., Laird, N. M. and Rubin, D. B. 1977. Maximum likelihood from incomplete data via the EM algorithm. *J. Royal Statistical Society, Series B* 34, 1-38.

Gailly, J. 1993. gzip program for unix.

Hinton, G. E., Dayan, P., Frey, B. J., Neal, R. M. 1995. The wake-sleep algorithm for unsupervised neural networks. *Science* 268, 1158-1161.

Neal, R. M. 1992. Connectionist learning of belief networks. *Artificial Intelligence* 56, 71-113.

Saul, L. K., Jaakkola, T., and Jordan, M. I. 1996. Mean field theory for sigmoid belief networks. Submitted to *Journal of Artificial Intelligence*.

Appendix

The average validation set cost per example and the associated learning time for each simulation are listed in tables 3 and 4. Architectures judged to be optimal according to validation performance are indicated by "*" and were used to produce the test results given in the body of this paper.

Table 3. Validation set cost (bits) and learning time (*min*) for the synthetic tasks.

	Model used to produce synthetic data									
	Mixture 20⇒100		BN 20⇒100		BN 5⇒10⇒ 15⇒20⇒100		MRF 10⇔20⇔100		MRF 10 x (10⇔10)	
gzip	61.6		98.1	0	92.3	0	35.6	0	60.0	0
Base rates	96.7	0	80.7	0	69.4	0	42.1	0	68.1	0
Mixture 20⇒100	44.6	3	75.6	3	63.9	4	19.2*	3	54.8	5
Mixture 40⇒100	36.8*	5	74.8	5	63.2	7	19.2	7	52.4	15
Mixture 60⇒100	36.8	7	74.4	7	62.9	8	19.2	8	51.0	17
Mixture 100⇒100	37.0	14	74.0*	12	62.7*	13	19.3	12	49.6*	22
GM 20⇒100	50.6	1187	63.9*	1639	58.1*	2084	26.1*	934	40.3*	1425
GM 50⇒100	68.8	2328	80.4	3481	76.4	5234	49.2	6472	56.5	3472
GM 10⇒20⇒100	44.1*	872	66.4	1771	59.8	3084	28.0	767	42.3	1033
GM 20⇒50⇒100	52.7	3476	91.3	7504	88.0	4647	55.3	3529	63.5	2781
MF 20⇒100	49.5	518	64.6	427	58.4*	497	19.4	862	39.2	471
MF 50⇒100	49.9	1644	64.8	1945	58.6	1465	20.4	1264	38.7*	2427
MF 10⇒20⇒100	46.0	306	64.6*	658	58.5	543	19.3*	569	38.9	882
MF 20⇒50⇒100	42.1*	1623	65.0	1798	58.6	1553	19.3	1778	38.8	1575
HM 20⇒100	50.0	41	65.2	28	58.8	41	19.7	15	38.6*	30
HM 50⇒100	50.7	81	65.5	66	59.4	78	20.2	27	38.9	46
HM 10⇒20⇒100	43.4	32	65.1*	38	58.5*	45	19.4*	21	38.9	46
HM 20⇒50⇒100	42.6*	308	67.2	69	59.2	93	19.5	64	39.4	102
FVBN	51.0	7	67.8	7	60.7	6	19.8	8	38.3	6

Table 4. Validation set cost (bits) and learning time (*min*) for the digit tasks.

Method	Single digits		Method	Digit pairs	
gzip	44.2	0	gzip	88.8	1
Base rates	59.0	0	Base rates	117.9	0
Mixture 16⇒64	43.2	1	Mixture 32⇒128	96.9	6
Mixture 32⇒64	40.0	4	Mixture 64⇒128	93.8	8
Mixture 64⇒64	38.0	5	Mixture 128⇒128	92.4*	14
Mixture 128⇒64	37.1*	6	Mixture 256⇒128	92.8	27
MF 16⇒24⇒64	39.9	341	MF 16⇒24⇒32⇒128	82.7	1335
MF 24⇒32⇒64	39.1*	845	MF 16⇒32⇒64⇒128	81.2	1441
MF 12⇒16⇒24⇒64	39.8	475	MF 12⇒16⇒24⇒32⇒128	82.8	896
MF 16⇒24⇒32⇒64	39.1	603	MF 12⇒16⇒32⇒64⇒128	80.1*	2586
HM 16⇒24⇒64	39.7	24	HM 16⇒24⇒32⇒128	83.8	76
HM 24⇒32⇒64	39.4	34	HM 16⇒32⇒64⇒128	80.1*	138
HM 12⇒16⇒24⇒64	40.4	16	HM 12⇒16⇒24⇒32⇒128	84.6	74
HM 16⇒24⇒32⇒64	38.9*	52	HM 12⇒16⇒32⇒64⇒128	80.1	135
FVBN	35.8	1	FVBN	72.5	7

PART V
IMPLEMENTATIONS

Improved Silicon Cochlea using Compatible Lateral Bipolar Transistors

André van Schaik, Eric Fragnière, Eric Vittoz
MANTRA Center for Neuromimetic Systems
Swiss Federal Institute of Technology
CH-1015 Lausanne
email: vschaik@di.epfl.ch

Abstract

Analog electronic cochlear models need exponentially scaled filters. CMOS Compatible Lateral Bipolar Transistors (CLBTs) can create exponentially scaled currents when biased using a resistive line with a voltage difference between both ends of the line. Since these CLBTs are independent of the CMOS threshold voltage, current sources implemented with CLBTs are much better matched than current sources created with MOS transistors operated in weak inversion. Measurements from integrated test chips are shown to verify the improved matching.

1. INTRODUCTION

Since the original publication of the "analog electronic cochlea" by Lyon and Mead in 1988 [1], several other analog VLSI models have been proposed which try to capture more of the details of the biological cochlear function [2],[3],[4]. In spite of the differences in their design, all these models use filters with exponentially decreasing cut-off frequencies. This exponential dependency is generally obtained using a linear decreasing voltage on the gates of MOS transistors operating in weak-inversion. In weak-inversion, the drain current of a saturated MOS transistor depends exponentially on its gate voltage. The linear decreasing voltage is easily created using a resistive polysilicon line; if there is a voltage difference between the two ends of the line, the voltage on the line will decrease linearly all along its length.

The problem of using MOS transistors in weak-inversion as current sources is that their drain currents are badly matched. An RMS mismatch of 12% in the drain current of two identical transistors with equal gate and source voltages is not exceptional [5], even when sufficient precautions, such as a good layout, are taken. The main cause of this mismatch is a variation of the threshold voltage between the two transistors. Since the threshold voltage and its variance are technology parameters, there is no good way to reduce the mismatch once the chip has been fabricated.

One can avoid this problem using Compatible Lateral Bipolar Transistors (CLBTs) [6] for the current sources. They can be readily made in a CMOS substrate, and their collector current also depends exponentially on their base voltage, while this current is completely independent of the CMOS technology's threshold voltage. The remaining mismatch is due to geometry mismatch of the devices, a parameter which is much better controlled than the variance of the threshold voltage. Therefore, the use of CLBTs can yield a large improvement in the regularity of the spacing of the cochlear filters. This regularity is especially important in a cascade of filters like the cochlea, since one filter can distort the input signal of all the following filters.

We have integrated an analog electronic cochlea as a cascade of second-order low-pass filters, using CLBTs as exponentially scaled current sources. The design of this cochlea is based on the silicon cochlea described in [7], since a number of important design issues, such as stability, dynamic range, device mismatch and compactness, have already been addressed in this design. In this paper, the design of [7] is briefly presented and some remaining possible improvements are identified. These improvements, notably the use of Compatible Lateral Bipolar Transistors as current sources, a differentiation that does not need gain correction and temperature independent biasing of the cut-off frequency, are then discussed in more detail. Finally, measurement results of a test chip will be presented and compared to the design without CLBTs.

2. THE ANALOG ELECTRONIC COCHLEA

The basic building block for the filters in all analog electronic cochlear models is the transconductance amplifier, operated in weak inversion. For input voltages smaller than about 60 mV$_{pp}$, the amplifier can be approximated as a linear transconductance:

$$I_{Out} = g_m(V_{In+} - V_{In-}) \tag{1}$$

with transconductance g_m given by:

$$g_m = \frac{I_0}{2nU_T} \tag{2}$$

where I_0 is the bias current, n is the slope factor, and the thermal voltage $U_T = kT/q = 25.6$ mV at room temperature.

This linear range is usually the input range used in the cochlear filters, yielding linear filters. In [7], a transconductance amplifier having a wider linear input range is proposed. This allows larger input signals to be used, up to about 140 mVpp. Furthermore, the wide range transconductance amplifier can be used to eliminate the large-signal instability shown to be present in the original second-order section [7]. This second-order section will be discussed in more detail in section 3.2.

The traditional techniques to improve matching [5], as for instance larger device sizes for critical devices and placing identical devices close together with identical orientation, are also discussed in [7] with respect to the implementation of the cochlear filter cascade. The transistors generating the bias current I_0 of the transconductance amplifiers in the second-order sections were identified as the most critical devices, since they have the largest effect on the cut-off frequency and the quality factor of each section. Therefore, extra area had to be devoted to these bias transistors. A further improvement is obtained in [7] by using a single resistive line to bias both the transconductance amplifiers controlling the cut-off frequency and the transconductance amplifier controlling the quality factor. The quality factor Q is then changed by varying the source of the transistor which biases the Q control amplifier. Instead of using two tilted resistive lines, this scheme uses only one tilted resistive line and a non-tilted Q control line, and therefore doesn't need to rely on an identical tilt on both resistive lines.

3. IMPROVED ANALOG ELECTRONIC COCHLEA

The design discussed in the previous section already showed a substantial improvement over the first analog electronic cochlea by Lyon and Mead. However, several improvements remain possible.

3.1 V_T VARIATION

The bias transistors have been identified as the major source of mismatch of the cochlea's parameters. This mismatch is mainly due to variation of the threshold voltage V_T of the MOS transistors. Since the drain current of a saturated MOS transistor in weak-inversion depends exponentially on the difference between its gate-source voltage and its threshold voltage, small variations in V_T introduce large variations in the drain current of these transistors, and since both the cut-off frequency and the quality factor of the filters are proportional to these drain currents, large parameter variations are generated by small V_T variations. This problem can be circumvented by the use of CMOS Compatible Lateral Bipolar transistors as bias transistors.

A CMOS Compatible Lateral Bipolar Transistor is obtained if the drain or source junction of a MOS transistor is forward-biased in order to inject minority carriers into the local substrate. If the gate voltage is negative enough (for an n-channel device), then no current can flow at the surface and the operation is purely bipolar [6]. Fig. 1 shows the major flows of current carriers in this mode of operation, with the source, drain and well terminals renamed emitter E, collector C and base B.

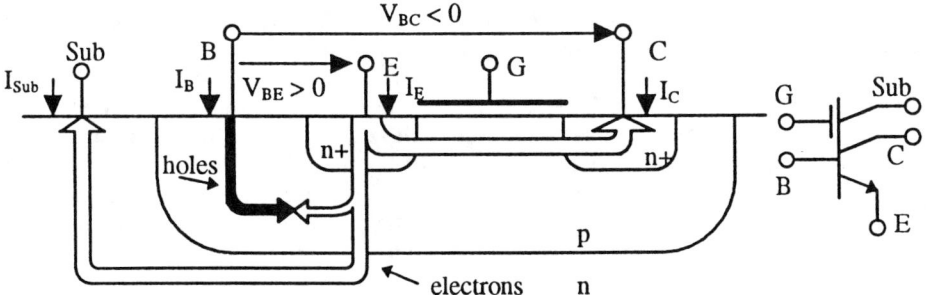

Fig. 1. : Bipolar operation of the MOS transistor : carrier flows and symbol.

Since there is no p+ buried layer to prevent injection to the substrate, this lateral npn bipolar transistor is combined with a vertical npn. The emitter current I_E is thus split into a base current I_B, a lateral collector current I_C and a substrate collector current I_{Sub}. Therefore, the common-base current gain $\alpha = -I_C/I_E$ cannot be close to 1. However, due to the very small rate of recombination inside the well and to the high emitter efficiency, the common-emitter current gain $\beta = I_C/I_B$ can be large. Maximum values of α and β are obtained in concentric structures using a minimum size emitter surrounded by the collector and a minimum lateral base width.

For $V_{CE} = V_{BE}-V_{BC}$ larger than a few hundred millivolts, this transistor is in active mode and the collector current is given, as for a normal bipolar transistor, by

$$I_C = I_{Sb} \, e^{\frac{V_{BE}}{U_T}} \tag{4}$$

where I_{Sb} is the specific current in bipolar mode, proportional to the cross-section of the emitter to collector flow of carriers. Since I_C is independent of the MOS transistor threshold voltage V_T, the main source of mismatch of distributed MOS current sources is suppressed, when CLBTs are used to create the current sources.

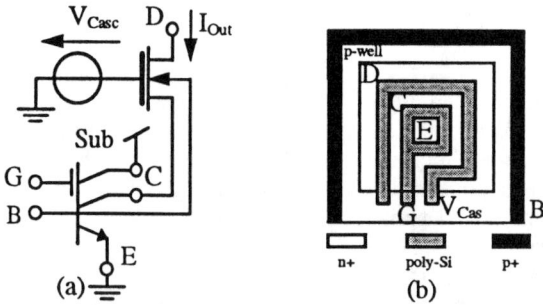

Fig. 2. CLBT cascode circuit (a) and its layout (b).

A disadvantage of the CLBT is its low Early voltage, i.e., the device has a low output resistance. Therefore, it is preferable to use a cascode circuit as shown in fig. 2. This yields an output resistance several hundred times larger than that of the single CLBT, whereas the area penalty, in a layout as shown in fig 2b, is acceptable.

Another disadvantage of the CLBTs, when biased using a resistive line, is their base current, which introduces an additional voltage drop on the resistive line. However, since the cut-off frequencies in the cochlea are controlled by the output current of the CLBTs and since these cut-off frequencies are relatively small, typically 20 kHz, the output current of the CLBTs will be small. If the common-emitter current gain β is much larger than 1, the base current of these CLBTs will be very small, and the voltage error introduced by the small base currents will be negligible. Furthermore, since the cut-off frequencies of the cochlea will typically span 2 decades with an exponentially decreasing cut-off frequency from the beginning to the end, only the first few filters will have any noticeable influence on the current drawn from the resistive line.

3.2 DIFFERENTIATION

The stabilized second-order section of [7] uses two wide range transconductance amplifiers (A1 and A2 in fig. 3) with equal bias current and equal capacitive load, to control the cut-off frequency. A basic transconductance amplifier (A3) is used in a feedback path to control the quality factor of the filter. The voltage V_{out} at the output of each second-order stage represents the basilar membrane displacement. Since the output of the biological cochlea is proportional to the velocity of the basilar membrane, the output of each second-order stage has to be differentiated. In [7] this is done by creating a copy of the output current I_{dif} of amplifier A2 at every stage. Since the voltage on a capacitor is proportional to the integral of the current onto the capacitor, I_{dif} is effectively proportional to the basilar membrane velocity. Yet, with equal displacement amplitudes, velocity will be much larger for high frequencies than for low frequencies, yielding output signals with an amplitude that decreases from the beginning of the cochlea to the end. This can be corrected by normalizing I_{dif} to give equal amplitude at every output. A second resistive line with identical tilt controlling the gain of the current mirrors that create the copies of I_{dif} at each stage is used for this purpose in [7]. However, if using a single resistive line for the control of the cut-off frequencies and the quality factor improves the performance of the chip, the same is true for the control of the current mirror gain.

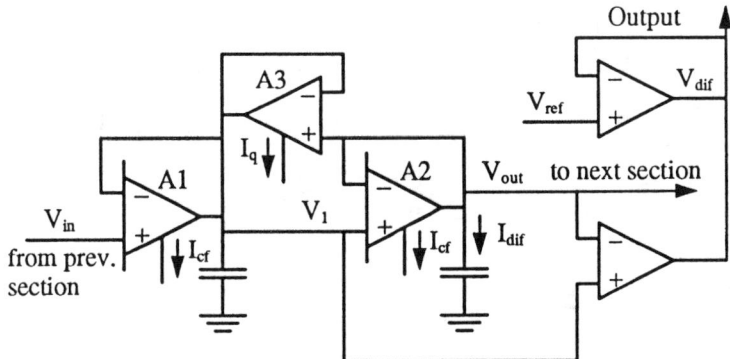

Fig. 3. One section of the cochlear cascade, with differentiator.

An alternative solution, which does not need normalization, is to take the difference between V_{Out} and V_1 (see fig. 3). This can be shown to be equivalent to differentiating V_{Out}, with 0dB gain at the cut-off frequency for all stages. This can be easily done with a combination of 2 transconductance amplifiers. These amplifiers can have a large bias current, so they can also be used to buffer the cascade voltages before connecting them to the output pins of the chip, to avoid charging the cochlear cascade with the extra capacitance introduced by the output pins.

3.3 TEMPERATURE SENSITIVITY

The cut-off frequency of the first and the last low-pass filter in the cascade can be set by applying voltages to both ends of the resistive line, and the intermediate filters will have a cut-off frequency decreasing exponentially from the beginning to the end. Yet, if we apply directly a voltage to the ends of the resistive line, the actual cut-off frequency obtained will depend on the temperature, since the current depends exponentially on the applied voltage *normalized* to the thermal voltage U_T (see(3). It is therefore better to create the voltages at both ends of the resistive line on-chip using a current biasing a CLBT with its base connected to its collector (or its drain connected to its gate if a MOS transistor is used). If this gate voltage is buffered, so that the current through the resistive line is not drawn from the input current, the bias currents of the first and last filter, and thus the cut-off frequency of all filters can be set, independent of temperature.

3.4 THE IMPROVED SILICON COCHLEA

The improved silicon cochlea is shown in figure 4. It uses the cochlear sections shown in figure 3, CLBTs as the bias transistors of each filter, and one resistive line to bias all CLBTs. The resistive line is biased using two bipolar current mirror structures and two voltage buffers, which allow temperature independent biasing of the cut-off frequencies of the cochlea. A similar structure is used to create the voltage source Vq to control, independent of temperature, the actual quality factor of each section. The actual bipolar current mirror implemented uses the cascode structure shown in figure 2a, however this is not shown in figure 4 for clarity.

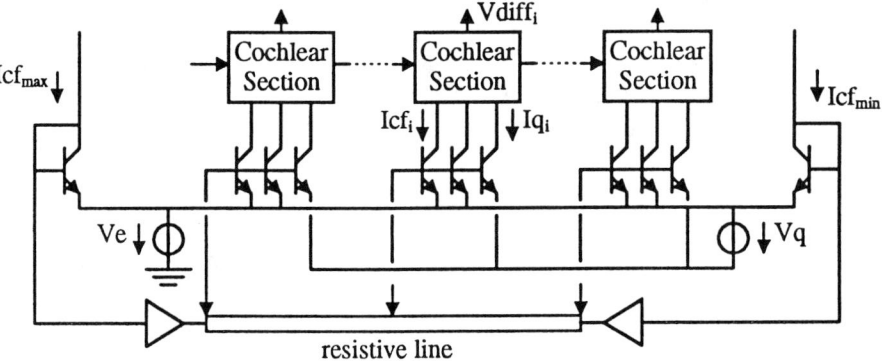

Fig 4. The improved silicon cochlea.

4. TEST RESULTS

The proposed silicon cochlea has been integrated using the ECPD15 technology at ES2 (Grenoble, France), containing 104 second-order stages, on a 4.77mm × 3.21mm die. Every second stage is connected to a pin, so its output voltage can be measured. In fig. 5, the frequency response curves after on-chip derivation are shown for the output taps of both the cochlea described in [7] (left), and our version (right). This clearly shows the improved regularity of the cut-off frequencies and the gain obtained using CLBTs. The drop-off in gain for the higher frequency stages (right) is a border effect, since at the beginning of the cochlea no accumulation of gain has yet taken place. In the figure on the left this is not visible, since the first nine outputs are not presented.

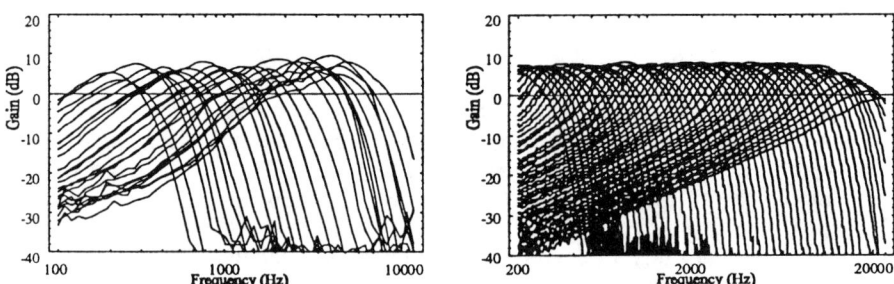

Fig.5. Measured frequency responses at the different taps.

In fig. 6 we show the cut-off frequency versus tap number of both chips. Ideally, this should be a straight line on a log-linear scale, since the cut-off frequency decreases exponentially with tap number. This also clearly shows the improved regularity using CLBTs as current sources.

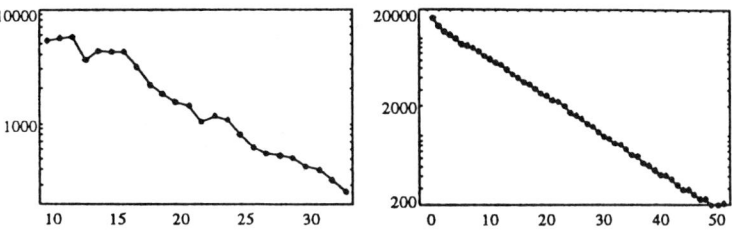

Fig.6. Cut-off frequency (Hz) versus tap number for both silicon cochleae.

5. CONCLUSIONS

Since the biological cochlea functions as a distributed filter, where the natural frequency decreases exponentially with the position along the basilar membrane, analog electronic cochlear models need exponentially scaled filters. The output current of a Compatible Lateral Bipolar Transistor depends exponentially on the base-emitter voltage. It is therefore easy to create exponentially scaled current sources using CLBTs biased with a resistive polysilicon line. Because the CLBTs are insensitive to variations of the CMOS threshold voltage V_T, current sources implemented with CLBTs are much better matched than current sources using MOS transistors in weak inversion.

Regularity is further improved using an on-chip differentiation that does not need a second resistive line to correct its gain, and therefore doesn't depend on identical tilt on both resistive lines. Better independence of temperature can be obtained by fixing the frequency domain of the cochlea using bias currents instead of voltages.

Acknowledgments

The authors would like to thank Felix Lustenberger for simulation and layout of the chip. We are also indebted to Lloyd Watts for allowing us to use his measurement data.

References

[1] R.F. Lyon and C.A. Mead, "An analog electronic cochlea," *IEEE Trans. Acoust., Speech, Signal Processing*, vol. 36, pp. 1119-1134, July 1988.

[2] R.F. Lyon, "Analog implementations of auditory models," *Proc. DARPA Workshop Speech and Natural Language*. San Mateo, CA:Morgan Kaufmann, 1991.

[3] W. Liu, et. al., "Analog VLSI implementation of an auditory periphery model," *Advances Res. VLSI, Proc. 1991 Santa Cruz Conf.*, MIT Press, 1991, pp. 153-163.

[4] L. Watts, "Cochlear Mechanics: Analysis and Analog VLSI," Ph.D. thesis, California Institute of Technology, Pasadena, 1992.

[5] E. Vittoz, "The design of high-performance analog circuits on digital CMOS chips," *IEEE J. Solid-State Circuits*, vol. SC-20, pp. 657-665, June 1985.

[6] E. Vittoz, "MOS transistors operated in the lateral bipolar mode and their application in CMOS technology," *IEEE J. Solid-State Circuits*, vol. SC-24, pp. 273-279, June 1983.

[7] L. Watts, et. al., "Improved implementation of the silicon cochlea," *IEEE J. Solid-State Circuits*, vol. SC-27, pp. 692-700, May 1992.

Adaptive Retina with Center-Surround Receptive Field

Shih-Chii Liu and Kwabena Boahen
Computation and Neural Systems
139-74 California Institute of Technology
Pasadena, CA 91125
shih@pcmp.caltech.edu, buster@pcmp.caltech.edu

Abstract

Both vertebrate and invertebrate retinas are highly efficient in extracting contrast independent of the background intensity over five or more decades. This efficiency has been rendered possible by the adaptation of the DC operating point to the background intensity while maintaining high gain transient responses. The center-surround properties of the retina allows the system to extract information at the edges in the image. This silicon retina models the adaptation properties of the receptors and the antagonistic center-surround properties of the laminar cells of the invertebrate retina and the outer-plexiform layer of the vertebrate retina. We also illustrate the spatio-temporal responses of the silicon retina on moving bars. The chip has 59x64 pixels on a 6.9x6.8mm^2 die and it is fabricated in 2 μm n-well technology.

1 Introduction

It has been observed previously that the initial layers of the vertebrate and invertebrate retina systems perform very similar processing functions on the incoming input signal[1]. The response versus log intensity curves of the receptors in invertebrate and vertebrate retinas look similar. The curves show that the receptors have a larger gain for changes in illumination than to steady illumination, i.e, the receptors adapt. This adaptation property allows the receptor to respond over a large input range without saturating.

Anatomically, the eyes of invertebrates differ greatly from that of vertebrates. Vertebrates normally have two simple eyes while insects have compound eyes. Each compound eye in the fly consists of 3000-4000 ommatidia and each ommatidium consists of 8 photoreceptors. Six of these receptors (which are also called R1-R6) are in a single spectral class. The other two receptors, R7 and R8 provide channels for wavelength discrimination and polarization.

The vertebrate eye is divided into the outer-plexiform layer and the inner-plexiform layer. The outer-plexiform layer consists of the rods and cones, horizontal cells and bipolar cells. Invertebrate receptors depolarise in response to an increase in light, in contrast to vertebrate receptors, which hyperpolarise to an increase in light intensity. Both vertebrate and invertebrate receptors show light adaptation over at least five decades of background illumination. This adaptation property allows the retina to maintain a high transient gain to contrast over a wide range of background intensities.

The invertebrate receptors project to the next layer which is called the lamina layer. This layer consists primarily of monopolar cells which show a similar response versus log intensity curve to that of vertebrate bipolar cells in the outer-plexiform layer. Both cells respond with graded potentials to changes in illumination. These cells also show a high transient gain to changes in illumination while ignoring the background intensity and they possess center-surround receptive fields. In vertebrates, the cones which are excited by the incoming light, activate the horizontal cells which in turn inhibit the cones. The horizontal cells thus mediate the lateral inhibition which produces the center-surround properties. In insects, a possible process of this lateral inhibition is done by current flow from the photoreceptors through the epithelial glial cells surrounding an ommatidium or the modulation of the local field potential in the lamina to influence the transmembrane potential of the photoreceptor[2]. The center-surround receptive fields allow contrasts to be accentuated since the surround computes a local mean and subtracts that from the center signal.

Mahowald[3] previously described a silicon retina with adaptive photoreceptors and Boahen et al.[4] recently described a compact current-mode analog model of the outer-plexiform layer of the vertebrate retina and analysed the spatio-temporal processing properties of this retina[5]. A recent array of photoreceptors from Delbrück[6] uses an adaptive photoreceptor circuit that adapts its operating point to the background intensity so that the pixel shows a high transient gain over 5 decades of background illumination. However this retina does not have spatial coupling between pixels.

The pixels in the silicon retina described here has a compact circuit that incorporates both spatial and temporal filtering with light adaptation over 5 decades of background intensity. The network exhibits center-surround behavior. Boahen *et al.*[4] in their current-mode diffusor retina, draw an analogy between parts of the diffusor circuit and the different cells in the outer-plexiform layer. While the same analogy cannot be drawn from this silicon retina to the invertebrate retina since the function of the cells are not completely understood, the output responses of the retina circuit are similar to the output responses of the photoreceptor and monopolar cells in invertebrates.

The circuit details are described in Section 2 and the spatio-temporal processing performed by the retina on stimulus moving at different speeds is shown in Section

2 Circuit

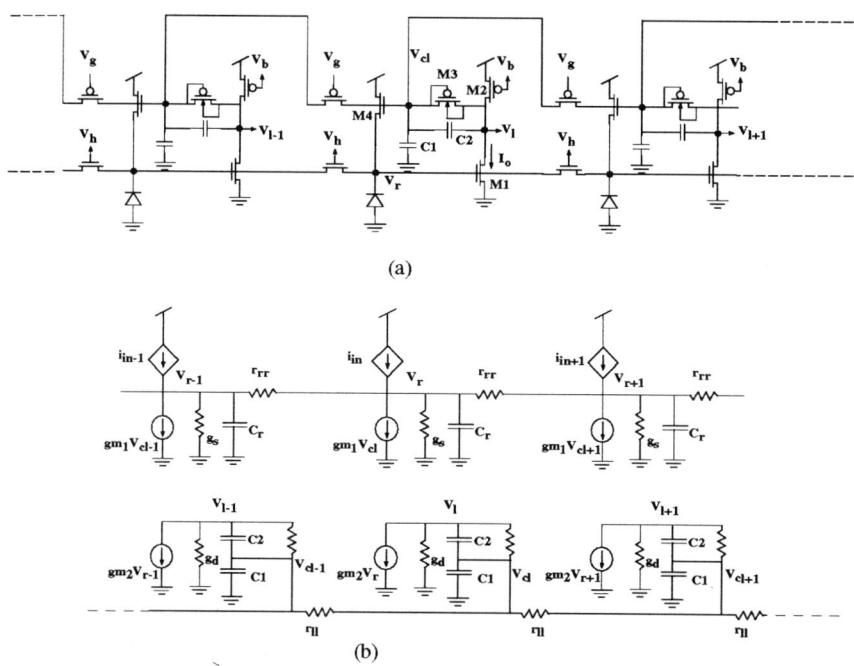

Figure 1: (a) One-dimensional version of the retina. (b) Small-signal equivalent of circuit in (a).

A one-dimensional version of the retina is shown in Figure 1(a). The retina consists of an adaptive photoreceptor circuit at each pixel coupled together with diffusors, controlled by voltages, V_g and V_h. The output of this network can either be obtained at the voltage output, V_l or at the current output, I_o but the outputs have different properties. Phototransduction is obtained by using a reverse-biased photodiode which produces current that is proportional to the incident light. The logarithmic properties are obtained by operating the feedback transistor shown in Figure 1(a) in the subthreshold region. The voltage change at the output photoreceptor, v_r, is proportional to a small contrast since

$$v_r = \frac{U_T}{\kappa} d(\log I) = \frac{U_T}{\kappa} \frac{dI}{I} = \frac{U_T}{\kappa} \frac{i}{I_{bg}}$$

where U_T is the thermal voltage, $\kappa = \frac{C_{ox}}{C_{ox}+C_d}$, C_{ox} is the oxide capacitance and C_d is the depletion capacitance of a transistor. The circuit works as follows: If the photocurrent through the photodiode increases, V_r will be pulled low and the output voltage at V_l increases by $v_l = Av_r$ where A is the amplifier gain of the output stage. This output change in V_l is coupled into V_{cl} through a capacitor divider ratio, $\frac{C_2}{C_1+C_2}$. The feedback transistor, M4, operates in the subthreshold region and supplies the current necessary to offset the photocurrent. The increase in V_{cl} (i.e. the gate voltage of M4) causes the current supplied by M3 to increase which pulls the node voltage, V_r, back to the voltage level needed by M1 to sink the bias current from transistor, M2.

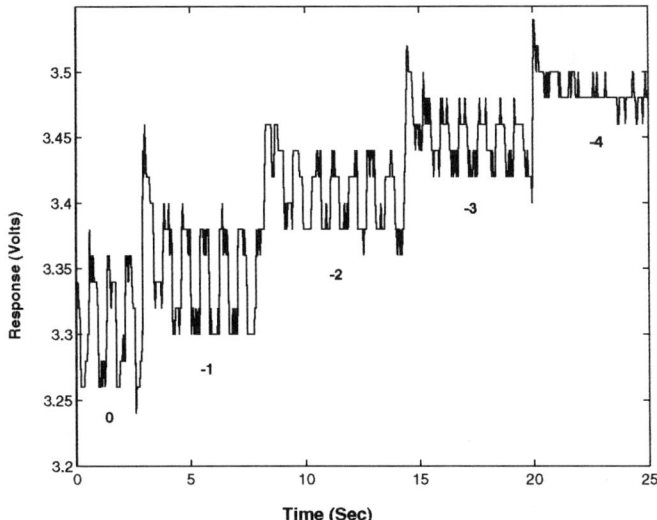

Figure 2: This figure shows the output response of the receptor to a variation of about 40% p-p in the intensity of a flickering LED light incident on the chip. The response shows that the high sensitivity of the receptor to the LED is maintained over 5 decades of differing background intensities. The numbers on the section of the curve indicate the log intensity of the mean value. 0 log is the absolute intensity from the LED.

The adaptive element, M3, has an I-V curve which looks like a hyperbolic sine. The small slope of the I-V curve in the middle means that for small changes of voltages across M3, the element looks like an open-circuit. With large changes of voltage across M3, the current through M3 becomes exponential and V_{cl} is charged or discharged almost instantaneously.

Figure 2 shows the output response of the photoreceptor to a square-wave variation of about 40% p-p in the intensity of a red LED (635 nm). The results show that the circuit is able to discern the small contrast over five decades of background intensity while the steady-state voltage of the photoreceptor output varies only about $15mV$. Further details of the photoreceptor circuit and its adaptation properties are described in Delbrück[6].

3 Spatio-Temporal Response

The spatio-temporal response of the network to different moving stimuli is explored in this section. The circuit shown in Figure 1(a) can be transferred to an equivalent network of resistors and capacitors as shown in Figure 1(b) to obtain the transfer function of the circuit. The capacitors at each node are necessary to model the

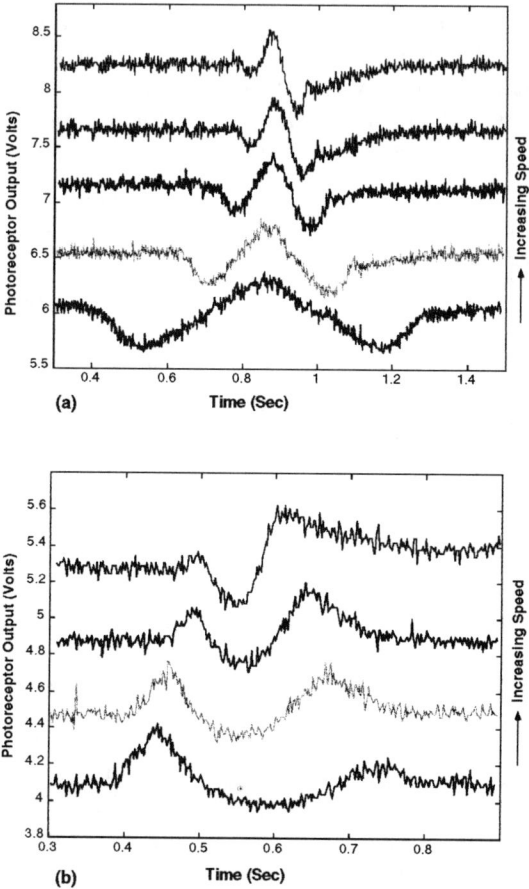

Figure 3: (a) Response of a pixel to a grey strip 2 pixels wide of gray-level "0.4" on a dark background of level "0" moving past the pixel at different speeds. (b) Response of a pixel to a dark strip of gray-level "0.6" on a white background of level "1" moving past the pixel at different speeds. The voltage shown on these curves is not the direct measurement of the voltage at V_l but rather V_l drives a current-sensing transistor and this current is then sensed by an offchip current sense-amplifier.

Adaptive Retina with Center-Surround Receptive Field

temporal responses of the circuit.

The chip results from the experiments below illustrate the center-surround properties of the network and the difference in time-constants between the surround and center.

3.1 Chip Results

Data from the 2D chip is shown in the next few figures. In these experiments, we are only looking at one pixel of the 2D array. A rotating circular fly-wheel stimulus with strips of alternating contrasts is mounted above the chip. The stimulus was created using Mathematica. Figure 3a shows the spatio-temporal impulse response of one pixel measured at V_l with a small strip at level "0.4" on a dark background of level "0" moving past the pixels on the row. At slow speeds, the impulse response shows a center-surround behavior where the pixel first receives inhibition from the preceding pixels which are excited by the stimulus. When the stimulus moves by the pixel of interest, it is excited and then it is inhibited by the subsequent pixels seeing the stimulus.

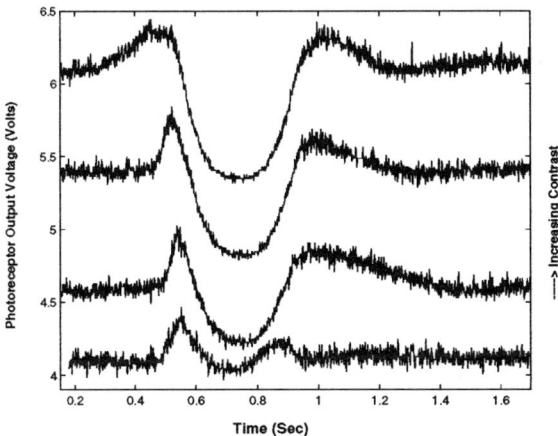

Figure 4: Response of a pixel to a strip of varying contrasts on a dark background moving past the pixel at a constant speed.

At faster speeds, the initial inhibition in the response grows smaller until at some even faster speed, the initial inhibition is no longer observed. This response comes about because the inhibition from the surround has a longer-time constant than the center. When the stimulus moves past the pixel of interest, the inhibition from the preceding pixels excited by the stimulus does not have time to inhibit the pixel of interest. Hence the excitation is seen first and then the inhibition comes into place when the stimulus passes by. Note that in these figures (Figures 3-4), the curves have been displaced to show the pixel response at different speeds of the moving stimulus. The voltage shown on these curves is not the direct measurement of the voltage at V_l but rather V_l drives a current-sensing transistor and this current is then sensed by an off-chip current sense-amplifier.

Figure 3b shows the spatio-temporal impulse response of one pixel with a similar size strip of level "0.6" on a light background of level "1" moving past the row of pixels. The same inhibition behavior is seen for increasing stimulus speeds. Figure 4 shows the output response at V_l for the same stimulus of gray-levels varying from "0.2" to "0.8" on a dark background of level "0" moving at one speed. The peak excitation response is plotted against the contrast in Figure 5. A level of "0.2" corresponds to a irradiance of $15mW/m^2$ while a level of "0.8" corresponds to a irradiance of $37.4mW/m^2$. These measurements are done with a photometer mounted about 1.5in above a piece of paper with the contrast which is being measured. The irradiance varies exponentially with increasing level.

4 Conclusion

In this paper, we described an adaptive retina with a center-surround receptive field. The system properties of this retina allows it to model functionally either the responses of the laminar cells in the invertebrate retina or the outer-plexiform layer of vertebrate retina. We show that the circuit shows adaptation to changes over 5 decades of background intensities. The center-surround property of the network can be seen from its spatio-temporal response to different stimulus speeds. This property serves to remove redundancy in space and time of the input signal.

Acknowledgements

We thank Carver Mead for his support and encouragement. SC Liu is supported by an NIMH fellowship and K Boahen is supported by a Sloan fellowship. We thank Tobias Delbrück for the inspiration and help in testing the design. We also thank Rahul Sarpeshkar and Bradley Minch for comments. Fabrication was provided by MOSIS.

References

[1] S. B. Laughlin, "Coding efficiency and design in retinal processing", In: *Facets of Vision* (D. G. Stavenga and R. C. Hardie, eds) pp. 213-234. Springer, Berlin, 1989.

[2] S. R. Shaw, "Retinal resistance barriers and electrical lateral inhibition", *Nature, Lond.***255**,: 480-483, 1975.

[3] M. A. Mahowald, "Silicon Retina with Adaptive Photoreceptors" in *SPIE/SPSE Symposium on Electronic Science and Technology: From Neurons to Chips.* Orlando, FL, April 1991.

[4] K. A. Boahen and A. G. Andreou, "A Contrast Sensitive Silicon Retina with Reciprocal Synapses", In D. S. Touretzky (ed.), *Advances in Neural Information Processing Systems 4*, 764-772. San Mateo, CA: Morgan Kaufmann, 1992.

[5] K. A. Boahen, "Spatiotemporal sensitivity of the retina: A physical model", *CNS Memo CNS-TR-91-06*, California Institute of Technology, Pasadena, CA 91125, June 1991.

[6] T. Delbrück, "Analog VLSI Phototransduction by continous-time, adaptive, logarithmic photoreceptor circuits", *CNS Memo No.30*, California Institute of Technology, Pasadena, CA 91125, 1994.

Neuron-MOS Temporal Winner Search Hardware for Fully-Parallel Data Processing

Tadashi SHIBATA, Tsutomu NAKAI, Tatsuo MORIMOTO
Ryu KAIHARA, Takeo YAMASHITA, and Tadahiro OHMI
Department of Electronic Engineering
Tohoku University
Aza-Aoba, Aramaki, Aobaku, Sendai 980-77 JAPAN

Abstract

A unique architecture of winner search hardware has been developed using a novel neuron-like high functionality device called Neuron MOS transistor (or νMOS in short) [1,2] as a key circuit element. The circuits developed in this work can find the location of the maximum (or minimum) signal among a number of input data on the continuous-time basis, thus enabling real-time winner tracking as well as fully-parallel sorting of multiple input data. We have developed two circuit schemes. One is an ensemble of self-loop-selecting νMOS ring oscillators finding the winner as an oscillating node. The other is an ensemble of νMOS variable threshold inverters receiving a common ramp-voltage for competitive excitation where data sorting is conducted through consecutive winner search actions. Test circuits were fabricated by a double-polysilicon CMOS process and their operation has been experimentally verified.

1 INTRODUCTION

Search for the largest (or the smallest) among a number of input data, i.e., the winner-take-all (WTA) action, is an essential part of intelligent data processing such as data retrieval in associative memories [3], vector quantization circuits [4], Kohonen's self-organizing maps [5] etc. In addition to the maximum or minimum search, data sorting also plays an essential role in a number of signal processing such as median filtering in image processing, evolutionary algorithms in optimizing problems [6] and so forth. Usually such data processing is carried out by software running on general purpose computers, but the computation time increases explosively with the increase in the volume of data. In order to build electronic systems having a real-time-response capability, the direct implementation of fully parallel algorithms on the integrated circuits hardware is critically demanded.

A variety of WTA [4, 7, 8] circuits have been implemented so far based on analog current-mode circuit technologies. A number of cells, each composed of a current source, competitively share the total current specified by a global current sink and the winner is identified through the current concentration toward the cell via tacit positive feedback mechanisms. The circuit implementations using MOSFET's operating in the subthreshold regime [4, 7] are ideal for large scale integration due to its ultra low power nature. Although they are inherently slow at circuit levels, the performance at a system level is far superior to digital counterparts owing to the flexible computing algorithms of analog. In order to achieve a high speed operation, MOSFET's biased at strong inversion is also utilized in Ref. [8]. However, cost must be traded off for increased power.

What we are presenting in this paper is a unique WTA architecture implemented by νMOS technology [1,2]. In νMOS circuits the summation of multiples of voltage signals is conducted on the νMOS floating gate (or better be called "temporary floating gate" when used in a clocked scheme [9]) via charge sharing among capacitors, and the result of the summation controls the transistor action. The voltage-mode summation capability of νMOS has been uniquely utilized to produce the WTA action. No DC current flows for the sum operation itself in contrast to the Kirchhoff sum. In νMOS transistors, however, DC current flows in a CMOS inverter configuration when the floating gate is biased in the transition region. Therefore the power consumption is larger than in the subthreshold circuitries. However, the νMOS WTA's presented in this article will give an opportunity of high speed operation at much less power consumption than current-mode circuitries operating in the strong inversion mode. In the following we present two kinds of winner search hardware featuring very fast operation. The winner can be tracked in a continuous-time regime with a detection delay time of about 100psec, while the sorting of multiple data is conducted in a fixed frame of time of about 100nsec.

2 NEURON-MOS CONTINUOUS-TIME WTA

Fig. 1(a) shows a schematic circuit diagram of a νMOS continuous-time WTA for four input signals. Each signal is fed to an input-stage νMOS inverter-A: a

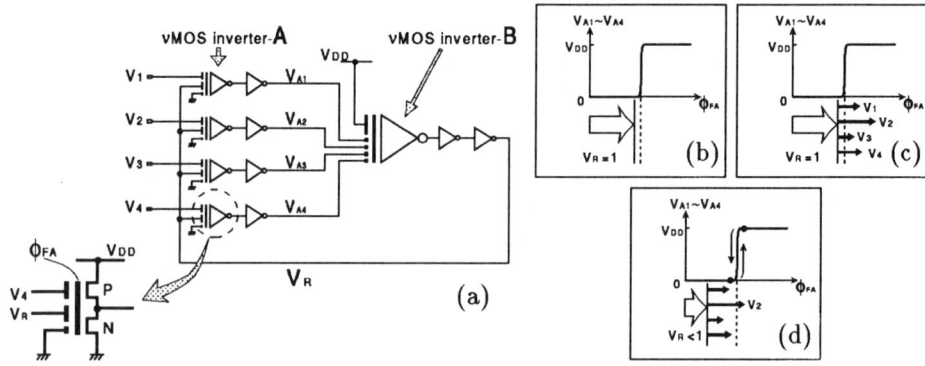

Figure 1: (a) Circuit diagram of νMOS continuous-time WTA circuit. (b)~(d) Response of $V_{A1} \sim V_{A4}$ as a function of the floating-gate potential of νMOS inverter-A.

CMOS inverter in which the common gate is made floating and its potential ϕ_{FA} is determined via capacitance coupling with three input terminals. $V_1(\sim V_4)$ and V_R are equally coupled to the floating gate and a small capacitance pulls down the floating gate to ground. The νMOS inverter-B is designed to turn on when the number of 1's in its inputs ($V_{A1} \sim V_{A4}$) is more than 1. When a feedback loop is formed as shown in the figure, it becomes a ring oscillator composed of odd-numbers of inverter stages.

When $V_1 \sim V_4 = 0$, the circuit is stable with $V_R = 1$ because inverter-A's do not turn on. This is because the small grounded capacitor pulls down the floating gate potential ϕ_{FA} a little smaller than its inverting threshold ($V_{DD}/2$) (see Fig. 1(b)). If non-zero signals are given to input terminals, more-than-one inverter-A's turn on (see Fig. 1(c)) and the inverter-B also turns on, thus initiating the transition of V_R from V_{DD} to 0. According to the decrease in V_R, some of the inverter-A's turn off but the inverter-B (number 1 detector) still stays at on-state until the last inverter-A turns off. When the last inverter-A, the one receiving the largest voltage input, turns off, the inverter-B also turns off and V_R begins to increase. As a result, ring oscillation occurs only in the loop including the largest-input inverter-A(Fig. 1(d)). In this manner, the winner is identified as an oscillating node. The inverter-B can be altered to a number "2" detector or a number "3" detector etc. by just reducing the input voltage to the largest coupling capacitor. Then it is possible for top two or top three to be winners.

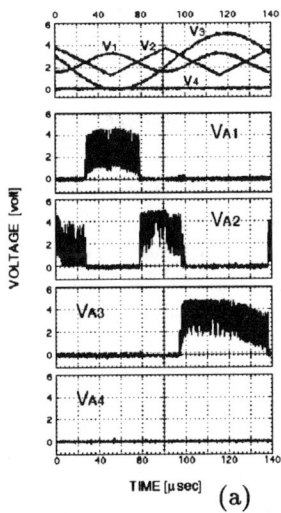 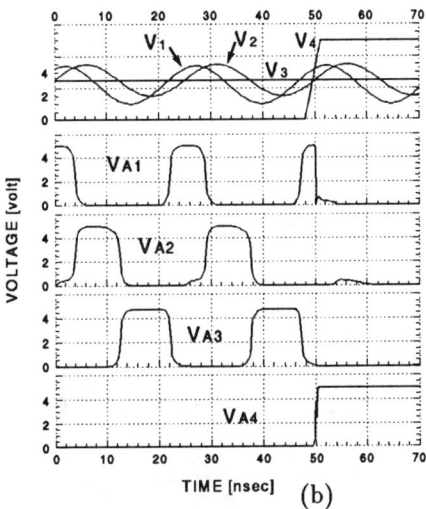

Figure 2: (a) Measured wave forms of four-input WTA as depicted in Fig. 1(a) (bread board experoment). (b) Simulation results for non-oscillating WTA explained in Fig. 3.

Fig. 2(a) demonstrates the measured wave forms of a bread-board test circuit composed of discrete components for verifying the circuit idea. It is clearly seen that ring oscillation occurs only at the temporal winner. However, the ring oscillation increases the power dissipation, and therefore, non-oscillating circuitry would be preferred. An example of simulation results for such a non-oscillating circuit is demonstrated in Fig. 2(b).

Fig. 3(a) gives the circuit diagram of a non-oscillating version of the νMOS

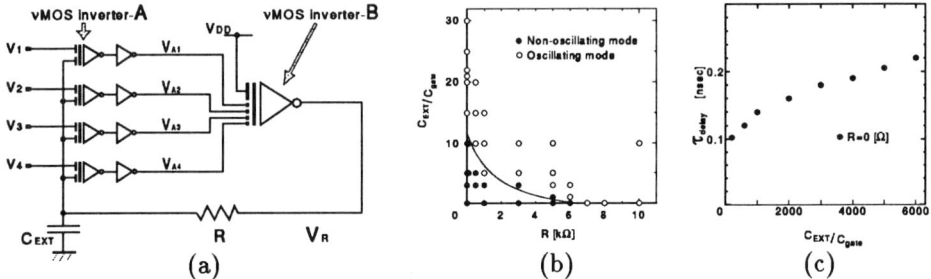

Figure 3: (a) Circuit diagram of non-oscillating-mode WTA. HSPICE simulation results: (b) combinations of R and C_{EXT} for non-oscillating mode; (c) winner detection delay as a function of capacitance load.

continuous-time WTA. In order to suppress the oscillation, the loop gain is reduced by removing the two-stage CMOS inverters in front of the inverter-B and RC delay element is inserted in the feedback loop. The small grounded capacitors were removed in inverter-A's. The waveforms demonstrated in Fig. 2(b) are the HSPICE simulation results with $R = 0$ and $C_{EXT} = 20C_{gate}$ (C_{gate}: input capacitance of elemental CMOS inverter=5.16fF) . The circuit was simulated assuming a typical double-poly 0.5-μm CMOS process. Fig. 3(b) indicates the combinations of R and C_{EXT} yielding the non-oscillating mode of operation obtained by HSPICE simulation. It is important to note that if $C_{EXT} \geq 15C_{gate}$, non-oscillating mode appears with $R = 0$. This means the output resistance of the inverter-B plays the role of R. When the number of inverter-A's is increased, the increased capacitance load serves as C_{EXT}. Therefore, WTA having more than 19 input signals can operate in the non-oscillating mode. Fig. 3(c) represents the detection delay as a function of C_{EXT}. It is known that the increase in C_{EXT}, therefore the increase in the number of input signals to the WTA, does not significantly increase the detection delay and that the delay is only in the range of 100 to 200psec.

A photomicrograph of a test circuit of the non-oscillating mode WTA fabricated by Tohoku-University standard double-polysilicon CMOS process on 3-μm design rules, and the measurement results are shown in Fig. 4(a) and (b), respectively.

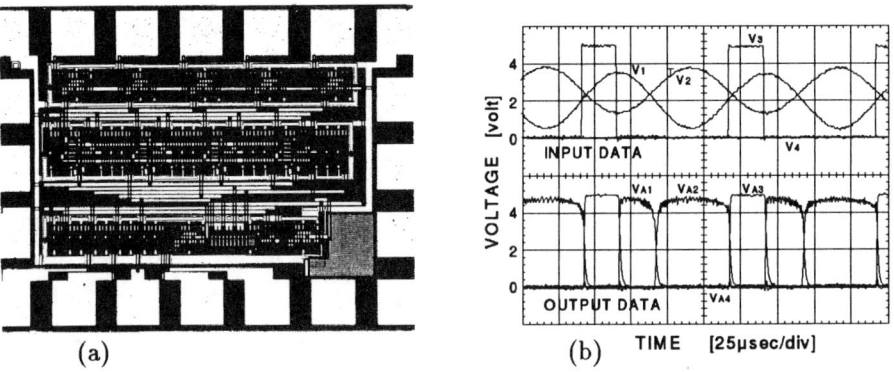

Figure 4: (a) Photomicrograph of a test circuit for 4-input continuous-time WTA. Chip size is 800μm×500μm including all peripherals (3-μm rules). The core circuit of Fig. 3(a) occupies approximately 0.12 mm^2. (b) Measured wave forms.

3   NEURON-MOS DATA SORTING CIRCUITRY

The elemental idea of this circuit was first proposed at ISSCC '93 [3] as an application of the νMOS WTA circuit. In the present work, a clocked-νMOS technique [9] was introduced to enhance the accuracy and reliability of νMOS circuit operation and test circuits were fabricated and their operation have been verified.

Fig. 5(a) shows the circuit diagram of a test circuit for sorting three analog data V_A, V_B, and V_C, and a photomicrograph of a fabricated test circuit designed on 3-μm rules is shown in Fig. 5(b). Each input stage is a νMOS inverter: a CMOS inverter in which the common gate is made floating and its potential ϕ_F is determined by two input voltages via equally-weighted capacitance coupling, namely $\phi_F = (V_A + V_{RAMP})/2$. The reset signal forces the floating node be grounded, thus cancelling the charge on the νMOS floating gate each time before sorting. This is quite essential in achieving long-term reliability of νMOS operation. In the second stage are flip-flop memory cells to store sorting results. The third stage is a circuit which counts the number of 1's at its three input terminals and outputs the result in binary code. The concept of the νMOS A/D converter design [10] has been utilized in the circuit.

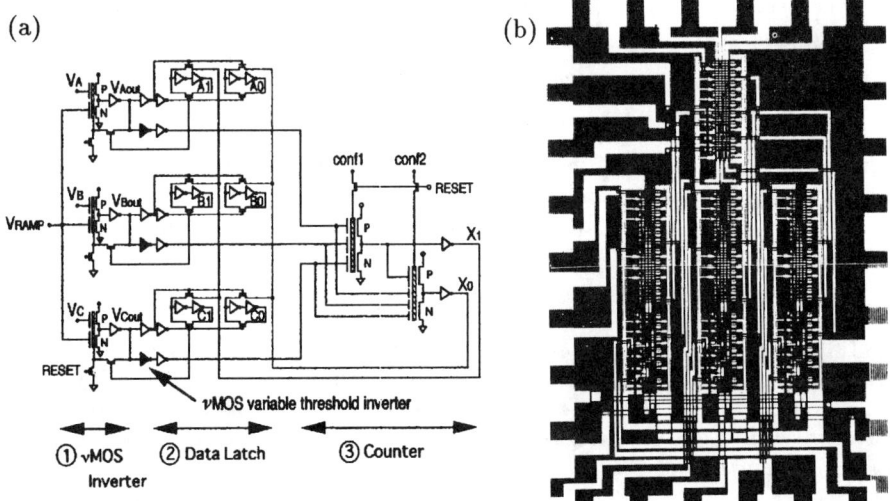

Figure 5: (a) Circuit diagram of νMOS data-soring circuit. (b)Photomicrograph of a test circuit fabricated by Tohoku Univ. Standard double-polysillicon CMOS process (3-μm rules). Chip size is 1250μm×800μm including all peripherals.

The sorting circuit is activated by ramping up V_{RAMP} from 0V to V_{DD}. Then the νMOS inverter receiving the largest input turns on first and the output data of the counter at this moment (0,0) is latched in the respective memory cells. The counter output changes to (0,1) after gate delays in the counter and this code is latched when the νMOS inverter receiving the second largest turns on. Then the counter counts up to (1,0). In this manner, the all input data are numbered according to the order of their magnitudes after a ramp voltage scan is completed.

The measurement results are demonstrated in Fig. 6(a) in comparison with the HSPICE simulation results. Simulation was carried out on the same architecture circuit designed on 0.5-μm design rules and operated under 3V power supply. For three analog input voltages: $V_A = 5V$, $V_B = 4V$, and $V_C = 2V$, (0,0), (0,1),

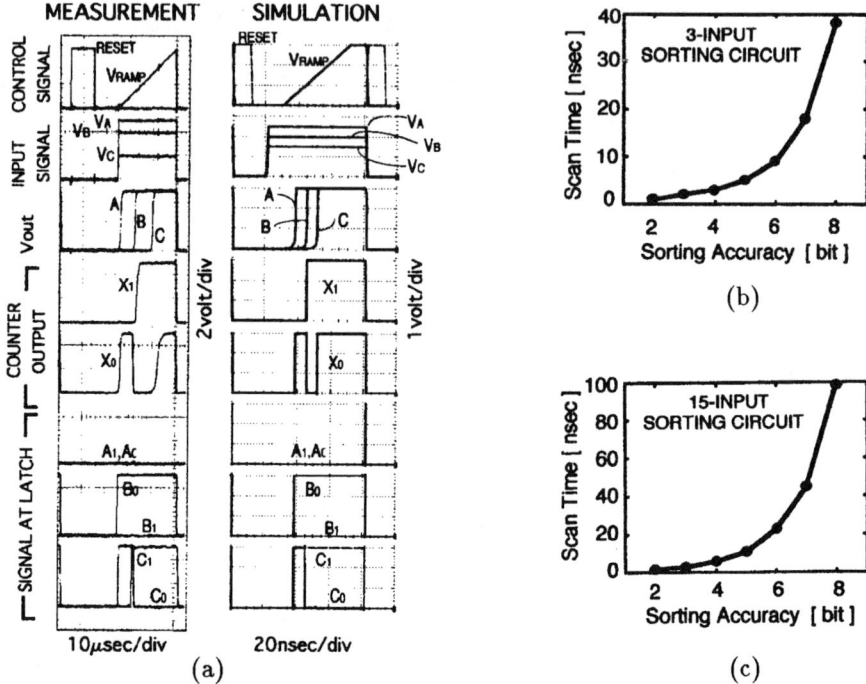

Figure 6: (a) Wave forms of the test circuit shown in Fig. 5(a) measured without buffer circuitry (left) and simulation results of a circuit designed with 0.5-μm rules (right). (b) Minimum scan time vs. sorting accuracy for a three-input sorter. (c) Minimum scan time vs. sorting accuracy for a 15-input sorter.

and (1,0) are latched, respectively, after the ramp voltage scan, thus accomplishing correct sorting. Slow operation of the test circuit is due to the loading effect caused by the direct probing of the node voltage without output buffer circuitries. The simulation with a 0.5-μm-design-rule circuit indicates the sorting is accomplished within the scan time of 40nsec.

In Fig. 6(b), the minimum scan time obtained by simulation is plotted as a function of the bit accuracy in sorting analog data. N-bit accuracy means the minimum voltage difference required for winner discrimination is $V_{DD}/2^2$. If the ramp rate is too fast, the νMOS inverter receiving the next largest data turns on before the correct counting results become available, leading to an erroneous operation. The scan time/accuracy relation in Fig. 6(b) is primarily determined by the response delay in the counter. It should be noted that the number of inverter stages in the counter (νMOS A/D converter) is always three indifferent to the number of output bits, namely, the delay would not increase significantly by the increase in the number of input data. In order to investigate this, a 15-input counter was designed and the delay time was evaluated by HSPICE simulation. It was 312 psec in comparison with 110 psec of the 3-input counter of Fig. 5(a). The scan time/accuracy relation for the 15-input sorting circuit is shown in Fig. 6(c), indicating the sorting of 15 input data can be accomplished in 100 nsec with 8-bit accuracy.

4 CONCLUSIONS

A novel neuron-like functional device νMOS has been successfully utilized in constructing intelligent electronic circuits which can carry out search for the temporal winner. As a result, it has become possible to perform data sorting as well as winner search in an instance, both requiring very time-consuming sequential data processing on a digital computer. The hardware algorithms presented here are typical examples of the νMOS binary-multivalue-analog merged computation scheme, which would play an important role in the future flexible data processing.

Acknowledgements

This work was partially supported by Grant-in-Aid for Scientific Research (06402038) from the Ministry of Education, Science, Sports, and Culture, Japan. A part of this work was carried out in the Super Clean Room of Laboratory for Electronic Intelligent Systems, Research Institute of Electrical communication, Tohoku University.

References

[1] T. Shibata and T. Ohmi, "A functional MOS transistor featuring gate-level weighted sum and threshold operations," IEEE Trans. Electron Devices, Vol. 39, No. 6, pp.1444-1455 (1992).

[2] T. Shibata, K. Kotani, T. Yamashita, H. Ishii, H. Kosaka, and T. Ohmi, "Implementing interlligence on silicon using neuron-like functional MOS transistors," in *Advances in Neural Information Processing Systems 6* (San Francisco, CA: Morgan Kaufmann 1994) pp. 919-926.

[3] T. Yamashita, T. Shibata, and T. Ohmi, "Neuron MOS winner-take-all circuit and its application to associative memory," in *ISSCC Dig. Tech. Papers*, Feb. 1993, FA 15.2, pp. 236-237.

[4] G. Gauwenberghs and V. Pedroni, "A charge-based CMOS parallel analog vector quantizer," in *Advances in Neural Information Processing Systems 7* (Cambridge, MA: The MIT Press 1995) pp. 779-786.

[5] T. Kohonen, *Self-Organization and Associative Memory*, 2nd ed. (New York: Springer-Verlag 1988).

[6] M. Kawamata, M. Abe, and T. Higuchi, "Evolutionary digital filters," in *Proc. Int. Workshop on Intelligent Signal Processing and Communication Systems*, seoul, Oct., 1994, pp. 263-268.

[7] J. Lazzaro, S. Ryckebusch, M. A. Mahowald, and C. A. Mead, "Winner-Take-All networks of O(N) complexity," in *Advances in Neural Information Processing Systems 1* (San Mateo, CA: Morgan Kaufmann 1989) pp. 703-711.

[8] J. Choi and B. J. Sheu, "A high-precision VLSI winner-take-all circuit for self-organizing neural networks," IEEE J. Solid State Circuits, Vol. 28, No. 5, pp.576-584 (1993).

[9] K. Kotani, T. Shibata, M. Imai, and T. Ohmi, "Clocked-Neuron-MOS logic circuits employing auto-threshold-adjustment," in *ISSCC Dig. Technical Papers*, Feb. 1995, FA 19.5, pp. 320-321.

[10] T. Shibata and T. Ohmi, "Neuron MOS binary-logic integrated circuits: Part II, Simplifying techniques of circuit configuration and their practical applications," IEEE Trans. Electron Devices, Vol. 40, No. 5, 974-979 (1993).

Analog VLSI Processor Implementing the Continuous Wavelet Transform

R. Timothy Edwards and Gert Cauwenberghs
Department of Electrical and Computer Engineering
Johns Hopkins University
3400 North Charles Street
Baltimore, MD 21218-2686
{tim,gert}@bach.ece.jhu.edu

Abstract

We present an integrated analog processor for real-time wavelet decomposition and reconstruction of continuous temporal signals covering the audio frequency range. The processor performs complex harmonic modulation and Gaussian lowpass filtering in 16 parallel channels, each clocked at a different rate, producing a multiresolution mapping on a logarithmic frequency scale. Our implementation uses mixed-mode analog and digital circuits, oversampling techniques, and switched-capacitor filters to achieve a wide linear dynamic range while maintaining compact circuit size and low power consumption. We include experimental results on the processor and characterize its components separately from measurements on a single-channel test chip.

1 Introduction

An effective mathematical tool for multiresolution analysis [Kais94], the wavelet transform has found widespread use in various signal processing applications involving characteristic patterns that cover multiple scales of resolution, such as representations of speech and vision. Wavelets offer suitable representations for temporal data that contain pertinent features both in the time and frequency domains; consequently, wavelet decompositions appear to be effective in representing wide-bandwidth signals interfacing with neural systems [Szu92].

The present system performs a continuous wavelet transform on temporal one-dimensional analog signals such as speech, and is in that regard somewhat related to silicon models of the cochlea implementing cochlear transforms [Lyon88], [Liu92], [Watt92], [Lin94]. The multiresolution processor we implemented expands on the architecture developed in [Edwa93], which differs from the other analog auditory processors in the way signal components in each frequency band are encoded. The signal is modulated with the center

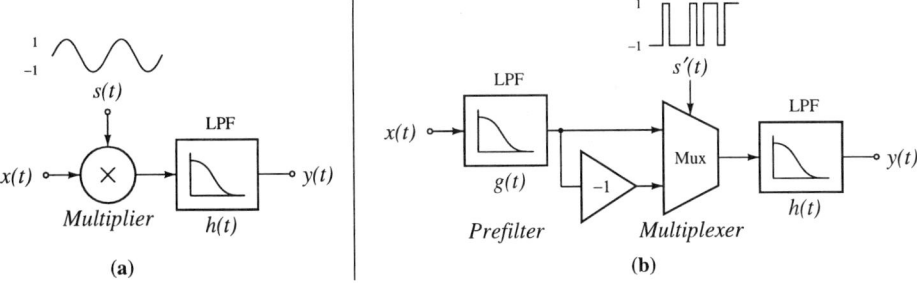

Figure 1: *Demodulation systems,* **(a)** *using multiplication, and* **(b)** *multiplexing.*

frequency of each channel and subsequently lowpass filtered, translating signal components taken around the center frequency towards zero frequency. In particular, we consider wavelet decomposition and reconstruction of analog continuous-time temporal data with a complex Gaussian kernel according to the following formulae:

$$y_k(t) = \int_{-\infty}^{t} x(\theta) \exp\left(j\omega_k\theta - \alpha(\omega_k(t-\theta))^2\right) d\theta$$

(decomposition) (1)

$$x'(t) = C \sum_k y'_k(t) \exp(-j\omega_k t)$$

(reconstruction)

where the center frequencies ω_k are spaced on a logarithmic scale. The constant α sets the relative width of the frequency bins in the decomposition, and can be adjusted (together with C) alter the shape of the wavelet kernel. Successive decomposition and reconstruction transforms yield an approximate identity operation; it cannot be exact as no continuous orthonormal basis function exists for the CWT [Kais94].

2 Architecture

The above operations are implemented in [Edwa93] using two demodulator systems per channel, one for the real component of (1), and another for the imaginary component, 90° out of phase with the first. Each takes the form of a sinusoidal modulator oscillating at the channel center frequency, followed by a Gaussian-shaped lowpass filter, as shown in Figure 1 (a). This arrangement requires a precise analog sine wave generator and an accurate linear analog multiplier. In the present implementation, we circumvent *both* requirements by using an oversampled binary representation of the modulation reference signal.

2.1 Multiplexing vs. Multiplying

Multiplication of an analog signal $x(t)$ with a binary (± 1) sequence is naturally implemented with high precision using a multiplexer, which alternates between presenting either the input or its inverse $-x(t)$ to the output. This principle is applied to simplify harmonic modulation, and is illustrated in Figure 1 (b). The multiplier has been replaced by an analog inverter followed by a multiplexer, where the multiplexer is controlled by an oversampled binary periodic sequence representing the sine wave reference. The oversampled binary sequence is chosen to approximate the analog sine wave as closely as possible, disregarding components at high frequency which are removed by the subsequent lowpass filter. The assumption made is that no high frequency components are present in the input signal

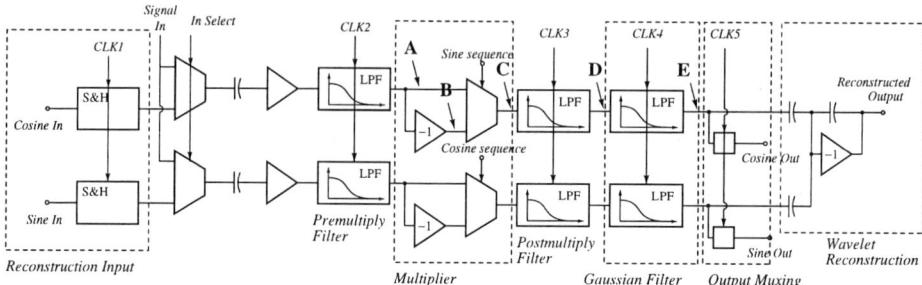

Figure 2: *Block diagram of a single channel in the wavelet processor, showing test points* **A** *through* **E**.

under modulation, which otherwise would convolve with corresponding high frequency components in the binary sequence to produce low frequency distortion components at the output. To that purpose, an additional lowpass filter is added in front of the multiplexer. Residual low-frequency distortion at the output is minimized by maximizing roll-off of the filters, placing proper constraints on their cutoff frequencies, and optimally choosing the bit sequence in the oversampled reference [Edwa95]. Clearly, the signal accuracy that can be achieved improves as the length N of the sequence is extended. Constraints on the length N are given by the implied overhead in required signal bandwidth, power dissipation, and complexity of implementation.

2.2 Wavelet Gaussian Function

The reason for choosing a Gaussian kernel in (1) is to ensure optimal support in both time and frequency [Gros89]. A key requirement in implementing the Gaussian filter is linear phase, to avoid spectral distortion due to non-uniform group delays. A worry-free architecture would be an analog FIR filter; however the number of taps required to accommodate the narrow bandwidth required would be prohibitively large for our purpose. Instead, we approximate a Gaussian filter by cascading several first-order lowpass filters. From probabilistic arguments, the obtained lowpass filter approximates a Gaussian filter increasingly well as the number of stages increases [Edwa93].

3 Implementation

Two sections of a wavelet processor, each containing 8 parallel channels, were integrated onto a single 4 mm × 6 mm die in 2 μm CMOS technology. Both sections can be configured to perform wavelet decomposition as well as reconstruction. The block diagram for one of the channels is shown in Figure 2. In addition, a separate test chip was designed which performs one channel of the wavelet function. Test points were made available at various points for either input or output, as indicated in boldface capitals, **A** through **E**, in Figure 2.

Each channel performs complex harmonic modulation and Gaussian lowpass filtering, as defined above. At the front end of the chip is a sample-and-hold section to sample time-multiplexed wavelet signals for reconstruction. In cases of both signal decomposition and reconstruction, each channel removes the input DC component removed, filters the result through the premultiplication lowpass (PML) filter, inverts the result, and passes both non-inverted and inverted signals onto the multiplexer. The multiplexer output is passed through a postmultiplication lowpass filter (PML, same architecture) to remove high frequency components of the oversampled sequence, and then passed through the Gaussian-shaped lowpass filter. The cutoff frequencies of all filters are controlled by the clock rates

(CLK1 to CLK4 in Figure 2). The remainder of the system is for reconstruction and for time-multiplexing the output.

3.1 Multiplier

The multiplier is implemented by use of the above multiplexing scheme, driven by an oversampled binary sequence representing a sine wave. The sequence we used was 256 samples in length, created from a 64-sample base sequence by reversal and inversion. The sequence length of 256 generates a modulator wave of 4 kHz (useful for speech applications) from a clock of about 1 MHz.

We derived a sequence which, after postfiltering through a 3rd-order lowpass filter of the form of the PML prefilter (see below), produces a sine wave in which all harmonics are more than 60 dB down from the primary [Edwa95]. The optimized 64-bit base sequence consists of 11 zeros and 53 ones, allowing a very simple implementation in which an address decoder decodes the "zero" bits. The binary sequence is shown in Figure 4. The magnitude of the prime harmonic of the sequence is approximately 1.02, within 2% of unity.

The process of reversing and inverting the sequence is simplified by using a gray code counter to produce the addresses for the sequence, with only a small amount of combinatorial logic needed to achieve the desired result [Edwa95]. It is also straightforward to generate the addresses for the cosine channel, which is 90° out of phase with the original.

3.2 Linear Filtering

All filters used are implemented as linear cascades of first-order, single-pole filter sections. The number of first-order sections for the PML filters is 3. The number of sections for the "Gaussian" filter is 8, producing a suitable approximation to a Gaussian filter response for all frequencies of interest (Figure 5).

Figure 3 shows one first-order lowpass section of the filters as implemented. This standard

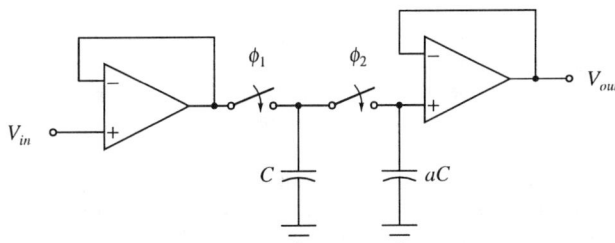

Figure 3: Single discrete-time lowpass filter section.

switched-capacitor circuit implements a transfer function containing a single pole, approximately located in the Laplace domain at $s = f_s/a$ for large values of the parameter a, with f_s being the sampling frequency. The value for this parameter a is fixed at the design stage as the ratio of two capacitors in Figure 3, and was set to be 15 for the The PML filters and 12 for the Gaussian filters.

4 Measured Results

4.1 Sine wave modulator

We tested the accuracy of the sine wave modulation signal by applying two constant voltages at test points **A** and **B**, such that the sine wave modulation signal is effectively multiplied

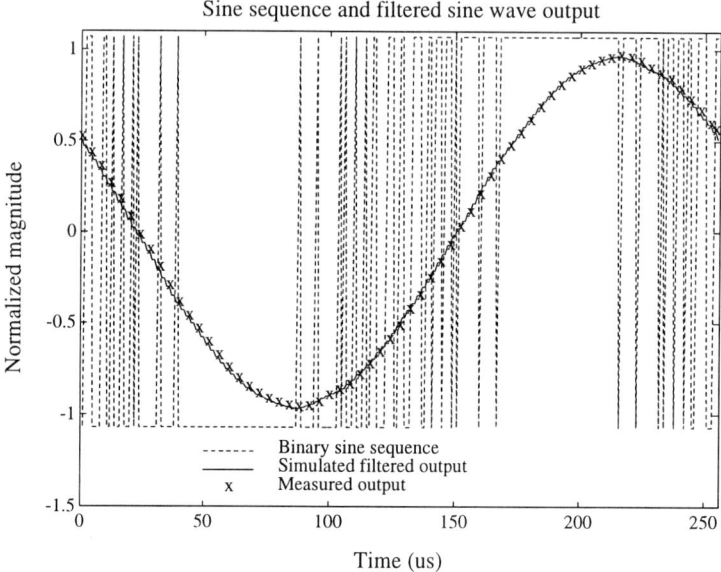

Figure 4: *Filtered sine wave output.*

by a constant. The output of the multiplier is filtered and the output taken at test point **D**, before the Gaussian filter. Figure 4 shows the (idealized) multiplexer output at test point **C**, which accurately creates the desired binary sequence. Figure 4 also shows the measured sine wave after filtering with the PML filter and the expected output from the simulation model, using a deviating value of 8.0 for the capacitor ratio a, as justified below. FFT analysis of Figure 4 has shown that the resulting sine wave has all harmonics below about −49 dB. This is in good agreement with the simulation model, provided a correction is made for the value of the capacitor ratio a to account for fringe and (large) parasitic capacitances. The best fit for the measured data from the postmultiplication filter is $a = 8.0$, compared to the desired value of $a = 15.0$. The transform of the simulated output shown in the figure takes into account the smaller value of a. Because the postmultiplication filter is followed by the Gaussian filter, the bandwidth of the output can be directly controlled by proper clocking of the Gaussian filter, so the distortion in the sine wave is ultimately much smaller than that measured at the output of the postmultiplication filter.

4.2 Gaussian filter

The Gaussian filter was tested by applying a signal at test point **D** and measuring the response at test point **E**. Figure 5 shows the response of the Gaussian filter as compared to expected responses. There are two sets of curves, one for a filter clocked at 64 kHz, and the other clocked at 128 kHz; these curves are normalized by plotting time relative to the clock frequency f_s. The solid line indicates the best match for an 8th-order lowpass filter, using the capacitor ratio, a, as a fitting parameter. The best-fit value of a is approximately 6.8. This is again much lower than the capacitor area ratio of 12 on the chip. The dotted line is the response of the ideal Gaussian characteristic $\exp(-\omega^2/(2a\omega_k^2))$ approximated by the cascade of first-order sections with capacitor ratio a.

Figure 5 (b) shows the measured phase response of the Gaussian filter for the 128 kHz clock. The phase response is approximately linear throughout the passband region.

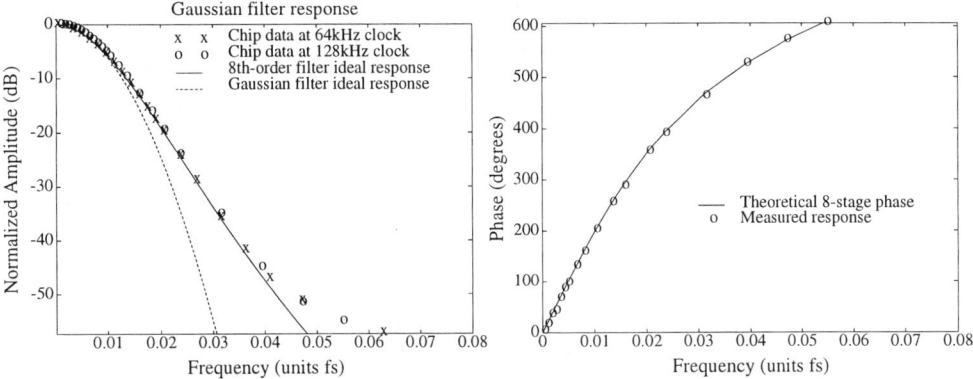

Figure 5: *Gaussian filter transfer functions: theoretical and actual. (a) Relative amplitude; (b) Phase.*

4.3 Wavelet decomposition

Figure 6 shows the test chip performing a wavelet transform on a simple sinusoidal input, illustrating the effects of (oversampled) sinusoidal modulation followed by lowpass filtering through the Gaussian filter. The chip multiplier system is clocked at 500 kHz. The input wave is approximately 3.1 kHz, close to the center frequency of the modulator signal, which is the clock rate divided by 128, or about 3.9 kHz (a typical value for the highest-frequency channel in an auditory application). The top trace in the figure shows the filtered and inverted input, taken from test point **B**. The middle trace shows the output of the multiplexer (test point **C**), wherein the output is multiplexed between the signal and its inverse. The bottom trace is taken from the system output (labeled *Cosine Out* in Figure 2) and shows the demodulated signal of frequency 800 Hz (= 3.9 kHz - 3.1 kHz). Not shown is the cosine output, which is 90° out of phase with the one shown. This demonstrates the proper operation of complex demodulation in a single channel configured for wavelet decomposition. In addition, we have tested the full 16-channel chip decomposition, and all individual parts function properly. The total power consumption of the 16-channel wavelet chip was measured to be less than 50 mW, of which a large fraction can be attributed to external interfacing and buffering circuitry at the periphery of the chip.

5 Conclusions

We have demonstrated the full functionality of an analog chip performing the continuous wavelet transform (decomposition). The chip is based on mixed analog/digital signal processing principles, and uses a demodulation scheme which is accurately implemented using oversampling methods. Advantages of the architecture used in the chip are an increased dynamic range and a precise control over lateral synchronization of wavelet components. An additional advantage inherent to the modulation scheme used is the potential to tune the channel bandwidths over a wide range, down to unusually narrow bands, since the cutoff frequency of the Gaussian filter and the center frequency of the modulator are independently adjustable and precisely controllable parameters.

References

G. Kaiser, *A Friendly Guide to Wavelets,* Boston, MA: Birkhäuser, 1994.

T. Edwards and M. Godfrey, "An Analog Wavelet Transform Chip," *IEEE Int'l Conf. on*

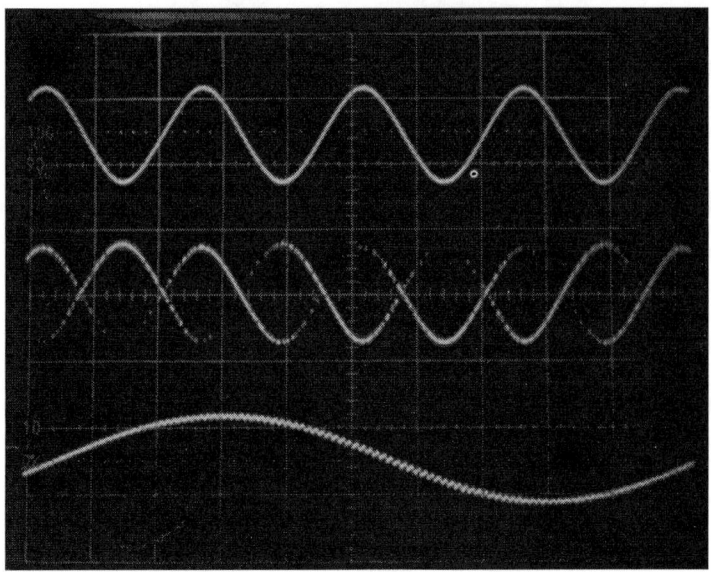

Figure 6: *Scope trace of the wavelet transform: filtered input (top), multiplexed signal (middle), and wavelet output (bottom).*

Neural Networks, vol. **III**, 1993, pp. 1247–1251.

T. Edwards and G. Cauwenberghs, "Oversampling Architecture for Analog Harmonic Modulation," to appear in *Electronics Letters*, 1996.

A. Grossmann, R. Kronland-Martinet, and J. Morlet, "Reading and understanding continuous wavelet transforms," *Wavelets: Time-Frequency Methods and Phase Space.* Springer-Verlag, 1989, pp. 2–20.

W. Liu, A.G. Andreou, and M.G. Goldstein, "Voiced-Speech Representation by an Analog Silicon Model of the Auditory Periphery," *IEEE T. Neural Networks,* vol. **3** (3), pp 477–487, 1992.

J. Lin, W.-H. Ki, T. Edwards, and S. Shamma, "Analog VLSI Implementations of Auditory Wavelet Transforms Using Switched-Capacitor Circuits," *IEEE Trans. Circuits and Systems—I,* vol.**41** (9), pp. 572–583, September 1994.

A. Lu and W. Roberts, "A High-Quality Analog Oscillator Using Oversampling D/A Conversion Techniques," *IEEE Trans. Circuits and Systems—II,* vol.**41** (7), pp. 437–444, July 1994.

R.F. Lyon and C.A. Mead, "An Analog Electronic Cochlea," *IEEE Trans. Acoustics, Speech and Signal Proc.,* vol. **36**, pp 1119–1134, 1988.

H.H. Szu, B. Tefler, and S. Kadembe, "Neural Network Adaptive Wavelets for Signal Representation and Classification," *Optical Engineering,* vol. **31** (9), pp. 1907–1916, September 1992.

L. Watts, D.A. Kerns, and R.F. Lyon, "Improved Implementation of the Silicon Cochlea," *IEEE Journal of Solid-State Circuits,* vol. **27** (5), pp 692–700, 1992.

Silicon Models for Auditory Scene Analysis

John Lazzaro and John Wawrzynek
CS Division
UC Berkeley
Berkeley, CA 94720-1776
lazzaro@cs.berkeley.edu, johnw@cs.berkeley.edu

Abstract

We are developing special-purpose, low-power analog-to-digital converters for speech and music applications, that feature analog circuit models of biological audition to process the audio signal before conversion. This paper describes our most recent converter design, and a working system that uses several copies of the chip to compute multiple representations of sound from an analog input. This multi-representation system demonstrates the plausibility of inexpensively implementing an auditory scene analysis approach to sound processing.

1. INTRODUCTION

The visual system computes multiple representations of the retinal image, such as motion, orientation, and stereopsis, as an early step in scene analysis. Likewise, the auditory brainstem computes secondary representations of sound, emphasizing properties such as binaural disparity, periodicity, and temporal onsets. Recent research in auditory scene analysis involves using computational models of these auditory brainstem representations in engineering applications.

Computation is a major limitation in auditory scene analysis research: the complete auditory processing system described in (Brown and Cooke, 1994) operates at approximately 4000 times real time, running under UNIX on a Sun SPARCstation 1. Standard approaches to hardware acceleration for signal processing algorithms could be used to ease this computational burden in a research environment; a variety of parallel, fixed-point hardware products would work well on these algorithms.

However, hardware solutions appropriate for a research environment may not be well suited for accelerating algorithms in cost-sensitive, battery-operated consumer products. Possible product applications of auditory algorithms include robust pitch-tracking systems for musical instrument applications, and small-vocabulary, speaker-independent wordspotting systems for control applications.

In these applications, the input takes an analog form: a voltage signal from a microphone or a guitar pickup. Low-power analog circuits that compute auditory representations have been implemented and characterized by several research groups – these working research prototypes include several generation of cochlear models (Lyon and Mead, 1988), periodicity models, and binaural models. These circuits could be used to compute auditory representations directly on the analog signal, in real-time, using these low-power, area-efficient analog circuits.

Using analog computation successfully in a system presents many practical difficulties; the density and power advantages of the analog approach are often lost in the process of system integration. One successful IC architecture that uses analog computation in a system is the special-purpose analog to digital converter, that includes analog, non-linear pre-processing before or during data conversion. For example, converters that include logarithmic waveform compression before digitization are commercially viable components.

Using this component type as a model, we have been developing special-purpose, low-power analog-to-digital converters for speech and audio applications; this paper describes our most recent converter design, and a working system that uses several copies of the chip to compute multiple representations of sound.

2. CONVERTER DESIGN

Figure 1 shows an architectural block diagram of our current converter design. The 35,000 transistor chip was fabricated in the 2μm, n-well process of Orbit Semiconductor, brokered through MOSIS; the circuit is fully functional. Below is a summary of the general architectural features of this chip; unless otherwise referenced, circuit details are similar to the converter design described in (Lazzaro et al., 1994).

- An analog audio signal serves as input to the chip; dynamic range is 40dB to 60dB (1-10mV to 1V peak, dependent on measurement criteria).

- This signal is processed by analog circuits that model cochlear processing (Lyon and Mead, 1988) and sensory transduction; the audio signal is transformed into 119 wavelet-filtered, half-wave rectified, non-linearly compressed audio signals. The cycle-by-cycle waveform of each signal is preserved; no temporal smoothing is performed.

- Two additional analog processing blocks follow this initial cochlear processing, a temporal autocorrelation processor and a temporal adaptation processor. Each block transforms the input array into a new representation of equal size; alternatively, the block can be programmed to pass its input vector to its output without alteration.

- The output circuits of the final processing block are pulse generators, which code the signal as a pattern of fixed-width, fixed-height spikes. All the information in the representation is contained in the onset times of the pulses.

- The activity on this array is sent off-chip via an asynchronous parallel bus. The converter chip acts as a sender on the bus; a digital host processor is the receiver. The converter initiates a transaction on the bus to communicate the onset of a pulse in the array; the data value on the bus is a number indicating which unit in the array pulsed. The time of transaction initiation carries essential information. This coding method is also known as the address-event representation.

- Many converters can be used in the same system, sharing the same asynchronous output bus (Lazzaro and Wawrzynek, 1995). No extra components are needed to implement bus sharing; the converter bus design includes extra signals and logic that implements multi-chip bus arbitration. This feature is a major difference between this design and (Lazzaro et al., 1994).

- The converter includes a digitally-controllable parameter storage and generation system; 25 tunable parameters control the behavior of the analog processing blocks. Programmability supports the creation of multi-converter systems that use a single chip design: each chip receives the same analog signal, but processes the signal in different ways, as determined by the parameter values for each chip.

- Non-volatile analog storage elements are used to store the parameters; parameters are changeable via Fowler-Nordhiem tunneling, using a 5V control input bus. Many converters can share the same control bus. Parameter values can be sensed by activating a control mode, which sends parameter information on the converter output bus. Apart from two high-voltage power supply pins, and a trimming input pin for tunneling pulse width, all control voltages used in this converter are generated on-chip.

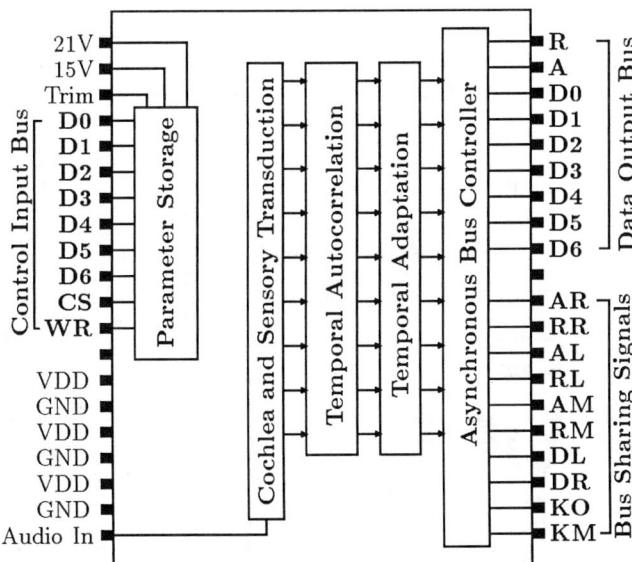

Figure 1. Block diagram of the converter chip. Most of the 40 pins of the chip are dedicated to the data output and control input buses, and to the control signals for coordinating bus sharing in multi-converter systems.

3. SYSTEM DESIGN

Figure 2 shows a block diagram of a system that uses three copies of the converter chip to compute multiple representations of sound; the system acts as a real-time audio input device to a Sun workstation. An analog audio input connects to each converter; this input can be from a pre-amplified microphone, for spontaneous input, or from the analog audio signal of the workstation, for controlled experiments.

The asynchronous output buses from the three chips are connected together, to produce a single output address space for the system; no external components are needed for output bus sharing and arbitration. The onset time of a transaction carries essential information on this bus; additional logic on this board adds a 16-bit timestamp to each bus transaction, coding the onset time with $20\mu s$ resolution. The control input buses for the three chips are also connected together to produce a single input address space, using external logic for address decoding. We use a commercial interface board to link the workstation with these system buses.

4. SYSTEM PERFORMANCE

We designed a software environment, **Aer**, to support real-time, low-latency data visualization of the multi-converter system. Using Aer, we can easily experiment with different converter tunings. Figure 3 shows a screen from Aer, showing data from the three converters as a function of time; the input sound for this screen is a short 800 Hz tone burst, followed by a sinusoid sweep from 300 Hz to 3 Khz. The top ("Spectral Shape") and bottom ("Onset") representations are raw data from converters 1 and 3, as marked on Figure 2, tuned for different responses. The output channel number is plotted vertically; each dot represents a pulse.

The top representation codes for periodicity-based spectral shape; for this representation, the temporal autocorrelation block (see Figure 1) is activated, and the temporal adaptation block is inactivated. Spectral frequency is mapped logarithmically on the vertical dimension, from 300 Hz to 4 Khz; the activity in each channel is the periodic waveform present at that frequency. The difference between a periodicity-based spectral method and a resonant spectral method can be seen in the response to the 800 Hz sinusoid onset: the periodicity representation shows activity only around the 800 Hz channels, whereas a spectral representation would show broadband transient activity at tone onset.

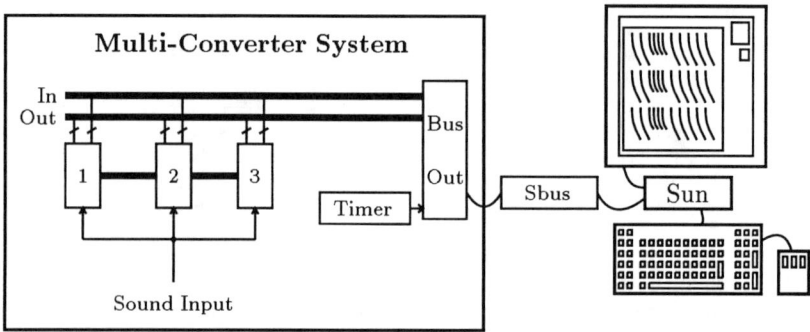

Figure 2. Block diagram of the multi-converter system.

Silicon Models for Auditory Scene Analysis

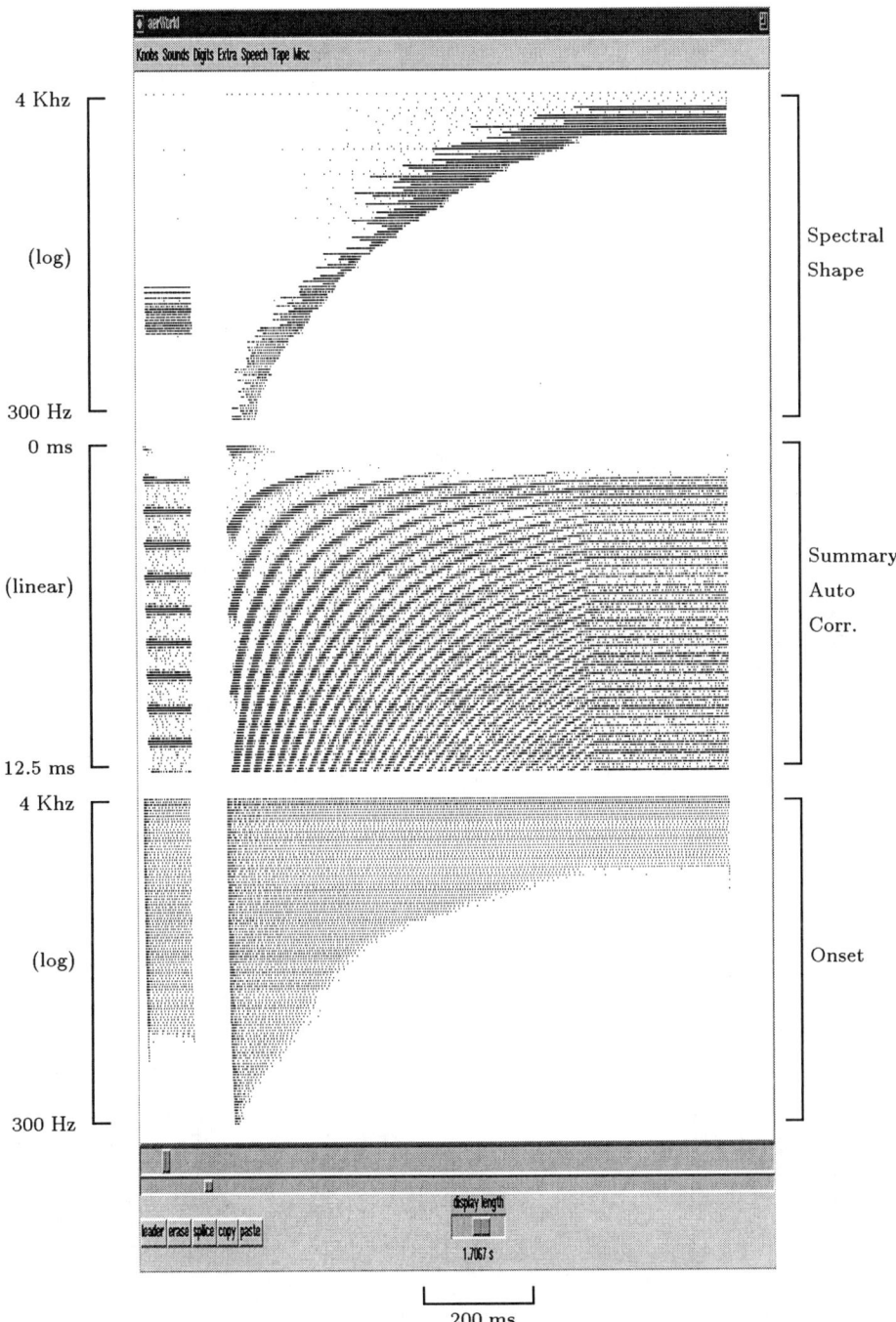

Figure 3. Data from the multi-converter system, in response to a 800-Hz pure tone, followed by a sinusoidal sweep from 300Hz to 3Khz.

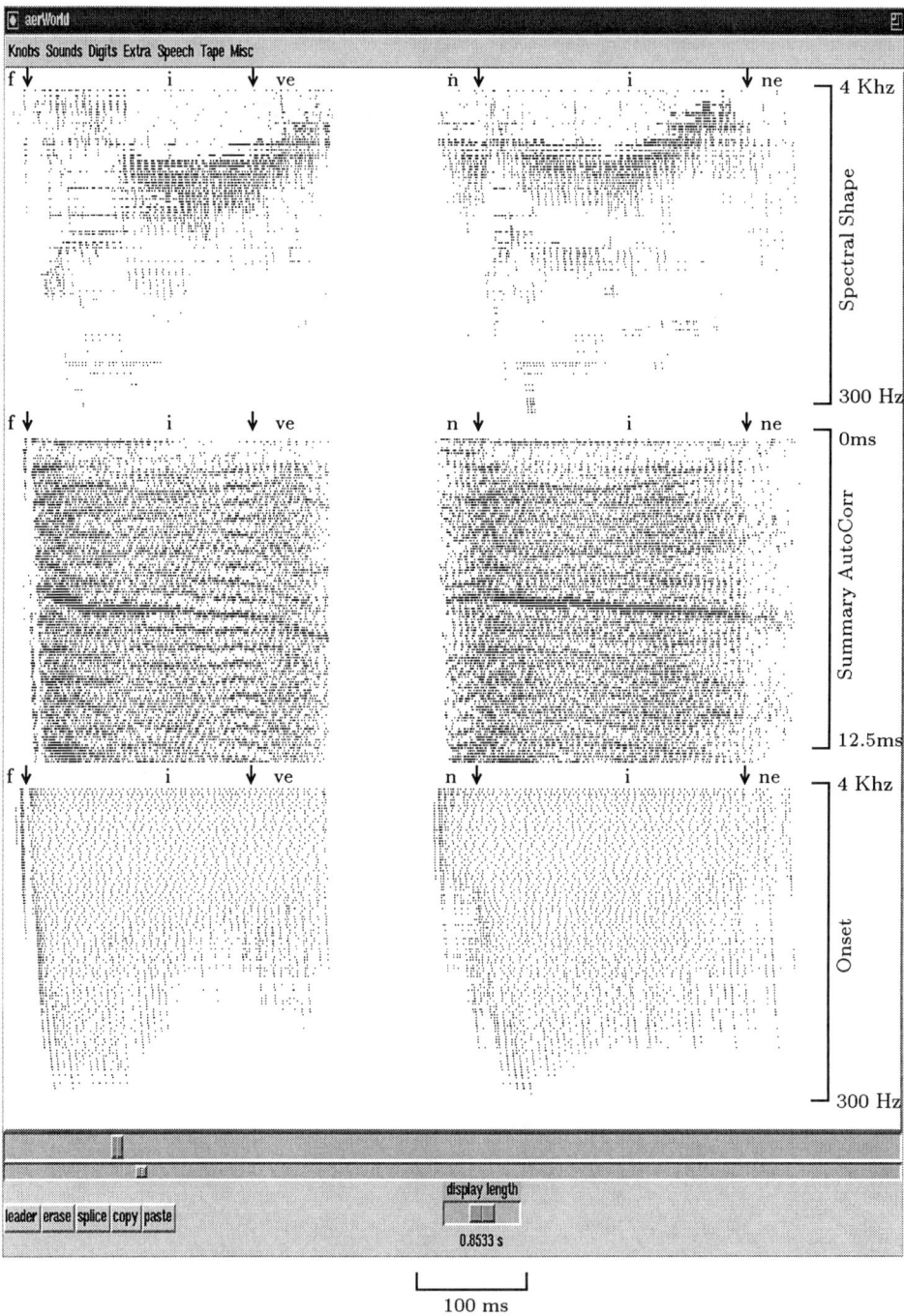

Figure 4. Data from the multi-converter system, in response to the word "five" followed by the word "nine".

The bottom representation codes for temporal onsets; for this representation, the temporal adaptation block is activated, and the temporal autocorrelation block is inactivated. The spectral filtering of the representation reflects the silicon cochlea tuning: a low-pass response with a sharp cutoff and a small resonant peak at the best frequency of the filter. The black, wideband lines at the start of the 800 Hz tone and the sinusoid sweep illustrate the temporal adaptation.

The middle ("Summary Auto Corr.") representation is a summary autocorrelogram, useful for pitch processing and voiced/unvoiced decisions in speech recognition. This representation is not raw data from a converter; software post-processing is performed on the converter output to produce the final result. The frequency response of converter 2 is set as in the bottom representation; the temporal adaptation response, however, is set to a 100 millisecond time constant. The converter output pulse rates are set so that the cycle-by-cycle waveform information for each output channel is preserved in the output.

To complete the representation, a set of running autocorrelation functions $x(t)x(t-\tau)$ is computed for $\tau = k\,105\mu s, k = 1\ldots 120$, for each of the 119 output channels. These autocorrelation functions are summed over all output channels to produce the final representation; τ is plotted as a linear function of time on the vertical axis. The correlation multiplication can be efficiently implemented by integer subtraction and comparison of pulse timestamps; the summation over channels is simply the merging of lists of bus transactions. The middle representation in Figure 3 shows the qualitative characteristics of the summary autocorrelogram: a repetitive band structure in response to periodic sounds.

Figure 4 shows the output response of the multi-converter system in response to telephone-bandwidth-limited speech; the phonetic boundaries of the two words, "five" and "nine", are marked by arrows. The vowel formant information is shown most clearly by the strong peaks in the spectral shape representation; the wideband information in the "f" of five is easily seen in the onset representation. The summary autocorrelation representation shows a clear texture break between vowels and the voiced "n" and "v" sounds.

Acknowledgements

Thanks to Richard Lyon and Peter Cariani for summary autocorrelogram discussions. Funded by the Office of Naval Research (URI-N00014-92-J-1672).

References

Brown, G.J. and Cooke, M. (1994). Computational auditory scene analysis. *Computer Speech and Language*, **8:4**, pp. 297-336.

Lazzaro, J. P. and Wawrzynek, J. (1995). A multi-sender asynchronous extension to the address-event protocol. In Dally, W. J., Poulton, J. W., Ishii, A. T. (eds), *16th Conference on Advanced Research in VLSI*, pp. 158–169.

Lazzaro, J. P., Wawrzynek, J., and Kramer, A (1994). Systems technologies for silicon auditory models. *IEEE Micro*, **14:3**. 7-15.

Lyon, R. F., and Mead, C. (1988). An analog electronic cochlea. *IEEE Trans. Acoust., Speech, Signal Processing* vol. 36, pp. 1119–1134.

VLSI Model of Primate Visual Smooth Pursuit

Ralph Etienne-Cummings
Department of Electrical Engineering,
Southern Illinois University, Carbondale,
IL 62901

Jan Van der Spiegel
Moore School of Electrical Engineering,
University of Pennsylvania, Philadelphia,
PA 19104

Paul Mueller
Corticon, Incorporated,
3624 Market Str, Philadelphia,
PA 19104

Abstract

A one dimensional model of primate smooth pursuit mechanism has been implemented in 2 μm CMOS VLSI. The model consolidates Robinson's negative feedback model with Wyatt and Pola's positive feedback scheme, to produce a smooth pursuit system which zero's the velocity of a target on the retina. Furthermore, the system uses the current eye motion as a predictor for future target motion. Analysis, stability and biological correspondence of the system are discussed. For implementation at the focal plane, a local correlation based visual motion detection technique is used. Velocity measurements, ranging over 4 orders of magnitude with < 15% variation, provides the input to the smooth pursuit system. The system performed successful velocity tracking for high contrast scenes. Circuit design and performance of the complete smooth pursuit system is presented.

1 INTRODUCTION

The smooth pursuit mechanism of primate visual systems is vital for stabilizing a region of the visual field on the retina. The ability to stabilize the image of the world on the retina has profound architectural and computational consequences on the retina and visual cortex, such as reducing the required size, computational speed and communication hardware and bandwidth of the visual system (Bandera, 1990; Eckert and Buchsbaum, 1993). To obtain similar benefits in active machine vision, primate smooth pursuit can be a powerful model for gaze control. The mechanism for smooth pursuit in primates was initially believed to be composed of a simple negative feedback system which attempts to zero the motion of targets on the fovea, figure 1(a) (Robinson, 1965). However, this scheme does not account for many psychophysical properties of smooth pursuit, which led Wyatt and Pola (1979) to proposed figure 1(b), where the eye movement signal is added to the target motion in a positive feed back loop. This mechanism results from their observation that eye motion or apparent target motion increases the magnitude of pursuit motion even when retinal motion is zero or constant. Their scheme also exhibited predictive qualities, as reported by Steinbach (1976). The smooth pursuit model presented in this paper attempts the consolidate the two models into a single system which explains the findings of both approaches.

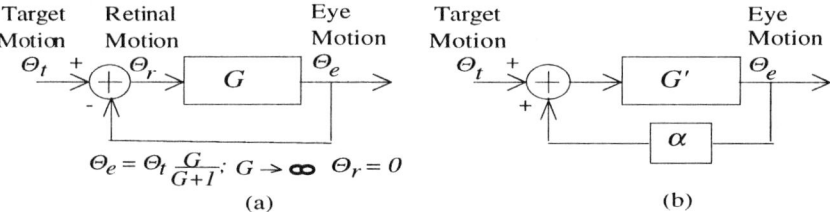

Figure 1: System Diagrams of Primate Smooth Pursuit Mechanism. (a) Negative feedback model by Robinson (1965). (b) Positive feedback model by Wyatt and Pola (1979).

The velocity based smooth pursuit implemented here attempts to zero the relative velocity of the retina and target. The measured retinal velocity, is zeroed by using positive feedback to accumulate relative velocity error between the target and the retina, where the accumulated value is the current eye velocity. Hence, this model uses the Robinson approach to match target motion, and the Wyatt and Pola positive feed back loop to achieve matching and to predict the future velocity of the target. Figure 2 shows the system diagram of the velocity based smooth pursuit system. This system is analyzed and the stability criterion is derived. Possible computational blocks for the elements in figure 1(b) are also discussed. Furthermore, since this entire scheme is implemented on a single 2 μm CMOS chip, the method for motion detection, the complete tracking circuits and the measured results are presented.

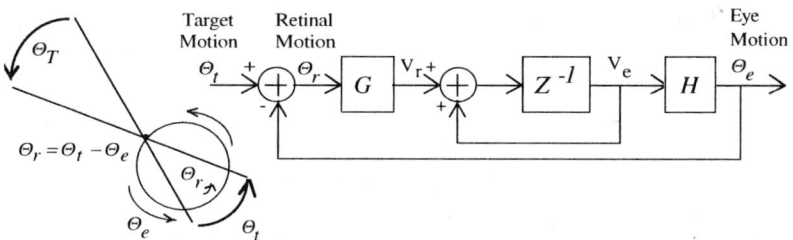

Figure 2: System Diagram of VLSI Smooth Pursuit Mechanism. Θ_T is target velocity in space, Θ_t is projected target velocity, Θ_e is the eye velocity and Θ_r is the measured retinal velocity.

2 VELOCITY BASED SMOOTH PURSUIT

Although figure 1(b) does not indicate how retinal motion is used in smooth pursuit, it provides the only measurement of the projected target motion. The very process of calculating retinal motion realizes negative feed back between the eye movement and the target motion, since retinal motion is the difference between project target and eye motion. If Robinson's model is followed, then the eye movement is simply the amplified version of the retinal motion. If the target disappears from the retina, the eye motion would be zero. However, Steinbach showed that eye movement does not cease when the target fades off and on, indicating that memory is used to predict target motion. Wyatt and Palo showed a direct additive influence of eye movement on pursuit. However, the computational blocks G' and α of their model are left unfilled.

In figure 2, the gain G models the internal gain of the motion detection system, and the internal representation of retinal velocity is then V_r. Under zero-slip tracking, the retinal velocity is zero. This is obtained by using positive feed back to correct the velocity error between target, Θ_t, and eye, Θ_e. The delay element represents a memory of the last eye velocity while the current retinal motion is measured. If the target disappears, the eye motion continues with the last value, as recorded by Steinbach, thus anticipating the position of the target in space. The memory also stores the current eye velocity during perfect pursuit. The internal representation of eye velocity, V_e, is subsequently amplified by H and used to drive the eye muscles. The impulse response of the system is given in equations (1). Hence, the relationship between eye velocity and target velocity is recursive and given by equations (2). To prove the stability of this system, the retinal velocity can be expressed in terms of the target motion as given in equations (3a). The ideal condition for accurate performance is for $GH = 1$. However, in practice, gains of different amplifiers

$$\frac{\theta_e}{\theta_r}(z) = GH \frac{z^{-1}}{1-z^{-1}} \quad (a); \quad \frac{\theta_e}{\theta_r}(n) = GH[-\delta(n) + u(n)] \quad (b) \tag{1}$$

$$\theta_e(n) = \theta_t(n) - \theta_r(n) = GH[-\delta(n) + u(n)] * \theta_r(n) = GH \sum_{k=0}^{n-1} \theta_r(k) \tag{2}$$

$$\theta_r(n) = \theta_t(n)(1-GH)^n \Rightarrow \theta_r(n) = 0 \text{ if } GH = 1 \Rightarrow \theta_e(n) = \theta_t(n) \quad (a)$$
$$\theta_r(n) \xrightarrow{n \to \infty} 0 \text{ if } |1-GH| < 1 \Rightarrow 0 < GH < 2 \text{ for stability} \quad (b) \tag{3}$$

are rarely perfectly matched. Equations (3b) shows that stability is assured for $0 < GH < 2$. Figure 3 shows a plot of eye motion versus updates for various choices of GH. At each update, the retinal motion is computed. Figure 3(a) shows the eye's motion at the on-set of smooth pursuit. For $GH = 1$, the eye movement tracks the target's motion exactly, and lags slightly only when the target accelerates. On the other hand, if $GH << 1$, the eye's motion always lags the target's. If $GH \to 2$, the system becomes increasing unstable, but converges for $GH < 2$. The three cases presented correspond to the smooth pursuit system being critically, over and under damped, respectively.

3 HARDWARE IMPLEMENTATION

Using the smooth pursuit mechanism described, a single chip one dimensional tracking system has been implemented. The chip has a multi-layered computational architecture, similar to the primate's visual system. Phototransduction, logarithmic compression, edge detection, motion detection and smooth pursuit control has been integrated at the focal-plane. The computational layers can be partitioned into three blocks, where each block is based on a segment of biological oculomotor systems.

3.1 IMAGING AND PREPROCESSING

The first three layers of the system mimics the photoreceptors, horizontal cells and bipolar cells of biological retinas. Similar to previous implementations of silicon retinas, the chip uses parasitic bipolar transistors as the photoreceptors. The dynamic range of photoreceptor current is compressed with a logarithmic response in low light and square root response in bright light. The range compress circuit represents 5-6 orders of magnitude of light intensity with 3 orders of magnitude of output current dynamic range. Subsequently, a passive resistive network is used to realize a discrete implementation of a Laplacian edge detector. Similar to the rods and cones system in primate retinas, the response time, hence the maximum detectable target speed, is ambient intensity dependent (160 (12.5) µs in 2.5 (250) µW/cm^2). However, this does prevent the system from handling fast targets even in dim ambient lighting.

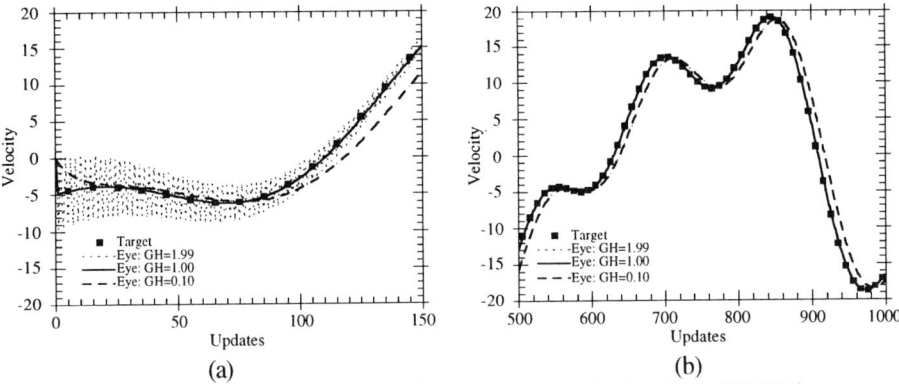

Figure 3: (a) The On-Set of Smooth Pursuit for Various GH Values.
(b) Steady-State Smooth Pursuit.

3.2 MOTION MEASUREMENT

This computational layer measures retinal motion. The motion detection technique implemented here differs from those believed to exist in areas V1 and MT of the primate visual cortex. Alternatively, it resembles the fly's and rabbit's retinal motion detection system (Reichardt, 1961; Barlow and Levick, 1965; Delbruck, 1993). This is not coincidental, since efficient motion detection at the focal plane must be performed in a small areas and using simple computational elements in both systems.

The motion detection scheme is a combination of local correlation for direction determination, and pixel transfer time measurement for speed. In this framework, motion is defined as the disappearance of an object, represented as the zero-crossings of its edges, at a pixel, followed by its re-appearance at a neighboring pixel. The (dis)appearance of the zero-crossing is determined using the (negative) positive temporal derivative at the pixel. Hence, motion is detected by AND gating the positive derivative of the zero-crossing of the edge at one pixel with the negative derivative at a neighboring pixel. The direction of motion is given by the neighboring pixel from which the edge disappeared. Provided that motion has been detected at a pixel, the transfer time of the edge over the pixel's finite geometry is inversely proportional to its speed.

Equation (4) gives the mathematical representation of the motion detection process for an object moving in $+x$ direction. In the equation, $f_t(I:k,y,t)$ is the temporal response of pixel k as the zero crossing of an edge of an object passes over its $2a$ aperture. Equation (4) gives the direction of motion, while equation (5) gives the speed. The schematic of

$$motion_{-x} = [\tfrac{\partial}{\partial t}f_t(I:k,y,t) > 0][\tfrac{\partial}{\partial t}f_t(I:k+1,y,t) < 0] = 0 \quad (a)$$

$$motion_{+x} = [\tfrac{\partial}{\partial t}f_t(I:k-1,y,t) < 0][\tfrac{\partial}{\partial t}f_t(I:k,y,t) > 0] \quad (b) \quad (4)$$

$$= \delta[t - \frac{2a(k-n)-a}{v_x}]\delta[x - 2ak]$$

$$Motion: t_m = \frac{2a(k-n)-a}{v_x}; \quad Disappear: t_d = \frac{2a(k-n)+a}{v_x}$$

$$Speed_{+x} = \frac{1}{t_d - t_m} = \frac{v_x}{2a} \quad (5)$$

the VLSI circuit of the motion detection model is shown in figure 4(a). Figure 4(b) shows reciprocal of the measured motion pulse-width for 1 D motion. The on-chip speed, Θ_t, is the projected target speed. The measured pulse-widths span 3-4 orders magnitude,

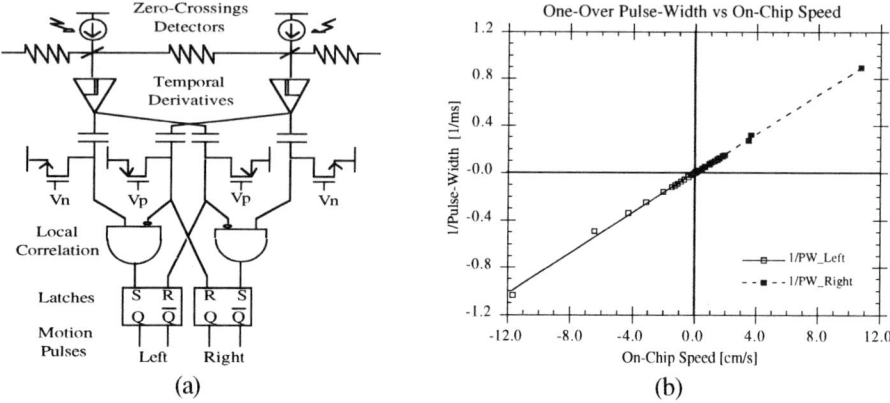

Figure 4: (a) Schematic of the Motion Detection Circuit. (b) Measured Output of the Motion Detection Circuit.

depending on the ambient lighting, and show less than 15% variation between chips, pixels, and directions (Etienne-Cummings, 1993).

3.3 THE SMOOTH PURSUIT CONTROL SYSTEM

The one dimensional smooth pursuit system is implemented using a 9 x 1 array of motion detectors. Figure 5 shows the organization of the smooth pursuit chip. In this system, only diverging motion is computed to reduce the size of each pixel. The outputs of the motion detectors are grouped into one global motion signal per direction. This grouping is performed with a simple, but delayed, OR, which prevents pulses from neighboring motion cells from overlapping. The motion pulse trains for each direction are XOR gated, which allows a single integrator to be used for both directions, thus limiting mis-match. The final value of the integrator is inversely proportional to the target's speed. The OR gates conserve the direction of motion. The reciprocal of the integrator voltage is next computed using the linear mode operation of a MOS transistor (Etienne-Cummings, 1993). The unipolar integrated pulse allows a single inversion circuit to be used for both directions of motion, again limiting mis-match. The output of the "one-over" circuit is amplified, and the polarity of the measured speed is restored. This analog voltage is proportional to retinal speed.

The measured retinal speed is subsequently added to the stored velocity. Figure 6 shows the schematic for the retinal velocity accumulation (positive feedback) and storage (analog

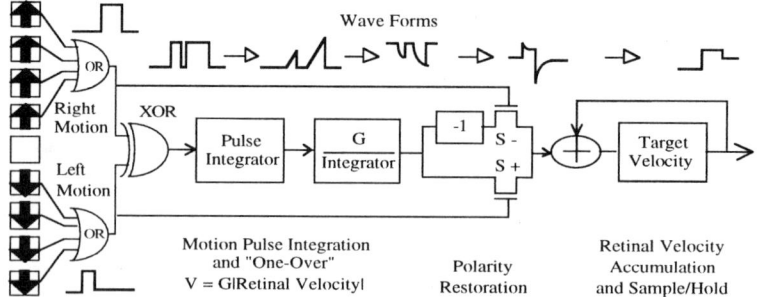

Figure 5: Architecture of the VLSI Smooth Pursuit System. Sketches of the wave forms for a fast leftward followed by a slow rightward retinal motion are shown.

memory). The output of the XOR gate in figure 5 is used by the sample-and-hold circuit to control sampling switches S1 and S2. During accumulation, the old stored velocity value, which is the current eye velocity, is isolated from the summed value. At the falling edge of the XOR output, the stored value on C2 is replaced by the new value on C1. This stored value is amplified using an off chip motor driver circuit, and used to move the chip. The gain of the motor driver can be finely controlled for optimal operation.

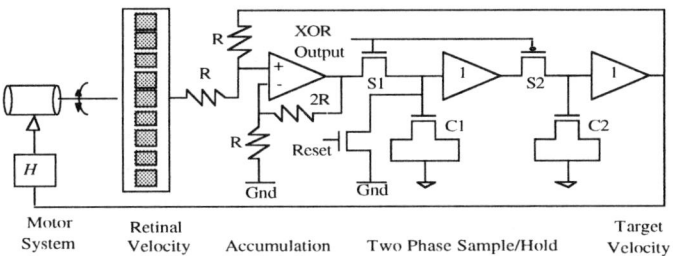

Figure 6: Schematic Retinal Velocity Error Accumulation, Storage and Motor Driver Systems.

Figure 7(a) shows a plot of one-over the measured integrated voltage as a function of on chip target speed. Due to noise in the integrator circuit, the dynamic range of the motion detection system is reduced to 2 orders of magnitude. However, the matching between left and right motion is unaffected by the integrator. The MOS "one-over" circuit, used to compute the analog reciprocal of the integrated voltage, exhibits only 0.06% deviation from a fitted line (Etienne-Cummings, 1993b). Figure 7(b) shows the measured increments in stored target velocity as a function of retinal (on-chip) speed. This is a test of all the circuit components of the tracking system. Linearity between retinal velocity increments and target velocity is observed, however matching between opposite motion has degraded. This is caused by the polarity restoration circuit since it is the only location where different circuits are used for opposite motion. On average, positive increments are a factor of 1.2 times larger than negative increments. The error bars shows the variation in velocity increments for different motion cells and different chips. The deviation is less than 15 %. The analog memory has a leakage of 10 mV/min and an asymmetric swing of 2 to -1 V, caused by the buffers. The dynamic range of the complete smooth pursuit system is measured to be 1.5 orders magnitude. The maximum speed of the system is adjustable by varying the integrator charging time. The maximum speed is ambient intensity dependent and ranges from 93 cm/s to 7 cm/s on-chip speed in

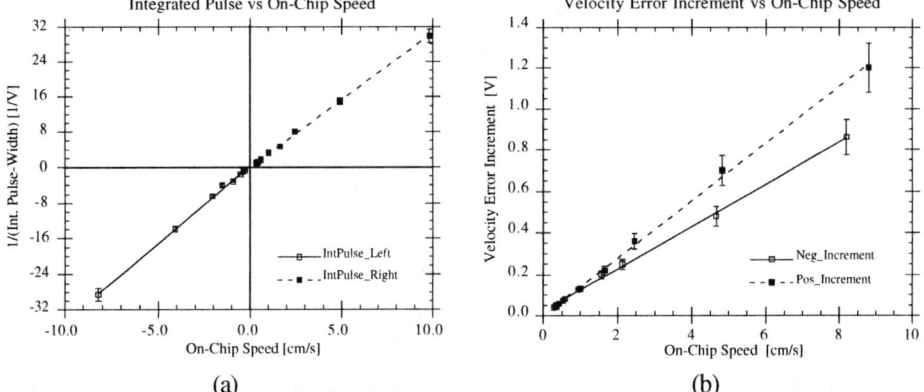

(a) (b)

Figure 7. (a) Measured integrated motion pulse voltage. (b) Measured output for the complete smooth pursuit system.

bright (250 µW/cm^2) and dim (2.5 µW/cm^2) lighting, respectively. However, for any maximum speed chosen, the minimum speed is a factor of 0.03 slower. The minimum speed is limited by the discharge time of the temporal differentiators in the motion detection circuit to 0.004 cm/s on chip. The contrast sensitivity of this system proved to be the stumbling block, and it can not track objects in normal indoor lighting. However, all circuits components tested successfully when a light source is used as the target. Additional measured data can be found in (Etienne-Cummings, 1995). Further work will improve the contrast sensitivity, combat noise and also consider two dimensional implementations with target acquisition (saccades) capabilities.

4 CONCLUSION

A model for biological and silicon smooth pursuit has been presented. It combines the negative feed back and positive feedback models of Robinson and Wyatt and Pola. The smooth pursuit system is stable if the gain product of the retinal velocity detection system and the eye movement system is less than 2. VLSI implementation of this system has been performed and tested. The performance of the system suggests that wide range (92.9 - 0.004 cm/s retinal speed) target tracking is possible with a single chip focal plane system. To improve this chip's performance, care must be taken to limit noise, improve matching and increase contrast sensitivity. Future design should also include a saccadic component to re-capture escaped targets, similar to biological systems.

References

C. Bandera, "Foveal Machine Vision Systems", *Ph.D. Thesis*, SUNY Buffalo, New York, 1990

H. Barlow and W. Levick, "The Mechanism for Directional Selective Units in Rabbit's Retina", *Journal of Physiology*, Vol. 178, pp. 477-504, 1965

T. Delbruck, "Silicon Retina with Correlation-Based, Velocity-Tuned Pixels", *IEEE Transactions on Neural Networks*, Vol. 4:3, pp. 529-41, 1993

M. Eckert and G. Buchsbaum, "Effect of Tracking Strategies on the Velocity Structure of Two-Dimensional Image Sequences", J. Opt. Soc. Am., Vol. A10:7, pp. 1582-85, 1993

R. Etienne-Cummings *et al.*, "A New Temporal Domain Optical Flow Measurement Technique for Focal Plane VLSI Implementation", *Proceedings of CAMP 93*, M. Bayoumi, L. Davis and K. Valavanis (Eds.), pp. 241-251, 1993

R. Etienne-Cummings, R. Hathaway and J. Van der Spiegel, "An Accurate and Simple CMOS 'One-Over' Circuit", *Electronic Letters*, Vol. 29-18, pp. 1618-1620, 1993b

R. Etienne-Cummings *et al.*, "Real-Time Visual Target Tracking: Two Implementations of Velocity Based Smooth Pursuit", *Visual Information Processing IV*, SPIE Vol. 2488, Orlando, 17-18 April 1995

W. Reichardt, "Autocorrelation, A Principle for the Evaluation of Sensory Information by the Central Nervous System", *Sensory Communication*, Wiley, New York, 1961

D. Robinson, "The Mechanism of Human Smooth Pursuit Eye Movement", *Journal of Physiology (London)* Vol. 180, pp. 569-591, 1965

M. Steinbach, "Pursuing the Perceptual Rather than the Retinal Stimuli", *Vision Research*, Vol. 16, pp. 1371-1376, 1976

H. Wyatt and J. Pola, "The Role of Perceived Motion in Smooth Pursuit Eye Movements", *Vision Research*, Vol. 19, pp. 613-618, 1979

Model Matching and SFMD Computation

Steve Rehfuss and Dan Hammerstrom
Department of Computer Science and Engineering
Oregon Graduate Institute of Science and Technology
P.O.Box 91000, Portland, OR 97291-1000 USA
stever@cse.ogi.edu, strom@asi.com

Abstract

In systems that process sensory data there is frequently a *model matching* stage where class hypotheses are combined to recognize a complex entity. We introduce a new model of parallelism, the *Single Function Multiple Data (SFMD)* model, appropriate to this stage. SFMD functionality can be added with small hardware expense to certain existing SIMD architectures, and as an incremental addition to the programming model. Adding SFMD to an SIMD machine will not only allow faster model matching, but also increase its flexibility as a general purpose machine and its scope in performing the initial stages of sensory processing.

1 INTRODUCTION

In systems that process sensory data there is frequently a post-classification stage where several independent class hypotheses are combined into the recognition of a more complex entity. Examples include matching word models with a string of observation probabilities, and matching visual object models with collections of edges or other features. Current parallel computer architectures for processing sensory data focus on the classification and pre-classification stages (Hammerstrom 1990). This is reasonable, as those stages likely have the largest potential for speedup through parallel execution. Nonetheless, the *model-matching* stage is also suitable for parallelism, as each model may be matched independently of the others.

We introduce a new style of parallelism, *Single Function Multiple Data (SFMD)*, that is suitable for the model-matching stage. The handling of interprocessor synchronization distinguishes the SFMD model from the SIMD and MIMD models: SIMD synchronizes implicitly at each instruction, SFMD synchronizes implicitly at conditional expression or loop boundaries, and MIMD synchronizes explicitly at arbitrary inter-processor communication points. Compared to MIMD, the use of implicit synchronization makes SFMD easier to program and cheaper to implement. Compared to SIMD, the larger granularity of synchronization gives SFMD increased flexibility and power.

SFMD functionality can be added with small hardware expense to SIMD architectures already having a high degree of processor autonomy. It can be presented as an incremental addition to programmer's picture of the machine, and applied as a compiler optimization to existing code written in an SIMD version of 'C'. Adding SFMD to an SIMD machine will not only allow faster model matching, but also increase its flexibility as a general purpose machine, and increase its scope in performing the initial stages of sensory processing.

2 SIMD ARCHITECTURE AND PROGRAMMING

As background, we first review SIMD parallelism. In SIMD, multiple processing elements, or *PE*'s, simultaneously execute identical instruction sequences, each processing different data. The instruction stream is produced by a controller, or *sequencer*. Generally, each PE has a certain amount of *local memory*, which only it can access directly. All PEs execute a given instruction in the stream at the same time, so are synchronized at each instruction. Thus synchronization is implicit, the hardware need not support it, and the programmer need (can) not manage it. SIMD architectures differ in the functionality of their PEs. If PEs can independently address local memory at differing locations, rather than all having to access the same address at a given step, the architecture is said to have *local addressing*. If PEs can independently determine whether to execute a given instruction, rather than having this determined by the sequencer, the architecture has *local conditional execution*. Note that all PEs see the same instruction stream, yet a given PE executes only one branch of any if-then-else, and so must idle while other PEs execute the other branch. This is the cost of synchronizing at each instruction.

3 MODEL MATCHING

We view models as pieces of *a priori* knowledge, interrelating their *components*. Models are *matched* against some *hypothesis set* of possible features. Matching produces a *correspondence* between components of the model and elements of the hypothesis set, and also *aligns* the model and the set ("pose estimation" in vision, and "time-alignment" in speech). An essential fact is that, because models are known *a priori*, in cases where there are many models it is usually possible and profitable to construct an *index* into the set of models. Use of the index at runtime restricts the set of models that need actually be matched to a few, high-probability ones.

Model-matching is a common stage in sensory data processing. Phoneme, character and word HMMs are models, where the hypothesis set is a string of observations and the matching process is either of the usual Viterbi or trellis procedures. For phonemes and characters, the HMMs used typically all have the same graph structure, so control flow in the matching process is not model-dependent and may be encoded in the instruction stream. Word models have differing structure, and control flow is model-dependent. In vision, model-matching has been used in a variety of complicated ways (cf. (Suetens, Fua & Hanson 1992)), for example, graph models may have constraints between node attribute values, to be resolved during matching.

4 DATA AND KNOWLEDGE PARALLELISM

SIMD is a type of computer architecture. At the algorithm level, it corresponds to *data parallelism*. Data parallelism, applying the same procedure in parallel to multiple pieces of data, is the most common explicit parallelization technique.and is the essence of the *Single Program Multiple Data (SPMD)* programming model. On a distributed memory machine, SPMD can be stylized as "given a limited amount of (algorithmic) knowledge to be applied to a large piece of data, distribute the data and broadcast the knowledge".

In sensory processing systems, conversely, one may have a large amount of knowledge (many models) that need to be applied to a (smallish) piece of data, for example, a speech signal frame or segment, or a restricted region of an image. In this case, it makes sense to "distribute the knowledge and broadcast the data". Model-matching often works well on an SIMD architecture, e.g. for identical phoneme models. However, when matching requires differing control flow between models, an SIMD implementation can be inefficient.

Data and knowledge parallelism are asymmetrical, however, in two ways. First, all data must normally be processed, while there are usually indexing techniques that greatly restrict the number of models that actually must be matched. Second, processing an array element frequently requires information about neighboring elements; when the data is partitioned among multiple processors, this may require inter-processor communication and synchronization. Conversely, models on different processors can be matched to data in their local memories without any inter-processor communication. The latter observation leads to the SFMD model.

5 PROGRAMMING MODEL

We view support for SFMD as functionality to be added to an existing SIMD machine to increase its flexibility, scope, and power. As such, the SFMD programming model should be an extension of the SIMD one. Given an SIMD architecture with the local addressing and local conditional execution, SFMD programming is made available at the assembly language level by adding three constructs:

distribute n tells the sequencer and PEs that the next n instructions are to be distributed for independent execution on the PEs. We call the next n instructions an *SFMD block*.

sync tells the individual PEs to suspend execution and signal the controller (barrier synchronization). This is a no-op if not within an SFMD block.

branch-local one or more local branch instruction(s), including a loop construct; the branch target must lie within the enclosing SFMD block. This is a no-op if not within an SFMD block.

We further require that *code within an SFMD block contain only references to PE-local memory*; none to global (sequencer) variables, to external memory or to the local memory of another PE. It must also contain no inter-PE communication.. When the PEs are independently executing an SFMD block, we say that the system is in *SFMD mode*, and refer to normal execution as *SIMD mode*.

When programming in a data-parallel 'C'-like language for an SIMD machine, use of SFMD functionality can be an optimization performed by the compiler, completely hidden from the user. Variable type and usage analysis can determine for any given block of code whether the constraints on non-local references are met, and emit code for SFMD execution if so. No new problems are introduced for debugging, as SFMD execution is semantically equivalent to executing on each PE sequentially, and can be executed this way during debugging.

To the programmer, SFMD ameliorates two inefficiencies of SIMD programming: (i) in conditionals, a PE need not be idle while other PEs execute the branch it didn't take, and (ii) loops and recursions may execute a processor-dependent number of times.

6 HARDWARE MODEL AND COST

We are interested in embedded, "delivery system" applications. Such systems must have few chips; scalability to 100's or 1000's of chips is not an issue. Parallelism is thus achieved with multiple PEs per chip. As off-chip I/O is always expensive compared to computation[1], such chips can contain only a relatively small number of processors. Thus, as feature size decreases, area will go to local memory and processor complexity, rather than more processors.

Adding SFMD functionality to an architecture whose PEs have local addressing and local conditional execution is straightforward. Here we outline an example implementation. Hardware for branch tests and decoding sequencer instructions in the instruction register (IR) already exists. Local memory is suitable for local addressing. A very simple "micro-sequencer" must be added, consisting essentially of a program counter (PC) and instruction buffer (IM), and some simple decode logic. The existing PE output path can be used for the barrier synchronization. A 1-bit path from the sequencer to each PE is added for interrupting local execution.

Execution of a `distribute n` instruction on a PE causes the next n instructions to be stored sequentially in IM, starting at the current address in the PC. The $(n+1)$'st instruction is executed in SPMD mode, it is typically either a `branch-local` to start execution, or possibly a `sync` if the instructions are just being cached[2].

Almost the entire cost of providing SFMD functionality is silicon area used by the IM. The IM contains inner loop code, or model-driven conditional code, which is likely to be small. For a 256 4-byte instruction buffer on the current ASI CNAPS 1064, having 64 PEs with 4KB memory each, this is about 11% of the chip area; for a hypothetical 16 PE, 16K per PE chip of the same size, it is 3%. These numbers are large, but as feature size decreases, the incremental cost of adding SFMD functionality to an SIMD architecture quickly becomes small.

7 PERFORMANCE

What performance improvement may be expected by adding SFMD to SIMD? There are two basic components, improvement on branches, and improvement on nested loops, where the inner loop count varies locally.

Unnested (equiprobable) branches speed up most when the branch bodies have the same size, with a factor of 2 improvement. For nested branches of depth d, the factor is 2^d, but these are probably unusual. An exception would be applying a decision tree classifier in a data-parallel way.

To examine improvement on nested loops, suppose we have a set of N models (or any independent tasks) to be evaluated on an architecture with P processors. On

---

[1] E.g., due to limited pin count, pad area, and slower clock off-chip.
[2] For example, if the distributed code is a subroutine that will be encountered again.

Model Matching and SFMD Computation

an SFMD architecture, we partition the set into P groups, assign each group to a processor, and have each processor evaluate all the models in its group. If evaluating the j'th model of the i'th group takes time $t_{ij}^{(sfmd)}$, then the total time is

$$T_{sfmd} = \max_{i=1}^{P} \sum_{j=1}^{N_i} t_{ij}^{(sfmd)} \qquad (1)$$

where N_i is the size of the i'th group, $\sum_{i=1}^{P} N_i = N$. On an SIMD architecture, we partition the set into $\lceil N/P \rceil$ groups of size P and sequentially evaluate each group in parallel. Each group has a model that takes the most time to evaluate; SIMD execution forces the whole group to have this time complexity. So, evaluating a single group, G_i, takes time $\max_j t_{ij}^{(simd)}$, where j indexes over the elements of the group, $1 \leq j \leq P$. The total time for SIMD execution is then

$$T_{simd} = \sum_{i=1}^{\lceil N/P \rceil} \max_{j=1}^{P} t_{ij}^{(simd)} \qquad (2)$$

Ignoring data-dependent branching and taking $t_{ij}^{(simd)} = t_{ij}^{(sfmd)} \doteq t_{ij}$, we see that optimal (i,j)-indexing of the N models for either case is a bin packing problem. As such, (i,j)-indexing will be heuristic, and we examine T_{simd}/T_{sfmd} by simulation. It should be clear that the expected improvement due to SFMD cannot be large unless the outer loop count is large. So, for model matching, improvement on nested loops is likely not an important factor, as usually only a few models are matched at once.

To examine the possible magnitude of the effect in general, we look instead at multiplication of an input vector by a large sparse matrix. Rows are partitioned among the PEs, and each PE computes all the row-vector inner products for its set of rows[3]. T_{sfmd} is given by equation (1), with $\{t_{ij}|1 \leq j \leq N_i\}$ the set of all rows for processor i. T_{simd} is given by equation (2), with $\{t_{ij}|1 \leq j \leq P\}$ the set of rows executed by all processors at time i. Here t_{ij} is the time to perform a row-vector inner product.

Under a variety of choices of matrix size (256 × 256 to 2048 × 2048), number of processors (16,32,64), distribution of elements (uniform, clustered around the diagonal), and sparsity (fraction of nonzero elements from 0.001 to 0.4) we get that the ratio T_{simd}/T_{sfmd} decreases from around 2.2-2.7 for sparsities near 0.001, to 1.2 for sparsities near 0.06, and to 1.1 or less for more dense matrices (Figure 1). The effect is thus not dramatic.

As an example of the potential utility of SFMD functionality for model matching, we consider *interpretation tree search (ITS)*, a technique used in vision[4]. ITS is a technique for establishing a correspondence between image and model features. It consists essentially of depth-first search (*DFS*), where a node on level d of the tree corresponds to a pairing of image features with the first d model features. The search is limited by a variety of unary and binary geometric constraints on the allowed pairings. Search complexity implies small models are matched to small

---

[3] We assume the assignment of rows to PEs is independent of the number of nonzero elements in the rows. If not, then for $N \gg P$, simply sorting rows by number of elements and then assigning row i to processor $i \bmod P$ is a good enough packing heuristic to make $T_{simd} \approx T_{sfmd}$.

[4] See (Grimson 1990) for a complete description of ITS and for the complexity results alluded to here.

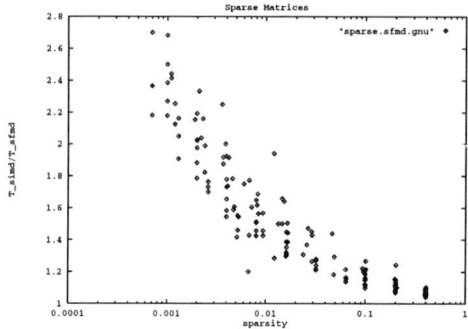

Figure 1: Sparse matrices: speedup vs. sparsity

numbers of data features, so distributing models and data to local memories is practical.

To examine the effect of SFMD on this form of model matching, we performed some simple simulations. To match a model with D features to a set of B data points, we attempt to match the first model feature with each data point in order, with some probability of success, p_{match}. If we succeed, we attempt to match the second model feature with one of the remaining $B-1$ data points, and so on. If we match all D features, we then check for global consistency of the correspondence, with some probability of success, p_{check}. This procedure is equivalent to DFS in a tree with branching factor $B-d$ at level d of the tree, $1 \leq d \leq D$, where the probability of expanding any given node is p_{match}, and the probability of stopping the search at any given leaf is $1 - p_{check}$.

By writing the search as an iteration managing an explicit stack, one obtains a loop with some common code and some code conditional on whether the current node has any child nodes left to be expanded. The bulk of the "no-child" code deals with leaf nodes, consisting of testing for global consistency and recording solutions. The relative performance of SIMD and SFMD thus depends mainly on the probability, p_{leaf}, that the node being traversed is a leaf. If, for each iteration, the time for the leaf code is taken to be 1, that for common code is t, and that for the non-leaf code is k, then

$$T_{simd}/T_{sfmd} = \frac{t+k+1}{t+(1-p)k+p}. \tag{3}$$

Panel 1 of figure 2 shows values of p from a variety of simulations of ITS, with $B, D \in \{8, 10, 12, 14, 16\}$, $p_{match} \in \{0.1, 0.2, 1/B\}$, $p_{check} \in \{0, 1\}$. Grimson (1990) reports searches on realistic data of around 5000-10000 expansions; this corresponds to $p \approx 0.2 - 0.4$. Panel 2 of figure 2 shows how equation 3 behaves for p in this regime and for realistic values of k. We see speedups in the range 2–4 unless the leaf code is very small. In fact, the code for global consistency checking is typically larger than that for local consistency, corresponding to $\log_2 k < 0$.

8 OTHER USES

There are a number of uses for SFMD, other than model matching. First, common "subroutines" involving branching may be kept in the IM. Analysis of code for IEEE floating point emulation on an SIMD machine shows an expected 2x improvement by

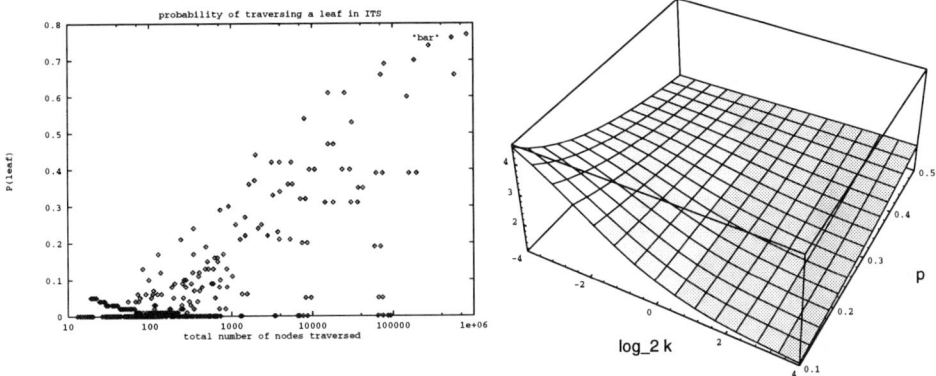

Figure 2: DFS speedup. Panel 1 shows the probability, p, of traversing a leaf. Panel 2 plots equation 3 for realistic values of p and k, with $t = 0.1$.

using SFMD. Second, simple PE-local searches and sorts should show a significant, sub-2x, improvement in expected time. Third, more speculatively, different PEs can execute entirely different tasks by having the SFMD block consist of a single (nested) if-then-else. This would allow a form of (highly synchronized) pipeline parallelism by communicating results in SIMD mode after the end of the SFMD block.

9 CONCLUSION

We have introduced the SFMD computation model as a natural way of implementing the common task of model matching, and have shown how it extends SIMD computing, giving it greater flexibility and power. SFMD functionality can easily, and relatively cheaply, be added to existing SIMD designs already having a high degree of processor autonomy. The addition can be made without altering the user's programming model or environment. We have argued that technology trends will force multiple-processor-per-chip systems to increase processor complexity and memory, rather than increase the number of processors model per chip, and believe that the SFMD model is a natural step in that evolution.

Acknowledgements

The first author gratefully acknowledges support under ARPA/ONR grants N00014-94-C-0130, N00014-92-J-4062, and N00014-94-1-0071.

References

Grimson, W. E. L. (1990), *Object Recognition by Computer: The Role of Geometric Constraints*, MIT Press.

Hammerstrom, D. (1990), A VLSI architecture for high-performance, low-cost, on-chip learning, *in* 'The Proceedings of the IJCNN'.

Suetens, P., Fua, P. & Hanson, A. J. (1992), 'Computational strategies for object recognition', *Computing Surveys* **24**(1), 5 – 61.

Parallel analog VLSI architectures for computation of heading direction and time-to-contact

Giacomo Indiveri
giacomo@klab.caltech.edu

Jörg Kramer
kramer@klab.caltech.edu

Christof Koch
koch@klab.caltech.edu

Division of Biology
California Institute of Technology
Pasadena, CA 91125

Abstract

We describe two parallel analog VLSI architectures that integrate optical flow data obtained from arrays of elementary velocity sensors to estimate heading direction and time-to-contact. For heading direction computation, we performed simulations to evaluate the most important qualitative properties of the optical flow field and determine the best functional operators for the implementation of the architecture. For time-to-contact we exploited the divergence theorem to integrate data from all velocity sensors present in the architecture and average out possible errors.

1 Introduction

We have designed analog VLSI velocity sensors invariant to absolute illuminance and stimulus contrast over large ranges that are able to achieve satisfactory performance in a wide variety of cases; yet such sensors, due to the intrinsic nature of analog processing, lack a high degree of precision in their output values. To exploit their properties at a system level, we developed parallel image processing architectures for applications that rely mostly on the qualitative properties of the optical flow, rather than on the precise values of the velocity vectors. Specifically, we designed two parallel architectures that employ arrays of elementary motion sensors for the computation of heading direction and time-to-contact. The application domain that we took into consideration for the implementation of such architectures, is the promising one of vehicle navigation. Having defined the types of images to be analyzed and the types of processing to perform, we were able to use *a priori* information to integrate selectively the sparse data obtained from the velocity sensors and determine the qualitative properties of the optical flow field of interest.

2 The elementary velocity sensors

A velocity sensing element, that can be integrated into relatively dense arrays to estimate in parallel optical flow fields, has been succesfully built [Kramer *et al.*, 1995]. Unlike most previous implementations of analog VLSI motion sensors, it unambiguously encodes 1-D velocity over considerable velocity, contrast, and illuminance ranges, while being reasonably compact. It implements an algorithm that measures the time of travel of features (here a rapid temporal change in intensity) stimulus between two fixed locations on the chip. In a first stage, rapid dark-to-bright irradiance changes or temporal ON edges are converted into short current pulses. Each current pulse then gives rise to a sharp voltage spike and a logarithmically-decaying voltage signal at each edge detector location. The sharp spike from one location is used to sample the analog voltage of the slowly-decaying signal from an adjacent location. The sampled output voltage encodes the relative time delay of the two signals, and therefore velocity, for the direction of motion where the onset of the slowly-decaying pulse precedes the sampling spike. In the other direction, a lower voltage is sampled. Each direction thus requires a separate output stage.

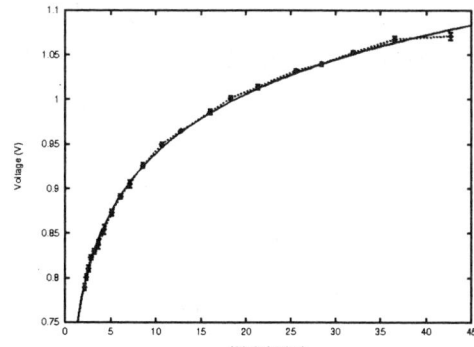

Figure 1: Output voltage of a motion sensing element for the preferred direction of motion of a sharp high-contrast ON edge versus image velocity under incandescent room illumination. Each data point represents the average of 5 successive measurements.

As implemented with a 2 μm CMOS process, the size of an elementary bi-directional motion element (including 30 transistors and 8 capacitances) is 0.045 mm^2. Fig. 1 shows that the experimental data confirms the predicted logarithmic encoding of velocity by the analog output voltage. The data was taken by imaging a moving high-contrast ON edge onto the chip under incandescent room illumination. The calibration of the image velocity in the focal plane is set by the 300 μm spacing of adjacent photoreceptors on the chip.

3 Heading direction computation

To simplify the computational complexity of the problem of heading direction detection we restricted our analysis to pure translational motion, taking advantage of the fact that for vehicle navigation it is possible to eliminate the rotational component of motion using lateral accelerometer measurements from the vehicle. Furthermore, to analyze the computational properties of the optical flow for typical vehicle navigation scenes, we performed software simulations on sequences of images obtained from a camera with a 64 × 64 pixel silicon retina placed on a moving truck (courtesy of B. Mathur at Rockwell Corporation). The optical flow fields have been computed

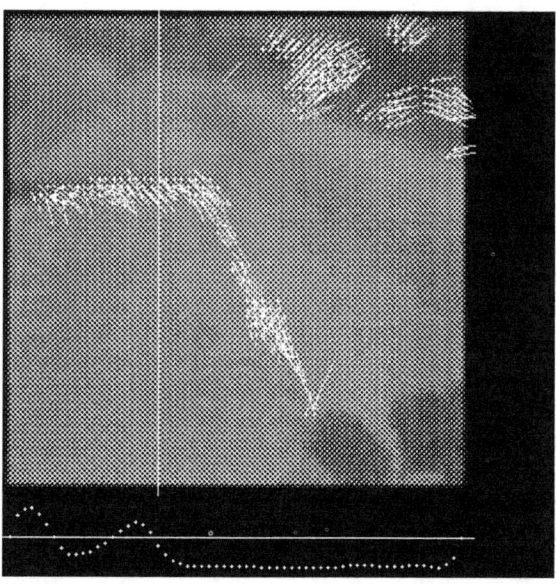

Figure 2: The sum of the horizontal components of the optical flow field is plotted on the bottom of the figure. The presence of more than one zero-crossing is due to different types of noise in the optical flow computation (e.g. quantization errors in software simulations or device mismatch in analog VLSI circuits). The coordinate of the heading direction is computed as the abscissa of the zero-crossing with maximum steepness and closest to the abscissa of the previously selected unit.

by implementing an algorithm based on the *image brightness constancy equation* [Verri et al., 1992] [Barron et al., 1994]. For the application domain considered and the types of optical flow fields obtained from the simulations, it is reasonable to assume that the direction of heading changes smoothly in time. Furthermore, being interested in determining, and possibly controlling, the heading direction mainly along the horizontal axis, we can greatly reduce the complexity of the problem by considering one-dimensional arrays of velocity sensors. In such a case, if we assign positive values to vectors pointing in one direction and negative values to vectors pointing in the opposite direction, the heading direction location will correspond to the point closest to the *zero-crossing*. Under these assumptions, the computation of the horizontal coordinate of the heading direction has been carried out using the following functional operators: thresholding on the horizontal components of the optical flow vectors; spatial smoothing on the resulting values; detection and evaluation of the steepness of the zero-crossings present in the array and finally selection of the zero-crossing with maximum steepness. The zero-crossing with maximum steepness is selected only if its position is in the neighborhood of the previously selected zero-crossing. This helps to eliminate errors due to noise and device mismatch and assures that the computed heading direction location will shift smoothly in time. Fig. 2 shows a result of the software simulations, on an image of a road with a shadow on the left side.

All of the operators used in the algorithm have been implemented with analog circuits (see Fig. 3 for a block diagram of the architecture). Specifically, we have

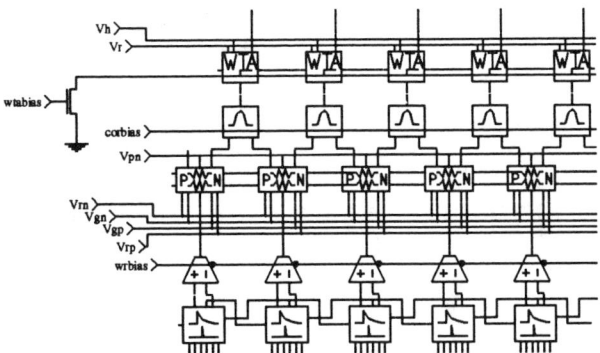

Figure 3: Block diagram of the architecture for detecting heading direction: the first layer of the architecture computes the velocity of the stimulus; the second layer converts the voltage output of the velocity sensors into a positive/negative current performing a threshold operation; the third layer performs a linear smoothing operation on the positive and negative halves of the input current; the fourth layer detects zero-crossings by comparing the intensity of positive currents from one pixel with negative currents from the neighboring pixel; the top layer implements a winner-take-all network with distributed excitation, which selects the zero-crossing with maximum steepness.

designed test chips in which the thresholding function has been implemented using a transconductance amplifier whose current represents the output signal [Mead, 1989], spatial smoothing has been obtained using a circuit that separates positive currents and negative currents into two distinct paths and feeds them into two layers of current-mode diffuser networks [Boahen and Andreou, 1992], the zero-crossing detection and evaluation of its steepness has been implemented using a newly designed circuit block based on a modification of the *simple current-correlator* [Delbrück, 1991], and the selection of the zero-crossing with maximum steepness closest to the previously selected unit has been implemented using a winner-take-all circuit with distributed excitation [Morris et al., 1995]. The schematics of the former three circuits, which implement the top three layers of the diagram of Fig. 3, are shown in Fig. 4.

Fig. 5 shows the output of a test chip in which all blocks up to the diffuser network (without the zero-crossing detection stages) were implemented. The velocity sensor layout was modified to maximize the number of units in the 1-D array. Each velocity sensor measures $60\mu m \times 802\mu m$. On a $(2.2mm)^2$ size chip we were able to fit 23 units. The shown results have been obtained by imaging on the chip expanding or contracting stimuli using black and white edges wrapped around a rotating drum and reflected by an adjacent tilted mirror. The point of contact between drum and mirror corresponding to the simulated heading direction has been imaged approximately onto the 15th unit of the array. As shown, the test chip considered does not achieve 100% correct performance due to errors that arise mainly from the presence of parasitic capacitors in the modified part of the velocity sensor circuits; nonetheless, at least from a qualitative point of view, the data confirms the results obtained from software simulations and demonstrates the validity of the approach considered.

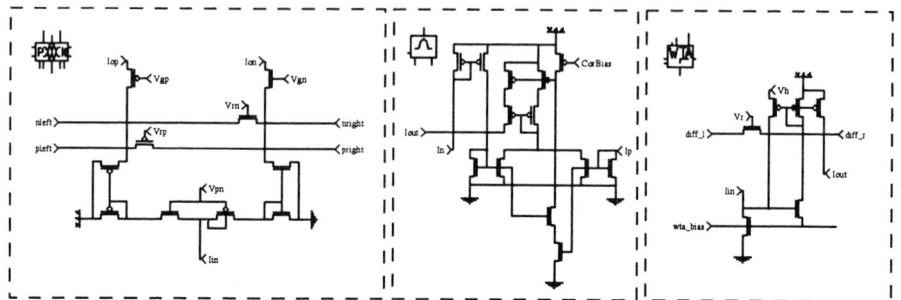

Figure 4: Circuit schematics of the smoothing, zero-detection and winner-take-all blocks respectively.

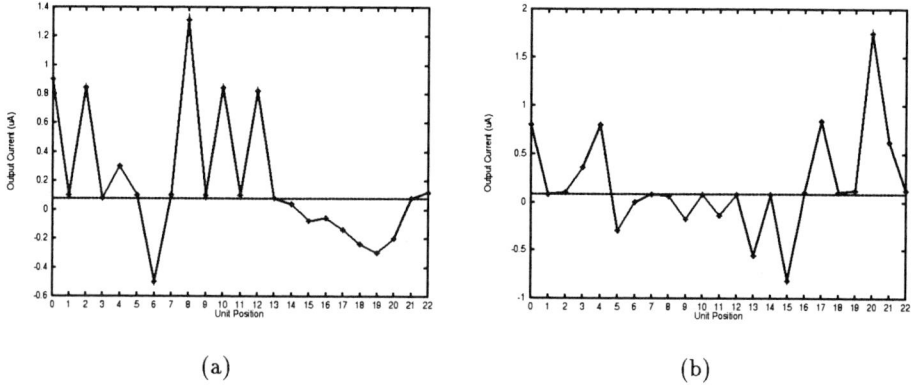

Figure 5: Zero crossings computed as difference between smoothed positive currents and smoothed negative currents: (a) for expanding stimuli; (b) for contracting stimuli. The "zero" axis is shifted due to is a systematic offset of 80 nA.

4 Time-to-contact

The time-to-contact can be computed by exploiting qualitative properties of the optical flow field such as expansion or contraction [Poggio et al., 1991]. The divergence theorem, or Gauss theorem, as applied to a plane, shows that the integral over a surface patch of the divergence of a vector field is equal to the line integral along the patch boundary of the component of the field normal to the boundary. Since a camera approaching a rigid object sees a linear velocity field, where the velocity vectors are proportional to their distance from the focus-of-expansion, the divergence is constant over the image plane. By integrating the radial component of the optical flow field along the circumference of a circle, the time-to-contact can thus be estimated, independently of the position of the focus-of-expansion.

We implemented this algorithm with an analog integrated circuit, where an array of twelve motion sensing elements is arranged on a circle, such that each element measures velocity radially. According to the Gauss theorem, the time-to-contact is then approximated by

$$\tau = \frac{N \cdot R}{\sum_{k=1}^{N} v_k}, \tag{1}$$

where N denotes the number of elements, R the radius of the circle, and v_k the radial velocity components at the locations of the elements. For each element, temporal aliasing is prevented by comparing the output voltages of the two directions of motion and setting the lower one, corresponding to the null direction, to zero. The output voltages are then used to control subthreshold transistor currents. Since these voltages are logarithmically dependent on velocity, the transistor currents are proportional to the measured velocities. The sum of the velocity components is thus calculated by aggregating the currents from all elements on two lines, one for outward motion and one for inward motion, and taking the difference of the total currents. The resulting bi-directional output current is an inverse function of the signed time-to-contact.

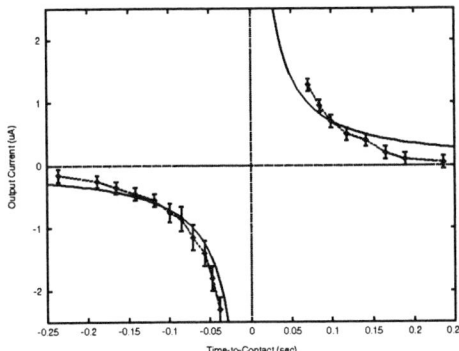

Figure 6: Output current of the time-to-contact sensor as a function of simulated time-to-contact under incandescent room illumination. The theoretical fit predicts an inverse relationship.

The circuit has been implemented on a chip with a size of $(2.2mm)^2$ using 2 μm technology. The photo diodes of the motion sensing elements are arranged on two concentric circles with radii of 400 μm and 600 μm respectively. In order to simulate an approaching or withdrawing object, a high-contrast spiral stimulus was printed onto a rotating disk. Its image was projected onto the chip with a microscope lens under incandescent room illumination. The focus-of-expansion was approximately centered with respect to the photo diode circles. The averaged output current is shown as a function of simulated time-to-contact with a theoretical fit in Fig. 6. The expected inverse relationship is qualitatively observed and the sign (expansion or contraction) is robustly encoded. However, the deviation of the output current from its average can be substantial: Since the output voltage of each motion sensing element decays slowly due to leak currents and since the spiral stimulus causes a serial update of the velocity values along the array, a step change in the output current is observed upon each update, followed by a slow decay. The effect is aggravated, if the individual motion sensing elements measure significantly differing velocities. This is generally the case, because the focus-of-expansion is usually not centered with respect to the sensor and because of inaccuracies in the velocity measurements due to circuit offsets, noise, and the *aperture problem* [Verri et al., 1992]. The integrative property of the algorithm is thus highly desirable, and more robust data would be obtained from an array with more elements and stimuli with higher edge densities.

5 Conclusions

We have developed parallel architectures for motion analysis that bypass the problem of low precision in analog VLSI technology by exploiting qualitative properties of the optical flow. The correct functionality of the devices built, at least from a qualitative point of view, have confirmed the validity of the approach followed and induced us to continue this line of research. We are now in the process of designing more accurate circuits that implement the operators used in the architectures proposed.

Acknowledgments

This work was supported by grants from ONR, ERC and Daimler-Benz AG. The velocity sensor was developed in collaboration with R. Sarpeshkar. The chips were fabricated through the MOSIS VLSI Fabrication Service.

References

[Barron et al., 1994] J.L. Barron, D.J. Fleet, and S.S. Beauchemin. Performance of optical flow techniques. *International Journal on Computer Vision*, 12(1):43–77, 1994.

[Boahen and Andreou, 1992] K.A. Boahen and A.G. Andreou. A contrast sensitive silicon retina with reciprocal synapses. In *NIPS91 Proceedings*. IEEE, 1992.

[Delbrück, 1991] T. Delbrück. "Bump" circuits for computing similarity and dissimilarity of analog voltages. In *Proc. IJCNN*, pages I-475–479, June 1991.

[Kramer et al., 1995] J. Kramer, R. Sarpeshkar, and C. Koch. An analog VLSI velocity sensor. In *Proc. Int. Symp. Circuit and Systems ISCAS '95*, pages 413–416, Seattle, WA, May 1995.

[Mead, 1989] C.A. Mead. *Analog VLSI and Neural Systems*. Addison-Wesley, Reading, 1989.

[Morris et al., 1995] T.G. Morris, D.M. Wilson, and S.P. DeWeerth. Analog VLSI circuits for manufacturing inspection. In *Conference for Advanced Research in VLSI-Chapel Hill, North Carolina*, March 1995.

[Poggio et al., 1991] T. Poggio, A. Verri, and V. Torre. Green theorems and qualitative properties of the optical flow. Technical report, MIT, 1991. Internal Lab. Memo 1289.

[Verri et al., 1992] A. Verri, M. Straforini, and V. Torre. Computational aspects of motion perception in natural and artificial vision systems. *Phil. Trans. R. Soc. Lond. B*, 337:429–443, 1992.

PART VI
SPEECH AND SIGNAL PROCESSING

Onset-based Sound Segmentation

Leslie S. Smith
CCCN/Department of Computer Science
University of Stirling
Stirling FK9 4LA
Scotland

Abstract

A technique for segmenting sounds using processing based on mammalian early auditory processing is presented. The technique is based on features in sound which neuron spike recording suggests are detected in the cochlear nucleus. The sound signal is bandpassed and each signal processed to enhance onsets and offsets. The onset and offset signals are compressed, then clustered both in time and across frequency channels using a network of integrate-and-fire neurons. Onsets and offsets are signalled by spikes, and the timing of these spikes used to segment the sound.

1 Background

Traditional speech interpretation techniques based on Fourier transforms, spectrum recoding, and a hidden Markov model or neural network interpretation stage have limitations both in continuous speech and in interpreting speech in the presence of noise, and this has led to interest in front ends modelling biological auditory systems for speech interpretation systems (Ainsworth and Meyer 92; Cosi 93; Cole et al 95).

Auditory modelling systems use similar early auditory processing to that used in biological systems. Mammalian auditory processing uses two ears, and the incoming signal is filtered first by the pinna (external ear) and the auditory canal before it causes the tympanic membrane (eardrum) to vibrate. This vibration is then passed on through the bones of the middle ear to the oval window on the cochlea. Inside the cochlea, the pressure wave causes a pattern of vibration to occur on the basilar membrane. This appears to be an active process using both the inner and outer hair cells of the organ of Corti. The movement is detected by the inner hair cells and turned into neural impulses by the neurons of the spiral ganglion. These pass down the auditory nerve, and arrive at various parts of the cochlear nucleus. From there, nerve fibres innervate other areas: the lateral and medial nuclei of the superior olive, and the inferior colliculus, for example. (See (Pickles 88)).

Virtually all modern sound or speech interpretation systems use some form of bandpass filtering, following the biology as far as the cochlea. Most use Fourier transforms to perform a calculation of the energy in each band over some time period, usually between 25 and 75 ms. This is not what the cochlea does. Auditory modelling front ends differ in the extent and length to which they follow animal early auditory processing, but the term generally implies at least that wideband filters are used, and that high temporal resolution is maintained in the initial stages. This means the use of filtering techniques, rather than Fourier transforms in the bandpass stage. Such filtering systems have been implemented by Patterson and Holdsworth (Patterson and Holdsworth 90; Slaney 93), and placed directly in silicon (Lazzaro and Mead 89; Lazzaro et al 93; Liu et al 93; Fragniere and van Schaik 94).

Some auditory models have moved beyond cochlear filtering. The inner hair cell has been modelled by either simple rectification (Smith 94) or has been based on the work of (Meddis 88) for example (Patterson and Holdsworth 90; Cosi 93; Brown 92). Lazzaro has experimented with a silicon version of Licklider's autocorrelation processing (Licklider 51; Lazzaro and Mead 89). Others such as (Wu et al 1989; Blackwood et al 1990; Ainsworth and Meyer 92; Brown 92; Berthommier 93; Smith 94) have considered the early brainstem nuclei, and their possible contribution, based on the neurophysiology of the different cell types (Pickles 88; Blackburn and Sachs 1989; Kim et al 90).

Auditory model-based systems have yet to find their way into mainstream speech recognition systems (Cosi 93). The work presented here uses auditory modelling up to onset cells in the cochlear nucleus. It adds a temporal neural network to clean up the segmentation produced. This part has been filed as a patent (Smith 95). Though the system has some biological plausibility, the aim is an effective data-driven segmentation technique implementable in silicon.

2 Techniques used

Digitized sound was applied to an auditory front end, (Patterson and Holdsworth 90), which bandpassed the sound into channels each with bandwidth $24.7(4.37F_c + 1)$Hz, where F_c is the centre frequency (in KHz) of the band (Moore and Glasberg 83). These were rectified, modelling the effect of the inner hair cells. The signals produced bear some resemblance to that in the auditory nerve. The real system has far more channels and each nerve channel carries spike-coded information. The coding here models the signal in a population of neighboring auditory nerve fibres.

2.1 The onset-offset filter

The signal present in the auditory nerve is stronger near the onset of a tone than later (Pickles 88). This effect is much more pronounced in certain cell types of the cochlear nucleus. These fire strongly just after the onset of a sound in the band to which they are sensitive, and are then silent. This emphasis on onsets was modelled by convolving the signal in each band with a filter which computes two averages, a more recent one, and a less recent one, and subtracts the less recent one from the more recent one. One biologically possible justification for this is to consider that a neuron is receiving the same driving input twice, one excitatorily, and the other inhibitorily; the excitatory input has a shorter time-constant than the inhibitory input. Both exponentially weighted averages, and averages formed using a Gaussian filter have been tried (Smith 94), but the former place too much emphasis on the most recent part of the signal, making the latter more effective.

The filter output for input signal $s(x)$ is

$$O(t, k, r) = \int_0^t (f(t-x, k) - f(t-x, k/r))s(x)dx \qquad (1)$$

where $f(x, y) = \sqrt{y}\exp(-yx^2)$. k and r determine the rise and fall times of the pulses of sound that the system is sensitive to. We used $k = 1000$, $r = 1.2$, so that the SD of the Gaussians are 24.49ms and 22.36ms. The convolving filter has a positive peak at 0, crosses 0 at 22.39ms, and is then negative. With these values, the system is sensitive to energy rises and falls which occur in the envelopes of everyday sounds. A positive onset-offset signal implies that the bandpassed signal is increasing in intensity, and a negative onset-offset signal implies that it is decreasing in intensity. The convolution used is a sound analog of the difference of Gaussians operator used to extract black/white and white/black edges in monochrome images (Marr and Hildreth 80). In (Smith 94) we performed sound segmentation directly on this signal.

2.2 Compressing the onset-offset signal

The onset-offset signal was divided into two positive-going signals, an onset signal consisting of the positive-going part, and an offset signal consisting of the inverted negative-going part. Both were compressed logarithmically (where $\log(x)$ was taken as 0 for $0 \leq x \leq 1$). This increases the dynamical range of the system, and models compressive biological effects. The compressed onset signal models the output of a population of onset cells. This technique for producing an onset signal is related to that of (Wu et al 1989; Cosi 93).

2.3 The integrate-and-fire neural network

To segment the sound using the onset and offset signals, they need to be integrated across frequency bands and across time. This temporal and tonotopic clustering was achieved using a network of integrate-and-fire units. An integrate-and-fire unit accumulates its weighted input over time. The activity of the unit A, is initially 0, and alters according to

$$\frac{dA}{dt} = I(t) - \gamma A \qquad (2)$$

where $I(t)$ is the input to the neuron and γ, the dissipation, describes the leakiness of the integration. When A reaches a threshold, the unit fires (i.e. emits a pulse), and A is reset to 0. After firing, there is a period of insensitivity to input, called the refractory period. Such neurons are discussed in, e.g. (Mirolla and Strogatz 90).

One integrate-and-fire neuron was used per channel: this neuron received input either from a single channel, or from a set of adjacent channels, all with equal positive weighting. The output of each neuron was fed back to a set of adjacent neurons, again with a fixed positive weight, one time step (here 0.5ms) later. Because of the leaky nature of the accumulation of activity, excitatory input to the neuron arriving when its activation is near threshold has a larger effect on the next firing time than excitatory input arriving when activation is lower. Thus, if similar input is applied to a set of neurons in adjacent channels, the effect of the inter-neuron connections is that when the first one fires, its neighbors fire almost immediately. This allows a network of such neurons to cluster the onset or offset signals, producing a sharp burst of spikes across a number of channels providing unambiguous onsets or offsets.

The external and internal weights of the network were adjusted so that onset or offset input alone allowed neurons to fire, while internal input alone was not enough to cause firing. The refractory period used was set to 50ms for the onset system, and 5ms for the offset system. For the onset system, the effect was to produce sharp onset firing responses across adjacent channels in response to a sudden increase in energy in some channels, thus grouping onsets both tonotopically and temporally. This is appropriate for onsets, as these are generally brief and clearly marked. The output of this stage we call the onset map. Offsets tend to be more gradual. This is due to physical effects: for example, a percussive sound will start suddenly, as the vibrating element starts to move, but die away slowly as the vibration ceases (see (Gaver 93) for a discussion). Even when the vibration does stop suddenly, the sound will die away more slowly due to echoes. Thus we cannot reliably mark the offset of a sound: instead, we reduce the refractory period of the offset neurons, and produce a train of pulses marking the duration of the offset in this channel. We call the output of this stage the offset map.

3 Results

As the technique is entirely data-driven, it can be applied to sound from any source. It has been applied to both speech and musical sounds. Figure 1 shows the effect of applying the techniques discussed to a short piece of speech. Fig 1c shows that the neural network integrates the onset timings across the channels, allowing these onsets to be used for segmentation. The simplest technique is to divide up the continuous speech at each onset: however,to ensure that the occasional onset in a single channel does not confuse the system, and that onsets which occur near to each other do not result in very short segments we demanded that a segmentation boundary have at least 6 onsets inside a period of 10ms, and the minimum segment length was set to 25ms.

The utterance *Neural information processing systems* has phonetic representation:

/njɯrlːənfərmeʃənprosɛsəŋsɪstəms/

and is segmented into the following 19 segments:

/n/, /jʉ/, /r/, /lə/, /ə/, /nf/, /ərm/, /e/, /ʃ/, /ən/, /pro/, /os/, /ɛs/, /əŋ/, /s/, /ɪ/, /st/, /əm/, /s/

The same text spoken more slowly (over 4.38s, rather than 2.31s) has phonetic representation:

/njuralːənfʊrmeʃənprosɛsʊŋsɪstəms/

Segmenting using this technique gives the following 25 segments:

/n/, /ju/, /u/, /r/, /a/, /al/, /l/, //, /ən/, /f/, /ʊrm/, /e/, /ʃ/, /ən/, /nː/, /pr/, /ro/, /os/, /ɛs/, /ʊŋ/, /s/, /ɪ/, /st/, /əm/, /s/

Although some phonemes are broken between segments, the system provides effective segmentation, and is relatively insensitive to speech rate. The system is also effective at finding speech inside certain types of noise (such as motor-bike noise), as can be seen in fig 1e and f.

The system has been used to segment sound from single musical instruments. Where these have clear breaks between notes this is straightforward: in (Smith 94) correct segmentation was achieved directly from the onset-offset signal but was not achieved for slurred sounds, in which the notes change smoothly. As is visible in figure 2c, the onsets here are clear using the network, and the segmentation produced is near-

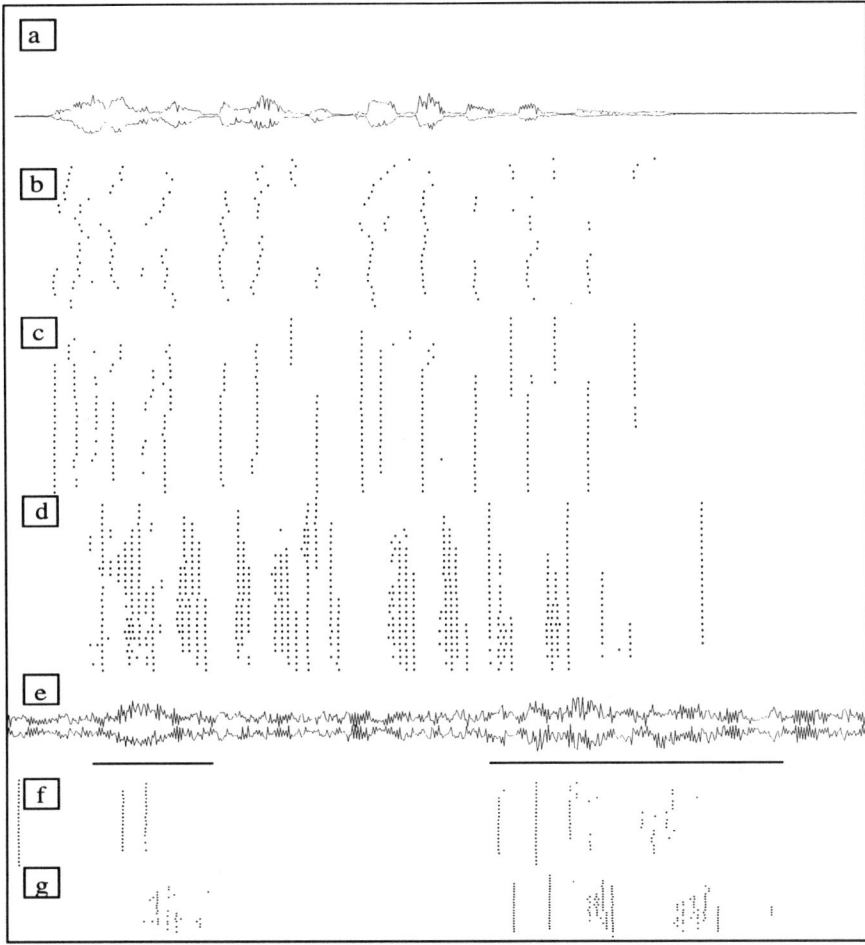

Figure 1: (a-d):Onset and Offset maps from author saying *Neural information processing systems* rapidly. a: envelope of original sound. b: onset map, from 28 channels, from 100Hz-6KHz. Onset filter parameters as in text; one neuron per channel, with no interconnection. Neuron refractory period is 50ms. c: as b, but network has input applied to 6 adjacent channels, and internal feedback to 10 channels. d: offset map produced similarly, with refractory period 5ms. e: envelope of *say, that's a nice bike* with motorbike noise in background (lines mark utterance). f, g: onset, offset maps for e.

perfect. Best results were obtained here when the input to the network is not spread across channels.

4 Conclusions and further work

An effective data driven segmentation technique based on onset feature detection and using integrate-and-fire neurons has been demonstrated. The system is relatively immune to broadband noise. Segmentation is not an end in itself: the effectiveness of any technique will depend on the eventual application.

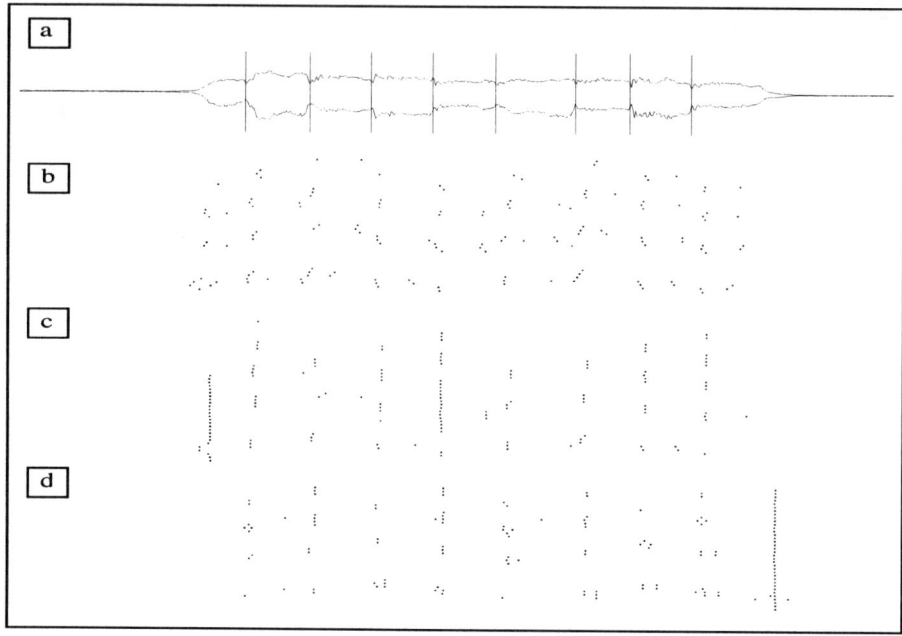

Figure 2: a: slurred flute sound, with vertical lines showing boundary between notes. b: onsets found using a single neuron per channel, and no interconnection. c: as b, but with internal feedback from each channel to 16 adjacent channels d: offsets found with refractory period 5ms.

The segmentation is currently not using the information on which bands the onsets occur in. We propose to extend this work by combining the segmentation described here with work streaming bands sharing same-frequency amplitude modulation. The aim of this is to extract sound segments from some subset of the bands, allowing segmentation and streaming to run concurrently.

Acknowledgements

Many thanks are due to the members of the Centre for Cognitive and Computational Neuroscience at the University of Stirling.

References

Ainsworth W, Meyer G. Speech analysis by means of a physiologically-based model of the cochlear nerve and cochlear nucleus, in *Visual representations of speech signals*, Cooke M, Beet S, eds, 1992.

Berthommier F., Modelling neural responses of the intermediate auditory system, in *Mathematics applied to biology and medicine*, Demongeot J, Capasso V, Wuertz Publishing, Canada, 1993.

Blackburn C.C., Sachs M.B. Classification of unit types in the anteroventral cochlear nucleus: PST histograms and regularity analysis, . *J. Neurophysiology*, 62, 6, 1989.

Blackwood N., Meyer G., Ainsworth W. A Model of the processing of voiced plosives in the auditory nerve and cochlear nucleus, *Proceedings Inst of Acoustics*, 12, 10, 1990.

Brown G. *Computational Auditory Scene Analysis*, TR CS-92-22, Department of Computing Science, University of Sheffield, England, 1992.

Cole R., et al, The challenge of spoken language systems: research directions of the 90's, *IEEE Trans Speech and Audio Processing*, 3, 1, 1995.

Cosi P. On the use of auditory models in speech technology, in *Intelligent Perceptual Models*, LNCS 745, Springer Verlag, 1993.

Fragniere E., van Schaik A., Linear predictive coding of the speech signal using an analog cochlear model, MANTRA Internal Report, 94/2, MANTRA Center for Neuro-mimetic systems, EPFL, Lausanne, Switzerland, 1994.

Gaver W.W. What in the world do we hear?: an ecological approach to auditory event perception, *Ecological Psychology*, 5(1), 1-29, 1993.

Kim D.O. ,Sirianni J.G., Chang S.O., Responses of DCN-PVCN neurons and auditory nerve fibres in unanesthetized decerebrate cats to AM and pure tones: analysis with autocorrelation/power-spectrum, *Hearing Research*, 45, 95-113, 1990.

Lazzaro J., Mead C., Silicon modelling of pitch perception, *Proc Natl. Acad Sciences*, USA, 86, 9597-9601, 1989.

Lazzaro J., Wawrzynek J., Mahowald M., Sivilotti M., Gillespie D., Silicon auditory processors as computer peripherals, *IEEE Trans on Neural Networks*, 4, 3, May 1993.

Licklider J.C.R., A Duplex theory of pitch perception, *Experentia*, 7, 128-133, 1951.

Liu W., Andreou A.G., Goldstein M.H., Analog cochlear model for multiresolution speech analysis, *Advances in Neural Information Processing Systems 5*, Hanson S.J., Cowan J.D., Lee Giles C. (eds), Morgan Kaufmann, 1993.

Marr D., Hildreth E. Theory of edge detection, *Proc. Royal Society of London B*, 207, 187-217, 1980.

Meddis R., Simulation of auditory-neural transduction: further studies, *J. Acoust Soc Am*, 83, 3, 1988.

Moore B.C.J., Glasberg B.R. Suggested formulae for calculating auditory-filter bandwidths and excitation patterns, *J Acoust Soc America*, 74, 3, 1983.

Mirollo R.E., Strogatz S.H. Synchronization of pulse-coupled biological oscillators, *SIAM J. Appl Math*, 50, 6, 1990.

Patterson R., Holdsworth J. (1990). *An Introduction to Auditory Sensation Processing*, in AAM HAP, Vol 1, No 1.

Pickles J.O. (1988). *An Introduction to the Physiology of Hearing*, 2nd Edition, Academic Press.

Slaney M., An efficient implementation of the Patterson-Holdsworth auditory filter bank, Apple technical report No 35, Apple Computer Inc, 1993.

Smith L.S. Sound segmentation using onsets and offsets, *J of New Music Research*, 23, 1, 1994.

Smith L.S. *Onset/offset coding for interpretation and segmentation of sound*, UK patent no 9505956.4, March 1995.

Wu Z.L., Schwartz J.L., Escudier P. A theoretical study of neural mechanisms specialized in the detection of articulatory-acoustic events, *Proc Eurospeech 89*, ed Tubach J.P., Mariani J.J., Paris, 1989.

Laterally Interconnected Self-Organizing Maps in Hand-Written Digit Recognition

Yoonsuck Choe, Joseph Sirosh, and Risto Miikkulainen
Department of Computer Sciences
The University of Texas at Austin
Austin, TX 78712
yschoe,sirosh,risto@cs.utexas.edu

Abstract

An application of laterally interconnected self-organizing maps (LISSOM) to handwritten digit recognition is presented. The lateral connections learn the correlations of activity between units on the map. The resulting excitatory connections focus the activity into local patches and the inhibitory connections decorrelate redundant activity on the map. The map thus forms internal representations that are easy to recognize with e.g. a perceptron network. The recognition rate on a subset of NIST database 3 is 4.0% higher with LISSOM than with a regular Self-Organizing Map (SOM) as the front end, and 15.8% higher than recognition of raw input bitmaps directly. These results form a promising starting point for building pattern recognition systems with a LISSOM map as a front end.

1 Introduction

Hand-written digit recognition has become one of the touchstone problems in neural networks recently. Large databases of training examples such as the NIST (National Institute of Standards and Technology) Special Database 3 have become available, and real-world applications with clear practical value, such as recognizing zip codes in letters, have emerged. Diverse architectures with varying learning rules have been proposed, including feed-forward networks (Denker et al. 1989; le Cun et al. 1990; Martin and Pittman 1990), self-organizing maps (Allinson et al. 1994), and dedicated approaches such as the neocognitron (Fukushima and Wake 1990).

The problem is difficult because handwriting varies a lot, some digits are easily confusable, and recognition must be based on small but crucial differences. For example, the digits 3 and 8, 4 and 9, and 1 and 7 have several overlapping segments, and the differences are often lost in the noise. Thus, hand-written digit recognition can be seen as a process of identifying the distinct features and producing an internal representation where the significant differences are magnified, making the recognition easier.

In this paper, the Laterally Interconnected Synergetically Self-Organizing Map architecture (LISSOM; Sirosh and Miikkulainen 1994, 1995, 1996) was employed to form such a separable representation. The lateral inhibitory connections of the LISSOM map *decorrelate* features in the input, retaining only those differences that are the most significant. Using LISSOM as a front end, the actual recognition can be performed by any standard neural network architecture, such as the perceptron.

The experiments showed that while direct recognition of the digit bitmaps with a simple perceptron network is successful 72.3% of the time, and recognizing them using a standard self-organizing map (SOM) as the front end 84.1% of the time, the recognition rate is 88.1% based on the LISSOM network. These results suggest that LISSOM can serve as an effective front end for real-world handwritten character recognition systems.

2 The Recognition System

2.1 Overall architecture

The system consists of two networks: a 20×20 LISSOM map performs the feature analysis and decorrelation of the input, and a single layer of 10 perceptrons the final recognition (Figure 1 (a)). The input digit is represented as a bitmap on the 32×32 input layer. Each LISSOM unit is fully connected to the input layer through the afferent connections, and to the other units in the map through lateral excitatory and inhibitory connections (Figure 1 (b)). The excitatory connections are short range, connecting only to the closest neighbors of the unit, but the inhibitory connections cover the whole map. The perceptron layer consists of 10 units, corresponding to digits 0 to 9. The perceptrons are fully connected to the LISSOM map, receiving the full activation pattern on the map as their input. The perceptron weights are learned through the delta rule, and the LISSOM afferent and lateral weights through Hebbian learning.

2.2 LISSOM Activity Generation and Weight Adaptation

The afferent and lateral weights in LISSOM are learned through Hebbian adaptation. A bitmap image is presented to the input layer, and the initial activity of the map is calculated as the weighted sum of the input. For unit (i,j), the initial response η_{ij} is

$$\eta_{ij} = \sigma \left(\sum_{a,b} \xi_{ab} \mu_{ij,ab} \right), \qquad (1)$$

where ξ_{ab} is the activation of input unit (a,b), $\mu_{ij,ab}$ is the afferent weight connecting input unit (a,b) to map unit (i,j), and σ is a piecewise linear approximation of the sigmoid activation function. The activity is then settled through the lateral connections. Each new activity $\eta_{ij}(t)$ at step t depends on the afferent activation and the lateral excitation and inhibition:

$$\eta_{ij}(t) = \sigma \left(\sum_{a,b} \xi_{ab} \mu_{ij,ab} + \gamma_e \sum_{k,l} E_{ij,kl} \eta_{kl}(t-1) - \gamma_i \sum_{k,l} I_{ij,kl} \eta_{kl}(t-1) \right), \qquad (2)$$

where $E_{ij,kl}$ and $I_{ij,kl}$ are the excitatory and inhibitory connection weights from map unit (k,l) to (i,j) and $\eta_{kl}(t-1)$ is the activation of unit (k,l) during the previous time step. The constants γ_e and γ_i control the relative strength of the lateral excitation and inhibition.

After the activity has settled, the afferent and lateral weights are modified according to the Hebb rule. Afferent weights are normalized so that the length of the weight

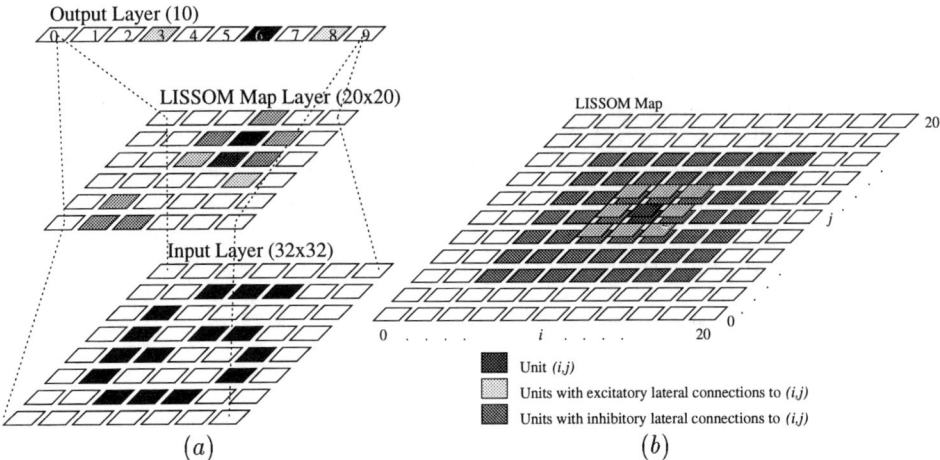

Figure 1: **The system architecture.** (a) The input layer is activated according to the bitmap image of digit 6. The activation propagates through the afferent connections to the LISSOM map, and settles through its lateral connections into a stable pattern. This pattern is the internal representation of the input that is then recognized by the perceptron layer. Through the connections from LISSOM to the perceptrons, the unit representing 6 is strongly activated, with weak activations on other units such as 3 and 8. (b) The lateral connections to unit (i,j), indicated by the dark square, are shown. The neighborhood of excitatory connections (lightly shaded) is elevated from the map for a clearer view. The units in the excitatory region also have inhibitory lateral connections (indicated by medium shading) to the center unit. The excitatory radius is 1 and the inhibitory radius 3 in this case.

vector remains the same; lateral weights are normalized to keep the sum of weights constant (Sirosh and Miikkulainen 1994):

$$\mu_{ij,mn}(t+1) = \frac{\mu_{ij,mn}(t) + \alpha_{\text{inp}} \eta_{ij} \xi_{mn}}{\sqrt{\sum_{mn} [\mu_{ij,mn}(t) + \alpha_{\text{inp}} \eta_{ij} \xi_{mn}]^2}}, \quad (3)$$

$$\omega_{ij,kl}(t+1) = \frac{\omega_{ij,kl}(t) + \alpha \eta_{ij} \eta_{kl}}{\sum_{kl} [\omega_{ij,kl}(t) + \alpha \eta_{ij} \eta_{kl}]}, \quad (4)$$

where $\mu_{ij,mn}$ is the afferent weight from input unit (m,n) to map unit (i,j), and α_{inp} is the input learning rate; $\omega_{ij,kl}$ is the lateral weight (either excitatory $E_{ij,kl}$ or inhibitory $I_{ij,kl}$) from map unit (k,l) to (i,j), and α is the lateral learning rate (either α_{exc} or α_{inh}).

2.3 Perceptron Output Generation and Weight Adaptation

The perceptrons at the output of the system receive the activation pattern on the LISSOM map as their input. The perceptrons are trained after the LISSOM map has been organized. The activation for the perceptron unit O_m is

$$O_m = C \sum_{i,j} \eta_{ij} \nu_{ij,m}, \quad (5)$$

where C is a scaling constant, η_{ij} is the LISSOM map unit (i,j), and $\nu_{ij,m}$ is the connection weight between LISSOM map unit (i,j) and output layer unit m. The delta rule is used to train the perceptrons: the weight adaptation is proportional to the map activity and the difference between the output and the target:

$$\nu_{ij,m}(t+1) = \nu_{ij,m}(t) + \alpha_{\text{out}} \eta_{ij} (\zeta_m - O_m), \quad (6)$$

where α_{out} is the learning rate of the perceptron weights, η_{ij} is the LISSOM map unit activity, ζ_m is the target activation for unit m. ($\zeta_m = 1$ if the correct digit $= m$, 0 otherwise).

Representation	Training	Test
LISSOM	93.0 / 0.76	88.1 / 3.10
SOM	84.5 / 0.68	84.1 / 1.71
Raw Input	99.2 / 0.06	72.3 / 5.06

Table 1: **Final Recognition Results.** The average recognition percentage and its variance over the 10 different splits are shown for the training and test sets. The differences in each set are statistically significant with $p > .9999$.

3 Experiments

A subset of 2992 patterns from the NIST Database 3 was used as training and testing data.[1] The patterns were normalized to make sure taht each example had an equal effect on the LISSOM map (Sirosh and Miikkulainen 1994). LISSOM was trained with 2000 patterns. Of these, 1700 were used to train the perceptron layer, and the remaining 300 were used as the validation set to determine when to stop training the perceptrons. The final recognition performance of the whole system was measured on the remaining 992 patterns, which neither LISSOM nor the perceptrons had seen during training. The experiment was repeated 10 times with different random splits of the 2992 input patterns into training, validation, and testing sets.

The LISSOM map can be organized starting from initially random weights. However, if the input dimensionality is large, as it is in case of the 32×32 bitmaps, each unit on the map is activated roughly to the same degree, and it is difficult to bootstrap the self-organizing process (Sirosh and Miikkulainen 1994, 1996). The standard Self-Organizing Map algorithm can be used to preorganize the map in this case. The SOM performs preliminary feature analysis of the input, and forms a coarse topological map of the input space. This map can then be used as the starting point for the LISSOM algorithm, which modifies the topological organization and learns lateral connections that decorrelate and represent a more clear categorization of the input patterns.

The initial self-organizing map was formed in 8 epochs over the training set, gradually reducing the neighborhood radius from 20 to 8. The lateral connections were then added to the system, and over another 30 epochs, the afferent and lateral weights of the map were adapted according to equations 3 and 4. In the beginning, the excitation radius was set to 8 and the inhibition radius to 20. The excitation radius was gradually decreased to 1 making the activity patterns more concentrated and causing the units to become more selective to particular types of input patterns. For comparison, the initial self-organized map was also trained for another 30 epochs, gradually decreasing the neighborhood size to 1 as well. The final afferent weights for the SOM and LISSOM maps are shown in figures 2 and 3.

After the SOM and LISSOM maps were organized, a complete set of activation patterns on the two maps were collected. These patterns then formed the training input for the perceptron layer. Two separate versions were each trained for 500 epochs, one with SOM and the other with LISSOM patterns. A third perceptron layer was trained directly with the input bitmaps as well.

Recognition performance was measured by counting how often the most highly active perceptron unit was the correct one. The results were averaged over the 10 different splits. On average, the final LISSOM+perceptron system correctly recognized 88.1% of the 992 pattern test sets. This is significantly better than the 84.1%

---

[1] Downloadable at **ftp://sequoyah.ncsl.nist.gov/pub/databases/**.

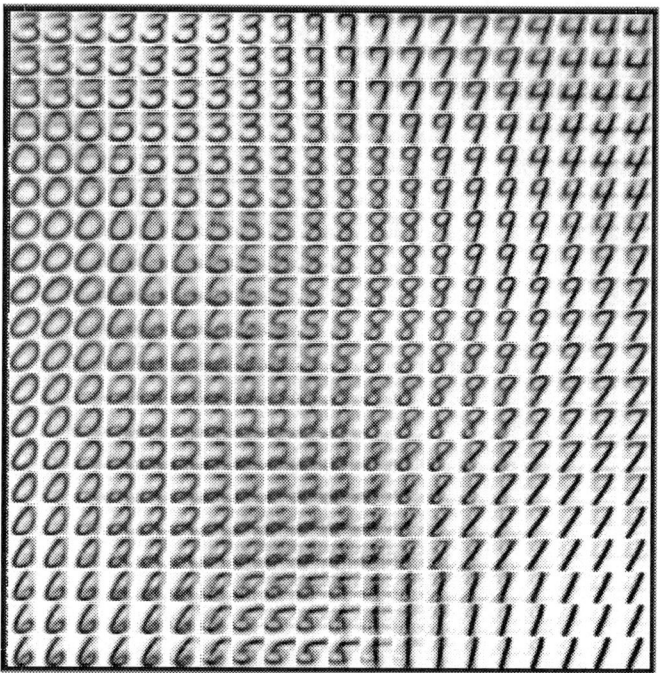

Figure 2: **Final Afferent Weights of the SOM map**. The digit-like patterns represent the afferent weights of each map unit projected on the input layer. For example, the lower left corner represents the afferent weights of unit (0,0). High weight values are shown in black and low in white. The pattern of weights shows the input pattern to which this unit is most sensitive (6 in this case). There are local clusters sensitive to each digit category.

of the SOM+perceptron system, and the 72.3% achieved by the perceptron layer alone (Table 1). These results suggest that the internal representations generated by the LISSOM map are more distinct and easier to recognize than the raw input patterns and the representations generated by the SOM map.

4 Discussion

The architecture was motivated by the hypothesis that the lateral inhibitory connections of the LISSOM map would decorrelate and force the map activity patterns to become more distinct. The recognition could then be performed by even the simplest classification architectures, such as the perceptron. Indeed, the LISSOM representations were easier to recognize than the SOM patterns, which lends evidential support to the hypothesis. In additional experiments, the perceptron output layer was replaced by a two-weight-layer backpropagation network and a Hebbian associator net, and trained with the same patterns as the perceptrons. The recognition results were practically the same for the perceptron, backpropagation, and Hebbian output networks, indicating that the internal representations formed by the LISSOM map are the crucially important part of the recognition system.

A comparison of the learning curves reveals two interesting effects (figure 4). First, even though the perceptron net trained with the raw input patterns initially performs well on the test set, its generalization decreases dramatically during training. This is because the net only learns to memorize the training examples, which does not help much with new noisy patterns. Good internal representations are therefore crucial for generalization. Second, even though initially the settling process of the LISSOM map forms patterns that are significantly easier to recognize than

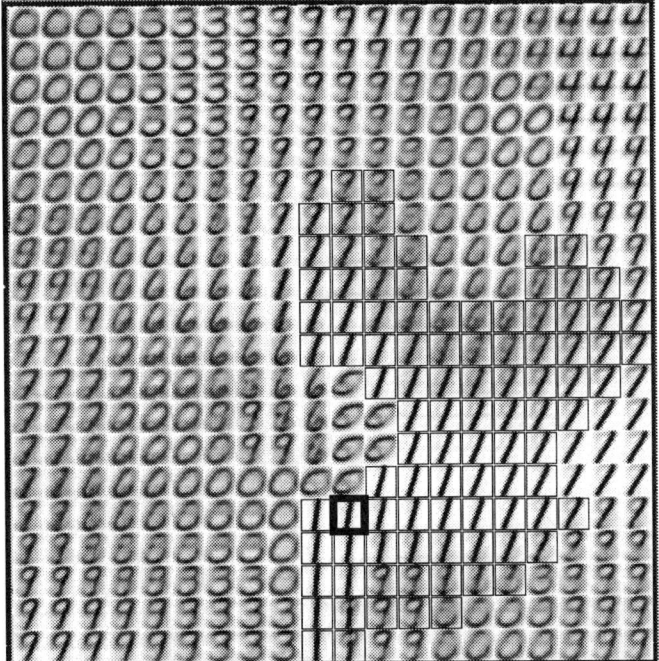

Figure 3: **Final Afferent Weights of the LISSOM map.** The squares identify the above-average inhibitory lateral connections to unit (10, 4) (indicated by the thick square). Note that inhibition comes mostly from areas of similar functionality (i.e. areas sensitive to similar input), thereby decorrelating the map activity and forming a sparser representation of the input.

the initial, unsettled patterns (formed through the afferent connections only), this difference becomes insignificant later during training. The afferent connections are modified according to the final, settled patterns, and gradually learn to anticipate the decorrelated internal representations that the lateral connections form.

5 Conclusion

The experiments reported in this paper show that LISSOM forms internal representations of the input patterns that are easier to categorize than the raw inputs and the patterns on the SOM map, and suggest that LISSOM can form a useful front end for character recognition systems, and perhaps for other pattern recognition systems as well (such as speech). The main direction of future work is to apply the approach to larger data sets, including the full NIST 3 database, to use a more powerful recognition network instead of the perceptron, and to increase the map size to obtain a richer representation of the input space.

Acknowledgements

This research was supported in part by National Science Foundation under grant #IRI-9309273. Computer time for the simulations was provided by the Pittsburgh Supercomputing Center under grants IRI930005P and IRI940004P, and by a High Performance Computer Time Grant from the University of Texas at Austin.

References

Allinson, N. M., Johnson, M. J., and Moon, K. J. (1994). Digital realisation of self-organising maps. In Touretzky, D. S., editor, *Advances in Neural Information Processing Systems 6*. San Mateo, CA: Morgan Kaufmann.

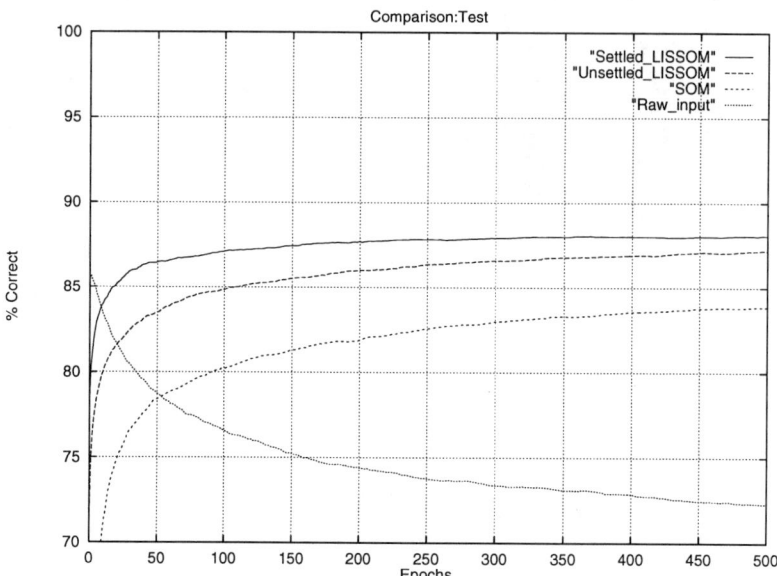

Figure 4: **Comparison of the learning curves.** A perceptron network was trained to recognize four different kinds of internal representations: the settled LISSOM patterns, the LISSOM patterns before settling, the patterns on the final SOM network, and raw input bitmaps. The recognition accuracy on the test set was then measured and averaged over 10 simulations. The generalization of the raw input + perceptron system decreases rapidly as the net learns to memorize the training patterns. The difference of using settled and unsettled LISSOM patterns diminishes as the afferent weights of LISSOM learn to take into account the decorrelation performed by the lateral weights.

Denker, J. S., Gardner, W. R., Graf, H. P., Henderson, D., Howard, R. E., Hubbard, W., Jackel, L. D., Baird, H. S., and Guyon, I. (1989). Neural network recognizer for hand-written zip code digits. In Touretzky, D. S., editor, *Advances in Neural Information Processing Systems 1*. San Mateo, CA: Morgan Kaufmann.

Fukushima, K., and Wake, N. (1990). Alphanumeric character recognition by neocognitron. In *Advanced Neural Computers*, 263–270. Elsevier Science Publishers B.V. (North-Holland).

le Cun, Y., Boser, B., Denker, J. S., Henderson, D., Howard, R. E., Hubbard, W., and Jackel, L. D. (1990). Handwritten digit recognition with a back-propagation network. In Touretzky, D. S., editor, *Advances in Neural Information Processing Systems 2*. San Mateo, CA: Morgan Kaufmann.

Martin, G. L., and Pittman, J. A. (1990). Recognizing hand-printed letters and digits. In Touretzky, D. S., editor, *Advances in Neural Information Processing Systems 2*. San Mateo, CA: Morgan Kaufmann.

Sirosh, J., and Miikkulainen, R. (1994). Cooperative self-organization of afferent and lateral connections in cortical maps. *Biological Cybernetics*, 71:66–78.

Sirosh, J., and Miikkulainen, R. (1995). Ocular dominance and patterned lateral connections in a self-organizing model of the primary visual cortex. In Tesauro, G., Touretzky, D. S., and Leen, T. K., editors, *Advances in Neural Information Processing Systems 7*. Cambridge, MA: MIT Press.

Sirosh, J., and Miikkulainen, R. (1996). Topographic receptive fields and patterned lateral interaction in a self-organizing model of the primary visual cortex. *Neural Computation* (in press).

Forward-backward retraining of recurrent neural networks

Andrew Senior [*] Tony Robinson
Cambridge University Engineering Department
Trumpington Street, Cambridge, England

Abstract

This paper describes the training of a recurrent neural network as the letter posterior probability estimator for a hidden Markov model, off-line handwriting recognition system. The network estimates posterior distributions for each of a series of frames representing sections of a handwritten word. The supervised training algorithm, backpropagation through time, requires target outputs to be provided for each frame. Three methods for deriving these targets are presented. A novel method based upon the forward-backward algorithm is found to result in the recognizer with the lowest error rate.

1 Introduction

In the field of off-line handwriting recognition, the goal is to read a handwritten document and produce a machine transcription. Such a system could be used for a variety of purposes, from cheque processing and postal sorting to personal correspondence reading for the blind or historical document reading. In a previous publication (Senior 1994) we have described a system based on a recurrent neural network (Robinson 1994) which can transcribe a handwritten document.

The recurrent neural network is used to estimate posterior probabilities for character classes, given frames of data which represent the handwritten word. These probabilities are combined in a hidden Markov model framework, using the Viterbi algorithm to find the most probable state sequence.

To train the network, a series of targets must be given. This paper describes three methods that have been used to derive these probabilities. The first is a naive bootstrap method, allocating equal lengths to all characters, used to start the training procedure. The second is a simple Viterbi-style segmentation method that assigns a single class label to each of the frames of data. Such a scheme has been used before in speech recognition using recurrent networks (Robinson 1994). This representation, is found to inadequately represent some frames which can represent two letters, or the ligatures between letters. Thus, by analogy with the forward-backward algorithm (Rabiner and Juang 1986) for HMM speech recognizers, we have developed a

---

[*] Now at IBM T.J.Watson Research Center, Yorktown Heights NY10598, USA.

forward-backward method for retraining the recurrent neural network. This assigns a probability distribution across the output classes for each frame of training data, and training on these 'soft labels' results in improved performance of the recognition system.

This paper is organized in four sections. The following section outlines the system in which the neural network is used, then section 3 describes the recurrent network in more detail. Section 4 explains the different methods of target estimation and presents the results of experiments before conclusions are presented in the final section.

2 System background

The recurrent network is the central part of the handwriting recognition system. The other parts are summarized here and described in more detail in another publication (Senior 1994). The first stage of processing converts the raw data into an invariant representation used as an input to the neural network. The network outputs are used to calculate word probabilities in a hidden Markov model.

First, the scanned page image is automatically segmented into words and then normalized. Normalization removes variations in the word appearance that do not affect its identity, such as rotation, scale, slant, slope and stroke thickness. The height of the letters forming the words is estimated, and magnifications, shear and thinning transforms are applied, resulting in a more robust representation of the word. The normalized word is represented in a compact canonical form encoding both the shape and salient features. All those features falling within a narrow vertical strip across the word are termed a frame. The representation derived consists of around 80 values for each of the frames, denoted x_t. The τ frames $(x_1, \ldots, x_\tau)$ for a whole word are written x_1^τ. Five frames would typically be enough to represent a single character. The recurrent network takes these frames sequentially and estimates the posterior character probability distribution given the data: $P(\Lambda_i | x_1^t)$, for each of the letters, a,..,z, denoted $\Lambda_0, \ldots, \Lambda_{25}$. These posterior probabilities are scaled by the prior class probabilities, and are treated as the emission probabilities in a hidden Markov model.

A separate model is created for each word in the vocabulary, with one state per letter. Transitions are allowed only from a state to itself or to the next letter in the word. The set of states in the models is denoted $Q = \{q_1, \ldots, q_N\}$ and the letter represented by q_i is given by $L(q_i), L : Q \mapsto \Lambda_0, \ldots, \Lambda_{25}$.

Word error rates are presented for experiments on a single-writer task tested with a 1330 word vocabulary[1]. Statistical significance of the results is evaluated using Student's t-test, comparing word recognition rates taken from a number of networks trained under the same conditions but with different random initializations. The results of the t-test are written: T(degrees of freedom) and the tabulated values: $t_{\text{significance}}$(degrees of freedom).

3 Recurrent networks

This section describes the recurrent error propagation network which has been used as the probability distribution estimator for the handwriting recognition system. Recurrent networks have been successfully applied to speech recognition (Robinson 1994) but have not previously been used for handwriting recognition, on-line or off-line. Here a left-to-right scanning process is adopted to map the frames of a word into a sequence, so adjacent frames are considered in consecutive instants.

---

[1] The experimental data are available in ftp://svr-ftp.eng.cam.ac.uk/pub/data

A recurrent network is well suited to the recognition of patterns occurring in a time-series because series of arbitrary length can be processed, with the same processing being performed on each section of the input stream. Thus a letter 'a' can be recognized by the same process, wherever it occurs in a word. In addition, internal 'state' units are available to encode multi-frame context information so letters spread over several frames can be recognized. The recurrent network

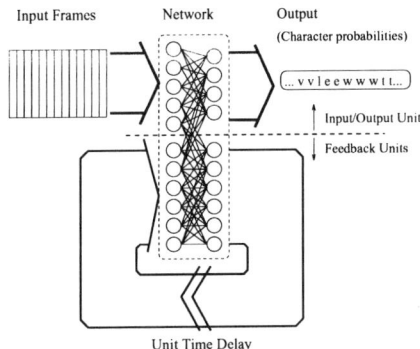

Figure 1: A schematic of the recurrent error propagation network. For clarity only a few of the units and links are shown.

architecture used here is a single layer of standard perceptrons with nonlinear activation functions. The output o_i of a unit i is a function of the inputs a_j and the network parameters, which are the weights of the links w_{ij} with a bias b_i:

$$o_i = f_i(\{\sigma_j\}), \quad (1) \qquad \sigma_i = b_i + \sum a_k w_{ik}. \quad (2)$$

The network is fully connected — that is, each input is connected to every output. However, some of the input units receive no external input and are connected one-to-one to corresponding output units through a unit time-delay (figure 1). The remaining input units accept a single frame of parametrized input and the remaining 26 output units estimate letter probabilities for the 26 character classes. The feedback units have a standard sigmoid activation function (3), but the character outputs have a 'softmax' activation function (4).

$$f_i(\{\sigma_j\}) = (1 + e^{-\sigma_i})^{-1} \quad (3) \qquad f_i(\{\sigma_j\}) = \frac{e^{\sigma_i}}{\sum_j e^{\sigma_j}}. \quad (4)$$

During recognition ('forward propagation'), the first frame is presented at the input and the feedback units are initialized to activations of 0.5. The outputs are calculated (1 and 2) and read off for use in the Markov model. In the next iteration, the outputs of the feedback units are copied to the feedback inputs, and the next frame presented to the inputs. Outputs are again calculated, and the cycle is repeated for each frame of input, with a probability distribution being generated for each frame.

To allow the network to assimilate context information, several frames of data are passed through the network before the probabilities for the first frame are read off, previous output probabilities being discarded. This input/output latency is maintained throughout the input sequence, with extra, empty frames of inputs being presented at the end to give probability distributions for the last frames of true inputs. A latency of two frames has been found to be most satisfactory in experiments to date.

3.1 Training

To be able to train the network the target values $\zeta_j(t)$ desired for the outputs $o_j(x_t)$ $j = 0, \ldots, 25$ for frame x_t must be specified. The target specification is dealt with in the next section. It is the discrepancy between the actual outputs and these targets which make up the objective function to be maximized by adjusting the internal weights of the network. The usual objective function is the mean squared error, but here the relative entropy, G, of the target and output distributions is used:

$$G = -\sum_t \sum_j \zeta_j(t) \log \frac{\zeta_j(t)}{o_j(x_t)}. \tag{5}$$

At the end of a word, the errors between the network's outputs and the targets are propagated back using the generalized delta rule (Rumelhart et al. 1986) and changes to the network weights are calculated. The network at successive time steps is treated as adjacent layers of a multi-layer network. This process is generally known as 'back-propagation through time' (Werbos 1990). After processing τ frames of data with an input/output latency, the network is equivalent to a (τ + latency) layer perceptron sharing weights between layers. For a detailed description of the training procedure, the reader is referred elsewhere (Rumelhart et al. 1986; Robinson 1994).

4 Target re-estimation

The data used for training are only labelled by word. That is, each image represents a single word, whose identity is known, but the frames representing that word are not labelled to indicate which part of the word they represent. To train the network, a label for each frame's identity must be provided. Labels are indicated by the state $S_t \in Q$ and the corresponding letter $L(S_t)$ of which a frame x_t is part.

4.1 A simple solution

To bootstrap the network, a naive method was used, which simply divided the word up into sections of equal length, one for each letter in the word. Thus, for an N-letter word of τ frames, x_1^τ, the first letter was assumed to be represented by frames $x_1^{\frac{\tau}{N}}$, the next by $x_{\frac{\tau}{N}+1}^{\frac{2\tau}{N}}$ and so on. The segmentation is mapped into a set of targets as follows:

$$\zeta_j(t) = \begin{cases} 1 \text{ if } L(S_t) = \Lambda_j \\ 0 \text{ otherwise.} \end{cases} \tag{6}$$

Figure 2a shows such a segmentation for a single word. Each line, representing $\zeta_j(t)$ for some j, has a broad peak for the frames representing letter Λ_j. Such a segmentation is inaccurate, but can be improved by adding prior knowledge. It is clear that some letters are generally longer than others, and some shorter. By weighting letters according to their a priori lengths it is possible to give a better, but still very simple, segmentation. The letters 'i, l' are given a length of $\frac{1}{2}$ and 'm, w' a length $\frac{3}{2}$ relative to other letters. Thus in the word 'wig', the first half of the frames would be assigned the label 'w', the next sixth 'i' and the last third the label 'g'. While this segmentation is constructed with no regard for the data being segmented, it is found to provide a good initial approximation from which it is possible to train the network to recognize words, albeit with high error rates.

4.2 Viterbi re-estimation

Having trained the network to some accuracy, it can be used to calculate a good estimate of the probability of each frame belonging to any letter. The probability of any state sequence can then be calculated in the hidden Markov model, and the most likely state sequence through the correct word S^* found using dynamic programming. This best state sequence S^* represents a new segmentation giving a label for each frame. For a network which models the probability distributions well, this segmentation will be better than the automatic segmentation of section 4.1

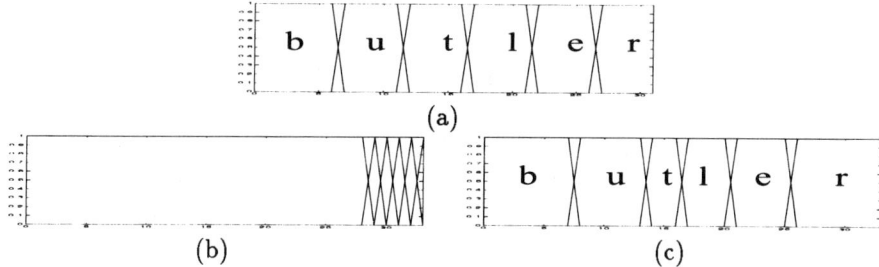

Figure 2: Segmentations of the word 'butler'. Each line represents $P(S_t = \Lambda_i | S)$ for one letter Λ_i and is high for frame t when $S_t^* = \Lambda_i$. (a) is the equal-length segmentation discussed in section 4.1 (b) is a segmentation of an untrained network. (c) is the segmentation re-estimated with a trained network.

since it takes the data into account. Finding the most probable state sequence S^* is termed a *forced alignment*. Since only the correct word model need be considered, such an alignment is faster than the search through the whole lexicon that is required for recognition. Training on this automatic segmentation gives a better recognition rate, but still avoids the necessity of manually segmenting any of the database.

Figure 2 shows two Viterbi segmentations of the word 'butler'. First, figure 2b shows the segmentation arrived at by taking the most likely state sequence before training the network. Since the emission probability distributions are random, there is nothing to distinguish between the state sequences, except slight variations due to initial asymmetry in the network, so a poor segmentation results. After training the network (2c), the durations deviate from the prior assumed durations to match the observed data. This re-estimated segmentation represents the data more accurately, so gives better targets towards which to train. A further improvement in recognition accuracy can be obtained by using the targets determined by the re-estimated segmentation. This cycle can be repeated until the segmentations do not change and performance ceases to improve. For speed, the network is not trained to convergence at each iteration.

It can be shown (Santini and Del Bimbo 1995) that, assuming that the network has enough parameters, the network outputs after convergence will approximate the posterior probabilities $P(\Lambda_i | x_1^t)$. Further, the approximation $P(\Lambda_i | x_1^t) \approx P(\Lambda_i | x_t)$ is made. The posteriors are scaled by the class priors $P(\Lambda_i)$ (Bourlard and Morgan 1993), and these scaled posteriors are used in the hidden Markov model in place of data likelihoods since, by Bayes' rule,

$$P(x_t | \Lambda_i) \propto \frac{P(\Lambda_i | x_t)}{P(\Lambda_i)}. \tag{7}$$

Table 1 shows word recognition error rates for three 80-unit networks trained towards fixed targets estimated by another network, and then retrained, re-estimating the targets at each iteration. The retraining improves the recognition performance ($T(2) = 3.91, t_{.95}(2) = 2.92$).

4.3 Forward-backward re-estimation

The system described above performs well and is the method used in previous recurrent network systems, but examining the speech recognition literature, a potential method of improvement can be seen. Viterbi frame alignment has so far been used to determine targets for training. This assigns one class to each frame, based on the most likely state sequence. A better approach might be to allow a distribution across all the classes indicating which are likely and which are not, avoiding a

Table 1: Error rates for 3 networks with 80 units trained with fixed alignments, and retrained with re-estimated alignments.

Training method	Error (%)	
	$\hat{\mu}$	$\hat{\sigma}$
Fixed targets	21.2	1.73
Retraining	17.0	0.68

'hard' classification at points where a frame may indeed represent more than one class (such as where slanting characters overlap), or none (as in a ligature). A 'soft' classification would give a more accurate portrayal of the frame identities.

Such a distribution, $\gamma_p(t) = P(S_t = q_p | x_1^\tau, W)$, can be calculated with the *forward-backward* algorithm (Rabiner and Juang 1986). To obtain $\gamma_p(t)$, the forward probabilities $\alpha_p(t) = P(S_t = q_p, x_1^t)$ must be combined with the *backward* probabilities $\beta_p(t) = P(S_t = q_p, x_{t+1}^\tau)$. The forward and backward probabilities are calculated recursively in the same manner.

$$\alpha_r(t+1) = \sum_p \alpha_p(t) P(x_t | L(q_p)) a_{p,r}, \qquad (8)$$

$$\beta_p(t-1) = \sum_r a_{p,r} P(x_t | S_t = q_r) \beta_r(t). \qquad (9)$$

Suitable initial distributions $\alpha_r(0) = \pi_r$ and $\beta_r(\tau+1) = \rho_r$ are chosen, e.g. π and ρ are one for respectively the first and last character in the word, and zero for the others. The likelihood of observing the data x_1^τ and being in state q_p at time t is then given by:

$$\xi_p(t) = \alpha_p(t) \beta_p(t). \qquad (10)$$

Then the probabilities $\gamma_p(t)$ of being in state q_p at time t are obtained by normalization and used as the targets $\zeta_j(t)$ for the recurrent network character probability outputs:

$$\gamma_p(t) = \frac{\xi_p(t)}{\sum_r \xi_r(t)}. \qquad (11) \qquad \zeta_j(t) = \sum_{p:L(q_p)=\Lambda_j} \gamma_p(t). \qquad (12)$$

Figure 3a shows the initial estimate of the class probabilities for a sample of the word '*butler*'. The probabilities shown are those estimated by the forward-backward algorithm when using an untrained network, for which the $P(x_t | S_t = q_p)$ will be independent of class. Despite the lack of information, the probability distributions can be seen to take reasonable shapes. The first frame must belong to the first letter, and the last frame must belong to the last letter, of course, but it can also be seen that half way through the word, the most likely letters are those in the middle of the word. Several class probabilities are non-zero at a time, reflecting the uncertainty caused since the network is untrained. Nevertheless, this limited information is enough to train a recurrent network, because as the network begins to approximate these probabilities, the segmentations become more definite. In contrast, using Viterbi segmentations from an untrained network, the most likely alignment can be very different from the true alignment (figure 2b). The segmentation is very definite though, and the network is trained towards the incorrect targets, reinforcing its error. Finally, a trained network gives a much more rigid segmentation (figure 3b), with most of the probabilities being zero or one, but with a boundary of uncertainty at the transitions between letters. This uncertainty, where a frame might truly represent parts of two letters, or a ligature between two, represents the data better. Just as with Viterbi training, the segmentations can be re-estimated after training and retraining results in improved performance. The final probabilistic segmentation can be stored with the data and used when subsequent networks are trained on the same data. Training is then significantly quicker than when training towards the approximate bootstrap segmentations and re-estimating the targets.

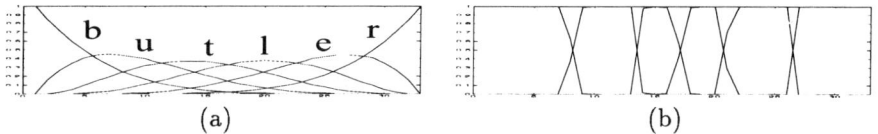

Figure 3: Forward-backward segmentations of the word *'butler'*. (a) is the segmentation of an untrained network with a uniform class prior. (b) shows the segmentation after training.

The better models obtained with the forward-backward algorithm give improved recognition results over a network trained with Viterbi alignments. The improvement is shown in table 2. It can be seen that the error rates for the networks trained with forward-backward targets are lower than those trained on Viterbi targets ($T(2) = 5.24, t_{.975}(2) = 4.30$).

Table 2: Error rates for networks with 80 units trained with Viterbi or Forward-Backward alignments.

Training method	Error (%)	
	$\hat{\mu}$	$\hat{\sigma}$
Viterbi	17.0	0.68
Forward-Backward	15.4	0.74

5 Conclusions

This paper has reviewed the training methods used for a recurrent network, applied to the problem of off-line handwriting recognition. Three methods of deriving target probabilities for the network have been described, and experiments conducted using all three. The third method is that of the forward-backward procedure, which has not previously been applied to recurrent neural network training. This method is found to improve the performance of the network, leading to reduced word error rates. Other improvements not detailed here (including duration models and stochastic language modelling) allow the error rate for this task to be brought below 10%.

Acknowledgments

The authors would like to thank Mike Hochberg for assistance in preparing this paper.

References

BOURLARD, H. and MORGAN, N. (1993) *Connectionist Speech Recognition: A Hybrid Approach*. Kluwer.

RABINER, L. R. and JUANG, B. H. (1986) An introduction to hidden Markov models. *IEEE ASSP magazine* **3** (1): 4–16.

ROBINSON, A. (1994) The application of recurrent nets to phone probability estimation. *IEEE Transactions on Neural Networks*.

RUMELHART, D. E., HINTON, G. E. and WILLIAMS, R. J. (1986) Learning internal representations by error propagation. In *Parallel Distributed Processing: Explorations in the Microstructure of Cognition*, ed. by D. E. Rumelhart and J. L. McClelland, volume 1, chapter 8, pp. 318–362. Bradford Books.

SANTINI, S. and DEL BIMBO, A. (1995) Recurrent neural networks can be trained to be maximum a posteriori probability classifiers. *Neural Networks* **8** (1): 25–29.

SENIOR, A. W., (1994) *Off-line Cursive Handwriting Recognition using Recurrent Neural Networks*. Cambridge University Engineering Department Ph.D. thesis. URL: ftp://svr-ftp.eng.cam.ac.uk/pub/reports/senior_thesis.ps.gz.

WERBOS, P. J. (1990) Backpropagation through time: What it does and how to do it. *Proceedings of the IEEE* **78**: 1550–60.

Context-Dependent Classes in a Hybrid Recurrent Network-HMM Speech Recognition System

Dan Kershaw   Tony Robinson   Mike Hochberg *
Cambridge University Engineering Department,
Trumpington Street, Cambridge CB2 1PZ, England.
Tel: [+44] 1223 332800, Fax: [+44] 1223 332662.
Email: djk, ajr @eng.cam.ac.uk

Abstract

A method for incorporating context-dependent phone classes in a connectionist-HMM hybrid speech recognition system is introduced. A modular approach is adopted, where single-layer networks discriminate between different context classes given the phone class and the acoustic data. The context networks are combined with a context-independent (CI) network to generate context-dependent (CD) phone probability estimates. Experiments show an average reduction in word error rate of 16% and 13% from the CI system on ARPA 5,000 word and SQALE 20,000 word tasks respectively. Due to improved modelling, the decoding speed of the CD system is more than twice as fast as the CI system.

INTRODUCTION

The ABBOT hybrid connectionist-HMM system performed competitively with many conventional hidden Markov model (HMM) systems in the 1994 ARPA evaluations of speech recognition systems (Hochberg, Cook, Renals, Robinson & Schechtman 1995). This hybrid framework is attractive because it is compact, having far fewer parameters than conventional HMM systems, whilst also providing the discriminative powers of a connectionist architecture.

It is well established that particular phones vary acoustically when they occur in different phonetic contexts. For example a vowel may become nasalized when following a nasal sound. The short-term contextual influence of co-articulation is

---

*Mike Hochberg is now at Nuance Communications, 333 Ravenswood Avenue, Building 110, Menlo Park, CA 94025, USA. Tel: [+1] 415 6148260.

handled in HMMs by creating a model for all sufficiently differing phonetic contexts with enough acoustic evidence. This modelling of phones in their particular phonetic contexts produces sharper probability density functions. This approach vastly improves HMM recognition accuracy over equivalent context-independent systems (Lee 1989). Although the recurrent neural network (RNN) model acoustic context internally (within the state vector), it does not model phonetic context. This paper presents an approach to improving the ABBOT system through phonetic context-dependent modelling.

In Cohen, Franco, Morgan, Rumelhart & Abrash (1992) separate sets of context-dependent output layers are used to model context effects in different states of HMM phone models. A set of networks discriminate between phones in 8 different broad-class left and right contexts. Training time is reduced by initialising from a CI multi-layer perceptron (MLP) and only changing the hidden-to-output weights during context-dependent training. This system performs well on the DARPA Resource Management Task. The work presented in Zhoa, Schwartz, Sroka & Makhoul (1995) followed along similar work to Cohen et al. (1992). A context-dependent mixture of experts (ME) system (Jordan & Jacobs 1994) based on the structure of the context-independent ME was built. For each state, the whole training data was divided into 46 parts according to its left or right context. Then, a separate ME model was built for each context.

Another approach to phonetic context-dependent modelling with MLPs was proposed by Bourlard & Morgan (1993). It was based on factoring the conditional probability of a phone-in-context given the data in terms of the phone given the data, and its context given the data and the phone. The approach taken in this paper is a mixture of the above work. However, this work augments a recurrent network (rather than an MLP) and concentrates on building a more compact system, which is more suited to our requirements. As a result, the context training scheme is fast and is implemented on a workstation (rather than a parallel processing machine as is used for training the RNN).

OVERVIEW OF THE ABBOT HYBRID SYSTEM

The basic framework of the ABBOT system is similar to the one described in Bourlard & Morgan (1994) except that a recurrent network is used as the acoustic model for the within the HMM framework. A more detailed description of the recurrent network for phone probability estimation is given in Robinson (1994). At each 16ms time frame, the acoustic vector $\mathbf{u}(t)$ is mapped to an output vector $\mathbf{y}(t)$, which represents an estimate of the posterior probability of each of the phone classes

$$y_i(t) \simeq \Pr(q_i(t)|\mathbf{u}_1^{t+4}), \qquad (1)$$

where $q_i(t)$ is phone class i at time t, and $\mathbf{u}_1^t = \{\mathbf{u}(1), \ldots, \mathbf{u}(t)\}$ is the input from time 1 to t. Left (past) acoustic context is modelled internally by a 256 dimensional state vector $\mathbf{x}(t)$, which can be envisaged as "storing" the information that has been presented at the input. Right (future) acoustic context is given by delaying the posterior probability estimation until four frames of input have been seen by the network. The network is trained using a modified version of error back-propagation through time (Robinson 1994).

Decoding with the hybrid connectionist-HMM approach is equivalent to conventional HMM decoding, with the difference being that the RNN models the state observations. Like typical HMM systems, the recognition process is expressed as finding the maximum *a posteriori* state sequence for the utterance. The decoding criterion specified above requires the computation of the likelihood of the acoustic data given a phone (state) sequence,

$$p(\mathbf{u}(t)|q_i(t)) = \frac{\Pr(q_i(t)|\mathbf{u}(t))p(\mathbf{u}(t))}{\Pr(q_i)}, \qquad (2)$$

where $p(\mathbf{u}(t))$ is the same for all phones, and hence drops out of the decoding process. Hence, the network outputs are mapped to scaled likelihoods by,

$$p(\mathbf{u}(t)|q_i(t)) \simeq \frac{y_i(t)}{\Pr(q_i)}, \qquad (3)$$

where the priors $\Pr(q_i)$ are estimated from the training data. Decoding uses the NOWAY decoder (Renals & Hochberg 1995) to compute the utterance model that is most likely to have generated the observed speech signal.

CONTEXT-DEPENDENT PROBABILITY ESTIMATION

The approach taken by this work is to augment the CI RNN, in a similar vein to Bourlard & Morgan (1993). The context-dependent likelihood, $p(\mathbf{U}_t|\mathbf{C}_t, \mathbf{Q}_t)$, can be factored as,

$$p(\mathbf{U}_t|\mathbf{C}_t, \mathbf{Q}_t) = \frac{\Pr(\mathbf{C}_t|\mathbf{U}_t, \mathbf{Q}_t)p(\mathbf{U}_t|\mathbf{Q}_t)}{\Pr(\mathbf{C}_t|\mathbf{Q}_t)}, \qquad (4)$$

where $\mathbf{C}$ is a set of context classes and $\mathbf{Q}$ is a set of context-independent phones or monophones. Substituting for the context independent probability density function, $p(\mathbf{U}_t|\mathbf{Q}_t)$, using (2), this becomes

$$p(\mathbf{U}_t|\mathbf{C}_t, \mathbf{Q}_t) = \frac{\Pr(\mathbf{C}_t|\mathbf{U}_t, \mathbf{Q}_t)\Pr(\mathbf{Q}_t|\mathbf{U}_t)}{\Pr(\mathbf{C}_t|\mathbf{Q}_t)\Pr(\mathbf{Q}_t)} p(\mathbf{U}_t). \qquad (5)$$

The term $p(\mathbf{U}_t)$ is constant for all frames, so this drops out of the decoding process and is ignored for all further purposes. This format is extremely appealing since $\Pr(\mathbf{C}_t|\mathbf{Q}_t)$ and $\Pr(\mathbf{Q}_t)$ are estimated from the training data and the CI RNN estimates $\Pr(\mathbf{Q}_t|\mathbf{U}_t)$. All that is then needed is an estimate of $\Pr(\mathbf{C}_t|\mathbf{U}_t, \mathbf{Q}_t)$. The approach taken in this paper uses a set of *context experts* or *modules* for each monophone class to augment the existing CI RNN.

TRAINING ON THE STATE VECTOR

An estimate of $\Pr(\mathbf{C}_t|\mathbf{U}_t, \mathbf{Q}_t)$ can be obtained by training a recurrent network to discriminate between contexts $c_j(t)$ for phone class $q_i(t)$, such that

$$y_{j|i}(t) \simeq \Pr(c_j(t)|\mathbf{u}_1^{t+4}, q_i(t)), \qquad (6)$$

where $y_{j|i}(t)$ is an estimate of the posterior probability of context class j given phone class i. However, training recurrent neural networks in this format would be expensive and difficult. For a recurrent format, the network must contain no discontinuities in the frame-by-frame acoustic input vectors. This implies all recurrent networks for all the phone classes i must be "shown" all the data. Instead, the assumption is made that since the state vector $\mathbf{x} = f(\mathbf{u})$, then

$$\underline{\mathbf{x}(t+4) \text{ is a good representation for } \mathbf{u}_1^{t+4}}.$$

Hence, a single-layer perceptron is trained on the state vectors corresponding to each monophone, q_i, to classify the different phonetic context classes. Finally, the likelihood estimates for the phonetic context class j for phone class i used in decoding are given by,

$$p(\mathbf{u}(t)|c_j(t), q_i(t)) \simeq \frac{\Pr(q_i(t)|\mathbf{u}_1^{t+4}) \Pr(c_j(t)|\mathbf{x}(t+4), q_i(t))}{\Pr(c_j(t)|q_i(t)) \Pr(q_i(t))},$$

$$\simeq \frac{y_i(t) y_{j|i}(t)}{\Pr(c_j|q_i) \Pr(q_i)}. \quad (7)$$

Embedded training is used to estimate the parameters of the CD networks and the training data is aligned using a Viterbi segmentation. Each context network is trained on a non-overlapping subset of the state vectors generated from all the Viterbi aligned training data. The context networks were trained using the RProp training procedure (Robinson 1994).

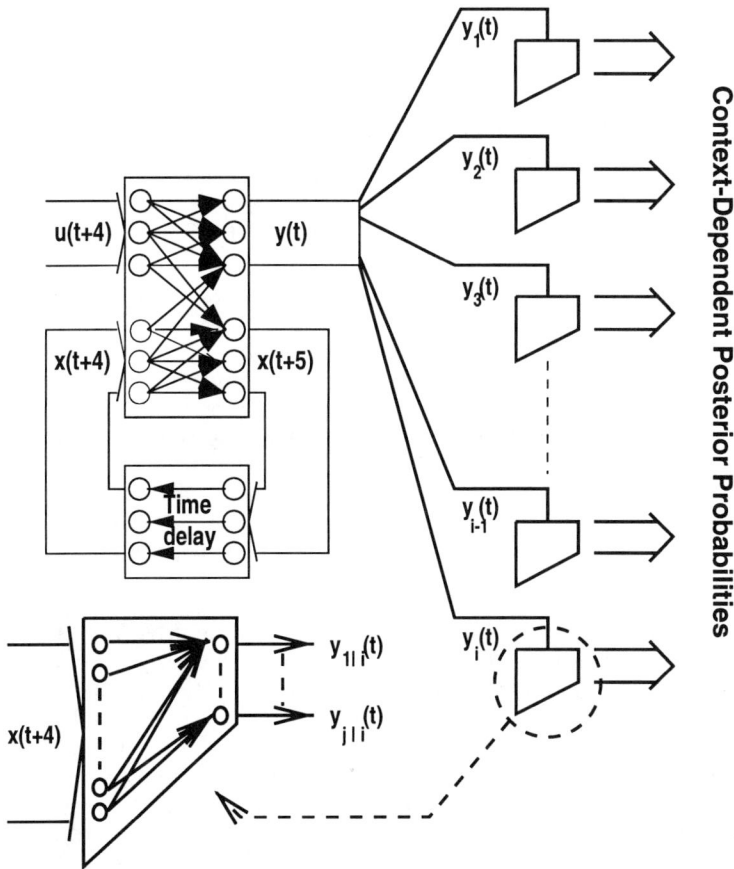

Figure 1: The Phonetic Context-Dependent RNN Modular System.

The frame-by-frame phonetic context posterior probabilities are required as input to the NOWAY decoder, i.e. all the outputs from the context modules on the right hand side of Figure 1. These posterior probabilities are calculated from the numerator of (7). The CI RNN stage operates in its normal fashion, generating frame-by-frame monophone posterior probabilities. At the same time the CD modules take the state vector generated by the RNN as input, in order to classify into a context class. The

RNN posterior probability outputs are multiplied by the module outputs to form context-dependent posterior probability estimates.

RELATIONSHIP WITH MIXTURE OF EXPERTS

This architecture has similarities with mixture of experts (Jordan & Jacobs 1994). During training, rather than making a "soft" split of the data as in the mixture of experts case, the Viterbi segmentation selects one expert at every exemplar. This means only one expert is responsible for each example in the data. This assumes that the Viterbi segmentation is a good approximation to the segmentation/selection process. Hence, each expert is trained on a small subset of the training data, avoiding the computationally expensive requirement for each expert to "see" all the data. During decoding, the RNN is treated as a gating network, smoothing the predictions of the experts, in an analogous manner to a standard mixture of experts gating network. For further description of the system see Kershaw, Hochberg & Robinson (1995).

CLUSTERING CONTEXT CLASSES

One of the problems faced by having a context-dependent system is to decide which context classes are to be included in the CD system. A method for overcoming this problem is a decision-tree based approach to cluster the context classes. This guarantees a full coverage of all phones in any context with the context classes being chosen using the acoustic evidence available. The tree clustering framework also allows for the building of a small number of context-dependent phones, keeping the new context-dependent connectionist system architecture compact. The tree building algorithm was based on Young, Odell & Woodland (1994), and further details can be found in Kershaw et al. (1995). Once the trees were built, they were used to relabel the training data and the pronunciation lexicon.

EVALUATION OF THE CONTEXT SYSTEM

The context-independent networks were trained on the ARPA Wall Street Journal SI84 Corpus. The phonetic context-dependent classes were clustered on the acoustic data according to the decision tree algorithm. Running the data through a recurrent network in a feed-forward fashion to obtain three million frames with 256 dimensional state vectors took approximately 8 hours on an HP735 workstation. Training all the context-dependent networks on all the training data takes between 4–6 hours (in total) on an HP735 workstation. The context-dependent modules were cross-validated on a development set at the word level.

Results for two context-dependent systems, compared with the context-independent baseline are shown in Table 1, where the 1993 spoke 5 test is used for cross-validation and development purposes.

The context-dependent systems were also applied to larger tasks such as the recent 1995 SQALE (a European multi-language speech recognition evaluation) 20,000 word development and evaluation sets. The American English context-dependent system (CD527) was extended to include a set of modules trained backwards in time (which were log-merged with the forward context), to augment a four way log-merged context-independent system (Hochberg, Cook, Renals & Robinson 1994).

Table 1: Comparison Of The CI System With The CD205 And CD527 Systems, For 5000 Word, Bigram Language Model Tasks.

1993 Test Sets	CI System WER	CD205 System WER	CD205 System Red^n WER	CD527 System WER	CD527 System Red^n WER
Spoke 5	16.0	14.0	12.7	13.6	14.9
Spoke 6	14.6	12.2	16.3	11.7	19.8
Eval.	15.7	14.3	8.4	13.7	12.6

Table 2: Comparison Of The Merged CI Systems With The CD527US And CD465UK Systems, For 20,000 Word Tasks. All Tests Use A Trigram Language Model. The CD527US And CD465UK Evaluation Results Have Been Officially Adjudicated.

1995 Test Sets	CI System WER	CD System WER	Red^n WER
US English dev_test	12.8	11.3	12.2
US English evl_test	14.5	12.9†	9.8
UK English dev_test	15.6	12.7	18.9
UK English evl_test	16.4	13.8†	15.7

Table 3: Comparison Of Average Utterance Decode Speed Of The CI Systems With The CD527US And CD465UK Systems On An HP735, For 20,000 Word Tasks. All Tests Use A Trigram Language Model, And The Same Pruning Levels.

Tests	CI Utterance Av. Decode Speed (s)	CD Utterance Av. Decode Speed (s)	Speedup
American English	67	31	2.16
British English	131	48	2.73

Table 4: The Number Of Parameters Used For The CI Systems As Compared With The CD527US And CD465UK Systems.

System	# CI Parameters	# CD Parameters	% Increase In Parameters
American English	341,000	612,000	79.0
British English	331,000	570,000	72.2

A similar system was built for British English (CD465). Table 2 shows the improvement gained by using context models. The daggers indicate the official entries for the 1995 SQALE evaluation. These figures represent the lowest reported word error rate for both the US and UK English tasks.

As a result of improved phonetic modelling and class discrimination the search space was reduced. This meant that decoding speed was over twice as fast as the context-dependent system, Table 3, even though there were roughly ten times as many context-dependent phones compared to the monophones.

The increase in the number of parameters due to the introduction of the context models for the SQALE evaluation system are shown in Table 4. Although this seems a large increase in the number of system parameters, it is still an order of magnitude less than any equivalent HMM system built for this task.

CONCLUSIONS

This paper has discussed a successful way of integrating phonetic context-dependent classes into the current ABBOT hybrid system. The architecture followed a modular approach which could be used to augment any current RNN-HMM hybrid system. Fast training of the context-dependent modules was achieved. Training on all of the SI84 corpus took between 4 and 6 hours. Utterance decoding was performed using the standard NOWAY decoder. The word error was significantly reduced, whilst the decoding speed of the context system was over twice as fast as the baseline system (for 20,000 word tasks).

References

Bourlard, H. & Morgan, N. (1993), 'Continuous Speech Recognition by Connectionist Statistical Methods', *IEEE Transactions on Neural Networks* **4**(6), 893–909.

Bourlard, H. & Morgan, N. (1994), *Connectionist Speech Recognition: A Hybrid Approach*, Kluwer Acedemic Publishers.

Cohen, M., Franco, H., Morgan, N., Rumelhart, D. & Abrash, V. (1992), Context-Dependent Multiple Distribution Phonetic Modeling with MLPs, *in* 'NIPS 5'.

Hochberg, M., Cook, G., Renals, S. & Robinson, A. (1994), Connectionist Model Combination for Large Vocabulary Speech Recognition, *in* 'Neural Networks for Signal Processing', Vol. IV, pp. 269–278.

Hochberg, M., Cook, G., Renals, S., Robinson, A. & Schechtman, R. (1995), The 1994 ABBOT Hybrid Connectionist-HMM Large-Vocabulary Recognition System, *in* 'Spoken Language Systems Technology Workshop', ARPA, pp. 170–6.

Jordan, M. & Jacobs, R. (1994), 'Hierarchical Mixtures of Experts and the EM Algorithm', *Neural Computation* **6**, 181–214.

Kershaw, D., Hochberg, M. & Robinson, A. (1995), Incorporating Context-Dependent Classes in a Hybrid Recurrent Network-HMM Speech Recognition System, F-INFENG TR217, Cambridge University Engineering Department.

Lee, K.-F. (1989), *Automatic Speech Recognition; The Development of the SPHINX System*, Kluwer Acedemic Publishers.

Renals, S. & Hochberg, M. (1995), Efficient Search Using Posterior Phone Probability Estimates, *in* 'ICASSP', Vol. 1, pp. 596–9.

Robinson, A. (1994), 'An Application of Recurrent Nets to Phone Probability Estimation.', *IEEE Transactions on Neural Networks* **5**(2), 298–305.

Young, S., Odell, J. & Woodland, P. (1994), 'Tree-Based State Tying for High Accuracy Acoustic Modelling', *Spoken Language Systems Technology Workshop*.

Zhoa, Y., Schwartz, R., Sroka, J. & Makhoul, J. (1995), Hierarchical Mixtures of Experts Methodology Applied to Continuous Speech Recognition, *in* 'NIPS 7'.

A New Learning Algorithm for Blind Signal Separation

S. Amari[*]
University of Tokyo
Bunkyo-ku, Tokyo 113, JAPAN
amari@sat.t.u-tokyo.ac.jp

A. Cichocki
Lab. for Artificial Brain Systems
FRP, RIKEN
Wako-Shi, Saitama, 351-01, JAPAN
cia@kamo.riken.go.jp

H. H. Yang
Lab. for Information Representation
FRP, RIKEN
Wako-Shi, Saitama, 351-01, JAPAN
hhy@koala.riken.go.jp

Abstract

A new on-line learning algorithm which minimizes a statistical dependency among outputs is derived for blind separation of mixed signals. The dependency is measured by the average mutual information (MI) of the outputs. The source signals and the mixing matrix are unknown except for the number of the sources. The Gram-Charlier expansion instead of the Edgeworth expansion is used in evaluating the MI. The natural gradient approach is used to minimize the MI. A novel activation function is proposed for the on-line learning algorithm which has an equivariant property and is easily implemented on a neural network like model. The validity of the new learning algorithm are verified by computer simulations.

1 INTRODUCTION

The problem of blind signal separation arises in many areas such as speech recognition, data communication, sensor signal processing, and medical science. Several neural network algorithms [3, 5, 7] have been proposed for solving this problem. The performance of these algorithms is usually affected by the selection of the activation functions for the formal neurons in the networks. However, all activation

---

[*]Lab. for Information Representation, FRP, RIKEN, Wako-shi, Saitama, JAPAN

functions attempted are monotonic and the selections of the activation functions are ad hoc. How should the activation function be determined to minimize the MI? Is it necessary to use monotonic activation functions for blind signal separation? In this paper, we shall answer these questions and give an on-line learning algorithm which uses a non-monotonic activation function selected by the independent component analysis (ICA) [7]. Moreover, we shall show a rigorous way to derive the learning algorithm which has the equivariant property, i.e., the performance of the algorithm is independent of the scaling parameters in the noiseless case.

2 PROBLEM

Let us consider unknown source signals $s^i(t), i = 1, \cdots, n$ which are mutually independent. It is assumed that the sources $s^i(t)$ are stationary processes and each source has moments of any order with a zero mean. The model for the sensor output is

$$\mathbf{x}(t) = \mathbf{A}\mathbf{s}(t)$$

where $\mathbf{A} \in \mathbf{R}^{n \times n}$ is an unknown non-singular mixing matrix, $\mathbf{s}(t) = [s^1(t), \cdots, s^n(t)]^T$ and $\mathbf{x}(t) = [x^1(t), \cdots, x^n(t)]^T$.

Without knowing the source signals and the mixing matrix, we want to recover the original signals from the observations $\mathbf{x}(t)$ by the following linear transform:

$$\mathbf{y}(t) = \mathbf{W}\mathbf{x}(t)$$

where $\mathbf{y}(t) = [y^1(t), \cdots, y^n(t)]^T$ and $\mathbf{W} \in \mathbf{R}^{n \times n}$ is a de-mixing matrix.

It is impossible to obtain the original sources $s^i(t)$ because they are not identifiable in the statistical sense. However, except for a permutation of indices, it is possible to obtain $c_i s^i(t)$ where the constants c_i are indefinite nonzero scalar factors. The source signals are identifiable in this sense. So our goal is to find the matrix $\mathbf{W}$ such that $[y^1, \cdots, y^n]$ coincides with a permutation of $[s^1, \cdots, s^n]$ except for the scalar factors. The solution $\mathbf{W}$ is the matrix which finds all independent components in the outputs. An on-line learning algorithm for $\mathbf{W}$ is needed which performs the ICA. It is possible to find such a learning algorithm which minimizes the dependency among the outputs. The algorithm in [6] is based on the Edgeworth expansion[8] for evaluating the marginal negentropy. Both the Gram-Charlier expansion[8] and the Edgeworth expansion[8] can be used to approximate probability density functions. We shall use the Gram-Charlier expansion instead of the Edgeworth expansion for evaluating the marginal entropy. We shall explain the reason in section 3.

3 INDEPENDENCE OF SIGNALS

The mathematical framework for the ICA is formulated in [6]. The basic idea of the ICA is to minimize the dependency among the output components. The dependency is measured by the Kullback-Leibler divergence between the joint and the product of the marginal distributions of the outputs:

$$D(\mathbf{W}) = \int p(\mathbf{y}) \log \frac{p(\mathbf{y})}{\prod_{a=1}^{n} p_a(y^a)} d\mathbf{y} \tag{1}$$

where $p_a(y^a)$ is the marginal probability density function (pdf). Note the Kullback-Leibler divergence has some invariant properties from the differential-geometrical point of view[1].

It is easy to relate the Kullback-Leibler divergence $D(\boldsymbol{W})$ to the average MI of $\mathbf{y}$:

$$D(\boldsymbol{W}) = -H(\mathbf{y}) + \sum_{a=1}^{n} H(y^a) \qquad (2)$$

where
$H(\mathbf{y}) = -\int p(\mathbf{y}) \log p(\mathbf{y}) d\mathbf{y}$,
$H(y^a) = -\int p_a(y^a) \log p_a(y^a) dy^a$ is the marginal entropy.

The minimization of the Kullback-Leibler divergence leads to an ICA algorithm for estimating $\boldsymbol{W}$ in [6] where the Edgeworth expansion is used to evaluate the negentropy. We use the truncated Gram-Charlier expansion to evaluate the Kullback-Leibler divergence. The Edgeworth expansion has some advantages over the Gram-Charlier expansion only for some special distributions. In the case of the Gamma distribution or the distribution of a random variable which is the sum of iid random variables, the coefficients of the Edgeworth expansion decrease uniformly. However, there is no such advantage for the mixed output y^a in general cases.

To calculate each $H(y^a)$ in (2), we shall apply the Gram-Charlier expansion to approximate the pdf $p_a(y^a)$. Since $E[\mathbf{y}] = E[\boldsymbol{W}\boldsymbol{A}\mathbf{s}] = 0$, we have $E[y^a] = 0$. To simplify the calculations for the entropy $H(y^a)$ to be carried out later, we assume $m_2^a = 1$. We use the following truncated Gram-Charlier expansion to approximate the pdf $p_a(y^a)$:

$$p_a(y^a) \approx \alpha(y^a)\{1 + \frac{\kappa_3^a}{3!} H_3(y^a) + \frac{\kappa_4^a}{4!} H_4(y^a)\} \qquad (3)$$

where $\kappa_3^a = m_3^a$, $\kappa_4^a = m_4^a - 3$, $m_k^a = E[(y^a)^k]$ is the k-th order moment of y^a, $\alpha(y) = \frac{1}{\sqrt{2\pi}} e^{-\frac{y^2}{2}}$, and $H_k(y)$ are Chebyshev-Hermite polynomials defined by the identity

$$(-1)^k \frac{d^k \alpha(y)}{dy^k} = H_k(y)\alpha(y).$$

We prefer the Gram-Charlier expansion to the Edgeworth expansion because the former clearly shows how κ_3^a and κ_4^a affect the approximation of the pdf. The last term in (3) characterizes non-Gaussian distributions. To apply (3) to calculate $H(y^a)$, we need the following integrals:

$$-\int \alpha(y) H_2(y) \log \alpha(y) dy = \frac{1}{4} \qquad (4)$$

$$\int \alpha(y)(H_2(y))^2 H_4(y) dy = 24. \qquad (5)$$

These integrals can be obtained easily from the following results for the moments of a Gaussian random variable N(0,1):

$$\int y^{2k+1} \alpha(y) dy = 0, \quad \int y^{2k} \alpha(y) dy = 1 \cdot 3 \cdots (2k-1). \qquad (6)$$

By using the expansion

$$\log(1+y) \approx y - \frac{y^2}{2} + O(y^3)$$

and taking account of the orthogonality relations of the Chebyshev-Hermite polynomials and (4)-(5), the entropy $H(y^a)$ is expanded as

$$H(y^a) \approx \frac{1}{2}\log(2\pi e) - \frac{(\kappa_3^a)^2}{2 \cdot 3!} - \frac{(\kappa_4^a)^2}{2 \cdot 4!} + \frac{5}{8}(\kappa_3^a)^2 \kappa_4^a + \frac{1}{16}(\kappa_4^a)^3. \qquad (7)$$

It is easy to calculate

$$-\int \alpha(y)\log \alpha(y)dy = \frac{1}{2}\log(2\pi e).$$

From $\mathbf{y} = \mathbf{Wx}$, we have $H(\mathbf{y}) = H(\mathbf{x}) + \log|det(\mathbf{W})|$. Applying (7) and the above expressions to (2), we have

$$D(\mathbf{W}) \approx -H(\mathbf{x}) - \log|det(\mathbf{W})| + \frac{n}{2}\log(2\pi e) - \sum_{a=1}^{n}[\frac{(\kappa_3^a)^2}{2\cdot 3!} + \frac{(\kappa_4^a)^2}{2\cdot 4!}$$
$$-\frac{5}{8}(\kappa_3^a)^2\kappa_4^a - \frac{1}{16}(\kappa_4^a)^3]. \qquad (8)$$

4 A NEW LEARNING ALGORITHM

To obtain the gradient descent algorithm to update $\mathbf{W}$ recursively, we need to calculate $\frac{\partial D}{\partial w_k^a}$ where w_k^a is the (a,k) element of $\mathbf{W}$ in the a-th row and k-th column.

Let $cof(w_k^a)$ be the cofactor of w_k^a in $\mathbf{W}$. It is not difficult to derive the followings:

$$\frac{\partial \log|det(\mathbf{W})|}{\partial w_k^a} = \frac{cof(w_k^a)}{det(\mathbf{W})} = (\mathbf{W}^{-T})_k^a$$

$$\frac{\partial \kappa_3^a}{\partial w_k^a} = 3E[(y^a)^2 x^k]$$

$$\frac{\partial \kappa_4^a}{\partial w_k^a} = 4E[(y^a)^3 x^k]$$

where $(\mathbf{W}^{-T})_k^a$ denotes the (a,k) element of $(\mathbf{W}^T)^{-1}$. From (8), we obtain

$$\frac{\partial D}{\partial w_k^a} \approx -(\mathbf{W}^{-T})_k^a + f(\kappa_3^a, \kappa_4^a)E[(y^a)^2 x^k] + g(\kappa_3^a, \kappa_4^a)E[(y^a)^3 x^k] \qquad (9)$$

where

$$f(y, z) = -\frac{1}{2}y + \frac{15}{4}yz, \quad g(y, z) = -\frac{1}{6}z + \frac{5}{2}y^2 + \frac{3}{4}z^2.$$

From (9), we obtain the gradient descent algorithm to update $\mathbf{W}$ recursively:

$$\frac{dw_k^a}{dt} = -\eta(t)\frac{\partial D}{\partial w_k^a}$$
$$= \eta(t)\{(\mathbf{W}^{-T})_k^a - f(\kappa_3^a, \kappa_4^a)E[(y^a)^2 x^k] - g(\kappa_3^a, \kappa_4^a)E[(y^a)^3 x^k]\} \qquad (10)$$

where $\eta(t)$ is a learning rate function. Replacing the expectation values in (10) by their instantaneous values, we have the stochastic gradient descent algorithm:

$$\frac{dw_k^a}{dt} = \eta(t)\{(\mathbf{W}^{-T})_k^a - f(\kappa_3^a, \kappa_4^a)(y^a)^2 x^k - g(\kappa_3^a, \kappa_4^a)(y^a)^3 x^k\}. \qquad (11)$$

We need to use the following adaptive algorithm to compute κ_3^a and κ_4^a in (11):

$$\frac{d\kappa_3^a}{dt} = -\mu(t)(\kappa_3^a - (y^a)^3)$$
$$\frac{d\kappa_4^a}{dt} = -\mu(t)(\kappa_4^a - (y^a)^4 + 3) \qquad (12)$$

where $\mu(t)$ is another learning rate function.

The performance of the algorithm (11) relies on the estimation of the third and fourth order cumulants performed by the algorithm (12). Replacing the moments of the random variables in (11) by their instantaneous values, we obtain the following algorithm which is a direct but coarse implementation of (11):

$$\frac{dw_k^a}{dt} = \eta(t)\{(\mathbf{W}^{-T})_k^a - f(y^a)x^k\} \qquad (13)$$

where the activation function $f(y)$ is defined by

$$f(y) = \frac{3}{4}y^{11} + \frac{25}{4}y^9 - \frac{14}{3}y^7 - \frac{47}{4}y^5 + \frac{29}{4}y^3. \qquad (14)$$

Note the activation function $f(y)$ is an odd function, not a monotonic function. The equation (13) can be written in a matrix form:

$$\frac{d\mathbf{W}}{dt} = \eta(t)\{\mathbf{W}^{-T} - \mathbf{f}(\mathbf{y})\mathbf{x}^T\}. \qquad (15)$$

This equation can be further simplified as following by substituting $\mathbf{x}^T\mathbf{W}^T = \mathbf{y}^T$:

$$\frac{d\mathbf{W}}{dt} = \eta(t)\{\mathbf{I} - \mathbf{f}(\mathbf{y})\mathbf{y}^T\}\mathbf{W}^{-T} \qquad (16)$$

where $\mathbf{f}(\mathbf{y}) = (f(y^1), \cdots, f(y^n))^T$. The above equation is based on the gradient descent algorithm (10) with the following matrix form:

$$\frac{d\mathbf{W}}{dt} = -\eta(t)\frac{\partial D}{\partial \mathbf{W}}. \qquad (17)$$

From information geometry perspective[1], since the mixing matrix $\mathbf{A}$ is non-singular we had better replace the above algorithm by the following natural gradient descent algorithm:

$$\frac{d\mathbf{W}}{dt} = -\eta(t)\frac{\partial D}{\partial \mathbf{W}}\mathbf{W}^T\mathbf{W}. \qquad (18)$$

Applying the previous approximation of the gradient $\frac{\partial D}{\partial \mathbf{W}}$ to (18), we obtain the following algorithm:

$$\frac{d\mathbf{W}}{dt} = \eta(t)\{\mathbf{I} - \mathbf{f}(\mathbf{y})\mathbf{y}^T\}\mathbf{W} \qquad (19)$$

which has the same "equivariant" property as the algorithms developed in [4, 5].

Although the on-line learning algorithms (16) and (19) look similar to those in [3, 7] and [5] respectively, the selection of the activation function in this paper is rational, not ad hoc. The activation function (14) is determined by the ICA. It is a non-monotonic activation function different from those used in [3, 5, 7].

There is a simple way to justify the stability of the algorithm (19). Let Vec($\cdot$) denote an operator on a matrix which cascades the columns of the matrix from the left to the right and forms a column vector. Note this operator has the following property:

$$\text{Vec}(\mathbf{ABC}) = (\mathbf{C}^T \otimes \mathbf{A})\text{Vec}(\mathbf{B}). \qquad (20)$$

Both the gradient descent algorithm and the natural gradient descent algorithm are special cases of the following general gradient descent algorithm:

$$\frac{d\text{Vec}(\mathbf{W})}{dt} = -\eta(t)\mathbf{P}\frac{\partial D}{\partial \text{Vec}(\mathbf{W})} \qquad (21)$$

where $\mathbf{P}$ is a symmetric and positive definite matrix. It is trivial that (21) becomes (17) when $\mathbf{P} = \mathbf{I}$. When $\mathbf{P} = \mathbf{W}^T\mathbf{W} \otimes \mathbf{I}$, applying (20) to (21), we obtain

$$\frac{d\text{Vec}(\mathbf{W})}{dt} = -\eta(t)(\mathbf{W}^T\mathbf{W} \otimes \mathbf{I})\frac{\partial D}{\partial \text{Vec}(\mathbf{W})} = -\eta(t)\text{Vec}(\frac{\partial D}{\partial \mathbf{W}}\mathbf{W}^T\mathbf{W})$$

and this equation implies (18). So the natural gradient descent algorithm updates $W(t)$ in the direction of decreasing the dependency $D(W)$. The information geometry theory[1] explains why the natural gradient descent algorithm should be used to minimize the MI.

Another on-line learning algorithm for blind separation using recurrent network was proposed in [2]. For this algorithm, the activation function (14) also works well. In practice, other activation functions such as those proposed in [2]-[6] may also be used in (19). However, the performance of the algorithm for such functions usually depends on the distributions of the sources. The activation function (14) works for relatively general cases in which the pdf of each source can be approximated by the truncated Gram-Charlier expansion.

5 SIMULATION

In order to check the validity and performance of the new on-line learning algorithm (19), we simulate it on the computer using synthetic source signals and a random mixing matrix. The extensive computer simulations have fully confirmed the theory and the validity of the algorithm (19). Due to the limit of space we present here only one illustrative example.

Example:

Assume that the following three unknown sources are mixed by a random mixing matrix A:

$$[s^1(t), s^2(t), s^3(t)] = [n(t), 0.1 sin(400t)cos(30t), 0.01 sign[sin(500t + 9cos(40t))]$$

where $n(t)$ is a noise source uniformly distributed in the range $[-1, +1]$, and $s_2(t)$ and $s_3(t)$ are two deterministic source signals. The elements of the mixing matrix A are randomly chosen in $[-1, +1]$. The learning rate is exponentially decreasing to zero as $\eta(t) = 250 exp(-5t)$.

A simulation result is shown in Figure 1. The first three signals denoted by X1, X2 and X3 represent mixing (sensor) signals: $x^1(t)$, $x^2(t)$ and $x^3(t)$. The last three signals denoted by O1, O2 and O3 represent the output signals: $y^1(t)$, $y^2(t)$, and $y^3(t)$. By using the proposed learning algorithm, the neural network is able to extract the deterministic signals from the observations after approximately 500 milliseconds.

The performance index E_1 is defined by

$$E_1 = \sum_{i=1}^{n}(\sum_{j=1}^{n} \frac{|p_{ij}|}{\max_k |p_{ik}|} - 1) + \sum_{j=1}^{n}(\sum_{i=1}^{n} \frac{|p_{ij}|}{\max_k |p_{kj}|} - 1)$$

where $P = (p_{ij}) = WA$.

6 CONCLUSION

The major contribution of this paper the rigorous derivation of the effective blind separation algorithm with equivariant property based on the minimization of the MI of the outputs. The ICA is a general principle to design algorithms for blind signal separation. The most difficulties in applying this principle are to evaluate the MI of the outputs and to find a working algorithm which decreases the MI. Different from the work in [6], we use the Gram-Charlier expansion instead of the Edgeworth expansion to calculate the marginal entropy in evaluating the MI. Using the natural gradient method to minimize the MI, we have found an on-line learning algorithm to find a de-mixing matrix. The algorithm has equivariant property and can be easily implemented on a neural network like model. Our approach provides a rational selection of the activation function for the formal neurons in the network. The algorithm has been simulated for separating unknown source signals mixed by a random mixing matrix. Our theory and the validity of the new learning algorithm are verified by the simulations.

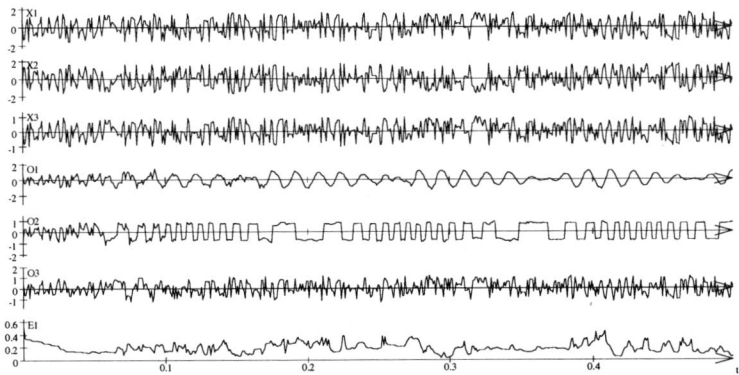

Figure 1: The mixed and separated signals, and the performance index

Acknowledgment

We would like to thank Dr. Xiao Yan SU for the proof-reading of the manuscript.

References

[1] S.-I. Amari. *Differential-Geometrical Methods in Statistics, Lecture Notes in Statistics vol.28.* Springer, 1985.

[2] S. Amari, A. Cichocki, and H. H. Yang. Recurrent neural networks for blind separation of sources. In *Proceedings 1995 International Symposium on Nonlinear Theory and Applications*, volume I, pages 37–42, December 1995.

[3] A. J. Bell and T. J. Sejnowski. An information-maximisation approach to blind separation and blind deconvolution. *Neural Computation*, 7:1129–1159, 1995.

[4] J.-F. Cardoso and Beate Laheld. Equivariant adaptive source separation. *To appear in IEEE Trans. on Signal Processing*, 1996.

[5] A. Cichocki, R. Unbehauen, L. Moszczyński, and E. Rummert. A new on-line adaptive learning algorithm for blind separation of source signals. In *ISANN94*, pages 406–411, Taiwan, December 1994.

[6] P. Comon. Independent component analysis, a new concept? *Signal Processing*, 36:287–314, 1994.

[7] C. Jutten and J. Herault. Blind separation of sources, part i: An adaptive algorithm based on neuromimetic architecture. *Signal Processing*, 24:1–10, 1991.

[8] A. Stuart and J. K. Ord. *Kendall's Advanced Theory of Statistics.* Edward Arnold, 1994.

Handwritten Word Recognition using Contextual Hybrid Radial Basis Function Network/Hidden Markov Models

Bernard Lemarié
La Poste/SRTP
10, Rue de l'île-Mabon
F-44063 Nantes Cedex France
lemarie@srtp.srt-poste.fr

Michel Gilloux
La Poste/SRTP
10, Rue de l'île-Mabon
F-44063 Nantes Cedex France
gilloux@srtp.srt-poste.fr

Manuel Leroux
La Poste/SRTP
10, Rue de l'île-Mabon
F-44063 Nantes Cedex France
leroux@srtp.srt-poste.fr

Abstract

A hybrid and contextual radial basis function network/hidden Markov model off-line handwritten word recognition system is presented. The task assigned to the radial basis function networks is the estimation of emission probabilities associated to Markov states. The model is contextual because the estimation of emission probabilities takes into account the left context of the current image segment as represented by its predecessor in the sequence. The new system does not outperform the previous system without context but acts differently.

1 INTRODUCTION

Hidden Markov models (HMMs) are now commonly used in off-line recognition of handwritten words (Chen et al., 1994) (Gilloux et al., 1993) (Gilloux et al. 1995a). In some of these approaches (Gilloux et al. 1993), word images are transformed into sequences of image segments through some explicit segmentation procedure. These segments are passed on to a module which is in charge of estimating the probability for each segment to appear when the corresponding hidden state is some state s (state emission probabilities). Model probabilities are generally optimized for the Maximum Likelihood Estimation (MLE) criterion.

MLE training is known to be sub-optimal with respect to discrimination ability when the underlying model is not the true model for the data. Moreover, estimating the emission probabilities in regions where examples are sparse is difficult and estimations may not be accurate. To reduce the risk of over training, images segments consisting of bitmaps are often replaced by feature vector of reasonable length (Chen et al., 1994) or even discrete symbols (Gilloux et al., 1993).

In a previous paper (Gilloux et al., 1995b) we described a hybrid HMM/radial basis function system in which emission probabilities are computed from full-fledged bitmaps though the use of a radial basis function (RBF) neural network. This system demonstrated better recognition rates than a previous one based on symbolic features (Gilloux et al., 1995b). Yet, many misclassification examples showed that some of the simplifying assumptions made in HMMs were responsible for a significant part of these errors. In particular, we observed that considering each segment independently from its neighbours would hurt the accuracy of the model. For example, figure 1 shows examples of letter *a* when it is segmented in two parts. The two parts are obviously correlated.

Figure 1: Examples of segmented *a*.

We propose a new variant of the hybrid HMM/RBF model in which emission probabilities are estimated by taking into account the context of the current segment. The context will be represented by the preceding image segment in the sequence.

The RBF model was chosen because it was proven to be an efficient model for recognizing isolated digits or letters (Poggio & Girosi, 1990) (Lemarié, 1993). Interestingly enough, RBFs bear close relationships with gaussian mixtures often used to model emission probabilities in markovian contexts. Their advantage lies in the fact that they do not directly estimate emission probabilities and thus are less prone to errors in this estimation in sparse regions. They are also trained through the Mean Square Error (MSE) criterion which makes them more discriminant.

The idea of using a neural net and in particular a RBF in conjunction with a HMM is not new. In (Singer & Lippman, 1992) it was applied to a speech recognition task. The use of context to improve emission probabilities was proposed in (Bourlard & Morgan, 1993) with the use of a discrete set of context events. Several neural networks are there used to estimate various relations between states, context events and current segment. Our point is to propose a different method without discrete context based on a adapted decomposition of the HMM likelihood estimation.This model is next applied to off-line handwritten word recognition.

The organization of this paper is as follows. Section 1 is an overview of the architecture of our HMM. Section 2 describes the justification for using RBF outputs in a contextual hidden Markov model. Section 3 describes the radial basis function network recognizer. Section 4 reports on an experiment in which the contextual model is applied to the recognition of handwritten words found on french bank or postal cheques.

2 OVERVIEW OF THE HIDDEN MARKOV MODEL

In an HMM model (Bahl et al., 1983), the recognition scores associated to words w are likelihoods

$$L(w|i_1...i_n) = p\left(i_1...i_n|w\right) \times p(w)$$

in which the first term in the product encodes the probability with which the model of each word w generates some image (some sequence of image segments) $i_1...i_n$. In the HMM paradigm, this term is decomposed into a sum on all paths (i.e. sequence of hidden states) of products of the probability of the hidden path by the probability that the path generated the image sequence:

$$p(i_1...i_n|w) = \sum_{path=\{s_1...s_n\}} p(i_1...i_n|s_1...s_n) \times p(s_1...s_n)$$

It is often assumed that only one path contributes significantly to this term so that

$$p(i_1...i_n \mid w) = p(i_1...i_n \mid s_1...s_n) \times p(s_1...s_n)$$

In HMMs, each sequence element is assumed to depend only on its corresponding state:

$$p(i_1...i_n \mid s_1...s_n) = \prod_{j=1}^{n} p(i_j \mid s_j)$$

Moreover, first-order Markov models assume that paths are generated by a first-order Markov chain so that

$$p(s_1...s_n) = \prod_{j=1}^{n} p(s_j \mid s_{j-1})$$

We have reported in previous papers (Gilloux et al., 1993) (Gilloux et al., 1995a) on several handwriting recognition systems based on this assumption. The hidden Markov model architecture used in all systems has been extensively presented in (Gilloux et al., 1995a). In that model, word letters are associated to three-states models which are designed to account for the situations where a letter is realized as 0, 1 or 2 segments. Word models are the result of assembling the corresponding letter models. This architecture is depicted on figure 2. We used here transition emission rather than state emission. However, this does not

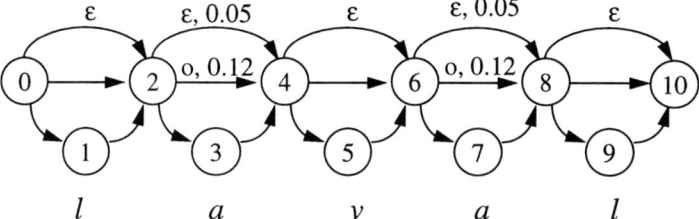

Figure 2: Outline of the model for "*laval*".

change the previous formulas if we replace states by transitions, i.e. pairs of states.

One of these systems was an hybrid RBF/HMM model in which a radial basis function network was used to estimate emission probabilities $p(i_j \mid s_j)$. The RBF outputs are introduced by applying Bayes rule in the expression of $p(i_1...i_n \mid s_1...s_n)$:

$$p(i_1...i_n \mid s_1...s_n) = \prod_{j=1}^{n} \frac{p(s_j \mid i_j) \times p(i_j)}{p(s_j)}$$

Since the product of a priori image segments probabilities $p(i_j)$ does not depend on the word hypothesis w, we may write:

$$p(i_1...i_n \mid s_1...s_n) \propto \prod_{j=1}^{n} \frac{p(s_j \mid i_j)}{p(s_j)}$$

In the above formula, terms of form $p(s_j \mid s_{j-1})$ are transition probabilities which may be estimated through the Baum-Welch re-estimation algorithm. Terms of form $p(s_j)$ are a priori probabilities of states. Note that for Bayes rule to apply, these probabilities have and only have to be estimated consistently with terms of form $p(s_j \mid i_j)$ since $p(i_j \mid s_j)$ is independent of the statistical distribution of states.

It has been proven elsewhere (Richard & Lippman, 1992) that systems trained through the MSE criterion tend to approximate Bayes probabilities in the sense that Bayes probabilities are optimal for the MSE criterion. In practice, the way in which a given system comes close to Bayes optimum is not easily predictable due to various biases of the trained system (initial parameters, local optimum, architecture of the net, etc.). Thus real output scores are generally not equal to Bayes probabilities. However, there exist different procedures which act as a post-processor for outputs of a system trained with the MSE and make them closer to Bayes probabilities (Singer & Lippman, 1992). Provided that such a post-processor is used, we will assume that terms $p(s_j|i_j)$ are well estimated by the post-processed outputs of the recognition system. Then, terms $p(s_j)$ are just the a priori probabilities of states on the set used to train the system or post-process the system outputs.

This hybrid handwritten word recognition system demonstrated better performances than previous systems in which word images were represented through sequences of symbolic features instead of full-fledged bitmaps (Gilloux et al., 1995b). However, some recognition errors remained, many of which could be explained by the simplifying assumptions made in the model. In particular, the fact that emission probabilities depend only on the state corresponding to the current bitmap appeared to be a poor choice. For example, on figure 3 the third and fourth segment are classified as two halves of the letter i. For letters

Figure 3: An image of *trente* classified as *mille*.

segmented in two parts, the second half is naturally correlated to the first (see figure 1). Yet, our Markov model architecture is designed so that both halves are assumed uncorrelated. This has two effects. Two consecutive bitmaps which cannot be the two parts of a unique letter are sometimes recognized as such like on figure 3. Also, the emission probability of the second part of a segmented letter is lower than if the first part has been considered for estimating this probability. The contextual model described in the next section is designed so has to make a different assumption on emission probabilities.

3 THE HYBRID CONTEXTUAL RBF/HMM MODEL

The exact decomposition of the emission part of word likelihoods is the following:

$$p(i_1...i_n|s_1...s_n) = p(i_1|s_1...s_n) \times \prod_{j=2}^{n} p(i_j|s_1...s_n, i_1...i_{j-1})$$

We assume now that bitmaps are conditioned by their state and the previous image in the sequence:

$$p(i_1...i_n|s_1...s_n) \cong p(i_1|s_1) \times \prod_{j=2}^{n} p(i_j|s_j, i_{j-1})$$

The RBF is again introduced by applying Bayes rule in the following way:

$$p(i_1...i_n|s_1...s_n) \cong \frac{p(s_1|i_1) \times p(i_1)}{p(s_1)} \times \prod_{j=2}^{n} \frac{p(s_j|i_j, i_{j-1}) \times p(i_j|i_{j-1})}{p(s_j|i_{j-1})}$$

Since terms of form $p(i_j|i_{j-1})$ do not contribute to the discrimination of word hypotheses, we may write:

$$p(i_1...i_n|s_1...s_n) \propto \frac{p(s_1|i_1)}{p(s_1)} \times \prod_{j=2}^{n} \frac{p(s_j|i_j, i_{j-1})}{p(s_j|i_{j-1})}$$

The RBF has now to estimate not only terms of form $p(s_j | i_j, i_{j-1})$ but also terms like $p(s_j | i_{j-1})$ which are no longer computed by mere counting. Two radial basis function networks are then used to estimate these probabilities. Their common architecture is described in the next section.

4 THE RADIAL BASIS FUNCTION MODEL

The radial basis function model has been described in (Lemarié, 1993). RBF networks are inspired from the theory of regularization (Poggio & Girosi, 1990). This theory studies how multivariate real functions known on a finite set of points may be approximated at these points in a family of parametric functions under some bias of *regularity*. It has been shown that when this bias tends to select smooth functions in the sense that some linear combination of their derivatives is minimum, there exist an analytical solution which is a linear combination of gaussians centred on the points where the function is known (Poggio & Girosi, 1990). It is straightforward to transpose this paradigm to the problem of learning probability distributions given a set of examples.

In practice, the theory is not tractable since it requires one gaussian per example in the training set. Empirical methods (Lemarié, 1993) have been developed which reduce the number of gaussian centres. Since the theory is no longer applicable when the number of centres is reduced, the parameters of the model (centres and covariance matrices for gaussians, weights for the linear combination) have to be trained by another method, in that case the gradient descent method and the MSE criterion. Finally, the resulting RBF model may be looked at like a particular neural network with three layers. The first is the input layer. The second layer is completely connected to the input layer through connections with unit weights. The transfer functions of cells in the second layer are gaussians applied to the weighed distance between the corresponding centres and the weighed input to the cell. The weight of the distance are analogous to the parameters of a diagonal covariance matrix. Finally, the last layer is completely connected to the second one through weighted connections. Cells in this layer just output the sum of their input.

In our experiments, inputs to the RBF are feature vectors of length 138 computed from the bitmaps of a word segment (Lemarié, 1993). The RBF that estimates terms of form $p(s_j | i_j, i_{j-1})$ uses to such vectors as input whereas the second RBF (terms $p(s_j | i_{j-1})$) is only fed with the vector associated to i_{j-1}. These vectors are inspired from "characteristic loci" methods (Gluksman, 1967) and encode the proportion of white pixels from which a bitmap border can be reached without meeting any black pixel in various of directions.

5 EXPERIMENTS

The model has been assessed by applying it to the recognition of words appearing in legal amounts of french postal or bank cheques. The size of the vocabulary is 30 and its perplexity is only 14.3 (Bahl et al., 1983). The training and test bases are made of images of amount words written by unknown writers on real cheques. We used 7 191 images during training and 2 879 different images for test. The image resolution was 300 dpi. The amounts were manually segmented into words and an automatic procedure was used to separate the words from the preprinted lines of the cheque form.

The training was conducted by using the results of the former hybrid system. The segmentation module was kept unchanged. There are 48 140 segments in the training set and 19 577 in the test set. We assumed that the base system is almost always correct when aligning segments onto letter models. We thus used this alignment to label all the segments in the training set and took these labels as the desired outputs for the RBF. We used a set of 63 different labels since 21 letters appear in the amount vocabulary and 3 types of segments are possible for each letter. The outputs of the RBF are directly interpreted as Bayes probabilities without further post-processing.

First of all, we assessed the quality of the system by evaluating its ability to recognize the class of a segment through the value of $p(s_j | i_j, i_{j-1})$ and compared it with that of the previous hybrid system. The results of this experiment are reported on table 1 for the test set. They demonstrate the importance of the context and thus its potential interest for a

Table 1: Recognition and confusion rates for segment classifiers

	Recognition rate	Confusion rate	Mean square error
RBF system without context	32.6%	67.4%	0.828
RBF system with context	41.7%	58.3%	0.739

word recognition system.

We next compare the performance on word recognition on the data base of 2878 images of words. Results are shown in table 2. The first remark is that the system without context

Table 2: Recognition and confusion rates for the word recognition systems

	Recognition rate	Confusion rate	# Confusions
RBF system without context	81,3%	16,7%	536
RBF system with context	76,3%	23,7%	683

present better results than the contextual system. Some of the difference between the systems with and without context are shown below in figures 4 and 5 and may explain why the contextual system remains at a lower level of performance. The word "huit" and "deux" of figure 4 are well recognized by the system without context but badly identified by the contextual system respectively as "trente" and "franc". The image of the word "huit", for example, is segmented into eight segments and each of the four letters of the word is thus necessarily considered as separated in two parts. The fifth and sixth segments are thus recognized as two halves of the letter "i" by the standard system while the contextual system avoids this decomposition of the letter "i". On the next image, the contextual system proposes "ra" for the second and third segments mainly because of the absence of information on the relative position of these segments. On the other hand, figure 5 shows examples where the contextual system outperforms the system without context. In the first case the latter proposed the class "trois" with two halves on the letter "i" on the fifth and sixth segments. In the second case the context is clearly useful for the recognition on the first letter of the word. Forthcoming experiments will try to combine the two systems so as to benefit of their respective characteritics.

 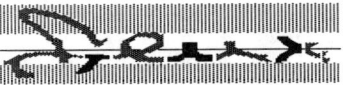

Figure 4 : some new confusions produced by the contextual system.

Experiments have also revealed that the contextual system remains very sensible to the numerical output values for the network which estimates $p(s_j | i_{j-1})$. Several approaches for solving this problem are currently under investigation. First results have yet been obtained by trying to approximate the network which estimates $p(s_j | i_{j-1})$ from the network which estimates $p(s_j | i_j, i_{j-1})$.

6 CONCLUSION

We have described a new application of a hybrid radial basis function/hidden Markov model architecture to the recognition of off-line handwritten words. In this architecture, the estimation of emission probabilities is assigned to a discriminant classifier. The estimation of emission probabilities is enhanced by taking into account the context as represented by the previous bitmap in the sequence to be classified. A formula have been derived introducing this context in the estimation of the likelihood of word scores. The ratio of the output values of two networks are now used so as to estimate the likelihood.

The reported experiments reveal that the use of context, if profitable at the segment recognition level, is not yet useful at the word recognition level. Nevertheless, the new system acts differently from the previous system without context and future applications will try to exploit this difference. The dynamic of the ratio networks output values is also very unstable and some solutions to stabilize it which will be deeply tested in the forthcoming experiences.

References

Bahl L, Jelinek F, Mercer R, (1983). A maximum likelihood approach to speech recognition. *IEEE Transactions on Pattern Analysis and Machine Intelligence* 5(2):179-190.

Bahl LR, Brown PF, de Souza PV, Mercer RL, (1986). Maximum mutual information estimation of hidden Markov model parameters for speech recognition. In: Proc of the Int Conf on Acoustics, Speech, and Signal Processing (ICASSP'86):49-52.

Bourlard, H., Morgan, N., (1993). Continuous speech recognition by connectionist statistical methods, *IEEE Trans. on Neural Networks*, vol. 4, no. 6, pp. 893-909, 1993.

Chen, M.-Y., Kundu, A., Zhou, J., (1994). Off-line handwritten word recognition using a hidden Markov model type stochastic network, *IEEE Trans. on Pattern Analysis and Machine Intelligence*, vol. 16, no. 5:481-496.

Gilloux, M., Leroux, M., Bertille, J.-M., (1993). Strategies for handwritten words recognition using hidden Markov models, Proc. of the 2nd Int. Conf. on Document Analysis and Recognition:299-304.

Gilloux, M., Leroux, M., Bertille, J.-M., (1995a). "Strategies for Cursive Script Recognition Using Hidden Markov Models", *Machine Vision & Applications*, Special issue on Handwriting recognition, R. Plamondon ed., accepted for publication.

Gilloux, M., Lemarié, B., Leroux, M., (1995b). "A Hybrid Radial Basis Function Network/Hidden Markov Model Handwritten Word Recognition System", Proc. of the 3rd Int. Conf. on Document Analysis and Recognition:394-397.

Gluksman, H.A., (1967). Classification of mixed font alphabetics by characteristic loci, 1st Annual IEEE Computer Conf.: 138-141.

Lemarié, B., (1993). Practical implementation of a radial basis function network for handwritten digit recognition, Proc. of the 2nd Int. Conf. on Document Analysis and Recognition:412-415.

Poggio, T., Girosi, F., (1990). Networks for approximation and learning, Proc. of the IEEE, vol 78, no 9.

Richard, M.D., Lippmann, R.P., (1991). "Neural network classifiers estimate bayesian a posteriori probabilities", *Neural Computation*, 3:461-483.

Singer, E, Lippmann, R.P., (1992). A speech recognizer using radial basis function networks in an HMM framework, Proc. of the Int. Conf. on acoustics, Speech, and Signal Processing.

Selective Attention for Handwritten Digit Recognition

Ethem Alpaydın
Department of Computer Engineering
Boğaziçi University
Istanbul, TR–80815 Turkey
alpaydin@boun.edu.tr

Abstract

Completely parallel object recognition is NP-complete. Achieving a recognizer with feasible complexity requires a compromise between parallel and sequential processing where a system selectively focuses on parts of a given image, one after another. Successive fixations are generated to sample the image and these samples are processed and abstracted to generate a temporal context in which results are integrated over time. A computational model based on a partially recurrent feedforward network is proposed and made credible by testing on the real-world problem of recognition of handwritten digits with encouraging results.

1 INTRODUCTION

For all-parallel bottom-up recognition, allocating one separate unit for each possible feature combination, i.e., conjunctive encoding, implies combinatorial explosion. It has been shown that completely parallel, bottom-up visual object recognition is NP-complete (Tsotsos, 1990). By exchanging space with time, systems with much less complexity may be designed. For example, to phone someone at the press of a button, one needs 10^7 buttons on the phone; the sequential alternative is to have 10 buttons on the phone and press one at a time, seven times.

We propose recognition based on selective attention where we analyze only a small part of the image in detail at each step, combining results in time. Noton and Stark's (1971) "scanpath" theory advocates that each object is internally represented as a feature-ring which is a temporal sequence of features extracted at each fixation and the positions or the motor commands for the eye movements in between. In this approach, there is an "eye" that looks at an image but which can really see only a small part of it. This part of the image that is examined in detail is the *fovea*. The

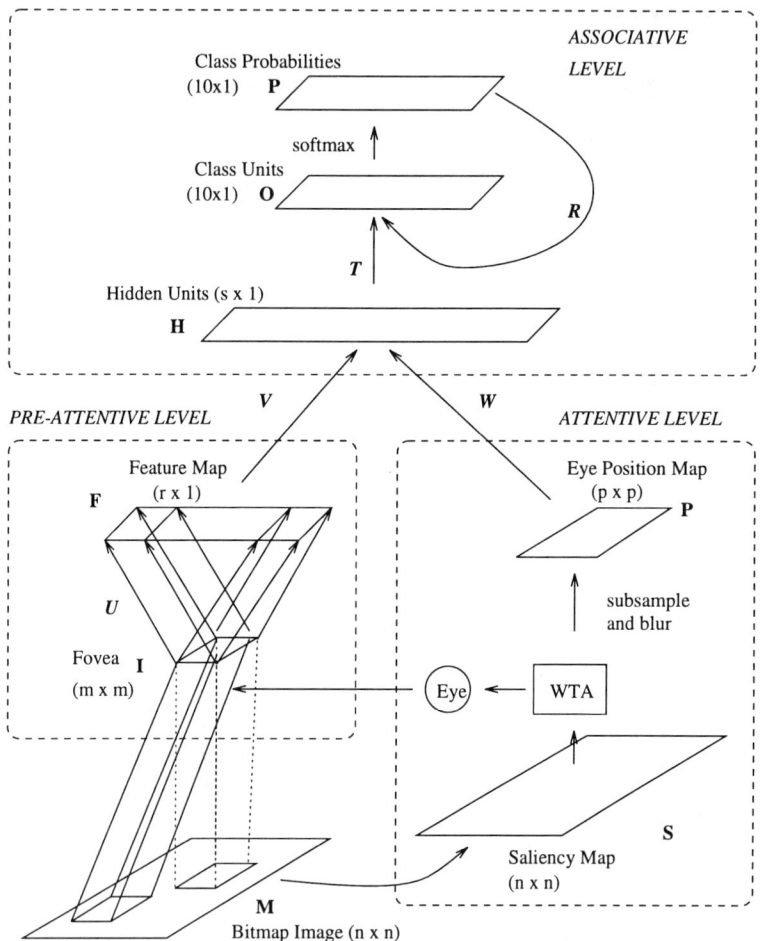

Figure 1: The block diagram of the implemented system.

fovea's content is examined by the *pre-attentive level* where basic feature extraction takes place. The features thus extracted are fed to an *associative* part together with the current eye position. If the accumulated information is not sufficient for recognition, the eye is moved to another part of the image, making a *saccade*. To minimize recognition time, the number of saccades should be minimized. This is done through defining a criterion of being "interesting" or saliency and by fixating only at the most interesting. Thus sucessive fixations are generated to sample the image and these samples are processed and abstracted to generate a temporal context in which results are integrated over time. There is a large amount of literature on selective attention in neuroscience and psychology; for reviews see respectively (Posner and Peterson, 1990) and (Treisman, 1988). The point stressed in this paper is that the approach is also useful in engineering.

2 AN EXAMPLE SYSTEM FOR OCR

The structure of the implemented system for recognition of handwritten digits is given in Fig. 1.

Selective Attention for Handwritten Digit Recognition

We have an $n \times n$ binary image in which the fovea is $m \times m$ with $m < n$. To minimize recognition time, the system should only attend to the parts of the image that carry discriminative information. We define a criterion of being "interesting" or saliency which is applied to all image locations in parallel to generate a *saliency map*, S. The saliency measure should be chosen to draw attention to parts that have the highest information content. Here, the saliency criterion is a low-pass filter which roughly counts the number of *on* pixels in the corresponding $m \times m$ region of the input image M. As the strokes in handwritten digits are mostly one or two pixels wide, a count of the *on* pixels is a good measure of the discontinuity (and thus information). It is also simple to compute:

$$S_{ij} = \sum_{k=i-\lfloor m/2 \rfloor}^{i+\lfloor m/2 \rfloor} \sum_{l=j-\lfloor m/2 \rfloor}^{j+\lfloor m/2 \rfloor} M_{kl} \mathcal{N}_2((i,j)^T, (\lfloor m/6 \rfloor)^2 * I), \quad i,j = 1 \ldots n$$

where $\mathcal{N}_2(\mu, \Sigma)$ is the bivariate normal with mean μ and the covariance Σ. Note that we want the convolution kernel to have effect up to $\lfloor m/2 \rfloor$ and also that the normal is zero after $\mu \pm 3\sigma$. In our simulations where n is 16 and m is 5 (typical for digit recognition), $\sigma \approx 1$. The location that is most salient is the position of the next fixation and as such defines the new center of the fovea. A location once attended to is no longer interesting; after each fixation, the saliency of all the locations that currently are in the scope of the fovea are set to 0 to inhibit another fixation there.

The attentive level thus controls the scope of the pre-attentive level. The maximum of the saliency map through a winner-take-all gives the eye position (i^*, j^*) at fixation t.

$$(i^*(t), j^*(t)) = \arg\max_{i,j} S_{ij}$$

By thus following the salient regions, we get an input-dependent emergent sequence in time.

Eye-Position Map

The *eye position map*, P, stores the position of the eye in the current fixation. It is $p \times p$. p is chosen to be smaller than n for dimensionality reduction for decreasing complexity and introducing an effect of regularization (giving invariance to small translations). When p is a factor of n, computations are also simpler. We also blur the immediate neighbors for a smoother representation:

$$P(t) = \text{blur}(\text{subsample}(\text{winner-take-all}(S)))$$

Pre-Attentive Level: Feature Extraction

The pre-attentive level extracts detailed features from the fovea to generate a *feature map*. This information and the current eye position is passed to the associative system for recognition. There is a trade-off between the fovea size and the number of saccades required for recognition: As the operation in the pre-attentive level is carried out in parallel, to minimize complexity the features extracted there should not be many and the fovea should not be large: Fovea is where the expensive computation takes place. On the other hand, the fovea should be large enough to extract discriminative features and thus complete recognition in a small amount of time. The features to be extracted can be learned through an supervised method when feedback is available.

The $m \times m$ region symmetrically around (i^*, j^*) is extracted as the fovea I and is fed to the feature extractors. The r features extracted there are passed on to the associative level as the feature map, F. r is typically 4 to 8. U_g denote the weights of feature g and F_g is the value of feature g that is found by convolving the fovea input with the feature weight vector ($f(\cdot)$ is the sigmoid function):

$$I_{ij}(t) = M_{i^*(t)-\lfloor m/2 \rfloor+i, j^*(t)-\lfloor m/2 \rfloor+j}, \quad i,j = 1\ldots m$$

$$F_{gij}(t) = f\left(\sum_i \sum_j U_{gij} I_{ij}(t)\right), \quad g = 1\ldots r$$

Associative Level: Classification

At each fixation, the associative level is fed the feature map from the pre-attentive level and the eye position map from the attentive level. As a number of fixations may be necessary to recognize an image, the associative system should have a short-term memory able to accumulate inputs coming through time. Learning similarly should be through time. When used for classification, the class units are organized so as to compete and during recognition the activations of the class units evolve till one class gets sufficiently active and suppresses the others. When a training set is available, a temporal supervised method can be used to train the associative level. Note that there may be more than one scanpath for each object and learning one sequence for each object fails. We see it is a task of accumulating two types of information through time: the "what" (features extracted) and the "where" (eye position).

The fovea map, F, and the eye position map, P, are concatenated to make a $r + p \times p$ dimensional input that is fed to the associative level. Here we use an artificial neural network with one hidden layer of s units. We have experimented with various architectures and noticed that recurrency at the output layer is the best. There are 10 output units.

$$H_h(t) = f\left(\sum_g V_{hg} F_g(t) + \sum_a \sum_b W_{hab} P_{ab}(t)\right), \quad h = 1\ldots s$$

$$O_c(t) = \sum_h T_{ch} H_h + \sum_k R_{ck} P_k(t-1), \quad c = 1\ldots 10$$

$$P_c(t) = \frac{\exp[O_c(t)]}{\sum_k \exp[O_k(t)]}$$

where P denotes the "softmax"ed output probabilities (Bridle, 1990) and $P(t-1)$ are the values in the preceding fixation (initially 0). We use the cross-entropy as the goodness measure:

$$C = \sum_t \frac{1}{t} \sum_c D_k \log P_c(t), \quad t \geq 1$$

D_c is the required output for class c. Learning is gradient-ascent on this goodness measure. The fraction $1/t$ is to give more weight to initial fixations than later ones. Connections to the output units are updated as follows (η is the learning factor):

$$\delta_c(t) = D_c - P_c(t) \quad \Delta T_{ch} = \frac{\eta}{t}\delta_c(t)H_h \quad R_{ck} = \frac{\eta}{t}\delta_c(t)P_k(t-1)$$

Note that we assume $\partial P_k(t-1)/\partial R_{ck} = 0$. For the connections to the hidden units we have:

$$\delta_h(t) = \sum_c \delta_c(t)T_{ch} \quad \Delta V_{hg}(t) = \frac{\eta}{t}\delta_h(t)F_g(t) \quad \Delta W_{hi}(t) = \frac{\eta}{t}\delta_h(t)P_i(t)$$

We can back-propagate one step more to train the feature extractors. Thus the update equations for the connections to feature units are:

$$\delta_g(t) = \sum_h \delta_h(t)V_{hg} \quad \Delta U_{gi}(t) = \frac{\eta}{t}\delta_g(t)I_i(t)$$

A series of fixations are made until one of the class units is sufficiently active: $\exists c, P_c > \theta$ (typically 0.99), or when the most salient point has a saliency less than a certain threshold (this condition is rarely met after the first few epochs). Then the computed changes are summed up and the updates are made like the exaple below:

$$\Delta T_{ch} = \sum_t \Delta T_{ch}(t)$$

Backpropagation through time where the recurrent connections are unfolded in time did not work well in this task because as explained before, for the same class, there is more than one scanpath. The above-mentioned approach is like real-time recurrent learning (Williams and Zipser, 1989) where the partial derivatives in the previous time step is 0, thus ignoring this temporal dependence.

3 RESULTS AND DISCUSSION

We have experimented with various parameter settings and finally chose the architecture given above: When input is 16 × 16 and there are 10 classes, the fovea is 5 × 5 with 8 features and there are 16 hidden units. There are 1,934 images for training, 946 for cross-validation and 943 for testing. Results are given in Table 1. ' It can be seen that by scanning less than half of the image, we get 80% generalization. Additional to the local high-resolution image provided by the fovea, a low-resolution image of the surrounding parafovea can be given to the associative level for better recognition. For example we low-pass filtered and undersampled the original image to get a 4 × 4 image which we fed to the class units additional to the attention-based hidden units. Success went up quite high and fewer fixations were necessary; compare rows 1 and 2 of the Table. The information provided by the 4 × 4 map is actually not much as can be seen from row 3 of the table where only that is given as input. Thus the idea is that when we have a coarse input, looking only at a quarter of the image in detail is sufficient to get 93% accuracy. Both features (what) and eye positions (where) are necessary for good recognition. When only one is used without the other, success is quite low as can be seen in rows 4 and 5. In the last row, we see the performance of a multi layer perceptron with 10 hidden units that does all-parallel recognition.

Beyond a certain network size, increasing the number of features do not help much. Decreasing θ, the certainty threshold, decreases the number of fixations necessary

Table 1: Results of handwritten digit recognition with selective attention. Values given are average and standard deviation of 10 independent runs. See text for comments.

METHOD	NO OF PARAMS	TEST SUCCESS	TRAINING EPOCHS	NO OF FIXATIONS
SA system	878	79.7, 1.8	74.5, 17.1	6.5, 0.2
SA+parafovea	1,038	92.5, 0.8	54.2, 10.2	3.9, 0.3
Only parafovea	170	86.9, 0.2	52.3, 8.2	1.0, 0.0
Only what info	622	49.0, 21.0	66.6, 30.6	7.5, 0.1
Only where info	440	54.2, 1.4	92.9, 6.5	7.6, 0.0
MLP, 10 hiddens	2,680	95.1, 0.6	13.5, 4.1	1.0, 0.0

which we want, but decreases success too which we don't. Smaller foveas decrease the number of free parameters but decrease success and require a larger number of fixations. Similarly larger foveas decrease the number of fixations but increase complexity.

The simple low-pass filter used here as a saliency measure is the simplest measure. Previously it has been used by Fukushima and Imagawa (1993) for finding the next character, i.e., segmentation, and also by Olshausen et al. (1992) for translation invariance. More robust measures at the expense of more computations, are possible; see (Rimey and Brown, 1990; Milanese et al., 1993). Salient regions are those that are conspicious, i.e., different from their surrounding where there is a change in X where X can be brightness or color (edges), orientation (corners), time (motion), etc. It is also possible that top-down, task-dependent saliency measures be integrated to minimize further recognition time implying a remembered explicit sequence analogous to skilled motor behaviour (probably gained after many repetitions).

Here a partially recurrent network is used for temporal processing. Hidden Markov Models like used in speech recognition are another possibility (Rimey and Brown, 1990; Hacısalihzade et al., 1992). They are probabilistic finite automata which can be trained to classify sequences and one can have more than one model for an object.

It should be noted here that better approaches for the same problem exists (Le Cun et al., 1989). Here we advocate a computational model and make it plausible by testing it on a real-world problem. It is necessary for more complicated problems where an all-parallel approach would not work. For example Le Cun et al.'s model for the same type of inputs has 2,578 free parameters. Here there are

$$\underbrace{(m \times m + 1) \times r}_{U} + \underbrace{(r + p \times p + 1) \times s}_{V+W} + \underbrace{(s+1) \times 10}_{T} + \underbrace{10 \times 10}_{R}$$

free parameters which make 878 when $m = 5, r = 8, s = 16$. This is the main advantage of selective attention which is that the complexity of the system is heavily reduced at the expense of slower recognition, both in overt form of attention through foveation and in its covert form, for binding features — For this latter type of attention not discussed here, see (Ahmad, 1992). Also note that low-level feature extraction operations like carried out in the pre-attentive level are local convolutions and are appropriate for parallel processing, e.g., on a SIMD machine. Higher-level operations require larger connectivity and are better carried out sequentially. Nature also seems to have taken this direction.

Acknowledgements

This work is supported by Tübitak Grant EEEAG-143 and Boğaziçi University Research Funds 95HA108. Cenk Kaynak prepared the handwritten digit database based on the programs provided by NIST (Garris et al., 1994).

References

S. Ahmad. (1992) VISIT: A Neural Model of Covert Visual Attention. In J. Moody, S. Hanson, R. Lippman (Eds.) *Advances in Neural Information Processing Systems 4*, 420–427. San Mateo, CA: Morgan Kaufmann.

J.S. Bridle. (1990) Probabilistic Interpretation of Feedforward Classification Network Outputs with Relationships to Statistical Pattern Recognition. In *Neurocomputing*, F. Fogelman-Soulié, J. Hérault, Eds. Springer, Berlin, 227–236.

K. Fukushima, T. Imagawa. (1993) Recognition and Segmentation of Connected Characters with Selective Attention, *Neural Networks*, **6**: 33–41.

M.D. Garris et al. (1994) NIST Form-Based Handprint Recognition System, NIS-TIR 5469, NIST Computer Systems Laboratory.

S.S. Hacısalihzade, L.W. Stark, J.S. Allen. (1992) Visual Perception and Sequences of Eye Movement Fixations: A Stochastic Modeling Approach, *IEEE SMC*, **22**, 474–481.

Y. Le Cun et al. (1991) Handwritten Digit Recognition with a Back-Propagation Network. In D.S. Touretzky (ed.) *Advances in Neural Information Processing Systems 2*, 396–404. San Mateo, CA: Morgan Kaufmann.

R. Milanese et al. (1994) Integration of Bottom-Up and Top-Down Cues for Visual Attention using Non-Linear Relaxation *IEEE Int'l Conf on CVPR*, Seattle, WA, USA.

D. Noton and L. Stark. (1971) Eye Movements and Visual Perception, *Scientific American*, **224**: 34–43.

B. Olshausen, C. Anderson, D. Van Essen. (1992) *A Neural Model of Visual Attention and Invariant Pattern Recognition*, CNS Memo 18, CalTech.

M.I. Posner, S.E. Petersen. (1990) The Attention System of the Human Brain, *Ann. Rev. Neurosci.*, **13**:25–42.

R.D. Rimey, C.M. Brown. (1990) *Selective Attention as Sequential Behaviour: Modelling Eye Movements with an Augmented Hidden Markov Model*, TR-327, Computer Science, Univ of Rochester.

A. Treisman. (1988) Features and Objects, *Quarterly Journ. of Exp. Psych.*, **40**: 201–237.

J.K. Tsotsos. (1990) Analyzing Vision at the Complexity Level, *Behav. and Brain Sci.* **13**: 423–469.

R.J. Williams, D. Zipser. (1989) A Learning Algorithm for Continually Running Fully Recurrent Neural Networks *Neural Computation*, **1**, 270–280.

KODAK IMAGELINK™ OCR
Alphanumeric Handprint Module

Alexander Shustorovich and Christopher W. Thrasher
Business Imaging Systems, Eastman Kodak Company, Rochester, NY 14653-5424

ABSTRACT

This paper describes the Kodak Imagelink ™ OCR alphanumeric handprint module. There are two neural network algorithms at its core: the first network is trained to find individual characters in an alphanumeric field, while the second one performs the classification. Both networks were trained on Gabor projections of the original pixel images, which resulted in higher recognition rates and greater noise immunity. Compared to its purely numeric counterpart (Shustorovich and Thrasher, 1995), this version of the system has a significant application specific postprocessing module. The system has been implemented in specialized parallel hardware, which allows it to run at 80 char/sec/board. It has been installed at the Driver and Vehicle Licensing Agency (DVLA) in the United Kingdom, and its overall success rate exceeds 96% (character level without rejects), which translates into 85% field rate. If approximately 20% of the fields are rejected, the system achieves 99.8% character and 99.5% field success rate.

1 INTRODUCTION

The system we describe below was designed to process alphanumeric fields extracted from forms. The major assumptions were that (1) the form layout and definition allows the system to capture the field image with a single line of characters, (2) the characters are handprinted capital letters and numerals, with possible addition of several special characters, and (3) the characters may occasionally touch, but generally they do not overlap. We also assume that some additional information about the contents of the field is available to assist in the process of disambiguation. Otherwise, it is virtually impossible to distinguish not only between " O " and zero, but also " I " and one, " Z " and two, " S " and five, etc.

A good example of such an application is the processing of vehicle registration forms at the Driver and Vehicle Licensing Agency (DVLA) in the United Kingdom. The alphanumeric field in question contains a license plate. There are 29 allowed patterns of character combinations, from two to seven characters long. For example, " A999AAA " is a valid license, whereas " A9A9A9 " is not (here " A " stands for any alpha character, " 9 " - for any numeric character). In addition, every field has a control character box on the right. This control character is computed as a remainder of the integer division by 37 of a linear combination of numeric values of the characters in the main field. Ambiguous characters, namely " O ", " I ", and " S " are not allowed in the role of the control character, so they are replaced here by " - ", " + ", and " / " (not a very good choice, and the 37th character used is the " % ". To make things more complicated, sometimes the control character is not available at the moment of filing the form (at a local post office), and this lack of knowledge is indicated by putting an asterisk instead. Later we will discuss possible ways to use this additional information in an application specific postprocessing module.

2 SEGMENTATION AND ALTERNATIVE APPROACHES

The most challenging problem for handprint OCR is finding individual characters in a field. A number of approaches to this problem can be found in the literature, the two most common being (1) segmentation (Gupta et al., 1993, as an example of a recent publication), and (2) combined segmentation and recognition (Keeler and Rumelhart, 1992).

The segmentation approach has difficulty separating touching characters, and recently the consensus of practitioners in the field started shifting towards combined segmentation and recognition. In this scheme, the algorithm moves a window of a certain width along the field, and confidence values of competing classification hypotheses are used (sometimes with a separate centered/noncentered node) to decide if the window is positioned on top of a character. In the Saccade system (Martin et al., 1993), for example, the neural network was trained not only to recognize characters in the center of the moving window (and whether there is a character centered in the window), but also to make corrective jumps (saccades) to the nearest character and, after classification, to the next character.

Still another variation on the theme is an arrangement when the classification window is duplicated with one- or several-pixel shifts along the field (Benjio et al., 1994). Then the outputs of the classifiers serve as input for a postprocessing module (in this paper, a Hidden Markov Model) used to decide which of the multitude of processing windows actually have centered characters in them.

All these approaches have deficiencies. As we mentioned earlier, touching characters are difficult for autonomous segmenters. The moving (and jumping) window with a single centered/noncentered node tends to miss narrow characters and sometimes to duplicate wide ones. The replication of a classifier together with postprocessing tends to be quite expensive computationally.

3 POSITIONING NETWORK

To do the positioning, we decided to introduce an array of output units corresponding to successive pixels in the middle portion of the window. These nodes signal if a center ("heart") of a character lies at the corresponding positions. Because the precision with which a human operator can mark the character heart is low (usually within one or two pixels at best), the target activations of three consecutive nodes are set to one if there is a character heart at a pixel position corresponding to the middle node. The rest of the target activations are set to zero.

The network is then trained to produce bumps of activation indicating the character hearts. Two buffer regions on the left and on the right of the window (pixels without corresponding output nodes) are necessary to allow all or most of the character centered at each of the output node positions to fit inside the window. The replacement of a single centered/noncentered node by an array allows us to average output activations, generated by different window shifts, while corresponding to the same position. This additional procedure allows us to slide the window several pixels at a time: the appropriate step is a trade-off between the processing speed and the required level of robustness. The final procedure involves thresholding of the activation-wave and the estimation of the predicted character position as the center of mass of the activation-bubble. The resulting algorithm is very effective: touching characters do not present significant problems, and only abnormally wide characters sometimes fool the system into false alarms.

The system works with preprocessed images. Each field is divided into subfields of disconnected groups of characters. These subfields are size-normalized to a height of 20 pixels. After that they are reassembled into a single field again, with 6 pixel gaps between them. Two blank rows are added both along the top and the bottom of the recombined field as preferred by the Gabor projection technique (Shustorovich, 1994). In our current system, the input nodes of a sliding window are organized in a 24 x 36 array. The first, intermediary, layer of the network implements the Gabor projections. It has 12 x 12 local receptive fields (LRFs) with fixed precomputed weights. The step between LRFs is 6 pixels in both directions. We work with 16 Gabor basis functions with circular Gaussian envelopes centered within each LRF; they are both sine and cosine wavelets in four orientations and two sizes. All 16 projections from each LRF constitute the input to a column of 20 hidden units, thus the second (first trainable) hidden layer is organized in a three-dimensional array 3 x 5 x 20. The third hidden layer of the network also has local receptive fields, they are three-dimensional 2 x 2 x 20 with the step 1 x 1 x 0. The units in the third hidden layer are also duplicated 20 times, thus this layer is organized in a three-dimensional array 2 x 4 x 20. The fourth hidden layer has 60 units fully connected to the third layer. Finally, the output layer has 12 units, also fully connected to the fourth layer.

The network was trained using a variant of the Back-Propagation algorithm. Both training and testing sets were drawn from the field data collected at DVLA. The training set contained approximately 60,000 characters from 8,000 fields, and about 5,000 characters from 650 fields were used for testing. On this test set, more than 92% of all character hearts were found within 1-pixel precision, and only 0.4% were missed by more than 4 pixels.

4 CLASSIFICATION NETWORK

The structure of the classification network resembles that of the positioning network. The Gabor projection layer works in exactly the same way, but the window size is smaller, only 24 x 24 pixels. We chose this size because after height normalization to 20 pixels, only occasionally the characters are wider than 24 pixels. Widening the window complicates training: it increases the dimensionality of the input while providing information, mostly about irrelevant pieces of adjacent characters. As a result, the second layer is organized as a 3 x 3 x 20 array of units with LRFs and shared weights, the third is a 2 x 2 x 20 array of units with LRFs, and there are 37 output units fully connected to the 80 units in the third layer. The number of output units in this variant of our system has been determined by the intended application. It was necessary to recognize uppercase letters, numerals, and also five special characters, namely plus (+), minus (-), slash (/), percent (%), and asterisk (*). Since additional information was available for the purposes of disambiguation, we combined " O " and zero, " I " and one, " Z " and two, " S " and five, and so the number of output classes became 26 (alpha) + 6 (numerals 3,4,6,7,8,9) + 5 (special characters) = 37.

Because we did not expect any positioning module to provide precision higher than 1 or 2 pixels, the classifier network was trained and tested on five copies of all centered characters in the database, with shifts of 0, 1, and 2 pixels, both left and right. On the same test set mentioned in the previous section, the corresponding character recognition rates averaged 93.0%, 95.5%, and 96.0% for characters normalized to the height of 18 to 20 pixels and placed in the middle of the window with shifts of 0 and 1 pixel up and down.

5 POSTPROCESSING MODULE

The postprocessing module is a rule-based algorithm. First, it monitors the width of each subfield and rejects it if the number of predicted character hearts is inconsistent with the width. For example, if the positioning system cannot find a single character in a subfield, the output of the system becomes a question mark. Second, the postprocessing module organizes competition between predicted character hearts if they are too close to each other. For example, it will kill a predicted center with a lower activation value if its distance from a competitor is less than ten pixels, but it may allow both to survive if one of the two labels is "one". It is especially sensitive to closely positioned centers with identical labels, and will remove the weaker one for wide characters such as " W " or " M ".

The rest of the postprocessing had to rely on the application knowledge. Since the alphanumeric fields on DVLA forms contain license plates, we could use the fact that there are exactly 29 allowed patterns of symbol combinations, and that correct strings should match control characters from the box on the right.

Because in this application rejection of individual characters is meaningless, we decided to keep and analyze all possible candidates for each detected position, that is, characters with output activations above a certain threshold (currently, 0.1). Of course, special characters are not allowed in the main field. The field as a whole is rejected if for any one position there is not even a single candidate character. All possible combinations of candidate characters are analyzed. A candidate string is rejected if it does not conform to any of allowed patterns, or if it does not match any of the candidate control characters. All remaining candidate strings are assigned confidences. Since a chain is no stronger than its weakest link, in the case of an asterisk (no control character information), the string confidence equals that of its least confident character. If there is a valid control character, then we can tolerate one low-confidence character, and so the string confidence equals that of its character with the second lowest individual confidence. If there are two or more candidate strings, the difference in confidence between the best and the second best is compared to another threshold (currently, 0.7) in order to pass the final round of rejects.

6 CONCLUSIONS

Kodak Imagelink™ OCR alphanumeric handprint module described in this paper uses one neural network to find individual characters in a field, and then the second network performs the classification. The outputs of both networks are interpreted by a postprocessing module that generates the final label string (Figure 1, Figure 2).

The algorithms were designed within the constraints of the planned hardware implementation. At the same time, they provide a high level of positioning accuracy as well as classification ability. One new feature of our approach is the use of an array of centered/noncentered nodes to significantly improve speed and robustness of the positioning scheme. The overall robustness of the system is further improved by noise resistance provided by a layer of Gabor projection units. The positioning module and the classification module are unified by the postprocessing module.

System-level testing was performed on a test set mentioned above. The image quality was generally very good, but the data included some fields with touching characters. The character level success rate (without rejects) achieved on this test exceeded 96%, which corresponded to above 85% field rate. With approximately 20% of the fields rejected, the system achieved 99.8% character and 99.5% field success rate.

In the testing mode, the preprocessing module would separate characters if it can reliably do so, normalize them individually, and place them with gaps of ten blank pixels, in order to simplify the job of both the positioning and the classification modules. When it is impossible to segment individual characters, our system is still able to perform on the level of approximately 94% (since it has been trained on such data). The robustness of our system is an important factor in its success. Most other systems have substantial difficulties trying to recover from errors in segmentation.

References

Benjio, Y., Le Cun, Y., and Henderson, D. (1994) Globally Trained Handwritten Word Recognizer Using Spatial Representation, Space Displacement Neural Networks and Hidden Markov Models. In Cowan, J.D., Tesauro, G., and Alspector, J. (eds.), *Advances in Neural Information Processing Systems 6,* pp. 937-944. San Mateo, CA: Morgan Kaufmann Publishers.

Gupta, A., Nagendraprasad, M.V., Liu, A., Wang, P.S.P., and Ayyadurai, S. (1993) An Integrated Architecture for Recognition of Totally Unconstrained Handwritten Numerals. *International Journal of Pattern Recognition and Artificial Intelligence* 7 (4), pp. 757-773.

Keeler, J. and Rumelhart, D.E. (1992) A Self-Organizing Integrated Segmentation and Recognition Neural Net. In Moody, J.E., Hanson, S.J., and Lippmann, R.P. (eds.), *Advances in Neural Information Processing Systems 4,* pp. 496-503. San Mateo, CA: Morgan Kaufmann Publishers.

Martin, G., Mosfeq, R., Chapman, D., and Pittman, J. (1993) Learning to See Where and What: Training a Net to Make Saccades and Recognize Handwritten Characters. In Hanson, S.J., Cowan, J.D., and Giles, C.L. (eds.), *Advances in Neural Information Processing Systems 5,* pp. 441-447. San Mateo, CA: Morgan Kaufmann Publishers.

Shustorovich, A. (1994) A Subspace Projection Approach to Feature Extraction: the Two-Dimensional Gabor Transform for Character Recognition. *Neural Networks* 7 (8), 1295-1301.

Shustorovich, A. and Thrasher, C.W. (1995) KODAK IMAGELINK^{TM} OCR Numeric Handprint Module: Neural Network Positioning and Classification. Proceedings of Session 11 (Document Processing) of the industrial conference of *ICANN-95* Paris, October 9-13, 1995.

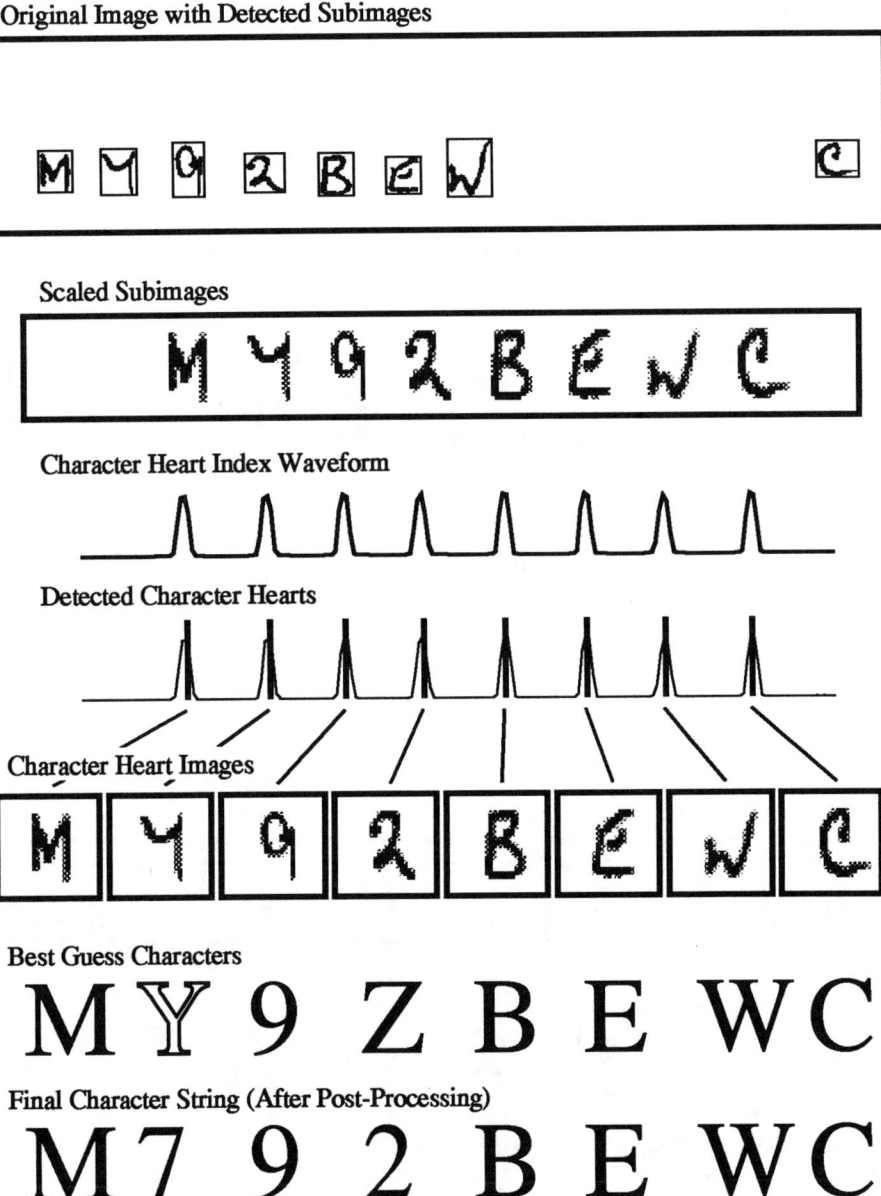

Figure 1: An Example of a Field Processed by the System
Outline characters indicate low confidence.

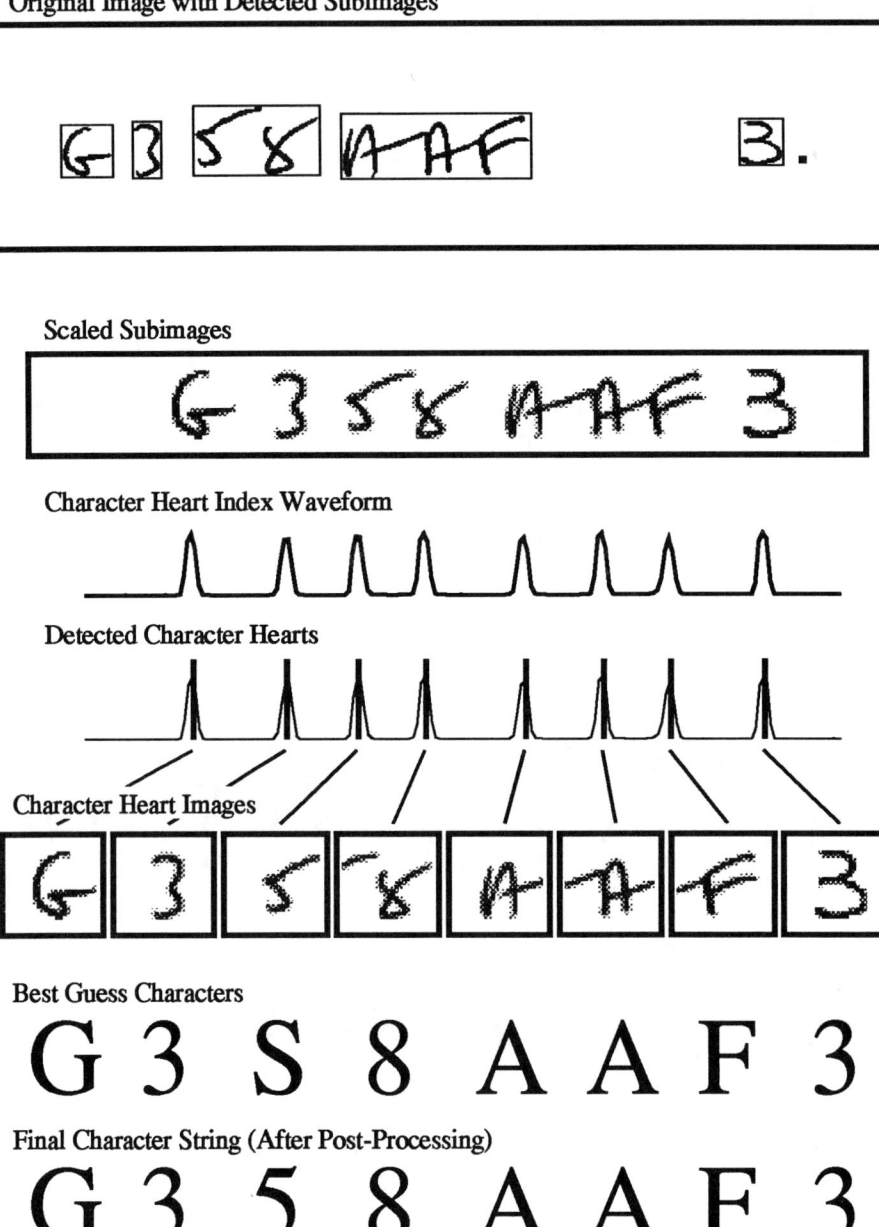

Figure 2: Another Example of a Field Processed by the System.

The Gamma MLP for Speech Phoneme Recognition

Steve Lawrence*, Ah Chung Tsoi, Andrew D. Back
{lawrence,act,back}@elec.uq.edu.au

Department of Electrical and Computer Engineering
University of Queensland
St. Lucia Qld 4072 Australia

Abstract

We define a Gamma multi-layer perceptron (MLP) as an MLP with the usual synaptic weights replaced by gamma filters (as proposed by de Vries and Principe (de Vries and Principe, 1992)) and associated gain terms throughout all layers. We derive gradient descent update equations and apply the model to the recognition of speech phonemes. We find that both the inclusion of gamma filters in all layers, and the inclusion of synaptic gains, improves the performance of the Gamma MLP. We compare the Gamma MLP with TDNN, Back-Tsoi FIR MLP, and Back-Tsoi IIR MLP architectures, and a local approximation scheme. We find that the Gamma MLP results in an substantial reduction in error rates.

1 INTRODUCTION

1.1 THE GAMMA FILTER

Infinite Impulse Response (IIR) filters have a significant advantage over Finite Impulse Response (FIR) filters in signal processing: the length of the impulse response is uncoupled from the number of filter parameters. The length of the impulse response is related to the memory depth of a system, and hence IIR filters allow a greater memory depth than FIR filters of the same order. However, IIR filters are

---
*http://www.neci.nj.nec.com/homepages/lawrence

not widely used in practical adaptive signal processing. This may be attributed to the fact that a) there could be instability during training and b) the gradient descent training procedures are not guaranteed to locate the global optimum in the possibly non-convex error surface (Shynk, 1989).

De Vries and Principe proposed using gamma filters (de Vries and Principe, 1992), a special case of IIR filters, at the input to an otherwise standard MLP. The gamma filter is designed to retain the uncoupling of memory depth to the number of parameters provided by IIR filters, but to have simple stability conditions.

The output of a neuron in a multi-layer perceptron is computed using[1] $y_k^l = f\left(\sum_{i=0}^{N_{l-1}} w_{ki}^l y_i^{l-1}\right)$. De Vries and Principe consider adding short term memory with delays: $y_k^l = f\left(\sum_{i=0}^{N_{l-1}} \sum_{j=0}^{K} g_{kij}^l(t-j) y_i^{l-1}(t-j)\right)$ where $g_{kij}^l = \frac{\mu_{ki}^l}{(j-1)!} t^{j-1} e^{-\mu_{ki}^l t}$ $j = 1, ..., K$. The depth of the memory is controlled by μ, and K is the order of the filter. For the discrete time case, we obtain the recurrence relation: $z_0(t) = x(t)$ and $z_j(t) = (1-\mu) z_j(t-1) + \mu z_{j-1}(t-1)$ for $j = 1, ..., K$. In this form, the gamma filter can be interpreted as a cascaded series of filter modules, where each module is a first order IIR filter with the transfer function $\frac{\mu}{q-(1-\mu)}$, where $qz_j(t) \triangleq z_j(t+1)$. We have a filter with K poles, all located at $1-\mu$. Thus, the gamma filter may be considered as a low pass filter for $\mu < 1$. The value of μ can be fixed, or it can be adapted during training.

2 NETWORK MODELS

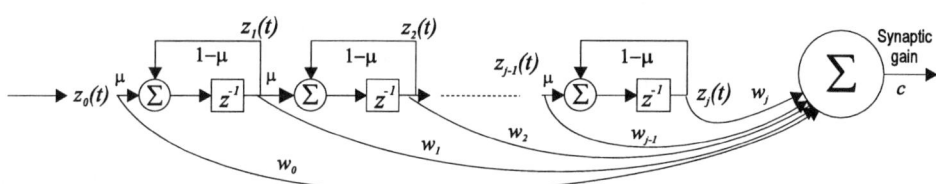

Figure 1: A gamma filter synapse with an associated gain term 'c'.

We have defined a gamma MLP as a multi-layer perceptron where every synapse contains a gamma filter and a gain term, as shown in figure 1. The motivation behind the inclusion of the gain term is discussed later. A separate μ parameter is used for each filter. Update equations are derived in a manner analogous to the standard MLP and can be found in Appendix A. The model is defined as follows.

---

[1]where y_k^l is the output of neuron k in layer l, N_l is the number of neurons in layer l, w_{ki}^l is the weight connecting neuron k in layer l to neuron i in layer $l-1$, $y_0^l = 1$ (bias), and f is commonly a sigmoid function.

The Gamma MLP for Speech Phoneme Recognition

Definition 1 A Gamma MLP with L layers excluding the input layer $(0, 1, ..., L)$, gamma filters of order K, and $N_0, N_1, ..., N_L$ neurons per layer, is defined as

$$
\begin{aligned}
y_k^l(t) &= f\left(x_k^l(t)\right) \\
x_k^l(t) &= \sum_{i=0}^{N_{l-1}} c_{ki}^l(t) \sum_{j=0}^{K} w_{kij}^l(t) z_{kij}^l(t) \\
z_{kij}^l(t) &= (1 - \mu_{ki}^l(t)) z_{kij}^l(t-1) + \mu_{ki}^l(t) z_{ki(j-1)}^l(t-1) \quad 1 \leq j \leq K \\
z_{kij}^l(t) &= y_i^{l-1}(t) \qquad\qquad\qquad\qquad\qquad\qquad\qquad\qquad j = 0
\end{aligned}
\tag{1}
$$

where $y(t)$ = neuron output, c_{ki}^l = synaptic gain, $f(\alpha) = \frac{e^{\alpha/2} - e^{-\alpha/2}}{e^{\alpha/2} + e^{-\alpha/2}}$, $k = 1, 2, ..., N_l$(neuron index), $l = 0, 1, ..., L$(layer), and $z_{kij}^l|_{i=0} = 1, w_{kij}^l|_{i=0, j \neq 0} = 0, c_{kij}^l|_{i=0} = 1$(bias).

□

For comparison purposes, we have used the TDNN (Time Delay Neural Network) architecture[2], the Back-Tsoi FIR[3] and IIR MLP architectures (Back and Tsoi, 1991a) where every synapse contains an FIR or IIR filter and a gain term, and the local approximation algorithm used by Casdagli (k-NN LA) (Casdagli, 1991)[4]. The Gamma MLP is a special case of the IIR MLP.

3 TASK

3.1 MOTIVATION

Accurate speech recognition requires models which can account for a high degree of variability in the data. Large amounts of data may be available but it may be impractical to use all of the information in standard neural network models.

Hypothesis: As the complexity of a problem increases (higher dimensionality, greater variety of training data), the error surface of a neural network becomes more complex. It may contain a number of local minima[5] many of which may be much worse than the global minimum. The training (parameter estimation) algorithms become "stuck" in local minima which may be increasingly poor compared to the global optimum. The problem suffers from the so called "curse of dimensionality" and the

---

[2] We use TDNN to refer to an MLP with a time window of inputs, not the replicated architecture introduced by Lang (Lang et al., 1990).

[3] We distinguish the Back-Tsoi FIR network from the Wan FIR network in that the Wan architecture has no synaptic gains, and the update algorithms are different. The Back-Tsoi update algorithm has provided better convergence in previous experiments.

[4] Casdagli created an affine model of the following form for each test pattern: $y^j = \alpha_0 + \sum_{i=1}^{n} \alpha_i x_i^j$, where k is the number of neighbors, $j = 1, \ldots, k$, and n is the input dimension. The resulting model is used to find y for the test pattern.

[5] We note that it can be difficult to distinguish a true local minimum from a long plateau in the standard backpropagation algorithm.

difficulty in optimizing a function with limited control over the nature of the error surface.

We can identify two main reasons why the application of the Gamma MLP may be superior to the standard TDNN for speech recognition: a) the gamma filtering operation allows consideration of the input data using different time resolutions and can account for more past history of the signal which can only be accounted for in an FIR or TDNN system by increasing the dimensionality of the model, and b) the low pass filtering nature of the gamma filter may create a smoother function approximation task, and therefore a smoother error surface for gradient descent[6].

3.2 TASK DETAILS

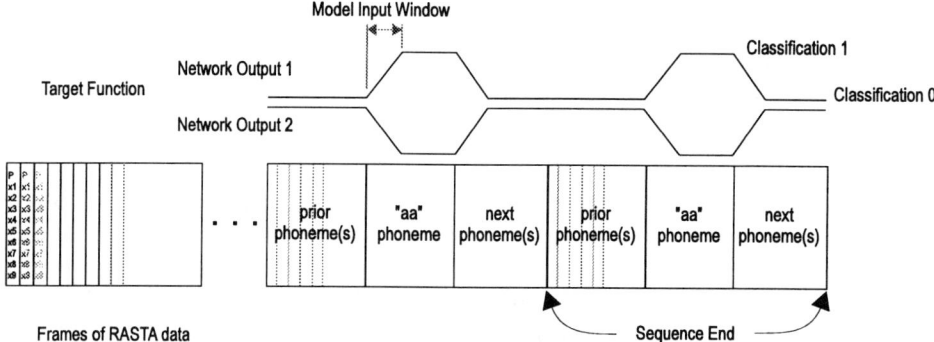

Figure 2: PLP input data format and the corresponding network target functions for the phoneme "aa".

Our data consists of phonemes extracted from the TIMIT database and organized as a number of sequences as shown in figure 2 (example for the phoneme "aa"). One model is trained for each phoneme. Note that the phonemes are classified in context, with a number of different contexts, and that the surrounding phonemes are labelled only as not belonging to the target phoneme class. Raw speech data was pre-processed into a sequence of frames using the RASTA-PLP v2.0 software[7]. We used the default options for PLP analysis. The analysis window (frame) was 20 ms. Each succeeding frame overlaps with the preceding frame by 10 ms. 9 PLP coefficients together with the signal power are extracted and used as features describing each frame of data. Phonemes used in the current tests were the vowel "aa" and the fricative "s". The phonemes were extracted from speakers coming from the same demographic region in the TIMIT database. Multiple speakers were used and the speakers used in the test set were not contained in the training set. The training set contained 4000 frames, where each phoneme is roughly 10 frames. The test set contained 2000 frames, and an additional validation set containing 2000 frames was used to control generalization.

---

[6]If we consider a very simple network and derive the relationship of the smoothness of the required function approximation to the smoothness of the error surface this statement appears to be valid. However, it is difficult to show a direct relationship for general networks.

[7]Obtained from ftp://ftp.icsi.berkeley.edu/pub/speech/rasta2.0.tar.Z.

The Gamma MLP for Speech Phoneme Recognition   789

4 RESULTS

Two outputs were used in the neural networks as shown by the target functions in figure 2, corresponding to the phoneme being present or not. A confidence criterion was used: $y_{max} \times (y_{max} - y_{min})$ (for softmax outputs). The initial learning rate was 0.1, 10 hidden nodes were used, FIR and Gamma orders were 5 (6 taps), the TDNN and k-NN models had an input window of 6 steps in time, the $tanh$ activation function was used, target outputs were scaled between -0.8 and 0.8, stochastic update was used, and initial weights were chosen from a set of candidates based on training set performance. The learning rate was varied over time according to the schedule:

$$\eta = \eta_0 / \left(\frac{n}{N/2} + \frac{c_1}{max\left(1, (c_1 - \frac{max(0, c_1(n - c_2 N))}{(1 - c_2)N}\right)} \right)$$

where η = learning rate, η_0 = initial learning rate, N = total epochs, n = current epoch, $c_1 = 50$, $c_2 = 0.65$. This is similar to the schedule proposed in (Darken and Moody, 1991) with an additional term to decrease the learning rate towards zero over the final epochs[8].

Train Error %	2-NN	5-NN	1st layer		All layers		Gains, 1st layer		Gains, all layers	
FIR MLP			17.6	0.43	14.5	1.5	27.2	0.59	40.9	19.8
Gamma MLP			7.78	0.39	5.73	0.88	6.07	0.12	5.63	1.68
TDNN									14.4	0.86
k-NN LA	0	0								

Test Error %	2-NN	5-NN	1st layer		All layers		Gains, 1st layer		Gains, all layers	
FIR MLP			22.2	0.97	20.4	0.61	29	0.14	41	21
Gamma MLP			14.7	0.16	13.5	0.33	12.8	1.0	12.7	0.50
TDNN									24.5	0.68
k-NN LA	31	28.4								

Test False +ve	2-NN	5-NN	1st layer		All layers		Gains, 1st layer		Gains, all layers	
FIR MLP			13.5	0.67	11.4	2.0	4.5	0.77	31.3	49.0
Gamma MLP			7.94	0.45	7.01	0.47	6.83	0.34	8.05	1.8
TDNN									13	0.27
k-NN LA	22.6	17.4								

Test False -ve	2-NN	5-NN	1st layer		All layers		Gains, 1st layer		Gains, all layers	
FIR MLP			44.9	2.6	44.1	5.6	92.9	2.4	66.4	53
Gamma MLP			32.2	1.2	30.4	2.2	28.4	2.8	24.7	4.4
TDNN									54.6	1.8
k-NN LA	53	56.8								

Table 1: Results comparing the architectures and the use of filters in all layers and synaptic gains for the FIR and Gamma MLP models. The NMSE is followed by the standard deviation. The TDNN results are listed under an arbitrary column heading (gains and 1st layer/all layers does not apply).

The results of the simulations are shown in table 1[9]. Each result represents an average over four simulations with different random seeds - the standard deviation of the four individual results is also shown. The FIR and Gamma MLP networks have been tested both with and without synaptic gains, and with and without filters in the output layer synapses. These results are for the models trained on the "s" phoneme, results for the "aa" phoneme exhibit the same trend. "Test false negative" is probably the most important result here, and is shown graphically in figure 3. This is the percentage of times a true classification (ie. the current

---

[8]Without this term we have encountered considerable parameter fluctuation over the last epoch.

[9]NMSE $= \sum_{k=1}^{N} (d(k) - y(k))^2 / \left(\sum_{k=1}^{N} \left(d(k) - \left(\sum_{k=1}^{N} d(k) \right) / N \right)^2 \right) / N$.

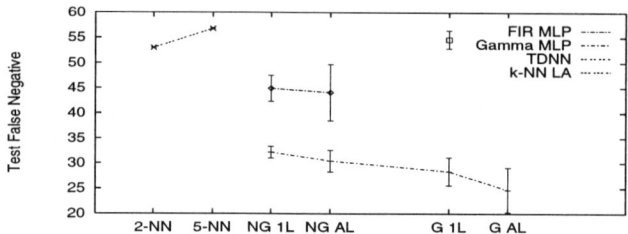

Figure 3: Percentage of false negative classifications on the test set. NG=No gains, G=Gains, 1L=filters in the first layer only, AL=filters in all layers. The error bars show plus and minus one standard deviation. The synaptic gains case for the FIR MLP is not shown as the poor performance compresses the remainder of the graph. Top to bottom, the lines correspond to: k-NN LA (left), TDNN, FIR MLP, and Gamma MLP.

phoneme is present) is incorrectly reported as false. From the table we can see that the Gamma MLP performs significantly better than the FIR MLP or standard TDNN models for this problem. Synaptic gains and gamma filters in all layers improve the performance of the Gamma MLP, while the inclusion of synaptic gains presented difficulty for the FIR MLP. Results for the IIR MLP are not shown - we have been unable to obtain significant convergence[10]. We investigated values of k not listed in the table for the k-NN LA model, but it performed poorly in all cases.

5 CONCLUSIONS

We have defined a Gamma MLP as an MLP with gamma filters and gain terms in every synapse. We have shown that the model performs significantly better on our speech phoneme recognition problem when compared to TDNN, Back-Tsoi FIR and IIR MLP architectures, and Casdagli's local approximation model. The percentage of times a phoneme is present but not recognized for the Gamma MLP was 44% lower than the closest competitor, the Back-Tsoi FIR MLP model.

The inclusion of gamma filters in all layers and the inclusion of synaptic gains improved the performance of the Gamma MLP. The improvement due to the inclusion of synaptic gains may be considered non-intuitive to many - we are adding degrees of freedom, but no additional representational power. The error surface will be different in each case, and the results indicate that the surface for the synaptic gains case is more amenable to gradient descent. One view of the situation is seen by Back & Tsoi with their FIR and IIR MLP networks (Back and Tsoi, 1991b): From a signal processing perspective the response of each synapse is determined by pole-zero positions. With no synaptic gains, the weights determine both the static gain and the pole-zero positions of the synapses. In an experimental analysis performed by Back & Tsoi it was observed that some synapses devoted themselves to model-

---

[10] Theoretically, the IIR MLP model is the most powerful model used here. Though it is prone to stability problems, the stability of the model can and was controlled in the simulations performed here (basically, by reflecting poles that move outside the unit circle back inside). The most obvious hypothesis for the difficulty in training the model is related to the error surface and the nature of gradient descent. We expect the error surface to be considerably more complex for the IIR MLP model, and for gradient descent update to experience increased difficulty optimizing the function.

ing the dynamics of the system in question, while others "sacrificed" themselves to provide the necessary static gains[11] to construct the required nonlinearity.

APPENDIX A: GAMMA MLP UPDATE EQUATIONS

$$\Delta w_{kij}^l(t) = -\eta \frac{\partial J(t)}{\partial w_{kij}^l(t)} = \eta \delta_k^l(t) c_{ki}^l(t) z_{kij}^l(t) \qquad (2)$$

$$\Delta c_{ki}^l(t) = -\eta \frac{\partial J(t)}{\partial c_{ki}^l(t)} = \eta \delta_k^l(t) \sum_{j=0}^{K} w_{kij}^l(t) z_{kij}^l(t) \qquad (3)$$

$$\Delta \mu_{ki}^l(t) = -\eta \frac{\partial J(t)}{\partial \mu_{ki}^l(t)} = \eta \delta_k^l(t) c_{ki}^l(t) \sum_{j=0}^{K} w_{kij}^l(t) \alpha_{kij}^l(t) \qquad (4)$$

$$\alpha_{kij}^l(t) = 0 \qquad j=0$$
$$= (1 - \mu_{ki}^l(t))\alpha_{kij}^l(t-1) + \mu_{ki}^l(t)\alpha_{ki(j-1)}^l(t-1) \qquad (5)$$
$$+ z_{ki(j-1)}^l(t-1) - z_{kij}^l(t-1) \qquad 1 \leq j \leq K$$

$$\delta_k^l(t) = -\frac{\partial J(t)}{\partial x_k^l(t)}$$
$$= e_k(t) f'(x_k^l(t)) \qquad l=L \qquad (6)$$
$$= f'\left(x_k^l(t)\right) \sum_{p=1}^{N_{l+1}} \delta_p^{l+1}(t) c_{pk}^{l+1}(t) \sum_{j=0}^{K} w_{pkj}^{l+1}(t) \beta_{pkj}^{l+1}(t) \qquad 1 \leq j \leq K$$

$$\beta_{pkj}^l(t) = 1 \qquad j=0$$
$$= (1 - \mu_{pk}^l(t))\beta_{pkj}^l(t-1) + \mu_{pk}^l(t)\beta_{pk(j-1)}^l(t-1) \qquad 1 \leq j \leq K \qquad (7)$$

Acknowledgments

This work has been partially supported by the Australian Research Council (ACT and ADB) and the Australian Telecommunications and Electronics Research Board (SL).

References

Back, A. and Tsoi, A. (1991a). FIR and IIR synapses, a new neural network architecture for time series modelling. *Neural Computation*, 3(3):337–350.

Back, A. D. and Tsoi, A. C. (1991b). Analysis of hidden layer weights in a dynamic locally recurrent network. In Simula, O., editor, *Proceedings International Conference on Artificial Neural Networks, ICANN-91*, volume 1, pages 967–976, Espoo, Finland.

Casdagli, M. (1991). Chaos and deterministic versus stochastic non-linear modelling. *J.R. Statistical Society B*, 54(2):302–328.

Darken, C. and Moody, J. (1991). Note on learning rate schedules for stochastic optimization. In *Neural Information Processing Systems 3*, pages 832–838. Morgan Kaufmann.

de Vries, B. and Principe, J. (1992). The gamma model - a new neural network for temporal processing. *Neural Networks*, 5(4):565–576.

Lang, K. J., Waibel, A. H., and Hinton, G. E. (1990). A time-delay neural network architecture for isolated word recognition. *Neural Networks*, 3:23–43.

Shynk, J. (1989). Adaptive IIR filtering. *IEEE ASSP Magazine*, pages 4–21.

---

[11] The neurons were observed to have gone into saturation, providing a constant output.

PART VII
VISION

A Framework for Non-rigid Matching and Correspondence

Suguna Pappu, Steven Gold, and Anand Rangarajan[1]
Departments of Diagnostic Radiology and Computer Science
and the Yale Neuroengineering and Neuroscience Center
Yale University New Haven, CT 06520-8285

Abstract

Matching feature point sets lies at the core of many approaches to object recognition. We present a framework for non-rigid matching that begins with a skeleton module, affine point matching, and then integrates multiple features to improve correspondence and develops an object representation based on spatial regions to model local transformations. The algorithm for feature matching iteratively updates the transformation parameters and the correspondence solution, each in turn. The affine mapping is solved in closed form, which permits its use for data of any dimension. The correspondence is set via a method for two-way constraint satisfaction, called *softassign*, which has recently emerged from the neural network/statistical physics realm. The complexity of the non-rigid matching algorithm with multiple features is the same as that of the affine point matching algorithm. Results for synthetic and real world data are provided for point sets in 2D and 3D, and for 2D data with multiple types of features and parts.

1 Introduction

A basic problem of object recognition is that of matching– how to associate sensory data with the representation of a known object. This entails finding a transformation that maps the features of the object model onto the image, while establishing a correspondence between the spatial features. However, a tractable class of transformation, e.g., affine, may not be sufficient if the object is non-rigid or has relatively independent parts. If there is noise or occlusion, spatial information alone may not be adequate to determine the correct correspondence. In our previous work in spatial point matching [1], the 2D affine transformation was decomposed into its

---
[1] e-mail address of authors: lastname-firstname@cs.yale.edu

physical component elements, which does not generalize easily to 3D, and so, only a rigid 3D transformation was considered.

We present a framework for non-rigid matching that begins with solving the basic affine point matching problem. The algorithm iteratively updates the affine parameters and correspondence in turn, each as a function of the other. The affine transformation is solved in closed form, which lends tremendous flexibility– the formulation can be used in 2D or 3D. The correspondence is solved by using a *softassign* [1] procedure, in which the two-way assignment constraints are solved without penalty functions. The accuracy of the correspondence is improved by the integration of multiple features. A method for non-rigid parameter estimation is developed, based on the assumption of a well-articulated model with distinct regions, each of which may move in an affine fashion, or can be approximated as such. Umeyama [3] has done work on parameterized parts using an exponential time tree search technique, and Wakahara [4] on local affine transforms, but neither integrates multiple features nor explicitly considers the non-rigid matching case, while expressing a one-to-one correspondence between points.

2 Affine Point Matching

The affine point matching problem is formulated as an optimization problem for determining the correspondence and affine transformation between feature points. Given two sets of data points $\hat{X}_j \in R^{n-1}$, $n = 3, 4 \ldots$, $j = 1, \ldots, J$, the image, and $\hat{Y}_k \in R^{n-1}$, $n = 3, 4, \ldots$, $k = 1, \ldots, K$, the model, find the correspondence and associated affine transformation that best maps a subset of the image points onto a subset of the model point set. These point sets are expressed in homogeneous coordinates, $X_j = (1, \hat{X}_j)$, $Y_k = (1, \hat{Y}_k)$. $\{a_{ij}\} = A \in R^{n \times n}$ is the affine transformation matrix. Note that $\{a_{1j} = 0 \; \forall j\}$ because of the homogeneous coordinates. Define the *match* variable M_{jk} where $M_{jk} \in [0, 1]$. For a given match matrix $\{M_{jk}\}$, transformation A and I, an identity matrix of dimension n, $\sum_{j,k} M_{jk} \|X_j - (A + I)Y_k\|^2$ expresses the similarity between the point sets. The term $-\alpha \sum_{j,k} M_{jk}$, with parameter $\alpha > 0$ is appended to this to encourage matches (else $M_{jk} = 0 \; \forall \; j, \; k$ minimizes the function). To limit the range of transformations, the terms of the affine matrix are regularized via a term $\lambda tr(A^T A)$ in the objective function, with parameter λ, where $tr(.)$ denotes the trace of the matrix. Physically, X_j may fully match to one Y_k, partially match to several, or may not match to any point. A similar constraint holds for Y_k. These are expressed as the constraints in the following optimization problem:

$$\min_{A,M} \sum_{j,k} M_{jk} \|X_j - (A + I)Y_k\|^2 + \lambda tr(A^T A) - \alpha \sum_{j,k} M_{jk} \quad (1)$$

$$\text{s.t.} \quad \sum_j M_{jk} \leq 1, \; \forall k, \; \sum_k M_{jk} \leq 1, \; \forall j \text{ and } M_{jk} \geq 0$$

To begin, slack variables $M_{j,K+1}$ and $M_{J+1,k}$ are introduced so that the inequality constraints can be transformed into equality constraints: $\sum_{j=1}^{J+1} M_{jk} = 1$, $\forall k$ and $\sum_{k=1}^{K+1} M_{jk} = 1$, $\forall j$. $M_{j,K+1} = 1$ indicates that X_j does not match to any point in Y_k. An equivalent unconstrained optimization problem to (2) is derived by relaxing the constraints via Lagrange parameters μ_j, ν_k, and introducing an $x \log x$ barrier function, indexed by a parameter β. A similar technique was used

[2] to solve the assignment problem. The energy function used is:

$$\min_{A,M} \max_{\mu,\nu} \sum_{j,k} M_{jk}\|X_j - (A+I)Y_k\|^2 + \lambda tr(A^T A) - \alpha \sum_{j,k} M_{jk} + \sum_{j}^{J} \mu_j(\sum_{k=1}^{K+1} M_{jk} - 1)$$

$$+ \sum_{k}^{K} \nu_k(\sum_{j=1}^{J+1} M_{jk} - 1) + \frac{1}{\beta}\sum_{j=1}^{J+1}\sum_{k=1}^{K+1} M_{jk}(\log M_{jk} - 1)$$

This is to be minimized with respect to the match variables and affine parameters while satisfying the constraints via Lagrange parameters. Using the recently developed *softassign* technique, we satisfy the constraints explicitly. When A is fixed, we have an assignment problem. Following the development in [1], the assignment constraints are satisfied using softassign, a technique for satisfying two-way (assignment) constraints without a penalty term that is analogous to softmax which enforces a one-way constraint. First, the match variables are initialized:

$$M_{jk}^*(A) = \exp(-\beta\|X_j - (I+A)Y_k\|^2 - \alpha) \qquad (2)$$

This is followed by repeated row-column normalization of the match variables until a stopping criterion is reached:

$$M_{jk} = \frac{M_{jk}}{\sum_{j'} M_{j'k}} \text{ then } M_{jk} = \frac{M_{jk}}{\sum_{k'} M_{jk'}} \qquad (3)$$

When the correspondence between the two point sets is fixed, A can be solved in closed form, by holding M fixed in the objective function, and differentiating and solving for A:

$$A = A^*(M) = (\sum_{j,k} M_{jk}(X_j Y_k^T - Y_k Y_k^T))(\sum_{j,k} M_{jk} Y_k Y_k^T + \lambda I)^{-1} \qquad (4)$$

The algorithm is summarized as:

1. INITIALIZE: Variables: $A = 0$, $M = 0$
   Parameters: β_{initial}, β_{update}, β_{final} T = Inner loop iterations, λ
2. ITERATE: Do T times for a fixed value of β
   Softassign: Re-initialize $M^*(A)$ and then (Eq. 2) until ΔM small
   $A^*(M)$ updated (Eq. 4)
3. UPDATE: While $\beta < \beta_{\text{final}}$, $\beta \leftarrow \beta * \beta_{\text{update}}$, Return to 2.

The complexity of the algorithm is $O(JK)$. Starting with small β_{initial} permits many partial correspondences in the initial solution for M. As β increases the correspondence becomes more refined. For large β_{final}, M approaches a permutation matrix (adjusting appropriately for the slack variables).

3 Nonrigid Feature Matching: Affine Quilts

Recognition of an object requires many different types of information working in concert. Spatial information alone may not be sufficient for representation, especially in the presence of noise. Additionally the affine transformation is limited in its inability to handle local variation in an object, due to the object's non-rigidity or to the relatively independent movement of its parts, e.g., in human movement.

The optimization problem (2) easily generalizes to integrate multiple invariant features. A representation with multiple features has a spatial component indicating the location of a feature element. At that location, there may be invariant geometric characteristics, e.g., this point belongs on a curve, or non-geometric invariant features such as color, and texture. Let X_{jr} be the value of feature r associated with point X_j. The *location* of point X_j is the null feature. There are R features associated with each point X_j and Y_k. Note that the match variable remains the same. The new objective function is identical to the original objective function, (2), appended by the term $\sum_{j,k,r} M_{jk} w_r (X_{jr} - Y_{kr})^2$. The $(X_{jr} - Y_{kr})^2$ quantity captures the similarity between invariant types of features, with w_r a weighting factor for feature r. Non-invariant features are not considered. In this way, the point matching algorithm is modified only in the re-initialization of $M(A)$: $M_{jk} = \exp(-\beta(\|X_j - (I + A)Y_k\|^2 + \sum_r w_r(X_{jr} - Y_{kr})^2 - \alpha))$ The rest of the algorithm remains unchanged.

Decomposition of spatial transformations motivates classification of the B individual regions of an object and use of a "quilt" of local affine transformations. In the multiple affine scenario, membership to a region is known on the well-articulated model, but not on the image set. It is assumed that all points that are members of one region undergo the same affine transformation. The model changes by the addition of one subscript to the affine matrix, $A_{\mathbf{b}(k)}$ where $\mathbf{b}(k)$ is an operator that indicates which transformation operates on point k. In the algorithm, during the $A(M)$ update, instead of a single update, B updates are done. Denote $K(b) = \{k | \mathbf{b}(k) = b\}$, i.e., all the points that are within region b. Then in the affine update, $A_b = A_b^*(M) = (\sum_{j,\ k \in K(b)} M_{jk}(X_j Y_k^T - Y_k Y_k^T))(\sum_{j,\ k \in K(b)} M_{jk} Y_k Y_k^T + \lambda_b I)^{-1}$ However, the theoretical complexity does not change, since the B updates still only require summing over the points.

4 Experimental Results: Hand Drawn and Synthetic

The speed for matching point sets of 50 points each is around 20 seconds on an SGI workstation with a R4400 processor. This is true for points in 2D, 3D and with extra features. This can be improved with a tradeoff in accuracy by adopting a looser schedule for the parameter β or by changing the stopping criterion.

In the hand drawn examples, the contours of the images are drawn, discretized and then expressed as a set of points in the plane. In Figure (1), the contours of the boy's face were drawn in two different positions, and a subset of the points were extracted to make up the point sets. In each set this was approximately 250 points. Note that even with the change in mood in the two pictures, the corresponding parts of the face are found. However, in Figure (2) spatial information alone is

Figure 1: Correspondence with simple point features

insufficient. Although the rotation of the head is not a true affine transformation, it is a weak perspective projection for which the approximation is valid. Each photo is outlined, generating approximately 225 points in each face. A point on a contour

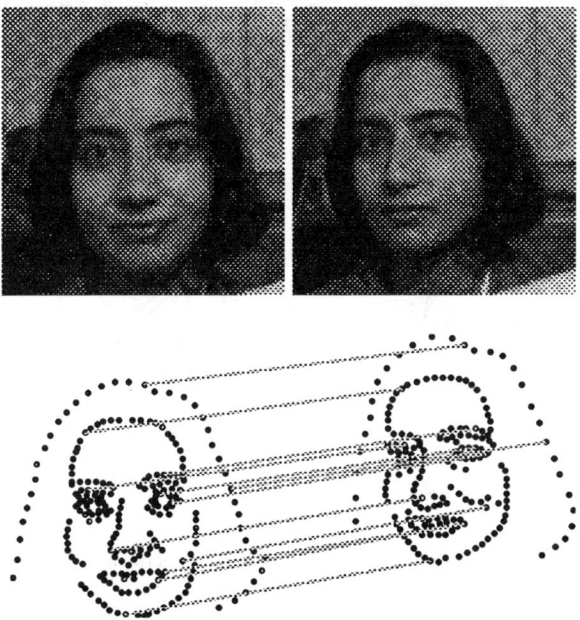

Figure 2: Correspondence with multiple features

has associated with it a feature marker indicating the incident textures. For a human face, we use a binary 4-vector, with a 1 in position r if feature r is present. Specifically, we have used a vector with elements [*skin, hair, lip, eye*]. For example, a point on the line marking the mouth segment the lip from the skin has a feature vector $[1, 0, 1, 0]$. Perceptual organization of the face motivates this type of feature marking scheme. The correspondence is depicted in Figure (2) for a small subset of matches.

Next, we demonstrate how the multiple affine works in recovering the correct correspondence and transformation. The points associated with the standing figure have a marker indicating its part membership. There are six parts in this figure: head, torso, each arm and each leg. The correspondence is shown in Figure (3).

For synthetic data, all 2D and 3D single part experiments used this protocol: The model set was generated uniformly on a unit square. A random affine matrix is generated, whose parameters, a_{ij} are chosen uniformly on a certain interval, which is used to generate the image set. Then, p_d image points are deleted, and Gaussian noise, $N(0, \sigma)$ is added. Finally, spurious points, p_s are added. For the multiple feature scenario, the elements of the feature vector are randomly mislabelled with probability, P_r, to represent distortion. For these experiments, 50 model points were generated, and a_{ij} are uniform on an interval of length 1.5. $\sigma \in \{0.01, 0.02, \ldots, 0.08\}$. Point deletions and spurious additions range from 0% to 50% of the image points. The random feature noise associated with non-spatial features has a probability of $P_r = 0.05$. The error measure we use is $e_a = c \sum_{i,j} |a_{ij} - \hat{a}_{ij}|$ where $c = \frac{3}{\text{\# parameters}} \frac{1}{\text{interval length}}$. a_{ij} and $\hat{a}_{ij}$ are the correct parameter and the computed value, respectively. The constant term c normalizes the measure so that the error equals 1 in the case that the a_{ij} and $\hat{a}_{ij}$ are chosen at random on this interval. The factor 3 in the numerator of this formula follows since

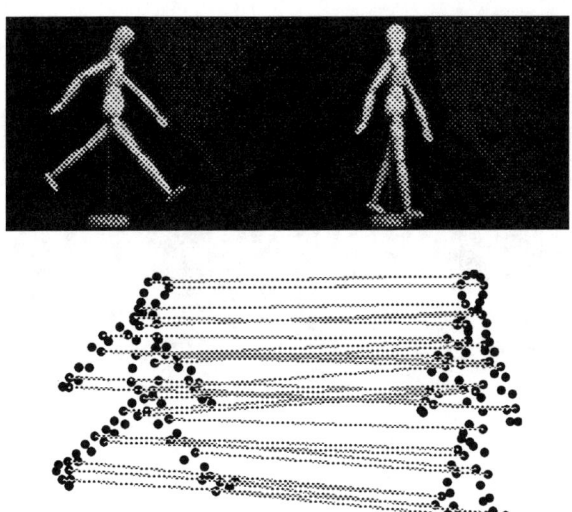

Figure 3: Articulated Matching: Figure with six parts

$E|x - y| = \frac{1}{3}$, when x and y are chosen randomly on the unit interval, and we want to normalize the error. The parameters used in all experiments were: $\beta_{\text{initial}} = .091$, $\beta_{\text{final}} = 100$, $\beta_{\text{update}} = 1.075$, and $T = 4$.

The model has four regions, 24 parameters. Points corresponding to part 1 were centered at $(.5, .5)$, and generated randomly with a diameter of 1.0. For the image set, an affine transformation was applied with a translation diameter of .5, i.e., for a_{21}, a_{22}, and the remaining four parameters have a diameter of 1. Points corresponding to regions 2, 3, and 4 were centered at $(-.5, .5), (-.5, -.5), (.5, -.5)$ with model points and transformations generated in a similar fashion. 120 points were generated for the model point set, divided equally among the four parts. Image points were deleted with equal probability from each region. Spurious point were not explicitly added, since the overlapping of parts provides implicit spurious points.

Results for the 2D and 3D (simple point) experiments are in Figure (4). Each data point represents 500 runs for a different randomly generated affine transformation. In all experiments, note that the error for small amounts of noise is approximately equal to that when there is no noise. We performed similar experiments for point sets that are 3-dimensional (12 parameters), but without any feature information. For the experiments with features, shown in Figure (5) we used $R = 4$ features, and $w_r = 0.2$, $\forall r$. Each data point represents 500 runs. As expected, the inclusion of feature information reduces the error, especially for large σ. Additionally, Figure (5) details synthetic results for experiments with multiple affines (2D). Each data point represents 70 runs.

5 Conclusion

We have developed an affine point matching module, robust in the presence of noise and able to accommodate data of any dimension. The module forms the basis for a non-rigid feature matching scheme in which multiple types of features interact to establish correspondence. Modeling an object in terms of its spatial regions and then using multiple affines to capture local transformations results in a tractable method for non-rigid matching. This non-rigid matching framework arising out of

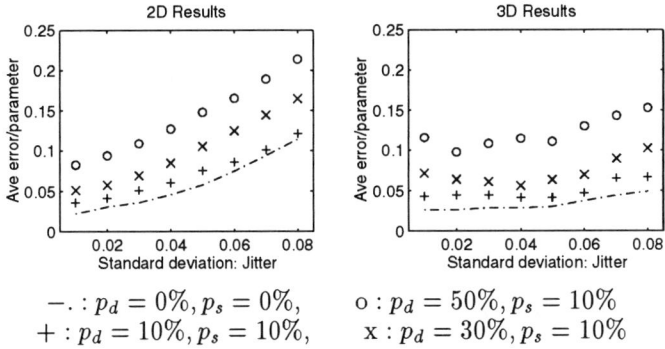

$-\cdot:p_d=0\%,p_s=0\%,$ $\circ:p_d=50\%,p_s=10\%$
$+:p_d=10\%,p_s=10\%,$ $\times:p_d=30\%,p_s=10\%$

Figure 4: Synthetic Experiments: 2D and 3D

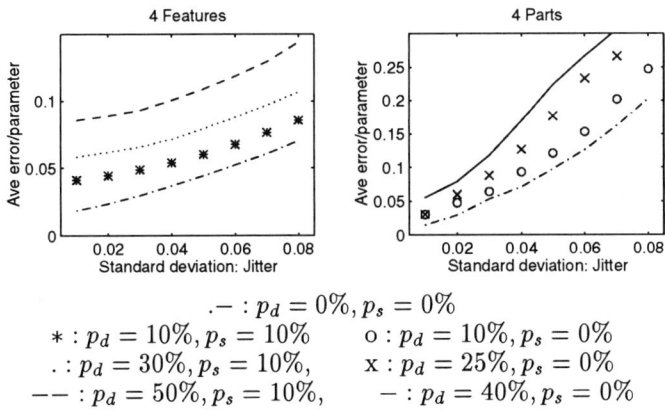

$\cdot-:p_d=0\%,p_s=0\%$
$*:p_d=10\%,p_s=10\%$ $\circ:p_d=10\%,p_s=0\%$
$\cdot:p_d=30\%,p_s=10\%,$ $\times:p_d=25\%,p_s=0\%$
$--:p_d=50\%,p_s=10\%,$ $-:p_d=40\%,p_s=0\%$

Figure 5: Synthetic Experiments: Multiple features and parts

neural computation is widely applicable in object recognition.

Acknowledgements: Our thanks to Eric Mjolsness for many interesting discussions related to the present work.

References

[1] S. Gold, C. P. Lu, A. Rangarajan, S. Pappu, and E. Mjolsness. New algorithms for 2D and 3D point matching: Pose estimation and correspondence. In G. Tesauro, D. Touretzky, and J. Alspector, editors, *Advances in Neural Information Processing Systems*, volume 7, San Francisco, CA, 1995. Morgan Kaufmann Publishers.

[2] J. Kosowsky and A. Yuille. The invisible hand algorithm: Solving the assignment problem with statistical physics. *Neural Networks*, 7:477–490, 1994.

[3] S. Umeyama. Parameterized point pattern matching and its application to recognition of object families. *IEEE Trans. on Pattern Analysis and Machine Intelligence*, 15:136–144, 1993.

[4] T. Wakahara. Shape matching using LAT and its application to handwritten numeral recognition. *IEEE Trans. in Pattern Analysis and Machine Intelligence*, 16:618–629, 1994.

Control of Selective Visual Attention: Modeling the "Where" Pathway

Ernst Niebur*
Computation and Neural Systems 139-74
California Institute of Technology

Christof Koch
Computation and Neural Systems 139-74
California Institute of Technology

Abstract

Intermediate and higher vision processes require selection of a subset of the available sensory information before further processing. Usually, this selection is implemented in the form of a spatially circumscribed region of the visual field, the so-called "focus of attention" which scans the visual scene dependent on the input and on the attentional state of the subject. We here present a model for the control of the focus of attention in primates, based on a saliency map. This mechanism is not only expected to model the functionality of biological vision but also to be essential for the understanding of complex scenes in machine vision.

1 Introduction: "What" and "Where" In Vision

It is a generally accepted fact that the computations of early vision are massively parallel operations, i.e., applied in parallel to all parts of the visual field. This high degree of parallelism cannot be sustained in intermediate and higher vision because of the astronomical number of different possible combination of features. Therefore, it becomes necessary to select only a part of the instantaneous sensory input for more detailed processing and to discard the rest. This is the mechanism of visual selective attention.

---

* Present address: Zanvyl Krieger Mind/Brain Institute and Department of Neuroscience, 3400 N. Charles Street, The Johns Hopkins University, Baltimore, MD 21218.

It is clear that similar selection mechanisms are also required in machine vision for the analysis of all but the simplest visual scenes. Attentional mechanisms are slowly introduced in this field; e.g., Yamada and Cottrell (1995) used sequential scanning by a "focus of attention" in the context of face recognition. Another model for eye scan path generation, which is characterized by a strong top-down influence, is presented by Rao and Ballard (this volume). Sequential scanning can be applied to more abstract spaces, like the dynamics of complex systems in optimization problems with large numbers of minima (Tsioutsias and Mjolsness, this volume).

Primate vision is organized along two major anatomical pathways. One of them is concerned mainly with object *recognition*. For this reason, it has been called the *What*–pathway; for anatomical reasons, it is also known as the ventral pathway. The principal task of the other major pathway is the determination of the *location* of objects and therefore it is called the *Where* pathway or, again for anatomical reasons, the dorsal pathway.

In previous work (Niebur & Koch, 1994), we presented a model for the implementation of the *What* pathway. The underlying mechanism is "temporal tagging:" it is assumed that the attended region of the visual field is distinguished from the unattended parts by the temporal fine-structure of the neuronal spike trains. We have shown that temporal tagging can be achieved by introducing moderate levels of correlation[1] between those neurons which respond to attended stimuli.

How can such synchronicity be obtained? We have suggested a simple, neurally plausible mechanism, namely common input to all cells which respond to attended stimuli. Such (excitatory) input will increase the propensity of postsynaptic cells to fire for a short time after receiving this input, and thereby increase the correlation between spike trains without necessarily increasing the average firing rate.

The subject of the present study is to provide a model of the control system which generates such modulating input. We will show that it is possible to construct an integrated system of attentional control which is based on neurally plausible elements and which is compatible with the anatomy and physiology of the primate visual system. The system scans a visual scene and identifies its most salient parts. A possible task would be "Find all faces in this image." We are confident that this model will not only further our understanding of the function of biological vision but that it will also be relevant for technical applications.

2 A Simple Model of The Dorsal Pathway

2.1 Overall Structure

Figure 1 shows an overview of the model *Where* pathway. Input is provided in the form of digitized images from an NTSC camera which is then analyzed in various feature maps. These maps are organized around the known operations in early visual cortices. They are implemented at different spatial scales and in a center-surround structure akin to visual receptive fields. Different spatial scales are implemented as Gaussian pyramids (Adelson, Anderson, Bergen, Burt, & Ogden, 1984). The center

---

[1]In (Niebur, Koch, & Rosin, 1993), a similar model was developed using periodic "40Hz" modulation. The present model can be adapted *mutatis mutandis* to this type of modulation.

of the receptive field corresponds to the value of a pixel at level n in the pyramid and the surround to the corresponding pixels at level $n+2$, level 0 being the image in normal size. The features implemented so far are the three principal components of primate color vision (intensity, red-green, blue-yellow), four orientations, and temporal change. Short descriptions of the different feature maps are presented in the next section (2.2).

We then (section 2.3) address the question of the integration of the input in the "saliency map," a topographically organized map which codes for the instantaneous conspicuity of the different parts of the visual field.

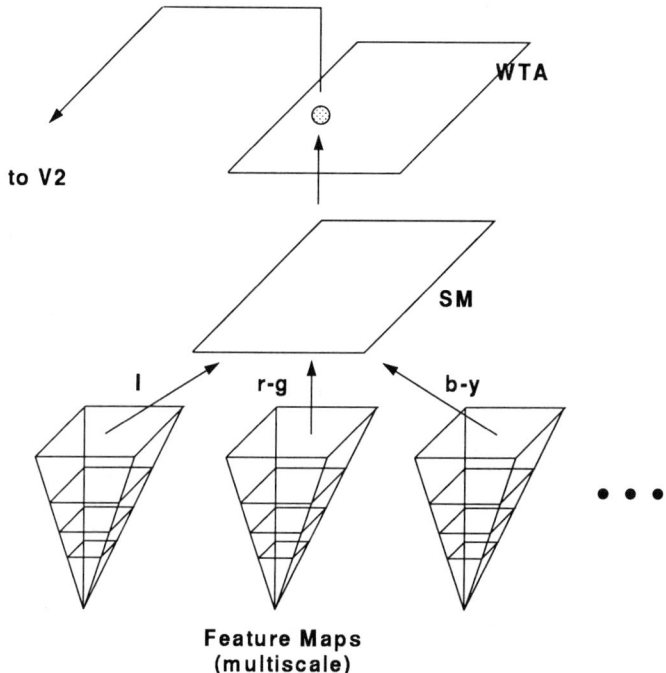

Figure 1: Overview of the model *Where* pathway. Features are computed as center-surround differences at 4 different spatial scales (only 3 feature maps shown). They are combined and integrated in the saliency map ("SM") which provides input to an array of integrate-and-fire neurons with global inhibition. This array ("WTA") has the functionality of a winner-take-all network and provides the output to the ventral pathway ("V2") as well as feedback to the saliency map (curved arrow).

2.2 Input Features

2.2.1 Intensity

Intensity information is obtained from the chromatic information of the NTSC signal. With R, G, and B being the red, green and blue channels, respectively, the intensity I is obtained as $I = (R + G + B)/3$. The entry in the feature map is the modulus of the contrast, i.e., $|I_{center} - I_{surround}|$. This corresponds roughly to the sum of two single-opponent cells of opposite phase, i.e. bright-center — dark-surround and vice-versa. Note, however, that the present version of the model does not reproduce the temporal behavior of ON and OFF subfields because we update the activities in the feature maps instantaneously with changing visual input. Therefore, we neglect the temporal filtering properties of the input neurons.

2.2.2 Chromatic Input

Red, green and blue are the pixel values of the RGB signal. Yellow is computed as $(R + G)/2$. At each pixel, we compute a quantity corresponding to the double-opponency cells in primary visual cortex. For instance, for the red-green filter, we first compute at each pixel the value of (red-green). From this, we then subtract (green-red) of the surround. Finally, we take the absolute value of the result.

2.2.3 Orientation

The intensity image is convolved with four Gabor patches of angles 0,45,90, and 135 degrees, respectively. The result of these four convolutions are four arrays of scalars at every level of the pyramid. The average orientation is then computed as a weighted vector sum. The components in this sum are the four unit vectors $\vec{u}_i, i = 1, ...4$ corresponding to the 4 orientations, each with the weight w_i. This weight is given by the result of its convolution of the respective Gabor patch with the image. Let $\vec{c}$ be this vector for the center pixel, then $\vec{c} = \sum_{i=1}^{4} w_i \vec{u}_i$.

The average orientation vector for the surround, $\vec{s}$, is computed analogously. What enters in the SM is the center-surround difference, i.e. the scalar product $\vec{c}(\vec{s} - \vec{c})$. This is a scalar quantity which corresponds to the center-surround difference in orientation at every location, and which also takes into account the relative "strength" of the oriented edges.

2.2.4 Change

The appearance of an object and the segregation of an object from its background have been shown to capture attention, even for stimuli which are equiluminant with the background (Hillstrom & Yantis, 1994). We incorporate the attentional capture by visual onsets and motion by adding the temporal derivative of the input image sequence, taking into account chromatic information. More precisely, at each pixel we compute at time t and for a time difference $\Delta t = 200ms$:

$$\frac{1}{3}\{|R(t) - R(t - \Delta t)| + |G(t) - G(t - \Delta t)| + |B(t) - B(t - \Delta t)|\} \quad (1)$$

2.2.5 Top-Down Information

Our model implements essentially bottom-up strategies for the rapid selection of conspicuous parts of the visual field and does not pretend to be a model for higher cognitive functions. Nevertheless, it is straightforward to incorporate some top-down influence. For instance, in a "Posner task" (Posner, 1980), the subject is instructed to attend selectively to one part of the visual field. This instruction can be implemented by additional input to the corresponding part of the saliency map.

2.3 The Saliency Map

The existence of a saliency map has been suggested by Koch and Ullman (1985); see also the "master map" of Treisman (1988). The idea is that of a topographically organized map which encodes information on *where* salient (conspicuous) objects are located in the visual field, but not *what* these objects are.

The task of the saliency map is the computation of the salience at every location in the visual field and the subsequent selection of the most salient areas or objects. At any time, only one such area is selected. The feature maps provide current input to the saliency map. The output of the saliency map consists of a spike train from neurons corresponding to this selected area in the topographic map which project to the ventral ("What") pathway. By this mechanism, they are "tagged" by modulating the temporal structure of the neuronal signals corresponding to attended stimuli (Niebur & Koch, 1994).

2.3.1 Fusion Of Information

Once all relevant features have been computed in the various feature maps, they have to be combined to yield the salience, i.e. a scalar quantity. In our model, we solve this task by simply adding the activities in the different feature maps, as computed in section 2.2, with constant weights. We choose all weights identical except for the input obtained from the temporal change. Because of the obvious great importance changing stimuli have for the capture of attention, we select this weight five times larger than the others.

2.3.2 Internal Dynamics And Trajectory Generation

By definition, the activity in a given location of the saliency map represents the relative conspicuity of the corresponding location in the visual field. At any given time, the maximum of this map is therefore the most salient stimulus. As a consequence, this is the stimulus to which the focus of attention should be directed next to allow more detailed inspection by the more powerful "higher" process which are not available to the massively parallel feature maps. This means that we have to determine the instantaneous maximum of this map.

This maximum is selected by application of a winner-take-all mechanism. Different mechanisms have been suggested for the implementation of neural winner-take-all networks (e.g., Koch & Ullman, 1985; Yuille & Grzywacz, 1989). In our model, we used a 2-dimensional layer of integrate-and-fire neurons with strong global inhibition in which the inhibitory population is reliably activated by any neuron in the layer. Therefore, when the first of these cells fires, it will inhibit all cells (including itself), and the neuron with the strongest input will generate a sequence of action potentials. All other neurons are quiescent.

For a static image, the system would so far attend continuously the most conspicuous stimulus. This is neither observed in biological vision nor desirable from a functional point of view; instead, after inspection of any point, there is usually no reason to dwell on it any longer and the next-most salient point should be attended.

We achieve this behavior by introducing feedback from the winner-take-all array. When a spike occurs in the WTA network, the integrators in the saliency map receive additional input with the spatial structure of an inverted Mexican hat, ie. a difference of Gaussians. The (inhibitory) center is at the location of the winner which becomes thus inhibited in the saliency map and, consequently, attention switches to the next-most conspicuous location. The function of the positive lobes of the inverted Mexican hat is to avoid excessive jumping of the focus of attention. If two locations are of nearly equal conspicuity and one of them is close to the present focus of attention, the next jump will go to the close location rather than to the distant one.

3 Results

We have studied the system with inputs constructed analogously to typical visual psychophysical stimuli and obtained results in agreement with experimental data. Space limitations prevent a detailed presentation of these results in this report. Therefore, in Fig. 2, we only show one example of a "real-world image." We choose, as an example, an image showing the Caltech bookstore and the trajectory of the focus of attention follows in our model. The most salient feature in this image is the red banner on the the wall of the building (in the center of the image). The focus of attention is directed first to this salient feature. The system then starts to scan the image in the order of decreasing saliency. Shown are the 3 jumps following the initial focussing on the red banner. The jumps are driven by a strong inhibition-of-return mechanism. Experimental evidence for such a mechanims has been obtained recently in area 7a of rhesus monkeys (Steinmetz, Connor, Constantinidis, & McLaughlin, 1994).

Figure 2: Example image. The black line shows the trajectory of the simulated focus of attention over a time of 140 ms which jumps from the center (red banner on wall of building) to three different locations of decreasing saliency.

4 Conclusion And Outlook

We present in this report a prototype for an integrated system mimicking the control of visual selective attention. Our model is compatible with the known anatomy and physiology of the primate visual system, and its different parts communicate by signals which are neurally plausible. The model identifies the most salient points in a visual scenes one-by-one and scans the scene autonomously in the order of decreasing saliency. This allows the control of a subsequently activated processor which is specialized for detailed object recognition.

At present, saliency is determined by combining the input from a set of feature maps with fixed weights. In future work, we will generalize our approach by introducing plasticity in these weights and thus adapting the system to the task at hand.

Acknowledgements

Work supported by the Office of Naval Research, the Air Force Office of Scientific Research, the National Science Foundation, the Center for Neuromorphic Systems Engineering as a part of the National Science Foundation Engineering Research Center Program, and by the Office of Strategic Technology of the California Trade and Commerce Agency.

References

Adelson, E., Anderson, C., Bergen, J., Burt, P., & Ogden, J. (1984). Pyramid methods in image processing. *RCA Engineer, Nov-Dec.*

Hillstrom, A. & Yantis, S. (1994). Visual motion and attentional capture. *Perception & Psychophysics, 55*(4), 399–411.

Koch, C. & Ullman, S. (1985). Shifts in selective visual attention: towards the underlying neural circuitry. *Human Neurobiol., 4*, 219–227.

Niebur, E. & Koch, C. (1994). A model for the neuronal implementation of selective visual attention based on temporal correlation among neurons. *Journal of Computational Neuroscience, 1*(1), 141–158.

Niebur, E., Koch, C., & Rosin, C. (1993). An oscillation-based model for the neural basis of attention. *Vision Research, 33*, 2789–2802.

Posner, M. (1980). Orienting of attention. *Quart. J. Exp. Psychol., 32*, 3–25.

Steinmetz, M., Connor, C., Constantinidis, C., & McLaughlin, J. (1994). Covert attention suppresses neuronal responses in area 7A of the posterior parietal cortex. *J. Neurophysiology, 72*, 1020–1023.

Treisman, A. (1988). Features and objects: the fourteenth Bartlett memorial lecture. *Quart. J. Exp. Psychol., 40A*, 201–237.

Tsioutsias, D. I. & Mjolsness, E. (1996). A Multiscale Attentional Framework for Relaxation Neural Networks. In Touretzky, D., Mozer, M. C., & Hasselmo, M. E. (Eds.), *Advances in Neural Information Processing Systems*, Vol. 8. MIT Press, Cambridge, MA.

Yamada, K. & Cottrell, G. W. (1995). A model of scan paths applied to face recognition. In *Proc. 17th Ann. Cog. Sci. Conf.* Pittsburgh.

Yuille, A. & Grzywacz, N. (1989). A winner-take-all mechanism based on presynaptic inhibition feedback. *Neural Computation, 2*, 334–344.

Unsupervised Pixel-prediction

William R. Softky
Math Research Branch
NIDDK, NIH
9190 Wisconsin Ave #350
Bethesda, MD 20814
bill@homer.niddk.nih.gov

Abstract

When a sensory system constructs a model of the environment from its input, it might need to verify the model's accuracy. One method of verification is multivariate time-series prediction: a good model could predict the near-future activity of its inputs, much as a good scientific theory predicts future data. Such a predicting model would require copious top-down connections to compare the predictions with the input. That feedback could improve the model's performance in two ways: by biasing internal activity toward expected patterns, and by generating specific error signals if the predictions fail. A proof-of-concept model—an event-driven, computationally efficient layered network, incorporating "cortical" features like all-excitatory synapses and local inhibition—was constructed to make near-future predictions of a simple, moving stimulus. After unsupervised learning, the network contained units not only tuned to obvious features of the stimulus like contour orientation and motion, but also to contour discontinuity ("end-stopping") and illusory contours.

1 Introduction

Somehow, brains make very accurate models of the outside world from their raw sensory input. How might brains check and improve those models? What signal is there to verify a model of the world?

The scientific method faces a similar problem: how to verify theories. In science, theories are verified by predicting *future* data, using the implicit assumption that good predictions can only result from good models. By analogy, it is possible that brains predict their afferent input (e.g. at the thalamus), and that making such predictions and using them as feedback is a unifying design principle of cortex. The proof-of-concept model presented here uses unsupervised Hebbian learning to predict, pixel-wise, the location of a moving pattern slightly in the future.

Why try prediction?

- Predicting future data usually requires a good generative model. For instance: to predict the brightness of individual TV pixels even a fraction of a second in advance, one would need models of contours, objects, motion, occlusion, shadow, etc.

- A successful prediction can help filter out input noise, like a Kalman filter.

- A failed prediction provides a specific, high-dimensional error signal.

- Prediction is not only possible in cortex—which has massive feedback connections—but necessary as well, because those feedback fibers, their target dendrites, and synaptic integration impose inevitable delays. So for a feedback signal to arrive at the cell body "on time," it would need to have been generated tens of milliseconds earlier, as a prediction of imminent activity.

- In this model, "prediction" means producing spikes in advance which will correlate with subsequent input spikes. Specifically, the network's goal is to produce at each grid point a train of spikes at times P_j which predicts the input train I_k, in the sense of maximizing their normalized cross-correlation. The objective function L ("likeness") can be expressed in terms of a smoothing "bump" function $B(t_x, t_y)$ (of spikes at times t_x and t_y) and a correlation function $C(train_1, train_2, \Delta t)$:

$$B(t_x, t_y) = \exp\left(\frac{-|t_x - t_y|}{\tau}\right)$$

$$C(P, I, \Delta T) = \sum_j \sum_k B(P_j + \Delta t, I_k)$$

$$L(P, I, \Delta T) = \frac{C(P, I, \Delta T)}{\sqrt{C(P, P, 0) C(I, I, 0)}}$$

- In order to avoid a trivial but useless prediction ("the weather tomorrow will be just like today"), one must ensure that a unit cannot usually predict its own firing (for example, pick $\Delta t \approx \tau$ greater than the autocorrelation time of a spike train).

2 Model

The input to the network is a 16 × 16 array of spike trains, with toroidal array boundary conditions. The spikes are driven by a "stimulus" bar of excitation one unit wide and seven units long, which moves smoothly perpendicular to its orientation behind the array (in a broad circle, so that all orientations and directions are represented; Fig. 1A). The stimulus point transiently generates spikes at each grid point there according to a Poisson process: the whole array of spikes can be visualized as a twinkling, moving contour.

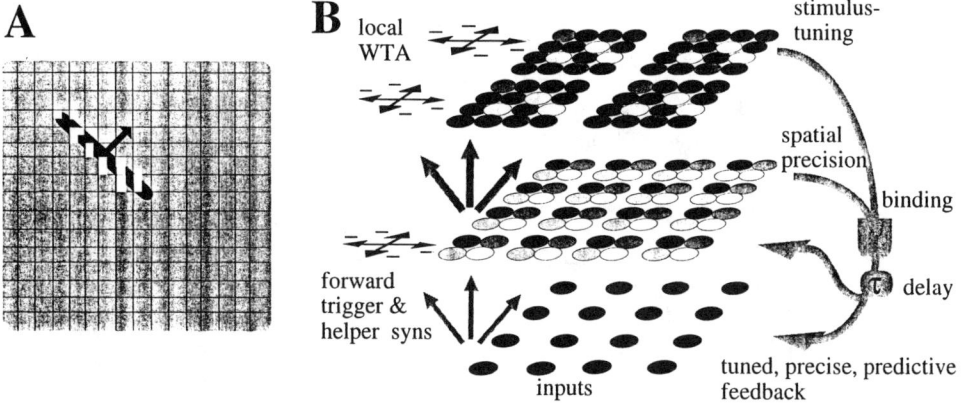

Figure 1: **A network predicts dynamic patterns.** **A** A moving pattern on a grid of spiking pixels describes a slow circle, and drives activity in a network above. **B** The three-layer network learns to predict that activity just before it occurs. Forward connections, evolving by Hebbian rules, produce top-level units with coarse receptive fields and fine stimulus-tuning (e.g. contour orientation and motion). Each spike from a top unit is "bound" (by coincidence detection) with the particular spike which triggered it, to produce feedback which is both stimulus-tuned and spatially specific. A Hebb rule determines how the delayed, predictive feedback will drive middle-layer units and be compared to input-layer units. Because all connections are excitatory, winner-take-all inhibition within local groups of units prevents runaway excitation.

2.1 Network Structure

The network has three layers. The bottom layer contains the spiking pixels, and the "surprise" units described below. The middle layer, having the same spatial resolution as the input, has four coarsely-tuned units per input pixel. And the top layer contains the most finely-tuned units, spaced at half the spatial resolution (at every fourth gridpoint, i.e. with coarser spatial resolution and larger receptive fields). The signal flow is bi-directional [10, 7], with both forward and feedback synaptic connections. All connections between units are excitatory, and excitation is kept in check by local winner-take-all inhibition (WTA). For example, a given input spike can only trigger one spike out of the 16 units directly above it in the top layer (Fig. 1B).

Unsupervised learning occurs through two local Hebb-like rules. Forward connections evolve to make nearby (competing) units strongly anticorrelated—for instance, units typically become tuned to different contour orientations and directions of motion—while feedback connections evolve to maximally correlate delayed feedback signals with their targets.

2.2 Binary multiplication in single units

While some neural models implement multiplication as a nonlinear function of the sum of the inputs, the spiking model used here implements multiplication as a binary operation on two distinct classes of synapses.

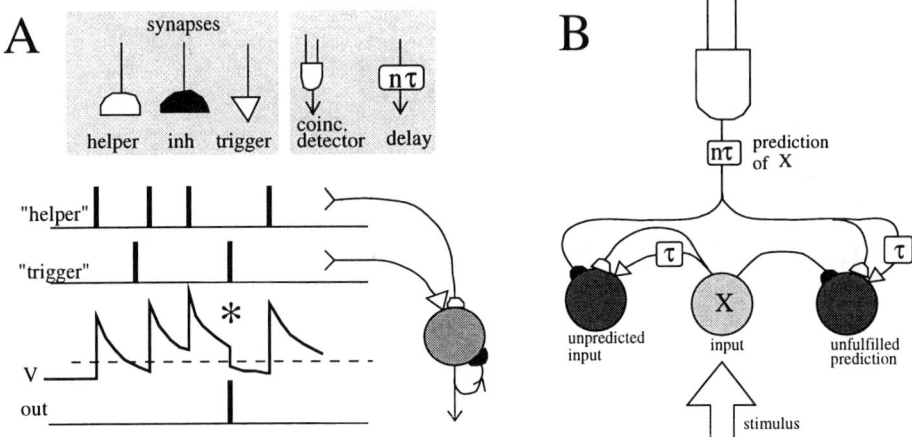

Figure 2: **Multiplicative synapses and surprise detection. A** A spiking unit multiplies two types of synaptic inputs: the "helper" type increments an internal bias without triggering a spike, and the "trigger" type can trigger a spike (*), without incrementing, but only if the bias is above a threshold. Spike propagation may be discretely delayed, and coincidences of two units fired by the same input spike can be detected. **B** Once the network has generated a (delayed) prediction of a given pixel's activity, the match of prediction and reality can be tested by special-purpose units: one type which detects unpredicted input, the other which detects unfulfilled predictions. The firing of either type can drive the network's learning rules, so units above can become tuned to consistent patters of failed predictions, as occur at discontinuities and illusory contours.

A *helper* synapse, when activated by a presynaptic spike, will increment or decrement the postsynaptic voltage without ever initiating a spike. A *trigger* synapse, on the other hand, can initiate a spike (if the voltage is above the threshold determined by its WTA neighbors), but cannot adjust the voltage (Fig. 2A; the helper type is loosely based on the weak, slow NMDA synapses on cortical apical dendrites, while triggers are based on strong, brief AMPA synapses on basal dendrites.) Thus, a unit can only fire when both synaptic types are active, so the output firing rate approximates the product of the rates of helpers and triggers. Each unit has two characteristic timescales: a slower voltage decay time, and the essentially instantaneous time necessary to trigger and propagate a spike.

This scheme has two advantages. One is that a single cell can implement a relatively "pure" multiplication of distinct inputs, as required for computations like motion-detection. The other advantage is that feedback signals, restricted to only helper synapses, cannot by themselves drive a cell, so closed positive-feedback loops cannot "latch" the network into a fixed state, independent of the input. Therefore, all trigger synapses in this network are forward, while all delayed, lateral, and feedback connections are of the helper type.

2.3 Feedback

There are two issues in feedback: How to construct tuned, specific feedback, and what to do with the feedback where it arrives.

An accurate prediction requires information about the input: both about its exact present state, and about its history over nearby space and recent time. In this model, those signals are distinct: spatial and temporal specificity is given by each input spike, and the spatio-temporal history is given by the stimulus-tuned responses of the slow, coarse-grained units in the top layer. Spatially-precise feedback requires recombining those signals. (Feedback from V1 cortical Layer VI to thalamus has recently been shown to fit these criteria, being both spatially refined and direction-selective; [3] Grieve & Sillito, 1995).

In this network, each feedback signal results from the AND of spikes from a input-layer spike (spatially specific) and the resulting top-layer spike it produces (stimulus-tuned). This "binding" across levels of specificity requires single-spike temporal precision, and may even be one of the perceptual uses for spike timing in cortex [1, 9].

2.4 Surprise detection

Once predictive feedback is learned, it can be used in two ways: biasing units toward expected activity, and comparing predictions against actual input. Feedback to the middle layer is used as a bias signal through *helper* synapses, by adding the feedback to the bias signal. But feedback to the bottom, input-layer is compared with actual input by means of special "surprise" units which subtract prediction from input (and vice versa).

Because both prediction and input are noisy signals, their difference is even noisier, and must be both temporally smoothed and thresholded to generate a mismatch-spike. In this model, these prediction/input differences are accomplished pixel-by-pixel using ad-hoc units designed for the purpose (Fig. 2B). There is no indication that cortex operates so simplistically, but there are indications that cortical cells are in general sensitive to mismatches between expectation and reality, such as discontinuities in space (edges), in time (on- and off-responses), and in context (saliency).

The resulting error vector can drive upper-layer units just as the input does, so that the network can learn patterns of failed predictions, which typically correspond to discontinuities in the stimulus. Learning consistent patterns of bad predictions is a completely generic recipe for discovering such discontinuitites, which often correspond closely to visually important features like contour ends, corners, illusory contours, and occlusion.

3 Results and Discussion

After prolonged exposure to the stimulus, the network produces a blurred cloud of spikes which anticipates the actual input spikes, but which also consistently predicts input beyond the bar's ends (leading to small clouds of surprise-unit activity tracking the ends). The top-level units, driven both by input signals and by feedback, become tuned either to different motions of the bar itself (due to Hebbian learning of the input), or to different motions of its *ends* (due to Hebbian learning of the surprise-units); see Fig. 3. Cells tuned to contour ends ("end-stopped") have been found in visual cortex [11], although the principles of their genesis are not known. Using the same parameters but a different stimlus, the network can also evolve units

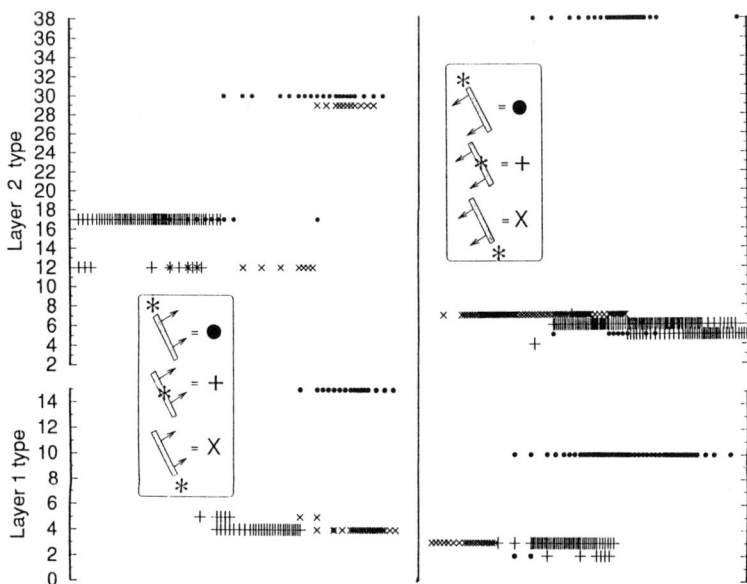

Figure 3: **Single units are highly stimulus-specific.** Spikes from all units at one location are shown (with time) as a stimulus bar (insets) passes them with six different relative positions and motions. Out of the many units available, only one or two are active in each layer for a given stimulus configuration. The inactive units are tuned to stimulus orientations not shown here. Some units are driven by "surprise" units (Figure 2 and text), and respond only to the bar's ends (• and ×), but not to its center (+). Such responses lag behind those of ordinary units, because they must temporally integrate to determine whether a significant mismatch exists between the noisy prediction and the noisy input. Spikes from five passes have been summed to show the units' reliability.

which detect the illusory contours present in certain moving gratings.

Several researchers propose that cortex (or similar networks) might use feedback pathways to recreate or regenerate their (static) input [7, 4, 10]. The approach here requires instead that the network forecast future (dynamic) input [8]. In a general sense, predicting the future is a better test of a model than predicting the present, in the same sense that scientific theories which predict future experimental data are more persuasive than theories which predict existing data. Prediction of the raw input has advantages over prediction of some higher-level signal [5, 6, 2]: the raw input is the only unprocessed "reality" available to the network, and comparing the prediction with that raw input yields the highest-dimensional error vector possible.

Spiking networks are likewise useful. As in cortex, spikes both truncate small inputs and contaminate them with quantization-noise, crucial practical problems which real-valued networks avoid. Spike-driven units can implement purely correlative computations like motion-detection, and can avoid parasitic positive-feedback loops. Spike timing can identify which of many possible inputs fired a given unit, thereby making possible a more specific feedback signal. The most practical benefit is that interactions among rare events (like spikes) are much faster to compute than real-valued ones; this particular network of 8000 units and 200,000 synapses runs faster than the workstation can display it.

This model is an ad-hoc network to illustrate some of the issues a brain might face in trying to predict its retinal inputs; it is not a model of cortex. Unfortunately, the hypothesis that cortex predicts its own inputs does not suggest any specific circuit or model to test. But two experimental tests may be sufficiently model-independent. One is that cortical "non-classical" receptive fields should have a temporal structure which reflects the temporal sequences of natural stimuli, so a given cell's activity will be either enhanced or suppressed when its input matches contextual expectations. Another is that feedback to a single cell in thalamus, or to an individual cortical apical dendrite, should arrive on average *earlier* than afferent input to the same cell.

References

[1] A. Engel, P. Koenig, A. Kreiter, T. Schillen, and W. Singer. Temporal coding in the visual cortex: New vistas on integration in the nervous system. *TINS*, 15:218–226, 1992.

[2] K. Fielding and D. Ruck. Recognition of moving light displays using hidden markov models. *Pattern Recognition*, 28:1415–1421, 1995.

[3] K. L. Grieve and A. M. Sillito. Differential properties of cells in the feline primary visual cortex providing the cortifugal feedback to the lateral geniculate nucleus and visual claustrum. *J. Neurosci.*, 15:4868–4874, 1995.

[4] G. Hinton, P. Dayan, B. Frey, and R. Neal. The wake-sleep algorithm for unsupervised neural networks. *Science*, 268:1158–1161, 1995.

[5] P. R. Montague and T. Sejnowski. The predictive brain: Temporal coincidence and temporal order in synaptic learning mechanisms. *Learning and Memory*, 1:1–33, 1994.

[6] P. Read Montague, Peter Dayan, Christophe Person, and T. Sejnowski. Bee foraging in uncertain environments using predictive hebbian learning. *Nature*, 377:725–728, 1995.

[7] D. Mumford. Neuronal architectures for pattern-theoretic problems. In C. Koch and J. Davis, editors, *Large-scale theories of the cortex*, pages 125–152. MIT Press, 1994.

[8] W. Softky. Could time-series prediction assist visual processing? *Soc. Neurosci. Abstracts*, 21:1499, 1995.

[9] W. Softky. Simple codes vs. efficient codes. *Current Opinion in Neurbiology*, 5:239–247, 1995.

[10] S. Ullman. Sequence-seeking and counterstreams: a model for bidirectional information flow in cortex. In C. Koch and J. Davis, editors, *Large-scale theories of the cortex*, pages 257–270. MIT Press, 1994.

[11] S. Zucker, A. Dobbins, and L. Iverson. Two stages of curve detection suggest two styles of visual computation. *Neural Computation*, 1:68–81, 1989.

Learning to Predict Visibility and Invisibility from Occlusion Events

Jonathan A. Marshall   Richard K. Alley
Robert S. Hubbard

Department of Computer Science, CB 3175, Sitterson Hall
University of North Carolina, Chapel Hill, NC 27599-3175, U.S.A.
marshall@cs.unc.edu, 919-962-1887, fax 919-962-1799

Abstract

Visual occlusion events constitute a major source of depth information. This paper presents a self-organizing neural network that learns to detect, represent, and predict the visibility and invisibility relationships that arise during occlusion events, after a period of exposure to motion sequences containing occlusion and disocclusion events. The network develops two parallel opponent channels or "chains" of lateral excitatory connections for every resolvable motion trajectory. One channel, the "On" chain or "visible" chain, is activated when a moving stimulus is visible. The other channel, the "Off" chain or "invisible" chain, carries a persistent, *amodal* representation that predicts the motion of a formerly visible stimulus that becomes invisible due to occlusion. The learning rule uses disinhibition from the On chain to trigger learning in the Off chain. The On and Off chain neurons can learn *separate* associations with object depth ordering. The results are closely related to the recent discovery (Assad & Maunsell, 1995) of neurons in macaque monkey posterior parietal cortex that respond selectively to inferred motion of invisible stimuli.

1 INTRODUCTION: LEARNING ABOUT OCCLUSION EVENTS

Visual occlusion events constitute a major source of depth information. Yet little is known about the neural mechanisms by which visual systems use occlusion events to infer the depth relations among visual objects. What is the structure of such mechanisms? Some possible answers to this question are revealed through an analysis of learning rules that can cause such mechanisms to self-organize.

Evidence from psychophysics (Kaplan, 1969; Nakayama & Shimojo, 1992; Nakayama, Shimojo, & Silverman, 1989; Shimojo, Silverman, & Nakayama, 1988, 1989; Yonas, Craton, & Thompson, 1987) and neurophysiology (Assad & Maunsell, 1995; Frost, 1993) suggests that the process of determining relative depth from occlusion events operates at an early stage of visual processing. Marshall (1991) describes evidence that suggests that the same early processing mechanisms maintain a representation of temporarily occluded objects for some amount of time after they have disappeared behind an occluder, and that these representations of invisible objects interact with other object representations, in much the same manner as do representations of visible objects. The evidence includes the phenomena of kinetic subjective contours (Kellman & Cohen, 1984), motion viewed through a slit (Parks' Camel) (Parks, 1965), illusory occlusion (Ramachandran, Inada, & Kiama, 1986), and interocular occlusion sequencing (Shimojo, Silverman, & Nakayama, 1988).

2 PERCEPTION OF OCCLUSION AND DISOCCLUSION EVENTS: AN ANALYSIS

The neural network model exploits the visual changes that occur at occlusion boundaries to form a mechanism for detecting and representing object visibility/invisibility information. The set of learning rules used in this model is an extended version of one that has been used before to describe the formation of neural mechanisms for a variety of other visual processing functions (Hubbard & Marshall, 1994; Marshall, 1989, 1990ac, 1991, 1992; Martin & Marshall, 1993).

Our analysis is derived from the following visual *predictivity principle*, which may be postulated as a fundamental principle of neural organization in visual systems: *Visual systems represent the world in terms of predictions of its appearance, and they reorganize themselves to generate better predictions*. To maximize the correctness and completeness of its predictions, a visual system would need to predict the motions and visibility/invisibility of all objects in a scene. Among other things, it would need to predict the disappearance of an object moving behind an occluder and the reappearance of an object emerging from behind an occluder.

A consequence of this postulate is that occluded objects must, at some level, continue to be represented even though they are invisible. Moreover, the representation of an object must distinguish whether the object is visible or invisible; otherwise, the visual system could not determine whether its representations predict visibility or invisibility, which would contravene the predictivity principle. Thus, simple single-channel prediction schemes like the one described by Marshall (1989, 1990a) are inadequate to represent occlusion and disocclusion events.

3 A MODEL FOR GROUNDED LEARNING TO PREDICT VISIBILITY AND INVISIBILITY

The initial structure of the Visible/Invisible network model is given in Figure 1A. The network self-organizes in response to a training regime containing many input sequences representing motion with and without occlusion and disocclusion events. After a period of self-organization, the specific connections that a neuron receives (Figure 1B) determine whether it responds to visible or invisible objects. A neuron that responds to visible objects would have strong bottom-up input connections, and it would also have strong time-delayed lateral excitatory input connections. A neuron that responds selectively to invisible objects would *not* have strong bottom-up connections, but it would have strong lateral excitatory input connections. These lateral inputs would transmit to the neuron evidence that a previously visible object existed. The neurons that respond to invisible objects must operate in a way that allows lateral input excitation alone to activate the neurons supraliminally, in the absence of bottom-up input excitation from actual visible objects.

4 SIMULATION OF A SIMPLIFIED NETWORK

4.1 INITIAL NETWORK STRUCTURE

The simulated network, shown in Figure 2, describes a simplified one-dimensional subnetwork (Marshall & Alley, 1993) of the more general two-dimensional network. Layer 1 is restricted to a set of motion-sensitive neurons corresponding to one rightward motion trajectory.

The L+ connections in the simulation have a signal transmission latency of one time unit. Restricting the lateral connections to a single time delay and to a single direction limits the simulation to representing a single speed and direction of motion; these results are therefore preliminary. This restriction reduced the number of connections and made the simulation much faster.

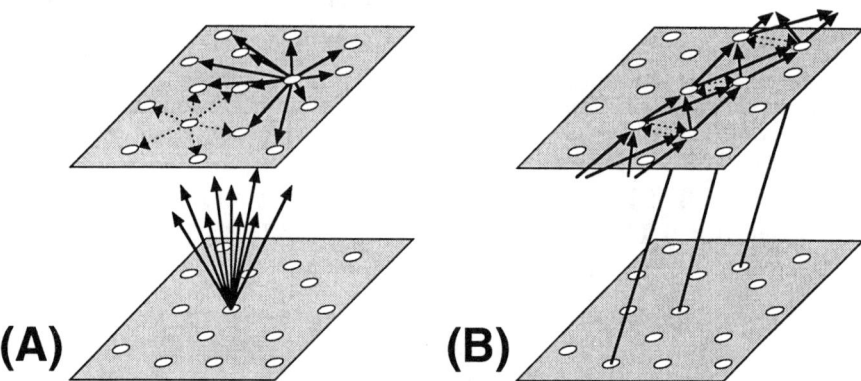

Figure 1: Model of a self-organized occlusion-event detector network. (A) Network is initially organized nonspecifically, so that each neuron receives roughly homogeneous input connections: feedforward, bottom-up excitatory ("B+") connections from a preprocessing stage of motion-tuned neurons (bottom-up solid arrows), lateral inhibitory ("L−") connections (dotted arrows), and time-delayed lateral excitatory ("L+") connections (lateral solid arrows). (B) After exposure during a developmental period to many motion sequences containing occlusion and disocclusion events, the network learns a highly specific connection structure. The previously homogeneous network bifurcates into two parallel opponent channels for every resolvable motion trajectory: some neurons keep their bottom-up connections and others lose them. The channels for one trajectory are shown. Neurons from the two opponent channels are strongly linked by lateral inhibitory connections (dotted arrows). Time-delayed lateral excitatory connections cause stimulus information (priming excitation, or "prediction signals") to propagate along the channels.

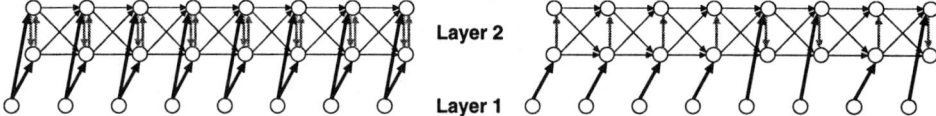

Figure 2: Simulation results. (Left) Simulated network structure before training. Neurons are wired homogeneously from the input layer. (Right) After training, some of the neurons lose their bottom-up input connections.

4.2 USING DISINHIBITION TO CONTROL THE LEARNING OF OCCLUSION RELATIONS

This paper describes one method for learning occlusion relations. Other methods may also work. The method involves extending the EXIN (excitatory+inhibitory) learning scheme described by Marshall (1992, 1995). The EXIN scheme uses a variant of a Hebb rule to govern learning in the bottom-up and time-delayed lateral excitatory connections, plus an anti-Hebb rule to govern learning in the lateral inhibitory connections.

The EXIN system was extended by letting inhibitory connections exert a *disinhibitory* effect under certain regulated conditions. The disinhibition rule was chosen because it constitutes a simple way that the unexpected failure of a neuron to become activated (e.g., when an object disappears behind an occluder) can cause some *other* neuron to become activated. That other neuron can then learn, becoming selective for invisible object motion. Thus, the representations of visible objects are protected from losing their bottom-up input connections during occlusion events.

In this way, the network can learn *separate* representations for visible and invisible stimuli. The representations of invisible objects are allowed to develop only to the extent that the neurons representing visible objects explicitly disclaim the "right" to represent the objects. These properties prevent the network from losing complete grounded contact with actual bottom-up visual input, while at the same time allowing *some* neurons to lose their direct bottom-up input connections.

The disinhibition produces an excitatory response at the target neurons. Disinhibition is generated according to the following rule: *When a neuron has strong,* active lateral excitatory input connections and strong but inactive bottom-up input connections, then it tends to disinhibit the neurons to which it projects inhibitory connections. This implements a type of differencing operation between lateral and bottom-up excitation. Because the disinhibition tends to excite the recipient neurons, it causes one (or possibly more) of the recipient neurons to become active and thereby enables that neuron to learn.

The lateral excitation that a neuron receives can be viewed as a prediction of the neuron's activation. If that prediction is not matched by actual bottom-up excitation, then a *shortfall* (prediction failure) has occurred, probably indicating an occlusion event.

Each neuron's disinhibition input was combined with its bottom-up excitatory input and its lateral excitatory input to form a total excitatory input signal. Either bottom-up excitation or disinhibition alone could contribute toward a neuron's excitation. However, lateral excitation could merely amplify the other signals and could not alone excite the neuron. This prevented neurons from learning in response to lateral excitation alone.

4.3 DISINHIBITION LETS THE NETWORK LEARN TO RESPOND TO INVISIBLE OBJECTS

During continuous motion sequences, without occlusion or disocclusion, the system operates similarly to a system with the standard EXIN learning rules (Marshall, 1990b, 1995): lateral excitatory "chains" of connections are learned across sequences of neurons along a motion trajectory. Marshall (1990a) showed that such chains form in 2-D networks with multiple speeds and multiple directions of motion.

During occlusion events, some predictive lateral excitatory signals reach neurons that have strong but inactive bottom-up excitatory connections. The neurons reached by this excitation pattern disinhibit, rather than inhibit, their competitor neurons. Over the course of many occlusion events, such neurons become increasingly selective for the inferred motion of an invisible object: their bottom-up input connections weaken, and their lateral inhibitory input connections strengthen.

More than one neuron receives L+ signals after every neuron activation; the recipients of each neuron's L+ output connections represent the (learned) possible sequents of the neuron's activation. But at most one of those sequents actually receives both B+ and L+ signals: the one that corresponds to the actual stimulus. This winner neuron receives the disinhibition from the other neurons receiving L+ excitation; its competitive advantage over the other neurons is thus reinforced.

4.4 SIMULATION TRAINING

The sequences of input training data consisted of a single visual feature moving with constant velocity across the 1-D visual field. When this stimulus was visible, its presence was indicated by strong activation of an input neuron in Layer 1. While occluded, the stimulus would produce no activation in Layer 1. The stimulus occasionally disappeared "behind" an occluder and reappeared at a later time and spatial position farther along the same trajectory. After some duration, the stimulus was removed and replaced by a new stimulus. The starting positions and lifetimes of the stimuli and occluders were varied randomly within a fixed range.

The network was trained for 25,000 input pattern presentations. The stability of the connection weights was verified by additional training for 50,000 presentations.

4.5 SIMULATION RESULTS: ARCHITECTURE

The second stage of neurons gradually underwent a self-organized *bifurcation* into two distinct pools of neurons, as shown in Figure 2B. These pools consist of two parallel opponent channels or "chains" of lateral excitatory connections for every resolvable motion trajectory. One channel, the "On" chain or "visible" chain, was active when a moving stimulus became visible. The other channel, the "Off" chain or "invisible" chain, was active when a formerly visible stimulus became invisible. The model is thus named the *Visible/Invisible* model. The bifurcation may be analogous to the activity-dependent stratification of cat retinal ganglion cells into separate On and Off layers, described by Bodnarenko and Chalupa (1993).

4.6 SIMULATION RESULTS: OPERATION

The On chain carries a predictive *modal* representation of the visible stimulus. The Off chain carries a persistent, *amodal* representation that predicts the motion of the invisible stimulus. The shading of the neurons in Figure 3 shows the neuron activations of the final, trained network simulation during an occlusion–disocclusion sequence. The following noteworthy behaviors were observed in the test.

- When the stimulus was visible, it was represented by activation in the On channel.
- When the stimulus became invisible, its representation was carried in the Off channel. The Off channel did not become active until the visible stimulus disappeared.
- The activations representing the visible stimulus became stronger (toward an asymptote) at successive spatial positions, because of the propagation of accumulating evidence for the presence of the stimulus (Martin & Marshall, 1993).
- The activation representing the invisible stimulus decayed at successive spatial positions. Thus, representations of invisible stimuli did not remain active indefinitely.
- When the stimulus reappeared (after a sufficiently brief occlusion), its activation in the On channel was greater than its initial activation in the On channel. Thus, the representation carried across the Off channel helps maintain the perceptual stability of the stimulus despite its being temporarily occluded along parts of its trajectory.

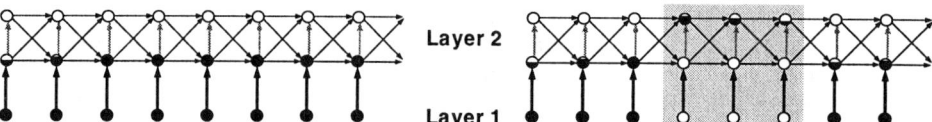

Figure 3: Simulated network operation after learning. The learning procedure causes the representation of each trajectory to split into two parallel opponent channels. The Visible and Invisible channel pair for a single trajectory are shown. The display has been arranged so that all the Visible channel neurons are on the same row (Layer 2, lower row); likewise the Invisible channel neurons (Layer 2, upper row). Solid arrows indicate excitatory connections. Gray arrows indicate lateral inhibitory connections. (Left) The network's responses to an unbroken rightward motion of the stimulus are shown. The activities of the network at successive moments in time have been combined into a single network display; each horizontal position in the figure represents a different moment in time as well as a different position in the network. The stimulus successively activates motion detectors (solid circles) in Layer 1. The activation of the responding neuron in the second layer builds toward an asymptote, reaching full activation by the fourth frame. (Right) The network's responses to a broken (occluded) rightward motion sequence are shown. When the stimulus reaches the region indicated by gray shading, it disappears behind a simulated occluder. The network responds by successively activating neurons in the Invisible channel. When the stimulus emerges from behind the occluder (end of gray shading), it is again represented by activation in the Visible channel.

5 DISCUSSION
5.1 PSYCHOPHYSICAL ISSUES AND PREDICTIONS

Several visual phenomena (Burr, 1980; Piaget, 1954; Shimojo, Silverman, & Nakayama, 1988) support the notion that early processing mechanisms maintain a dynamic representation of temporarily occluded objects for some amount of time after they disappear (Marshall, 1991). In general, the duration of such representations should vary as a function of many factors, including top-down cognitive expectations, stimulus complexity, and Gestalt grouping.

5.2 ALTERNATIVE MECHANISMS

Another model besides the Visible/Invisible model was studied extensively: a *Visible/Virtual* system, which would develop some neurons that respond to visible objects and others that respond to both visible and invisible objects (i.e., to "virtual" objects). There is a functional equivalence between such a Visible/Virtual system and a Visible/Invisible system: the same information about visibility and invisibility can be determined by examining the activations of the neurons. Activity in a Virtual channel neuron, paired with inactivity in a corresponding Visible channel neuron, would indicate the presence of an invisible stimulus.

5.3 NEUROPHYSIOLOGICAL CORRELATES

Assad and Maunsell (1995) recently described their remarkable discovery of neurons in macaque monkey posterior parietal cortex that respond selectively to the inferred motion of invisible stimuli. This type of neuron responded more strongly to the disappearance and reappearance of a stimulus in a task where the stimulus' "inferred" trajectory would pass through the neuron's receptive field than in a task where the stimulus would disappear and reappear in the same position. Most of these neurons also had a strong off-response, which in the present models is closely correlated with inferred motion. Thus, the results of Assad and Maunsell (1995) are more directly consistent with the Visible/Virtual model than with the Visible/Invisible model. Although this paper describes only one of these models, both models merit investigation.

5.4 LEARNING ASSOCIATIONS BETWEEN VISIBILITY AND RELATIVE DEPTH

The activation of neurons in the Off channels is highly correlated with the activation of other neurons elsewhere in the visual system, specifically neurons whose activation indicates the presence of other objects acting as occluders. Simple associative Hebb-type learning lets such occluder-indicator neurons and the Off channel neurons gradually establish reciprocal excitatory connections to each other.

After such reciprocal excitatory connections have been learned, activation of occluder-indicator neurons at a given spatial position causes the network to favor the Off channel in its predictions – i.e., to predict that a moving object will be invisible at that position. Thus, the network learns to use occlusion information to generate better predictions of the visibility/invisibility of objects.

Conversely, the activation of Off channel neurons causes the occluder-indicator neurons to receive excitation. The disappearance of an object excites the representation of an occluder at that location. If the representation of the occluder was not previously activated, then the excitation from the Off channel may even be strong enough to activate it alone. Thus, disappearance of moving visual objects constitutes evidence for the presence of an inferred occluder. These results will be described in a later paper.

5.5 LIMITATIONS AND FUTURE WORK

The Visible/Invisible model presented in this paper describes some of the processes that may be involved in detecting and representing depth from occlusion events. There are other major issues that have not been addressed in this paper. For example, how can the system handle real 2-D or 3-D objects, composed of many visual features grouped together across space, instead of mere point stimuli? How can it handle partial occlusion of objects? How can it handle nonlinear trajectories? How exactly can the associative links between occluding and occluded objects be formed? How can it handle transparency?

6 CONCLUSIONS

Perception of relative depth from occlusion events is a powerful, useful, but poorly-understood capability of human and animal visual systems. We have presented an analysis based on predictivity: a visual system that can predict the visibility/invisibility of objects during occlusion events possesses (*ipso facto*) a good representation of relative depth. The analysis implies that the representations for visible and invisible objects must be distinguishable. We have implemented a model system in which distinct representations for visible and invisible features self-organize in response to exposure to motion sequences containing simulated occlusion and disocclusion events. When a moving feature fails to appear approximately where and when it is predicted to appear, the mismatch between prediction and the actual image triggers an unsupervised learning rule. Over many motions, the learning leads to a bifurcation of a network layer into two parallel opponent channels of neurons. Prediction signals in the network are carried along motion trajectories by specific chains of lateral excitatory connections. These chains also cause the representation of invisible features to propagate for a limited time along the features' trajectories. The network uses shortfall (differencing) and disinhibition to maintain grounding of the representations of invisible features.

Acknowledgements
Supported in part by ONR (N00014-93-1-0208), NEI (EY09669), a UNC-CH Junior Faculty Development Award, an ORAU Junior Faculty Enhancement Award from Oak Ridge Associated Universities, the Univ. of Minnesota Center for Research in Learning, Perception, and Cognition, NICHHD (HD-07151), and the Minnesota Supercomputer Institute.

We thank Kevin Martin, Stephen Aylward, Eliza Graves, Albert Nigrin, Vinay Gupta, George Kalarickal, Charles Schmitt, Viswanath Srikanth, David Van Essen, Christof Koch, and Ennio Mingolla for valuable discussions.

References

Assad JA, Maunsell JHR (1995) Neuronal correlates of inferred motion in macaque posterior parietal cortex. *Nature* 373:518–521.

Bodnarenko SR, Chalupa LM (1993) Stratification of On and Off ganglion cell dendrites depends on glutamate-mediated afferent activity in the developing retina. *Nature* 364:144–146.

Burr D (1980) Motion smear. *Nature* 284:164–165.

Frost BJ (1993) Subcortical analysis of visual motion: Relative motion, figure-ground discrimination and induced optic flow. *Visual Motion and Its Role in the Stabilization of Gaze*, Miles FA, Wallman J (Eds). Amsterdam: Elsevier Science, 159–175.

Hubbard RS, Marshall JA (1994) Self-organizing neural network model of the visual inertia phenomenon in motion perception. Technical Report 94-001, Department of Computer Science, University of North Carolina at Chapel Hill. 26 pp.

Kaplan GA (1969) Kinetic disruption of optical texture: The perception of depth at an edge. *Perception & Psychophysics* 6:193–198.

Kellman PJ, Cohen MH (1984) Kinetic subjective contours. *Perception & Psychophysics* 35:237–244.

Marshall JA (1989) Self-organizing neural network architectures for computing visual depth from motion parallax. *Proceedings of the International Joint Conference on Neural Networks*, Washington DC, II:227–234.

Marshall JA (1990a) Self-organizing neural networks for perception of visual motion. *Neural Networks* 3:45–74.

Marshall JA (1990b) A self-organizing scale-sensitive neural network. *Proceedings of the International Joint Conference on Neural Networks*, San Diego, CA, III:649–654.

Marshall JA (1990c) Adaptive neural methods for multiplexing oriented edges. *Intelligent Robots and Computer Vision IX: Neural, Biological, and 3-D Methods*, Casasent DP (Ed), Proceedings of the SPIE 1382, Boston, MA, 282–291.

Marshall JA (1991) Challenges of vision theory: Self-organization of neural mechanisms for stable steering of object-grouping data in visual motion perception. *Stochastic and Neural Methods in Signal Processing, Image Processing, and Computer Vision*, Chen SS (Ed), Proceedings of the SPIE 1569, San Diego, CA, 200–215.

Marshall JA (1992) Unsupervised learning of contextual constraints in neural networks for simultaneous visual processing of multiple objects. *Neural and Stochastic Methods in Image and Signal Processing*, Chen SS (Ed), Proceedings of the SPIE 1766, San Diego, CA, 84–93.

Marshall JA (1995) Adaptive perceptual pattern recognition by self-organizing neural networks: Context, uncertainty, multiplicity, and scale. *Neural Networks* 8:335–362.

Marshall JA, Alley RK (1993) A self-organizing neural network that learns to detect and represent visual depth from occlusion events. *Proceedings of the AAAI Fall Symposium on Machine Learning and Computer Vision*, Bowyer K, Hall L (Eds), 70–74.

Martin KE, Marshall JA (1993) Unsmearing visual motion: Development of long-range horizontal intrinsic connections. *Advances in Neural Information Processing Systems, 5*, Hanson SJ, Cowan JD, Giles CL (Eds). San Mateo, CA: Morgan Kaufmann Publishers, 417–424.

Nakayama K, Shimojo S (1992) Experiencing and perceiving visual surfaces. *Science* 257:1357–1363.

Nakayama K, Shimojo S, Silverman GH (1989) Stereoscopic depth: Its relation to image segmentation, grouping, and the recognition of occluded objects. *Perception* 18:55–68.

Parks T (1965) Post-retinal visual storage *American Journal of Psychology* 78:145–147.

Piaget J (1954) *The Construction of Reality in the Child*. New York: Basic Books.

Ramachandran VS, Inada V, Kiama G (1986) Perception of illusory occlusion in apparent motion. *Vision Research* 26:1741–1749.

Shimojo S, Silverman GH, Nakayama K (1989) Occlusion and the solution to the aperture problem for motion. *Vision Research* 29:619–626.

Yonas A, Craton LG, Thompson WB (1987) Relative motion: Kinetic information for the order of depth at an edge. *Perception & Psychophysics* 41:53–59.

Classifying Facial Action

**Marian Stewart Bartlett, Paul A. Viola,
Terrence J. Sejnowski, Beatrice A. Golomb**
Howard Hughes Medical Institute
The Salk Institute, La Jolla, CA 92037
marni, viola, terry, beatrice @salk.edu

Jan Larsen
The Niels Bohr Institute
2100 Copenhagen
Denmark
jlarsen@fys.ku.dk

Joseph C. Hager
Network Information Research Corp
Salt Lake City, Utah
jchager@ibm.net

Paul Ekman
University of California San Francisco
San Francisco, CA 94143
ekmansf@itsa.ucsf.edu

Abstract

The Facial Action Coding System, (FACS), devised by Ekman and Friesen (1978), provides an objective means for measuring the facial muscle contractions involved in a facial expression. In this paper, we approach automated facial expression analysis by detecting and classifying facial actions. We generated a database of over 1100 image sequences of 24 subjects performing over 150 distinct facial actions or action combinations. We compare three different approaches to classifying the facial actions in these images: Holistic spatial analysis based on principal components of graylevel images; explicit measurement of local image features such as wrinkles; and template matching with motion flow fields. On a dataset containing six individual actions and 20 subjects, these methods had 89%, 57%, and 85% performances respectively for generalization to novel subjects. When combined, performance improved to 92%.

1 INTRODUCTION

Measurement of facial expressions is important for research and assessment psychiatry, neurology, and experimental psychology (Ekman, Huang, Sejnowski, & Hager, 1992), and has technological applications in consumer-friendly user interfaces, interactive video and entertainment rating. The Facial Action Coding System (FACS) is a method for measuring facial expressions in terms of activity in the underlying facial muscles (Ekman & Friesen, 1978). We are exploring ways to automate FACS.

Rather than classifying images into emotion categories such as happy, sad, or surprised, the goal of this work is instead to detect the muscular actions that comprise a facial expression.

FACS was developed in order to allow researchers to measure the activity of facial muscles from video images of faces. Ekman and Friesen defined 46 distinct action units, each of which correspond to activity in a distinct muscle or muscle group, and produce characteristic facial distortions which can be identified in the images. Although there are static cues to the facial actions, dynamic information is a critical aspect of facial action coding.

FACS is currently used as a research tool in several branches of behavioral science, but a major limitation to this system is the time required to both train human experts and to manually score the video tape. Automating the Facial Action Coding System would make it more widely accessible as a research tool, and it would provide a good foundation for human-computer interactions tools.

Why Detect Facial Actions?

Most approaches to facial expression recognition by computer have focused on classifying images into a small set of emotion categories such as happy, sad, or surprised (Mase, 1991; Yacoob & Davis, 1994; Essa & Pentland, 1995). Real facial signals, however, consist of thousands of distinct expressions, that differ often in only subtle ways. These differences can signify not only which emotion is occurring, but whether two or more emotions have blended together, the intensity of the emotion(s), and if an attempt is being made to control the expression of emotion (Hager & Ekman, 1995).

An alternative to training a system explicitly on a large number of expression categories is to detect the facial actions that comprise the expressions. Thousands of facial expressions can be defined in terms of this smaller set of structural components. We can verify the signal value of these expressions by reference to a large body of behavioral data relating facial actions to emotional states which have already been scored with FACS. FACS also provides a means for obtaining reliable training data. Other approaches to automating facial measurement have mistakenly relied upon voluntary expressions, which tend to contain exaggerated and redundant cues, while omitting some muscular actions altogether (Hager & Ekman, 1995).

2 IMAGE DATABASE

We have collected a database of image sequences of subjects performing specified facial actions. The full database contains over 1100 sequences containing over 150 distinct actions, or action combinations, and 24 different subjects. The sequences contain 6 images, beginning with a neutral expression and ending with a high intensity muscle contraction (Figure 1). For our initial investigation we used data from 20 subjects and attempted to classify the six individual upper face actions illustrated in Figure 2. The information that is available in the images for detecting and discriminating these actions include distortions in the shapes and relative positions of the eyes and eyebrows, the appearance of wrinkles, bulges, and furrows, in specific regions of the face, and motion of the brows and eyelids.

Prior to classifying the images, we manually located the eyes, and we used this information to crop a region around the upper face and scale the images to 360 x 240. The images were rotated so that the eyes were horizontal, and the luminance was normalized. Accurate image registration is critical for principal components based approaches. For the holistic analysis and flow fields, the images were further scaled to 22 x 32 and 66 x 96, respectively. Since the muscle contractions are frequently asymmetric about the face, we doubled the size of our data set by reflecting each image about the vertical axis, giving a total of 800 images.

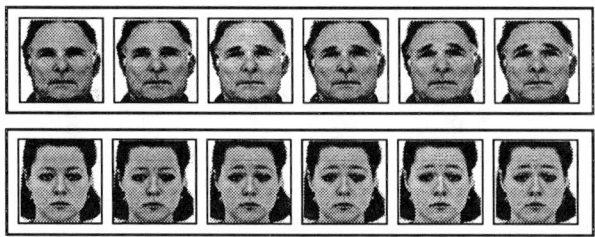

Figure 1: Example action sequences from the database.

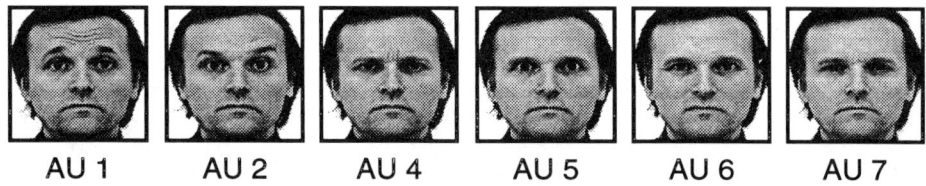

Figure 2: Examples of the six actions used in this study. AU 1: Inner brow raiser. 2: Outer brow raiser. 4: Brow lower. 5: Upper lid raiser (widening the eyes). 6: Cheek raiser. 7: Lid tightener (partial squint).

3 HOLISTIC SPATIAL ANALYSIS

The Eigenface (Turk & Pentland, 1991) and Holon (Cottrell & Metcalfe, 1991) representations are holistic representations based on principal components, which can be extracted by feed forward networks trained by back propagation. Previous work in our lab and others has demonstrated that feed forward networks taking such holistic representations as input can successfully classify gender from facial images (Cottrell & Metcalfe, 1991; Golomb, Lawrence, & Sejnowski, 1991). We evaluated the ability of a back propagation network to classify facial actions given principal components of graylevel images as input.

The primary difference between the present approach and the work referenced above is that we take the principal components of a set of difference images, which we obtained by subtracting the first image in the sequence from the subsequent images (see Figure 3). The variability in our data set is therefore due to the facial distortions and individual differences in facial distortion, and we have removed variability due to surface-level differences in appearance.

We projected the difference images onto the first N principal components of the dataset, and these projections comprised the input to a 3 layer neural network with 10 hidden units, and six output units, one per action (Figure 3.) The network is feed forward and fully connected with a hyperbolic tangent transfer function, and was trained with conjugate gradient descent. The output of the network was determined using winner take all, and generalization to novel subjects was determined by using the leave-one-out, or jackknife, procedure in which we trained the network on 19 subjects and reserved all of the images from one subject for testing. This process was repeated for each of the subjects to obtain a mean generalization performance across 20 test cases.

We obtained the best performance with 50 component projections, which gave 88.6% correct across subjects. The benefit obtained by using principal components over the 704-dimensional difference images themselves is not large. Feeding the difference images directly into the network gave a performance of 84% correct.

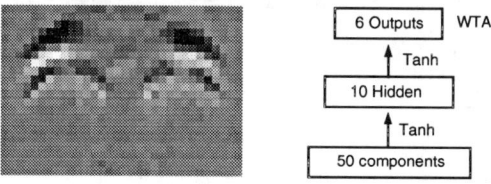

Figure 3: Left: Example difference image. Input values of -1 are mapped to black and 1 to white. Right: Architecture of the feed forward network.

4 FEATURE MEASUREMENT

We turned next to explicit measurement of local image features associated with these actions. The presence of wrinkles in specific regions of the face is a salient cue to the contraction of specific facial muscles. We measured wrinkling at the four facial positions marked in Figure 4a, which are located in the image automatically from the eye position information. Figure 4b shows pixel intensities along the line segment labeled A, and two major wrinkles are evident.

We defined a wrinkle measure P as the sum of the squared derivative of the intensity values along the segment (Figure 4c.) Figure 4d shows P values along line segment A, for a subject performing each of the six actions. Only AU 1 produces wrinkles in the center of the forehead. The P values remain at zero except for AU 1, for which it increases with increases in action intensity. We also defined an eye opening measure as the area of the visible sclera lateral to the iris. Since we were interested in changes in these measures from baseline, we subtract the measures obtained from the neutral image.

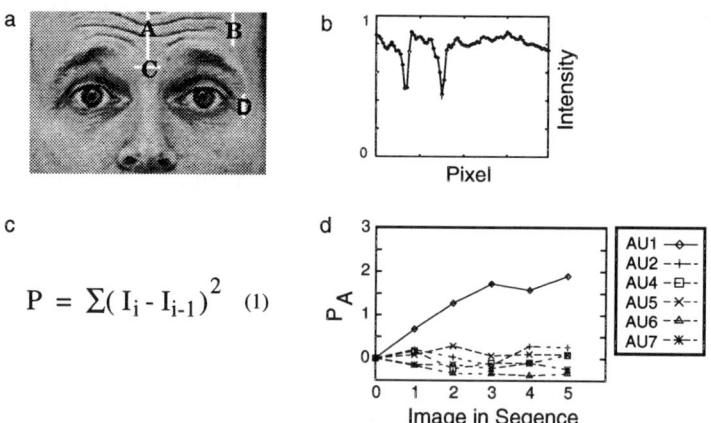

$$P = \sum (I_i - I_{i-1})^2 \quad (1)$$

Figure 4: a) Wrinkling was measured at four image locations, A-D. b) Smoothed pixel intensities along the line labeled A. c) Wrinkle measure. d) P measured at image location A for one subject performing each of the six actions.

We classified the actions from these five feature measures using a 3-layer neural net with 15 hidden units. This method performs well for some subjects but not for

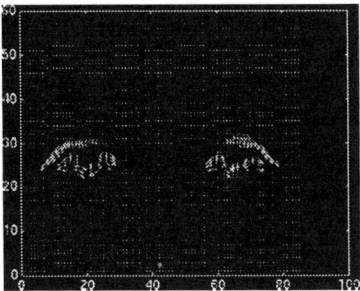

Figure 5: Example flow field for a subject performing AU 7, partial closure of the eyelids. Each flow vector is plotted as an arrow that points in the direction of motion. Axes give image location.

others, depending on age and physiognomy. It achieves an overall generalization performance of 57% correct.

5 OPTIC FLOW

The motion that results from facial action provides another important source of information. The third classifier attempts to classify facial actions based only on the pattern of facial motion. Motion is extracted from image pairs consisting of a neutral image and an image that displays the action to be classified. An approximation to flow is extracted by implementing the brightness constraint equation (2) where the velocity (v_x, v_y) at each image point is estimated from the spatial and temporal gradients of the image I. The velocities can only be reliably extracted at points of large gradient, and we therefore retain only the velocities from those locations. One of the advantages of this simple local estimate of flow is speed. It takes 0.13 seconds on a 120 MHz Pentium to compute one flow field. A resulting flow image is illustrated in Figure 5.

$$v_x \frac{\partial I(x,y,t)}{\partial x} + v_y \frac{\partial I(x,y,t)}{\partial y} + \frac{\partial I(x,y,t)}{\partial t} = 0 \qquad (2)$$

We obtained weighted templates for each of the actions by taking mean flow fields from 10 subjects. We compared novel flow patterns, f^n to the template f^t by the similarity measure S (3). S is the normalized dot product of the novel flow field with the template flow field. This template matching procedure gave 84.8% accuracy for novel subjects. Performance was the same for the ten subjects used in the training set as for the ten in the test set.

$$S(f^n, f^t) = \frac{\sum_i f_i^n \cdot f_i^t}{\sqrt{\sum_i f_i^n \cdot f_i^n} \sqrt{\sum_i f_i^t \cdot f_i^t}} \qquad (3)$$

6 COMBINED SYSTEM

Figure 6 compares performance for the three individual methods described in the previous sections. Error bars give the standard deviation for the estimate of generalization to novel subjects. We obtained the best performance when we combined all three sources of information into a single neural network. The classifier is a

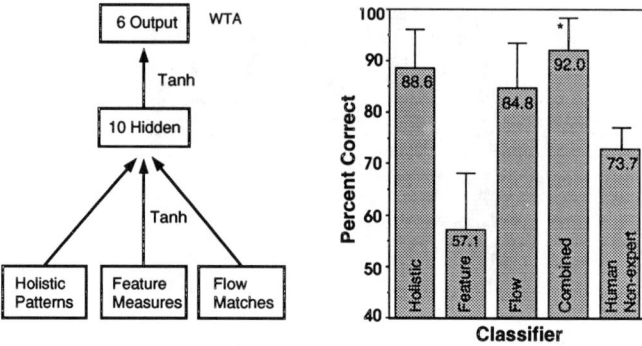

Figure 6: Left: Combined system architecture. Right: Performance comparisons.

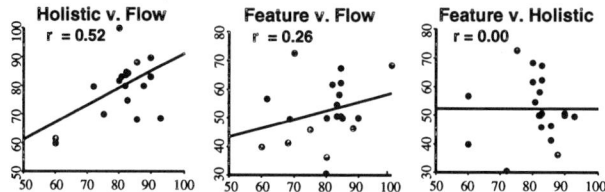

Figure 7: Performance correlations among the three individual classifiers. Each data point is performance for one of the 20 subjects.

feed forward network taking 50 component projections, 5 feature measures, and 6 template matches as input (see Figure 6.)

The combined system gives a generalization performance of 92%, which is an improvement over the best individual method at 88.6%. The increase in performance level is statistically significant by a paired t-test. While the improvement is small, it constitutes about 30% of the difference between the best individual classifier and perfect performance. Figure 6 also shows performance of human subjects on this same dataset. Human non-experts can correctly classify these images with about 74% accuracy. This is a difficult classification problem that requires considerable training for people to be able to perform well.

We can examine how the combined system benefits from multiple input sources by looking at the correlations in performance of the three individual classifiers. Combining estimators is most beneficial when the individual estimators make very different patterns of errors.[1] The performance of the individual classifiers are compared in Figure 7.

The holistic and the flow field classifiers are correlated with a coefficient of 0.52. The feature based system, however, has a more independent pattern of errors from the two template-based methods. Although the stand-alone performance of the feature-based system is low, it contributes to the combined system because it provides estimates that are independent from the two template-based systems. Without the feature measures, we lose 40% of the improvement. Since we have only a small number of features, this data does not address questions about whether templates are *better* than features, but it does suggest that local features plus templates may be superior to either one alone, since they may have independent patterns of errors.

---

[1] Tom Dietterich, Connectionists mailing list, July 24, 1993.

7 DISCUSSION

We have evaluated the performance of three approaches to image analysis on a difficult classification problem. We obtained the best performance when information from holistic spatial analysis, feature measurements, and optic flow fields were combined in a single system. The combined system classifies a face in less than a second on a 120 MHz Pentium.

Our initial results are promising since the upper facial actions included in this study represent subtle distinctions in facial appearance that require lengthy training for humans to make reliably. Our results compare favorably with facial expression recognition systems developed by Mase (1991), Yacoob and Davis (1994), and Padgett and Cottrell (1995), who obtained 80%, 88%, and 88% accuracy respectively for classifying up to six full face expressions. The work presented here differs from these systems in that we attempt to detect individual muscular actions rather than emotion categories, we use a dataset of labeled facial actions, and our dataset includes low and medium intensity muscular actions as well as high intensity ones. Essa and Pentland (1995) attempt to relate facial expressions to the underlying musculature through a complex physical model of the face. Since our methods are image-based, they are more adaptable to variations in facial structure and skin elasticity in the subject population.

We intend to apply these techniques to the lower facial actions and to action combinations as well. A completely automated method for scoring facial actions from images would have both commercial and research applications and would reduce the time and expense currently required for manual scoring by trained observers.

Acknowledgments

This research was supported by Lawrence Livermore National Laboratories, Intra-University Agreement B291436, NSF Grant No. BS-9120868, and Howard Hughes Medical Institute. We thank Claudia Hilburn for image collection.

References

Cottrell, G., & Metcalfe, J. (1991): Face, gender and emotion recognition using holons. In *Advances in Neural Information Processing Systems 3,* D. Touretzky, (Ed.) San Mateo: Morgan & Kaufman. 564 - 571.

Ekman, P., & Friesen, W. (1978): Facial Action Coding System: A Technique for the Measurement of Facial Movement. Palo Alto, CA: *Consulting Psychologists Press.*

Ekman, P., Huang, T., Sejnowski, T., & Hager, J. (1992): Final Report to NSF of the Planning Workshop on Facial Expression Understanding. Available from HIL-0984, UCSF, San Francisco, CA 94143.

Essa, I., & Pentland, A. (1995). Facial expression recognition using visually extracted facial action parameters. *Proceedings of the International Workshop on Automatic Face- and Gesture-Recognition.* University of Zurich, Multimedia Laboratory.

Golomb, B., Lawrence, D., & Sejnowski, T. (1991). SEXnet: A neural network identifies sex from human faces. In *Advances in Neural Information Processing Systems 3,* D. Touretzky, (Ed.) San Mateo: Morgan & Kaufman: 572 - 577.

Hager, J., & Ekman, P., (1995). The essential behavioral science of the face and gesture that computer scientists need to know. *Proceedings of the International Workshop on Automatic Face- and Gesture-Recognition.* University of Zurich, Multimedia Laboratory.

Mase, K. (1991): Recognition of facial expression from optical flow. *IEICE Transactions E* 74(10): 3474-3483.

Padgett, C., Cottrell, G., (1995). Emotion in static face images. *Proceedings of the Institute for Neural Computation Annual Research Symposium, Vol 5.* La Jolla, CA.

Turk, M., & Pentland, A. (1991): Eigenfaces for Recognition. *Journal of Cognitive Neuroscience* 3(1): 71 - 86.

Yacoob, Y., & Davis, L. (1994): Recognizing human facial expression. *University of Maryland Center for Automation Research Technical Report No. 706.*

Modeling Saccadic Targeting in Visual Search

Rajesh P. N. Rao
Computer Science Department
University of Rochester
Rochester, NY 14627
rao@cs.rochester.edu

Gregory J. Zelinsky
Center for Visual Science
University of Rochester
Rochester, NY 14627
greg@cvs.rochester.edu

Mary M. Hayhoe
Center for Visual Science
University of Rochester
Rochester, NY 14627
mary@cvs.rochester.edu

Dana H. Ballard
Computer Science Department
University of Rochester
Rochester, NY 14627
dana@cs.rochester.edu

Abstract

Visual cognition depends critically on the ability to make rapid eye movements known as *saccades* that orient the fovea over targets of interest in a visual scene. Saccades are known to be ballistic: the pattern of muscle activation for foveating a prespecified target location is computed prior to the movement and visual feedback is precluded. Despite these distinctive properties, there has been no general model of the saccadic targeting strategy employed by the human visual system during visual search in natural scenes. This paper proposes a model for saccadic targeting that uses iconic scene representations derived from oriented spatial filters at multiple scales. Visual search proceeds in a *coarse-to-fine* fashion with the largest scale filter responses being compared first. The model was empirically tested by comparing its performance with actual eye movement data from human subjects in a natural visual search task; preliminary results indicate substantial agreement between eye movements predicted by the model and those recorded from human subjects.

1 INTRODUCTION

Human vision relies extensively on the ability to make saccadic eye movements. These rapid eye movements, which are made at the rate of about three per second, orient the high-acuity foveal region of the eye over targets of interest in a visual scene. The high velocity of saccades, reaching up to 700° per second for large movements, serves to minimize the time in flight; most of the time is spent fixating the chosen targets.

The objective of saccades is currently best understood for reading text [13] where the eyes fixate almost every word, sometimes skipping over small function words. In general scenes, however, the purpose of saccades is much more difficult to analyze. It was originally suggested that

Modeling Saccadic Targeting in Visual Search

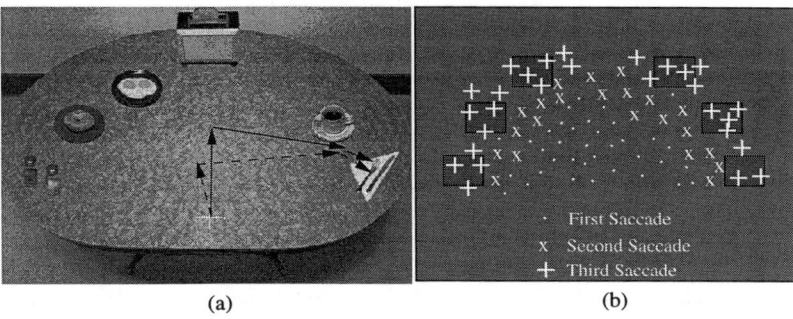

(a) (b)

Figure 1: **Eye Movements in Visual Search**. (a) shows the typical pattern of multiple saccades (shown here for two different subjects) elicited during the course of searching for the object composed of the fork and knife. The initial fixation point is denoted by '+'. (b) depicts a summary of such movements over many experiments as a function of the six possible locations of a target object on the table.

the movements and their resultant fixations formed a visual-motor memory (or "scan-paths") of objects [11] but subsequent work has suggested that the role of saccades is more tightly coupled to the momentary problem solving strategy being employed by the subject. In chess, it has been shown that saccades are used to assess the current situation on the board in the course of making a decision to move, but the exact information that is being represented is not yet known [5]. In a task involving the copying of a model block pattern located on a board, fixations have been shown to be used in accessing crucial information for different stages of the copying task [2]. In natural language processing, there has been recent evidence that fixations reflect the instantaneous parsing of a spoken sentence [18]. However, none of the above work addresses the important question of what possible computational mechanisms underlie saccadic targeting.

The complexity of the targeting problem can be illustrated by the saccades employed by subjects to solve a natural visual search task. In this task, subjects are given a 1 second preview of a single object on a table and then instructed to determine, in the shortest possible amount of time, whether the previewed object is among a group of one to five objects on the same table in a subsequent view. The typical eye movements elicited are shown in Figure 1 (a). Rather than a single movement to the remembered target, several saccades are typical, with each successive saccade moving closer to the goal object (Figure 1 (b)).

The purpose of this paper is to describe a mechanism for programming saccades that can approximately model the saccadic targeting method used by human subjects. Previous models of human visual search have focused on simple search tasks involving elementary features such as horizontal/vertical bars of possibly different color [1, 4, 8] or have relied exclusively on bottom-up input-driven saliency criteria for generating scan-paths [10, 19]. The proposed model achieves targeting in arbitrary visual scenes by using bottom-up scene representations in conjunction with previously memorized top-down object representations; both of these representations are iconic, based on oriented spatial filters at multiple scales.

One of the difficult aspects of modeling saccadic targeting is that saccades are ballistic, i.e., their final location is computed prior to making the movement and the movement trajectory is uninterrupted by incoming visual signals. Furthermore, owing to the structure of the retina, the central 1.5° of the visual field is represented with a resolution that is almost 100 times greater than that of the periphery. We resolve these issues by positing that the targeting computation proceeds sequentially with coarse resolution information being used in the computation of target coordinates prior to fine resolution information. The method is compared to actual eye movements made by human subjects in the visual search task described above; the eye movements predicted by the model are shown to be in close agreement with observed human eye movements.

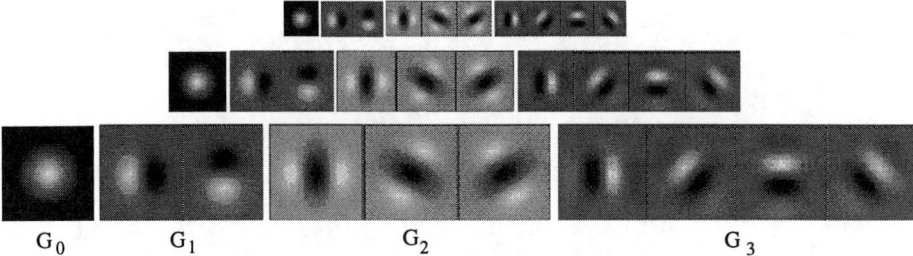

G_0 G_1 G_2 G_3

Figure 2: **Multiscale Natural Basis Functions.** The 10 oriented spatial filters used in our model to generate iconic scene representations, shown here at three octave-separated scales. These filters resemble the receptive field profiles of cells in the primate visual cortex [20] and have been shown to approximate the dominant eigenvectors of natural image distributions as obtained from *principal component analysis* [7, 17].

2 ICONIC REPRESENTATIONS

The current implementation of our model uses a set of non-orthogonal basis functions as given by a zeroth order Gaussian G_0 and nine of its oriented derivatives as follows [6]:

$$G_n^{\theta_n}, n = 1, 2, 3, \theta_n = 0, \ldots, m\pi/(n+1), m = 1, \ldots, n \qquad (1)$$

where n denotes the order of the filter and θ_n refers to the preferred orientation of the filter (Figure 2). The response of an image patch I centered at (x_0, y_0) to a particular basis filter $G_i^{\theta_j}$ can be obtained by convolving the image patch with the filter:

$$r_{i,j}(x_0, y_0) = \iint G_i^{\theta_j}(x_0 - x, y_0 - y) I(x, y) dx\, dy \qquad (2)$$

The iconic representation for the local image patch centered at (x_0, y_0) is formed by combining into a high-dimensional vector the responses from the ten basis filters at different scales:

$$\mathbf{r_s}(x_0, y_0) = [r_{i,j,s}(x_0, y_0)] \qquad (3)$$

where $i = 0, 1, 2, 3$ denotes the order of the filter, $j = 1, \ldots, i+1$ denotes the different filters per order, and $s = s_{min}, \ldots, s_{max}$ denotes the different scales as given by the levels of a Gaussian image pyramid.

The use of multiple scales is crucial to the visual search model (see Section 3). In particular, the larger the number of scales, the greater the perspicuity of the representation as depicted in Figure 3. A multiscale representation also allows interpolation strategies for scale invariance. The high-dimensionality of the vectors makes them remarkably robust to noise due to the *orthogonality* inherent in high-dimensional spaces: given any vector, most of the other vectors in the space tend to be relatively uncorrelated with the given vector. The iconic representations can also be made invariant to rotations in the image plane (for a fixed scale) without additional convolutions by exploiting the property of *steerability* [6]. Rotations about an image plane axis are handled by storing feature vectors from different views. We refer the interested reader to [14] for more details regarding the above properties.

3 THE VISUAL SEARCH MODEL

Our model for visual search is derived from a model for vision that we previously proposed in [14]. This model decomposes visual behaviors into sequences of two visual routines, one for identifying the visual image near the fovea (the "what" routine), and another for locating a stored prototype on the retina (the "where" routine).

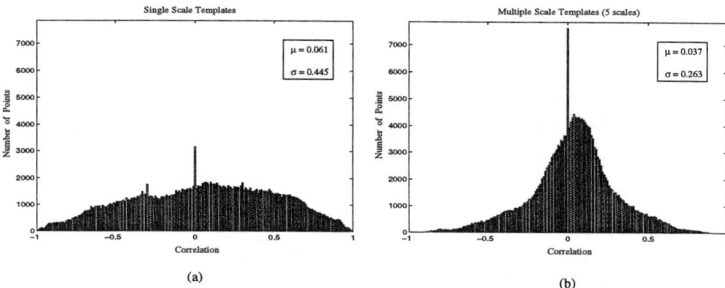

Figure 3: **The Effect of Scale.** The distribution of distances (in terms of correlations) between the response vector for a selected model point in the dining table scene and all other points in the scene is shown for single scale response vectors (a) and multiple scale vectors (b). Using responses from multiple scales (five in this case) results in greater perspicuity and a sharper peak near 0.0; only one point (the model point) had a correlation greater than 0.94 in the multiple scale case (b) whereas 936 candidate points fell in this category in the single scale case (a).

The visual search model assumes the existence of three independent processes running concurrently: (a) a *targeting process* (similar to the "where" routine of [14]) that computes the next location to be fixated; (b) an *oculomotor process* that accepts target locations and executes a saccade to foveate that location (see [16] for more details); and (c) a *decision process* that models the cortico-cortical dynamics of the $V1 \leftrightarrow V2 \leftrightarrow V4 \leftrightarrow IT$ pathway related to the identification of objects in the fovea (see [15] for more details).

Here, we focus on the saccadic targeting process. Objects of interest to the current search task are assumed to be represented by a *set* of previously memorized iconic feature vectors r_s^m where s denotes the scale of the filters. The targeting algorithm computes the next location to be foveated as follows:

1. Initialize the routine by setting the current scale of analysis k to the largest scale i.e. $k = max$; set $S_m(x,y) = 0$ for all (x,y).

2. Compute the current *saliency image* S_m as
$$S_m(x,y) = \sum_{s=k}^{max} ||r_s^i(x,y) - r_s^m||^2 \tag{4}$$

3. Find the location to be foveated by using the following *weighted population averaging (or soft max) scheme*:
$$(\hat{x}, \hat{y}) = \sum_{(x,y)} F(S_m(x,y))(x,y) \tag{5}$$
where F is an interpolation function. For the experiments, we chose:
$$F(S_m(x,y)) = \frac{e^{-S_m(x,y)/\lambda(k)}}{\sum_{(x,y)} e^{-S_m(x,y)/\lambda(k)}} \tag{6}$$
This choice is attractive since it allows an interpretation of our algorithm as computing *maximum likelihood estimates* (cf. [12]) of target locations. In the above, $\lambda(k)$ is decreased with k.

4. Iterate step (2) and (3) above with $k = max\text{-}1, max\text{-}2, \ldots$ until either the target object has been foveated or the number of scales has been exhausted.

Figure 4 illustrates the above targeting procedure. The case where multiple model vectors are used per object proceeds in an analogous manner with the target location being averaged over all the model vectors.

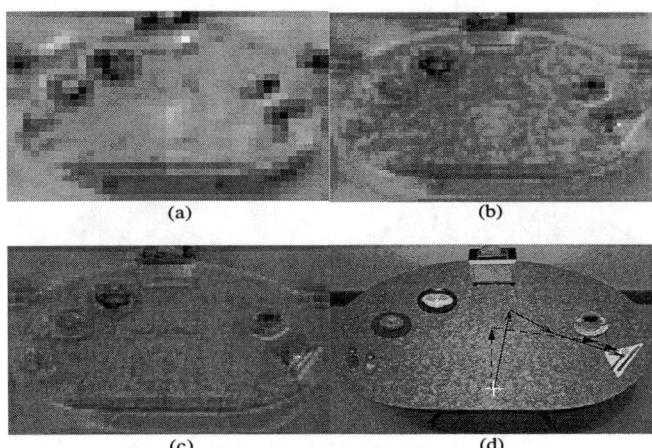

Figure 4: **Illustration of Saccadic Targeting.** The saliency image after the inclusion of the largest (a), intermediate (b), and smallest scale (c) as given by image distances to the prototype (the fork and knife); the lightest points are the closest matches. (d) shows the predicted eye movements as determined by the weighted population averaging scheme (for comparison, saccades from a human subject are given by the dotted arrows).

4 EXPERIMENTAL RESULTS AND DISCUSSION

Eye movements from four human subjects were recorded for the search task described in Section 1 for three different scenes (dining table, work bench, and a crib) using an *SRI Dual Purkinje* Eyetracker. The model was implemented on a pipeline image processor, the Datacube MV200, which can compute convolutions at frame rate ($30/sec$). Figure 5 compares the model's performance to the human data. As the results show, there is remarkably good correspondence between the eye movements observed in human subjects and those generated by the model on the same data sets. The model has only one important parameter: the scaling function used to rate the peaks in the saliency map. In the development of the algorithm, this was adjusted to achieve an approximate fit to the human data.

Our model relies crucially on the existence of a coarse-to-fine matching mechanism. The main benefit of a coarse-to-fine strategy is that it allows continuous execution of the decision/oculomotor processes, thereby increasing the probability of an early match. Coarse-to-fine strategies have enjoyed recent popularity in computer vision with the advent of image pyramids in tasks such as motion detection [3]. Although these methods show that considerable speedup can be achieved by decreasing the size of window of analysis as resolution increases, our preliminary experiments suggest that this might be an inappropriate strategy for visual search: limiting search to a small window centered on the coarse location estimate obtained from a larger scale often resulted in significant errors since the targets frequently lay outside the search window. A possible solution is to adaptively select the size of the search window based on the current scene but this would require additional computational machinery.

A key question that remains is the source of sequential application of the filters in the human visual system. A possible source is the variation in resolution of the retina. Since only very high resolution information is at the fovea, and since this resolution falls off with distance, fine spatial scales may be ineffective purely because the fixation point is distant from the target. However, our preliminary experiments with modeling the variation in retinal resolution suggest that this is probably not the sole cause. The variations at middle distances from the fovea are too small to explain the dramatic improvement in target location experienced with the second saccade. Thus,

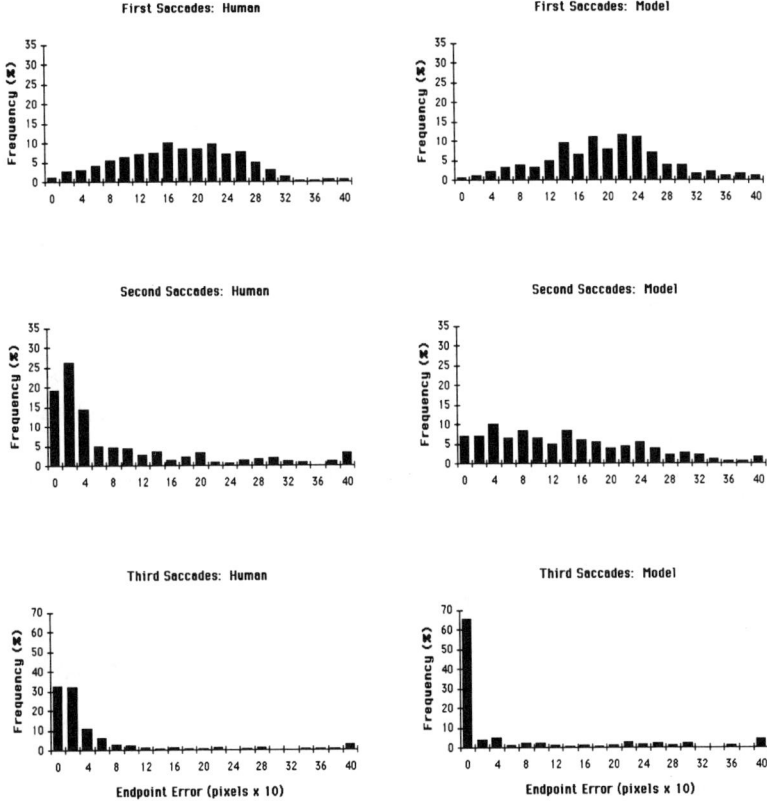

Figure 5: **Experimental Results.** The graphs compare the distribution of endpoint errors (in terms of frequency histograms) for three consecutive saccades as predicted by the model for 180 trials (on the right) and as observed with four human subjects for 676 trials (left). Each of the trials contained search scenes with one to five objects, one of the objects being the previewed model.

there are two remaining possibilities: (a) the resolution fall-off in the cortex is different from the retinal variation in a way that supports the data, or (b) the cortical machinery is set up to match the larger scales first. In the latter case, the observed data would result from the fact that the oculomotor system is ready to move before all the scales can be matched, and thus the eyes move to the current best target position. This interpretation of the data is appealing in two aspects. First, it reflects a long history of observations on the priority of large scale channels [9], and second, it reflects current thinking about eye movement programming suggesting that fixation times are approximately constant and that the eyes are moved as soon as they can be during the course of visual problem solving. The above questions can however be definitively answered only through additional testing of human subjects followed by subsequent modeling. We expect our saccadic targeting model to play a crucial role in this process.

Acknowledgments

This research was supported by NIH/PHS research grants 1-P41-RR09283 and 1-R24-RR06853-02, and by NSF research grants IRI-9406481 and IRI-8903582.

References

[1] Subutai Ahmad and Stephen Omohundro. Efficient visual search: A connectionist solution. In *Proceeding of the 13th Annual Conference of the Cognitive Science Society, Chicago*, 1991.

[2] Dana H. Ballard, Mary M. Hayhoe, and Polly K. Pook. Deictic codes for the embodiment of cognition. Technical Report 95.1, National Resource Laboratory for the study of Brain and Behavior, University of Rochester, January 1995.

[3] P.J. Burt. Attention mechanisms for vision in a dynamic world. In *ICPR*, pages 977–987, 1988.

[4] David Chapman. *Vision, Instruction, and Action*. PhD thesis, MIT Artificial Intelligence Laboratory, 1990. (Technical Report 1204).

[5] W.G. Chase and H.A. Simon. Perception in chess. *Cognitive Psychology*, 4:55–81, 1973.

[6] William T. Freeman and Edward H. Adelson. The design and use of steerable filters. *IEEE PAMI*, 13(9):891–906, September 1991.

[7] Peter J.B. Hancock, Roland J. Baddeley, and Leslie S. Smith. The principal components of natural images. *Network*, 3:61–70, 1992.

[8] Michael C. Mozer. *The perception of multiple objects : A connectionist approach*. Cambridge, MA: MIT Press, 1991.

[9] D. Navon. Forest before trees: The precedence of global features in visual perception. *Cognitive Psychology*, 9:353–383, 1977.

[10] Ernst Niebur and Christof Koch. Control of selective visual attention: Modeling the "where" pathway. This volume, 1996.

[11] D. Noton and L. Stark. Scanpaths in saccadic eye movements while viewing and recognizing patterns. *Vision Reseach*, 11:929–942, 1971.

[12] Steven J. Nowlan. Maximum likelihood competitive learning. In *Advances in Neural Information Processing Systems 2*, pages 574–582. Morgan Kaufmann, 1990.

[13] J.K. O'Regan. Eye movements and reading. In E. Kowler, editor, *Eye Movements and Their Role in Visual and Cognitive Processes*, pages 455–477. New York: Elsevier, 1990.

[14] Rajesh P.N. Rao and Dana H. Ballard. An active vision architecture based on iconic representations. *Artificial Intelligence (Special Issue on Vision)*, 78:461–505, 1995.

[15] Rajesh P.N. Rao and Dana H. Ballard. Dynamic model of visual memory predicts neural response properties in the visual cortex. Technical Report 95.4, National Resource Laboratory for the study of Brain and Behavior, Computer Sci. Dept., University of Rochester, November 1995.

[16] Rajesh P.N. Rao and Dana H. Ballard. Learning saccadic eye movements using multiscale spatial filters. In G. Tesauro, D.S. Touretzky, and T.K. Leen, editors, *Advances in Neural Information Processing Systems 7*, pages 893–900. Cambridge, MA: MIT Press, 1995.

[17] Rajesh P.N. Rao and Dana H. Ballard. Natural basis functions and topographic memory for face recognition. In *Proc. of IJCAI*, pages 10–17, 1995.

[18] M. Tanenhaus, M. Spivey-Knowlton, K. Eberhard, and J. Sedivy. Integration of visual and linguistic information in spoken language comprehension. To appear in Science, 1995.

[19] Keiji Yamada and Garrison W. Cottrell. A model of scan paths applied to face recognition. In *Proc. 17th Annual Conf. of the Cognitive Science Society*, 1995.

[20] R.A. Young. The Gaussian derivative theory of spatial vision: Analysis of cortical cell receptive field line-weighting profiles. *General Motors Research Publication GMR-4920*, 1985.

A model of transparent motion and non-transparent motion aftereffects

Alexander Grunewald*
Max-Planck Institut für biologische Kybernetik
Spemannstraße 38
D-72076 Tübingen, Germany

Abstract

A model of human motion perception is presented. The model contains two stages of direction selective units. The first stage contains broadly tuned units, while the second stage contains units that are narrowly tuned. The model accounts for the motion aftereffect through adapting units at the first stage and inhibitory interactions at the second stage. The model explains how two populations of dots moving in *slightly* different directions are perceived as a single population moving in the direction of the vector sum, and how two populations moving in *strongly* different directions are perceived as transparent motion. The model also explains why the motion aftereffect in both cases appears as non-transparent motion.

1 INTRODUCTION

Transparent motion can be studied using displays which contain two populations of moving dots. The dots within each population have the same direction of motion, but directions can differ between the two populations. When the two directions are very similar, subjects report seeing dots moving in the average direction (Williams & Sekuler, 1984). However, when the difference between the two directions gets large, subjects perceive two overlapping sheets of moving dots. This percept is called transparent motion. The occurrence of transparent motion cannot be explained by direction averaging, since that would result in a single direction of perceived motion.

Rather than just being a quirk of the human visual system, transparent motion is an important issue in motion processing. For example, when a robot is moving its

---
* Present address: Caltech, Mail Code 216-76, Pasadena, CA 91125.

motion leads to a velocity field. The ability to detect transparent motion within that velocity field enables the robot to detect other moving objects at the same time that the velocity field can be used to estimate the heading direction of the robot. Without the ability to code multiple directions of motion at the same location, i.e. without the provision for transparent motion, this capacity is not available. Traditional algorithms have failed to properly process transparent motion, mainly because they assigned a unique velocity signal to each location, instead of allowing the possibility for multiple motion signals at a single location. Consequently, the study of transparent motion has recently enjoyed widespread interest.

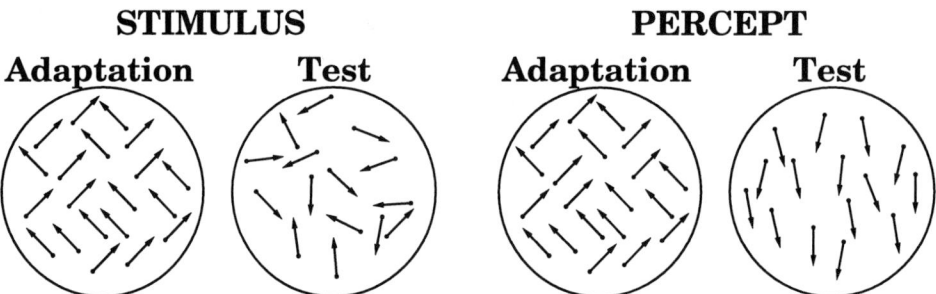

Figure 1: Two populations of dots moving in different directions during an adaptation phase are perceived as transparent motion. Subsequent viewing of randomly moving dots during a test phase leads to an illusory percept of unidirectional motion, the motion aftereffect (MAE). Stimulus and percept in both phases are shown.

After prolonged exposure to an *adaptation* display containing dots moving in one direction, randomly moving dots in a *test* display appear to be moving in the opposite direction (Hiris & Blake, 1992; Wohlgemuth, 1911). This illusory percept of motion is called the motion aftereffect (MAE). Traditionally this is explained by assuming that pairs of oppositely tuned direction selective units together code the presence of motion. When both are equally active, no motion is seen. Visual motion leads to stronger activation of one unit, and thus an imbalance in the activity of the two units. Consequently, motion is perceived. Activation of that unit causes it to fatigue, which means its response weakens. After motion offset, the previously active unit sends out a reduced signal compared to its partner due to adaptation. Thus adaptation generates an imbalance between the two units, and therefore illusory motion, the MAE, is perceived. This is the *ratio model* (Sutherland, 1961).

Recent psychophysical results show that after prolonged exposure to transparent motion, observers perceive a MAE of a single direction of motion, pointing in the vector average of the adaptation directions (Mather, 1980; Verstraten, Fredericksen, & van de Grind, 1994). Thus adaptation to transparent motion leads to a non-transparent MAE. This is illustrated in Figure 1. This result cannot be accounted for by the ratio model, since the non-transparent MAE does not point in the direction opposite to either of the adaptation directions. Instead, this result suggests that direction selective units of all directions interact and thus contribute to the MAE. This explanation is called the *distribution-shift model* (Mather, 1980). However, thus far it has only been vaguely defined, and no demonstration has been given that shows how this mechanism might work.

This study develops a model of human motion perception based on elements from both the ratio and the distribution-shift models for the MAE. The model is also applicable to the situation where two directions of motion are present. When the directions differ slightly, only a single direction is perceived. When the directions differ a lot, transparent motion is perceived. Both cases lead to a unitary MAE.

2 OUTLINE OF THE MODEL

The model consists of two stages. Both stages contain units that are direction selective. The architecture of the model is shown in Figure 2.

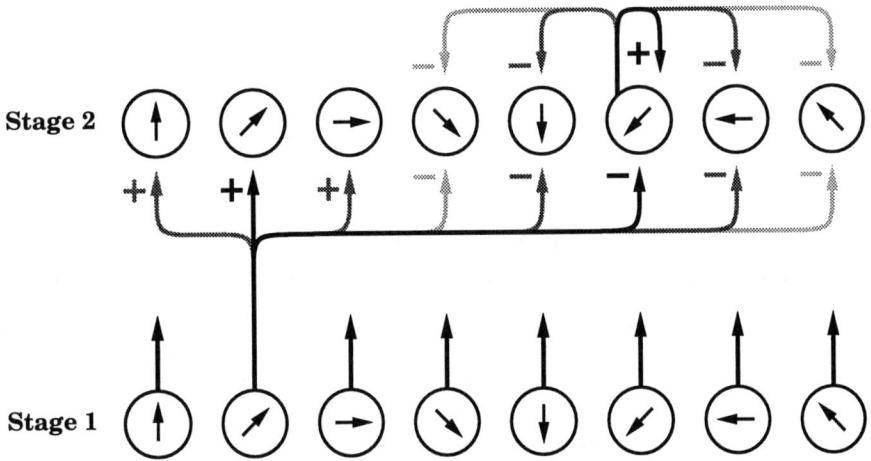

Figure 2: The model contains two stages of direction selective units. Units at stage 1 excite units of like direction selectivity at stage 2, and inhibit units of opposite directions. At stage 2 recurrent inhibition sharpens directional motion responses. The grey level indicates the strength of interaction between units. Strong influence is indicated by black arrows, weak influence is indicated by light grey arrows.

Units in stage 1 are broadly tuned motion detectors. In the present study the precise mechanism of motion detection is not central, and hence it has not been modeled. It is assumed that the bandwidth of motion detectors at this stage is about 30 degrees (Raymond, 1993; Williams, Tweten, & Sekuler, 1991). In the absence of any visual motion, all units are active at a baseline level; this is equivalent to neuronal noise. Whenever motion of a particular direction is present in the input, the activity of the corresponding unit (v_i) is activated maximally ($v_i = 9$), and units of similar direction selectivity are weakly activated ($v_i = 3$). The activities of all other units decrease to zero. Associated with each unit i at stage 1 is a weight w_i that denotes the adaptational state of unit i to fire a unit at stage 2. During prolonged exposure to motion these weights adapt, and their strength decreases. The equation governing the strength of the weights is given below:

$$\frac{dw_i}{dt} = R(1 - w_i) - v_i w_i,$$

where $R = 0.5$ denotes the rate of recovery to the baseline weight. When $w_i = 1$ the corresponding unit is not adapted. The further w_i is reduced from 1, the more the corresponding unit is adapted. The products $v_i w_i$ are transmitted to stage 2. Each unit of stage 1 excites units coding similar directions at stage 2, and inhibits units coding opposite directions of motion. The excitatory and inhibitory effects between units at stages 1 and 2 are caused by kernels, shown in Figure 3.

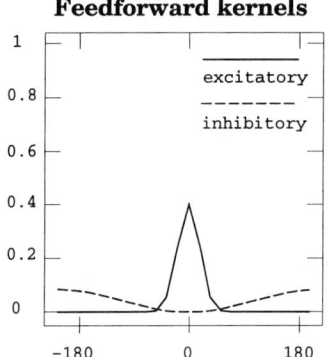

Figure 3: Kernels used in the model. Left: excitatory and inhibitory kernels between stages 1 and 2; right: excitatory and inhibitory feedback kernels within stage 2.

Activities at stage 2 are highly tuned for the direction of motion. The broad activation of motion signals at stage 1 is directionally sharpened at stage 2 through the interactions between recurrent excitation and inhibition. Each unit in stage 2 excites itself, and interacts with other units at stage 2 through recurrent inhibition. This inhibition is maximal for close directions, and falls off as the directions become more dissimilar. The kernels mediating excitatory and inhibitory interactions within stage 2 are shown in Figure 3. Through these inhibitory interactions the directional tuning of units at stage 2 is sharpened; through the excitatory feedback it is ensured that one unit will be maximally active. Activities of units at stage 2 are given by $M_i = \max^4(m_i, 0)$, where the behavior of m_i is governed by:

$$\frac{dm_i}{dt} = -m_i + (1 - m_i)(F_i^+ + B_i^+) - (1 + m_i)(F_i^- + B_i^-).$$

F_i^+ and F_i^- denote the result of convolving the products of the activities at stage 1 and the corresponding adaptation level, $v_j w_j$, with excitatory and inhibitory feedforward kernels respectively. Similarly, B_i^+ and B_i^- denote the convolution of the activities M_j at stage 2 with the feedback kernels.

3 SIMULATIONS OF PSYCHOPHYSICAL RESULTS

In the simulations there were 24 units at each stage. The model was simulated dynamically by integrating the differential equations using a fourth order Runge-Kutta method with stepsize $H = 0.01$ time units. The spacing of units in direction space was 15 degrees at both stages. Spatial interactions were not modeled. In the simulations shown, a motion stimulus is present until $t = 3$. Then the motion stimulus ceases. Activity at stage 2 after $t = 3$ corresponds to a MAE.

3.1 UNIDIRECTIONAL MOTION

When adapting to a single direction of motion, the model correctly generates a motion signal for that particular direction of motion. After offset of the motion input, the unit coding the opposite direction of motion is activated, as in the MAE. A simulation of this is shown in Figure 4.

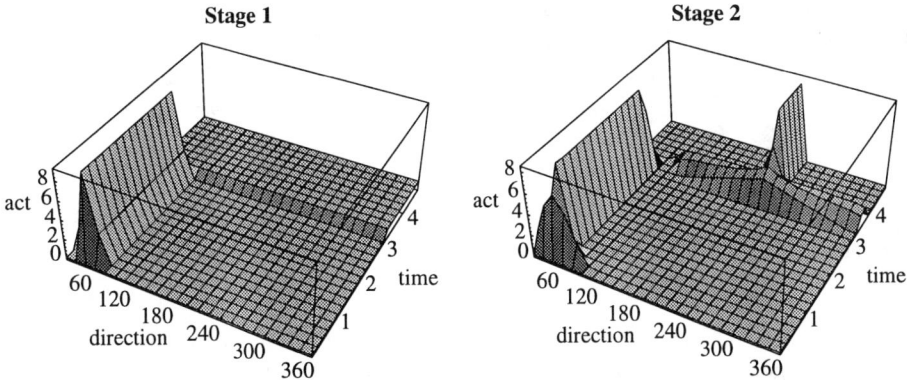

Figure 4: Simulation of single motion input and resulting MAE. Motion input is presented until $t = 3$.

During adaptation the motion stimulus excites the corresponding units at stage 1, which in turn activate units at stage 2. Due to recurrent inhibition only one unit at stage 2 remains active (Grossberg, 1973), and thus a very sharp motion signal is registered at stage 2. During adaptation the weights associated with the units that receive a motion input decrease. After motion offset, all units receive the same baseline input. Since the weights of the previously active units are decreased, the corresponding cells at stage 2 receive less feedforward excitation. At the same time, the previously active units receive strong feedforward inhibition, since they receive inhibition from units tuned to very different directions of motion and whose weights did not decay during adaptation. Similarly, the units coding the opposite direction of motion as those previously active receive more excitation and less inhibition. Through recurrent inhibition the unit at stage 2 coding the opposite direction to that which was active during adaptation is activated after motion offset: this activity corresponds to the MAE. Thus the MAE is primarily an effect of disinhibition.

3.2 TRANSPARENT MOTION: SIMILAR DIRECTIONS

Two populations of dots moving in different, but very similar, directions lead to bimodal activation at stage 1. Since the feedforward excitatory kernel is broadly tuned, and since the directions of motion are similar, the ensuing distribution of activities at stage 2 is unimodal, peaking halfway between the two directions of motion. This corresponds to the vector average of the directions of motion of the two populations of dots. A simulation of this is shown in Figure 5.

During adaptation the units at stage 1 corresponding to the input adapt. As before this means that after motion offset the previously active units receive less excitatory input and more inhibitory input. As during adaptation this signal is unimodal. Also, the unit at stage 2 coding the opposite direction to that of the stimulus receives

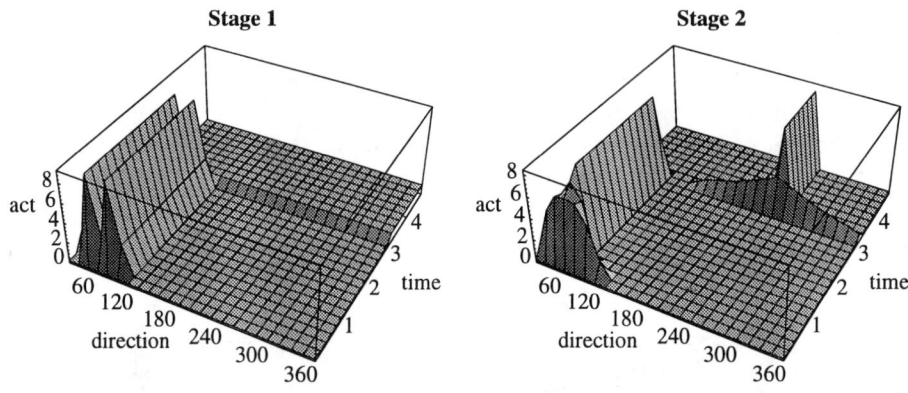

Figure 5: Simulation of two close directions of motion. Stage 2 of the network model registers unitary motion and a unitary MAE.

less inhibition and more excitation. Through the recurrent activities within stage 2, that unit gets maximally activated. A unimodal MAE results.

3.3 TRANSPARENT MOTION: DIFFERENT DIRECTIONS

When the directions of the two populations of dots in a transparent motion display are sufficiently distinct, the distribution of activities at stage 2 is no longer unimodal, but bimodal. Thus, recurrent inhibition leads to activation of two units at stage 2. They correspond to the two stimulus directions. A simulation is shown in Figure 6.

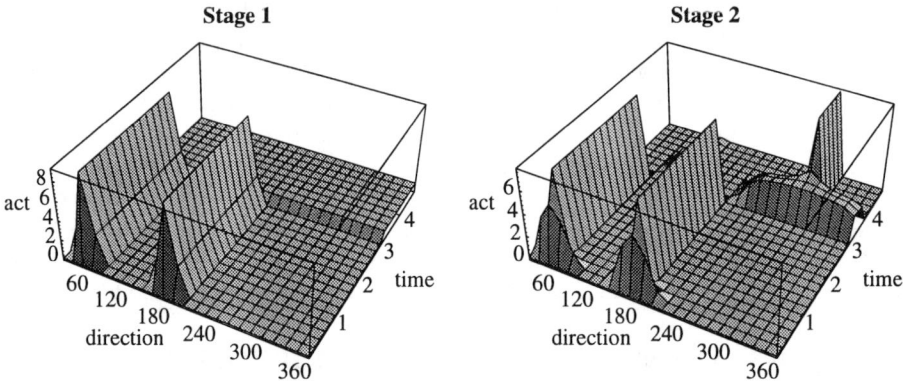

Figure 6: Simulation of two distinct directions of motion. Stage 2 of the model registers transparent motion during adaptation, but the MAE is unidirectional.

Feedforward inhibition is tuned much broader than feedforward excitation, and as a consequence the inhibitory signal during adaptation is unimodal, peaking at the unit of stage 2 coding the opposite direction of the average of the two previously active directions. Therefore that unit receives the least amount of inhibition after motion offset. It receives the same activity from stage 1 as units coding nearby directions, since the corresponding weights at stage 1 did not adapt. Due to recurrent activities at stage 2 that unit becomes active: non-transparent motion is registered.

4 DISCUSSION

Recently Snowden, Treue, Erickson, and Andersen (1991) have studied the effect of transparent motion stimuli on neurons in areas V1 and MT of macaque monkey. They simultaneously presented two populations of dots, one of which was moving in the preferred direction of the neuron under study, and the other population was moving in a different direction. They found that neurons in V1 were barely affected by the second population of dots. Neurons in MT, on the other hand, were inhibited when the direction of the second population differed from the preferred direction, and inhibition was maximal when the second population was moving opposite to the preferred direction. These results support key mechanisms of the model. At stage 1 there is no interaction between opposing directions of motion. The feedforward inhibition between stages 1 and 2 is maximal between opposite directions. Thus activities of units at stage 1 parallel neural activities recorded at V1, and activities of units at stage 2 parallels those neural activities recorded in area MT.

Acknowledgments

This research was carried out under HFSP grant SF-354/94.

Reference

Grossberg, S. (1973). Contour enhancement, short term memory, and constancies in reverberating neural networks. *Studies in Applied Mathematics, LII*, 213-257.

Hiris, E., & Blake, R. (1992). Another perspective in the visual motion aftereffect. *Proceedings of the National Academy of Sciences USA, 89*, 9025-9028.

Mather, G. (1980). The movement aftereffect and a distribution-shift model for coding the direction of visual movement. *Perception, 9*, 379-392.

Raymond, J. E. (1993). Movement direction analysers: independence and bandwidth. *Vision Research, 33*(5/6), 767-775.

Snowden, R. J., Treue, S., Erickson, R. G., & Andersen, R. A. (1991). The response of area MT and V1 neurons to transparent motion. *Journal of Neuroscience, 11*(9), 2768-2785.

Sutherland, N. S. (1961). Figural after-effects and apparent size. *Quarterly Journal of Experimental Psychology, 13*, 222-228.

Verstraten, F. A. J., Fredericksen, R. E., & van de Grind, W. A. (1994). Movement aftereffect of bi-vectorial transparent motion. *Vision Research, 34*, 349-358.

Williams, D., Tweten, S., & Sekuler, R. (1991). Using metamers to explore motion perception. *Vision Research, 31*(2), 275-286.

Williams, D. W., & Sekuler, R. (1984). Coherent global motion percept from stochastic local motions. *Vision Research, 24*(1), 55-62.

Wohlgemuth, A. (1911). On the aftereffect of seen movement. *British Journal of Psychology (Monograph Supplement), 1*, 1-117.

A Neural Network Model of 3-D Lightness Perception

Luiz Pessoa
Federal Univ. of Rio de Janeiro
Rio de Janeiro, RJ, Brazil
pessoa@cos.ufrj.br

William D. Ross
Boston University
Boston, MA 02215
bill@cns.bu.edu

Abstract

A neural network model of 3-D lightness perception is presented which builds upon the FACADE Theory Boundary Contour System/Feature Contour System of Grossberg and colleagues. Early ratio encoding by retinal ganglion neurons as well as psychophysical results on constancy across different backgrounds (background constancy) are used to provide functional constraints to the theory and suggest a *contrast negation hypothesis* which states that ratio measures between coplanar regions are given more weight in the determination of lightness of the respective regions. Simulations of the model address data on lightness perception, including the coplanar ratio hypothesis, the Benary cross, and White's illusion.

1 INTRODUCTION

Our everyday visual experience includes surface color constancy. That is, despite 1) variations in scene lighting and 2) movement or displacement across visual contexts, the color of an object appears to a large extent to be the same. Color constancy refers, then, to the fact that surface color remains largely constant despite changes in the intensity and composition of the light reflected to the eyes from both the object itself and from surrounding objects. This paper discusses a neural network model of 3D lightness perception — i.e., only the achromatic or black to white dimension of surface color perception is addressed. More specifically, the problem of *background constancy* (see 2 above) is addressed and mechanisms to accomplish it in a system exhibiting *illumination constancy* (see 1 above) are proposed.

A landmark result in the study of lightness was an experiment reported by Wallach (1948) who showed that for a disk-annulus pattern, lightness is given by the ratio of disk and annulus luminances (i.e., independent of overall illumination); the so-called ratio principle. In another study, Whittle and Challands (1969) had subjects perform brightness matches in a haploscopic display paradigm. A striking result was that subjects always matched decrements to decrements, or increments to increments, but never increments to decrements. Whittle and Challands' (1969) results provide psychophysical support to the notion that the early visual system codes luminance ratios and not absolute luminance. These psychophysical results are in line with results from neurophysiology indicating that cells at early stages of the visual system encode local luminance contrast (Shapley and Enroth-Cugell, 1984). Note that lateral inhibition mechanisms are sensitive to local ratios and can be used as part of the explanation of illumination constancy.

Despite the explanatory power of the ratio principle, and the fact that the early stages of the visual system likely code contrast, several experiments have shown that, in general, ratios are insufficient to account for surface color perception. Studies of background constancy (Whittle and Challands, 1969; Land and McCann, 1971; Arend and Spehar, 1993), of the role of 3-D spatial layout and illumination arrangement on lightness perception (e.g., Gilchrist, 1977) as well as many other effects, argue against the sufficiency of local contrast measures (e.g., Benary cross, White's, 1979 illusion). The neural network model presented here addresses these data using several fields of neurally plausible mechanisms of lateral inhibition and excitation.

2 FROM LUMINANCE RATIOS TO LIGHTNESS

The *coplanar ratio hypothesis* (Gilchrist, 1977) states that the lightness of a given region is determined predominantly in relation to other coplanar surfaces, and not by equally weighted relations to all retinally adjacent regions. We propose that in the determination of lightness, contrast measures between non-coplanar adjacent surfaces are partially negated in order to preserve background constancy.

Consider the Benary Cross pattern (input stimulus in Fig. 2). If the gray patch on the cross is considered to be at the same depth as the cross, while the other gray patch is taken to be at the same depth as the background (which is below the cross), the gray patch on the cross should look lighter (since its lightness is determined in *relation* to the black cross), and the other patch darker (since its lightness is determined in *relation* to the white background). White's (1979) illusion can be discussed in similar terms (see the input stimulus in Fig. 3).

The mechanisms presented below implement a process of *partial contrast negation* in which the initial retinal contrast code is modulated by depth information such that the retinal contrast consistent with the depth interpretation is maintained while the retinal contrast not supported by depth is negated or attenuated.

3 A FILLING-IN MODEL OF 3-D LIGHTNESS

Contrast/Filling-in models propose that initial measures of boundary contrast followed by spreading of neural activity within filling-in compartments produce a response profile isomorphic with the percept (Gerrits & Vendrik, 1970; Cohen & Grossberg, 1984; Grossberg & Todorović, 1988; Pessoa, Mingolla, & Neumann, 1995). In this paper we develop a neural network model of lightness perception in the tradition of contrast/filling-in theories. The neural network developed here is an extension of the Boundary Contour System/Feature Contour System (BCS/FCS) proposed by Cohen and Grossberg (1984) and Grossberg and Mingolla (1985) to explain 3-D lightness data.

A fundamental idea of the BCS/FCS theory is that lateral inhibition achieves illumination constancy but requires the recovery of lightness by the filling-in, or diffusion, of *featural* quality ("lightness" in our case). The final diffused activities correspond to lightness, which is the outcome of interactions between boundaries and featural quality, whereby boundaries control the process of filling-in by forming gates of variable resistance to diffusion.

How can the visual system construct 3-D lightness percepts from contrast measures obtained by retinotopic lateral inhibition? A mechanism that is easily instantiated in a neural model and provides a straightforward modification to the contrast/filling-in proposal of Grossberg and Todorović (1988) is the use of depth-gated filling-in. This can be accomplished through a pathway that modulates boundary strength for boundaries between surfaces or objects across depth. The use of permeable or "leaky" boundaries was also used by Grossberg and Todorović (1988) for 2-D stimuli. In the current usage, permeability is actively increased at depth boundaries to partially negate the contrast effect — since filling-in proceeds more freely — and thus preserve lightness constancy across backgrounds. Figure 1 describes the four computational stages of the system.

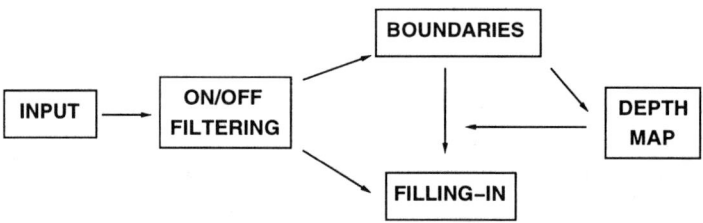

Figure 1: Model components.

Stage 1: Contrast Measurement. At this stage both ON and OFF neural fields with lateral inhibitory connectivity measure the strength of contrast at image regions — in uniform regions a contrast measurement of zero results. Formally, the ON field is given by

$$\frac{dy_{ij}^+}{dt} = -\alpha y_{ij}^+ + (\beta - y_{ij}^+)C_{ij}^+ - (y_{ij}^+ + \gamma)E_{ij}^+ \tag{1}$$

where α, β and γ are constants; C_{ij}^+ is the total excitatory input to y_{ij}^+ and E_{ij}^+ is the total inhibitory input to y_{ij}^+. These terms denote discrete convolutions of the input I_{ij} with Gaussian weighting functions, or kernels. An analogous equation specifies y_{ij}^- for the OFF field. Figure 2 shows the ON-contrast minus the OFF-contrast.

Stage 2: 2-D Boundary Detection. At Stage 2, oriented odd-symmetric boundary detection cells are excited by the oriented sampling of the ON and OFF Stage 1 cells. Responses are maximal when ON activation is strong on one side of a cell's receptive field and OFF activation is strong on the opposite side. In other words, the cells are tuned to ON/OFF contrast co-occurrence, or juxtaposition (see Pessoa et al., 1995). The output at this stage is the sum of the activations of such cells at each location for all orientations. The output responses are sharpened and localized through lateral inhibition across space; an equation similar to Equation 1 is used. The final output of Stage 2 is given by the signals z_{ij} (see Fig. 2, Boundaries).

Stage 3: Depth Map. In the current implementation a simple scheme was employed for the determination of the depth configuration. Initially, four types of

T-junction cells detect such configurations in the image. For example,

$$T_{ij} = z_{i-d,j} \times z_{i+d,j} \times z_{i,j+d}, \qquad (2)$$

where d is a constant, detects T-junctions, where left, right, and top positions of the boundary stage are active; similar cells detect T-junctions of different orientations. The activities of the T-junction cells are then used in conjunction with boundary signals to define complete boundaries. Filling-in within these depth boundaries results in a depth map (see Fig. 2, Depth Map).

Stage 4: Depth-modulated Filling-in. In Stage 4, the ON and OFF contrast measures are allowed to diffuse across space within respective filling-in regions. Diffusion is blocked by boundary activations from Stage 2 (see Grossberg & Todorović, 1988, for details). The diffusion process is further modulated by depth information. The depth map provides this information; different activities code different depths. In a full blown implementation of the model, depth information would be obtained by the depth segmentation of the image supported by both binocular disparity and monocular depth cues.

Depth-modulated filling-in is such that boundaries across depths are reduced in strength. This allows a small percentage of the contrast on either side of the boundary to leak across it resulting in partial contrast negation, or reduction, at these boundaries. ON and OFF filling-in domains are used which receive the corresponding ON and OFF contrast activities from Stage 1 as inputs (see Fig. 2, Filled-in).

4 SIMULATIONS

The present model can account for several important phenomena, including 2 - D effects of lightness constancy and contrast (see Grossberg and Todorović, 1988). The simulations that follow address 3 -D lightness effects.

4.1 Benary Cross

Figure 2 shows the simulation for the Benary Cross. The plotted gray level values for filling-in reflect the activities of the ON filling-in domain minus the OFF domain. The model correctly predicts that the patch on the cross appears lighter than the patch on the background. This result is a direct consequence of contrast negation. The depth relationships are such that the patch on the cross is at the same depth as the cross and the patch on the background is at the same depth as the background (see Fig. 2, Depth Map). Therefore, the ratio of the background to the patch on the cross (across a depth boundary) and the ratio of the cross to the patch on the background (also across a depth boundary), are given a smaller weight in the lightness computation. Thus, the background will have a stronger effect on the appearance of the patch on the background, which will appear darker. At the same time, the cross will have a greater effect on the appearance of the patch on the cross, which will appear lighter.

4.2 White's Illusion

White's (1979) illusion (Fig. 3) is such that the gray patches on the black stripes appear lighter than the gray patches on the white stripes. This effect is considered a puzzling violation of *simultaneous contrast* since the contour length of the gray patches is larger for the stripes they do not lie on. Simultaneous contrast would predict that the gray patches on the black stripes appear lighter than the ones on white.

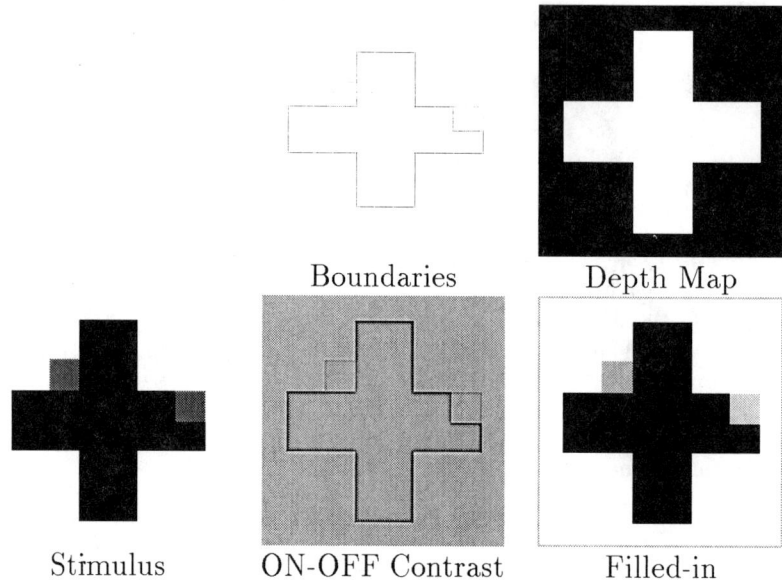

Figure 2: Benary Cross. The filled-in values of the gray patch on the cross are higher than the ones for the gray patch on the background. Gray levels code intensity; darker grays code lower values, lighter grays code higher values.

Figure 3 shows the result of the model for White's effect. The T-junction information in the stimulus determines that the gray patches are coplanar with the patches they lie on. Therefore, their appearance will be determined in relation to the contrast of their respective backgrounds. This is obtained, again, through contrast modulation, where the contrast of, say, the gray patch on a black stripe is preserved, while the contrast of the same patch with the white is partially negated (due to the depth arrangement).

4.3 Coplanar Hypothesis

Gilchrist (1977) showed that the perception of lightness is *not* determined by retinal adjacency, and that depth configuration and spatial layout help specify lightness. More specifically, it was proposed that the ratio of coplanar surfaces, not necessarily retinally adjacent, determines lightness, the so-called coplanar ratio hypothesis. Gilchrist was able to convincingly demonstrate this by comparing the perception of lightness in two equivalent displays (in terms of luminance values), aside from the *perceived* depth relationships in the displays.

Figure 4 shows computer simulations of the coplanar ratio effect. The same stimulus is given as input in two simulations with different depth specifications. In one (Depth Map 1), the depth map specifies that the rightmost patch is at a different depth than the two leftmost patches which are coplanar. In the other (Depth Map 2), the two rightmost patches are coplanar and at a different depth than the leftmost patch. In all, the depth organization alters the lightness of the central region, which should appear darker in the configuration of Depth Map 1 than the one for Depth Map 2. For Depth Map 1, since the middle patch is coplanar with a white patch, this patch is darkened by simultaneous contrast. For Depth Map 2, the middle patch will be lightened by contrast since it is coplanar with a black patch. It should be noted that the depth maps for the simulations shown in Fig. 4 were given as input.

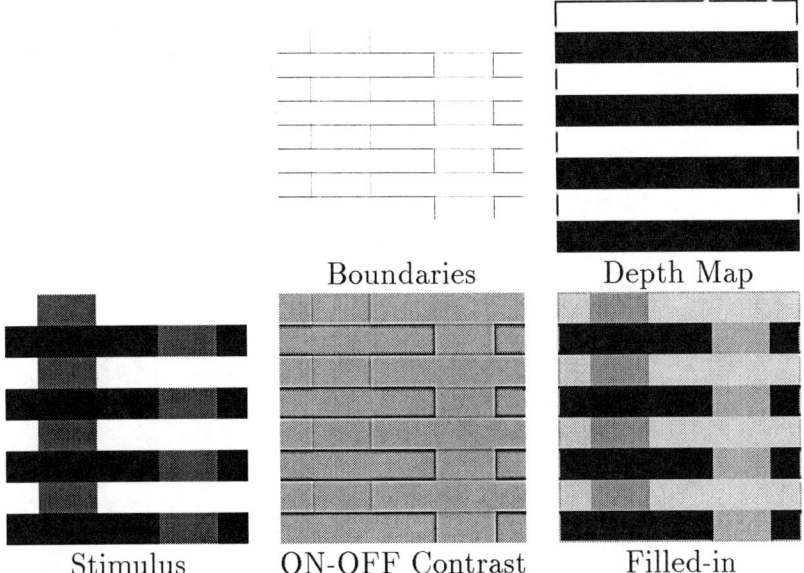

Figure 3: White's effect. The filled-in values of the gray patches on the black stripes are higher than the ones for the gray patches on white stripes.

The current implementation cannot recover depth trough binocular disparity and only employs monocular cues as in the previous simulations.

5 CONCLUSIONS

In this paper, data from experiments on lightness perception were used to extend the BCS/FCS theory of Grossberg and colleagues to account for several challenging phenomena. The model is an initial step towards providing an account that can take into consideration the complex factors involved in 3-D vision — see Grossberg (1994) for a comprehensive account of 3-D vision.

Acknowledgements

The authors would like to than Alan Gilchrist and Fred Bonato for their suggestions concerning this work. L. P. was supported in part by Air Force Office of Scientific Research (AFOSR F49620-92-J-0334) and Office of Naval Research (ONR N00014-91-J-4100); W. R. was supported in part by HNC SC-94-001.

Reference

Arend, L., & Spehar, B. (1993) Lightness, brightness, and brightness contrast: 2. Reflectance variation. *Perception & Psychophysics* **54**:4576-468.

Cohen, M., & Grossberg, S. (1984) Neural dynamics of brightness perception: Features, boundaries, diffusion, and resonance. *Perception & Psychophysics* **36**:428-456.

Gerrits, H. & Vendrik, A. (1970) Simultaneous contrast, filling-in process and information processing in man's visual system. *Experimental Brain Research* **11**:411-430.

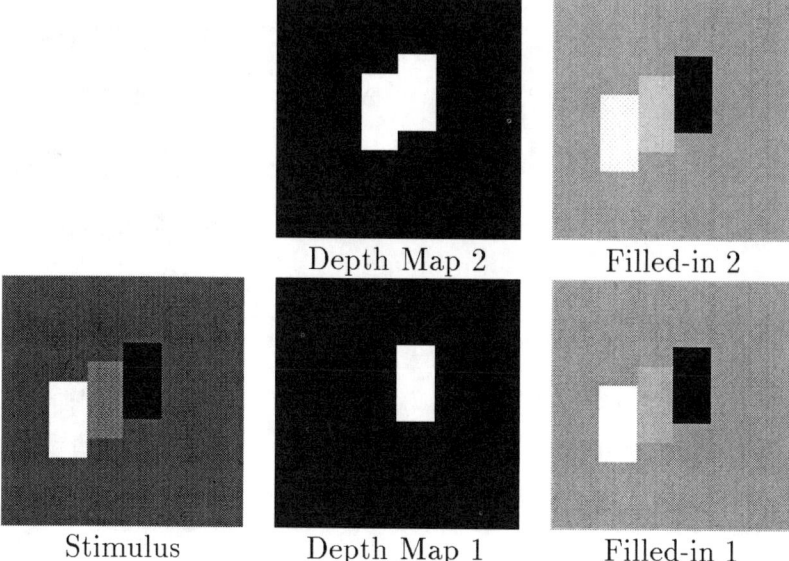

Figure 4: Gilchrist's coplanarity. The Filled-in values for the middle patch on top are higher than on bottom.

Gilchrist, A. (1977) Perceived lightness depends on perceived spatial arrangement. *Science* **195**:185-187.

Grossberg, S. (1994) 3-D vision and figure-ground separation by visual cortex. *Perception & Psychophysics* **55**:48-120.

Grossberg, S., & Mingolla, E. (1985) Neural dynamics of form perception: Boundary completion, illusory figures, and neon color spreading. *Psychological Review* **92**:173-211.

Grossberg, S., & Todorović. D. (1988). Neural dynamics of 1-D and 2-D brightness perception: A unified model of classical and recent phenomena. *Perception & Psychophysics* **43**:241-277.

Land, E., & McCann, J. (1971). Lightness and retinex theory. *Journal of the Optical Society of America* **61**:1-11.

Pessoa, L., Mingolla, E., & Neumann, H. (1995) A contrast- and luminance-driven multiscale network model of brightness perception. *Vision Research* **35**:2201-2223.

Shapley, R., & Enroth-Cugell, C. (1984) Visual adaptation and retinal gain controls. In N. Osborne and G. Chader (eds.), *Progress in Retinal Research*, pp. 263-346. Oxford: Pergamon Press.

Wallach, H. (1948) Brightness constancy and the nature of achromatic colors. *Journal of Experimental Psychology* **38**: 310-324.

White, M. (1979) A new effect of pattern on perceived lightness. *Perception* **8**:413-416.

Whittle, P., & Challands, P. (1969) The effect of background luminance on the brightness of flashes. *Vision Research* **9**:1095-1110.

Empirical Entropy Manipulation for Real-World Problems

Paul Viola,* Nicol N. Schraudolph, Terrence J. Sejnowski
Computational Neurobiology Laboratory
The Salk Institute for Biological Studies
10010 North Torrey Pines Road
La Jolla, CA 92037-1099
viola@salk.edu

Abstract

No finite sample is sufficient to determine the density, and therefore the entropy, of a signal directly. Some assumption about either the functional form of the density or about its smoothness is necessary. Both amount to a prior over the space of possible density functions. By far the most common approach is to assume that the density has a parametric form.

By contrast we derive a differential learning rule called EMMA that optimizes entropy by way of kernel density estimation. Entropy and its derivative can then be calculated by sampling from this density estimate. The resulting parameter update rule is surprisingly simple and efficient.

We will show how EMMA can be used to detect and correct corruption in magnetic resonance images (MRI). This application is beyond the scope of existing parametric entropy models.

1 Introduction

Information theory is playing an increasing role in unsupervised learning and visual processing. For example, Linsker has used the concept of information maximization to produce theories of development in the visual cortex (Linsker, 1988). Becker and Hinton have used information theory to motivate algorithms for visual processing (Becker and Hinton, 1992). Bell and Sejnowski have used information maximization

---

*Author to whom correspondence should be addressed. Current address: M.I.T., 545 Technology Square, Cambridge, MA 02139.

to solve the "cocktail party" or signal separation problem (Bell and Sejnowski, 1995). In order to simplify analysis and implementation, each of these techniques makes specific assumptions about the nature of the signals used, typically that the signals are drawn from some parametric density. In practice, such assumptions are very inflexible.

In this paper we will derive a procedure that can effectively estimate and manipulate the entropy of a wide variety of signals using non-parametric densities. Our technique is distinguished by is simplicity, flexibility and efficiency.

We will begin with a discussion of principal components analysis (PCA) as an example of a simple parametric entropy manipulation technique. After pointing out some of PCA's limitation, we will then derive a more powerful non-parametric entropy manipulation procedure. Finally, we will show that the same entropy estimation procedure can be used to tackle a difficult visual processing problem.

1.1 Parametric Entropy Estimation

Typically parametric entropy estimation is a two step process. We are given a parametric model for the density of a signal and a sample. First, from the space of possible density functions the most probable is selected. This often requires a search through parameter space. Second, the entropy of the most likely density function is evaluated.

Parametric techniques can work well when the assumed form of the density matches the actual data. Conversely, when the parametric assumption is violated the resulting algorithms are incorrect. The most common assumption, that the data follow the Gaussian density, is especially restrictive. An entropy maximization technique that assumes that data is Gaussian, but operates on data drawn from a non-Gaussian density, may in fact end up minimizing entropy.

1.2 Example: Principal Components Analysis

There are a number of signal processing and learning problems that can be formulated as entropy maximization problems. One prominent example is *principal component analysis* (PCA). Given a random variable X, a vector v can be used to define a new random variable, $Y_v = X \cdot v$ with variance $\text{Var}(Y_v) = E[(X \cdot v - E[X \cdot v])^2]$. The principal component $\hat{v}$ is the unit vector for which $\text{Var}(Y_{\hat{v}})$ is maximized.

In practice neither the density of X nor Y_v is known. The projection variance is computed from a finite sample, A, of points from X,

$$\text{Var}(Y_v) \approx \text{Var}_A(Y_v) \equiv E_A[(X \cdot v - E_A[X \cdot v])^2] \ , \tag{1}$$

where $\text{Var}_A(Y_v)$ and $E_A[\cdot]$ are shorthand for the empirical variance and mean evaluated over A. Oja has derived an elegant on-line rule for learning $\hat{v}$ when presented with a sample of X (Oja, 1982).

Under the assumption that X is Gaussian is is easily proven that $Y_{\hat{v}}$ has maximum entropy. Moreover, in the absence of noise, $Y_{\hat{v}}$, contains maximal information about X. However, when X is *not* Gaussian $Y_{\hat{v}}$ is generally not the most informative projection.

2 Estimating Entropy with Parzen Densities

We will now derive a general procedure for manipulating and estimating the entropy of a random variable from a sample. Given a sample of a random variable X, we can construct another random variable $Y = F(X, v)$. The entropy, $h(Y)$, is a function of v and can be manipulated by changing v. The following derivation assumes that Y is a vector random variable. The joint entropy of a two random variables, $h(W_1, W_2)$, can be evaluated by constructing the vector random variable, $Y = [W_1, W_2]^T$ and evaluating $h(Y)$.

Rather than assume that the density has a parametric form, whose parameters are selected using maximum likelihood estimation, we will instead use Parzen window density estimation (Duda and Hart, 1973). In the context of entropy estimation, the Parzen density estimate has three significant advantages over maximum likelihood parametric density estimates: (1) it can model the density of any signal provided the density function is smooth; (2) since the Parzen estimate is computed directly from the sample, there is no search for parameters; (3) the derivative of the entropy of the Parzen estimate is simple to compute.

The form of the Parzen estimate constructed from a sample A is

$$P^*(y, A) = \frac{1}{N_A} \sum_{y_A \in A} R(y - y_A) = E_A[R(y - y_A)], \qquad (2)$$

where the Parzen estimator is constructed with the window function $R(\cdot)$ which integrates to 1. We will assume that the Parzen window function is a Gaussian density function. This will simplify some analysis, but it is *not* necessary. Any differentiable function could be used. Another good choice is the Cauchy density.

Unfortunately evaluating the entropy integral

$$h(Y) \approx -E[\log P^*(Y, A)] = -\int_{-\infty}^{\infty} \log P^*(y, A) dy$$

is inordinately difficult. This integral can however be approximated as a sample mean:

$$h(Y) \approx h^*(Y) \equiv -E_B[\log P^*(Y, A)] \qquad (3)$$

where $E_B[\ ]$ is the sample mean taken over the sample B. The sample mean converges toward the true expectation at a rate proportional to $1/\sqrt{N_B}$ (N_B is the size of B). To reiterate, two samples can be used to estimate the entropy of a density: the first is used to estimate the density, the second is used to estimate the entropy[1]. We call $h^*(Y)$ the EMMA estimate of entropy[2].

One way to extremize entropy is to use the derivative of entropy with respect to v. This may be expressed as

$$\frac{d}{dv} h(Y) \approx \frac{d}{dv} h^*(Y) = -\frac{1}{N_B} \sum_{y_B \in B} \frac{\sum_{y_A \in A} \frac{d}{dv} g_\psi(y_B - y_A)}{\sum_{y_A \in A} g_\psi(y_B - y_A)} \qquad (4)$$

$$= \frac{1}{N_B} \sum_{y_B \in B} \sum_{y_A \in A} W_y(y_B, y_A) \frac{d}{dv} \frac{1}{2} D_\psi(y_B - y_A), \qquad (5)$$

$$\text{where } W_y(y_1, y_2) \equiv \frac{g_\psi(y_1 - y_2)}{\sum_{y_A \in A} g_\psi(y_1 - y_A)}, \qquad (6)$$

$D_\psi(y) \equiv y^T \psi^{-1} y$, and $g_\psi(y)$ is a multi-dimensional Gaussian with covariance ψ. $W_y(y_1, y_2)$ is an indicator of the degree of match between its arguments, in a "soft"

---

[1] Using a procedure akin to leave-one-out cross-validation a single sample can be used for both purposes.

[2] EMMA is a random but pronounceable subset of the letters in the words "Empirical entropy Manipulation and Analysis".

sense. It will approach one if y_1 is significantly closer to y_2 than any element of A. To reduce entropy the parameters v are adjusted such that there is a reduction in the average squared distance between points which W_y indicates are nearby.

2.1 Stochastic Maximization Algorithm

Both the calculation of the EMMA entropy estimate and its derivative involve a double summation. As a result the cost of evaluation is quadratic in sample size: $O(N_A N_B)$. While an accurate estimate of empirical entropy could be obtained by using all of the available data (at great cost), a stochastic estimate of the entropy can be obtained by using a random subset of the available data (at quadratically lower cost). This is especially critical in entropy manipulation problems, where the derivative of entropy is evaluated many hundreds or thousands of times. Without the quadratic savings that arise from using smaller samples entropy manipulation would be impossible (see (Viola, 1995) for a discussion of these issues).

2.2 Estimating the Covariance

In addition to the learning rate λ, the covariance matrices of the Parzen window functions, g_ψ, are important parameters of EMMA. These parameters may be chosen so that they are optimal in the maximum likelihood sense. For simplicity, we assume that the covariance matrices are diagonal, $\psi = \text{DIAG}(\sigma_1^2, \sigma_2^2, \ldots)$. Following a derivation almost identical to the one described in Section 2 we can derive an equation analogous to (4),

$$\frac{d}{d\sigma_k} h^*(Y) = \frac{1}{N_B} \sum_{y_B \in b} \sum_{y_A \in a} W_y(y_B, y_A) \left(\frac{1}{\sigma_k}\right) \left(\frac{[y]_k^2}{\sigma_k^2} - 1\right) \quad (7)$$

where $[y]_k$ is the kth component of the vector y. The optimal, or most likely, ψ minimizes $h^*(Y)$. In practice both v and ψ are adjusted simultaneously; for example, while v is adjusted to maximize $h^*(Y_v)$, ψ is adjusted to minimize $h^*(Y_v)$.

3 Principal Components Analysis and Information

As a demonstration, we can derive a parameter estimation rule akin to principal components analysis that truly maximizes information. This new EMMA based component analysis (ECA) manipulates the entropy of the random variable $Y_v = X \cdot v$ under the constraint that $|v| = 1$. For any given value of v the entropy of Y_v can be estimated from two samples of X as: $h^*(Y_v) = -E_B[\log E_A[g_\psi(x_B \cdot v - x_A \cdot v)]]$, where ψ is the variance of the Parzen window function. Moreover we can estimate the derivative of entropy:

$$\frac{d}{dv} h^*(Y_v) = \frac{1}{N_B} \sum_B \sum_A W_y(y_B, y_A) \psi^{-1}(y_B - y_A)(x_B - x_A) ,$$

where $y_A = x_A \cdot v$ and $y_B = x_B \cdot v$. The derivative may be decomposed into parts which can be understood more easily. Ignoring the weighting function $W_y \psi^{-1}$ we are left with the derivative of some unknown function $f(Y_v)$:

$$\frac{d}{dv} f(Y_v) = \frac{1}{N_B N_A} \sum_B \sum_A (y_B - y_A)(x_B - x_A) \quad (8)$$

What then is $f(Y_v)$? The derivative of the squared difference between samples is: $\frac{d}{dv}(y_B - y_A)^2 = 2(y_B - y_A)(x_B - x_A)$. So we can see that

$$f(Y_v) = \frac{1}{2 N_B N_A} \sum_B \sum_A (y_B - y_A)^2$$

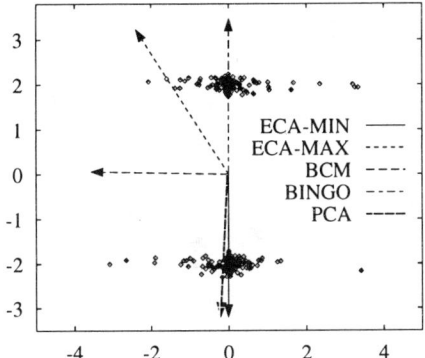

Figure 1: See text for description.

is one half the expectation of the squared difference between pairs of trials of Y_v.

Recall that PCA searches for the projection, Y_v, that has the largest sample variance. Interestingly, $f(Y_v)$ is precisely the sample variance. Without the weighting term $W_y \psi^{-1}$, ECA would find exactly the same vector that PCA does: the maximum variance projection vector. However because of W_y, the derivative of ECA does not act on all points of A and B equally. Pairs of points that are far apart are forced no further apart. Another way of interpreting ECA is as a type of robust variance maximization. Points that might best be interpreted as outliers, because they are very far from the body of other points, play a very small role in the minimization. This robust nature stands in contrast to PCA which is very sensitive to outliers.

For densities that are Gaussian, the maximum entropy projection is the first principal component. In simulations ECA effectively finds the same projection as PCA, and it does so with speeds that are comparable to Oja's rule. ECA can be used both to find the entropy maximizing (ECA-MAX) and minimizing (ECA-MIN) axes. For more complex densities the PCA axis is very different from the entropy maximizing axis. To provide some intuition regarding the behavior of ECA we have run ECA-MAX, ECA-MIN, Oja's rule, and two related procedures, BCM and BINGO, on the same density. BCM is a learning rule that was originally proposed to explain development of receptive fields patterns in visual cortex (Bienenstock, Cooper and Munro, 1982). More recently it has been argued that the rule finds projections that are far from Gaussian (Intrator and Cooper, 1992). Under a limited set of conditions this is equivalent to finding the minimum entropy projection. BINGO was proposed to find axes along which there is a bimodal distribution (Schraudolph and Sejnowski, 1993).

Figure 1 displays a 400 point sample and the projection axes discussed above. The density is a mixture of two clusters. Each cluster has high kurtosis in the horizontal direction. The *oblique* axis projects the data so that it is most uniform and hence has the highest entropy; ECA-MAX finds this axis. Along the *vertical* axis the data is clustered and has low entropy; ECA-MIN finds this axis. The vertical axis also has the highest variance. Contrary to published accounts, the first principal component can in fact correspond to the *minimum* entropy projection. BCM, while it may find minimum entropy projections for some densities, is attracted to the kurtosis along the *horizontal* axis. For this distribution BCM neither minimizes nor maximizes entropy. Finally, BINGO successfully discovers that the *vertical* axis is very bimodal.

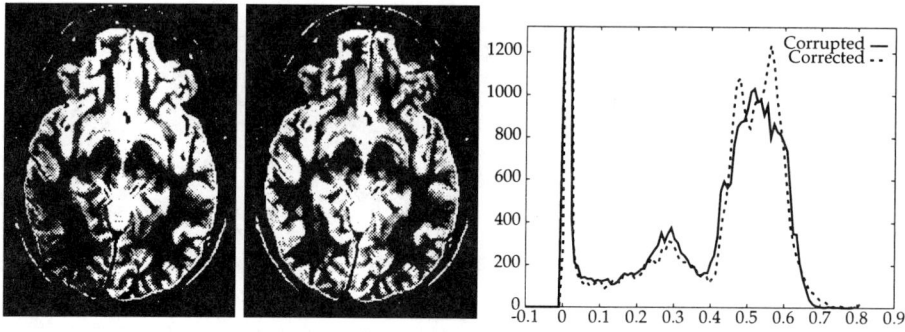

Figure 2: At left: A slice from an MRI scan of a head. Center: The scan after correction. Right: The density of pixel values in the MRI scan before and after correction.

4 Applications

EMMA has proven useful in a number of applications. In object recognition EMMA has been used align 3D shape models with video images (Viola and Wells III, 1995). In the area of medical imaging EMMA has been used to register data that arises from differing medical modalities such as magnetic resonance images, computed tomography images, and positron emission tomography (Wells, Viola and Kikinis, 1995).

4.1 MRI Processing

In addition, EMMA can be used to process magnetic resonance images (MRI). An MRI is a 2 or 3 dimensional image that records the density of tissues inside the body. In the head, as in other parts of the body, there are a number of distinct tissue classes including: bone, water, white matter, grey matter, and fat. In principle the density of pixel values in an MRI should be clustered, with one cluster for each tissue class. In reality MRI signals are corrupted by a bias field, a multiplicative offset that varies slowly in space. The bias field results from unavoidable variations in magnetic field (see (Wells III et al., 1994) for an overview of this problem).

Because the densities of each tissue type cluster together tightly, an uncorrupted MRI should have relatively low entropy. Corruption from the bias field perturbs the MRI image, increasing the values of some pixels and decreasing others. The bias field acts like noise, adding entropy to the pixel density. We use EMMA to find a low-frequency *correction* field that when applied to the image, makes the pixel density have a lower entropy. The resulting corrected image will have a tighter clustering than the original density.

Call the uncorrupted scan $s(x)$; it is a function of a spatial random variable x. The corrupted scan, $c(x) = s(x) + b(x)$ is a sum of the true scan and the bias field. There are physical reasons to believe $b(x)$ is a low order polynomial in the components of x. EMMA is used to minimize the entropy of the corrected signal, $h(c(x) - \hat{b}(x, v))$, where $\hat{b}(x, v)$, a third order polynomial with coefficients v, is an estimate for the bias corruption.

Figure 2 shows an MRI scan and a histogram of pixel intensity before and after correction. The difference between the two scans is quite subtle: the uncorrected scan is brighter at top right and dimmer at bottom left. This non-homogeneity makes constructing automatic tissue classifiers difficult. In the histogram of the original scan white and grey matter tissue classes are confounded into a single peak ranging from about 0.4 to 0.6. The histogram of the corrected scan shows much better separation between these two classes. For images like this the correction field takes between 20 and 200 seconds to compute on a Sparc 10.

5 Conclusion

We have demonstrated a novel entropy manipulation technique working on problems of significant complexity and practical importance. Because it is based on non-parametric density estimation it is quite flexible, requiring no strong assumptions about the nature of signals. The technique is widely applicable to problems in signal processing, vision and unsupervised learning. The resulting algorithms are computationally efficient.

Acknowledgements

This research was support by the Howard Hughes Medical Institute.

References

Becker, S. and Hinton, G. E. (1992). A self-organizing neural network that discovers surfaces in random-dot stereograms. *Nature*, 355:161-163.

Bell, A. J. and Sejnowski, T. J. (1995). An information-maximisation approach to blind separation. In Tesauro, G., Touretzky, D. S., and Leen, T. K., editors, *Advances in Neural Information Processing*, volume 7, Denver 1994. MIT Press, Cambridge.

Bienenstock, E., Cooper, L., and Munro, P. (1982). Theory for the development of neuron selectivity: Orientation specificity and binocular interaction in visual cortex. *Journal of Neuroscience*, 2.

Duda, R. and Hart, P. (1973). *Pattern Classification and Scene Analysis*. Wiley, New York.

Intrator, N. and Cooper, L. N. (1992). Objective function formulation of the bcm theory of visual cortical plasticity: Statistical connections, stability conditions. *Neural Networks*, 5:3-17.

Linsker, R. (1988). Self-organization in a perceptual network. *IEEE Computer*, pages 105-117.

Oja, E. (1982). A simplified neuron model as a principal component analyzer. *Journal of Mathematical Biology*, 15:267-273.

Schraudolph, N. N. and Sejnowski, T. J. (1993). Unsupervised discrimination of clustered data via optimization of binary information gain. In Hanson, S. J., Cowan, J. D., and Giles, C. L., editors, *Advances in Neural Information Processing*, volume 5, pages 499-506, Denver 1992. Morgan Kaufmann, San Mateo.

Viola, P. A. (1995). *Alignment by Maximization of Mutual Information*. PhD thesis, Massachusetts Institute of Technology. MIT AI Laboratory TR 1548.

Viola, P. A. and Wells III, W. M. (1995). Alignment by maximization of mutual information. In *Fifth Intl. Conf. on Computer Vision*, pages 16-23, Cambridge, MA. IEEE.

Wells, W., Viola, P., and Kikinis, R. (1995). Multi-modal volume registration by maximization of mutual information. In *Proceedings of the Second International Symposium on Medical Robotics and Computer Assisted Surgery*, pages 55 – 62. Wiley.

Wells III, W., Grimson, W., Kikinis, R., and Jolesz, F. (1994). Statistical Gain Correction and Segmentation of MRI Data. In *Proceedings of the Computer Society Conference on Computer Vision and Pattern Recognition*, Seattle, Wash. IEEE , Submitted.

Active Gesture Recognition using Learned Visual Attention

Trevor Darrell and Alex Pentland
Perceptual Computing Group
MIT Media Lab
20 Ames Street, Cambridge MA, 02138
trevor,sandy@media.mit.edu

Abstract

We have developed a foveated gesture recognition system that runs in an unconstrained office environment with an active camera. Using vision routines previously implemented for an interactive environment, we determine the spatial location of salient body parts of a user and guide an active camera to obtain images of gestures or expressions. A hidden-state reinforcement learning paradigm is used to implement visual attention. The attention module selects targets to foveate based on the goal of successful recognition, and uses a new multiple-model Q-learning formulation. Given a set of target and distractor gestures, our system can learn where to foveate to maximally discriminate a particular gesture.

1 INTRODUCTION

Vision has numerous uses in the natural world. It is used by many organisms in navigation and object recognition tasks, for finding resources or avoiding predators. Often overlooked in computational models of vision, however, and particularly relevant for humans, is the use of vision for communication and interaction. In these domains visual perception is an important communication modality, either in addition to language or when language cannot be used. In general, people place considerable weight on visual signals from another individual, such as facial expression, hand gestures, and body language. We have been developing neurally-inspired methods which combine low-level vision and learning to model these visual abilities.

Previously, we presented a method for view-based recognition of spatio-temporal hand gestures [2] and a similar mechanism for the analysis/real-time tracking of facial expressions [4]. These methods offered real-time performance and a relatively high level of accuracy, but required foveated images of the object performing the gesture. There are many domains/tasks for which these are not unreasonable assumptions, such as interaction with a single user workstation or an automobile with a single driver. However the method had limited usefulness in unconstrained domains, such as "intelligent rooms" or interactive virtual environments, when the identity and location of the user are unknown.

In this paper, we expand our gesture recognition method to include an active component, utilizing a foveated image sensor that can selectively track a person's hand or face as they walk through a room. The camera tracking and model selection routines are guided by an action-selection system that implements visual attention based on reinforcement learning. Using on a simple reward schedule, this attention system learns the appropriate object (hand, head) to foveate in order to maximize recognition performance.

2   FOVEATED GESTURE ANALYSIS

Our system for foveated gesture recognition combines person tracking routines, an active, high-resolution camera, and view-based normalized correlation analysis. First we will briefly describe the person tracking module and view-based analysis, then discuss their use with an active camera.

We have implemented vision routines to track a user in in an office setting as part of our ALIVE system, an Artificial Life Interactive Video Environment[3]. This system can track people and identify head/hand locations as they walk about a room, and provides the contextual environment within which view-based gesture analysis methods can be successfully applied. The ALIVE system assumed little prior knowledge of the user, and operated on coarse-scale images.[1] ALIVE allows a user to interact with virtual artificial life creatures, through the use of a "magic-mirror" metaphor in which user sees him/herself presented in a video display along with virtual creatures. A wide field-of-view video camera acquires an image of the user, which is then combined with computer graphics imagery and projected on a large screen in front of the user. Vision routines in ALIVE compute figure/ground segmentation and analyze the user's silhouette to determine the location of head, hands, and other salient body features. We use only a single, calibrated, wide field-of-view camera to determine the 3-D position of these features.[2] For details of our person tracking method see [14].

In our approach to real-time expression matching/tracking, a set of view-based correlation models is used to represent spatio-temporal gesture patterns. We take a sequence of images representing the gesture to be trained, and build a set of view models that are sufficient to track the object as it performs the gesture. Our view models are normalized correlation templates, and can either be intensity-based or based on band-pass or wavelet-based signal representations.[3] We applied our model to the problem of hand gesture recognition [2] as well as for tracking facial expressions [4]. For facial tracking, we implemented an interpolation paradigm to map view-based correlation scores to facial motor controls. We used the Radial Basis Function (RBF) method[7]; interpolation was performed using a set of exemplars consisting of pairs of real faces and model faces in different expressions, which were

---

[1] A simple mechanism for recognition of hand gestures was implemented in the original ALIVE system but made no use of high-resolution view models, and could only recognize pointing and waving motions defined by the motion of the centroid of the hand.

[2] By assuming the the user is sitting or standing on the ground plane, we use the imaging and ground plane geometry to compute the location of the user in 3-D.

[3] The latter have the advantage of being less dependent on illumination direction.

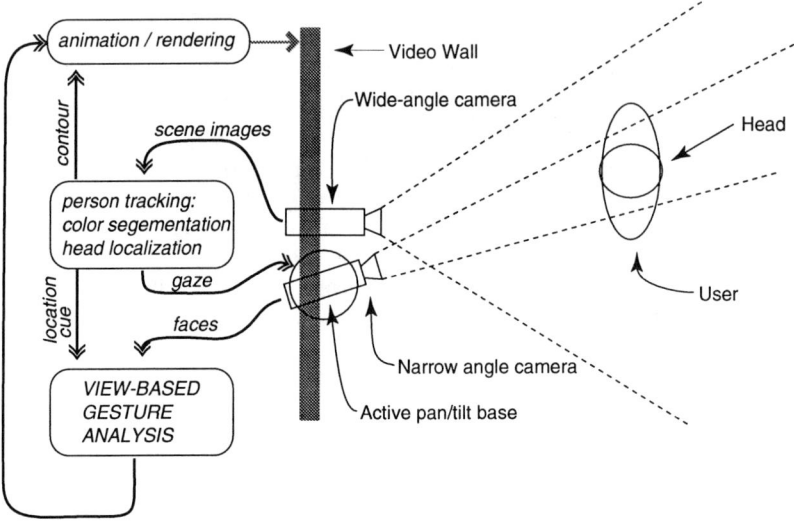

Figure 1: Overview of system for person tracking and active gesture recognition. Static, wide-field-of-view, camera tracks user's head and hands, which drives gaze control of active narrow-field-of-view camera. Foveated images are used for view-based gesture analysis and recognition. Graphical objects are rendered on video wall and can react to user's position, pose, and gestures.

obtained by generating a 3-D model face and asking the user to match it. With this simple formalism, we were able to track expressions of a real user and interpolate equivalent 3-D model faces in real-time.

This view-based analysis requires detailed imagery, which cannot be obtained from a single, fixed camera as the user walks about a room. To provide high resolution images for gesture recognition, we augment the wide field-of-view camera in our interactive environment with an active, narrow-field-of-view camera, as shown in Figure 1. Information about head/hand location from the existing ALIVE routines is used to drive the motor control parameters of the narrow field camera. Currently the camera can be directed to autonomously track head or hands. Using a highly simplified, two expression model of facial expression (neutral and surprised), we have been able to track facial expressions as users move about the room and the narrow angle camera followed the face. For details on this foveated gesture recognition see [5]

3 VISUAL ATTENTION FOR RECOGNITION

The visual routines in the ALIVE system can be used to track the head and hands of a user, and the active camera can provide foveated images for gesture recognition. If we know a priori which body part will produce the gesture of interest, or if we have a sufficient number of active cameras to track all body parts, then we have solved the problem. Of course, in practice there are more possible loci of gesture performance than there are active cameras, and we have to address the problem of action selection for visual routines, i.e., attention. In our active gesture recognition system, we have adopted an action selection model based on reinforcement learning.

3.1 THE ACTIVE GESTURE RECOGNITION PROBLEM

We define an Active Gesture Recognition (AGR) task as follows. First, we assume primitive routines exist to provide the continuous valued control and tracking of the different body parts that perform gestures. Second, we assume that body pose and hand/face state is represented as a feature set, based on the representation produced by our body tracker and view-based recognition system, and we define a gesture to be a configuration of the user's body pose and hand/face expression. Third, we assume that, in addition to there being actions for foveating all the relevant body parts, there is also a special action labeled **accept**, and that the execution of this action by the AGR system signifies detection of the gesture. Finally, the goal of the AGR task is to execute the **accept** action whenever the user is in the target gesture state, and not to perform that action when the user is in any other (e.g. distractor) state. The AGR system should use the foveation actions to optimally discriminate the target pattern from distractor patterns, even when no single view of the user is sufficient to decide what gesture the user is performing.

An important problem in applying reinforcement learning to this task is that our perceptual observations may not provide a complete description of the user's state. Indeed, because we have a foveated image sensor we know that the user's true gestural state will be hidden whenever the user is performing a gesture and the camera is not foveated on the appropriate body part. By definition, a system for perceptual action selection must not assume a full observation of state is available, otherwise there would be no meaningful perception taking place.

The AGR task can be considered as a Partially Observable Markov Decision Process (POMDP), which is essentially a Markov Decision Process without direct access to state[11, 9]. Rather than attempt to solve them explicitly, we look to techniques for hidden state reinforcement learning to find a solution [10, 8, 6, 1]. A POMDP consists of a set of states in the world $\mathcal{S}$, a set of observations $\mathcal{O}$, a set of actions $\mathcal{A}$, a reward function R. After executing an action a, the likelihood of transitioning between two states s, s' is given by $T(s, a, a')$, an observation o is generated with probability $O(s, a, o)$. In practice, T and O are not easily obtainable, and we use reinforcement learning methods which do not require them *a priori*.

Our state is defined by the users pose, facial expression, and hand configurations, expressed in nine variables. Three are boolean and are provided directly by the person tracker: **person-present**, **left-arm-extended**, and **right-arm-extended**. Three more are provided by the foveated gesture recognition system, (**face, left-hand, right-hand**), and take on an integer number of values according to the number of view-based expressions/hand-poses: in our first experiments **face** can be one of **neutral, smile**, or **surprise**, and the hands can each be one of **neutral, point**, or **grab**. In addition, three boolean features represent the internal state of the vision system: **head-foveated, left-hand-foveated, right-hand-foveated**. At each time step, the world is defined by a state $s \in \mathcal{S}$, which is defined by these features. An observation, $o \in \mathcal{O}$, consists of the same feature variables, except that those provided by the foveated gesture system (e.g., head and hands) are only observable when foveated. Thus the **face** variable is hidden unless the **head-foveated** variable is set, the **left-hand** variable hidden unless the **left-hand-foveated** variable set, and similarly with the right hand. Hidden variables are set to a **undefined** value.

The set of actions, $\mathcal{A}$, available to the AGR system are 4 foveation commands: **look-body, look-head, look-left-hand**, and **look-right-hand** plus the special **accept** action. Each foveation command causes the active camera to follow the respective body part, and sets the internal foveation feature bits accordingly.

The reward function provides a unit positive reward whenever the accept action is performed and the user is in the target state (as defined by an oracle, external to the AGR system), and a fixed negative reward of magnitude α when performed and the user is in a distractor (non-target) state. Zero reward is given whenever a foveation action is performed.

3.2 HIDDEN-STATE REINFORCEMENT LEARNING

We have implemented a instance-based method for hidden state reinforcement learning, based on earlier work by McCallum [10]. The instance-based approach to reinforcement learning replaces the absolute state with a distributed memory-based state representation. Given a history of action, reward, and observation tuples, $(a[t], r[t], o[t])$, $0 \leq t \leq T$, a Q-value is also stored with each time step, $q[t]$, and Q-learning[12, 13] is performed by evaluating the similarity of recently observed tuples with sequences farther back in the history chain. Q-values are computed, and the Q-learning update rule applied, maintaining this distributed, memory-based representation of Q-values.

As in traditional Q-learning, at each time step the utility of each action in the current state is evaluated. If full access to the state was available and a table used to represent Q values, this would simply be a table look-up operation, but in a POMDP we do not have full access to state. Using a variation on the instance based approach employed by McAllum's Nearest Sequence Memory (NSM) algorithm, we instead find the K nearest neighbors in the history list relative to the current time point, and compute their average Q value. For each element on the history list, we compute the sequence match criteria with the current time point, $M(i, T)$, where

$$M(i,j) = S(i,j) + M(i-1, j-1) \quad \text{if } S(i,j) > 0 \text{ and } i > 0 \text{ and } j > 0$$
$$0 \quad \text{otherwise}.$$

We define $S(i,j)$ to be 1 if $o[i] = o[j]$ or $a[i] = a[j]$, 2 if both are equal, and 0 otherwise. Using a superscript in parentheses to denote the action index of a Q-value, we then compute

$$Q^{(a)}[T] = (1/K) \sum_{i=0}^{T} v^{(a)}[i] q[t], \quad (1)$$

where $v^{(a^*)}[i]$ indicates whether the history tuple at time step i votes when computing the Q-value of a new action a^*: $v^{(a^*)}[i]$ is set to 1 when $a[i] = a^*$ and $M(i-1, T)$ is among the K largest match values for all k which have $a[k] = a^*$, otherwise it is set to 0. Given Q values for each action the optimal policy is simply

$$\pi[T] = \arg\max_{a \in \mathcal{A}} Q^{(a)}[T]. \quad (2)$$

The new action $a[T+1]$ is chosen either according to this policy or based on an exploration strategy. In either case, the action is executed yielding an observation and reward, and a new tuple added to the history. The new Q-value is set to be the Q value of the chosen action, $q[T+1] = Q^{(a[T+1])}[T]$. The update step of Q learning is then computed, evaluating

$$U[T+1] = \max_{a \in \mathcal{A}} Q^{(a)}[T+1], \quad (3)$$

$$q[i] \leftarrow (1-\beta)q[i] + \beta(r[i] + \gamma U[T+1]), \quad (4)$$

for each i such that $v^{(a[T+1])}[i] = 1$.

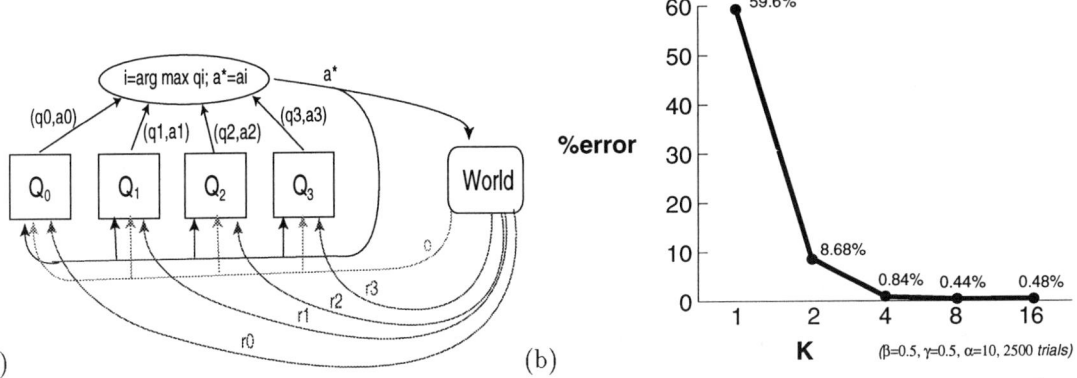

Figure 2: (a) Multiple model Q-learning: one Q-learning agent for each target gesture to be recognized, with coupled observation and action but separate reward and Q-value. (b) Results on recognition task with 8 gesture targets; graph shows error rate after convergence plotted as a function of number of nearest neighbors used in learning algorithm.

4 MULTIPLE MODEL Q-LEARNING

In general, we have found the simple, instance-based hidden state reinforcement learning described above to be an effective way to perform action selection for foveation when the task is recognition of a single object from a set of distractors. However, we did not find that this type of system performed well when the AGR task was extended to include more than one target gesture. When multiple **accept** actions were added to enumerate the different targets, we were not able to find exploration strategies that would converge in reasonable time.

This is not unexpected, since the addition of multiple causes of positive reward makes the Q-value space considerably more complex. To remedy this problem, we propose a multiple model Q-learning system. In a multiple model approach to the AGR problem, separate learning agents model the task from each targets perspective. Conceptually, a separate Q-learning agent exists for each target, maintains it's own Q-value and history structure, and is coupled to the other agents via shared observations. Since we can interpret the Q-value of an individual AGR agent as a confidence value that its target is present, we can mediate among the actions predicted by the different agents by selecting the action from the agent with highest Q-value (Figure 2).

Formally, in our multiple model Q-learning system all agents share the same observation and selected action, but have different reward and Q-values. Thus they can be considered a single Q-learning system, but with vector reward and Q-values. Our multiple model learning system is thus obtained by rewriting Eqs. (1)-(4) with vector $q[t]$ and $r[t]$. Using a subscript j to indicate the target index, we have

$$Q_j^{(a)}[T] = (1/K) \sum_{i=0}^{T} v^{(a)}[i] q_j[t] , \quad \pi[T] = \arg\max_{a \in \mathcal{A}} \left(\max_j Q_j^{(a)}[T] \right) . \quad (5)$$

Rewards are computed with: if $a[T] =$ **accept** then $r_j[T] = R(j,T)$ else $r_j[T] = 0$; $R(j,T) = 1$ if gesture j was present at time T, else $R(j,T) = -\alpha$. Further,

$$U_j[T+1] = \max_{a \in \mathcal{A}} Q_j^{(a)}[T+1] , \quad (6)$$

$$q_j[i] \leftarrow (1-\beta)q_j[i] + \beta(r_j[i] + \gamma U_j[T+1]) \quad \forall \ i \ \text{s.t.} \ v^{(a[T+1])}[i] = 1 \ . \quad (7)$$

Note that our sequence match criteria, unlike that in [10], does not depend on $r[t]$; this allows considerable computational savings in the multiple model system since $v^{(a)}$ need not depend on j.

We ran the multiple model learning system on the AGR task using 8 targets, with $\beta = 0.5, \gamma = 0.5, \alpha = 10$. Results summed over 2500 trials are shown in Figure 2(b), with classification error plotted against the number of nearest neighbors used in the NSM algorithm. The error rate shown is after convergence; we ran the algorithm with a period of deterministic exploration before following the optimal policy. (The system deterministically explored each action/accept pair.) As can be seen from the graph, for any non-degenerate value of K reasonable performance was obtained; for $K > 2$, the system performed almost perfectly.

References

[1] A. Cassandra, L. P. Kaelbling, and M. Littman. Acting optimally in partially observable stochastic domains. In *Proc. AAAI-94*, pages 1023–1028. Morgan Kaufmann, 1994.

[2] T. Darrell and A. P. Pentland. Classification of Hand Gestures using a View-Based Distributed Representation In *Advances in Neural Information Processing Systems 6*, Morgan Kauffman, 1994.

[3] T. Darrell, P. Maes, B. Blumberg, and A. P. Pentland, A Novel Environment for Situated Vision and Behavior, *Proc. IEEE Workshop for Visual Behaviors*, IEEE Comp. Soc. Press, Los Alamitos, CA, 1994

[4] T. Darrell, I. Essa, and A. P. Pentland, Correlation and Interpolation Networks for Real-time Expression Analysis/Synthesis, In *Advances in Neural Information Processing Systems 7*, MIT Press, 1995.

[5] T. Darrell and A. Pentland, A., Attention-driven Expression and Gesture Analysis in an Interactive Environment, in *Proc. Intl. Workshop on Automatic Face and Gesture Recognition (IWAFGR '95)*, Zurich, Switzerland, 1995.

[6] T. Jaakkola, S. Singh, and M. Jordan. Reinforcement Learning Algorithm for Partially Observable Markov Decision Problems. In *Advances In Neural Information Processing Systems 7*, MIT Press, 1995.

[7] T. Poggio and F. Girosi, A Theory of Networks for Approximation and Learning. MIT AI Lab TR-1140, 1989.

[8] L. Lin and T. Michell. Reinforcement learning with hidden states. In *Proc. AAAI-92*. Morgan Kaufmann, 1992.

[9] W. Lovejoy. A survey of algorithmic methods of partially observed markov decision processes. *Annals of Operation Reserach*, 28:47–66, 1991.

[10] R. A. McCallum. Instance-based State Identification for Reinforcement Learning. In *Advances In Neural Information Processing Systems 7*, MIT Press, 1995.

[11] Edward J. Sondik. The optimal control of partially observable markov processes over the infinite horizon: Discounted costs. *Operations Reserach*, 26(2):282–304, 1978.

[12] R. S. Sutton. Learning to predict by the method of temporal differences. *Machine Learning*, 3:9–44, 1988.

[13] C. Watkins and P. Dayan. Q-learning. *Machine Learning*, 8:279–292, 1992.

[14] C. Wren, A. Azarbayejani, T. Darrell, and A. Pentland, Pfinder: Real-Time Tracking of the Human Body, Media Lab Per. Comp. TR-353, 1994

SEEMORE: A View-Based Approach to 3-D Object Recognition Using Multiple Visual Cues

Bartlett W. Mel
Department of Biomedical Engineering
University of Southern California
Los Angeles, CA 90089
mel@quake.usc.edu

Abstract

A neurally-inspired visual object recognition system is described called SEEMORE, whose goal is to identify common objects from a large known set—independent of 3-D viewing angle, distance, and non-rigid distortion. SEEMORE's database consists of 100 objects that are rigid (shovel), non-rigid (telephone cord), articulated (book), statistical (shrubbery), and complex (photographs of scenes). Recognition results were obtained using a set of 102 color and shape feature channels within a simple feedforward network architecture. In response to a test set of 600 novel test views (6 of each object) presented individually in color video images, SEEMORE identified the object correctly 97% of the time (chance is 1%) using a nearest neighbor classifier. Similar levels of performance were obtained for the subset of 15 non-rigid objects. Generalization behavior reveals emergence of striking natural category structure not explicit in the input feature dimensions.

1 INTRODUCTION

In natural contexts, visual object recognition in humans is remarkably fast, reliable, and viewpoint invariant. The present approach to object recognition is "view-based" (e.g. see [Edelman and Bulthoff, 1992]), and has been guided by three main dogmas.

First, the "natural" object recognition problem faced by visual animals involves a large number of objects and scenes, extensive visual experience, and no artificial distinctions among object classes, such as rigid, non-rigid, articulated, etc.

Second, when an object is recognized in the brain, the "heavy lifting" is done by the first wave of action potentials coursing from the retina to the inferotemporal cortex (IT) over a period of 100 ms [Oram and Perrett, 1992]. The computations carried out during this time can be modeled as a shallow but very wide feedforward network of simple image filtering operations. Shallow means few processing levels, wide means a sparse, high-dimensional representation combining cues from multiple visual submodalities, such as color, texture, and contour [Tanaka et al., 1991].

Third, more complicated processing mechanisms, such as those involving focal attention, segmentation, binding, normalization, mental rotation, dynamic links, parts recognition, etc., may exist and may enhance recognition performance but are not necessary to explain rapid, robust recognition with objects in normal visual situations.

In this vein, the main goal of this project has been to explore the limits of performance of a shallow—but very wide—feedforward network of simple filtering operations for viewpoint-invariant 3-D object recognition, where the filter "channels" themselves have been loosely modeled after the shape- and color-sensitive visual response properties seen in the higher levels of the primate visual system [Tanaka et al., 1991]. Architecturally similar approaches to vision have been most often applied in the domain of optical character recognition [Fukushima et al., 1983, Le Cun et al., 1990]. SEEMORE'S architecture is also similar in spirit to the color histogramming approach of [Swain and Ballard, 1991], but includes spatially-structured features that provide also for shape-based generalization.

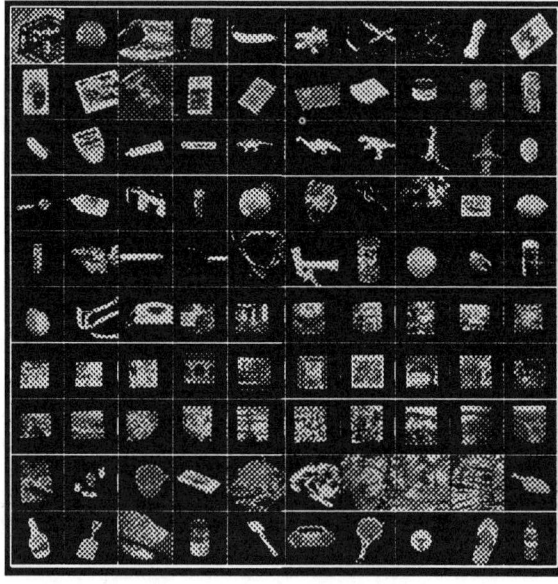

Figure 1: The database includes 100 objects of many different types, including rigid (soup can), non-rigid (necktie), statistical (bunch of grapes), and photographs of complex indoor and outdoor scenes.

2 SEEMORE'S VISUAL WORLD

SEEMORE's database contains 100 common 3-D objects and photogaphs of scenes, each represented by a set of pre-segmented color video images (fig. 1). The training set consisted of 12–36 views of each object as follows. For rigid objects, 12 training views were chosen at roughly 60° intervals in depth around the viewing sphere, and each view was then scaled to yield a total of three images at 67%, 100%, and 150%. Image plane orientation was allowed to vary arbitrarily. For non-rigid objects, 12 training views were chosen in random poses.

During a recognition trial, SEEMORE was required to identify novel test images of the database objects. For rigid objects, test images were drawn from the viewpoint intersices of the training set, excluding highly foreshortened views (e.g. bottom of can). Each test view could therefore be presumed to be correctly recognizable, but never closer than roughly 30° in orientation in depth or 22% in scale to the nearest training view of the object, while position and orientation in the image plane could vary arbitrarily. For non-rigid objects, test images consisted of novel random poses. Each test view depicted the isolated object on a smooth background.

2.1 FEATURE CHANNELS

SEEMORE's internal representation of a view of an object is encoded by a set of feature channels. The ith channel is based on an elemental nonlinear filter $f_i(x, y, \theta_1, \theta_2, \ldots)$, parameterized by position in the visual field and zero or more internal degrees of freedom. Each channel is by design relatively sensitive to changes in the image that are strongly related to object identity, such as the object's shape, color, or texture, while remaining relatively insensitive to changes in the image that are unrelated to object identity, such as are caused by changes in the object's pose. In practice, this invariance is achieved in a straightforward way for each channel by subsampling and summing the output of the elemental channel filter over the entire visual field and one or more of its internal degrees of freedom, giving a channel output $F_i = \sum_{x,y,\theta_1,\ldots} f_i()$. For example, a particular shape-sensitive channel might "look" for the image-plane projections of right-angle corners, over the entire visual field, 360° of rotation in the image plane, 30° of rotation in depth, one octave in scale, and tolerating partial occlusion and/or slight misorientation of the elemental contours that define the right angle. In general, then, F_i may be viewed as a "cell" with a large receptive field whose output is an estimate of the number of occurences of distal feature i in the workspace over a large range of viewing parameters.

SEEMORE's architecture consists of 102 feature channels, whose outputs form an input vector to a nearest-neighbor classifer. Following the design of the individual channels, the channel vector $\mathbf{F} = \{F_1, \ldots F_{102}\}$ is (1) insensitive to changes in image plane position and orientation of the object, (2) modestly sensitive to changes in object scale, orientation in depth, or non-rigid deformation, but (3) highly sensitive to object "quality" as pertains to object identity. Within this representation, total memory storage for all views of an object ranged from 1,224 to 3,672 integers.

As shown in fig. 2, SEEMORE's channels fall into in five groups: (1) 23 color channels, each of which responds to a small blob of color parameterized by "best" hue and saturation, (2) 11 coarse-scale intensity corner channels parameterized by open angle, (3) 12 "blob" features, parameterized by the shape (round and elongated) and size (small, medium, and large) of bright and dark intensity blobs, (4) 24 contour shape features, including straight angles, curve segments of varying radius, and parallel and oblique line combinations, and (5) 16 shape/texture-related features based on the outputs of Gabor functions at 5 scales and 8 orientations. The implementations of the channel groups were crude, in the interests of achieving a working, multiple-cue system with minimal development time. Images were grabbed using an off-the-shelf Sony S-Video Camcorder and SunVideo digitizing board.

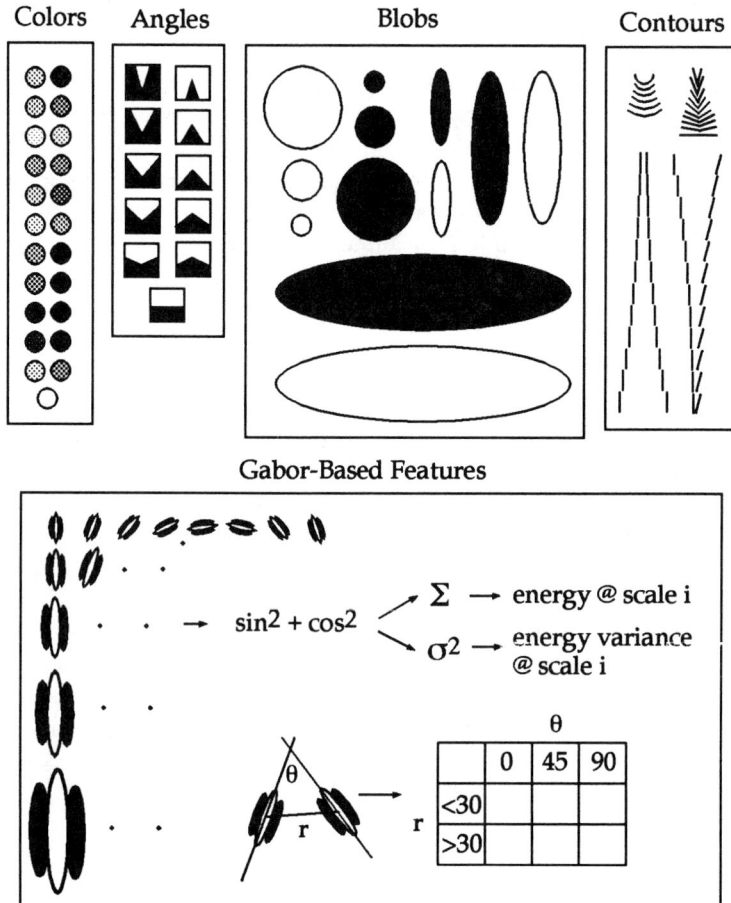

Figure 2: SEEMORE's 102 channels fall into 5 groups, sensitive to (1) colors, (2) intensity corners, (3) circular and elongated intensity blobs, (4) contour shape features, and (5) 16 oriented-energy and relative-orientation features based on the outputs of Gabor functions at several scales and orientations.

3 RECOGNITION

SEEMORE's recognition performance was assesed quantitatively as follows. A test set consisting of 600 novel views (100 objects x 6 views) was culled from the database, and presented to SEEMORE for identification. It was noted empirically that a compressive transform on the feature dimensions (histogram values) led to improved classification performance; prior to all learning and recognition operations,

SEEMORE: A View-based Approach to 3-D Object Recognition

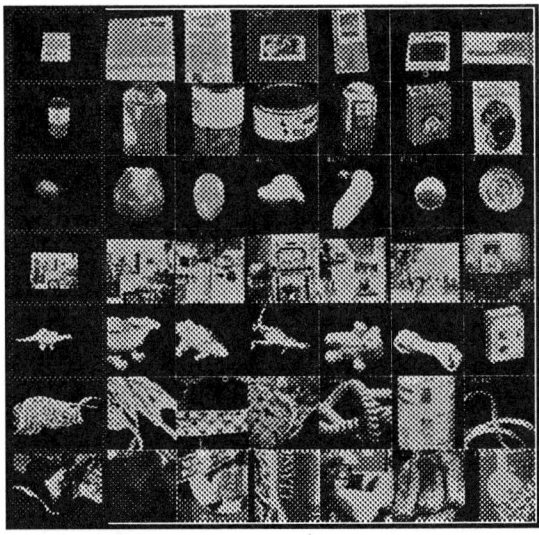

Figure 3: Generalization using only shape-related channels. In each row, a novel test view is shown at far left. The sequence of best matching training views (one per object) is shown to right, in order of decreasing similarity.

therefore, each feature value was replaced by its natural logarithm (0 values were first replaced with a small positive constant to prevent the logarithm from blowing up). For each test view, the city-block distance was computed to every training view in the database and the nearest neighbor was chosen as the best match. The log transform of the feature dimensions thus tied this distance to the ratios of individual feature values in two images rather than their differences.

4 RESULTS

Recognition time on a Sparc-20 was 1-2 minutes per view; the bulk of the time was devoted to shape processing, with under 2 seconds required for matching.

Recognition results are reported as the proportion of test views that were correctly classified. Performance using all 102 channels for the 600 novel object views in the intact test set was 96.7%; the chance rate of correct classification was 1%. Across recognition conditions, second-best matches usually accounted for approximately half the errors. Results were broken down in terms of the separate contributions to recognition performance of color-related vs. shape-related feature channels. Performance using only the 23 color-related channels was 87.3%, and using only the 79 shape-related channels was 79.7%. Remarkably, very similar performance figures were obtained for the subset of 90 test views of the non-rigid objects, which included several scarves, a bike chain, necklace, belt, sock, necktie, maple-leaf cluster, bunch of grapes, knit bag, and telephone cord. Thus, a novel random configuration of a telephone cord was as easily recognized as a novel view of a shovel.

5 GENERALIZATION BEHAVIOR

Numerical indices of recognition performance are useful, but do not explicitly convey the similarity structure of the underlying feature space. A more qualitative but extremely informative representation of system performance lies in the sequence of images in order of increasing distance from a test view. Records of this kind are shown in fig. 3 for trials in which only shape-related channels were used. In each, a test view is shown at the far left, and the ordered set of nearest neighbors is shown to the right. When a test view's nearest neighbor (second image from left) was not the correct match, the trial was classified as an error.

As shown in row (1), a view of a book is judged most similar to a series of other books (or the bottom of a rectangular cardboard box)—each a view of a rectangular object with high-frequency surface markings. A similar sequence can be seen in subsequent rows for (2) a series of cans, each a right cylinder with detailed surface markings, (3) a series of smooth, not-quite-round objects, (4) a series of photographs of complex scenes, and (5) a series of dinosaurs (followed by a teddy bear). In certain cases, SEEMORE's shape-related similarity metric was more difficult to visually interpret or verbalize (last two rows), or was different from that of a human observer.

6 DISCUSSION

The ecology of natural object vision gives rise to an apparent contradiction: (i) generalization in shape-space must in some cases permit an object whose global shape has been grossly perturbed to be matched to itself, such as the various tangled forms of a telephone cord, but (ii) quasi-rigid basic-level shape categories (e.g. chair, shoe, tree) must be preserved as well, and distinguished from each other.

A partial resolution to this conundrum lies in the observation that locally-computed shape statistics are in large part preserved under the global shape deformations that non-rigid common objects (e.g. scarf, bike-chain) typically undergo. A feature-space representation with an emphasis on locally-derived shape channels will therefore exhibit a significant degree of invariance to global nonrigid shape deformations. The definition of shape similarity embodied in the present approach is that two objects are similar if they contain similar profiles (histograms) of their shape measures, which emphasize locality. One way of understanding the emergence of global shape categories, then, such as "book", "can", "dinosaur", etc., is to view each as a set of instances of a single canonical object whose local shape statistics remain quasi-stable as it is warped into various global forms. In many cases, particularly within rigid object categories, exemplars may share longer-range shape statistics as well.

It is useful to consider one further aspect of SEEMORE's shape representation, pertaining to an apparent mismatch between the simplicity of the shape-related feature channels and the complexity of the shape categories that can emerge from them. Specifically, the order of binding of spatial relations within SEEMORE's shape channels is relatively low, i.e. consisting of single simple open or closed curves, or conjunctions of two oriented contours or Gabor patches. The fact that shape categories, such as "photographs of rooms", or "smooth lumpy objects", cluster together in a feature space of such low binding order would therefore at first seem surprising. This phenomenon relates closely to the notion of "wickelfeatures" (see [Rumelhart and McClelland, 1986], ch. 18), in which features (relating to phonemes) that bind spatial information only locally are nonetheless used to represent global patterns (words) with little or no residual ambiguity.

The presegmentation of objects is a simplifying assumption that is clearly invalid in the real world. The advantage of the assumption from a methodological perspective is that the object similarity structure induced by the feature dimensions can be studied independently from the problem of segmenting or indexing objects imbedded in complex scenes. In continuing work, we are pursuing a leap to sparse very-high-dimensional space (e.g. 10,000 dimensions), whose advantages for classification in the presence of noise (or clutter) have been discussed elsewhere [Kanerva, 1988, Califano and Mohan, 1994].

Acknowledgements

Thanks to József Fiser for useful discussions and for development of the Gabor-based channel set, to Dan Lipofsky and Scott Dewinter for helping in the construction of the image database, and to Christof Koch for providing support at Caltech where this work was initiated. This work was funded by the Office of Naval Research, and the McDonnell-Pew Foundation.

References

[Califano and Mohan, 1994] Califano, A. and Mohan, R. (1994). Multidimensional indexing for recognizing visual shapes. *IEEE Trans. on PAMI*, 16:373–392.

[Edelman and Bulthoff, 1992] Edelman, S. and Bulthoff, H. (1992). Orientation dependence in the recognition of familiar and novel views of three-dimensional objects. *Vision Res.*, 32:2385–2400.

[Fukushima et al., 1983] Fukushima, K., Miyake, S., and Ito, T. (1983). Neocognitron: A neural network model for a mechanism of visual pattern recognition. *IEEE Trans. Sys. Man & Cybernetics*, SMC-13:826–834.

[Kanerva, 1988] Kanerva, P. (1988). *Sparse distributed memory*. MIT Press, Cambridge, MA.

[Le Cun et al., 1990] Le Cun, Y., Matan, O., Boser, B., Denker, J., Henderson, D., Howard, R., Hubbard, W., Jackel, L., and Baird, H. (1990). Handwritten zip code recognition with multilayer networks. In *Proc. of the 10th Int. Conf. on Patt. Rec.* IEEE Computer Science Press.

[Oram and Perrett, 1992] Oram, M. and Perrett, D. (1992). Time course of neural responses discriminating different views of the face and head. *J. Neurophysiol.*, 68(1):70–84.

[Rumelhart and McClelland, 1986] Rumelhart, D. and McClelland, J. (1986). *Parallel distributed processing*. MIT Press, Cambridge, Massachusetts.

[Swain and Ballard, 1991] Swain, M. and Ballard, D. (1991). Color indexing. *Int. J. Computer Vision*, 7:11–32.

[Tanaka et al., 1991] Tanaka, K., Saito, H., Fukada, Y., and Moriya, M. (1991). Coding visual images of objects in the inferotemporal cortex of the macaque monkey. *J. Neurophysiol.*, 66:170–189.

PART VIII
APPLICATIONS

Human Face Detection in Visual Scenes

Henry A. Rowley
har@cs.cmu.edu

Shumeet Baluja
baluja@cs.cmu.edu

Takeo Kanade
tk@cs.cmu.edu

School of Computer Science, Carnegie Mellon University, Pittsburgh, PA 15213, USA

Abstract

We present a neural network-based face detection system. A retinally connected neural network examines small windows of an image, and decides whether each window contains a face. The system arbitrates between multiple networks to improve performance over a single network. We use a bootstrap algorithm for training, which adds false detections into the training set as training progresses. This eliminates the difficult task of manually selecting non-face training examples, which must be chosen to span the entire space of non-face images. Comparisons with another state-of-the-art face detection system are presented; our system has better performance in terms of detection and false-positive rates.

1 INTRODUCTION

In this paper, we present a neural network-based algorithm to detect frontal views of faces in gray-scale images. The algorithms and training methods are general, and can be applied to other views of faces, as well as to similar object and pattern recognition problems.

Training a neural network for the face detection task is challenging because of the difficulty in characterizing prototypical "non-face" images. Unlike in face *recognition*, where the classes to be discriminated are different faces, in face *detection*, the two classes to be discriminated are "images containing faces" and "images not containing faces". It is easy to get a representative sample of images which contain faces, but much harder to get a *representative sample* of those which do not. The size of the training set for the second class can grow very quickly.

We avoid the problem of using a huge training set of non-faces by selectively adding images to the training set as training progresses [Sung and Poggio, 1994]. This "bootstrapping" method reduces the size of the training set needed. Detailed descriptions of this training method, along with the network architecture are given in Section 2. In Section 3 the performance of the system is examined. We find that the system is able to detect 92.9% of faces with an acceptable number of false positives. Section 4 compares this system with a similar system. Conclusions and directions for future research are presented in Section 5.

2 DESCRIPTION OF THE SYSTEM

Our system consists of two major parts: a set of neural network-based filters, and a system to combine the filter outputs. Below, we describe the design and training of the filters, which scan the input image for faces. This is followed by descriptions of algorithms for arbitrating among multiple networks and for merging multiple overlapping detections.

2.1 STAGE ONE: A NEURAL NETWORK-BASED FILTER

The first component of our system is a filter that receives as input a small square region of the image, and generates an output ranging from 1 to -1, signifying the presence or absence of a face, respectively. To detect faces anywhere in the input, the filter must be applied at every location in the image. To allow detection of faces larger than the window size, the input image is repeatedly reduced in size (by subsampling), and the filter is applied at each size. The set of scaled input images is known as an "image pyramid", and is illustrated in Figure 1. The filter itself must have some invariance to position and scale. The amount of invariance in the filter determines the number of scales and positions at which the filter must be applied.

With these points in mind, we can give the filtering algorithm (see Figure 1). It consists of two main steps: a preprocessing step, followed by a forward pass through a neural network. The preprocessing consists of lighting correction, which equalizes the intensity values across the window, followed by histogram equalization, which expands the range of intensities in the window [Sung and Poggio, 1994]. The preprocessed window is used as the input to the neural network. The network has retinal connections to its input layer; the receptive fields of each hidden unit are shown in the figure. Although the figure shows a single hidden unit for each subregion of the input, these units can be replicated. Similar architectures are commonly used in speech and character recognition tasks [Waibel *et al.*, 1989, Le Cun *et al.*, 1989].

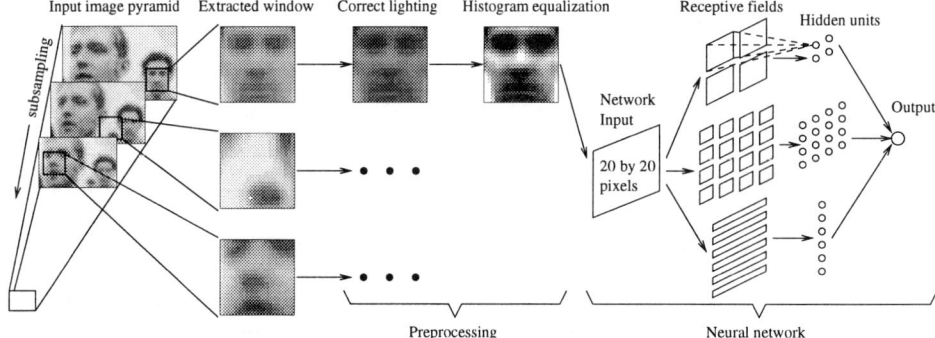

Figure 1: The basic algorithm used for face detection.

Examples of output from a single filter are shown in Figure 2. In the figure, each box represents the position and size of a window to which the neural network gave a positive response. The network has some invariance to position and scale, which results in multiple boxes around some faces. Note that there are some false detections; we present methods to eliminate them in Section 2.2. We next describe the training of the network which generated this output.

2.1.1 Training Stage One

To train a neural network to serve as an accurate filter, a large number of face and non-face images are needed. Nearly 1050 face examples were gathered from face databases at CMU and Harvard. The images contained faces of various sizes, orientations, positions, and intensities. The eyes and upper lip of each face were located manually, and these points were used to normalize each face to the same scale, orientation, and position. A 20-by-20 pixel region containing the face is extracted and preprocessed (by apply lighting correction and histogram equalization). In the training set, 15 faces were created from each original image, by slightly rotating (up to 10°), scaling (90%–110%), translating (up to half a pixel),

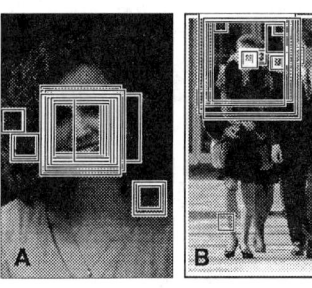

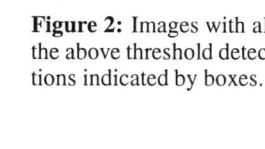

Figure 2: Images with all the above threshold detections indicated by boxes.

Figure 3: Example face images, randomly mirrored, rotated, translated, and scaled by small amounts.

and mirroring each face. A few example images are shown in Figure 3.

It is difficult to collect a *representative* set of non-faces. Instead of collecting the images before training is started, the images are collected during training, as follows [Sung and Poggio, 1994]:

1. Create 1000 non-face images using random pixel intensities.
2. Train a neural network to produce an output of 1 for the face examples, and -1 for the non-face examples.
3. Run the system on an image of scenery which contains no faces. Collect subimages in which the network incorrectly identifies a face (an output activation > 0).
4. Select up to 250 of these subimages at random, and add them into the training set. Go to step 2.

Some examples of non-faces that are collected during training are shown in Figure 4. We used 120 images for collecting negative examples in this bootstrapping manner. A typical training run selects approximately 8000 non-face images from the 146,212,178 subimages that are available at all locations and scales in the scenery images.

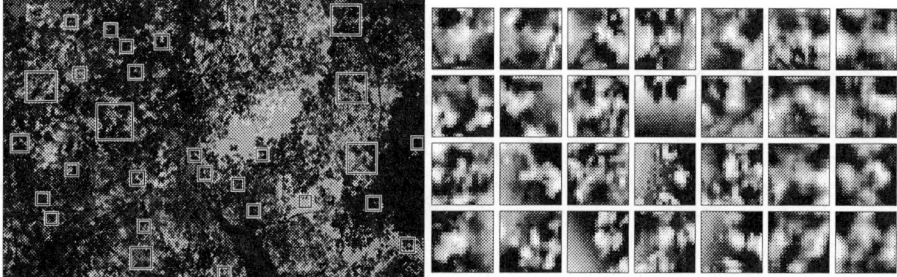

Figure 4: Some non-face examples which are collected during training.

2.2 STAGE TWO: ARBITRATION AND MERGING OVERLAPPING DETECTIONS

The examples in Figure 2 showed that just one network cannot eliminate all false detections. To reduce the number of false positives, we apply two networks, and use arbitration to produce the final decision. Each network is trained in a similar manner, with random initial weights, random initial non-face images, and random permutations of the order of presentation of the scenery images. The detection and false positive rates of the individual networks are quite close. However, because of different training conditions and because of self-selection of negative training examples, the networks will have different biases and will make different errors.

For the work presented here, we used very simple arbitration strategies. Each detection by a filter at a particular position and scale is recorded in an image pyramid. One way to combine two such pyramids is by ANDing. This strategy signals a detection only if both networks detect a face at precisely the same scale and position. This ensures that, if a particular false detection is made by only one network, the combined output will not have that error. The disadvantage is that if an actual face is detected by only one network, it will be lost in the combination. Similar heuristics, such as ORing the outputs, were also tried.

Further heuristics (applied either before or after the arbitration step) can be used to improve the performance of the system. Note that in Figure 2, most faces are detected at multiple nearby positions or scales, while false detections often occur at single locations. At each location in an image pyramid representing detections, the number of detections within a specified neighborhood of that location can be counted. If the number is above a threshold, then that location is classified as a face. These detections are then collapsed down to a single point, located at their centroid. When this is done before arbitration, the centroid locations rather than the actual outputs from the networks are ANDed together.

If we further assume that a position is correctly identified as a face, then all other detections which overlap it are likely to be errors, and can therefore be eliminated. There are relatively few cases in which this heuristic fails; however, one such case is illustrated in the left two faces in Figure 2B, in which one face partially occludes another. Together, the steps of combining multiple detections and eliminating overlapping detections will be referred to as *merging detections*. In the next section, we show that by merging detections and arbitrating among multiple networks, we can reduce the false detection rate significantly.

3 EMPIRICAL RESULTS

A large number of experiments were performed to evaluate the system. Because of space restrictions only a few results are reported here; further results are presented in [Rowley et al., 1995]. We first show an analysis of which features the neural network is using to detect faces, and then present the error rates of the system over two large test sets.

3.1 SENSITIVITY ANALYSIS

In order to determine which part of the input image the network uses to decide whether the input is a face, we performed a sensitivity analysis using the method of [Baluja and Pomerleau, 1995]. We collected a test set of face images (based on the training database, but with different randomized scales, translations, and rotations than were used for training), and used a set of negative examples collected during the training of an earlier version of the system. Each of the 20-by-20 pixel input images was divided into 100 two-by-two pixel subimages. For each subimage in turn, we went through the test set, replacing that subimage with random noise, and tested the neural network. The sum of squared errors made by the network is an indication of how important that portion of the image is for the detection task. Plots of the error rates for two networks we developed are shown in Figure 5.

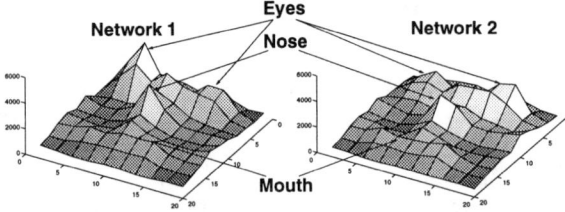

Figure 5: Sum of squared errors (z-axis) on a small test resulting from adding noise to various portions of the input image (horizontal plane), for two networks. Network 1 uses two sets of the hidden units illustrated in Figure 1, while network 2 uses three sets.

The networks rely most heavily on the eyes, then on the nose, and then on the mouth (Figure 5). Anecdotally, we have seen this behavior on several real test images: the network's accuracy decreases more when an eye is occluded than when the mouth is occluded. Further, when both eyes of a face are occluded, it is rarely detected.

3.2 TESTING

The system was tested on two large sets of images. Test Set A was collected at CMU, and consists of 42 scanned photographs, newspaper pictures, images collected from the World Wide Web, and digitized television pictures. Test set B consists of 23 images provided by Sung and Poggio; it was used in [Sung and Poggio, 1994] to measure the accuracy of their system. These test sets require the system to analyze 22,053,124 and 9,678,084 windows, respectively. Table 1 shows the performance for the two networks working alone, the effect of overlap elimination and collapsing multiple detections, and the results of using ANDing and ORing for arbitration. Each system has a better false positive rate (but a worse detection rate) on Test Set A than on Test Set B, because of differences in the types of images in the two sets. Note that for systems using arbitration, the ratio of false detections to windows examined is extremely low, ranging from 1 in 146,638 to 1 in 5,513,281, depending on the type of arbitration used. Figure 6 shows some example output images from the system, produced by merging the detections from networks 1 and 2, and ANDing the results. Using another neural network to arbitrate among the two networks gives about the same performance as the simpler schemes presented above [Rowley et al., 1995].

Table 1: Detection and Error Rates

Type	System	Test Set A # miss / Detect rate False detects / Rate		Test Set B # miss / Detect rate False detects / Rate	
	0) Ideal System	0/169	100.0%	0/155	100.0%
		0	0/22053124	0	0/9678084
Single network, no heuristics	1) Network 1 (52 hidden units, 2905 connections)	17	89.9%	11	92.9%
		507	1/43497	353	1/27417
	2) Network 2 (78 hidden units, 4357 connections)	20	88.2%	10	93.5%
		385	1/57281	347	1/27891
Single network, with heuristics	3) Network 1 → merge detections	24	85.8%	12	92.3%
		222	1/99338	126	1/76810
	4) Network 2 → merge detections	27	84.0%	13	91.6%
		179	1/123202	123	1/78684
Arbitrating among two networks	5) Networks 1 and 2 → AND → merge detections	52	69.2%	34	78.1%
		4	1/5513281	3	1/3226028
	6) Networks 1 and 2 → merge detections → AND	36	78.7%	20	87.1%
		15	1/1470208	15	1/645206
	7) Networks 1 and 2 → merge → OR → merge	26	84.6%	11	92.9%
		90	1/245035	64	1/151220

4 COMPARISON TO OTHER SYSTEMS

[Sung and Poggio, 1994] reports a face-detection system based on clustering techniques. Their system, like ours, passes a small window over all portions of the image, and determines whether a face exists in each window. Their system uses a supervised clustering method with six "face" and six "non-face" clusters. Two distance metrics measure the distance of an input image to the prototype clusters. The first metric measures the "partial" distance between the test pattern and the cluster's 75 most significant eigenvectors. The second distance metric is the Euclidean distance between the test pattern and its projection in the 75 dimensional subspace. These distance measures have close ties with Principal Components Analysis (PCA), as described in [Sung and Poggio, 1994]. The last step in their system is to use either a perceptron or a neural network with a hidden layer, trained to classify points using the two distances to each of the clusters (a total of 24 inputs). Their system is trained with 4000 positive examples, and nearly 47500 negative examples collected in the "bootstrap" manner. In comparison, our system uses approximately 16000 positive examples and 8000 negative examples.

Table 2 shows the accuracy of their system on Test Set B, along with the results of our

Figure 6: Output produced by System 6 in Table 1. For each image, three numbers are shown: the number of faces in the image, the number of faces detected correctly, and the number of false detections. Some notes on specific images: Although the system was not trained on hand-drawn faces, it detects them in K and R. One false detect is present in both D and R. Faces are missed in D (removed because a false detect overlapped it), B (one due to occlusion, and one due to large angle), and in N (babies with fingers in their mouths are not well represented in training data). Images B, D, F, K, L, and M were provided by Sung and Poggio at MIT. Images A, G, O, and P were scanned from photographs, image R was obtained with a CCD camera, images J and N were scanned from newspapers, images H, I, and Q were scanned from printed photographs, and image C was obtained off of the World Wide Web. Images P and B correspond to Figures 2A and 2B.

system using a variety of arbitration heuristics. In [Sung and Poggio, 1994], only 149 faces were labelled in the test set, while we labelled 155 (some are difficult for either system to detect). The number of missed faces is therefore six more than the values listed in their paper. Also note that [Sung and Poggio, 1994] check a slightly smaller number of windows over the entire test set; this is taken into account when computing the false detection rates. The table shows that we can achieve higher detection rates with fewer false detections.

Table 2: Comparison of [Sung and Poggio, 1994] and Our System on Test Set B

System	Missed faces	Detect rate	False detects	Rate
5) Networks 1 and 2 → AND → merge	34	78.1%	3	1/3226028
6) Networks 1 and 2 → merge → AND	20	87.1%	15	1/645206
7) Networks 1 and 2 → merge → OR → merge	11	92.9%	64	1/151220
[Sung and Poggio, 1994] (Multi-layer network)	36	76.8%	5	1/1929655
[Sung and Poggio, 1994] (Perceptron)	28	81.9%	13	1/742175

5 CONCLUSIONS AND FUTURE RESEARCH

Our algorithm can detect up to 92.9% of faces in a set of test images with an acceptable number of false positives. This is a higher detection rate than [Sung and Poggio, 1994]. The system can be made more conservative by varying the arbitration heuristics or thresholds.

Currently, the system does not use temporal coherence to focus attention on particular portions of the image. In motion sequences, the location of a face in one frame is a strong predictor of the location of a face in next frame. Standard tracking methods can be applied to focus the detector's attention. The system's accuracy might be improved with more positive examples for training, by using separate networks to recognize different head orientations, or by applying more sophisticated image preprocessing and normalization techniques.

Acknowledgements

The authors thank Kah-Kay Sung and Dr. Tomaso Poggio (at MIT), Dr. Woodward Yang (at Harvard), and Michael Smith (at CMU) for providing training and testing images. We also thank Eugene Fink, Xue-Mei Wang, and Hao-Chi Wong for comments on drafts of this paper.

This work was partially supported by a grant from Siemens Corporate Research, Inc., and by the Department of the Army, Army Research Office under grant number DAAH04-94-G-0006. Shumeet Baluja was supported by a National Science Foundation Graduate Fellowship. The views and conclusions in this document are those of the authors, and should not be interpreted as necessarily representing official policies or endorsements, either expressed or implied, of the sponsoring agencies.

References

[Baluja and Pomerleau, 1995] Shumeet Baluja and Dean Pomerleau. Encouraging distributed input reliance in spatially constrained artificial neural networks: Applications to visual scene analysis and control. Submitted, 1995.

[Le Cun et al., 1989] Y. Le Cun, B. Boser, J. S. Denker, D. Henderson, R. E. Howard, W. Hubbard, and L. D. Jackel. Backpropagation applied to handwritten zip code recognition. *Neural Computation*, 1:541–551, 1989.

[Rowley et al., 1995] Henry A. Rowley, Shumeet Baluja, and Takeo Kanade. Human face detection in visual scenes. CMU-CS-95-158R, Carnegie Mellon University, November 1995. Also available at http://www.cs.cmu.edu/~har/faces.html.

[Sung and Poggio, 1994] Kah-Kay Sung and Tomaso Poggio. Example-based learning for view-based human face detection. A.I. Memo 1521, CBCL Paper 112, MIT, December 1994.

[Waibel et al., 1989] Alex Waibel, Toshiyuki Hanazawa, Geoffrey Hinton, Kiyohiro Shikano, and Kevin J. Lang. Phoneme recognition using time-delay neural networks. *Readings in Speech Recognition*, pages 393–404, 1989.

Improving Committee Diagnosis with Resampling Techniques

Bambang Parmanto
Department of Information Science
University of Pittsburgh
Pittsburgh, PA 15260
parmanto@lis.pitt.edu

Paul W. Munro
Department of Information Science
University of Pittsburgh
Pittsburgh, PA 15260
munro@lis.pitt.edu

Howard R. Doyle
Pittsburgh Transplantation Institute
3601 Fifth Ave, Pittsburgh, PA 15213
doyle@vesalius.tzs.med.pitt.edu

Abstract

Central to the performance improvement of a committee relative to individual networks is the error correlation between networks in the committee. We investigated methods of achieving error independence between the networks by training the networks with different resampling sets from the original training set. The methods were tested on the sinwave artificial task and the real-world problems of hepatoma (liver cancer) and breast cancer diagnoses.

1 INTRODUCTION

The idea of a neural net committee is to combine several neural net predictors to perform collective decision making, instead of using a single network (Perrone, 1993). The potential of a committee in improving classification performance has been well documented. Central to this improvement is the extent to which the errors tend to coincide. Committee errors occur where the misclassification sets of individual networks overlap. On the one hand, if all errors of committee members coincide, using a committee does not improve performance. On the other hand, if errors do not coincide, performance of the committee dramatically increases and asymptotically approaches perfect performance. Therefore, it is beneficial to make the errors among the networks in the committee less correlated in order to improve the committee performance.

One way of making the networks less correlated is to train them with different sets of data. Decreasing the error correlation by training members of the committee using different sets of data is intuitively appealing. Networks trained with different data sets have a higher probability of generalizing differently and tend to make errors in different places in the problem space.

The idea is to split the data used in the training into several sets. The sets are not necessarily mutually exclusive, they may share part of the set (overlap). This idea resembles resampling methods such as cross-validation and bootstrap known in statistics for estimating the error of a predictor from limited sets of available data. In the committee framework, these techniques are recast to construct different training sets from the original training set. David Wolpert (1992) has put forward a general framework of training the committee using different partitions of the data known as stacked generalization. This approach has been adopted to the regression environment and is called stacked regression (Breiman, 1992). Stacked regression uses cross-validation to construct different sets of regression functions. A similar idea of using a bootstrap method to construct different training sets has been proposed by Breiman (1994) for classification and regression trees predictors.

2 THE ALGORITHMS

2.1 BOOTSTRAP COMMITTEE (BOOTC)

Consider a total of N items are available for training. The approach is to generate K replicates from the original set, each containing the same number of item as the original set. The replicates are obtained from the original set by drawing at random *with replacement*. See Efron & Tibshirani (1993) for background on bootstrapping. Use each replicate to train each network in the committee.

Using this bootstrap procedure, each replicate is expected to include roughly 36 % duplicates (due to replacement during sampling). Only the distinct fraction is used for training and the leftover fraction for early stopping, if necessary (notice slight difference from the standard bootstrapping and from Breiman's bagging). Early stopping usually requires a fraction of the data to be taken from the original training set, which might degrade the performance of the neural network. The advantage of a BOOTC is that the leftover sample is already available.

Algorithm:

1. Generate bootstrap replicates $L^1, \ldots, L^K$ from the original set.

2. For each bootstrap replicate, collect unsampled items into leftover sample sets, giving: $l^{*1}, \ldots, l^{*K}$.

3. For each L^k, train a network. Use the leftover set l^{*k} as validation stopping criteria if necessary. Giving K neural net predictors: $f(x; L^k)$

4. Build a committee from the bootstrap networks using a simple averaging procedure: $f_{com}(x) = \frac{1}{K} \sum_{k=1}^{K} f(x; L^k)$

There is no rule as to how many bootstrap replicates should be used to achieve a good performance. In error estimation, the number ranges from 20 to 200. It is beneficial to keep the number of replicates, hence the number of networks, small to reduce training time. Unless the networks are trained on a parallel machine, training time increases proportionally to the number of networks in the committee. In this experiment, 20 bootstrap training replicates were constructed for 20 networks in the committee. Twenty replicates were chosen since beyond this number there is no significant improvement on the performance.

2.2 CROSS-VALIDATION COMMITTEE (CVC)

The algorithm is quite similar to the procedure used in prediction error estimation. First, generate replicates from the original training set by removing a fraction of the data. Let D denote the original data, and D^{-v} denote the data with subset v removed. The procedure revolves so that each item is in the removed fraction at least once. Generate replicates $D_1^{-v1}, \ldots D_K^{-vk}$ and train each network in the committee with one replicate.

An important issue in the CVC is the degree of data overlap between the replicates. The degree of overlap depends on the number of replicates and the size of a removed fraction from the original sample. For example, if the committee consists of 5 networks and 0.5 of the data are removed for each replicate, the minimum fraction of overlap is 0 (calculation: $(v \times 2) - 1.0$) and the maximum is $\frac{4}{5}$ (calculation: $1.0 - \frac{1}{K}$).

Algorithm:

1. Divide data into v-fractions $d_1, \ldots, d_v$
2. Leave one fraction d_k and train network f_k with the rest of the data $(D - d_k)$.
3. Use d_k as a validation stopping criteria, if necessary.
4. Build a committee from the networks using a simple averaging procedure.

The fraction of data overlap determines the trade-off between the individual network performance and error correlation between the networks. Lower correlation can be expected if the networks train with less overlapped data, which means a larger removed fraction and smaller fraction for training. The smaller the training set size, the lower the individual network performance that can be expected.

We investigated the effect of data overlap on the error correlations between the networks and the committee performance. We also studied the effect of training size on the individual performance. The goal was to find an optimal combination of data overlap and individual training size.

3 THE BASELINE & PERFORMANCE EVALUATION

To evaluate the improvement of the proposed methods on the committee performance, they should be compared with existing methods as the baseline. The common method for constructing a committee is to train an ensemble of networks independently. The networks in the committee are initialized with different sets of weights. This type of committee has been reported as achieving significant improvement over individual network performances in regression (Hashem, 1993) and classification tasks (Perrone, 1993; Parmanto et al., 1994).

The baseline, BOOTC, and CVC were compared using exactly the same architecture and using the same pair of training-test sets. Performance evaluation was conducted using 4-fold exhaustive cross-validation where 0.25 fraction of the original data is used for the test set and the remainder of the data is used for the training set. The procedure was repeated 4 times so that all items were once on the test set. The performance was calculated by averaging the results of 4 test sets. The simulations were conducted several times using different initial weights to exclude the possibility that the improvement was caused by chance.

4 EXPERIMENTS

4.1 SYNTHETIC DATA: SINWAVE CLASSIFICATION

The sinwave task is a classification problem with two classes, a negative class represented as 0 and a positive class represented as 1. The data consist of two input variables, $x = (x_1, x_2)$. The entire space is divided equally into two classes with the separation line determined by the curve $x_2 = \sin(\frac{2\pi}{3} x_1)$. The upper half of the rectangle is the positive class, while the lower half is the negative one (see Fig. 1).

Gaussian noise along the perfect boundary with variance of 0.1 is introduced to the clean data and is presented in Fig. 1 (middle). Let z be a vector drawn from the Gaussian distribution with variance η, then the classification rule is given by equation:

$$y(x) \begin{cases} 1 & \text{if}(x_2 + z_1) \geq \sin(\frac{2\pi}{3}(x_1 + z_2)) \\ 0 & \text{if}(x_2 + z_1) < \sin(\frac{2\pi}{3} x_1 + z_2) \end{cases} \quad (1)$$

A similar artificial problem is used to analyze the bias-variance trade-offs by Geman et al. (1992).

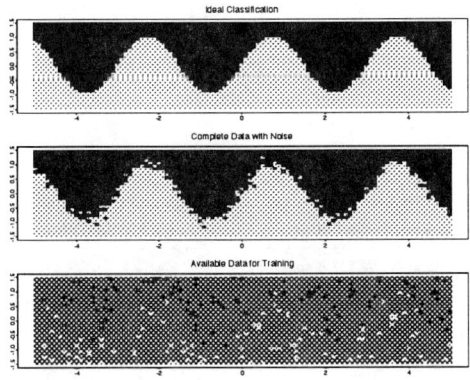

Figure 1: Complete and clean data/without noise (top), complete data with noise (middle), and a small fraction used for training (bottom).

The population contains 3030 data items, since a grid of 0.1 is used for both x_1 and x_2. In the real world, we usually have no access to the entire population. To mimic this situation, the training set contained only a small fraction of the population. Fig. 1 (bottom) visualizes a training set that contains 200 items with 100 items for each class. The training set is constructed by randomly sampling the population. The performance of the predictor is measured with respect to the test set. The population (3030 items) is used as the test set.

4.2 HEPATOMA DETECTION

Hepatoma is a very important clinical problem in patients who are being considered for liver transplantation for its high probability of recurrence. Early hepatoma detection may improve the ultimate outlook of the patients since special treatment can be carried out. Unfortunately, early detection using non-invasive procedures can be difficult, especially in the presence of cirrhosis. We have been developing neural network classifiers as a detection system with minimum imaging or invasive studies (Parmanto et al., 1994).

The task is to detect the presence or absence (binary output) of a hepatoma given variables taken from an individual patient. Each data item consists of 16 variables, 7 of which are continuous variables and the rest are binary variables, primarily blood measurements.

For this experiment, 1172 data items with their associated diagnoses are available. Out of 1172 itmes, 693 items are free from missing values, 309 items contain missing values only on the categorical variables, and 170 items contain missing values on both types of variables. For this experiment, only the fraction without missing values and the fraction with missing values on the categorical variables were used, giving the total item of 1002. Out of the 1002 items, 874 have negative diagnoses and the remaining 128 have positive diagnoses.

4.3 BREAST CANCER

The task is to diagnose if a breast cytology is benign or malignant based on cytological characteristics. Nine input variables have been established to differentiate between the benign and malignant samples which include clump thickness, marginal adhesion, the uniformity of cell size and shape, etc.

The data set was originally obtained from the University of Wisconsin Hospitals and currently stored at the UCI repository for machine learning (Murphy & Aha, 1994). The current size of the data set is 699 examples.

5 THE RESULTS

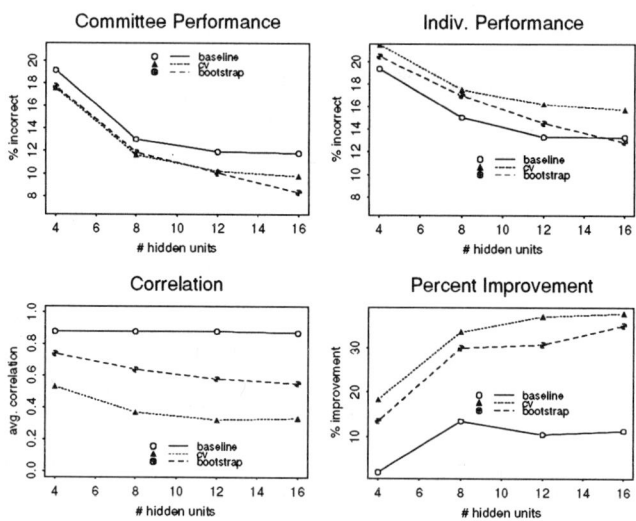

Figure 2: **Results on the sinwave classif. task.** Performances of individual nets and the committee (top); error correlation and committee improvement (bottom).

Figure 2. (top) and Table 1. show that the performance of the committee is always better than the average performance of individual networks in all three committees.

Task	Methods	Indiv. Nets % error	Error Corr	Committee % error	Improv. to Indiv.	Improv. to baseline
Sinwave (2 vars)	Baseline	13.31	.87	11.8	11 %	-
	BOOTC	12.85	.57	8.36	35 %	29 %
	CVC	15.72	.33	9.79	38 %	17 %
Cancer (9 vars)	Baseline	2.7	.96	2.5	5 %	-
	BOOTC	3.14	.83	2.0	34 %	20 %
	CVC	3.2	.80	1.63	49 %	35 %
Hepatoma (16 vars)	Baseline	25.95	.89	23.25	10.5 %	-
	BOOTC	26.00	.70	19.72	24 %	15.2 %
	CVC	26.90	.55	19.05	29 %	18 %

Table 1: Error rate, correlation, and performance improvement *calculated based on the best architecture for each method*. Reduction of misclassification rates compare to the baseline committee

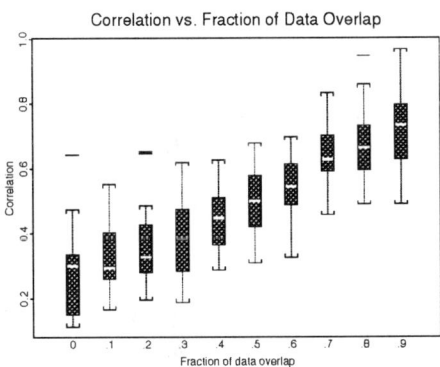

Figure 3: Error correlation and fraction of overlap in training data (results from the sinwave classification task).

The CVC and BOOTC are always better than the baseline even when the individual network performance is worse. Figure 2 (bottom) and the table show that the improvement of a committee over individual networks is proportional to the error correlation between the networks in the committee. The CVC consistently produces significant improvement over its individual network performance due to the low error correlation, while the baseline committee only produces modest improvement. This result confirms the basic assumption of this research: committee performance can be improved by decorrelating the errors made by the networks.

The performance of a committee depends on two factors: individual performance of the networks and error correlation between the networks. The gain of using BOOTC or CVC depends on how the algorithms can reduce the error correlations while still maintaining the individual performance as good as the individual performance of the baseline. The BOOTC produced impressive improvement (29 %) over the baseline on the sinwave task due to the lower correlation and good individual performance. The performances of the BOOTC on the other two tasks were not as impressive due to the modest reduction of error correlation and slight decrease in individual performance. The performances were still significantly better than the baseline committee. The CVC, on the other hand, consistently reduced the correlation and improved the committee performance. The improvement on the sinwave task was not as good as the BOOTC due to the low individual performance.

The individual performance of the CVC and BOOTC in general are worse than the baseline. The individual performance of CVC is 18 % and 19 % lower than the baseline on the sinwave and cancer tasks respectively, while the BOOTC suffered significant reduction of individual performance only on the cancer task (16 %). The degradation of individual performance is due to the smaller training set for each network on the CVC and the BOOTC. The detrimental effect of a small training set, however, is compensated by low correlation between the networks. The effect of a smaller training set depends on the size of the original training set. If the data size is large, using a smaller set may not be harmful. On the contrary, if the data set is small, using an even smaller data set can significantly degrade the performance.

Another interesting finding of this experiment is the relationship between the error correlation and the overlap fraction in the training set. Figure 3 shows that small data overlap causes the networks to have low correlation to each other.

6 SUMMARY

Training committees of networks using different set of data resampled from the original training set can improve committee performance by reducing the error correlation among the networks in the committee. Even when the individual network performances of the BOOTC and CVC degrade from the baseline networks, the committee performance is still better due to the lower correlation.

Acknowledgement

This study is supported in part by Project Grant DK 29961 from the National Institutes of Health, Bethesda, MD. We would like to thank the Pittsburgh Transplantation Institute for providing the data for this study.

References

Breiman, L, (1992) *Stacked Regressions*, TR 367, Dept. of Statistics., UC. Berkeley.

Breiman, L, (1994) *Bagging Predictors*, TR 421, Dept. of Statistics, UC. Berkeley.

Efron, B., & Tibshirani, R.J. (1993) *An Introd. to the Bootstrap*. Chapman & Hall.

Hashem, S. (1994). *Optimal Linear Combinations of Neural Networks*. PhD Thesis, Purdue University.

Geman, S., Bienenstock, E., and Doursat, R. (1992) Neural networks and the bias/variance dilemma. *Neural Computation*, 4(1), 1-58.

Murphy, P. M., & Aha, D. W. (1994). *UCI Repository of machine learning databases* [ftp: ics.uci.edu/pub/machine-learning-databases/]

Parmanto, B., Munro, P.W., Doyle, H.R., Doria, C., Aldrighetti, L., Marino, I.R., Mitchel, S., and Fung, J.J. (1994) Neural network classifier for hepatoma detection. *Proceedings of the World Congress of Neural Networks 1994* San Diego, June 4-9.

Perrone, M.P. (1993) *Improving Regression Estimation: Averaging Methods for Variance Reduction with Extension to General Convex Measure Optimization*. PhD Thesis, Department of Physics, Brown University.

Wolpert, D. (1992). Stacked generalization, *Neural Networks*, 5, 241-259.

Primitive Manipulation Learning with Connectionism

Yoky Matsuoka
The Artificial Intelligence Laboratory
NE43-819
Massachusetts Institute of Techonology
Cambridge, MA 02139

Abstract

Infants' manipulative exploratory behavior within the environment is a vehicle of cognitive stimulation[McCall 1974]. During this time, infants practice and perfect sensorimotor patterns that become behavioral modules which will be seriated and imbedded in more complex actions. This paper explores the development of such primitive learning systems using an embodied light-weight hand which will be used for a humanoid being developed at the MIT Artificial Intelligence Laboratory[Brooks and Stein 1993]. Primitive grasping procedures are learned from sensory inputs using a connectionist reinforcement algorithm while two submodules preprocess sensory data to recognize the hardness of objects and detect shear using competitive learning and back-propagation algorithm strategies, respectively. This system is not only consistent and quick during the initial learning stage, but also adaptable to new situations after training is completed.

1 INTRODUCTION

Learning manipulation in an unpredictable, changing environment is a complex task. It requires a nonlinear controller to respond in a nonlinear system that contains a significant amount of sensory inputs and noise[Miller, et al 1990]. Investigating the human manipulation learning system and implementing it in a physical system has not been done due to its complexity and too many unknown parameters. Conventional adaptive control theory assumes too many parameters that are constantly changing in a real environment [Sutton, et al 1991, Williams 1988]. For an embodied hand, even the simplest form of learning process requires a more intelligent control network. Wiener [Wiener 1948] has proposed the idea of "Connectionism", which suggests that a muscle is controlled by affecting the gain of the "efferent-

Figure 1: A four fingered hand, using a novel tendon driven design for the fingers, was constructed for these experiments. It includes four motors and 36 sensors. The hand, unlike almost every other robot hand, is fully self contained with integrated motors and an onboard microprocessor for local motor and sensory processing. A parallel port connects this processor to a Motorola 68332 for learning and high level control.

nerve – muscle – kinesthetic-end-body – afferent nerve – central-spinal-synapse – efferent-nerve" loop. Each system within the loop such as an efferent nerve contains its own feedback loop system. This kind of loop is inherently nonlinear with the capability of handling many noisy inputs and may be implemented in a physical hand. For this paper, only primitive manipulation grasping learning that occurs without communicating with other features such as eyes and ears is considered.

1.1 THE HARDWARE SETUP

This project uses an anthropomorphic scale hand which has three fingers and an opposing thumb as shown in Figure 1. There are four motors, one controlling each finger, each of which has two coupled joints that are controlled by a cable. Motors are integrated with rotational potentiometers to detect the motor positions. Force/pressure sensors cover the surface of all fingers and the palm has four additional touch position sensors. All the sensory readings are multiplexed and converted to digital signals at a Motorola 6811 microcontroller which is integrated on the top of the palm.

2 THE STRUCTURE OF THE MODEL

Using connectionist ideas, a grasping network was implemented using a internal self reinforcement system, Grasping Action Network, GAN, and two trained neural network components, Hardness Recognition Network, HRN, and Slip Detection Network, SDN, as shown in Figure 2.

In the grasping action network, the Reinforced Probability Net, RPN, takes the classified information, $H(x)$, from HRN and a set of actions, $A = \{a_1, a_2, ..., a_z \mid a(j) \equiv$ a set of actuator inputs of jth action$\}$, and outputs an action merit vector, $M(A)$, that assigns a value to each action. Then, the stochastic Action

Primitive Manipulation Learning with Connectionism

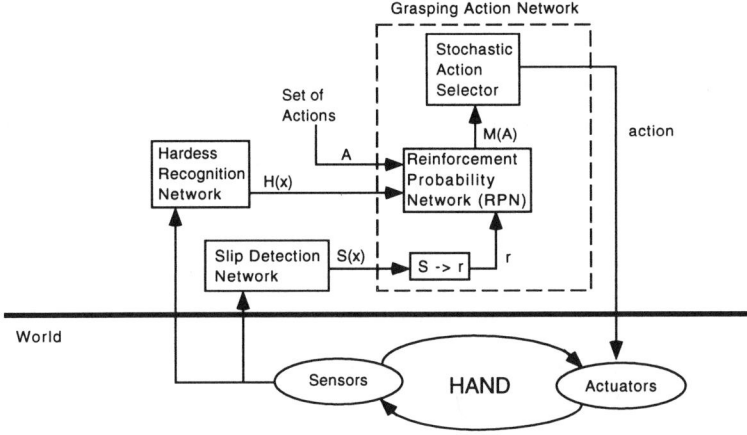

Figure 2: Grasping Network Block Diagram

Selector takes $M(A)$ and selects an action sending the information to the actuators. According to the action given, the shear detection network gives an output, $S(x)$, the probability of slip existence, which can be converted to an immidiate payoff value, r. RPN is reinforced using TD methods, back-propagating a reinforced correction vector, $RC(n)$. The simplified algorithm is as follows:

1. $H(x) \leftarrow$ current hardness class; for each action $a(j)$, $M(a(j)) \leftarrow RPN(H(x), a(j))$;
2. $a \leftarrow SAS(M(A))$;
3. Perform action a;
4. Send new sensory information to hardness recognition network and shear detection network; $(H(x), S(x)) \leftarrow$ new hardness class and shear value;
5. $r = -2S(x) + 1$;
6. $RC = M(A) + (\xi r)$; where ξ is a damping constant.
7. Adjust the RPN by back-propagating RC;
8. Go to 1;

Each network is described below separately.

2.1 HARDNESS RECOGNITION NETWORK

Competitive learning theory is used to categorize the hardness of objects over time. An experiment was conducted with eight different objects of the same size and different compressibilities. Each object is touched by curling one finger around the object very slowly, precisely taking three seconds to fold fingers fully, hold for two seconds, and straighten the finger taking three seconds. The sensory readings are taken from both force sensors on the finger and the potentiometer reading, $p(t)$, of the motor controlling the finger which are converted to an eight bit digital information, recorded at 7 hertz. As the finger curls, the motor moves at a constant rate when the finger does not contact the object surface. At this stage, $dp(t)/dt$ is a non zero constant. When the object is firmly grasped, the finger stops curling and results in $dp(t)/dt \to 0$. The significant difference between different hardness object can be seen in the stage where $dp(t)/dt$ is not constant. This stage signifies

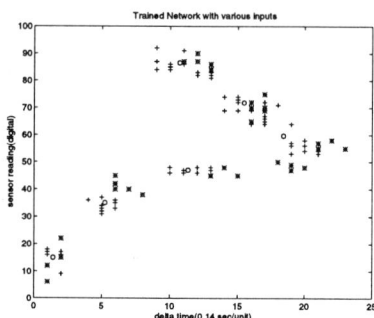

Figure 3: Competitive learning trained network with testing inputs: '+' are inputs, 'o' are the neurons, and '*' are testing inputs(all the test inputs are clustered around the existing trained neurons)

that the object and the finger are in contact, but the object's compliancy is letting the finger continue to move.

2.1.1 Training and Results

For each curling experiment, two numbers are extracted and recorded. The first is the duration of $dp(t)/dt$ non constant time, Δt. It is expressed in digital units where one unit is 0.14 seconds. The other is the maximum force sensor reading expressed in a seven bit digital number. Using those data as inputs, a 2 layer, 6 neuron competitive network is constructed with random initial synaptic weights and trained. Once the network is trained, different inputs can be fed to the network to find the category of the touched object. This strategy works well for this purpose since there is no clear cut way to categorize objects. The trained network was tested with data taken from objects not used for training and shown in Figure 3. With very diverse test objects, the sensory readings fell close to the trained neurons. Initially training the network with six diverse hardness categories gives a good distribution of graspable objects. Even if an object with dramatically different compliancy is found, it only takes roughly 10 experiments to take data and 500 epochs to retrain, all of which takes less than one minute to do.

2.2 SLIP DETECTION NETWORK

Shear is locally detectable sensory information if there exist multiple rows of pressure sensors perpendicular to the direction of slip. With the way the robot hand for this research is oriented, the palm is perpendicular to the ground and fingers are horizontal, which makes the three fingers orthogonal to the direction of slip. In order to simulate the shear learning process, sensory data from the fingers are used as inputs and the visual feedback about the existence of shear is used as the desired output to train a feedforward network. Since shear is a time dependent process, the input signals have to contain multiple time space sensor readings. Two discrete time steps with the step size 0.28 seconds is satisfactory since slipping is not a reversible operation without an external force applied. The size of input vector needs to be minimized in order to speed up the learning operation. As a solution, the number of sensory reading levels m, which has 128 levels straight out of the controller, is reduced to numbers between 5 and 0, where 5 is for the reading level between 81 and 127 and 0 is for the reading level 0. These are the only information needed to train a back-propagation classifier because it can generalize the numbers between

Primitive Manipulation Learning with Connectionism

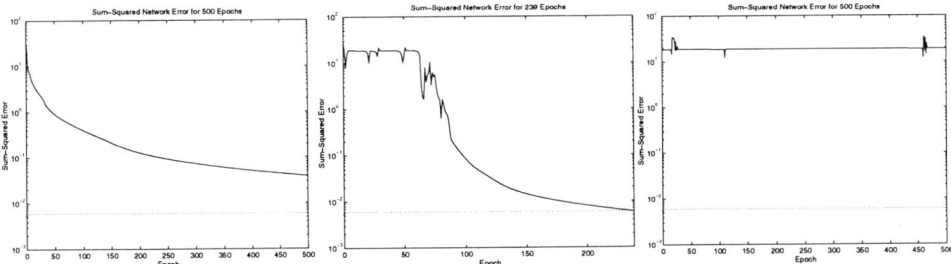

Figure 4: Six neuron hidden layer training result: left, $\eta = 0.1$; middle, $\eta = 1.01$; right, $\eta = 3.0$.

maximum and minimum well with an optimal number of layers and without overtraining. When the data is overtrained, the inputs are overfitted and cannot adapt the values between 4 and 1. Reducing m to two still contains enough information conserving the physics of shear and makes the calculation much simpler and faster. The desired output data is one bit information, 1 being shear detected and 0 being no shear.

2.2.1 Training and Results

Having six input nodes and one output neuron, a four layer with two hidden layer feedforward network is constructed. A four layer network was found most optimal for the generalization to occur accordingly. When slip is not detected the computer is given a default signal 0, and when it is detected through visual feedback, 1 is input. In the training session, the number of hidden layer neurons and the learning rate η were varied to find the optimal back-propagated networks. It was found that the network converges consistently and optimally by having 6 neurons for both hidden layers with learning rate 1.01 as shown in Figure 4. The desired sum-squared network error was set to 0.006. Intuitively, all the networks converges faster when the learning rate is increased. However, as soon as the learning rate exceeds the fastest convergent point, the systems never converge and seem to get stuck in a local minima. Even if the system converges at the end, the error does not stably decrease when the learning rate is higher. This makes the system unreliable since depending on the inputs, the system has a possibility of finding a local minima and never converging. Average outputs of a trained network are taken under many operations containing slips. The average output with slip was 0.9863 and the average output without slip was 0.0003.

2.3 GRASPING ACTION NETWORK

Finally the whole system can be integrated with a reinforcement learning strategy connecting the networks previously trained in the last sections. The Q-learning algorithm assumes that the system can observe the next input vector x_{n+1} at each time step. However, since grasping is a one way operation(meaning $open \rightarrow close$, not $open \leftrightarrow close$), x_{n+1} cannot be seen at the end of the iteration, n. Moreover, x_n is already analyzed and categorized using competitive learning networks. Therefore, a connectionist self-imposed reinforcement learning system is constructed as shown in Figure 2. There are two plausible ways of implementing RPN. The first, classified RPN is shown in Figure 5. There are only two layers in the network with an additional neuron selector at the output. This allows the $M(A)$ to converge faster for each class, though when a new hardness category is added, it has to relearn by

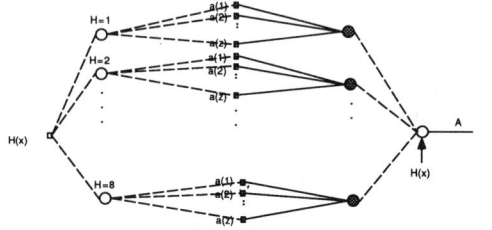

Figure 5: Classified RPN(Back-propagated on the Solid Lines)

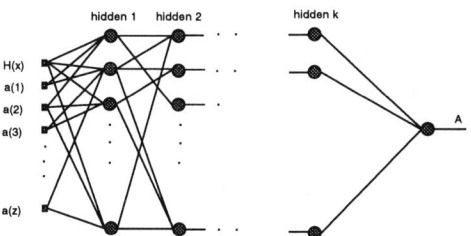

Figure 6: Multiple Hidden Layer RPN

adding unattached neurons into the network and start from scratch. The second implementation strategy is Mutiple Layer RPN which uses more hidden layers and feed $H(x)$ with the action vector as shown in Figure 6. For this system, only synaptic weight adjustment is made for the existing neurons. This method varies in the time of retraining depending on the newly given object. For the experiment in this paper, the classified RPN was chosen to use due to the calculation speed and limited object hardness categories.

2.3.1 Training and Results

A six set classified RPN has been constructed with six categories from the hardness recognition network. Since each set gives a similar training result, only one class, $H(x) = 3$ is shown in this paper. The set of actions has been determined to have eight cases of grasping potential positions. The initial weights are set in a way that each action has equal probability of being chosen at the beginning. For the Classified RPN method, the number of epochs can be quite small to achieve an optimally trained network. There are two variable constants, learning rate η and damping constant ξ, to change to achieve different ways of training the network. The learning graphs with different constant values in a short period of training are plotted in Figure 7. When ξ is too small, the network never gets trained as desired because the system is not reinforced strongly enough. Though as long as ξ is large, η does not need to be large to learn quickly and correctly. When both ξ and η are too large, the system falls into a local minimum and does not converge. For a well trained network, 15 iterations were conducted and it chose the most optimal grasping action 97.5% of the experimental trials.

3 CONCLUSION

A connectionism learning process with 3 separate neural network blocks was constructed and tested in this paper. The advantage of this system is that once the

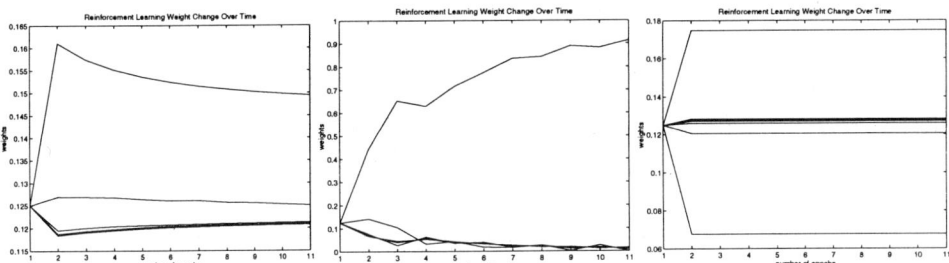

Figure 7: Changes in synaptic weights over short period of time for different learning rates and damping constant: left: $\xi = 0.1$, $\eta = 5$; middle: $\xi = 5$, $\eta = 0.1$; right: $\xi = 5$, $\eta = 5$.

networks are trained within the desired square-sum errors, as long as the damping constant and learning rate are optimally small, the system can adapt to any new objects that are to be grasped.

Acknowledgements

This reasearch was funded by NASA and by ARPA.

References

[Brooks and Stein 1993] Brooks, Rodney A., and Stein, Lynn A., "Building Brains for Bodies", A.I. Memo No. 1439, Cambridge, MA. 1993.

[Lin 1992] Lin, Long-Ji, "Reinforcement Learning for Robots Using Neural Networks", Ph.D thesis, Carnegie Mellon University, Pittsburgh, PA. 1992.

[McCall 1974] McCall, Robert B., "Exploratory Manipulation And Play In the Human Infant", Monographs: Society of research in child development, Unversity of Chicago Press, No. 155, Vol. 39, No.2, 1974.

[Miller, et al 1990] Miller, W. Thomas, Sutton, Richard S., and Werbos, Paul J., "Neural Networks for Control", The MIT Press, Cambridge, MA. 1990.

[Sutton, et al 1991] Sutton, Richard S., Barto, Andrew G., and Williams, Ronald J., "Reinforcement Learning is Direct Adaptice Optimal Control", American Control Conference, Boston, MA. 1991.

[Watkins 1989] Watkins, C.J.C.H., "Learning from Delayed Rewards", Ph.D thesis, King's College, Cambridge, 1989.

[Wiener 1948] Wiener, N., "Cybernetics", Cambridge, MA: MIT Press, 1948.

[Williams 1988] Williams, Ronald J., "One the Use of Backpropagation in Associative Reinforcement Learning", IEEE International Conference on Neural Networks, 1988.

Beating a Defender in Robotic Soccer: Memory-Based Learning of a Continuous Function

Peter Stone
Department of Computer Science
Carnegie Mellon University
Pittsburgh, PA 15213

Manuela Veloso
Department of Computer Science
Carnegie Mellon University
Pittsburgh, PA 15213

Abstract

Learning how to adjust to an opponent's position is critical to the success of having intelligent agents collaborating towards the achievement of specific tasks in unfriendly environments. This paper describes our work on a Memory-based technique for to choose an action based on a continuous-valued state attribute indicating the position of an opponent. We investigate the question of how an agent performs in nondeterministic variations of the training situations. Our experiments indicate that when the random variations fall within some bound of the initial training, the agent performs better with some initial training rather than from a tabula-rasa.

1 Introduction

One of the ultimate goals subjacent to the development of intelligent agents is to have multiple agents collaborating in the achievement of tasks in the presence of hostile opponents. Our research works towards this broad goal from a Machine Learning perspective. We are particularly interested in investigating how an intelligent agent can choose an action in an adversarial environment. We assume that the agent has a specific goal to achieve. We conduct this investigation in a framework where teams of agents compete in a game of robotic soccer. The real system of model cars remotely controlled from off-board computers is under development. Our research is currently conducted in a simulator of the physical system.

Both the simulator and the real-world system are based closely on systems designed by the Laboratory for Computational Intelligence at the University of British Columbia [Sahota et al., 1995, Sahota, 1993]. The simulator facilitates the control of any number of cars and a ball within a designated playing area. Care has been taken to ensure that the simulator models real-world responses (friction, conservation of momentum, etc.) as closely as possible. Figure 1(a) shows the simulator graphics.

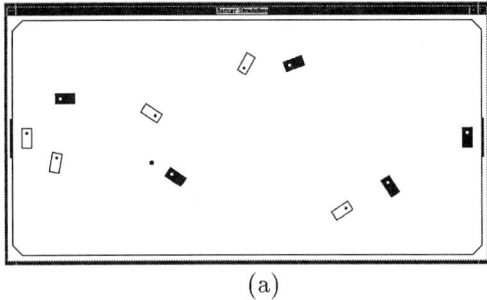
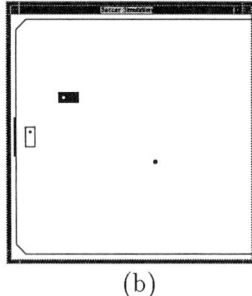

Figure 1: (a) the graphic view of our simulator. (b) The initial position for all of the experiments in this paper. The teammate (black) remains stationary, the defender (white) moves in a small circle at different speeds, and the ball can move either directly towards the goal or towards the teammate. The position of the ball represents the position of the learning agent.

We focus on the question of learning to choose among actions in the presence of an adversary. This paper describes our work on applying memory-based supervised learning to acquire strategy knowledge that enables an agent to decide how to achieve a goal. For other work in the same domain, please see [Stone and Veloso, 1995b]. For an extended discussion of other work on incremental and memory-based learning [Aha and Salzberg, 1994, Kanazawa, 1994, Kuh et al., 1991, Moore, 1991, Salganicoff, 1993, Schlimmer and Granger, 1986, Sutton and Whitehead, 1993, Wettschereck and Dietterich, 1994, Winstead and Christiansen, 1994], particularly as it relates to this paper, please see [Stone and Veloso, 1995a].

The input to our learning task includes a continuous-valued range of the position of the adversary. This raises the question of how to discretize the space of values into a set of learned features. Due to the cost of learning and reusing a large set of specialized instances, we notice a clear advantage to having an appropriate degree of generalization. For more details please see [Stone and Veloso, 1995a].

Here, we address the issue of the effect of differences between past episodes and the current situation. We performed extensive experiments, training the system under particular conditions and then testing it (with learning continuing incrementally) in nondeterministic variations of the training situation. Our results show that when the random variations fall within some bound of the initial training, the agent performs better with some initial training rather than from a tabula-rasa. This intuitive fact is interestingly well- supported by our empirical results.

2 Learning Method

The learning method we develop here applies to an agent trying to learn a function with a continuous domain. We situate the method in the game of robotic soccer.

We begin each trial by placing a ball and a stationary car acting as the "teammate" in specific places on the field. Then we place another car, the "defender," in front of the goal. The defender moves in a small circle in front of the goal at some speed and begins at some random point along this circle. The learning agent must take one of two possible actions: *shoot* straight towards the goal, or *pass* to the teammate so that the ball will rebound towards the goal. A snapshot of the experimental setup is shown graphically in Figure 1(b).

The task is essentially to learn two functions, each with one continuous input variable, namely the defender's position. Based on this position, which can be represented unambiguously as the angle at which the defender is facing, ϕ, the agent tries to learn the probability of scoring when shooting, $P_s^*(\phi)$, and the probability of scoring when passing, $P_p^*(\phi)$.[1] If these functions were learned completely, which would only be possible if the defender's motion were deterministic, then both functions would be binary partitions: $P_s^*, P_p^* : [0.0, 360.0) \mapsto \{-1, 1\}$.[2] That is, the agent would know without doubt for any given ϕ whether a shot, a pass, both, or neither would achieve its goal. However, since the agent cannot have had experience for every possible ϕ, and since the defender may not move at the same speed each time, the learned functions must be approximations: $P_s, P_p : [0.0, 360.0) \mapsto [-1.0, 1.0]$.

In order to enable the agent to learn approximations to the functions P_s^* and P_p^*, we gave it a memory in which it could store its experiences and from which it could retrieve its current approximations $P_s(\phi)$ and $P_p(\phi)$. We explored and developed appropriate methods of storing to and retrieving from memory and an algorithm for deciding what action to take based on the retrieved values.

2.1 Memory Model

Storing every individual experience in memory would be inefficient both in terms of amount of memory required and in terms of generalization time. Therefore, we store P_s and P_p only at discrete, evenly-spaced values of ϕ. That is, for a memory of size M (with M dividing evenly into 360 for simplicity), we keep values of $P_p(\theta)$ and $P_s(\theta)$ for $\theta \in \{360n/M \mid 0 \leq n < M\}$. We store memory as an array "**Mem**" of size M such that **Mem**$[n]$ has values for both $P_p(360n/M)$ and $P_s(360n/M)$. Using a fixed memory size precludes using memory-based techniques such as K-Nearest-Neighbors (kNN) and kernel regression which require that every experience be stored, choosing the most relevant only at decision time. Most of our experiments were conducted with memories of size 360 (low generalization) or of size 18 (high generalization), i.e. $M = 18$ or $M = 360$. The memory size had a large effect on the rate of learning [Stone and Veloso, 1995a].

2.1.1 Storing to Memory

With M discrete memory storage slots, the problem then arises as to how a specific training example should be generalized. Training examples are represented here as $E_{\phi,a,r}$, consisting of an angle ϕ, an action a, and a result r where ϕ is the initial position of the defender, a is "s" or "p" for "shoot" or "pass," and r is "1" or "-1" for "goal" or " miss" respectively. For instance, $E_{72.345,p,1}$ represents a pass resulting in a goal for which the defender started at position $72.345°$ on its circle.

Each experience with $\theta - 360/2M \leq \phi < \theta + 360/2M$ affects **Mem**$[\theta]$ in proportion to the distance $|\theta - \phi|$. In particular, **Mem**$[\theta]$ keeps running sums of the magnitudes of scaled results, **Mem**$[\theta]$.*total-a-results*, and of scaled positive results, **Mem**$[\theta]$.*positive-a-results*, affecting $P_a(\theta)$, where "a" stands for "s" or "p" as before. Then at any given time, $P_a(\theta) = -1 + 2 * \frac{positive-a-results}{total-a-results}$. The "-1" is for

---

[1] As per convention, P^* represents the target (optimal) function.
[2] Although we think of P_s^* and P_p^* as functions from angles to probabilities, we will use -1 rather than 0 as the lower bound of the range. This representation simplifies many of our illustrative calculations.

the lower bound of our probability range, and the "2*" is to scale the result to this range. Call this our *adaptive* memory storage technique:

Adaptive Memory Storage of $E_{\phi,a,r}$ in **Mem**$[\theta]$
- $r' = r * (1 - \frac{|\phi - \theta|}{360/M})$.
- **Mem**$[\theta]$.*total-a-results* += r'.
- If $r' > 0$ Then **Mem**$[\theta]$.*positive-a-results* += r'.
- $P_a(\theta) = -1 + 2 * \frac{positive-a-results}{total-a-results}$.

For example, $E_{110,p,1}$ would set both *total-p-results* and *positive-p-results* for **Mem**$[120]$ (and **Mem**$[100]$) to 0.5 and consequently $P_p(120)$ (and $P_p(100)$) to 1.0. But then $E_{125,p,-1}$ would increment *total-p-results* for **Mem**$[120]$ by .75, while leaving *positive-p-results* unchanged. Thus $P_p(120)$ becomes $-1 + 2 * \frac{.5}{1.25} = -.2$.

This method of storing to memory is effective both for time-varying concepts and for concepts involving random noise. It is able to deal with conflicting examples within the range of the same memory slot.

Notice that each example influences 2 different memory locations. This memory storage technique is similar to the kNN and kernel regression function approximation techniques which estimate $f(\phi)$ based on $f(\theta)$ possibly scaled by the distance from θ to ϕ for the k nearest values of θ. In our linear continuum of defender position, our memory generalizes training examples to the 2 nearest memory locations.[3]

2.1.2 Retrieving from Memory

Since individual training examples affect multiple memory locations, we use a simple technique for retrieving $P_a(\phi)$ from memory when deciding whether to shoot or to pass. We round ϕ to the nearest θ for which **Mem**$[\theta]$ is defined, and then take $P_a(\theta)$ as the value of $P_a(\phi)$. Thus, each **Mem**$[\theta]$ represents $P_a(\phi)$ for $\theta - 360/2M \leq \phi < \theta + 360/2M$. Notice that retrieval is much simpler when using this technique than when using kNN or kernel regression: we look directly to the closest fixed memory position, thus eliminating the indexing and weighting problems involved in finding the k closest training examples and (possibly) scaling their results.

2.2 Choosing an Action

The action selection method is designed to make use of memory to select the action most probable to succeed, and to fill memory when no useful memories are available. For example, when the defender is at position ϕ, the agent begins by retrieving $P_p(\phi)$ and $P_s(\phi)$ as described above. Then, it acts according to the following function:

If $P_p(\phi) = P_s(\phi)$ (no basis for a decision), shoot or pass randomly.
  else If $P_p(\phi) > 0$ and $P_p(\phi) > P_s(\phi)$, pass.
    else If $P_s(\phi) > 0$ and $P_s(\phi) > P_p(\phi)$, shoot.
      else If $P_p(\phi) = 0$, (no previous passes) pass.
        else If $P_s(\phi) = 0$, (no previous shots) shoot.
          else $(P_p(\phi), P_s(\phi) < 0)$ shoot or pass randomly.

An action is only selected based on the memory values if these values indicate that one action is likely to succeed and that it is better than the other. If, on the other hand, neither value $P_p(\phi)$ nor $P_s(\phi)$ indicate a positive likelihood of success, then an action is chosen randomly. The only exception to this last rule is when one of

---

[3] For particularly large values of M it is useful to generalize training examples to more memory locations, particularly at the early stages of learning. However for the values of M considered in this paper, we always generalize to the 2 nearest memory locations.

the values is zero,[4] suggesting that there has not yet been any training examples for that action at that memory location. In this case, there is a bias towards exploring the untried action in order to fill out memory.

3 Experiments and Results

In this section, we present the results of our experiments. We explore our agent's ability to learn time-varying and nondeterministic defender behavior.

While examining the results, keep in mind that even if the agent used the functions P_s^* and P_p^* to decide whether to shoot or to pass, the success rate would be significantly less than 100% (it would differ for different defender speeds): there were many defender starting positions for which neither shooting nor passing led to a goal (see Figure 2). For example, from our experiments with the defender moving

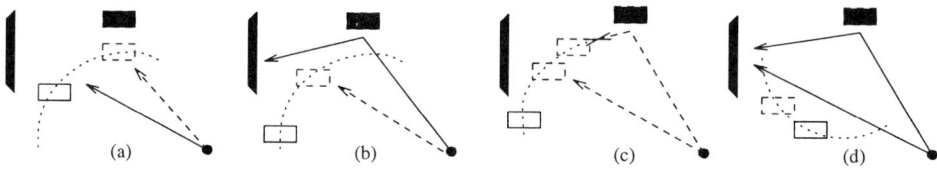

Figure 2: For different defender starting positions (solid rectangle), the agent can score when (a) shooting, (b) passing, (c) neither, or (d) both.

at a constant speed of 50,[5] we found that an agent acting optimally scores 73.6% of the time; an agent acting randomly scores only 41.3% of the time. These values set good reference points for evaluating our learning agent's performance.

3.1 Coping with Changing Concepts

Figure 3 demonstrates the effectiveness of adaptive memory when the defender's speed changes. In all of the experiments represented in these graphs, the agent

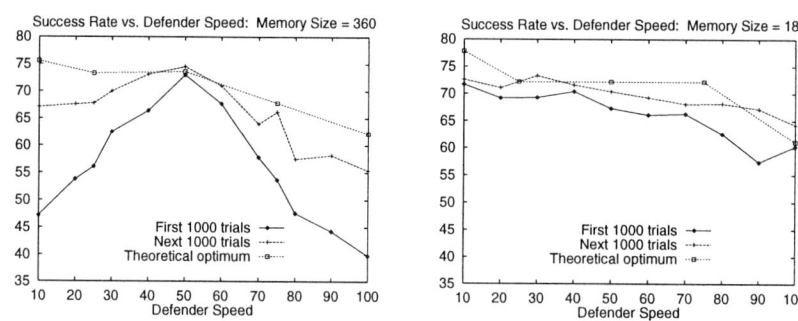

Figure 3: For all trials shown in these graphs, the agent began with a memory trained for a defender moving at constant speed 50.

started with a memory trained by attempting a single pass and a single shot with the defender starting at each position θ for which **Mem**$[\theta]$ is defined and moving in

---

[4] Recall that a memory value of 0 is equivalent to a probability of .5, representing no reason to believe that the action will succeed or fail.

[5] In the simulator, "50" represents 50 cm/s. Subsequently, we omit the units.

its circle at speed 50. We tested the agent's performance with the defender moving at various (constant) speeds.

With adaptive memory, the agent is able to unlearn the training that no longer applies and approach optimal behavior: it *re-learns* the new setup. During the first 1000 trials the agent suffers from having practiced in a different situation (especially for the less generalized memory, $M = 360$), but then it is able to approach optimal behavior over the next 1000 trials. Remember that optimal behavior, represented in the graph, leads to roughly a 70% success rate, since at many starting positions, neither passing nor shooting is successful.

From these results we conclude that our adaptive memory can effectively deal with time-varying concepts. It can also perform well when the defender's motion is nondeterministic, as we show next.

3.2 Coping with Noise

To model nondeterministic motion by the defender, we set the defender's speed randomly within a range. For each attempt this speed is constant, but it varies from attempt to attempt. Since the agent observes only the defender's initial position, from the point of view of the agent, the defender's motion is nondeterministic.

This set of experiments was designed to test the effectiveness of adaptive memory when the defender's speed was both nondeterministic and different from the speed used to train the existing memory. The memory was initialized in the same way as in Section 3.1 (for defender speed 50). We ran experiments in which the defender's speed varied between 10 and 50. We compared an agent with trained memory against an agent with initially empty memories as shown in Figure 4.

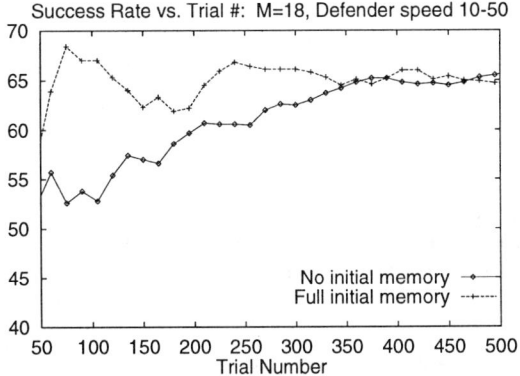

Figure 4: A comparison of the effectiveness of starting with an empty memory versus starting with a memory trained for a constant defender speed (50) different from that used during testing. Success rate is measured as goal percentage thus far.

The agent with full initial memory outperformed the agent with initially empty memory in the short run. The agent learning from scratch did better over time since it did not have any training examples from when the defender was moving at a fixed speed of 50; but at first, the training examples for speed 50 were better than no training examples. Thus, when you would like to be successful immediately upon entering a novel setting, adaptive memory allows training in related situations to be effective without permanently reducing learning capacity.

4 Conclusion

Our experiments demonstrated that online, incremental, supervised learning can be effective at learning functions with continuous domains. We found that adaptive memory made it possible to learn both time-varying and nondeterministic concepts. We empirically demonstrated that short-term performance was better when acting with a memory trained on a concept related to but different from the testing concept, than when starting from scratch. This paper reports experimental results on our work towards multiple learning agents, both cooperative and adversarial, in a continuous environment.

Future work on our research agenda includes simultaneous learning of the defender and the controlling agent in an adversarial context. We will also explore learning methods with several agents where teams are guided by planning strategies. In this way we will simultaneously study cooperative and adversarial situations using reactive and deliberative reasoning.

Acknowledgements

We thank Justin Boyan and the anonymous reviewers for their helpful suggestions. This research is sponsored by the Wright Laboratory, Aeronautical Systems Center, Air Force Materiel Command, USAF, and the Advanced Research Projects Agency (ARPA) under grant number F33615-93-1-1330. The views and conclusions contained in this document are those of the authors and should not be interpreted as necessarily representing the official policies or endorsements, either expressed or implied, of Wright Laboratory or the U. S. Government.

References

[Aha and Salzberg, 1994] David W. Aha and Steven L. Salzberg. Learning to catch: Applying nearest neighbor algorithms to dynamic control tasks. In P. Cheeseman and R. W. Oldford, editors, *Selecting Models from Data: Artificial Intelligence and Statistics IV*. Springer-Verlag, New York, NY, 1994.

[Kanazawa, 1994] Keiji Kanazawa. Sensible decisions: Toward a theory of decision-theoretic information invariants. In *Proceedings of the Twelfth National Conference on Artificial Intelligence*, pages 973–978, 1994.

[Kuh et al., 1991] A. Kuh, T. Petsche, and R.L. Rivest. Learning time-varying concepts. In *Advances in Neural Information Processing Systems 3*, pages 183–189. Morgan Kaufman, December 1991.

[Moore, 1991] A.W. Moore. Fast, robust adaptive control by learning only forward models. In *Advances in Neural Information Processing Systems 3*. Morgan Kaufman, December 1991.

[Sahota et al., 1995] Michael K. Sahota, Alan K. Mackworth, Rod A. Barman, and Stewart J. Kingdon. Real-time control of soccer-playing robots using off-board vision: the dynamite testbed. In *IEEE International Conference on Systems, Man, and Cybernetics*, pages 3690–3663, 1995.

[Sahota, 1993] Michael K. Sahota. Real-time intelligent behaviour in dynamic environments: Soccer-playing robots. Master's thesis, University of British Columbia, August 1993.

[Salganicoff, 1993] Marcos Salganicoff. Density-adaptive learning and forgetting. In *Proceedings of the Tenth International Conference on Machine Learning*, pages 276–283, 1993.

[Schlimmer and Granger, 1986] J.C. Schlimmer and R.H. Granger. Beyond incremental processing: Tracking concept drift. In *Proceedings of the Fiffth National Conference on Artificial Intelligence*, pages 502–507. Morgan Kaufman, Philadelphia, PA, 1986.

[Stone and Veloso, 1995a] Peter Stone and Manuela Veloso. Beating a defender in robotic soccer: Memory-based learning of a continuous function. Technical Report CMU-CS-95-222, Computer Science Department, Carnegie Mellon University, 1995.

[Stone and Veloso, 1995b] Peter Stone and Manuela Veloso. Broad learning from narrow training: A case study in robotic soccer. Technical Report CMU-CS-95-207, Computer Science Department, Carnegie Mellon University, 1995.

[Sutton and Whitehead, 1993] Richard S. Sutton and Steven D. Whitehead. Online learning with random representations. In *Proceedings of the Tenth International Conference on Machine Learning*, pages 314–321, 1993.

[Wettschereck and Dietterich, 1994] Dietrich Wettschereck and Thomas Dietterich. Locally adaptive nearest neighbor algorithms. In J. D. Cowan, G. Tesauro, and J. Alspector, editors, *Advances in Neural Information Processing Systems 6*, pages 184–191, San Mateo, CA, 1994. Morgan Kaufmann.

[Winstead and Christiansen, 1994] Nathaniel S. Winstead and Alan D. Christiansen. Pinball: Planning and learning in a dynamic real-time environment. In *AAAI-94 Fall Symposium on Control of the Physical World by Intelligent Agents*, pages 153–157, New Orleans, LA, November 1994.

Visual gesture-based robot guidance with a modular neural system

E. Littmann,
Abt. Neuroinformatik, Fak. f. Informatik
Universität Ulm, D-89069 Ulm, FRG
enno@neuro.informatik.uni-ulm.de

A. Drees, and H. Ritter
AG Neuroinformatik, Techn. Fakultät
Univ. Bielefeld, D-33615 Bielefeld, FRG
andrea,helge@techfak.uni-bielefeld.de

Abstract

We report on the development of the modular neural system "SEE-EAGLE" for the visual guidance of robot pick-and-place actions. Several neural networks are integrated to a single system that visually recognizes human hand pointing gestures from stereo pairs of color video images. The output of the hand recognition stage is processed by a set of color-sensitive neural networks to determine the cartesian location of the target object that is referenced by the pointing gesture. Finally, this information is used to guide a robot to grab the target object and put it at another location that can be specified by a second pointing gesture. The accuracy of the current system allows to identify the location of the referenced target object to an accuracy of 1 cm in a workspace area of 50x50 cm. In our current environment, this is sufficient to pick and place arbitrarily positioned target objects within the workspace. The system consists of neural networks that perform the tasks of image segmentation, estimation of hand location, estimation of 3D-pointing direction, object recognition, and necessary coordinate transforms. Drawing heavily on the use of learning algorithms, the functions of all network modules were created from data examples only.

1 Introduction

The rapidly developing technology in the fields of robotics and virtual reality requires the development of new and more powerful interfaces for configuration and control of such devices. These interfaces should be intuitive for the human advisor and comfortable to use. Practical solutions so far require the human to wear a device that can transfer the necessary information. One typical example is the data glove [14, 12]. Clearly, in the long run solutions that are contactless will be much more desirable, and vision is one of the major modalities that appears especially suited for the realization of such solutions.

In the present paper, we focus on a still restricted but very important task in robot control, the guidance of robot pick-and-place actions by unconstrained human pointing gestures in a realistic laboratory environment. The input of target locations by pointing gestures provides a powerful, very intuitive and comfortable functionality for a vision-based man-machine interface for guiding robots and extends previous work that focused on the detection of hand location or the discrimination of a small, discrete number of hand gestures only [10, 1, 2, 8]. Besides two color cameras, no special device is necessary to evaluate the gesture of the human operator.

A second goal of our approach is to investigate how to build a neural system for such a complex task from several neural modules. The development of advanced artificial neural systems challenges us with the task of finding architectures for the cooperation of multiple functional modules such that part of the structure of the overall system can be designed at a useful level of abstraction, but at the same time learning can be used to create or fine-tune the functionality of parts of the system on the basis of suitable training examples.

To approach this goal requires to shift the focus from exploring the properties of single networks to exploring the properties of entire *systems of neural networks*. The work on "mixtures of experts" [3, 4] is one important contribution along these lines. While this is a widely applicable and powerful approach, there clearly is a need to go beyond the exploration of strictly hierarchical systems and to gain experience with architectures that admit more complex types of information flow as required e.g. by the inclusion of features such as control of focal attention or reentrant processing branches. The need for such features arose very naturally in the context of the task described above, and in the following section we will report our results with a system architecture that is crucially based on the exploitation of such elements.

2 System architecture

Our system, described in fig. 1, is situated in a complex laboratory environment. A robot arm with manipulator is mounted at one side of a table with several objects of different color placed on it. A human operator is positioned at the next side to the right of the robot. This scenery is watched by two cameras from the other two sides from high above. The cameras yield a stereo color image of the scene (images I0). The operator points with one hand at one of the objects on the table. On the basis of the image information, the object is located and the robot grabs it. Then, the operator points at another location, where the robot releases the object.[1]

The system consists of several hardware components: a PUMA 560 robot arm with six axes and a three-fingered manipulator [2]; two single-chip PULNIX color cameras; two ANDROX vision boards with software for data acquisition and processing; a work space consisting of a table with a black grid on a yellow surface. Robot and person refer to the same work space. Both cameras must show both the human hand and the table with the objects. Within this constraint, the position of the cameras can be chosen freely as long as they yield significantly different views.

An important prerequisite for the recognition of the pointing direction is the segmentation of the human hand from the background scenery. This task is solved by a LLM network (S1) trained to yield a probability value for each image pixel to belong to the hand region. The training is based on the local color information. This procedure has been investigated in [7].

An important feature of the chosen method is the great reliability and robustness of both the classification performance and the localization accuracy of the searched object. Furthermore, the performance is quite constant over a wide range of image resolutions. This allows a fast two-step procedure: First, the images are segmented in low resolution (S1: I1 → A1) and the hand position is extracted. Then, a small

---

[1]In analogy to the sea eagle who watches its prey from high above, shoots down to grab the prey, and then flies to a safe place to feed, we nicknamed our system "SEE-EAGLE".
[2]Development by Prof. Pfeiffer, TU Munich

Visual Gesture-based Robot Guidance with a Modular Neural System

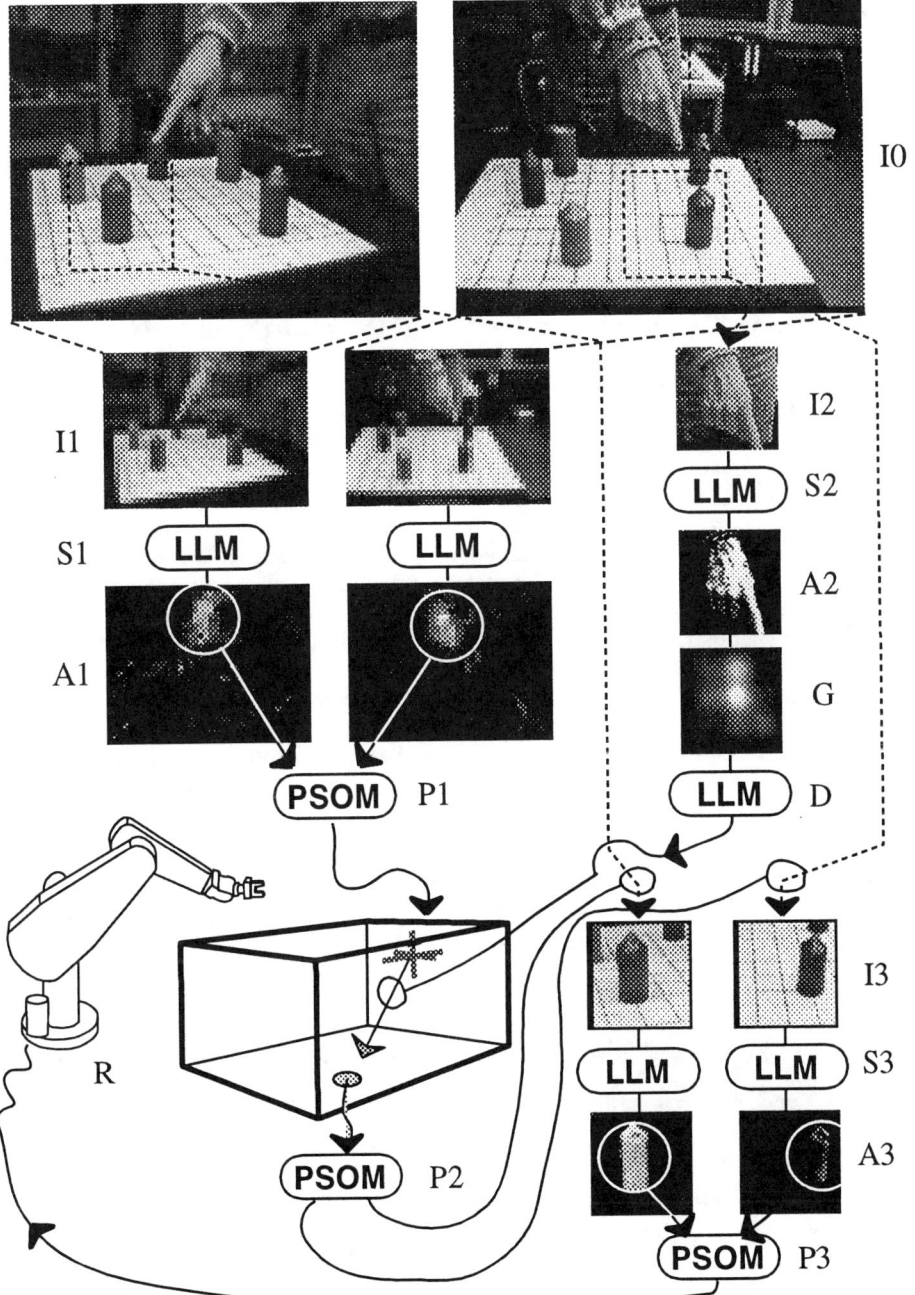

Fig. 1: System architecture. From two color camera images I0 we extract the hand position (I1 ▷ S1 ▷ A1 (pixel coord.) ▷ P1 ▷ cartesian hand coord.). In a subframe centered on the hand location (I2) we determine the pointing direction (I2 ▷ S2 ▷ A2 (pixel coord.) ▷ G ▷ D ▷ pointing angles). Pointing direction and hand location define a cartesian target location that is mapped to image coord. that define the centers of object subframes (I0 ▷ P2 ▷ I3). There we determine the target object (I3 ▷ S3 ▷ A3) and map the pixel coord. of its centers to world coord. (A3 ▷ P3 ▷ world target loc.). These coordinates are used to guide the robot R to the target object.

subframe (I2) around the estimated hand position is processed in high resolution by another dedicated LLM network (S2: I2 → A2). For details of the segmentation process, refer to [6].

The extraction of hand information by LLMs on the basis of Gabor masks has already been studied for hand posture [9] and orientation [5]. The method is based on a segmented image containing the hand only (A2). This image is filtered by 36 Gabor masks that are arranged on a 3x3 grid with 4 directions per grid position and centered on the hand. The filter kernels have a radius of 10 pixels, the distance between the grid points is 20 pixels. The 36 filter responses (G) form the input vector for a LLM network (D). Further details of the processing are reported in [6].

The network yields the pointing direction of the hand (D: I2 → G → pointing direction). Together with the hand position which is computed by a parametrized self-organizing map ("PSOM", see below and [11, 13]) (P1: A1 → cartesian hand position), a (cartesian) target location in the workspace can be calculated. This location can be retransformed by the PSOM into pixel coordinates (P2: cartesian target location → target pixel coordinates). These coordinates define the center of an "attention region" (I3) that is searched for a set of predefined target objects. This object recognition is performed by a set of LLM color segmentation networks (S3: I3 → A3), each previously trained for one of the defined targets. A ranking procedure is used to determine the target object. The pixel coordinates of the target in the segmented image are mapped by the PSOM to world coordinates (P3: A3 → cartesian target position). The robot R now moves to above these world coordinates, moves vertically down, grabs whatever is there, and moves upward again. Now, the system evaluates a second pointing gesture that specifies the place where to place the object. This time, the world coordinates calculated on the basis of the pointing direction from network D and the cartesian hand location from PSOM P1 serve directly as target location for the robot.

For our processing we must map corresponding pixels in the stereo images to cartesian world coordinates. For these transformations, training data was generated with aid of the robot on a precise sampling grid. We automatically extract the pixel coordinates of a LED at the tip of the robot manipulator from both images. The seven-dimensional feature vector serves as training input for an PSOM network [11]. By virtue of its capability to represent a transformation in a symmetric, "multiway"-fashion, this offers the additional benefit that both the camera-to-world mapping *and* its inverse can be obtained with a single network trained only once on a data set of 27 calibration positions of the robot. A detailed description for such a procedure can be found in [13].

3 Results

3.1 System performance

The accuracy of the current system allows to estimate the pointing target to an accuracy of 1 ± 0.4 cm (average over $N = 7$ objects at randomly chosen locations in the workspace) in a workspace area of 50x50 cm. In our current environment, this is sufficient to pick and place any of the seven defined target objects at any location in the workspace. This accuracy can only be achieved if we use the object recognition module described in sec. 2. The output of the pointing direction module approximates the target location with an considerably lower accuracy of 3.6 ± 1.6 cm.

3.2 Image segmentation

The problem to evaluate these preprocessing steps has been discussed previously [7], especially the relation of specifity and sensitivity of the network for the given task. As the pointing recognition is based on a subframe centered on the hand center, it is very sensitive to deviations from this center so that a good localization accuracy is even more important than the classification rate. The localization accuracy is calculated by measuring the pixel distance between the centers determined manually on the original image and as the center of mass in the image obtained after application of the neural network. Table 1 provides quantitative results.

On the whole, the two-step cascade of LLM networks yields for *399 out of 400 images* an activity image precisely centered on the human hand. Only in one image, the first LLM net missed the hand completely, due to a second hand in the image that could be clearly seen in this view. This image was excluded from further processing and from the evaluation of the localization accuracy.

	Camera A		Camera B	
	Pixel deviation	NRMSE	Pixel deviation	NRMSE
Person A	0.8 ± 1.2	0.03 ± 0.06	0.8 ± 2.2	0.03 ± 0.09
Person B	1.3 ± 1.4	0.06 ± 0.11	2.2 ± 2.8	0.11 ± 0.21

Table 1: *Estimation error of the hand localization on the test set. Absolute error in pixels and normalized error for both persons and both camera images.*

3.3 Recognition performance

One major problem in recognizing human pointing gestures is the variability of these gestures and their measurement for the acquisition of reliable training information. Different persons follow different strategies where and how to point (fig. 2 (center) and (right)). Therefore, we calculate this information indirectly. The person is told to point at a certain grid position with known world coordinates. From the camera images we extract the pixel positions of the hand center and map them to world coordinates using the PSOM net (P1 in fig. 1). Given these coordinates the angles of the intended pointing vector with the basis vectors of the world coordinate system can be calculated trigonometrically. These angles form the target vector for the supervised training of a LLM network (D in fig. 1).

After training, the output of the net is used to calculate the point where the pointing vector intersects the table surface. For evaluation of the network performance we measure the Euclidian distance between this point and the actual grid point where the person intended to point at. Fig. 3 *(left)* shows the mean euclidean error MEE of the estimated target position as a function of the number of learning steps. The error on the training set can be considerably reduced, whereas on the test set the improvement stagnates after some 500 training steps. If we perform even more training steps the performance might actually suffer from overfitting. The graph compares training and test results achieved on images obtained by two different ways of determining the hand center. The "manual" curves show the performance that can be achieved if the Gabor masks are manually centered on the hand. For the "neuronal" curves, the center of mass calculated in the fine-segmented and post-processed subframe was used. This allows us to study the influence of the error of the segmentation and localization steps on the pointing recognition. This influence is rather small. The MEE increases from 17 mm for the optimal method to 19 mm for the neural method, which is hardly visible in practice.

The curves in fig. 3 *(center)* are obtained if we apply the networks to images of another person. The MEE is considerably larger but a detailed analysis shows that part of this deviation is due to systematic differences in the pointing strategy as shown in fig. 2 *(right)*. Over a wide range, the number of nodes used for the LLM network has only minor influence on the performance. While obviously the performance on the training set can be arbitrarily improved by spending more nodes, the differences in the MEE on the test set are negligible in a range of 5 to 15 nodes. Using more nodes is problematic as the training data consists of 50 examples only. If not indicated otherwise, we use LLM networks with 10 nodes. Further results,

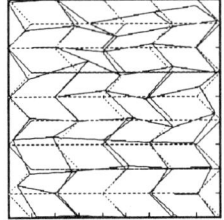 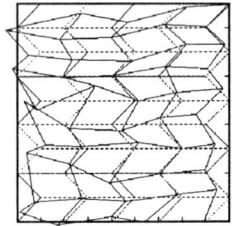 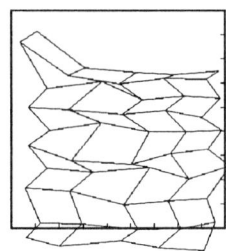

Fig. 2: The table grid points can be reconstructed according to the network output. The target grid is dotted. Reconstruction of training grid (left) and test grid (center) for one person, and of the test grid for another person (right).

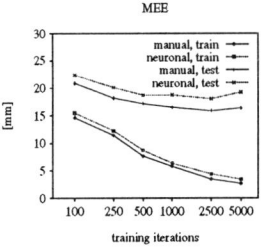 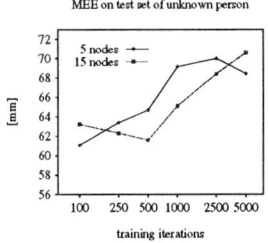

Fig. 3: The euclidean error of estimated target point calculated using the network output depends on the preprocessing (left), and the person (center).

comparing the pointing recognition based on only one of the camera images, indicate that the method works better if the camera takes a lateral view rather than a frontal view. All evaluations were done for both persons. The performance was always very similar.

4 Discussion

While we begin to understand many properties of neural networks at the single network level, our insight into principled ways of how to build *neural systems* is still rather limited. Due to the complexity of this task, theoretical progress is (and probably will continue to be) very slow. What we can do in the mean time, however, is to experiment with different design strategies for neural systems and try to "evolve" useful approaches by carefully chosen case studies.

The current work is an effort along these lines. It is focused on a challenging, practically important vision task with a number of generic features that are shared with vision tasks for which biological vision systems were evolved.

One important issue is how to achieve robustness at the different processing levels of the system. There are only very limited possibilities to study this issue in simulations, since practically nothing is known about the statistical properties of the various sources of error that occur when dealing with real world data. Thus, a real implementation that works with actual data is practically the only way to study the robustness issue in a realistic fashion. Therefore, the demonstrated integration of several functional modules that we had developed previously in more restricted settings [7, 6] was a non-trivial test of the feasability of having these functions cooperate in a larger, modular system. It also gives confidence that the scaling problem can be dealt with successfully if we apply modular neural nets.

A related and equally important issue was the use of a processing strategy in which earlier processing stages *incrementally restrict the search space* for the subsequent stages. Thus, the responsibility for achieving the goal is not centralized in any single module and subsequent modules have always the chance to compensate for limited errors of earlier stages. This appears to be a generally useful strategy for achieving robustness and for cutting computational costs that is related to the use of "focal attention", which is clearly an important element of many biological vision systems.

A third important point is the extensive use of learning to build the essential constituent functions of the system from data examples. We are not yet able to train the assembled system as a whole. Instead, different modules are trained separately and are integrated only later. Still, the experience gained with assembling a complex system via this "engineering-type" of approach will be extremely valuable for gradually developing the capability of crafting larger functional building blocks by learning methods.

We conclude that carefully designed experiments with modular neural systems that are based on the use of real world data and that focus on similar tasks for which also biological neural systems were evolved can make a significant contribution in tackling the challenge that lies ahead of us: to develop a reliable technology for the construction of *large-scale artificial neural systems* that can solve complex tasks in real world environments.

Acknowledgements

We want to thank Th. Wengerek (robot control), J. Walter (PSOM implementation), and P. Ziemeck (image acquisition software). This work was supported by BMFT Grant No. ITN9104AO.

References

[1] T. J. Darell and A. P. Pentland. Classifying hand gestures with a view-based distributed representation. In J. D. Cowan, G. Tesauro, and J. Alspector, editors, *Neural Information Processing Systems 6*, pages 945–952. Morgan Kaufman, 1994.

[2] J. Davis and M. Shah. Recognizing hand gestures. In J.-O. Eklundh, editor, *Computer Vision — ECCV '94*, volume 800 of *Lecture Notes in Computer Science*, pages 331–340. Springer-Verlag, Berlin Heidelberg New York, 1994.

[3] R.A. Jacobs, M.I. Jordan, S.J. Nowlan, and G.E. Hinton. Adaptive mixtures of local experts. *Neural Computation*, 3:79–87, 1991.

[4] M.I. Jordan and R.A. Jacobs. Hierarchical mixtures of experts and the EM algorithm. *Neural Computation*, 6(2):181–214, 1994.

[5] F. Kummert, E. Littmann, A. Meyering, S. Posch, H. Ritter, and G. Sagerer. A hybrid approach to signal interpretation using neural and semantic networks. In *Mustererkennung 1993*, pages 245–252. Springer, 1993.

[6] E. Littmann, A. Drees, and H. Ritter. Neural recognition of human pointing gestures in real images. Submitted to *Neural Processing Letters*, 1996.

[7] E. Littmann and H. Ritter. Neural and statistical methods for adaptive color segmentation — a comparison. In G. Sagerer, S. Posch, and F. Kummert, editors, *Mustererkennung 1995*, pages 84–93. Springer-Verlag, Heidelberg, 1995.

[8] C. Maggioni. A novel device for using the hand as a human-computer interface. In *Proceedings HCI'93 — Human Control Interface*, Loughborough, Great Britain, 1993.

[9] A. Meyering and H. Ritter. Learning 3D shape perception with local linear maps. In *Proc. of the IJCNN*, volume IV, pages 432–436, Baltimore, MD, 1992.

[10] Steven J. Nowlan and John C. Platt. A convolutional neural network hand tracker. In *Neural Information Processing Systems 7*. Morgan Kaufman Publishers, 1995.

[11] H. Ritter. Parametrized self-organizing maps for vision learning tasks. In P. Morasso, editor, *ICANN '94*. Springer-Verlag, Berlin Heidelberg New York, 1994.

[12] K. Väänänen and K. Böhm. Gesture driven interaction as a human factor in virtual environments – an approach with neural networks. In R. Earnshaw, M. Gigante, and H. Jones, editors, *Virtual reality systems*, pages 93–106. Academic Press, 1993.

[13] J. Walter and H. Ritter. Rapid learning with parametrized self-organizing maps. *Neural Computing*, 1995. Submitted.

[14] T. G. Zimmermann, J. Lanier, C. Blanchard, S. Bryson, and Y. Harvill. A hand gesture interface device. In *Proc. CHI+GI*, pages 189–192, 1987.

A Novel Channel Selection System in Cochlear Implants Using Artificial Neural Network

Marwan A. Jabri   &   Raymond J. Wang
Systems Engineering and Design Automation Laboratory
Department of Electrical Engineering
The University of Sydney
NSW 2006, Australia
{marwan,jwwang}@sedal.usyd.edu.au

Abstract

State-of-the-art speech processors in cochlear implants perform channel selection using a spectral maxima strategy. This strategy can lead to confusions when high frequency features are needed to discriminate between sounds. We present in this paper a novel channel selection strategy based upon pattern recognition which allows "smart" channel selections to be made. The proposed strategy is implemented using multi-layer perceptrons trained on a multi-speaker labelled speech database. The input to the network are the energy coefficients of N energy channels. The output of the system are the indices of the M selected channels.

We compare the performance of our proposed system to that of spectral maxima strategy, and show that our strategy can produce significantly better results.

1 INTRODUCTION

A cochlear implant is a device used to provide the sensation of sound to those who are profoundly deaf by means of electrical stimulation of residual auditory neurons. It generally consists of a directional microphone, a wearable speech processor, a head-set transmitter and an implanted receiver-stimulator module with an electrode array which all together provide an electrical representation of the speech signal to the residual nerve fibres of the peripheral auditory system (Clark et al, 1990).

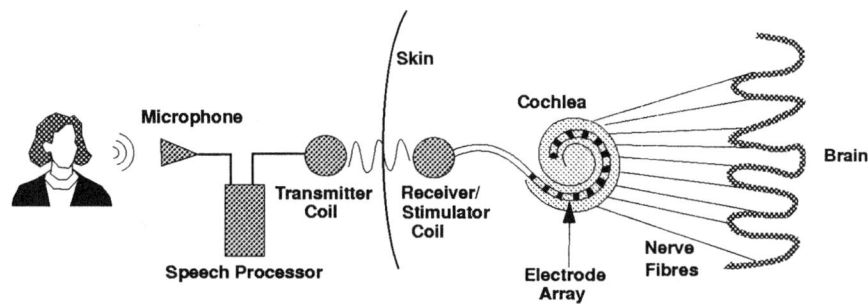

Figure 1: A simplified schematic diagram of the cochlear implants

A simplified schematic diagram of the cochlear implants is shown in Figure 1. Speech sounds are picked up by the directional microphone and sent to the speech processor. The speech processor amplifies, filters and digitizes these signals, and then selects and codes the appropriate sound information. The coded signal contains information as to which electrode to stimulate and the intensity level required to generate the appropriate sound sensations. The signal is then sent to the receiver/stimulator via the transmitter coil. The receiver/stimulator delivers electrical impulses to the appropriate electrodes in the cochlea. These stimulated electrodes then directly activate the hearing nerve in the inner ear, creating the sensation of sound, which is then forwarded to the brain for interpretation. The entire process happens in milliseconds.

For multi-channel cochlear implants, the task of the speech processor is to compute the spectral energy of the electrical signals it receives, and to quantise them into different levels. The energy spectrum is commonly divided into separate bands using a filter bank of N (typically 20) bandpass filters with centre frequencies ranging from 250 Hz to 10 KHz. The bands of energy are allocated to electrodes in the patient's implant on a one-to-one basis. Usually the most-apical bipolar electrode pairs are allocated to the channels in tonotopic order. The limitations of implant systems usually require only a selected number of the quantised energy levels to be fed to the implanted electrode array (Abbas, 1993; Schouten, 1992).

The state-of-the-art speech processor for multi-channel implants performs channel selection using spectral maxima strategy (McDermott et al, 1992; Seligman & McDermott, 1994). The maxima strategy selects the M (about 6) largest spectral energy of the frequency spectrum as stimulation channels from a filter bank of N (typically 20) bandpass. It is believed that compared to other channel selection techniques (F0F2, F0F1F2, MPEAK ...), the maxima strategy increases the amount of spectral information and improves the speech perception and recognition performance.

However, maxima strategy relies heavily on the highest energies. This often leads to the same levels being selected for different sounds, as the energy levels that distinguish them are not high enough to be selected. For some speech signals, it does not cater for confusions and cannot discriminate between high frequency features.

We present in this paper Artificial Neural Networks (ANN) techniques for implementing "smart" channel selection for cochlear implant systems. The input to the proposed channel selection system consists of the energy coefficients (18 in our experiments) and the output the indices of the selected channels (6 in our experiments). The neural network based selection system is trained on a multi-speaker labelled speech and has been evaluated on a separated multi-speaker database not used in the training phase. The most important feature of our ANN based channel selection system is its ability to select the channels for stimulation on the basis of the overall morphology of the energy spectrum and not only on the basis of the maximal energy values.

2 THE PATTERN RECOGNITION BASED CHANNEL SELECTION STRATEGY

Speech is the most natural form of human communication. The speech information signal can be divided into phonemes, which share some common acoustic properties with one another for a short interval of time. The phonemes are typically divided into two broad classes: (a) vowels, which allow unrestricted airflow in the vocal tract, and (b) consonants, which restrict airflow at some point and are weaker than vowels. Different phonemes have different morphology in the energy spectrum. Moreover, for different speakers and different speech sentences, the same phonemes have different energy spectrum morphologies (Kent & Read, 1992). Therefore, simple methods to select some of the most important channels for all the phoneme patterns will not perform as good as the method that considers the spectrum in its entirety.

The existing maxima strategy only refers to the spectrum amplitudes found in the entire estimated spectrum without considering the morphology. Typically several of the maxima results can be obtained from a single spectral peak. Therefore, for some phoneme patterns, the selection result is good enough to represent the original phoneme. But for some others, some important features of the phoneme are lost. This usually happens to those phonemes with important features in the high frequency region. Due to the low amplitude of the high frequency in the spectrum morphology, maxima methods are not capable to extract those high frequency features. The relationship between the desired M output channels and the energy spectrum patterns is complex, and depending on the conditions, may be influenced by many factors. As mentioned in the Introduction, channel selection methods that make use of local information only in the energy spectrum are bound to produce channel sub-sets where sounds may be confused. The confusions can be reduced if "global" information of the energy spectrum is used in the selection process.

The channel selection approach we are proposing makes use of the overall energy spectrum. This is achieved by turning the selection problem into that of a spectrum morphology pattern recognition one and hence, we call our approach Pattern Recognition based Channel Selection (PRCS).

2.1 PRCS STRATEGY

The PRCS strategy is implemented using two cascaded neural networks shown in Figure 2:

- Spectral morphological classifier: Its inputs are the spectrum energy amplitudes of all the channels and its outputs all the transformations of the inputs. The transformation between input and output can be seen as a recognition, emphasis, and/or decaying of the inputs. The consequence is that some inputs are amplified and some decayed, depending on the morphology of the spectrum. The classifier performs a non-linear mapping.

- M strongest of N classifier: It receives the output of morphological classifier and applies a M strongest selection rule.

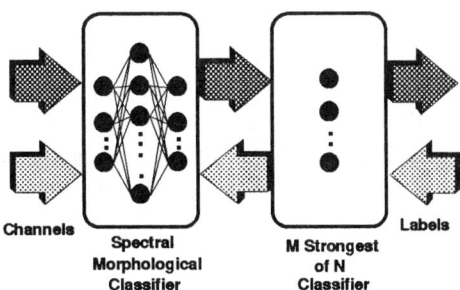

Figure 2: The pattern recognition based channel selection architecture

2.2 TRAINING AND TESTING DATA

The most difficult task in developing the proposed PRCS is to set up the labelled training and testing data for the spectral morphological classifier.

The training and testing data sets have been constructed using the process shown in Figure 3.

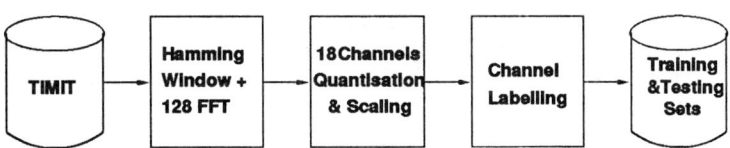

Figure 3: The process of generating training and testing sets

The sounds in the data sets are speech extracted from the DARPA TIMIT multispeaker speech corpus (Fisher et al, 1987) which contains a total of 6300 sentences, 10 sentences spoken by each of 630 speakers. The speech signal is sampled at 16KHz rate with 16 bit precision. As the speech is nonstationary, to produce the energy spectrum versus channel numbers, a short-time speech analysis method is used.

The Fast Fourier Transform with $8ms$ smooth Hamming window technique is applied to yield the energy spectrum. The hamming window has the shape of a raised cosine pulse:

$$h(n) = \begin{cases} 0.54 - 0.46 \cos\left(\frac{2\pi n}{N-a}\right) & \text{for } 0 \leq n \leq N-1 \\ 0 & \text{otherwise} \end{cases}$$

The time frame on which the speech analysis is performed is $4ms$ long and the successive time frame windows overlap by 50%.

Using frequency allocations similar to that used in commercial cochlear implant speech processors, the frequency range in the spectrum is divided into 18 channels with each channel having the center frequencies of *250, 450, 650, 850 1050, 1250, 1450, 1650, 1895, 2177, 2500, 2873, 3300, 3866, 4530, 5307, 6218* and *7285Hz* respectively. Each energy spectrum from a time frame is quantised into these 18 frequency bands. The energy amplitude for each level is the sum of the amplitude value of the energy for all the frequency components in the level.

The quantised energy spectrum is then labelled using a graphics based tool, called LABEL, developed specially for this application. LABEL displays the spectrum pattern including the unquantised spectrum, the signal source, speaker's name, speech sentence, phoneme, signal pre-processing method and FFT results. All these information assists labelling experts to allocate a score (1 to 18) to each channel. The score reflects the importance of the information provided by each of the bands. Hence, if six channels are only to be selected, the channels with the score 1 to 6 can be used and are highlighted. The labelling is necessary as a supervised neural network training method is being used.

A total of 5000 energy spectrum patterns have been labelled. They are from 20 different speakers and different spoken sentences. Of the 5000 example patterns, 4000 patterns are allocated for training and 1000 patterns for testing.

3 EXPERIMENTAL RESULTS

We have implemented and tested the PRCS system as described above and our experiments show that it has better performance than channel selection systems used in present cochlear implant processors.

The PRCS system is effectively constructed as a multi-module neural network using MUME (Jabri et al, 1994). The back-propagation algorithm in an on-line mode is used to train the MLP. The training patterns input components are the energy amplitudes of the 18 channels and the teacher component consists of a "1" for a channel to be selected and "0" for all others. The MLP is trained for up to 2000 epochs or when a minimum total mean squared error is reached. A learning rate η of 0.01 is used (no weight decay).

We show the average performance of our PRCS in Table 1 where we also show the performance of a leading commercial spectral maxima strategy called SPEAK on the same test set. In the first column of this table we show the number of channels that matched out of the 6 desired channels. For example, the first row corresponds to the case where all 6 channels match the desired 6 channels in the test data base, and so on. As Table 1 shows, the PRCS produces a significantly better performance than the commercial strategy on the speech test set.

The selection performance to different phonemes is listed in Table 2. It clearly

Table 1: The comparison of average performance between commercial and PRCS system

The Channel Selections from the two different methods		
	PRCS results	Commercial technique results
Fully matched	22 %	4 %
5 matched	80 %	25 %
4 matched	98 %	57 %
3 matched	100 %	93 %
2 matched	100 %	99 %
1 matched	100 %	100 %

Table 2: PRCS channel selecting performance on different phoneme patterns

The PRCS results for different phoneme patterns				
Phoneme	Fully matched	5 matched	4 matched	3 matched
Stops	19 %	69 %	96 %	100 %
Fricatives	18 %	66 %	92 %	100 %
Nasals	14 %	66 %	96 %	100 %
Semivowels & Glides	14 %	79 %	95 %	100 %
Vowels	25 %	84 %	98 %	100 %

shows that the PRCS strategy can cater for the features of all the speech spectrum patterns.

To compare the practical performance of the PRCS with the maxima strategies we have developed a direct performance test system which allows us to play the synthesized speech of the selected channels through post-speech synthesizer. Our test shows that the PRCS produces more intelligible speech to the normal ears. Sixteen different sentences spoken by sixteen people are tested using both maxima and PRCS methods. It is found that the synthesized speech from PRCS has much more high frequency features than that of the speech produced by the maxima strategy. All listeners who were asked to take the test agreed that the quality of the speech sound from PRCS is much better than those from the commercial maxima channel selection system. The tape recording of the synthesized speech will be available at the conference.

4 CONCLUSION

A pattern recognition based channel selection strategy for Cochlear Implants has been presented. The strategy is based on a 18-72-18 MLP strongest selector. The proposed channel selection strategy has been compared to a leading commercial technique. Our simulation and play back results show that our machine learning based technique produces significantly better channel selections.

Reference

Abbas, P. J. (1993) Electrophysiology. *"Cochlear Implants: Audiological Foundations" edited by R. S. Tyler, Singular Publishing Group*, pp.317–355.

Clark, G. M., Tong, Y. C.& Patrick, J. F. (1990) Cochlear Prosthesis. *Edinborough: Churchill Living stone.*

Fisher, W. M., Zue, V., Bernstein, J. & Pallett, D. (1987) An Acoustic-Phonetic Data Base. *In 113th Meeting of Acoust Soc Am*, May 1987

Jabri, M. A., Tinker, E. A. & Leerink, L. (1994) MUME — A Multi-Net Multi-Architecture Neural Simulation Environment. *"Neural Network Simulation Environments", J. Skrzypek ed.*, Kluwer Academic Publishers.

Kent, R. D. & Read, C. (1992) The Acoustic Analysis of Speech. *Whurr Publishers.*

McDermott, H. J., McKay, C. M. & Vandali, A. E. (1992) A new portable sound processor for the University of Melbourne / Nucleus Limited multielectrode cochlear implant. *J. Acoust. Soc. Am.* 91(6), June 1992, pp.3367-3371

Schouten, M. E. H edited (1992) The Auditory Processing of Speech — From Sounds to Words. *Speech Research 10, Mouton de Gruyter.*

Seligman, P. & McDermott, H. (1994) Architecture of the SPECTRA 22 Speech Processor. *International Cochlear Implant, Speech and Hearing Symposium*, Melbourne, October, 1994, p.254.

Prediction of Beta Sheets in Proteins

Anders Krogh
The Sanger Centre
Hinxton, Cambs CB10 1RQ, UK.
Email: krogh@sanger.ac.uk

Søren Kamaric Riis
Electronics Institute, Building 349
Technical University of Denmark
2800 Lyngby, Denmark
Email: riis@ei.dtu.dk

Abstract

Most current methods for prediction of protein secondary structure use a small window of the protein sequence to predict the structure of the central amino acid. We describe a new method for prediction of the non-local structure called β-sheet, which consists of two or more β-strands that are connected by hydrogen bonds. Since β-strands are often widely separated in the protein chain, a network with two windows is introduced. After training on a set of proteins the network predicts the sheets well, but there are many false positives. By using a global energy function the β-sheet prediction is combined with a local prediction of the three secondary structures α-helix, β-strand and coil. The energy function is minimized using simulated annealing to give a final prediction.

1 INTRODUCTION

Proteins are long sequences of amino acids. There are 20 different amino acids with varying chemical properties, *e.g.*, some are hydrophobic (dislikes water) and some are hydrophilic [1]. It is convenient to represent each amino acid by a letter and the sequence of amino acids in a protein (the *primary structure*) can be written as a string with a typical length of 100 to 500 letters. A protein chain folds back on itself, and the resulting 3D structure (the *tertiary structure*) is highly correlated to the function of the protein. The prediction of the 3D structure from the primary structure is one of the long-standing unsolved problems in molecular biology. As an important step on the way a lot of work has been devoted to predicting the local conformation of the protein chain, which is called the *secondary structure*. Neural network methods are currently the most successful for predicting secondary structure. The approach was pioneered by Qian and Sejnowski [2] and Bohr *et al.* [3], but later extended in various ways, see *e.g.* [4] for an overview. In most of this work, only the two regular secondary structure elements α-helix and β-strand are being distinguished, and everything else is labeled coil. Thus, the methods based

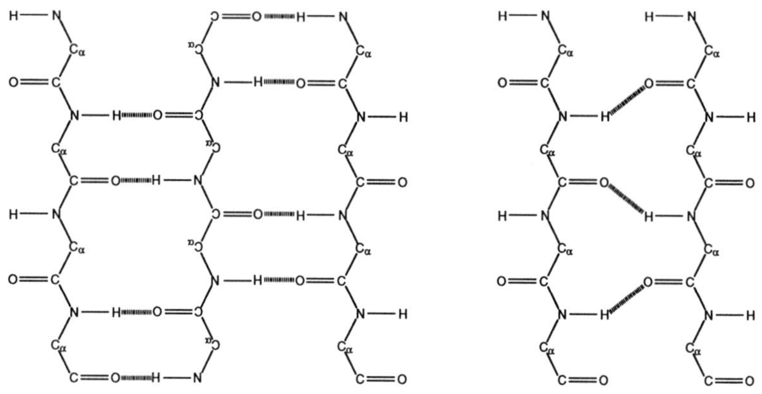

Figure 1: Left: Anti-parallel β-sheet. The vertical lines correspond to the backbone of the protein. An amino acid consists of N–C$_\alpha$–C and a side chain on the C$_\alpha$ that is not shown (the 20 amino acids are distinguished by different side chains). In the anti-parallel sheet the directions of the strands alternate, which is here indicated quite explicitly by showing the middle strand up-side down. The H-bonds between the strands are shown by ||||||||. A sheet has two or more strands, here the anti-parallel sheet is shown with three strands. Right: Parallel β-sheet consisting of two strands.

on a local window of amino acids give a three-state prediction of the secondary structure of the central amino acid in the window.

Current predictions of secondary structure based on single sequences as input have accuracies of about 65-66%. It is widely believed that this accuracy is close to the limit of what can be done from a local window (using only single sequences as input) [5], because interactions between amino acids far apart in the protein chain are important to the structure. A good example of such non-local interactions are the β-sheets consisting of two or more β-strands interconnected by H-bonds, see fig. 1. Often the β-strands in a sheet are widely separated in the sequence, implying that only part of the available sequence information about a β-sheet can be contained in a window of, say, 13 amino acids. This is one of the reasons why the accuracy of β-strand predictions are generally lower than the accuracy of α-helix predictions. The aim of this work is to improve prediction of secondary structures by combining local predictions of α-helix, β-strand and coil with a non-local method predicting β-sheets.

Other work along the same directions include [6] in which β-sheet predictions are done by linear methods and [7] where a so-called density network is applied to the problem.

2 A NEURAL NETWORK WITH TWO WINDOWS

We aim at capturing correlations in the β-sheets by using a neural network with two windows, see fig. 2. While window 1 is centered around amino acid number i (a_i), window 2 slides along the rest of the chain. When the amino acids centered in each of the two windows sit opposite each other in a β-sheet the target output is 1, and otherwise 0. After the whole protein has been traversed by window 2, window 1 is moved to the next position ($i+1$) and the procedure is repeated. If the protein is L amino acids long this procedure yields an output value for each of the $L(L-1)/2$

Figure 2: Neural network for predicting β-sheets. The network employs weight sharing to improve the encoding of the amino acids and to reduce the number of adjustable parameters.

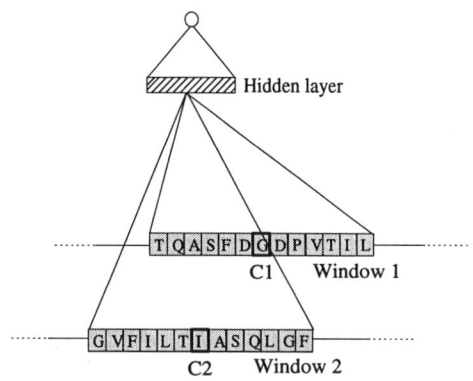

pairs of amino acids. We display the output in a $L \times L$ gray-scale image as shown in fig. 3. We assume symmetry of sheets, *i.e.*, if the two windows are interchanged, the output does not change. This symmetry is ensured (approximately) during training by presenting all inputs in both directions.

Each window of the network sees K amino acids. An amino acid is represented by a vector of 20 binary numbers all being zero, except one, which is 1. That is, the amino acid A is represented by the vector $1, 0, 0, \ldots, 0$ and so on. This coding ensures that the input representations are uncorrelated, but it is a very inefficient coding, since 20 amino acids could in principle be represented by only 5 bit. Therefore, we use *weight sharing* [8] to learn a better encoding [4]. The 20 input units corresponding to one window position are fully connected to three hidden units. The $3 \times (20 + 1)$ weights to these units are shared by all window positions, *i.e.*, the activation of the 3 hidden units is a new *learned* encoding of the amino acids, so instead of being represented by 20 binary values they are represented by 3 real values. Of course the number of units for this encoding can be varied, but initial experiments showed that 3 was optimal [4]. The two windows of the network are made the same way with the same number of inputs *etc.*. The first layer of hidden units in the two windows are fully connected to a hidden layer which is fully connected to the output unit, see fig. 2. Furthermore, two structurally identical networks are used: one for parallel and one for anti-parallel β-sheets.

The basis for the training set in this study is the set of 126 non-homologous protein chains used in [9], but chains forming β-sheets with *other* chains are excluded. This leaves us with 85 proteins in our data set. For a protein of length L only a very small fraction of the $L(L-1)/2$ pairs are positive examples of β-sheet pairs. Therefore it is very important to balance the positive and negative examples to avoid the situation where the network always predicts no β-sheet. Furthermore, there are several types of negative examples with quite different occurrences: 1) two amino acids of which none belong to a β-sheet; 2) one in a β-sheet and one which is not in a β-sheet; 3) two sitting in β-sheets, but not opposite to each other. The balancing was done in the following way. For each positive example selected at random a negative example from each of the three categories were selected at random.

If the network does not have a second layer of hidden units, it turns out that the result is no better than a network with only one input window, *i.e.*, the network cannot capture correlations between the two windows. Initial experiments indicated that about 10 units in the second hidden layer and two identical input windows of size $K = 9$ gave the best results. In fig. 3(left) the prediction of anti-parallel sheets is shown for the protein identified as 1acx in the Brookhaven Protein Data Bank

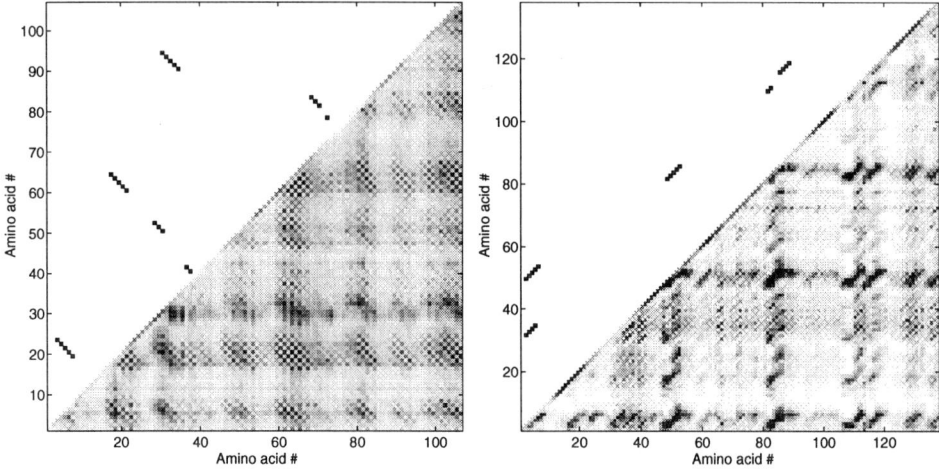

Figure 3: Left: The prediction of anti-parallel β-sheets in the protein 1acx. In the upper triangle the correct structure is shown by a black square for each β-sheet pair. The lower triangle shows the prediction by the two-window network. For any pair of amino acids the network output is a number between zero (white) and one (black), and it is displayed by a linear gray-scale. The diagonal shows the prediction of α-helices. Right: The same display for parallel β-sheets in the protein 4fxn. Notice that the correct structure are lines parallel to the diagonal, whereas they are perpendicular for anti-parallel sheets. For both cases the network was trained on a training set that did *not* contain the protein for which the result is shown.

[10]. First of all, one notices the checker board structure of the prediction of β-sheets. This is related to the structure of β-sheets. Many sheets are hydrophobic on one side and hydrophilic on the other. The side chains of the amino acids in a strand alternates between the two sides of the sheet, and this gives rise to the periodicity responsible for the pattern.

Another network was trained on *parallel* β-sheets. These are rare compared to the anti-parallel ones, so the amount of training data is limited. In fig. 3(right) the result is shown for protein 4fxn. This prediction seems better than the one obtained for anti-parallel sheets, although false positive predictions still occurs at some positions with strands that do not pair. Strands that bind in parallel β-sheets are generally more widely separated in the sequence than strands in anti-parallel sheets. Therefore, one can imagine that the strands in parallel sheets have to be more correlated to find each other in the folding process, which would explain the better prediction accuracy.

The results shown in fig. 3 are fairly representative. The network misses some of the sheets, but false positives present a more severe problem. By calculating correlation coefficients we can show that the network *does* capture some correlations, but they seem to be weak. Based on these results, we hypothesize that the formation of β-sheets is only weakly dependent on correlations between corresponding β-strands. This is quite surprising. However weak these correlations are, we believe they can still improve the accuracy of the three state secondary structure prediction. In order to combine local methods with the non-local β-sheet prediction, we introduce a global energy function as described below.

3 A GLOBAL ENERGY FUNCTION

We use a newly developed local neural network method based on *one* input window [4] to give an initial prediction of the three possible structures. The output from this network is constrained by softmax [11], and can thus be interpreted as the probabilities for each of the three structures. That is, for amino acid a_i, it yields three numbers $p_{i,n}$, $n = 1, 2$ or 3 indicating the probability of α-helix ($p_{i,1}$), β-sheet ($p_{i,2}$), or coil ($p_{i,3}$). Define $s_{i,n} = 1$ if amino acid i is assigned structure n and $s_{i,n} = 0$ otherwise. Also define $h_{i,n} = \log p_{i,n}$. We now construct the 'energy function'

$$H_3(s) = -\sum_i \sum_n u_n h_{i,n} s_{i,n}, \tag{1}$$

where weights u_n are introduced for later usage. Assuming the probabilities $p_{i,n}$ are independent for any two amino acids in a sequence, this is the negative log likelihood of the assigned secondary structure represented by s, provided that $u_n = 1$. As it stands, alone, it is a fairly trivial energy function, because the minimum is the assignment which corresponds to the prediction with the maximum $p_{i,n}$ at each position i — the assignment of secondary structure that one would probably use anyway.

For amino acids a_i and a_j the logarithm of the output of the β-sheet network described previously is called q_{ij}^p for parallel β-sheets and q_{ij}^a for anti-parallel sheets. We interpret these numbers as the gain in energy if a β-sheet pair is formed. (As more terms are added to the energy, the interpretation as a log-likelihood function is gradually fading.) If the two amino acids form a pair in a parallel β-sheet, we set the variable T_{ij}^p equal to 1, and otherwise to 0, and similarly with T_{ij}^a for anti-parallel sheets. Thus the T_{ij}^a and T_{ij}^p are sparse binary matrices. Now the total energy of the β-sheets can be expressed as

$$H_\beta(s, T^a, T^p) = -\sum_{ij}[C_a q_{ij}^a T_{ij}^a + C_p q_{ij}^p T_{ij}^p], \tag{2}$$

where C_a and C_p determine the weights of the two terms in the function. Since an amino acid can only be in one structure, the dynamic T and s variables are constrained: Only T_{ij}^a or T_{ij}^p can be 1 for the same (i, j), and if any of them is 1 the amino acids involved must be in a β-sheet, so $s_{i,2} = s_{j,2} = 1$. Also, $s_{i,2}$ can only be 1 if there exists a j with either T_{ij}^a or T_{ij}^p equal to 1. Because of these constraints we have indicated an s dependence of H_β.

The last term in our energy function introduces correlations between neighboring amino acids. The above assumption that the secondary structure of the amino acids are independent is of course a bad assumption, and we try to repair it with a term

$$H_n(s) = \sum_i \sum_{nm} J_{nm} s_{i,n} s_{i+1,m}, \tag{3}$$

that introduces nearest neighbor interactions in the chain. A negative J_{11}, for instance, means that α following α is favored, and e.g., a positive J_{12} discourages a β following an α.

Now the total energy is

$$H_{\text{total}}(s, T^a, T^p) = H_3(s) + H_\beta(s, T^a, T^p) + H_n(s). \tag{4}$$

Since β-sheets are introduced in two ways, through $h_{i,2}$ and q_{ij}, we need the weights u_n in (1) to be different from 1.

The total energy function (4) has some resemblance with a so-called Potts glass in an external field [12]. The crucial difference is that the couplings between the 'spins' s_i are dependent on the dynamic variables T. Another analogy of the energy function is to image analysis, where couplings like the T's are sometimes used as edge elements.

3.1 PARAMETER ESTIMATION

The energy function contains a number of parameters, u_n, C_a, C_p and J_{nm}. These parameters were estimated by a method inspired by Boltzmann learning [13]. In the Boltzmann machine the estimation of the weights can be formulated as a minimization of the difference between the free energy of the 'clamped' system and that of the 'free-running' system [14]. If we think of our energy function as a free energy (at zero temperature), it corresponds to minimizing the difference between the energy of the correct protein structure and the minimum energy,

$$C = \sum_{\mu=1}^{p} \left[H_{\text{total}}\left(s(\mu), T^a(\mu), T^p(\mu)\right) - H_{\text{total}}\left(\hat{s}(\mu), \hat{T}^a(\mu), \hat{T}^p(\mu)\right) \right], \quad (5)$$

where p is the total number of proteins in the training set. Here the *correct* structure of protein μ is called $s(\mu), T^a(\mu), T^p(\mu)$, whereas $\hat{s}(\mu), \hat{T}^a(\mu), \hat{T}^p(\mu)$ represents the structure that minimizes the energy H_{total}. By definition the second term of C is less than the first, so C is bounded from below by zero.

The cost function C is minimized by gradient descent in the parameters. This is in principle straightforward, because all the parameters appear linearly in H_{total}. However, a problem with this approach is that C is minimal when all the parameters are set to zero, because then the energy is zero. It is cured by constraining some of the parameters in H_{total}. We chose the constraint $\sum_n u_n = 1$. This may not be the perfect solution from a theoretical point of view, but it works well. Another problem with this approach is that one has to find the minimum of the energy H_{total} in the dynamic variables in each iteration of the gradient descent procedure. To globally minimize the function by simulated annealing each time would be very costly in terms of computer time. Instead of using the (global) minimum of the energy for each protein, we use the energy obtained by minimizing the energy from the correct structure. This minimization is done by a greedy algorithm in the following way. In each iteration the change in s, T^a, T^p which results in the largest decrease in H_{total} is carried out. This is repeated until any change will increase H_{total}. This algorithm works towards a *local stability* of the protein structures in the training set. We believe it is not only an efficient way of doing it, but also a very sensible way. In fact, the method may well be applicable in other models, such as Boltzmann machines.

3.2 STRUCTURE PREDICTION BY SIMULATED ANNEALING

After estimation of the parameters on which the energy function H_{total} depends, we can proceed to predict the structure of new proteins. This was done using simulated annealing and the EBSA package [15]. The total procedure for prediction is,

1. A neural net predicts α-helix, β-strand or coil. The logarithm of these predictions give all the $h_{i,n}$ for that protein.
2. The two-window neural networks predict the β-sheets. The result is the q_{ij}^a from one network and the q_{ij}^p from the other.
3. A random configuration of s, T^a, T^p variables is generated from which the simulated annealing minimization of H_{total} was started. During annealing, all constraints on s, T^a, T^p variables are strictly enforced.

4. The final minimum configuration $\hat{s}$ is the prediction of the secondary structure. The β-sheets are predicted by $\hat{T}^a$ and $\hat{T}^p$.

Using the above scheme, an average secondary structure accuracy of 66.5% is obtained by seven-fold cross validation. This should be compared to 66.3% obtained by the local neural network based method [4] on the same data set. Although these preliminary results do not represent a significant improvement, we consider them very encouraging for future work. Because the method not only predicts the secondary structure, but also which strands actually binds to form β-sheets, even a modest result may be an important step on the way to full 3D predictions.

4 CONCLUSION

In this paper we introduced several novel ideas which may be applicable in other contexts than prediction of protein structure. Firstly, we described a neural network with two input windows that was used for predicting the non-local structure called β-sheets. Secondly, we combined local predictions of α-helix, β-strand and coil with the β-sheet prediction by minimization of a global energy function. Thirdly, we showed how the adjustable parameters in the energy function could be estimated by a method similar to Boltzmann learning.

We found that correlations between β-strands in β-sheets are surprisingly weak. Using the energy function to combine predictions improves performance a little. Although we have not solved the protein folding problem, we consider the results very encouraging for future work. This will include attempts to improve the performance of the two-window network as well as experimenting with the energy function, and maybe add more terms to incorporate new constraints.

Acknowledgments: We would like to thank Tim Hubbard, Richard Durbin and Benny Lautrup for interesting comments on this work and Peter Salamon and Richard Frost for assisting with simulated annealing. This work was supported by a grant from the Novo Nordisk Foundation.

References

[1] C. Branden and J. Tooze, *Introduction to Protein Structure* (Garland Publishing, Inc., New York, 1991).
[2] N. Qian and T. Sejnowski, Journal of Molecular Biology **202**, 865 (1988).
[3] H. Bohr et al., FEBS Letters **241**, 223 (1988).
[4] S. Riis and A. Krogh, Nordita Preprint 95/34 S, submitted to J. Comp. Biol.
[5] B. Rost, C. Sander, and R. Schneider, J Mol. Biol. **235**, 13 (1994).
[6] T. Hubbard, in *Proc. of the 27th HICSS*, edited by R. Lathrop (IEEE Computer Soc. Press, 1994), pp. 336–354.
[7] D. J. C. MacKay, in *Maximum Entropy and Bayesian Methods, Cambridge 1994*, edited by J. Skilling and S. Sibisi (Kluwer, Dordrecht, 1995).
[8] Y. Le Cun et al., Neural Computation **1**, 541 (1989).
[9] B. Rost and C. Sander, Proteins **19**, 55 (1994).
[10] F. Bernstein et al., J Mol. Biol. **112**, 535 (1977).
[11] J. Bridle, in *Neural Information Processing Systems 2*, edited by D. Touretzky (Morgan Kaufmann, San Mateo, CA, 1990), pp. 211–217.
[12] K. Fisher and J. Hertz, *Spin glasses* (Cambridge University Press, 1991).
[13] D. Ackley, G. Hinton, and T. Sejnowski, Cognitive Science **9**, 147 (1985).
[14] J. Hertz, A. Krogh, and R. Palmer, *Introduction to the Theory of Neural Computation* (Addison-Wesley, Redwood City, 1991).
[15] R. Frost, SDSC EBSA, C Library Documentation, version 2.1. SDSC Techreport.

A Neural Network Autoassociator for Induction Motor Failure Prediction

Thomas Petsche, Angelo Marcantonio, Christian Darken,
Stephen J. Hanson, Gary M. Kuhn and Iwan Santoso
[PETSCHE, ANGELO, DARKEN, JOSE, GMK, NIS]@SCR.SIEMENS.COM
Siemens Corporate Research, Inc.
755 College Road East
Princeton, NJ 08853

Abstract

We present results on the use of neural network based autoassociators which act as novelty or anomaly detectors to detect imminent motor failures. The autoassociator is trained to reconstruct spectra obtained from the healthy motor. In laboratory tests, we have demonstrated that the trained autoassociator has a small reconstruction error on measurements recorded from healthy motors but a larger error on those recorded from a motor with a fault. We have designed and built a motor monitoring system using an autoassociator for anomaly detection and are in the process of testing the system at three industrial and commercial sites.

1 Introduction

An unexpected breakdown of an electric induction motor can cause financial loss significantly in excess of the cost of the motor. For example, the breakdown of a motor in a production line during a production run can cause the loss of work in progress as well as loss of production time.

When a motor does fail, it is not uncommon to replace it with an oversized motor based on the assumption that if a motor is not running at its design limit then it will survive longer. While this is frequently effective, this leads to significantly lower operating efficiencies and higher initial and operating costs.

The primary motivation behind this project is the observation that if a motor breakdown and be predicted before the actual breakdown occurs, then the motor can be replaced in a more orderly way, with minimal interruption of the process in which it is involved. The goal is to produce a system that is conceptually similar to a fuel gauge on an automobile. When the system detects conditions that indicate that the motor is approaching its end-of-life, the operators are notified that a replacement is necessary in the near future.

2 Background

At present, motors in critical operations that are subject to mechanical failures - for example, fire pump motors on US Navy vessels - are typically monitored by a human expert who periodically listens to the vibrations of the motor and, based on experience, determines whether the motor sounds healthy or sounds like a problem is developing. Since mechanical problems in motors typically lead to increased or changed vibrations, this technique can work well. Unfortunately, it depends on a competent and expensive expert.

In an attempt to automate motor monitoring, several vendors have "automated motor monitoring" equipment available. For mechanical failure monitoring, such systems typically rely on several accelerometers to measure the vibration of the motor at various points and along various axes. The systems then display information, primarily about the vibration spectrum, to an operator who determines whether the motor is functioning properly. These systems are expensive since they rely on several accelerometers, each of which is itself expensive, as well as data collection hardware and a computer. Further, the systems require an expert operator and frequently require that the motor be tested only when it is driving a known load.

Neither the human motor expert nor the existing motor monitoring systems provide an affordable solution for continuous on-line mechanical failure monitoring. However, the success of the human expert and existing vibration monitors does demonstrate that in fact, there is sufficient information in the vibration of an electric induction motor to detect imminent mechanical failures.

Siemens Energy and Automation has proposed a new product, the Siemens Advanced Motor Master System II (SAMMS II), that will continuously monitor and protect an electric induction motor while it is operating on-line. Like the presently available SAMMS, the SAMMS II is designed to provide protection against thermal and electrical overload an, in addition, it will provide detection of insulation deterioration and mechanical fault monitoring.

In contrast to existing systems and techniques, the SAMMS II is designed to (1) require no human expert to determine if a motor is developing problems; (2) be inexpensive; and (3) provide continuous, on-line monitoring of the motor in normal operation.

The requirements for the SAMMS II, in particular the cost constraint, require that several issues be resolved. First, in order to produce a low cost system, it is necessary to eliminate the need for expensive accelerometers. Second, wiring should be limited to the motor control center, i.e., it should not be necessary to run new signal wires from the motor control center to the motor. Third, the SAMMS II is to provide continuous on-line monitoring, so the system must adapt to or factor out the effect of changing loads on the motor. Finally since the SAMMS II would not necessarily be bundled with a motor and so might be used to control and monitor an arbitrary motor from an arbitrary manufacturer, the design can not assume that a full description of the motor construction is available.

3 Approach

The first task was to determine how to eliminate the accelerometers. Based on work done elsewhere (Schoen, Habetler & Bartheld, 1994), SE&A determined that it might be possible to use measurements of the current on a single phase of the power supply to estimate the vibration of the motor. This depends on the assumption that any vibration of the motor will cause the rotor to move radially relative to the stator which will cause changes in the airgap which, in turn, will induce changes in the current.

Experiments were done at the Georgia Institute of Technology to determine the feasibility of this idea using the same sort of data collection system described later. Early experiments indicated that, for a single motor driving a variety of loads, it is possible to distinguish

Table 1: Loads for motors #1 and #2.

Load type	Load Magnitude
constant	half and full rated
sinusoidal oscillation at rotating frequency	half and full rated
sinusoidal oscillation at twice the rotating frequency	full rated
switching load (50% duty cycle) at rotating frequency	full rated
sinusoidal oscillation 28 Hz	half and full rated
sinusoidal oscillation at 30 Hz	full rated
switching load (50% duty cycle) at 30 Hz	full rated

Table 2: Neural network classifier experiment.

Features (N)	48	63	64	110	320
Performance on motor #1	100%	100%	92%	100%	100%
Performance on motor #2	—	30%	25%	55%	37%

between a current spectrum obtained from the motor while it is healthy and another obtained when the motor contains a fault. Moreover, it is also possible to automatically generate a classifiers that correctly determine the presence or absence of a fault in the motor.

The first, obvious approach to this monitoring task would seem to be to build a classifier that would be used to distinguish between a healthy motor and one that has developed a fault that is likely to lead to a breakdown. Unfortunately, this approach does not work.

As described above, we have successfully built classifiers of various sorts using manual and automatic techniques to distinguish between current spectra obtained from a motor when it is healthy and those obtained when it contains a fault.

However, since the SAMMS II will be connected to a motor before it fails and will be asked to identify a failure without ever seeing a labeled example of a failure from that motor, a classifier can only be used if it can be trained on data collected from one or more motors and then used to monitor the motor of interest. Unfortunately, experiments indicate that this will not work.

One of these experiments is illustrated in table 2. Several feedforward neural network classifiers were trained using examples from a single motor under four conditions: (1) healthy, (2) unbalanced, (3) containing a broken rotor bar and (4) containing a hole in the outer bearing race. The ten different loads listed in table 1 were applied to the motor for each of these conditions.

The networks contained N inputs (where N is given in table 2); 9 hidden units and 4 outputs. There were 40 training examples where each example is the average of 50 distinct magnitude scaled FFTs obtained from motor #1 from a single load/fault combination. The test data for which the results are reported in the table consisted of 40 averaged FFTs from motor #1 and 20 averaged FFTs (balanced and unbalanced only) from motor #2. The test set for motor #1 is completely distinct from the training set.

In the case where $n = 110$, the FFT components were selected to include the frequencies identified by the theory of motor physics as interesting for the three fault conditions and exclude all other components. This led to an improvement over the other cases where a single contiguous set of components was chosen, but the performance still degrades to about random chance instead of 100%.

This experiment clearly illustrates that is is possible to distinguish between healthy and faulty spectra obtained from the same motor. However, it also clearly illustrates that a

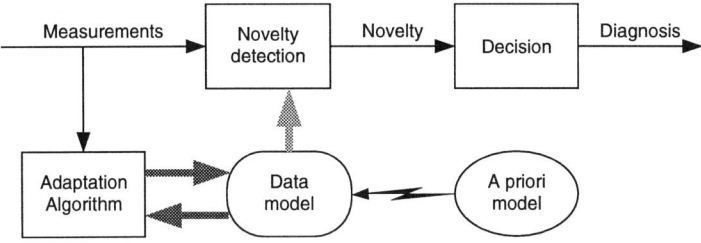

Figure 1: The basic form of an anomaly detection system.

classifier trained on one motor does not perform well on another motor since the error rates increase immensely. Based on results such as these, we have concluded that it is not feasible to build a single classifier that would be trained once and then placed in the field to monitor a motor. Instead we are pursuing an alternative based on anomaly detection which adapts a monitor to the particular motor for which it is responsible.

4 Anomaly detection

The basic notion of anomaly detection for monitoring is illustrated in figure 1. Statistical anomaly detection centers around a model of the data that was seen while the motor was operating normally. This model is produced by collecting spectra from the motor while it is operating normally. Once trained, the system compares each new spectrum to the model to determine how similar to or different from the training set it is. This similarity is described by an "anomaly metric" which, in the simplest case, can be thresholded to determine whether the motor is still normal or has developed a fault. Once the "anomaly metric" has been generated, various statistical techniques can be used to determine if there has been a change in the distribution of values.

5 A Neural Network-based Anomaly Detector

The core of the most successful monitoring system we have built to date is a neural network designed to function as an autoassociator (Rumelhart, Hinton & Williams, 1986, called it an "encoder"). We use a simple three layer feedforward network with N inputs, N outputs and $K < N$ hidden units. The input layer is fully connected to the hidden layer which is fully connected to the output layer. Each unit in the hidden and output layers computes $x_i = \sigma\left(\sum_{j=0}^{M_i} w_{i,j} x_j\right)$, where x_i is the output of neuron i which receives inputs from M_i other neurons and $w_{i,j}$ is the weight on the connection from neuron j to neuron i. The network is trained using the backpropagation algorithm to reconstruct the input vector on the output units. Specifically, if x_i is one of n input vectors and $\hat{x}_i$ is the corresponding output vector, the network is trained to minimize the sum of squared errors $E = \sum_{i=1}^{n} \|x_i - \hat{x}_i\|^2$. Once training is complete, the anomaly metric is $m_i = \|x_i - \hat{x}_i\|^2$.

6 Anomaly Detection Test

We have tested the effectiveness of the neural network autoassociator as an anomaly detector on several motors. For all these tests, the autoasociator had 20 hidden units. The hidden layer size was chosen after some experimentation and data analysis on motor #1, but no attempt was made to tune the hidden layer size for motor #2 or motor #3.

Motor #1 was tested using the ten different loads listed in table 1 and four different

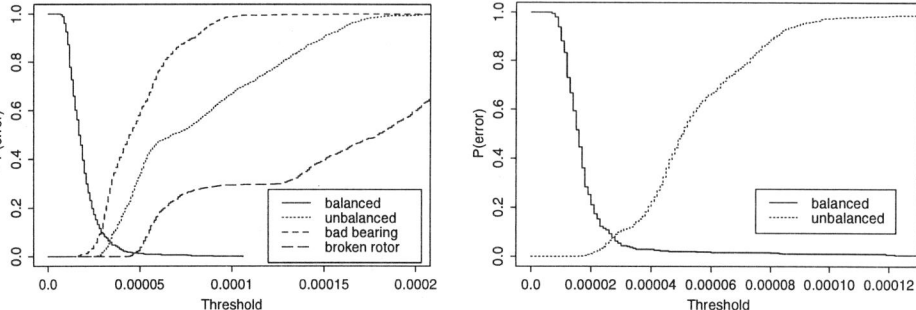

Figure 2: Probability of error as a function of threshold using individual FFTs on (a) motor #1 with 319 inputs and (b) motor #2 with 320 inputs.

health/fault conditions: healthy (balanced); unbalanced; broken rotor bar; and a hole in the outer bearing race. Motor #2 was tested while driving the same ten loads, but for one healthy and one faulty condition: healthy (balanced) and unbalanced.

For both motors #1 and #2, recordings of a single current phase were made as follows. For each fault condition, a load was selected and applied and the motor was run and the current signal recorded for five minutes. Then a new load was introduced and the motor was run again. The load was constant during any five minute recording session.

Motor #3 was tested using thirteen different loads, but only two fault conditions: healthy (balanced) and unbalanced. In this case, however, load changes occurred at random times. We preprocessed this data to to identify where the load changes occurred to generate the training set and the healthy motor test sets.

6.1 Preprocessing

Recordings were made on a digital audio tape (DAT). The current on a single phase was measured with a current transformer, amplified, notch filtered to reduce the magnitude of the 60Hz component, amplified again and then applied as input to the DAT. The notch filter was a switched capacitor filter which reduced the magnitude at 60Hz by about 30dB.

The time series obtained from the DAT was processed to reduce the sampling rate and then dividing the data into non-overlapping blocks and computing the FFT of each block. A subset of the FFT magnitude coefficients was selected and for each FFT, independent of any other FFT, the components were linearly scaled and translated to the interval $[\varepsilon, 1 - \varepsilon]$ (typically $\varepsilon = 0.02$). That is, for each FFT consisting of coefficients $f_0, \ldots, f_{n-1}$, we selected a subset, $\mathcal{F}$, (the same for all FFTs) of the components and computed $a = (1 - 2\varepsilon)(\max_{i \in \mathcal{F}} f_i - \min_{i \in \mathcal{F}} f_i)^{-1}$ and $b = \min_{i \in \mathcal{F}} f_i$. Then the input vector, x, to the network is $x_j = a(f_{i_j} - b) + \varepsilon$ where, for all $j < k$: $i_j, i_k \in \mathcal{F}$ and $i_j < i_k$.

6.2 Experimental Results

In figure 2a, we illustrate the results of a typical anomaly detection experiment on motor #1 using an autoassociator with 319 inputs and 20 hidden units. This graph illustrates the performance (false alarm and miss rates) of a very simple anomaly detection system which thresholds the anomaly metric to determine if the motor is good or bad. The decreasing curve that starts at threshold = 0, P(error) = 1 is the false alarm rate as a function of the threshold. Each increasing curve is the miss rate for a particular fault type.

In figure 2b we illustrate the performance of an autoassociator on motor #2 using an

A Neural Network Autoassociator for Induction Motor Failure Prediction

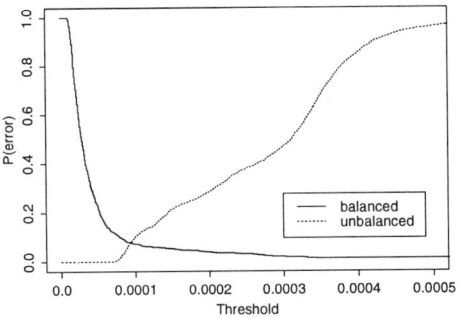

Figure 3: Probability of error for motor #3 using individual FFTs and 319 inputs.

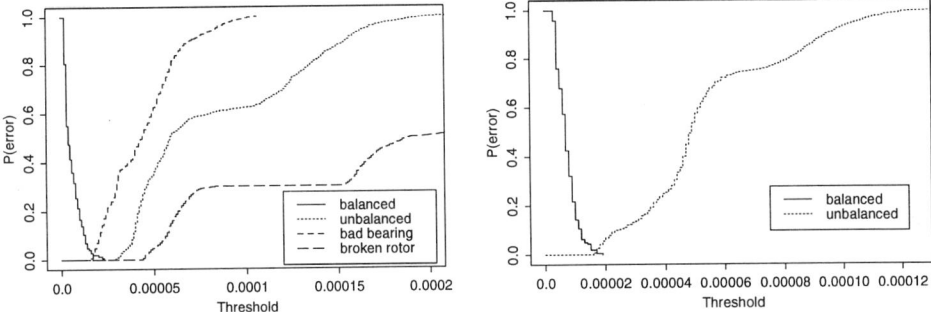

Figure 4: Probability of error using averaged FFTs for (a) motor #1 and 319 inputs (b) motor #2 and 320 inputs.

autoassociator with 320 inputs and 20 hidden units. Figure 3 shows our results on motor #3 using an autoassociator with 319 inputs.

We have found significant performance improvements by averaging several consecutive FFTs. In figure 4 we show the results for motors #1 and #2 when we averaged 11 FFTs to produce the input features. Compare these curves to those in figure 2. In particular, notice that the probability of error is much lower for the averaged FFTs when the good motor curve crosses any one of the faulty motor curves.

7 Candor System Design

Based on our experiments with autoassociators, we designed a prototype mechanical motor condition monitoring system. The functional system architecture is shown in figure 5. In order to control costs, the system is implemented on a PC. The system is designed so that each PC can monitor up to 128 motors using one 16-bit analog to digital converter. The signals are collected, filtered and multiplexed on custom external signal processing cards. Each card supports up to eight motors (with up to 16 cards per PC).

The system records current measurements from one motor at a time. For each motor, measurements are collected, four FFTs are computed on non-overlapping time series, and the four FFTs are averaged to produce a vector that is input to the neural network. The system reports that a motor is bad only if more than five of the last ten averaged FFTs produced an anomaly metric more than five standard deviations greater than the mean metric computed on the training set. Otherwise the motor is reported to be normal. In addition to monitoring the motors, the prototype systems are designed to record all measurements on tape to support

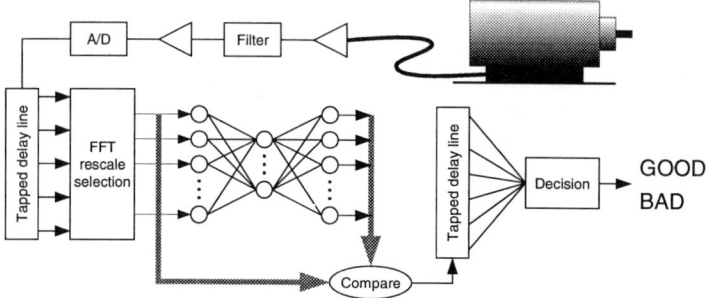

Figure 5: Functional architecture of Candor.

future experiments with alternative algorithms and tuning to improve performance.

To date, three monitoring systems have been installed: in an oil refinery, in a testing laboratory and on an office building ventilation system. The system has correctly detected the only failure it has seen so far: when a filter on the inlet to a water circulation pump became clogged the spectrum changed so much that the average daily novelty metric jumped from less than one standard deviation above the training set average to more than twenty standard deviations. We hope to have further test results in a year or so.

8 Related work

Gluck and Myers (1993) proposed a model of learning in the hippocampus based in part on an autoassociator which is used to detect novel stimuli and to compress the representation of the stimuli. This model has accurately predicted many of the classical conditioning behaviors that have been observed in normal and hippocampal-damaged animals. Based on this work, Japkowicz, Myers and Gluck (1995) independently derived an autoassociator-based novelty detector for machine learning tasks similar to that used in our system.

Together with Gluck, we have tested an autoassociator based anomaly detector on helicopter gearbox failures for the US Navy. In this case, the autoassociator is given 512 inputs consisting of 64 vibration based features from each of 8 accelerometers mounted at different locations on the gearbox. In a blind test, the autoassociator was able to correctly distinguish between feature vectors taken from a damaged gearbox and other feature vectors taken from normal gearboxes, all recorded in flight. Our anomaly detector will be included in test flights of a gearbox monitoring system later this year.

References

Gluck, M. A. & Myers, C. E. (1993). Hippocampal mediation of stimulus representation: A compuational theory. *Hippocampus*, *3*(4), 491–561.

Japkowicz, N., Myers, C., & Gluck, M. A. (1995). A novelty detection approach to classification. In *Proceedings of the Fourteenth International Joint Conference on Artificial Intelligence*.

Rumelhart, D., Hinton, G., & Williams, R. (1986). Learning internal representations by error propagation. In D. Rumelhart & J. McClelland (Eds.), *Parallel Distributed Processing* (pp. 318–362). MIT Press.

Schoen, R., Habetler, T., & Bartheld, R. (1994). Motor bearing damage detection using stator current monitoring. In *Proceedings of the IEEE IAS Annual Meeting*.

Using Feedforward Neural Networks to Monitor Alertness from Changes in EEG Correlation and Coherence

Scott Makeig
Naval Health Research Center, P.O. Box 85122
San Diego, CA 92186-5122

Tzyy-Ping Jung
Naval Health Research Center and
Computational Neurobiology Lab
The Salk Institute, P.O. Box 85800
San Diego, CA 92186-5800

Terrence J. Sejnowski
Howard Hughes Medical Institute and
Computational Neurobiology Lab
The Salk Institute, P.O. Box 85800
San Diego, CA 92186-5800

Abstract

We report here that changes in the normalized electroencephalographic (EEG) cross-spectrum can be used in conjunction with feedforward neural networks to monitor changes in alertness of operators continuously and in near-real time. Previously, we have shown that EEG spectral amplitudes covary with changes in alertness as indexed by changes in behavioral error rate on an auditory detection task [6, 4]. Here, we report for the first time that increases in the frequency of detection errors in this task are also accompanied by patterns of increased and decreased spectral coherence in several frequency bands and EEG channel pairs. Relationships between EEG coherence and performance vary between subjects, but within subjects, their topographic and spectral profiles appear stable from session to session. Changes in alertness also covary with changes in correlations among EEG waveforms recorded at different scalp sites, and neural networks can also estimate alertness from correlation changes in spontaneous and unobtrusively-recorded EEG signals.

1 Introduction

When humans become drowsy, EEG scalp recordings of potential oscillations change dramatically in frequency, amplitude, and topographic distribution [3]. These changes are complex and differ between subjects [10]. Recently, we have shown that using principal components analysis in conjunction with feedforward neural networks, minute-scale changes in performance on a sustained auditory detection task can be estimated in near real-time from changes in the EEG spectrum at one or more scalp channels [4, 6]. Here, we report, first, that loss of alertness during auditory detection task performance is also accompanied by changes in spectral coherence of EEG signals recorded at different scalp sites. The extent, topography, and frequency content of coherence changes linked to changes in alertness differ between subjects, but within subjects they appear stable from session to session. Second, since most coherence changes linked to alertness are not associated with significant phase differences, moving correlation measures applied to wideband or bandlimited EEG waveforms also covary with changes in alertness. Incorporating coherence and/or correlation information into neural network algorithms for estimating alertness from the EEG spectrum should enhance their accuracy and robustness and contribute to the design of practical neural human-system interfaces performing real-time monitoring of changes in operator alertness.

2 Methods

Concurrent EEG and behavioral data were collected for the purpose of developing a method of objectively monitoring the alertness of operators of complex systems [6]. Ten adult volunteers participated in three or more half-hour sessions during which they pushed one button whenever they detected an above-threshold auditory target stimulus (a brief increase in the level of the continuously-present background noise). To maximize the chance of observing alertness decrements, sessions were conducted in a small, warm, and dimly-lit experimental chamber, and subjects were instructed to keep their eyes closed.

Targets were 350 ms increases in the intensity of a 62 dB white noise background, 6 dB above their threshold of detectability, presented at random time intervals at a mean rate of 10/min. Short, and task-irrelevant probe tones of two frequencies (568 and 1098 Hz) were interspersed between the target noise bursts at 2-4 s intervals. EEG was collected from thirteen electrodes located at sites of the Internation 10-20 System, referred to the right mastoid, at a sampling rate of 312.5 Hz. A bipolar diagonal electrooculogram (EOG) channel was also recorded for use in eye movement artifact correction and rejection. Two sessions each from three of the subjects were chosen for analysis on the basis of their including more than 50 detection lapses.

A continuous performance measure, local error rate, was computed by convolving an irregularly-spaced performance index (hit=0/lapse=1) with a 95 s smoothing window advanced through the performance data in 1.64 s steps. Target hits were defined as targets responded to within a 100-3000 ms window; other targets were called lapses. After eye movement artifacts were removed from the data using a selective regression procedure [5], and data containing other large artifacts were rejected from analysis, complex EEG spectra were computed by advancing a 512-point (1.64 s) data window through the data in 0.41 s steps, multiplying by a Hanning window, and converting to frequency domain using an FFT.

Complex coherence was then computed for each channel pair in 1.64 s spectral epochs. In the coherence studies, error rate was smoothed with a bell-shaped Papoulis window; a 36 s rectangular window was used to smooth the coherence estimates. Finally, complex coherence was converted to coherence amplitude and phase and results were correlated with local error rate. A moving correlation measure between (1-20 Hz) bandlimited EEG waveforms was computed for each channel pair in a moving 1.64 s smoothing window, and then smoothed using a causal 95-s exponential window. The same window was used to smooth the error rate time series for the correlation studies.

3 Results

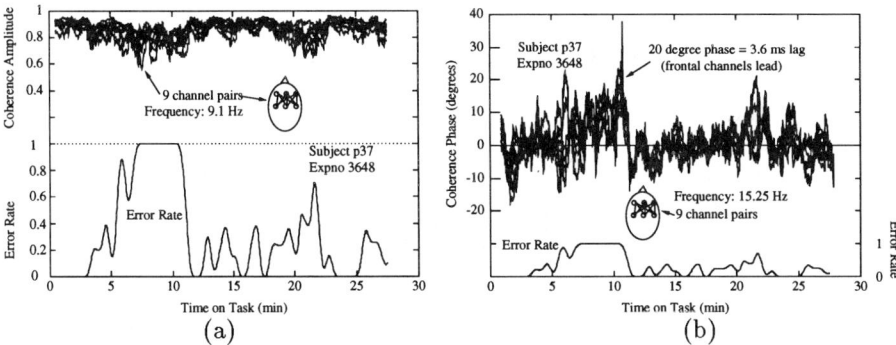

Figure 1: (a) Changes in coherence amplitude at 9.1 Hz (*upper traces*) are correlated with simultaneous changes in error rate during a half auditory detection task (*lower trace*) in nine indicated central-frontal channel pairs. (b) Concurrent changes in coherence phase at 15.25 Hz (*upper traces*) and local error rate (*lower trace*) for the same session and channel-pairs.

3.1 Relation of Coherence Changes to Detection Performance.

During the first 2-3 minutes of the session shown in Fig. 1a, the subject detected all targets presented, and coherence amplitudes remained high (0.9). In minutes 8-10, however, when the subject failed to make a single detection response(*lower trace*), coherence amplitude fell to as low as 0.6. Overall correlations for this session between the coherence and error rate time series in these channel pairs ranged from -0.590 to -0.776.

In the same session, coherence phase at 15 Hz also covaried with performance (Fig. 1b). During low-error portions of the session, there was no detectable coherence phase lag at 15 Hz within the same nine channel pairs, whereas while the subject performed poorly, a 20 degree phase lag appeared during which 15 Hz activity at frontal sites lead activity at frontal sites by 3 ms. Overall correlations for this session between coherence phase and error rate for these channel pairs ranged from 0.416 to 0.689. Correlations between coherence amplitude and error rate at 80 EEG frequencies (Fig. 2a, *upper traces*) included two broad bands of strong negative correlations (3-12 Hz and 15-20 Hz), while appreciable correlations between coherence phase and performance were confined to much narrower frequency bands (*lower traces*).

To estimate the significance of these coherence correlations, surrogate moving coherence records were collected 10 times using randomly-selected, asynchronous blocks of contiguous EEG data for each channel. Correlations between the resulting surrogate moving coherence time series and error rate were computed, and the 99.936th percentile of the distribution of (absolute) correlations was determined. For the subject whose data is shown here, this value was 0.485. Under conservative assumptions of complete independence of adjacent frequencies, this should give the (p=0.05) significance level for the maximum absolute correlation in each 80-bin correlation spectrum. (The heuristic estimate of this significance level from the surrogate data was 0.435). In the two sessions from this subject, however, more than 20% of all the 78 channel-pair coherence correlations were larger in absolute value than 0.485, implying that coherence amplitude changes at many scalp sites and frequencies are significantly related to changes in alertness in this subject.

3.2 Spectral and Topographic Stability

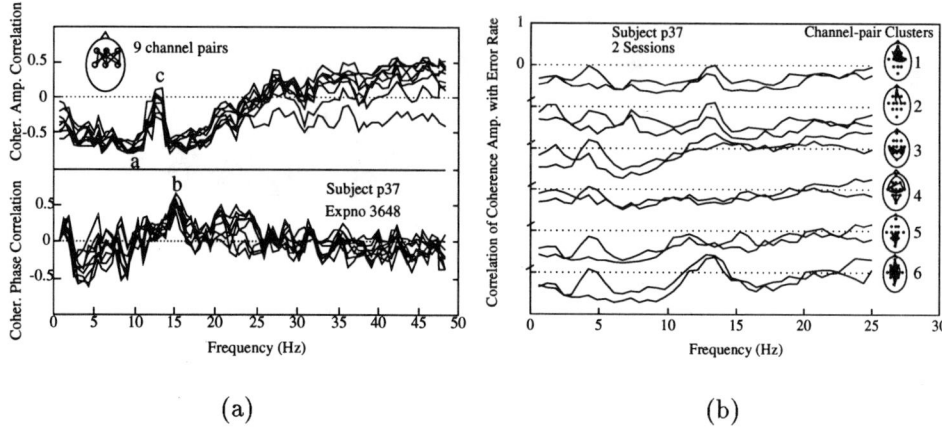

Figure 2: (a) Correlation spectra showing correlations between moving-average coherence and error rate for the same session and channel-pairs. Small letters 'a,b,c' indicate the frequencies analyzed in Figs. 1 and 3. (b) Cluster analysis of correlations between coherence amplitude and error rate at 41 frequencies (0.6 Hz to 25 Hz). Means of six sets of channel pairs derived from cluster analysis of 78 similar coherence correlation spectra from all pairs of 13 scalp channels; superimposed on the same means for a second session from the same subject.

The sign, size, and spectral and topographic structure of correlations between coherence amplitude and error rate at each frequency were stable across two sessions for most channel pairs and frequency bands. Fig. 2b shows mean spectral correlations in both sessions from the same subject for six clusters of similar channel-pair correlation spectra identified by cluster analysis on results of the first session. Except near 5 Hz, the size and structure of the correlation spectra for the second session replicate results of the first session. The spectral stability of monotonic relationships between EEG coherence and auditory detection performance suggests that coherence may be used to predict changes in performance level from spontaneous EEG data collected continuously and unobtrusively from two or more scalp channels.

3.3 EEG Waveform Correlations and Performance

In most cases, coherence phase lags in these data are small, and correlations between changes in phase lag and performance were insignificant. We therefore investigated whether moving-average correlations between band-limited EEG signals in different scalp channels might also be used to predict changes in alertness, possibly at a lower computational cost, by studying the relationship between error rate and changes in moving-average correlations of time-domain EEG waveforms (1-20 Hz bandpass) in the same 6 sessions. Again, we found that the strength and topographic structure of significant relationships between moving-correlation and performance measures are stable within, and variable between subjects. For each subject, we selected 8 EEG channel pairs whose moving-correlation time series correlated most highly with error rate, and used these to train a multilinear regression network and three feedforward three-layer perceptrons to estimate error rate from moving-average correlations. The feedforward neural networks had 3, 4, and 5 hidden units, respectively. Weights and biases of the network were adjusted using the error backpropagation algorithm [9]. Conjugate gradient descent was used to minimize the mean-squared error between network output and the actual error rate time series. Cross-validation [7] was used to prevent the network from overfitting the training data. For each of the 6 training-testing session pairs and each neural network architecture, the time course of error rate was estimated five times using different random initial weights between -0.3 and 0.3. We tested the generalization ability of the models on second sessions from the same subjects. The procedure simulated potential real-world alertness monitoring applications in which pilot data for each operator would be used to train a network to estimate his or her alertness in subsequent sessions from unobtrusively-recorded EEG data.

Accuracy of error rate estimation in the test sessions was almost identical for neural networks with 3, 4, and 5 hidden units. Each was more accurate than multivariate linear regression. Figure 3 shows the time courses of actual and estimated error rate in one pair of training (*top panel*) and test sessions. Results for two other subjects were equivalent. Table 1 shows the average correlations and root-mean-squared estimation error between actual and estimated error rate time series for 6 sessions, 2 each on 3 subjects using a feedforward neural network with 3 hidden units. Results using 4 or 5 hidden units are equivalent. Diagonal cells show results for training sessions, off-diagonal cells for test sessions. The nonlinear adaptability of three-layer perceptrons give improved estimation performance over multivariate linear regression, reducing the RMS estimation error in the test sessions from 0.255 to 0.225 ($F(1,5) = 1234.29; p \leq 0.0001$), and increasing the mean correlation between actual and estimated error rate time series from 0.63 to 0.67 ($F(1,5) = 549.5; p \leq 0.0001$).

4 Discussion

Spectral coherence of EEG waveforms at different scalp sites has been measured for nearly 30 years [11]. and is the subject of a steadily increasing number of clinical, behavioral, and developmental EEG studies. Coherence values are known to be higher in sleep than in waking [8], and wake-sleep transitions have been noted to be preceded by increased coherence at some frequencies [2]. Our results, from data on three subjects performing a sustained auditory detection task under soporific conditions, suggest that during drowsiness, coherence may either increase or decrease, depending on the subject, analysis frequency, and electrode sites analyzed. However, in individual subjects the spectral and topographic structure of alertness-related coherence changes appears stable from session to session.

EEG correlation and coherence are intimately related: changes in moving-average correlations of EEG waveforms reflect changes in broad-band, zero-lag coherence of activity at the same sites. The possibility of using moving-average correlation measures of electrophysiological activity to monitor state changes in animals was discussed by Arduini [1], but to our knowledge this approach has not previously been applied to human EEG.

The origin and function of nonstationarity in EEG synchrony are not yet understood. Decreased EEG coherence during drowsiness might result from inactivation of subcortical brain systems coordinating activity in separate cortical EEG generators during wakefulness, or from emergence of drowsiness-related EEG activity projecting preferentially to one part of the scalp surface. Similarly, increases in coherence in drowsiness might either result from increased synchrony between cortical generators, or from volume conduction of enhanced activity generated at a single cortical or subcortical site. Measuring changes in EEG coherence and correlation during other cognitive tasks give clues to the possible role of variable EEG synchrony in brain and cognitive dynamics.

We are now investigating to what extent moving EEG coherence and/or correlation measures, in combination with spectral amplitude measures [4], will allow practical, robust, continuous, and near-real time estimation of alertness level in auditory detection and other task environments.

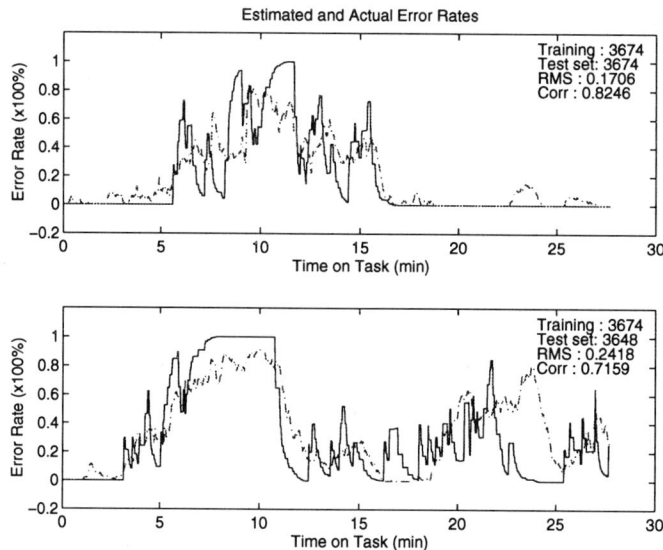

Figure 3: Changes in detection rate (95-s exponential window) and their estimate using a feedforward three-layer perceptron on moving correlations between (1-20 Hz) band passed EEG signals for 8 selected pairs of 7 scalp channels. The top panel shows the training session, the bottom panel the testing session. Solid lines show the actual error rate time course; dashed lines, the estimate. Correlation and RMS error between the two are indicated.

Table 1: The results of alertness monitoring using moving EEG pairwise correlation.

Subject A

Test set	Training Set	
	3648	3674
3648	rms : 0.17 corr : 0.87	rms : 0.26 corr : 0.68
3674	rms : 0.21 corr: 0.73	rms : 0.17 corr: 0.83

Subject B

Test set	Training Set	
	3654	3656
3654	rms : 0.17 corr : 0.83	rms : 0.22 corr : 0.73
3656	rms : 0.25 corr : 0.54	rms : 0.14 corr: 0.76

Subject C

Test set	Training Set	
	3665	3673
3665	rms : 0.19 corr : 0.76	rms : 0.23 corr : 0.65
3673	rms : 0.18 corr : 0.67	rms : 0.17 corr: 0.70

Acknowledgments

This work was supported by a grant (ONR.Reimb.30020.6429) to the Naval Health Research Center by the Office of Naval Research. The views expressed in this article are those of the authors and do not reflect the official policy or position of the Department of the Navy, Department of Defense, or the U.S. Government. We acknowledge the contributions of Keith Jolley, F.Scot Elliott, and Mark Postal in collecting and processing the data, and thank Tony Bell for suggestions.

References

[1] Arduini A.. 1979. In-phase brain activity and sleep. *Electroencephalog clin Neurophysiol* 47, 441-9

[2] Borodkin SM, Grindel' OM, Boldyreva GN, Zaitsev VA & Luk'ianov V.I. 1987. Dynamics of the spectral-coherent characteristics of the human EEG in healthy subjects and brain pathology. *Zh Vyssh Nerv Deiat* 37, 22-30

[3] Davis H., Davis P.A., Loomis A.L., Harvey E.N., & Hobart G. 1938. Human brain potentials during the onset of sleep. *J Neurophysiol* 1, 24-38

[4] Jung T-P, Makeig S., Stensmo M., & Sejnowski T. Estimating alertness from the EEG power spectrum, submitted for publication.

[5] Kenemans J.L., Molenaar P.C.M., Verbaten M.N. & Slangen J.L. 1991. Removal of the ocular artifact from the EEG: a comparison of time and frequency domain methods with simulated and real data. *Psychophysiolog* 28, 114-121

[6] Makeig S. & Inlow M. 1993. Lapses in alertness: Coherence of fluctuations in performance and EEG spectrum. *Electroencephalog clin Neurophysiol* 86, 23-35

[7] Morgan N., & Bourlard H. 1990. Generalization and parameter estimation in feedforward nets: some experiments. *Neural Information Processing Systems,* 2, 630-637.

[8] Nielsen T, Abel A, Lorrain D, & Montplaisir J. 1990. Interhemispheric EEG coherence during sleep and wakefulness in left- and right-handed subjects. *Brain and Cognition* 14, 113-25

[9] Rumelhart D, Hinton G, & Williams R, 1986. Learning internal representation by error propagation, *Parallel distributed processing, Chap. 8.*

[10] Santamaria J. & Chiappa K.H. 1987. The EEG of drowsiness in normal adults. *J Clin Neurophysiol* 4, 327-82

[11] Walter D.O. 1968. Coherence as a measure of relationship between EEG records. *Electroencephalog clin Neurophysiol* 24, 282

A Neural Network Classifier for the I1000 OCR Chip

John C. Platt and Timothy P. Allen
Synaptics, Inc.
2698 Orchard Parkway
San Jose, CA 95134
platt@synaptics.com, tpa@synaptics.com

Abstract

This paper describes a neural network classifier for the I1000 chip, which optically reads the E13B font characters at the bottom of checks. The first layer of the neural network is a hardware linear classifier which recognizes the characters in this font. A second software neural layer is implemented on an inexpensive microprocessor to clean up the results of the first layer. The hardware linear classifier is mathematically specified using constraints and an optimization principle. The weights of the classifier are found using the active set method, similar to Vapnik's separating hyperplane algorithm. In 7.5 minutes of SPARC 2 time, the method solves for 1523 Lagrange multipliers, which is equivalent to training on a data set of approximately 128,000 examples. The resulting network performs quite well: when tested on a test set of 1500 real checks, it has a 99.995% character accuracy rate.

1 A BRIEF OVERVIEW OF THE I1000 CHIP

At Synaptics, we have created the I1000, an analog VLSI chip that, when combined with associated software, optically reads the E13B font from the bottom of checks. This E13B font is shown in figure 1. The overall architecture of the I1000 chip is shown in figure 2. The I1000 recognizes checks hand-swiped through a slot. A lens focuses the image of the bottom of the check onto the retina. The retina has circuitry which locates the vertical position of the characters on the check. The retina then sends an image vertically centered around a possible character to the classifier.

The classifier in the I1000 has a tough job. It must be very accurate and immune to noise and ink scribbles in the input. Therefore, we decided to use an integrated segmentation and recognition approach (Martin & Pittman, 1992)(Platt, et al., 1992). When the classifier produces a strong response, we know that a character is horizontally centered in the retina.

A Neural Network Classifier for the I1000 OCR Chip

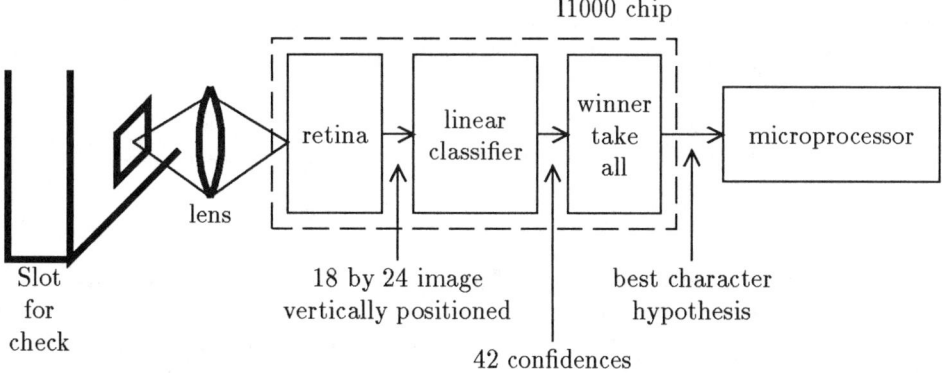

Figure 1: The E13B font, as seen by the I1000 chip

Figure 2: The overall architecture of the I1000 chip

We decided to use analog VLSI to minimize the silicon area of the classifier. Because of the analog implementation, we decided to use a linear template classifier, with fixed weights in silicon to minimize area. The weights are encoded as lengths of transistors acting as current sources. We trained the classifier using only the specification of the font, because we did not have the real E13B data at the time of classifier design. The design of the classifier is described in the next section.

As shown in figure 2, the input to the classifier is an 18 by 24 pixel image taken from the retina at a rate of 20 thousand frames per second. The templates in the classifier are 18 by 22 pixels. Each template is evaluated in three different vertical positions, to allow the retina to send a slightly vertically mis-aligned character. The output of the classifier is a set of 42 confidences, one for each of the 14 characters in the font in three different vertical positions. These confidences are fed to a winner-take-all circuit (Lazzaro, et al., 1989), which finds the confidence and the identity of the best character hypothesis.

2 SPECIFYING THE BEHAVIOR OF THE CLASSIFIER

Let us consider the training of one template corresponding to one of the characters in the font. The template takes a vector of pixels as input. For ease of analog implementation, the template is a linear neuron with no bias input:

$$O = \sum_i W_i I_i \qquad (1)$$

where O is the output of the template, W_i are the weights of the template, and I_i are the input pixels of the template.

We will now mathematically express the training of the templates as three types of constraints on the weights of the template. The input vectors used by these constraints are the ideal characters taken from the specification of the font.

The first type of constraint on the template is that the output of the template should be above 1 when the character that corresponds to the template is centered

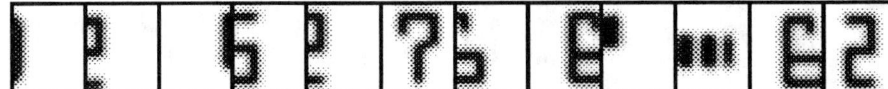

Figure 3: Examples of images from the bad set for the templates trained to detect the zero character. These images are E13B characters that have been horizontally and vertically offset from the center of the image. The black border around each of the characters shows the boundary of the input field. Notice the variety of horizontal and vertical shifts of the different characters.

in the horizontal field. Call the vector of pixels of this centered character G_i. This constraint is stated as:

$$\sum_i W_i G_i \geq 1 \qquad (2)$$

The second type of constraint on the template is to have an output much lower than 1 when incorrect or offset characters are applied to the template. We collect these incorrect and offset characters into a set of pixel vectors $\vec{B}^j$, which we call the "bad set." The constraint that the output of the template be lower than a constant c for all of the vectors in the bad set is expressed as:

$$\sum_i W_i B_i^j \leq c \quad \forall j \qquad (3)$$

Together, constraints (2) and (3) permit use of a simple threshold to distinguish between a positive classifier response and a negative one.

The bad set contains examples of the correct character for the template that are horizontally offset by at least two pixels and vertically offset by up to one pixel. In addition, examples of all other characters are added to the bad set at every horizontal offset and with vertical offsets of up to one pixel (see figure 3). Vertically offset examples are added to make the classifier resistant to characters whose baselines are slightly mismatched.

The third type of constraint on the template requires that the output be invariant to the addition of a constant to all of the input pixels. This constraint makes the classifier immune to any changes in the background lighting level, k. This constraint is equivalent to requiring the sum of the weights to be zero:

$$\sum_i W_i (I_i + k) = \sum_i W_i I_i \quad \Rightarrow \quad \sum_i W_i = 0 \qquad (4)$$

Finally, an optimization principle is necessary to choose between all possible weight vectors that fulfill constraints (2), (3), and (4). We minimize the perturbation of the output of the template given uncorrelated random noise on the input. This optimization principle is similar to training on a large data set, instead of simply the ideal characters described by the specification. This optimization principle is equivalent to minimizing the sum of the square of the weights:

$$\min \sum_i W_i^2 \qquad (5)$$

Expressing the training of the classifier as a combination of constraints and an optimization principle allows us to compactly define its behavior. For example, the combination of constraints (3) and (4) allows the classifier to be immune to situations when two partial characters appear in the image at the same time. The confluence of two characters in the image can be described as:

$$I_i^{\text{overlap}} = k + B_i^l + B_i^r \qquad (6)$$

where k is a background value and B_i^l and B_i^r are partial characters from the bad set that appears on the left side and right side of the image, respectively. The output of the template is then:

$$O^{\text{overlap}} = \sum_i W_i(k + B_i^l + B_i^r) = \sum_i W_i k + \sum_i W_i B_i^l + \sum_i W_i B_i^r < 2c \qquad (7)$$

Constraints (3) and (4) thus limit the output of the neuron to less than $2c$ when two partial characters appear in the input. Therefore, we want c to be less than 0.5. In order to get a 2:1 margin, we choose $c = 0.25$.

The classifier is trained only on individual partial characters instead of all possible combinations of partial characters. Therefore, we can specify the classifier using only 1523 constraints, instead of creating a training set of approximately 128,000 possible combinations of partial characters. Applying these constraints is therefore much faster than back-propagation on the entire data set.

Equations (2), (3) and (5) describe the optimization problem solved by Vapnik (Vapnik, 1982) for constructing a hyperplane that separates two classes. Vapnik solves this optimization problem by converting it into a dual space, where the inequality constraints become much simpler. However, we add the equality constraint (4), which does not allow us to directly use Vapnik's dual space method. To overcome this limitation, we use the active set method, which can fulfill any extra linear equality or inequality constraints. The active set method is described in the next section.

3   THE ACTIVE SET METHOD

Notice that constraints (2), (3), and (4) are all linear in W_i. Therefore, minimizing (5) with these constraints is simply quadratic programming with a mixture of equality and inequality constraints. This problem can be solved using the active set method from optimization theory (Gill, et al., 1981).

When the quadratic programming problem is solved, some of the inequality constraints and all of the equality constraints will be "active." In other words, the active constraints affect the solution as equality constraints. The system has "bumped into" these constraints. All other constraints will be inactive; they will not affect the solution.

Once we know which constraints are active, we can easily solve the quadratic minimization problem with equality constraints via Lagrange multipliers. The solution is a saddle point of the function:

$$\frac{1}{2} \sum_i W_i^2 + \sum_k \lambda_k (\sum_j A_{kj} W_j - C_k) \qquad (8)$$

where λ_k is the Lagrange multiplier of the kth active constraint, and A_{kj} and C_k are the linear and constant coefficients of the kth active constraint. For example, if constraint (2) is the kth active constraint, then $\vec{A}_k = \vec{G}$ and $C_k = 1$. The saddle point can be found via the set of linear equations:

$$W_i = -\sum_k \lambda_k A_{ki} \qquad (9)$$

$$\lambda_k = -\sum_j (\sum_i A_{ji} A_{ki})^{-1} C_j \qquad (10)$$

The active set method determines which inequality constraints belong in the active set by iteratively solving equation (10) above. At every step, one inequality constraint is either made active, or inactive. A constraint can be moved to the active

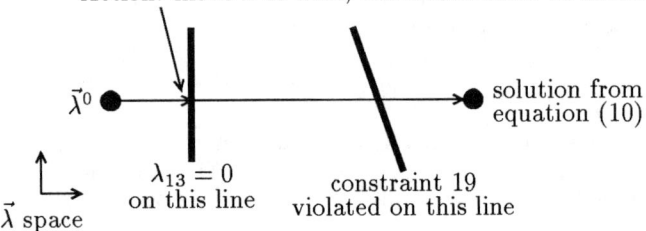

Figure 4: The position along the step where the constraints become violated or the Lagrange multipliers become zero can be computed analytically. The algorithm then takes the largest possible step without violating constraints or having the Lagrange multipliers become zero.

set if the inequality constraint is violated. A constraint can be moved off the active set if its Lagrange multiplier has changed sign[1].

Each step of the active set method attempts to adjust the vector of Lagrange multipliers to the values provided by equation (10). Let us parameterize the step from the old to the new Lagrange multipliers via a parameter α:

$$\vec{\lambda} = \vec{\lambda}^0 + \alpha \Delta \vec{\lambda} \qquad (11)$$

where $\vec{\lambda}^0$ is the vector of Lagrange multipliers before the step, $\Delta \vec{\lambda}$ is the step, and when $\alpha = 1$, the step is completed. Now, the amount of constraint violation and the Lagrange multipliers are linear functions of this α. Therefore, we can analytically derive the α at which a constraint is violated or a Lagrange multiplier changes sign (see figure 4). For currently inactive constraints, the α for constraint violation is:

$$\alpha_k = -\frac{C_k + \sum_j \lambda_j^0 \sum_i A_{ji} A_{ki}}{\sum_j \Delta \lambda_j \sum_i A_{ji} A_{ki}} \qquad (12)$$

For a currently active constraint, the α for a Lagrange multiplier sign change is simply:

$$\alpha_k = -\frac{\lambda_k^0}{\Delta \lambda_k} \qquad (13)$$

We choose the constraint that has a smallest positive α_k. If the smallest α_k is greater than 1, then the system has found the solution, and the final weights are computed from the Lagrange multipliers at the end of the step. Otherwise, if the kth constraint is active, we make it inactive, and vice versa. We then set the Lagrange multipliers to be the interpolated values from equation (11) with $\alpha = \alpha_k$. We finally re-evaluate equation (10) with the updated active set[2].

When this optimization algorithm is applied to the E13B font, the templates that result are shown in figure 5. When applied to characters that obey the specification, the classifier is guaranteed to give a 2:1 margin between the correct peak and any false peak caused by the confluence of two partial characters. Each template has 1523 constraints and takes 7.5 minutes on a SPARC 2 to train. Back-propagation on the 128,000 training examples that are equivalent to the constraints would obviously require much more computation time.

---

[1] The sign of the Lagrange multiplier indicates on which side of the inequality constraint the constrained minimum lies.

[2] For more details on active set methods, such as how to recognize infeasible constraints, consult (Gill, et al., 1981).

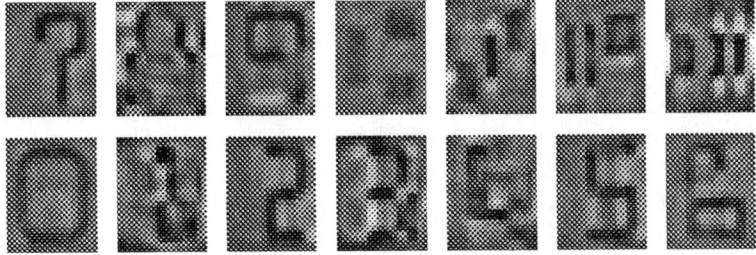

Figure 5: The weights for the fourteen E13B templates. The light pixels correspond to positive weights, while the dark pixels correspond to negative weights.

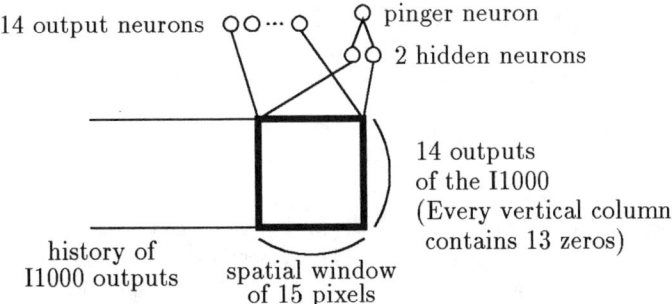

Figure 6: The software second layer

4 THE SOFTWARE SECOND LAYER

As a test of the linear classifier, we fabricated the I1000 and tested it with E13B characters on real checks. The system worked when the printing on the check obeyed the contrast specification of the font. However, some check printing companies use very light or very dark printing. Therefore, there was no single threshold that could consistently read the lightly printed checks without hallucinating characters on the dark checks. The retina shown in figure 2 does not have automatic gain control (AGC). One solution would have been to refabricate the chip using an AGC retina. However, we opted for a simpler solution.

The output of the I1000 chip is a 2-bit confidence level and a character code that is sent to an inexpensive microprocessor every 50 microseconds. Because this output bandwidth is low, it is feasible to put a small software second layer into this microprocessor to post-process and clean up the output of the I1000.

The architecture of this software second layer is shown in figure 6. The input to the second layer is a linearly time-warped history of the output of the I1000 chip. The time warping makes the second layer immune to changes in the velocity of the check in the slot. There is one output neuron that is a "pinger." That is, it is trained to turn on when the input to the I1000 chip is centered over any character (Platt, et al., 1992) (Martin & Pittman, 1992). There are fourteen other neurons that each correspond to a character in the font. These neurons are trained to turn on when the appropriate character is centered in the field, and otherwise turn off. The classification output is the output of the fourteen neurons only when the pinger neuron is on. Thus, the pinger neuron aids in segmentation.

Considering the entire network spanning both the hardware first layer and software second layer, we have constructed a non-standard TDNN (Waibel, et. al., 1989) which recognizes characters.

We trained the second layer using standard back-propagation, with a training set gathered from real checks. Because the I1000 output bandwidth is quite low, collecting the data and training the network was not onerous. The second layer was trained on a data set of approximately 1000 real checks.

5 OVERALL PERFORMANCE

When the hardware first layer in the I1000 is combined with the software second layer, the performance of the system on real checks is quite impressive. We gathered a test set of 1500 real checks from across the country. This test set contained a variety of light and dark checks with unusual backgrounds. We swiped this test set through one system. Out of the 1500 test checks, the system only failed to read 2, due to staple holes in important locations of certain characters. As such, this test yielded a 99.995% character accuracy on real data.

6 CONCLUSIONS

For the I1000 analog VLSI OCR chip, we have created an effective hardware linear classifier that recognizes the E13B font. The behavior of this classifier was specified using constrained optimization. The classifier was designed to have a predictable margin of classification, be immune to lighting variations, and be resistant to random input noise. The classifier was trained using the active set method, which is an enhancement of Vapnik's separating hyperplane algorithm. We used the active set method to find the weights of a template in 7.5 minutes of SPARC 2 time, instead of training on a data set with 128,000 examples. To make the overall system resistant to contrast variation, we separately trained a software second layer on top of this first hardware layer, thereby constructing a non-standard TDNN.

The application discussed in this paper shows the utility of using the active set method to very rapidly create either a stand-alone linear classifier or a first layer of a multi-layer network.

References

P. Gill, W. Murray, M. Wright (1981), *Practical Optimization*, Section 5.2, Academic Press.

J. Lazzaro, S. Ryckebusch, M. Mahowald, C. Mead (1989), "Winner-Take-All Networks of $O(N)$ Complexity," *Advances in Neural Information Processing Systems*, **1**, D. Touretzky, ed., Morgan-Kaufmann, San Mateo, CA.

G. Martin, M. Rashid (1992), "Recognizing Overlapping Hand-Printed Characters by Centered-Object Integrated Segmentation and Recognition," *Advances in Neural Information Processing Systems*, **4**, Moody, J., Hanson, S., Lippmann, R., eds., Morgan-Kaufmann, San Mateo, CA.

J. Platt, J. Decker, and J. LeMoncheck (1992), Convolutional Neural Networks for the Combined Segmentation and Recognition of Machine Printed Characters, *USPS 5th Advanced Technology Conference*, **2**, 701-713.

V. Vapnik (1982), *Estimation of Dependencies Based on Empirical Data*, Addendum I, Section 2, Springer-Verlag.

A. Waibel, T. Hanazawa, G. Hinton, K. Shikano, K. Lang (1989), "Phoneme Recognition Using Time-Delay Neural Networks," *IEEE Transactions on Acoustics, Speech, and Signal Processing*, vol. 37, pp. 328–339.

Predictive Q-Routing: A Memory-based Reinforcement Learning Approach to Adaptive Traffic Control

Samuel P.M. Choi, Dit-Yan Yeung
Department of Computer Science
Hong Kong University of Science and Technology
Clear Water Bay, Kowloon, Hong Kong
{pmchoi,dyyeung}@cs.ust.hk

Abstract

In this paper, we propose a memory-based Q-learning algorithm called *predictive Q-routing* (PQ-routing) for adaptive traffic control. We attempt to address two problems encountered in Q-routing (Boyan & Littman, 1994), namely, the inability to fine-tune routing policies under low network load and the inability to learn new optimal policies under decreasing load conditions. Unlike other memory-based reinforcement learning algorithms in which memory is used to keep past experiences to increase learning speed, PQ-routing keeps the best experiences learned and reuses them by predicting the traffic trend. The effectiveness of PQ-routing has been verified under various network topologies and traffic conditions. Simulation results show that PQ-routing is superior to Q-routing in terms of both learning speed and adaptability.

1 INTRODUCTION

The adaptive traffic control problem is to devise routing policies for controllers (i.e. routers) operating in a non-stationary environment to minimize the average packet delivery time. The controllers usually have no or only very little prior knowledge of the environment. While only local communication between controllers is allowed, the controllers must cooperate among themselves to achieve the common, global objective. Finding the optimal routing policy in such a distributed manner is very difficult. Moreover, since the environment is non-stationary, the optimal policy varies with time as a result of changes in network traffic and topology.

In (Boyan & Littman, 1994), a distributed adaptive traffic control scheme based on reinforcement learning (RL), called *Q-routing*, is proposed for the routing of packets in networks with dynamically changing traffic and topology. Q-routing is a variant of Q-learning (Watkins, 1989), which is an incremental (or asynchronous) version of dynamic programming for solving multistage decision problems. Unlike the original Q-learning algorithm, Q-routing is distributed in the sense that each communication node has a separate local controller, which does not rely on global information of the network for decision making and refinement of its routing policy.

2 EXPLORATION VERSUS EXPLOITATION

As in other RL algorithms, one important issue Q-routing must deal with is the tradeoff between exploration and exploitation. While exploration of the state space is essential to learning good routing policies, continual exploration without putting the learned knowledge into practice is of no use. Moreover, exploration is not done at no cost. This dilemma is well known in the RL community and has been studied by some researchers, e.g. (Thrun, 1992).

One possibility is to divide learning into an exploration phase and an exploitation phase. The simplest exploration strategy is random exploration, in which actions are selected randomly without taking the reinforcement feedback into consideration. After the exploration phase, the optimal routing policy is simply to choose the next network node with minimum Q-value (i.e. minimum estimated delivery time). In so doing, Q-routing is expected to learn to avoid congestion along popular paths.

Although Q-routing is able to alleviate congestion along popular paths by routing some traffic over other (possibly longer) paths, two problems are reported in (Boyan & Littman, 1994). First, Q-routing is not always able to find the shortest paths under low network load. For example, if there exists a longer path which has a Q-value less than the (erroneous) estimate of the shortest path, a routing policy that acts as a minimum selector will not explore the shortest path and hence will not update its erroneous Q-value. Second, Q-routing suffers from the so-called hysteresis problem, in that it fails to adapt to the optimal (shortest) path again when the network load is lowered. Once a longer path is selected due to increase in network load, a minimum selector is no longer able to notice the subsequent decrease in traffic along the shortest path. Q-routing continues to choose the same (longer) path unless it also becomes congested and has a Q-value greater than some other path. Unless Q-routing continues to explore, the shortest path cannot be chosen again even though the network load has returned to a very low level. However, as mentioned in (Boyan & Littman, 1994), random exploration may have very negative effects on congestion, since packets sent along a suboptimal path tend to increase queue delays, slowing down all the packets passing through this path.

Instead of having two separate phases for exploration and exploitation, one alternative is to mix them together, with the emphasis shifting gradually from the former to the latter as learning proceeds. This can be achieved by a probabilistic scheme for choosing next nodes. For example, the Q-values may be related to probabilities by the Boltzmann-Gibbs distribution, involving a randomness (or pseudo-temperature) parameter T. To guarantee sufficient initial exploration and subsequent convergence, T usually has a large initial value (giving a uniform probability distribution) and decreases towards 0 (degenerating to a deterministic minimum selector) during the learning process. However, for a continuously operating network with dynamically changing traffic and topology, learning must be continual and hence cannot be controlled by a prespecified decay profile for T. An algorithm which automatically adapts between exploration and exploitation is therefore necessary. It is this very reason which led us to develop the algorithm presented in this paper.

3 PREDICTIVE Q-ROUTING

A memory-based Q-learning algorithm called *predictive Q-routing* (PQ-routing) is proposed here for adaptive traffic control. Unlike *Dyna* (Peng & Williams, 1993) and *prioritized sweeping* (Moore & Atkeson, 1993) in which memory is used to keep past experiences to increase learning speed, PQ-routing keeps the best experiences (best Q-values) learned and reuses them by predicting the traffic trend. The idea is as follows. Under low network load, the optimal policy is simply the shortest path routing policy. However, when the load level increases, packets tend to queue up along the shortest paths and the simple shortest path routing policy no longer performs well. If the congested paths are not used for a period of time, they will recover and become good candidates again. One should therefore try to utilize these paths by occasionally sending packets along them. We refer to such controlled exploration activities as *probing*. The probing frequency is crucial, as frequent probes will increase the load level along the already congested paths while infrequent probes will make the performance little different from Q-routing. Intuitively, the probing frequency should depend on the congestion level and the processing speed (recovery rate) of a path. The congestion level can be reflected by the current Q-value, but the recovery rate has to be estimated as part of the learning process.

At first glance, it seems that the recovery rate can be computed simply by dividing the difference in Q-values from two probes by the elapse time. However, the recovery rate changes over time and depends on the current network traffic and the possibility of link/node failure. In addition, the elapse time does not truly reflect the actual processing time a path needs. Thus this noisy recovery rate should be adjusted for every packet sent. It is important to note that the recovery rate in the algorithm should not be positive, otherwise it may increase the predicted Q-value without bound and hence the path can never be used again.

Predictive Q-Routing Algorithm

TABLES:
    $Q_x(d, y)$ - estimated delivery time from node x to node d via neighboring node y
    $B_x(d, y)$ - best estimated delivery time from node x to node d via neighboring node y
    $R_x(d, y)$ - recovery rate for path from node x to node d via neighboring node y
    $U_x(d, y)$ - last update time for path from node x to node d via neighboring node y

TABLE UPDATES: (after a packet arrives at node y from node x)
    $\Delta Q = $ (transmission delay + queueing time at y + $\min_z\{Q_y(d, z)\}) - Q_x(d, y)$
    $Q_x(d, y) \leftarrow Q_x(d, y) + \alpha \Delta Q$
    $B_x(d, y) \leftarrow \min(B_x(d, y), Q_x(d, y))$
    if $(\Delta Q < 0)$ then
        $\Delta R \leftarrow \Delta Q$ / (current time $- U_x(d, y)$)
        $R_x(d, y) \leftarrow R_x(d, y) + \beta \Delta R$
    else if $(\Delta Q > 0)$ then
        $R_x(d, y) \leftarrow \gamma R_x(d, y)$
    end if
    $U_x(d, y) \leftarrow$ current time

ROUTING POLICY: (packet is sent from node x to node y)
    $\Delta t =$ current time $- U_x(d, y)$
    $Q'_x(d, y) = \max(Q_x(d, y) + \Delta t \, R_x(d, y), B_x(d, y))$
    $y \leftarrow \arg\min_y\{Q'_x(d, y)\}$

There are three learning parameters in the PQ-routing algorithm. α is the Q-function learning parameter as in the original Q-learning algorithm. In PQ-routing, this parameter should be set to 1 or else the accuracy of the recovery rate may be affected. β is used for learning the recovery rate. In our experiments, the value of 0.7 is used. γ is used for controlling the decay of the recovery rate, which affects the probing frequency in a congested path. Its value is usually chosen to be larger than β. In our experiments, the value of 0.9 is used.

PQ-learning is identical to Q-learning in the way the Q-function is updated. The major difference is in the routing policy. Instead of selecting actions based solely on the current Q-values, the recovery rates are used to yield better estimates of the Q-values before the minimum selector is applied. This is desirable because the Q-values on which routing decisions are based may become outdated due to the ever-changing traffic.

4 EMPIRICAL RESULTS

4.1 A 15-NODE NETWORK

To demonstrate the effectiveness of PQ-routing, let us first consider a simple 15-node network (Figure 1(a)) with three sources (nodes 12 to 14) and one destination (node 15). Each node can process one packet per time step, except nodes 7 to 11 which are two times faster than the other nodes. Each link is bidirectional and has a transmission delay of one time unit. It is not difficult to see that the shortest paths are $12 \to 1 \to 4 \to 15$ for node 12, $13 \to 2 \to 4 \to 15$ for node 13, and $14 \to 3 \to 4 \to 15$ for node 14. However, since each node along these paths can process only one packet per time step, congestion will soon occur in node 4 if all source nodes send packets along the shortest paths.

One solution to this problem is that the source nodes send packets along different paths which share no common nodes. For instance, node 12 can send packets along path $12 \to 1 \to 5 \to 6 \to 15$ while node 13 along $13 \to 2 \to 7 \to 8 \to 9 \to 10 \to 11 \to 15$ and node 14 along $14 \to 3 \to 4 \to 15$. The optimal routing policy depends on the traffic from each source node. If the network load is not too high, the optimal routing policy is to alternate between the upper and middle paths in sending packets.

4.1.1 PERIODIC TRAFFIC PATTERNS UNDER LOW LOAD

For the convenience of empirical analysis, we first consider periodic traffic in which each source node generates the same traffic pattern over a period of time. Figure 1(b) shows the average delivery time for Q-routing and PQ-routing. PQ-routing performs better than Q-routing after the initial exploration phase (25 time steps), despite of some slight oscillations. Such oscillations are due to the occasional probing activities of the algorithm. When we examine Q-routing more closely, we can find that after the initial learning, all the source nodes try to send packets along the upper (shortest) path, leading to congestion in node 4. When this occurs, both nodes 12 and 13 switch to the middle path, which subsequently leads to congestion in node 5. Later, nodes 12 and 13 detect this congestion and then switch to the lower path. Since the nodes along this path have higher (two times) processing speed, the Q-values become stable and Q-routing will stay there as long as the load level does not increase. Thus, Q-routing fails to fine-tune the routing policy to improve it. PQ-routing, on the other hand, is able to learn the recovery rates and alternate between the upper and middle paths.

Predictive Q-Routing

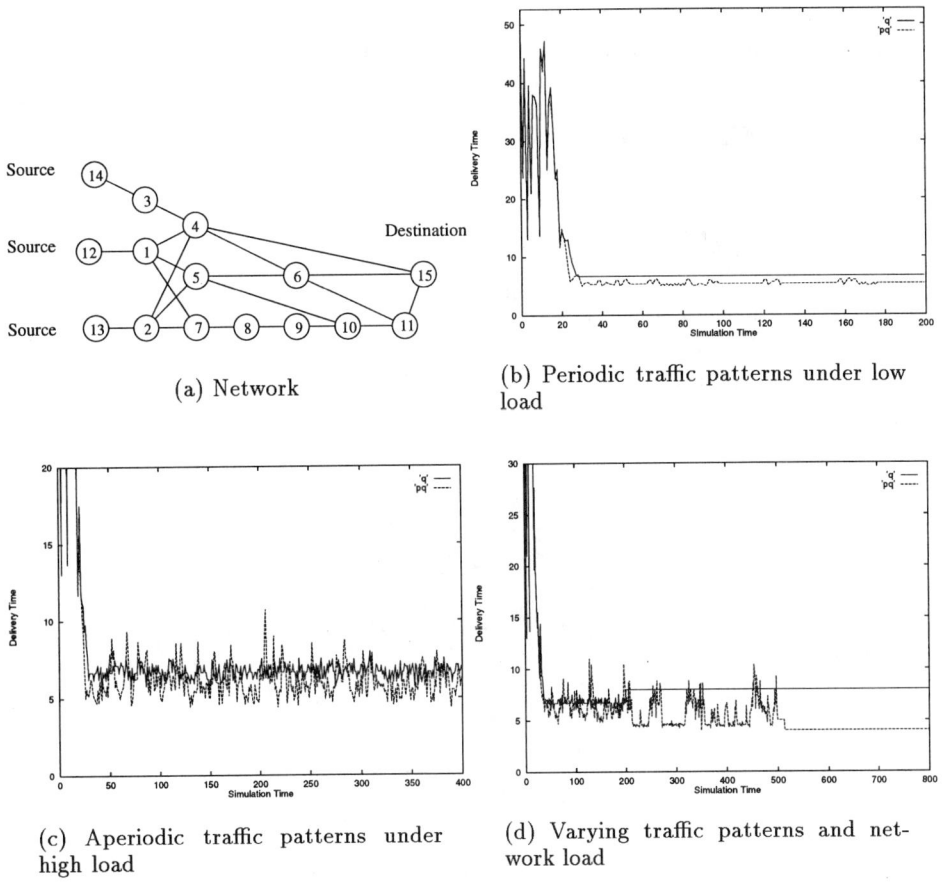

Figure 1: A 15-Node Network and Simulation Results

4.1.2 APERIODIC TRAFFIC PATTERNS UNDER HIGH LOAD

It is not realistic to assume that network traffic is strictly periodic. In reality, the time interval between two packets sent by a node varies. To simulate varying intervals between packets, a probability of 0.8 is imposed on each source node for generating packets. In this case, the average delivery time for both algorithms oscillates. Figure 1(c) shows the performance of Q-routing and PQ-routing under high network load. The difference in delivery time between Q-routing and PQ-routing becomes less significant, as there is less available bandwidth in the shortest path for interleaving. Nevertheless, it can be seen that the overall performance of PQ-routing is still better than Q-routing.

4.1.3 VARYING TRAFFIC PATTERNS AND NETWORK LOAD

In the more complicated situation of varying traffic patterns and network load, PQ-routing also performs better than Q-routing. Figure 1(d) shows the hysteresis problem in Q-routing under gradually changing traffic patterns and network load. After an initial exploration phase of 25 time steps, the load level is set to medium from time step 26 to 200. From step 201 to 500, node 14 ceases to send packets and nodes 12 and 13 slightly increase their load level. In this case, although the shortest path becomes available again, Q-routing is not able to notice the change in traffic and still uses the same routing policy, but PQ-routing is able to utilize the optimal paths. After step 500, node 13 also ceases to send packets. PQ-routing is successful in adapting to the optimal path $12 \to 1 \to 4 \to 15$.

4.2 A 6x6 GRID NETWORK

Experiments have been performed on some larger networks, including a 32-node hypercube and some random networks, with results similar to those above. Figures 2(b) and 2(c) depict results for Boyan and Littman's 6x6 grid network (Figure 2(a)) under varying traffic patterns and network load.

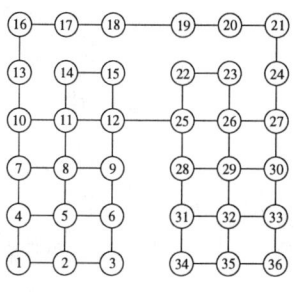

(a) Network

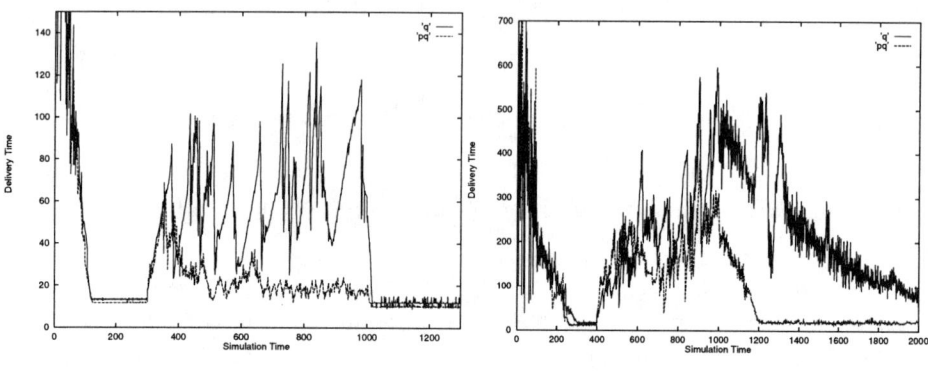

(b) Varying traffic patterns and network load

(c) Varying traffic patterns and network load

Figure 2: A 6x6 Grid Network and Simulation Results

In Figure 2(b), after an initial exploration for 50 time steps, the load level is set to low. From step 51 to 300, the load level increases to medium but with the same periodic traffic patterns. PQ-routing performs slightly better. From step 301 to 1000, the traffic patterns change dramatically under high network load. Q-routing cannot learn a stable policy in this (short) period of time, but PQ-routing becomes more stable after about 200 steps. From step 1000 onwards, the traffic patterns change again and the load level returns to low. PQ-routing still performs better.

In Figure 2(c), the first 100 time steps are for initial exploration. After this period, packets are sent from the bottom right part of the grid to the bottom left part with low network load. PQ-routing is found to be as good as the shortest path routing policy, while Q-routing is slightly poorer than PQ-routing. From step 400 to 1000, packets are sent from both the left and right parts of the grid to the opposite sides at high load level. Both the two bottleneck paths become congested and hence the average delivery time increases for both algorithms. From time step 1000 onwards, the network load decreases to a more manageable level. We can see that PQ-routing is faster than Q-routing in adapting to this change.

5 DISCUSSIONS

PQ-learning is generally better than Q-learning under both low and varying network load conditions. Under high load conditions, they give comparable performance. In general, Q-routing prefers stable routing policies and tends to send packets along paths with higher processing power, regardless of the actual packet delivery time. This strategy is good under extremely high load conditions, but may not be optimal under other situations. PQ-routing, on the contrary, is more aggressive. It tries to minimize the average delivery time by occasionally probing the shortest paths. If the load level remains extremely high with the patterns unchanged, PQ-routing will gradually degenerate to Q-routing, until the traffic changes again. Another advantage PQ-routing has over Q-routing is that shorter adaptation time is generally needed when the traffic patterns change, since the routing policy of PQ-routing depends not only on the current Q-values but also on the recovery rates. In terms of memory requirement, PQ-routing needs more memory for recovery rate estimation. It should be noted, however, that extra memory is needed only for the visited states. In the worst case, it is still in the same order as that of the original Q-routing algorithm. In terms of computational cost, recovery rate estimation is computationally quite simple. Thus the overhead for implementing PQ-routing should be minimal.

References

J.A. Boyan & M.L. Littman (1994). Packet routing in dynamically changing networks: a reinforcement learning approach. *Advances in Neural Information Processing Systems 6*, 671–678. Morgan Kaufmann, San Mateo, California.

M. Littman & J. Boyan (1993). A distributed reinforcement learning scheme for network routing. *Proceedings of the First International Workshop on Applications of Neural Networks to Telecommunications*, 45–51. Lawrence Erlbaum, Hillsdale, New Jersey.

A.W. Moore & C.G. Atkeson (1993). Memory-based reinforcement learning: efficient computation with prioritized sweeping. *Advances in Neural Information Processing Systems 5*, 263–270. Morgan Kaufmann, San Mateo, California.

A.W. Moore & C.G. Atkeson (1993). Prioritized sweeping: reinforcement learning with less data and less time. *Machine Learning*, 13:103–130.

J. Peng & R.J. Williams (1993). Efficient learning and planning within the Dyna framework. *Adaptive Behavior*, 1:437–454.

S. Thrun (1992). The role of exploration in learning control. In *Handbook of Intelligent Control: Neural, Fuzzy, and Adaptive Approaches*, D.A. White & D.A. Sofge (eds). Van Nostrand Reinhold, New York.

C.J.C.H. Watkins (1989). *Learning from delayed rewards*. PhD Thesis, University of Cambridge, England.

Optimal Asset Allocation using Adaptive Dynamic Programming

Ralph Neuneier[*]
Siemens AG, Corporate Research and Development
Otto-Hahn-Ring 6, D-81730 München, Germany

Abstract

In recent years, the interest of investors has shifted to computerized asset allocation (portfolio management) to exploit the growing dynamics of the capital markets. In this paper, asset allocation is formalized as a *Markovian Decision Problem* which can be optimized by applying *dynamic programming* or reinforcement learning based algorithms. Using an artificial exchange rate, the asset allocation strategy optimized with reinforcement learning (*Q-Learning*) is shown to be equivalent to a policy computed by dynamic programming. The approach is then tested on the task to invest liquid capital in the German stock market. Here, neural networks are used as value function approximators. The resulting asset allocation strategy is superior to a heuristic benchmark policy. This is a further example which demonstrates the applicability of neural network based reinforcement learning to a problem setting with a high dimensional state space.

1 Introduction

Billions of dollars are daily pushed through the international capital markets while brokers shift their investments to more promising assets. Therefore, there is a great interest in achieving a deeper understanding of the capital markets and in developing efficient tools for exploiting the dynamics of the markets.

---

[*] Ralph.Neuneier@zfe.siemens.de, http://www.siemens.de/zfe_nn/homepage.html

Asset allocation (portfolio management) is the investment of liquid capital to various trading opportunities like stocks, futures, foreign exchanges and others. A portfolio is constructed with the aim of achieving a maximal expected return for a given risk level and time horizon. To compose an optimal portfolio, the investor has to solve a difficult optimization problem consisting of two phases (Brealy, 1991). First, the expected yields are estimated simultaneously with a certainty measure. Second, based on these estimates, a portfolio is constructed obeying the risk level the investor is willing to accept (*mean-variance* techniques). The problem is further complicated if transaction costs must be considered and if the investor wants to revise the decision at every time step. In recent years, neural networks (NN) have been successfully used for the first task. Typically, a NN delivers the expected future values of a time series based on data of the past. Furthermore, a confidence measure which expresses the certainty of the prediction is provided.

In the following, the modeling phase and the search for an optimal portfolio are combined and embedded in the framework of *Markovian Decision Problems*, MDP. That theory formalizes control problems within stochastic environments (Bertsekas, 1987, Elton, 1971). If the discrete state space is small and if an accurate model of the system is available, MDP can be solved by conventional *Dynamic Programming*, DP. On the other extreme, reinforcement learning methods, e.g. *Q-Learning*, QL, can be applied to problems with large state spaces and with no appropriate model available (Singh, 1994).

2 Portfolio Management is a Markovian Decision Problem

The following simplifications do not restrict the generalization of the proposed methods with respect to real applications but will help to clarify the relationship between MDP and portfolio optimization.

- There is only one possible asset for a Deutsch-Mark based investor, say a foreign currency called Dollar, US-$.

- The investor is small and does not influence the market by her/his trading.

- The investor has no risk aversion and always invests the total amount.

- The investor may trade at each time step for an infinite time horizon.

MDP provide a model for multi-stage decision making problems in stochastic environments. MDP can be described by a finite state set $S = 1, \ldots, n$, a finite set $U(i)$ of admissible control actions for every state $i \in S$, a set of transition probabilities p_{ij}^π, which describe the dynamics of the system, and a return function[1] $r(i, j, u(i))$, with $i, j \in S, u(i) \in U(i)$. Furthermore, there is a stationary policy $\pi(i)$, which delivers for every state an admissible action $u(i)$. One can compute the value-function V_i^π of a given state and policy,

$$V_{i_0}^\pi = E[\sum_{t=0}^\infty \gamma^t R(i_t, \pi(i_t))], \qquad (1)$$

---

[1] In the MDP-literature, the return often depends only on the current state i, but the theory extends to the case of $r = r(i, j, u(i))$ (see Singh, 1994).

where E indicates the expected value, γ is the discount factor with $0 \leq \gamma < 1$, and where R are the expected returns, $R = E_j(r(i,j,u(i)))$. The aim is now to find a policy π^* with the optimal value-function $V_i^* = \max_\pi V_i^\pi$ for all states.

In the context discussed here, a state vector consists of elements which describe the financial time series, and of elements which quantify the current value of the investment. For the simple example above, the state vector is the triple of the exchange rate, x_t, the wealth of the portfolio, c_t, expressed in the basis currency (here DM), and a binary variable b, representing the fact that currently the investment is in DM or US-\$.

Note, that out of the variables which form the state vector, the exchange rate is actually independent of the portfolio decisions, but the wealth and the returns are not. Therefore, asset allocation is a control problem and may not be reduced to pure prediction.[2] This problem has the attractive feature that, because the investments do not influence the exchange rate, we do not need to invest real money during the training phase of QL until we are convinced that our strategy works.

3 Dynamic Programming: Off-line and Adaptive

The optimal value function V^* is the unique solution of the well-known Bellman equation (Bertsekas, 1987). According to that equation one has to maximize the expected return for the next step and follow an optimal policy thereafter in order to achieve global optimal behavior (Bertsekas, 1987). An optimal policy can be easily derived from V^* by choosing a $\pi(i)$ which satisfies the Bellman equation. For nonlinear systems and non-quadric cost functions, V^* is typically found by using an iterative algorithm, *value iteration*, which converges asymptotically to V^*. Value iteration applies repeatedly the operator T for all states i,

$$T_i(V) = \max_{u(i) \in U(i)} (R(i, u(i)) + \gamma \sum_{j \in S} p_{ij}^\pi V_j). \qquad (2)$$

Value iteration assumes that the expected return function $R(i, u(i))$ and the transition probabilities p_{ij}^π (i. e. the model) are known. Q-Learning, (QL), is a *reinforcement-learning* method that does not require a model of the system but optimizes the policy by sampling state-action pairs and returns while interacting with the system (Barto, 1989). Let's assume that the investor executes action $u(i)$ at state i, and that the system moves to a new state j. Let $r(i,j,u(i))$ denote the actual return. QL then uses the update equation

$$\begin{aligned} Q(i, u(i)) &= (1-\eta)Q(i,u(i)) + \eta(r(i,j,u(i)) + \gamma \max_{u(j)} Q(j, u(j))) \\ Q(k,v) &= Q(k,v), \text{ for all } k \neq i \text{ and } v \neq u(i) \end{aligned} \qquad (3)$$

where η is the learning rate and $Q(i, u(i))$ are the tabulated Q-values. One can prove, that this relaxation algorithm converges (under some conditions) to the optimal Q-values (Singh, 1994).

---

[2] To be more precise, the problem only becomes a multi-stage decision problem if the transaction costs are included in the problem.

The selection of the action $u(i)$ should be guided by the trade-off between exploration and exploitation. In the beginning, the actions are typically chosen randomly (exploration) and in the course of training, actions with larger Q-values are chosen with increasingly higher probability (exploitation). The implementation in the following experiments is based on the Boltzmann-distribution using the actual Q-values and a slowly decreasing temperature parameter (see Barto, 1989).

4 Experiment I: Artificial Exchange Rate

In this section we use an exchange-rate model to demonstrate how DP and Q-Learning can be used to optimize asset allocation.

The artificial exchange rate x_t is in the range between 1 and 2 representing the value of 1 US-\$ in DM. The transition probabilities p_{ij} of the exchange rate are chosen to simulate a situation where the x_t follows an increasing trend, but with higher values of x_t, a drop to very low values becomes more and more probable. A realization of the time series is plotted in the upper part of fig. 2. The random state variable c_t depends on the investor's decisions u_t, and is further influenced by x_t, x_{t+1}, and c_{t-1}. A complete state vector consists of the current exchange rate x_t and the capital c_t, which is always calculated in the basis currency (DM). Its sign represents the actual currency, i. e., $c_t = -1.2$ stands for an investment in US-\$ worth of 1.2 DM, and $c_t = 1.2$ for a capital of 1.2 DM. c_t and x_t are discretized in 10 bins each. The transaction costs $\xi = 0.1 + |c/100|$ are a combination of fixed (0.1) and variable costs ($|c/100|$). Transactions only apply, if the currency is changed from DM to US-\$. The immediate return $r_t(x_t, c_t, x_{t+1}, u_t)$ is computed as in table 1. If the decision has been made to change the portfolio into DM or to keep the actual portfolio in DM, $u_t = $ DM, then the return is always zero. If the decision has been made to change the portfolio into US-\$ or to keep the actual portfolio in US-\$, $u_t = $ US-\$, then the return is equal to the relative change of the exchange rate weighted with c_t. That return is reduced by the transaction costs ξ, if the investor has to change into US-\$.

Table 1: The immediate return function.

$r_t(x_t, c_t, x_{t+1}, u_t)$	$u_t = $ DM	$u_t = $ US-\$
$c_t \in $ DM	0	$r_t = (x_{t+1}/x_t)(c_t - \xi) - c_t$
$c_t \in $ US-\$	0	$r_t = (x_{t+1}/x_t - 1)c_t$

The success of the strategies was tested on a realization (2000 data points) of the exchange rate. The initial investment is 1 DM, at each time step the algorithm has to decide to either change the currency or remain in the present currency.

As a reinforcement learning method, QL has to interact with the environment to learn optimal behavior. Thus, a second set of 2000 data was used to learn the Q-values. The training phase is divided into epochs. Each epoch consists of as many trials as data exist in the training set. At every trial the algorithm looks at x_t, chooses randomly a portfolio value c_t and selects a decision. Then the immediate return and the new state is evaluated to apply eq. 3. The Q-values were initialized with zero, the learning rate η was 0.1. Convergence was achieved after 4 epochs.

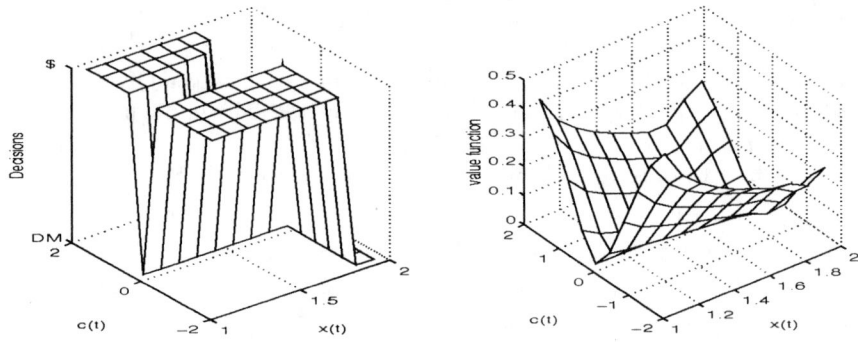

Figure 1: The optimal decisions (left) and value function (right).

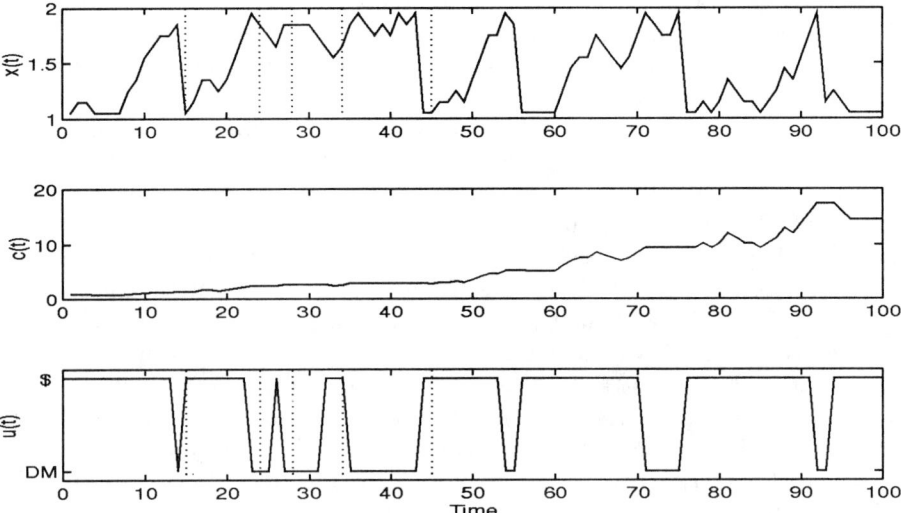

Figure 2: The exchange rate (top), the capital and the decisions (bottom).

To evaluate the solution QL has found, the DP-algorithm from eq. 2 was implemented using the given transition probabilities. The convergence of DP was very fast. Only 5 iterations were needed until the average difference between successive value functions was lower than 0.01. That means 500 updates in comparison to 8000 updates with QL.

The solutions were identical with respect to the resulting policy which is plotted in fig. 1, left. It can clearly be seen, that there is a difference between the policy of a DM-based and a US-$-based portfolio. If one has already changed the capital to US-$, then it is advisable to keep the portfolio in US-$ until the risk gets too high, i. e. $x_t \in \{1.8, 1.9\}$. On the other hand, if c_t is still in DM, the risk barrier moves to lower values depending on the volume of the portfolio. The reason is that the potential gain by an increasing exchange rate has to cover the fixed and variable transaction costs. For very low values of c_t, it is forbidden to change even at low x_t because the fixed transaction costs will be higher than any gain. Figure 2 plots the exchange rate x_t, the accumulated capital c_t for 100 days, and the decisions u_t.

Let us look at a few interesting decisions. At the beginning, $t = 0$, the portfolio was changed immediately to US-$ and kept there for 13 steps until a drop to low rates x_t became very probable. During the time steps 35-45, the exchange rate oscillated at higher exchange rates. The policy insisted on the DM portfolio, because the risk was too high. In contrary, looking at the time steps 24 to 28, the policy first switched back to DM, then there was a small decrease of x_t which was sufficient to let the investor change again. The following increase justified that decision. The success of the resulting strategy can be easily recognized by the continuous increase of the portfolio. Note, that the ups and downs of the portfolio curve get higher in magnitude at the end because the investor has no risk aversion and always the whole capital is traded.

5 Experiment II: German Stock Index DAX

In this section the approach is tested on a real world task: assume that an investor wishes to invest her/his capital into a block of stocks which behaves like the German stock index DAX. We based the benchmark strategy (short: MLP) on a NN model which was build to predict the daily changes of the DAX (for details, see Dichtl, 1995). If the prediction of the next day DAX difference is positive then the capital is invested into DAX otherwise in DM. The input vector of the NN model was carefully optimized for optimal prediction. We used these inputs (the DAX itself and 11 other influencing market variables) as the market description part of the state vector for QL. In order to store the value functions two NNs, one for each action, with 8 nonlinear hidden neurons and one linear output are used.

The data is split into a training (from 2. Jan. 1986 to 31. Dec. 1992) and a test set (from 2. Jan. 1993 to 18. Oct. 1995). The return function is defined in the same way as in section 4 using 0.4% as proportional costs and 0.001 units as fixed costs, which are realistic for financial institutions. The training proceeds as outlined in the previous section with $\eta = 0.001$ for 1000 epochs.

In fig. 3 the development of a reinvested capital is plotted for the optimized (upper line) and the MLP strategy (middle line). The DAX itself is also plotted but with a scaling factor to fit it into the figure (lower line). The resulting policy by QL clearly beats the benchmark strategy because the extra return amounts to 80% at the end of the training period and to 25% at the end of the test phase. A closer look at some statistics can explain the success. The QL policy proposes almost as often as the MLP policy to invest in DAX, but the number of changes from DM to DAX and v. v. is much lower (see table 2). Furthermore, it seems that the QL strategy keeps the capital out of the market if there is no significant trend to follow and the market shows too much volatility (see fig. 3 with straight horizontal lines of the capital development curve indicating no investments). An extensive analysis of the resulting strategy will be the topic of future research.

In a further experiment the NNs which store the Q-values are initialized to imitate the MLP strategy. In some runs the number of necessary epochs were reduced by a factor of 10. But often the QL algorithm took longer to converge because the initialization ignores the input elements which describe the investor's capital and therefore led to a bad starting point in the weight space.

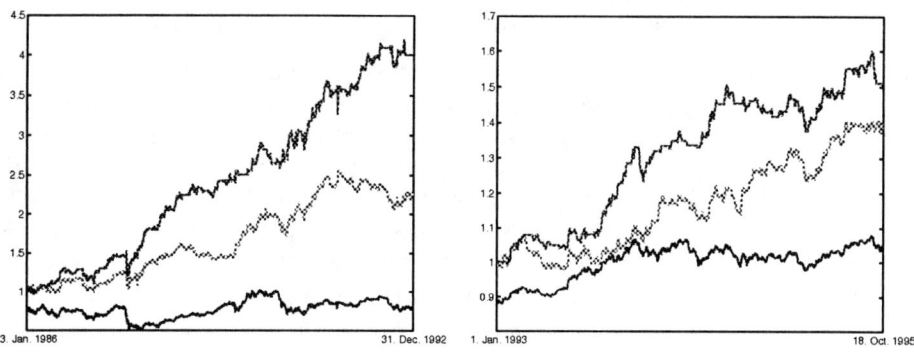

Figure 3: The development of a reinvested capital on the training (left) and test set (right). The lines from top to bottom: QL-strategy, MLP-strategy, scaled DAX.

Table 2: Some statistics of the policies.

		DAX investments		position changes	
	Data	MLP Policy	QL-Policy	MLP Policy	QL-Policy
Training set	1825	1020	1005	904	284
Test set	729	434	395	344	115

6 Conclusions and Future Work

In this paper, the task of asset allocation/portfolio management was approached by reinforcement learning algorithms. QL was successfully utilized in combination with NNs as value function approximators in a high dimensional state space.

Future work has to address the possibility of several alternative investment opportunities and to clarify the connection to the classical mean-variance approach of professional brokers. The benchmark strategy in the real world experiment is in fact a neuro-fuzzy model which allows the extraction of useful rules after learning. It will be interesting to use that network architecture to approximate the value function in order to achieve a deeper insight in the resulting optimized strategy.

References

Barto A. G., Sutton R. S. and Watkins C. J. C. H. (1989), Learning and Sequential Decision Making, COINS TR 89-95.
Bertsekas D. P. (1987), Dynamic Programming, NY: Wiley.
Singh, P. S. (1993), Learning to Solve Markovian Decision Processes, CMPSCI TR 93-77.
Neuneier R. (1995), Optimal Strategies with Density-Estimating Neural Networks, ICANN 95, Paris.
Brealy, R. A., Myers, S. C. (1991), Principles of Corporate Finance, McGraw-Hill.
Watkins C. J., Dayan, P. (1992), Technical Note: Q-Learning, Machine Learning 8, 3/4.
Elton, E. J. , Gruber, M. J. (1971), Dynamic Programming Applications in Finance, The Journal of Finance, 26/2.
Dichtl, H. (1995), Die Prognose des DAX mit Neuro-Fuzzy, masterthesis, engl. abstract in preparation.

Using the Future to "Sort Out" the Present: Rankprop and Multitask Learning for Medical Risk Evaluation

Rich Caruana, Shumeet Baluja, and Tom Mitchell
School of Computer Science, Carnegie Mellon University, Pittsburgh, PA 15213
(caruana, baluja, mitchell)@cs.cmu.edu

Abstract

A patient visits the doctor; the doctor reviews the patient's history, asks questions, makes basic measurements (blood pressure, ...), and prescribes tests or treatment. The prescribed course of action is based on an assessment of patient risk—patients at higher risk are given more and faster attention. It is also sequential—it is too expensive to immediately order all tests which might later be of value. This paper presents two methods that together improve the accuracy of backprop nets on a pneumonia risk assessment problem by 10-50%. *Rankprop* improves on backpropagation with sum of squares error in ranking patients by risk. *Multitask learning* takes advantage of *future* lab tests available in the training set, but not available in practice when predictions must be made. Both methods are broadly applicable.

1 Background

There are 3,000,000 cases of pneumonia each year in the U.S., 900,000 of which are admitted to the hospital for treatment and testing. Most pneumonia patients recover given appropriate treatment, and many can be treated effectively without hospitalization. Nonetheless, pneumonia is serious: 100,000 of those hospitalized for pneumonia die from it, and many more are at elevated risk if not hospitalized.

1.1 The Problem

A primary goal of medical decision making is to accurately, swiftly, and economically identify patients at high risk from diseases like pneumonia so they may be hospitalized to receive aggressive testing and treatment; patients at low risk may be more comfortably, safely, and economically treated at home. Note that the diagnosis of pneumonia has already been made; the goal is not to determine the illness, but how much risk the illness poses to the patient. Some of the most useful tests for doing this require hospitalization and will be available only if preliminary assessment indicates it is warranted. Low risk patients can safely be treated as outpatients and can often be identified using measurements made prior to admission.

The problem considered in this paper is to learn to rank pneumonia patients according to their probability of mortality. We present two learning methods that combined outperform standard backpropagation by 10-50% in identifying groups of patients with least mortality risk. These methods are applicable to domains where the goal is to rank instances according to a probability function and where useful attributes do not become available until after the prediction must be made. In addition to medical decision making, this class includes problems as diverse as investment analysis in financial markets and autonomous vehicle navigation.

1.2 The Pneumonia Database

The Medis Pneumonia Database [6] contains 14,199 pneumonia cases collected from 78 hospitals in 1989. Each patient in the database was diagnosed with pneumonia and hospitalized. 65 measurements are available for most patients. These include 30 basic measurements typically acquired prior to hospitalization such as age, sex, and pulse, and 35 lab results such as blood counts or gases not available until after hospitalization. The database indicates how long each patient was hospitalized and whether the patient lived or died. 1,542 (10.9%) of the patients died.

1.3 The Performance Criterion

The Medis database indicates which patients lived or died. The most useful decision aid for this problem would predict which patients will live or die. But this is too difficult. In practice, the best that can be achieved is to estimate a probability of death (POD) from the observed symptoms. In fact, it is sufficient to learn to *rank* patients by POD so lower risk patients can be discriminated from higher risk patients. The patients at least risk may then be considered for outpatient care.

The performance criterion used by others working with the Medis database [4] is the accuracy with which one can select a prespecified fraction of the patient population that do not die. For example, given a population of 10,000 patients, find the 20% of this population at *least* risk. To do this we learn a risk model and a threshold for this model that allows 20% of the population (2000 patients) to fall below it. If 30 of the 2000 patients below this threshold died, the error rate is $30/2000 = 0.015$. We say that the error rate for FOP 0.20 is 0.015 for this model ("FOP" stands for fraction of population). In this paper we consider FOPs 0.1, 0.2, 0.3, 0.4, and 0.5. Our goal is to learn models and model thresholds, such that the error rate at each FOP is minimized. Models with acceptably low error rates might then be employed to help determine which patients do not require hospitalization.

2 Methodology

The Medis database is unusually large, with over 14K training patterns. Because we are interested in developing methods that will be effective in other domains where databases of this size are not available, we perform our experiments using small training sets randomly drawn from the 14K patterns and use the remaining patterns as test sets. For each method we run ten trials. For each trial we randomly sample 2K patterns from the 14K pool for training. The 2K training sample is further split into a 1K backprop set used to train the net and a 1K halting set used to determine when to halt training.[1] Once the network is trained, we run the 1K halt set through the model again to find the threshold that passes 10%, 20%, 30%, 40%, and 50% of the halt set. The performance of the model is evaluated on the 12K unused patterns by determining how many of the cases that fall below threshold in this test set die. This is the error rate for that model at that FOP.

3 The Traditional Approach: SSE on 0/1 Targets

Sections 3-5 present three neural net approaches to pneumonia risk prediction. This section presents the standard approach: using backpropagation on sum of squares errors (SSE) with 0=lives/1=dies to predict mortality. This works well if early stopping is used to prevent overfitting. Section 4 presents rankprop (SSE on ranks instead of 0/1 targets). Rankprop, which learns to rank patients by risk instead of directly predicting mortality, works better. Section 5 uses multitask learning (MTL) to benefit from tests in the database that in practice will not be available until after deciding to admit the patient. Rankprop with MTL works even better.

The straightforward approach to this problem is to use backprop to train a net to learn to predict which patients live or die, and then use the real-valued predictions of this net to sort patients by risk. This net has 30 inputs, 1 for each of the observed patient measurements, a hidden layer with 8 units[2], and a single output trained with 0=lived, 1=died.[3] Given an infinite training set, a net trained this way should learn to predict the probability of death for each patient, not which patients live or die. In the real world, however, where we rarely have an infinite number of training cases, a net will overtrain and begin to learn a very nonlinear function that outputs values near 0/1 for cases in the training set, but which does not generalize well. In this domain it is critical to use early stopping to halt training before this happens.

Table 1 shows the error rates of nets trained with SSE on 0/1 targets for the five FOPs. Each entry is the mean of ten trials. The first entry in the table indicates that on average, in the 10% of the test population predicted by the nets to be at least risk, 1.4% died. We do not know the best achievable error rates for this data.

Table 1: Error Rates of SSE on 0/1 Targets

FOP	0.1	0.2	0.3	0.4	0.5
Error Rate	.0140	.0190	.0252	.0340	.0421

4 Using Rankprop to Rank Cases by Risk

Because the goal is to find the fraction of the population least likely to die, it is sufficient just to learn to rank patients by risk. Rankprop learns to rank patients without learning to predict mortality. "Rankprop" is short for "backpropagation using sum of squares errors on estimated ranks". The basic idea is to sort the training set using the target values, scale the ranks from this sort (we scale uniformly to [0.25,0.75] with sigmoid output units), and use the scaled ranks as target values for standard backprop with SSE instead of the 0/1 values in the database.

---

[1] Performance at different FOPs sometimes peaks at different epochs. We halt training separately for each FOP in all the experiments to insure this does not confound results.

[2] To make comparisons between methods fair, we first found hidden layer sizes and learning parameters that performed well for each method.

[3] Different representations such as 0.15/0.85 and different error metrics such as cross entropy did not perform better than SSE on 0/1 targets.

Ideally, we'd rank the training set by the true probabilities of death. Unfortunately, all we know is which patients lived or died. In the Medis database, 89% of the target values are 0's and 11% are 1's. There are many possible sorts consistent with these values. Which sort should backprop try to fit? It is the large number of possible sorts of the training set that makes backpropagating ranks challenging. Rankprop solves this problem by using the net model *as it is being learned* to order the training set *when target values are tied*. In this database, where there are many ties because there are only two target values, finding a proper ranking of the training set is a serious problem. Rankprop learns to adjust the target ranks *of* the training set at the same time it is learning to predict ranks *from* that training set.

How does rankprop do this? Rankprop alternates between rank passes and backprop passes. On the rank pass it records the output of the net for each training pattern. It then sorts the training patterns using the *target* values (0 or 1 in the Medis database), *but using the network's predictions for each pattern as a* **secondary** *sort key to break ties.* The basic idea is to find the legal rank of the target values (0 or 1) maximally consistent with the ranks the current model predicts. This *closest match* ranking of the target values is then used to define the target ranks used on the next backprop pass through the training set. Rankprop's pseudo code is:

```
foreach epoch do {
   foreach pattern do {
      network_output[pattern] = forward_pass(pattern)}
   target_rank = sort_and_scale_patterns(target_value, network_output)
   foreach pattern do {
      backprop(target_rank[pattern] - network_output[pattern])}}
```

where "sort_and_scale_patterns" sorts and ranks the training patterns using the sort keys specified in its arguments, the second being used to break ties in the first.

Table 2 shows the mean rankprop performance using nets with 8 hidden units. The bottom row shows improvements over SSE on 0/1 targets. All differences are statistically significant. See Section 7.1 for discussion of why rankprop works better.

Table 2: Error Rates of Rankprop and Improvement Over Standard Backprop

FOP	0.1	0.2	0.3	0.4	0.5
Error Rate	.0083	.0144	.0210	.0289	.0386
% Change	-40.7%	-24.2%	-16.7%	-15.0%	-8.3%

5 Learning From the Future with Multitask Learning

The Medis database contains results from 36 lab tests that will be available only after patients are hospitalized. Unfortunately, these results will not be available when the model is used because the patients will not yet have been admitted. Multitask learning (MTL) improves generalization by having a learner simultaneously learn sets of related tasks with a shared representation; what is learned for each task might benefit other tasks. In this application, we use MTL to benefit from the future lab results. The extra lab values are used as extra backprop *outputs* as shown in Figure 1. The extra outputs bias the shared hidden layer towards representations that better capture important features of the domain. See [2][3][9] for details about MTL and [1] for other ways of using extra outputs to bias learning.

The MTL net has 64 hidden units. Table 3 shows the mean performance of ten runs of MTL with rankprop. The bottom row shows the improvement over rankprop

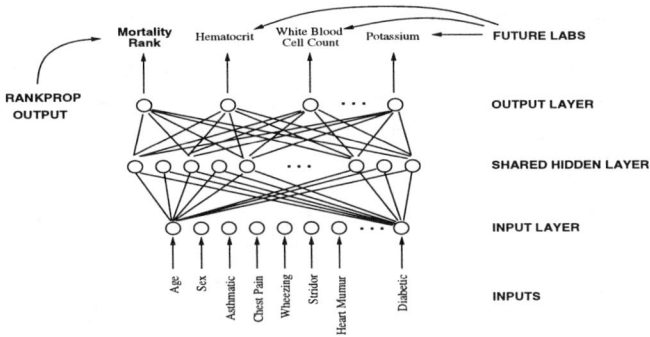

Figure 1: Using Future Lab Results as Extra Outputs To Bias Learning

alone. Although MTL lowers error at each FOP, only the differences at FOP = 0.3, 0.4, and 0.5 are statistically significant with ten trials. Feature nets [7], a competing approach that trains nets to predict the missing future labs and uses the predictions as extra net *inputs* does not yield benefits comparable to MTL on this problem.

Table 3: Error Rates of Rankprop+MTL and Improvement Over Rankprop Alone

FOP	0.1	0.2	0.3	0.4	0.5
Error Rate	.0074	.0127	.0197	.0269	.0364
% Change	-10.8%	-11.8%	-6.2%	-6.9%	-5.7%

6 Comparison of Results

Table 4 compares the performance of backprop using SSE on 0/1 targets with the combination of rankprop and multitask learning. On average, Rankprop+MTL reduces error more than 25%. This improvement is not easy to achieve—experiments with other learning methods such as Bayes Nets, Hierarchical Mixtures of Experts, and K-Nearest Neighbor (run not by us, but by experts in their use) indicate SSE on 0/1 targets is an excellent performer on this domain[4].

Table 4: Comparison Between SSE on 0/1 Targets and Rankprop+MTL

FOP	0.1	0.2	0.3	0.4	0.5
SSE on 0/1	.0140	.0190	.0252	.0340	.0421
Rankprop+MTL	.0074	.0127	.0197	.0269	.0364
% Change	-47.1%	-33.2%	-21.8%	-20.9%	-13.5%

7 Discussion

7.1 Why Does Rankprop Work?

We are given data from a target function $f(x)$. Suppose the goal is not to learn a model *of* $f(x)$, but to learn to sort patterns *by* $f(x)$. Must we learn a model of $f(x)$ and use its predictions for sorting? No. It suffices to learn a function $g(x)$ such that for all $x_1, x_2, [g(x_1) \leq g(x_2)] \rightarrow [f(x_1) \leq f(x_2)]$. There can be many such functions $g(x)$ for a given $f(x)$, and some of these may be easier to learn than $f(x)$.

Consider the probability function in Figure 2.1 that assigns to each x the probability $p = f(x)$ that the outcome is 1; with probability $1 - p$ the outcome is 0. Figure 2.2 shows a training set sampled from this distribution. Where the probability is low, there are many 0's. Where the probability is high, there are many 1's. Where the probability is near 0.5, there are 0's and 1's. *This region causes problems for backprop using SSE on 0/1 targets: similar inputs are mapped to dissimilar targets.*

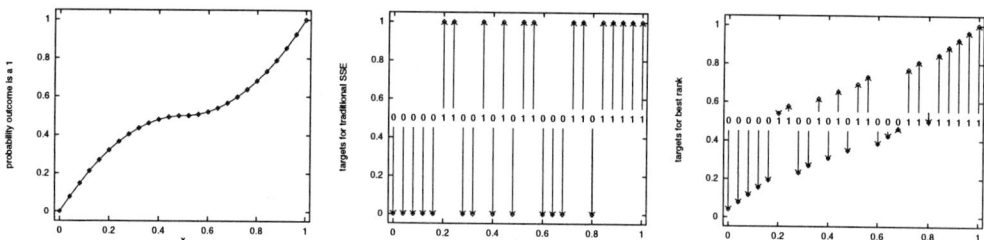

Figure 2: SSE on 0/1 Targets and on Ranks for a Simple Probability Function

Backprop learns a very nonlinear function if trained on Figure 2.2. This is unfortunate: Figure 2.1 is smooth and maps similar inputs to similar outputs. If the goal is to learn to rank the data, we can learn a simpler, *less nonlinear* function instead. There exists a ranking of the training data such that if the ranks are used as backprop target values, the resulting function is less nonlinear than the original target function. Figure 2.3 shows these target rank values. Similar input patterns have more similar rank target values than the original target values.

Rankprop tries to learn *simple* functions that directly support ranking. One difficulty with this is that rankprop must learn a ranking of the training data while also training the model to predict ranks. We do not yet know under what conditions this parallel search will converge. We conjecture that when rankprop does converge, it will often be to simpler models than it would have learned from the original target values (0/1 in Medis), and that these simpler models will often generalize better.

7.2 Other Applications of Rankprop and Learning From the Future

Rankprop is applicable wherever a relative assessment is more useful or more learnable than an absolute one. One application is domains where quantitative measurements are not available, but relative ones are[8]. For example, a game player might not be able to evaluate moves quantitatively , but might excel at relative move evaluation[10]. Another application is where the goal is to learn to order data drawn from a probability distribution, as in medical risk prediction. But it can also be applied wherever the goal is to order data. For example, in information filtering it is usually important to present more useful information to the user first, not to predict how important each is[5].

MTL is a general method for using related tasks. Here the extra MTL tasks are future measurements. Future measurements are available in many offline learning problems where there is opportunity to collect the measurements for the training set. For example, a robot or autonomous vehicle can more accurately measure the size, location, and identity of objects when it passes near them—road stripes can be detected reliably as a vehicle passes alongside them, but detecting them far ahead of a vehicle is hard. Since driving brings future road into the car's present, stripes can be measured accurately when passed and used as extra features in the training set. They can't be used as *inputs* for learning to drive because they will not be available until too late when driving. As MTL outputs, though, they provide information that improves learning without requiring they be available at run time[2].

8 Summary

This paper presents two methods that can improve generalization on a broad class of problems. This class includes identifying low risk pneumonia patients. The first method, rankprop, tries to learn simple models that support ranking future cases while simultaneously learning to rank the training set. The second, multitask learning, uses lab tests available only during training, as additional target values to bias learning towards a more predictive hidden layer. Experiments using a database of pneumonia patients indicate that together these methods outperform standard backpropagation by 10-50%. Rankprop and MTL are applicable to a large class of problems in which the goal is to learn a relative ranking over the instance space, and where the training data includes features that will not be available at run time. Such problems include identifying higher-risk medical patients as early as possible, identifying lower-risk financial investments, and visual analysis of scenes that become easier to analyze as they are approached in the future.

Acknowledgements

We thank Greg Cooper, Michael Fine, and other members of the Pitt/CMU Cost-Effective Health Care group for help with the Medis Database. This work was supported by ARPA grant F33615-93-1-1330, NSF grant BES-9315428, Agency for Health Care Policy and Research grant HS06468, and an NSF Graduate Student Fellowship (Baluja).

References

[1] Y.S. Abu-Mostafa, "Learning From Hints in Neural Networks," *Journal of Complexity* 6:2, pp. 192-198, 1989.

[2] R. Caruana, "Learning Many Related Tasks at the Same Time With Backpropagation," *Advances in Neural Information Processing Systems 7*, pp. 656-664, 1995.

[3] R. Caruana, "Multitask Learning: A Knowledge-Based Source of Inductive Bias," *Proceedings of the 10th International Conference on Machine Learning*, pp. 41-48, 1993.

[4] G. Cooper, et al., "An Evaluation of Machine Learning Methods for Predicting Pneumonia Mortality," submitted to *AI in Medicine*, 1995.

[5] K. Lang, "NewsWeeder: Learning to Filter News," *Proceedings of the 12th International Conference on Machine Learning*, pp. 331-339, 1995.

[6] M. Fine, D. Singer, B. Hanusa, J. Lave, and W. Kapoor, "Validation of a Pneumonia Prognostic Index Using the MedisGroups Comparative Hospital Database," *American Journal of Medicine*, **94** 1993.

[7] I. Davis and A. Stentz, "Sensor Fusion For Autonomous Outdoor Navigation Using Neural Networks," *Proceedings of IEEE's Intelligent Robots and Systems Conference*, 1995.

[8] G.T. Hsu, and R. Simmons, "Learning Footfall Evaluation for a Walking Robot," *Proceedings of the 8th International Conference on Machine Learning*, pp. 303-307, 1991.

[9] S.C. Suddarth and A.D.C. Holden, "Symbolic-neural Systems and the Use of Hints for Developing Complex Systems," *International Journal of Man-Machine Studies* 35:3, pp. 291-311, 1991.

[10] P. Utgoff and S. Saxena, "Learning a Preference Predicate," *Proceedings of the 4th International Conference on Machine Learning*, pp. 115-121, 1987.

Stock Selection via Nonlinear Multi-Factor Models

Asriel U. Levin
BZW Barclays Global Investors
Advanced Strategies and Research Group
45 Fremont Street
San Francisco CA 94105
email: asriel.levin@bglobal.com

Abstract

This paper discusses the use of multilayer feedforward neural networks for predicting a stock's excess return based on its exposure to various technical and fundamental factors. To demonstrate the effectiveness of the approach a hedged portfolio which consists of equally capitalized long and short positions is constructed and its historical returns are benchmarked against T-bill returns and the S&P500 index.

1 Introduction

Traditional investment approaches (Elton and Gruber, 1991) assume that the return of a security can be described by a multifactor linear model:

$$R_i = a_i + u_{i1}F_1 + u_{i2}F_2 + \ldots + u_{iL}F_L + e_i \qquad (1)$$

where R_i denotes the return on security i, F_l are a set of factor values and u_{il} are security i exposure to factor l, a_i is an intercept term (which under the CAPM framework is assumed to be equal to the risk free rate of return (Sharpe, 1984)) and e_i is a random term with mean zero which is assumed to be uncorrelated across securities.

The factors may consist of any set of variables deemed to have explanatory power for security returns. These could be aspects of macroeconomics, fundamental security analysis, technical attributes or a combination of the above. The value of a factor is the expected excess return above risk free rate of a security with unit exposure to the factor and zero exposure to all other factors. The choice of factors can be viewed as a proxy for the "state of the world" and their selection defines a metric imposed on the universe of securities: Once the factors are set, the model assumption is that, on average, two securities with similar factor loadings (u_{il}) will behave in a similar manner.

The factor model (1) was not originally developed as a predictive model, but rather as an explanatory model, with the returns R_i and the factor values F_l assumed to be contemporaneous. To utilize (1) in a predictive manner, each factor value must be replaced by an estimate, resulting in the model

$$R_i = a_i + u_{i1}\hat{F}_1 + u_{i2}\hat{F}_2 + \ldots + u_{iL}\hat{F}_L + e_i \qquad (2)$$

where R_i is a security's future return and $\hat{F}_l$ is an estimate of the future value of factor l, based on currently available information. The estimation of $\hat{F}_l$ can be approached with varying degree of sophistication ranging from a simple use of the historical mean to estimate the factor value (setting $\hat{F}_l(t) = \bar{F}_l$), to more elaborate approaches attempting to construct a time series model for predicting the factor values.

Factor models of the form (2) can be employed both to control risk and to enhance return. In the first case, by capturing the major sources of correlation among security returns, one can construct a well balanced portfolio which diversifies specific risk away. For the latter, if one is able to predict the likely future value of a factor, higher return can be achieved by constructing a portfolio that tilts toward "good" factors and away from "bad" ones.

While linear factor models have proven to be very useful tools for portfolio analysis and investment management, the assumption of linear relationship between factor values and expected return is quite restrictive. Specifically, the use of linear models assumes that each factor affects the return independently and hence, they ignore the possible interaction between different factors. Furthermore, with a linear model, the expected return of a security can grow without bound as its exposure to a factor increases. To overcome these shortcomings of linear models, one would have to consider more general models that allow for nonlinear relationship among factor values, security exposures and expected returns.

Generalizing (2), while maintaining the basic premise that the state of the world can be described by a vector of factor values and that the expected return of a security is determined through its coordinates in this factor world, leads to the nonlinear model:

$$R_i = \tilde{f}(u_{i1}, u_{i2}, \ldots, u_{iL}, \hat{F}_1, \hat{F}_2, \ldots, \hat{F}_L) + e_i \qquad (3)$$

where $\tilde{f}(\cdot)$ is a nonlinear function and e_i is the noise unexplained by the model, or "security specific risk".

The prediction task for the nonlinear model (3) is substantially more complex than in the linear case since it requires both the estimation of future factor values as well as a determination of the unknown function $\tilde{f}$. The task can be somewhat simplified if factor estimates are replaced with their historical means:

$$\begin{aligned} R_i &= \tilde{f}(u_{i1}, u_{i2}, \ldots, u_{iL}, \bar{F}_1, \bar{F}_2, \ldots, \bar{F}_L) + e_i \\ &\triangleq f(u_{i1}, u_{i2}, \ldots, u_{iL}) + e_i \end{aligned} \qquad (4)$$

where now u_{il} are the security's factor exposure at the beginning of the period over which we wish to predict.

To estimate the unknown function $f(\cdot)$, a family of models needs to be selected, from which a model is to be identified. In the following we propose modeling the relationship between factor exposures and future returns using the class of multilayer feedforward neural networks (Hertz et al., 1991). Their universal approximation capabilities (Cybenko, 1989; Hornik et al., 1989), as well as the existence of an effective parameter tuning method (the backpropagation algorithm (Rumelhart et al., 1986)) makes this family of models a powerful tool for the identification of nonlinear mappings and hence a natural choice for modeling (4).

2   The stock selection problem

Our objective in this paper is to test the ability of neural network based models of the form (4) to differentiate between attractive and unattractive stocks. Rather than trying to predict the total return of a security, the objective is to predict its performance relative to the market, hence eliminating the need to predict market directions and movements.

The data set consists of monthly historical records (1989 through 1995) for the largest 1200-1300 US companies as defined by the BARRA HiCap universe. Each data record ($\approx$1300 per month) consists of an input vector composed of a security's factor exposures recorded at the beginning of the month and the corresponding output is the security's return over the month. The factors used to build the model include Earning/Price, Book/Price, past price performance, consensus of analyst sentiments etc, which have been suggested in the financial literature as having explanatory power for security returns (e.g. (Fama and French, 1992)). To minimize risk, exposure to other unwarranted factors is controlled using a quadratic optimizer.

3   Model construction and testing

Potentially, changes in a price of a security are a function of a very large number of forces and events, of which only a small subset can be included in the factor model (4). All other sources of return play the role of noise whose magnitude is probably much larger than any signal that can be explained by the factor exposures. When this information is used to train a neural network, the network attempts to replicate the examples it sees and hence much of what it tries to learn will be the particular realizations of noise that appeared in the training set.

To minimize this effect, both a validation set and regularization are used in the training. The validation set is used to monitor the performance of the model with data on which it has not been trained on. By stopping the learning process when validation set error starts to increase, the learning of noise is minimized. Regularization further limits the complexity of the function realized by the network and, through the reduction of model variance, improves generalization (Levin et al., 1994).

The stock selection model is built using a rolling train/test window. First, M "two layer" feedforward networks are built for each month of data (result is rather insensitive to the particular choice of M). Each network is trained using stochastic gradient descent with one quarter of the monthly data (randomly selected) used as a validation set. Regularization is done using principal component pruning (Levin et al., 1994). Once training is completed, the models constructed over N consecutive month of data (again, result is insensitive to particular choice of N) are combined (thus increasing the robustness of the model (Breiman, 1994)) to predict the returns in the following month. Thus the predicted (out of sample) return of stock i in month k is given by

$$\hat{R}_i(k) = \frac{1}{N*M} \sum_{j=1}^{N*M} NN_{k-j}(u_{i1}^k, u_{i2}^k, \ldots, u_{iL}^k) \quad (5)$$

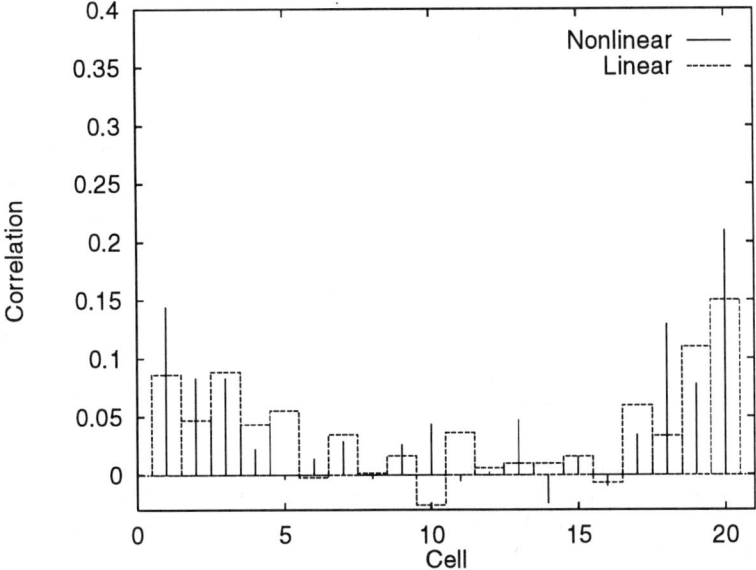

Figure 1: Average correlation between predicted alphas and realized returns for linear and nonlinear models

where $\hat{R}_i(k)$ is stock's i predicted return, $NN_{k-j}(\cdot)$ denoted the neural network model built in month $k-j$ and u_{il}^k are stock's i factor exposures as measured at the beginning of month k.

4 Benchmarking to linear

As a first step in evaluating the added value of the nonlinear model, its performance was benchmarked against a generalized least squares linear model. Each model was run over three universes: all securities in the HiCap universe, the extreme 200 stocks (top 100, bottom 100 as defined by each model), and the extreme 100 stocks. As a comparative performance measure we use the Sharpe ratio (Elton and Gruber, 1991). As shown in Table 4, while the performance of the two models is quite comparable over the whole universe of stocks, the neural network based model performs better at the extremes, resulting in a substantially larger Sharpe ratio (and of course, when constructing a portfolio, it is the extreme alphas that have the most impact on performance).

Portfolio\Model	Linear	Nonlinear
All HiCap	6.43	6.92
100 long/100 short	4.07	5.49
50 long/50 short	3.07	4.23

Table 1: Ex ante Sharpe ratios: Neural network vs. linear

While the numbers in the above table look quite impressive, it should be emphasised that they do not represent returns of a practical strategy: turnover is huge and the figures do not take transaction costs into account. The main purpose of the table is to compare the information that can be captured by the different models and specifically to show the added value of the neural network at the extremes. A practical implementation scheme and the associated performance will be discussed in the next section.

Finally, some insight as to the reason for the improved performance can be gained by looking at the correlation between model predictions and realized returns for different values of model predictions (commonly referred to as *alphas*). For that, the alpha range was divided to 20 cells, 5% of observations in each and correlations were calculated separately for each cell. As is shown in figure 1, while both neural network and linear model seem to have more predictive power at the extremes, the network's correlations are substantially larger for both positive and negative alphas.

5 Portfolio construction

Given the superior predictive ability of the nonlinear model at the extremes, a natural way of translating its predictions into an investment strategy is through the use of a long/short construct which fully captures the model information on both the positive as well as the negative side.

The long/short portfolio (Jacobs and Levy, 1993) is constructed by allocating equal capital to long and short positions. By monitoring and controlling the risk characteristics on both sides, one is able to construct a portfolio that has zero correlation with the market ($\beta = 0$) - a "market neutral" portfolio. By construction, the return of a market neutral portfolio is insensitive to the market up or down swings and its only source of return is the performance spread between the long and short positions, which in turn is a direct function of the model (5) discernment ability.

Specifically, the translation of the model predictions into a realistically implementable strategy is done using a quadratic optimizer. Using the model predicted returns and incorporating volatility information about the various stocks, the optimizer is utilized to construct a portfolio with the following characteristics:

- Market neutral (equal long and short capitalization).
- Total number of assets in the portfolio $<= 200$.
- Average (one sided) monthly turnover $\approx 15\%$.
- Annual active risk $\approx 5\%$.

In the following, all results are test set results (out of sample), net of estimated transaction costs (assumed to be 1.5% round trip). The standard benchmark for a market neutral portfolio is the return on 3 month T-bill and as can be seen in Table 2, over the test period the market neutral portfolio has consistently and decisively outperformed its benchmark. Furthermore, the results reported for 1995 were recorded in real-time (simulated paper portfolio).

An interesting feature of the long/short construct is its ease of transportability (Jacobs and Levy, 1993). Thus, while the base construction is insensitive to market movement, if one wishes, full exposure to a desired market can be achieved through the use of futures or swaps (Hull, 1993). As an example, by adding a permanent S&P500 futures overlay in an amount equal to the invested capital, one is fully exposed to the equity market at all time, and returns are the sum of the long/short performance spread and the profits or losses resulting from the market price movements. This form of a long/short strategy is referred to as an "equitized" strategy and the appropriate benchmark will be overlayed index. The relative performance

Statistics	T-Bill	Neutral	S&P500	Equitized
Total Return(%)	27.8	131.5	102.0	264.5
Annual total(Yr%)	4.6	16.8	10.4	27.0
Active Return(%)	-	103.7	-	162.5
Annual active(Yr%)	-	12.2	-	16.6
Active risk(Yr%)	-	4.8	-	4.8
Max draw down(%)	-	3.2	13.9	10.0
Turnover(Yr%)	-	198.4	-	198.4

Table 2: Comparative summary of ex ante portfolio performance (net of transaction costs) 8/90 - 12/95

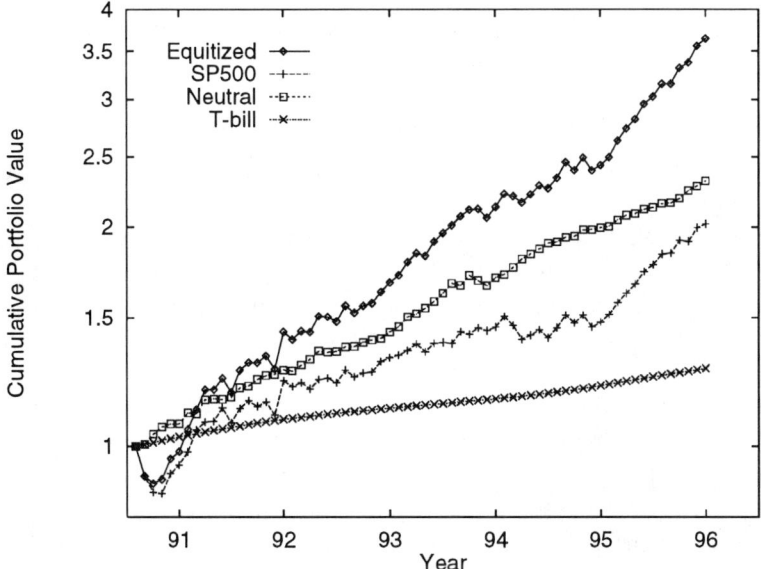

Figure 2: Cumulative portfolio value 8/90 - 12/95 (net of estimated transaction costs)

of the equitized strategy with an S&P500 futures overlay is presented in Table 2. Summary of the accumulated returns over the test period for the market neutral and equitized portfolios compared to T-bill and S&P500 are given in Figure 2.

Finally, even though the performance of the model is quite good, it is very difficult to convince an investor to put his money on a "black box". A rather simple way to overcome this problem of neural networks is to utilize a CART tree (Breiman et al., 1984) to explain the model's structure. While the performance of the tree on the raw data in substantially inferior to the network's, it can serve as a very effective tool for analyzing and interpreting the information that is driving the model.

6 Conclusion

We presented a methodology by which neural network based models can be used for security selection and portfolio construction. In spite of the very low signal to noise ratio of the raw data, the model was able to extract meaningful relationship between factor exposures and expected returns. When utilized to construct hedged portfolios, these predictions achieved persistent returns with very favorable risk characteristics.

The model is currently being tested in real time and given its continued consistent performance, is expected to go live soon.

References

Anderson, J. and Rosenfeld, E., editors (1988). *Neurocomputing: Foundations of Research*. MIT Press, Cambridge.

Breiman, L. (1994). Bagging predictors. Technical Report 416, Department of Statistics, UCB, Berkeley, CA.

Breiman, L., Friedman, J., Olshen, R., and Stone, C. (1984). *Classification and Regression Trees*. Chapman & Hall.

Cybenko, G. (1989). Approximation by superpositions of a sigmoidal function. *Mathematics of Control, Signals, and Systems*, 2:303–314.

Elton, E. and Gruber, M. (1991). *Modern Portfolio Theory and Investment Analysis*. John Wiley.

Fama, E. and French, K. (1992). The cross section of expected stock returns. *Journal of Finance*, 47:427–465.

Hertz, J., Krogh, A., and Palmer, R. (1991). *Introduction to the theory of neural computation*, volume 1 of *Santa Fe Institute studies in the sciences of complexity*. Addison Wesley Pub. Co.

Hornik, K., Stinchcombe, M., and White, H. (1989). Multilayer feedforward networks are universal approximators. *Neural Networks*, 2:359–366.

Hull, J. (1993). *Options, Futures and Other Derivative Securities*. Prentice-Hall.

Jacobs, B. and Levy, K. (1993). Long/short equity investing. *Journal of Portfolio Management*, pages 52–63.

Levin, A. U., Leen, T. K., and Moody, J. E. (1994). Fast pruning using principal components. In Cowan, J. D., Tesauro, G., and Alspector, J., editors, *Advances in Neural Information Processing Systems*, volume 6. Morgan Kaufmann. to apear.

Rumelhart, D., Hinton, G., and Williams, R. (1986). Learning representations by back-propagating errors. *Nature*, 323:533–536. Reprinted in (Anderson and Rosenfeld, 1988).

Sharpe, W. (1984). Factor models, CAPMs and the APT. *Journal of Portfolio Management*, pages 21–25.

Experiments with Neural Networks for Real Time Implementation of Control

P. K. Campbell, M. Dale, H. L. Ferrá and A. Kowalczyk

Telstra Research Laboratories
770 Blackburn Road Clayton, Vic. 3168, Australia
{p.campbell, m.dale, h.ferra, a.kowalczyk}@trl.oz.au

Abstract

This paper describes a neural network based controller for allocating capacity in a telecommunications network. This system was proposed in order to overcome a "real time" response constraint. Two basic architectures are evaluated: 1) a feedforward network-heuristic and; 2) a feedforward network-recurrent network. These architectures are compared against a linear programming (LP) optimiser as a benchmark. This LP optimiser was also used as a teacher to label the data samples for the feedforward neural network training algorithm. It is found that the systems are able to provide a traffic throughput of 99% and 95%, respectively, of the throughput obtained by the linear programming solution. Once trained, the neural network based solutions are found in a fraction of the time required by the LP optimiser.

1 Introduction

Among the many virtues of neural networks are their efficiency, in terms of both execution time and required memory for storing a structure, and their practical ability to approximate complex functions. A typical drawback is the usually "data hungry" training algorithm. However, if training data can be computer generated off line, then this problem may be overcome. In many applications the algorithm used to generate the solution may be impractical to implement in real time. In such cases a neural network substitute can become crucial for the feasibility of the project. This paper presents preliminary results for a non-linear optimization problem using a neural network. The application in question is that of capacity allocation in an optical communications network. The work in this area is continuing and so far we have only explored a few possibilities.

2 Application: Bandwidth Allocation in SDH Networks

Synchronous Digital Hierarchy (SDH) is a new standard for digital transmission over optical fibres [3] adopted for Australia and Europe equivalent to the SONET (Synchronous Optical NETwork) standard in North America. The architecture of the particular SDH network researched in this paper is shown in Figure 1 (a).

1) Nodes at the periphery of the SDH network are switches that handle individual calls.

2) Each switch concentrates traffic for another switch into a number of streams.

3) Each stream is then transferred to a Digital Cross-Connect (DXC) for switching and transmission to its destination by allocating to it one of several alternative virtual paths.

The task at hand is the dynamic allocation of capacities to these virtual paths in order to maximize SDH network throughput.

This is a non-linear optimization task since the virtual path capacities and the constraints, i.e. the physical limit on capacity of links between DXC's, are quantized, and the objective function (Erlang blocking) depends in a highly non-linear fashion on the allocated capacities and demands. Such tasks can be solved 'optimally' with the use of classical linear programming techniques [5], but such an approach is time-consuming - for large SDH networks the task could even require hours to complete.

One of the major features of an SDH network is that it can be remotely reconfigured using software controls. Reconfiguration of the SDH network can become necessary when traffic demands vary, or when failures occur in the DXC's or the links connecting them. Reconfiguration in the case of failure must be extremely fast, with a need for restoration times under 60 ms [1].

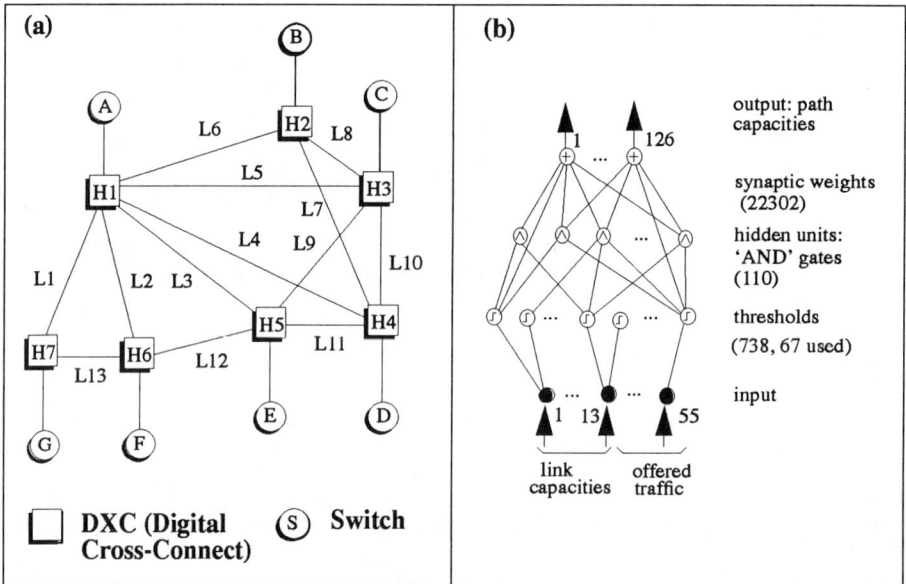

Figure 1
(a) Example of an Inter-City SDH/SONET Network Topology used in experiments.
(b) Example of an architecture of the mask perceptron generated in experiments.

In our particular case, there are three virtual paths allocated between any pair of switches, each using a different set of links between DXC's of the SDH network. Calls from one switch to another can be sent along any of the virtual paths, leading to 126 paths in total (7 switches to 6 other switches, each with 3 paths).

The path capacities are normally set to give a predefined throughput. This is known as the "steady state". If links in the SDH network become partially damaged or completely cut, the operation of the SDH network moves away from the steady state and the path capacities must be reconfigured to satisfy the traffic demands subject to the following constraints:

(i) Capacities have integer values (between 0 and 64 with each unit corresponding to a 2 Mb/s stream, or 30 Erlangs),

(ii) The total capacity of all virtual paths through any one link of the SDH network cannot exceed the physical capacity of that link.

The neural network training data consisted of 13 link capacities and 42 traffic demand values, representing situations in which the operation of one or more links is degraded (completely or partially). The output data consisted of 126 integer values representing the difference between the steady state path capacities and the final allocated path capacities.

3 Previous Work

The problem of optimal SDH network reconfiguration has been researched already. In particular Gopal et. al. proposed a heuristic greedy search algorithm [4] to solve this non-linear integer programming problem. Herzberg in [5] reformulated this non-linear integer optimization problem as a linear programming (LP) task, Herzberg and Bye in [6] investigated application of a simplex algorithm to solve the LP problem, whilst Bye [2] considered an application of a Hopfield neural network for this task, and finally Leckie [8] used another set of AI inspired heuristics to solve the optimization task.

All of these approaches have practical deficiencies; the linear programming is slow, while the heuristic approaches are relatively inaccurate and the Hopfield neural network method (simulated on a serial computer) suffers from both problems.

In a previous paper Campbell et al. [10] investigated application of a mask perceptron to the problem of reconfiguration for a "toy" SDH network. The work presented here expands on the work in that paper, with the idea of using a second stage mask perceptron in a recurrent mode to reduce link violations/underutilizations.

4 The Neural Controller Architecture

Instead of using the neural network to solve the optimization task, e.g. as a substitute for the simplex algorithm, it is taught to replicate the optimal LP solution provided by it.

We decided to use a two stage approach in our experiments. For the first stage we developed a feedforward network able to produce an approximate solution. More precisely, we used a collection of 2000 random examples for which the linear programming solution of capacity allocations had been pre-computed to develop a feedforward neural network able to approximate these solutions.

Then, for a new example, such an "approximate" neural network solution was rounded to the nearest integer, to satisfy constraint (i), and used to seed the second stage providing refinement and enforcement of constraint (ii).

For the second stage experiments we initially used a heuristic module based on the Gopal et al. approach [4]. The heuristic firstly reduces the capacities assigned to all paths which cause a physical capacity violation on any links, then subsequently increases the capacities assigned to paths across links which are being under-utilized.

We also investigated an approach for the second stage which uses another feedforward neural network. The teaching signal for the second stage neural network is the difference between the outputs from the first stage neural network alone and the combined first stage neural network/heuristic solution. This time the input data consisted of 13 link usage values (either a link violation or underutilization) and 42 values representing the amount of traffic lost per path for the current capacity allocations. The second stage neural network had 126 outputs representing the correction to the first stage neural network's outputs.

The second stage neural network is run in a recurrent mode, adjusting by small steps the currently allocated link capacities, thereby attempting to iteratively move closer to the combined neural-heuristic solution by removing the link violations and under-utilizations left behind by the first stage network.

The setup used during simulation is shown in Figure 2. For each particular instance tested the network was initialised with the solution from the first stage neural network. The offered traffic (demand) and the available maximum link capacities were used to determine the extent of any link violations or underutilizations as well as the amount of lost traffic (demand satisfaction). This data formed the initial input to the second stage network. The outputs of the neural network were then used to check the quality of the solution, and iteration continued until either no link violations occurred or a preset maximum number of iterations had been performed.

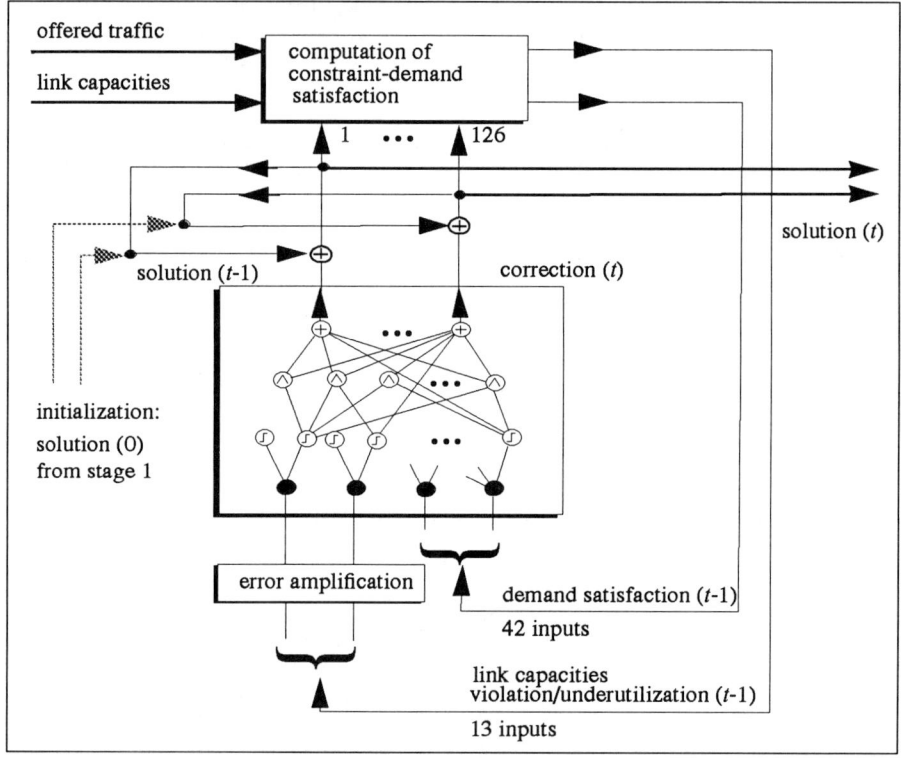

Figure 2. Recurrent Network used for second stage experiments.

When computing the constraint satisfaction the outputs of the neural network where combined and rounded to give integer link violations/under-utilizations. This means that in many cases small corrections made by the network are discarded and no further improvement is possible. In order to overcome this we introduced a scheme whereby errors (link violations/under-utilizations) are occasionally amplified to allow the network a chance of removing them. This scheme works as follows:

1) an instance is iterated until it has either no link violations or until 10 iterations have been performed;

2) if any link violations are still present then the size of the errors are multiplied by an amplification factor (>1);

3) a further maximum of 10 iterations are performed;

4) if subsequently link violations persist then the amplification factor is increased;

the procedure repeats until either all link violations are removed or the amplification factor reaches some fixed value.

5 Description of Neural Networks Generated

The first stage feedforward neural network is a mask perceptron [7], c.f. Figure 1 (b). Each input is passed through a number of arbitrarily chosen binary threshold units. There were a total of 738 thresholds for the 55 inputs. The task for the mask perceptron training algorithm [7] is to select a set of useful thresholds and hidden units out of thousands of possibilities and then to set weights to minimize the mean-square-error on the training set.

The mask perceptron training algorithm automatically selected 67 of these units for direct connection to the output units and a further 110 hidden units ("AND" gates) whose outputs are again connected to the neural network outputs, giving 22,302 connections in all.

Such neural networks are very rapid to simulate since the only operations required are comparison and additions.

For the recurrent network used in the second stage we also used a mask perceptron. The training algorithm used for the recurrent network was the same as for the first stage, in particular note that no gradual adaptation was employed. The inputs to the network are passed through 589 arbitrarily chosen binary threshold units. Of these 35 were selected by the training algorithm for direct connection to the output units via 4410 weighted links.

6 Results

The results are presented in Table 1 and Figure 3. The values in the table represent the traffic throughput of the SDH network, for the respective methods, as a percentage of the throughput determined by the LP solution. Both the neural networks were trained using 2000 instances and tested against a different set of 2000 instances. However for the recurrent network approximately 20% of these cases still had link violations after simulation so the values in Table 1 are for the 80% of valid solutions obtained from either the training or test set.

Solution type	Training	Test
Feedforward Net/Heuristic	99.08%	98.90%,
Feedforward Net/Recurrent Net	94.93% (*)	94.76%(*)
Gopal-S	96.38%	96.20%
Gopal-0	85.63%	85.43%

(*) these numbers are for the 1635 training and 1608 test instances (out of 2000) for which the recurrent network achieved a solution with no link violations after simulation as described in Section 3.

Table 1. Efficiency of solutions measured by average fraction of the 'optimal' throughput of the LP solution

As a comparison we implemented two solely heuristic algorithms. We refer to these as Gopal-S and Gopal-0. Both employ the same scheme described earlier for the Gopal et al. heuristic. The difference between the two is that Gopal-S uses the steady state solution as an initial starting point to determine virtual path capacities for a degraded network, whereas Gopal-0 starts from a point where all path capacities are initially set to zero.

Referring to Figure 3, *link capacity ratio* denotes the total link capacity of the degraded SDH network relative to the total link capacity of the steady state SDH network. A low value of link capacity ratio indicates a heavily degraded network. The *traffic throughput ratio* denotes the ratio between the throughput obtained by the method in question, and the throughput of the steady state solution.

Each dot in the graphs in Figure 3 represents one of the 2000 test set cases. It is clear from the figure that the neural network/heuristic approach is able to find better solutions for heavily degraded networks than each of the other approaches. Overall the clustering of dots for the neural network/heuristic combination is tighter (in the y-direction) and closer to 1.00 than for any of the other methods. The results for the recurrent network are very encouraging being qualitatively quite close to those for the Gopal-S algorithm.

All experiments were run on a SPARCStation 20. The neural network training took a few minutes. During simulation the neural network took an average of 9 ms per test case with a further 36.5 ms for the heuristic, for a total of 45.5 ms. On average the Gopal-S algorithm required 55.3 ms and the Gopal-0 algorithm required 43.7 ms per test case. The recurrent network solution required an average of 55.9 ms per test case. The optimal solutions calculated using the linear programming algorithm took between 2 and 60 seconds per case on a SPARCStation 10.

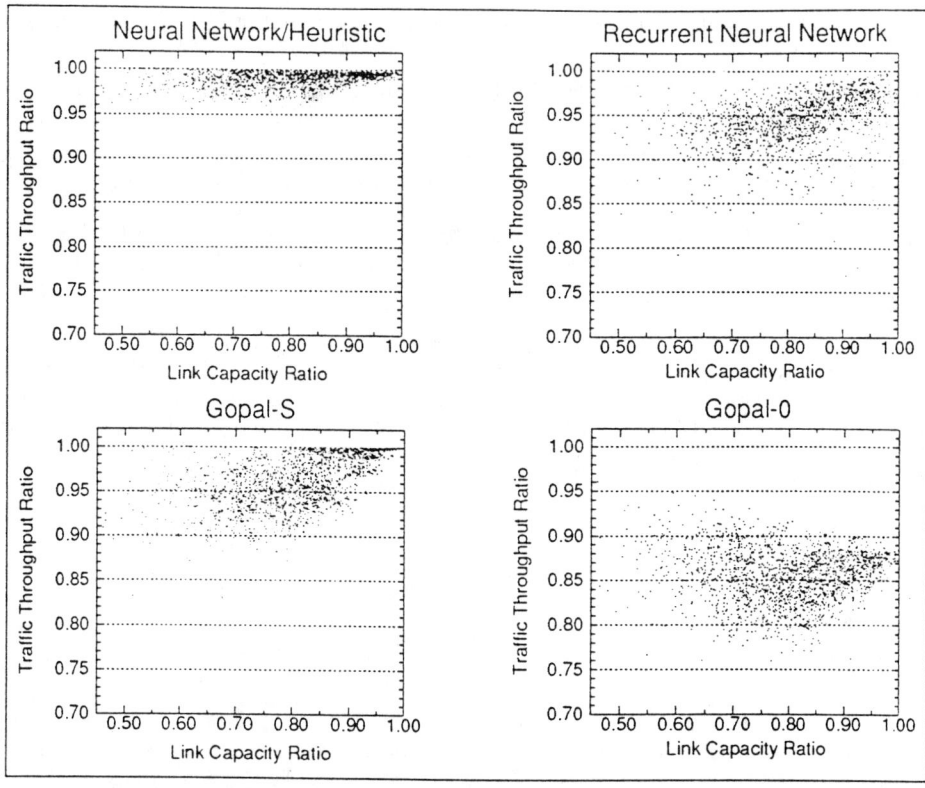

Figure 3. Experimental results for the Inter-City SDH network (Fig. 1) on the independent test set of 2000 random cases. On the x axis we have the ratio between the total link capacity of the degraded SDH network and the steady state SDH network. On the y axis we have the ratio between the throughput obtained by the method in question, and the throughput of the steady state solution.

Fig 3. (a) shows results for the neural network combined with the heuristic second stage. Fig 3. (b) shows results for the recurrent neural network second stage. Fig 3. (c) shows results for the heuristic only, initialised by the steady state (Gopal-S) and Fig 3. (d) has the results for the heuristic initialised by zero (Gopal-0).

7 Discussion and Conclusions

The combined neural network/heuristic approach performs very well across the whole range of degrees of SDH network degradation tested. The results obtained in this paper are consistent with those found in [10]. The average accuracy of ~99% and fast solution generation times (< 60 ms) highlight this approach as a possible candidate for implementation in a real system, especially when one considers the easily achievable speed increase available from parallelizing the neural network. The mask perceptron used in these experiments is well suited for simulation on a DSP (or other hardware): the operations required are only comparisons, calculation of logical "AND" and the summation of synaptic weights (no multiplications or any non-linear transformations are required).

The interesting thing to note is the relatively good performance of the recurrent network, namely that it is able to handle over 80% of cases achieving very good performance when compared against the neural network/heuristic solution (95% of the quality of the teacher). One thing to bear in mind is that the heuristic approach is highly tuned to producing a solution which satisfies the constraints, changing the capacity of one link at a time until the desired goal is achieved. On the other hand the recurrent network is generic and does not target the constraints in such a specific manner, making quite crude global changes in one hit, and yet is still able to achieve a reasonable level of performance. While the speed for the recurrent network was lower on average than for the heuristic solution in our experiments, this is not a major problem since many improvements are still possible and the results reported here are only preliminary, but serve to show what is possible. It is planned to continue the SDH network experiment in the future; with more investigation on the recurrent network for the second stage and also more complex SDH architectures.

Acknowledgments

The research and development reported here has the active support of various sections and individuals within the Telstra Research Laboratories (TRL), especially Dr. C. Leckie, Mr. P. Sember, Dr. M. Herzberg, Mr. A. Herschtal and Dr. L. Campbell. The permission of the Managing Director, Research and Information Technology, Telstra, to publish this paper is acknowledged.

The research and development reported here has the active support of various sections and individuals within the Telstra Research Laboratories (TRL), especially Dr. C. Leckie and Mr. P. Sember who were responsible for the creation and trialling of the programs designed to produce the testing and training data.

The SDH application was possible due to co-operation of a number of our colleagues in TRL, in particular Dr. L. Campbell (who suggested this particular application), Dr. M. Herzberg and Mr. A. Herschtal.

The permission of the Managing Director, Research and Information Technology, Telstra, to publish this paper is acknowledged.

References

[1] E. Booker, Cross-connect at a Crossroads, Telephony, Vol. 215, 1988, pp. 63-65.

[2] S. Bye, A Connectionist Approach to SDH Bandwidth Management, *Proceedings of the 19th International Conference on Artificial Neural Networks (ICANN-93)*, Brighton Conference Centre, UK, 1993, pp. 286-290.

[3] R. Gillan, Advanced Network Architectures Exploiting the Synchronous Digital Hierarchy, Telecommunications Journal of Australia 39, 1989, pp. 39-42.

[4] G. Gopal, C. Kim and A. Weinrib, Algorithms for Reconfigurable Networks, *Proceedings of the 13th International Teletraffic Congress (ITC-13)*, Copenhagen, Denmark, 1991, pp. 341-347.

[5] M. Herzberg, Network Bandwidth Management - A New Direction in Network Management, *Proceedings of the 6th Australian Teletraffic Research Seminar*, Wollongong, Australia, pp. 218-225.

[6] M. Herzberg and S. Bye, Bandwidth Management in Reconfigurable Networks, *Australian Telecommunications Research* 27, 1993, pp 57-70.

[7] A. Kowalczyk and H.L. Ferra, Developing Higher Order Networks with Empirically Selected Units, *IEEE Transactions on Neural Networks*, pp. 698-711, 1994.

[8] C. Leckie, A Connectionist Approach to Telecommunication Network Optimisation, in *Complex Systems: Mechanism of Adaptation*, R.J. Stonier and X.H. Yu, eds., IOS Press, Amsterdam, 1994.

[9] M. Schwartz, *Telecommunications Networks,* Addison-Wesley, Readings, Massachusetts, 1987.

[10] P. Campbell, H.L. Ferra, A. Kowalczyk, C. Leckie and P. Sember, Neural Networks in Real Time Decision Making, *Proceedings of the International Workshop on Applications of Neural Networks to Telecommunications 2 (IWANNT-95)*, Ed. J Alspector et. al. Lawrence Erlbaum Associates, New Jersey, 1995, pp. 273-280.

High-Speed Airborne Particle Monitoring Using Artificial Neural Networks

Alistair Ferguson
ERDC, Univ. of Hertfordshire
A.Ferguson@herts.ac.uk

Theo Sabisch
Dept. Electrical and Electronic Eng.
Univ. of Hertfordshire

Paul Kaye
ERDC, Univ. of Hertfordshire

Laurence C. Dixon
NOC, Univ. of Hertfordshire

Hamid Bolouri
ERDC, Univ. of Hertfordshire, Herts, AL10 9AB, UK

Abstract

Current environmental monitoring systems assume particles to be spherical, and do not attempt to classify them. A laser-based system developed at the University of Hertfordshire aims at classifying airborne particles through the generation of two-dimensional scattering profiles. The performances of template matching, and two types of neural network (HyperNet and *semi-linear units*) are compared for image classification. The neural network approach is shown to be capable of comparable recognition performance, while offering a number of advantages over template matching.

1 Introduction

Reliable identification of low concentrations of airborne particles requires high speed monitoring of large volumes of air, and incurs heavy computational overheads. An instrument to detect particle shape and size from spatial light scattering profiles has previously been described [6]. The system constrains individual particles to traverse a laser beam. Thus, spatial distributions of the light scattered by individual particles may be recorded as two dimensional grey-scale images.

Due to their highly distributed nature, Artificial Neural Networks (ANNs) offer the possibility of high-speed non-linear pattern classification. Their use in particulate classification has already been investigated. The work by Kohlus [7] used contour data extracted from microscopic images of particles, and so was not real-time. While using laser scattering data to allow real-time analysis, Bevan [2] used only three photomultipliers, from which very little shape information can be collected.

This paper demonstrates the plausibility of particle classification based on shape recognition using an ANN. While capable of similar recognition rates, the neural networks are shown to offer a number of advantages over template matching.

2 The HyperNet Architecture

HyperNet is the term used to denote the hardware model of a RAM-based sigma-pi neural architecture developed by Gurney [5]. The architecture is similar in nature to the pRAM of Gorse and Taylor (references in [4]). The amenability of these nodes to hardware realisation has been extensively investigated, leading to custom VLSI implementations of both nodes [3, 4]. Each HyperNet node is termed a multi-cube unit (MCU), and consists of a number of subunits, each with an arbitrary number of inputs. j references the nodes, with $i = 1, \ldots, I^j$ indexing the subunits. μ denotes the site addresses, and is the set of bit strings $\mu_1, \ldots, \mu_n$ where n denotes the number of inputs to the subunit. z_c refers to the cth real-valued input, with $z_c \in [0, 1]$ and $\hat{z}_c \equiv (1 - z_c)$. For each of the 2^n site store locations, two sets are defined: $c \in M^{ij}_{\mu 0}$ if $\mu_c = 0$; $c \in M^{ij}_{\mu 1}$ if $\mu_c = 1$. The access probability $P(\mu^{ij})$ for location μ in subunit i of hidden layer node j is therefore

$$P(\mu^{ij}) = \prod_{c \in M^{ij}_{\mu 0}} \hat{z}_c \prod_{c \in M^{ij}_{\mu 1}} z_c \qquad (1)$$

The activation (a^j) is formed by accumulating the proportional site values $(S_{\mu^{ij}})$ from every subunit. The activation is then passed through a sigmoidal transfer function to yield the node output (y^j).

$$a^j = \frac{1}{I^j} \sum_{i=1}^{I^j} \sum_{\mu^{ij}} S_{\mu^{ij}} P(\mu^{ij}) \qquad (2)$$

$$y^j = \sigma(a^j) = \frac{1}{1 + e^{a^j/\rho}} \qquad (3)$$

where ρ is a positive parameter determining the steepness of the sigmoidal curve. By combining equations (1) and (2), it becomes apparent that the node is a *higher-order* or *sigma-pi* node [9]. A wide variety of learning algorithms have been tailored for these nodes, notably reward-penalty and back-propagation [5].

3 Description of the Particle Monitoring System

The instrument draws air through the laser scattering chamber at approximately 1.5 min^{-1}, and is constrained to a column of approximately 0.8mm diameter at the intersection with the laser beam. Light scattered into angles between 30° and 141° to the beam direction is reflected through the optics and onto the photocathode of an intensified CCD (charge-coupled device), thus giving rise to the scattering profile. The imaging device used has a pixel resolution of 385 × 288, which is quantised into 256^2 8-bit pixels by the frame grabbing processor card of the host computer.

Data was collected on eight particle types, namely: long and short caffeine fibres; 3μm and 12μm micro-machined silicon dioxide fibres; copper flakes (2–5μm in length and 0.1μm thick); 3μm and 4.3μm polystyrene spheres; and salt crystals. An exemplar profile for each class is given in figure 1. Almost all the image types are highly variable. In particular, the scattering profile obtained for a fibrous particle is affected by its orientation as it passes through the laser beam. The scattering profiles are intrinsically centred, with the scaling giving important information regarding the size of the particle. The experiments reported here use 100 example scattering profiles for each of the eight particle classes. For each class, 50 randomly selected images were used to construct the templates or train the neural network (training set), and the remainder used to test the performance of the pattern classifiers.

4 Experimental Results

The performance of template matching is compared to both HyperNet and networks of semi-linear units. In all experiments, high-speed classification is emphasised by

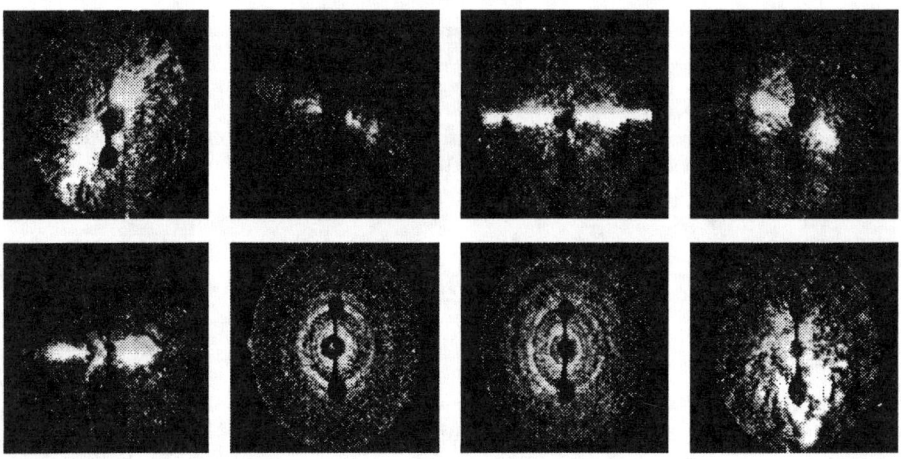

Figure 1: Exemplar Image Profile For Each Of The Eight Benchmark Classes

avoiding image preprocessing operations such as transformation to the frequency domain, histogram equalisation, and other filtering operations. Furthermore, all experiments use the scatter profile image as input, and include no other information.

The current monitoring system produces a 256^2 8-bit pixel image. The sensitivity of the camera is such that a single pixel can represent the registration of a single photon of light. Two possible methods of reducing computation, implementable through the use of a cheaper, less sensitive camera were investigated. The first grouped neighbouring pixels to form a single average intensity value. The neighbourhood size was restricted to powers of two, producing images ranging in size from 256^2 to 4^2 pixels. The second banded grey levels into groups, again in powers of two. Each pixel could therefore range from eight bits down to one.

4.1 Template Matching Results

The construction of reference templates is crucial to successful classification. Two approaches to template construction were investigated

① Single reference image for each class. Various techniques were applied ranging from individual images, to mode, median, and mean averaged templates. Mean averaged templates were found to lead to the highest classification rates. In this approach, each pixel location in the template takes on the averaged value of that location across the 50 training images.

② Multiple templates per class. A K-means clustering algorithm [1] was used to identify clusters of highly correlated images within each class. The initial cluster centres were hand selected. The maximum number of clusters within each class was limited to six. For each cluster, the reference template was constructed using the mean averaging approach above.

Tables 1 and 2 summarise the recognition rates achieved using single, and multiple mean averaged templates for each particle class. In both cases, the best average recognition rate using this approach was gained with 128^2 3-bit pixel images. With a single template this lead to a recognition rate of 78.2%, increasing to 85.2% for multiple templates. However, the results for both 16^2 and 8^2 pixel images are reasonable approximations of the best performance, and represent an acceptable trade-off between computational cost and performance. With few exceptions, multiple templates per class led to higher recognition rates than for the corresponding single template results. This is attributable to the variability of the particles within a class. As expected, the effect of grey level quantisation is inversely proportional to that of local averaging.

In order to evaluate the efficiency of the template construction methods, every image in the training set was used as a reference template. 256^2 8-bit, 128^2 3-bit, and 64^2 2-bit pixel images were used for these experiments. However, the recognition rate did not exceed 85%, demonstrating the success of the template generation schemes previously employed.

Table 1: Single Template Per Class % Recognition Rates

grey levels	image size						
	256^2	128^2	64^2	32^2	16^2	8^2	4^2
256	73.5	75.0	74.7	74.7	74.7	75.0	67.2
128	73.5	75.0	74.7	74.7	74.5	75.0	**68.5**
64	73.0	75.0	74.5	74.5	74.2	74.7	66.2
32	73.0	74.7	75.2	75.5	74.7	74.2	66.5
16	74.0	76.0	76.7	76.0	75.0	**75.5**	56.0
8	**75.5**	**78.2**	**77.5**	**77.5**	**76.0**	73.7	38.7
4	68.4	69.7	71.0	70.7	69.7	58.5	18.7
2	69.7	68.7	65.5	66.2	46.2	23.0	16.6

Table 2: Multiple Templates Per Class % Recognition Rates

grey levels	image size						
	256^2	128^2	64^2	32^2	16^2	8^2	4^2
256	78.0	80.0	80.2	80.5	79.0	76.7	**70.2**
128	78.5	80.2	80.5	80.5	79.0	77.0	69.7
64	78.7	80.2	80.2	80.5	79.2	76.0	69.2
32	78.2	81.2	81.7	80.0	78.7	76.7	67.7
16	80.2	83.5	83.0	81.2	79.5	78.5	56.0
8	**82.2**	**85.2**	**84.5**	**84.7**	**81.0**	**80.0**	43.5
4	72.7	74.5	72.2	72.2	69.5	61.2	39.2
2	69.7	70.2	70.7	62.7	51.7	51.7	0.03

4.2 Neural Network Results

A fully connected three layer feed-forward network was used in all experiments. The number of hidden layer neurons was equal to the square root of the number of pixels. The target patterns were chosen to minimise the number of output layer nodes, while ensuring an equitable distribution of zeros and ones. Six output layer neurons were used to give a minimum Hamming distance of two between target patterns. The classification of a pattern was judged to be the particle class whose target pattern was closest (lowest difference error). The HyperNet architecture was trained using steepest descent, though the line search was hardware based and inexact. The semi-linear network was trained using a variety of back-propagation type algorithms, with the best results obtained reported. Both networks were randomly initialised. Due to the enormous training overhead, only 16^2 and 8^2 pixel images were tried. The recognition rates achieved are given in table 3.

Both neural networks are significantly better than the single, and some of the multiple template matching results. With optimisation of the network structures, it is likely that the ANNs could exceed the performance of multiple templates.

Table 3: Neural Network % Recognition Rates

Classifier	Quantisation Levels			
	16^2 4 bit	16^2 3-bit	8^2 4-bit	8^2 3-bit
HyperNet	83.8	82.3	83.0	76.8
Semi-linear	84.5	86.3	77.8	76.0

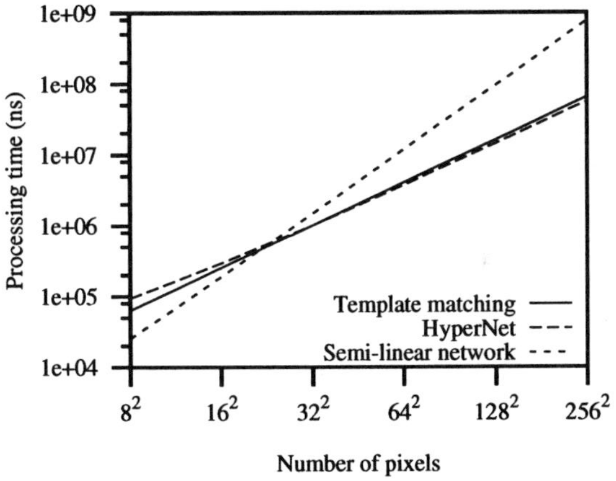

Figure 2: Hardware classification speeds for a single pattern against image size

5 Speed Considerations

Single processor, pipelined hardware implementations of the three classification techniques have been considered. A fast (45ns) multiply-accumulate chip (Logic Devices Ltd, LMA2010) was utilised for semi-linear units. Both template matching and HyperNet were implemented using the Logic Devices LGC381 ALU (26ns per accumulate). The cost of these devices is approximately the same (£10–20). The HyperNet implementation uses a bit-stream approach to eliminate the probability multiplications [8], with a stream length of 256 bits. Figure 2 plots single pattern processing time for each classifier against image size.

For small image resolutions, the semi-linear network offers the best performance, being almost three times faster than template matching. However, template matching and HyperNet yield faster performance at higher image resolutions. At the optimum (indicated by template matching results (§4.1); 128^2 pixels), HyperNet is almost seven times faster than the comparable implementation of semi-linear units. While the hardware performance of template matching is similar to HyperNet, it suffers from a number of disadvantages to which the neural approaches are immune

① Recognition rate is dependent on the choice of reference images.

② Multiple reference images must be used to achieve good recognition rates which drastically increases the amount of computation required.

③ New reference images must be found whenever a new class is introduced.

④ Difficult to make behaviour adaptive, ie. respond to changing conditions.

6 Conclusions

The feasibility of constructing an airborne particle monitoring system capable of reliable particle identification at high speeds has been demonstrated. Template matching requires multiple reference images and is cumbersome to develop. The neural networks offer easier training procedures and equivalent recognition rates. In addition, HyperNet has the advantage of high speed operation at large image sizes.

Acknowledgements

The authors would like to thank Dr. Eric Dykes and Dr. Edwin Hirst at the University of Hertfordshire, Dr. Kevin Gurney at Brunel University, and the EPSRC and the Royal Society for financial support.

References

[1] Stephen Banks. *Signal Processing, Image Processing, and Pattern Recognition.* Prentice Hall, 1990.

[2] A V Bevan et al. The application of neural networks to particle shape classification. *Journal of Aerosol Science*, 23(Suppl. 1):329–332, 1992.

[3] Hamid Bolouri et al. Design, manufacture, and evaluation of a scalable high-performance neural system. *Electronics Letters*, 30(5):426–427, 3 March 1994.

[4] T G Clarkson et al. The pRAM: An adaptive VLSI chip. *IEEE Transactions on Neural Networks*, 4(3):408–412, May 1993.

[5] Kevin N Gurney. *Learning in networks of structured hypercubes.* PhD thesis, Department of Electrical Engineering, UK, 1995.

[6] Paul H Kaye et al. Airborne particle shape and size classification from spatial light scattering profiles. *Journal of Aerosol Science*, 23(6):597–611, 1992.

[7] R Kohlus et al. Particle shape analysis as an example of knowledge extraction by neural nets. *Part. Part. Syst. Charact.*, 10:275–278, 1993.

[8] Paul Morgan et al. Hardware implementation of a real-valued sigma-pi network. In *Artificial Neural Networks 5*, volume 2, pages 351–356, North-Holland, 1995.

[9] David E Rumelhart et al. *Parallel Distributed Processing: Explorations in the Macrostructure of Cognition*, volume 1. MIT Press, 1986.

PART IX
CONTROL

A Dynamical Systems Approach for a Learnable Autonomous Robot

Jun Tani and Naohiro Fukumura
Sony Computer Science Laboratory Inc.
Takanawa Muse Building, 3-14-13 Higashi-gotanda, Shinagawa-ku,Tokyo, 141 JAPAN

Abstract

This paper discusses how a robot can learn goal-directed navigation tasks using local sensory inputs. The emphasis is that such learning tasks could be formulated as an embedding problem of dynamical systems: desired trajectories in a task space should be embedded into an adequate sensory-based internal state space so that an unique mapping from the internal state space to the motor command could be established. The paper shows that a recurrent neural network suffices in self-organizing such an adequate internal state space from the temporal sensory input. In our experiments, using a real robot with a laser range sensor, the robot navigated robustly by achieving dynamical coherence with the environment. It was also shown that such coherence becomes structurally stable as the global attractor is self-organized in the coupling of the internal and the environmental dynamics.

1 Introduction

Conventionally, robot navigation problems have been formulated assuming a global view of the world. Given a detailed map of the workspace, described in a global coordinate system, the robot navigates to the specified goal by following this map. However, in situations where robots have to acquire navigational knowledge based on their own behaviors, it is important to describe the problems from the internal views of the robots.

[Kuipers 87], [Mataric 92] and others have developed an approach based on landmark detection. The robot acquires a graph representation of landmark types as a topological modeling of the environment through its exploratory travels using the local sensory inputs. In navigation, the robot can identify its topological position by anticipating the landmark types in the graph representation obtained. It is, however, considered that this navigation strategy might be susceptible to erroneous landmark-matching. If the robot is once lost by such a catastrophe, its recoverance of the positioning might be difficult. We need certain mechanisms by which the robot can recover autonomously from such failures.

We study the above problems by using the dynamical systems approach, expecting that this approach would provide an effective representational and computational framework. The approach focuses on the fundamental dynamical structure that arises from coupling the internal and the environmental dynamics [Beer 95]. Here, the objective of learning is to adapt the internal dynamical function such that the resultant dynamical structure might generate the desired system behavior. The system's performance becomes structurally stable if the dynamical structure maintains a sufficiently large basin of attraction against possible perturbations.

We verify our claims through the implementation of our scheme on *YAMABICO* mobile robot equipped with a laser range sensor. The robot conducts navigational tasks under the following assumptions and conditions. (1) The robot cannot access its global position, but it navigates depending on its local sensory (range image) input. (2) There is no explicit landmarks accessible to the robot in the adopted workspace. (3) The robot learns tasks of *cyclic routing* by following guidance of a trainer. (4) The navigation should be robust enough against possible noise in the environment.

2 NAVIGATION ARCHITECTURE

The *YAMABICO* mobile robot [Yuta and Iijima 90] was used as an experimental platform. The robot can obtain range images by a range finder consisting of laser projectors and three CCD cameras. The ranges for 24 directions, covering a 160 degree arc in front of the robot, are measured every 150 milliseconds. In our formulation, maneuvering commands are generated as the output of a composite system consisting of two levels [Tani and Fukumura 94]. The control level generates a collision-free, smooth trajectory using the range image, while the navigation level directs the control level in a macroscopic sense, responding to the sequential branching that appears in the sensory flows. The control level is fixed; the navigation level, on the other hand, can be adapted through learning. Firstly, let us describe the control level. The robot can sense the forward range readings of the surrounding environment, given in robot-centered polar coordinates by $r_i\,(1 \leq i \leq N)$. The angular range profile R_i is obtained by smoothing the original range readings through applying an appropriate Gaussian filter. The maneuvering focus of the robot is the maximum (the angular direction of the largest range) in this range profile. The robot proceeds towards the maximum of the profile (an open space in the environment). The navigation level focuses on the topological changes in the range profile as the robot moves. As the robot moves through a given workspace, the profile gradually changes until another local peak appears when the robot reaches a branching point. At this moment of branching the navigation level decides whether to transfer the focus to the new local peak or to remain with the current one. It is noted that this branching could be quite undeterministic one if applied to rugged obstacle environment. The robot is likely to fail to detect branching points frequently in such environment.

The navigation level determines the branching by utilizing the range image obtained at branch points. Since the pertinent information in the range profile at a given moment is assumed to be only a small fraction of the total, we employ a vector quantization technique, known as the Kohonen network [Kohonen 82], so that the information in the profile may be compressed into specific lower-dimensional data. The Kohonen network employed here consists of an l-dimensional lattice with m nodes along each dimension (l=3 and m=6 for the experiments with *YAMABICO*). The range image consisting of 24 values is input to the lattice, then the most

A Dynamical Systems Approach for a Learnable Autonomous Robot

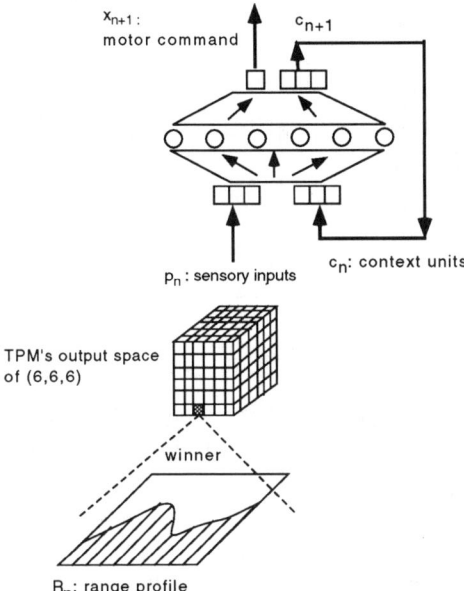

Figure 1: Neural architecture for skill-based learning.

highly activated unit in the lattice, the "winner" unit, is found. The address of the winner unit in the lattice denotes the output vector of the network. Therefore, the navigation level receives the sensory input compressed into three dimensional data. The next section will describe how the robot can generate right branching sequences upon receiving the compressed range image.

3 Formulation

3.1 Learning state-action map

The neural adaptation schemes are applied to the navigation level so that it can generate an adequate state-action map for a given task. Although some might consider that such map can be represented by using a layered feed-forward network with the inputs of the sensory image and the outputs of the motor command, this is not always true. The local sensory input does not always correspond uniquely to the true state of the robot (the sensory inputs could be the same for different robot positions). Therefore, there exists an ambiguity in determining the motor command solely from sensory inputs. This is a typical example of so-called non-Markovian problems which have been discussed by Lin and Mitchell [Lin and Mitchell 92]. In order to solve this ambiguity, a representation of contexts which are memories of past sensory sequences is required. For this purpose, a recurrent neural network (RNN) [Elman 90] was employed since its recurrent context states could represent the memory of past sequences. The employed neural architecture is shown in Figure. 1. The sensory input p_n and the context units c_n determine the appropriate motor command x_{n+1}. The motor command x_n takes a binary value of 0 (staying at the current branch) or 1 (a transit to a new branch). The RNN learning of sensory-motor (p_n, x_{n+1}) sequences, sampled through the supervised training, can build the desired state-action map by self-organizing adequate internal representation in time.

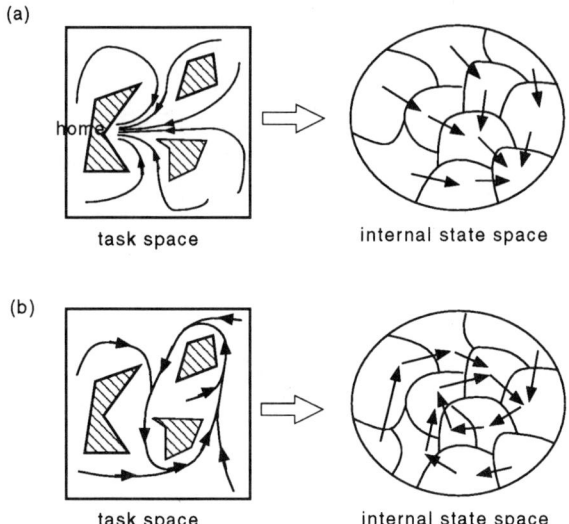

Figure 2: The desired trajectories in the task space and its mapping to the internal state space.

3.2 Embedding problem

The objective of the neural learning is to embed a task into certain global attractor dynamics which are generated from the coupling of the internal neural function and the environment. Figure 2 illustrates this idea. We define the internal state of the robot by the state of the RNN. The internal dynamics, which are coupled with the environmental dynamics through the sensory-motor loop, evolve as the robot travels in the task space. We assume that the desired vector field in the task space forms a global attractor, such as a fixed point for a homing task or limit cycling for a cyclic routing task. All that the robot has to do is to follow this vector flow by means of its internal state-action map. This requires a condition: the vector field in the internal state space should be self-organized as being topologically equivalent to that in the task space in order that the internal state determine the action (motor command) uniquely. This is the embedding problem from the task space to the internal state space, and RNN learning can attain this, using various training trajectories. This analysis conjectured that the trajectories in the task space can always converge into the desired one as long as the task is embedded into the global attractor in the internal state space.

4 Experiment

4.1 Task and training procedure

Figure 3 shows an example of the navigation task, (which is adopted for the physical experiment in a later section). The task is for the robot to repeat looping of a figure of '8' and '0' in sequence. The task is not trivial because at the branching position A the robot has to decide whether to go '8' or '0' depending on its memory of the last sequence.

The robot learns this navigation task through supervision by a trainer. The trainer repeatedly guides the robot to the desired loop from a set of arbitrarily selected

A Dynamical Systems Approach for a Learnable Autonomous Robot

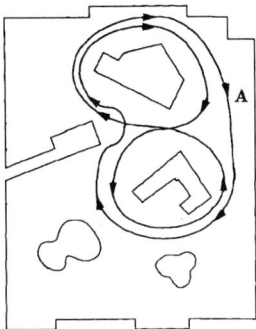

Figure 3: Cyclic routing task, in which *YAMABICO* has to trace a figure of eight followed by a single loop.

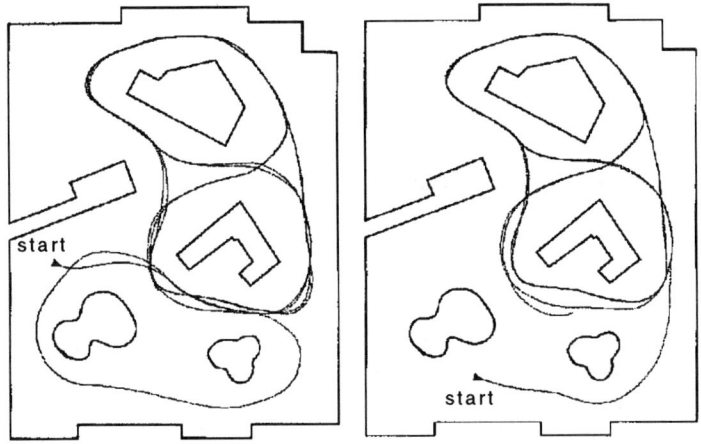

Figure 4: Trace of test travels for cyclic routing.

initial locations. (The training was conducted with starting the robot from 10 arbitrarily selected initial locations in the workspace.) In actual training, the robot moves by the navigation of the control level and stops at each branching point, where the branching direction is taught by the trainer. The sequence of range images and teaching branching commands at those bifurcation points are fed into the neural architecture as training data. The objective of training RNN is to find the optimal weight matrix that minimizes the mean square error of the training output (branching decision) sequences associating with sensory inputs (outputs of Kohonen network). The weight matrix can be obtained through an iterative calculation of back-propagation through time (BPTT) [Rumelhart et al. 86].

4.2 Results

After the training, we examined how the robot achieves the trained task. The robot was started from arbitrary initial positions for this test. Fig. 4 shows example test travels. The result showed that the robot always converged to the desired loop regardless of its starting position. The time required to converge, however, took a

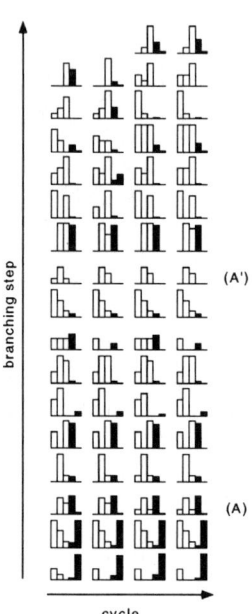

Figure 5: The sequence of activations in input and context units during the cycling travel.

certain period that depended on the case. The RNN initially could not function correctly because of the arbitrary initial setting of the context units. However, while the robot wandered around the workspace, the RNN became *situated* (recovered the context) as it encountered pre-learned sensory sequences. Thereafter, its navigation converged to the cycling loop.

Even after convergence, the robot could, by chance, leave the loop, under the influence of noise. However, the robot always came back to the loop after a while. These observations indicate that the robot learned the objective navigational task as embedded in a global attractor of limit cycling.

It is interesting to examine how the task is encoded in the internal dynamics of the RNN. We investigated the activation patterns of RNN after its convergence into the loop. The results are shown in Fig. 5. The input and context units at each branching point are shown as three white and two black bars, respectively. One cycle (the completion of two routes of '0' and '8') are aligned vertically as one column. The figure shows those of four continuous cycles. It can be seen that robot navigation is exposed to much noise; the sensing input vector becomes unstable at particular locations, and the number of branchings in one cycle is not constant (i.e. some branching points are undeterministic). The rows labeled as (A) and (A') are branches to the routes of '0' and '8', respectively. In this point, the sensory input receives noisy chattering of different patterns independent of (A) or (A'). The context units, on the other hand, is completely identifiable between (A) and (A'), which shows that the task sequence between two routes (a single loop and an eight) is rigidly encoded internally, even in a noisy environment. In further experiments in more rugged obstacle environments, we found that this sort of structural stability could not be always assured. When the undeterministicity in the branching exceeds a certain limit, the desired dynamical structure cannot be preserved.

5 Summary and Discussion

The navigation learning problem was formulated from the dynamical systems perspective. Our experimental results showed that the robot can learn the goal-directed navigation by embedding the desired task trajectories in the internal state space through the RNN training. It was also shown that the robot achieves the navigational tasks in terms of convergence of attractor dynamics which emerge in the coupling of the internal and the environmental dynamics. Since the dynamical coherence arisen in this coupling leads to the robust navigation of the robot, the intrinsic mechanism presented here is characterized by the term "autonomy".

Finally, it is interesting to study how robots can obtain analogical models of the environment rather than state-action maps for adapting to flexibly changed goals. We discuss such formulation based on the dynamical systems approach elsewhere [Tani 96].

References

[Beer 95] R.D. Beer. A dynamical systems perspective on agent-environment interaction. *Artificial Intelligence*, Vol. 72, No. 1, pp.173–215, 1995.

[Elman 90] J.L. Elman. Finding structure in time. *Cognitive Science*, Vol. 14, pp.179–211, 1990.

[Kohonen 82] T. Kohonen. Self-Organized Formation of Topographically Correct Feature Maps. *Biological Cybernetics*, Vol. 43, pp.59–69, 1982.

[Kuipers 87] B. Kuipers. A Qualitative Approach to Robot Exploration and Map Learning. In *AAAI Workshop Spatial Reasoning and Multi-Sensor Fusion (Chicago)*, 1987.

[Lin and Mitchell 92] L.-J. Lin and T.M. Mitchell. Reinforcement learning with hidden states. In *Proc. of the Second Int. Conf. on Simulation of Adaptive Behavior*, pp. 271–280, 1992.

[Mataric 92] M. Mataric. Integration of Representation into Goal-driven Behavior-based Robot. *IEEE Trans. Robotics and Automation*, Vol. 8, pp.304–312, 1992.

[Rumelhart et al. 86] D.E. Rumelhart, G.E. Hinton, and R.J. Williams. Learning Internal Representations by Error Propagation. In *Parallel Distributed Processing*. MIT Press, 1986.

[Tani 96] J. Tani. Model-Based Learning for Mobile Robot Navigation from the Dynamical Systems Perspective. *IEEE Trans. System, Man and Cybernetics Part B, Special issue on robot learning*, Vol. 26, No. 3, 1996.

[Tani and Fukumura 94] J. Tani and N. Fukumura. Learning goal-directed sensory-based navigation of a mobile robot. *Neural Networks*, Vol. 7, No. 3, pp.553–563, 1994.

[Yuta and Iijima 90] S. Yuta and J. Iijima. State Information Panel for Inter-Processor Communication in an Autonomous Mobile Robot Controller. In *proc. of IROS'90*, 1990.

Parallel Optimization of Motion Controllers via Policy Iteration

J. A. Coelho Jr., R. Sitaraman, and R. A. Grupen
Department of Computer Science
University of Massachusetts, Amherst, 01003

Abstract

This paper describes a policy iteration algorithm for optimizing the performance of a harmonic function-based controller with respect to a user-defined index. Value functions are represented as potential distributions over the problem domain, being control policies represented as gradient fields over the same domain. All intermediate policies are intrinsically safe, i.e. collisions are not promoted during the adaptation process. The algorithm has efficient implementation in parallel SIMD architectures. One potential application – travel distance minimization – illustrates its usefulness.

1 INTRODUCTION

Harmonic functions have been proposed as a uniform framework for the solution of several versions of the motion planning problem. Connolly and Grupen [Connolly and Grupen, 1993] have demonstrated how harmonic functions can be used to construct smooth, complete artificial potentials with no local minima. In addition, these potentials meet the criteria established in [Rimon and Koditschek, 1990] for *navigation functions*. This implies that the gradient of harmonic functions yields smooth ("realizable") motion controllers.

By construction, harmonic function-based motion controllers will always command the robot from any initial configuration to a goal configuration. The intermediate configurations adopted by the robot are determined by the boundary constraints and conductance properties set for the domain. Therefore, it is possible to tune both factors so as to extremize user-specified performance indices (e.g. travel time or energy) without affecting controller completeness.

Based on this idea, Singh et al. [Singh et al., 1994] devised a policy iteration method for combining two harmonic function-based control policies into a controller that minimized travel time on a given environment. The two initial control policies were derived from solutions to two distinct boundary constraints (Neumann and Dirichlet constraints). The *policy space* spawned by the two control policies was parameterized by a mixing coefficient, that ultimately determined the obstacle avoidance behavior adopted by the robot. The resulting controller preserved obstacle avoidance, ensuring safety at every iteration of the learning procedure.

This paper addresses the question of how to adjust the conductance properties associated with the problem domain Ω, such as to extremize an user-specified performance index. Initially, conductance properties are homogeneous across Ω, and the resulting controller is optimal in the sense that it minimizes collision probabilities at every step [Connolly, 1994][1]. The method proposed is a policy iteration algorithm, in which the policy space is parameterized by the set of node conductances.

2 PROBLEM CHARACTERIZATION

The problem consists in constructing a path controller $\vec{\pi}_0$ that maximizes an integral performance index $\mathcal{P}$ defined over the set of all possible paths on a lattice for a closed domain $\Omega \subset \Re^n$, subjected to boundary constraints. The controller $\vec{\pi}_0$ is responsible for generating the sequence of configurations from an initial configuration q_0 on the lattice to the goal configuration q_G, therefore determining the performance index $\mathcal{P}$. In formal terms, the performance index $\mathcal{P}$ can be defined as follows:

Def. 1 *Performance index $\mathcal{P}$:*

$$\mathcal{P} = \sum_q \mathcal{P}_{q,\vec{\pi}} \quad \text{for all } q \in L(\Omega), \text{ where } \quad \mathcal{P}_{q_0,\vec{\pi}} = \sum_{q=q_0}^{q_G} f(q).$$

$L(\Omega)$ *is a lattice over the domain Ω, q_0 denotes an arbitrary configuration on $L(\Omega)$, q_G is the goal configuration, and $f(q)$ is a function of the configuration q.*

For example, one can define $f(q)$ to be the available joint range associated with the configuration q of a manipulator; in this case, $\mathcal{P}$ would be measuring the available joint range associated with all paths generated within a given domain.

2.1 DERIVATION OF REFERENCE CONTROLLER

The derivation of $\vec{\pi}_0$ is very laborious, requiring the exploration of the set of all possible paths. Out of this set, one is primarily interested in the subset of smooth paths. We propose to solve a simpler problem, in which the derived controller $\vec{\pi}$ is a numerical approximation to the optimal controller $\vec{\pi}_0$, and (1) generates smooth paths, (2) is admissible, and (3) locally maximizes $\mathcal{P}$. To guarantee (1) and (2), it is assumed that the control actions of $\vec{\pi}$ are proportional to the gradient of a harmonic function ϕ, represented as the voltage distribution across a resistive lattice that tessellates the domain Ω. The condition (3) is achieved through incremental changes in the set G of internodal conductances; such changes maximize $\mathcal{P}$ locally.

Necessary condition for optimality: Note that $\mathcal{P}_{q_0,\vec{\pi}}$ defines a scalar field over $L(\Omega)$. It is assumed that there exists a well-defined neighborhood $\mathcal{N}(q)$ for node q; in fact, it is assumed that every node q has two neighbors across each dimension. Therefore, it is possible to compute the gradient over the scalar field $\mathcal{P}_{q_0,\vec{\pi}}$ by locally approximating its rate of change across all dimensions. The gradient $\vec{\nabla} \mathcal{P}_{q_0}$ defines

---

[1]This is exactly the control policy derived by the TD(0) reinforcement learning method, for the particular case of an agent travelling in a grid world with absorbing obstacle and goal states, and being rewarded only for getting to the goal states (see [Connolly, 1994]).

a *reference controller*; in the optimal situation, the actions of the controller $\vec{\pi}$ will parallel the actions of the reference controller. One can now formulate a policy iteration algorithm for the synthesis of the reference controller:

1. Compute $\vec{\pi} = -\vec{\nabla}\phi$, given conductances G;
2. Evaluate $\vec{\nabla}\mathcal{P}_q$:
   – for each cell, compute $\mathcal{P}_{q,\vec{\phi}}$.
   – for each cell, compute $\vec{\nabla}\mathcal{P}_q$.
3. Change G incrementally, minimizing the approx. error $\epsilon = f(\vec{\pi}, \vec{\nabla}\mathcal{P}_q)$;
4. If ϵ is below a threshold ϵ^0, stop. Otherwise, return to (1).

On convergence, the policy iteration algorithm will have derived a control policy that maximizes $\mathcal{P}$ globally, and is capable of generating smooth paths to the goal configuration. The key step on the algorithm is step (3), or how to reduce the current approximation error by changing the conductances G.

3 APPROXIMATION ALGORITHM

Given a set of internodal conductances, the approximation error ϵ is defined as

$$\epsilon = -\sum_{q \in L(\Omega)} \cos(\vec{\pi}, \vec{\nabla}\mathcal{P}) \qquad (1)$$

or the sum over $L(\Omega)$ of the cosine of the angle between vectors $\vec{\pi}$ and $\vec{\nabla}\mathcal{P}$. The approximation error ϵ is therefore a function of the set G of internodal conductances.

There exist $\Theta(nd^n)$ conductances in a n-dimensional grid, where d is the discretization adopted for each dimension. Discrete search methods for the set of conductance values that minimizes ϵ are ruled out by the cardinality of the search space: $\Theta(k^{nd^n})$, if k is the number of distinct values each conductance can assume. We will represent conductances as real values and use gradient descent to minimize ϵ, according to the approximation algorithm below:

1. Evaluate the approximation error ϵ;
2. Compute the gradient $\vec{\nabla}\epsilon = \frac{\partial \epsilon}{\partial G}$;
3. Update conductances, making $G = G - \alpha \vec{\nabla}\epsilon$;
4. Normalize conductances, such that minimum conductance $g_{min} = 1$;

Step (4) guarantees that every conductance $g \in G$ will be strictly positive. The conductances in a resistive grid can be normalized without constraining the voltage distribution across it, due to the linear nature of the underlying circuit. The complexity of the approximation algorithm is dominated by the computation of the gradient $\vec{\nabla}\epsilon(G)$. Each component of the vector $\vec{\nabla}\epsilon(G)$ can be expressed as

$$\frac{\partial \epsilon}{\partial g_i} = -\sum_{q \in L(\Omega)} \frac{\partial \cos(\vec{\pi}_q, \vec{\nabla}\mathcal{P}_q)}{\partial g_i}. \qquad (2)$$

By assumption, $\vec{\pi}$ is itself the gradient of a harmonic function ϕ that describes the voltage distribution across a resistive lattice. Therefore, the calculation of $\frac{\partial \epsilon}{\partial g_i}$ involves the evaluation of $\frac{\partial \phi_q}{\partial g_i}$ over all domain $L(\Omega)$, or how the voltage ϕ_q is affected by changes in a certain conductance g_i.

For n-dimensional grids, $\frac{\partial \phi}{\partial g_i}$ is a matrix with d^n rows and $\Theta(nd^n)$ columns. We posit that the computation of every element of $\frac{\partial \phi}{\partial g_i}$ is unnecessary: the effects of changing

Parallel Optimization of Motion Controllers via Policy Iteration

g_i will be more pronounced in a certain grid neighborhood of it, and essentially negligible for nodes beyond that neighborhood. Furthermore, this simplification allows for breaking up the original problem into smaller, independent sub-problems suitable to simultaneous solution in parallel architectures.

3.1 THE LOCALITY ASSUMPTION

The first simplifying assumption considered in this work establishes bounds on the neighborhood affected by changes on conductances at node i; specifically, we will assume that changes in elements of g_i affect only the voltage at nodes in $\mathcal{N}(i)$, being $\mathcal{N}(i)$ the set composed of node i and its direct neighbors. See [Coelho Jr. et al., 1995] for a discussion on the validity of this assumption. In particular, it is demonstrated that the effects of changing one conductance decay exponentially with grid distance, for infinite 2D grids. Local changes in resistive grids with higher dimensionality will be confined to even smaller neighborhoods.

The locality assumption simplifies the calculation of $\frac{\partial \epsilon}{\partial g_i}$ to

$$\frac{\partial \epsilon}{\partial g_i} = -\sum_{q \in \mathcal{N}(i)} \frac{\partial \cos(\vec{\pi}, \vec{\nabla}\mathcal{P})}{\partial g_i} = -\sum_{q \in \mathcal{N}(i)} \frac{\partial}{\partial g_i}\left[\frac{\vec{\pi} \cdot \vec{\nabla}\mathcal{P}}{|\vec{\pi}||\vec{\nabla}\mathcal{P}|}\right].$$

But

$$\frac{\partial}{\partial g_i}\left[\frac{\vec{\pi} \cdot \vec{\nabla}\mathcal{P}}{|\vec{\pi}||\vec{\nabla}\mathcal{P}|}\right] = \frac{1}{|\vec{\pi}||\vec{\nabla}\mathcal{P}|}\left[\frac{\partial \vec{\pi}}{\partial g_i} \cdot \vec{\nabla}\mathcal{P} - \frac{\vec{\pi} \cdot \vec{\nabla}\mathcal{P}}{|\vec{\pi}|^2}\left(\frac{\partial \vec{\pi}}{\partial g_i} \cdot \vec{\pi}\right)\right].$$

Note that in the derivation above it is assumed that changes in G affects primarily the control policy $\vec{\pi}$, leaving $\vec{\nabla}\mathcal{P}$ relatively unaffected, at least in a first order approximation.

Given that $\vec{\pi} = -\vec{\nabla}\phi$, it follows that the component π_j at node q can be approximated by the change of potential across the dimension j, as measured by the potential on the corresponding neighboring nodes:

$$\pi_j|_q = \frac{\phi_{q-} - \phi_{q+}}{2\Delta^2}, \quad \text{and} \quad \frac{\partial \pi_j}{\partial g_i} = \frac{1}{2\Delta^2}\left[\frac{\partial \phi_{q-}}{\partial g_i} - \frac{\partial \phi_{q+}}{\partial g_i}\right],$$

where Δ is the internodal distance on the lattice $L(\Omega)$.

3.2 DERIVATION OF $\frac{\partial \phi}{\partial g_i}$

The derivation of $\frac{\partial \phi}{\partial g_i}$ involves computing the Thévenin equivalent circuit for the resistive lattice, when every conductance g connected to node i is removed. For clarity, a 2D resistive grid was chosen to illustrate the procedure. Figure 1 depicts the equivalence warranted by Thévenin's theorem [Chua et al., 1987] and the relevant variables for the derivation of $\frac{\partial \phi_q}{\partial g_i}$. As shown, the equivalent circuit for the resistive grid consists of a four-port resistor, driven by four independent voltage sources. The relation between the voltage vector $\vec{\phi} = [\phi_1 \dots \phi_4]^T$ and the current vector $\vec{i} = [i_1 \dots i_4]^T$ is expressed as

$$\vec{\phi} = R\vec{i} + \vec{\omega}, \tag{3}$$

where R is the impedance matrix for the grid equivalent circuit and $\vec{\omega}$ is the vector of open-circuit voltage sources. The grid equivalent circuit behaves exactly like the whole resistive grid; there is no approximation error.

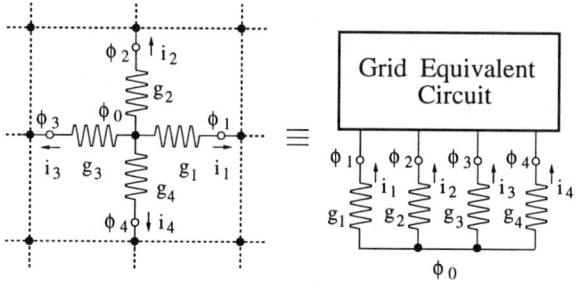

Figure 1: Equivalence established by Thévenin's theorem.

The derivation of the 20 parameters (the elements of R and $\vec{\omega}$) of the equivalent circuit is detailed in [Coelho Jr. et al., 1995]; it involves a series of relaxation operations that can be efficiently implemented in SIMD architectures. The total number of relaxations for a grid with n^2 nodes is exactly $6n - 12$, or an average of $1/2n$ relaxations per link. In the context of this paper, it is assumed that R and $\vec{\omega}$ are known. Our primary interest is to compute how changes in conductances g_k affect the voltage vector $\vec{\phi}$, or the matrix

$$\frac{\partial \phi}{\partial g} = \left| \frac{\partial \phi_j}{\partial g_k} \right|, \quad \text{for} \quad \begin{cases} j = 1, \ldots, 4 \\ k = 1, \ldots, 4. \end{cases}$$

The elements of $\frac{\partial \phi}{\partial g}$ can be computed by derivating each of the four equality relations in Equation 3 with respect to g_k, resulting in a system of 16 linear equations, and 16 variables – the elements of $\frac{\partial \phi}{\partial g}$. Notice that each element of $\vec{i}$ can be expressed as a linear function of the potentials $\vec{\phi}$, by applying Kirchhoff's laws [Chua et al., 1987]:

$$i_j = g_j \left[\frac{\sum_{k=1}^{4} g_k \phi_k}{\sum_{k=1}^{4} g_k} - \phi_j \right].$$

4 APPLICATION EXAMPLE

A robot moves repeatedly toward a goal configuration. Its initial configuration is not known in advance, and every configuration is equally likely of being the initial configuration. The problem is to construct a motion controller that minimizes the overall travel distance for the whole configuration space. If the configuration space Ω is discretized into a number of cells, define the combined travel distance $D(\vec{\pi})$ as

$$D(\vec{\pi}) = \sum_{q \in L(\Omega)} d_{q,\vec{\pi}}, \qquad (4)$$

where $d_{q,\vec{\pi}}$ is the travel distance from cell q to the goal configuration q_G, and robot displacements are determined by the controller $\vec{\pi}$. Figure 2 depicts an instance of the travel distance minimization problem, and the paths corresponding to its optimal solution, given the obstacle distribution and the goal configuration shown.

A resistive grid with 17×17 nodes was chosen to represent the control policies generated by our algorithm. Initially, the resistive grid is homogeneous, with all internodal resistances set to 1Ω. Figure 3 indicates the paths the robot takes when commanded by $\vec{\pi}^0$, the initial control policy derived from an homogeneous resistive grid.

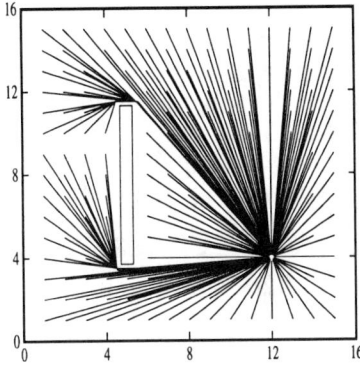 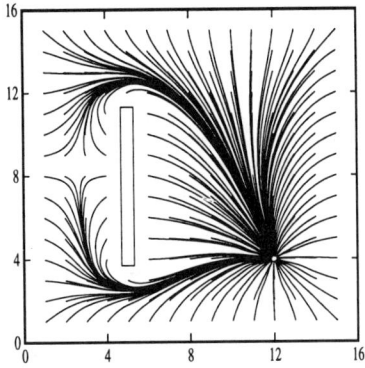

Figure 2: Paths for optimal solution of the travel distance minimization problem.

Figure 3: Paths for the initial solution of the same problem.

The conductances in the resistive grid were then adjusted over 400 steps of the policy iteration algorithm, and Figure 4 is a plot of the overall travel distance as a function of the number of steps. It also shows the optimal travel distance (horizontal line), corresponding to the optimal solution depicted in Figure 2. The plot shows that convergence is initially fast; in fact, the first 140 iterations are responsible for 90% of the overall improvement. After 400 iterations, the travel distance is within 2.8% of its optimal value. This residual error may be explained by the approximation incurred in using a discrete resistive grid to represent the potential distribution.

Figure 5 shows the paths taken by the robot after convergence. The final paths are straightened versions of the paths in Figure 3. Notice also that some of the final paths originating on the left of the I-shaped obstacle take the robot south of the obstacle, resembling the optimal paths depicted in Figure 2.

5 CONCLUSION

This paper presented a policy iteration algorithm for the synthesis of provably correct navigation functions that also extremize user-specified performance indices. The algorithm proposed solves the optimal feedback control problem, in which the final control policy optimizes the performance index over the whole domain, assuming that every state in the domain is as likely of being the initial state as any other state.

The algorithm modifies an existing harmonic function-based path controller by incrementally changing the conductances in a resistive grid. Departing from an homogeneous grid, the algorithm transforms an optimal controller (i.e. a controller that minimizes collision probabilities) into another optimal controller, that extremizes locally the performance index of interest. The tradeoff may require reducing the safety margin between the robot and obstacles, but collision avoidance is preserved at each step of the algorithm.

Other Applications: The algorithm presented can be used (1) in the synthesis of time-optimal velocity controllers, and (2) in the optimization of non-holonomic path controllers. The algorithm can also be a component technology for Intelligent Vehicle Highway Systems (IVHS), by combining (1) and (2).

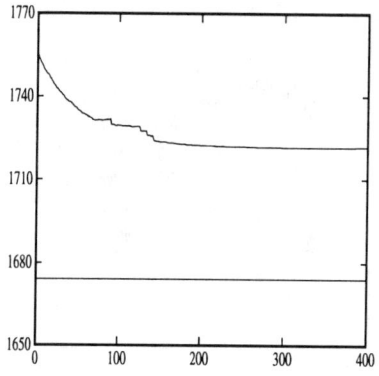 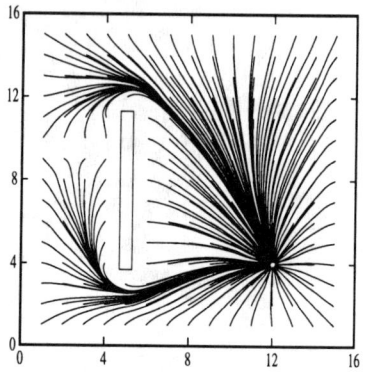

Figure 4: Overall travel distance, as a function of iteration steps.

Figure 5: Final paths, after 800 policy iteration steps.

Performance on Parallel Architectures: The proposed algorithm is computationally demanding; however, it is suitable for implementation on parallel architectures. Its sequential implementation on a SPARC 10 workstation requires $\approx$ 30 sec. per iteration, for the example presented. We estimate that a parallel implementation of the proposed example would require $\approx$ 4.3 ms per iteration, or 1.7 seconds for 400 iterations, given conservative speedups available on parallel architectures [Coelho Jr. et al., 1995].

Acknowledgements

This work was supported in part by grants NSF CCR-9410077, IRI-9116297, IRI-9208920, and CNPq 202107/90.6.

References

[Chua et al., 1987] Chua, L., Desoer, C., and Kuh, E. (1987). *Linear and Nonlinear Circuits.* McGraw-Hill, Inc., New York, NY.

[Coelho Jr. et al., 1995] Coelho Jr., J., Sitaraman, R., and Grupen, R. (1995). Control-oriented tuning of harmonic functions. Technical Report CMPSCI Technical Report 95-112, Dept. Computer Science, University of Massachusetts.

[Connolly, 1994] Connolly, C. I. (1994). Harmonic functions and collision probabilities. In *Proc. 1994 IEEE Int. Conf. Robotics Automat.*, pages 3015–3019. IEEE.

[Connolly and Grupen, 1993] Connolly, C. I. and Grupen, R. (1993). The applications of harmonic functions to robotics. *Journal of Robotic Systems*, 10(7):931–946.

[Rimon and Koditschek, 1990] Rimon, E. and Koditschek, D. (1990). Exact robot navigation in geometrically complicated but topologically simple spaces. In *Proc. 1990 IEEE Int. Conf. Robotics Automat.*, volume 3, pages 1937–1942, Cincinnati, OH.

[Singh et al., 1994] Singh, S., Barto, A., Grupen, R., and Connolly, C. (1994). Robust reinforcement learning in motion planning. In *Advances in Neural Information Processing Systems 6*, pages 655–662, San Francisco, CA. Morgan Kaufmann Publishers.

Learning Fine Motion by Markov Mixtures of Experts

Marina Meilă
Dept. of Elec. Eng. and Computer Sci.
Massachussetts Inst. of Technology
Cambridge, MA 02139
mmp@ai.mit.edu

Michael I. Jordan
Dept.of Brain and Cognitive Sciences
Massachussetts Inst. of Technology
Cambridge, MA 02139
jordan@psyche.mit.edu

Abstract

Compliant control is a standard method for performing fine manipulation tasks, like grasping and assembly, but it requires estimation of the state of contact (s.o.c.) between the robot arm and the objects involved. Here we present a method to learn a model of the movement from measured data. The method requires little or no prior knowledge and the resulting model explicitly estimates the s.o.c. The current s.o.c. is viewed as the hidden state variable of a discrete HMM. The control dependent transition probabilities between states are modeled as parametrized functions of the measurement. We show that their parameters can be estimated from measurements at the same time as the parameters of the movement in each s.o.c. The learning algorithm is a variant of the EM procedure. The E step is computed exactly; solving the M step exactly is not possible in general. Here, gradient ascent is used to produce an increase in likelihood.

1 INTRODUCTION

For a large class of robotics tasks, such as assembly tasks or manipulation of relatively light-weight objects, under appropriate damping of the manipulator the dynamics of the objects can be neglected. For these tasks the main difficulty is in having the robot achieve its goal despite uncertainty in its position relative to the surrounding objects. Uncertainty is due to inaccurate knowledge of the geometric shapes and positions of the objects, of their physical properties (surface friction coefficients), or to positioning errors in the manipulator. The standard solution to this problem is *controlled compliance* first introduced in (Mason, 1981). Under compliant motion, the task is performed in stages; in each stage the robot arm maintains contact with a selected surface or feature of the environment; the stage ends when contact with the feature corresponding to the next stage is made.

Decomposing the given task into subtasks and specifying each goal or subgoal in terms of contact constraints has proven to be a particularly fertile idea, from which a fair number of approaches have evolved. But each of them have to face and solve the problem of estimating the *state of contact* (i.e. checking if the contact with the correct surface is achieved), a direct consequence of dealing with noisy measurements. Additionally, most approaches assume prior geometrical and physical knowledge of the environment.

In this paper we present a method to *learn* a model of the environment which will serve to estimate the s.o.c. and to predict future positions from noisy measurements. It associates to each state of contact the coresponding *movement model* (m.m.); that is: a relationship between positions, nominal and actual velocities that holds over a domain of the position-nominal velocity space. The current m.m. is viewed as the hidden state variable of a discrete Hidden Markov Model (HMM) with transition probabilities that are parametrized functions of the measurement. We call this model *Markov Mixture of Experts* (MME) and show how its parameters can be estimated. In section 2 the problem is defined, section 3 introduces the learning algorithm, section 4 presents a simulated example and 5 discusses other aspects relevant to the implementation.

2 REACHABILITY GRAPHS AND MARKOV MIXTURES OF EXPERTS

For any ensemble of objects, the space of all the relative degrees of freedom of the objects in the ensemble is called the *configuration space* (C-space). Every possible configuration of the ensemble is represented by a unique point in the C-space and movement in the real space maps into continuous trajectories in the C-space (Lozano-Perez, 1983). The sets of points corresponding to each state of contact create a partition over the C-space. Because trajectories are continuous, a point can move from a s.o.c. only to a neighboring s.o.c. This can be depicted by a directed graph with vertices representing states of contact and arcs for the possible transitions between them, called the *reachability graph*. If no constraints on the velocities are imposed, then in the reachability graph each s.o.c. is connected to all its neighbours. But if the range of velocities is restricted, the connectivity of the graph decreases and the connections are generally non-symmetric. Figure 1 shows an example of a C-space and its reachability graph for velocities with only positive components.

Ideally, in the absence of noise, the states of contact can be perfectly observed and every transition through the graph is thus deterministic. To deal with the uncertainty in the measurements, we will attach probabilities to the arcs of the graph in the following way: Let us denote by Q_i the set of configurations corresponding to s.o.c. i and let the movement of a point x with uniform nominal velocity v for a time ΔT be given by $x(t + \Delta T) = f^*(x, v, \Delta T)$; both x and v are vectors of same dimension as the C-space. Now, let x', v' be the noisy measurements of the true values x, v, $x \in Q_j$ and $P[x, v|x', v', j]$ the posterior distribution of (x, v) given the measurements and the s.o.c. Then, the probability of transition to a state i from a given state j in time T_s can be expressed as:

$$P[i|x', v', j] = \int_{\{x,v|x \in Q_j, f^*(x,v,T_s) \in Q_i\}} P[x, v|x', v', j] dx\, dv = a_{ij}(x', v') \tag{1}$$

Defining the transition probability matrix $A = [a_{ji}]_{i,j=1}^m$ and assuming measurement

Learning Fine Motion by Markov Mixtures of Experts

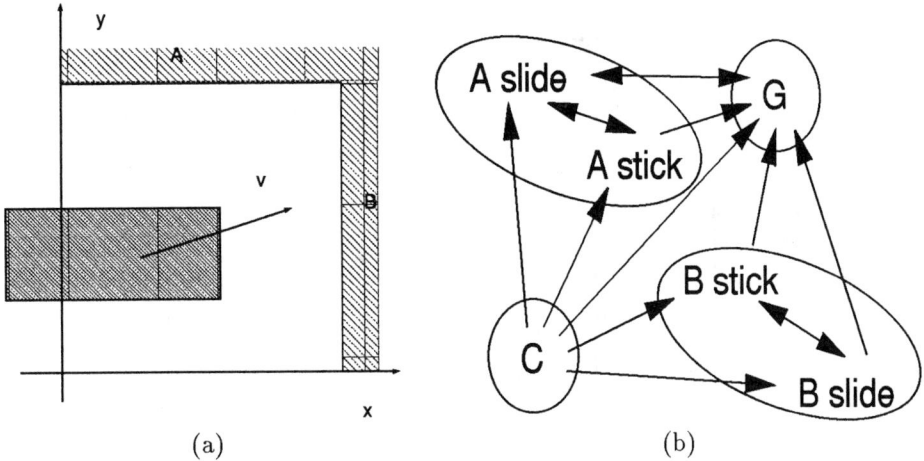

Figure 1: A configuration space (a) and its reachability graph (b). The nodes represent movement models: C is the free space, A and B are surfaces with static and dynamic friction, G represents jamming in the corner. The velocity V has positive components.

noise $P[x'|q = i, x \in Q_i]$ leads to an HMM with output x having a continuous emission probability distribution and where the s.o.c. plays the role of a hidden state variable. Our main goal is to estimate this model from observed data.

To give a general statement of the problem we will assume that all the position, velocity and force measurements are represented by the input vector u; the output vector y of dimensionality n_y contains the future position (which our model will learn to predict). Observations are made at moments which are integer multiples of T_s, indexed by $t = 0, 1, .., T$. If T_s is a constant sampling time the dependency of the transition probability on T_s can be ignored. For the purpose of the parameter estimation, the possible dependence between $u(t)$ and $y(t+1)$ will also be ignored, but it should be considered when the trained model is used for prediction.

Throughout the following section we will also assume that the input-output dependence is described by a Gaussian conditional density $p(y(t)|u(t), q(t) = k)$ with mean $f(u(t), \theta_k)$ and variance $\Sigma = \sigma^2 I$. This is equivalent to assuming that given the s.o.c. all noise is additive Gaussian output noise, which is obviously an approximation. But this approximation will allow us to derive certain quantities in closed form in an effective way.

The function $f(u, \theta_k)$ is the m.m. associated with state of contact k (with θ_k its parameter vector) and q is the selector variable representing it. Sometimes we will find it useful to partition the domain of a m.m. into subdomains and to represent it by a different function (i.e. a different set of parameters θ_k) on each of the subdomains; then, the name *movement model* will be extended to them.

The evolution of q is controlled by a Markov chain which depends on u and of a set of parameters W:

$$a_{ij}(u(t), W) = Pr[q(t+1) = i | q(t) = j, u(t)] \quad t = 0, 1, \ldots$$

with

$$\sum_i a_{ij}(u, W) = 1 \quad \forall u, W, j = 1, \ldots, m. \quad (2)$$

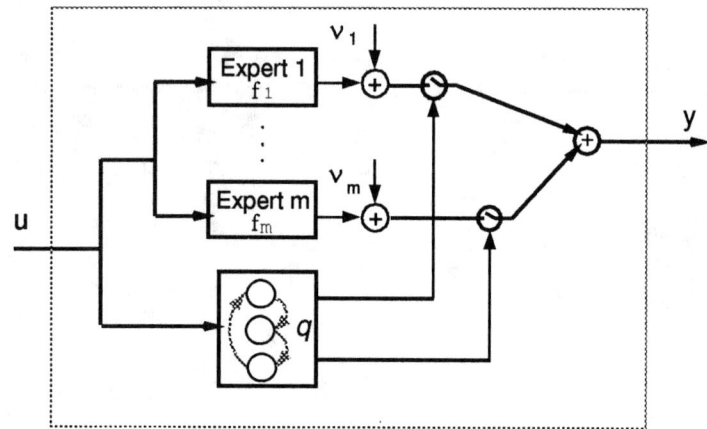

Figure 2: The Markov Mixture of Experts architecture

Fig. 2 depicts this architecture. It can be easily seen that this model generalizes the mixture of experts (ME) architecture (Jacobs, et al., 1991), to which it reduces in the case where a_{ij} are independent of j (the columns of A are all equal). It becomes the model of (Bengio and Frasconi, 1995) when A and f are neural networks.

3 AN EM ALGORITHM FOR MME

To estimate the values of the unknown parameters σ^2, W_k, θ_k, $k = 1, \ldots, m$ given the sequence of observations $\{(u(t), y(t))\}_{t=0}^{T}$, $T > 0$ the *Expectation Maximization* (EM) algorithm will be used. The states $\{q(t)\}_{t=0}^{T}$ play the role of the unobserved variables. More about EM can be found in (Dempster et al., 1977) while aspects specific to this algorithm are in (Meila and Jordan, 1994).

The E step computes the probability of each state and of every transition to occur at $t \in \{0, \ldots, T\}$ given the observations and an initial parameter set. This can be done efficiently by the *forward-backward* algorithm (Rabiner and Juang, 1986).

$$\gamma_k(t) = Pr[q(t) = k \mid \{(u(t), y(t))\}_{t=0}^{T}, W, \theta, \sigma^2] \quad (3)$$
$$\xi_{ij}(t) = Pr[q(t) = j, q(t+1) = i \mid \{(u(t), y(t))\}_{t=0}^{T}, W, \theta, \sigma^2]$$

In the M step the new estimates of the parameters are found by maximizing the average *complete log-likelihood* J, which in our case has the form

$$J(\theta, \sigma^2, W) = \sum_{t=0}^{T-1} \sum_{i,j=1}^{m} \xi_{ij}(t) \ln a_{ij}(u(t), W) -$$

$$- \frac{1}{2\sigma^2} \sum_{t=0}^{T} \sum_{k=1}^{m} \gamma_k(t) \|y(t) - f(u(t), \theta_k)\|^2 - \frac{T+1}{2} n_y \ln(\sigma^2) + \text{ct.} \quad (4)$$

Since each parameter appears in only one term of J the maximization is equivalent to:

$$\theta_k^{new} = \underset{\theta_k}{\operatorname{argmin}} \sum_{t=0}^{T} \gamma_k(t) \|y(t) - f(u(t), \theta_k)\|^2 \quad (5)$$

$$W^{new} = \underset{W}{\operatorname{argmax}} \sum_{t=0}^{T-1} \sum_{ij} \xi_{ij}(t) \ln\left(a_{ij}(u(t), W)\right) \qquad (6)$$

$$\sigma^{2\,new} = \frac{1}{n_y(T+1)} \sum_{t=0}^{T} \sum_{k=0}^{m} \gamma_k(t) \left\| y(t) - f(u(t), \theta_k) \right\|^2 \qquad (7)$$

There is no general closed form solution to (5) and (6). Their difficulty depends on the form of f and a_{ij}. The complexity of the m.m. is determined by the geometrical shape of the objects' surfaces. For planar surfaces and no rotational degrees of freedom f is linear in θ_k. Then, (5) becomes a weighted least squares problem which can be solved in closed form.

The functions in A depend both on the movement and of the noise models. Because the noise is propagated through non-linearities to the output, an exact form as in (1) may be hard to compute analytically. Moreover, a correct noise model for each of the possible uncertainties is rarely available (Eberman, 1995). A common practical approach is to trade accuracy for computability and to parametrize A in a form which is easy to update but deprived of physical meaning. In all the cases where maximization cannot be performed exactly, one can resort to *Generalized EM* by merely *increasing* J. In particular, gradient ascent in parameter space is a technique which can replace maximization. This modification will not affect the overall convergence of the EM iteration but can significantly reduce its speed.

Because EM only finds *local* maxima of the likelihood, the initialization is important. If $f(u, \theta_k)$ correspond to physical movement models, good initial estimates for their parameters can be available. The same applies to those components of W which bear physical significance. A complementary approach is to reduce the number of parameters by explicitly setting the probabilities of impossible transitions to 0.

4 SIMULATION RESULTS

Simulations have been run on the C-space shown in fig. 1. The inputs were the 4-dimensional vectors of position (x, y) and nominal velocity (V_x, V_y); the output was the predicted position. The coordinate range was $[0, 10]$ and the admissible velocities were confined to the upper right quadrant ($V_{max} \geq V_x, V_y \geq V_{min} > 0$). The restriction in direction implied that the trajectories remain in the coordinate domain; it also appeared in the topology of the reachability graph, which has no transition to the free space from another state.

This model was implemented by a MME. The m.m. are linear in the parameters, corresponding to the piecewise linearity of the true model. To implement the transition matrix A we used a bank of *gating networks*, one for each s.o.c., consisting of 2 layer perceptrons with softmax[1] output. There are 230 free parameters in the gating networks and 64 in the m.m.

The training set included $N = 5000$ data points, in sequences of length $T \leq 6$, all starting in free space. The starting position of the sequence and the nominal velocities at each step were picked randomly. We found that a more uniform distribution of the data points over the states of contact is necessary for successful learning. Since this is not expected to happen in applications (where, e.g., *sticking* occurs less often than *sliding*), the obtained models were tested also on a distribution that

---

[1] The *softmax function* is given by: $\operatorname{softmax}_i(x) = \frac{\exp(W_i^T x)}{\sum_j \exp(W_j^T x)}$, $i = 1, ..m$ with W_j, x vectors of the same dimension.

Table 1: Performance of MME versus ME

(a) Model Prediction Standard Error $(MSE)^{1/2}$

Test set	Training distribution					Uniform V distribution				
noise level	0	.1	.2	.3	.4	0	.1	.2	.3	.4
MME, $\sigma = .2$	.024	.113	.222	.332	.443	.023	.11	.219	.327	.437
MME, $\sigma = 0$	.003	.114	.228	.343	.456	.010	.109	.218	.327	.435
ME, $\sigma = .2$	.052	.133	.25	.37	.493	.044	.129	.247	.367	.488
ME, $\sigma = 0$	.047	.131	.25	.37	.49	.034	.126	.245	.366	.488

(b) State Misclassification Error [%]

Test set	Training distribution					Uniform V distribution				
noise level	0	.1	.2	.3	.4	0	.1	.2	.3	.4
MME, $\sigma = .2$	5.15	5.2	5.5	5.9	6.4	3.45	3.5	3.8	4.2	4.6
MME, $\sigma = 0$	.78	1.40	2.35	3.25	4.13	.89	1.19	1.70	2.30	2.88
ME, $\sigma = .2$	6.46	6.60	7.18	7.73	8.13	3.85	3.90	4.38	4.99	5.65
ME, $\sigma = 0$	6.25	6.45	6.98	7.61	8.15	3.84	3.98	4.53	5.05	5.70

was uniform over velocities (and consequently, highly non-uniform over states of contact). Gaussian noise with $\sigma=0.2$ or 0 was added to the (x, y) training data.

In the M step, the parameters of the gating networks were updated by gradient ascent. For the m.m. least squares estimation was used. To ensure that models and gates are correctly coupled, initial values for θ are chosen around the true values. As discussed in the previous section, this is not an unrealistic assumption. W was initialized with small random values. Each simulation was run until convergence.

We used two criteria to measure the performance of the learning algorithm: square root of prediction MSE and hidden state misclassificaton. The results are summarized in table 1. The test set size is 50,000 in all cases. Input noise is Gaussian with levels between 0 and 0.4. Comparisons were made with a ME model with the same number of states.

The simulations show that the MME architecture is tolerant to input noise, although it is not taking it into account explicitly. The MME consistently outperforms the ME model in both prediction and state estimation accuracy.

5 DISCUSSION

An algorithm to estimate the parameters of composite movement models in the presence of noisy measurements has been presented. The algorithm exploits the physical decomposability of the problem and the temporal relationship between the data points to produce estimates of both the model's parameters and the s.o.c. It requires only imprecise initial knowledge about the geometry and physical properties of the system.

Prediction via MME The trained model can be used either as an estimator for the state of contact or as a forward model in predicting the next position. For the former goal the forward part of the forward-backward algorithm can be used to implement a recursive estimator or the methods in (Eberman, 1995) can be used. The obtained $\gamma_k(t)$, combined with the outputs of the movement models, will produce a predicted output $\hat{y}$. An improved posterior estimate of y can be obtained by combining $\hat{y}$ with the current measurement.

Scaling issues. Simulations have shown that relatively large datasets are required for training even for a small number of states. But, since the states represent physical entities, the model will inherit the geometrical locality properties thereof. Thus, the number of possible transitions from a state will be bounded by a small constant when the number of states grows, keeping the data complexity linear in m.

As a version of EM, our algorithm is batch. It follows that parameters are not adapted on line. In particular, the discretization time T_s must be fixed prior to training. But small changes in T_s can be accounted for by rescaling the velocities V. For the other changes, inasmuch as they are local, relearning can be confined to those components of the architecture which are affected.

References

Bengio, Y. and Frasconi, P. (1995). An input output HMM architecture. In G. Tesauro, D. Touretzky, & T. Leen (Eds.), *Neural Information Processing Systems 7*, Cambridge, MA: MIT Press, pp. 427–435.

Dempster, A. P., Laird, N. M., and Rubin, D. B. (1977). Maximum likelihood from incomplete data via the EM algorithm. *Journal of the Royal Statistical Society, B*, 39:1–38.

Eberman, B. S. (1995). *A sequential decision approach to sensing manipulation contact features.* PhD thesis, M.I.T., Dept. of Electrical Engineering.

Jacobs, R. A., Jordan, M. I., Nowlan, S., & Hinton, G. E. (1991). Adaptive mixtures of local experts. *Neural Computation, 3*, 1–12.

Lozano-Perez, T. (1983). Spatial planning: a configuration space approach. *IEEE Transactions on Computers*.

Mason, M. T. (1981). Compliance and force control for computer controlled manipulation. *IEEE Trans. on Systems, Man and Cybernetics*.

Meila, M. and Jordan, M. I. (1994). Learning the parameters of HMMs with auxilliary input. Technical Report 9401, MIT Computational Cognitive Science, Cambridge, MA.

Rabiner, R. L. and Juang, B. H. (1986). An introduction to hidden Markov models. *ASSP Magazine*, 3(1):4–16.

Neural Control for Nonlinear Dynamic Systems

Ssu-Hsin Yu
Department of Mechanical Engineering
Massachusetts Institute of Technology
Cambridge, MA 02139
Email: hsin@mit.edu

Anuradha M. Annaswamy
Department of Mechanical Engineering
Massachusetts Institute of Technology
Cambridge, MA 02139
Email: aanna@mit.edu

Abstract

A neural network based approach is presented for controlling two distinct types of nonlinear systems. The first corresponds to nonlinear systems with parametric uncertainties where the parameters occur nonlinearly. The second corresponds to systems for which stabilizing control structures cannot be determined. The proposed neural controllers are shown to result in closed-loop system stability under certain conditions.

1 INTRODUCTION

The problem that we address here is the control of general nonlinear dynamic systems in the presence of uncertainties. Suppose the nonlinear dynamic system is described as $\dot{x} = f(x, u, \theta)$, $y = h(x, u, \theta)$ where u denotes an external input, y is the output, x is the state, and θ is the parameter which represents constant quantities in the system. The control objectives are to stabilize the system in the presence of disturbances and to ensure that reference trajectories can be tracked accurately, with minimum delay. While uncertainties can be classified in many different ways, we focus here on two scenarios. One occurs because the changes in the environment and operating conditions introduce uncertainties in the system parameter θ. As a result, control objectives such as regulation and tracking, which may be realizable using a continuous function $u = \gamma(x, \theta)$ cannot be achieved since θ is unknown. Another class of problems arises due to the complexity of the nonlinear function f. Even if θ, f and h can be precisely determined, the selection of an appropriate γ that leads to stabilization and tracking cannot be made in general. In this paper, we present two methods based on neural networks which are shown to be applicable to both the above classes of problems. In both cases, we clearly outline the assumptions made, the requirements for adequate training of the neural network, and the class of engineering problems where the proposed methods are applicable. The proposed approach significantly expands the scope of neural controllers in relation to those proposed in (Narendra and Parthasarathy, 1990; Levin and Narendra, 1993; Sanner and Slotine, 1992; Jordan and Rumelhart, 1992).

Neural Control for Nonlinear Dynamic Systems

The first class of problems we shall consider includes nonlinear systems with parametric uncertainties. The field of adaptive control has addressed such a problem, and over the past thirty years, many results have been derived pertaining to the control of both linear and nonlinear dynamic systems (Narendra and Annaswamy, 1989). A common assumption in almost all of the published work in this field is that the uncertain parameters occur linearly. In this paper, we consider the control of nonlinear dynamic systems with nonlinear parametrizations. We design a neural network based controller that adapts to the parameter θ and show that closed-loop system stability can be achieved under certain conditions. Such a controller will be referred to as a θ-adaptive neural controller. Pertinent results to this class are discussed in section 2.

The second class of problems includes nonlinear systems, which despite being completely known, cannot be stabilized by conventional analytical techniques. The obvious method for stabilizing nonlinear systems is to resort to linearization and use linear control design methods. This limits the scope of operation of the stabilizing controller. Feedback linearization is another method by which nonlinear systems can be stably controlled (Isidori, 1989). This however requires fairly stringent set of conditions to be satisfied by the functions f and h. Even after these conditions are satisfied, one cannot always find a closed-form solution to stabilize the system since it is equivalent to solving a set of partial differential equations. We consider in this paper, nonlinear systems, where system models as well as parameters are known, but controller structures are unknown. A neural network based controller is shown to exist and trained so that a stable closed-loop system is achieved. We denote this class of controllers as a stable neural controller. Pertinent results to this class are discussed in section 3.

2 θ-ADAPTIVE NEURAL CONTROLLER

The focus of the nonlinear adaptive controller to be developed in this paper is on dynamic systems that can be written in the d-step ahead predictor form as follows:

$$y_{t+d} = f_r(\omega_t, u_t, \theta) \tag{1}$$

where $\omega_t^T = [y_t, \cdots, y_{t-n+1}, u_{t-1}, \cdots, u_{t-m-d+1}]$, $n \geq 1$, $m \geq 0$, $d \geq 1$, $m + d = n$, $\mathcal{Y}_1, \mathcal{U}_1 \subset \Re$ containing the origin and $\Theta_1 \subset \Re^k$ are open, $f_r : \mathcal{Y}_1^n \times \mathcal{U}_1^{m+d} \times \Theta_1 \to \Re$, y_t and u_t are the output and the input of the system at time t respectively, and θ is an unknown parameter and occurs nonlinearly in f_r.[1] The goal is to choose a control input u such that the system in (1) is stabilized and the plant output is regulated around zero.

Let $x_t^T \triangleq [y_{t+d-1}, \cdots, y_{t+1}, \omega_t^T]^T$, $A_m = [e_2, \cdots, e_{n+d-1}, 0, e_{n+d+1}, \cdots, e_{n+m+2d-2}, 0]$, $B_m = [e_1, e_{n+d}]$, where e_i is an unit vector with the i-th term equal to 1. The following assumptions are made regarding the system in Eq. (1).

(A1) For every $\theta \in \Theta_1$, $f_r(0, 0, \theta) = 0$.

(A2) There exist open and convex neighborhoods of the origin $\mathcal{Y}_2 \subset \mathcal{Y}_1$ and $\mathcal{U}_2 \subset \mathcal{U}_1$, an open and convex set $\Theta_2 \subset \Theta_1$, and a function $K : \Omega_2 \times \mathcal{Y}_2 \times \Theta_2 \to \mathcal{U}_1$ such that for every $\omega_t \in \Omega_2$, $y_{t+d} \in \mathcal{Y}_2$ and $\theta \in \Theta_2$, Eq. (1) can be written as $u_t = K(\omega_t, y_{t+d}, \theta)$, where $\Omega_2 \triangleq \mathcal{Y}_2^n \times \mathcal{U}_2^{m+d-1}$.

(A3) K is twice differentiable and has bounded first and second derivatives on $E_1 \triangleq \Omega_2 \times \mathcal{Y}_2 \times \Theta_2$, while f_r is differentiable and has a bounded derivative on $\Omega_2 \times K(E_1) \times \Theta_2$.

(A4) There exists $\delta_g > 0$ such that for every $y_1 \in f_r(\Omega_2, K(\Omega_2, 0, \Theta_2), \Theta_2)$, $\omega \in \Omega_2$ and $\theta, \widehat{\theta} \in \Theta_2$, $|1 - (\frac{\partial K(\omega, y, \theta)}{\partial y} - \frac{\partial K(\omega, y, \widehat{\theta})}{\partial y})|_{y=y_1} \cdot \frac{\partial f_r(\omega, u, \theta)}{\partial u}|_{u=u_1}| > \delta_g$.

---

[1] Here, as well as in the following sections, A^n denotes the n-th product space of the set A.

(A5) There exist positive definite matrices P and Q of dimensions $(n + m + 2d - 2)$ such that $x_t^T(A_m^T P A_m - P)x_t + \bar{K}^T B_m^T P B_m \bar{K} + 2x_t^T A_m^T P B_m \bar{K} \leq -x_t^T Q x_t$, where $\bar{K} = [0, K(\omega_t, 0, \theta)]^T$.

Since the objective is to control the system in (1) where θ is unknown, in order to stabilize the output y at the origin with an estimate $\hat{\theta}_t$, we choose the control input as

$$u_t = K(\omega_t, 0, \hat{\theta}_t) \qquad (2)$$

2.1 PARAMETER ESTIMATION SCHEME

Suppose the estimation algorithm for updating $\hat{\theta}_t$ is defined recursively as $\Delta\hat{\theta}_t \triangleq \hat{\theta}_t - \hat{\theta}_{t-1} = R(y_t, \omega_{t-d}, u_{t-d}, \hat{\theta}_{t-1})$ the problem is to determine the function R such that $\hat{\theta}_t$ converges to θ asymptotically. In general, R is chosen to depend on y_t, ω_{t-d}, u_{t-d} and $\hat{\theta}_{t-1}$ since they are measurable and contain information regarding θ. For example, in the case of linear systems which can be cast in the input predictor form, $u_t = \phi_t^T \theta$, a well-known linear parameter estimation method is to adjust $\Delta\hat{\theta}$ as (Goodwin and Sin, 1984) $\Delta\hat{\theta}_t = \frac{\phi_{t-d}}{1+\phi_{t-d}^T\phi_{t-d}}[u_{t-d} - \phi_{t-d}^T\hat{\theta}_{t-1}]$. In other words, the mechanism for carrying out parameter estimation is realized by R. In the case of general nonlinear systems, the task of determining such a function R is quite difficult, especially when the parameters occur nonlinearly. Hence, we propose the use of a neural network parameter estimation algorithm denoted θ-adaptive neural network (TANN) (Annaswamy and Yu, 1996). That is, we adjust $\hat{\theta}_t$ as

$$\hat{\theta}_t = \begin{cases} \hat{\theta}_{t-1} + N(y_t, \omega_{t-d}, u_{t-d}, \hat{\theta}_{t-1}) & \text{if } \Delta V_{d_t} < -\epsilon \\ \hat{\theta}_{t-1} & \text{otherwise} \end{cases} \qquad (3)$$

where the inputs of the neural network are y_t, ω_{t-d}, u_{t-d} and $\hat{\theta}_{t-1}$, the output is $\Delta\hat{\theta}_t$, and ϵ defines a dead-zone where parameter adaptation stops.

The neural network is to be trained so that the resulting network can improve the parameter estimation over time for any possible θ in a compact set. In addition, the trained network must ensure that the overall system in Eqs. (1), (2) and (3) is stable. Toward this end, N in TANN algorithm is required to satisfy the following two properties: (P1) $|N(y_t, \omega_{t-d}, u_{t-d}, \hat{\theta}_{t-1})|^2 \leq a\frac{|C(\bar{\phi}_{t-d})|^2}{(1+|C(\bar{\phi}_{t-d})|^2)^2}\tilde{u}_{t-d}^2$, and (P2) $\Delta V_t - \Delta V_{d_t} < \epsilon_1$, $\epsilon_1 > 0$, where $\Delta V_t = |\tilde{\theta}_t|^2 - |\tilde{\theta}_{t-1}|^2$, $\tilde{\theta}_t = \hat{\theta}_t - \theta$, $\Delta V_{d_t} = -a\frac{2+|C(\bar{\phi}_{t-d})|^2}{(1+|C(\bar{\phi}_{t-d})|^2)^2}\tilde{u}_{t-d}^2$,

$C(\bar{\phi}_t) = \left(\frac{\partial K}{\partial \theta}(\omega_t, y_{t+d}, \theta)\big|_{\theta=\theta_0}\right)^T$, $\tilde{u}_t = u_t - K(\omega_t, y_{t+d}, \hat{\theta}_{t+d-1})$, $\bar{\phi}_t = [\omega_t^T, y_{t+d}]^T$, $a \in (0, 1)$ and θ_0 is the point where K is linearized and often chosen to be the mean value of parameter variation.

2.2 TRAINING OF TANN FOR CONTROL

In the previous section, we proposed an algorithm using a neural network for adjusting the control parameters. We introduced two properties (P1) and (P2) of the identification algorithm that the neural network needs to possess in order to maintain stability of the closed-loop system. In this section, we discuss the training procedure by which the weights of the neural network are to be adjusted so that the network retains these properties.

The training set is constructed off-line and should compose of data needed in the training phase. If we want the algorithm in Eq. (3) to be valid on the specified sets $\mathcal{Y}_3$ and $\mathcal{U}_3$ for various θ and $\hat{\theta}$ in Θ_3, the training set should cover those variables appearing in Eq. (3) in their respective ranges. Hence, we first sample ω in the set $\mathcal{Y}_3^n \times \mathcal{U}_3^{m+d-1}$, and θ, $\widehat{\theta}$ in the set Θ_3. Their values are, say, ω_1, θ_1 and $\widehat{\theta}_1$ respectively. For the particular $\widehat{\theta}_1$ and θ_1 we sample $\widehat{\theta}$ again in the set $\{\theta \in \Theta_3| |\theta - \theta_1| \leq |\widehat{\theta}_1 - \theta_1|\}$, and its value is, say, $\widehat{\theta}_1^d$. Once ω_1, θ_1, $\widehat{\theta}_1$ and $\widehat{\theta}_1^d$ are sampled, other data can then be calculated, such as $u_1 = K(\omega_1, 0, \widehat{\theta}_1)$ and $y_1 = f_r(\omega_1, u_1, \theta_1)$. We can also obtain the corresponding $C(\bar{\phi}_1) = \frac{\partial K}{\partial \theta}(\omega_1, y_1, \theta_0)$, $\Delta V_{d_1} = -a\frac{2+|C(\bar{\phi}_1)|^2}{(1+|C(\bar{\phi}_1)|^2)^2}(u_1 - \widehat{u}_1)^2$ and $L_1 = a\frac{|C(\bar{\phi}_1)|^2}{(1+|C(\bar{\phi}_1)|^2)^2}(u_1 - \widehat{u}_1)^2$, where $\bar{\phi}_1 = [\omega_1^T, y_1]^T$ and $\widehat{u}_1 = K(\omega_1, y_1, \widehat{\theta}_1^d)$. A data element can then be formed as $(y_1, \omega_1, u_1, \widehat{\theta}_1^d, \theta_1, \Delta V_{d_1}, L_1)$. Proceeding in the same manner, by choosing various ω_s, θ_s, $\widehat{\theta}_s$ and $\widehat{\theta}_s^d$ in their respective ranges, we form a typical training set $T_{train} = \left\{(y_s, \omega_s, u_s, \widehat{\theta}_s^d, \theta_s, \Delta V_{d_s}, L_s)\middle| 1 \leq s \leq M\right\}$, where M denotes the total number of patterns in the training set. If the quadratic penalty function method (Bertsekas, 1995) is used, properties (P1) and (P2) can be satisfied by training the network on the training set to minimize the following cost function:

$$\min_W J \triangleq \min_W \frac{1}{2}\sum_{i=1}^{M}\left\{(\max\{0,\Delta V_{e_i}\})^2 + \frac{1}{b^2}(\max\{0, |N_i(W)|^2 - L_i\})^2\right\} \quad (4)$$

To find a W which minimizes the above unconstrained cost function J, we can apply algorithms such as the gradient method and the Gauss-Newton method.

2.3 STABILITY RESULT

With the plant given by Eq. (1), the controller by Eq. (2), and the TANN parameter estimation algorithm by Eq. (3), it can be shown that the stability of the closed-loop system is guaranteed.

Based on the assumptions of the system in (1) and properties (P1) and (P2) that TANN satisfies, the stability result of the closed-loop system can be concluded in the following theorem. We refer the reader to (Yu and Annaswamy, 1996) for further detail.

Theorem 1 *Given the compact sets $\mathcal{Y}_3^{n+1} \times \mathcal{U}_3^{m+d} \times \Theta_3$ where the neural network in Eq. (3) is trained. There exist $\epsilon_1, \epsilon > 0$ such that for any interior point θ of Θ_3, there exist open sets $\mathcal{Y}_4 \subset \mathcal{Y}_3$, $\mathcal{U}_4 \subset \mathcal{U}_3$ and a neighborhood Θ_4 of θ such that if $y_0, \cdots, y_{n+d-2} \in \mathcal{Y}_4$, $u_0, \cdots, u_{n-2} \in \mathcal{U}_4$, and $\widehat{\theta}_{n-1}, \cdots, \widehat{\theta}_{n+d-2} \in \Theta_4$, then all the signals in the closed-loop system remain bounded and y_t converges to a neighborhood of the origin.*

2.4 SIMULATION RESULTS

In this section, we present a simulation example of the TANN controller proposed in this section. The system is of the form $y_{t+1} = \frac{\theta y_t(1-y_t)}{1+e^{-0.05\theta y_t}} + u_t$, where θ is the parameter to be determined on-line. Prior information regarding the system is that $\theta \in [4, 10]$. Based on Eq. (2), the controller was chosen to be $u_t = -\frac{\widehat{\theta}_t y_t(1-y_t)}{1+e^{-0.05\widehat{\theta}_t y_t}}$, where $\widehat{\theta}_t$ denotes the parameter estimate at time t. According to Eq. (3), θ was estimated using the TANN algorithm with inputs y_{t+1}, y_t, u_t and $\widehat{\theta}_t$, and $\epsilon = 0.01$. N is a Gaussian network with 700 centers. The training set and the testing set were composed of 6,040 and 720 data elements respectively.

After the training was completed, we tested the TANN controller on the system with six different values of θ, 4.5, 5.5, 6.5, 7.5, 8.5 and 9.5, while the initial parameter estimate and the initial output were chosen as $\widehat{\theta}_1 = 7$ and $y_0 = -0.9$ respectively. The results are plotted in Figure 1. It can be seen that y_t can be stabilized at the origin for all these values of θ. For comparison, we also simulated the system under the same conditions but with $\widehat{\theta}$

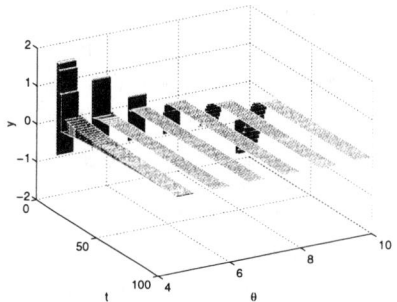

Figure 1: y_t (TANN Controller)

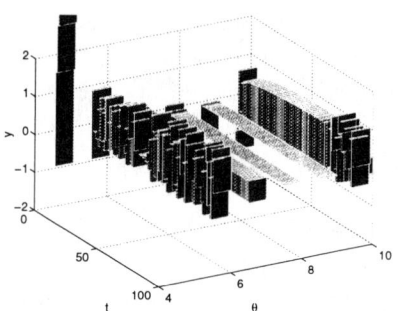

Figure 2: y_t (Extended Kalman Filter)

estimated using the extended Kalman filter (Goodwin and Sin, 1984). Figure 2 shows the output responses. It is not surprising that for some values of θ, especially when the initial estimation error is large, the responses either diverge or exhibit steady state error.

3 STABLE NEURAL CONTROLLER

3.1 STATEMENT OF THE PROBLEM

Consider the following nonlinear dynamical system

$$\dot{x} = f(x, u), \qquad y = h(x) \tag{5}$$

where $x \in R^n$ and $u \in R^m$. Our goal is to construct a stabilizing neural controller as $u = N(y; W)$ where N is a neural network with weights W, and establish the conditions under which the closed-loop system is stable.

The nonlinear system in (5) is expressed as a combination of a higher-order linear part and a nonlinear part as $\dot{x} = Ax + Bu + R_1(x, u)$ and $y = Cx + R_2(x)$, where $f(0, 0) = 0$ and $h(0) = 0$. We make the following assumptions: (A1) f, h are twice continuously differentiable and are completely known. (A2) There exists a K such that $(A - BKC)$ is asymptotically stable.

3.2 TRAINING OF THE STABLE NEURAL CONTROLLER

In order for the neural controller in Section 3.1 to result in an asymptotically stable closed-loop system, it is sufficient to establish that a continuous positive definite function of the state variables decreases monotonically through output feedback. In other words, if we can find a scalar definite function with a negative definite derivative of all points in the state space, we can guarantee stability of the overall system. Here, we limit our choices of the Lyapunov function candidates to the quadratic form, i.e. $V = x^T P x$, where P is positive definite, and the goal is to choose the controller so that $\dot{V} < 0$ where $\dot{V} = 2x^T P f(x, N(h(x), W))$. Based on the above idea, we define a "desired" time-derivative $\dot{V}_d$ as $\dot{V}_d = -x^T Q x$ where $Q = Q^T > 0$. We choose P and Q matrices as follows. First, according to (A1), we can find a matrix K to make $(A - BKC)$ asymptotically stable. We can then find a (P, Q) pair by choosing an arbitrary positive definite matrix Q and solving the Lyapunov equation, $(A - BKC)^T P + P(A - BKC) = -Q$ to obtain a positive definite P.

Neural Control for Nonlinear Dynamic Systems

With the controller of the form in Section 3.1, the goal is to find W in the neural network which yields $\dot{V} \leq \dot{V}_d$ along the trajectories in a neighborhood $\mathcal{X} \subset \Re^n$ of the origin in the state space. Let x_i denote the value of a sample point where i is an index to the sample variable $x \in \mathcal{X}$ in the state space. To establish $\dot{V} \leq \dot{V}_d$, it is necessary that for every x_i in a neighborhood $\mathcal{X} \subset \Re^n$ of the origin, $\dot{V}_i \leq \dot{V}_{d_i}$, where $\dot{V}_i = 2x_i^T P f(x_i, N(h(x_i), W))$ and $\dot{V}_{d_i} = -x_i^T Q x_i$. That is, the goal is to find a W such that the inequality constraints $\Delta V_{e_i} \leq 0$, where $i = 1, \cdots, M$, is satisfied, where $\Delta V_{e_i} = \dot{V}_i - \dot{V}_{d_i}$ and M denotes the total number of sample points in $\mathcal{X}$. As in the training of TANN controller, this can also be posed as an optimization problem. If the same quadratic penalty function method is used, the problem is to find W to minimize the following cost function over the training set, which is described as $T_{train} = \{(x_i, y_i, \dot{V}_{d_i}) | 1 \leq i \leq M\}$:

$$\min_W J \triangleq \min_W \frac{1}{2} \sum_{i=1}^M (\max\{0, \Delta V_{e_i}\})^2 \tag{6}$$

3.3 STABILITY OF THE CLOSED-LOOP SYSTEM

Assumptions (A1) and (A2) imply that a stabilizing controller $u = -Ky$ exists so that $V = x^T P x$ is a candidate Lyapunov function. More generally, suppose a continuous but unknown function $\gamma(y)$ exists such that for $V = x^T P x$, a control input $u = \gamma(y)$ leads to $\dot{V} \leq -x^T Q x$, then we can find a neural network $N(y)$ which approximates $\gamma(y)$ arbitrarily closely in a compact set leading to closed-loop stability. This is summarized in Theorem 2 (Yu and Annaswamy, 1995).

Theorem 2 *Let there be a continuous function $\gamma(h(x))$ such that $2x^T P f(x, \gamma(h(x))) + x^T Q x \leq 0$ for every $x \in \mathcal{X}$ where $\mathcal{X}$ is a compact set containing the origin as an interior point. Then, given a neighborhood $\mathcal{O} \subset \mathcal{X}$ of the origin, there exists a neural controller $u = N(h(x); W)$ and a compact set $\mathcal{Y} \in \mathcal{X}$ such that the solutions of $\dot{x} = f(x, N(h(x); W))$ converge to $\mathcal{O}$, for every initial condition $x(t_0) \in \mathcal{Y}$.*

3.4 SIMULATION RESULTS

In this section, we show simulation results for a discrete-time nonlinear systems using the proposed neural network controller in Section 3, and compare it with a linear controller to illustrate the difference. The system we considered is a second-order nonlinear system $x_t = f(x_{t-1}, u_{t-1})$, where $f = [f_1, f_2]^T$, $f_1 = x_{1_{t-1}} \times (1 + x_{2_{t-1}}) + x_{2_{t-1}} \times (1 - u_{t-1} + u_{t-1}^2)$ and $f_2 = x_{1_{t-1}}^2 + 2x_{2_{t-1}} + u_{t-1}(1 + x_{2_{t-1}})$. It was assumed that x is measurable, and we wished to stabilize the system around the origin. The controller is of the form $u_t = N(x_{1_t}, x_{2_t})$. The neural network N used is a Gaussian network with 120 centers. The training set and the testing set were composed of 441 and 121 data elements respectively.

After the training was done, we plotted the actual change of the Lyapunov function, ΔV, using the linear controller $u = -Kx$ and the neural network controller in Figures 3 and 4 respectively. It can be observed from the two figures that if the neural network controller is used, ΔV is negative definite except in a small neighborhood of the origin, which assures that the closed-loop system would converge to vicinity of the origin; whereas, if the linear controller is used, ΔV becomes positive in some region away from the origin, which implies that the system can be unstable for some initial conditions. Simulation results confirmed our observation.

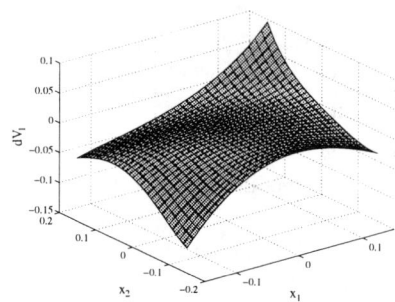
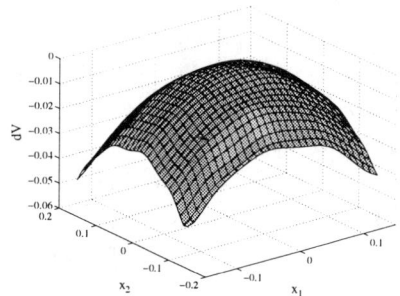

Figure 3: $\Delta V(u = -Kx)$

Figure 4: $\Delta V(u = N(x))$

Acknowledgments

This work is supported in part by Electrical Power Research Institute under contract No. 8060-13 and in part by National Science Foundation under grant No. ECS-9296070.

References

[1] A. M. Annaswamy and S. Yu. θ-adaptive neural networks: A new approach to parameter estimation. *IEEE Transactions on Neural Networks*, (to appear) 1996.

[2] D. P. Bertsekas. *Nonlinear Programming*. Athena Scientific, Belmont, MA, 1995.

[3] G. C. Goodwin and K. S. Sin. *Adaptive Filtering Prediction and Control*. Prentice-Hall, Inc., 1984.

[4] A. Isidori. *Nonlinear Control Systems*. Springer-Verlag, New York, NY, 1989.

[5] M. I. Jordan and D. E. Rumelhart. Forward models: Supervised learning with a distal teacher. *Cognitive Science*, 16:307–354, 1992.

[6] A. U. Levin and K. S. Narendra. Control of nonlinear dynamical systems using neural networks: Controllability and stabilization. *IEEE Transactions on Neural Networks*, 4(2):192–206, March 1993.

[7] K. S. Narendra and A. M. Annaswamy. *Stable Adaptive Systems*. Prentice-Hall, Inc., 1989.

[8] K. S. Narendra and K. Parthasarathy. Identification and control of dynamical systems using neural networks. *IEEE Transactions on Neural Networks*, 1(1):4–26, March 1990.

[9] R. M. Sanner and J.-J. E. Slotine. Gaussian networks for direct adaptive control. *IEEE Transactions on Neural Networks*, 3(6):837–863, November 1992.

[10] S. Yu and A. M. Annaswamy. Adaptive control of nonlinear dynamic systems using θ-adaptive neural networks. Technical Report 9601, Adaptive Control Laboratory, Department of Mechanical Engineering, M.I.T., 1996.

[11] S.-H. Yu and A. M. Annaswamy. Control of nonlinear dynamic systems using a stability based neural network approach. In *Technical report 9501, Adaptive Control Laboratory, MIT, Submitted to Proceedings of the 34th IEEE Conference on Decision and Control*, New Orleans, LA, 1995.

Improving Elevator Performance Using Reinforcement Learning

Robert H. Crites
Computer Science Department
University of Massachusetts
Amherst, MA 01003-4610
crites@cs.umass.edu

Andrew G. Barto
Computer Science Department
University of Massachusetts
Amherst, MA 01003-4610
barto@cs.umass.edu

Abstract

This paper describes the application of reinforcement learning (RL) to the difficult real world problem of elevator dispatching. The elevator domain poses a combination of challenges not seen in most RL research to date. Elevator systems operate in continuous state spaces and in continuous time as discrete event dynamic systems. Their states are not fully observable and they are nonstationary due to changing passenger arrival rates. In addition, we use a team of RL agents, each of which is responsible for controlling one elevator car. The team receives a global reinforcement signal which appears noisy to each agent due to the effects of the actions of the other agents, the random nature of the arrivals and the incomplete observation of the state. In spite of these complications, we show results that in simulation surpass the best of the heuristic elevator control algorithms of which we are aware. These results demonstrate the power of RL on a very large scale stochastic dynamic optimization problem of practical utility.

1 INTRODUCTION

Recent algorithmic and theoretical advances in reinforcement learning (RL) have attracted widespread interest. RL algorithms have appeared that approximate dynamic programming (DP) on an incremental basis. Unlike traditional DP algorithms, these algorithms can perform with or without models of the system, and they can be used online as well as offline, focusing computation on areas of state space that are likely to be visited during actual control. On very large problems, they can provide computationally tractable ways of approximating DP. An example of this is Tesauro's TD–Gammon system (Tesauro, 1992; 1994; 1995), which used RL techniques to learn to play strong masters level backgammon. Even the best human experts make poor teachers for this class of problems since they do not always know the best actions. Even if they did, the state space is so large that it would be difficult for experts to provide sufficient training data. RL algorithms are naturally suited to this class of problems, since they learn on the basis of their own experience. This paper describes the application of RL to elevator dispatching, another problem where classical DP is completely intractable. The elevator domain poses a number of difficulties that were not present in backgammon. In spite of these complications, we show results that surpass the best of the heuristic elevator control algorithms of which we are aware. The following sections describe the elevator dispatching domain, the RL algorithm and neural network architectures that were used, the results, and some conclusions.

2 THE ELEVATOR SYSTEM

The particular elevator system we examine is a simulated 10-story building with 4 elevator cars (Lewis, 1991; Bao et al, 1994). Passenger arrivals at each floor are assumed to be Poisson, with arrival rates that vary during the course of the day. Our simulations use a traffic profile (Bao et al, 1994) which dictates arrival rates for every 5-minute interval during a typical afternoon down-peak rush hour. Table 1 shows the mean number of passengers arriving at each floor (2-10) during each 5-minute interval who are headed for the lobby. In addition, there is inter-floor traffic which varies from 0% to 10% of the traffic to the lobby.

Time	00	05	10	15	20	25	30	35	40	45	50	55
Rate	1	2	4	4	18	12	8	7	18	5	3	2

Table 1: The Down-Peak Traffic Profile

The system dynamics are approximated by the following parameters:

- Floor time (the time to move one floor at the maximum speed): 1.45 secs.
- Stop time (the time needed to decelerate, open and close the doors, and accelerate again): 7.19 secs.
- Turn time (the time needed for a stopped car to change direction): 1 sec.
- Load time (the time for one passenger to enter or exit a car): random variable from a $20th$ order truncated Erlang distribution with a range from 0.6 to 6.0 secs and a mean of 1 sec.
- Car capacity: 20 passengers.

The state space is continuous because it includes the elapsed times since any hall calls were registered. Even if these real values are approximated as binary values, the size of the state space is still immense. Its components include 2^{18} possible combinations of the 18 hall call buttons (up and down buttons at each landing except the top and bottom), 2^{40} possible combinations of the 40 car buttons, and 18^4 possible combinations of the positions and directions of the cars (rounding off to the nearest floor). Other parts of the state are not fully observable, for example, the desired destinations of the passengers waiting at each floor. Ignoring everything except the configuration of the hall and car call buttons and the approximate position and direction of the cars, we obtain an extremely conservative estimate of the size of a discrete approximation to the continuous state space:

$$2^{18} \cdot 2^{40} \cdot 18^4 \approx 10^{22} \text{ states.}$$

Each car has a small set of primitive actions. If it is stopped at a floor, it must either "move up" or "move down". If it is in motion between floors, it must either "stop at the next floor" or "continue past the next floor". Due to passenger expectations, there are two constraints on these actions: a car cannot pass a floor if a passenger wants to get off there and cannot turn until it has serviced all the car buttons in its present direction. We have added three additional action constraints in an attempt to build in some primitive prior knowledge: a car cannot stop at a floor unless someone wants to get on or off there, it cannot stop to pick up passengers at a floor if another car is already stopped there, and given a choice between moving up and down, it should prefer to move up (since the down–peak traffic tends to push the cars toward the bottom of the building). Because of this last constraint, the only real choices left to each car are the stop and continue actions. The actions of the elevator cars are executed asynchronously since they may take different amounts of time to complete.

The performance objectives of an elevator system can be defined in many ways. One possible objective is to minimize the average *wait* time, which is the time between the arrival of a passenger and his entry into a car. Another possible objective is to minimize the average *system* time, which is the sum of the wait time and the travel time. A third possible objective is to minimize the percentage of passengers that wait longer than some dissatisfaction threshold (usually 60 seconds). Another common objective is to minimize the sum of *squared* wait times. We chose this latter performance objective since it tends to keep the wait times low while also encouraging fair service.

3 THE ALGORITHM AND NETWORK ARCHITECTURE

Elevator systems can be modeled as *discrete event* systems, where significant events (such as passenger arrivals) occur at discrete times, but the amount of time between events is a real–valued variable. In such systems, the constant discount factor γ used in most discrete–time reinforcement learning algorithms is inadequate. This problem can be approached using a variable discount factor that depends on the amount of time between events (Bradtke & Duff, 1995). In this case, returns are defined as integrals rather than as infinite sums, as follows:

$$\sum_{t=0}^{\infty} \gamma^t r_t \quad \text{becomes} \quad \int_0^{\infty} e^{-\beta\tau} r_\tau d\tau,$$

where r_t is the immediate cost at discrete time t, r_τ is the instantaneous cost at continuous time τ (e.g., the sum of the squared wait times of all waiting passengers), and β controls the rate of exponential decay.

Calculating reinforcements here poses a problem in that it seems to require knowledge of the waiting times of all waiting passengers. There are two ways of dealing with this problem. The simulator knows how long each passenger has been waiting. It could use this information to determine what could be called *omniscient* reinforcements. The other possibility is to use only information that would be available to a real system online. Such *online* reinforcements assume only that the waiting time of the first passenger in each queue is known (which is the elapsed button time). If the Poisson arrival rate λ for each queue is estimated as the reciprocal of the last inter–button time for that queue, the Gamma distribution can be used to estimate the arrival times of subsequent passengers. The time until the nth subsequent arrival follows the Gamma distribution $\Gamma(n, \frac{1}{\lambda})$. For each queue, subsequent arrivals will generate the following expected penalties during the first b seconds after the hall button has been pressed:

$$\sum_{n=1}^{\infty} \int_0^b (\text{prob } n^{th} \text{ arrival occurs at time } \tau) \cdot (\text{penalty given arrival at time } \tau) \, d\tau$$

$$= \sum_{n=1}^{\infty} \int_0^b \frac{\lambda^n \tau^{n-1} e^{-\lambda \tau}}{(n-1)!} \int_0^{b-\tau} w^2 e^{-\beta(w+\tau)} dw \, d\tau = \int_0^b \int_0^{b-\tau} \lambda w^2 e^{-\beta(w+\tau)} dw \, d\tau.$$

This integral can be solved by parts to yield expected penalties. We found that using online reinforcements actually produced somewhat better results than using omniscient reinforcements, presumably because the algorithm was trying to learn average values anyway.

Because elevator system events occur randomly in continuous time, the branching factor is effectively infinite, which complicates the use of algorithms that require explicit lookahead. Therefore, we employed a team of discrete-event Q-learning agents, where each agent is responsible for controlling one elevator car. $Q(x, a)$ is defined as the expected infinite discounted return obtained by taking action a in state x and then following an optimal policy (Watkins, 1989). Because of the vast number of states, the Q-values are stored in feedforward neural networks. The networks receive some state information as input, and produce Q-value estimates as output. We have tested two architectures. In the parallel architecture, the agents share a single network, allowing them to learn from each other's experiences and forcing them to learn identical policies. In the fully decentralized architecture, the agents have their own networks, allowing them to specialize their control policies. In either case, none of the agents have explicit access to the actions of the other agents. Cooperation has to be learned indirectly via the global reinforcement signal. Each agent faces added stochasticity and nonstationarity because its environment contains other learning agents. Other work on team Q-learning is described in (Markey, 1994).

The algorithm calls for each car to select its actions probabilistically using the Boltzmann distribution over its Q-value estimates, where the temperature is lowered gradually during training. After every decision, error backpropagation is used to train the car's estimate of $Q(x, a)$ toward the following target output:

$$\int_{t_x}^{t_y} e^{-\beta(\tau - t_x)} r_\tau d\tau + e^{-\beta(t_y - t_x)} \min_b \hat{Q}(y, b),$$

where action a is taken by the car from state x at time t_x, the next decision by that car is required from state y at time t_y, and r_τ and β are defined as above. $e^{-\beta(t_y - t_x)}$ acts as a variable discount factor that depends on the amount of time between events. The learning rate parameter was set to 0.01 or 0.001 and β was set to 0.01 in the experiments described in this paper.

After considerable experimentation, our best results were obtained using networks for pure down traffic with 47 input units, 20 hidden sigmoid units, and two linear output units (one for each action value). The input units are as follows:

- 18 units: Two units encode information about each of the nine down hall buttons. A real-valued unit encodes the elapsed time if the button has been pushed and a binary unit is on if the button has not been pushed.

- 16 units: Each of these units represents a possible location and direction for the car whose decision is required. Exactly one of these units will be on at any given time.
- 10 units: These units each represent one of the 10 floors where the other cars may be located. Each car has a "footprint" that depends on its direction and speed. For example, a stopped car causes activation only on the unit corresponding to its current floor, but a moving car causes activation on several units corresponding to the floors it is approaching, with the highest activations on the closest floors.
- 1 unit: This unit is on if the car whose decision is required is at the highest floor with a waiting passenger.
- 1 unit: This unit is on if the car whose decision is required is at the floor with the passenger that has been waiting for the longest amount of time.
- 1 unit: The bias unit is always on.

4 RESULTS

Since an optimal policy for the elevator dispatching problem is unknown, we measured the performance of our algorithm against other heuristic algorithms, including the best of which we were aware. The algorithms were: SECTOR, a sector–based algorithm similar to what is used in many actual elevator systems; DLB, Dynamic Load Balancing, attempts to equalize the load of all cars; HUFF, Highest Unanswered Floor First, gives priority to the highest floor with people waiting; LQF, Longest Queue First, gives priority to the queue with the person who has been waiting for the longest amount of time; FIM, Finite Intervisit Minimization, a receding horizon controller that searches the space of admissible car assignments to minimize a load function; ESA, Empty the System Algorithm, a receding horizon controller that searches for the fastest way to "empty the system" assuming no new passenger arrivals. ESA uses queue length information that would not be available in a real elevator system. ESA/nq is a version of ESA that uses arrival rate information to estimate the queue lengths. For more details, see (Bao et al, 1994). These receding horizon controllers are very sophisticated, but also very computationally intensive, such that they would be difficult to implement in real time. RLp and RLd denote the RL controllers, parallel and decentralized. The RL controllers were each trained on 60,000 hours of simulated elevator time, which took four days on a 100 MIPS workstation. The results are averaged over 30 hours of simulated elevator time. Table 2 shows the results for the traffic profile with down traffic only.

Algorithm	AvgWait	SquaredWait	SystemTime	Percent>60 secs
SECTOR	21.4	674	47.7	1.12
DLB	19.4	658	53.2	2.74
BASIC HUFF	19.9	580	47.2	0.76
LQF	19.1	534	46.6	0.89
HUFF	16.8	396	48.6	0.16
FIM	16.0	359	47.9	0.11
ESA/nq	15.8	358	47.7	0.12
ESA	15.1	338	47.1	0.25
RLp	14.8	320	41.8	0.09
RLd	14.7	313	41.7	0.07

Table 2: Results for Down–Peak Profile with Down Traffic Only

Table 3 shows the results for the down–peak traffic profile with up and down traffic, including an average of 2 up passengers per minute at the lobby. The algorithm was trained on down–only traffic, yet it generalizes well when up traffic is added and upward moving cars are forced to stop for any upward hall calls.

Algorithm	AvgWait	SquaredWait	SystemTime	Percent>60 secs
SECTOR	27.3	1252	54.8	9.24
DLB	21.7	826	54.4	4.74
BASIC HUFF	22.0	756	51.1	3.46
LQF	21.9	732	50.7	2.87
HUFF	19.6	608	50.5	1.99
ESA	18.0	524	50.0	1.56
FIM	17.9	476	48.9	0.50
RLp	16.9	476	42.7	1.53
RLd	16.9	468	42.7	1.40

Table 3: Results for Down–Peak Profile with Up and Down Traffic

Table 4 shows the results for the down–peak traffic profile with up and down traffic, including an average of 4 up passengers per minute at the lobby. This time there is twice as much up traffic, and the RL agents generalize extremely well to this new situation.

Algorithm	AvgWait	SquaredWait	SystemTime	Percent>60 secs
SECTOR	30.3	1643	59.5	13.50
HUFF	22.8	884	55.3	5.10
DLB	22.6	880	55.8	5.18
LQF	23.5	877	53.5	4.92
BASIC HUFF	23.2	875	54.7	4.94
FIM	20.8	685	53.4	3.10
ESA	20.1	667	52.3	3.12
RLd	18.8	593	45.4	2.40
RLp	18.6	585	45.7	2.49

Table 4: Results for Down–Peak Profile with Twice as Much Up Traffic

One can see that both the RL systems achieved very good performance, most notably as measured by system time (the sum of the wait and travel time), a measure that was not directly being minimized. Surprisingly, the decentralized RL system was able to achieve as good a level of performance as the parallel RL system. Better performance with nonstationary traffic profiles may be obtainable by providing the agents with information about the current traffic context as part of their input representation. We expect that an additional advantage of RL over heuristic controllers may be in buildings with less homogeneous arrival rates at each floor, where RL can adapt to idiosyncracies in their individual traffic patterns.

5 CONCLUSIONS

These results demonstrate the utility of RL on a very large scale dynamic optimization problem. By focusing computation onto the states visited during simulated trajectories, RL avoids the need of conventional DP algorithms to exhaustively sweep the state set. By storing information in artificial neural networks, it avoids the need to maintain large lookup tables. To achieve the above results, each RL system experienced 60,000 hours of simulated elevator time, which took four days of computer time on a 100 MIPS processor. Although this is a considerable amount of computation, it is negligible compared to what any conventional DP algorithm would require. The results also suggest that approaches to decentralized control using RL have considerable promise. Future research on the elevator dispatching problem will investigate other traffic profiles and further explore the parallel and decentralized RL architectures.

Acknowledgements

We thank John McNulty, Christos Cassandras, Asif Gandhi, Dave Pepyne, Kevin Markey, Victor Lesser, Rod Grupen, Rich Sutton, Steve Bradtke, and the ANW group for assistance with the simulator and for helpful discussions. This research was supported by the Air Force Office of Scientific Research under grant F49620-93-1-0269.

References

G. Bao, C. G. Cassandras, T. E. Djaferis, A. D. Gandhi, and D. P. Looze. (1994) *Elevator Dispatchers for Down Peak Traffic*. Technical Report, ECE Department, University of Massachusetts, Amherst, MA.

S. J. Bradtke and M. O. Duff. (1995) Reinforcement Learning Methods for Continuous-Time Markov Decision Problems. In: G. Tesauro, D. S. Touretzky and T. K. Leen, eds., *Advances in Neural Information Processing Systems 7*, MIT Press, Cambridge, MA.

J. Lewis. (1991) *A Dynamic Load Balancing Approach to the Control of Multiserver Polling Systems with Applications to Elevator System Dispatching*. PhD thesis, University of Massachusetts, Amherst, MA.

K. L. Markey. (1994) Efficient Learning of Multiple Degree-of-Freedom Control Problems with Quasi-independent Q-agents. In: M. C. Mozer, P. Smolensky, D. S. Touretzky, J. L. Elman and A. S. Weigend, eds., *Proceedings of the 1993 Connectionist Models Summer School*. Erlbaum Associates, Hillsdale, NJ.

G. Tesauro. (1992) Practical Issues in Temporal Difference Learning. *Machine Learning* **8**:257–277.

G. Tesauro. (1994) TD-Gammon, a Self-Teaching Backgammon Program, Achieves Master-Level Play. *Neural Computation* **6**:215–219.

G. Tesauro. (1995) Temporal Difference Learning and TD-Gammon. *Communications of the ACM* **38**:58–68.

C. J. C. H. Watkins. (1989) *Learning from Delayed Rewards*. PhD thesis, Cambridge University.

High-Performance Job-Shop Scheduling With A Time-Delay $TD(\lambda)$ Network

Wei Zhang and Thomas G. Dietterich
Department of Computer Science
Oregon State University
Corvallis, Oregon 97331-3202
{zhangw, tgd}@research.cs.orst.edu

Abstract

Job-shop scheduling is an important task for manufacturing industries. We are interested in the particular task of scheduling payload processing for NASA's space shuttle program. This paper summarizes our previous work on formulating this task for solution by the reinforcement learning algorithm $TD(\lambda)$. A shortcoming of this previous work was its reliance on hand-engineered input features. This paper shows how to extend the time-delay neural network (TDNN) architecture to apply it to irregular-length schedules. Experimental tests show that this TDNN-$TD(\lambda)$ network can match the performance of our previous hand-engineered system. The tests also show that both neural network approaches significantly outperform the best previous (non-learning) solution to this problem in terms of the quality of the resulting schedules and the number of search steps required to construct them.

1 Introduction

In Tesauro's 1992 landmark work on TD-gammon, he showed that the temporal difference algorithm $TD(\lambda)$ [Sutton, 1988] can learn an excellent evaluation function for the game of backgammon. This is the most successful application of reinforcement learning to date. The goal of our research is to determine whether this success can be duplicated in an application of industrial importance: Job-shop scheduling.

We are interested in a particular scheduling problem: space shuttle payload processing for NASA. The goal is to schedule a set of tasks to satisfy a set of temporal and resource constraints while also seeking to minimize the total duration (makespan) of the schedule. The best existing method for this task is an iterative repair scheduler that combines heuristics with simulated annealing [Zweben et al., 1994]. In [Zhang and Dietterich, 1995], we report initial results showing that a neural network-based $TD(\lambda)$ scheduler can out-perform this iterative repair algorithm.

To obtain those results, we hand-engineered a set of input features. An advantage of neural network algorithms, however, is that they can often learn good "features" (i.e., hidden units) from more primitive, raw features. The work described in this paper shows how to apply the time-delay neural network architecture [Lang et al., 1990, LeCun et al., 1989] to this task to learn from raw features and thereby eliminate hand-engineering.

In the following sections, we first describe the scheduling task and show how this task can be formulated for $TD(\lambda)$. We then discuss the problem of schedule representation and our network architecture. Following this, we present experiments on a set of simulated problems and discuss the results. These results show that the time-delay network using low level features can not only match the performance of the hand-engineered features—it can actually perform slightly better.

2 The NASA Domain and $TD(\lambda)$ for the Task

The NASA space shuttle payload processing (SSPP) domain requires scheduling the tasks that must be performed to install and test the payloads that are placed in the cargo bay of the space shuttle. In job-shop scheduling terminology, each shuttle mission is a job, which has a fixed launch date. Each job consists of a partially-ordered set of tasks that must be performed. Most of these tasks are "pre-tasks" that must be performed prior to launch, but some are "post-tasks" that take place after the shuttle has landed. Each task has a duration and a list of resource requirements. The resources are grouped into resource pools. For each task and each type of resource, the required amount of the resource must be obtained from a single resource pool. A complete schedule must specify the start time of each task and the resource pool by which each resource requirement of each task is satisfied. A key goal of the scheduling system is to minimize the total duration of the schedule. This is much more challenging than simply finding a *feasible* schedule.

Zweben et al. [1994] developed the following iterative repair method for solving this scheduling problem. First, a critical path schedule is constructed by working backward and forward from the launch and landing dates; resource constraints are ignored. This critical-path schedule serves as the starting state for a state-space search. In each state of this problem space, there are two possible operators that can be applied. The REASSIGN-POOL operator changes the pool assignment for one of the resource requirements of a task. It is only applied when the pool reassignment would allow the resource requirement to be successfully satisfied. The MOVE operator moves a task to a different time and then reschedules all of the temporal dependents of the task using the critical path method (leaving the resource pool assignments of the dependents unchanged). The MOVE operator is only applied to move a task to the first earlier or the first later time at which the violated resource requirement can be satisfied. The iterative repair method uses a combination of three heuristics to choose a task to repair. It prefers to move the task that (a) requires an amount of resource nearly equal to the amount that is over allocated, (b) has few temporal dependents, and (c) needs to be moved only a short distance to satisfy the resource request. The overall control structure of the algorithm applies simulated annealing to minimize a designated cost function. The search continues until a schedule is found that has no constraint violations.

To view the scheduling problem as a reinforcement learning problem, we must describe the problem space and the reinforcement function. We employ the same problem space as Zweben et al. The starting state s_0 is the critical path schedule as discussed above. We define the reinforcement function $R(s)$ to give a reinforcement of -0.001 for each schedule s that still contains constraint violations. This assesses a small penalty for each scheduling action, and it is intended to encourage reinforcement learning to prefer actions that *quickly* find a good schedule. For any schedule s that is free of violations, the reinforcement is the negative of the *resource dilation factor*, $-RDF(s, s_0)$. The RDF attempts to provide a scale-independent measure of the length of the schedule, and this final reinforcement is intended to encourage reinforcement learning to find short final schedules.

The RDF is defined as follows. Let $capacity(i)$ be the capacity of resource type i—that is, the combined capacity of all resource pools of resource type i. At each time t in the schedule, let $u(i, t)$ be the current utilization of resources of type i. We define the *resource utilization index* $RUI(i, t)$ for resource type i at time t to be $RUI(i, t) = \max\left\{1, \frac{u(i,t)}{capacity(i)}\right\}$. If the resource is not over-allocated, $RUI(i, t)$ is 1; otherwise it is the fraction of overallocation. The *total resource utilization index* ($TRUI$) for a schedule of length l is the sum of the resource utilization index taken over all n resources and all l times: $TRUI = \sum_{i=1}^{n} \sum_{t=1}^{l} RUI(i, t)$. Given these definitions, the resource dilation factor is defined as $RDF(s, s_0) = \frac{TRUI(s)}{TRUI(s_0)}$.

Now that we have specified how to view repair-based scheduling as a reinforcement learning problem, we turn our attention to the learning algorithm. Suppose at a given point in the learning process we have developed policy π, which says that in state s the action to select is $a = \pi(s)$. We can define an associated function f_π, called the *value function*, such that $f_\pi(s)$ tells the cumulative reward that we will receive if we follow policy π from state s onward. Formally, $f_\pi(s) = \sum_{j=0}^{N} R(s_{j+1})$, where N is the number of steps until a conflict-free schedule is found.

As in most reinforcement learning work, we will attempt to learn the value function of the optimal policy π^*, denoted $f^* = f_{\pi^*}$, rather than directly learning π^*. Once we have learned this optimal value function, we can transform it into the optimal policy via a simple one-step lookahead search. To learn the value function, we apply $TD(\lambda)$ as a form of value iteration. $TD(\lambda)$ is applied online to the sequences of states and reinforcements that result from choosing actions according to the current estimated value function, $\hat{f}$. At each state s during learning, we conduct a one-step lookahead search using the current estimated value function $\hat{f}$ to evaluate the states resulting from applying each possible operator. We then select the action that maximizes the predicted value of the resulting state s'. After applying this action and receiving the reward, we update our estimate of $\hat{f}$ to reflect the difference between the value of $\hat{f}(s)$ and the more informed value $R(s') + \hat{f}(s')$.

3 Schedule Representation and Network Design

The main challenge for designing a schedule representation is that virtually all methods for learning evaluation functions can only be applied to fixed-length vectors of features. However, the length of schedules varies depending on the number of tasks and the complexity of their temporal and resource constraints. In our previous work, we hand-engineered a fixed set of features that summarized the structure of the schedule. We included such features as the RDF of the current schedule, the mean and standard deviation of the unused resource capacity of each resource pool (negative if the pool is over-allocated), the mean and standard deviation of the slack times (idle times between temporal dependents), and so on. However,

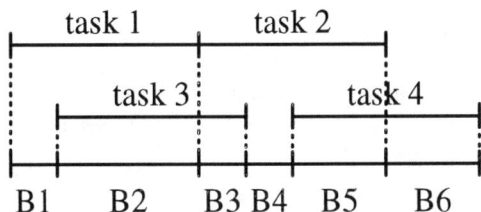

Figure 1: The definition of "blocks".

hand-engineering increases the cost of creating a new application and reduces the autonomy of the learning system. Therefore, we wish to develop a method that can automatically learn good input features.

The time-delay neural network [Lang et al., 1990] has proved to be very effective in learning good position-independent features in visual- and speech-recognition tasks. In speech recognition, it is applied to convert an input sequence of speech frames into a "hidden sequence" of extracted features. A classifier then walks along this hidden sequence and classifies each position in the sequence. The mapping from a particular position in the input sequence to a particular position in the hidden sequence is performed by a "kernel" neural network, which is scanned along the input sequence. It examines a sliding window of adjacent positions in the sequence. The kernel network has a single set of weights that are applied at all positions in the sequence, although each position may have its own bias weight.

To apply this architecture to scheduling, we must solve two problems. First, we must define what a "position" means in the schedule. Second, we must decide how to use the "hidden sequence" of computed features.

To define "positions", we subdivide the schedule into a sequence of "blocks." Each block is a maximal time interval in which the current tasks and resource assignments do not change (see Figure 1). For each block, we can compute primitive features such as the number of resource units available in each pool, and whether each pool is over-allocated. We also say that a task is "inside" a block if that task starts at the beginning of the block. Given this definition, we can compute additional primitive features of the tasks inside the block: minimum and average slack time, number of dependents, and number of tasks inside the block. If there are multiple tasks inside a block, we compute the average values of these features. A total of 12 primitive features are computed for each block.

We then define five kernels, each of which examines a single "current block" and computes a hidden "feature" from this block. These five kernels are scanned along the entire schedule, and they create a derived sequence containing five "hidden features" for each block. How should this derived sequence be processed to compute the estimated value function?

One approach would be to scan a network along the hidden sequence and take the maximum value output by that network. However, because our goal is to estimate the RDF of the final schedule, it seems wiser to view the kernels as learning to recognize "bad conflicts" and "opportunities". By summing (or averaging) the "hidden features", the network can effectively count the number of opportunities and conflicts and estimate how much more the RDF will change before the conflicts are eliminated. Hence, we take the following approach.

The sequence of "hidden features" is split into thirds. Within each third, five features are computed by finding the mean value of each of the five hidden features over the blocks in this third. This gives a total of 15 features. These features, along with two other "global" features—the RDF of the current schedule and the resource utilization of the starting schedule—are input to a network having 40 hidden units. The output of that network is taken as the estimated value for the current schedule.

To recap, the network has three hidden layers named H1, H2, and H3. Layer H1 has 5 kernels (each with 12 weights). There are 15 biases, one for each feature in each third of the schedule. So H1 has a total of 75 parameters. H2 has 17 units; 15 of these are hidden units (3 sets of 5) averaged from H1 and 2 of these are the two global input features. H2 has no adjustable parameters. H3 has 40 hidden units fully connected to H2, for a total of 720 parameters. The output layer has 8 units fully connected to H3 and encoding the predicted RDF using the technique of overlapping gaussian ranges [Pomerleau, 1991]. The output layer has $328 (= 8 \cdot (40 + 1))$ parameters. Therefore, this net has a total of 1123 parameters. All units in H1, H3, and the output layer use sigmoidal transfer functions.

4 Experiments

We constructed an artificial problem set based on specifications for the NASA SSPP problem. Space constraints do not permit a complete description of the problems or the training procedure (see [Zhang and Dieterich, 1995] for full details). 100 scheduling problems were generated. These were subdivided into 50 problems for final testing, 20 problems for validation testing, and three training sets of 10 problems each. An ensemble of 6 networks was constructed by training a separate network for each of these three training sets and for $\lambda = 0.2$ and $\lambda = 0.7$. Training was monitored by testing on the validation set every 100 epochs. Training was halted when the validation test showed no further change. For each of the 6 networks, the final set of weights and the set of weights giving the best validation score were retained for a total of 12 networks.

Figure 2 compares the test set performance of six different scheduling configurations. G1TDN is the mean test set RDF of the best single TDNN $TD(\lambda)$ network (as determined by validation set performance). G12TDN is the mean RDF of all 12 learned networks. Analogously, G1N is the best single network trained using our hand-engineering features and G12N is the mean RDF of 12 hand-engineered networks. IR-V and IR-RDF are Zweben's iterative repair algorithms using the number of violations and the RDF (respectively) as the error function to be minimized via simulated annealing. From this we can see that G1TDN produces schedules with better average RDF than any of the other methods. In particular the F test shows that it is significantly better than all other algorithms except G12TDN.

Figure 3 compares the mean number of repairs required by each algorithm to find a solution. For the IR algorithms only repairs accepted by simulated annealing were counted. This shows that the neural network methods have learned very good evaluation functions—they are able to find a good solution much more directly than the simulated annealing methods. According to the F tests, the networks with engineered features are slightly better than the TDNN networks, but all of the networks are significantly better than simulated annealing.

A shortcoming of these figures, however, is that they only record the mean results of *single runs*. Better results are typically obtained from simulated annealing if the algorithm is run many times and the best solution retained. Figures 4 and 5 show the mean RDF of the best schedule as a function of the number of schedule repairs and CPU time expended. IR-V and IR-RDF were each run 50 times; G12N and

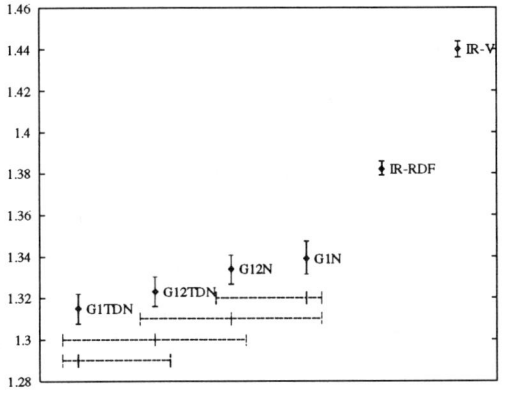 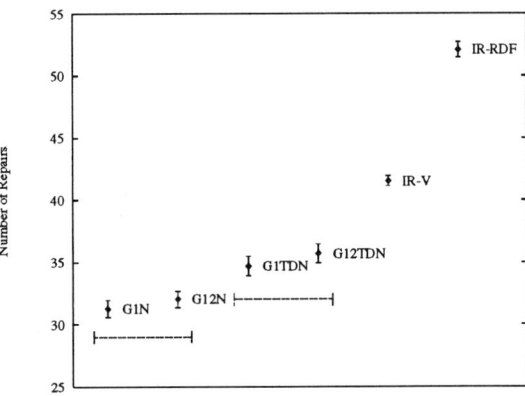

Figure 2: Mean RDF values. Vertical error bars show 95% confidence intervals. Horizontal bars group together algorithms that cannot be distinguished based on ANOVA F-tests at $p < 0.05$.

Figure 3: Mean number of repairs. Vertical error bars show 95% confidence intervals. Horizontal bars group together algorithms that cannot be distinguished based on ANOVA F-tests at $p < 0.05$.

G12TDN show the results of running each of the 12 networks once on each test problem. G1N and G1TDN show the results of running the best single net 10 times on each test problem. Because evaluation function ties are broken randomly, these 10 repetitions usually generate different schedules. Each time a network finds an improved solution to a problem, a point is plotted on the graph.

The graphs show that the learned networks clearly out-perform Zweben's IR algorithms. Figure 4 shows that the networks perform many fewer repairs to find schedules of the same quality as the IR algorithms. Note that the horizontal axis is plotted on a log scale—the networks maintain a constant *factor* advantage over IR. For a schedule of a year's duration, this improvement would translate into several days (and hundreds of thousands of dollars) saved.

Ultimately, G12TDN does slightly better than G12N. After 12 iterations and 21,676 repairs, G12TDN produced solutions with an average RDF of 1.196. By comparison, G12N performs 19,406 repairs and produces an average RDF of 1.202.

Figure 5 illustrates a problem with the neural network approach: the networks spend more CPU time selecting each repair. This reduces the differences between the methods. G12N exhibits the best tradeoff between CPU time and schedule quality, although G12TDN attains the best final schedule quality.

The major CPU cost of G12TDN is the cost of breaking the schedule into blocks and convolving the kernel networks with the blocks. There are many opportunities to make this more efficient by taking advantage of the fact that each repair changes only parts of the schedule, and therefore, only parts of the neural network calculation need to be updated.

5 Conclusions

This paper has shown how to apply temporal difference learning to job shop scheduling problems by formulating them as iterative repair problem spaces. The paper has also presented a modification of the TDNN architecture appropriate for schedul-

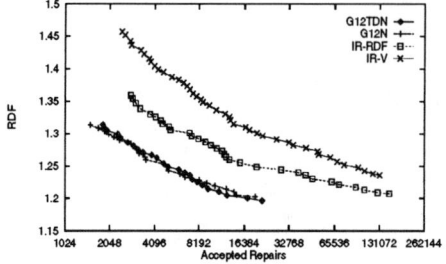 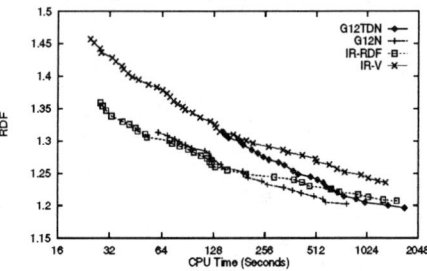

Figure 4: Comparison of Accepted Schedule Repairs

Figure 5: Comparison in CPU time

ing problems. The combined TDNN-$TD(\lambda)$ architecture can learn very powerful search heuristics that significantly out-perform all previous algorithms in terms of the quality of the resulting schedules. The TDNN architecture achieves this high performance with much less "feature-engineering" than our previous neural network approach. This demonstrates once again the superior ability of neural networks to learn useful higher-level features from raw input features.

Both of our neural-net-based methods demonstrate that the impressive performance of Tesauro's TD-gammon system can carry over to an important industrial application. Temporal difference learning is able to learn a very effective evaluation function for job shop scheduling. Using this function, a scheduler can find better schedules and find them in fewer search steps than the best previous methods.

Acknowledgments

The authors thank Rich Sutton and Monte Zweben for several helpful discussions. The authors gratefully acknowledge the support of NASA grant NAG 2-630 from NASA Ames Research Center. Additional support was provided by NSF grants CDA-9216172 and IRI-9204129.

References

[Lang et al., 1990] K. J. Lang, A. H. Waibel, and G. E. Hinton. A time-delay neural network architecture for isolated word recognition. *Neural Networks*, 3:33–43, 1990.

[LeCun et al., 1989] Y. LeCun, B. Boser, J. S. Deniker, and D. Henderson et al. Backpropagation applied to handwritten zip code recognition. *Neural Computation*, 1:541–551, 1989.

[Pomerleau, 1991] D. A. Pomerleau. Efficient training of artificial neural networks for autonomous navigation. *Neural Computation*, 3(1):88–97, 1991.

[Sutton, 1988] R. S. Sutton. Learning to predict by the methods of temporal differences. *Machine Learning*, 3(1):9–44, August 1988.

[Tesauro, 1992] G. J. Tesauro. Practical issues in temporal difference learning. *Machine Learning*, 8(3/4):257–277, 1992.

[Zhang and Dietterich, 1995] W. Zhang and T. Dietterich. A reinforcement learning approach to job-shop scheduling. In *IJCAI-95*, pages 1114–1120, 1995.

[Zweben et al., 1994] M. Zweben, B. Daun, and M. Deal. Scheduling and rescheduling with iterative repair. In M. Zweben and M. S. Fox, editors, *Intelligent Scheduling*, chapter 8, pages 241–255. Morgan Kaufmann, 1994.

Competence Acquisition in an Autonomous Mobile Robot using Hardware Neural Techniques.

Geoff Jackson and Alan F. Murray
Department of Electrical Engineering
Edinburgh University
Edinburgh, EH9 3JL
Scotland, UK
gbj@ee.ed.ac.uk,afm@ee.ed.ac.uk

Abstract

In this paper we examine the practical use of hardware neural networks in an autonomous mobile robot. We have developed a hardware neural system based around a custom VLSI chip, EPSILON II[1], designed specifically for embedded hardware neural applications. We present here a demonstration application of an autonomous mobile robot that highlights the flexibility of this system. This robot gains basic mobility competence in very few training epochs using an "instinct-rule" training methodology.

1 INTRODUCTION

Though neural networks have been shown as an effective solution for a diverse range of real-world problems, applications and especially hardware implementations have been few and slow to emerge. For example in the DARPA neural networks study of 1988; of the 77 neural network applications investigated only 4 had resulted in field tested systems [Widrow, 1988]. Furthermore, none of these used dedicated neural network hardware. It is our view that this lack of tangible successes can be summarised by the following points:

- Most neural applications will be served optimally by fast, generic digital computers.
- Dedicated digital neural accelerators have a limited lifetime as "the fastest", as standard computers develop so rapidly.

---

[1] Edinburgh Pulse Stream Implemenation of a Learning Oriented Network.

- Analog neural VLSI is a niche technology, optimally applied at the interface between the real world and higher-level digital processing.

This attitude has some profound implications with respect to the size, nature and constraints we place on new hardware neural designs. After several years of research into hardware neural network implementation, we have now concentrated on the areas in which analog neural network technology has an "edge" over well established digital technology.

Within the pulse stream neural network research at the University of Edinburgh, the EPSILON chip's areas of strength can be summarised as:

- Analog or digital inputs, digital outputs.
- Scaleable and cascadeable design.
- Modest size.
- Compact, low power.

This list points naturally and strongly to problems on the boundary of the real, analog world and digital processing, such as pre-processing/interpretation of analog sensor data. Here a modest neural network can act as an *intelligent analog-to-digital converter* presenting preprocessed information to its host. We are now engaged in a two pronged approach, whereby development of technology to improve the performance of pulse stream neural network chips is occurring concurrently with a search and development of applications to which this technology can be applied. The key requirements of this technological development are that devices must:

- Work directly with analog signals.
- Provide a moderate size network.
- Have the potential for a fully integrated solution.

In working with the above constraints and goals we have developed a new chip, EPSILON II, and a bus based processor card incorporating it. It is our aim to use this system to develop applications. As our first demonstration the EPSILON processor card has been mounted on an autonomous mobile robot. In this case the network utilises a mixture of analog and digital sensor information and performs a mapping between input/sensor space, a mixture of analog and digital signals, and output motor control.

2 THE EPSILON II CHIP

The EPSILON II chip has been designed around the requirements of an application based system. It follows on from an earlier generation of pulse stream neural network chip, the EPSILON chip [Murray, 1992].

The EPSILON II chip represents neural states as a pulse encoded signal. These pulse encoded signals have digital signal levels which make them highly immune to noise and ideal for inter and intra-chip communication, facilitating efficient cascading of chips to form larger systems. The EPSILON II chip can take as inputs either pulse encoded signals or analog voltage levels, thus facilitating the fusing of analog and digital data in one system. Internally the chip is analog in nature allowing the synaptic multiplication function to be carried out in compact and efficient analog cells [Jackson, 1994].

Table 1 shows the principal specifications of the EPSILON II chip. The EPSILON II chip is based around a 32x32 synaptic matrix allowing efficient interfacing to digital systems. Several features of the device have been developed specifically for applications based usage. The first of these is a programmable input mode. This

Table 1: EPSILON II Specifications

EPSILON II Chip Specifications	
No. of state input pins	32
Input modes	Analog, PW or PF
Input mode programmability	Bit programmable
No. of state outputs	32 pinned out
Output modes	PW or PF
Digital recovery of analog I/P	Yes - PW encoded
No. of Synapses	1024
Additional *autobias* synapses	4 per output neuron
Weight storage	Dynamic
Programmable activity voltage	Yes
Die size	$6.9mm \times 7mm$

allows each of the network inputs to be programmed as either a direct analog input or a digital pulse encoded input. We believe that this is vital for application based usage where it is often necessary to *fuse* real–world analog data with historical or control data generated digitally. The second major feature is a pulse recovery mode. This allows conversion of any analog input into a digital value for direct use by the host system. Both these features are utilised in the robotics application described in section 4 of this paper.

3 EPSILON PROCESSOR CARD

The need to embed the EPSILON chip in a processor card is driven by several considerations. Firstly, working with pulse encoded signals requires substantial processing to interface directly to digital systems. If the neural processor is to be transparent to the host system and is not to become a substantial processing overhead, then all pulse support operations must be carried out independently of the host system. Secondly, to respond to further chip level advances and allow rapid prototyping of new applications as they emerge, a certain amount of flexibility is needed in the system. It is with these points in mind that the design of the flexible EPSILON Processor Card (EPC) was undertaken.

3.1 DESIGN SPECIFICATION

The EPC has been designed to meet the following specifications. The card must:

- Operate on a conventional digital bus system.
- Be transparent to the host processor, that is carry out all the necessary pulse encoding and decoding.
- Carry out the refresh operations of the dynamic weights stored on the EPSILON chip.
- Generate the ramp waveforms necessary for pulse width coding.
- Support the operation of multiple EPC's.
- Allow direct input of analog signals.

As all data used and generated by the chip is effectively of 8-bit resolution, the STE bus, an industry standard 8-bit bus, was chosen for the bus system. This is also cost effective and allows the use of readily available support cards such as processors, DSP cards and analog and digital signal conditioning cards.

To allow the transparency of operation the card must perform a variety of functions. A block diagram indicating these functions is shown in figure 1.

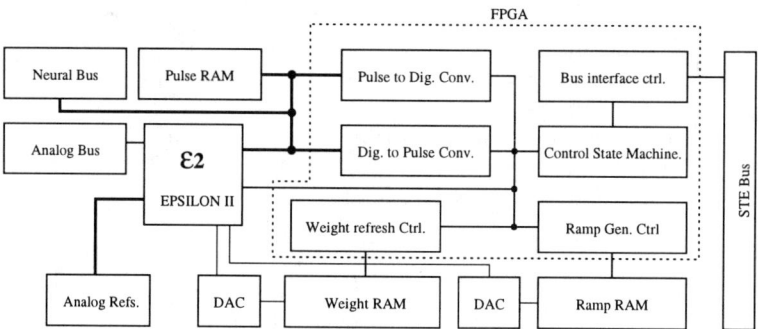

Figure 1: EPSILON Processor Card

A substantial amount of digital processing is required by the card, especially in the pulse conversion circuitry. To conform to the *Eurocard* standard size of the STE specification an FPGA device is used to "absorb" most of the digital logic. A twin mother/daughter board design is also used to isolate sensitive analog circuitry from the digital logic. The use of the FPGA makes the card extremely versatile as it is now easily reconfigurable to adapt to specialist application. The dotted box of figure 1 shows functions implemented by the FPGA device. An on board EPROM can hold multiple FPGA configurations such that the board can be reconfigured "on the fly". All EPSILON support functions, such as ramp generation, weight refresh, pulse conversion and interface control are carried out on the card. Also the use of the FPGA means that new ideas are easily tested as all digital signal paths go via this device. Thus a card of new functionality can be designed without the need to design a new PCB.

3.2 SPECIALIST BUSES

The digital pulse bus is buffered out under control of the FPGA to the neural bus along with two control signals. Handshaking between EPC's is done over these lines to allow the transfer of pulse stream data between processors. This implies that larger networks can be implemented with little or no increase in computation time or overhead. A separate analog bus is included to bring analog inputs directly onto the chip.

4 APPLICATIONS DEVELOPMENT

The over-riding reason for the development of the EPC is to allow the easy development of hardware neural network applications. We have already indicated that we believe that this form of neural technology will find its niche where its advantages of direct sensor interface, compactness and cost-effectiveness are of prime importance. As a good and intrinsically interesting example of this genre of applications, we have chosen autonomous mobile robotic control as a first test for EPSILON II. The object of this demonstrator is not to advance the state-of-the-art in robotics.

Rather it is to demonstrate analog neural VLSI in an appropriate and stimulating context.

4.1 "INSTINCT-RULE" ROBOT

The "instinct-rule" robotic control philosophy is based on a software-controlled exemplar from the University's Department of Artificial Intelligence [Nehmzow, 1992]. The robot incorporates an EPC which interfaces all the analog sensor signals and provides the programmable neural link between sensor/input space and the motor drive actuators.

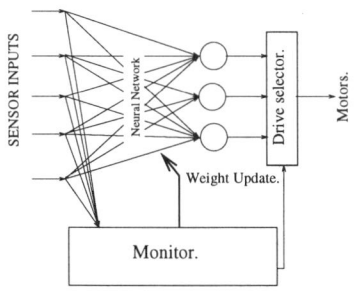

a) Controller Architecture.　　　　　　　　b) Instinct rule robot.

Figure 2: "Instinct Rule" Robot

The controller architecture is shown in figure 2. The neural network implemented on the EPC is the *plastic* element that determines the mapping between sensory data and motor actions. The majority of the monitor section is currently implemented on a host processor and monitors the performance of the neural network. It does this by regularly evaluating a set of *instinct rules*. These rules are simple behaviour based axioms. For example, we use two rules to promote simple obstacle avoidance competence in the robot, as listed in column one of table 2

Table 2: Instinct Rules

Simple obstacle avoidance.		Wall following	
1.	**Keep crash sensors inactive.**	1.	**Keep crash sensors inactive.**
2.	**Move forward.**	2.	**Keep side sensors active.**
		3.	**Move forward.**

If an instinct rule is violated the drive selector then chooses the next strongest output (motor action) from the neural network. This action is then performed to see if it relieves the violation. If it does, it is used as targets to train the neural network. If it does not, the next strongest action is tried. The mechanism to accomplish this will be described in more detail in section 4.2.

Using this scheme the robot can be initialised with random weights (i.e. no mapping between sensors and motor control) and within a few epochs obtains basic obstacle avoidance competence.

It is a relatively easy matter to promote more complex behaviour with the addition of other rules. For example to achieve a wall following behaviour a third rule is introduced as shown in column two of table 2. Navigational tasks can be accomplished with the addition of a **"maximise navigational signal"** rule. An example of this is a light sensor mounted on the robot producing a behaviour to move towards a light source. Equally, a signal from a more complex, higher level, navigational system could be used. Thus the instinct rule controller handles basic obstacle avoidance competence and motor/sensory interface tasks leaving other resources free for intensive navigational tasks.

4.2 INSTINCT RULE EVALUATION USING SOMATIC TENSION

The original instinct rule robot used binary sensor signals and evaluated performance of alternative actions for fixed, and progressively longer, periods of time [Nehmzow, 1992]. With the EPC interfacing directly to analog sensors an improved scheme has been developed. If we sum all sensors onto a neuron with fixed and equal weights we gain a measure of total sensory activity. Let us call this *somatic tension* as an analogy to biological signal aggregation on the soma. If we have an instinct violation and an alternative action is performed we can monitor this somatic tension to gauge the performance of this action. If tension decreases significantly we continue the action. If it increases significantly we choose an alternative action. If tension remains high and roughly the same, we are in a *tight* situation, for example say a corner. In this case we perform actions for progressively longer periods continuing to monitor somatic tension for a drop.

4.3 RESULTS AND DISCUSSION

The instinct rule robot has been constructed and its performance is comparable with software-controlled predecessors. Unfortunately direct comparisons are not possible due to unavailability of the original exemplars and differing physical characteristics of the robots themselves. In developing the application several observations were made concerning the behaviour of the system that would not have come to light in a simulated environment.

In any system including real mechanics and real analog signals, imperfections and noise are present. For example, in a real robot we cannot guarantee that a forward motion directive will result in perfect forward motion due to inherent asymmetries in the system. The instinct rule architecture does not assume a-priori knowledge such as this so behaviour is not affected adversely. This was tested by retarding one drive motor of the robot to give it a bias to one side.

In early development, as the monitor was being *tuned*, the robot showed a tendency to oscillatory motion, thus exhibiting undesirable behaviour that satisfies its instincts. It could, for example, oscillate back and forth at a corner. In a simulated environment this continues indefinitely. However, with real mechanics and noisy analog sensors the robot breaks out of this undesirable behaviour.

These observations strengthen the arguments for hardware development aimed at embedded systems. The robot application is but an example of the different, and often surprising conditions that pertain in a "real" system. If neural networks are to find applications in real-world, low-cost and analog-interface applications, these are the conditions we must deal with, and appropriate, analog hardware is the optimal medium for a solution.

5 CONCLUSIONS

This paper has described pulse stream neural networks that have been developed to a system level to aid development of applications. We have therefore defined areas of strengths of this technology along with suggestions of where this is best applied. The strengths of this system include:

1. Direct interfacing to analog signals.
2. The ability to fuse direct analog sensor data with digital sensor data processed elsewhere in the system.
3. Distributed processing. Several EPC's may be embedded in a system to allow multiple networks and/or multi layer networks.
4. The EPC represents a flexible system level development environment. It is easily reconfigured for new applications or improved chip technology.
5. The EPC requires very little computational overhead from the host system and can operate independently if needed.

A demonstration application of an instinct rule robot has been presented highlighting the use of neural networks as an interface between real-world analog signals and digital control.

In conclusion we believe that the immediate future of neural analog VLSI is in small applications based systems that interface directly to the real-world. We see this as the primary niche area where analog VLSI neural networks will replace conventional digital systems.

Acknowledgements

Thanks are due to Ulrich Nehmzow, University of Manchester, for discussions and information on the instinct-rule controller and the loan of his original robot – Alder.

References

[Caudell, 1990] Caudell, M. and Butler, C. (1990). *Naturally Intelligent Systems*. MIT Press, Cambridge, Ma.

[Jackson, 1994] Jackson, G., Hamilton, A., and Murray, A. F. (1994). Pulse stream VLSI neural systems: into robotics. In *Proceedings ISCAS'94*, volume 6, pages 375–378. IEEE Press.

[Maren, 1990] Maren, A., Harston, C., and Pap, R. (1990). *Handbook of Neural Computing Applications*. Academic Press, San Diego, Ca.

[Murray, 1992] Murray, A. F., Baxter, D. J., Churcher, S., Hamilton, A., Reekie, H. M., and Tarassenko, L. (1992). The Edinburgh pulse stream implementation of a learning-oriented network (EPSILON) chip. In *Neural Information Processing Systems (NIPS) Conference*.

[Nehmzow, 1992] Nehmzow, U. (1992). *Experiments in Competence Acquisition for Autonomous Mobile Robots*. PhD thesis, University of Edinburgh.

[Widrow, 1988] Widrow, B. (1988). *DARPA Neural Network Study*. AFCEA International Press.

Generalization in Reinforcement Learning: Successful Examples Using Sparse Coarse Coding

Richard S. Sutton
University of Massachusetts
Amherst, MA 01003 USA
rich@cs.umass.edu

Abstract

On large problems, reinforcement learning systems must use parameterized function approximators such as neural networks in order to generalize between similar situations and actions. In these cases there are no strong theoretical results on the accuracy of convergence, and computational results have been mixed. In particular, Boyan and Moore reported at last year's meeting a series of negative results in attempting to apply dynamic programming together with function approximation to simple control problems with continuous state spaces. In this paper, we present positive results for all the control tasks they attempted, and for one that is significantly larger. The most important differences are that we used sparse-coarse-coded function approximators (CMACs) whereas they used mostly global function approximators, and that we learned online whereas they learned offline. Boyan and Moore and others have suggested that the problems they encountered could be solved by using actual outcomes ("rollouts"), as in classical Monte Carlo methods, and as in the TD(λ) algorithm when $\lambda = 1$. However, in our experiments this always resulted in substantially poorer performance. We conclude that reinforcement learning can work robustly in conjunction with function approximators, and that there is little justification at present for avoiding the case of general λ.

1 Reinforcement Learning and Function Approximation

Reinforcement learning is a broad class of optimal control methods based on estimating value functions from experience, simulation, or search (Barto, Bradtke & Singh, 1995; Sutton, 1988; Watkins, 1989). Many of these methods, e.g., dynamic programming and temporal-difference learning, build their estimates in part on the basis of other estimates. This may be worrisome because, in practice, the estimates never become exact; on large problems, parameterized function approximators such as neural networks must be used. Because the estimates are imperfect, and because they in turn are used as the targets for other estimates, it seems possible that the ultimate result might be very poor estimates, or even divergence. Indeed some such methods have been shown to be unstable in theory (Baird, 1995; Gordon, 1995; Tsitsiklis & Van Roy, 1994) and in practice (Boyan & Moore, 1995). On the other hand, other methods have been proven stable in theory (Sutton, 1988; Dayan, 1992) and very effective in practice (Lin, 1991; Tesauro, 1992; Zhang & Dietterich, 1995; Crites & Barto, 1996). What are the key requirements of a method or task in order to obtain good performance? The experiments in this paper are part of narrowing the answer to this question.

The reinforcement learning methods we use are variations of the *sarsa* algorithm (Rummery & Niranjan, 1994; Singh & Sutton, 1996). This method is the same as the TD(λ) algorithm (Sutton, 1988), except applied to state-action pairs instead of states, and where the predictions are used as the basis for selecting actions. The learning agent estimates action-values, $Q^\pi(s, a)$, defined as the expected future reward starting in state s, taking action a, and thereafter following policy π. These are estimated for all states and actions, and for the policy currently being followed by the agent. The policy is chosen dependent on the current estimates in such a way that they jointly improve, ideally approaching an optimal policy and the optimal action-values. In our experiments, actions were selected according to what we call the ϵ-*greedy policy*. Most of the time, the action selected when in state s was the action for which the estimate $\hat{Q}(s, a)$ was the largest (with ties broken randomly). However, a small fraction, ϵ, of the time, the action was instead selected randomly uniformly from the action set (which was always discrete and finite). There are two variations of the sarsa algorithm, one using conventional *accumulate* traces and one using *replace* traces (Singh & Sutton, 1996). This and other details of the algorithm we used are given in Figure 1.

To apply the sarsa algorithm to tasks with a continuous state space, we combined it with a sparse, coarse-coded function approximator known as the CMAC (Albus, 1980; Miller, Gordon & Kraft, 1990; Watkins, 1989; Lin & Kim, 1991; Dean et al., 1992; Tham, 1994). A CMAC uses multiple overlapping tilings of the state space to produce a feature representation for a final linear mapping where all the learning takes place. See Figure 2. The overall effect is much like a network with fixed radial basis functions, except that it is particularly efficient computationally (in other respects one would expect RBF networks and similar methods (see Sutton & Whitehead, 1993) to work just as well). It is important to note that the tilings need not be simple grids. For example, to avoid the "curse of dimensionality," a common trick is to ignore some dimensions in some tilings, i.e., to use hyperplanar slices instead of boxes. A second major trick is "hashing"—a consistent random collapsing of a large set of tiles into a much smaller set. Through hashing, memory requirements are often reduced by large factors with little loss of performance. This is possible because high resolution is needed in only a small fraction of the state space. Hashing frees us from the curse of dimensionality in the sense that memory requirements need not be exponential in the number of dimensions, but need merely match the real demands of the task.

2   Good Convergence on Control Problems

We applied the sarsa and CMAC combination to the three continuous-state control problems studied by Boyan and Moore (1995): *2D gridworld*, *puddle world*, and *mountain car*. Whereas they used a model of the task dynamics and applied dynamic programming backups offline to a fixed set of states, we learned *online*, without a model, and backed up whatever states were encountered during complete trials. Unlike Boyan

1. Initially: $w_a(f) := \frac{Q_o}{c}$, $e_a(f) := 0$, $\forall a \in Actions$, $\forall f \in CMAC\text{-}tiles$.

2. Start of Trial: $s := random\text{-}state()$;
   $F := features(s)$;
   $a := \epsilon\text{-}greedy\text{-}policy(F)$.

3. Eligibility Traces: $e_b(f) := \lambda e_b(f)$, $\forall b$, $\forall f$;
   3a. Accumulate algorithm: $e_a(f) := e_a(f) + 1$, $\forall f \in F$.
   3b. Replace algorithm: $e_a(f) := 1$, $e_b(f) := 0$, $\forall f \in F$, $\forall b \neq a$.

4. Environment Step:
   Take action a; observe resultant reward, r, and next state, s'.

5. Choose Next Action:
   $F' := features(s')$, unless s' is the terminal state, then $F' := \emptyset$;
   $a' := \epsilon\text{-}greedy\text{-}policy(F')$.

6. Learn: $w_b(f) := w_b(f) + \frac{\alpha}{c}[r + \sum_{f \in F'} w_{a'} - \sum_{f \in F} w_a]e_b(f)$, $\forall b, \forall f$.

7. Loop: $a := a'$; $s := s'$; $F := F'$; if s' is the terminal state, go to 2; else go to 3.

Figure 1: The sarsa algorithm for finite-horizon (trial based) tasks. The function ϵ-greedy-policy(F) returns, with probability ϵ, a random action or, with probability $1-\epsilon$, computes $\sum_{f \in F} w_a$ for each action a and returns the action for which the sum is largest, resolving any ties randomly. The function features(s) returns the set of CMAC tiles corresponding to the state s. The number of tiles returned is the constant c. Q_0, α, and λ are scalar parameters.

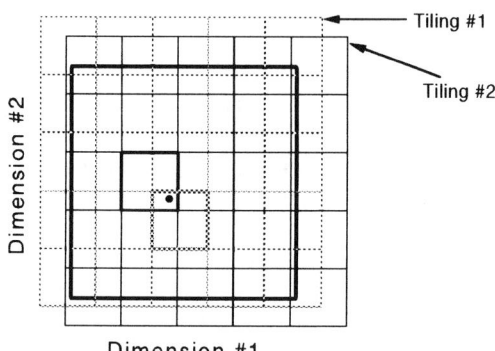

Figure 2: CMACs involve multiple overlapping tilings of the state space. Here we show two 5 × 5 regular tilings offset and overlaid over a continuous, two-dimensional state space. Any state, such as that shown by the dot, is in exactly one tile of each tiling. A state's tiles are used to represent it in the sarsa algorithm described above. The tilings need not be regular grids such as shown here. In particular, they are often hyperplanar slices, the number of which grows sub-exponentially with dimensionality of the space. CMACs have been widely used in conjunction with reinforcement learning systems (e.g., Watkins, 1989; Lin & Kim, 1991; Dean, Basye & Shewchuk, 1992; Tham, 1994).

and Moore, we found robust good performance on all tasks. We report here results for the puddle world and the mountain car, the more difficult of the tasks they considered.

Training consisted of a series of trials, each starting from a randomly selected non-goal state and continuing until the goal region was reached. On each step a penalty (negative reward) of -1 was incurred. In the puddle-world task, an additional penalty was incurred when the state was within the "puddle" regions. The details are given in the appendix. The 3D plots below show the estimated cost-to-goal of each state, i.e., $\max_a \hat{Q}(s,a)$. In the puddle-world task, the CMACs consisted of 5 tilings, each 5×5, as in Figure 2. In the mountain-car task we used 10 tilings, each 9×9.

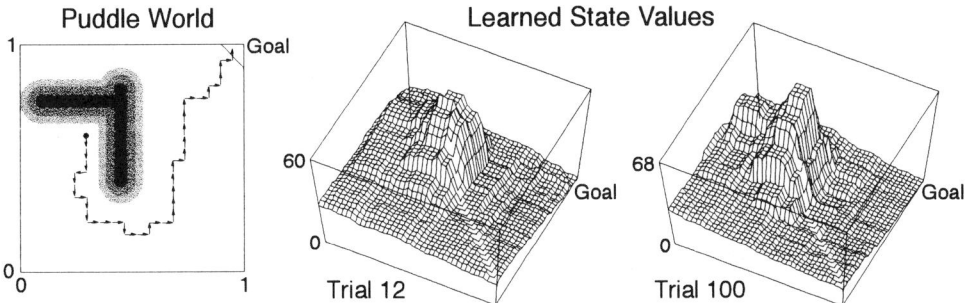

Figure 3: The puddle task and the cost-to-goal function learned during one run.

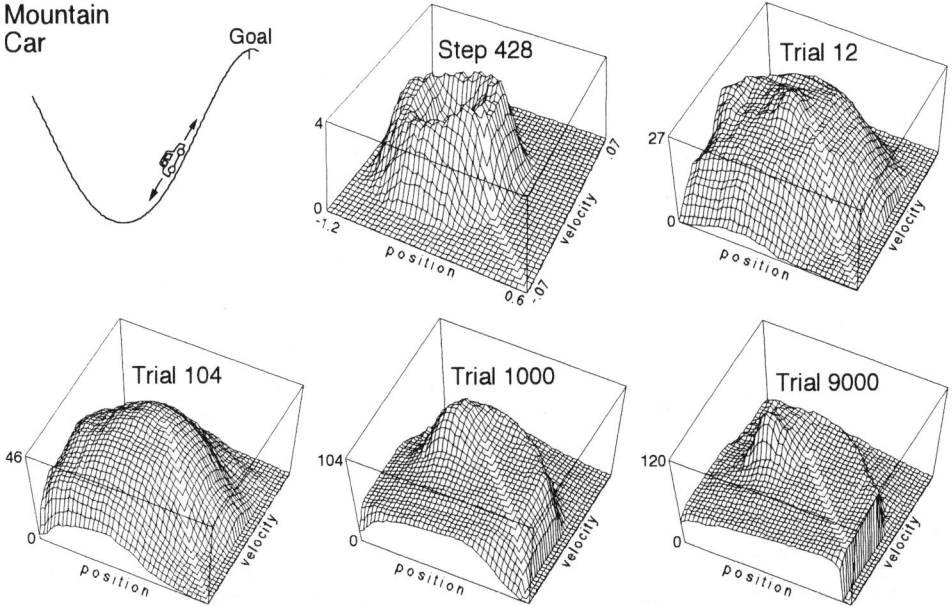

Figure 4: The mountain-car task and the cost-to-goal function learned during one run. The engine is too weak to accelerate directly up the slope; to reach the goal, the car must first move away from it. The first plot shows the value function learned before the goal was reached even once.

We also experimented with a larger and more difficult task not attempted by Boyan and Moore. The *acrobot* is a two-link under-actuated robot (Figure 5) roughly analogous to a gymnast swinging on a highbar (Dejong & Spong, 1994; Spong & Vidyasagar, 1989). The first joint (corresponding to the gymnast's hands on the bar) cannot exert

The object is to swing the endpoint (the feet) above the bar by an amount equal to one of the links. As in the mountain-car task, there are three actions, positive torque, negative torque, and no torque, and reward is −1 on all steps. (See the appendix.)

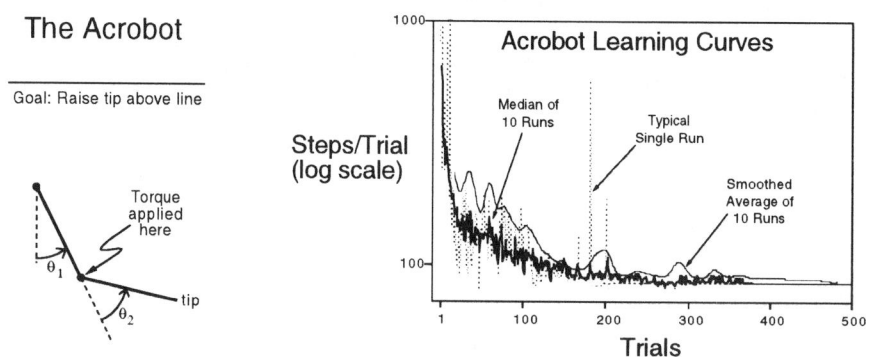

Figure 5: The Acrobot and its learning curves.

3 The Effect of λ

A key question in reinforcement learning is whether it is better to learn on the basis of actual outcomes, as in Monte Carlo methods and as in TD(λ) with $\lambda = 1$, or to learn on the basis of interim estimates, as in TD(λ) with $\lambda < 1$. Theoretically, the former has asymptotic advantages when function approximators are used (Dayan, 1992; Bertsekas, 1995), but empirically the latter is thought to achieve better learning rates (Sutton, 1988). However, hitherto this question has not been put to an empirical test using function approximators. Figures 6 shows the results of such a test.

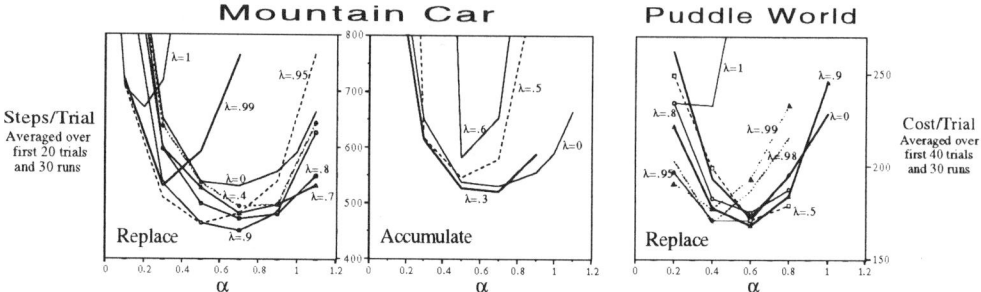

Figure 6: The effects of λ and α in the Mountain-Car and Puddle-World tasks.

Figure 7 summarizes this data, and that from two other systematic studies with different tasks, to present an overall picture of the effect of λ. In all cases performance is an inverted-U shaped function of λ, and performance degrades rapidly as λ approaches 1, where the worst performance is obtained. The fact that performance improves as λ is increased from 0 argues for the use of eligibility traces and against 1-step methods such as TD(0) and 1-step Q-learning. The fact that performance improves rapidly as λ is reduced below 1 argues against the use of Monte Carlo or "rollout" methods. Despite the theoretical asymptotic advantages of these methods, they are appear to be inferior in practice.

Acknowledgments
The author gratefully acknowledges the assistance of Justin Boyan, Andrew Moore, Satinder Singh, and Peter Dayan in evaluating these results.

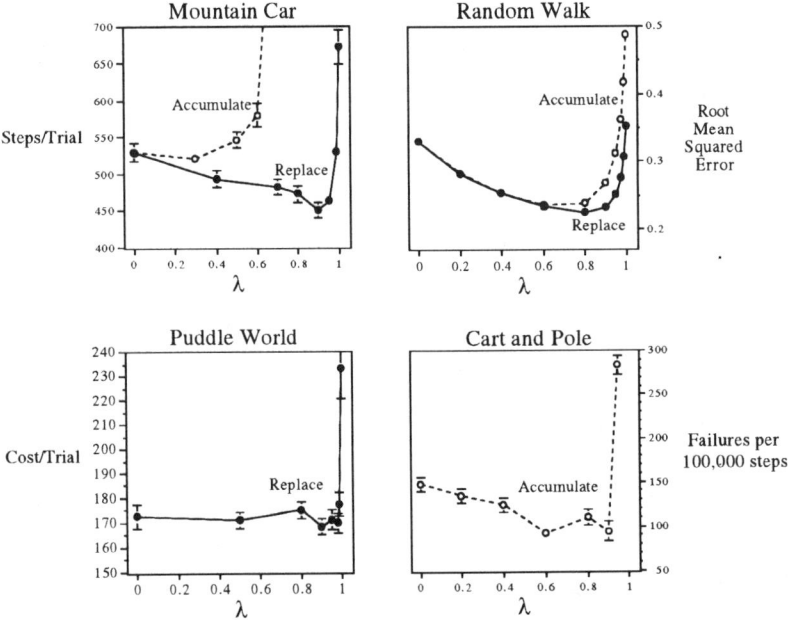

Figure 7: Performance versus λ, at best α, for four different tasks. The left panels summarize data from Figure 6. The upper right panel concerns a 21-state Markov chain, the objective being to predict, for each state, the probability of terminating in one terminal state as opposed to the other (Singh & Sutton, 1996). The lower left panel concerns the pole balancing task studied by Barto, Sutton and Anderson (1983). This is previously unpublished data from an earlier study (Sutton, 1984).

References

Albus, J. S. (1981) *Brain, Behavior, and Robotics*, chapter 6, pages 139–179. Byte Books.

Baird, L. C. (1995) Residual Algorithms: Reinforcement Learning with Function Approximation. *Proc. ML95*. Morgan Kaufman, San Francisco, CA.

Barto, A. G., Bradtke, S. J., & Singh, S. P. (1995) Real-time learning and control using asynchronous dynamic programming. *Artificial Intelligence*.

Barto, A. G., Sutton, R. S., & Anderson, C. W. (1983) Neuronlike elements that can solve difficult learning control problems. *Trans. IEEE SMC*, 13, 835–846.

Bertsekas, D. P. (1995) A counterexample to temporal differences learning. *Neural Computation*, 7, 270–279.

Boyan, J. A. & Moore, A. W. (1995) Generalization in reinforcement learning: Safely approximating the value function. *NIPS-7*. San Mateo, CA: Morgan Kaufmann.

Crites, R. H. & Barto, A. G. (1996) Improving elevator performance using reinforcement learning. *NIPS-8*. Cambridge, MA: MIT Press.

Dayan, P. (1992) The convergence of TD(λ) for general λ. *Machine Learning*, 8, 341–362.

Dean, T., Basye, K. & Shewchuk, J. (1992) Reinforcement learning for planning and control. In S. Minton, *Machine Learning Methods for Planning and Scheduling*. Morgan Kaufmann.

DeJong, G. & Spong, M. W. (1994) Swinging up the acrobot: An example of intelligent control. In *Proceedings of the American Control Conference, pages 2158–2162*.

Gordon, G. (1995) Stable function approximation in dynamic programming. *Proc. ML95*.

Lin, L. J. (1992) Self-improving reactive agents based on reinforcement learning, planning and teaching. *Machine Learning*, 8(3/4), 293–321.

Lin, C-S. & Kim, H. (1991) CMAC-based adaptive critic self-learning control. *IEEE Trans. Neural Networks*, 2, 530–533.

Miller, W. T., Glanz, F. H., & Kraft, L. G. (1990) CMAC: An associative neural network alternative to backpropagation. *Proc. of the IEEE*, 78, 1561–1567.

Rummery, G. A. & Niranjan, M. (1994) On-line Q-learning using connectionist systems. Technical Report CUED/F-INFENG/TR 166, Cambridge University Engineering Dept.

Singh, S. P. & Sutton, R. S. (1996) Reinforcement learning with replacing eligibility traces. *Machine Learning*.

Spong, M. W. & Vidyasagar, M. (1989) *Robot Dynamics and Control*. New York: Wiley.

Sutton, R. S. (1984) *Temporal Credit Assignment in Reinforcement Learning*. PhD thesis, University of Massachusetts, Amherst, MA.

Sutton, R. S. (1988) Learning to predict by the methods of temporal differences. *Machine Learning*, 3, 9–44.

Sutton, R. S. & Whitehead, S. D. (1993) Online learning with random representations. *Proc. ML93*, pages 314–321. Morgan Kaufmann.

Tham, C. K. (1994) *Modular On-Line Function Approximation for Scaling up Reinforcement Learning*. PhD thesis, Cambridge Univ., Cambridge, England.

Tesauro, G. J. (1992) Practical issues in temporal difference learning. *Machine Learning*, 8(3/4), 257–277.

Tsitsiklis, J. N. & Van Roy, B. (1994) Feature-based methods for large-scale dynamic programming. Techical Report LIDS-P2277, MIT, Cambridge, MA 02139.

Watkins, C. J. C. H. (1989) *Learning from Delayed Rewards*. PhD thesis, Cambridge Univ.

Zhang, W. & Dietterich, T. G., (1995) A reinforcement learning approach to job-shop scheduling. *Proc. IJCAI95*.

Appendix: Details of the Experiments

In the puddle world, there were four actions, up, down, right, and left, which moved approximately 0.05 in these directions unless the movement would cause the agent to leave the limits of the space. A random gaussian noise with standard deviation 0.01 was also added to the motion along both dimensions. The costs (negative rewards) on this task were -1 for each time step plus additional penalties if either or both of the two oval "puddles" were entered. These penalties were -400 times the distance into the puddle (distance to the nearest edge). The puddles were 0.1 in radius and were located at center points (.1, .75) to (.45, .75) and (.45, .4) to (.45, .8). The initial state of each trial was selected randomly uniformly from the non-goal states. For the run in Figure 3, $\alpha = 0.5$, $\lambda = 0.9$, $c = 5$, $\epsilon = 0.1$, and $Q_0 = 0$. For Figure 6, $Q_0 = -20$.

Details of the mountain-car task are given in Singh & Sutton (1996). For the run in Figure 4, $\alpha = 0.5$, $\lambda = 0.9$, $c = 10$, $\epsilon = 0$, and $Q_0 = 0$. For Figure 6, $c = 5$ and $Q_0 = -100$.

In the acrobot task, the CMACs used 48 tilings. Each of the four dimensions were divided into 6 intervals. 12 tilings depended in the usual way on all 4 dimensions. 12 other tilings depended only on 3 dimensions (3 tilings for each of the four sets of 3 dimensions). 12 others depended only on two dimensions (2 tilings for each of the 6 sets of two dimensions. And finally 12 tilings depended each on only one dimension (3 tilings for each dimension). This resulted in a total of $12 \cdot 6^4 + 12 \cdot 6^3 + 12 \cdot 6^2 + 12 \cdot 6 = 18,648$ tiles. The equations of motion were:

$$\ddot{\theta}_1 = -d_1^{-1}(d_2\ddot{\theta}_2 + \phi_1)$$

$$\ddot{\theta}_2 = \left(m_2 l_{c2}^2 + I_2 - \frac{d_2^2}{d_1}\right)^{-1} \left(\tau + \frac{d_2}{d_1}\phi_1 - \phi_2\right)$$

$$d_1 = m_1 l_{c1}^2 + m_2(l_1^2 + l_{c2}^2 + 2l_1 l_{c2} \cos\theta_2) + I_1 + I_2)$$

$$d_2 = m_2(l_{c2}^2 + l_1 l_{c2} \cos\theta_2) + I_2$$

$$\phi_1 = -m_2 l_1 l_{c2} \dot{\theta}_2^2 \sin\theta_2 - 2m_2 l_1 l_{c2} \dot{\theta}_2 \dot{\theta}_1 \sin\theta_2 + (m_1 l_{c1} + m_2 l_1)g \cos(\theta_1 - \pi/2) + \phi_2$$

$$\phi_2 = m_2 l_{c2} g \cos(\theta_1 + \theta_2 - \pi/2)$$

where $\tau \in \{+1, -1, 0\}$ was the torque applied at the second joint, and $\Delta = 0.05$ was the time increment. Actions were chosen after every four of the state updates given by the above equations, corresponding to 5 Hz. The angular velocities were bounded by $\dot{\theta}_1 \in [-4\pi, 4\pi]$ and $\dot{\theta}_2 \in [-9\pi, 9\pi]$. Finally, the remaining constants were $m1 = m2 = 1$ (masses of the links), $l_1 = l_2 = 1$ (lengths of links), $l_{c1} = l_{c2} = 0.5$ (lengths to center of mass of links), $I_1 = I_2 = 1$ (moments of inertia of links), and $g = 9.8$ (gravity). The parameters were $\alpha = 0.2$, $\lambda = 0.9$, $c = 48$, $\epsilon = 0$, $Q_0 = 0$. The starting state on each trial was $\theta_1 = \theta_2 = 0$.

Stable Linear Approximations to Dynamic Programming for Stochastic Control Problems with Local Transitions

Benjamin Van Roy and John N. Tsitsiklis
Laboratory for Information and Decision Systems
Massachusetts Institute of Technology
Cambridge, MA 02139
e-mail: bvr@mit.edu, jnt@mit.edu

Abstract

We consider the solution to large stochastic control problems by means of methods that rely on compact representations and a variant of the value iteration algorithm to compute approximate cost–to–go functions. While such methods are known to be unstable in general, we identify a new class of problems for which convergence, as well as graceful error bounds, are guaranteed. This class involves linear parameterizations of the cost–to–go function together with an assumption that the dynamic programming operator is a contraction with respect to the Euclidean norm when applied to functions in the parameterized class. We provide a special case where this assumption is satisfied, which relies on the locality of transitions in a state space. Other cases will be discussed in a full length version of this paper.

1 INTRODUCTION

Neural networks are well established in the domains of pattern recognition and function approximation, where their properties and training algorithms have been well studied. Recently, however, there have been some successful applications of neural networks in a totally different context – that of sequential decision making under uncertainty (stochastic control).

Stochastic control problems have been studied extensively in the operations research and control theory literature for a long time, using the methodology of dynamic programming [Bertsekas, 1995]. In dynamic programming, the most important object is the *cost–to–go (or value) function*, which evaluates the expected future cost to be incurred, as a function of the current state of a system. Such functions can be used to guide control decisions.

Dynamic programming provides a variety of methods for computing cost–to–go functions. Unfortunately, dynamic programming is computationally intractable in the context of many stochastic control problems that arise in practice. This is because a cost–to–go value is computed and stored for each state, and due to the curse of dimensionality, the number of states grows exponentially with the number of variables involved.

Due to the limited applicability of dynamic programming, practitioners often rely on *ad hoc* heuristic strategies when dealing with stochastic control problems. Several recent success stories – most notably, the celebrated Backgammon player of Tesauro (1992) – suggest that neural networks can help in overcoming this limitation. In these applications, neural networks are used as compact representations that approximate cost–to–go functions using far fewer parameters than states. This approach offers the possibility of a systematic and practical methodology for addressing complex stochastic control problems.

Despite the success of neural networks in dynamic programming, the algorithms used to tune parameters are poorly understood. Even when used to tune the parameters of linear approximators, algorithms employed in practice can be unstable [Boyan and Moore, 1995; Gordon, 1995; Tsitsiklis and Van Roy, 1994].

Some recent research has focused on establishing classes of algorithms and compact representation that guarantee stability and graceful error bounds. Tsitsiklis and Van Roy (1994) prove results involving algorithms that employ feature extraction and interpolative architectures. Gordon (1995) proves similar results concerning a closely related class of compact representations called *averagers*. However, there remains a huge gap between these simple approximation schemes that guarantee reasonable behavior and the complex neural network architectures employed in practice.

In this paper, we motivate an algorithm for tuning the parameters of linear compact representations, prove its convergence when used in conjunction with a class of approximation architectures, and establish error bounds. Such architectures are not captured by previous results. However, the results in this paper rely on additional assumptions. In particular, we restrict attention to Markov decision problems for which the dynamic programming operator is a contraction with respect to the Euclidean norm when applied to functions in the parameterized class. Though this assumption on the combination of compact representation and Markov decision problem appears restrictive, it is actually satisfied by several cases of practical interest. In this paper, we discuss one special case which employs affine approximations over a state space, and relies on the locality of transitions. Other cases will be discussed in a full length version of this paper.

2   MARKOV DECISION PROBLEMS

We consider infinite horizon, discounted Markov decision problems defined on a finite state space $S = \{1, \ldots, n\}$ [Bertsekas, 1995]. For every state $i \in S$, there is a finite set $U(i)$ of possible control actions, and for each pair $i, j \in S$ of states and control action $u \in U(i)$ there is a probability $p_{ij}(u)$ of a transition from state i to state j given that action u is applied. Furthermore, for every state i and control action $u \in U(i)$, there is a random variable c_{iu} which represents the one-stage cost if action u is applied at state i.

Let $\beta \in [0, 1)$ be a discount factor. Since the state spaces we consider in this paper are finite, we choose to think of cost–to–go functions mapping states to cost–to–go values in terms of cost–to–go vectors whose components are the cost–to–go values of various states. The optimal cost–to–go vector $V^* \in \Re^n$ is the unique solution to Bellman's equation:

$$V_i^* = \min_{u \in U(i)} \left(E[c_{iu}] + \beta \sum_{j \in S} p_{ij}(u) V_j^* \right), \qquad \forall i \in S. \tag{1}$$

If the optimal cost–to–go vector is known, optimal decisions can be made at any state i as follows:

$$u^* = \arg \min_{u \in U(i)} \left(E[c_{iu}] + \beta \sum_{j \in S} p_{ij}(u) V_j^* \right), \qquad \forall i \in S.$$

There are several algorithms for computing V^* but we only discuss the value iteration algorithm which forms the basis of the approximation algorithm to be considered later on. We start with some notation. We define the *dynamic programming operator* as the mapping $T : \Re^n \mapsto \Re^n$ with components $T_i : \Re^n \mapsto \Re$ defined by

$$T_i(V) = \min_{u \in U(i)} \left(E[c_{iu}] + \beta \sum_{j \in S} p_{ij}(u) V_j \right), \qquad \forall i \in S. \tag{2}$$

It is well known and easy to prove that T is a maximum norm contraction. In particular,

$$\|T(V) - T(V')\|_\infty \leq \beta \|V - V'\|_\infty, \qquad \forall V, V' \in \Re^n.$$

The value iteration algorithm is described by

$$V(t+1) = T(V(t)),$$

where $V(0)$ is an arbitrary vector in $\Re^n$ used to initialize the algorithm. It is easy to see that the sequence $\{V(t)\}$ converges to V^*, since T is a contraction.

3 APPROXIMATIONS TO DYNAMIC PROGRAMMING

Classical dynamic programming algorithms such as value iteration require that we maintain and update a vector V of dimension n. This is essentially impossible when n is extremely large, as is the norm in practical applications. We set out to overcome this limitation by using compact representations to approximate cost-to-go vectors. In this section, we develop a formal framework for compact representations, describe an algorithm for tuning the parameters of linear compact representations, and prove a theorem concerning the convergence properties of this algorithm.

3.1 COMPACT REPRESENTATIONS

A *compact representation* (or *approximation architecture*) can be thought of as a scheme for recording a high–dimensional cost–to–go vector $V \in \Re^n$ using a lower–dimensional parameter vector $w \in \Re^m$ ($m \ll n$). Such a scheme can be described by a mapping $\tilde{V} : \Re^m \mapsto \Re^n$ which to any given parameter vector $w \in \Re^m$ associates a cost–to–go vector $\tilde{V}(w)$. In particular, each component $\tilde{V}_i(w)$ of the mapping is the ith component of a cost–to–go vector represented by the parameter vector w. Note that, although we may wish to represent an arbitrary vector $V \in \Re^n$, such a scheme allows for exact representation only of those vectors V which happen to lie in the range of $\tilde{V}$.

In this paper, we are concerned exclusively with linear compact representations of the form $\tilde{V}(w) = Mw$, where $M \in \Re^{n \times m}$ is a fixed matrix representing our choice of approximation architecture. In particular, we have $\tilde{V}_i(w) = M_i w$, where M_i (a row vector) is the ith row of the matrix M.

3.2 A STOCHASTIC APPROXIMATION SCHEME

Once an appropriate compact representation is chosen, the next step is to generate a parameter vector w such that $\tilde{V}(w)$ approximates V^*. One possible objective is to minimize squared error of the form $\|Mw - V^*\|_2^2$. If we were given a fixed set of N samples $\{(i_1, V_{i_1}^*), (i_2, V_{i_2}^*), ..., (i_N, V_{i_N}^*)\}$ of an optimal cost-to-go vector V^*, it seems natural to choose a parameter vector w that minimizes $\sum_{j=1}^{N}(M_{i_j}w - V_{i_j}^*)^2$. On the other hand, if we can actively sample as many data pairs as we want, one at a time, we might consider an iterative algorithm which generates a sequence of parameter vectors $\{w(t)\}$ that converges to the desired parameter vector. One such algorithm works as follows: choose an initial guess $w(0)$, then for each $t \in \{0, 1, ...\}$ sample a state $i(t)$ from a uniform distribution over the state space and apply the iteration

$$w(t+1) = w(t) - \alpha(t)\Big(M_{i(t)}w(t) - V_{i(t)}^*\Big)M_{i(t)}^T, \qquad (3)$$

where $\{\alpha(t)\}$ is a sequence of diminishing step sizes and the superscript T denotes a transpose. Such an approximation scheme conforms to the spirit of traditional function approximation – the algorithm is the common stochastic gradient descent method. However, as discussed in the introduction, we do not have access to such samples of the optimal cost-to-go vector. We therefore need more sophisticated methods for tuning parameters.

One possibility involves the use of an algorithm similar to that of Equation 3, replacing samples of $V_{i(t)}^*$ with $T_{i(t)}(V(t))$. This might be justified by the fact that $T(V)$ can be viewed as an improved approximation to V^*, relative to V. The modified algorithm takes on the form

$$w(t+1) = w(t) - \alpha(t)\Big(M_{i(t)}w(t) - T_{i(t)}(Mw(t))\Big)M_{i(t)}^T. \qquad (4)$$

Intuitively, at each time t this algorithm treats $T(Mw(t))$ as a "target" and takes a steepest descent step as if the goal were to find a w that would minimize $\|Mw - T(Mw(t))\|_2^2$. Such an algorithm is closely related to the TD(0) algorithm of Sutton (1988). Unfortunately, as pointed out in Tsitsiklis and Van Roy (1994), such a scheme can produce a diverging sequence $\{w(t)\}$ of weight vectors even when there exists a parameter vector w^* that makes the approximation error $V^* - Mw^*$ zero at every state. However, as we will show in the remainder of this paper, under certain assumptions, such an algorithm converges.

3.3 MAIN CONVERGENCE RESULT

Our first assumption concerning the step size sequence $\{\alpha(t)\}$ is standard to stochastic approximation and is required for the upcoming theorem.

Assumption 1 *Each step size $\alpha(t)$ is chosen prior to the generation of $i(t)$, and the sequence satisfies $\sum_{t=0}^{\infty} \alpha(t) = \infty$ and $\sum_{t=0}^{\infty} \alpha^2(t) < \infty$.*

Our second assumption requires that $T : \Re^n \mapsto \Re^n$ be a contraction with respect to the Euclidean norm, at least when it operates on value functions that can be represented in the form Mw, for some w. This assumption is not always satisfied, but it appears to hold in some situations of interest, one of which is to be discussed in Section 4.

Assumption 2 *There exists some $\beta' \in [0, 1)$ such that*

$$\|T(Mw) - T(Mw')\|_2 \leq \beta'\|Mw - Mw'\|_2, \qquad \forall w, w' \in \Re^m.$$

Stable Linear Approximations to Programming for Stochastic Control Problems

The following theorem characterizes the stability and error bounds associated with the algorithm when the Markov decision problem satisfies the necessary criteria.

Theorem 1 *Let Assumptions 1 and 2 hold, and assume that M has full column rank. Let $\Pi = M(M^T M)^{-1} M^T$ denote the projection matrix onto the subspace $\mathcal{X} = \{Mw | w \in \Re^m\}$. Then,*
(a) With probability 1, the sequence $w(t)$ converges to w^*, the unique vector that solves:
$$Mw^* = \Pi T(Mw^*).$$
(b) Let V^* be the optimal cost-to-go vector. The following error bound holds:
$$\|Mw^* - V^*\|_2 \leq \frac{(1+\beta)\sqrt{n}}{1-\beta'} \|\Pi V^* - V^*\|_\infty.$$

3.4 OVERVIEW OF PROOF

Due to space limitations, we only provide an overview of the proof of Theorem 1. Let $s : \Re^m \mapsto \Re^m$ be defined by
$$s(w) = E\left[\left(M_i w - T_i(Mw(t))\right) M_i^T\right],$$
where the expectation is taken over i uniformly distributed among $\{1, \ldots, n\}$. Hence,
$$E[w(t+1)|w(t), \alpha(t)] = w(t) - \alpha(t) s(w(t)),$$
where the expectation is taken over $i(t)$. We can rewrite s as
$$s(w) = \frac{1}{n}\left(M^T Mw - M^T T(Mw)\right),$$
and it can be thought of as a vector field over $\Re^m$. If the sequence $\{w(t)\}$ converges to some w, then $s(w)$ must be zero, and we have
$$M^T Mw = M^T T(Mw)$$
$$Mw = \Pi T(Mw).$$
Note that
$$\|\Pi T(Mw) - \Pi T(Mw')\|_2 \leq \beta' \|Mw - Mw'\|_2, \quad \forall w, w' \in \Re^m,$$
due to Assumption 2 and the fact that projection is a nonexpansion of the Euclidean norm. It follows that $\Pi T(\cdot)$ has a unique fixed point $w^* \in \Re^m$, and this point uniquely satisfies
$$Mw^* = \Pi T(Mw^*).$$
We can further establish the desired error bound:
$$\begin{aligned}
\|Mw^* - V^*\|_2 &\leq \|Mw^* - \Pi T(\Pi V^*)\|_2 + \|\Pi T(\Pi V^*) - \Pi V^*\|_2 + \|\Pi V^* - V^*\|_2 \\
&\leq \beta' \|Mw^* - V^*\|_2 + \|T(\Pi V^*) - V^*\|_2 + \|\Pi V^* - V^*\|_2 \\
&\leq \beta' \|Mw^* - V^*\|_2 + (1+\beta)\sqrt{n} \|\Pi V^* - V^*\|_\infty,
\end{aligned}$$
and it follows that
$$\|Mw^* - V^*\|_2 \leq \frac{(1+\beta)\sqrt{n}}{1-\beta'} \|\Pi V^* - V^*\|_\infty.$$

Consider the potential function $U(w) = \frac{1}{2}\|w - w^*\|_2^2$. We will establish that $(\nabla U(w))^T s(w) \geq \gamma U(w)$, for some $\gamma > 0$, and we are therefore dealing with a "pseudogradient algorithm" whose convergence follows from standard results on stochastic approximation [Polyak and Tsypkin, 1972]. This is done as follows:

$$\begin{aligned}(\nabla U(w))^T s(w) &= \frac{1}{n}\left(w - w^*\right)^T M^T \left(Mw - T(Mw)\right) \\ &= \frac{1}{n}\left(w - w^*\right)^T M^T \left(Mw - \Pi T(Mw) - (I - \Pi)T(Mw)\right) \\ &= \frac{1}{n}\left(Mw - Mw^*\right)^T \left(Mw - \Pi T(Mw)\right),\end{aligned}$$

where the last equality follows because $M^T \Pi = M^T$. Using the contraction assumption on T and the nonexpansion property of projection mappings, we have

$$\begin{aligned}\|\Pi T(Mw) - Mw^*\|_2 &= \|\Pi T(Mw) - \Pi T(Mw^*)\|_2 \\ &\leq \beta' \|Mw - Mw^*\|_2,\end{aligned}$$

and applying the Cauchy–Schwartz inequality, we obtain

$$\begin{aligned}(\nabla U(w))^T s(w) &\geq \frac{1}{n}(\|Mw - Mw^*\|_2^2 - \|Mw - Mw^*\|_2 \|Mw^* - \Pi T(Mw)\|_2) \\ &\geq \frac{1}{n}(1 - \beta')\|Mw - Mw^*\|_2^2.\end{aligned}$$

Since M has full column rank, it follows that $(\nabla U(w))^T s(w) \geq \gamma U(w)$, for some fixed $\gamma > 0$, and the proof is complete.

4 EXAMPLE: LOCAL TRANSITIONS ON GRIDS

Theorem 1 leads us to the next question: are there some interesting cases for which Assumption 2 is satisfied? We describe a particular example here that relies on properties of Markov decision problems that naturally arise in some practical situations.

When we encounter real Markov decision problems we often interpret the states in some meaningful way, associating more information with a state than an index value. For example, in the context of a queuing network, where each state is one possible queue configuration, we might think of the state as a vector in which each component records the current length of a particular queue in the network. Hence, if there are d queues and each queue can hold up to k customers, our state space is a finite grid $\mathcal{Z}_k^d$ (i.e., the set of vectors with integer components each in the range $\{0, \ldots, k-1\}$).

Consider a state space where each state $i \in \{1, \ldots, n\}$ is associated to a point $x^i \in \mathcal{Z}_k^d$ ($n = k^d$), as in the queuing example. We might expect that individual transitions between states in such a state space are local. That is, if we are at a state x^i the next visited state x^j is probably close to x^i in terms of Euclidean distance. For instance, we would not expect the configuration of a queuing network to change drastically in a second. This is because one customer is served at a time so a queue that is full can not suddenly become empty.

Note that the number of states in a state space of the form $\mathcal{Z}_k^d$ grows exponentially with d. Consequently, classical dynamic programming algorithms such as value iteration quickly become impractical. To efficiently generate an approximation to the cost-to-go vector, we might consider tuning the parameters $w \in \Re^d$ and $a \in \Re$ of an affine approximation $\tilde{V}_i(w, a) = w^T x^i + a$ using the algorithm presented in the previous section. It is possible to show that, under the following assumption concerning the state space topology and locality of transitions, Assumption 2 holds with $\beta' = \sqrt{\beta^2 + \frac{6}{k-3}}$, and thus Theorem 1 characterizes convergence properties of the algorithm.

Assumption 3 *The Markov decision problem has state space $S = \{1, \ldots, k^d\}$, and each state i is uniquely associated with a vector $x^i \in \mathcal{Z}_k^d$ with $k \geq 6(1-\beta^2)^{-1} + 3$. Any pair $x^i, x^j \in \mathcal{Z}_k^d$ of consecutively visited states either are identical or have exactly one unequal component, which differs by one.*

While this assumption may seem restrictive, it is only one example. There are many more candidate examples, involving other approximation architectures and particular classes of Markov decision problems, which are currently under investigation.

5 CONCLUSIONS

We have proven a new theorem that establishes convergence properties of an algorithm for generating linear approximations to cost–to–go functions for dynamic programming. This theorem applies whenever the dynamic programming operator for a Markov decision problem is a contraction with respect to the Euclidean norm when applied to vectors in the parameterized class. In this paper, we have described one example in which such a condition holds. More examples of practical interest will be discussed in a forthcoming full length version of this paper.

Acknowledgments

This research was supported by the NSF under grant ECS 9216531, by EPRI under contract 8030-10, and by the ARO.

References

Bertsekas, D. P. (1995) *Dynamic Programming and Optimal Control*. Athena Scientific, Belmont, MA.

Boyan, J. A. & Moore, A. W. (1995) Generalization in Reinforcement Learning: Safely Approximating the Value Function. In J. D. Cowan, G. Tesauro, and D. Touretzky, editors, *Advances in Neural Information Processing Systems 7*. Morgan Kaufmann.

Gordon, G. J. (1995) Stable Function Approximation in Dynamic Programming. Technical Report: CMU-CS-95-103, Carnegie Mellon University.

Polyak, B. T. & Tsypkin, Y. Z., (1972) Pseudogradient Adaptation and Training Algorithms. *Avtomatika i Telemekhanika*, 3:45-68.

Sutton, R. S. (1988) Learning to Predict by the Method of Temporal Differences. *Machine Learning*, 3:9-44.

Tesauro, G. (1992) Practical Issues in Temporal Difference Learning. *Machine Learning*, 8:257-277.

Tsitsiklis, J. & Van Roy, B. (1994) Feature–Based Methods for Large Scale Dynamic Programming. Technical Report: LIDS-P-2277, Laboratory for Information and Decision Systems, Massachusetts Institute of Technology. Also to appear in *Machine Learning*.

Stable Fitted Reinforcement Learning

Geoffrey J. Gordon
Computer Science Department
Carnegie Mellon University
Pittsburgh PA 15213
ggordon@cs.cmu.edu

Abstract

We describe the reinforcement learning problem, motivate algorithms which seek an approximation to the Q function, and present new convergence results for two such algorithms.

1 INTRODUCTION AND BACKGROUND

Imagine an agent acting in some environment. At time t, the environment is in some state x_t chosen from a finite set of states. The agent perceives x_t, and is allowed to choose an action a_t from some finite set of actions. The environment then changes state, so that at time $(t + 1)$ it is in a new state x_{t+1} chosen from a probability distribution which depends only on x_t and a_t. Meanwhile, the agent experiences a real-valued cost c_t, chosen from a distribution which also depends only on x_t and a_t and which has finite mean and variance.

Such an environment is called a Markov decision process, or MDP. The reinforcement learning problem is to control an MDP to minimize the expected discounted cost $\sum_t \gamma^t c_t$ for some discount factor $\gamma \in [0, 1]$. Define the function Q so that $Q(x, a)$ is the cost for being in state x at time 0, choosing action a, and behaving optimally from then on. If we can discover Q, we have solved the problem: at each step, we may simply choose a_t to minimize $Q(x_t, a_t)$. For more information about MDPs, see (Watkins, 1989, Bertsekas and Tsitsiklis, 1989).

We may distinguish two classes of problems, online and offline. In the offline problem, we have a full model of the MDP: given a state and an action, we can describe the distributions of the cost and the next state. We will be concerned with the online problem, in which our knowledge of the MDP is limited to what we can discover by interacting with it. To solve an online problem, we may approximate the transition and cost functions, then proceed as for an offline problem (the indirect approach); or we may try to learn the Q function without the intermediate step (the direct approach). Either approach may work better for any given problem: the direct approach may not extract as much information from each observation, but the indirect approach may introduce additional errors with its extra approximation step. We will be concerned here only with direct algorithms.

Watkins' (1989) Q-learning algorithm can find the Q function for small MDPs, either online or offline. Convergence with probability 1 in the online case was proven in (Jaakkola et al., 1994, Tsitsiklis, 1994). For large MDPs, exact Q-learning is too expensive: representing the Q function requires too much space. To overcome this difficulty, we may look for an inexpensive approximation to the Q function. In the offline case, several algorithms for this purpose have been proven to converge (Gordon, 1995a, Tsitsiklis and Van Roy, 1994, Baird, 1995). For the online case, there are many fewer provably convergent algorithms. As Baird (1995) points out, we cannot even rely on gradient descent for large, stochastic problems, since we must observe two independent transitions from a given state before we can compute an unbiased estimate of the gradient. One of the algorithms in (Tsitsiklis and Van Roy, 1994), which uses state aggregation to approximate the Q function, can be modified to apply to online problems; the resulting algorithm, unlike Q-learning, must make repeated small updates to its control policy, interleaved with comparatively lengthy periods of evaluation of the changes. After submitting this paper, we were advised of the paper (Singh et al., 1995), which contains a different algorithm for solving online MDPs. In addition, our newer paper (Gordon, 1995b) proves results for a larger class of approximators.

There are several algorithms which can handle restricted versions of the online problem. In the case of a Markov chain (an MDP where only one action is available at any time step), Sutton's TD(λ) has been proven to converge for arbitrary linear approximators (Sutton, 1988, Dayan, 1992). For decision processes with linear transition functions and quadratic cost functions (the so-called linear quadratic regulation problem), the algorithm of (Bradtke, 1993) is guaranteed to converge. In practice, researchers have had mixed success with approximate reinforcement learning (Tesauro, 1990, Boyan and Moore, 1995, Singh and Sutton, 1996).

The remainder of the paper is divided into four sections. In section 2, we summarize convergence results for offline Q-learning, and prove some contraction properties which will be useful later. Section 3 extends the convergence results to online algorithms based on TD(0) and simple function approximators. Section 4 treats nondiscounted problems, and section 5 wraps up.

2 OFFLINE DISCOUNTED PROBLEMS

Standard offline Q-learning begins with an MDP M and an initial Q function $q^{(0)}$. Its goal is to learn $q^{(n)}$, a good approximation to the optimal Q function for M. To accomplish this goal, it performs the series of updates $q^{(i+1)} = T_M(q^{(i)})$, where the component of $T_M(q^{(i)})$ corresponding to state x and action a is defined to be

$$[T_M(q^{(i)})]_{xa} \equiv c_{xa} + \gamma \sum_y P_{xay} \min_b q^{(i)}_{yb}$$

Here c_{xa} is the expected cost of performing action a in state x; P_{xay} is the probability that action a from state x will lead to state y; and γ is the discount factor.

Offline Q-learning converges for discounted MDPs because T_M is a contraction in max norm. That is, for all vectors q and r,

$$\| T_M(q) - T_M(r) \| \leq \gamma \| q - r \|$$

where $\| q \| \equiv \max_{x,a} |q_{xa}|$. Therefore, by the contraction mapping theorem, T_M has a unique fixed point q^*, and the sequence $q^{(i)}$ converges linearly to q^*.

It is worth noting that a weighted version of offline Q-learning is also guaranteed to converge. Consider the iteration

$$q^{(i+1)} = (I + \alpha D(T_M - I))(q^{(i)})$$

where α is a positive learning rate and D is an arbitrary fixed nonsingular diagonal matrix of weights. In this iteration, we update some Q values more rapidly than others, as might occur if for instance we visited some states more frequently than others. (We will come back to this possibility later.) This weighted iteration is a max norm contraction, for sufficiently small α: take two Q functions q and r, with $\|q - r\| = l$. Suppose α is small enough that the largest element of αD is $B < 1$, and let $b > 0$ be the smallest diagonal element of αD. Consider any state x and action a, and write d_{xa} for the corresponding element of αD. We then have

$$\begin{aligned}
{[(I - \alpha D)q - (I - \alpha D)r]_{xa}} &\leq (1 - d_{xa})l \\
[T_M q - T_M r]_{xa} &\leq \gamma l \\
[\alpha D T_M q - \alpha D T_M r]_{xa} &\leq d_{xa} \gamma l \\
[(I - \alpha D + \alpha D T_M)q - (I - \alpha D + \alpha D T_M)r]_{xa} &\leq (1 - d_{xa})l + d_{xa} \gamma l \\
&\leq (1 - b(1 - \gamma))l
\end{aligned}$$

so $(I - \alpha D + \alpha D T_M)$ is a max norm contraction with factor $(1 - b(1 - \gamma))$. The fixed point of weighted Q-learning is the same as the fixed point of unweighted Q-learning: $T_M(q^*) = q^*$ is equivalent to $\alpha D(T_M - I)q^* = 0$.

The difficulty with standard (weighted or unweighted) Q-learning is that, for MDPs with many states, it may be completely infeasible to compute $T_M(q)$ for even one value of q. One way to avoid this difficulty is fitted Q-learning: if we can find some function M_A so that $M_A \circ T_M$ is much cheaper to compute than T_M, we can perform the fitted iteration $q^{(i+1)} = M_A(T_M(q^{(i)}))$ instead of the standard offline Q-learning iteration. The mapping M_A implements a function approximation scheme (see (Gordon, 1995a)); we assume that $q^{(0)}$ can be represented as $M_A(q)$ for some q. The fitted offline Q-learning iteration is guaranteed to converge to a unique fixed point if M_A is a nonexpansion in max norm, and to have bounded error if $M_A(q^*)$ is near q^* (Gordon, 1995a).

Finally, we can define a fitted weighted Q-learning iteration:

$$q^{(i+1)} = (I + \alpha M_A D(T_M - I))(q^{(i)})$$

If M_A is a max norm nonexpansion and $M_A^2 = M_A$ (these conditions are satisfied, for example, by state aggregation), then fitted weighted Q-learning is guaranteed to converge:

$$\begin{aligned}
(I + \alpha M_A D(T_M - I))q &= ((I - M_A) + M_A(I + \alpha D(T_M - I)))q \\
&= M_A(I + \alpha D(T_M - I))q
\end{aligned}$$

since $M_A q = q$ for q in the range of M_A. (Note that $q^{(i+1)}$ is guaranteed to be in the range of M_A if $q^{(i)}$ is.) The last line is the composition of a max norm nonexpansion with a max norm contraction, and so is a max norm contraction.

The fixed point of fitted weighted Q-learning is not necessarily the same as the fixed point of fitted Q-learning, unless M_A can represent q^* exactly. However, if M_A is linear, we have that

$$(I + \alpha M_A D(T_M - I))(q + c) = c + M_A(I + \alpha D(T_M - I))(q + c)$$

for any q in the range of M_A and c perpendicular to the range of M_A. In particular, if we take c so that $q^* - c$ is in the range of M_A, and let $q = M_A q$ be a fixed point of the weighted fitted iteration, then we have

$$\begin{aligned}
\| q^* - q \| &= \| (I + \alpha M_A D(T_M - I))q^* - (I + \alpha M_A D(T_M - I))q \| \\
&= \| c + M_A(I + \alpha D(T_M - I)))q^* - M_A(I + \alpha D(T_M - I)))q \| \\
&\leq \| c \| + (1 - b(1 - \gamma)) \| q^* - q \|
\end{aligned}$$

$$\| q^* - q \| \leq \frac{\| c \|}{b(1 - \gamma)}$$

That is, if M_A is linear in addition to the conditions for convergence, we can bound the error for fitted weighted Q-learning.

For offline problems, the weighted version of fitted Q-learning is not as useful as the unweighted version: it involves about the same amount of work per iteration, the contraction factor may not be as good, the error bound may not be as tight, and it requires $M_A^2 = M_A$ in addition to the conditions for convergence of the unweighted iteration. On the other hand, as we shall see in the next section, the weighted algorithm can be applied to online problems.

3 ONLINE DISCOUNTED PROBLEMS

Consider the following algorithm, which is a natural generalization of TD(0) (Sutton, 1988) to Markov decision problems. (This algorithm has been called "sarsa" (Singh and Sutton, 1996).) Start with some initial Q function $q^{(0)}$. Repeat the following steps for i from 0 onwards. Let $\pi^{(i)}$ be a policy chosen according to some predetermined tradeoff between exploration and exploitation for the Q function $q^{(i)}$. Now, put the agent in M's start state and allow it to follow the policy $\pi^{(i)}$ for a random number of steps $L^{(i)}$. If at step t of the resulting trajectory the agent moves from the state x_t under action a_t with cost c_t to a state y_t for which the action b_t appears optimal, compute the estimated Bellman error

$$e_t = (c_t + \gamma [q^{(i)}]_{y_t b_t}) - [q^{(i)}]_{x_t a_t}$$

After observing the entire trajectory, define $e^{(i)}$ to be the vector whose xa-th component is the sum of e_t for all t such that $x_t = x$ and $a_t = a$. Then compute the next weight vector according to the TD(0)-like update rule with learning rate $\alpha^{(i)}$

$$q^{(i+1)} = q^{(i)} + \alpha^{(i)} M_A e^{(i)}$$

See (Gordon, 1995b) for a comment on the types of mappings M_A which are appropriate for online algorithms.

We will assume that $L^{(i)}$ has the same distribution for all i and is independent of all other events related to the i-th and subsequent trajectories, and that $E(L^{(i)})$ is bounded. Define $d_{xa}^{(i)}$ to be the expected number of times the agent visited state x and chose action a during the i-th trajectory, given $\pi^{(i)}$. We will assume that the policies are such that $d_{xa}^{(i)} > \epsilon$ for some positive ϵ and for all i, x, and a. Let $D^{(i)}$ be the diagonal matrix with elements $d_{xa}^{(i)}$. With this notation, we can write the expected update for the sarsa algorithm in matrix form:

$$E(q^{(i+1)} \mid q^{(i)}) = (I + \alpha^{(i)} M_A D^{(i)}(T_M - I))q^{(i)}$$

With the exception of the fact that $D^{(i)}$ changes from iteration to iteration, this equation looks very similar to the offline weighted fitted Q-learning update. However, the sarsa algorithm is not guaranteed to converge even in the benign case

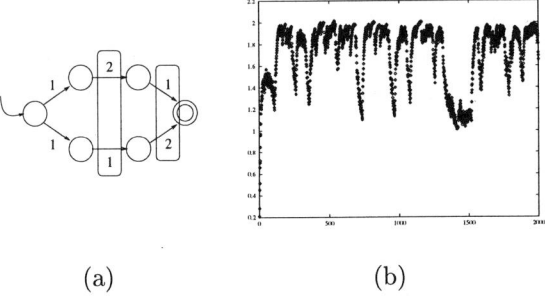

(a)   (b)

Figure 1: A counterexample to sarsa. (a) An MDP: from the start state, the agent may choose the upper or the lower path, but from then on its decisions are forced. Next to each arc is its expected cost; the actual costs are randomized on each step. Boxed pairs of arcs are aggregated, so that the agent must learn identical Q values for arcs in the same box. We used a discount $\gamma = .9$ and a learning rate $\alpha = .1$. To ensure sufficient exploration, the agent chose an apparently suboptimal action 10% of the time. (Any other parameters would have resulted in similar behavior. In particular, annealing α to zero wouldn't have helped.) (b) The learned Q value for the right-hand box during the first 2000 steps.

where the Q-function is approximated by state aggregation: when we apply sarsa to the MDP in figure 1, one of the learned Q values oscillates forever. This problem happens because the frequency-of-update matrix $D^{(i)}$ can change discontinuously when the Q function fluctuates slightly: when, by luck, the upper path through the MDP appears better, the cost-1 arc into the goal will be followed more often and the learned Q value will decrease, while when the lower path appears better the cost-2 arc will be weighted more heavily and the Q value will increase. Since the two arcs out of the initial state always have the same expected backed-up Q value (because the states they lead to are constrained to have the same value), each path will appear better infinitely often and the oscillation will continue forever.

On the other hand, if we can represent the optimal Q function q^*, then no matter what $D^{(i)}$ is, the expected sarsa update has its fixed point at q^*. Since the smallest diagonal element of $D^{(i)}$ is bounded away from zero and the largest is bounded above, we can choose an α and a $\gamma' < 1$ so that $(I + \alpha M_A D^{(i)}(T_M - I))$ is a contraction with fixed point q^* and factor γ' for all i. Now if we let the learning rates satisfy $\sum_i \alpha^{(i)} = \infty$ and $\sum_i (\alpha^{(i)})^2 < \infty$, convergence w.p.1 to q^* is guaranteed by a theorem of (Jaakkola et al., 1994). (See also the theorem in (Tsitsiklis, 1994).)

More generally, if M_A is linear and can represent $q^* - c$ for some vector c, we can bound the error between q^* and the fixed point of the expected sarsa update on iteration i: if we choose an α and a $\gamma' < 1$ as in the previous paragraph,

$$\| E(q^{(i+1)} \mid q^{(i)}) - q^* \| \leq \gamma' \| q^{(i)} - q^* \| + 2\|c\|$$

for all i. A minor modification of the theorem of (Jaakkola et al., 1994) shows that the distance from $q^{(i)}$ to the region

$$\left\{ q \,\middle|\, \| q - q^* \| \leq 2\|c\| \frac{1}{1-\gamma'} \right\}$$

converges w.p.1 to zero. That is, while the sequence $q^{(i)}$ may not converge, the worst it will do is oscillate in a region around q^* whose size is determined by how accurately we can represent q^* and how frequently we visit the least frequent (state, action) pair.

Finally, if we follow a fixed exploration policy on every trajectory, the matrix $D^{(i)}$ will be the same for every i; in this case, because of the contraction property proved in the previous section, convergence w.p.1 for appropriate learning rates is guaranteed again by the theorem of (Jaakkola et al., 1994).

4 NONDISCOUNTED PROBLEMS

When M is not discounted, the Q-learning backup operator T_M is no longer a max norm contraction. Instead, as long as every policy guarantees absorption w.p.1 into some set of cost-free terminal states, T_M is a contraction in some weighted max norm. The proofs of the previous sections still go through, if we substitute this weighted max norm for the unweighted one in every case. In addition, the random variables $L^{(i)}$ which determine when each trial ends may be set to the first step t so that x_t is terminal, since this and all subsequent steps will have Bellman errors of zero. This choice of $L^{(i)}$ is not independent of the i-th trial, but it does have a finite mean and it does result in a constant $D^{(i)}$.

5 DISCUSSION

We have proven new convergence theorems for two online fitted reinforcement learning algorithms based on Watkins' (1989) Q-learning algorithm. These algorithms, sarsa and sarsa with a fixed exploration policy, allow the use of function approximators whose mappings M_A are max norm nonexpansions and satisfy $M_A^2 = M_A$. The prototypical example of such a function approximator is state aggregation. For similar results on a larger class of approximators, see (Gordon, 1995b).

Acknowledgements

This material is based on work supported under a National Science Foundation Graduate Research Fellowship and by ARPA grant number F33615-93-1-1330. Any opinions, findings, conclusions, or recommendations expressed in this publication are those of the author and do not necessarily reflect the views of the National Science Foundation, ARPA, or the United States government.

References

L. Baird. Residual algorithms: Reinforcement learning with function approximation. In *Machine Learning (proceedings of the twelfth international conference)*, San Francisco, CA, 1995. Morgan Kaufmann.

D. P. Bertsekas and J. N. Tsitsiklis. *Parallel and Distributed Computation: Numerical Methods*. Prentice Hall, 1989.

J. A. Boyan and A. W. Moore. Generalization in reinforcement learning: safely approximating the value function. In G. Tesauro and D. Touretzky, editors, *Advances in Neural Information Processing Systems*, volume 7. Morgan Kaufmann, 1995.

S. J. Bradtke. Reinforcement learning applied to linear quadratic regulation. In S. J. Hanson, J. D. Cowan, and C. L. Giles, editors, *Advances in Neural Information Processing Systems*, volume 5. Morgan Kaufmann, 1993.

P. Dayan. The convergence of TD(λ) for general lambda. *Machine Learning*, 8(3–4):341–362, 1992.

G. J. Gordon. Stable function approximation in dynamic programming. In *Machine Learning (proceedings of the twelfth international conference)*, San Francisco, CA, 1995. Morgan Kaufmann.

G. J. Gordon. Online fitted reinforcement learning. In J. A. Boyan, A. W. Moore, and R. S. Sutton, editors, *Proceedings of the Workshop on Value Function Approximation*, 1995. Proceedings are available as tech report CMU-CS-95-206.

T. Jaakkola, M. I. Jordan, and S. P. Singh. On the convergence of stochastic iterative dynamic programming algorithms. *Neural Computation*, 6(6):1185–1201, 1994.

S. P. Singh, T. Jaakkola, and M. I. Jordan. Reinforcement learning with soft state aggregation. In G. Tesauro and D. Touretzky, editors, *Advances in Neural Information Processing Systems*, volume 7. Morgan Kaufmann, 1995.

S. P. Singh and R. S. Sutton. Reinforcement learning with replacing eligibility traces. *Machine Learning*, 1996.

R. S. Sutton. Learning to predict by the methods of temporal differences. *Machine Learning*, 3(1):9–44, 1988.

G. Tesauro. Neurogammon: a neural network backgammon program. In *IJCNN Proceedings III*, pages 33–39, 1990.

J. N. Tsitsiklis and B. Van Roy. Feature-based methods for large-scale dynamic programming. Technical Report P-2277, Laboratory for Information and Decision Systems, 1994.

J. N. Tsitsiklis. Asynchronous stochastic approximation and Q-learning. *Machine Learning*, 16(3):185–202, 1994.

C. J. C. H. Watkins. *Learning from Delayed Rewards*. PhD thesis, King's College, Cambridge, England, 1989.

Improving Policies without Measuring Merits

Peter Dayan[1]
CBCL
E25-201, MIT
Cambridge, MA 02139
dayan@ai.mit.edu

Satinder P Singh
Harlequin, Inc
1 Cambridge Center
Cambridge, MA 02142
singh@harlequin.com

Abstract

Performing policy iteration in dynamic programming should only require knowledge of relative rather than absolute measures of the utility of actions (Werbos, 1991) – what Baird (1993) calls the *advantages* of actions at states. Nevertheless, most existing methods in dynamic programming (including Baird's) compute some form of absolute utility function. For smooth problems, advantages satisfy two differential consistency conditions (including the requirement that they be free of curl), and we show that enforcing these can lead to appropriate policy improvement solely in terms of advantages.

1 Introduction

In deciding how to change a policy at a state, an agent only needs to know the differences (called advantages) between the total return based on taking each action a for one step and then following the policy forever after, and the total return based on always following the policy (the conventional *value* of the state under the policy). The advantages are like differentials – they do not depend on the local levels of the total return. Indeed, Werbos (1991) defined Dual Heuristic Programming (DHP), using these facts, learning the derivatives of these total returns with respect to the state. For instance, in a conventional undiscounted maze problem with a

---

[1] We are grateful to Larry Saul, Tommi Jaakkola and Mike Jordan for comments, and Andy Barto for pointing out the connection to Werbos' DHP. This work was supported by NSERC, MIT, and grants to Professor Michael I Jordan from ATR Human Information Processing Research and Siemens Corporation.

penalty for each move, the advantages for the actions might typically be $-1, 0$ or 1, whereas the values vary between 0 and the maximum distance to the goal. Advantages should therefore be easier to represent than absolute value functions in a generalising system such as a neural network and, possibly, easier to learn. Although the advantages are differential, existing methods for learning them, notably Baird (1993), require the agent simultaneously to learn the total return from each state. The underlying trouble is that advantages do not appear to satisfy any form of a Bellman equation. Whereas it is clear that the value of a state should be closely related to the value of its neighbours, it is not obvious that the advantage of action a at a state should be equally closely related to its advantages nearby.

In this paper, we show that under some circumstances it is possible to use a solely advantage-based scheme for policy iteration using the spatial derivatives of the value function rather than the value function itself. Advantages satisfy a particular consistency condition, and, given a model of the dynamics and reward structure of the environment, an agent can use this condition to directly acquire the spatial derivatives of the value function. It turns out that the condition alone may not impose enough constraints to specify these derivatives (this is a consequence of the problem described above) – however the value function is like a potential function for these derivatives, and this allows extra constraints to be imposed.

2 Continuous DP, Advantages and Curl

Consider the problem of controlling a deterministic system to minimise $V^*(\mathbf{x}_0) = \min_{\mathbf{u}(t)} \int_0^\infty r(\mathbf{y}(t), \mathbf{u}(t)) dt$, where $\mathbf{y}(t) \in \Re^n$ is the state at time t, $\mathbf{u}(t) \in \Re^m$ is the control, $\mathbf{y}(0) = \mathbf{x}_0$, and $\dot{\mathbf{y}}(t) = \mathbf{f}((\mathbf{y}(t), \mathbf{u}(t)))$. This is a simplified form of a classic variational problem since r and $\mathbf{f}$ do not depend on time t explicitly, but only through $\mathbf{y}(t)$ and there are no stopping time or terminal conditions on $\mathbf{y}(t)$ (see Peterson, 1993; Atkeson, 1994, for recent methods for solving such problems). This means that the optimal $\mathbf{u}(t)$ can be written as a function of $\mathbf{y}(t)$ and that $V(\mathbf{x}_0)$ is a function of $\mathbf{x}_0$ and not t. We do not treat the cases in which the infinite integrals do not converge comfortably and we will also assume adequate continuity and differentiability.

The solution by advantages: This problem can be solved by writing down the Hamilton-Jacobi-Bellman (HJB) equation (see Dreyfus, 1965) which $V^*(\mathbf{x})$ satisfies:

$$0 = \min_{\mathbf{u}} \left[r(\mathbf{x}, \mathbf{u}) + \mathbf{f}(\mathbf{x}, \mathbf{u}) \cdot \nabla_\mathbf{x} V^*(\mathbf{x}) \right] \qquad (1)$$

This is the continuous space/time analogue of the conventional Bellman equation (Bellman, 1957) for discrete, non-discounted, deterministic decision problems, which says that for the optimal value function V^*, $0 = \min_a \left[r(x, a) + V^*(f(x, a)) - V^*(x) \right]$, where starting the process at state x and using action a incurs a cost $r(x, a)$ and leaves the process in state $f(x, a)$. This, and its obvious stochastic extension to Markov decision processes, lie at the heart of temporal difference methods for reinforcement learning (Sutton, 1988; Barto, Sutton & Watkins, 1989; Watkins, 1989). Equation 1 describes what the *optimal* value function must satisfy. Discrete dynamic programming also comes with a method called value iteration which starts with any function $V_0(\mathbf{x})$, improves it sequentially, and converges to the optimum.

The alternative method, policy iteration (Howard, 1960), operates in the space of policies, ie functions $\mathbf{w}(\mathbf{x})$. Starting with $\mathbf{w}(\mathbf{x})$, the method requires evaluating everywhere the value function $V^{\mathbf{w}}(\mathbf{x}) = \int_0^\infty r(\mathbf{y}(t), \mathbf{w}(\mathbf{y}(t))) dt$, where $\mathbf{y}(0) = \mathbf{x}$, and $\dot{\mathbf{y}}(t) = \mathbf{f}(\mathbf{y}(t), \mathbf{w}(\mathbf{y}(t)))$. It turns out that $V^{\mathbf{w}}$ satisfies a close relative of equation 1:

$$0 = r(\mathbf{x}, \mathbf{w}(\mathbf{x})) + \mathbf{f}(\mathbf{x}, \mathbf{w}(\mathbf{x})) \cdot \nabla_{\mathbf{x}} V^{\mathbf{w}}(\mathbf{x}) \qquad (2)$$

In policy iteration, $\mathbf{w}(\mathbf{x})$ is improved, by choosing the maximising action:

$$\mathbf{w}'(\mathbf{x}) = \mathrm{argmax}_{\mathbf{u}} \left[r(\mathbf{x}, \mathbf{u}) + \mathbf{f}(\mathbf{x}, \mathbf{u}) \cdot \nabla_{\mathbf{x}} V^{\mathbf{w}}(\mathbf{x}) \right] \qquad (3)$$

as the new action. For discrete Markov decision problems, the equivalent of this process of policy improvement is guaranteed to improve upon $\mathbf{w}$.

In the discrete case and for an analogue of value iteration, Baird (1993) defined the optimal advantage function $A^*(x, a) = [Q^*(x, a) - \max_b Q^*(x, b)]/\delta t$, where δt is effectively a characteristic time for the process which was taken to be 1 above, and the optimal Q function (Watkins, 1989) is $Q^*(x, a) = r(x, a) + V^*(f(x, a))$, where $V^*(y) = \max_b Q^*(y, b)$. It turns out (Baird, 1993) that in the discrete case, one can cast the whole of policy iteration in terms of advantages. In the continuous case, we define advantages directly as

$$A^{\mathbf{w}}(\mathbf{x}, \mathbf{u}) = r(\mathbf{x}, \mathbf{u}) + \mathbf{f}(\mathbf{x}, \mathbf{u}) \cdot \nabla_{\mathbf{x}} V^{\mathbf{w}}(\mathbf{x}) \qquad (4)$$

This equation indicates how the spatial derivatives of $V^{\mathbf{w}}$ determine the advantages. Note that the consistency condition in equation 2 can be written as $A^{\mathbf{w}}(\mathbf{x}, \mathbf{w}(\mathbf{x})) = 0$. Policy iteration can proceed using

$$\mathbf{w}'(\mathbf{x}) = \mathrm{argmax}_{\mathbf{u}} A^{\mathbf{w}}(\mathbf{x}, \mathbf{u}). \qquad (5)$$

Doing without $V^{\mathbf{w}}$: We can now state more precisely the intent of this paper: a) the consistency condition in equation 2 provides constraints on the spatial derivatives $\nabla_{\mathbf{x}} V^{\mathbf{w}}(\mathbf{x})$, at least given a model of r and $\mathbf{f}$; b) equation 4 indicates how these spatial derivatives can be used to determine the advantages, again using a model; and c) equation 5 shows that the advantages *tout court* can be used to improve the policy. Therefore, one apparently should have no need to know $V^{\mathbf{w}}(x)$ but just its spatial derivatives in order to do policy iteration.

Didactic Example — LQR: To make the discussion more concrete, consider the case of a one-dimensional linear quadratic regulator (LQR). The task is to minimise $V^*(x_0) = \int_0^\infty \alpha x(t)^2 + \beta u(t)^2 dt$ by choosing $u(t)$, where $\alpha, \beta > 0$, $\dot{x}(t) = -[ax(t) + u(t)]$ and $x(0) = x_0$. It is well known (eg Athans & Falb, 1966) that the solution to this problem is that $V^*(x) = k^* x^2/2$ where $k^* = (\alpha + \beta(u^*)^2)/(a + u^*)$ and $u(t) = (-a + \sqrt{a^2 + \alpha/\beta}) x(t)$. Knowing the form of the problem, we consider policies w that make $u(t) = wx(t)$ and require $h(x, k) \equiv \nabla_x V^w(x) = kx$, where the correct value of $k = (\alpha + \beta w^2)/(a + w)$. The consistency condition in equation 2 evaluated at state x implies that $0 = (\alpha + \beta w^2)x^2 - h(x, k)(a + w)x$. Doing online gradient descent in the square inconsistency at samples x_n gives $k_{n+1} = k_n - \epsilon \partial \left[(\alpha + \beta w^2)x_n^2 - k_n x_n(a + w)x_n\right]^2 / \partial k_n$, which will reduce the square inconsistency for small enough ϵ unless $x = 0$. As required, the square inconsistency can only be zero for all values of x if $k = (\alpha + \beta w^2)/((a + w))$. The advantage of performing action v (note this is *not* vx) at state x is, from equation 4, $A^w(x, v) = \alpha x^2 + \beta v^2 - (ax + v)(\alpha + \beta w^2)x/(a + w)$, which, minimising over v (equation 5) gives $u(x) = w'x$ where $w' = (\alpha + \beta w^2)/(2\beta(a + w))$, which is the Newton-Raphson iteration to solve the quadratic equation that determines the optimal policy. In this case, without ever explicitly forming $V^w(x)$, we have been able to learn an optimal policy. This was based, at least conceptually, on samples x_n from the interaction of the agent with the world.

The curl condition: The astute reader will have noticed a problem. The consistency condition in equation 2 constrains the spatial derivatives $\nabla_x V^w$ in only one direction at every point – along the route $\mathbf{f}(\mathbf{x}, \mathbf{w}(\mathbf{x}))$ taken according to the policy there. However, in evaluating actions by evaluating their advantages, we need to know $\nabla_x V^w$ in all the directions accessible through $\mathbf{f}(\mathbf{x}, \mathbf{u})$ at state $\mathbf{x}$. The quadratic regulation task was only solved *because* we employed a function approximator (which was linear in this case $h(x, k) = kx$). For the case of LQR, the restriction that $\mathbf{h}$ be linear allowed information about $\mathbf{f}(\mathbf{x}', \mathbf{w}(\mathbf{x}')) \cdot \nabla_{x'} V^w(\mathbf{x}')$ at distant states $\mathbf{x}'$ and for the policy actions $\mathbf{w}(\mathbf{x}')$ there to determine $\mathbf{f}(\mathbf{x}, \mathbf{u}) \cdot \nabla_x V^w(\mathbf{x})$ at state $\mathbf{x}$ but for non-policy actions $\mathbf{u}$. If we had tried to represent $h(x, k)$ using a more flexible approximator such as radial basis functions, it might not have worked. In general, if we didn't know the form of $\nabla_x V^w(\mathbf{x})$, we cannot rely on the function approximator to generalize correctly.

There is one piece of information that we have yet to use – function $\mathbf{h}(\mathbf{x}, \mathbf{k}) \equiv \nabla_x V^w(\mathbf{x})$ (with parameters $\mathbf{k}$, and in general non-linear) is the gradient of something – it represents a conservative vector field. Therefore its curl should vanish ($\nabla_x \times \mathbf{h}(\mathbf{x}, \mathbf{k}) = 0$). Two ways to try to satisfy this are to represent $\mathbf{h}$ as a suitably weighted combination of functions that satisfy this condition or to use its square as an additional error during the process of setting the parameters $\mathbf{k}$. Even in the case of the LQR, but in more than one dimension, it turns out to be essential to use the curl condition. For the multi-dimensional case we know that $V^w(\mathbf{x}) = \mathbf{x}^T K^w \mathbf{x}/2$ for some symmetric matrix K^w, but enforcing zero curl is the only way to enforce this symmetry.

The curl condition says that knowing how some component of $\nabla_x V^w(\mathbf{x})$ *changes* in some direction (*eg* $\partial \nabla_x V^w(\mathbf{x})_2/\partial x_1$) does provide information about how some other component *changes* in a different direction (*eg* $\partial \nabla_x V^w(\mathbf{x})_1/\partial x_2$). This information is only useful up to constants of integration, and smoothness conditions will be necessary to apply it.

3 Simulations

We tested the method of approximating $\mathbf{h}^w(\mathbf{x}) = \nabla_x V^w(\mathbf{x})$ as a linearly weighted combination of local conservative vector fields $\mathbf{h}^w(\mathbf{x}) = \sum_{i=1}^n c_i^w \nabla_x \phi(\mathbf{x}, \mathbf{z}_i)$, where c_i^w are the approximation weights that are set by enforcing equation 2, and $\phi(\mathbf{x}, \mathbf{z}_i) = e^{-\alpha |\mathbf{x} - \mathbf{z}_i|^2}$ are standard radial basis functions (Broomhead & Lowe, 1988; Poggio & Girosi, 1990). We enforced this condition at a discrete set $\{\mathbf{x}_k\}$ of 100 points scattered in the state space, using as a policy, explicit vectors $\mathbf{u}_k$ at those locations, and employed 49 similarly scattered centres $\mathbf{z}_i$. Issues of learning to approximate conservative and non-conservative vector fields using such sums have been discussed by Mussa-Ivaldi (1992). One advantage of using this representation is that $\psi(\mathbf{x}) = \sum_{i=1}^n c_i^w \phi(\mathbf{x}, \mathbf{z}_i)$ can be seen as the system's effective policy evaluation function $V^w(\mathbf{x})$, at least modulo an arbitrary constant (we call this an un-normalised value function).

We chose two 2-dimensional problems to prove that the system works. They share the same dynamics $\dot{x}(t) = -\mathbf{x}(t) + \mathbf{u}(t)$, but have different cost functions:

$$r_{\text{LQR}}(\mathbf{x}(t), \mathbf{u}(t)) = 5|\mathbf{x}(t)|^2 + |\mathbf{u}(t)|^2 \quad , \quad r_{\text{SP}}(\mathbf{x}(t), \mathbf{u}(t)) = |\mathbf{x}(t)|^2 + \sqrt{1 + |\mathbf{u}(t)|^2} \tag{6}$$

r_{LQR} makes for a standard linear quadratic regulation problem, which has a quadratic optimal value function and a linear optimal controller as before (although now we are using limited range basis functions instead of using the more appropriate linear form). r_{SP} has a mixture of a quadratic term in $\mathbf{x}(t)$, which encourages the state to move towards the origin, and a more nearly linear cost term in $\mathbf{u}(t)$, which would tend to encourage a constant speed. All the sample points $\mathbf{x}_k$ and radial basis function centres $\mathbf{z}_i$ were selected within the $\{-1, 1\}^2$ square. We started from a randomly chosen policy with both components of $\mathbf{u}_k$ being samples from the uniform distribution $\mathcal{U}(-.25, .25)$. This was chosen so that the overall dynamics of the system, including the $-\mathbf{x}(t)$ component should lead the agent towards the origin.

Figure 1a shows the initial values of $\mathbf{u}_k$ in the regulator case, where the circles are at the leading edges of the local policies which point in the directions shown with relative magnitudes given by the length of the lines, and (for scale) the central object is the square $\{-0.1, 0.1\}^2$. The 'policy' lines are centred at the 100 $\mathbf{x}_k$ points. Using the basis function representation, equation 2 is an over-determined linear system, and so, the standard Moore-Penrose pseudo-inverse was used to find an approximate solution. The un-normalised approximate value function corresponding to this policy is shown in figure 1b. Its bowl-like character is a feature of the optimal value function. For the LQR case, it is straightforward to perform the optimisation in equation 5 analytically, using the values for $\mathbf{h}^{\mathbf{w}}(\mathbf{x}_k)$ determined by the $c_i^{\mathbf{w}}$. Figure 1c,d show the policy and its associated un-normalised value function after 4 iterations. By this point, the policy and value functions are essentially optimal – the policy shows the agent moves inwards from all $\mathbf{x}_k$ and the magnitudes are linearly related to the distances from the centre. Figure 1e,f show the same at the end point for r_{SP}. One major difference is that we performed the optimisation in equation 5 over a discrete set of values for $\mathbf{u}_k$ rather than analytically. The tendency for the agent to maintain a constant speed is apparent except right near the origin. The bowl is not centred exactly at $(0, 0)$ – which is an approximation error.

4 Discussion

This paper has addressed the question of whether it is possible to perform policy iteration using just differential quantities like advantages. We showed that using a conventional consistency condition and a curl constraint on the spatial derivatives of the value function it is possible to learn enough about the value function for a policy to improve upon that policy. Generalisation can be key to the whole scheme. We showed this working on an LQR problem and a more challenging non-LQR case. We only treated 'smooth' problems – addressing discontinuities in the value function, which imply undifferentiability, is clearly key. Care must be taken in interpreting this result. The most challenging problem is the error metric for the approximation. The consistency condition may either under-specify or over-specify the parameters. In the former case, just as for standard approximation theory, one needs prior information to regularise the gradient surface. For many problems there may be spatial discontinuities in the policy evaluation, and therefore this is particularly difficult. If the parameters are over-specified (and, for good generalisation, one would generally be working in this regime), we need to evaluate inconsistencies. Inconsistencies cost exactly to the degree that the optimisation in equation 5 is compromised – but this is impossible to quantify. Note that this problem is not

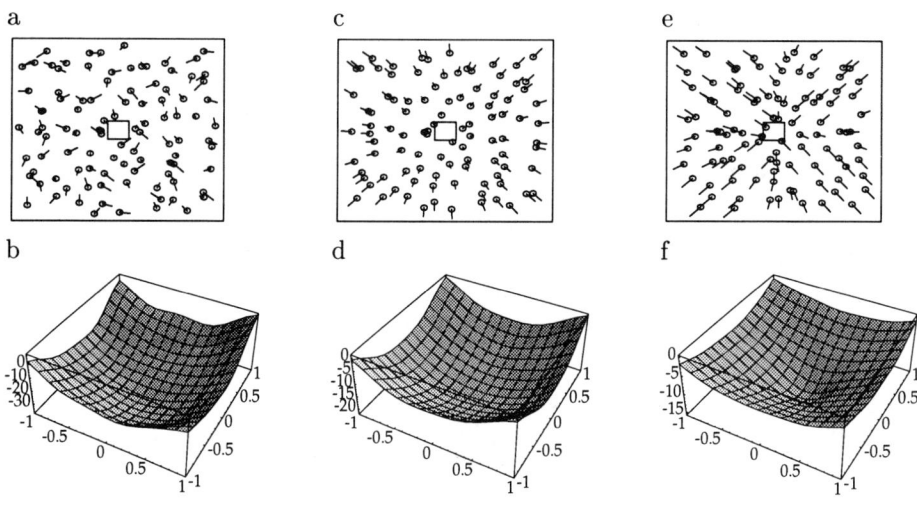

Figure 1: a-d) Policies and un-normalised value functions for the r_{LQR} and e-f) for the r_{SP} problem.

confined to the current scheme of learning the derivatives of the value function – it also impacts algorithms based on learning the value function itself. It is also unreasonable to specify the actions u_k only at the points x_k. In general, one would either need a parameterised function for $u(x)$ whose parameters would be updated in the light of performing the optimisations in equation 5 (or some sort of interpolation scheme), or alternatively one could generate u on the fly using the learned values of $h(x)$.

If there is a discount factor, ie $V^*(x_0) = \min_{u(t)} \int_0^\infty e^{-\lambda t} r(y(t), u(t))dt$, then $0 = r(x, w(x)) - \lambda V^w(x) + f(x, w(x)) \cdot \nabla_x V^w(x)$ is the equivalent consistency condition to equation 2 (see also Baird, 1993) and so it is no longer possible to learn $\nabla_x V^w(x)$ without ever considering $V^w(x)$ itself. One can still optimise parameterised forms for V^w as in section 3, except that the once arbitrary constant is no longer free.

The discrete analogue to the differential consistency condition in equation 2 amounts to the tautology that given current policy π, $\forall x$, $A^\pi(x, \pi(x)) = 0$. As in the continuous case, this only provides information about $V^\pi(f(x, \pi(x))) - V^\pi(x)$ and not $V^\pi(f(x, a)) - V^\pi(x)$ for other actions a which are needed for policy improvement. There is an equivalent to the curl condition: if there is a cycle in the undirected transition graph, then the weighted sum of the advantages for the actions along the cycle is equal to the equivalently weighted sum of payoffs along the cycle, where the weights are $+1$ if the action respects the cycle and -1 otherwise. This gives a consistency condition that A^π has to satisfy – and, just as in the constants of integration for the differential case, it requires grounding: $A^\pi(z, a) = 0$ for some z in the cycle. It is certainly not true that all discrete problems will have sufficient cycles to specify A^π completely – in an extreme case, the undirected version of the directed transition graphs might contain no cycles at all. In the continuous case, if the updates are sufficiently smooth, this is not possible. For stochastic problems, the consistency condition equivalent to equation 2 will involve an integral, which, if doable, would permit the application of our method.

Werbos's (1991) DHP and Mitchell and Thrun's (1993) explanation-based Q-learning also study differential forms of the Bellman equation based on differentiating the discrete Bellman equation (or its Q-function equivalent) with respect to the state. This is certainly fine as an *additional* constraint that V^* or Q^* must satisfy (as used by Mitchell and Thrun and Werbos' Globalized version of DHP), but by itself, it does not enforce the curl condition, and is insufficient for the whole of policy improvement.

References

Athans, M & Falb, PL (1966). *Optimal Control.* New York, NY: McGraw-Hill.

Atkeson, CG (1994). Using Local Trajectory Optimizers To Speed Up Global Optimization in Dynamic Programming. In *NIPS 6*.

Baird, LC, IIIrd (1993). *Advantage Updating.* Technical report, Wright Laboratory, Wright-Patterson Air Force Base.

Barto, AG, Bradtke, SJ & Singh, SP (1995). Learning to act using real-time dynamic programming. *Artificial Intelligence,* **72**, 81-138.

Barto, AG, Sutton, RS & Watkins, CJCH (1990). Learning and sequential decision making. In M Gabriel & J Moore, editors, *Learning and Computational Neuroscience: Foundations of Adaptive Networks.* Cambridge, MA: MIT Press, Bradford Books.

Bellman, RE (1957). *Dynamic Programming.* Princeton, NJ: Princeton University Press.

Broomhead, DS & Lowe, D (1988). Multivariable functional interpolation and adaptive networks. *Complex Systems,* **2**, 321-55.

Dreyfus, SE (1965). *Dynamic Programming and the Calculus of Variations.* New York, NY: Academic Press.

Howard, RA (1960). *Dynamic Programming and Markov Processes.* New York, NY: Technology Press & Wiley.

Mitchell, TM & Thrun, SB (1993). Explanation-based neural network learning for robot control. In *NIPS 5*.

Mussa-Ivaldi, FA (1992). From basis functions to basis fields: Vector field approximation from sparse data. *Biological Cybernetics,* **67**, 479-489.

Peterson, JK (1993). On-Line estimation of optimal value functions. In *NIPS 5*.

Poggio, T & Girosi, F (1990). A theory of networks for learning. *Science,* **247**, 978-982.

Sutton, RS (1988). Learning to predict by the methods of temporal difference. *Machine Learning,* **3**, pp 9-44.

Watkins, CJCH (1989). *Learning from Delayed Rewards.* PhD Thesis. University of Cambridge, England.

Werbos, P (1991). A menu of designs for reinforcement learning over time. In WT Miller IIIrd, RS Sutton & P Werbos, editors, *Neural Networks for Control.* Cambridge, MA: MIT Press, 67-96.

Memory-based Stochastic Optimization

Andrew W. Moore and Jeff Schneider
School of Computer Science
Carnegie-Mellon University
Pittsburgh, PA 15213

Abstract

In this paper we introduce new algorithms for optimizing noisy plants in which each experiment is very expensive. The algorithms build a global non-linear model of the expected output at the same time as using Bayesian linear regression analysis of locally weighted polynomial models. The local model answers queries about confidence, noise, gradient and Hessians, and use them to make automated decisions similar to those made by a practitioner of Response Surface Methodology. The global and local models are combined naturally as a locally weighted regression. We examine the question of whether the global model can really help optimization, and we extend it to the case of time-varying functions. We compare the new algorithms with a highly tuned higher-order stochastic optimization algorithm on randomly-generated functions and a simulated manufacturing task. We note significant improvements in total regret, time to converge, and final solution quality.

1 INTRODUCTION

In a stochastic optimization problem, noisy samples are taken from a plant. A sample consists of a chosen control **u** (a vector of real numbers) and a noisy observed response y. y is drawn from a distribution with mean and variance that depend on **u**. y is assumed to be independent of previous experiments. Informally the goal is to quickly find control **u** to maximize the expected output $E[y \mid \mathbf{u}]$. This is different from conventional numerical optimization because the samples can be very noisy, there is no gradient information, and we usually wish to avoid ever performing badly (relative to our start state) even during optimization. Finally and importantly: **each experiment is very expensive** and there is **ample computational time** (often many minutes) for deciding on the next experiment. The following questions are both interesting and important: how should this computational time best be used, and how can the data best be used?

Stochastic optimization is of real industrial importance, and indeed one of our reasons for investigating it is an association with a U.S. manufacturing company that has many new examples of stochastic optimization problems every year.

The discrete version of this problem, in which **u** is chosen from a discrete set, is the well known k-armed bandit problem. Reinforcement learning researchers have recently applied bandit-like algorithms to efficiently optimize several discrete problems [Kaelbling, 1990, Greiner and Jurisica, 1992, Gratch *et al.*, 1993, Maron and Moore, 1993]. This paper considers extensions to the continuous case in which **u** is a vector of reals. We anticipate useful applications here too. Continuity implies a formidable number of arms (uncountably infinite) but permits us to assume smoothness of $E[y \mid \mathbf{u}]$ as a function of **u**.

The most popular current techniques are:

- **Response Surface Methods (RSM).** Current RSM practice is described in the classic reference [Box and Draper, 1987]. Optimization proceeds by cautious steepest ascent hill-climbing. A region of interest (ROI) is established at a starting point and experiments are made at positions within the region that can best be used to identify the function properties with low-order polynomial regression. A large portion of the RSM literature concerns *experimental design*—the decision of where to take data points in order to acquire the lowest variance estimate of the local polynomial coefficients in a fixed number of experiments. When the gradient is estimated with sufficient confidence, the ROI is moved accordingly. Regression of a quadratic locates optima within the ROI and also diagnoses ridge systems and saddle points.

  The strength of RSM is that it is careful not to change operating conditions based on inadequate evidence, but moves once the data justifies. A weakness of RSM is that human judgment is needed: it is not an algorithm, but a manufacturing methodology.

- **Stochastic Approximation methods.** The algorithm of [Robbins and Monro, 1951] does root finding without the use of derivative estimates. Through the use of successively smaller steps convergence is proven under broad assumptions about noise. Keifer-Wolfowitz (KW) [Kushner and Clark, 1978] is a related algorithm for optimization problems. From an initial point it estimates the gradient by performing an experiment in each direction along each dimension of the input space. Based on the estimate, it moves its experiment center and repeats. Again, use of decreasing step sizes leads to a proof of convergence to a local optimum.

  The strength of KW is its aggressive exploration, its simplicity, and that it comes with convergence guarantees. However, it has more of a danger of attempting wild experiments in the presence of noise, and effectively discards the data it collects after each gradient estimate is made. In practice, higher order versions of KW are available in which convergence is accelerated by replacing the fixed step size schedule with an adaptive one [Kushner and Clark, 1978]. Later we compare the performance of our algorithms to such a higher-order KW.

2 MEMORY-BASED OPTIMIZATION

Neither KW nor RSM uses old data. After a gradient has been identified the control **u** is moved up the gradient and the data that produced the gradient estimate is discarded. Does this lead to inefficiencies in operation? This paper investigates one way of using old data: build a global non-linear plant model with it.

We use locally weighted regression to model the system [Cleveland and Delvin, 1988, Atkeson, 1989, Moore, 1992]. We have adapted the methods to return posterior distributions for their coefficients and noise (and thus, indirectly, their predictions) based on very broad priors, following the Bayesian methods for global linear regression described in [DeGroot, 1970].

We estimate the coefficients $\beta = \{\beta_1 \ldots \beta_m\}$ of a local polynomial model in which the data was generated by the polynomial and corrupted with gaussian noise of variance σ^2, which we also estimate. Our prior assumption will be that β is distributed according to a multivariate gaussian of mean $\mathbf{0}$ and covariance matrix Σ. Our prior on σ is that $1/\sigma^2$ has a gamma distribution with parameters α and β.

Assume we have observed n pieces of data. The jth polynomial term for the ith data point is X_{ij} and the output response of the ith data point is Y_i. Assume further that we wish to estimate the model local to the query point $\mathbf{x}_q$, in which a data point at distance d_i from the the query point has weight $w_i = \exp(-d_i^2/K)$. K, the *kernel width* is a fixed parameter that determines the degree of localness in the local regression. Let $\mathbf{W} = \text{Diag}(w_1, w_2 \ldots w_n)$.

The marginal posterior distribution of β is a t distribution with mean $\bar{\beta} = (\Sigma^{-1} + X^T W^2 X)^{-1}(X^T W^2 Y)$ covariance

$$(2\beta + (Y^T - \beta^T X^T)W^2 Y^T)(\Sigma^{-1} + X^T W^2 X)^{-1} / (2\alpha + \sum_{i=1}^n w_i^2) \quad (1)$$

and $\alpha + \sum_{i=1}^n w_i^2$ degrees of freedom.

We assume a wide, weak, prior $\Sigma = \text{Diag}(20^2, 20^2, \ldots 20^2), \alpha = 0.8, \beta = 0.001$, meaning the prior assumes each regression coefficient independently lies with high probability in the range -20 to 20, and the noise lies in the range 0.01 to 0.5.

Briefly, we note the following reasons that Bayesian locally weighted polynomial regression is particularly suited to this application:

- We can directly obtain meaningful confidence estimates of the joint pdf of the regressed coefficients and predictions. Indirectly, we can compute the probability distribution of the steepest gradient, the location of local optima and the principal components of the local Hessian.

- The Bayesian approach allows meaningful regressions even with fewer data points than regression coefficients—the posterior distribution reveals enormous lack of confidence in some aspects of such a model but other useful aspects can still be predicted with confidence. This is crucial in high dimensions, where it may be more effective to head in a known positive gradient without waiting for all the experiments that would be needed for a precise estimate of steepest gradient.

- Other pros and cons of locally weighted regression in the context of control can be found in [Moore et al., 1995].

Given the ability to derive a plant model from data, how should it best be used? The true optimal answer, which requires solving an infinite-dimensional Markov decision process, is intractable. We have developed four approximate algorithms that use the learned model, described briefly below.

- **AutoRSM.** Fully automates the (normally manual) RSM procedure and incorporates weighted data from the model; not only from the current design. It uses online experimental design to pick ROI design points to maximize information about local gradients and optima. Space does not permit description of the linear algebraic formulations of these questions.

- **PMAX.** This is a greedy, simpler approach that uses the global non-linear model from the data to jump immediately to the model optimum. This is similar to the technique described in [Botros, 1994], with two extensions. First, the Bayesian

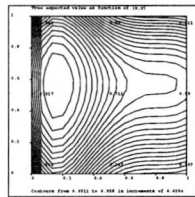 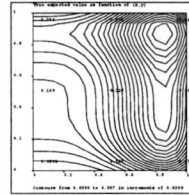 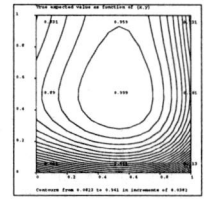

Figure 1: Three examples of 2-d functions used in optimization experiments

priors enable useful decisions before the regression becomes full-rank. Second, local quadratic models permit second-order convergence near an optimum.

- **IEMAX.** Applies Kaelbling's IE algorithm [Kaelbling, 1990] in the continuous case using Bayesian confidence intervals.

$$\mathbf{u}_{\text{chosen}} = \underset{\mathbf{u}}{\text{argmax}}\ \hat{f}_{\text{opt}}(\mathbf{u}) \qquad (2)$$

where $\hat{f}_{\text{opt}}(\mathbf{u})$ is the top of the 95th %-ile confidence interval. The intuition here is that we are encouraged to explore more aggressively than PMAX, but will not explore areas that are confidently below the best known optimum.

- **COMAX.** In a real plant we would never want to apply PMAX or IEMAX. Experiments must be cautious for reasons of safety, quality control, and managerial peace of mind. COMAX extends IEMAX thus:

$$\mathbf{u}_{\text{chosen}} = \underset{\mathbf{u}\ \in\ SAFE}{\text{argmax}}\ \hat{f}_{\text{opt}}(\mathbf{u}); \mathbf{u} \in SAFE \Leftrightarrow \hat{f}_{\text{pess}}(\mathbf{u}) > \text{disaster threshold} \qquad (3)$$

Analysis of these algorithms is problematic unless we are prepared to make strong assumptions about the form of $E[Y \mid \mathbf{u}]$. To examine the general case we rely on Monte Carlo simulations, which we now describe.

The experiments used randomly generated nonlinear unimodal (but not necessarily convex) d-dimensional functions from $[0,1]^d \to [0,1]$. Figure 1 shows three example 2-d functions. Gaussian noise ($\sigma = 0.1$) is added to the functions. This is large noise, and means several function evaluations would be needed to achieve a reliable gradient estimate for a system using even a large step size such as 0.2.

The following optimization algorithms were tested on a sample of such functions.

Vary-KW	The best performing KW algorithm we could find varied step size and adapted gradient estimation steps to avoid undue regret at optima.
Fixed-KW	A version of KW that keeps its gradient-detecting step size fixed. This risks causing extra regret at a true optima, but has less chance of becoming delayed by a non-optimum.
Auto-RSM	The best performing version thereof.
Passive-RSM	Auto-RSM continues to identify the precise location of the optimum when it's arrived at that optimum. When Passive-RSM is confident (greater than 99%) that it knows the location of the optimum to two significant places, it stops experimenting.
Linear RSM	A linear instead of quadratic model, thus restricted to steepest ascent.
CRSM	Auto-RSM with conservative parameters, more typical of those recommended in the RSM literature.
Pmax, IEmax and Comax	As described above.

Figures 2a and 2b show the first sixty experiments taken by AutoRSM and KW respectively on their journeys to the goal.

(a)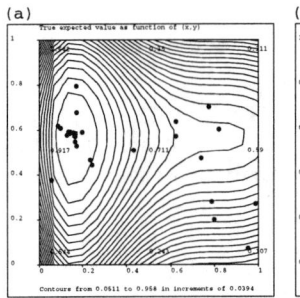
(b)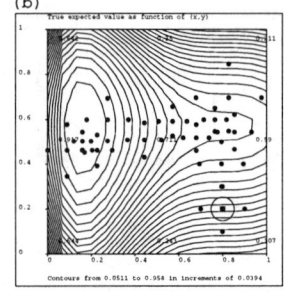

Figure 2a: The path taken (start at (0.8,0.2)) by AutoRSM optimizing the given function with added noise of standard deviation 0.1 at each experiment.

Figure 2b: The path taken (start at (0.8,0.2)) by KW. KW's path looks deceptively bad, but remember it is continually buffeted by considerable noise.

(a) Regret incurred during first 60 steps
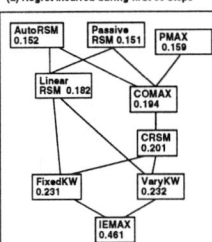

(b) Percent of "disastrous" steps, all trials
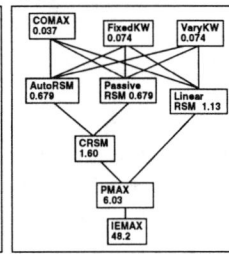

(c) No. of steps until within 0.05 of optimum
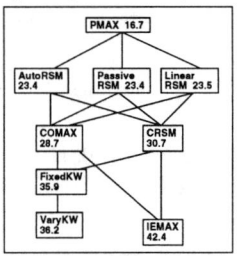

(d) Mean regret of FINAL ten steps
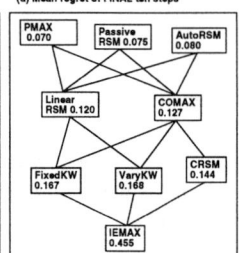

Figure 3: Comparing nine stochastic optimization algorithms by four criteria: (a) Regret, (b) Disasters, (c) Speed to converge (d) Quality at convergence. The partial order depicted shows which results are significant at the 99% level (using blocked pairwise comparisons). The outputs of the random functions range between 0–1 over the input domain. The numbers in the boxes are means over fifty 5-d functions. (a) Regret is defined as the mean $y_{opt} - y_i$—the cost incurred during the optimization compared with performance if we had known the optimum location and used it from the beginning. With the exception of IEMAX, model-based methods perform significantly better than KW, with reduced advantage for cautious and linear methods. (b) The %-age of steps which tried experiments with more than 0.1 units worse performance than at the search start. This matters to a risk averse manager. AutoRSM has fewer than 1% disasters, but COMAX and the model-free methods do better still. PMAX's aggressive exploration costs it. (c) The number of steps until we reach within 0.05 units of optimal. PMAX's aggressiveness wins. (d) The quality of the "final" solution between steps 50 and 60 of the optimization.

Results for 50 trials of each optimization algorithms for five-dimensional randomly generated functions are depicted in Figure 3. Many other experiments were performed in other dimensionalities and for modified versions of the algorithm, but space does not permit detailed discussion here.

Finally we performed experiments with the simulated power-plant process in Figure 4. The catalyst controller adjusts the flow rate of the catalyst to achieve the goal chemical A content. Its actions also affect chemical B content. The temperature controller adjusts the reaction chamber temperature to achieve the goal chemical B content. The chemical contents are also affected by the flow rate which is determined externally by demand for the product.

The task is to find the optimal values for the six controller parameters that minimize the total squared deviation from desired values of chemical A and chemical B contents. The feedback loops from sensors to controllers have significant delay. The controller gains on product demand are feedforward terms since there is significant delay in the effects of demand on the process. Finally, the performance of the system may also depend on variations over time in the composition of the input chemicals which can not be directly sensed.

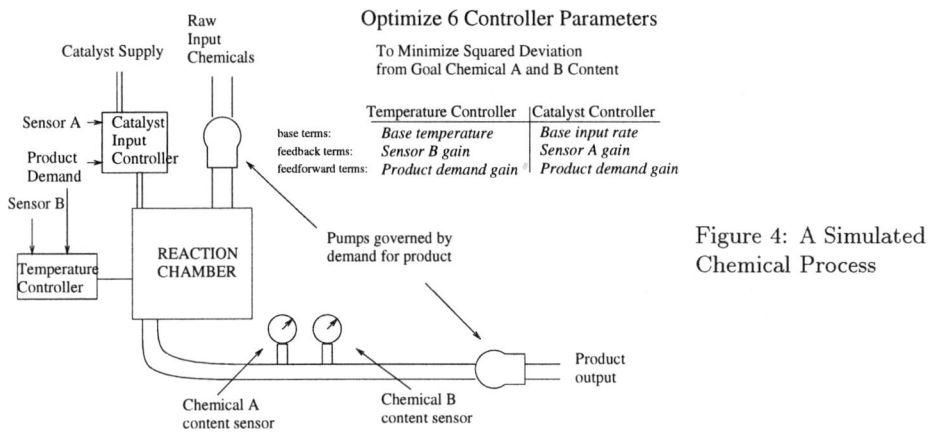

Figure 4: A Simulated Chemical Process

The total summed regrets of the optimization methods on 200 simulated steps were:

StayAtStart	FixedKW	AutoRSM	PMAX	COMAX
10.86	2.82	1.32	3.30	4.50

In this case AutoRSM is best, considerably beating the best KW algorithm we could find. In contrast PMAX and COMAX did poorly: in this plant wild experiments are very costly to PMAX and COMAX is too cautious. StayAtStart is the regret that would be incurred if all 200 steps were taken at the initial parameter setting.

3 UNOBSERVED DISTURBANCES

An apparent danger of learning a model is that if the environment changes, the out of date model will mean poor performance and very slow adaptation. The model-free methods, which use only recent data, will react more nimbly. A simple but unsatisfactory answer to this is to use a model that implicitly (e.g. a neural net) or explicitly (e.g. local weighted regression of the fifty most recent points) forgets. An interesting possibility is to learn a model in a way that automatically determines whether a disturbance has occurred, and if so, how far back to forget.

The following "adaptive forgetting" (AF) algorithm was added to the AutoRSM algorithm: At each step, use all the previous data to generate 99% confidence intervals on the output value at the current step. If the observed output is outside the intervals assume that a large change in the system has occured and forget all previous data. This algorithm is good for recognizing jumps in the plant's operating characteristics and allows AutoRSM to respond to them quickly, but is not suitable for detecting and handling process drift.

We tested our algorithm's performance on the simulated plant for 450 steps. Operation began as before, but at step 150 there was an unobserved change in the composition of the raw input chemicals. The total regrets of the optimization methods were:

StayAtStart	FixedKW	AutoRSM	PMAX	AutoRSM/AF
11.90	5.31	8.37	9.23	2.75

AutoRSM and PMAX do poorly because all their decisions after step 150 are based partially on the invalid data collected before then. The AF addition to AutoRSM solves the problem while beating the best KW by a factor of 2. Furthermore, AutoRSM/AF gets 1.76 on the invariant task, thus demonstrating that it can be used safely in cases where it is not known if the process is time varying.

4 DISCUSSION

Botros' thesis [Botros, 1994] discusses an algorithm similar to PMAX based on local linear regression. [Salganicoff and Ungar, 1995] uses a decision tree to learn a model. They use Gittins indices to suggest experiments: we believe that the memory-based methods can benefit from them too. They, however, do not use gradient information, and so require many experiments to search a 2D space.

IEmax performed badly in these experiments, but optimism-guided exploration may prove important in algorithms which check for potentially superior local optima.

A possible extension is self tuning optimization. Part way through an optimization, to estimate the best optimization parameters for an algorithm we can run monte-carlo simulations which run on sample functions from the posterior global model given the current data.

This paper has examined the question of how much can learning a Bayesian memory-based model accelerate the convergence of stochastic optimization. We have proposed four algorithms for doing this, one based on an autonomous version of RSM; the other three upon greedily jumping to optima of three criteria dependent on predicted output and uncertainty. Empirically the model-based methods provide significant gains over a highly tuned higher order model-free method.

References

[Atkeson, 1989] C. G. Atkeson. Using Local Models to Control Movement. In *Proceedings of Neural Information Processing Systems Conference*, November 1989.

[Botros, 1994] S. M. Botros. Model-Based Techniques in Motor Learning and Task Optimization. PhD. Thesis, MIT Dept. of Brain and Cognitive Sciences, February 1994.

[Box and Draper, 1987] G. E. P. Box and N. R. Draper. *Empirical Model-Building and Response Surfaces*. Wiley, 1987.

[Cleveland and Delvin, 1988] W. S. Cleveland and S. J. Delvin. Locally Weighted Regression: An Approach to Regression Analysis by Local Fitting. *Journal of the American Statistical Association*, 83(403):596–610, September 1988.

[DeGroot, 1970] M. H. DeGroot. *Optimal Statistical Decisions*. McGraw-Hill, 1970.

[Gratch et al., 1993] J. Gratch, S. Chien, and G. DeJong. Learning Search Control Knowledge for Deep Space Network Scheduling. In *Proceedings of the 10th International Conference on Machine Learning*. Morgan Kaufmann, June 1993.

[Greiner and Jurisica, 1992] R. Greiner and I. Jurisica. A statistical approach to solving the EBL utility problem. In *Proceedings of the Tenth International Conference on Artificial Intelligence (AAAI-92)*. MIT Press, 1992.

[Kaelbling, 1990] L. P. Kaelbling. Learning in Embedded Systems. PhD. Thesis; Technical Report No. TR-90-04, Stanford University, Department of Computer Science, June 1990.

[Kushner and Clark, 1978] H. Kushner and D. Clark. *Stochastic Approximation Methods for Constrained and Unconstrained Systems*. Springer-Verlag, 1978.

[Maron and Moore, 1993] O. Maron and A. Moore. Hoeffding Races: Accelerating Model Selection Search for Classification and Function Approximation. In *Advances in Neural Information Processing Systems 6*. Morgan Kaufmann, December 1993.

[Moore et al., 1995] A. W. Moore, C. G. Atkeson, and S. Schaal. Memory-based Learning for Control. Technical report, CMU Robotics Institute, Technical Report CMU-RI-TR-95-18 *(Submitted for Publication)*, 1995.

[Moore, 1992] A. W. Moore. Fast, Robust Adaptive Control by Learning only Forward Models. In J. E. Moody, S. J. Hanson, and R. P. Lippman, editors, *Advances in Neural Information Processing Systems 4*. Morgan Kaufmann, April 1992.

[Robbins and Monro, 1951] H. Robbins and S. Monro. A stochastic approximation method. *Annals of Mathematical Statistics*, 22:400–407, 1951.

[Salganicoff and Ungar, 1995] M. Salganicoff and L. H. Ungar. Active Exploration and Learning in Real-Valued Spaces using Multi-Armed Bandit Allocation Indices. In *Proceedings of the 12th International Conference on Machine Learning*. Morgan Kaufmann, 1995.

Temporal Difference Learning in Continuous Time and Space

Kenji Doya
doya@hip.atr.co.jp
ATR Human Information Processing Research Laboratories
2-2 Hikaridai, Seika-cho, Soraku-gun, Kyoto 619-02, Japan

Abstract

A continuous-time, continuous-state version of the temporal difference (TD) algorithm is derived in order to facilitate the application of reinforcement learning to real-world control tasks and neurobiological modeling. An optimal nonlinear feedback control law was also derived using the derivatives of the value function. The performance of the algorithms was tested in a task of swinging up a pendulum with limited torque. Both the "critic" that specifies the paths to the upright position and the "actor" that works as a nonlinear feedback controller were successfully implemented by radial basis function (RBF) networks.

1 INTRODUCTION

The temporal-difference (TD) algorithm (Sutton, 1988) for delayed reinforcement learning has been applied to a variety of tasks, such as robot navigation, board games, and biological modeling (Houk et al., 1994). Elucidation of the relationship between TD learning and dynamic programming (DP) has provided good theoretical insights (Barto et al., 1995). However, conventional TD algorithms were based on discrete-time, discrete-state formulations. In applying these algorithms to control problems, time, space and action had to be appropriately discretized using a priori knowledge or by trial and error. Furthermore, when a TD algorithm is used for neurobiological modeling, discrete-time operation is often very unnatural.

There have been several attempts to extend TD-like algorithms to continuous cases. Bradtke et al. (1994) showed convergence results for DP-based algorithms for a discrete-time, continuous-state linear system with a quadratic cost. Bradtke and Duff (1995) derived TD-like algorithms for continuous-time, discrete-state systems (semi-Markov decision problems). Baird (1993) proposed the "advantage updating" algorithm by modifying Q-learning so that it works with arbitrary small time steps.

In this paper, we derive a TD learning algorithm for continuous-time, continuous-state, nonlinear control problems. The correspondence of the continuous-time version to the conventional discrete-time version is also shown. The performance of the algorithm was tested in a nonlinear control task of swinging up a pendulum with limited torque.

2 CONTINUOUS-TIME TD LEARNING

We consider a continuous-time dynamical system (plant)

$$\dot{\mathbf{x}}(t) = f(\mathbf{x}(t), \mathbf{u}(t)) \tag{1}$$

where $\mathbf{x} \in X \subset \mathbf{R}^n$ is the state and $\mathbf{u} \in U \subset \mathbf{R}^m$ is the control input (action). We denote the immediate reinforcement (evaluation) for the state and the action as

$$r(t) = r(\mathbf{x}(t), \mathbf{u}(t)). \tag{2}$$

Our goal is to find a feedback control law (policy)

$$\mathbf{u}(t) = \mu(\mathbf{x}(t)) \tag{3}$$

that maximizes the expected reinforcement for a certain period in the future. To be specific, for a given control law μ, we define the "value" of the state $\mathbf{x}(t)$ as

$$V^\mu(\mathbf{x}(t)) = \int_t^\infty \frac{1}{\tau} e^{-\frac{s-t}{\tau}} r(\mathbf{x}(s), \mathbf{u}(s)) ds, \tag{4}$$

where $\mathbf{x}(s)$ and $\mathbf{u}(s)$ ($t < s < \infty$) follow the system dynamics (1) and the control law (3). Our problem now is to find an optimal control law μ^* that maximizes $V^\mu(\mathbf{x})$ for any state $\mathbf{x} \in X$. Note that τ is the time scale of "imminence-weighting" and the scaling factor $\frac{1}{\tau}$ is used for normalization, i.e., $\int_t^\infty \frac{1}{\tau} e^{-\frac{s-t}{\tau}} ds = 1$.

2.1 TD ERROR

The basic idea in TD learning is to predict future reinforcement in an on-line manner. We first derive a local consistency condition for the value function $V^\mu(\mathbf{x})$. By differentiating (4) by t, we have

$$\tau \frac{d}{dt} V^\mu(\mathbf{x}(t)) = V^\mu(\mathbf{x}(t)) - r(t). \tag{5}$$

Let $P(t)$ be the prediction of the value function $V^\mu(\mathbf{x}(t))$ from $\mathbf{x}(t)$ (output of the "critic"). If the prediction is perfect, it should satisfy $\tau \dot{P}(t) = P(t) - r(t)$. If this is not satisfied, the prediction should be adjusted to decrease the inconsistency

$$\hat{r}(t) = r(t) - P(t) + \tau \dot{P}(t). \tag{6}$$

This is a continuous version of the temporal difference error.

2.2 EULER DIFFERENTIATION: TD(0)

The relationship between the above continuous-time TD error and the discrete-time TD error (Sutton, 1988)

$$\hat{r}(t) = r(t) + \gamma P(t) - P(t - \Delta t) \tag{7}$$

can be easily seen by a backward Euler approximation of $\dot{P}(t)$. By substituting $\dot{P}(t) = (P(t) - P(t - \Delta t))/\Delta t$ into (6), we have

$$\hat{r} = r(t) + \frac{\tau}{\Delta t}\left[(1 - \frac{\Delta t}{\tau})P(t) - P(t - \Delta t)\right].$$

This coincides with (7) if we make the "discount factor" $\gamma = 1 - \frac{\Delta t}{\tau} \simeq e^{-\frac{\Delta t}{\tau}}$, except for the scaling factor $\frac{\tau}{\Delta t}$.

Now let us consider a case when the prediction of the value function is given by

$$P(t) = \sum_i v_i b_i(\mathbf{x}(t)), \qquad (8)$$

where $b_i()$ are basis functions (e.g., sigmoid, Gaussian, etc) and v_i are the weights. The gradient descent of the squared TD error is given by

$$\Delta v_i \propto -\frac{\partial \frac{1}{2}\hat{r}^2(t)}{\partial v_i} \propto -\hat{r}(t)\left[(1 - \frac{\Delta t}{\tau})\frac{\partial P(t)}{\partial v_i} - \frac{\partial P(t - \Delta t)}{\partial v_i}\right].$$

In order to "back-up" the information about the future reinforcement to correct the prediction in the past, we should modify $P(t - \Delta t)$ rather than $P(t)$ in the above formula. This results in the learning rule

$$\Delta v_i \propto \hat{r}(t)\frac{\partial P(t - \Delta t)}{\partial v_i} = \hat{r}(t)b_i(\mathbf{x}(t - \Delta t)). \qquad (9)$$

This is equivalent to the TD(0) algorithm that uses the "eligibility trace" from the previous time step.

2.3 SMOOTH DIFFERENTIATION: TD(λ)

The Euler approximation of a time derivative is susceptible to noise (e.g., when we use stochastic control for exploration). Alternatively, we can use a "smooth" differentiation algorithm that uses a weighted average of the past input, such as

$$\dot{P}(t) \simeq \frac{P(t) - \bar{P}(t)}{\tau_c} \quad \text{where} \quad \tau_c \frac{d}{dt}\bar{P}(t) = P(t) - \bar{P}(t)$$

and τ_c is the time constant of the differentiation. The corresponding gradient descent algorithm is

$$\Delta v_i \propto -\frac{\partial \frac{1}{2}\hat{r}^2(t)}{\partial v_i} \propto \hat{r}(t)\frac{\partial \bar{P}(t)}{\partial v_i} = \hat{r}(t)\bar{b}_i(t), \qquad (10)$$

where $\bar{b}_i$ is the eligibility trace for the weight

$$\tau_c \frac{d}{dt}\bar{b}_i(t) = b_i(\mathbf{x}(t)) - \bar{b}_i(t). \qquad (11)$$

Note that this is equivalent to the TD(λ) algorithm (Sutton, 1988) with $\lambda = 1 - \frac{\Delta t}{\tau_c}$ if we discretize the above equation with time step Δt.

3 OPTIMAL CONTROL BY VALUE GRADIENT

3.1 HJB EQUATION

The value function V^* for an optimal control μ^* is defined as

$$V^*(\mathbf{x}(t)) = \max_{\mathbf{u}[t,\infty)}\left[\int_t^\infty \frac{1}{\tau} e^{-\frac{s-t}{\tau}} r(\mathbf{x}(s), \mathbf{u}(s))ds\right]. \qquad (12)$$

According to the principle of dynamic programming (Bryson and Ho, 1975), we consider optimization in two phases, $[t, t+\Delta t]$ and $[t+\Delta t, \infty)$, resulting in the expression

$$V^*(\mathbf{x}(t)) = \max_{\mathbf{u}[t,t+\Delta t)}\left[\int_t^{t+\Delta t} \frac{1}{\tau} e^{-\frac{s-t}{\tau}} r(\mathbf{x}(s), \mathbf{u}(s))ds + e^{-\frac{\Delta t}{\tau}} V^*(\mathbf{x}(t + \Delta t))\right].$$

By Taylor expanding the value at $t + \Delta t$ as

$$V^*(\mathbf{x}(t+\Delta t)) = V^*(\mathbf{x}(t)) + \frac{\partial V^*}{\partial \mathbf{x}(t)} f(\mathbf{x}(t), \mathbf{u}(t)) \Delta t + O(\Delta t)$$

and then taking Δt to zero, we have a differential constraint for the optimal value function

$$V^*(t) = \max_{\mathbf{u}(t) \in U} \left[r(\mathbf{x}(t), \mathbf{u}(t)) + \tau \frac{\partial V^*}{\partial \mathbf{x}} f(\mathbf{x}(t), \mathbf{u}(t)) \right]. \tag{13}$$

This is a variant of the Hamilton-Jacobi-Bellman equation (Bryson and Ho, 1975) for a discounted case.

3.2 OPTIMAL NONLINEAR FEEDBACK CONTROL

When the reinforcement $r(\mathbf{x}, \mathbf{u})$ is convex with respect to the control $\mathbf{u}$, and the vector field $f(\mathbf{x}, \mathbf{u})$ is linear with respect to $\mathbf{u}$, the optimization problem in (13) has a unique solution. The condition for the optimal control is

$$\frac{\partial r(\mathbf{x}, \mathbf{u})}{\partial \mathbf{u}} + \tau \frac{\partial V^*}{\partial \mathbf{x}} \frac{\partial f(\mathbf{x}, \mathbf{u})}{\partial \mathbf{u}} = 0. \tag{14}$$

Now we consider the case when the cost for control is given by a convex potential function $G_j()$ for each control input

$$f(\mathbf{x}, \mathbf{u}) = r_x(\mathbf{x}) - \sum_j G_j(u_j),$$

where reinforcement for the state $r_x(\mathbf{x})$ is still unknown. We also assume that the input gain of the system

$$\mathbf{b}_j(\mathbf{x}) = \frac{\partial f(\mathbf{x}, \mathbf{u})}{\partial u_j}$$

is available. In this case, the optimal condition (14) for u_j is given by

$$-G'_j(u_j) + \tau \frac{\partial V^*}{\partial \mathbf{x}} \mathbf{b}_j(\mathbf{x}) = 0.$$

Noting that the derivative $G'()$ is a monotonic function since $G()$ is convex, we have the optimal feedback control law

$$u_j = (G')^{-1} \left(\tau \frac{\partial V^*}{\partial \mathbf{x}} \mathbf{b}(\mathbf{x}) \right). \tag{15}$$

Particularly, when the amplitude of control is bounded as $|u_j| \leq u_j^{\max}$, we can enforce this constraint using a control cost

$$G_j(u_j) = c_j \int_0^{\frac{u_j}{u_j^{\max}}} g^{-1}(s) ds, \tag{16}$$

where $g^{-1}()$ is an inverse sigmoid function that diverges at ± 1 (Hopfield, 1984). In this case, the optimal feedback control law is given by

$$u_j = u_j^{\max} g \left(\frac{u_j^{\max}}{c_j} \tau \frac{\partial V^*}{\partial \mathbf{x}} \mathbf{b}_j(\mathbf{x}) \right). \tag{17}$$

In the limit of $c_j \to 0$, this results in the "bang-bang" control law

$$u_j = u_j^{\max} \text{sign} \left[\frac{\partial V^*}{\partial \mathbf{x}} \mathbf{b}_j(\mathbf{x}) \right]. \tag{18}$$

Temporal Difference in Learning in Continuous Time and Space

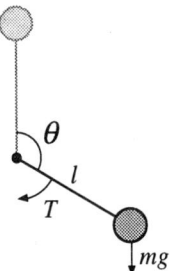

Figure 1: A pendulum with limited torque. The dynamics is given by $ml\ddot{\theta} = -\mu\dot{\theta} + mgl\sin\theta + T$. Parameters were $m = l = 1$, $g = 9.8$, and $\mu = 0.01$.

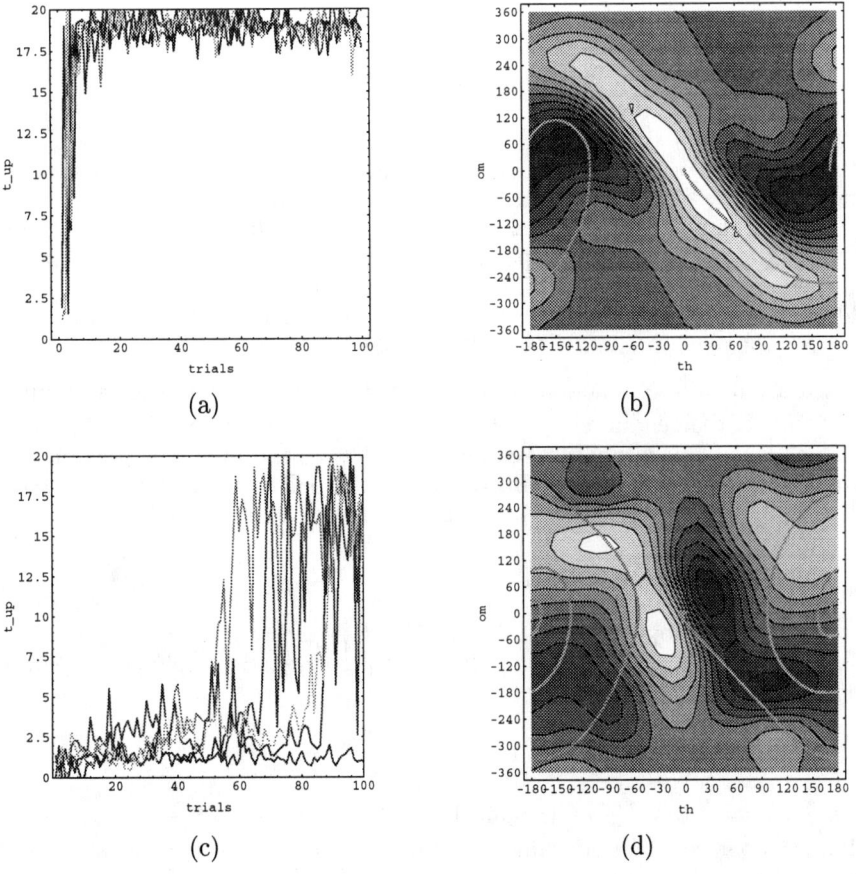

Figure 2: Left: The learning curves for (a) optimal control and (c) actor-critic. t_up: time during which $|\theta| < 90°$. Right: (b) The predicted value function P after 100 trials of optimal control. (d) The output of the controller after 100 trials with actor-critic learning. The thick gray line shows the trajectory of the pendulum. th: θ (degrees), om: $\dot{\theta}$ (degrees/sec).

4 ACTOR-CRITIC

When the information about the control cost, the input gain of the system, or the gradient of the value function is not available, we cannot use the above optimal control law. However, the TD error (6) can be used as "internal reinforcement" for training a stochastic controller, or an "actor" (Barto et al., 1983).

In the simulation below, we combined our TD algorithm for the critic with a reinforcement learning algorithm for real-valued output (Gullapalli, 1990). The output of the controller was given by

$$u_j(t) = u_j^{\max} g\left(\sum_i w_{ji} b_i(\mathbf{x}(t)) + \sigma n_j(t)\right), \tag{19}$$

where $n_j(t)$ is normalized Gaussian noise and w_{ji} is a weight. The size of this perturbation was changed based on the predicted performance by $\sigma = \sigma_0 \exp(-P(t))$. The connection weights were changed by

$$\Delta w_{ji} \propto \hat{r}(t) n_j(t) b_i(\mathbf{x}(t)). \tag{20}$$

5 SIMULATION

The performance of the above continuous-time TD algorithm was tested on a task of swinging up a pendulum with limited torque (Figure 1). Control of this one-degree-of-freedom system is trivial near the upright equilibrium. However, bringing the pendulum near the upright position is not if we set the maximal torque $T^{\max}$ smaller than mgl. The controller has to swing the pendulum several times to build up enough momentum to bring it upright. Furthermore, the controller has to decelerate the pendulum early enough to avoid falling over.

We used a radial basis function (RBF) network to approximate the value function for the state of the pendulum $\mathbf{x} = (\theta, \dot{\theta})$. We prepared a fixed set of 12×12 Gaussian basis functions. This is a natural extension of the "boxes" approach previously used to control inverted pendulums (Barto et al., 1983). The immediate reinforcement was given by the height of the tip of the pendulum, i.e., $r_x = \cos\theta$.

5.1 OPTIMAL CONTROL

First, we used the optimal control law (17) with the predicted value function P instead of V^*. We added noise to the control command to enhance exploration. The torque was given by

$$T = T^{\max} g\left(\frac{T^{\max}}{c} \tau \frac{\partial P(\mathbf{x})}{\partial \mathbf{x}} \mathbf{b} + \sigma n(t)\right),$$

where $g(x) = \frac{2}{\pi} \tan^{-1}(\frac{\pi}{2} x)$ (Hopfield, 1984). Note that the input gain $\mathbf{b} = (0, 1/ml^2)^T$ was constant. Parameters were $T^{\max} = 5$, $c = 0.1$, $\sigma_0 = 0.01$, $\tau = 1.0$, and $\tau_c = 0.1$.

Each run was started from a random θ and was continued for 20 seconds. Within ten trials, the value function P became accurate enough to be able to swing up and hold the pendulum (Figure 2a). An example of the predicted value function P after 100 trials is shown in Figure 2b. The paths toward the upright position, which were implicitly determined by the dynamical properties of the system, can be seen as the ridges of the value function. We also had successful results when the reinforcement was given only near the goal: $r_x = 1$ if $|\theta| < 30°$, -1 otherwise.

5.2 ACTOR-CRITIC

Next, we tested the actor-critic learning scheme as described above. The controller was also implemented by a RBF network with the same 12 × 12 basis functions as the critic network. It took about one hundred trials to achieve reliable performance (Figure 2c). Figure 2d shows an example of the output of the controller after 100 trials. We can see nearly linear feedback in the neighborhood of the upright position and a non-linear torque field away from the equilibrium.

6 CONCLUSION

We derived a continuous-time, continuous-state version of the TD algorithm and showed its applicability to a nonlinear control task. One advantage of continuous formulation is that we can derive an explicit form of optimal control law as in (17) using derivative information, whereas a one-ply search for the best action is usually required in discrete formulations.

References

Baird III, L. C. (1993). Advantage updating. Technical Report WL-TR-93-1146, Wright Laboratory, Wright-Patterson Air Force Base, OH 45433-7301, USA.

Barto, A. G., Bradtke, S. J., and Singh, S. P. (1995). Learning to act using real-time dynamic programming. *Artificial Intelligence*, 72:81–138.

Barto, A. G., Sutton, R. S., and Anderson, C. W. (1983). Neuronlike adaptive elements that can solve difficult learning control problems. *IEEE Transactions on System, Man, and Cybernetics*, SMC-13:834–846.

Bradtke, S. J. and Duff, M. O. (1995). Reinforcement learning methods for continuous-time Markov decision problems. In Tesauro, G., Touretzky, D. S., and Leen, T. K., editors, *Advances in Neural Information Processing Systems 7*, pages 393–400. MIT Press, Cambridge, MA.

Bradtke, S. J., Ydstie, B. E., and Barto, A. G. (1994). Adaptive linear quadratic control using policy iteration. CMPSCI Technical Report 94-49, University of Massachusetts, Amherst, MA.

Bryson, Jr., A. E. . and Ho, Y.-C. (1975). *Applied Optimal Control*. Hemisphere Publishing, New York, 2nd edition.

Gullapalli, V. (1990). A stochastic reinforcement learning algorithm for learning real-valued functions. *Neural Networks*, 3:671–192.

Hopfield, J. J. (1984). Neurons with graded response have collective computational properties like those of two-state neurons. *Proceedings of National Academy of Science*, 81:3088–3092.

Houk, J. C., Adams, J. L., and Barto, A. G. (1994). A model of how the basal ganglia generate and use neural signlas that predict renforcement. In Houk, J. C., Davis, J. L., and Beiser, D. G., editors, *Models of Information Processing in the Basal Ganglia*, pages 249–270. MIT Press, Cambrigde, MA.

Sutton, R. S. (1988). Learning to predict by the methods of temporal difference. *Machine Learning*, 3:9–44.

Reinforcement Learning by Probability Matching

Philip N. Sabes
sabes@psyche.mit.edu

Michael I. Jordan
jordan@psyche.mit.edu

Department of Brain and Cognitive Sciences
Massachusetts Institute of Technology
Cambridge, MA 02139

Abstract

We present a new algorithm for associative reinforcement learning. The algorithm is based upon the idea of matching a network's output probability with a probability distribution derived from the environment's reward signal. This Probability Matching algorithm is shown to perform faster and be less susceptible to local minima than previously existing algorithms. We use Probability Matching to train mixture of experts networks, an architecture for which other reinforcement learning rules fail to converge reliably on even simple problems. This architecture is particularly well suited for our algorithm as it can compute arbitrarily complex functions yet calculation of the output probability is simple.

1 INTRODUCTION

The problem of learning associative networks from scalar reinforcement signals is notoriously difficult. Although general purpose algorithms such as REINFORCE (Williams, 1992) and Generalized Learning Automata (Phansalkar, 1991) exist, they are generally slow and have trouble with local minima. As an example, when we attempted to apply these algorithms to mixture of experts networks (Jacobs et al., 1991), the algorithms typically converged to the local minimum which places the entire burden of the task on one expert.

Here we present a new reinforcement learning algorithm which has faster and more reliable convergence properties than previous algorithms. The next section describes the algorithm and draws comparisons between it and existing algorithms. The following section details its application to Gaussian units and mixtures of Gaussian experts. Finally, we present empirical results.

2 REINFORCEMENT PROBABILITY MATCHING

We begin by formalizing the learning problem. Given an input $\mathbf{x} \in \mathcal{X}$ from the environment, the network must select an output $\mathbf{y} \in \mathcal{Y}$. The network then receives a scalar reward signal r, with a mean $\bar{r}$ and distribution that depend on $\mathbf{x}$ and $\mathbf{y}$. The goal of the learner is to choose an output which maximizes the expected reward. Due to the lack of an explicit error signal, the learner must choose its output stochastically, exploring for better rewards. Typically the learner starts with a parameterized form for the conditional output density $p_\theta(\mathbf{y}|\mathbf{x})$, and the learning problem becomes one of finding the parameters θ which maximize the expected reward:

$$J_r(\theta) = \int_{\mathcal{X},\mathcal{Y}} p(\mathbf{x}) p_\theta(\mathbf{y}|\mathbf{x}) \bar{r}(\mathbf{x},\mathbf{y}) d\mathbf{y} d\mathbf{x}.$$

We present an alternative route to the maximum expected reward cost function, and in doing so derive a novel learning rule for updating the network's parameters. The learner's task is to choose from a set of conditional output distributions based on the reward it receives from the environment. These rewards can be thought of as inverse energies; input/output pairs that receive high rewards are low energy and are preferred by the environment. Energies can always be converted into probabilities through the Boltzmann distribution, and so we can define the environment's conditional distribution on $\mathcal{Y}$ given $\mathbf{x}$,

$$p^*(\mathbf{y}|\mathbf{x}) = \frac{\exp(-T^{-1}E(\mathbf{x},\mathbf{y}))}{Z_T(\mathbf{x})} = \frac{\exp(T^{-1}\bar{r}(\mathbf{x},\mathbf{y}))}{Z_T(\mathbf{x})},$$

where T is a temperature parameter and $Z_T(\mathbf{x})$ is a normalization constant which depends on T. This distribution can be thought of as representing the environment's ideal input-output mapping, high reward input-output pairs being more typical or likely than low reward pairs. The temperature parameter determines the strength of this preference: when T is infinity all outputs are equally likely; when T is zero only the highest reward output is chosen. This new distribution is a purely theoretical construct, but it can be used as a target distribution for the learner. If the θ are adjusted so that $p_\theta(\mathbf{y}|\mathbf{x})$ is nearly equal to $p^*(\mathbf{y}|\mathbf{x})$, then the network's output will typically result in high rewards.

The agreement between the network and environment conditional output densities can be measured with the Kullback-Liebler (KL) divergence:

$$KL(p \| p^*) = -\int_{\mathcal{X},\mathcal{Y}} p(\mathbf{x}) p_\theta(\mathbf{y}|\mathbf{x}) \left[\log p^*(\mathbf{y}|\mathbf{x}) - \log p_\theta(\mathbf{y}|\mathbf{x})\right] d\mathbf{y} d\mathbf{x} \quad (1)$$

$$= -\frac{1}{T}\int_{\mathcal{X},\mathcal{Y}} p(\mathbf{x}) p_\theta(\mathbf{y}|\mathbf{x}) \left[\bar{r}(\mathbf{x},\mathbf{y}) - T\hat{r}_\theta(\mathbf{x},\mathbf{y})\right] d\mathbf{y} d\mathbf{x} + \int_{\mathcal{X}} p(\mathbf{x}) \log Z_T(\mathbf{x}) d\mathbf{x},$$

where $\hat{r}_\theta(\mathbf{x},\mathbf{y})$ is defined as the logarithm of the conditional output probability and can be thought of as the network's estimate of the mean reward. This cost function is always greater than or equal to zero, with equality only when the two probability distributions are identical.

Keeping only the part of Equation 1 which depends on θ, we define the Probability Matching (PM) cost function:

$$J_{PM}(\theta) = -\int_{\mathcal{X},\mathcal{Y}} p(\mathbf{x}) p_\theta(\mathbf{y}|\mathbf{x}) \left[\bar{r}(\mathbf{x},\mathbf{y}) - T\hat{r}_\theta(\mathbf{x},\mathbf{y})\right] d\mathbf{y} d\mathbf{x} = -J_r(\theta) - TS(p_\theta)$$

The PM cost function is analogous to a free energy, balancing the energy, in the form of the negative of the average reward, and the entropy $S(p_\theta)$ of the output

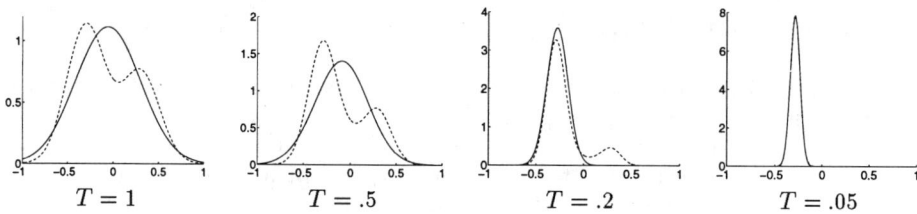

Figure 1: p^*'s (dashed) and PM optimal Gaussians (solid) for the same bimodal reward function and various temperatures. Note the differences in scale.

distribution. A higher T corresponds to a smoother target distribution and tilts the balance of the cost function in favor of the entropy term, making diffuse output distributions more favorable. Likewise, a small T results in a sharp target distribution placing most of the weight on the reward dependent term of cost function, which is always optimized by the singular solution of a spike at the highest reward output.

Although minimizing the PM cost function will result in sampling most often at high reward outputs, it will not optimize the overall expected reward if $T > 0$. There are two reasons for this. First, the output $\mathbf{y}$ which maximizes $\hat{r}_\theta(\mathbf{x}, \mathbf{y})$ may not maximize $\bar{r}(\mathbf{x}, \mathbf{y})$. Such an example is seen in the first panel of Figure 1: the network's conditional output density is a Gaussian with adjustable mean and variance, and the environment has a bimodal reward function and $T = 1$. Even in the realizable case, however, the network will choose outputs which are suboptimal with respect to its own predicted reward, with the probability of choosing output $\mathbf{y}$ falling off exponentially with $\hat{r}_\theta(\mathbf{x}, \mathbf{y})$. The key point here is that early in learning this non-optimality is exactly what is desired. The PM cost function forces the learner to maintain output density everywhere the reward, as measure by $p^{*1/T}$, is not much smaller than its maximum. When T is high, the rewards are effectively flattened and even fairly small rewards look big. This means that a high temperature ensures that the learner will explore the output space.

Once the network is nearly PM optimal, it would be advantageous to "sharpen up" the conditional output distribution, sampling more often at outputs with higher predicted rewards. This translates to decreasing the entropy of the output distribution or lowering T. Figure 1 shows how the PM optimal Gaussian changes as the temperature is lowered in the example discussed above; at very low temperatures the output is almost always near the mode of the target distribution. In the limit of $T = 0$, J_{PM} becomes original reward maximization criterion J_r. The idea of the Probability Matching algorithm is to begin training with a large T, say unity, and gradually decrease it as the performance improves, effectively shifting the bias of the learner from exploration to exploitation.

We now must find an update rule for θ which minimizes $J_{PM}(\theta)$. We proceed by looking for a stochastic gradient descent step. Differentiating the cost function gives

$$\nabla_\theta J_{PM}(\theta) = -\int_{\mathcal{X}, \mathbf{y}} p(\mathbf{x}) p_\theta(\mathbf{y}|\mathbf{x}) \left[\bar{r}(\mathbf{x}, \mathbf{y}) - T\hat{r}_\theta(\mathbf{x}, \mathbf{y})\right] \nabla_\theta \hat{r}_\theta(\mathbf{x}, \mathbf{y}) dy dx.$$

Thus, if after every action the parameters are updated by the step

$$\Delta \theta = \alpha \left[r - T\hat{r}_\theta(\mathbf{x}, \mathbf{y})\right] \nabla_\theta \hat{r}_\theta(\mathbf{x}, \mathbf{y}), \qquad (2)$$

where alpha is a constant which can vary over time, then the parameters will on average move down the gradient of the PM cost function. Note that any quantity which does not depend on **y** or r can be added to the difference in the update rule, and the expected step will still point along the direction of the gradient.

The form of Equation 2 is similar to the REINFORCE algorithm (Williams, 1992), whose update rule is

$$\Delta \theta = \alpha (r - b) \nabla_\theta \log p_\theta(\mathbf{y}|\mathbf{x}),$$

where b, the reinforcement baseline, is a quantity which does not depend on **y** or r. Note that these two update rules are identical when T is zero.[1] The advantage of the PM rule is that it allows for an early training phase which encourages exploration without forcing the output distribution to converge on suboptimal outputs. This will lead to striking qualitative differences in the performance of the algorithm for training mixtures of Gaussian experts.

3 UPDATE RULES FOR GAUSSIAN UNITS AND MIXTURES OF GAUSSIAN EXPERTS

We employ Gaussian units with mean $\boldsymbol{\mu} = \mathbf{w}^T \mathbf{x}$ and covariance $\sigma^2 \mathbf{I}$. The learner must select the matrix **w** and scalar σ which minimize $J_{PM}(\mathbf{w}, \sigma)$. Applying the update rule in Equation 2, we get

$$\Delta \mathbf{w} = \alpha [r - T\hat{r}(\mathbf{x}, \mathbf{y})] \frac{1}{\sigma^2} (\mathbf{y} - \boldsymbol{\mu})^T \mathbf{x}$$

$$\Delta \sigma = \alpha [r - T\hat{r}(\mathbf{x}, \mathbf{y})] \frac{1}{\sigma^2} \left(\frac{\|\mathbf{y} - \boldsymbol{\mu}\|^2}{\sigma^2} - 1 \right).$$

In practice, for both single Gaussian units and the mixtures presented below we avoid the issue of constraining $\sigma > 0$ by updating $\log \sigma$ directly.

We can generalize the linear model by considering a conditional output distribution in the form of a mixture of Gaussian experts (Jacobs et al., 1991),

$$p(\mathbf{y}|\mathbf{x}) = \sum_{i=1}^{N} g_i(\mathbf{x}) (2\pi \sigma_i^2)^{-\frac{1}{2}} \exp\left(-\frac{1}{2\sigma_i^2} \|\mathbf{y} - \boldsymbol{\mu}_i\|^2\right).$$

Expert i has mean $\boldsymbol{\mu}_i = \mathbf{w}_i^T \mathbf{x}$ and covariance $\sigma_i^2 \mathbf{I}$. The prior probability given **x** of choosing expert i, $g_i(\mathbf{x})$, is determined by a single layer gating network with weight matrix **v** and softmax output units. The gating network learns a soft partitioning of the input space into regions for which each expert is responsible.

Again, we can apply Equation 2 to get the PM update rules:

$$\Delta \mathbf{v}_i = \alpha [r - T\hat{r}(\mathbf{x}, \mathbf{y})] (h_i - g_i) \mathbf{x}$$

$$\Delta \mathbf{w}_i = \alpha [r - T\hat{r}(\mathbf{x}, \mathbf{y})] h_i \frac{1}{\sigma_i^2} (\mathbf{y} - \boldsymbol{\mu}_i)^T \mathbf{x}$$

$$\Delta \sigma_i = \alpha [r - T\hat{r}(\mathbf{x}, \mathbf{y})] h_i \frac{1}{\sigma_i^2} \left(\frac{\|\mathbf{y} - \boldsymbol{\mu}_i\|^2}{\sigma_i^2} - 1 \right),$$

where $h_i = g_i p_i(\mathbf{y}|\mathbf{x})/p(\mathbf{y}|\mathbf{x})$ is the posterior probability of choosing expert i given **y**. We note that the PM update rules are equivalent to the supervised learning gradient descent update rules in (Jacobs et al., 1991) modulated by the difference between the actual and expected rewards.

---

[1] This fact implies that the REINFORCE step is in the direction of the gradient of $J_R(\theta)$, as shown by (Williams, 1992). See Williams and Peng, 1991, for a similar REINFORCE plus entropy update rule.

Table 1: Convergence times and gate entropies for the linear example (standard errors in parentheses). Convergence times: An experiment consisting of 50 runs was conducted for each algorithm, with a wide range of learning rates and both reward functions. Best results for each algorithm are reported. Entropy: Values are averages over the last 5,000 time steps of each run. 20 runs of 50,000 time steps were conducted.

Algorithm	Convergence Time	Entropy
PM, $T = 1$	1088 (43)	.993 (.001)
PM, $T = .5$	—	.97 (.02)
PM, $T = .1$	—	.48 (.04)
REINFORCE	2998 (183)	.21 (.03)
REINF-COMP	1622 (46)	.21 (.03)

Both the h_i and $\hat{r}$ depend on the overall conditional probability $p(\mathbf{y}|\mathbf{x})$, which in turn depends on each $p_i(\mathbf{y}|\mathbf{x})$. This adds an extra step to the training procedure. After receiving the input $\mathbf{x}$, the network chooses an expert based on the priors $g_i(\mathbf{x})$ and an output $\mathbf{y}$ from the selected expert's output distribution. The output is then sent back to each of the experts in order to compute the likelihood of their having generated it. Given the set of p_i's, the network can update its parameters as above.

4 SIMULATIONS

We present three examples designed to explore the behavior of the Probability Matching algorithm. In each case, networks were trained using Probability Matching, REINFORCE, and REINFORCE with reinforcement comparison (REINF-COMP), where a running average of the reward is used as a reinforcement baseline (Sutton, 1984). In the first two examples an optimal output function $\mathbf{y}^*(\mathbf{x})$ was chosen and used to calculate a noisy error, $\varepsilon = \|\mathbf{y} - \mathbf{y}^*(\mathbf{x}) - \mathbf{z}\|$, where $\mathbf{z}$ was i.i.d. zero-mean Gaussian with $\sigma = .1$. The error signal determined the reward by one of two functions, $r = -\varepsilon^2/2$ or $\exp(-\varepsilon^2/2)$. When the RMSE between the network mean and the optimal output was less that .05 the network was said to have converged.

4.1 A Linear Example

In this example $\mathbf{x}$ was chosen uniformly from $[-1, 1]^2 \times \{1\}$, and the optimal output was $\mathbf{y}^* = A\mathbf{x}$, for a 2×3 matrix A. A mixture of three Gaussian experts was trained. The details of the simulation and results for each algorithm are shown in Table 1. Probability Matching with constant $T = 1$ shows almost a threefold reduction in training time compared to REINFORCE and about a 50% improvement over REINF-COMP.

The important point of this example is the manner in which the extra Gaussian units were employed. We calculated the entropy of the gating network, normalized so that a value of one means that each expert has equal probability of being chosen and a value of zero means that only one expert is ever chosen. The values after 50,000 time steps are shown in the second column of Table 1. When $T \approx 1$, the Probability Matching algorithm gives the three experts roughly equal priors. This is due to the fact that small differences in the experts' parameters lead to increased output entropy if all experts are used. REINFORCE on the other hand always converges to a solution which employs only one expert. This difference in the behavior of the algorithms will have a large qualitative effect in the next example.

Table 2: Results for absolute value. The percentage of trials that converged and the average time to convergence for those trials. Standard errors are in parentheses. 50 trials were conducted for a range of learning rates and with both reward functions; the best results for each algorithm are shown.

Algorithm	Successful Trials	Convergence Time
PM	100%	6,052 (313)
REINFORCE	48%	76,775 (3,329)
REINF-COMP	38%	42,105 (3,869)

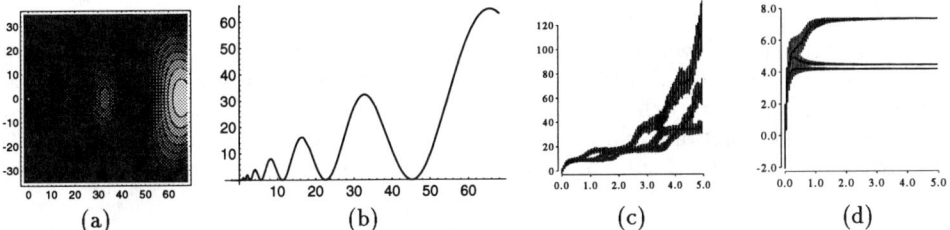

Figure 2: Example 4.3. The environment's probability distribution for $T = 1$: (a) density plot of p^* vs. $\mathbf{y}/x$, (b) cross-sectional view with $y_2 = 0$. Locally weighted mean and variance of y_2/x over representative runs: (c) $T = 1$, (d) $T = 0$ (i.e. REINFORCE).

4.2 Absolute Value

We used a mixture of two Gaussian units to learn the absolute value function. The details of the simulation and the best results for each algorithm are shown in Table 2. Probability Matching with constant $T = 1$ converged to criterion on every trial, in marked contrast to the REINFORCE algorithm. With no reinforcement baseline, REINFORCE converged to criterion in only about half of the cases, less with reinforcement comparison. In almost all of the trials that didn't converge, only one expert was active on the domain of the input. Neither version of REINFORCE ever converged to criterion in less than 14,000 time steps.

This example highlights the advantage of the Probability Matching algorithm. During training, all three algorithms initially use both experts to capture the overall mean of the data. REINFORCE converges on this local minimum, cutting one expert off before it has a chance to explore the rest of the parameter space. The Probability Matching algorithm keeps both experts in use. Here, the more conservative approach leads to a stark improvement in performance.

4.3 An Example with Many Local Maxima

In this example, the learner's conditional output distribution was a bivariate Gaussian with $\boldsymbol{\mu} = [w_1, w_2]^T x$, and the environment's rewards were a function of $\mathbf{y}/x$. The optimal output distribution $p^*(\mathbf{y}/x)$ is shown in Figures 2(a,b). These figures can also be interpreted as the expected value of p^* for a given $\mathbf{w}$. The weight vector is initially chosen from a uniform distribution over $[-.2, .2]^2$, depicted as the very small white dot in Figure 2(a). There are a series of larger and larger local maxima off to the right, with a peak of height 2^n at $w_1 = 2^n$.

The results are shown in Table 3. REINFORCE, both with and without reinforcement comparison, never got past third peak; the variance of the Gaussian unit would

Table 3: Results for Example 4.3. These values represent 20 runs for 50,000 time steps each. The first and second columns correspond to number of the peak the learner reached.

Algorithm	Mean Final $\log_2 w_1$	Range of Final $\log_2 w_1$'s	Mean Final σ
PM, $T = 2$	28,8	[19.1,51.0]	$> 10^5$
PM, $T = 1$	6.34	[5.09,8.08]	13.1
PM, $T = .5$	3.06	[3.04,3.07]	.40
REINFORCE	2.17	[2.00,2.90]	.019
REINF-COMP	2.05	[2.05,2.06]	.18

very quickly close down to a small value making further exploration of the output space impossible. Probability Matching, on the other hand, was able to find greater and greater maxima, with the variance growing adaptively to match the local scale of the reward function. These differences can be clearly seen in Figures 2(c,d), which show typical behavior for the Probability Matching algorithm with $T = 1$ and $T = 0$.

5 CONCLUSION

We have presented a new reinforcement learning algorithm for associative networks which converges faster and more reliably than existing algorithms. The strength of the Probability Matching algorithm is that it allows for a better balance between exploration of the output space and and exploitation of good outputs. The parameter T can be adjusted during learning to allow broader output distributions early in training and then to force the network to sharpen up its distribution once nearly optimal parameters have been found.

Although the applications in this paper were restricted to networks with Gaussian units, the Probability Matching algorithm can be applied to any reinforcement learning task and any conditional output distribution. It could easily be employed, for example, on classification problems using logistic or multinomial (softmax) output units or mixtures of such units. Finally, the simulations presented in this paper are of simple examples. Preliminary results indicate that the advantages of the Probability Matching algorithm scale up to larger, more interesting problems.

References

Jacobs, R. A., Jordan, M. I., Nowlan, S. J., and Hinton, G. E. (1991). Adaptive mixtures of local experts. *Neural Computation*, 3:79–87.

Phansalkar, V. V. (1991). *Learning automata algorithms for connectionist systems – local and global convergence.* PhD Thesis, Dept. of Electrical Engineering, India Institute of Science, Bangalore.

Sutton, R. S. (1984). *Temporal credit assignment in reinforcement learning.* PhD Thesis, Dept. of Computer and Information Science, University of Massachusetts, Amherst, MA.

Williams, R. J. (1992). Simple statistical gradient-following algorithms for connectionist reinforcement learning. *Machine Learning*, 8:229–256.

Williams, R. J. and Peng, J. (1991). Function optimization using connectionist reinforcement learning algorithms. *Connection Science*, 3:241–268.

Author Index

Abdallah, C.T., 274
Allen, T.P., 938
Alley, R.K., 816
Alpaydin, E., 771
Amari, S., 176, 757
Annaswamy, A.M., 1010
Asanovic, K., 619
Atkeson, C.C., 605
Auer, P., 316

Back, A.D., 785
Bair, W., 68
Baldi, P., 451
Ballard, D.H., 830
Baluja, S., 875, 959
Bartlett, M.S., 823
Bartlett, P.L., 344
Barto, A.G., 138, 1017
Baxter, J., 169
Beck, J., 619
Bell, A.J., 145
Bengio, Y., 395, 493
Bialek, W., 281
Bishop, C.M., 465
Blair, H.T., 152
Blatt, M., 416
Boahen, K., 678
Boes, S., 218
Bohossian, V., 246
Bolouri, H., 980
Botelho, F., 372
Bourlard, H., 388
Bruck, J., 246
Buckingham, J.T., 138

Campbell, P., 973
Caruana, R., 959
Cauwenberghs, G., 692
Cekic, M., 131
Cherkauer, K.J., 45
Choe, Y., 736
Choi, S.P.M., 945
Cichocki, A., 757

Coelho, J.A., 996
Coenen, O.J.M., 89
Coolen, A.C.C., 253
Cortes, C., 479
Craven, M.W., 24, 654
Crites, R.H., 1017

Dale, M., 973
Darken, C., 924
Darrell, T., 858
Dasgupta, B., 204
Dayan, P., 661, 1059
Denham, M.J., 52
Deweese, M., 281
Dietterich, T.G., 1024
Dixon, L.C., 980
Dodier, R., 365
Domany, E., 416
Doya, K., 38, 1073
Doyle, H.R., 882
Drees, A., 903
Drucker, H., 479

Edwards, R.T., 692
Ekman, P., 823
Elman, J.L., 549
Etienne-Cummings, R., 706

Ferguson, A., 980
Ferra, H.L., 973
Finch, S., 330
Finke, M., 176
Flake, G.W., 556
Flash, T., 117
Fragniere, E., 671
Frey, B.J., 661
Fry, C.L., 110
Fukumizu, K., 295
Fukumura, N., 989
Furukawa, T., 159

Garzon, M., 372
Gersho, A., 591

Gerstner, W., 124
Ghahramani, Z., 472
Giles, C.L., 577
Gilloux, M., 764
Gingras, F., 395
Gold, S., 626, 795
Goodhill, G.J., 330
Gordon, G.J., 1052
Gourley, R., 31
Grunewald, A., 837
Grupen, R.A., 996

Hadjifaradji, S., 288
Hager, J.C., 823
Hammerstrom, D., 713
Handzel, A.A., 117
Hansen, L.K., 521
Hanson, S.J., 924
Hasselmo, M., 131
Hastie, T., 409
Hayhoe, M.M., 830
Heileman, G.L., 274
Helmbold, D.P., 309
Herbster, M., 316
Hihi, S.E., 493
Hinton, G., 507, 661
Hochberg, M.M., 750
Hofmann, R., 500
Horne, B.G., 577
Hornik, K., 451
Houk, J.C., 138
Howse, J.W., 274
Hubbard, R.S., 816

Indiveri, G., 720

Jaakkola, T., 528
Jabri, M.A., 910
Jackson, G., 1031
Jackson, J.C., 654
Jagota, A., 372
Johnson, D., 619
Jordan, M.I., 472, 486, 528, 1003, 1080
Joseph, S.R.H., 96
Juels, A., 430
Jung, T., 145, 931

Kadirkamanathan, M., 239
Kadirkamanathan, V., 239
Kaihara, R., 685
Kanade, T., 875
Kaye, P., 980
Kearns, M., 183
Kempter, R., 124
Kershaw, D.J., 750
Kingsbury, B., 619

Kivinen, J., 309
Koch, C., 68, 720, 802
Koiran, P., 197
Konig, Y., 388
Kowalczyk, A., 344, 973
Kramer, J., 720
Kremer, S.C., 612
Krogh, A., 190, 917
Kuhn, G.M., 924

Larsen, J., 521, 823
Laughton, S.N., 253
Lawrence, S., 785
Lazzaro, J., 699
Lemarie, B., 764
Leroux, M., 764
Levin, A.U., 966
Littmann, E., 903
Lin, T., 577
Liu, S., 678

Maass, W., 211
Mackay, D., 351
Makeig, S., 145, 931
Mansour, Y., 259
Marcantonio, A., 924
Marchand, M., 288
Marshall, J.A., 816
Martin, G.L., 10
Matsuoka, Y., 889
McCabe, S.L., 52
Meila, M., 1003
Mel, B.W., 865
Meyer-Baese, A., 337
Miikkulainen, R., 736
Miller, O., 591
Mitchell, T., 959
Mjolsness, E., 633
Moody, J., 458
Moore, A.W., 1066
Morgan, N., 388, 619
Morimoto, T., 685
Mueller, K., 176
Munro, P.W., 882
Murata, N., 176
Murray, A.F., 1031

Nakahara, H., 38
Nakai, T., 685
Neuneier, R., 952
Niebur, E., 802

Ohmi, T., 685
Ohl, F., 337
Omohundro, S.M., 402
Opitz, D.W., 535

Ormoneit, D., 542

Pappu, S., 795
Parmanto, B., 882
Parra, L.C., 437
Pedersen, M.W., 521
Pentland, A., 858
Pessoa, L., 844
Peterson, R.S., 82
Petsche, T., 924
Platt, J.C., 938
Pouget, A., 10

Rangarajan, A., 626, 795
Rao, A., 591
Rao, R.P.N., 830
Rasmussen, C.E., 598
Rebotier, T., 549
Redish, A.D., 61
Rehfuss, S., 713
Revow, M., 507
Riis, S.K., 917
Ritter, H., 570, 903
Robinson, A.J., 351, 584, 743, 750
Rose, K., 591
Ross, W., 844
Rowley, H.A., 875
Roy, B.V., 1045
Rueger, S.M., 225

Saad, D., 302, 323
Sabes, P.N., 1080
Sabisch., T., 980
Sahar, S., 260
Santoso, I., 924
Sato, A., 423
Saul, L.K., 486, 528
Schaal, S., 605
Scheich, H., 337
Schneider, J., 1066
Schraudolph, N.N., 563, 851
Sejnowski, T.J., 10, 89, 145, 563, 823, 851, 931
Semenov, S.A., 358
Senior, A., 743
Shavlik, J.W., 24, 45, 535
Shawe-Taylor, J., 267
Sherrington, D., 253
Shibata, T., 685
Shustorovich, A., 778
Shuvalova, I.B., 358
Singer, Y., 381
Singh, S.P., 1059
Sirosh, J., 736
Sitaramen, R., 996
Smith, L.S., 729

Snapp, R.R., 232
Softky, W.R., 809
Solla, S.A., 302
Sollich, P., 190
Sontag, E.D., 197, 204
Stevens, C., 75, 103
Stone, P., 896
Sutton, R.S., 1038
Svensen, M., 465
Szymanski, J., 344

Tani, J., 989
Taylor, J.G., 82
Tenenbaum, J.B., 3
Thrasher, C.W., 778
Thrun, S., 640
Tibshirani, R., 409
Tino, P., 577
Touretzky, D.S., 61
Towell, G., 647
Tresp, V., 500, 542
Tsioutsias, O.I., 633
Tsitsiklis, J.N., 1045
Tsoi, A.C., 785

Van der Spiegel, J., 706
Van Hemmen, J.L., 124
Van Schaik, A., 671
Veloso, M., 896
Viola, P.A., 823, 851
Vittoz, E., 671

Wagner, H., 124
Walter, J., 570
Wang, R.J., 910
Wang, X., 372
Warmuth, M.K., 309, 316
Waterhouse, S.R., 351, 584
Wattenberg, M., 430
Wawrzynek, J., 619, 699
West, A.H.L., 323
Williams, C.K.I., 465, 514
Williamson, R.C., 344
Willshaw, D.J., 96
Wiseman, S., 416
Wu, L., 458

Xu, L., 444
Xu, T., 232

Yamada, K., 423
Yamashita, T., 685
Yang, H., 176, 757
Yasui, S., 159
Yeung, D., 945
Yu, S., 1010

Zador, A., 75, 103
Zelinsky, G.J., 830
Zhang, W., 1024
Zhao, J., 267
Zohary, E., 68

Keyword Index

acetylcholine, 131
active learning, 295
active set method, 938
active vision, 858
actor-critic, 1073
adaptation, 678, 837
adaptive algorithms, 381
adaptive back-propagation, 323
adaptive behavior, 38
adaptive control, 1010
adaptive learning, 896
adaptive metric, 409
adaptive routing, 945
ADDEMUP, 535
additive clustering (ADCLUS), 3
advantage updating, 1059
adverserial learning, 896
alertness, 931
alphanumeric fields, 778
amodal completion, 816
analog circuits, 671
analog VLSI, 699, 720, 938
animal cognition, 61
anomaly detection, 528, 924
anterior thalamus, 152
applications, 1031
approximation rate, 183
architectural limitations, 612
area MT, 68
ARMAX processes, 204
articulated matching, 795
articulated objects, 795
asset allocation, 952
assimilation, 844
associative memory, 131
associative networks, 1080
asymptotic stability, 225, 372
asymptotic theory, 176, 295
asynchronous data, 395

attention, 633, 802
attention dynamics, 38
attractor dynamics, 989
attractor networks, 253
audition, 699
auditory modelling, 729
auditory perception, 110
auditory scene analysis, 699
auditory streaming, 52
auditory system, 124
auditory template hypothesis, 110
autoassociator, 402, 924
automatic relevance determination, 514
autonomous robot, 989, 1031

background constancy, 844
backpropagation through time
 (BPTT), 577, 743
backpropagation training, 159, 225, 619
bagging, 535, 542
barn owl, 124
basis functions, 10
Baum-Welch, 472
Bayes classifier, 542
Bayes risk, 232
Bayesian analysis, 514
Bayesian-Kullback, 444
Bayesian learning, 402, 598
Bayesian methods, 351
Bayesian networks, 500
Bayesian penalty terms, 542
Bayesian regression, 1066
belief network, 528, 661
Benary Cross, 844
beta sheet prediction, 917
bias learning, 169
bifurcation (saddle-node bifurcation), 38
binary tree, 507

binding, 809
bipolar cell, 159
birdsong learning, 110
bit stream neural networks, 267
blind separation, 757
blurring, 45
boolean functions, 260
boosting, 479
bootstrap, 882
brain lesions, 10
brain stem, 89

C4.5, 24, 654
capacity, 556
CART, 507
CART analysis, 966
center-surround opponent receptive field, 159, 678
cerebellum, 89, 138
channel selection, 910
character recognition, 423
check reader, 938
classification, 197
classification tree, 507
classifiers, 176
clustering, 3, 416
CMAC, 1038
CMOS, 685
coarticulation, 486
cochlea, 910
cochlear implants, 910
cognitive modeling, 3, 10

Cohen-Grossberg model, 337
coherence, 931
color constancy, 844
color segmentation, 903
combinatorial optimization, 626
combining classifiers, 535
combining estimators, 190
committee, 882
compact representations, 1045
transistors, 671
competence acquisition, 1031
competition, 837
competitive networks, 82
complexity, 246, 549
complexity regularization, 183
compliant control, 1003
comprehensibility, 24, 654
computational complexity, 211

computational learning theory, 288
computational power, 612
computer vision, 875
condition monitoring, 924
confidence levels, 260
conjugate gradient, 633
coincidence detection, 124
conjugate prior, 542
connectionist reinforcement algorithm, 889
constrained optimization, 938
context-dependency, 750
context dependent learning, 570
context free grammars, 31
continuous activations, 197
continuous-function learning, 896
continuous-time model, 1073
continuous variables, 500
continuous wavelet transform, 692
contrast-filling-in, 844
control, 973
control, direct, 1052
control, online, 1052
convergence, 423
convergent learning, 274
cooperation, 1017
correlations, 917, 931
correspondence, 795
cortical reorganization, 82, 131
cost functions, 423
covariance function, 514
CRAWL model, 61
cross-correlation, 68
cross-validation, 176, 183, 190, 218, 882
cumulants, 437, 757
curse of dimensionality, 10, 409, 1045

data association, 591
data classification, 416
data compression, 661
data sorting circuit, 685
DAX stock index, 952
decentralized control, 1017
decision trees, extraction of 24, 45
decorrelation, 736
delta-bar-delta, 563
density estimation, 465, 528, 661
depth perception, 816
deterministic annealing, 591, 626
development, 96
dichotomics, 556
digital flitering, 204

Keyword Index

dimensionality reduction, 10, 330
discrete event dynamic systems, 1017
discretized models, 372
discriminant analysis, 409
discriminant training, 388
discriminitive learning, 591
disinhibition, 816
Donders' law, 117
dorsal pathway, 802
drowsiness, 931
dual constraint model, 96
dual space method, 938
dynamic parameter adaptation, 225
dynamic programming, 952, 1017, 1038, 1045, 1059, 1073
dynamic wave model, 549
dynamical systems approach, 989
dynamics, 253

early stopping, 176, 218, 365, 959
EBNN, 640
edge detection, 159
EEG, 145, 931
elastic net algorithm, 330
elevator control, 1017
EM algorithm, 3, 351, 444, 465, 472, 486, 528, 542, 647, 1003
embedding problem, 989
EMMA, 851
energy, 31
energy bands labelling, 910
energy minimization, 917
ensemble, 479, 535, 598, 882
ensemble learning, 190, 351
entropy, 458, 1080
equilibrium points, 337
equivariant property, 757
error attenuation, 563
estimation rate, 183
eutropic loss, 316
evoked response, 145
evolution of complexity, 549
evolutionary programming, 38
exact identification, 288
expectation-maximization, 395, 402
experiment design, 1066
exploration, 945
exponentiated gradient algorithm, 309
extra outputs, 959

face detection, 875

Facial Action Coding System (FACS), 823
facial expression recognition, 823
factor analysis, 465
factorization, 437
family discovery, 402
family relations task, 563
fan-in/fan-out of nodes, 563
feature discovery, 3
feature extraction, 1024
feature measurement, 823
feature selection, 45, 232
feature space models, 330
feedback, 809
feedforward networks, 145, 176, 197, 218, 246, 323, 931
finite automata, 211
finite state automata, 612
focus of attention, 802
focus of expansion, 720
Fokker- Planck equation, 103
forward-backward algorithm, 743
Fourier transform, 260
free energy, 351, 661
function approximation, 1038, 1045
fusion of information, 802

gabor projections, 778
gain fields, 10
gamma memory, 785
gamma MLP, 785
gamma filter, 785
Gaussian, 556
Gaussian mixtures, 395, 542
Gaussian processes, 514
generalization, 169, 176, 218, 267, 423, 458, 521, 598, 959, 1038
generalization error, 344
genetic algorithms, 430, 535
genetic programming, 430
gesture recognition, 858, 903
Gibbs sampling, 472, 500, 514
global convergence, 372
GLVQ, 423
gradient descent, 302, 309, 316
gradient dynamics, 274
Gram-Charlier expansion, 757
grammatical induction, 612
graph partitioning, 626

Hamilton, Jacobi, Bellman elevation, 1059

Hamiltonian dynamics, 274
hand recognition, 903
handprint recognition, 778
handwriting recognition, 743, 771, 736, 764
hard competition, 239
hardware, 1031
hardware implantation, 699
harmonic functions, 996
harmony, 31
head direction cell, 61, 152
Hebbian learning, 124, 131
Helmholtz free energy, 591
Helmholtz machine, 444, 661
hemineglect, 10
hidden Markov models, 472, 485, 493, 750, 1003
hidden state, 858
hierarchical architectures, 493
hierarchical mixtures of experts, 351, 584
hierarchical network, 570
hierarchical priors, 598
higher order statistics, 437
hillclimbing, 430
hippocampus, 61, 152
HJB equation, 1073
Horwitz-matrix, 337
human reading, 10
humanoid hand, 889
HVC, 110
hybrid Monte Carlo, 514, 598
Models, 764
HyperNet, 980
hyperparameters, 598
hypothesis boosting, 654

I1000 chip, 938
ICA, 145
ID2-of-3, 24
ID3leaves, 45
illumination constancy, 844
image classification, 409
image processing, 633
image recognition, 823
image understanding, 875
improved current precision, 671
incremental learning, 605, 896
independent component analysis, 757
index of resoluability, 183
industrial production, 458
information, 145

information conservation, 437
information matrix, 295
information theory, 75, 281
inhibition, 68, 837
inhibition of return, 802
input cycles, 612
input/output hidden Markov models, 493
input representations, 45
instinct-rules, 1031
integrate-and-fire neurons, 75, 103, 124, 729
intelligent sensory processing, 52
internal representation, 736
invariances, 640
inverse problems, 145
investment learning, 570
irregular computation, 713

job-shop scheduling, 1024

KBANN, 535
Kalman filter estimation, 239
knowledge-based neural networks, 535
Kohonen networks, 110
kriging, 514

latent variable, 465, 661
lateral connections , 736
learning, 851, 875
learning curves, 344
learning dynamics, 302
learning from examples, 302
learning invariances, 640
learning rates, 563
learning-rate adaptation, 225
learning representations, 640
learning rule, 337
learning theory, 260, 323, 365
learning with queries, 24
lie algebra, 117
lifelong learning, 640
lightness perception, 844
likelihood bounds, 528
limit cycling, 989
linear models, 365
linear networks, 190
linear threshold element, 246
LISSOM, 736
Listing's law, 117
local bias, 605
local distance metric, 605
local feature detection, 605

Keyword Index

local learning, 605
local linear map, 903
local minima, 309, 316
locally weighted regression, 1066
long/short strategy, 966
long-term dependencies, 493, 577
LVQ, 423
Lyapunov function, 337

manipulation learning, 889
man-machine interface, 903
MAP estimation, 388
Markov decision problems, 952
Markov decision process, 1052
mask perceptron, 973
matching loss function, 309, 316
matrix perturbation theory, 337
maximum entropy, 591
maximum information, 444
maximum liklihood, 528, 591
McCulloch-Pitts neurons, 211
mean field theory, 472, 486, 661
medical diagnosis, 882
medical risk, 959
memory-based learning, 640, 896, 945, 1066
minimum description length, 507
missing data, 395, 465, 647
missing values, 395
mixture models, 381, 472, 1003
mixture of experts, 351, 584, 1080
MLP, 556
model-based recognition, 713
model selection, 183
modular networks, 239
modular system, 903
modulation, 131, 692
morphogenesis, 96
motion, 68, 809
motion control, 996
motion detection, 706
motion perception, 837
motion sensor, 720
motors, 924
motor control, 138
mountain car, 1038
multifactor models, 966
multilayer perceptron, 295, 323
multiple models, 239, 858
multiple time scales, 493
multiplication, 809
multiscale, 633

multiscale filters, 591
multitask learning, 959
mutual information, 757
mutual neighborhood value, 416

NARX networks, 577
natural basis functions, 591
natural gradient, 757
navigation, 61, 152, 989
neural hardware engineering, 671
near-neighbor classification, 409
nearest neighbor, 232, 640
network averaging, 542
network structure, 288, 563
neural coding, 75, 281
neural controller, 1010
neural development, 816
neural field theory, 82
neural integration, 152
neuro-fuzzy, 952
neuromodulation, 131
neuromorphic architectures, 720
neuromuscular junction, 96
neuron, 152
neuron gains, 372
neuron MOS transistor, 685
neuronal coding, 211
new learning models, 444
noise robustness, 211
non-Gaussian distributions, 437
non-linear, 500
non-linear systems, 1010
non-parametric clustering, 416
nonlinear control, 1073
nonlinear feature extraction, 437
nonlinear perceptron, 316
nonlinear system identification, 274
nonparametric statistics, 605
non-rigid matching, 795
novelty detection, 924
nuisance parameters, 521

OBD, 521
OBS, 521
object detection, 875
object recognition, 795, 865
occlusion, 816
OCR, 10, 479, 938
ocular dominance columns, 330

oculomotor control, 117
oculomotor system, 89
on-line learning, 302, 309, 381, 757
onset cells, 729
onset-offset filter, 729
opponent processing, 816
optic flow, 720, 823
optical character recognition, 10
optimal design, 295
optimization, 330, 372, 430, 851, 1066
Ornstein-Uhlenbeck Process, 103
oscillators, 451
otoliths, 89
overfitting, 176, 190, 218, 458
oversampling, 692
overtraining, 176, 458

PAC learning, 197, 204, 267, 288, 344, 654
parallel architectures, 996
parallel and sequential dynamics, 372
parallel hardware processing, 720
parameter adaptation, 225
parameterized models, 402
parameterized self-organizing map, 570, 903
parametric uncertainty, 1010
parietal cortex, 10
particle monitoring, 980
Parzen windows, 500
path integration, 61
path planning, 996
path pruning, 584
pattern recognition, 232, 253, 736, 875
perceptron, 218
performance comparison, 598
period-doubling bifurcation, 372
phase transition, 416
phase locking, 124
phoneme recognition, 785
physiology, 837
piecewise affine transformations, 795
piriform cortex, 131
pixel classification, 232
place cells, 61, 152
pneumonia, 959
point matching, 795
Poisson model, 103
portfolio management, 952
positioning, 778
Potts model, 416
prediction, 138, 809
predictive Q-routing, 945

predictivity, 816
presynaptic inhibition, 131
principal components, 437, 465, 823
principal component pruning, 966
probabilistic networks, 486, 528
probabilistic transducers, 381
probing, 945
product distributions, 288
promoter recognition, 647
protein structure prediction, 917
pruning, 521
pseudo-dimension, 204
PSOM, 570
psychophysics, 837
pulse stream, 1031

Q-learning, 858, 945, 952, 1017
Q-routing, 945
quadratic assignment, 626

radial basis functions, 239, 591
RAM-based nodes, 980
rankprop, 959
rapid learning, 570
rat, 61, 131, 152
read-once formulas, 288
reading, 10
real-world data, 598
receptive fields, 10, 605
recurrent cascade correlation, 612
recurrent networks, 38, 89, 204, 253, 274, 395, 458, 493, 577, 612, 743, 750, 771, 837, 973, 989
recurrent perceptrons, 204
recursive estimation, 239
recursive model selection, 239
reference frames, 10
REGENT, 535
regression, 514
regularization, 190, 458
reinforcement learning, 110, 858, 945, 1017, 1024, 1038, 1045, 1052, 1073, 1080
relaxation, 633
relaxing network, 395
representation quality, 45
representation selection, 45
resampling techniques, 882
response function, 190
response surface methods, 1066
retina, 159
ring oscillator, 685

Keyword Index

ridge function, 556
robot guidance, 903
robot learning, 570, 605
robotic control, 1031
robotic soccer, 896
rotation group, 117
rule extraction, 24

saccades, 117, 591
saliency, 521
saliency map, 591, 802
saliency measure, 633
sample complexity, 197, 204
sample sizes, 267
sarsa, 1038, 1052
scheduling, 430
second-order low-pass filters, 671
secondary structure prediction, 917
segmentation, 743, 778
selective attention, 771
self-organization, 110, 131, 500
self-organizing algorithms, 330
self-organizing map, 736
sensory signal processing, 713
sequence classification, 388
sequential associations, 52
sequential data, 395, 493
shunting of error signals, 563
sigma-pi nodes, 980
sigmoid, 218
sigmoidal networks, 197
sigmoidal transfer function, 316
Signal-to-Noise Ratio (SNR)-dependent plasticity, 159
signal processing, 851
silicon audition, 699
silicon cochlea, 671, 699
silicon retina, 678, 706
SIMD/MIMD hybrid, 713
similarity, 3
simple neuron, 316
simulated annealing, 917
single neuron, 309
singularity, 295
sleep, 931
sliding window, 778
small training data set, 570
smooth regularizers, 458
soft assign, 626, 795
soft competition, 239
soft max function, 591, 626

somatosensory cortex, 82, 131
song sparrow, 110
sorting, 959
sound segmentation, 729
source analysis, 145
sparse perceptrons, 654
spatial reasoning, 61
spatial representations, 10
spatio-temporal receptive field, 159, 678
spectral classification, 910
speech processing, 910
speech recognition, 388, 402, 486, 750, 785, 910
SPERT, 619
SPERT-II, 619
spike coding, 75, 124, 281, 699
spike trains, 68
spiking, 809
spiking neurons, 211
splice junction determination, 647
SPMD, 713
square loss, 316
stability, 1010
stability criterion, 225
stable dynamic parameter adaptation, 225
state of contact estimation, 1003
statistical mechanics, 218, 302, 323, 416
statistical methods, 288
statistical physics, 626
statistics, 851
steepest descent, 423
stochastic, 430
stochastic approximation, 1045
stochastic computing, 267
stochastic control, 1045
stock selection, 966
strong unimodality, 288
structure learning, 500
sub threshold, 671
suffix trees, 381
supervised learning, 591
suppression, 131
surface learning, 402
symbolic representations, 24
symmetric networks, 372
symmetry breaching, 323
synaptic competition, 96
synaptic modification, 131
synchronous digital hierarchy (SDH), 973
synchronous optical network (SONET), 973
system identification, 1010

TANN, 1010
target tracking, 706
TD learning, 1024
teams, 1017
telecommunications, 973
tempering, 563
templates, 938
template matching, 823
temporal dependencies, 493
temporal difference, 1073
temporal difference learning, 1038
temporal winner search, 685
tensor representation, 31
thalamocortical, 152
theoretical analysis, 612
threshold circuits, 211
time-delay neural network, 1024
time series, 472
time-to-contact, 720
TIMIT database, 910
topographic map, 82, 330, 465
tracking chip, 706
trade-off theorem for backpropagation, 225
training-test split, 183
trajectory learning, 274, 451
transfer functions, 309
transfer in learning, 640
transparency measures, 45
traveling salesman problem, 626
tree, 479
tree growing, 584
TREPAN, 24
trust region, 633

unified learning scheme, 444
uniform convergence, 169
universal approximation, 451
unlabeled data, 647
unsupervised, 444, 809
unsupervised learning, 124, 416, 661

value function, 1073
value function approximator, 952
Vapnik-Chervonenkis dimension, 183
VC dimension, 197, 204, 267, 344
vector processor, 619
vehicle havigation, 720
vergence, 89
vestibular nucleus, 89
vestibulo-ocular reflex (VOR), 89

video indexing, 875
view-based approach, 865
vigilance, 931
vision, 633, 851, 865, 875
vision, primate, 802
vision chip for tracking, 706
visual adaptation, 159
visual attention, 771, 858
visual cortex, 68,,330, 591, 809, 816, 865
visual motion chip, 706
visual processing, 837, 858
visual search, 591
visual smooth pursuit, 706
visualization, 465
Viterbi algorithm, 743
VLSI, 699, 1031
VLSI model of smooth pursuit, 706
volume conservation, 437

weak inversion, 671
weight decay, 458
weight sharing, 917
weight size, 246
"where" pathway, 802
White's illusion, 844
winner search hardware, 685
winner take all circuit, 685
word recognition, 10
word sense resolution, 647
worst-case loss bounds, 309

Ying-Yang machine, 444